Poverty Trends for the
General Population and
for the Population 65
and Older*

*Poverty statistics for the
elderly were not
published for the period
1960–1965.

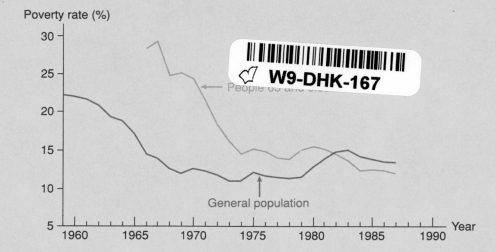

People 65 and older

General population

ve Income of
Families

age income of
operator households
d by average
e of all
holds.

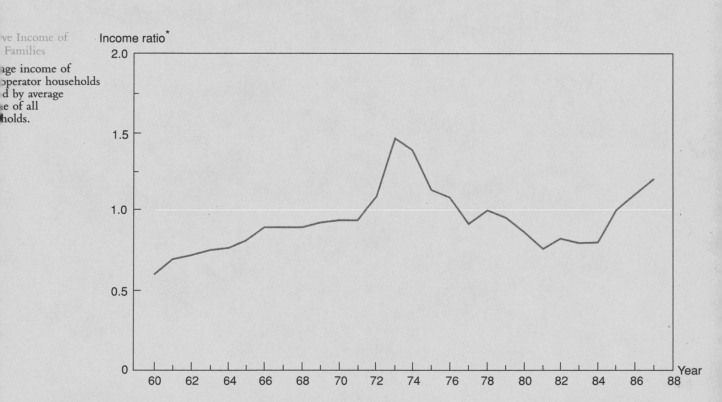

PRINCIPLES OF ECONOMICS

JAMES F. RAGAN, JR.
Kansas State University

LLOYD B. THOMAS, JR.
Kansas State University

Harcourt Brace Jovanovich, Publishers
and its subsidiary, ACADEMIC PRESS
San Diego New York Chicago Austin Washington, D.C.
London Sydney Tokyo Toronto

ISBN: 0-15-571598-4
Library of Congress Catalog Card Number: 89-84695
Printed in the United States of America

ILLUSTRATION CREDITS

Bio photo of James F. Ragan, Jr., Blaker Studio Royal, Manhattan, Kansas; bio photo of Lloyd B. Thomas, Jr., Creative Image Portrait Design, Pullman, Washington; page 4, Bart Bartholemew/NYT Pictures; page 8, The Bettmann Archive; page 60, The Bettmann Archive; page 62, Stephen P. Allen/Gamma Liaison; page 219, courtesy of The Institute for Social Research and Department of Economics, The University of Michigan; page 244, The Bettmann Archive; page 268, José Lopez/NYT Pictures; page 301, Art Stein/Photo Researchers; page 337, Wide World Photos; page 373, Richards/Magnum Photos; page 423, courtesy of Robert J. Barro/photo by Robert J. Gordon; page 479 (top), courtesy of James Tobin/photo by T. Charles Erickson; page 479 (bottom), courtesy of Robert M. Solow; page 500, Nina Leen/TIME Magazine; page 519, Jeff Share; page 590, courtesy of Joan Robinson; page 630, Tony Freeman/Photoedit; page 643, © George Olson/ Photofile; page 667, courtesy of The Walt Disney Company; page 756, Robert Burroughs; page 831, Brad Bower/Picture Group.

For Gail—my wife and dear friend—who, despite amazement that anyone would freely choose to write a textbook, has graciously supported the endeavor and sacrificed so that it might be completed.

James F. Ragan, Jr.

For Sally—whose love, absolute generosity, and indomitable spirit sustained the inspiration that made this book possible.

Lloyd B. Thomas, Jr.

PREFACE

Economics is not totally foreign to beginning students. Everyone who has struggled with a budget, followed a political campaign, or read the headlines—on poverty, trade deficits, and inflation—has acquired some familiarity with economic issues. What is often missing is an economic way of thinking—a framework for organizing thoughts, analyzing economic events, and separating economic fact from fiction. Economic literacy is important because economic decisions shape the future of the nation and affect the well-being of its citizens. For these reasons and others, it is essential that economics be made accessible to students. Students may open an economics book, but how far they read depends on what is in the book and how it is presented.

Aware of this, we have attempted to convey both the importance of economics and our enthusiasm for the subject. We do not expect students to read economics for the joy of understanding. Rather, our philosophy is that we must first convince students that what they are reading is relevant. Toward that end, at the start of each chapter we raise critical policy issues and pose key questions to which students can relate. To sustain interest throughout the chapter, we include many examples and applications, and provide historical background on the variables at issue—so they become more than abstract theoretical concepts. Economic theory is never presented for its own sake; there is always a payoff. Economic theory is integrated with empirical evidence, and the implications of the theory are clearly spelled out. Our goal here is to have students develop a feel for the way economic principles relate to the real world around them.

In determining just how much theory to present, we have resisted the encyclopedic approach of some authors and the decision of others to provide broad coverage of technical concepts at the frontiers of economics. Too often the readers of such books receive an extensive but shallow background in economics or become familiar with the latest economic theories without developing a firm grounding in basic economic analysis. Instead, we emphasize the bread-and-butter concepts of economics (supply and demand, efficiency, opportunity cost, and so forth), ensuring that students acquire sufficient background in these seminal concepts before moving on to more advanced topics.

Traditionally, international issues are relegated to the back of the book. Given an increasingly interrelated world, this approach is no longer defensible. Agricultural problems cannot be discussed intelligently without considering exchange rates, world production, and protectionism. Market structure and antitrust policy cannot be studied as if competition came only from domestic producers. Similarly, analyses of interest rates, inflation, monetary and fiscal policy, economic growth, and numerous other topics require an understanding of the interrelationships among national economies. For this reason, gains from trade, trade restrictions, and related concepts are introduced at the beginning of the book, allowing us to integrate global issues with what are customarily considered domestic topics. By the time the student encounters the more technical concepts of international economics near the end of the book, he or she has already gained a familarity with and an appreciation of international economics.

Another basic feature of this book is its thorough treatment of critical economic policy issues. Entire chapters are devoted to inflation, budget deficits and national debt, alternative viewpoints on stabilization policies, externalities and the environment, and discrimination and differences in labor market outcomes. Although this latter subject can be deleted in the event of time constraints, our classroom experience indicates that students respond enthusiastically to this material. The topics—including pay differentials, affirmative action, and comparable worth—underscore the book's commitment to real-world issues and policies.

The organization of this book does not differ dramatically from that of most other principle texts. However, for those adopting a paperback split, one difference should be noted—the present text contains an unusually comprehensive set of core chapters common to both *Principles of Macroeconomics* and *Principles of Microeconomics*. This feature is designed to give instructors greater choice in topic selection.

Typically, macro splits do not contain information on elasticity (Chapter 5), despite the fact that many instructors want to acquaint their students with at least the price elasticity of demand. Similarly, most macro splits omit a chapter on the business firm (Chapter 6), even though its topics—including balance sheets, bonds, and the stock market—are often relevant to macro classes. The final core chapter (Chapter 7), on government, treats such topics as rationale for government intervention, growth of the government sector, and principles of taxation. Usually these topics appear in several macro chapters and are ignored in the micro split or they are covered in a public-finance section of microeconomics and ignored in the macro split. Because these subjects are appropriate for macroeconomics or microeconomics, we include them in the core so that instructors have the option of including them in either course. At the same time, we realize that not all instructors wish to cover every topic in the core. Accordingly, the core chapters following supply and demand are structured so that they are not prerequisites for later chapters. Any or all of these chapters may be deleted when appropriate.

LEARNING AIDS

Among the pedagogical features of this book are the **Exhibits** (boxed inserts) interspersed throughout the chapters. Exhibits perform a variety of functions—illustrating real-life economic events, assessing current policy, and providing background on great economists. Through exhibits students learn about the importance of elasticity of demand in determining broadcast revenues for team sports, the impact of agricultural supply restrictions on the rural Missouri economy, the evolution of the U.S. savings and loan crisis, the effect of macroeconomic conditions on political elections, and the role of *perestroika* in motivating Soviet entrepreneurship. Exhibits are written in a lively fashion to be both educational and entertaining.

To foster student involvement, we include the **Your-Turn** feature, in which the student is quizzed on a subject just presented. (Answers to these quizzes appear at the end of the chapter.) These quizzes provide immediate feedback on how well the student has mastered the material and inform the student as to whether he or she is ready to move on to the next topic.

To assist the student in learning the economist's vocabulary, key terms appear in boldface print when first introduced, and most are defined in the margins. These definitions are arranged alphabetically in a glossary at the end of the book for easy student access. Other important concepts (not quite key terms) are emphasized with italics.

At the end of each chapter, a summary organizes and highlights the important points of the preceding pages. This is followed by a list of the chapter's key terms (arranged in order of presentation) and by study questions and problems. The questions are designed to test comprehension and ability to apply the concepts and principles of the chapter. Following answers to the Your-Turn quizzes, most chapters conclude with a set of carefully selected references.

Figures and tables are used liberally to illustrate economic concepts, to facilitate analysis, and to provide historical background. The figures are accompanied by captions that convey the message independent of the text discussion.

ANCILLARY PACKAGE

Principles of Economics is supported by the following supplementary materials:

1. *Instructor's Manual*—written by Robert Ley, Bemidji State University, and Kathryn A. Nantz, Fairfield University, featuring 100 transparency masters.
2. *Study Guide*—written by Roger Trenary (an experienced teacher of principles of economics and recipient of the Kansas State University Outstanding Teaching Award in Arts and Sciences).
3. *Testbook-A*—written by Roger Trenary, contains 2000 test items (also available on computerized disk).
4. *Testbook-B*—written by John Sondey, University of Idaho, contains 2000 test items (also available on computerized disk).
5. *Transparencies*—approximately 80 four-color transparencies featuring key figures and tables from the text.
6. *Eco-Talk*—HBJ computer tutorial.

ACKNOWLEDGMENTS

As with any project of this magnitude, credit must be shared with many individuals, starting with our publishing team at Harcourt Brace Jovanovich. The entire HBJ staff has impressed us with their knowledge and dedication. Among those deserving special recognition are John Carey and Rick Hammonds (acquisitions editors), Robert C. Miller (manuscript editor), Cindy Simpson (production editor), Diane Pella and Don Fujimoto (designers), Stacy Simpson and Avery Hallowell (art editors), and Mandy Van Dusen (production manager).

We have also benefited greatly from the comments of our colleagues, many of whom offered suggestions in their area of expertise. These include Arlo Biere, Wayne Nafziger, Bryan Schurle, Carol Tremblay, and Jeff Williams. We are especially indebted to Roger Trenary who, in addition to writing the *Study Guide* and *Testbook-A*, diligently reviewed the entire manuscript. Patrick Gormely of Kansas State University and John Knudsen of the University of Idaho made indispensable contributions in their areas of expertise, Chapters 38 and 39, respectively. The authors also extend thanks to Karen Gillespie, Al Grant, Jeanette

Harold, Diane Landoll, and Susan Koch for typewriting, computer, and other assistance.

Our reviewers have played a special role, providing an objective assessment of our proposed material and making many helpful suggestions. We extend our appreciation to Jack E. Adams, University of Arkansas; Paul Barkley, Washington State University; George S. Bohler, Florida Junior College at Jacksonville; Thomas Bonsor, Eastern Washington University; Michael Brusin, College of San Mateo; Bobby N. Corcoran, Middle Tennessee State University; Vernon Dobis, Moorhead State University; Michael G. Ellis, New Mexico State University; John L. Fizel, Pennsylvania State University (Behrend College); Richard B. Hansen, University of Northern Iowa; David Hula, Kansas State University; Walter Johnson, University of Missouri at Columbia; Robert Keller, Colorado State University; Kathy Kemper, Everman, Texas; Susan N. Koenigsberg, San Francisco State University; Michael Kupilik, University of Montana; Stephen E. Lile, Western Kentucky University; Charles Link, University of Delaware; Barbara Morgan, San Francisco State University; Glenn Perrone, Pace University; Louis F. Pisciottoli, California State University at Fresno; Jerry Riddle, Central Virginia Community College; Janet Rivers, University of Northern Iowa; Keith Rowley, Baylor University; Lynda Rush, California State Polytechnic University at Pomona; Peter Schwartz, University of North Carolina-Charlotte; John Scoggins, California State University-Long Beach; Lee Spector, Ball State University; Ed Stuart, Northeastern Illinois University; James L. Swofford, University of South Alabama; Tom TenHoeve, Iowa State University; Victor Tremblay, Kansas State University; Roger Trenary, Kansas State University; Arthur L. Welsh, Pennsylvania State University.

Finally, we acknowledge the support of our families. In addition to our wives—to whom we dedicate this book—we are indebted to our parents for their years of support, their love, and their confidence in us. Our children—Elizabeth Thomas and Emily, Patrick, and Laura Ragan—have also sacrificed so that this book could be written. They too have our gratitude.

READER INPUT

As we learned throughout the review process, the comments of others can strengthen a book. Accordingly, we encourage readers to share their thoughts and insights with us. Please write us in care of Harcourt Brace Jovanovich, College Department, 1250 Sixth Avenue, San Diego, California 92101.

James F. Ragan, Jr.
Lloyd B. Thomas, Jr.

CONTENTS

Contents

xiii

James F. Ragan, Jr., is Professor of Economics at Kansas State University. Prior to joining the faculty there, he worked as a research economist for the Federal Reserve Bank of New York. He has also been a visiting scholar at the Federal Reserve Bank of Kansas City and a visiting associate professor at Washington University. He earned a B.A. in economics from the University of Missouri in 1971 and a Ph.D. in economics from Washington University (St. Louis) in 1975.

Professor Ragan has published in such journals as *Review of Economics and Statistics, Economic Inquiry, Journal of Human Resources*, and *Southern Economic Journal*. He has presented papers before numerous groups, including the National Commission on Youth, the Conference on U.S. Productive Capacity, the National Commission for Employment Policy, and the American Enterprise Institute Conference on Legal Minimum Wages. His work has been cited in such publications as *The Wall Street Journal, Business Week,* and *U.S. News & World Report*.

Professor Ragan's special interests lie in labor economics, microeconomics, and public policy. He has taught principles of economics on a regular basis since 1977.

Lloyd B. Thomas, Jr., is Professor of Economics at Kansas State University. He earned a B.A. and an M.A. in economics from the University of Missouri in 1963 and 1964 and a Ph.D. from Northwestern University in 1970.

Professor Thomas has conducted extensive research within his academic interests—primarily the areas of macroeconomic policy and international finance—and has published in numerous economic journals. He is the author of a best-selling textbook entitled *Money, Banking, and Economic Activity* (Prentice-Hall, 1986), now in its third edition.

Recognized as an excellent teacher, Professor Thomas continues to make undergraduate instruction in principles of economics, money and banking, and intermediate economic theory an important focus of his professional career. He teaches graduate courses primarily in the areas of monetary theory and policy.

Professor Thomas has taught at Florida State University, Northwestern University, the University of California at Berkeley, the University of Delaware, and the University of Idaho.

PART I

THE
BASICS

CHAPTER 1

ECONOMICS AND ECONOMIC THINKING

Economics is the academic discipline most discussed by the general public. It is also one of the least understood.[1]

Economics can be understood in terms of the questions it asks and the approach it uses to answer these questions. Economic issues abound. Why do women generally earn less than men? How successful are government programs designed to aid the needy? Should the government's budget be balanced? How does trade affect a nation's standard of living?

On a personal level, you make economic decisions throughout life. Is college a good investment? Compared to a state university, is a degree from an expensive private college worth the added expense? Which job should you take? How can you best spend your income? Should you buy or rent a house?

If you enter business you confront numerous economic decisions—including what to produce, how to produce, and in what quantities. In politics you face different economic issues. Given its limited ability to respond to societal wants, how much should a nation spend on defense, on care for the elderly, on environmental cleanup? Even as a voter, you evaluate candidates partly on the basis of their economic views. Opinion polls consistently rank economic problems—such as unemployment, inflation, and the deficit—high on the list of public concerns.

No one escapes the forces of economics; we must deal with them, intelligently or otherwise. Accordingly, it is important to build an understanding of economics. The principal goal of this book is to help build that understanding. With discipline and effort, one soon develops an inventory of economic facts and principles and, more importantly, develops an economic way of thinking. A word of caution: resist the temptation to dismiss economic theory. As the great English economist John Maynard Keynes observed, those who disdain economic theory "are usually the slaves of some defunct economist."

---

[1]James B. Ramsey, *Economic Forecasting—Models or Markets?* (London: The Institute of Economic Affairs, 1977), p. 11.

RESOURCES AND OUTPUT

Now that a sample of economic issues has been presented, the more basic question becomes: What is economics? However, before answering the question in detail, it is appropriate to introduce a few terms.

Each country has certain finite **resources,** which economists generally divide into three categories: land, capital, and labor. *Land* is a general term encompassing more than a country's soil. **Land** includes all natural resources—timber, minerals, rivers, and the like. **Capital** refers to inputs produced by humans—factories, tools, roads, and so forth. This book constitutes capital. So do a sports arena, an oil refinery, and a calculator.

Labor consists of the physical and mental abilities of workers—the production potential of miners, secretaries, accountants, and all others willing to contribute to output. The most accurate measure of labor is a country's labor force, in terms of both quantity and composition. Labor consists of more than the number of people available for work; it also encompasses the skills of workers. Those with more education or experience can generally produce more output than workers with fewer skills. Table 1-1 lists certain resources available to the United States in a recent year.

Sometimes *entrepreneurship* is considered a fourth resource category, although it is commonly viewed as a subset of labor. The hallmarks of an **entrepreneur** are innovation and risk taking. An entrepreneur organizes resources for production, attempting to take advantage of what is viewed as an opportunity. An entrepreneur may introduce a new product or attempt a new technique of production. When successful, an entrepreneur may reap substantial financial rewards—but success is by no means guaranteed. Those who introduce the wrong product—the proverbial lead balloon—can expect to lose money on their venture. Exhibit 1-1 (page 4) provides information on some recent entrepreneurs.

Resources
Inputs (land, capital, and labor) used to produce goods and services.
Land
A country's natural resources.
Capital
Inputs produced by humans.
Labor
The physical and mental abilities of workers.

Entrepreneur
An individual who organizes resources for production, introduces new products or techniques of production, and reaps the rewards/bears the consequences of such endeavors.

Table 1-1		
SELECTED U.S. RESOURCES		
Land	**Capital**	**Labor**
3.6 million square miles of surface, including: 482 million acres of commercial timberland 476 billion short tons of proven coal reserves 152 million metric tons of proven sulphur reserves	3.9 million miles of highway 4.7 million farm tractors 3.9 million commercial buildings 100 nuclear reactors	124 million people in the labor force: among those 25–64 years old, 26% have completed at least 4 years of college and 20% have completed 1–3 years.

Sources: U.S. Bureau of the Census, *Statistical Abstract of the United States: 1988;* U.S. Department of Agriculture, *Agricultural Statistics: 1987;* U.S. Department of Energy, Energy Information Administration, *Annual Energy Review: 1987;* U.S. Bureau of Labor Statistics, *News,* USDL 88-423 (August 1988) and *Employment and Earnings (1989).*

EXHIBIT 1–1

THE SWEET SMELL OF SUCCESS—ENTREPRENEURS WITH A VISION

Vini Bergeman had an idea. Traditional limousines were boring. They could comfortably transport only four passengers and they failed to provide the amenities for which some wealthy customers were prepared to pay handsomely. What the world needed was his Ultra Limousine Corporation, which he founded in 1979. The company custom designs and builds roomy and luxurious limousines. Take the four-wheel-drive vehicle designed for a businessman with a passion for rabbit hunting. Through its sunroofs, as many as 18 hunters can take aim at every rabbit stopping to gawk. Among Mr. Bergeman's other creations is a limousine 92 feet long that accommodates 35 passengers. With an emphasis on comfort, this particular vehicle sports a swimming pool, a big-screen TV, and of course a putting green.

Mr. Bergeman gambled that there were enough companies and individuals willing to pay big bucks for big limos. He won. With sales doubling each year, the entrepreneur has carved out a small but lucrative niche in the automotive industry.

John Walker and Daniel Drake saw a different untapped market—software designed to help ar-

Ultra Limousine Corporation's
92-Footer
Source: *New York Times,* June 15, 1986, p. 1F.

chitects and engineers with their drawings. In 1982, the two computer programmers created Autodesk Inc. Within three years the company's AutoCad program was available in seven languages and could be run on most desktop computers. Profits in 1988 amounted to $20.5 million on sales of $79.3 million. Clearly, their vision had paid off.

Sources: Adapted from N. R. Kleinfield, "The Art of Selling to the Very Rich," *The New York Times,* June 15, 1986, p. 8F; Richard Brandt, "Autodesk," *Business Week,* May 26, 1986, p. 96.

Economic resources are sometimes called *factors of production* in order to emphasize their role in producing goods and services:

$$\text{resources} \xrightarrow{\text{production}} \text{goods and services}$$

The distinction between goods and services is based on whether the *output*—what is produced—is tangible or intangible. Clothes, sporting goods, beverages, and other tangible products are termed *goods.* Examples of *services* include haircuts, income tax preparation, and computer repair.

Sometimes the term "good" is used loosely to include both goods and services. For example, the expression **economic good** refers to any product that is *scarce.* That is, at a price of zero (if the good were free) the amount desired would exceed the quantity available. In contrast, a **free good** is any product so abundant that even at a zero price the amount available would fully satisfy all wants. Within a desert, sand is likely to be a free good. On many mountain ranges snow is a free good, although not always. If snowfall is insufficient for good skiing, the amount freely available may fall short of the amount desired. Ski resorts frequently pay for the creation of artificial snow.

At some colleges baseball games are free goods. Despite free admission, more seats are available than spectators. Of course, conditions can change. When a team contends for a national championship, interest in the game may swell so dramatically

Economic Good
A good that is scarce. At a price of zero the amount of the good desired exceeds the quantity available.
Free Good
A good that is not scarce.

that some fans must be turned away. In that event, the college baseball game is no longer a free good—*even when no admission is charged.* Available seating is now insufficient to permit all who want to watch the game to see it—seats are scarce. For this reason the game becomes an economic good.

ECONOMICS AS A STUDY OF SCARCITY AND CHOICE

Naturally, we want more from life than baseball. In fact, human wants are seemingly unlimited. Although we may initially ask only for life's necessities, once they are within reach we tend to crave richer foods, more stylish clothing, larger homes, and assorted luxuries. Even then our wish list continues to grow. No matter how affluent the individual, invariably something else is desired.

Scarcity of Resources
Insufficient resources are available to produce all goods and services desired by consumers.

While desires appear endless, economic resources are **scarce**—finite. Therein lies the rub. No society has sufficient resources to satisfy all human wants. *Because resources are limited, what can be produced is also limited.*

Contrary to the Michelob slogan, it is not true that we "can have it all." Actually, we must choose among competing options. *What* will be produced? Which wants will be met? Which will go unsatisfied? Should society build more shelter for the homeless and fewer roads and parks? Should we allocate fewer resources to consumer goods (such as VCRs) and transfer additional resources to the production of business computers and other forms of capital? Which do we prefer—more steel or cleaner air?

In addition to determining which goods and services are produced, there is the question of *how*. Which production technique do we use? Should we generate electricity with coal, natural gas, or nuclear power? How do we grow our crops? For example, should we economize on labor, making farming more capital-intensive?

Moreover, there are allocation decisions. How are the goods and services to be distributed? *Who* are fed? *Who* go hungry? *Who* receive heart transplants? *Who* drive Mercedes? *Who* get the Yugos? *Who* must walk? Such issues are at the heart of **economics.**

Economics
The study of how scarce resources are allocated among competing uses.

Scarcity limits options and forces choice. In a world without scarcity there would be no economic goods, only free goods. No one would need to do without. But that world—the Michelob world—is not where you were born. Here on earth society is forced to choose among competing options—and so are you. Consequently, such choices carry a cost: foregone opportunities, what we sacrifice as the consequence of our decisions. This is the essence of **opportunity cost.**

Opportunity Cost
The best alternative to the option chosen.

What would you do if you skipped your next class—earn money by working? share a Coke with a friend? sleep? What is your best alternative? Whatever it is, that is the opportunity cost of attending class. You may want both a bicycle and stereo speakers, but you cannot afford both. The opportunity cost of the bicycle is the speakers; the opportunity cost of the speakers is the bicycle.

So it is for society. Selecting one option requires forgoing another—perhaps not eliminating a program entirely, but at least reducing its size. If society chooses to reduce pollution by slicing student financial aid, the opportunity cost of a cleaner environment is fewer students receiving a college education. Similarly, if the government decides to lay claim to a greater percentage of the nation's output, the cost is a reduced share of output for the private, nongovernment sector. The opportunity cost of an aircraft carrier, for example, may be additional housing and consumer goods.

According to government statistics, over 30 million people in the United States live in *poverty:* they possess insufficient purchasing power to maintain what the government considers an adequate standard of living. Can poverty be reduced? Certainly. But at what cost? What is society willing to sacrifice to remove another million people from the poverty rolls? Choices are not always easy, but must be made.

YOUR TURN   POVERTY

Are poverty and scarcity the same concept? Assume the government waged a successful *war on poverty,* wiping out poverty in this country. Would that eliminate scarcity?

ECONOMIC THINKING

Despite differences in the questions they pose, economists share a common approach to problems—an economic way of thinking—based on certain principles. The first such principle has just been articulated: *scarcity forces choice.* Other economic principles involve the ways in which decision makers behave and the processes through which choices are made. Finally, economic thinking starts with the status quo and considers the consequences of change. When you understand these basic economic principles—when you understand how economists think—then the arguments of economists are easier to follow and the subject of economics is easier to master.

Rational Behavior

Rational Behavior
Acting in a manner consistent with a decision maker's objectives.

A basic tenet of economic thinking is that decision makers behave *rationally.* In other words, decision makers establish a particular goal or objective and then choose purposefully in an attempt to achieve that goal. For consumers, the assumed goal is to maximize happiness or well-being—what economists call *utility.* Here **rational behavior** simply means making choices that the consumer believes maximize utility. For example, if a consumer prefers brand X to brand Y and both are the same price, the consumer does not choose brand Y.

Rational behavior does not mean consumers never make what, in retrospect, was a bad decision. A consumer may try *new and improved* brand Y, only to discover that it too falls short of brand X. Such experimentation is not irrational. What is irrational is to continue purchasing brand Y after determining that brand X is the better buy (provides more utility for the money).

Producers are also presumed to behave purposefully. Economists assume that the goal of every producer is to maximize *profit:* the difference between income earned from selling a product and the cost incurred in producing it. For instance, when a farmer sells a crop for $50,000 that cost $48,000 to produce, the farmer earns $2000 profit. An implication of profit maximization is that a producer uses the fewest resources necessary to produce the output. Using more resources than necessary increases production costs and reduces profit.

Decision Making—A Matter of Costs and Benefits

Economic thinking also involves assumptions about how decisions are made. Economists assume that decision makers are guided by the perceived costs and benefits of an action. For example, when it comes to seat belts, economists assume that consumers *buckle up* if the perceived benefit (reduced risk of injury) outweighs the cost (time spent buckling and unbuckling). On the other hand, if the cost is viewed as greater than the benefit, seat belts will not be used.

Because costs and benefits differ among individuals, decisions also differ, but in a predictable manner. Consider the traveler who can either leave the airport immediately by taxi or wait for a bus which, after numerous stops, reaches the same destination. Which does the traveler choose? The answer, of course, depends on how the benefits of the taxi (including time saved) stack up against the costs (e.g., higher fare). Not everyone reaches the same conclusion. A lawyer who charges clients $200 per hour likely places a higher value on time savings than does a poor student. Therefore, the lawyer is more likely to choose the taxi than is the student.

Given this view of the decision-making process, a change in costs or benefits affects outcomes—again in a predictable manner. If taxi fares decrease and bus fares stay the same, one expects the number of travelers choosing taxi service to increase. Similarly, if the government increases the costs of not wearing a seat belt—by imposing stiff fines on beltless drivers—one expects more drivers to buckle up. What emerges is the view that decision makers respond to incentives. As the benefits of an action increase or its costs decrease, that action becomes more likely. This scenario gives economists a powerful framework for analyzing human behavior and for predicting consequences of programs that alter costs or benefits.

YOUR TURN   RESPONDING TO INCENTIVES

(a) Even such addictive behavior as cigarette smoking is amenable to economic incentives. Cite at least one policy that has reduced or could reduce cigarette smoking in the United States. (b) Incentives also affect career decisions. Explain how incentives can be used to convince more people to enter the nursing profession.

Marginal Analysis

Marginal Analysis
An examination of what occurs when current conditions change.

Economic thinking often involves **marginal analysis**—considering the effects of change. For example, one relies on marginal analysis when deciding to spend six hours this week studying economics rather than five hours. One simply determines that the benefits of the additional hour (greater understanding of economics and possibly a higher grade) exceed the costs (less leisure, less sleep, or perhaps a lower grade in another course). Had one reached a different conclusion, the extra time would not be allotted to economics.

Similarly, producers make marginal calculations. For example, a farmer may ask: How much more corn can I grow if I apply additional fertilizer? How much will the additional fertilizer increase my costs of production? Will the additional fertilizer increase or decrease my profit? In each case the farmer considers the consequences of changing current operations.

Marginal analysis is also appropriate for assessing government policy. Before a government raises tax rates, it is useful to know how the change will affect the economy. Similarly, if a government is concerned about poverty, it can make more-enlightened decisions when it knows how changes in various government programs are likely to alter poverty. Because decision making frequently deals with change, marginal analysis plays a central role in economic thinking.

METHODOLOGY

In addition to a common way of thinking, economists share a common methodology. In the tradition of Sherlock Holmes, economists approach problems scientifically.

How did Holmes solve a mystery? Relying on his keen sense of observation, he began by gathering important facts. Holmes then tied these facts together to form a coherent **theory,** thereby attempting to explain their underlying relationships. His next step was to test the theory. This testing involved examining one or more of the theory's **hypotheses** to determine their consistency with the evidence.

For example, in one of his celebrated cases, Sherlock Holmes sought to identify the thief of a jeweled crown—the so-called beryl coronet. After gathering bits of relevant evidence, Holmes theorized that the culprit was one Sir George Burnwell. A basic hypothesis of this theory was that the soles of Sir George's shoes would match tracks found in the snow at the scene of the crime. If the shoes did not fit, Holmes would be forced to reject the theory, or at least reformulate it to explain why the soles of the shoes did not match the tracks. On the other hand, a finding that the shoes did match would support the theory but not prove it, since alternative theories might also be consistent with the evidence. (The soles of other shoes might also match the impressions left in the snow.)[2]

Good theories make the world appear elementary: they ignore less important bits of information and focus on central relationships. Theories abstract and simplify. They do not attempt to explain every thought in a villain's mind nor every action—only the major events and relationships. Theories are built on a set of assumptions (for example, assumptions about the motives of the people involved). From these assumptions various conclusions are derived. Theories are then judged in terms of the quality of these conclusions—that is, in terms of the ability to explain and predict.

Interestingly, criminologists are not alone in using the **scientific method:** developing theories, gathering evidence (data), and determining whether the theories are consistent with the evidence. Theories also play a major role in economics: helping us learn cause-and-effect relationships and understand our complex world. For example, economists are interested in knowing why prices rise. The rate at which a nation's average prices rise is termed the **inflation rate.**

The inflation rate fluctuates over time. In the United States, prices rose an average of 13.5 percent in 1980 but only 1.9 percent in 1986 (Figure 1-1). With millions of goods and tens of millions of consumers, how can we ever hope to uncover the determinants of inflation? Obviously, we must simplify the task and concentrate on the key factors. In other words, we need a theory of inflation.

Actually, several theories have been advanced. Among them, one holds that inflation is a monetary phenomenon—the result of too much money chasing too few goods. According to this theory, inflation is directly related to growth in the money supply: the faster government prints money, the faster prices rise. Alternative theories of inflation stress the role of other (nonmonetary) factors.

Theories are sometimes presented in terms of graphical or mathematical **models.** For example, Figure 1-2 (page 10) presents a monetary model of inflation, according to which each 1-percent increase in growth in the money supply leads to a

Theory
A formulation of underlying relationships in an attempt to explain certain phenomena.

Hypothesis
A proposition concerning a particular relationship or event—often part of a theory.

Inflation Rate
The rate at which a nation's average prices rise over time.

Model
A formal presentation of a theory, often mathematical or graphical.

---

[2]For a solution to the mystery, see A. Conan Doyle, *The Adventures of Sherlock Holmes* (New York: A&W Visual Library, 1975), pp. 261-288.

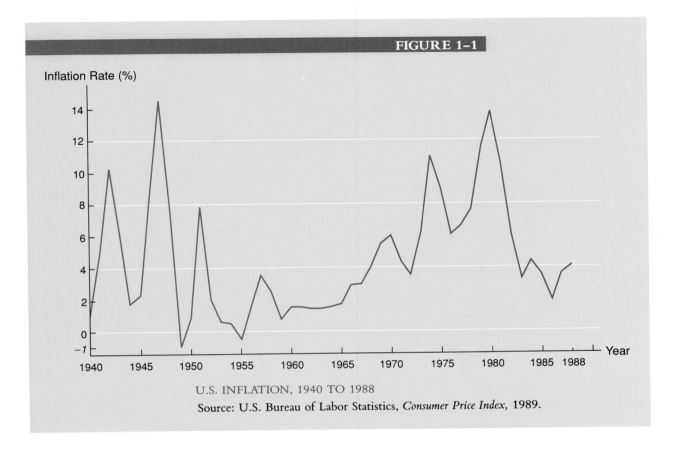

FIGURE 1-1

Inflation Rate (%)

U.S. INFLATION, 1940 TO 1988

Source: U.S. Bureau of Labor Statistics, *Consumer Price Index*, 1989.

1-percent increase in inflation. (For a review on interpreting graphs, see Appendix 1A at the end of this chapter.)

Given competing theories of inflation, which are credible and which are not? How are theories evaluated? As a starting point, an acceptable theory must be consistent with available evidence. Recall the scientific method, whereby theories are subjected to possible refutation. The monetary theory predicts that an increase in the growth of money is followed by an increase in the inflation rate. Is it? If not, we must either abandon the theory or reformulate it so that it is consistent with the evidence—and then test the new version.

What if two or more theories are consistent with the same data? Which theory is best? Because the answer is not always clear, economists often rely on statistics to help choose among competing theories. Assume the reason you are interested in a theory of inflation is so that you can forecast future inflation. One approach is to choose the theory with the smallest forecast error—the theory that, on average, comes closest to predicting the actual rate of inflation.

Assume that on average the monetary theory is off, in one direction or the other, by 10 percent, whereas all competing theories are off by at least 20 percent. Using the preceding decision rule, the monetary theory is selected for forecasting. No theory permits perfect forecasting at all times. Despite this, as long as one theory forecasts better than others, it remains the best choice for forecasting.

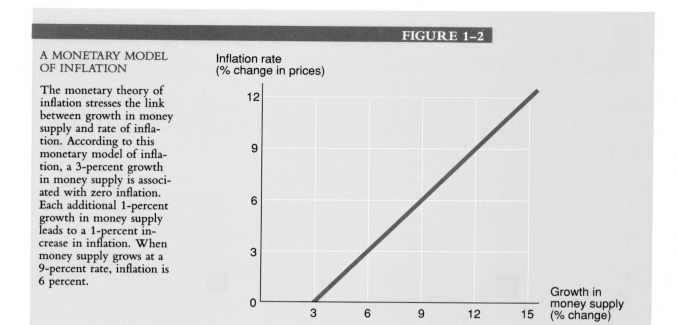

FIGURE 1–2

A MONETARY MODEL OF INFLATION

The monetary theory of inflation stresses the link between growth in money supply and rate of inflation. According to this monetary model of inflation, a 3-percent growth in money supply is associated with zero inflation. Each additional 1-percent growth in money supply leads to a 1-percent increase in inflation. When money supply grows at a 9-percent rate, inflation is 6 percent.

HAZARDS TO CLEAR THINKING

Economic theory helps one analyze and predict. By increasing knowledge of how the world *works,* it aids policymakers in formulating beneficial programs and in avoiding costly mistakes. But like any tool, economic theory must be used with care. Consider three of the most common stumbling blocks for would-be economists: the other-things-equal assumption, causality, and the fallacy of composition.

Other Things Equal

Other Things (being) Equal
A condition in which only the specific variables under consideration change; all other variables remain constant.

Generally, economic theories are built on the assumption of **other things (being) equal:** all variables are assumed to remain unchanged except those variables specifically under consideration. For example, ski-lift operators may have developed a theory that, other things (being) equal, consumers will purchase more ski-lift tickets if their price is reduced. Assume the price of ski-lift tickets decreases from one year to the next, yet consumers purchase *fewer* tickets. Should the ski-lift operators discard their theory?

Think carefully. The number of tickets purchased depends on factors other than ticket price. Perhaps snowfall was considerably lighter the second year, so that there were fewer days to ski. In that event, the change in the number of tickets purchased reflected changes in both snowfall and ticket price. After all, the theory does not predict that a lower price will increase the number of tickets purchased regardless of snowfall. Rather, the theory claims that other things (being) equal, including snowfall, a lower price will spur the purchase of additional tickets. If snowfall changes, other things are *not* equal and a basic assumption of the theory is violated. A theory cannot be tested legitimately unless its assumptions are satisfied. Accordingly, if snowfall changes, ski-lift operators have no legitimate basis for rejecting their theory.

Correlation versus Causation

Abuse of the other-things-equal assumption is not the only hurdle to clear economic thinking; another is the concept of causality. Having uncovered a relationship between two or more variables, some read into this relationship more than is actually there.

Demographic data indicate that married men consistently have lower unemployment rates than single men of the same age and education. Does this mean that marriage *causes* lower unemployment in men? Put another way, is a lower unemployment rate the direct consequence of being married? One could argue that the responsibilities of marriage cause workers to search harder for jobs and to hold on to jobs that single men might walk away from. In that event, marriage would indeed lead to a lower unemployment rate. But this is not the only feasible explanation for the statistical correlation (or association) between marriage and unemployment.

An alternative view is that married men and single men tend to differ in characteristics other than marriage. According to this scenario, unemployment differences result from these differences, not from marriage. Some men have poor health; others are emotionally unstable, irresponsible, and poorly adjusted. Such men are less likely to be married and more likely to be unemployed. The same characteristics that *turn off* women also *turn off* employers. If true, the difference in unemployment rates between married men and single men has nothing to do with marriage per se but instead is the consequence of poor health or personality quirks. Marital status and unemployment are correlated, but marital status has no impact on unemployment. We leave it to the reader to evaluate this theory. (It made little sense to the authors when they were single, but has become more appealing with time and family.)

The game of football can also help differentiate between correlation and causation. Each January the champions of the American Football Conference (AFC) and the National Football Conference (NFC) meet in the Super Bowl. A simplistic theory holds that a win by the NFC team causes the stock market to rise, whereas a win by the AFC team causes the stock market to fall.[3] What do the data show? Through 1988, 22 Super Bowl games had been played. For 20 of the 22 years the data actually support the theory—that is, the stock market advanced when the NFC team won and retreated when the AFC team won (Table 1-2, page 12). Undeniably, stock prices have been highly correlated with the outcome of the Super Bowl, but does anyone really believe that the Super Bowl *caused* the stock market to advance or decline? Sometimes two variables are correlated by chance: the fact that one event follows another does not necessarily mean that the first event caused the second.

The Fallacy of Composition

It is tempting to conclude that what is true for the individual is also true for the group. After all, the group simply consists of the individuals in it. But if this is your reasoning, you are guilty of the **fallacy of composition**. As an individual you may speak louder so others can hear you better. Does it therefore follow that when everyone in a room talks louder they can all be heard better? To the contrary, it is

Fallacy of Composition Falsely concluding that what is true for the individual must be true for the group.

[3]More precisely, the theory categorizes teams in terms of their original football conference. This means that the Pittsburgh Steelers and the Indianapolis (formerly Baltimore) Colts are classified as members of the NFC even though the teams have since moved to the AFC.

Table 1-2

IS THE SUPER BOWL RESPONSIBLE FOR SWINGS IN THE STOCK MARKET?

Year	Winning team	Original conference	Percentage change in stock market*
1967	Green Bay Packers	NFC	15.2
1968	Green Bay Packers	NFC	4.3
1969	New York Jets	AFC	−15.2
1970	Kansas City Chiefs	AFC	4.8
1971	Baltimore Colts	NFC**	6.1
1972	Dallas Cowboys	NFC	14.6
1973	Miami Dolphins	AFC	−16.6
1974	Miami Dolphins	AFC	−27.6
1975	Pittsburgh Steelers	NFC**	38.3
1976	Pittsburgh Steelers	NFC**	17.9
1977	Oakland Raiders	AFC	−17.3
1978	Dallas Cowboys	NFC	− 3.1
1979	Pittsburgh Steelers	NFC**	4.2
1980	Pittsburgh Steelers	NFC**	14.9
1981	Oakland Raiders	AFC	− 9.2
1982	San Francisco 49ers	NFC	19.6
1983	Washington Redskins	NFC	20.3
1984	Los Angeles Raiders	AFC	− 3.7
1985	San Francisco 49ers	NFC	27.7
1986	Chicago Bears	NFC	22.6
1987	New York Giants	NFC	2.3
1988	Washington Redskins	NFC	11.8

*From end of prior year as measured by the Dow-Jones Industrial Average.

**Now members of AFC.

According to a naive theory (first offered by a stockbroker), the stock market advances when a team from the (original) National Football Conference wins the Super Bowl and declines when a team from the American Football Conference wins. Although this theory enjoys an admirable track record, its success is attributable to chance.

Source: Adapted from Manufacturers Hanover Corporation, *Financial Digest* (January 16, 1987), p. 1. Updated by authors.

likely that each speaker simply drowns out the others. What is true for you as an individual, acting alone, does not hold true when everyone in the group does the same thing.

As a further example, consider an individual wheat farmer. The more wheat harvested by an individual farmer in a given year the larger the farmer's income. It does not follow, however, that aggregate income of wheat farmers increases whenever aggregate wheat production increases. An individual farmer produces such a miniscule share of the total wheat crop that the price of wheat received by the farmer can be taken as given. When the farmer produces twice as much wheat, the farmer's income from wheat doubles. But this is not true for wheat farmers as a group. Doubling the aggregate wheat crop causes wheat prices to plummet (unless the government intervenes to stabilize prices). If prices fall sufficiently, total income of wheat farmers may drop despite the higher volume of output.

WHY DO ECONOMISTS DISAGREE?

If economists are careful to avoid such pitfalls as the ones just discussed, then why do they disagree so often? According to an old saying, if all economists were placed end to end they still would not reach a conclusion. Actually, economists agree more than is commonly believed. According to one poll, 97 percent of economists agree that restricting trade between countries "reduces general economic welfare." And 98 percent conclude that limiting the ability of landlords to raise rents "reduces the quantity and quality of housing available."[4]

Disagreements, where they occur, sometimes arise because data fail to demonstrate convincingly the superiority of one theory. One data set may suggest that theory X is better, whereas other evidence favors theory Y. In such cases, disagreements among economists are not surprising. Fortunately, additional research sometimes leads to a consensus.

Differences also exist in the area of forecasts. A forecast can be thought of as a conditional statement: if event A occurs, event B will follow. Economic forecasts, however, often diverge because of differences in assumptions—for example, about whether or not event A will even occur. Two economists may agree that if the money supply grows 9 percent this year then prices will rise about 6 percent next year. Nonetheless, their predictions about inflation may differ markedly because one economist believes the money supply will grow 9 percent, whereas the other economist expects a much slower growth. Even a good model cannot forecast accurately when the assumptions on which it is based do not hold.

Certain disagreements among economists are attributable to differences in ideology. Some economists, like some noneconomists, are liberal; other economists are conservative. Liberals tend to have greater confidence than conservatives in the ability of government to solve problems. Therefore, it should come as no surprise that liberals tend to favor heavier doses of government intervention. If you hear two economists debate a proposal to scale back the size of government, realize that their differences arise not because economists cannot agree on how much government is optimal, but because conservatives and liberals cannot agree.

Normative versus Positive Economics

Normative Economics
Deals with value judgments.

Statements in **normative economics** cannot be tested—cannot be shown to be true or false. Instead, they reflect value judgments—subjective preferences of an individual. Because normative statements cannot be tested, they are not scientific. Examples of normative statements include: *spending on national defense should be increased* and *lotteries are a good way for a state to raise revenues.*

Positive Economics
Involves statements based on fact.

In contrast, statements in **positive economics** deal with facts. Such statements are either true or false. In principle they can be tested and, if not supported by the evidence, rejected. Factual statements about the past and predictions about the future both fall within the realm of positive economics. Examples include: *spending on national defense outpaced the inflation rate during President Reagan's Administration* and *a Kansas lottery, if enacted, would generate at least $50 million a year in revenue for the state.* Note that the second statement makes no claim about whether or not Kansas should have a lottery, only about what would occur if there were a lottery.

Economists, of course, sometimes make normative statements. If you are chairman of the Council of Economic Advisors, you cannot very well turn down the President's request that you develop a set of policy recommendations. If Dan Rather, with the cameras rolling, asks for an assessment of a tax proposal, he is likely to

---

[4]J. R. Kearl, C. L. Pope, G. C. Whiting, and L. T. Wimmer, "What Economists Think," *American Economic Review* (May 1979), p. 30.

receive an opinion. Most economics, however, focuses on positive economics—as does this book. This is where economists make their greatest contribution. By formulating and testing theories, economists provide valuable information to individuals, businesses, unions, politicians, and other interested groups. But once the facts are on the table, economists can no better determine optimal policy than informed noneconomists can.

Consider the case of unemployment insurance, a program in which workers who lose their jobs may qualify for weekly unemployment insurance (UI) benefits while they are out of work. Economic research has uncovered certain findings such as:

1. For many workers UI benefits replace more than one-half their lost wages.
2. Unemployed workers spend less time looking for a job if they are receiving UI benefits.
3. On average, the higher weekly UI benefits are, the longer a person remains unemployed.
4. The UI system causes employers to lay off more workers than they otherwise would.

These findings do not indicate whether the UI program is good or bad; they do not tell policymakers whether UI laws should be amended, repealed, or left as is. What economic research does is heighten political awareness of the consequences of UI laws. Armed with such information, legislators frequently adjust previously enacted laws. As one economist observed:

> The congressional staff personnel I interviewed, none of whom had formal training in economics, indicated that economic research provided part of the impetus for changing the UI program.[5]

MACROECONOMICS VERSUS MICROECONOMICS

Macroeconomics
The study of the aggregate economy.
Microeconomics
The study of the individual units that comprise the economy.
Gross National Product (GNP)
A measure of the total output of the economy.

Economics consists of two main branches: **macroeconomics** and **microeconomics.** Macroeconomics studies the big picture, the economy as a whole. Microeconomics focuses on smaller economic units, including consumers and business firms. If macroeconomics is the forest, microeconomics is the trees.

Consider production. Macroeconomics is concerned with aggregate output of the entire economy—what economists call **gross national product (GNP).** How fast is GNP growing? What can society do to promote more rapid growth in the future? If growth turns negative, so that less output is being produced this year than last year, what can be done to soften the blow and alleviate economic hardship? In contrast, microeconomics examines the amount of output produced by individual industries and by the companies within those industries. It also addresses the question of whether the price and the volume of an industry's output depend on the number of business firms producing that product. In other words, what difference does it make whether a single company or 1000 companies produce the product?

Output often flows across a country's borders. *Exports* are goods produced in one country but sold elsewhere. *Imports* are goods brought in from other countries. Macroeconomists compare the volume of exports and imports (Figure 1-3) and monitor how differences in the size of these flows affect the value of the U.S. dollar

[5]Daniel Hamermesh, "The Interaction Between Research and Policy: the Case of Unemployment Insurance," *American Economic Review* (May 1982), p. 240.

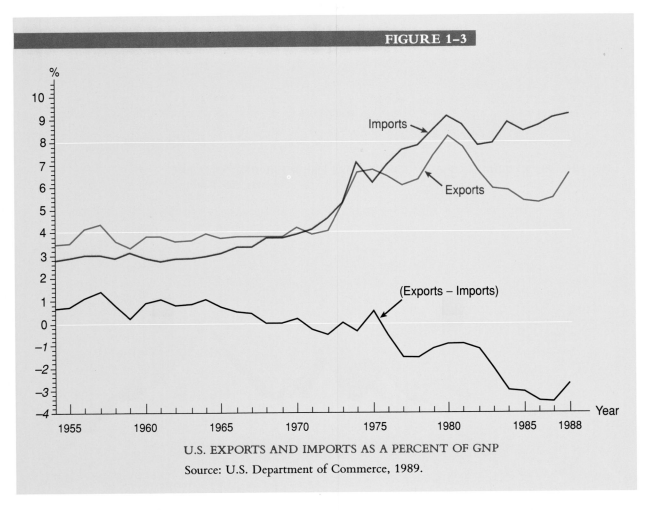

FIGURE 1–3

U.S. EXPORTS AND IMPORTS AS A PERCENT OF GNP
Source: U.S. Department of Commerce, 1989.

compared to foreign currencies. Of late, macroeconomists are examining why U.S. imports are so much greater than U.S. exports and analyzing the effect this has on the overall economy. Microeconomists focus on how trade restrictions affect particular groups and industries. For example, how do trade barriers affect employment of textile workers, income of farmers, or the standard of living of the average consumer? Similarly, in other fields of economics, macroeconomists study aggregate conditions while microeconomists focus on individual components.

WHAT DO ECONOMISTS DO?

Economists hold a variety of jobs. For example, macroeconomists may be employed to forecast economic activity over the coming year, to predict the effects of higher oil prices, to analyze the economic impact of tax reform. Some microeconomists forecast sales and profits for the company employing them. Others work for government agencies (e.g., advising a state commission on the rate a public utility should be allowed to charge for electricity). Still others work as consultants (e.g., helping a jury assess the economic loss a worker may have experienced from an injury or providing and interpreting evidence at a wage discrimination trial).

EXHIBIT 1–2

FORECASTING MACROECONOMIC VARIABLES

It is no secret that forecasts of the economy are fallible. As a nonexperimental social science, economics cannot achieve the degree of precision that physicists attain in measuring the speed of light or even the lower degree achieved by meteorologists in predicting tomorrow's precipitation. It is less widely understood that, despite several notable mistakes, economic forecasters have been able to predict some, though not all, important economic variables better than simple rules of thumb and that their accuracy seems to have increased over time.

A long period of time is required to assess whether forecasting accuracy has changed. The longest documented history of economic forecasts with which I am familiar is the real GNP forecasts issued each November by the University of Michigan.[6] The accompanying chart displays these forecasts along with the actual GNP results since 1952. The forecasting errors made since 1969 are smaller on average than those made before, even though the changes in real GNP growth have been greater. Improved forecast accuracy has also been found by Mervin Daub for forecasts of real GNP in Canada and by Sir Terence Burns for two year-ahead forecasts of both real growth and inflation rates in Britain.

A cynic might say that these errors are still too large, but an absolute standard is inappropriate for evaluating forecasts because levels of uncertainty vary over time. Small errors—more than half of which are less than one percentage point—are not a sign of great skill if other forecasts are even more accurate. The "huge" errors (more than a percentage point) made by the University of Michigan forecasters and shown in the chart (the recessions of 1974 and 1982 and the early recoveries in 1955 and 1959) might constitute brilliant forecasts if everyone else were even farther off the mark. The point is, that without any sensible absolute standard, forecast evaluation must be taken as relative. If no superior record can be established, describing these errors as too large simply expresses the wish that the future should be less uncertain.

---

[6]*Real GNP* measures output growth net of inflation—that is, after adjusting for price changes. An alternative measure, *nominal GNP,* is discussed in Chapter 9.

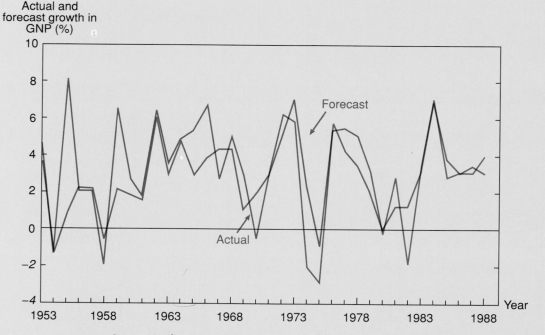

Sources: Stephen K. McNees, "The Accuracy Keeps Improving," *The New York Times,* January 10, 1988, p. F2. Data for chart from Stephen K. McNees, "How Accurate Are Macroeconomic Forecasts?" *New England Economic Review,* July/August, 1988, p. 16. Copyright © 1988 by The New York Times Company. Reprinted by permission.

Table 1-3
DISTRIBUTION OF ECONOMISTS BY EMPLOYER AND SALARY, 1982

Employer	Percent employed by	Median annual salary
Business and industry	49.7	$40,900
4-year colleges and universities	25.4	36,800
2-year colleges	2.9	29,600
Nonprofit organizations	2.9	46,600
Federal government	11.3	40,800
State government	1.8	28,800
Other*	6.0	60,900

*Includes those not reporting type of employer.

Source: National Science Foundation, *The 1982 Postcensal Survey of Scientists and Engineers,* Surveys of Science Resource Series (NSF 84-330), 1984.

As Table 1-3 indicates, about one-half of economists are employed in business and industry, working for such large corporations as General Electric and Citibank or for small businesses. Unlike many social sciences, economics offers substantial employment opportunities outside of teaching. Nevertheless, colleges and universities are the second-largest employer of economists, followed by the federal government. As might be expected, salaries vary by sector of employment (as well as by educational level and years of experience). Although salaries have risen since 1982—for the country at large average earnings have increased more than 30 percent—today's relative salaries are not substantially different from the pattern reported in Table 1-3. According to these numbers, academic jobs and state government pay the least.

SUMMARY

1. Economic resources consist of land, capital, and labor. Because these resources are limited, what society can produce is also limited; there are insufficient resources to satisfy all human wants.
2. Given resource scarcity, society must choose among alternatives: what to produce, how to produce it, and for whom. These issues are at the heart of economics.
3. When we choose one course we must forgo another. The opportunity cost of an action is what we give up to pursue our decision—that is, the best alternative to the choice we make.
4. Economists assume that economic decision makers behave rationally, that they choose purposefully in an attempt to achieve a given objective. For consumers the assumed goal is utility maximization; for producers it is profit maximization. In making choices, decision makers are assumed to compare the costs and benefits of a given action.
5. Marginal analysis is the study of change. In approaching economic problems, economists rely heavily on marginal analysis. Economic thinking also involves the principles of scarcity and choice, rational behavior, and the weighing of costs and benefits.
6. Economists construct theories to explain economic behavior and to predict economic events. A theory does not replicate the world precisely; instead, it simplifies, focusing on the most important relationships. A model is a formal version of a theory, often mathematical or graphical.
7. Economics relies on the scientific approach. After a theory is formulated, evidence is gathered to determine whether it is consistent with the theory. If not, the theory must be revised or rejected.
8. To interpret evidence correctly, one must avoid certain pitfalls. Remember that:
   a. A theory cannot be tested when its "other-things-equal" assumption is violated.

    b. Correlation does not imply causation.

    c. What is true for the individual is not necessarily true for the group.

9. Statements in normative economics reflect value judgments; statements in positive economics deal with facts. Only issues in positive economics can be tested. Therefore, only positive economics is scientific.

10. Economics consists of two main branches. Macroeconomics focuses on the aggregate economy, analyzing such issues as inflation and the overall growth rate of the economy. Microeconomics focuses on smaller units of the economy, such as individual business firms and consumers.

KEY TERMS

resources	hypothesis
land	inflation rate
capital	scientific method
labor	model
entrepreneur	other things (being) equal
economic good	fallacy of composition
free good	normative economics
scarcity	positive economics
opportunity cost	macroeconomics
rational behavior	microeconomics
marginal analysis	gross national product (GNP)
theory	

STUDY QUESTIONS AND PROBLEMS

1. Which of the following are scarce economic resources?

    a. a bank teller   f. a library

    b. fertilizer   g. a telephone

    c. air   h. a lake

    d. a baseball game   i. an ice cream cone

    e. an ax

2. Are the following arguments legitimate? If not, indicate the source of the error.

    a. Because I washed my car yesterday, it rained today.

    b. If I leave the concert 10 minutes before it ends, I can avoid the traffic. If the entire audience leaves 10 minutes early, we can all avoid the traffic.

    c. Consumers purchased fewer Cabbage Patch dolls in 1989 than in 1985 despite the lower 1989 price. This proves consumers are insensitive to price.

    d. A former coach of the Boston Celtics used to light a cigar in the closing minutes of a game if his team was well ahead. After the cigar was lit, the Celtics always won. Lighting the cigar assured victory.

    e. With record output this year, farmers are assured their highest income ever.

3. An agronomist developed a new strain of corn. To test his claim that its yield exceeds that of an older strain, he conducted the following experiment. He planted the new corn in rich soil, fertilized liberally, and watered as needed. He planted the older corn in heavy, clay soil, which he neither watered nor fertilized. The yield for his new strain of corn was 20 percent higher. Has the agronomist demonstrated that the new corn has a higher yield? Explain.

4. (a) Assume the stock you purchase in a company later becomes worthless. Does this imply that your initial purchase was irrational? Explain. (b) Assume an insurance agent offers you the opportunity to purchase either $20,000 or $30,000 of life insurance. The two policies

are identical except for the level of coverage. If both cost $200 per year, is it rational to purchase the $20,000 policy? Explain.

5. "Economics cannot be scientific as long as economists have differing views of what is good and bad." Do you agree? Why or why not?

6. Which of the following are statements in normative economics? Which are statements in positive economics?
   a. The President's economic policies make good sense.
   b. Unemployment is a more serious problem than inflation.
   c. The United States exported a larger share of its output last year than did Canada.
   d. Other things equal, if the price of housing falls more people will buy houses.
   e. There are more farmers in the United States today than 100 years ago.
   f. Poverty in the United States should be reduced.
   g. Inflation next year will be higher in Italy than in Spain.

7. (a) Does the economic cost of attending college include more than tuition and other direct expenses? What else might a student forego? (b) Tuition and fees at a state university are $4000 per year. If Amy starts college this year she must quit her $35,000-per-year job as a computer programmer. If Sam starts he loses the $12,000 he would earn as a farm worker. From an economic perspective, is the cost of attending college the same for Amy as for Sam?

8. "Economic forecasts are rarely on target. Therefore, economists should stop forecasting." Do you agree? Defend your answer. Why do businesses and governments pay for forecasts that might be wrong?

ANSWERS TO YOUR TURN

POVERTY

Poverty and scarcity are different concepts. Scarcity exists because there are insufficient resources to satisfy all human wants. Even if poverty were eliminated, scarcity would remain. Although everyone might be guaranteed a minimally acceptable standard of living, society still would have inadequate resources to produce everything desired.

ANSWERS TO YOUR TURN

RESPONDING TO INCENTIVES

(a) Anything that reduces the perceived benefits of smoking or increases its perceived costs can be expected to reduce the level of smoking. The Surgeon General has attempted to alter perceived costs through public announcements that cigarette smoking harms the health of smokers, their families, and even babies born to pregnant smokers. Federal and state governments have increased the cost of smoking by subjecting cigarettes to federal and state taxes. Even employers have altered incentives by paying employees to stop smoking and by forcing those who do smoke to leave the workplace before "lighting up." (b) More people will enter the nursing profession if the benefits of becoming a nurse increase (e.g., because of higher pay for nurses) or if the costs of becoming a nurse decrease (e.g., because of scholarships).

SELECTED REFERENCES

Gary S. Becker, *The Economic Approach to Human Behavior* (Chicago: University of Chicago Press, 1976), Chapter 1.

Kenneth E. Boulding, *Economics as a Science* (New York: McGraw-Hill, 1970).

Milton Friedman, *Essays in Positive Economics* (Chicago: University of Chicago Press, 1953).

Joan V. Robinson, *Introduction to the Theory of Employment*, 2d ed. (London: Macmillan, 1969), Chapter 13.

APPENDIX 1A

USE OF GRAPHS IN ECONOMICS— A PICTURE IS WORTH A THOUSAND WORDS

Interpreting graphs is essential to the process of learning economics. Because modern economics is a quantitative discipline, much of economic analysis involves examining relationships among variables. A graph can be defined as a visual mechanism for illustrating the quantitative relationship between two variables. This book contains hundreds of graphs, and facility in interpreting the graphs inevitably benefits your progress in this course. Beyond that, you will encounter a multitude of graphs in other college courses, in your professional career, and during your leisure as you read journals and newspapers.

Graphs are often more efficient than words or tables in that they display a relatively large amount of data with precision and often more easily facilitate interpretation of that data. A good graph illuminates key facts and casts important relationships into sharp relief. Thus, a good graph is an excellent learning device; a bad graph confuses and misleads.

In Appendix 1A we outline certain key aspects of graphs as they pertain to economics and cover two types of graphs commonly used in economics. In addition, we offer some tips for getting the most from graphs and we caution against certain important pitfalls in interpreting them.

Two types of graphs pervade economic analysis in general and this book in particular: two-variable graphs and time-series graphs. You will undoubtedly recognize both types of graphs from previous work in high school or college—especially in mathematics, physical sciences, and social sciences.

TWO-VARIABLE GRAPHS

As its name implies, a two-variable graph illustrates the relationship between two variables. Frequently one variable (**dependent variable**) moves *in response to* or *because of* changes in another variable (**independent variable**).

Dependent Variable
Variable whose behavior depends upon, or moves in response to, some other variable (independent variable).

Independent Variable
Variable that causes or influences the behavior of some other variable (dependent variable).

The horizontal axis of a graph is the *x-axis;* the vertical axis is the *y-axis.* These axes meet perpendicularly at the **origin.** In mathematics, convention displays the independent variable on the horizontal axis (*x*-axis) and the dependent variable on the vertical axis (*y*-axis). (Economists occasionally ignore this convention, thereby confusing students.)

Origin
The point where the two axes of a graph meet. At the origin, both variables equal zero.

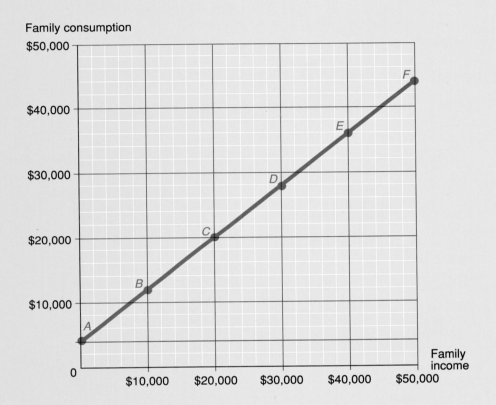

FIGURE 1A–1

RELATIONSHIP BETWEEN FAMILY INCOME AND FAMILY CONSUMPTION SPENDING

Family consumption expenditures depend on family income. The consumption function graph indicates the nature of this relationship. For example, as family income rises from $20,000 to $30,000, family consumption increases from $20,000 to $28,000 (points *C* and *D*).

Source: Table 1A-1 (hypothetical data).

To illustrate construction of a typical two-variable graph in economics, consider the data in Table 1A-1 (page 22), which indicate the relationship between income and consumption spending for different families.

Figure 1A-1 graphically illustrates the consumption-function data given in Table 1A-1—the relationship between family income and family consumption spending. Family income, the independent variable, is measured along the *x*-axis. Family consumption, the dependent variable, is measured along the *y*-axis. Changes in family income induce changes in family expenditures on consumer goods. Each point (*A, B, C, D, E, F*) on the graph depicts one income-consumption observation given in Table 1A-1. Join-

Table 1A-1

FAMILY INCOME AND CONSUMPTION
PATTERNS

Family income	Family consumption
0	$ 4,000
$10,000	$12,000
$20,000	$20,000
$30,000	$28,000
$40,000	$36,000
$50,000	$44,000

ing these points by a straight line forms the consumption function. Point A ($4000) is the *y-intercept*—the magnitude of *y* (consumption) when *x* (family income) is zero.[1]

Occasionally in economics the axes for the dependent and independent variables are reversed. An example is the *demand curve*—the relationship between the price of a good and the quantity consumers would like to purchase. A hypothetical demand curve for grapefruit is shown in Figure 1A-2. In the case of a demand curve, quantity demanded of an item depends upon its price. The price, shown on the *vertical axis,* is the independent variable. Quantity demanded is shown on the horizontal axis. Changes in price bring about changes in quantity demanded (dependent variable).

In some instances a relationship may be depicted wherein it is unclear which variable is the independent variable and which is the dependent variable. Many variables in economics are *interdependent*—causation goes both ways. For example, a strong economy might lead to rising stock prices, but a rising stock market might also stimulate economic activity. Two variables may affect, and be affected by, each other. A graph or diagram may illustrate a relationship between two variables without implying any direction of causation.

Movement Along a Relationship versus Shift in the Relationship

It is important to recognize that a two-variable diagram in economics is constructed under the as-

sumption of *ceteris paribus*—other things (being) equal. For example, consider the consumption function in Figure 1A-1. The figure shows the relationship between family income and family consumption, *assuming that all other factors besides family income that influence family consumption remain unchanged.* If any of these other factors change, the entire relationship between family income and family consumption changes. The relationship *shifts.* As an example, family consumption is influenced by attitudes toward thrift and by several other factors in addition to family income. Assume that when families become more concerned about their future well being, they become more thrifty. Such families spend less on consumer goods at each income level in order to save and provide for the future. Accordingly, the entire income-consumption relationship in Figure 1A-1 shifts downward.

Consider also Figure 1A-2. In reality, many factors besides the price of grapefruit influence the quantity of grapefruit demanded. The nation's population and level of per-capita income are obvious examples. The demand curve for grapefruit in Figure 1A-2 is constructed under the assumption that population and per-capita income remain constant. However, assume that both per-capita income and population increase in the next year. Accordingly, the position of the demand curve in Figure 1A-2 shifts rightward or upward. In other words, more grapefruit is demanded at each and every price level.

Positive and Negative Relationships in Two-Variable Graphs

Economic relationships are typically either positive or negative in nature. When an increase in one variable is associated with an increase in the other, the variables are said to be *positively* or *directly* related. An example is the consumption function in Figure 1A-1. An increase in family income gives rise to an increase in family consumption; thus family consumption is directly or positively related to family income. When an increase in one variable is associated with a decrease in the other variable, the variables are *negatively* or *inversely* related. An example is the demand curve in Figure 1A-2. An increase in the price of grapefruit leads to a decrease in the quantity demanded; thus price and quantity demanded are negatively or inversely related.

A substantial part of economics concerns the discovery of independent variables that cause fluctua-

[1]A straight line can be described by the equation $y = a + bx$, where *y* is the dependent variable, *x* is the independent variable, *b* is the slope, and *a* is the *y*-intercept (the magnitude of *y* when *x* is zero). The data in Table 1A-1 and Figure 1A-1 may be expressed in equation form as $y = $4000 + 0.8x$, where *y* is family consumption and *x* is family income.

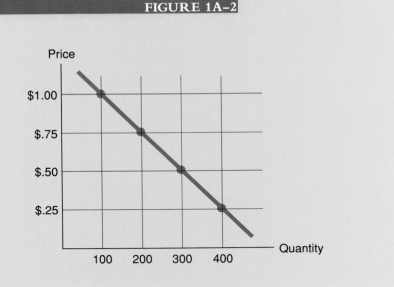

FIGURE 1A–2

DEMAND CURVE FOR GRAPEFRUIT

The demand curve for grapefruit shows the quantity of grapefruit that consumers would purchase at each price. In this instance, the independent variable (price) is measured along the vertical axis, whereas the dependent variable (quantity demanded) is measured along the horizontal axis. If the price of grapefruit were to fall from $1.00 to $0.50, quantity demanded would increase from 100 to 300.

---

tions in key dependent variables. For example, economists attempt to find the determinants of birthrates, immigration patterns, exchange-rate movements, and housing starts. In fact, economists usually go beyond simply finding the appropriate independent variable(s) to explain key phenomena; they also attempt to pin down the approximate quantitative nature of the relationship. This brings us to the important concept of the *slope* of a graph.

The Slope of a Graph

A graph may be either linear (straight-line) or nonlinear (curvilinear). In either case, the slope provides quantitative information about the nature of the relationship. Slope shows *how much* one variable changes in response to a one-unit change in the other variable. Specifically, slope is the ratio of the vertical change to the horizontal change on the graph.

$$\text{slope} = \frac{\text{rise}}{\text{run}} = \frac{\Delta y}{\Delta x} \text{ where } \Delta \text{ means } change\ in$$

$$\frac{\Delta y}{\Delta x} = \frac{y_2 - y_1}{x_2 - x_1}$$

Slope indicates the change in y (vertical axis) divided by the change in x (horizontal axis).

Slope
The ratio of the vertical change to the corresponding horizontal change as we move left to right along the line (i.e., the ratio of the *rise* to the *run*).

Slope of a Linear Relationship

The consumption-function example illustrates slope in a linear relationship, such as Figure 1A-3 (page 24) where the slope is constant at all points along the line. To measure slope in this instance, simply choose any two points along the line, measure the rise and the run, and compute their ratio. In Figure 1A-3 we see that as family income increases from $10,000 to $20,000, family consumption increases from $12,000 to $20,000. Hence, the *rise* or increase in consumption (ΔC) = $8000 and the *run* or increase in income (ΔY) = $10,000. The slope = $\Delta C / \Delta Y$ = $8000/$10,000 = 0.80. Each one-dollar increase in income induces the family to increase consumption by 80 cents. Note that the slope is positive in this example because the variables are directly or positively related.

Slope may be positive, negative, zero, or infinite; Figure 1A-4 provides examples of each. Remembering that slope = rise/run or $\Delta y/\Delta x$, you can confirm each slope category shown in Figure 1A-4 (page 24). In (a) the two variables vary directly or positively; hence, an increase in x gives rise to an increase in y. Because Δy and Δx are both positive as you move left to right along the line, so too is their ratio (the slope). In Figure 1A-4(b) the variables are negatively or inversely related; hence, an increase in x leads to a decrease in y. Because Δy and Δx are of opposite signs, their ratio (slope) is negative. In Figure 1A-4(c), y is

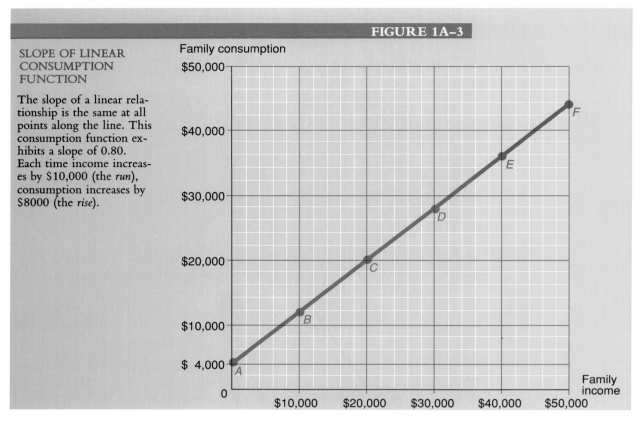

FIGURE 1A-3

SLOPE OF LINEAR CONSUMPTION FUNCTION

The slope of a linear relationship is the same at all points along the line. This consumption function exhibits a slope of 0.80. Each time income increases by $10,000 (the *run*), consumption increases by $8000 (the *rise*).

constant irrespective of x; hence, whenever x changes y remains unchanged. The slope is $\Delta y/\Delta x = 0/\Delta x =$ zero. In Figure 1A-4(d) x never changes—Δx is always zero. Therefore, the slope of the line is $\Delta y/\Delta x = \Delta y/0$, which is undefined or infinity. You encounter each of these four relationships in the study of economics.

A Ray Through the Origin

There is a straight line of special significance in economics that has a y-intercept of zero. This line is

termed a "ray through the origin" or simply a "ray." Figure 1A-5 illustrates four rays of differing slopes.

Ray
A straight line of any slope that emanates from the origin. A straight line with a y-intercept of zero.

Given the grid on which the four *rays* of Figure 1A-5 are drawn, you can confirm the slope of each ray. Of particular significance in economics is the ray of slope = 1. Because this line has a slope of one and passes through the origin, it depicts the set of points

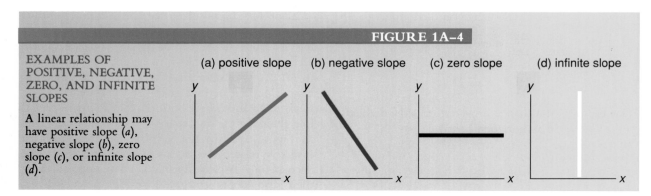

FIGURE 1A-4

EXAMPLES OF POSITIVE, NEGATIVE, ZERO, AND INFINITE SLOPES

A linear relationship may have positive slope (*a*), negative slope (*b*), zero slope (*c*), or infinite slope (*d*).

(a) positive slope   (b) negative slope   (c) zero slope   (d) infinite slope

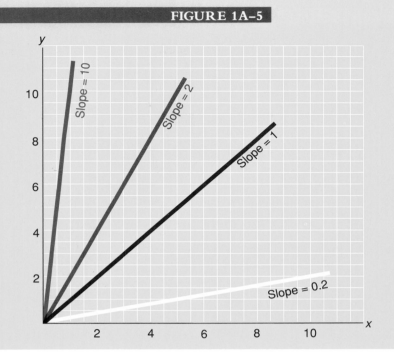

FIGURE 1A–5

FOUR RAYS AND THEIR SLOPES

A ray is a straight line that begins at the origin. It may have any slope. Of special usefulness in economics is the 45-degree line—a ray with slope of plus 1. This line marks off all points at which the variables on the x- and y-axes have the same values (assuming both variables are measured in the same units). The 45-degree line is often used as a guideline or reference line.

at which x and y are equal. The ray of slope = 1 is a 45-degree line emanating from the origin. Any point lying above this ray indicates that y exceeds x; any point lying below the ray indicates that y is less than x. Any point on the 45-degree line indicates that y and x are equal. Accordingly, the ray of slope = 1 is commonly used in graphs as a guideline or line of equality of the two variables.

45-Degree Line
A ray with slope of (positive) one. It indicates points where the two variables have equal values if both variables are measured in the same units.

Slope of a Nonlinear Relationship

Calculating the slope of a curvilinear relationship (a curved line) is more complex. The slope of such a relationship, unlike a linear one, changes as you move along the curve. This is illustrated in Figure 1A-6 (page 26).

To measure the slope of a curve at some particular point, construct a straight-line *tangent* to the curve at that point. A tangent is the unique line that *touches but does not intersect* the curve. Then measure the slope of the straight-line tangent by calculating the rise/run of the tangent. In Figure 1A-6, the line drawn tangent

to the curve at point A exhibits a rise/run of 3/2 or 1.5; the slope of the curve at point A is therefore 1.5. At points B and D, the tangents are horizontal; therefore, the slope of the curve is zero at each of these points.[2] Can you confirm that the slope of the curve at point C is negative 1?

What to Do When You See a Two-Variable Graph

When you encounter a two-variable graph in economics, it is important to adopt an active mode of thinking. When you do, the graph substantially facilitates your understanding of the material under discussion. Try proceeding in the following manner:

1. Immediately look at the variables given on the horizontal and vertical axes and briefly consider the nature of the relationship portrayed. Is the relationship positive (direct) or negative (inverse)? Is it linear or nonlinear?

2. Consider the probable causation involved, if any. Using intuition, does it seem plausible that

---

[2]Whenever a curve changes from a positive to a negative slope or vice versa, it must experience a zero slope. Whenever a curve experiences a *maximum* or *minimum*, its slope at such points is zero.

FIGURE 1A–6

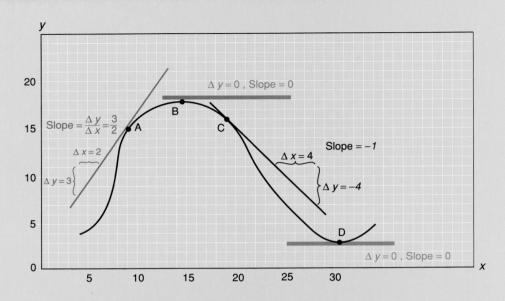

SLOPE OF A CURVE

The slope of a curve changes as you move along the curve. At any point on the curve, the slope of the curve is the slope of the *tangent* drawn to the curve at that point. Hence, the slope of Figure 1A-6 at point *A* is the slope of the line drawn tangent at point *A*. Note that this slope is rise/run or $\Delta y/\Delta x$ or 3/2 = 1.5

a. the variable on the horizontal axis influences the variable on the vertical axis?

b. the variable on the vertical axis influences the variable on the horizontal axis?

c. causation is running both ways—the variables are interdependent?

d. there is no causation involved—the variables are related only by chance?

3. Think about the *slope* of the graph. What is the *economic interpretation* of this slope?

4. Put the graph into words that explain precisely what the graph tells you.

5. Remember that a two-variable graph, like an economic model, *abstracts from reality*—it isolates the relationship between two variables *while all other factors are conceptually held constant.* Can you think of one such factor that, if changed, would alter the entire *position* of the relationship depicted in the graph?

TIME-SERIES GRAPHS

A time-series graph simply plots the behavior of an important variable over time. Units of time (e.g., years or months) are shown on the horizontal axis; the

YOUR TURN   ANALYZING A GRAPH: THE LAFFER CURVE

Given the graph in Figure 1A-7, known as a Laffer Curve, respond in writing to the preceding five suggestions.

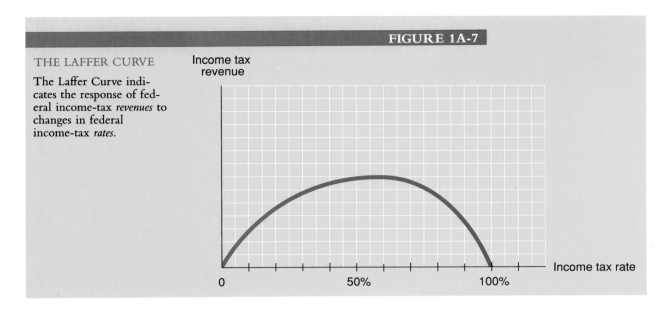

FIGURE 1A-7

THE LAFFER CURVE

The Laffer Curve indicates the response of federal income-tax *revenues* to changes in federal income-tax *rates*.

other variable is shown on the vertical axis. Figure 1A-8 is an example of a time-series graph, illustrating the course of the nation's annual unemployment rate from 1900 to 1988.

Time-Series Graph

Shows how a particular variable changes over time.

Time-series graphs are very informative because they efficiently convey historical information about a particular variable. In Figure 1A-8, the behavior of the U.S. unemployment rate since 1900 tells us a lot about our economic history. Note, for example, what happened to the unemployment rate in the 1930s.

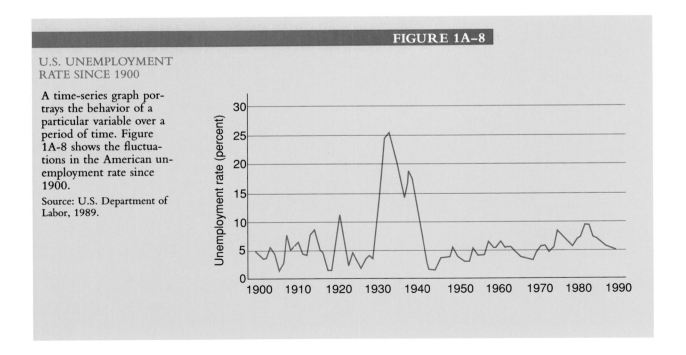

FIGURE 1A–8

U.S. UNEMPLOYMENT RATE SINCE 1900

A time-series graph portrays the behavior of a particular variable over a period of time. Figure 1A-8 shows the fluctuations in the American unemployment rate since 1900.

Source: U.S. Department of Labor, 1989.

This period, the "Great Depression," was a time of severe economic hardship.

PITFALLS IN INTERPRETING GRAPHS

When properly used, a graph is an efficient and effective means of conveying information. However, graphs can be used to distort facts and sometimes even to consciously misinform.[3] Candidates for political office, advertisers, and others have been known to deliberately mislead by manipulating graphs. Moreover, researchers may inadvertently mislead themselves as well as their readers by the faulty construction of a graph.

Because it is essential to be able to correctly interpret the information conveyed in a graph, we now warn readers of certain perils involved in reading graphs.

Steepness of a Graph and Choice of Units

The appearance of a graph may be altered dramatically at the discretion of the person constructing the graph by simply changing the units on the axes. For this reason, the apparent steepness of the rise or fall of a graphical relationship is not always a reliable indicator of the strength of the relationship between the two variables. Consider the factual information provided in Table 1A-2.

Table 1A-2 gives the level of the nation's consumer price index (CPI) and the nation's real output (real GNP) during each year from 1981 to 1987. The CPI

Table 1A-2

BEHAVIOR OF CPI AND REAL GNP, 1981–1987

Year	CPI	Real GNP ($)
1981	90.9	$3249
1982	96.5	3166
1983	99.6	3279
1984	103.9	3501
1985	107.6	3608
1986	109.6	3713
1987	113.6	3821

Source: *Economic Indicators,* U.S. Government Printing Office, 1988.

[3]For more on this, see Darrell Huff and Irving Geis, *How to Lie with Statistics* (New York: Norton, 1954).

measures changes in the general level of prices, whereas real GNP measures the value of the nation's annual output adjusted for changes in the price level. Growth in real GNP is highly desirable because it normally indicates there are more jobs and income available. On the other hand, rising prices are undesirable because they imply that each dollar of income purchases fewer goods and services. People love higher incomes and hate higher prices.

In the 1988 U.S. presidential campaign, Michael Dukakis (Democrat) ran against George Bush (Republican). Bush had been vice-president during the 1980s in the Reagan Administration. As the candidate of the incumbent party, Bush had a natural incentive to portray a "glowing" picture of the nation's economic performance during the 1980s. Dukakis, the challenger, had a natural incentive to portray the economic performance as "less than glowing." Here's how the Bush and Dukakis campaign staffs might hypothetically have portrayed the identical data from Table 1A-2 to support their own agendas (Figure 1A-9).

The Bush campaign graphs, *at first glance,* appear to demonstrate outstanding economic performance—a quite modest increase in prices and a robust expansion (except for the 1982 recession) in the nation's output. The Dukakis graphs appear to show just the opposite results—a sharp increase in the consumer price index and rather anemic growth in real GNP. Neither side cheated or fudged the data in Table 1A-2. All each side did was construct the scales on the vertical axes of the two graphs in a manner conducive to convincing naive or unsophisticated viewers as to the validity of the case they were attempting to portray. The moral: Look carefully at the gradation on the axes before drawing inferences about the magnitude of the change of a variable over time or about the strength of the relationship between two variables.

Interpreting Growth Trends

Aggregative economic data are frequently characterized by growth over time. For example, the nation's population, price level, and level of real output or GNP all rise persistently over time. To obtain a useful perspective on time-series data over time, it is frequently helpful to look at a particular variable *relative to some other key relevant variable* in the economy. Instead of looking at the level of wages over time, economists typically look at *real* wages (wages adjust-

Bush

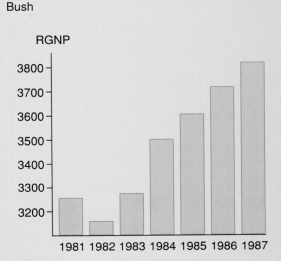

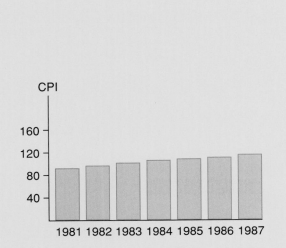

Dukakis

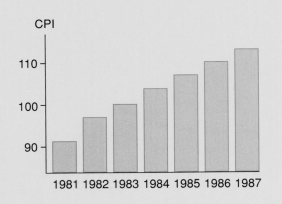

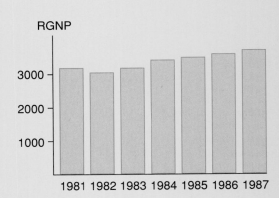

BUSH AND DUKAKIS GRAPHIC PORTRAYALS OF ECONOMIC
PERFORMANCE, 1981–1987

By changing the units along the vertical axis of a graph, the *apparent* relationship may
be altered dramatically. The Bush graphs *seem* to indicate a relatively stable price level
performance (CPI) and a strong economic growth performance (RGNP). The Dukakis
graphs *seem* to show the opposite. Actually, both candidates' graphs depict the same
information (i.e., the data of Table 1A-2). In interpreting a graph, always carefully note
the gradation of the units along the axes.

Source: Table 1A-2.

ed for changes in the price level). Instead of looking at real income in India, economists frequently look at real income *per capita*. Instead of looking at growth in the national debt, economists often look at growth in the debt *relative to the nation's GNP*.

Figure 1A-10 is a time-series graph that shows American defense spending since 1960, together with the percentage of the nation's gross income (GNP) spent on defense in the same period. An alarmist might use the top portion of the figure to emphasize the apparent *runaway growth* in defense spending. Indeed, defense spending increased by more than 500 percent during 1960-1988. However, this analysis neglects to mention that the nation's output (GNP) increased even faster during the same period. As a

result, the fraction of the nation's output allocated to defense was lower in the 1980s than in the 1960s, as indicated in the lower portion of Figure 1A-10.

One can frequently obtain a better perspective on the growth of a time-series variable by viewing its growth relative to a key macroeconomic indicator—dividing it by the nation's GNP or the price level, for example. Be careful in interpreting the meaning of a graph that merely plots the growth in the dollar value of a variable over time.

Distortion of Trend by Choice of the Time Period

Those who use data must constantly be wary of the potential distortion of the trend of time-series data by

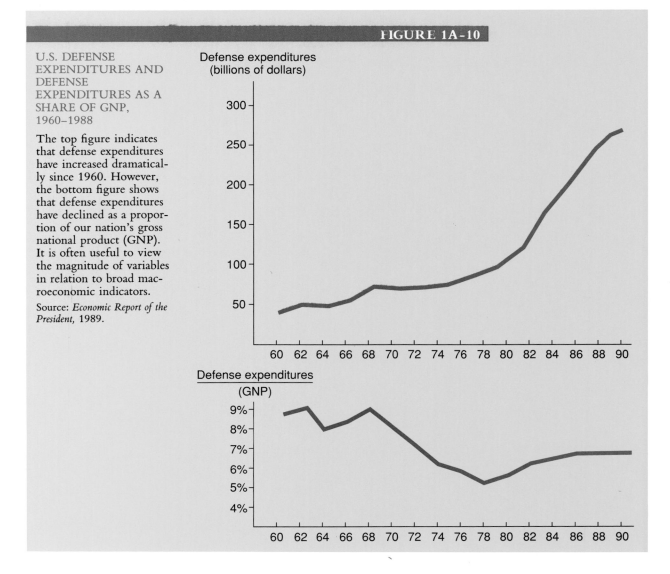

FIGURE 1A-10

U.S. DEFENSE EXPENDITURES AND DEFENSE EXPENDITURES AS A SHARE OF GNP, 1960–1988

The top figure indicates that defense expenditures have increased dramatically since 1960. However, the bottom figure shows that defense expenditures have declined as a proportion of our nation's gross national product (GNP). It is often useful to view the magnitude of variables in relation to broad macroeconomic indicators.

Source: *Economic Report of the President,* 1989.

the selection of the starting point or ending point in the series. The Dukakis supporter of 1988, in attempting to convince viewers of the *sluggish performance* of the U.S. economy during the 1980s, could begin the GNP graph at the point representing the previous peak or high point of the business cycle. A Bush supporter could best make the case for *robust growth* by beginning the GNP series at the low point of the business cycle.

Assume someone wants to make the case that common stocks are a poor investment. U.S. stock-market performance during the past 25 years is shown in Figure 1A-11. On October 19, 1987 the Dow-Jones Industrials average plummeted by a record-setting 509 points. One could begin the graph shortly prior to the crash and bring it up to the present. This graph would indicate a relatively weak performance of stock prices since mid-1987. Such a graph would

be misleading because the Dow-Jones Industrials average increased by more than 1500 points from 1982 until the 1987 crash. If one starts the graph in the early 1980s, the stock market's performance appears quite impressive for the decade in spite of the *Great Meltdown* of 1987. But that choice of starting point also distorts the facts and is misleading because the stock market did rather poorly during 1966-1982. In fact, the Dow-Jones Industrials average of stock prices was actually lower in 1982 than in late 1965— 17 years earlier.

To present time-series data objectively, it is usually best to show a long time span and to update the series to the most recent observations. In this way viewers may obtain an objective view of what actually happened. Portrayal of time-series data for a brief time span removes the data from historical context and runs the risk of misleading the viewer.

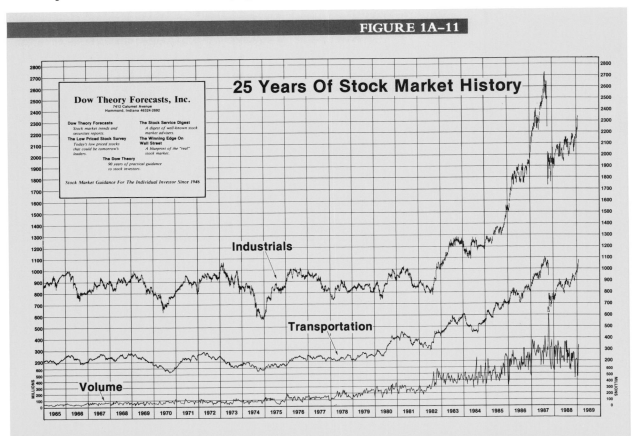

U.S. STOCK-MARKET PERFORMANCE FOR RECENT DECADES
(DOW-JONES AVERAGES)

Reprinted by permission of Dow Theory Forecasts, Inc.

**ANSWER TO
YOUR TURN**

ANALYZING A GRAPH: THE LAFFER CURVE

1. The Laffer Curve relates income-tax rates and income-tax revenues. The relationship is nonlinear. At tax rates from zero to about 60 percent, the relationship is direct or positive. At tax rates above 60 percent, the relationship is inverse or negative.
2. The income-tax rate is the independent variable and income-tax revenue, i.e., income-tax receipts, is the dependent variable. The direction of causation runs from the income-tax rate to the income-tax revenue. Changes in income-tax rates give rise to changes in income-tax revenue.
3. The slope reveals the additional tax revenue (positive or negative) per unit increase in the income-tax rate.
4. The graph tells us that with zero- or 100-percent income-tax rates, there is no income-tax revenue. As the income-tax rate increases from zero to about 60 percent, income-tax revenues increase. However, as the income-tax rate rises from 60 percent to 100 percent, income-tax revenues decline. Maximum income-tax revenues are generated when the income-tax rate is about 60 percent.
5. The Laffer Curve is drawn for a given point of time and therefore a given size of economy—a given national income or gross national product. If the nation's income rises, the Laffer Curve moves upward. However, zero- and 100-percent income-tax rates always yield zero income-tax revenue. So the Laffer Curve is likely to gradually *bow increasingly upward* over time as the economy grows.

CHAPTER 2

PRODUCTION POSSIBILITIES, TRADE, AND ECONOMIC SYSTEMS

We are the largest producers of shoes in the world. But if you come to Moscow you won't find a pair of decent shoes. . . . We are building new tractor factories. But we now produce 10 or 15 times more tractors than the United States. We don't need those tractors and they are still building new factories to produce more. That means we are using our capital to do the wrong things.[1]

—Soviet economist
STANISLAV MENSHIKOV

[1]Joel Kurtzman, "Is This the Second Russian Revolution?" *The New York Times,* May 29, 1988, p. 2F. Copyright © 1988 by The New York Times Company. Reprinted by permission.

[2]Robert Gillette, "Creaking Economy Needs More than a Little Repair," *Los Angeles Times,* reprinted in *Kansas City Times,* November 26, 1987, p. N–3.

As noted in Chapter 1, all countries must confront the fundamental economic problem—scarcity. Lacking sufficient resources to satisfy all wants, nations must decide what goods to produce, how to produce them, and for whom. Different countries, of course, rely on different economic systems to answer these questions.

In the Soviet Union, for example, government planners decided to produce large quantities of shoes and tractors. At the same time, citizens in many Soviet cities are limited to one kilogram (2.2 pounds) of meat each month and must wait an entire year for delivery of a television set. And even though shoes are plentiful, quality shoes are not: "From Riga to Vladivostock, shoppers wait for hours to snatch up the 100 million pairs of shoes the state buys abroad each year."[2]

Unlike in the Soviet system, in the United States most economic decisions are made in markets rather than in government ministries. Consumers, through spending, determine how much meat is produced and whether the quality of shoes is upgraded. Similarly, business firms, not government, generally determine how goods are produced.

Chapter 2 develops a model with which to analyze certain of the economic decisions facing a country and considers how different economic systems make these decisions—focusing on the U.S. and Soviet economies. Finally, Chapter 2 extends the discussion to include trade between countries. Just as the Soviet Union imports quality shoes from abroad, the United States imports various items from abroad. In turn, both countries export some of the output they produce. Why do countries trade? Does trade benefit both trading partners, or just one?

33

THE PRODUCTION POSSIBILITIES CURVE

Production Possibilities Curve
A line revealing the maximum combinations of two goods that can be produced with a given quantity of resources, assuming that technology is fixed.

Technology
The body of knowledge encompassing techniques for transforming resources into output.

The **production possibilities curve** is an example of a model. Underlying this model are the assumptions that the quantity of resources is fixed, the resources can be used to produce either of two goods, and the country's **technology** or technical expertise is constant. Under these conditions, the production possibilities curve indicates the maximum combinations of the two goods that can be produced with available resources. Figure 2-1 depicts a hypothetical production possibilities curve for tractors and corn. According to Figure 2-1, the hypothetical country can produce 50 tractors (if it devotes all its resources to this activity), 4 million bushels of corn (if it produces only corn), or intermediate combinations of tractors and corn (if it divides resources between these two products).

Note that the production possibilities curve is not perfectly realistic; the assumption that a country produces only corn and tractors is, of course, simplistic. Nevertheless, recall that abstraction and simplicity are the hallmarks of a model. A model is judged on how well it explains and predicts—and on such criteria the production possibilities curve must be judged a success. The production possibilities curve demonstrates such concepts as scarcity, efficient production, trade-offs, opportunity cost, the law of increasing costs, and economic growth.

Scarcity

The production possibilities curve is the boundary between feasible outcomes and nonfeasible outcomes. No matter how resources are used, the hypothetical country

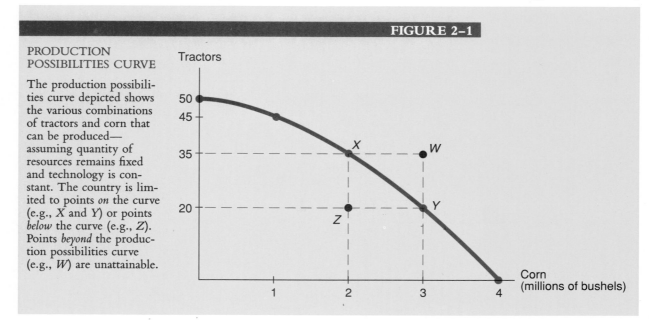

FIGURE 2–1

PRODUCTION POSSIBILITIES CURVE

The production possibilities curve depicted shows the various combinations of tractors and corn that can be produced—assuming quantity of resources remains fixed and technology is constant. The country is limited to points *on* the curve (e.g., *X* and *Y*) or points *below* the curve (e.g., *Z*). Points *beyond* the production possibilities curve (e.g., *W*) are unattainable.

cannot reach point *W* (Figure 2-1). If the country produces 3 million bushels of corn, its remaining resources are insufficient to produce 35 tractors. Given the country's limited resources, point *W* and all other points that lie beyond the production possibilities curve are unattainable. *Because of scarcity, a country is limited to points on or below its production possibilities curve.*

Efficient Production

Inefficient Production
Producing less than maximum output due to leaving resources idle or using them ineffectively.

Although points below the production possibilities curve are feasible (Figure 2-1), they are in some sense unattractive. In particular, the points signify **inefficient production.** Production is said to be *efficient* when a country achieves maximum output from its resources. Clearly, point *Z* is inefficient. If the country desires to produce 2 million bushels of corn, it can also produce 35 tractors. To produce only 20 tractors—which is what the country does when it operates at point *Z*—means that the country is not achieving maximum output from its resources. Either it has idle resources (e.g., unemployed workers and closed plants) or it is not putting its resources to their best use (e.g., farmers produce tractors while transportation workers grow corn). Only points on the production possibilities curve signify **efficient production.** Thus, *the production possibilities curve consists of all combinations of output that are both feasible and produced efficiently.*

Efficient Production
Achieving maximum feasible output from a given amount of resources.

Trade-Offs

If production is efficient, the only way a country can produce more of one good is to give up some of the other good. Efficient production means operating on the production possibilities curve—that is, gaining maximum output from a country's resources. Therefore, the only way a country can produce more of one good is to devote additional resources to that good. But this means that resources must be diverted from the other good and, in the process, production of the other good must fall. In other words, the country faces a trade-off: additional corn means fewer tractors and, conversely, more tractors mean less corn.

Opportunity Cost

The cost of additional corn is the number of tractors sacrificed to produce that corn (Figure 2-1). Consider what happens as the hypothetical country moves from point *X* on the production possibilities curve to point *Y*. Production of corn rises from 2 million bushels to 3 million while production of tractors falls from 35 units to 20 units. Therefore, the opportunity cost of the additional 1 million bushels of corn is 15 tractors.

The Law of Increasing Costs

Law of Increasing Costs
The hypothesis that the opportunity cost of a good rises as the quantity of the good produced increases.

Observe that the opportunity cost of one million bushels of corn depends on a country's location along its production possibilities curve. Starting at the upper-left corner (Figure 2-1), the cost of moving from no corn to 1 million bushels is 5 tractors (50 − 45). Once the country produces the first million bushels, the cost of a second million is 10 tractors (45 − 35) and, as we have just seen, the cost of a third million bushels is higher yet—15 tractors. In other words, the cost of producing additional corn rises as the country devotes additional resources to the production of this good. These events reflect a proposition in economics known as the **law of increasing costs.**

The law of increasing costs holds that the opportunity cost of a good increases as more of the good is produced. In other words, a country must give up ever-increasing amounts of one good to achieve a given increase in the other good. Diagrammatically, the law of increasing costs implies that the production possibilities curve assumes a *bowed* shape—that is, the curve becomes steeper as the country moves down the curve.

The law of increasing costs can be explained in terms of specialization of resources. In general, resources are not perfectly adaptable to the production of both goods. As a country increases its production of one good, it must divert resources from the production of the other good. At first the cost of doing so is relatively minor. For example, when a country produces relatively little corn, the only resources employed in this activity are resources that are very proficient at producing corn—prime farmland, experienced farmers, and agricultural equipment. However, as a country increases production of corn, it must employ resources that are relatively less suited for growing corn. Ultimately, a country must transfer to farming those resources most suitable for producing tractors—industrial sites, skilled transportation workers, and manufacturing equipment. As resources that are less and less proficient at producing corn are transferred to this activity, the number of tractors given up to produce additional one million bushels of corn rises. In other words, the opportunity cost of producing corn rises.

Nevertheless, production is not always subject to increasing costs. When resources are perfectly adaptable, production is characterized by *constant costs*. For example, assume resources are equally adept at producing tables and chairs. As Figure 2-2 illustrates, the production possibilities curve in this case is a straight line. The cost of producing another table is always two chairs—regardless of how many

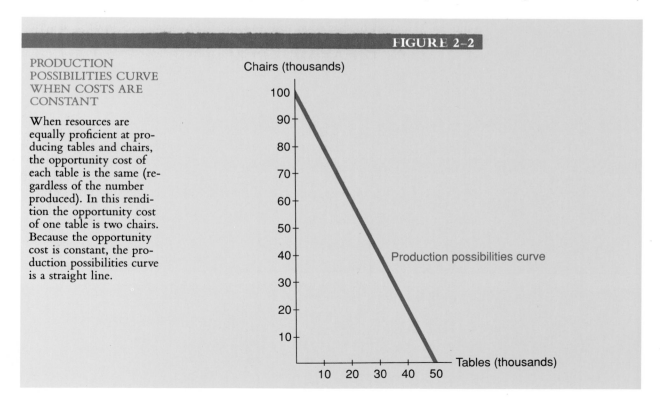

FIGURE 2-2

PRODUCTION POSSIBILITIES CURVE WHEN COSTS ARE CONSTANT

When resources are equally proficient at producing tables and chairs, the opportunity cost of each table is the same (regardless of the number produced). In this rendition the opportunity cost of one table is two chairs. Because the opportunity cost is constant, the production possibilities curve is a straight line.

tables are produced. Because the opportunity cost does not change, the slope of the production possibilities curve is constant.

Empirical evidence indicates that increasing costs, rather than constant costs, are the norm. Therefore, production possibilities curves are traditionally drawn with a bowed shape.

Shifting the Production Possibilities Curve

The production possibilities curve is drawn on the assumption that resources are fixed and technology is constant. But what happens when we relax these assumptions? If a country's resources or technology changes, so must its production possibilities curve. Because the amount of output a country can produce is limited by its resources, an increase in resources shifts the production possibilities curve outward. With additional resources a country can produce previously unattainable levels of output; this is illustrated in Figure 2-3(a).

A country's potential output is similarly constrained by available technology. If technological progress occurs, allowing a country to gain additional output from its resources, the result is again an increase (outward shift) in the production possibilities curve. That is, if technological advances increase productivity of resources by ten percent, it is possible to increase output by ten percent [Figure 2-3(a)].

In reality, technological progress tends to occur unevenly across sectors, so that gains from technology are similarly spread unevenly. Figure 2-3(b) illustrates a case where technological progress occurs in the production of corn (due, for example, to the development of a new high-yielding strain of corn). As a result, if the

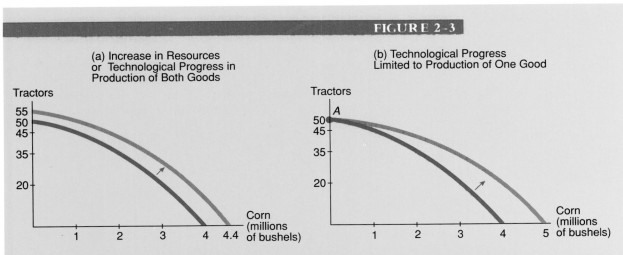

INCREASING A COUNTRY'S PRODUCTION POSSIBILITIES CURVE

A production possibilities curve shifts rightward when a country acquires additional resources or when technological progress allows a country to obtain increased output from existing resources (a). The special situation in which technological progress is limited to the production of corn is depicted in (b). Both the initial production possibilities curve and the new production possibilities curve share the common end point *A*, reflecting the fact that when resources are used solely to produce tractors the country does not benefit from the technological advance.

hypothetical country devotes all its resources to the production of corn, it can now produce 5 million bushels of corn, rather than 4 million. However, the new strain of corn does not increase the number of tractors that can be produced with a given amount of resources. Consequently, if the country chooses to produce only tractors, it is still limited to 50 tractors. Therefore, the production possibilities curve rotates outward, remaining anchored at point *A*.

YOUR TURN   TECHNOLOGICAL ADVANCES IN TRACTOR PRODUCTION
Assume technological progress occurs only in the production of tractors. (a) Draw a new production possibilities curve, indicating how it differs from the original production possibilities curve of Figure 2-3. (b) When a country initially produces both corn and tractors, does a technological advance in tractor production permit it to produce more tractors *and more corn*? Explain.

Economic Growth

Economic Growth
The ability of a country to produce greater levels of output—represented by an outward shift of its production possibilities curve.

An outward shift in the production possibilities curve represents **economic growth,** the ability of a country to increase its output. Because countries have been able to raise their standards of living through economic growth, not surprisingly they sometimes attempt to accelerate growth. But how can countries accomplish this?

The production possibilities model indicates that growth occurs when a country increases its resources or develops new technologies. Therefore, economic growth depends on the rate at which a country acquires additional resources and the speed of its technological progress. Both factors, in turn, depend on a country's current production decisions—that is, on how it uses its resources in the present period.

Capital Goods
Output used to produce other goods.
Consumer Goods
Output consumed directly, rather than used to produce other goods.

At this point in our discussion it is important to distinguish between *capital goods* and *consumer goods*. **Capital goods** are goods built in order to produce other goods and services. That is, capital goods—including factories, tools, and other equipment—contribute to *future* consumption. In contrast, **consumer goods**—such as food and clothing—are consumed directly. If a country is willing to defer consumption—to produce more capital goods and fewer consumer goods—it can accelerate economic growth. This is illustrated in Figure 2-4.

Because tractors represent a capital good and corn a consumer good, the mix of tractors and corn produced during this period determines production possibilities in the future (Figure 2-4). By increasing tractor production, a country adds to its stock of capital and therefore to its ability to produce additional output next period. For example, if a country operates at point *Y,* producing 20 tractors this year, its production possibilities curve expands only slightly (a). On the other hand, if it operates at point *X,* producing 35 tractors in the present year, its production possibilities curve shifts farther outward next period (b). In summary, *by increasing the ratio of capital goods to consumer goods a country accelerates economic growth.*

Economic growth also depends on the pace of technological progress, something that society can influence. Because technological progress derives from research and development, *an increase in the amount of resources committed to research and development permits more rapid economic growth.*

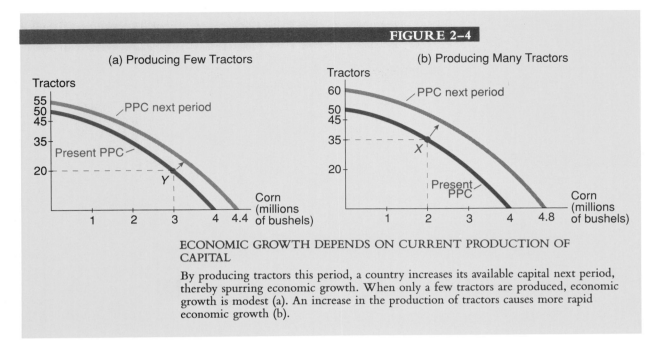

FIGURE 2-4

(a) Producing Few Tractors

(b) Producing Many Tractors

ECONOMIC GROWTH DEPENDS ON CURRENT PRODUCTION OF CAPITAL

By producing tractors this period, a country increases its available capital next period, thereby spurring economic growth. When only a few tractors are produced, economic growth is modest (a). An increase in the production of tractors causes more rapid economic growth (b).

Optimal Combination of Output

What quantities of tractors and corn should society produce? Would it be better off operating at point X on its production possibilities curve or at point Y (Figure 2-4)? Although point X permits more rapid economic growth, such growth carries a cost. In particular, the cost of operating at point X rather than at point Y is the additional one million bushels of corn that must be sacrificed this year. Therefore, the issue is whether society places a higher value on the additional 15 tractors or the additional million bushels of corn.

Alternatively, because the additional tractors permit additional consumption in the future, the issue can be recast in terms of the trade-off between present consumption and future consumption. How much additional corn must society receive in the future to induce it to forego consumption of one million bushels of corn in the present period? As important as this question is, the production possibilities curve cannot provide the answer—it contains no information about societal preferences. The production possibilities curve indicates which choices are available to society, but not how to make them. This is something society must decide for itself and, as Exhibit 2-1 (page 40) reveals, such decisions are sometimes difficult.

ALTERNATIVE ECONOMIC SYSTEMS

Each society must decide which combination of goods to produce—that is, where to operate on its production possibilities curve. In the process, it must choose how to produce such goods. When a country fails to use its resources efficiently, it is forced to a point beneath the production possibilities curve. Finally, each country must decide how to allocate these goods to the various members of its society—that is, who gets the output after it is produced?

EXHIBIT 2–1

TRADE-OFF
BETWEEN JOBS
AND FISH

Until it closed, a paper mill in Mechanic Falls, Maine, was the town's largest employer. Although the plant closing initially brought despair to the town's residents, the mood brightened after an employer was found who was willing to purchase and reopen the paper mill. But before the deal could be consummated, the prospective owner needed to obtain a waste-discharge license—and that proved to be a major obstacle.

The State Department of Environmental Protection and various private environmental groups opposed issuing a license on the grounds that the water discharged from the mill would warm the Little Androscoggin River, thereby reducing the river's population of brook trout. If the water discharges went unchecked, some claimed that all the trout would die. An alternative favored by environmentalists was to force the company to cool the water to its original temperature before returning it to the river, a costly procedure. If forced to do this, the would-be employer vowed that the mill would remain closed.

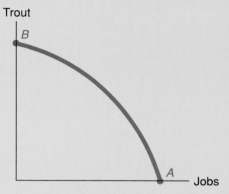

Other options included forcing the company to cool the water but not to the river's initial temperature. Less stringent cooling requirements would ease the financial burden on the company, allowing it to reopen the mill. As allowable water temperatures rose, the company would expand production, adding more and more jobs—but losses to the trout population would also mount. The production possibilities curve depicted illustrates the various options. Not surprisingly, different groups had different opinions regarding the optimal point on the production possibilities curve. Most town residents favored a point close to *A;* most environmental groups proposed operating near point *B*.

Source: Adapted from *The New York Times,* "120 Jobs May Rest on Effect on Fish," February 15, 1987, p. 15.

Economic System
An Institutional arrangement for determining what goods are produced, how they are produced, and for whom.

The way a society answers these questions depends on the **economic system** adopted by that country. Although there are different ways to categorize economic systems, one convention, at least for modern economies, is to define economic systems in terms of who owns the country's resources and how economic decisions are made. On this basis, two fundamental economic systems emerge: pure capitalism and the command economy.[3]

[3]Certain less developed countries rely on economic systems that emphasize tradition or heredity. Accordingly, when dealing with such countries it is often necessary to categorize economic systems using an alternative, more elaborate approach.

Pure Capitalism
An economic system in which property is privately owned and markets rather than central authorities coordinate economic decisions.

Market
A mechanism through which buyers and sellers are brought together for the purpose of exchanging some good or resource.

Command Economy
An economic system in which property is publicly owned and central authorities coordinate economic decisions.

Mixed Economy
An economic system that mixes pure capitalism and a command economy. Some resources are owned privately, others publicly. Some economic decisions are made in markets, others by central authorities.

Pure capitalism is characterized by private ownership of resources and by reliance on **markets,** in which buyers and sellers come together and determine what quantities of goods and resources are sold and at what price. Here no central authority oversees production and consumption. Rather, economic decisions are coordinated by the actions of large numbers of consumers and producers, each operating in his or her own self-interest. Because property is privately owned, it can be used in whatever manner its owner chooses.

At the opposite extreme, a **command economy** is an economic system in which resources are publicly (collectively) owned and where central authorities (government agencies) dictate how such resources are used. In particular, the questions of *what, how,* and *for whom* are answered through government planning. Production takes place in government-owned companies whose output decisions are determined as part of the government's central economic plan. Companies are assigned specific output goals and allocated a certain quantity of resources with which to carry out the goals. The output is then distributed in accordance with government objectives.

Both purely capitalistic and command economies are theoretical extremes, unobserved in reality. All modern economies are classified as **mixed economies;** they contain elements of both economic systems, differing only in terms of the extent to which resources are privately owned and the role accorded to markets. For example, even though the economy of the United States is highly capitalistic, some resources are publicly owned (national parks, highways, public schools). Similarly, despite heavy reliance on markets, the U.S. government makes certain economic decisions (determining the amount of resources devoted to national defense and ordering companies to reduce pollution). On the other hand, the Soviet economy—which approximates a command economy—exhibits certain capitalistic tendencies. Consider that Soviet farmers, although they spend most of their time producing for the state, are given small plots of land and permitted to sell the produce from that land in markets.

Because modern economic systems are hybrids of pure capitalism and a command economy, it is useful to understand how economic decisions are made under each of these theoretical systems. Actually, an appreciation of pure capitalism is essential for an understanding of the U.S. economy. Similarly, the Soviet economy—and the enormity of the economic problems confronting Soviet planners—cannot be comprehended until one understands the mechanics of a command economy. For this reason, we now consider how pure capitalism and a command economy answer the basic economic questions of *what, how,* and *for whom.* In the process, we illustrate how the mechanics of pure capitalism and of a command economy manifest themselves, respectively, in the American and Soviet economies.

How Capitalistic Economies Answer the Basic Economic Questions

Consumer Sovereignty
The principle that consumers, through spending decisions, determine how much of each good is produced.

A purely capitalistic system operates on the principle of **consumer sovereignty:** consumers determine which goods are produced and in what quantities. Consumers reveal preferences through their spending; in a sense, they vote with their dollars. Because companies are in business to make profit, they pay attention to what consumers want—to how they vote.

You see this happening frequently in the United States. When U.S. consumers decide they want more poultry and less beef, producers duly respond, raising more chickens and turkeys while reducing herd size. Similarly, when—in the face of rising energy rates—consumers indicate they want more-energy-efficient houses, builders construct such houses. The actual mechanism through which consumer preferences are revealed and output levels are determined is explained more fully in Chapters 3 and 4. But this much should be clear: in capitalistic economies, when it comes to determining what is produced, the consumer is king.

Although determining how to produce is the responsibility of individual firms, the market provides signals—rewarding firms that choose the best production techniques and penalizing those that do not. To maximize profit, a company must select the technique that minimizes the costs of producing a given output. Companies that waste resources or that use them inefficiently inflate costs and sacrifice profit. Companies that fail to cover costs lose money—the market's way of indicating that better alternatives exist for the resources. Thus capitalism promotes efficient production.

In a capitalistic economy, the distribution of output is based on the distribution of income. Those whose labor is valued highly or who own large quantities of property are able to purchase more goods and services than those receiving lower wages and owning less property. It all boils down to this: those willing and able to pay the market price obtain the output; those without sufficient income leave the market empty handed. Because resources are distributed unevenly and because market prices for labor and other resources vary greatly, the distribution of goods and services in a capitalistic economy is also highly uneven. In capitalistic-oriented countries, such as the United States, some dine on caviar and pheasant while others scavenge for scraps.

How Command Economies Answer the Basic Economic Questions

In a command economy, government agencies (central planners) replace the market as arbiter of economic decisions. The government decides which goods are produced, which state companies produce them, which production techniques are used, and how the output is distributed.

Those who favor this type of economic system argue that a command economy overcomes various deficiencies of a capitalistic economy. For example, central planners can ensure that everyone, even those unable to contribute to production, are provided adequate food and shelter. Central planners can also guarantee that goods vital to the nation, including national defense, are adequately provided.[4] In Chapter 3, where the capitalistic system is discussed in greater detail, we illustrate how private markets sometimes fail to produce as much of certain goods as society desires and how at other times they produce output in socially unacceptable ways. For example, market producers may use heavily polluting fuels because of their lower cost even though society prefers that producers use more-expensive but cleaner fuels.

However, even supporters of a command economy concede it is fraught with problems. For example, if the government does not arrange to have enough or the right size of bolts produced, companies that require bolts as an input cannot meet their production goals. In an effort to avoid such problems, the government must fashion a detailed economic plan that coordinates the production activities of all firms. With hundreds of thousands of companies and products, however, such coordination is difficult to achieve—mistakes are inevitable. For example, due to a lack of communication, Soviet repair crews undertook extensive rehabilitation and

---

[4]For a further discussion of the strengths of a command economy, see E. Wayne Nafziger, *The Economics of Developing Countries* (Belmont, CA: Wadsworth, 1984), pp. 453–54.

remodeling of an apartment complex just months before it was scheduled to be torn down. Similarly, Soviet planners have erred in deciding where to locate facilities by building factories in remote regions, far from workers and raw materials, and by constructing hydroelectric dams in regions that already had ample electricity.[5]

Another problem of command economies involves stipulating how production is to occur. Because central authorities are far removed from actual production sites, they are often less informed than plant managers and therefore may assign production techniques that fail to minimize costs. Inefficiencies arise for other reasons as well. Because managers and workers receive a bonus if their company meets its production goals, they have an incentive to request more resources from the state than they actually need. From their perspective, it is better to be on the safe side and be able to handle any emergency that may arise. But excess resources assigned to one enterprise are unavailable elsewhere, which reduces the amount of output the country can produce.

Indicative of such waste, some Soviet collective farms are given so much fertilizer that it lies unused in ever-growing hills. Other collective farms burn fertilizer to conceal from central authorities the fact that their allocation is more than they can use. At the same time, other farms are left without adequate fertilizer—since available stocks are fully distributed (the cupboard is bare).

Quality and variety of output also suffer in a command economy. Because state enterprises are not motivated by profit, there is little incentive to produce goods of the type and quality demanded by consumers. When a factory is ordered to produce 100,000 pairs of shoes, it is easier to meet this goal—thereby earning bonuses for the manager and workers—if the factory produces identical, low-quality shoes than if it sets rigorous quality-control standards and introduces a variety of styles and colors.

Compared to capitalism, command economies foster a more equal distribution of output, but the process by which output is distributed is more complex. While

[5]These and other examples of problems confronting Soviet planners are found in Robert G. Kaiser, *Russia* (New York: Simon & Schuster, 1976), Chapter 9.

capitalism relies on the price system to allocate—those who can pay the market price receive the goods—prices do not serve the same allocative function in a command economy, where prices are administered by the state and often bear scant relationship to the value consumers attach to additional units of a good. Frequently the amount consumers want to buy at the government-determined price exceeds the amount produced. Therefore, the government must resort to measures other than price rationing to distribute output.

Among such measures, the Soviet Union relies on queues. People line up to buy a product, and when available stocks are depleted those still in line are turned away. It has been estimated that Soviet families typically spend from 20 to 40 hours each week standing in line. In fact the appearance of a long line often attracts passing shoppers, who ask what is for sale only after securing a place in line. For other products there is a waiting list. For example, Soviet automobiles are so scarce that consumers must pay cash *up front,* forfeit choice of color, and still wait years for delivery. Families fortunate enough to obtain cars go to great lengths to protect them. Given shortages of auto parts, it is common for owners to lock windshield wipers and other removable parts inside their cars before parking them.

Aware of the problems inherent in command economies, the Soviet Union recently increased the role of market forces. The economic reforms instituted under Mikhail Gorbachev's *perestroika* (restructuring) program loosen the reins of Soviet central planners. In some cases, managers now make their own production decisions, choose which companies to buy inputs from, and even negotiate over input prices. The role of incentives is also greater, with workers' pay rising with increased output or cost savings and falling when quality is substandard. Finally, a 1987 law permits some Soviet citizens to become entrepreneurs—to set up their own private enterprises (Exhibit 2-2). It is important to remember, however, that most enterprises and resources are state-owned, that shortages continue, and that central planning still plays an important if reduced role. Thus, despite economic reforms under way, the Soviet economic system remains much closer to a command economy than to capitalism.

TRADE

International Trade
The exchange of goods or resources between countries.

Regardless of the economic system chosen, each country must decide how to use its resources. In the absence of international trade, each country is limited to points on its production possibilities curve. But what if two countries trade? Is it possible for each country to increase the amount of output available to its citizens? Can trade push a country beyond its production possibilities curve?

Why Countries Trade

Specialization
An arrangement in which persons or countries concentrate on the production of a limited number of goods or activities, rather than becoming self-sufficient.

Some consider trade to be a zero-sum game. According to this view, trade cannot create value: if one party benefits from trade, the other party must lose. In fact, the amount the first party gains must coincide exactly with the amount the second party loses.

This view is incorrect. Trade is often a positive-sum game in which both parties gain. For example, both the butcher and the baker may benefit when one trades meat to the other for bread. Although both parties may be able to bake bread and butcher meat, there are reasons for each to specialize in the production of just one good: one party may have a natural gift for baking bread, the other for

EXHIBIT 2–2

ECONOMIC REFORM OPENS THE DOOR FOR SOVIET ENTREPRENEURS

Woolen tights, and the first blush of economic reform in the Soviet Union, have changed Lydia Petrovna's life. Only a few months ago Petrovna, a 42-year-old mother of two, was working as a loom operator in a Moscow textile factory, bringing home a monthly salary of 100 rubles, about $160. Then, with little to lose but her poverty-level income, Petrovna decided to gamble on the success of Soviet leader Mikhail S. Gorbachev's program to reorganize, decentralize and modernize the Soviet economy.

With a 200-ruble membership fee in hand, Petrovna joined 19 other women at her factory in forming a cooperative—a form of semiprivate enterprise permitted under new legislation that the Soviet leadership hopes will breathe life and vigor into the nation's primitive consumer economy. In the new cooperative, sponsored by her factory but managed by the members themselves, Petrovna now works at home in her apartment on an imported Japanese knitting machine rented from the factory, turning out 70 pairs of woolen tights a month. For each pair of tights, a Soviet version of cold-weather pantyhose, she gets 4.5 rubles. The cooperative then sells them from a booth in one of Moscow's farmers' markets for the exorbitant price of 25 rubles.

"That's a lot, but the fact is you can't buy tights anywhere else in Moscow," Petrovna said the other day. "You should see the women pushing and pulling to get their hands on them." More important for Petrovna, even after paying taxes to the state, she has nearly tripled her monthly income, to 280 rubles, or $448. And along with her co-workers, she is entertaining thoughts of building up capital, buying the knitting machines and opening a new business selling made-to-order knitwear. "When I think about it," she said, "I don't know why anyone would want to work in a state factory anymore."

Petrovna's knitting enterprise is one of 3,000 small cooperatives, most of them cafes and food shops, that have been organized across the country in the last few months. Under legislation that took effect May 1, several thousand additional family-owned shops with no links to state enterprises also have sprung up, offering services from hair styling to automobile repair. These miniature businesses—licensed, taxed and closely watched by the authorities—are more restricted than similar small businesses in Poland and Hungary. But their emergence marks the first tentative blossoming of legal private and semi-private enterprise in the Soviet Union since Vladimir I. Lenin's comparatively liberal New Economic Policy—instituted in 1921 in the face of widespread discontent amid severe shortages—ended in 1928–29 with the consolidation of Josef Stalin's dictatorship.

By such steps, in its 70th anniversary year, the Soviet leadership has begun a partial dismantling of the rigidly centralized economic structure that Stalin erected half a century ago to carry out his crash program of industrialization. In its place, Gorbachev and his allies in the ruling Politburo are reaching back and borrowing features of the more benign and flexible New Economic Policy, which mixed elements of a market economy in consumer goods with state control of the "commanding heights" of industry.

Source: Robert Gillette, "Creaking Economy Needs More than a Little Repair," *Los Angeles Times;* reprinted in *Kansas City Times,* November 26, 1987, p. N-1. Reprinted by permission.

butchering meat. In addition, by specializing in one line of work each trader gains the experience necessary to become highly proficient in that work. Finally, with specialization there is no unnecessary duplication of capital—it is not necessary for each party to have an oven and a meat grinder. Instead, each obtains specialized equipment for just one line of work—which may reduce the butcher's cost of preparing a pound of meat and the baker's cost of producing a loaf of bread.

For the preceding reasons, the total amounts of bread and meat produced may be greater when each party specializes in a single line of production. For example, rather than each producing 10 pounds of meat and 10 loaves of bread per hour, through specialization the butcher may be able to produce 30 pounds of meat and the baker 30 loaves of bread. In that event, the total amounts of bread and meat both increase (Table 2-1). With greater output to divide, it is possible for both parties to increase their consumption. *Specialization and trade increase total output and therefore permit a higher standard of living.*

The same logic applies to specialization and trade by countries. Under certain conditions trade increases total output, allowing citizens of each country to increase their average level of consumption. In particular, trade benefits both countries if the opportunity costs of the goods they trade differ by country.

Consider the following hypothetical example. Assume each unit of a resource in the United States can produce either 2 hams or 6 bottles of vodka, regardless of the quantities of each already produced. In this event, the opportunity cost of 2 hams is 6 bottles of vodka. Equivalently, the opportunity cost of 1 ham is 3 bottles of vodka. Assume further that each resource in the Soviet Union can produce either 1 ham or 5 bottles of vodka. Comparing the two countries, it is apparent that the opportunity cost of ham is lower in the United States—the United States must sacrifice 3 bottles of vodka for each ham whereas the Soviet Union must sacrifice 5. Because of the lower opportunity cost, the United States is said to have a **comparative advantage** in the production of ham.

Comparative Advantage
The ability of one country to produce a particular good at a lower opportunity cost than a second country.

Because the United States is relatively more proficient at producing ham, both the United States and the Soviet Union can benefit when the United States specializes in the production of ham and the Soviet Union in the production of vodka. The United States can trade some of the additional ham produced as a result of specialization to the Soviet Union for some of the additional vodka produced there. Under these conditions, both the United States and the Soviet Union realize greater output than when each country is self-sufficient in the production of the two goods.

To extend the example one step further, assume the two countries agree that the United States will export 1 ham for every 4 bottles of vodka imported from the Soviet Union. In that event, the United States is better off importing vodka than producing it. By trading with the Soviet Union, the United States obtains 4 bottles of vodka for each ham—one more bottle than it would receive if the vodka were produced in the United States (Table 2-2). The Soviet Union also gains, since the cost of a ham imported from the United States (4 bottles of vodka) is less than the cost of a ham produced in the Soviet Union (5 bottles of vodka).

Table 2-1

SPECIALIZATION MAY INCREASE THE OUTPUT OF BOTH GOODS

| | Amount of meat and bread produced in one hour | | | |
| | (a) without specialization | | (b) with specialization | |
	Meat*	Bread**	Meat*	Bread**
Worker 1	10	10	30	0
Worker 2	10	10	0	30
Total	20	20	30	30

*Pounds.
**Loaves.

Table 2-2

HOW TRADE BENEFITS BOTH THE UNITED STATES AND THE SOVIET UNION

Country	The opportunity cost of 1 ham	
	(a) without trade	(b) with trade
United States	3 bottles of vodka	4 bottles of vodka
Soviet Union	5 bottles of vodka	4 bottles of vodka

If the United States produces one less ham it has sufficient resources to produce an additional 3 bottles of vodka. Alternatively, the U.S. can produce the ham and trade it to the Soviet Union for 4 bottles of vodka. Because the United States receives one extra bottle of vodka for each ham exported to the Soviet Union, trade benefits the United States. From the Soviet perspective, trade lowers the cost of a ham from 5 bottles of vodka (if produced in the Soviet Union) to 4 bottles (if imported from the United States). Thus, trade is also advantageous to the Soviet Union.

In conclusion, trade permits each country to specialize in the production of goods for which it is relatively more proficient—that is, goods for which it has a comparative advantage. By producing goods in countries where the opportunity cost is lower and then trading the goods, both countries gain additional output. Thus trade creates value—output combinations not possible when a country is self-sufficient become possible when a country trades. In graphical terms, trade allows a country to move beyond its production possibilities curve.

YOUR TURN

HOW TRADE ALLOWS A COUNTRY TO MOVE BEYOND ITS PRODUCTION POSSIBILITIES CURVE

Assume the United States has one million units of a resource and that each unit can produce either 2 hams or 6 bottles of vodka. (a) If the United States uses all its resources to produce ham, how much ham can it produce? (b) If the U.S. uses one-half its resources to produce ham and one-half to produce vodka, how much of each good can it produce? (c) Draw the appropriate production possibilities curve. (d) The Soviet Union agrees to trade 4 bottles of vodka for each ham the United States exports. As a result, the United States decides to produce only ham. If the U.S. keeps one-half the ham it produces and trades the other one-half to the Soviet Union, how much vodka will the United States receive? (e) Add one point to the diagram drawn in (c) to represent the combination of ham and vodka available to the United States after trade. Is this combination of ham and vodka attainable without trade?

Transaction Costs Reduce the Gains from Trade

Transaction Costs
The costs associated with the exchange of a good or resource.

For expediency, the preceding discussion ignored **transaction costs**—the costs associated with exchange. But, as you know, the exchange of goods often consumes resources. For example, when a homeowner hires a realtor to advertise and show the home, appraise its market value, handle the necessary paperwork, and otherwise assist in the sale of the home, the realtor collects a fee for services rendered. On the sale of a $100,000 home, the realtor may collect $6000 or, in some markets, even more. This fee drives a wedge between the price paid by the buyer ($100,000) and the price received by the seller ($94,000).

Import Quota

A restriction limiting the amount of a foreign good that may enter a country legally.

Similarly, the exchange of goods and resources between countries often involves transaction costs. Businesses may need to establish foreign offices for making contacts with other countries, hire lawyers to negotiate contracts, and employ lobbyists to fight such impediments to trade as **import quotas**—limits on the quantity of a good that may be imported into a country. Transaction costs also include transportation costs (e.g., the costs of shipping a good from one country to another). Where transaction costs are substantial, they often prevent countries from reaching agreements on trade. And where trade does occur, transaction costs reduce the gains from such trade. Therefore, anything that facilitates trade—from a reduction in transportation costs to the elimination of quotas—tends to magnify the volume of trade and the benefits derived from such trade.

Volume of Trade

Despite the existence of transaction costs, countries still find trade advantageous. Currently, international trade exceeds $2 trillion per year. Table 2-3 lists volume of trade for selected countries, including the United States, the world's largest trading country (as measured by volume of imports). Much of the United States trade is with adjacent countries (Canada and Mexico) and with Japan. Trade with the Soviet Union is extremely modest.

West Germany, on the other hand, trades more with the Soviet Union than with Canada and Mexico combined. The West German scenario illustrates the importance of transportation costs. Because transportation costs tend to rise with distance (other things equal), a country is more likely to trade with neighboring countries than with more distant countries. Of course, the magnitude of output is also important. The economies of some countries are so huge—including those of the United States, West Germany, and Japan—that they export enormous volumes of output even to distant countries.

Table 2-3

1988 TRADE VOLUME FOR SELECTED COUNTRIES
(billions of U.S. dollars)

Country	Total imports	U.S.	Imports from Canada	Imports from Mexico	Japan	USSR
U.S.	441	—	81	23	90	1
Canada	107	70	—	1	8	*
Japan	188	42	8	2	—	3
West Germany	251	17	2	*	16	4
U.K.	189	19	4	*	12	1

*Less than $0.5 billion.

Source: Organization for Economic Cooperation and Development, *Monthly Statistics of Foreign Trade* (Paris, May 1989).

Looking Ahead

Although various components of international trade are discussed in subsequent chapters, the more subtle points are deferred to Part X (on world economy), after you have acquired the tools and background necessary to a more careful consideration of these issues. The next task is to attain a deeper understanding of how markets work or, in some cases, why markets fail. This is the focus of Chapter 3.

SUMMARY

1. A production possibilities curve portrays the combinations of output that can be produced with a given technology and fixed resources, assuming the resources are used efficiently. When a country fails to put its resources to their best use, or leaves them unused, it fails to reach its production possibilities curve.

2. When a country is *on* its production possibilities curve, the only way it can produce more of one good is to divert resources from the production of a second good. The amount of the second good sacrificed indicates the opportunity cost involved.

3. The law of increasing costs predicts that the opportunity cost of a good rises as output of the good increases. The principle is based on the argument that, as more and more of one good is produced, it is necessary to use resources less and less suited for production of that good. Where the law of increasing costs holds, the production possibilities curve is bowed.

4. When a country's stock of resources increases or when technological progress occurs, the country's production possibilities curve shifts outward, denoting economic growth. To spur economic growth a country can produce relatively more capital goods, and relatively fewer consumer goods, or increase the amount of resources devoted to research and development.

5. Different societies choose different economic systems for deciding what is produced, how it is produced, and for whom. Pure capitalism rests on private ownership of resources and use of markets. At the opposite extreme, a command economy is one where resources are publicly owned and decisions are made by central authorities. All modern economic systems are, to varying degrees, mixes of pure capitalism and a command economy. For that reason they are called mixed economies.

6. Capitalism is guided by consumer sovereignty—firms produce the combinations of goods demanded by consumers. To maximize profit, firms are induced to produce such goods at the lowest possible cost. Under capitalism, output is distributed on the basis of ability to pay.

7. In a command economy, central planners develop an elaborate scheme to determine what is produced. These central planners next assign production goals to companies and allocate resources. Finally, the government determines how output is distributed.

8. Through specialization and trade it is possible to increase the amount of output produced and therefore to raise standards of living. When trading, countries and individuals should specialize in the production of goods for which they enjoy a comparative advantage—that is, goods they can produce at a lower opportunity cost.

9. Transaction costs reduce the gains from trade and, when large enough, prevent two potential traders from making an exchange. An increase in the amount of resources required to effect an exchange reduces the incentive to trade.

10. International trade currently exceeds $2 trillion per year. The United States alone imports in excess of $400 billion annually. Because exchange costs tend to increase with distance, most countries conduct a disproportionate amount of trade with neighboring countries.

KEY TERMS

production possibilities curve
technology
inefficient production

efficient production
law of increasing costs
economic growth

command economy

mixed economy

consumer sovereignty

capital goods

consumer goods

economic system

pure capitalism

market

international trade

zero-sum game

positive-sum game

specialization

comparative advantage

transaction costs

import quota

STUDY QUESTIONS AND PROBLEMS

1. For each of the following, explain whether the production possibilities curve shifts outward, shifts inward, or remains unchanged:
   a. average educational attainment of the population increases by one year
   b. due to war, one-third of a country's capital is depleted
   c. the government decides to reduce spending on defense and instead to devote more resources to public housing
   d. because of a declining birthrate, a country's working-age population shrinks

2. For each of the following, indicate whether output increases or decreases. If output rises, specify whether the rise is due to greater efficiency in the economy or to economic growth.
   a. a previously idle automobile plant is back in operation
   b. a government pays farmers to idle cropland—that is, to remove land from production
   c. a new technique is discovered for converting industrial waste into energy
   d. an experienced builder temporarily employed as a cashier finds a construction job; a cashier temporarily working on a construction crew finds employment as a cashier

3. (a) Assume U.S. consumers want to buy more red convertibles than are currently available in dealer showrooms. How would you expect this situation to affect production of red convertibles? Why? (b) Assume Soviet citizens also desire more red convertibles. Would you expect the same production response in the Soviet Union as in the United States? Explain.

4. Economists argue that production tends to be more efficient in capitalistic economies than in command economies. Analyze this argument.

5. In Mexico each unit of a resource can produce either one professional computer (with business and scientific applications) or three computer-game systems. Mexico has 100,000 units of this resource.
   a. Draw Mexico's production possibilities curve.
   b. What is the opportunity cost of one professional computer?
   c. Is the production of professional computers subject to constant or increasing costs?
   d. Which of the two goods being produced is considered a capital good?
   e. In the absence of trade, should Mexico increase production of professional computers or computer-game systems if it desires more rapid economic growth?

6. In Japan each unit of a resource can produce either two professional computers or eight computer-game systems.
   a. Based on the figures for Japan and Mexico (see problem 5), which country enjoys a comparative advantage in the production of professional computers?
   b. To increase world output, which country should specialize in the production of professional computers?
   c. Which country should export computer-game systems?

7. Tom can paint one window frame or two walls in one hour. In the same time, Sally can paint either two window frames or three walls.
   a. For whom is the opportunity cost of painting window frames lower?
   b. If Tom and Sally desire to minimize the time spent painting, who should specialize in painting window frames and who should specialize in painting walls?

8. Indicate whether each of the following increases or decreases the volume of world trade:

a. a decline in the price of oil reduces transportation costs between countries
b. the development of a new telecommunications system reduces the cost of obtaining information about both the availability of foreign goods and foreign interest in the goods produced in a country
c. a country levies a tax on all imported goods
d. a new law requires companies to obtain permits to export their products and to hire additional staff to complete necessary paperwork

9. Assume that the New York Yankees have two outstanding first basemen but only mediocre catchers. Assume further that the Los Angeles Dodgers have two outstanding catchers but only mediocre first basemen. If the Yankees trade one outstanding first baseman to the Dodgers for one outstanding catcher, is the trade more likely to be a zero-sum game or a positive-sum game? Explain.

ANSWERS TO YOUR TURN

TECHNOLOGICAL ADVANCES IN THE PRODUCTION OF TRACTORS

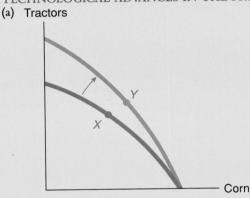

(a) Tractors

(b) Yes. Technological progress enables the country to produce more tractors with fewer resources. With additional resources available for growing corn, the country can also increase its production of corn. This is illustrated by the movement from point X to point Y.

ANSWERS TO YOUR TURN

HOW TRADE ALLOWS A COUNTRY TO MOVE BEYOND ITS PRODUCTION POSSIBILITIES CURVE

(a) 2 million hams.
(b) 1 million hams and 3 million bottles of vodka.
(c) Hams (millions)

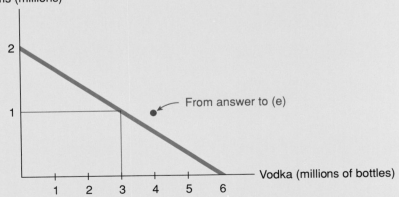

From answer to (e)

(d) 4 million bottles.
(e) No. Without trade it is not possible to obtain both 1 million hams and 4 million bottles of vodka.

CHAPTER 3

THE PRICE SYSTEM

Chapter 2 introduced the concept of markets, noting their crucial role in such largely capitalistic countries as the United States. Even in such decidedly noncapitalistic economies as that of the Soviet Union, the virtues of markets are being rediscovered. Accordingly, it is important to take a closer look at markets, examining both how they work and why market outcomes are sometimes deemed unacceptable and are therefore modified by government.

Prices are to guide and direct the economic activities of the people. Prices are to tell them what to do.[1]

---

[1]Benjamin M. Anderson, *Economics and the Public Welfare* (New York: Van Nostrand, 1949), p. 550.

THE PARTICIPANTS

We begin with a discussion of the major participants in the economy: consumers, firms, and government.

Consumers

Consumers earn income from their labor and from the property they own. For example, an employed person who also leases land to others receives both wage income and rental income. With their incomes, consumers buy various goods and services. Table 3-1 presents the spending pattern of urban consumers in the United States. Notice that, on average, housing is the largest expenditure. Altogether, housing, food, and clothing constitute about two-thirds of the spending of the typical urban consumer.

The term "household" is sometimes used in place of consumer, especially when economic decisions are made within a family setting. Clearly, some economic

TABLE 3-1

SPENDING PATTERN OF U.S. CONSUMERS*

Category		Percent of Spending
Food and beverages		17.6
food at home	9.9	
food away from home	6.2	
alcoholic beverages	1.5	
Housing		42.5
shelter	27.8	
fuel and other utilities	7.7	
household furnishings and operation	7.0	
Apparel		6.3
Transportation		17.5
Medical care		5.8
Entertainment		4.4
Other goods and services		5.9
tobacco	1.3	
nontobacco	4.6	____
TOTAL		100.0

*Average for urban consumers (excludes rural consumers).

Source: U.S. Department of Labor, Bureau of Labor Statistics, *The Consumer Price Index*, 1989.

decisions—for example, whether both husband and wife should work and where to vacation—are based on the input of more than one individual. As previously observed, consumers are generally assumed to maximize their well-being or what economists dub "utility."

Firms

Firms or businesses are the unit of production. They hire workers and pay for the use of various property owned by consumers. Firms use these resources to produce the goods and services consumers buy.

Firms come in all sizes, from a company run and operated by one individual to such multinational giants as Toyota and Exxon. Although firms operate in all industries, Table 3-2 demonstrates that the industries with the most firms are the service sector (which includes hospitals, automobile repair, legal services, and so forth) and retail trade (which includes restaurants, grocery stores, department stores, and other shopping outlets). Altogether, the U.S. economy has approximately 17 million firms.

Regardless of size and the industry in which they operate, all firms share a common feature—the pursuit of profit.[2] Indeed, economists generally assume that profit maximization is the single goal of firms.

TABLE 3-2

DISTRIBUTION OF FIRMS BY INDUSTRY

Industry	Number of firms (thousands)
Agriculture, forestry, fishing*	558
Mining	279
Construction	1829
Manufacturing	633
Transportation, public utilities	709
Wholesale trade	618
Retail trade	2733
Finance, insurance, real estate	2376
Services	6812
Miscellaneous	373
TOTAL	16,920

*Excludes farm proprietorships.

Source: U.S. Department of Commerce, *Statistical Abstract of the United States, 1989* (1989), Table 848.

[2]Public schools, churches, and other not-for-profit institutions employ resources and produce goods and services; however, because they lack the profit motive, they are not classified as firms.

	TABLE 3-3		
GOVERNMENT STATISTICS BY TYPE OF GOVERNMENT, 1987			
Type of government	Number of government units	Millions of employees	Spending (billions of dollars)
Federal	1	2.9	$1067.1
State and Local	83,216	14.1	607.1
state	50	4.0	N/A
local	83,166	10.1	N/A
TOTAL	83,217	17.0	$1674.2

N/A = Not available.

Sources: U.S. Department of Commerce, *Statistical Abstract of the United States, 1989,* Table 445; *Survey of Current Business* (1988); U.S. Department of Labor, *Employment and Earnings,* 1988, Table B-1.

Government

The term **government** is used broadly to include all government and quasi-government bodies at the federal, state, and local levels. Although the local sector has the largest number of government units and the most employees, spending is greatest at the federal level (see Table 3-3). American government agencies include the Federal Reserve System (which oversees the nation's money supply), the Post Office, the Internal Revenue Service, state highway patrols, mayoral offices, various regulatory commissions, and many more. Unlike consumers and firms, government is not assumed to have a single, overriding goal or even to behave consistently. Government agencies may have conflicting agendas, and government officials may be motivated by private as well as public interests.

In a purely capitalistic economy, the government is limited to such activities as law enforcement. Individual consumers and firms are left to buy and sell as they see fit in the marketplace. In reality, government involvement is more extensive—as governments of all countries restrict, to varying degrees, the activities of both firms and consumers. Reasons for government involvement are addressed at the end of the chapter. Until then we ignore the role of government in order to concentrate on the interplay between firms and consumers in unrestricted markets.

TWO TYPES OF MARKETS

Product Market
A market in which a particular good or service is bought and sold.
Resource (factor) Market
A market in which a particular resource (factor of production) is bought and sold.

Markets can be divided into two categories: *product markets* and *resource* (or *factor*) *markets.* The difference relates to what is bought and sold. In **product markets** goods and services are exchanged; in **resource markets** the focus is on labor and other factors of production. Regardless of the type of market, buyers and sellers make contact, reach terms on the amount of an item to be exchanged, and agree on a price.

THE ROLE OF MONEY

Prices are usually stated in monetary terms. For example, a plumber might charge $100 to fix a leaky faucet. In this case the plumber performs a service and, in return,

Barter
A system of exchange whereby goods and services are traded directly without the use of money.

receives a certain amount of money ($100). An alternative method of exchange is **barter,** in which goods or services are traded without the use of money. For example, a nearsighted plumber might repair a faucet in return for a new pair of eyeglasses.

Although money is not necessary for exchange, it greatly facilitates exchange. Think of the difficulties involved in a barter economy. A plumber who wants glasses must first locate an optician with a leaky faucet. To eat, the plumber must find a farmer or grocer in need of plumbing services. The time spent searching for parties with whom to trade may well exceed the time spent plumbing. With money, exchanges are so much simpler. The plumber sells his or her services to whoever needs them and uses the money earned from this work to buy eyeglasses, food, or whatever else is desired. Simply put, money eliminates the need to find someone who has what you want and who also wants something you have. As a consequence, money reduces the transaction costs of exchange.

Governments issue the coins and currency we commonly associate with money, but it is important to realize that money is created even in the absence of government. In primitive economies, shells, stones, and sundry other goods have served as money. In modern economies, most money consists of checking accounts, which are issued not by governments but by private financial institutions. The main requirement is that the good serving as money, whatever it is, be generally accepted as a means of payment—a person accepting a good as money must be confident that this good will, in turn, be accepted by others. In prisoner-of-war camps during World War II, cigarettes became the accepted medium of exchange and therefore functioned as money (see Exhibit 3-1).

THE CIRCULAR FLOW OF INCOME

The interplay between the type of markets (product and resource), the market participants (consumers and firms), and the terms of exchange (money for goods or resources) is illustrated with a model known as the **circular flow of income** (see Figure 3–1, page 58). Consumers sell their resources to firms and, in return, receive income payments (wages, rent, interest, and profit). These transactions take place in resource markets, which are depicted in the lower half of the diagram. Firms then combine these resources to produce goods and services, which they sell to consumers. Transactions in product markets are depicted in the upper half of the diagram. Note that firms and consumers participate in both resource and product markets, but in different capacities. In resource markets firms are on the buying (demand) side, whereas consumers are on the selling (supply) side. In product markets the roles are reversed.

The outer arrows in Figure 3-1 represent the flow of resources and products; the inner arrows depict monetary flows. Note the circular nature of these flows. Money flows from firms to consumers (in resource markets) and then back to firms (in product markets). In each case these monetary flows are balanced by flows of resources or products in the opposite direction.

As a model, the circular flow diagram simplifies reality. For example, it considers only markets for *final products*—the goods and services purchased by consumers. But sometimes firms sell their output to other firms, as when steel companies sell steel sheeting to appliance makers. These transactions—the buying and selling of *intermediate products*—do not directly appear in the circular flow diagram.

EXHIBIT 3–1

THE EMERGENCE OF MARKETS AND MONEY IN POW CAMPS

The economy of a prisoner-of-war camp is typically very simple. There is no production of marketable goods and services and no buying and selling of resources. The principal economic activity is consumption. Still, economic decisions must be made, the paramount issue involving how to divide consumption among the prisoners.

During World War II, prisoners received weekly rations from their captors and various goods from the Red Cross. Although these were distributed equally, the values of the goods differed from prisoner to prisoner. Some smoked cigarettes, others did not. Some preferred tea, others coffee. Such differences in preferences meant that prisoners could increase their well-being (utility) by trading among themselves.

Trade initially consisted of barter; but over time markets became increasingly sophisticated, with cigarettes emerging as the medium of exchange. One former prisoner of war recounts these developments:

> Very soon after capture people realized that it was both undesirable and unnecessary, in view of the limited size and the equality of supplies, to give away or to accept gifts of cigarettes or food. "Goodwill" developed into trading as a more equitable means of maximizing individual satisfaction.
>
> We reached a transit camp in Italy about a fortnight after capture and received one-quarter of a Red Cross food parcel each a week later. At once exchanges, already established, multiplied in volume. Starting with simple direct barter, such as a non-smoker giving a smoker friend his cigarette issue in exchange for a chocolate ration, more complex exchanges soon became an accepted custom. Stories circulated of a padre who started off round the camp with a tin of cheese and five cigarettes and returned to his bed with a complete parcel in addition to his original cheese and cigarettes; the market was not yet perfect. Within a week or two, as the volume of trade grew, rough scales of exchange values came into existence. Sikhs, who had at first exchanged tinned beef for practically any other foodstuff, began to insist on jam and margarine. It was realized that a tin of jam was worth one-half pound of margarine plus something else, that a cigarette issue was worth several chocolate issues, and a tin of diced carrots was worth practically nothing.

> In this camp we did not visit other bungalows very much and prices varied from place to place; hence the germ of truth in the story of the itinerant priest. By the end of a month, when we reached our permanent camp, there was a lively trade in all commodities and their relative values were well known, and expressed not in terms of one another—one didn't quote bully [canned corned beef] in terms of sugar—but in terms of cigarettes. The cigarette became the standard of value. In the permanent camp people started by wandering through the bungalows calling their offers—"cheese for seven" (cigarettes)—and the hours after parcel issue were bedlam. The inconvenience of this system soon led to its replacement by an Exchange and Mart notice board in every bungalow, where under the headings "name," "room number," "wanted" and "offered" sales and wants were advertised. When a deal went through, it was crossed off the board. The public and semipermanent records of transactions led to cigarette prices being well known and thus tending to equality throughout the camp, although there were always opportunities for an astute trader to make a profit from arbitrage. With this development everyone, including nonsmokers was willing to sell for cigarettes, using them to buy at another time and place. Cigarettes became the normal currency, though, of course, barter was never extinguished. . . .
>
> The permanent camps in Germany saw the highest level of commercial organisation. In addition to the Exchange and Mart notice boards, a shop was organized as a public utility, controlled by representatives of the Senior British Officer, on a no profit basis. People left their surplus clothing, toilet requisites, and food there until they were sold at a fixed price in cigarettes. Only sales in cigarettes were accepted—there was no barter—and there was no haggling. For food at least there were standard prices. . . . Thus the cigarette attained its fullest currency status, and the market was almost completely unified.

Source: R. A. Radford, "The Economic Organisation of a P.O.W. Camp," *Economica* (November 1945), pp. 189-201. Reprinted by permission of Basil Blackwell, publisher, and the author.

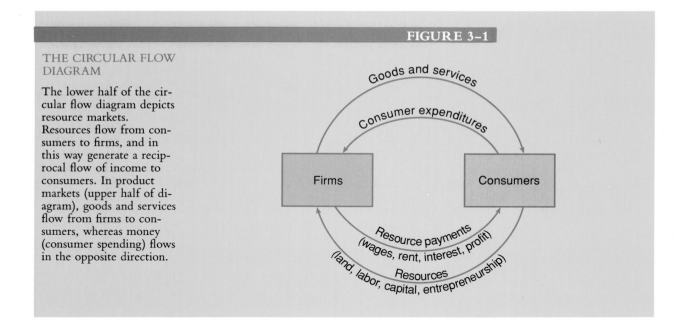

FIGURE 3–1

THE CIRCULAR FLOW DIAGRAM

The lower half of the circular flow diagram depicts resource markets. Resources flow from consumers to firms, and in this way generate a reciprocal flow of income to consumers. In product markets (upper half of diagram), goods and services flow from firms to consumers, whereas money (consumer spending) flows in the opposite direction.

The circular flow diagram also ignores taxes and saving, which represent *leakages* of income from the system. Because income that consumers save or pay in taxes is not available for consumption, the flow of output from firms to consumers is reduced. (Such complications are addressed later in the text.) But even if the circular flow model does not perfectly mirror reality, it is still useful in illustrating the interdependence of product and resource markets, the relationships between firms and consumers, and the role of money.

THE PRICE SYSTEM

Although the circular flow diagram provides an overview of capitalistic economies, it does not address a fundamental question: How do they work? With potentially millions of firms and consumers, each acting in their own self-interest, how is anything accomplished? In the absence of central authorities to guide the economy, what prevents the economy from grinding to a halt? What mechanism organizes production, links decisions of producers and consumers in a mutually consistent manner, and brings order rather than chaos to the economy?

In a capitalistic economy, economic activities are coordinated through the price system. In product markets, prices signal consumer preferences. In resource markets, prices indicate relative scarcity, telling firms which resources to buy and how to combine them.

Price System
A mechanism for coordinating economic decisions in which prices are determined in markets and used to allocate resources and output.

The key to the **price system** is the adjustment of prices and the response triggered by that adjustment. When consumers want more of a good than firms are willing to sell, their competition for this good forces up price (more on this in Chapter 4). This induces firms to produce more of the good since, other things equal, a higher price indicates an opportunity for increased profits. Conversely, if consumers want less than firms wish to sell, firms are forced to lower price. This, in turn, provides a signal to reduce production of the good.

Prices send similar signals in resource markets. Prices tell resource owners where to employ their resources—namely, in those activities where the returns are the greatest. Prices also tell firms how to combine resources. For example, if the price of labor rises while the price of computers falls, this alerts producers that they can lower production costs by using additional computers and fewer workers. Similarly, skyrocketing oil prices send a signal to switch to energy-saving techniques of production.

In summary, in a capitalistic economy prices convey information about the value of resources and output. The pattern of product and resource prices tells firms what to produce and how. Similarly, the pattern shapes the decisions of consumers concerning their supply of resources and their purchases of goods and services. Whenever conditions change—on either the buying or selling side of the market—prices also change, thereby sending new information to firms and consumers. In the process, the price system coordinates economic activity, distributing resources where they are valued most highly, and linking the decisions of firms and consumers.

YOUR TURN | Suppose consumers want additional strawberries. (a) How are these preferences conveyed to producers? (b) Why do firms have an incentive to produce additional strawberries? (c) If strawberry producers need additional strawberry pickers, how can they induce additional individuals to pick strawberries?

THE INVISIBLE HAND

Adam Smith, the eighteenth-century economist, described the price system as an "invisible hand" guiding economic decision makers. Recognizing that consumers and firms tend to act in their own self-interest, he addressed an important social issue: Will the price system lead to socially optimal outcomes? It is not obvious that what is in the interest of private parties—consumers and firms—is also in the best interest of society. But Smith argued that, in the presence of competition among both firms and consumers, the price system guides private parties to do what is best for society.

Smith explains this argument in a famous passage from his book, *The Wealth of Nations*:

> Every individual necessarily labours to render the annual revenue of the society as great as he can. He generally, indeed, neither intends to promote the public interest, nor knows how much he is promoting it. By . . . directing that industry in such a manner as its produce may be of the greatest value, he intends only his own gain, and he is in this, as in many other cases, led by an *invisible hand* to promote an end which was no part of his intention. Nor is it always the worse for the society that it was no part of it. By pursuing his own interest he frequently promotes that of the society more effectually than when he really intends to promote it.[3]

The convergence of private and public interests can be illustrated with several examples. A firm minimizes the costs of producing a given output so that it may maximize its profits. But minimizing costs also benefits society because, when firms

---

[3]Adam Smith, *An Inquiry into the Nature and Causes of the Wealth of Nations* (New York: Random House, 1937), p. 423 [originally published in 1776].

produce efficiently, society obtains the greatest output possible from its limited resources. Profit maximization also forces firms to produce those goods valued most highly by consumers. Again, there is harmony of public and private interests. Similarly, individuals toil so that they may increase their consumption. But through their labor they also benefit others by expanding the amount of output available for society. In summary, Smith argued that private parties are motivated by self-interest and that, through an invisible hand, pursuit of self-interest promotes the public good. Exhibit 3-2 provides additional background on the famous economist and his views.

EXHIBIT 3–2

ADAM SMITH

Adam Smith is widely recognized as the founder of economics. Although much of Smith's work built upon the ideas of others, he expanded their arguments and integrated various strands of thought, blending theory with empirical observation.

Born in Scotland in 1723, Smith was educated at the University of Glasgow and later studied, at his own direction, at Oxford University. Upon completing his studies, he accepted a position at the University of Glasgow, initially as professor of logic and later as professor of moral philosophy, the discipline from which economics evolved. After publishing *The Theory of Moral Sentiment* in 1759, Smith was heralded as one of the prominent philosophers of his time. Although a popular and provocative lecturer, Smith left the university to become the highly paid tutor for a young duke. It was during his service as tutor in France that Smith began work on *The Wealth of Nations,* which, though it had limited impact in its first few years, is now regarded as one of the greatest treatises ever written in political economy.

In the book, Smith preached a *laissez-faire* or "hands-off" approach by the government. He argued that government involvement should be limited to those activities that promote the public good and that cannot be adequately provided by the market (e.g., maintaining law and order, preserving national defense, and providing public education).

Smith's views were a sharp attack on the prevailing *mercantilist* philosophy, which favored massive government intervention as a means to increase a nation's wealth. Because mercantilists believed that a nation's wealth was a function of its gold and silver, they favored policies to promote exports and restrict imports, arguing that the gold and silver accumulated as a result of exports would benefit the entire country. Smith rejected this argument, pointing out that it is capital, rather than gold and silver, that increases a country's productive capacity.

Smith also presented a labor theory of value, which held that the value of all output was ultimately derived from labor—an argument later picked up and expanded upon by Karl Marx. Another theme of *The Wealth of Nations* was that output could be expanded through the division of labor, whereby individual workers specialize in narrowly defined activities. Before he died in 1790, Adam Smith had received worldwide acclaim; *The Wealth of Nations* was in its fifth edition and had been translated into French, Spanish, Italian, German, and Danish.[4]

---

[4]For a more detailed analysis of the life and influence of Adam Smith, see Robert L. Heilbroner, *The Worldly Philosophers,* 6th ed. (New York: Simon & Schuster, 1986), Chapter 3.

LIMITATIONS OF THE PRICE SYSTEM

The preceding discussion has painted a highly favorable picture of the price system. Individuals and firms are free to pursue the activities of their choice and yet, in so doing, they advance the interests of society. The price system leads to efficient production, so that society gains the maximum possible output from its resources. Moreover, resources are allocated across industries in just the right mix. Firms produce neither more nor less of a good than society wants. Thanks to an *invisible hand,* society receives the optimal amount of each good.

The preceding story is, however, incomplete. Despite its strengths, the price system has certain limitations, as Smith himself was aware. Indeed, it is because of these limitations that no country relies exclusively on capitalism to make its economic decisions.

Competition

It is the price system *plus competition* that leads to harmony of public and private interests. In the absence of competition, the invisible hand fails. Take away competition, and firms are free to thwart the signals of the price system.

For example, high prices are a signal to increase production of a good—and when firms compete against one another, that is exactly what happens. But Adam Smith warned that rather than compete against one another, producers would often attempt to limit competition—to work together to keep production artificially low and prices artificially high:

> People of the same trade seldom meet together, even for merriment and diversion, but the conversation ends in a conspiracy against the public, or in some contrivance to raise prices.[5]

Clearly in cases where firms raise prices and restrict output, they do not serve the interests of society.

Similarly, buyers of a resource (e.g., hospitals) might conspire to limit their use of a resource (e.g., nurses) in order to keep down the price of this resource. Although this may benefit resource buyers, it harms society by leading to an underutilization of the resource (i.e., society has too few nurses).

In conclusion, competition in both product markets and resource markets is essential if the price system is to promote the interests of society. But competition may not be the natural outcome of unrestricted markets. Instead, individual groups of buyers or sellers may succeed in restraining competition for their own personal gain, in which event the price system fails to deliver socially optimal outcomes. In such cases, government intervention may be necessary to keep competition strong and to keep the price system functioning properly.

Market Failure

Market Failure
A situation in which unrestricted markets produce either more or less of a good than is socially optimal.

Even when markets are competitive, the price system may still fail to produce the socially optimal amount of a good—a phenomenon known as **market failure.** Markets fail in two principal areas: provision of *public goods* and production in the presence of *externalities.*

---

[5]Same as 3, p. 128.

Public Goods   A public good is one that is consumed collectively. Once produced, a public good is available to all consumers. Examples include national defense and the judicial system. Because individuals derive benefits from a public good whether or not they pay for it, they have no incentive to spend their income on public goods. Therefore, the price system cannot be counted on to provide sufficient quantities of public goods. Instead, the government must ensure the adequate support of national defense, the judicial system, and other public goods.

Externalities   Externalities (sometimes known as "spillover effects") refer to the side effects of an economic activity; they arise when the production or consumption of a good affects others not in the market. As an example, consider pollution—an externality associated with the production of certain goods. Pollution imposes costs on society above and beyond those incurred by firms. Such costs include health problems, damage to wildlife, and loss of recreational facilities. Because firms do not bear these costs, they have an incentive to use production methods that pollute the environment, despite the harm done to society. The price system breaks down because it allows those imposing costs on others to escape the consequences of their actions. When externalities exist, government intervention may improve market outcomes (e.g., by forcing firms to reduce pollution).

Income Inequality

Under the price system, the distribution of income is based on consumers' command over resources and the market value of those resources. Consumers without property and without labor to sell receive no income. Consumers with great wealth or with highly valued skills earn high incomes. Witness the lofty salary of Bill Cosby and other top entertainers (see Exhibit 3-3).

If society seeks some minimum standard of living for all its citizens, government intervention is necessary to achieve this goal. For example, the government

---

EXHIBIT 3–3

IS BILL COSBY
WORTH MORE
THAN CHILDREN'S
HOSPITAL?

Bill Cosby earned an estimated $57 million in 1987 and almost as much the following year.[6] This is more than the entire budget for some hospitals and school districts. Indeed, based on workers' average pay in 1987, Cosby's salary was equivalent to the earnings of 4325 nurses, 3158 elementary and secondary teachers, 1552 engineers, or 2912 construction workers. Although some wince at the idea of paying such staggering sums of money to select individuals while others go malnourished, the price system does not recognize hunger.

In economies that rely on the price system, an individual's income depends on the market's valuation of his or her services. When an individual produces highly valued services, that individual will be compensated commensurately. This is the case with Bill Cosby, who provides entertainment for millions of viewers, advertising revenues for his network, ticket sales for movie theaters, and book sales for publishers. Given the strong demand for his services, the price system rewards the talented entertainer with an eight-figure income. As shocking as it may be, the answer to the question posed above is: Yes, from the market's perspective, Bill Cosby is worth more than the entire staff of Children's Hospital.

[6]Peter Newcomb, "The New Aristocracy," *Forbes,* October 3, 1988, p. 115.

may wish to tax those with high incomes to provide support for the poor, in the process creating a more equal distribution of income. Although there can be disagreement over how much *equity* or equality the government should attempt to achieve, the price system disregards equity entirely, focusing instead on *efficiency*—resource owners are rewarded on the basis of how much they contribute to output, not on the basis of how much they need. Therefore, when equity is a consideration, distribution of income under the price system is unacceptable.

Economic Instability

Capitalistic economies are generally viewed as inherently unstable. During some periods, unemployment rises to socially unacceptable levels. During other periods, capitalistic economies overheat, leading to inflationary pressures. If the government can promote greater economic stability, it may be able to reduce unemployment and mitigate inflationary pressures. This is a major issue of macroeconomics.

Conclusion

Despite its strengths, the price system has certain major limitations. The price system works well only when markets are competitive, and even then it fails to produce the socially optimal amount of output in the presence of public goods or externalities. The price system also results in a highly unequal distribution of income, failing to guarantee a basic standard of living for all consumers. Finally, economies that rely on the price system are characterized by considerable economic instability. For such reasons, governments have seen fit to modify market outcomes—to redirect the invisible hand. The extent of government and its functions are addressed in Chapter 7. However, before taking up this issue, it is essential to develop a deeper understanding of the process through which prices are determined. With this in mind, Chapter 4 introduces the economist's most important tools: supply and demand.

SUMMARY

1. Consumers earn income by providing resources to firms. Firms earn profit by combining those resources to produce goods and services. Economists generally assume that consumers attempt to maximize utility and that firms attempt to maximize profits.
2. Consumers and firms interact in both resource and product markets. As the circular flow diagram illustrates, firms buy resources from consumers and consumers buy goods and services from firms.
3. In a monetary economy resource owners receive money for the resources they supply, whereas firms receive money for the goods and services they sell. Compared to barter, the use of money reduces transaction costs, thereby facilitating exchange. Money is any good generally accepted as a means of payment, not just coins and currency.
4. In a capitalistic economy the price system coordinates economic activity, reconciling the decisions of buyers and sellers. Product prices reveal consumer preferences; resource prices indicate the relative scarcity of resources.
5. Higher product prices send a signal to increase production, lower prices to decrease production. In resource markets a higher price tells firms to economize on the use of a resource, a lower price to use the input more intensively.
6. Under certain conditions the price system operates as an invisible hand promoting public well-being. When these conditions are satisfied, individual firms and consumers, acting in their own self-interest, pursue policies that are also in the best interest of society. The

price system, while preserving personal freedom, directs firms to produce the socially optimal amount of each good and to produce it efficiently (at minimum cost).

7. To work well, the price system requires competition in both product markets and resource markets. When competition is lacking, government intervention may be necessary to promote a competitive environment.

8. Because consumers have no incentive to voluntarily spend their income on public goods (such as national defense), the price system fails to provide adequate quantities of public goods—even when markets are competitive. Nor are market outcomes likely to be optimal in the presence of externalities, such as pollution. Because of such instances of market failure, government intervention may advance the interests of society.

9. Yet another source of dissatisfaction with the price system is the distribution of income. The price system rewards consumers on the basis of how much they contribute to output, not on the basis of need. Those without property and without labor to sell receive no income. If society values equity, it will modify the distribution of income generated by the price system.

10. The price system is also characterized by economic instability. Because of this, government intervention may offer the potential to reduce unemployment and to mitigate inflationary pressures.

KEY TERMS

consumer	barter
firm	circular flow of income
government	price system
product market	market failure
resource market	

STUDY QUESTIONS AND PROBLEMS

1. (a) What is the difference between a product market and a resource market? (b) Provide an example of something sold in a product market and something sold in a resource market.

2. What advantage does a monetary economy have over a barter economy? If money is not necessary for trade, why was it created?

3. In the circular flow diagram, what is the relationship between firms and consumers?

4. What message is the price system sending to college students when the starting salary of engineers rises and the starting salary of mathematicians falls? Assuming that students are motivated in part by income, how would you expect this change in salaries to affect the pattern of college majors?

5. Assume the price of whole wheat bread increases. In the absence of other changes, how does this affect the profitability of baking and selling whole wheat bread? What signal does this send to bakers?

6. It is not from the benevolence of the butcher, the brewer, or the baker, that we expect our dinner, but from their regard to their own interest. We address ourselves, not to their humanity but to their self-love.[7]

What does Adam Smith mean by this passage? What motivates the butcher—self-interest or public interest? Who benefits from the butcher's work?

7. A former executive at General Motors once proclaimed: "What is good for General Motors is good for the country."[8] (a) Under what conditions would this be true? (b) Suppose

---

[7]Same as 3, p. 14.
[8]Charles E. Wilson, appearance before a Congressional committee, 1952.

General Motors conspires with Ford and Chrysler to drive up the price of automobiles. Would this be good for the country?

8. Is the price system consistent with the philosophy: "From each according to his abilities; to each according to his needs"? Explain.

9. Provide three reasons why government intervention might be socially desirable.

(a) Through higher strawberry prices. (b) Other things equal, a higher price for strawberries increases the profits from growing strawberries. (c) By offering a higher wage to strawberry pickers—that is, by increasing the price for this resource.

CHAPTER 4

SUPPLY AND DEMAND

Why does a 1952 Mickey Mantle baseball card sell for $5000 or a 1909 Honus Wagner card for $36,000? Why did prices for baseball cards rise more rapidly in the late 1980s than prices for stocks and bonds or other collectibles, including dolls and stamps? The answer in each case is the same: supply and demand. The price of baseball cards depends on how strongly buyers want the cards and on how willing collectors, card stores, and dealers are to sell their cards.

In the 1980s, demand exploded as more people started collecting cards and as investors became convinced that the cards they purchased today could be sold at vastly inflated prices in the future. As buyers competed for available cards, they drove prices higher. Of course, there is no guarantee that prices will continue their recent rise. If card collecting turns out to be a fad, prices may tumble in the future.

The price of baseball cards also depends on their supply. One reason a rookie Mickey Mantle card sells for $5000 is that it was issued late in 1952 and therefore fewer cards were printed of Mantle that year than of other players. Conversely, an increase in supply can be expected to dampen price. With production of cards nearly doubling in 1988, the prices of these cards are likely to remain below the prices of cards issued in prior years.

Supply and demand are equally important in determining the prices of other goods. Accordingly, it is important to understand which factors determine the amount of a good buyers want to purchase and the amount sellers wish to provide. Under what conditions are the desires of buyers and sellers compatible? What happens when they are not?

Sometimes markets are not allowed to operate freely: governments set minimum legal prices for some goods, maximum legal prices for others. What are the immediate effects of price controls, and how do market participants respond? Chapter 4 provides answers to these questions, answers that allow you to

In what has amounted to an explosion of value, [baseball] cards bought for mere pennies as part of bubble-gum packs just a few years ago have skyrocketed in price, with the rookie cards of some superstars now selling for more than $100 and even those of common players commanding prices many times their original cost. "Over the last two years it's been just awesome," said Frank Barning, the editor of the San Diego-based *Baseball Hobby News,* one of a number of periodicals that have sprung up to cater to the burgeoning interest in card collecting.

Industry estimates indicate there are now about 1 million serious collectors, and more than 100 card shows and fairs every *week.* From a handful no more than five years ago, there are now more than 3,500 retail card stores and more than 10,000 dealers.

As unabashed investors have joined

begin mastering the basic tools of the economics trade: supply and demand. After presenting demand and supply separately, we bring the two together. Finally, we explore the consequences of government price controls.

hobbyists in fueling the boom, the market for baseball cards has begun to take on the trappings of Wall Street.[1]

DEMAND

As Chapter 3 observed, consumers are on the buying side of product markets. Given their limited incomes, consumers must decide how much of each good they wish to buy. These decisions are based on various factors, including the good's price.

THE LAW OF DEMAND

The price of a good influences the amount consumers want to buy. High prices discourage consumption, which may be one reason you are driving that clunker instead of a BMW. In contrast, low prices spur additional purchases. This explains why businesses sometimes put their merchandise *on sale*—they have found that customers buy greater quantities once the price is reduced. Such observations lead to an economic principle known as the **law of demand:**

Other things (being) equal, when the price of a good rises the quantity demanded falls; when the price falls the quantity demanded rises.

Quantity Demanded
The amount of a good that consumers wish to buy at a particular price.

While the law of demand has an intuitive appeal, economists offer two explanations for the inverse relationship between price and **quantity demanded.** The first explanation rests on substitutability. A BMW and a Chevrolet are substitutes—both provide transportation. Likewise, butter and margarine are substitutes. As the price of a good falls, it becomes cheaper relative to its substitutes. The lower price induces some consumers to buy more of that good and less of the substitutes. Accordingly, consumption patterns change.

If the price of imported vehicles falls relative to the price of domestic vehicles, imports can be expected to carve out a larger share of the market. Or consider a price cut by Apple Computer. At a lower relative price, an Apple is more attractive than before. The price cut may be sufficient to convince some consumers to buy an Apple rather than an IBM or other substitute. Of course, the reverse holds for higher prices. If Apple raises prices, it loses potential customers to competing brands.

In addition to the substitution effect, there is a second reason for predicting a negative relation between price and quantity demanded. For any given income, a lower price increases consumer purchasing power: less income is now required to buy a given bundle of goods. As a result, consumers can increase consumption of

---

[1]Robert McG. Thomas, Jr., "Investors Hope a Rich Future Is in the Cards," *The New York Times,* April 10, 1988, pp. 19-20. Copyright © 1988 by The New York Times Company. Reprinted by permission.

various goods, including the good whose price has fallen. Conversely, a higher price reduces consumer purchasing power, which can be expected to reduce the quantity demanded of many goods.

Demand Schedule
A table showing the relationship between the price of a good and the quantity demanded per period of time, other things equal.

Demand Curve
A diagram showing the relationship between the price of a good and the quantity demanded per period of time, other things equal.

Consider a specific example. Suppose the **demand schedule** in Figure 4-1 represents the demand for fish in Harbortown.[2] Consistent with the law of demand, the quantity demanded rises as price falls. For example, when the price of fish decreases from $2.40 to $2.20 per pound, the quantity demanded rises from 6 million pounds to 8 million pounds per month. The **demand curve** is obtained by plotting the points of the demand schedule. Notice that the demand curve is expressed in terms of a specific period of time, in this case, a month. To say that consumers want 8 million pounds of fish is vague. In other words, is this the quantity demanded per week, per month, per year, or some other period of time? We must specify.

For simplicity we present a straight-line (linear) demand curve (Figure 4-1). But often demand curves are actually *curved.* If you become a corporate economist, one of your responsibilities may be to estimate the shape of the demand curves for your company's products.

SHIFTS IN THE DEMAND CURVE

The amount of a good that consumers stand ready to buy depends on more than the price of that good. Other relevant factors include income, prices of other goods, number of potential buyers, tastes, and expectations. The demand curve is drawn on the assumption that *other things are equal.* This assumption allows us to isolate the

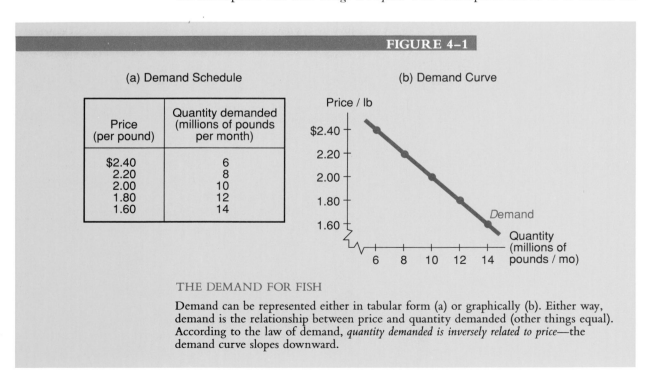

FIGURE 4–1

(a) Demand Schedule

Price (per pound)	Quantity demanded (millions of pounds per month)
$2.40	6
2.20	8
2.00	10
1.80	12
1.60	14

(b) Demand Curve

THE DEMAND FOR FISH

Demand can be represented either in tabular form (a) or graphically (b). Either way, demand is the relationship between price and quantity demanded (other things equal). According to the law of demand, *quantity demanded is inversely related to price—the* demand curve slopes downward.

---

[2]Actually, separate demand curves could be drawn for cod, lobster, perch, and the like. To keep the discussion general, we do not specify the type of fish.

relationship between price and the quantity demanded. That is, it indicates the effect of a price change provided that income, expectations, and all the other relevant factors affecting demand remain constant. Whenever one of these other variables changes, the result is a new demand curve—**a shift in demand.** We now discuss the major causes of such shifts.

Income

Generally, an increase in income increases demand for a good—shifts the demand curve rightward. With a higher income, consumers can afford to buy more of the good. Sometimes, however, consumption falls in response to a higher income. For example, as incomes rise consumers may decrease consumption of inexpensive foods (perhaps day-old bread, TV dinners, and generic brands) while expanding consumption of preferred foods (perhaps fresh bread, restaurant meals, and deli products). These responses are illustrated in Figure 4-2. An increase in income bolsters demand for **normal goods** (e.g., fresh bread) while reducing demand for **inferior goods** (e.g., day-old bread). A decrease in income has the opposite effect.

Prices of Substitutes

In satisfying their wants, consumers can generally substitute one good for another—fish for meat, apples for pears, sweaters for jackets. Given such options, the demand for a good depends on the prices of **substitute goods.** For example, when the price of beef rises, consumers can be expected to eat less beef and more fish. In other words, a higher price for beef increases the demand for fish (Figure 4-3a, page 70). In contrast, when the price of beef falls, consumers want to buy less fish. As consumers increase their purchases of beef, the demand for fish decreases (shifts leftward).

Prices of Complements

Complementary goods are goods that tend to be used together—for example, automobiles and gasoline, cameras and film, computer hardware and software. Because complements are used in tandem, a change in the price of one good alters

Normal Good
A good for which demand increases in response to a higher income.

Inferior Good
A good for which demand falls in response to a higher income.

Substitute Goods
Goods that are substitutable in consumption. Two goods are substitutes when an increase in the price of one good increases demand for the other.

Complementary Goods
Goods that are consumed together. Two goods are complements when an increase in the price of one good reduces demand for the other.

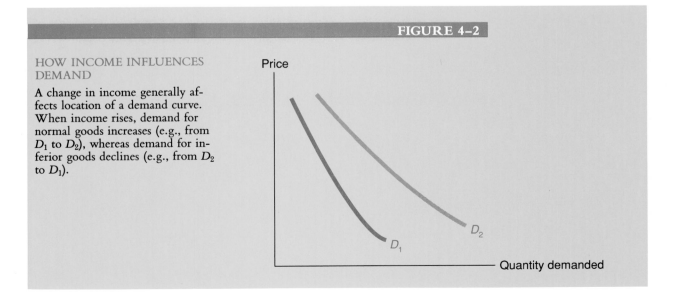

FIGURE 4–2

HOW INCOME INFLUENCES DEMAND

A change in income generally affects location of a demand curve. When income rises, demand for normal goods increases (e.g., from D_1 to D_2), whereas demand for inferior goods declines (e.g., from D_2 to D_1).

demand for the other. But whereas an increase in the price of a substitute shifts demand outward, an increase in the price of a complement shifts demand inward (see Figure 4-3b). When the price of tennis balls skyrockets, one expects consumers to demand fewer tennis racquets. Some continue to play tennis but less frequently, prolonging the life of their racquets. Others decide that tennis is now too expensive and turn to jogging, swimming, or other sports. Some may even give up exercise altogether (switching from court time to Miller time). A reduction in the price of tennis balls should have the opposite effect—encouraging more tennis and, in the process, increasing demand for tennis racquets.

Number of Potential Buyers

Another variable affecting demand is the number of consumers in the market. If a state were to lower the legal driving age, demand for automobiles would likely increase. Some who previously could not legally drive in the state would take advantage of the law and visit an automobile dealer. States also regulate alcoholic beverages, with many states raising the legal drinking age in recent years. Although liquor laws are frequently broken, they do have an impact. These laws make it more difficult for minors to obtain alcohol and they introduce a new deterrent (penalties if caught). This is enough to influence the behavior of some young people, thereby reducing demand for alcohol.

Tastes

Demand also depends on the tastes or preferences of consumers. A recent government report, criticized by ranchers, suggests that U.S. consumers eat too much red meat. Some research links high consumption of red meat to heart disease

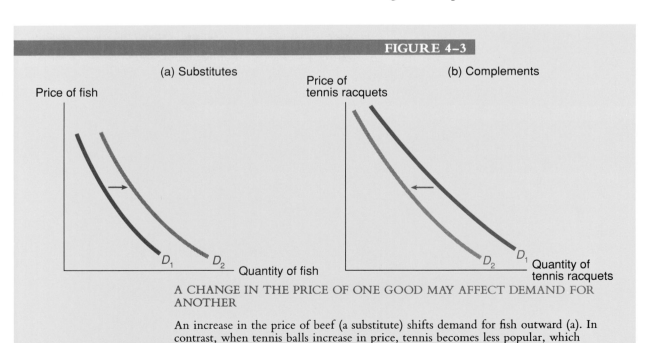

FIGURE 4–3

(a) Substitutes

(b) Complements

A CHANGE IN THE PRICE OF ONE GOOD MAY AFFECT DEMAND FOR ANOTHER

An increase in the price of beef (a substitute) shifts demand for fish outward (a). In contrast, when tennis balls increase in price, tennis becomes less popular, which dampens demand for tennis racquets (b).

and strokes. Other studies conclude that fried hamburgers contain carcinogens (cancer-causing agents). At the same time, many nutritionists tout the benefits of fish and poultry. Such reports can be expected to alter consumer buying patterns, augmenting the demand for fish and poultry while depressing the demand for red meat (see Figure 4-4).

Expectations

A belief that market conditions will change in the future can influence demand today. How do consumers react when they hear that stores may run out of bathroom tissue, that coffee prices will soon jump, or that production of their favorite beverage is being discontinued? Many try to beat the price hike or empty shelves by stocking up on the item now—buying more in the current period than they otherwise would. The result is an increase in current demand.

DISTINGUISHING BETWEEN CHANGES IN DEMAND AND CHANGES IN THE QUANTITY DEMANDED

Because the events described in Figures 4-5(a) and (b) (page 72) clearly differ, they must be given different names, so we can distinguish between them without confusion. The names economists have chosen to denote Figures 4-5(a) and (b), respectively, are **a change in demand** and **a change in quantity demanded.**

The expression "a change in demand" refers to a *shift in the demand curve*—the relationship between price and quantity demanded has been modified. At any given price, the quantity demanded is now different: it is higher if demand increases, lower if demand falls (see Figure 4-5a). *Again,* the major reasons for a change in demand: a change in income, different expectations, and so on.

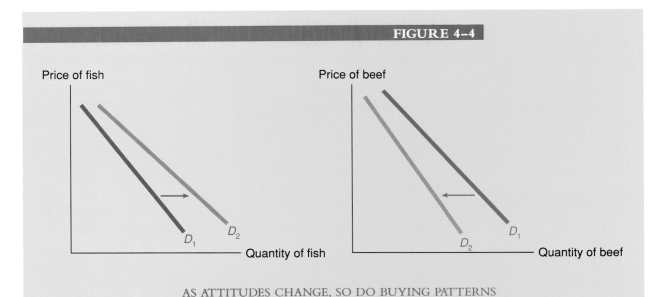

FIGURE 4–4

AS ATTITUDES CHANGE, SO DO BUYING PATTERNS

When published reports convince consumers they should eat more fish, while cutting back on beef, demand for fish increases and demand for beef falls.

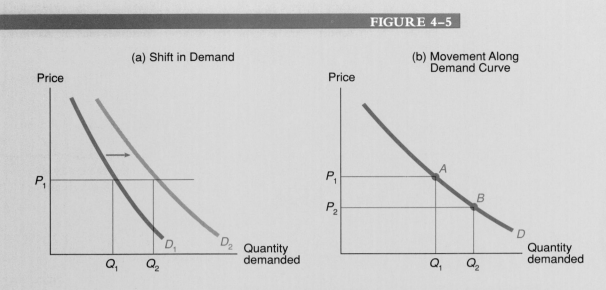

FIGURE 4–5

A SHIFT IN DEMAND VERSUS A MOVEMENT ALONG A DEMAND CURVE
A shift in demand (a) occurs when some determinant of demand changes, other than a good's own price. An increase in demand means that at each price (e.g., P_1) a greater quantity is now demanded (Q_2 rather than Q_1). A movement along a demand curve (b) occurs in response to a change in the price of the good. When price falls from P_1 to P_2, the quantity demanded increases from Q_1 to Q_2.

Note carefully that a change in the good's own price does *not* cause a change in demand. When the price of a good changes, the quantity demanded either rises (if price falls) or falls (if price rises). But the demand curve does not shift. Instead, a change in a good's own price can be represented as a *movement along the demand curve* (see Figure 4-5b). There has been a change in quantity demanded, but not a change in demand.

This is an important point, one you are expected to master: *A change in a good's own price leads to a movement along a given demand curve (a change in quantity demanded); a change in any other variable results in a new demand curve (a change in demand).*

YOUR TURN   RECOGNIZING SHIFTS IN DEMAND
How, if at all, do the following factors affect the demand for record players?

(a) The price of records falls.
(b) The price of compact disc players falls.
(c) The price of record players falls.
(d) The country's population increases.
(e) Consumers decide to spend more time watching music videos and less time listening to records.

SUPPLY

Despite its importance, demand alone determines neither price nor quantity purchased. A market must have sellers as well as buyers; otherwise, there can be no transactions. Accordingly, it is essential to consider the supply side of the market. What determines the amount of a good that sellers are willing to bring to market? Several factors are important, including price of the good.

THE LAW OF SUPPLY

Quantity Supplied
The amount of a good that firms wish to sell at a particular price.

The **law of supply** predicts a positive relationship between price and the **quantity supplied:**

Other things (being) equal, a higher price for a good increases the quantity supplied; a lower price reduces the quantity supplied.

Price is an inducement, the carrot that prompts sellers to bring a good to market. As price rises, the incentive to sell intensifies. Not only do existing firms want to provide more of the good, but new firms may also be drawn into the market now that the reward for selling the product has been sweetened.

When the price of fish rises, additional resources are drawn into fishing. Boats and equipment that were idle at low prices are called into service. Vessels ordinarily used for other purposes (e.g., sightseeing or recreation) may be converted to fishing boats. Crews put in more hours, fishing some waters more intensively as well as traveling farther out to sea. New fishing operations may be started because of more favorable market conditions. All these responses contribute to a greater quantity supplied.

A higher price achieves similar results on land. When the price of corn rises, other things equal, farmers grow more corn. Some land is switched from less profitable crops to production of corn. Low-grade land that previously was idle is planted with corn. Not only does acreage increase, but so does yield per acre—due to more intensive use of fertilizer, pesticides, and irrigation.[3]

Supply Schedule
A table showing the relationship between the price of a good and the quantity supplied per period of time, other things equal.
Supply Curve
A diagram showing the relationship between the price of a good and the quantity supplied per period of time, other things equal.

As is true for demand curves, supply curves are drawn on the assumption that other things are equal—that the other factors influencing supply do not change. Under these conditions, there is a unique functional relationship between price and the quantity supplied. That relationship can be expressed in terms of either a **supply schedule** or a **supply curve.** A hypothetical supply schedule and the corresponding supply curve are presented in Figure 4-6 (page 74).

Analogous to the case of demand, a change in price leads to a *movement along the supply curve.* For example, in Figure 4-6, raising the price of fish from $1.60/pound to $1.80/pound increases the quantity of fish supplied from 8 million pounds to 9 million pounds per month. A change in the value of any other determinant of supply (besides the good's own price) results in a new supply curve: *a shift in supply.* When the supply curve shifts leftward, supply has decreased—at each price a lower quantity is now brought to market. When the supply curve shifts rightward, supply has increased. This is illustrated in Figure 4-7 (page 74).

---

[3]For corn and other crops, empirical studies estimate that the increase in yield per acre exceeds the increase in acreage.

FIGURE 4-6

(a) Supply Schedule

Price (per pound)	Quantity supplied (millions of pounds per month)
$2.40	12
2.20	11
2.00	10
1.80	9
1.60	8

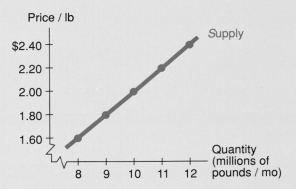

(b) Supply Curve

SUPPLY OF FISH

The supply schedule (a) and supply curve (b) indicate that the quantity of fish supplied is a positive function of price (other things equal). This is consistent with the law of supply.

FIGURE 4-7

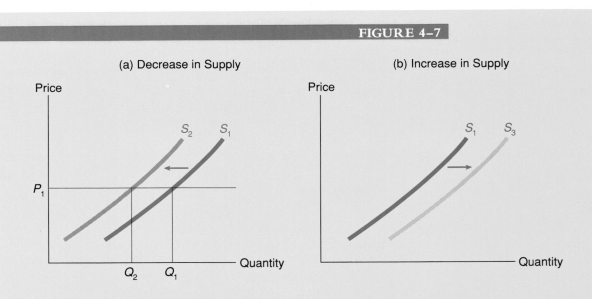

SHIFTS IN SUPPLY

Supply decreases when costs of production rise (e.g., due to higher input prices), when prices of other goods (the firm could produce) increase, or when producers anticipate higher prices. At any given price (e.g., P_1) a smaller quantity is now supplied (Q_2 rather than Q_1). In contrast, supply increases (b) when production costs fall, when prices of other goods decline, or when producers anticipate lower prices.

SHIFTS IN SUPPLY

The major forces responsible for changes in supply are costs of production, prices of other goods, and expectations.

Costs of Production

Whereas a higher price increases the reward for production, higher costs reduce the incentive to produce. The result is a decrease in supply. Conversely, developments that make production less costly increase supply. Costs may change for several reasons, notably *a change in input prices, taxes,* and *technological change.*

Higher input prices add to the costs of production. Assume the prices of fuel and boats rise, so that it costs more to catch fish. Some who fish may decide to leave the sea now that fishing is less lucrative. Others remain, but fish less. At each price suppliers are willing to sell fewer fish now that costs have increased. As this example illustrates, higher input prices reduce supply.

The imposition of a tax on output (or an increase in an existing tax) likewise adds to production costs.[4] Again the result is a leftward shift in the supply curve—the tax reduces the quantity that producers are willing to supply at each price.

Production costs, when they change, do not always head skyward. Sometimes they fall. When this happens the result is an increase in supply. Supply increases when input prices are reduced, when taxes on producers are lowered, or when costs otherwise decline. Technological advance provides an example of how production costs can fall, even if input prices and taxes do not. Technological advances have increased agricultural yields per acre, lowered the cost of radios, and permitted computers to be manufactured more cheaply. The result: greater supplies of food, radios, and computers.

Prices of Other Goods the Firm Could Produce

Resources often can be diverted from the production of one good to another. For example, land may be suitable for growing both corn and wheat. For that reason, the supply of corn depends on the price of wheat. An increase in the price of wheat makes growing corn less attractive (the opportunity cost rises). As some land is switched from production of corn to wheat, the supply of corn falls (the supply curve shifts leftward). Conversely, more corn is grown when the price of wheat falls (the supply curve of corn shifts rightward).

Expectations of Producers

Expectations may affect producers as well as consumers, supply as well as demand. For some goods the expectation of higher prices provides producers with an incentive to reduce supply in the present period, deferring sales to the future. For example, oil producers may withhold oil from the market in the current period in anticipation of sharply higher prices in subsequent months. So for any given price, the amount supplied in the current period declines. Or suppose oil prices are

---

[4]Taxes are discussed more fully in Chapter 5.

EXHIBIT 4–1

A NEW NUMBER ONE CROP?

The National Organization for the Reform of Marijuana Laws (NORML) claims that in 1985 marijuana became the largest revenue-producing crop in the United States. Officials at the U.S. Department of Agriculture insist that corn remains king. Because marijuana growers are understandably reluctant to report their harvests, the debate is not likely to be resolved. But even if marijuana is only the second- or third-largest crop, it is clearly big business. Does our discussion of supply hold for illegal goods such as marijuana? Yes, the same forces operate.

Consider the law of supply as applied to marijuana. In response to a higher price, existing growers can be expected to raise larger crops. Some may take less profitable crops out of production in order to grow more marijuana. Some previously

idle land may also be planted. Lured by high potential profits, new producers are likely to enter the market. Some consumers may even decide to grow their own and become sellers. A higher price for marijuana leads to a greater quantity supplied.

A change in costs of production also has the predicted effect: a shift in supply. Because of heightened concern over controlled substance abuse, the federal government recently stepped up enforcement of drug laws. Heightened enforcement caused suppliers to spend more on security in order to avoid detection and to switch to more elaborate and expensive means of transportation. Both actions drove up the costs of marijuana production. As a consequence, the supply of marijuana decreased. How did this reduction in supply affect the price of marijuana? Read on.

---

expected to fall. Producers may want to increase supply now, before conditions deteriorate.

For other goods supply is independent of price expectations. An anticipated increase in the price of haircuts is unlikely to affect the current supply of haircuts. The central difference between oil and haircuts is that oil is storable, haircuts are not.[5] Oil not sold today can be sold later. In contrast, haircuts cannot be inventoried. Sales not made this period may be lost forever.

THE INTERACTION OF SUPPLY AND DEMAND

Thus far we have dealt separately with demand and supply; it is now time to bring the two together and explain how prices are determined. We restrict our analysis to competitive markets, which contain a large number of buyers and sellers, none large enough to influence price. In such markets firms compete against each other for customers, and consumers compete for the available output. (For now we ignore government intervention, but consider the effect of government price controls later in the chapter.)

For a given price, the demand curve reveals the quantity demanded, the supply curve the quantity supplied. Neither curve, by itself, sheds any light on the price that will prevail. But bring supply and demand together and it is a different matter,

---

[5]Because of the *storable* nature of oil, it is important to distinguish between *production* of oil and *supply* of oil. The expectation of higher oil prices induces producers to cut back current supply—to reduce the amount they are willing to sell this period at any given price. But current production does not necessarily decline. It may even increase as oil producers build up inventories.

as can be seen with the aid of the supply and demand schedules for fish given in Table 4-1.

Consider a price of $1.60/lb. At this price the quantity demanded (14 million pounds) exceeds the quantity supplied (8 million pounds)—there is an excess demand, or **shortage,** of 6 million pounds. This situation cannot persist. Rivalry among consumers will push up prices. Rather than accept less than they want, some fish-hungry consumers will offer sellers a higher price. Those who fish, finding that they can sell their product at a higher price, are only too happy to raise their prices. Higher prices reduce the shortage for two reasons: consumers reduce the amount of fish they want to buy while suppliers increase the amount they are willing to sell. At a price of $1.80/lb, the shortage shrinks to 3 million pounds. But as long as a shortage exists, upward pressure on prices will continue.

Now consider a price of $2.40/lb. At this price the quantity supplied (12 million pounds) exceeds the quantity demanded (6 million pounds). The market is characterized by an excess supply, or a **surplus,** of 6 million pounds. Such conditions cannot persist over time. Unable to sell as much as they would like, some who fish will cut prices in order to spur sales. (Would you want to be stuck with a load of smelly fish?) As prices fall, consumers will want to buy more fish; producers will want to sell less. Both forces cause the surplus to dwindle. The market will exert downward pressure on prices until the surplus is eliminated.

EQUILIBRIUM

Having peeked at Table 4-1, you realize that a price exists ($2.00) for which there is neither a shortage of fish nor a surplus. This is the **equilibrium price.** At this price the amount consumers wish to buy coincides exactly with the amount producers wish to sell. The market is in **equilibrium,** a state of balance. Producers have no incentive to lower prices; they are selling all they want at this price. Nor do consumers have any reason to bid up prices; at the equilibrium price they are consuming the amount desired. As long as supply and demand remain unchanged, there is no reason for price to move away from the equilibrium price.

Equilibrium can also be depicted graphically as the intersection of the supply and demand curves. In Figure 4-8 (page 78), the equilibrium price is $2.00 and the equilibrium quantity is 10 million pounds per month.

Shortage
The amount by which quantity demanded exceeds quantity supplied at a given price.

Surplus
The amount by which quantity supplied exceeds quantity demanded at a given price.

Equilibrium Price
The price for which the quantity demanded equals the quantity supplied.
Equilibrium
A state of balance; a market is in equilibrium when the quantity demanded equals the quantity supplied.

TABLE 4-1			
DEMAND AND SUPPLY OF FISH			
Price per pound	Quantity demanded (Q^d)*	Quantity supplied (Q^s)*	$(Q^d - Q^s)$*
$2.40	6	12	−6 ⎫ surplus
2.20	8	11	−3 ⎭
2.00	10	10	0 equilibrium
1.80	12	9	3 ⎫ shortage
1.60	14	8	6 ⎭

*Millions of pounds per month.

FIGURE 4–8

EQUILIBRIUM IN THE
FISH MARKET

Equilibrium occurs where
supply and demand curves
intersect. Here the equi-
librium price is $2.00 and
the equilibrium quantity
is 10 million pounds per
month. At any higher
price (e.g., $2.40) there is
a surplus, which exerts
downward pressure on
price. When the price is
below $2.00, the resulting
shortage causes the price
to increase.

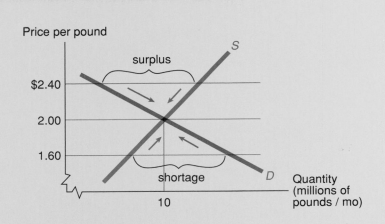

DISEQUILIBRIUM

Disequilibrium Price
Any price for which the
quantity demanded differs
from the quantity supplied.
Disequilibrium
A state of imbalance; a
market is in disequilibrium
when the quantity
demanded does not
coincide with the quantity
supplied.

Any price for which quantity demanded and quantity supplied diverge is called a
disequilibrium price. In unrestricted, competitive markets, disequilibrium prices
cannot be maintained. Whenever the actual price exceeds the equilibrium price it
falls, as producers attempt to unload unwanted surpluses. In contrast, whenever the
actual price is below the equilibrium price, consumers respond to the shortage by
bidding up the price.

As demand or supply changes, what previously was an equilibrium price
becomes a **disequilibrium** price, and the market moves to its new equilibrium.
How rapidly prices adjust depends on the market. In some markets price changes are
almost instantaneous. For example, on the Minneapolis Grain Exchange, grain
prices respond immediately to changes in buying or selling plans. In other markets
adjustments may be more sluggish and, as we see later, the government sometimes
impedes a market's movement to equilibrium.

CHANGES IN THE EQUILIBRIUM PRICE

Equilibrium corresponds to the intersection of supply and demand curves. Both
supply and demand are crucial (see Exhibit 4-2); if either changes, the result is a new
equilibrium. We now consider, in turn, a shift in demand, a shift in supply, and a
shift in both demand and supply curves.

A Change in Demand

Earlier we explained why demand might change. Let us now consider the
consequences of such change. As Figure 4-9 illustrates, an increase in demand leads
to an increase in both the equilibrium price and quantity. As demand increases from
D_1 to D_2, the equilibrium price rises from P_1 to P_2 and the equilibrium quantity from
Q_1 to Q_2. Analysis of a decrease in demand is symmetric: when demand falls, so do
the equilibrium price and quantity.

EXHIBIT 4–2

THE TWO BLADES OF A PAIR OF SCISSORS

Early economists debated the relative importance of supply and demand in determining market price. Emphasizing costs of production, classical economists (such as David Ricardo) gave top billing to supply. A later school of thought, marginalism, focused on consumer utility or demand. According to the marginalist view, the price of a good is determined by the utility or satisfaction to consumers of an additional unit of that good. Alfred Marshall resolved the controversy by explaining that price depends critically on both supply and demand. In a famous passage comparing supply and demand to the two blades of a pair of scissors, Marshall writes:

> We might as reasonably dispute whether it is the upper or under blade of a pair of scissors that cuts a piece of paper, as whether value is governed by utility [demand] or cost of production [supply].

Another contribution of Marshall was explaining consumer responsiveness to price changes. Marshall presented certain principles that indicate why price changes have a disproportionately large effect on the quantity demanded of some goods but relatively little effect on the quantity demanded of others.[6]

Marshall was born in London in 1842. Despite pressure from his father to enter the ministry, Marshall studied mathematics and later turned to economics. He taught at Cambridge and Bristol, where he shaped the thinking of the next generation of English economists.

A gifted mathematician, Marshall went against the tide by attempting to keep economics comprehensible to the lay audience. He argued that "when a great many symbols have to be used, they become very laborious to any one but the writer himself." Marshall's highly influential book, *Principles of Economics,* went through eight editions before his death in 1924. It is still being sold today.

---

[6]The technical term for this "responsiveness" is the "price elasticity of demand." This concept is discussed in Chapter 5. Marshall's work was not restricted to consumer goods. Extending his analysis to the demand for labor, Marshall also examined the responsiveness of employers to changes in the price of labor (the wage rate).

FIGURE 4–9

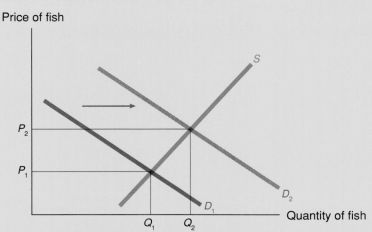

A CHANGE IN DEMAND GENERATES A NEW EQUILIBRIUM
An increase in the demand for fish (e.g., due to reports recommending more fish in consumers' diets) increases the equilibrium price and quantity of fish.

A Change in Supply

Like an increase in demand, a greater supply also puts upward pressure on quantity (Figure 4-10). The difference is that a greater supply depresses price. Given an increase in supply from S_1 to S_2, the equilibrium price falls from P_1 to P_2 while the equilibrium quantity rises from Q_1 to Q_2. A decrease in supply has the opposite effect: the equilibrium price rises and the equilibrium quantity falls.

A Change in Both Demand and Supply

Now that you appreciate the effect of a change in demand or supply, let's muddy the waters. Assume both the demand and supply curves shift. What happens to equilibrium price and quantity? For example, suppose the demand for fish and the supply of fish both increase. In that event, the new equilibrium quantity is higher—increases in demand and supply both exert upward pressure on quantity. But what happens to price? The answer is not obvious, since an increase in demand tends to raise price, whereas an increase in supply has the opposite effect.

Whether price rises, falls, or remains unchanged depends on the magnitude of the shift in demand relative to the shift in supply. This is shown in Figure 4-11. When supply increases to S_2, price is higher at the new equilibrium. When the supply curve shifts all the way to S_4 (c), the new equilibrium price is lower. Finally, when supply increases to S_3 (so that at P_1 supply and demand shift by the same horizontal amount), the equilibrium price does not change. In analogous fashion, when demand and supply both decline, the equilibrium quantity falls; however, barring information on the extent to which demand and supply have changed, the effect on price is ambiguous.

When demand and supply curves shift in opposite directions, the effect on price is clear, but the effect on quantity is indeterminate. A simultaneous increase in demand and decrease in supply raise the equilibrium price. A reduction in demand

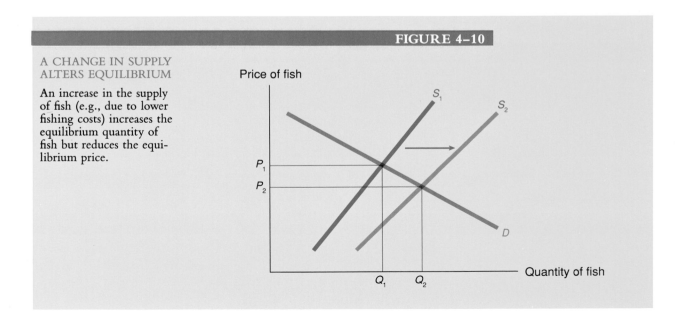

FIGURE 4–10

A CHANGE IN SUPPLY ALTERS EQUILIBRIUM

An increase in the supply of fish (e.g., due to lower fishing costs) increases the equilibrium quantity of fish but reduces the equilibrium price.

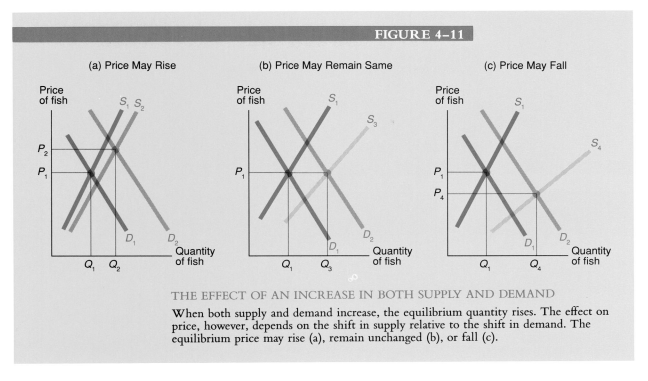

FIGURE 4-11

(a) Price May Rise · (b) Price May Remain Same · (c) Price May Fall

THE EFFECT OF AN INCREASE IN BOTH SUPPLY AND DEMAND

When both supply and demand increase, the equilibrium quantity rises. The effect on price, however, depends on the shift in supply relative to the shift in demand. The equilibrium price may rise (a), remain unchanged (b), or fall (c).

coupled with growth in supply push the equilibrium price lower. Whether quantity rises, falls, or remains unchanged depends on the relative shifts of the demand and supply curves.

YOUR TURN APPLYING SUPPLY AND DEMAND ANALYSIS TO AUTOMOBILE EXPORT RESTRICTIONS

As a result of intense pressure from Congress, Japan agreed to limit the number of automobiles shipped to the United States. (a) How has this "voluntary export restriction" affected the supply of automobiles imported by the United States and the price paid by U.S. consumers for imported automobiles? (b) How and why does a change in the price of imported automobiles affect the demand for domestic automobiles (i.e., automobiles produced in the United States)? (c) Given your answers to (a) and (b), how have voluntary export restrictions affected the price of domestic automobiles?

PRICE CONTROLS

Price Ceiling
The maximum legal price that may be charged for a good.

Price Floor
The minimum legal price that must be paid for a good.

So far we have assumed that markets operate free of government intervention. But sometimes governments erect barriers that may prevent equilibrium from being attained. A primary example is *price controls,* which may take the form of either a **price ceiling** or a **price floor.** A price ceiling refers to the maximum legal price at which a good may be sold. A price floor is the minimum legal price.

Examples of price controls abound. Rent controls place a lid on rents, usury laws provide a cap on interest rates (the price paid for borrowing money). Federal minimum wage laws mandate that employers covered by these laws cannot hire labor at less than a specified rate of pay ($3.35 per hour in 1989). In many agricultural markets, price supports place a lower limit on prices.

Price controls are often imposed for political reasons. Sometimes buyers pressure politicians to limit the price they must pay (as in the case of rent controls). In other instances sellers convince government officials to guarantee a minimum price for their product (as in the case of agricultural price supports). Given the frequency with which price controls are imposed, it is important to examine their impact. We begin with price ceilings.

PRICE CEILINGS

Assume the government sets a maximum legal price for some good. To be specific, assume the price of gasoline is subject to an upper limit (as was true during part of the 1970s). What is the impact of this government decree? The answer depends on whether the maximum price is set above or below the equilibrium price:

A price ceiling set above the equilibrium price has no impact. A price ceiling set below the equilibrium price tends to create a shortage.

These two statements can be visualized with the aid of Figure 4-12. Assume the government establishes a maximum legal price of P_1. Despite this action, motorists find it unnecessary to pay a price this high. Any station owner attempting to extract the maximum legal price from consumers loses customers to companies charging a lower price. Thus a maximum price set above the equilibrium price does not prevent the equilibrium price from being attained. Although the government rules out prices above P_1, these prices would not have prevailed even in the absence of a price ceiling.

On a more whimsical note, consider a proposal made in the late 1970s, when resentment toward OPEC was high: a bushel of wheat should sell for more than a barrel of oil. ("You can't eat oil.") At the time, oil was trading for about $30 per barrel and wheat at about $4 per bushel. Suppose the U.S. government, taking the

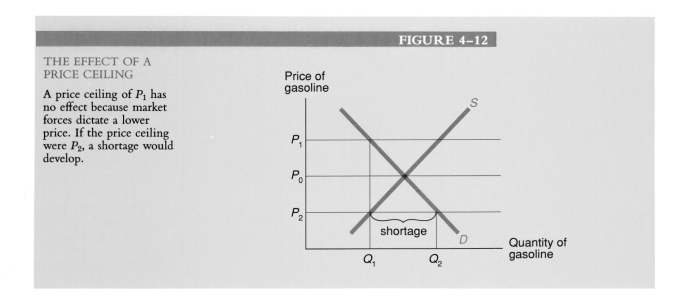

FIGURE 4-12

THE EFFECT OF A PRICE CEILING

A price ceiling of P_1 has no effect because market forces dictate a lower price. If the price ceiling were P_2, a shortage would develop.

Price of gasoline

P_1

P_0

P_2

shortage

S

D

Quantity of gasoline

Q_1 Q_2

recommendation seriously, sternly announced that it would not tolerate a price of wheat in excess of $30 per bushel. Would this pronouncement affect either the price or the quantity of wheat sold? Obviously not. Even without this "protection," no buyer would be foolish enough to pay more than dictated by the market—let alone $30 per bushel. All the government would be doing in this case is forbidding prices that the market had already ruled out.

Figure 4-12 also illustrates what happens when a price ceiling is set below the equilibrium price. A maximum price of P_2, if effectively enforced, creates a shortage of $Q_2 - Q_1$. Although the low price is considered attractive to consumers, producers are unwilling to supply more than Q_1 to the market.

In an unrestricted market, price rations out of the market those unwilling or unable to pay the equilibrium price. With price constrained below the equilibrium level, this rationing function is thwarted. Buyers unwilling to pay the equilibrium price remain in the market. How then will the available output be allocated? Given excess demand, who will leave the market satisfied and who will leave frustrated?

When price is frozen below the equilibrium level, the primary methods of allocating goods are *first-come first-served, government mandate,* and *sellers' choice.* In some situations the last may be first, but not when it comes to shortages. If there is not enough gasoline to go around at the price ceiling, one method of distributing the quantity available is on the basis of who is first in line at the pump. When the pumps run dry, those still in line are out of luck.

Alternatively, the government could decide which consumers receive how much. Under the Carter Administration, the government considered methods of allocating gasoline in the event of a severe shortage. For example, each driver might be permitted to purchase a specified number of gallons of gasoline per week. This is the approach commonly adopted during wartime. Not only is money required to purchase a product, but the consumer must also have a *ration ticket,* which conveys the right to buy a good.

Another option is to allow sellers to decide who can buy the good and who cannot. Under such circumstances the owner of a gasoline station is likely to give top priority to employees, friends, and regular customers. (If so, the owner may be surprised to discover how many friends he or she has.) Alternatively, given excess demand at the legal price, the owner might refuse to sell to members of a particular race, nationality, or sex. In other words, a price ceiling creates an environment conducive to discrimination.

Regardless of the nonprice method of allocation, many consumers will be thwarted in their attempts to purchase the product. Some may be willing to offer suppliers a little extra—either directly in the form of a price above the legal ceiling or indirectly by providing the seller with something else of value. In fact, when gasoline shortages developed in California during the "oil crisis," the press reported instances of service station attendants being offered personal favors in return for the opportunity to purchase gasoline. At the same time that some consumers are willing to pay more than the legal price rather than do without, suppliers have an incentive to sell at a price in excess of the price ceiling, thereby earning extra profits.[7] It should

---

[7]Note that a price ceiling could actually lead to a *higher* price than would occur in an unregulated market. In the extreme case, when controls effectively limit the quantity supplied to Q_1 (Figure 4-12), firms may be able to sell (illegally) their output for as much as P_1. Further note that when sellers differ in terms of their inclination to obey the law, a price floor is more likely to drive law-abiding suppliers from the market. Suppliers unwilling to charge more than the legal price earn less than those willing to break the law.

Black Market
A market in which goods are bought and sold at prices above the legal maximum.

therefore come as no surprise that exchanges sometimes occur illegally in what is known as the **black market.**

Nonprice rationing occasionally crops up in markets that are not regulated by the government. For instance, recently a builder in California completed a subdivision and then offered all the houses for sale at a specified price. So many people wanted to purchase his houses that the builder resorted to a lottery to determine the lucky buyers. What this indicates is that the builder set the price too low: he could have sold all the houses at a higher price and therefore earned greater profits. Although the builder did not know the equilibrium or market-clearing price, he could have discovered it. Had he auctioned the houses, each would have sold to the buyer willing to pay the highest price.

Universities sometimes set prices for athletic events at levels that do not yield maximum profits. For example, every football game at the University of Nebraska is a sellout, and fans must be turned away. The university could generate additional revenues by raising ticket prices, but profit maximization is not a goal of universities. Still, economic forces do play a role. Universities generally find tickets for those contributing to their athletic programs (sellers' choice).

Price ceilings can do more than create allocation problems. Consider the case of rent controls, which keep the price of rental housing below market levels. Although often supported as a way to protect low-income tenants, the negative repercussions of rent controls abound. Housing quality declines. Owners have little incentive to maintain housing, let alone make improvements, since the cost cannot be passed on to consumers through higher rents. By accelerating the rate at which housing deteriorates, controls reduce the stock of housing in the long run, exacerbating the shortage. Rent-controlled housing becomes difficult to find, so consumers are forced to spend more time searching for it, lower their standards (e.g., accept lower-quality housing or housing in a nonpreferred location), and often make side payments, effectively raising the price above the legal maximum. Market values for rent-controlled housing plunge, which lowers the amount cities collect in real-estate taxes. Sometimes property values become negative, as costs exceed rental income, inducing landlords to abandon their property.

PRICE FLOORS

Rather than set a maximum legal price, sometimes a government mandates a minimum price. As was the case for price ceilings, the ultimate impact depends on the value of the price floor relative to the equilibrium price:

A price floor set below the equilibrium price has no impact. A price floor set above the equilibrium price tends to create a surplus.

Consider the market for sugar depicted in Figure 4-13. When the price floor (P_1) is set below the equilibrium price (P_0), neither price nor quantity is affected. Because suppliers can sell their output at a price in excess of P_1, the price floor does not hinder attainment of equilibrium.

This is not the case when the minimum legal price exceeds the equilibrium price. A price floor of P_2 creates a surplus of $Q_2 - Q_1$. Producers want to sell more than the equilibrium quantity; consumers want to buy less. Unless the government buys the surplus, producers have an incentive to shave the price. Extra income can be earned by those willing to violate the law or clever enough to get around it (see Exhibit 4-3).

FIGURE 4–13

THE EFFECT OF A PRICE FLOOR

A price floor of P_1 rules out all lower prices. However, because the equilibrium price is higher than P_1, the price floor has no effect. A price floor of P_2, which lies above the equilibrium price, tends to create a surplus.

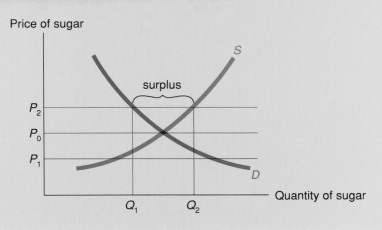

EXHIBIT 4–3

A SWEET DEAL

In 1982, the federal government established price supports for sugar. Recently, while raw (unrefined) sugar was selling for as little as 3 cents per pound in world markets, the U.S. government enforced a minimum price of 22 cents per pound for sugar produced in the United States. To prevent buyers from switching to foreign-produced sugar, the government restricted sugar imports.

The cost advantage of up to 19 cents per pound for imports tempted more than a few producers to smuggle sugar into the United States. One of the favorite scams was to take advantage of a loophole in the law. In essence, raw sugar could be purchased legally at low prices in foreign markets and then brought into the United States for refining, provided that the refined sugar was sold outside the United States. Customs officials and agents for the Justice Department discovered that the volume of refined sugar leaving the United States was much less than the volume of raw sugar entering the country. The difference, estimated to be as much as one million tons since 1982, was being sold illegally in the United States at premium prices. Some companies allegedly filed false shipping documents, claiming they were exporting their refined sugar, while they were actually selling it in the United States. More than a dozen companies were indicted on charges of smuggling and falsifying documents.

Smuggling was not the only tactic for obtaining cheap sugar—potential profits spur creativity. Some U.S. companies actually imported candy, melted it down, and then extracted the sugar! Whenever a law sets prices at artificial levels, it creates incentives to violate the law—either in letter or in spirit.

SUMMARY

1. According to the law of demand, the quantity demanded is inversely related to price—demand curves slope downward. A lower price induces consumers to buy relatively more of a good and less of substitutes. In addition, a lower price increases consumers' purchasing power, enabling them to buy more of the good.

2. Demand is the relationship between the price of a good and the amount consumers want to buy, other things equal. A change in the price leads to a change in the quantity

demanded—a movement along the demand curve. A change in any other variable (income, tastes, and the like) results in a change in demand—a shift of the demand curve.

3. A higher income boosts demand for normal goods but dampens demand for inferior goods. A lower income has the opposite effect.

4. A change in the price of one good may affect demand for another. If two goods are substitutes, a rise in the price of one increases demand for the other. In the case of complements, a higher price for one good reduces demand for the other.

5. Demand also depends on the number of potential buyers, tastes, and expectations.

6. The law of supply states that, other things equal, the quantity supplied is a positive function of price—supply curves slope upward.

7. Changes in costs of production, prices of other goods, and expectations lead to a change in supply—a shift of the supply curve.

8. Equilibrium occurs when the quantity demanded equals the quantity supplied. When price is above the equilibrium price, a surplus results, putting downward pressure on price. When price is below the equilibrium price, a shortage develops, putting upward pressure on price. A change in demand or supply results in a new equilibrium.

9. A price ceiling set below the equilibrium price tends to create a shortage. In response, a black market is likely to emerge. When price is not allowed to ration the available quantity, alternative methods of allocation must be used—for example, first-come first-served, government mandate, or sellers' choice. A price ceiling set above the equilibrium price has no impact.

10. A price floor set above the equilibrium price tends to create a surplus. Given excess supply, the price floor may be difficult to maintain. A price floor set below the equilibrium price has no impact.

KEY TERMS

law of demand	supply schedule
quantity demanded	supply curve
demand schedule	a shift in supply
demand curve	shortage
a shift in demand	surplus
normal good	equilibrium price
inferior good	equilibrium
substitute good	disequilibrium
complementary good	disequilibrium price
a change in demand	price ceiling
a change in quantity demanded	price floor
law of supply	black market
quantity supplied	

STUDY QUESTIONS AND PROBLEMS

1. (a) Why do demand curves slope downward? (b) Why do supply curves slope upward?

2. (a) List several factors that would be expected to increase the demand for turkey. (b) List several factors that would be expected to increase the supply of turkey.

3. Would an increase in the price of hamburgers change the supply of hamburgers? Would it change the quantity supplied? Explain.

4. The following graph depicts the demand for and supply of VCR tape rentals in Pleasantville:

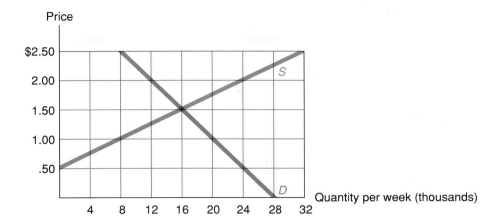

a. At which price is the quantity demanded equal to 8000 tapes per week?
b. At which price is the quantity supplied equal to 8000 tapes per week?
c. What is the equilibrium price for renting a tape? What is the equilibrium quantity?
d. If the rental price is $2 per tape, what is the quantity demanded? How many tapes are supplied at this price?
e. Will a price of $2 per tape lead to a shortage or a surplus of tapes?
f. At which price is there a shortage of 12,000 tapes per week?

5. Explain how each of the following affects the equilibrium price and the equilibrium quantity of trucking services. In each case, indicate whether the changes are due to a shift in the demand for trucking services or a shift in supply.
a. The tax on diesel fuel is raised.
b. Insurance rates for truckers are reduced.
c. The number of households seeking to move furniture and other possessions increases.
d. The price for shipping freight by rail (an alternative mode of transportation) is reduced.
e. The speed limit for trucks is increased, reducing the time required to make deliveries.
f. Engineers discover ways to increase the gas mileage of trucks without increasing the price of trucks.

6. Assume that a freeze damages this year's crop of oranges.
a. What effect does this have on the supply of oranges and on the price of oranges?
b. How does this change in the price of oranges affect the demand for apples?
c. Given your answer to (b), how does the price of apples change, other things equal?

7. In December 1988, the Ford Motor Company announced that it was developing a catalytic converter that could be manufactured without platinum. At the time, *one-third* of the world's platinum output was used in the manufacture of catalytic converters.
a. How would Ford's new catalytic converters affect the demand for platinum?
b. Assume that new platinum deposits are discovered. How would this affect the supply of platinum?
c. How would the shifts in supply and demand just discussed affect the equilibrium price of platinum?
d. How would these changes in supply and demand affect the equilibrium output of platinum? Explain.

8. Assume the quantity of houses demanded exceeds the quantity supplied. In the absence of price controls, how would you expect prices to adjust? As housing prices change, what happens to the quantity demanded and to the quantity supplied?

9. The government's price-support program guarantees farmers a minimum price per bushel of wheat.

     a. What impact does this program have when the minimum price is set below the equilibrium price of wheat?

     b. What impact does this program have when the minimum price is set above the equilibrium price of wheat?

10. Assume the equilibrium price of pens is higher in 1991 than in 1990, and the equilibrium price of pencils is lower. If the government imposed a price ceiling that prevented prices from rising in 1991, what impact would this have on the market for pens and on the market for pencils? Explain.

11. Can you spot the flaw in the following argument?

> An increase in the demand for pretzels increases their price. Consumers respond to a higher price by reducing the number of pretzels they buy. Therefore, an increase in the demand for pretzels results in consumers buying fewer pretzels.

    What mistake does the author make?

ANSWERS TO YOUR TURN

RECOGNIZING SHIFTS IN DEMAND

(a) A lower price for records, a complement, *increases* the demand for record players. (b) A lower price for compact disk players, a substitute, *decreases* the demand for record players. (c) A lower price for record players has *no effect* on the demand for record players; it simply increases the quantity demanded (a movement along the demand curve). (d) A greater population can be expected to *increase* the demand for record players. (e) A change in tastes that makes listening to records less fashionable *decreases* the demand for record players.

ANSWERS TO YOUR TURN

APPLYING SUPPLY AND DEMAND ANALYSIS TO AUTOMOBILE EXPORT RESTRICTIONS

(a) Restrictions on the number of automobiles allowed to enter the United States reduce the supply of imported automobiles and increase their price. (b) A higher price for imported automobiles increases demand for domestic automobiles, since they are substitutes. (c) Voluntary export restrictions have increased the price of domestic automobiles. (According to some studies, these restrictions have raised the price of domestic automobiles by more than $600 per vehicle.)

SELECTED REFERENCES

The Margin [a magazine published by the University of Colorado that applies supply and demand analysis to current policy issues].

Alfred Marshall, *Principles of Economics,* 8th ed. (London: Macmillan, 1920) [a text first published 100 years ago that even today offers insights into the operation of markets].

Robert Schuettinger and Eamonn Butler, *Forty Centuries of Wage and Price Controls* (Washington, DC: The Heritage Foundation, 1979) [a historical perspective on the problems associated with price controls].

DEMAND AND SUPPLY ELASTICITIES

Consumer responses to the energy price increases of the 1970s convinced the general public of what economists had long preached: "Price matters." However, neither economists nor the public have been very satisfied with the answers to the more difficult question: "But by how much?"[1]

Demand curves slope downward; supply curves slope upward. So say the laws of demand and supply. While this information may be useful, it is often of limited value. More important is knowing the sensitivity of quantity demanded (or supplied) to a change in price. By how much will quantity change?

It matters a great deal to AT&T whether demand for its long-distance telephone service looks like D_1 or D_2 in Figure 5-1(a). In both cases a lower price increases consumer willingness to "reach out and touch someone." But there is more reaching out and touching with D_2 than with D_1.

Public policy is also influenced by the perceived responsiveness of consumers. For example, in the late 1970s many in Congress advocated a tax on oil in order to reduce U.S. dependence on foreign supplies. They argued that, by raising prices, the tax would make consumers considerably more frugal in their use of gasoline, heating oil, and other petroleum products. Critics of the proposed tax countered that consumers were not very responsive to prices of such products and, consequently, consumption would scarcely be affected. To help resolve this debate, what was needed was information on consumer responsiveness to energy prices. Recent economic studies have attempted to meet this need.

Producer responsiveness is also crucial. At the same time that Congress was debating the merits of an energy tax, it was grappling with the issue of whether the price of natural gas should be set by the market or by the government.[2] Some in Congress (especially

---

[1] Forward to Douglas Bohi, *Analyzing Demand Behavior: A Study of Energy Elasticities* (Baltimore: The Johns Hopkins University Press, 1981).

[2] Congress initially chose to regulate the price of natural gas but later began phasing out price controls. (U.S. energy policy is discussed in Chapter 34.)

conservatives and members from gas-producing states) argued that the volume of natural gas supplied was highly sensitive to price. Compared to the case of a government-enforced price ceiling, the price of natural gas would, they asserted, be slightly higher in an unrestricted market but production would be greatly expanded. Shortages would be eliminated and, with greater availability of natural gas, our dependence on imported oil would diminish.

Others saw things differently, contending that the price of natural gas would soar in the absence of price controls, with little additional production. At issue was whether the supply of natural gas was more closely approximated by S_1 or S_2 in Figure 5-1 (b). If Congress is to fashion a sensible energy policy, it must know how consumers and producers respond to prices—it needs to know the price elasticities of demand and supply.

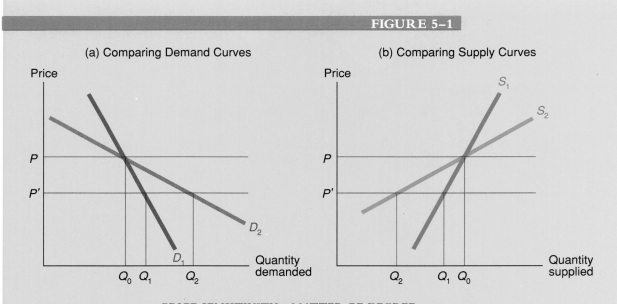

FIGURE 5–1

(a) Comparing Demand Curves

(b) Comparing Supply Curves

PRICE SENSITIVITY—MATTER OF DEGREE

Demand curve D_2 is more sensitive to price changes than is demand curve D_1. That is, for a given change in price, the change in quantity demanded is greater for D_2 than for D_1. For example, when price falls from P to P', quantity demanded increases from Q_0 to Q_2 if demand is D_2, but from Q_0 to Q_1 (a much smaller increase) if demand is D_1. Similarly, S_2 is more sensitive to price changes than is S_1.

Knowledge of these elasticities is important for other reasons. Suppose a tax is levied on producers. To what extent will the tax be absorbed by producers, and to what extent will it be passed on to consumers in the form of higher prices? The answer depends on the price elasticities of demand and supply. Or consider a university's decision to raise ticket prices for its varsity's basketball games. Will higher prices increase or decrease basketball revenues? The price elasticity of demand holds the key.

Among the other issues considered are how the quantity demanded of one good responds to a change in the price of a second good (the cross elasticity of demand) and how quantity demanded varies with income (the income elasticity of demand). For example, how much business can MCI be expected to lose if AT&T's long-distance rates are reduced? As incomes rise, how much more will consumers spend on long-distance telephone calls?

Chapter 5 presents the various demand elasticities just introduced and then analyzes the elasticity of supply. In the process it provides estimates of the elasticities for various goods, discusses the determinants of these elasticities, and explains the relevance of these numbers to consumers, businesses, and governments.

PRICE ELASTICITY OF DEMAND

Elasticity is a measure of responsiveness. Assume the price of a good rises by 10%. Other things equal, the quantity demanded should fall. But by how much—1%, 10%, 100% . . . ? The answer is given by the **price elasticity of demand:**

$$E_d = \frac{\text{percentage change in quantity demanded}}{\text{percentage change in price}}$$

Strictly speaking, the numbers generated by this formula are negative, since price and quantity demanded move in opposite directions. By convention the negative sign is dropped.

If a 10% change in price leads to a 1% change in quantity demanded, the price elasticity of demand is 0.1 ($E_d = 1\% \div 10\%$). But if the quantity demanded changes by 100%, the elasticity is 10 ($E_d = 100\% \div 10\%$). Alternatively, if the elasticity is known, information about a price change permits a prediction of how much quantity demanded will change:

$$\frac{\text{percentage change in}}{\text{quantity demanded}} = \frac{\text{percentage change in quantity demanded}}{\text{percentage change in price}} \times \text{percentage change in price}$$

$$= E_d \times \text{percentage change in price}$$

For example, if the price elasticity of demand for cigarettes is 0.5, we can predict that, other things equal, a 10% increase in the price of cigarettes will reduce the quantity demanded by 5% (i.e., 0.5 × 10%).

THE MIDPOINT FORMULA

Consider the demand curve for Charlie's Deluxe Hamburgers given in Figure 5-2 (page 92). At a price of $1.80, 1200 burgers are demanded each week. But if the price rises to $2.20, consumers will want to buy only 800 burgers. Given these figures, what is the price elasticity of demand? To answer this we must compute the percentage change in both price and quantity demanded and then plug these numbers into the elasticity formula. But first we must agree on some terminology. How do we define "percentage change"?

Suppose we take $P_1 = \$1.80$ and $Q_1 = 1200$ as our reference point (point A on the demand curve in Figure 5-2). Then an increase in the price of hamburgers from $\$1.80$ to $\$2.20$ constitutes a price change of 22%: $(P_2 - P_1)/P_1 = (\$2.20 - \$1.80)/\$1.80 = .22$ or 22%. Similarly, a reduction in the number of hamburgers purchased from 1200 to 800 constitutes a change in the quantity demanded of 33%: $(Q_1 - Q_2)/Q_1 = (1200 - 800)/1200 = .33$ or 33%. Based on these numbers, the elasticity of demand between points A and B is $E_d = 33/22 = 1.5$.

Someone else could just as easily take $P_2 = \$2.20$ and $Q_2 = 800$ as the reference point and compute the elasticity by considering a movement from point B to point A on the demand curve in Figure 5-2. In that event, the change in price is 18% $[(\$2.20 - \$1.80)/\$2.20 = .18]$ and the change in quantity demanded is 50% $[(1200 - 800)/800 = .50]$. According to these numbers, the elasticity of demand is $E_d = 50/18 = 2.8$, which differs from the prior calculation ($E_d = 1.5$).

A definition should be consistent. Different people working with the same numbers should not obtain different answers. To avoid this possibility, our definition requires greater precision: we must specify a reference point. But should it be point A or point B? The convention adopted by economists is to use neither endpoint, but instead to use the midpoint (point C in Figure 5-2): the average of the two prices and the average of the two quantities.[3] The price elasticity of demand is then defined as:

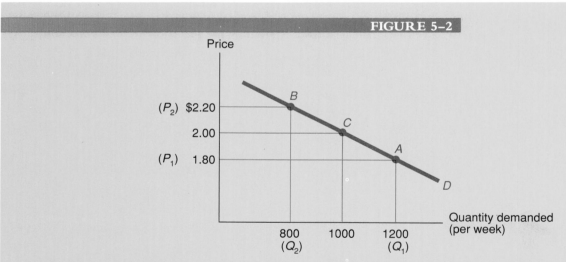

FIGURE 5-2

CALCULATING THE ELASTICITY OF DEMAND FOR CHARLIE'S DELUXE HAMBURGERS

Price elasticity of demand between points A and B is calculated on the basis of average price ($\$2.00$) and average quantity demanded (1000). The percentage change in price is 20% $[(\$2.20 - \$1.80)/\$2.00 = .20]$; the percentage change in quantity demanded is 40% $[(1200 - 800)/1000 = .40]$. Consequently, $E_d = 40/20 = 2.0$.

[3]The average price is defined as $(P_1 + P_2)/2$, the average quantity demanded is $(Q_1 + Q_2)/2$. In this example, the average price is $(\$1.80 + \$2.20)/2 = \$2.00$; the average quantity demanded is $(1200 + 800)/2 = 1000$.

$$E_d = \frac{\text{change in quantity demanded}}{\text{average quantity demanded}} \div \frac{\text{change in price}}{\text{average price}}$$

Return now to our example. Given an average price of $2.00 and an average quantity demanded of 1000, the percentage change in price is 20% [($2.20 − $1.80)/$2.00 = .20] and the percentage change in quantity demanded is 40% [(1200 − 800)/1000 = .40]. Therefore, the price elasticity of demand over this range of the demand curve is 2.0.

YOUR TURN   DETERMINING THE PRICE ELASTICITY OF DEMAND
To help raise money for a local charity, you agree to produce and sell a calendar. Based on preliminary analysis, you estimate that 900 calendars will be sold this year if the price is $5, but only 700 calendars if the price is $7. Given these figures, compute (a) the change in quantity demanded, average quantity demanded, change in price, average price, and (b) the price elasticity of demand.

CATEGORIZING ELASTICITIES

Elastic Demand
Demand is elastic when $E_d > 1$.

Inelastic Demand
Demand is inelastic when $E_d < 1$.

Unit Elastic Demand
Demand is unit elastic when $E_d = 1$.

Economists often label demand for a good on the basis of its price elasticity. When $E_d > 1$, demand is said to be **elastic.** With an elastic demand curve, the change in quantity demanded is greater, *in percentage terms,* than the change in price. For example, demand for Charlie's Deluxe Hamburgers is elastic. A 20% change in price generated a 40% change in quantity demanded.

When $E_d < 1$, demand is termed **inelastic**—meaning that each 1% change in price leads to a change in quantity demanded of less than 1%. A third possibility is that $E_d = 1$, in which case demand is classified as **unit elastic.** In such cases, price and quantity demanded change by equal percentages. For example, a 10% increase in the price of a good reduces quantity demanded by 10%.

The same good may have an elastic demand for some set of prices, yet be inelastic over a different price range. This is illustrated in Figure 5-3 (page 94). Over the five segments for which the elasticity is calculated, the price elasticity of demand ranges from 9 to 0.11. As the figure indicates, for *linear* (straight-line) demand curves the price elasticity of demand becomes smaller as you move down the demand curve. This is also true for demand curves that are nearly linear.[4] The only exceptions are depicted in Figure 5-4 (page 94), which illustrates linear demand curves that do not slope downward.

---

[4]For some nonlinear demand curves, E_d does not fall as you move down the curve. In fact, for the nonlinear curve depicted (a rectangular hyperbola), demand at every segment is unit elastic.

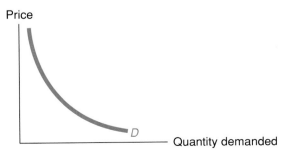

Price

D   Quantity demanded

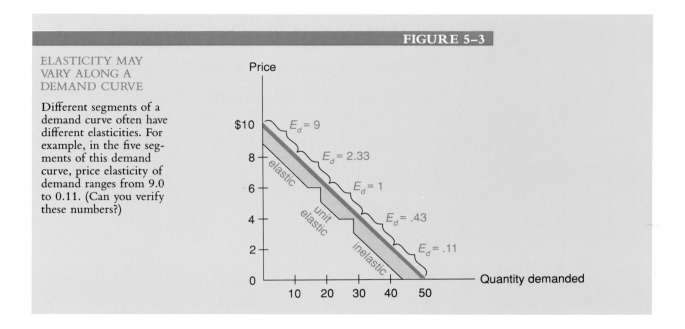

FIGURE 5–3

ELASTICITY MAY VARY ALONG A DEMAND CURVE

Different segments of a demand curve often have different elasticities. For example, in the five segments of this demand curve, price elasticity of demand ranges from 9.0 to 0.11. (Can you verify these numbers?)

Although most demand curves have negative slopes, in extreme cases the law of demand may be violated. Figure 5-4(a) presents the case where demand is **perfectly inelastic** ($E_d = 0$). Assume you are being held hostage in some foreign country. Your demand for airline tickets out of this foreign country may look like Figure 5-4(a)—assuming the tickets convey safe passage. If the price per ticket is $10,000, you want to buy one ticket. If the price is reduced to $10, you still want one ticket only. Even at this bargain price you are not likely to want to return to this country

Perfectly Inelastic Demand
A demand that is totally unresponsive to price—represented by a vertical demand curve.

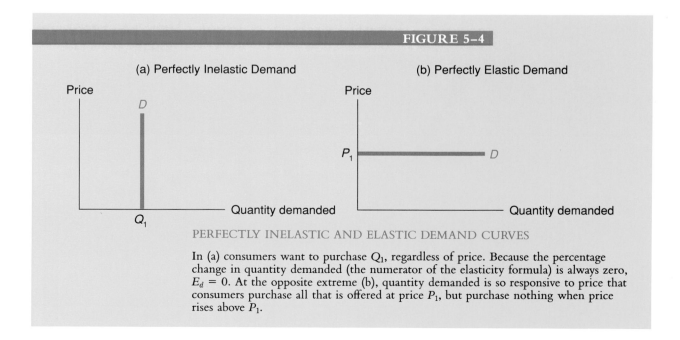

FIGURE 5–4

(a) Perfectly Inelastic Demand

(b) Perfectly Elastic Demand

PERFECTLY INELASTIC AND ELASTIC DEMAND CURVES

In (a) consumers want to purchase Q_1, regardless of price. Because the percentage change in quantity demanded (the numerator of the elasticity formula) is always zero, $E_d = 0$. At the opposite extreme (b), quantity demanded is so responsive to price that consumers purchase all that is offered at price P_1, but purchase nothing when price rises above P_1.

anytime soon. (And a round-trip ticket is out of the question.) Thus quantity demanded is not responsive to price, and demand is perfectly inelastic.

Perfectly Elastic Demand
A demand that is infinitely responsive to price—represented by a horizontal demand curve.

The demand curve in Figure 5-4(b) is **perfectly elastic.** Consumers are so responsive to price (E_d is so high) that they buy as much as they can at P_1, but nothing at prices above P_1. As we discuss in Chapter 24, the demand curve facing the typical wheat farmer is perfectly elastic. At the market price, buyers purchase as much wheat as the farmer wants to sell, but they buy nothing from the farmer if he or she attempts to charge more than the market price.

EXHIBIT 5–1

ELASTICITY VERSUS SLOPE

From a casual inspection of Figures 5-5(a) and (b), you might be tempted to conclude that D_2 is more elastic than D_1. Don't. Even though the slopes differ, over each price range the elasticities are identical. Both curves depict the same relationship between price of milk and quantity demanded. The only difference is that quantity is measured in gallons for (a) and in quarts for (b).

That slope and elasticity of demand are different concepts can also be driven home by computing elasticity at different places along a linear demand curve. Although the slope is the same everywhere, elasticity varies from one segment of the curve to another (as shown in Figure 5-3). Whereas slope is based on absolute changes in price and quantity, elasticity is based on relative changes.[5]

[5]Slope of a demand curve is defined as $\Delta P / \Delta Q$ where Δ is the symbol for *change in*. Elasticity is:

$$\frac{\Delta Q/Q}{\Delta P/P} = \frac{\Delta Q}{\Delta P} \times \frac{P}{Q} = \frac{P}{Q} \div \text{slope}$$

FIGURE 5–5

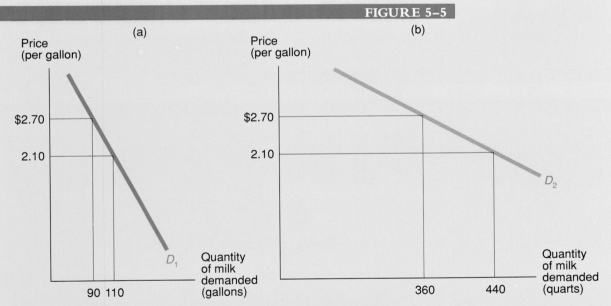

DIFFERENT SLOPES, SAME ELASTICITY

Although D_2 initially may appear more elastic than D_1, any difference is illusory. D_1 has a steeper slope because its quantity is measured in gallons rather than quarts. When price falls from $2.70/gallon to $2.10/gallon (25% drop), the quantity demanded increases from 90 gallons to 110 gallons or, equivalently, from 360 quarts to 440 quarts. Whether measured in gallons or quarts, the quantity demanded rises by 20%. In either case, $E_d = 0.80$.

ELASTICITY AND TOTAL REVENUE

Total Revenue
The price of a good times the quantity sold
$(TR = P \times Q)$.

Elasticity of demand is more than a formula, more than a number; it has a variety of applications. One is revealing the effect of a change in price on *total revenue*. **Total revenue** is defined as total spending on a good: the product of price times quantity sold. Equivalently, from the buyers' perspective, total spending is price times quantity purchased.

A change in price has two effects on total revenue. A higher price means that each unit sold now contributes more to total revenue. On the other hand, given a downward-sloping demand curve, fewer units are sold at the higher price. Whether total revenue rises or falls (or remains unchanged) depends on which effect is stronger: the increase in revenue per unit (price) or the decrease in the volume of sales. This, in turn, hinges on the price elasticity of demand.

The relationship among elasticity, price, and total revenue is presented in Table 5-1. When demand is elastic, cutting price raises total revenue and increasing price lowers total revenue. Quantity demanded is so responsive to price that, when price changes, the volume of sales changes by a relatively larger amount, causing price and total revenue to move in opposite directions. In other words, the change in revenue per unit is swamped by a relatively greater change in the volume of sales. When demand is inelastic, the percentage change in price exceeds the percentage change in quantity demanded. Therefore, price and total revenue move in the same direction. Finally, for unit elastic demand, changes in price and quantity demanded offset one another. Whether price rises or falls, total revenue remains the same.

The role played by elasticity can also be illustrated diagrammatically. Because total revenue is the product of price and quantity purchased, it can be represented as an area beneath the demand curve, with sides corresponding to price and quantity demanded. Consider the demand curve in Figure 5-6 (reproduced from Figure 5-3). In (a), for $P_1 = \$6$ total revenue is given by the rectangle $0P_1AQ_1 = \$120$, and for $P_2 = \$8$ the total revenue rectangle is $0P_2BQ_2 = \$80$. Because $E_d > 1$, raising price diminishes total revenue (in this case by $40). When $E_d < 1$, case (b), a price hike raises total revenue. Finally, when $E_d = 1$, case (c), a price change has no impact on total revenue.

The preceding discussion has important implications. For example, assume a university wishes to maximize the total revenue generated by its varsity basketball

TABLE 5-1		
ELASTICITY OF DEMAND AND THE RELATIONSHIP BETWEEN PRICE AND TOTAL REVENUE		
Category of demand	**Relative change in price (P) and quantity demanded (Q^d)**	**Effect on total revenue**
Elastic $(E_d > 1)$	% change in Q^d > % change in P	$\downarrow P(\uparrow Q^d) \rightarrow \uparrow TR$ $\uparrow P(\downarrow Q^d) \rightarrow \downarrow TR$
Inelastic $(E_d < 1)$	% change in Q^d < % change in P	$\downarrow P(\uparrow Q^d) \rightarrow \downarrow TR$ $\uparrow P(\downarrow Q^d) \rightarrow \uparrow TR$
Unit elastic $(E_d = 1)$	% change in Q^d = % change in P	$\downarrow P(\uparrow Q^d) \rightarrow$ TR does not change $\uparrow P(\downarrow Q^d) \rightarrow$ TR does not change

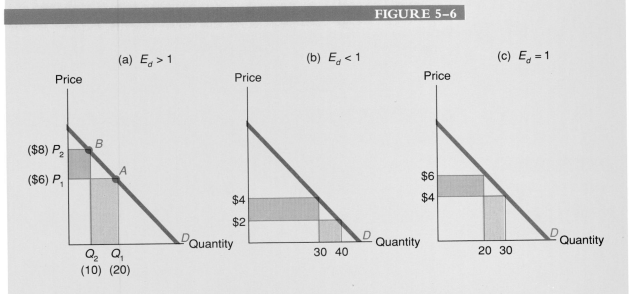

A GRAPHICAL REPRESENTATION OF THE RELATIONSHIP BETWEEN E_d AND TOTAL REVENUE

A price increase has a two-fold effect on total revenue. (1) The gain in revenue resulting from a higher revenue per unit is shown by the gray-shaded area. (2) The loss associated with reduced purchases is shown by the color-shaded area. When $E_d > 1$, (a), revenue loss exceeds revenue gain—a higher price lowers total revenue. When $E_d < 1$, (b), revenue gain exceeds revenue loss—a higher price increases total revenue. When $E_d = 1$, (c), the shaded areas are equal—implying that total revenue does not change.

program. Further assume that basketball games are not sellouts.[6] Should the university raise or lower the price of tickets? A lower price translates into greater ticket sales, a higher price into fewer sales. The crucial question is how responsive fans are to ticket price. In other words, what is the price elasticity of demand? If the university is operating on an inelastic portion of its demand curve, revenue is enhanced by raising price. In contrast, if demand is elastic the solution is to lower price. The same reasoning can be applied to other issues confronting the university—for example, setting rates for parking permits and dormitory rooms.

Concern about total revenue extends beyond a university's borders. Now that the U.S. airline industry is deregulated, carriers have the ability to set airline fares. The general tendency has been for fares to drop following deregulation, reflecting the belief that demand for air travel tends to be elastic. Although this may be true for households, there is evidence that demand by business travelers is inelastic. In that event, the ticket price that maximizes total revenue in the business segment of the market exceeds the price that maximizes total revenue in the nonbusiness segment.

---

[6] If every game sold out and patrons were turned away, the university should clearly raise price. The university would make more money filling an arena and charging a high price than filling an arena and charging a low price.

Accordingly, airlines have an incentive to charge a higher price for business travel than for personal travel. To a considerable extent, airlines have been able to do exactly that. Households generally are better able to plan in advance when they want to fly. Vacation dates, holidays, the school calendar, and other occasions that may call for travel are often known well ahead of time. Business travel, in contrast, is more likely to be in response to short-term developments. Airlines generally offer deep discounts for reservations booked in advance, say 30 days before the start of travel. Because households are more likely to meet these purchase deadlines, the result is a lower fare, on average, for these customers than for business travelers.

YOUR TURN   MAXIMIZING TOTAL REVENUE

In the previous Your Turn it is assumed that you are printing and selling a calendar. Suppose a local business agrees to pay the costs of production, so that all receipts from sales of the calendar go to charity. Based on the information contained in the previous Your Turn and assuming you wish to maximize the funds raised for charity, should you charge a price of $5 or $7 per calendar? Why?

EXHIBIT 5–2

ELASTICITIES AND REVENUES FOR TV SPORTS

Is the demand for TV sports entertainment inelastic? For some sports the evidence suggests that it is.

The National Collegiate Athletic Association (NCAA) long held exclusive control over TV contracts for college football. When the U.S. Supreme Court eliminated this monopoly power in 1984, the result was an explosion of televised football games. With more games broadcast, TV networks were willing to pay less per game. For example, when UCLA played Nebraska several years ago, the schools collected half of what they would have received under the old NCAA contract. The athletic director for the University of Nebraska estimated that TV revenues at his institution would plunge 40 percent. An NCAA official predicted that the loss at most schools would be at least 50 percent. More games on the tube meant lower total revenues—demand was inelastic.

Aware of what had happened in football, the National Basketball Association (NBA) adopted a different strategy, permitting fewer games to be televised. This increased the price networks were willing to pay per game and the total broadcast revenue collected by the NBA. As one reporter observed:

> Cutting the NBA's exposure has boosted the value of commercial time. As a result, the league will show a 16% increase in TV revenues this year while airing half as many games.

Sources: Adapted from "It Finally Happened: Too Much College Football on TV," *Business Week*, October 8, 1984, pp. 71 and 75; Brent Wellington, "Why Basketball Is Having a Championship Season," *Business Week*, March 4, 1985, pp. 75–76.

WHAT DETERMINES E_d?

Price elasticity of demand depends on several factors. The following four are generally considered to be the most important.

Availability of Substitutes

When good substitutes are readily available, consumers tend to be sensitive to price changes—E_d tends to be high. For example, there are numerous brands of tissue (e.g., Kleenex, Puffs, Scotts). Each brand is generally considered a good substitute for the others. In addition, other products can readily be substituted for tissue (e.g., handkerchiefs, cotton balls for removing makeup). Accordingly, the demand for any given brand of tissue can be expected to be highly elastic.

When substitution possibilities are limited—as is the case for gasoline—E_d tends to be low. This does not imply, however, that elasticity of demand at Bob's Texaco station is low. If Bob raises the price of gasoline relative to that of competitors, he is likely to lose a substantial share of business. While there are few good substitutes for gasoline in general, many substitutes exist for Bob's Texaco gasoline—Kim's Texaco, Gabriel's Shell, Kathy's Exxon. As a general rule: the more narrowly defined a good, the more substitutes exist and therefore, the more elastic is demand.

Degree of Necessity

Goods viewed as necessities tend to have a low price elasticity of demand. We would find it difficult to get by without food, heating fuel in the winter,[7] or essential medical care.[8] As such, elasticity of demand for these goods and services is low: consumers are relatively insensitive to price. This is not the case for vacations, restaurant meals, or various luxuries: consumers can survive without them. Because of this low degree of necessity, E_d is high.

Share of Budget Spent on the Good

Typically, *the less of a consumer's budget devoted to a good, the less elastic is demand.* Because the average consumer spends such a minuscule portion of income on toothpicks, a price hike of, say, 20 percent is likely to have little effect on the quantity demanded. The budget can easily be stretched to accommodate spending a few cents more on toothpicks. Compare that to a 20-percent increase in the price of a new car. Given an average sticker price of $15,000, that translates into an increase of several thousand dollars—which is not so easy to work into the budget. For that reason, big-ticket items, such as cars, tend to have a relatively high elasticity of demand.

Time Period

A longer time period allows for greater responsiveness on the part of consumers and, consequently, leads to a greater elasticity of demand. Consider the demand for gasoline. If

---

[7]Those living in Miami or Honolulu may ignore this argument.

[8]The emphasis is on *essential*. Certain medical treatment (e.g., elective cosmetic surgery) is difficult to call necessary. Demand for medical care tends to be more price elastic the less *necessary* it is. Consistent with this proposition, two economists found that the demand for physician house calls is more elastic than the demand for physician office visits, which in turn is more elastic than the demand for hospital admissions. See Charles E. Phelps and Joseph P. Newhouse, *Coinsurance and the Demand for Medical Services* (Santa Monica, CA: Rand Corp., October 1974), Table 12, cited in Robert Helms, "Contemporary Health Policy: Dealing with the Cost of Care," in William Fellner, ed., *Contemporary Economic Problems* (Washington, DC: American Enterprise Institute, 1978), p. 344.

the price of gasoline shoots up, as it did in the 1970s, consumers initially make few adjustments. In the months immediately following a price hike, consumers may cut back on pleasure driving, combine trips, and do more carpooling, but these adjustments make only a modest dent in gasoline consumption. As time passes, however, consumers adapt their behavior in more fundamental ways. Cars wear out and are replaced with vehicles boasting better gas mileage. Greater use is made of nontraditional vehicles (e.g., cars and trucks powered by compressed natural gas). Alternative energy sources (e.g., gasohol, which is made from corn-based ethanol) are substituted for gasoline. As households move, they are more likely to locate close to work or to rail and subway stops. Public transportation is substituted for private automobile use. Accordingly, demand for gasoline can be expected to be more elastic in the long run (after consumers have had a chance to complete their adjustments) than in the short run. As the estimates of Table 5-2 indicate, price elasticity of demand is indeed greater in the long run (for gasoline as well as other products).[9]

OTHER ELASTICITIES OF DEMAND

Quantity demanded depends on a good's own price but on other factors too—for example, on income and prices of other goods.[10] A key issue concerns the degree of responsiveness of demand to these other variables. This responsiveness is measured by the following two elasticities.

TABLE 5-2

ESTIMATED PRICE ELASTICITIES OF DEMAND FOR THE UNITED STATES

Good	Elasticity	
	Short run	Long run
Owner-occupied housing	0.04	1.22
Medical care and hospital insurance	0.31	0.92
Shoe repair	1.31	1.81
China and glassware	1.54	2.55
Flowers and plants	0.82	2.65
Radio and TV repair	0.47	3.84
Motion pictures	0.87	3.67
Theater and opera	0.18	0.31
Commuter rail travel	0.72	0.91
Intercity rail travel	1.42	3.19
Foreign travel	0.14	1.77
Residential natural gas	0.1	0.5
Gasoline	0.2	0.7

Sources: Adapted from H. S. Houthakker and L. D. Taylor, *Consumer Demand in the United States: Analysis and Projections* (Cambridge: Harvard University Press, 1970), Table 4.2; (for natural gas and gasoline) Douglas R. Bohi, *Analyzing Demand Behavior* (Baltimore: The Johns Hopkins University Press, 1981), Table 7.1. Reprinted by permission.

[9]The estimates of Table 5-2 are based on observed prices (i.e., the segment of the demand curve that, given the past history of prices, is most relevant). For a different range of prices, different estimates of E_d can be expected. For example, if we were to move up the demand curve to uncharted areas of higher prices, E_d for gasoline might be considerably higher than the values given in Table 5-2.
[10]Recall from Chapter 4 that when any of these other relevant factors change the result is a shift in the demand curve and consequently, for any given price, a change in the quantity demanded.

The Income Elasticity of Demand

What happens when income rises? For **normal goods** demand increases—so that at any given price a higher quantity is now demanded. For **inferior goods** demand falls—consumers reduce purchases of inferior goods by substituting preferred goods (which they are now better able to afford). In addition to the question of whether demand rises or falls, there is also the question of the magnitude of any change. Both issues can be addressed with a concept known as the **income elasticity of demand.** Holding price constant, the income elasticity of demand is given by the following formula:

$$E_d^y = \frac{\text{percentage change in quantity demanded}}{\text{percentage change in income}}$$

The income elasticity of demand is positive for a normal good, negative for an inferior good.[11]

    Normal goods are often subclassified in terms of their income elasticity of demand. According to a commonly adopted convention, **luxuries** are defined as goods whose income elasticity of demand exceeds 1. Examples include cars, food away from home, and books. **Necessities** are normal goods for which $E_d^y < 1$. Examples are food, electricity, and cigarettes. According to this conventional definition, necessity does not mean "required for survival." Consumers could extinguish their cigarette habit without life going up in smoke. Even so, economists classify cigarettes as necessities because of their low income elasticity of demand.

    Perhaps a more intuitive way to distinguish between necessities and luxuries is in terms of how consumption patterns change with income. When income doubles consumers can buy twice as much of each good, but there is evidence that they do not. Instead, consumers spend more than twice as much on entertainment (for example) but less than twice as much on food. Necessities are the first priority. When income is low necessities absorb a large share of the budget. As income rises consumers spend a few more dollars on necessities, but *as a percentage of the budget* expenditures on necessities fall (see Table 5-3). With a higher income consumers can devote a growing share of their income to other, less essential goods. It is these goods that economists dub "luxuries."

    In forecasting consumer demand, many companies rely on estimates of income elasticity. Such estimates help the Coca-Cola Company, for example, gauge the likely effects of growing income on demand for its beverages. Or consider an

Luxury
A good for which the income elasticity of demand is greater than 1.

Necessity
A good for which the income elasticity of demand is greater than 0 but less than 1.

TABLE 5-3

CLASSIFICATION OF GOODS BASED ON INCOME ELASTICITY OF DEMAND

Type of good	Income elasticity	Effect of a 10% gain in income
Normal	Positive	Quantity demanded rises
Luxury	Greater than 1	Quantity demanded rises in excess of 10%
Necessity	Less than 1	Quantity demanded rises by under 10%
Inferior	Negative	Quantity demanded falls

---

[11]The negative sign is not dropped for income elasticity of demand (as it is for price elasticity of demand). This is so we can distinguish between normal goods ($E_d^y > 0$) and inferior goods ($E_d^y < 0$).

investor who anticipates rapid income growth in the economy. Given this bullish outlook, the investor may want to purchase stock in growth industries—those likely to experience the most rapid advance in sales. Which industries are these? Income elasticities of demand provide important clues.

The Cross Elasticity of Demand

Suppose the Anheuser-Busch Company lowers the price of its Busch beer. Will this cannibalize sales of Budweiser (also produced by Anheuser-Busch)? Despite possibly higher revenue from the sales of Busch beer (if $E_d > 1$), a lower price might reduce overall company revenue by heavily tapping into sales of Budweiser. How sensitive is quantity demanded of one good (e.g., Budweiser) to price of a second good (e.g., Busch)? The answer is provided by the **cross elasticity of demand:**

$$E_{1,2} = \frac{\text{percentage change in quantity demanded of good 1}}{\text{percentage change in price of good 2}}$$

Substitute Goods
Goods for which the cross elasticity of demand is positive.

Complementary Goods
Goods for which the cross elasticity of demand is negative.

Independent Goods
Goods for which the cross elasticity of demand is zero.

The value of the cross elasticity indicates the relationship between two goods. When the cross elasticity is positive, the goods are **substitute goods** (e.g., Budweiser and Busch). When the price of one good falls, consumers buy relatively more of it at the expense of the second (substitute) good. That is, quantity demanded of the second good falls. When the cross elasticity is negative, the goods are **complementary goods** (e.g., cameras and film). Consumers want more, not only of the good whose price has fallen, but also of the second (complementary) good. Finally, when the cross elasticity equals zero, the goods are **independent goods** (e.g., pencils and automobiles). The quantity demanded of one good does not depend on the price of the other. Exhibits 5-3 and 5-4 illustrate the relevance of cross elasticities to producers and jurists.

EXHIBIT 5-3

IT ONLY HURTS WHEN YOU DRINK

In 1985, the federal excise tax on distilled spirits was raised from $10.50/gallon to $12.50/gallon, leading to an increase in the price of hard liquor. The tax on beer and wine was not raised. How would the price increase for hard liquor affect demand for beer and wine? Liquor producers and distributors were thirsty for an answer.

Estimated cross elasticities are close to zero, indicating that the demands for beer and wine are each insensitive to the price of spirits.[12] Anheuser-Busch need not schedule an extra production shift. Liquor stores need not stock up on wine. A higher price for spirits will have little if any effect on the demand for beer and wine.

[12]One study estimates that the demand for wine is independent of the price of spirits (the cross elasticity of demand is zero). Nor does it find evidence that a higher price for spirits leads consumers to switch to beer. A second study estimates that a 10-percent change in the price of spirits affects demand for beer and wine each by less than one percent. See James Johnson and Ernest Oksanen, "Estimation of Demand for Alcoholic Beverages in Canada . . ." *Review of Economics and Statistics* (February 1977), pp. 113–17; Kenneth Clements and Lester Johnson, "The Demand for Beer, Wine, and Spirits: A Systemwide Analysis," *Journal of Business* (July 1983), Table 8.

ELASTICITY OF SUPPLY

Elasticity of supply is, in many ways, analogous to (price) elasticity of demand. The central difference is that, whereas elasticity of demand considers the percentage

---

EXHIBIT 5–4

CROSS ELASTICITIES IN THE COURTROOM

Economists and producers are not the only parties concerned with how changes in the price of one good affect demand for another. Cross elasticities have played major roles in the courtroom. Two of the more famous cases involve duPont and the Brown Shoe Company.

U.S. antitrust laws are designed to prevent a company from dominating the market it serves.[13] In 1947, the U.S. Department of Justice brought suit against duPont charging the company with ". . . conspiracy to monopolize interstate commerce in cellophane. . . ." As evidence, the Justice Department presented figures showing that almost 75 percent of the cellophane sold in the United States was produced by duPont.

DuPont countered that the relevant market included Pliofilm™, aluminum foil, waxed paper, and other flexible wrapping materials. With less than 20 percent of this broader market, duPont contended that it faced considerable competition. To prove its case, duPont presented evidence that the cross elasticity of demand between cellophane and other packaging materials was positive and high.

Accepting these cross-elasticity figures, the U.S. Supreme Court ruled in favor of duPont:

If a slight decrease in the price of cellophane causes a considerable number of customers of other flexible wrappings to switch to cellophane, it would be an indication that a high cross-elasticity of demand exists between them; that the products compete in the same market. The court below upheld that the "[g]reat sensitivity of customers in the flexible packaging markets to price or quality changes" prevented duPont from possessing monopoly control over price. . . . The record sustains these findings. . . .

In the Brown Shoe Case (1962), the U.S. Department of Justice sued to prevent the Brown Shoe Company from acquiring the Kinney Shoe Company. The government claimed that if the merger were allowed it would seriously lessen competition in the shoe industry. Not so, claimed lawyers for Brown; the two companies compete in separate markets. To support their claim, Brown's lawyers presented evidence that the Brown Shoe Company produced a higher-grade, higher-price shoe than Kinney. But the Department of Justice refuted this argument by demonstrating that the cross elasticity of demand between the two brands of shoes was significantly greater than zero. This implied that the two brands were close substitutes and therefore were being sold in the *same* market. Accepting these cross-elasticity figures, the court denied the merger.

[13]U.S. antitrust policy is discussed in Chapter 27.

Source: Adapted from United States v. E. I. duPont de Nemours and Company, 351 U.S. 377 (1956), United States v. Brown Shoe Company, 370 U.S. 294 (1962).

---

change in quantity *demanded,* **elasticity of supply** focuses on quantity *supplied.* Thus, the formula for the elasticity of supply is:

$$E_s = \frac{\text{percentage change in quantity supplied}}{\text{percentage change in price}}$$

Certain terminology also carries over from our discussion of elasticity of demand. For example:

> supply is *elastic* when $E_s > 1$
> supply is *inelastic* when $E_s < 1$
> supply is *unit elastic* when $E_s = 1$

Perfectly Inelastic Supply
A supply that is totally unresponsive to price—represented by a vertical supply curve.

Perfectly Elastic Supply
A supply that is infinitely responsive to price—represented by a horizontal supply curve.

A vertical supply curve is said to be **perfectly inelastic,** a horizontal supply curve **perfectly elastic.**

The main determinant of E_s is the time period. *The longer the time period, the more elastic supply is.* Based on the time dimension, supply decisions can be studied in three different periods: the market period, the short run, and the long run.

Market Period
A period of time during which the quantity supplied cannot be changed—represented by a perfectly inelastic supply curve.

Short Run
A period of time during which at least one input is fixed.

Long Run
A period of time long enough to change the quantities of all inputs.

The **market period** can be thought of as a time period so short that the quantity supplied cannot be changed—that is, supply is perfectly inelastic (see Figure 5-7a). Consider the supply of apples. In the market period, the apples have already been picked. The growers take their crops to market, selling them for whatever they can get. Although a high price is obviously preferred, growers do not hold back apples even when the price is low—rotten apples have no value.

Next consider a one-year period, which in this example can be considered the **short run**.[14] Over this period, apple growers are responsive to price (see Figure 5-7b). When price is high, producers may use more water, fertilizer, and fungicides in order to increase the quantity of marketable apples. Even hard-to-reach apples will be picked. Still, the number of apples is limited by the number of fruit-bearing trees. In the short run, quantity supplied can be changed, but responsiveness is limited because some of the inputs necessary for production (e.g., trees) cannot be changed.

Over a longer period of time, quantity supplied is even more responsive to price, since new orchards can be planted (see Figure 5–7c). In the **long run**, no inputs are fixed, not even the number of fruit-bearing trees. Given differences in ability of producers to respond to price changes, a given change in demand will have the greatest effect on quantity supplied in the long run and the smallest effect (no change) in the market period.

Empirically, how responsive is quantity supplied to price? Table 5-4 presents estimates for various agricultural products. According to this table, the supplies of

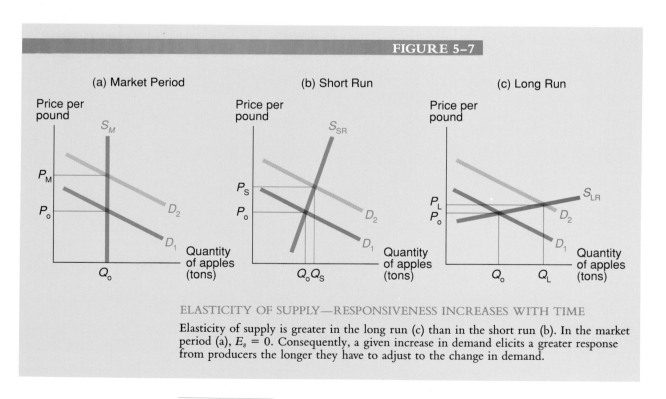

FIGURE 5–7

(a) Market Period   (b) Short Run   (c) Long Run

ELASTICITY OF SUPPLY—RESPONSIVENESS INCREASES WITH TIME

Elasticity of supply is greater in the long run (c) than in the short run (b). In the market period (a), $E_s = 0$. Consequently, a given increase in demand elicits a greater response from producers the longer they have to adjust to the change in demand.

---

[14]The calendar provides no simple rule for distinguishing among time periods. A given length of time (say one year) might be considered the short run in one industry but the long run in a second industry.

TABLE 5-4

ESTIMATED PRICE ELASTICITIES OF SUPPLY
FOR THE UNITED STATES

Good	Elasticity	
	Short run*	**Long run**
Aggregate farm output**	0.25	1.79
Livestock	0.38	2.90
Crops	0.17	1.56
Individual crops:		
Green lima beans	0.10	1.7
Cabbage	0.36	1.2
Carrots	0.14	1.0
Cucumbers	0.29	2.2
Lettuce	0.03	0.16
Onions	0.34	1.0
Green peas	0.31	4.4
Green peppers	0.07	0.26
Tomatoes	0.16	0.90
Watermelons	0.23	0.48

*Short run is defined as two years by Tweeten (top three lines), one year by Nerlove and Addison (individual crops).

**Weighted average of crops and livestock.

Sources: Data from Luther G. Tweeten, *Foundations of Farm Policy* (Lincoln: University of Nebraska Press, 1979), Table 9.5; Marc Nerlove and William Addison, "Statistical Estimation of Long-Run Elasticities of Supply and Demand," *Journal of Farm Economics* (November 1958), Table 3.

livestock and most crops are highly inelastic in the short run but generally elastic in the long run.

TAX INCIDENCE

Governments tax the sales of many items. One reason—especially with regard to *sin taxes*—is to discourage activities (e.g., smoking, drinking, gambling) that some legislators consider unhealthy or of questionable morality. A second reason for such taxes is to raise revenue for the government. Sometimes producers are forced to absorb the bulk of any tax. In other cases they are able to pass on most of the tax to consumers in the form of higher prices. How the tax burden is shared between producers and consumers—the **tax incidence**—depends on the price elasticities of demand and supply.

Tax Incidence
The distribution of the tax burden—that is, who ultimately pays the tax.

The Role of Elasticities

Suppose the government levies a fixed tax on each unit of output sold, say, $.50 per pack of cigarettes. (A constant per-unit tax is called a *specific tax*.) Assuming the tax is collected from producers, the tax can be viewed as increasing the cost of production, which shifts the supply curve up and to the left (the supply curve shifts by a vertical amount equal to the tax). If, in the absence of any tax, producers are willing to supply Q_1 cigarettes at $1.00 per pack, they are now willing to supply this same quantity only if they receive $1.50 per pack (see Figure 5-8). The extra $.50 just compensates producers for the tax they must pay—that is, the $1.50 price is equivalent to $1.00 per pack net of taxes.

It does not follow, however, that a $.50 tax raises the price of cigarettes by $.50. Unless demand for cigarettes is perfectly inelastic (Figure 5-8a), the new equilibrium price is less than $1.50 per pack. In the limiting case of a perfectly elastic

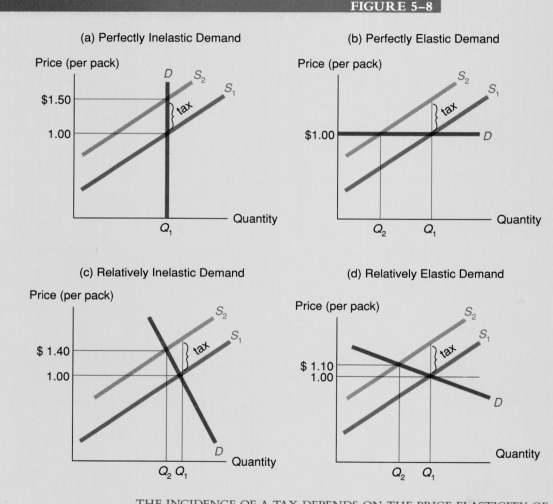

FIGURE 5–8

(a) Perfectly Inelastic Demand

(b) Perfectly Elastic Demand

(c) Relatively Inelastic Demand

(d) Relatively Elastic Demand

THE INCIDENCE OF A TAX DEPENDS ON THE PRICE ELASTICITY OF DEMAND

The less sensitive quantity demanded is to price, the more of a tax producers pass on to consumers. In (a) the entire tax is passed on—price increases by the full amount of the tax ($ .50). In (b) none of the tax is passed on. In (c) consumers bear more of the tax than do consumers in (d)—$ .40 versus $ .10—because demand is relatively more inelastic in (c) than in (d).

demand curve (Figure 5-8b), price does not rise at all. Given a downward-sloping demand curve (Figure 5-8c and d), price rises—but by an amount less than the tax. How much price rises depends on the price elasticity of demand. The higher the elasticity of demand, the smaller the price increase induced by the tax. In other words: *given supply, the more elastic demand is, the less of a tax is passed on to consumers.* On the other hand, a higher elasticity of demand leads to a greater change in quantity.

Tax incidence also hinges on elasticity of supply. As illustrated in Figure 5-9, the higher the elasticity of supply, the larger the price increase resulting from a tax. That is: *given demand, the more elastic supply is, the more of a tax is shouldered by consumers.*

Because demand and supply elasticities vary from one good to another, the effect of a tax similarly varies. This suggests, depending on the goal of the tax, that some goods may be better candidates for taxation than others. If the goal is to generate tax receipts for the government, a tax is more effective the lower the price elasticity of demand. With a high elasticity, quantity demanded falls more precipitously and, since the government receives tax revenues only on units actually sold, tax receipts suffer. Lawmakers may find the cigarette tax an appealing vehicle for raising government revenues precisely because the elasticity of demand for cigarettes is so low. On the other hand, if the reason for taxing cigarettes is to reduce consumption, the low elasticity of demand implies that the tax will not be very successful. The lower the price elasticity of demand, the more effective a tax is at raising government revenue; the less effective it is at curtailing consumption.

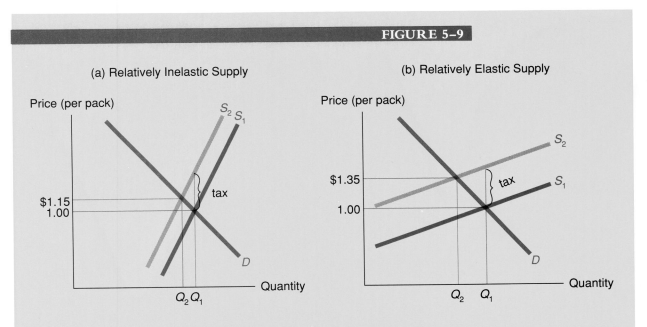

FIGURE 5–9

(a) Relatively Inelastic Supply

(b) Relatively Elastic Supply

THE INCIDENCE OF A TAX DEPENDS ON THE PRICE ELASTICITY OF SUPPLY

The more elastic supply is, the more of a tax producers pass on to consumers. Accordingly, price rises by a greater amount in (b), where supply is relatively more elastic.

OBTAINING RELIABLE ESTIMATES OF ELASTICITY[15]

Before moving on to Chapter 6, it is necessary to underscore the importance of obtaining accurate information on supply and demand. Because elasticities are

---

EXHIBIT 5–5

IDENTIFYING
DEMAND—
PRICE/QUANTITY
COMBINATIONS
DO NOT A
DEMAND CURVE
MAKE

To estimate the price elasticity of demand, it is necessary to have information about the demand curve. How can that information be obtained?

One possibility is to gather data on various price/quantity combinations. For example, a company may observe that when it charges a price of P_1 consumers purchase the quantity Q_1. Suppose the company raises price to P_2 and, at the higher price, finds that consumers buy only Q_2. The company might be tempted to infer that its demand curve intersects these two points (A and B in Figure 5-10). But this would be a valid conclusion only if all the other variables affecting demand remained unchanged.

FIGURE 5–10

THE IDENTIFICATION
PROBLEM

When demand curves shift over time, observed price/quantity combinations such as (P_1/Q_1) and (P_2/Q_2) do not identify a demand curve. To estimate actual demand curves (e.g., D_1 and D_2), one must know how other variables (e.g., income and population) changed between the two periods.

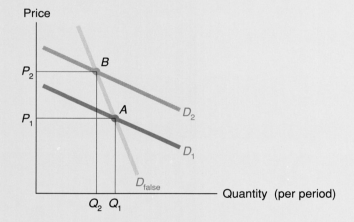

Another possibility is that, in addition to price changing between the two periods, the demand curve also shifted. This would happen, for instance, if income or population changed or if prices of substitutes or complements were different in the two periods. For such reasons, the demand curve in the first period may actually be given by D_1, the demand curve in the second period by D_2. The company could make a serious mistake by inferring that D_{false} is its demand curve. By so doing it would be underestimating the sensitivity of quantity demanded to price—that is, the company would be underestimating the price elasticity of demand. In that event the company would lose more customers than anticipated each time it raised price.

To estimate actual demand curves, such as D_1 and D_2, the researcher must account for changes in any variable that causes the demand curve to shift (e.g., changes in income or population). Fortunately, there are statistical procedures that do this, that net out the effects of shifts in demand. Although such procedures are outside the scope of this course, it is important to realize that the different price/quantity combinations observed in actual experience do not necessarily lie on the same demand curve.

---

[15]Some instructors may wish to delete this section due to the technical nature of the material.

computed from supply and demand curves, any errors made in estimating these curves lead to corresponding errors in the elasticity calculations. Exhibit 5-5 discusses one of the more common errors made when estimating demand curves. Remember: elasticity estimates are only as reliable as the supply and demand curves on which they are based.

SUMMARY

1. Price elasticity of demand measures responsiveness of quantity demanded to price. In particular, price elasticity of demand is defined as the percentage change in quantity demanded divided by the percentage change in price. Percentages are calculated using average price and average quantity.
2. Price elasticity of demand generally varies from one segment of a demand curve to another. For linear (or nearly linear) demand curves, elasticity becomes progressively smaller as one moves down the demand curve.
3. When demand is elastic ($E_d > 1$), price and total revenue move in opposite directions. When demand is inelastic ($E_d < 1$), price and total revenue are positively related. When demand is unit elastic ($E_d = 1$), total revenue is unaffected by price.
4. Price elasticity of demand tends to be lower when good substitutes are not readily available, when the good is considered a necessity, and when the share of the budget spent on this good is small. Elasticity is also lower the less time consumers have to adjust to a price change—that is, the shorter the time period.
5. The income elasticity of demand measures the percentage change in quantity demanded divided by the percentage change in income. The income elasticity of demand is positive for normal goods and negative for inferior goods. Within the class of normal goods, the income elasticity is greater than 1 for luxuries, less than 1 for necessities. The income elasticity of demand enables us to predict how consumption patterns will respond to a change in income, and hence to long-term economic growth.
6. The cross elasticity of demand measures, in percentage terms, how the quantity demanded of one good responds to a change in the price of a second good. For substitutes the cross elasticity is positive, for complements it is negative, and for independent goods it is zero.
7. Elasticity of supply is defined as the percentage change in quantity supplied divided by the percentage change in price. The longer producers have to adjust to price changes, the greater the elasticity of supply is. Consequently, supply is more elastic in the long run than in the short run and, in turn, more elastic in the short run than in the market period.
8. The incidence of a tax depends on the price elasticities of both supply and demand. More of a tax is passed on to consumers (and less is borne by producers) the less elastic demand is and the more elastic supply is.
9. Because of shifts in demand, various price/quantity combinations observed in actual experience may not lie on the same demand curve. Failure to account for shifts in demand leads to incorrect inferences about the true relationship between price and quantity demanded.

KEY TERMS

price elasticity of demand
perfectly inelastic demand
perfectly elastic demand
total revenue
normal goods
inferior goods
income elasticity of demand

unit elastic demand
substitute goods
complementary goods
independent goods
elasticity of supply
perfectly inelastic supply
perfectly elastic supply

luxuries

necessities

cross elasticity of demand

elastic demand

inelastic demand

market period

short run

long run

tax incidence

STUDY QUESTIONS AND PROBLEMS

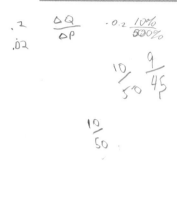

1. Assume the short-run price elasticity of demand for cigarettes is 0.2. (a) How much does a 10% hike in the price of cigarettes curtail the quantity demanded? (b) How large a price hike is required to achieve a 10% reduction in quantity demanded?

2. In the early 1980s, an elected representative from California spoke out against increasing the tax on oil producers. He argued that any higher tax "will end up on the backs of consumers. You can't sock it to the big oil companies . . . they'll just pass [all of it] along to the consumers." (a) What was the representative implying about the price elasticity of demand for oil? (b) Does available evidence support his claim? (c) If the representative were correct and if a new tax were imposed, how much less oil would be demanded?

3. Which of the following products has the lowest price elasticity of demand? For which product would you expect price elasticity to be highest? Why?
   a. food
   b. dairy products
   c. yogurt
   d. peach yogurt

4. Consider the following demand schedule:

Price	Quantity demanded
$11	16
9	24
7	32
5	40

What is the price elasticity of demand between:
   a. $P = \$11$ and $P = \$9$
   b. $P = \$\ 9$ and $P = \$7$
   c. $P = \$\ 7$ and $P = \$5$

5. (a) Suppose a friend spends $50 per month on jeans, regardless of the price of jeans. What is her price elasticity of demand for jeans? (b) A second friend spends more on jeans when the price is low, while reducing spending when the price is high. Is her demand for jeans elastic or inelastic?

6. (a) Provide examples of several goods that you expect to have an inelastic demand. For each good, explain why you think demand is inelastic. (b) Provide examples of several goods that you expect to have an elastic demand. For each good, explain why you think demand is elastic.

7. The following editorial recently appeared in a collegiate newspaper:

> Residence hall occupancy is at its lowest rate ever. . . . What everyone on campus didn't know was that [the department of] housing is once again discussing raising the rates to stay in residence halls. Simple rules of supply and demand discredit the reasoning behind consideration of raising housing fees. When demand is down, producers lower prices to attract customers.

Evaluate this editorial. Would raising housing rates be a sign that university officials do not understand economics? Would "lower[ing] prices to attract customers" generate more housing revenue for the university? On what does the answer depend?

8. In 1982, a Chicago commuter railroad reduced fares by 40 percent. According to *The Wall Street Journal,* ridership increased by 50 percent. Assume the increase in railroad travel was the direct response by riders to the fare cut—that is, assume that the lower fare caused quantity demanded to increase by 50 percent. (a) In that event, what is the price elasticity of demand? (b) If the 50-percent increase in ridership was the short-run response, would you predict a relatively larger or smaller response in the long run?

9. Suppose the demand for grapes increases. Will the resulting change in price be greatest in the market period, the short run, or the long run? What about the change in the quantity actually sold?

10. Consider the following quotation from *The Wall Street Journal* (August 20, 1982; p. 1):
    > To U.S. farmers this year, a bountiful harvest is not something to rejoice over. So the news last week that the Agriculture Department is predicting a mammoth fall crop exceeding previous expectations was a shock to this farmland hamlet.

    What is the problem? Why would higher output levels diminish farm revenue? What can we infer about the price elasticity of demand for agricultural products?

11. Rent controls have led to housing shortages in certain cities. (a) How would the quantity of housing demanded and the quantity supplied be affected if rent controls were eliminated? (b) Other things equal, would rents rise more if price elasticity of demand were low or high? (c) Would rents tend to rise more if elasticity of supply were low or high?

12. Elasticities can also be computed for the labor market. The price elasticity of the demand for labor is defined as the percentage change in the quantity of labor demanded divided by the percentage change in the price of labor (the wage rate). (a) In recent years, workers at various companies have accepted pay cuts in an effort to expand employment. This strategy has been more successful in some companies than in others. Discuss the role of the price elasticity of demand for labor in determining the effect of a pay cut on the level of employment. (b) Will an increase in the minimum wage have a greater effect on employment if demand for labor is elastic or inelastic?

13. The short-run cross elasticity of demand for residential electricity with respect to a change in the price of natural gas is estimated to be 0. The long-run cross elasticity is put at 0.5.[16] (a) Based on these numbers, are electricity and natural gas substitutes, complements, or independent in the long run? (b) What about the short run? (c) Why is the relationship between these two goods different in the short run than in the long run?

14. Assume a state currently taxes gasoline at the rate of 8 cents per gallon. A state legislator claims that doubling the tax, to 16 cents per gallon, would double gasoline tax receipts for the state. Do you agree? Why or why not?

15. A *subsidy* can be viewed as a negative tax. Rather than taxing a producer (and increasing costs), the government may provide financial support through a subsidy, thereby lowering costs of production. Suppose the government subsidizes production of cheese. (a) How will this affect the price of cheese? (b) Will the magnitude of any price change depend on the price elasticity of demand? Explain.

16. Assume more people attend concerts this year than last year, despite higher prices. Does this imply that the demand for concerts is upward sloping? Explain.

17. Reread question 8 in light of the arguments appearing in Exhibit 5-5. (a) Can we be confident that the increase in ridership was completely attributable to the fare cut? Explain. (b) If some other factor were involved, would the elasticity computed in 8(a) be accurate? (c) Why might it be important to obtain an accurate estimate of the elasticity of demand for railroad travel?

---

[16]T. R. Lakshmanan and William Anderson, "Residential Energy Demand in the United States," *Regional Science & Urban Economics* (August 1980), pp. 383 and 385.

ANSWERS TO YOUR TURN

DETERMINING THE PRICE ELASTICITY OF DEMAND
(a) 200, 800, $2.00, $6.00. (b) 0.75.

ANSWERS TO YOUR TURN

MAXIMIZING TOTAL REVENUE
A price of $7 raises $4900 for the charity, compared to only $4500 when the price is $5. The higher price raises more revenue because $E_d < 1$.

BUSINESS FIRMS IN THE AMERICAN ECONOMY

The business of America is business.

—CALVIN COOLIDGE

Business firms are where the action is in the U.S. economy. Firms produce almost all our goods and services, hire most of our workers, and issue the stocks and bonds that constitute a large portion of the nation's wealth. Their decisions about investment, pollution control, and output influence our current and future quality of life. In Chapter 6, we discuss the various forms of business organization (i.e., proprietorships, partnerships, and corporations) and look at the distribution of America's business activity across the different forms and sizes of business firms. In addition, the causes and possible consequences of the recent wave of corporation takeovers are analyzed. We then look at the types of securities issued by firms and provide a framework for understanding the forces that produce fluctuations in stock and bond prices. Finally, we overview certain basic elements of business-firm accounting by scanning the nature of the balance sheet and income statement.

SIZE CHARACTERISTICS OF AMERICAN FIRMS

The American business sector consists of millions of very small firms that control only a minor portion of the nation's productive capacity, many intermediate-size firms, and a few hundred huge corporations that have great economic power, as indicated by their assets, sales, and employment figures. There are approximately 18 million firms in America. The largest 500 of these firms—less than one-hundredth of one percent of all firms—produce almost half the nation's output of goods and services. The sales of General Motors Corporation—the nation's largest firm, with annual revenues in excess of $100 billion—exceed the gross national product of such nations as Austria, Belgium, and Sweden. The combined annual receipts of America's five largest firms exceed the combined gross national products of Greece, Netherlands, Switzerland, and Taiwan.

TABLE 6-1

THE 25 LARGEST U.S. INDUSTRIAL CORPORATIONS, 1988
(ranked by annual sales)

Rank 1988	Rank 1987	Company	1988 sales ($ billions)
1	1	General Motors (Detroit)	121.1
2	3	Ford Motor Company (Dearborn, MI)	92.4
3	2	Exxon (New York)	79.6
4	4	International Business Machines (Armonk, NY)	59.7
5	6	General Electric (Fairfield, CT)	49.4
6	5	Mobil (New York)	48.2
7	10	Chrysler (Highland Park, MI)	35.5
8	7	Texaco (White Plains, NY)	33.5
9	9	E.I. du Pont de Nemours (Wilmington, DE)	32.5
10	12	Philip Morris (New York)	25.9
11	11	Chevron (San Francisco)	25.2
12	14	Amoco (Chicago)	21.2
13	13	Shell Oil (Houston)	21.1
14	16	Occidental Petroleum (Los Angeles)	19.4
15	17	Proctor and Gamble (Cincinnati)	19.3
16	15	United Technologies (Hartford)	18.1
17	18	Atlantic Richfield (Los Angeles)	17.6
18	25	Eastman Kodak (Rochester, NY)	17.0
19	20	Boeing (Seattle)	17.0
20	19	RJR Nabisco (Atlanta)	17.0
21	24	Dow Chemical (Midland, MI)	16.7
22	34	Xerox (Stanford, CT)	16.4
23	23	USX (Pittsburgh)	15.8
24	21	Tenneco (Houston)	15.7
25	26	McDonnell Douglas (St. Louis)	15.1

Source: *Fortune,* April 24, 1989. Reprinted by permission of Fortune 500. © 1989 by Time Inc. All rights reserved.

America's 25 largest industrial corporations, ranked by annual sales, are listed in Table 6-1. No doubt you are familiar with most of these giant firms.

At the other end of the spectrum are millions of small firms with a tiny share of the nation's total receipts. The smallest 80 percent of American firms produce only about 10 percent of the nation's output. Small firms tend to be relatively risky and short-lived, exhibiting an average lifetime of roughly five years. Table 6–2 indicates the number of firms and total receipts of firms arranged according to industry.

Approximately one-half of all firms are located in the broadly classified industries of agriculture and services. Such firms tend to be small—the family farm, the shoe repair shop, the barbershop. Firms in these sectors constitute approximately one-half of all firms, but account for only about 10 percent of the receipts of all firms. Although roughly 14 percent of all firms are in agriculture, they account for only about 2 percent of total receipts of firms. On the other hand, the 3 percent of firms engaged in manufacturing receive more than one-third of total receipts. Manufacturing firms tend to be large, agricultural and service firms small.

FAILURES OF BUSINESS FIRMS

Figure 6-1 (page 116) indicates the failure rate of American corporations from 1970 to 1986. In the 1980s roughly one percent of the nation's corporations failed each year. Note the rather dramatic increase during the 1980s. This is due partly to a liberalization of bankruptcy laws, which has enticed more firms to declare bankruptcy. In addition, the 1980s witnessed periods of hardship for certain sectors of the economy such as agriculture and petroleum. Severe problems in these sectors have ripple effects—spilling over and dragging down businesses in other sectors. Although tens of thousands of firms go under each year, the number of firms in existence continues to increase significantly.

FORMS OF BUSINESS ENTERPRISE

The three primary forms of business organization are the proprietorship, the partnership, and the corporation. The relative numbers of these three forms of

TABLE 6-2

DISTRIBUTION OF FIRMS AND RECEIPTS BY INDUSTRY*

Industry	Number of firms (millions)	Receipts of firms ($ billions)
Agriculture, forestry, fisheries	2.5	170
Mining	0.3	143
Construction	1.7	416
Manufacturing	0.6	2,645
Transportation, communication	0.7	733
Wholesale and retail trade	3.5	2,519
Financial	2.3	555
Services	6.2	695
TOTAL	17.8	7,876

*This table (unlike Table 6-3) includes farm proprietorships.
Source: *Statistical Abstract of the United States,* 1988. Figures are based on income-tax returns filed with the Internal Revenue Service.

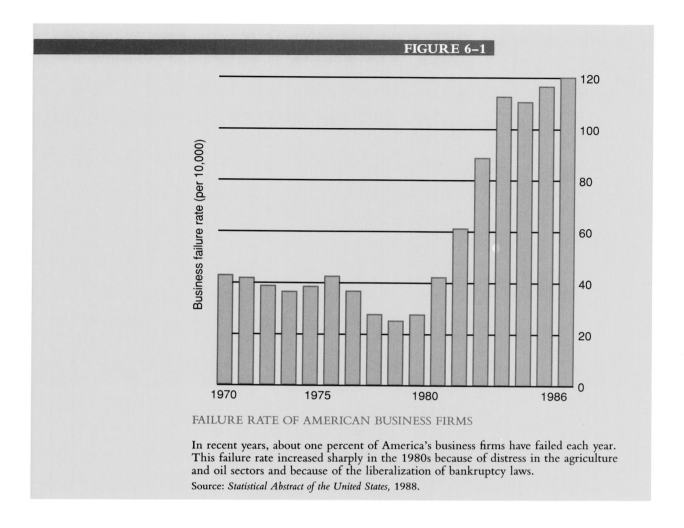

FIGURE 6-1

FAILURE RATE OF AMERICAN BUSINESS FIRMS

In recent years, about one percent of America's business firms have failed each year. This failure rate increased sharply in the 1980s because of distress in the agriculture and oil sectors and because of the liberalization of bankruptcy laws.

Source: *Statistical Abstract of the United States, 1988.*

business enterprise among the 18 million American firms, along with their shares of total sales in America, are illustrated in Figure 6-2. The key point is that proprietorships and partnerships are extremely numerous but contribute only a small portion of total national output. Proprietorships, for example, make up 70 percent of all firms but receive only 6 percent of all sales. Corporations constitute one-fifth of all firms but reap 90 percent of total sales. America's business is distributed highly unevenly among firms.

Table 6-3 (page 118) provides a more detailed breakdown of the number of firms in each organizational category by revenue and average size (farm proprietorships are not included). Note that the average corporation is more than 10 times larger than the average partnership and nearly 50 times larger than the average nonfarm proprietorship. More than 75 percent of all firms (all three classifications combined) have annual revenues of less than $100,000. Less than 4 percent of all firms have annual sales in excess of $1 million. Even within the corporate category, less than 20 percent of firms exceed the $1 million sales level. The point is that while almost all America's large firms are corporations, many corporations are surprisingly small.

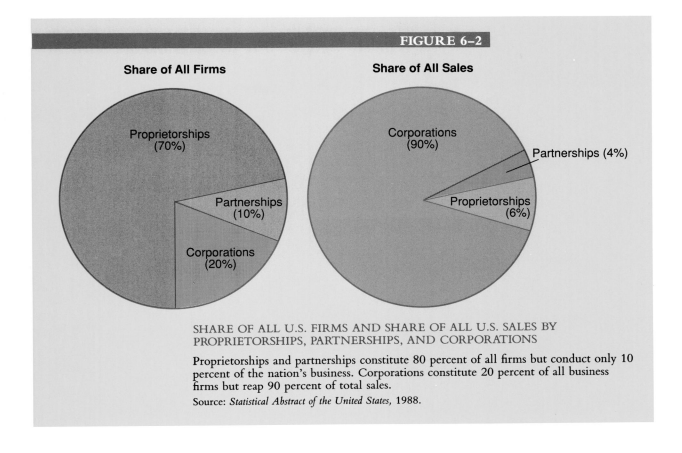

SHARE OF ALL U.S. FIRMS AND SHARE OF ALL U.S. SALES BY
PROPRIETORSHIPS, PARTNERSHIPS, AND CORPORATIONS

Proprietorships and partnerships constitute 80 percent of all firms but conduct only 10
percent of the nation's business. Corporations constitute 20 percent of all business
firms but reap 90 percent of total sales.

Source: *Statistical Abstract of the United States,* 1988.

Proprietorships

Proprietorship
A firm owned by a single
individual who has
unlimited liability for the
firm's debts.

The most prevalent form of business organization, and the form involving the fewest
legal complications, is the individual **(sole) proprietorship.** In a proprietorship,
the firm is owned by a single individual. Many people dream of owning and running
their own business; proprietors have total control over their businesses. No
stockholders or partners must be consulted when a proprietor wishes to change
advertising policy, hire new workers, or alter the nature of the business in a minor or
major way. Proprietorships are especially prevalent in farming, construction, and
wholesale and retail trade. Think of the small businesses in your hometown—
drugstores, dry cleaners, restaurants, service stations. Most are likely to be proprietorships. Roughly 90 percent of all farming operations are organized as proprietorships.

The ease of establishing a proprietorship—basically just hang out your shingle
and announce you are in business—helps explain its popularity. The total discretion
the owner exerts over the business and the possibility of earning healthy financial
rewards via wise decisions and hard work are very appealing. In fact, many
proprietors continue in business even though they could earn more working for
someone else. A proprietor's income is taxed by the Internal Revenue Service as
personal income.

TABLE 6-3			

NUMBERS, TOTAL REVENUES, AND AVERAGE SIZE OF AMERICAN
FIRMS—NONFARM PROPRIETORSHIPS, PARTNERSHIPS, AND
CORPORATIONS* 1984

	Number of firms	Total revenue ($ billions)	Average size
Nonfarm proprietorships			
Revenues under $100,000	10,154,000	$171	$ 16,840
Revenues of $100,000–$1,000,000	1,070,000	264	246,728
Revenues of $1,000,000 and above	37,000	81	$2,189,000
All nonfarm proprietorships	11,261,000	$516	$ 45,822
Partnerships			
Revenues under $100,000	1,217,000	$ 14	$ 11,504
Revenues of $100,000–$1,000,000	374,000	73	195,187
Revenues of $1,000,000 and above	52,000	232	$4,462,000
All partnerships	1,643,000	$319	$ 194,157
Corporations			
Revenues under $100,000	1,238,000	$ 33	$ 26,655
Revenues of $100,000–$1,000,000	1,429,000	499	349,152
Revenues of $1,000,000 and above	505,000	$6,417	$12,707,000
All corporations	3,172,000	$6,949	$ 2,190,731

*This table excludes the nation's approximately two million farm proprietorships, as does Table 3-2 in Chapter 3.
Source: *Statistical Abstract of the United States,* 1988, Table Number 824. Figures based on returns filed with the Internal Revenue Service.

There are two significant drawbacks to the proprietorship form of business organization. First, proprietors are personally liable for all debts of the firm. This means the owner's home, car, and other personal belongings may legally be confiscated to cover the firm's liabilities in the event of extreme financial problems incurred by the firm. Second, it is difficult to raise large amounts of financial support with a proprietorship. For this reason, proprietorships are limited to small-capitalized types of enterprises. You do not see this form of business organization in such large-scale industries as steel and automobiles.

Partnerships

Partnership
An unincorporated firm with two or more owners who have unlimited liability for the firm's debts.

The **partnership** is more complex than the proprietorship, but closer in its legal nature to the proprietorship than to the corporation. In a partnership, two or more individuals agree to own and operate a business. Each partner agrees to contribute a specified portion of the resources—labor and financial capital—to the firm and agrees to receive (or absorb) a certain portion of the profits (or losses). The partnership is a common type of business organization in such areas as law, medicine, accounting services, and investment banking in states whose laws prevent professional groups in these fields from forming corporations. Partnerships are typically larger than proprietorships but smaller than corporations. However, some of the larger partnerships are vastly more powerful—both in size and influence—than are millions of the nation's smaller corporations.

A partnership can bring together the financial resources and expertise of several individuals. This mix allows the firm to be larger and more efficient than would be possible in a proprietorship. For example, partners in a large accounting firm, law firm, or medical practice can specialize in a particular area of expertise. When one needs considerable financial capital—say $1 million—to start up a firm, most individuals must find partners in order to get started. Like the proprietorship, the partnership's income is taxed as personal income.

The partnership form of organization has certain severe drawbacks. Like the proprietor, each partner is personally liable for the debts of the firm. Also, partnerships are usually unable to raise huge amounts of financial capital. Perhaps the most troublesome aspect of the partnership, however, is the problem of decision making. In this regard, the partnership may be the least efficient form of business organization. The corporation selects officers who make key decisions; the sole proprietor makes decisions unilaterally. In a partnership, it is often necessary for each partner to agree before the firm can implement important decisions. This often causes problems.[1]

A partnership has been likened to a marriage arrangement entered into chiefly for the financial benefit of the participants—there is likely to be undue haggling over the terms. Further, the death or departure of one partner may result in the dissolution of the firm. In that event, remaining partners may commence a renegotiation of the terms of the new partnership. Moreover, a partner leaving the firm may experience difficulties or delays in obtaining financial settlement: a new partner must be found or remaining partners must be willing to buy out the departing partner.

Corporations

Corporation
A firm that takes the form of an independent legal entity with ownership divided into shares and each owner's liability limited to his or her investment in the firm.

Common Stock
A certificate of partial ownership of a corporation that gives its holder a vote in the selection of the firm's directors and a residual claim on the assets and profits of the firm.

A **corporation** is a more complex form of business organization than either the proprietorship or the partnership. The key legal distinction is that a corporation is treated as a fictitious individual, separate and distinct from its actual owners. As a result of this distinction, the owners have **limited liability**—their personal assets are not at risk in the event of financial disaster of the corporation. On the other hand, this form of organization leads to **double taxation.** First, the corporation's profits are taxed by the federal government via the corporate income tax. Second, the dividend income paid from after-tax profits by the corporation to its individual owners (stockholders) is taxed via the individual income tax.[2]

A corporation is formed when a state's corporation commissioner approves legal papers specifying the general nature of the activities in which the firm seeks to engage. Corporations are owned by stockholders. **Common stock** consists of certificates that signify ownership. This stock is issued in the form of *shares* to its owners in exchange for cash. Each share of common stock entitles its owner to one

[1]Remember that each partner is personally accountable for the liabilities of the firm, including those resulting from unwise actions by the other partners. The more wealthy partners therefore have a natural incentive to pursue more conservative or risk-averse business policies than the less affluent partners. The wealthy partners have more to lose.

[2]Income earned by corporations that pay no dividends but reinvest all profits in the corporation is not subject to double taxation. See Chapter 7 for a discussion of the corporate income tax and the individual income tax.

vote. A large corporation may have perhaps 400 million shares of stock outstanding, a single individual owning 10 shares or 40 million shares. A *board of directors* of the corporation, elected by its stockholders, selects the top management and oversees the general activities of the firm.

The corporate form of business has major advantages not available to proprietorships and partnerships. As indicated, the owners (stockholders) have limited liability in the event of adverse circumstances of the firm. When you purchase 10 shares of common stock in IBM Corporation, you become one of its owners. In the event of insolvency of the firm, the most you can lose is the amount you paid for your 10 shares: laws prohibit the corporation's creditors from coming after your personal assets. Also, unlike partnerships and proprietorships, which typically terminate with the death of an owner, the corporation potentially has eternal life. Such considerations explain why the corporation is a superior business organization when it comes to raising large amounts of financial capital. Millions of individual investors all around the world are willing to purchase shares in corporations because they stand to participate in the success of the firms and yet cannot conceivably lose any more than the value of the shares they own. Also, because of their continuity, corporations normally find it easier to borrow large amounts of funds than do partnerships and proprietorships.

The drawbacks to the corporate form of business organization include the possibility of conflicting goals of owners and management, the double taxation of income, and the relative high cost and difficulty of forming a corporation. State laws differ somewhat in this area, but services of attorneys and substantial fees are normally involved. These costs rule out consideration of the corporate form of business for millions of small or temporary business ventures. (See Table 6-4.)

OWNERSHIP VERSUS CONTROL IN CORPORATE AMERICA

Corporations are run by hired managers—a president, vice presidents, a board of directors, and others. Legally these executives are the employees of the owners of such firms—the stockholders. This arrangement has the pragmatic advantage of avoiding the indecision and haggling over day-to-day operations typical of partnerships. However, many observers are increasingly concerned over the separation of *ownership* and *control* in corporate America. These critics charge that the managers tend to look after their own interests instead of those of the owners of the corporation.

Stockholders' (owners') interests are best served when the firm maximizes profits. Maximum profits keep the price of stock as high as possible, thereby maximizing the wealth of the individual shareholders. Management, however, may be more interested in maximizing its own power, income, and job security. In pursuit of these goals, management has an incentive to expand the firm beyond the size that maximizes shareholder wealth. The *power* of management is related to the amount of resources under its control—the size of its *empire*. Payment of profits to stockholders reduces resources in the hands of management. Moreover, the compensation of management seems related to the *size* or *growth* of the firm rather than to its efficiency or current profits. Management may therefore have a further incentive to maximize the *size* of the firm rather than remain *lean and mean* in order to maximize profits. When this is true, management may use current profits to build

	TABLE 6-4	

ADVANTAGES AND DISADVANTAGES OF THE THREE PRIMARY TYPES OF BUSINESS ORGANIZATIONS

Type of Firm	Advantages	Disadvantages
Proprietorship	1. Firm is easy to set up 2. Decision making is simple; owner has total control 3. Income is taxed only once—as personal income	1. Owner has unlimited personal liability for obligations of the firm 2. Difficulty in raising financial capital
Partnership	1. Firm is easy to set up 2. Access to more financial capital than proprietorship 3. Some specialization is possible; more management skills available 4. Income is taxed only once	1. Decision-making problems 2. Unlimited liability for partners 3. Legal complications when any change in ownership occurs
Corporation	1. Limited liability of owners for obligations of firm 2. Access to large blocks of financial capital via issuing stocks and bonds 3. Firm can hire professional management and replace management when necessary 4. Firm potentially has eternal life as distinguished from owners' lives	1. Double taxation of income of firm 2. Possibility of conflicting goals of owners and management 3. More costly to establish than proprietorship or partnership

unnecessary facilities or to acquire new divisions rather than to pay out dividends to the stockholders.

THE CORPORATE TAKEOVER MOVEMENT

The bulk of the shares of common stock of many large American corporations are owned by a large number of relatively small shareholders. Managers of corporations are technically agents of their stockholders. In principle, when stockholders are dissatisfied with management's performance, they can replace them with a new team. In practice, however, stockholders frequently have neither sufficient knowledge of the firm's day-to-day operations nor the initiative to oust ineffective management. Many individuals hold shares of stock in 5, 10, or 30 different corporations. When these stockholders are unhappy with a firm's performance, they can attend stockholder's meetings, voice their views, and attempt to elect a new board of directors. However, it is usually less aggravating to just sell the shares and invest in companies with more satisfactory management.

When such stockholder dissatisfaction becomes widespread, the price of the stock drops significantly below the value of the assets of the firm. Investor-entrepreneurs are likely to see this discrepancy and to implement a *takeover bid,* which may be waged by an individual, a group, or most commonly, another corporation. This investor-entrepreneur (*raider*) buys up shares of stock in the company by making a **tender offer** to shareholders (i e., an offer to purchase the shares at a premium to the current market price of the shares). In this way the raider attempts to gain voting control of the *target firm.* Management may be replaced and peripheral or unimportant divisions may be sold off in order to help pay for the acquisition or make the business more profitable.

Corporate Mergers in America

Hostile Takeover
A merger accomplished by purchasing controlling interest directly from the stockholders of the target firm, against the wishes of its management.

Historically, merger movements in America have come in great waves. Surges of merger activity occurred in the 1890s, 1920s, 1960s, and in the past decade. In earlier periods mergers were almost always *friendly,* both firms favoring the merger. The distinguishing aspect of the recent merger movement is the **hostile takeover**— acquisitions in which the purchasing company (raider) bypasses the target company's management and purchases controlling interest in the company directly from its stockholders.

In such industries as airlines, takeovers have resulted in consolidation within the industry—fewer firms in operation. Many takeovers result in divestment (selling off) of peripheral operations and a focusing of efforts on the largest or most profitable divisions. Such *spin-offs* often increase efficiency by allowing management to concentrate efforts on a limited range of operations. However, other mergers are motivated by diversification—purchasing businesses unrelated to mainline operations.

In terms of the number and magnitude of transactions, the merger movement of the 1980s has exceeded those of the past. Annual transactions involved in mergers averaged more than $100 billion throughout the 1980s, with the figure approaching $200 billion per year in the second half of the decade. Of the hundred largest mergers in American history, fewer than 10 percent occurred prior to the 1980s.

Causes of the Recent Takeover Movement

Several factors have joined to explain the *merger mania* of the past decade. An easing of enforcement of antitrust statutes occurred as a more tolerant attitude toward merger activity became prevalent. The globalization of markets and the increasing U.S. market penetration by large foreign firms has led to the view that larger and more efficient American firms are required to compete with foreign giants. Larger firms often benefit from **economies of scale**—efficiencies attributable to larger size—that allow them to produce goods and services at lower cost than smaller firms.

In addition, a dynamic world economy, advances in technology, or changes in market conditions sometimes require a major restructuring of corporate assets and activities. It is often easier for new management, with its fresh viewpoint and lack of ties with current employees or the community, to come in and implement difficult but essential changes. Innovations in financing tactics have made possible many mergers that formerly would not have been feasible.

Finally, the stock market price of a company's shares is sometimes low relative to the replacement costs of the plant, equipment, and other resources owned by the firm. It is frequently much cheaper to purchase an existing operation than to build from scratch. This was especially true in the 1970s and early 1980s, when stock prices were depressed.

Consequences of the Takeover Movement

Many economists—probably most—have a *laissez-faire* philosophy about the corporate takeover phenomenon. They believe takeovers usually benefit both stockholders and society. Other economists, however, are more skeptical about the consequences. They believe that not all the effects are beneficial and that we would be wise to reserve judgment on the merits of the movement until the smoke clears.

Positive Arguments   The view is commonly expressed that the ever-present possibility of a corporate takeover serves the purpose of motivating existing management to do its utmost to serve stockholders by maximizing efficiency and profitability. When management is incompetent, lazy, or pursues objectives at odds with the goals of stockholders, the price of the company's stock is likely to reflect this fact. In this event both the stockholders and society at large suffer. Stockholders are cheated because the stock's price is lower than it should be; society loses because the presence of inefficiency implies that the nation is operating below its production possibilities curve.

When management does its job properly, this is reflected in the price of the company's stock. In principle, there is no incentive for corporate raiders to attempt a takeover. Hence, the possibility of a corporate takeover is viewed as a beneficial mechanism that forces management to behave itself and to look after the interests of its stockholders.

Wall Street evidently believes acquisitions are beneficial: stock prices of acquired firms typically rise by some 30 percent after takeover. It is estimated that gains to shareholders of acquired companies averaged about $35 billion annually during the decade ending in 1986. To place this figure in perspective, it is equivalent to about one-half of total cash dividends paid out annually by corporations.

Acquired firms may grow to become more profitable as new management directs operations toward areas more compatible with consumer demand. New management is believed more likely to shut down unprofitable and inefficient operations and to sell off peripheral divisions to more specialized firms. In the American steel and textile industries, hostile takeovers have facilitated important wage concessions needed in order to compete with less-expensive imports. In the oil industry, takeovers have held down what many observers believe to be a propensity of management to invest excessive resources in exploration. *Bust-up takeovers* of conglomerate firms have led to the sale of peripheral divisions to specialized firms better equipped to operate them.

Negative Arguments   Critics of the takeover movement believe that the constant threat of takeover makes it harder for management to take the *long view.* In other words, management is forced to attempt to keep *current* profits high in order to maximize the price of the company's stock and to minimize the company's vulnerability to raiders. Corporate investment projects are allegedly biased by the threat of takeover toward those with immediate and obvious payoffs, and away from research and development and projects yielding long-term benefits. Longer-term investments often result in new technologies that raise living standards.

In addition, the takeover movement may have adverse side effects on the nation's financial structure and macroeconomy. Firms typically finance acquisitions by borrowing (i.e., by issuing new debt). The money raised by borrowing is used to acquire the stock of the company being purchased. The merger movement, by increasing the debt of many firms, has increased the vulnerability of firms to financial problems in the event of a severe business downturn. This is because the firms are obligated to continue paying interest on their debt (debt service) at a time when their sales and revenues are declining.

On the human level, takeovers can result in wrenching changes in the lives of employees, managers, customers, and suppliers of the firm. Takeovers can result in layoffs, pay cuts, and plant closings. Entire communities are sometimes devastated. Of course, supporters of the takeover movement point out that these transitional costs are simply manifestations of changing technology and changing markets in a dynamic economy.

Defensive Ploys to Avoid a Takeover

The defensive tactics employed by management of target firms to avoid hostile takeovers are often destructive and costly to both stockholders and society at large. A firm may sell off desirable assets to obtain funds with which to purchase its own shares on the market, thereby making them unavailable to raiders. Even worse, a firm may sell off its *crown jewels*—the firm's most attractive assets—in a destructive effort to reduce potential raiders' interest in attempting a takeover. A firm may repurchase stock from hostile raiders at a price significantly higher than the market price to get them to drop the takeover effort—a form of bribery dubbed **greenmail.** Firms may also issue **poison pills** to deter raiders—rights granted existing shareholders to purchase additional stock (usually at half price) in the event of a hostile takeover bid. These *pills* greatly raise the takeover cost, thus *poisoning* the firm to hostile raiders. In an environment of widespread takeovers, corporate management's attention is partially diverted from the socially desirable goal of producing to the wasteful task of fending off raiders.

Supporters of the takeover movement acknowledge the detrimental effects of these defensive tactics. However, they view these tactics as evidence of management's contempt for stockholders. The sooner such deceitful management is ousted, the better!

CORPORATIONS—THE FINANCIAL SIDE

Corporate Securities

Corporations require outside funds in order to finance plant construction, equipment purchases, and inventories of goods. Corporations raise funds by issuing equities and debt instruments. Equities are ownership claims consisting of *common stock* and *preferred stock.* On balance, corporations are net debtors or deficit-spending units. Forms of corporate debt include *bonds, bank loans,* and *commercial paper*—short-term IOUs issued in large denominations by large corporations of impeccable financial reputation. Of special interest are three important instruments of equity and debt finance—common stocks, preferred stocks, and bonds.

Common Stock   Common stock represents claims of ownership in the corporation. Holders of common stock own a pro-rata share of the firm, the share of each stockholder being the number of shares owned relative to the total number of shares of common stock outstanding. Generally, the stockholders share in the firm's annual profits. Each corporation's board of directors meets periodically and declares a **dividend**—a payout based on the firm's recent and prospective future profits.[3]

---

[3]Some firms pay out the bulk of their annual profits in dividends. Others, especially rapidly growing firms, pay little or no dividend. They choose instead to plow back most or all of the profits into the firm for financing expansion or research and development.

Dividends are typically paid quarterly, though in some cases they are paid less frequently. Dividends are a form of income that stockholders receive on a regular basis. In addition, shareholders may eventually benefit from selling their shares at a higher price than they originally paid for them. Such income is known as **capital gains.** Once issued, many common stocks are traded on organized exchanges such as the New York Stock Exchange or the American Stock Exchange, or through an informal over-the-counter (OTC) network of dealers. The prices of thousands of these stocks are quoted daily in major newspapers. Other companies are privately owned (i.e., the shares of their stock are not available for purchase by the public). Prices of such stock are not made public information.

Preferred Stock **Preferred stock** represents a hybrid sort of claim that involves payment of a relatively high dividend but carries no voting rights and no prospects of participating in the long-term growth of the firm via capital gains. Consider

EXHIBIT 6–1

BUYING COMMON STOCKS

Considering that nearly 40 million Americans own common stocks, two things are apparent. First, you don't have to be rich to purchase stocks. Second, owning stocks is appealing to many people. When you buy shares of stock, you purchase a share of the company's profits or losses in the future. You own a piece of the company and directly participate in the future success or failure of the firm.

Suppose you are considering the purchase of a few shares of Ford Motor Company. To find its current price and other relevant information, turn to the financial pages of any major newspaper. On Monday, April 17, 1989, *The Wall Street Journal* revealed the following data on Ford Motor's stock, together with corresponding information on thousands of other stocks, for the Friday before.

52 Weeks Hi	Lo	Stock	Sym	Div	Yld %	PE	Vol 100s	Hi	Lo	Close	Net Chg
28	22¼	FooteCone	FCB	1.20	5.1	15	139	24	23½	23¾	...
8½	6¼	FoothillGp	FGI	.28	3.4	6	24	8⅛	8⅛	8⅛	...
56⅝	44	FordMotor	F	3.00	6.3	4	10390	48¼	47¼	48	+1
23	8⅛	Formica	FOR		...	7	650	18¾	18⅝	18¾	+ ⅛

Reading from the left, the first two columns reveal the highest and lowest prices at which Ford traded in the last 52 weeks. Ford ranged from a high of $56 5/8 to a low of $44 a share. The stock pays a dividend of $3 annually per share ($0.75 quarterly), which represents a yield of 6.3 percent based on its most recent price ($48). The price-earnings ratio (P-E) of 4 indicates the stock is selling at a price that is four times the company's annual earnings or profits. The next column indicates the number of shares traded that day, in hundreds. Shares of Ford traded totalled 1,039,000. The next three columns reveal the highest, lowest, and closing prices of the stock for the most recent trading day (April 14, 1989). Ford traded as high as 48 1/4 and as low as 47 1/4. It closed at 48, for a gain of one dollar per share on the day (final column).

To determine whether Ford is currently a sound stock to purchase, you would be well advised to obtain as much information as possible about the company's prospects for the next few years. The price of common stock is closely related to Ford's current and expected future profits. If profits expand sharply over the years, the price of its stock will probably do so also. The modest price/earnings ratio of Ford (4) indicates that the consensus of investors is that Ford's future is not expected to be blessed with *rapid growth.* More glamorous, rapid growth stocks often sell at a P–E ratio of 20 or 30.

This does not mean that Ford is a poor stock to buy. Each stock's price already reflects the marketplace's opinion of the company's prospects. If you are smarter, more perceptive, or more diligent than the market as a whole, you may be able to select stocks that will outperform broad market averages. Although some are able to do this on a consistent basis, it is extremely difficult. Again, that is because the stock market tends to be *efficient*—it already reflects all readily available information about each company's future prospects.

Source: Data on Ford Motor's stock from *The Wall Street Journal,* April 17, 1989. Reprinted by permission of *The Wall Street Journal.* © 1989, Dow Jones & Company, Inc. All rights reserved.

Harcourt Brace Jovanovich (HBJ)—the publisher of this book. Owners of HBJ preferred stock receive $1.62 per share each year as long as the firm earns enough to pay this dividend. HBJ cannot legally pay dividends on its common stock until dividends on its preferred stock are paid in full. Owners of HBJ preferred stock are *preferred* stockholders in the sense that they have prior claim (over common stockholders) on the firm's profits and assets. To the investor, this makes the preferred stock less risky than the common stock. On the other hand, preferred stockholders do not benefit from the long-term growth in the firm's profits, whereas common stockholders do (via increased dividends and capital appreciation). Preferred stock is a more conservative investment than common stock.

Corporate Bond

An IOU or evidence of debt issued by a corporation that carries a specified schedule of interest payments to be made to the bondholder (lender) and a date for redemption of the principal face value.

Bonds   Bonds are a distinctly different animal than common and preferred stocks. **Bonds** are *debts* of corporations—a type of long-term IOU issued by corporations. Unlike stockholders, bondholders do *not* own a piece of the firm; they are creditors and receive *interest payments* instead of dividends. Semi-annual interest payments continue until the bond matures, at which time the original *principal* is repaid to the bondholder. Bonds are typically sold in $1000 denominations. Consider Texaco 8 7/8 bonds due in the year 2005. This bond is a contractual agreement to pay the bondholder 8 7/8 dollars per one-hundred dollar face amount ($88.75 per $1000 denomination) each year and also to pay back the $1000 original principal at maturity in the year 2005. A corporation is obligated to pay the interest and principal as scheduled, or the firm may be declared bankrupt. Bondholders are legally entitled to the full amount they are owed before stockholders receive a penny.

Stocks and Bonds as Inflation Hedges

From the investor's viewpoint, bonds are less risky than preferred stock, which is in turn less risky than common stock. However, there is another important consideration—inflation. The tendency for the U.S. price level to rise persistently over time implies that bondholders are usually paid off (at maturity) in dollars with considerably less purchasing power than the dollars initially loaned to the firm. In contrast, common stock prices have a strong tendency to rise sufficiently in the long run to keep pace with increases in the nation's price level. During this century, while the American price level has increased by perhaps 800 percent, common stocks have increased even more. Common stock has been a good hedge against inflation when viewed from the perspective of several decades. This is because stock prices follow corporation profits, which tend to increase over time in line with the price level. But consider the investor who purchases bonds—the Texaco 8 7/8s of 2005. This investor will receive exactly $1000 per bond when they mature in the year 2005, no matter how high the U.S. price level has risen by that year. Hence, unless the annual interest payment is commensurately high, bonds tend to be a poor long-term investment in an era of high inflation.[4]

[4]Actually, the market price (and hence yield) of existing bonds fluctuates to compensate potential new investors for the expected depreciation in the real value of the principal due to expected inflation. If the outlook for inflation worsens, the current market price of the Texaco 8 7/8s of 2005 (and all other existing bonds) will decline sufficiently to entice investors to be willing to buy and hold the bonds. In 1981, with inflation in double-digit territory, the price of high-quality bonds fell dramatically. Bond prices fell so low that astute investors were able to lock in 12–15 percent yields. In principle, bonds are a good inflation hedge if yields are high enough. Historically, bonds generally have not been a good hedge against inflation when viewed from the perspective of several decades. Returns from common stocks have significantly exceeded returns from bonds over the long haul.

DISCOUNTING EXPECTED FUTURE RETURNS TO COMPUTE PRESENT VALUE

We now present a general approach to understanding how the market places a specific price on any particular stock, bond, or other financial asset. This framework helps one understand intuitively why stocks and bonds fluctuate in price. Consider Equation 6-1.

$$\text{PV (or price)} = \frac{R_1}{1 + i} + \frac{R_2}{(1 + i)^3} + \frac{R_3}{(1 + i)^3} + \cdots + \frac{R_n}{(1 + i)^n} \qquad (6\text{-}1)$$

In Equation 6-1, PV represents the present value (or price) of the asset; R_1, $R_2 \ldots R_n$ indicate the annual returns (flows of income) currently expected from the asset in years 1, 2 . . . n; i represents the interest rate used to discount these expected future returns (discussed later).

Every financial asset holds the promise of yielding a stream of returns in future years ($R_1, R_2 \ldots R_n$). For some securities the promise may involve only one return to be received in one year (R_1) or perhaps in 40 years (R_{40}).[5] Most bonds promise a finite series of annual returns, involving constant payments for 10, 20, or 30 years. Common stocks, preferred stocks, and some rare types of bonds issued in foreign countries potentially involve an infinite number of annual returns—they are expected to yield returns *in perpetuity* or as long as the corporation is in existence.

For common stocks, expected returns consist of annual dividends and perhaps some appreciation in the price of the stock (capital gains). For bonds, returns consist of fixed annual interest payments. For common stocks there is considerable uncertainty about future returns (Rs) because firms have no legal obligation to pay any specific dividend and because the financial condition of the corporation can change considerably over time. For bonds the Rs are subject to less uncertainty because the corporation issuing the bonds enters a contractual agreement with the bondholder to pay a specific stream of Rs over time. Hence, in the case of common stocks, market participants revise the expected stream of Rs on a daily basis. This is not generally the case with bondholders, although this does occur when financial problems of the corporation increase sufficiently to raise the prospect of default.

Present Value
The value now of one or a series of payments to be received in the future; often referred to as the *discounted present value* of future payments.

To find the **present value** (today's value, or PV) of a return (R) expected to be received *in the future,* one must *discount* that return. The present value of a promise to receive one dollar in the future is less than one dollar. If you have one dollar today you can invest the dollar at interest in a risk-free asset, such as a savings account, and accumulate more than a dollar in the future. The rate of discount—the interest rate—is indicated by i in the denominator of Equation 6-1. The present value of each expected future return ($R_1, R_2 \ldots R_n$) is less than its face value by an amount that depends on the level of the interest rate and the number of years in the future that the return will be received.

Figure 6-3 (page 128) summarizes the relationship between the present value of one dollar, the number of years in the future that the dollar will be received, and the interest rate used to discount the future return.

What is the present value of the promise to receive one dollar in 10 years when the rate of discount is 5 percent? Answer: $\$1/(1.05)^{10} = 61$¢. What is the present value of the promise to receive one dollar in 20 years when the rate of discount is 15

---

[5]Examples of securities promising a single lump-sum payment of principal in 1 year and in 40 years, respectively, are a one-year U.S. Treasury bill (issued by the U.S. Government) and a 40-year zero-coupon bond (issued by corporations and other entities). A zero-coupon bond is a long-term bond that pays no annual interest but instead pays a specific sum of money (usually in thousand-dollar denominations) at some distant future date. It sells at a price considerably below its future face value.

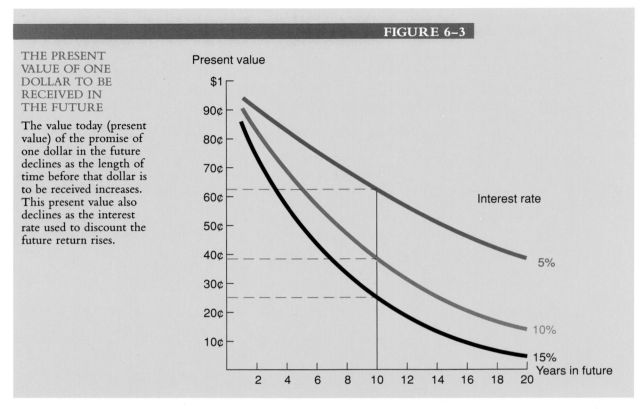

FIGURE 6–3

THE PRESENT
VALUE OF ONE
DOLLAR TO BE
RECEIVED IN
THE FUTURE

The value today (present
value) of the promise of
one dollar in the future
declines as the length of
time before that dollar is
to be received increases.
This present value also
declines as the interest
rate used to discount the
future return rises.

percent? Answer: $\$1/(1.15)^{20} = 6$¢! Note that the present value of one dollar tails off rapidly as you increase the length of time into the future that it is to be received. This is especially true when the interest rate is high. The present value of one dollar to be received in 10 years falls from 61¢ to 39¢ to 25¢ as the discount rate increases from 5 percent to 10 percent to 15 percent, respectively.

The current price of a share of IBM stock is the sum of the present values of the unlimited number of future annual returns expected from each share of stock. In reality, because the present value tails off rapidly with time into the future, the price of IBM stock is dominated by the returns expected in the next five or ten years.

You now have the tools with which to understand why the prices of individual stocks and the stock market in general fluctuate significantly over time. As new information becomes available each day, market participants revise their estimates for the Rs of Equation 6-1. In addition, interest rates fluctuate over time. An increase in interest rates, unless accompanied by a compensating increase in the Rs expected from stocks, depresses stock market prices. For bonds an increase in interest rates unambiguously decreases bond prices because the Rs are fixed by contractual arrangement and do not fluctuate once the bond is issued. A decline in interest rates unambiguously increase bond prices. A decline also increases stock prices unless the same forces that depress interest rates also depress the returns (Rs) expected from stocks commensurately.[6]

---

[6]In recessions, interest rates typically fall. Other things equal, this causes stock prices to go up. However, recessions are associated with a significant drop in corporation profits. Hence, the Rs of Equation 6-1 are revised downward. Because recessions result in a decrease in both the numerator and denominator of Equation 6-1, the net effect on stock prices is ambiguous. Severe recessions usually cause a decline in the stock market because corporation profits (and the Rs of Equation 6-1) drop sharply.

BEHAVIOR OF STOCK PRICES IN RECENT DECADES

Figure 6-4 illustrates the behavior of Standard & Poors 500, a broad index of common-stock prices, over the 1971–1988 period. Figure 6-4 also indicates the range of the price–earnings ratio for the basket of stocks in the index for each year.

Figure 6-4 reveals that although stocks were basically flat during 1971–1982, the 1982–1987 period witnessed a strong bull market. From the 1982 lows to the 1987 highs, the index increased by some 200 percent or almost 25 percent per year. Using the framework of Equation 6-1, it is clear that this bull market was driven by persistent upward revisions in the returns expected from stocks (Rs) and by a sustained decline in interest rates (i). The Reagan Administration's policies were perceived by market participants as bullish for stocks. Income-tax rates (individual and corporate) were slashed significantly; inflation was brought down sharply below rates of the 1970s and was maintained at modest levels; deregulatory measures were implemented; and corporate profits increased strongly after 1982. The duration of the economic recovery beginning in late 1982 set a new record.

Note in Figure 6-4 that the price–earnings ratio of stocks increased considerably during 1981–1987: market participants were willing to pay more and more for each

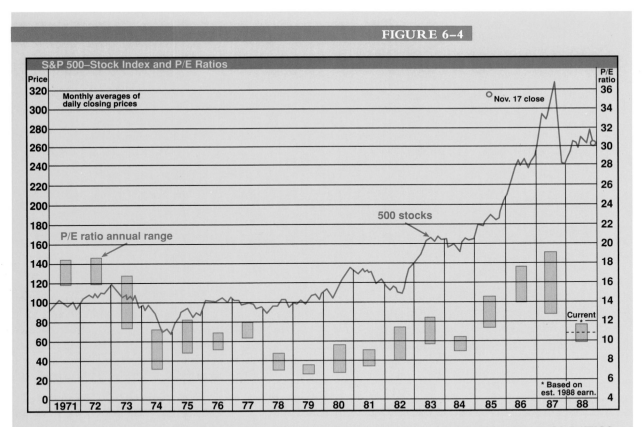

FIGURE 6–4

STANDARD & POORS 500—STOCK INDEX AND PRICE–EARNINGS RATIOS

After remaining flat in the 1970s, common stock prices more than doubled in the 1980s (left-hand vertical axis).

Source: Standard & Poors, *The Outlook*, November 23, 1988. Reprinted by permission.

dollar of current profits earned by corporations. This willingness can be explained partly by the persistent upward revisions of the prospective returns (Rs) expected from stocks owing to the gradually improving perception of the U.S. economic environment and partly by the sustained decline in interest rates in the U.S. economy. Since stocks compete with bonds and other interest-bearing instruments for investor attention, a decline in interest rates makes stocks more attractive. Investors are willing to pay more (higher share prices) for each dollar of current profits because bonds become less desirable when interest rates decline.

Note the "Crash of '87" in Figure 6-4. On October 19, 1987, stock prices plunged by approximately 20 percent! This episode illustrates that herd psychology can be a powerful force and that people can lose an awful lot of money in a very short period of time. Nevertheless, even if one computes returns using the *highs* of 1980–1981 to the *lows* of the late 1980s, stocks were an excellent investment in the decade of the 1980s. However, resist concluding that stocks will necessarily be a good investment during the 1990s. Before aggressively converting your life's savings into shares of common stock, ponder the experience of the 1970s (Figure 6-4). Or, for an even more sobering admonishment, study the period 1929–1933. Common stocks lost some 90 percent of their value in the Great Depression.

YOUR TURN Assume OPEC (Organization of Petroleum Exporting Countries) announces an agreement to sharply reduce output of oil, leading to expectations of considerably higher oil prices. Analyze, via the framework of Equation 6-1, the probable effect of this *announcement* on (a) the price of common stock of oil companies and (b) the Dow-Jones (and other) stock market averages.

FUNDAMENTAL ACCOUNTING ELEMENTS—BALANCE SHEETS AND INCOME STATEMENTS

The economic status of any firm is summarized in two key documents—the balance sheet and the income statement. Both documents provide important information about the financial condition of the firm. Financial analysts and stock-market investment advisors scrutinize both documents with care.

The Balance Sheet

Balance sheet
A financial report listing a firm's assets and liabilities at a moment in time.

Assets
Items that the firm owns and claims that the firm has upon entities external to the firm.

Liabilities
Debts of the firm or claims that outsiders have on the firm.

The firm's **balance sheet** is a statement of its assets and liabilities at a given point of time. The firm's **assets** are comprised of items that the firm owns and of claims that the firm has against outside entities. Its **liabilities** are claims that outside entities have against resources of the firm (i.e., what the firm *owes*). It is essential to recognize that the balance sheet is a snapshot—it looks at the *stock* of assets and liabilities *at a given time.* The balance sheet changes from day-to-day as the value of assets and liabilities fluctuate.

The balance sheet summarizes the current financial position of a firm by comparing its assets and its liabilities.

Consider the hypothetical balance sheet of the fictitious company, California Computer Corporation.

BALANCE SHEET—CALIFORNIA COMPUTER CORPORATION (December 31, 1989).

Assets		Liabilities	
Cash	$1,000,000	Accounts payable	$5,000,000
Accounts receivable	$4,000,000	Short-term bank loans	$3,000,000
Inventory	$6,000,000	Long-term debts (mortgages and bonds)	$15,000,000
Real estate, plant, and equipment	$20,000,000		
Total assets	$31,000,000	Total liabilities	$23,000,000
		Net worth	$ 8,000,000

Assets of California Computer include cash on hand (chiefly checking and savings accounts); accounts receivable (monies owed the firm by its customers); inventories of computers and other items; and the firm's real estate, plant, and equipment. California Computer's assets sum to $31 million. Its liabilities consist of accounts payable (monies owed by California Computer to its suppliers and others), bank loans, and long-term debt such as bonds issued and mortgages on its buildings. Total liabilities sum to $23 million.

Total assets of any solvent firm (that is, any firm that is not bankrupt) exceed total liabilities. For California Computer, total assets exceed total liabilities by $8 million. This difference, known as **net worth,** is the owners' equity in the business or the owners' claim against the assets of the firm. The $8 million net worth of California Computer means that if the firm were to cease operations, sell off all its assets at full value, and pay off its liabilities, it would still have $8 million. These funds would accrue to the owners of the firm.

Net Worth
The difference between a firm's assets and its liabilities; net worth is the residual equity or claim of the owners of the firm.

Accounting Identities

1. **net worth = total assets − total liabilities**
2. **total assets = total liabilities + net worth**

The first accounting identity is simply a definition; the second identity follows from the definition of net worth (1). Because net worth is the difference between total assets and total liabilities, it follows logically that total assets are equal to total liabilities plus net worth. For solvent firms, net worth is positive—total assets exceed total liabilities. When net worth is negative, the firm is technically bankrupt—liabilities exceed assets.

As a firm grows over time, the entries on its balance sheet increase. As the firm becomes larger, it normally requires additional plant and equipment and a larger stock of inventories. Moreover, as the firm does business with more customers, its cash requirements and accounts receivable typically expand.

From the second identity (2), we know that the firm's liabilities or net worth, or both, must grow as its assets increase. A firm's profits may be either paid out in dividends or retained by the firm. If the firm is highly profitable, it can finance much of its growth via *retained earnings* (i.e., by plowing profits back into the business). To the extent that the firm does this, its assets expand without a compensating increase in its liabilities. And, therefore, the firm's net worth increases, together with the owners' stake in the firm. If the firm does not earn and retain sufficient profits to finance expansion, it must seek outside financing. The firm may issue new equity shares—ownership claims—by taking in new partners (if it is a partnership) or new shareholders (if it is a corporation). Or, the firm can issue debt (i.e., borrow funds from banks or float new bonds to obtain financial capital).

The Income Statement

As time goes by, California Computer Corporation is productively engaged in the enterprise of manufacturing and selling computers. To know the firm's flow of income over one year or one quarter, we consult the firm's **income statement,** or its statement of profit or loss.

Income Statement
A financial report showing the revenues, costs, and profits from the firm's activities over a specified period of time.

The income statement for a specified interval shows the firm's revenues from sales during that period, the expenses of the firm, and its net income—the profits remaining after expenses are deducted from sales.

INCOME STATEMENT—CALIFORNIA COMPUTER CORPORATION
(January 1, 1990—December 31, 1990)

Total sales		$8,000,000
Less		
Materials	$2,000,000	
Labor costs	$3,000,000	
Depreciation	$1,000,000	
Miscellaneous costs	$ 500,000	
Total cost of goods sold	$6,500,000	$6,500,000
Gross profit		$1,500,000
Less: sales and administrative costs		100,000
Net operating profit		$1,400,000
Less: state and local taxes and interest expense		200,000
Net income before income taxes		$1,200,000
Less: corporate income tax		400,000
Net income after taxes		$ 800,000
Less: dividends paid on common stock		$ 200,000
Addition to retained earnings		$ 600,000

To begin with, focus on the column of items farthest right and ignore the individual items contributing to the cost of goods sold. Total sales receipts of California Computer were $8 million in 1990. Deducting the cost of goods sold of $6.5 million, we calculate a gross profit of $1.5 million. When we subtract sales and administrative costs, interest expense on the firm's debts, and state and local taxes, we obtain net income before federal taxes of $1,200,000. After paying $400,000 in corporate income taxes to the Internal Revenue Service, California Computer Corporation earned $800,000 in 1990. One-fourth of these profits were paid out in dividends to the owners of common stock in California Computer. The remaining

$600,000 (retained earnings) were plowed back into the firm. The 1990 profitability of the firm raised its net worth by $600,000.[7]

Turning briefly to the individual costs of goods sold, the materials, labor, and miscellaneous costs of producing computers are obvious; only depreciation requires elaboration. Firms require the use of capital goods—equipment, plants, trucks, and so forth—to produce their output. These capital goods do not last forever; they have a finite lifetime, wearing out gradually. The accounting charge for the annual cost of such capital assets as equipment and buildings is known as **depreciation.** Rather than attributing all this cost to the year in which the capital goods are installed, accountants reduce or depreciate the value of the assets over a period of time estimated to reflect their lifetime. For example, if a new building costing $10 million is erected in 1990 and is expected to have a useful life of 20 years, the firm might claim a depreciation cost of $500,000 annually for 20 consecutive years. This depreciation cost, like other costs, may be deducted from the firm's revenues for purposes of figuring its taxable income.

SUMMARY

1. The magnitude of business activity is distributed highly unevenly across American business firms. The smallest 80 percent of the nation's 18 million firms produce only 10 percent of output. The largest one-hundredth of 1 percent of American firms produce more than one-half our output.
2. The three forms of business enterprise are the individual proprietorship, the partnership, and the corporation. Eighty percent of America's firms are proprietorships and partnerships, but they collectively account for only ten percent of the nation's sales.
3. A sole proprietorship is a nonincorporated business owned by one person. Easy to set up, its decision making is simple and its income is taxed once by the IRS—as personal income of the owner. Drawbacks include the unlimited personal financial liability of the owner and the difficulty of raising large amounts of funds from outside sources.
4. A partnership is an unincorporated business owned by two or more persons, each of whom has a financial interest in the business. Its advantages and disadvantages are similar to those of the proprietorship. However, decision making is more cumbersome because of the need for all partners to reach agreement on policy decisions.
5. A corporation is a business that is legally incorporated under state laws. Chief advantages include the limited liability of its owners for the debts of the corporation and the superior access to large blocks of financial capital. Drawbacks include the costs of setting up the corporation, the double taxation of its income by the federal government, and the difficulties caused by conflicting goals of management and owners (stockholders).
6. When a corporation is poorly managed, the price of its stock declines relative to the true value of its assets. This, in turn, makes the company attractive to corporate *raiders*—firms that purchase a majority share of the company's stock and take over operations of the firm. A *market for corporate control* emerged with the hostile takeover movement of the 1980s. During 1985–1988, roughly ten corporate mergers were announced each day, on average.
7. Many economists applaud the corporate takeover movement, viewing the potential threat of takeover as a beneficial mechanism forcing corporate management to work hard to look after the interests of the stockholders. Other economists are more reserved. They worry that the takeover movement induces firms to place excessive emphasis on short-term

---

[7]Of course, the net worth of the firm during 1990 may have increased by more than $600,000 or may even have decreased. The values of individual assets and liabilities fluctuate throughout the year, producing changes in net worth. Given the 1990 retained earnings of $600,000, we *can* state that the net worth of California Computer is higher at the end of 1990 by $600,000 than it would have been if it had no retained earnings in 1990.

profits at the expense of long-run considerations. Also, by stimulating an increase in corporate indebtedness, the takeover movement probably has increased the fragility of America's financial structure.

8. To obtain funds above and beyond those generated internally, firms issue equities and debt instruments. Common stocks are equities—claims of ownership in the form of shares. Stockholders receive dividends and the possibility of capital gains—appreciation in the market price of the shares. Debt instruments issued by firms include bonds. A corporate bond is a contractual agreement by the firm to pay interest to the lender on the principal at a specified rate for a specified period and to return the principal at maturity. The bondholder has no ownership claim on the firm, but has a prior claim on the firm's assets above stockholders in the event of financial problems.

9. The present value of any asset—a stock, bond, factory, apartment building—is the sum of the discounted stream of future returns currently anticipated from the asset. In the case of common stocks and many other assets, these future returns are not known with certainty. To discount these future returns, the interest rate is used. An increase in interest rate, unless offset by a corresponding increase in expected returns, inevitably reduces the present value (and price) of the asset.

10. A steady upward revision in the market's perception of the future returns expected from stocks, combined with a major decline in interest rates, generated a bull market in stocks in the 1980s. From the low of 1982 to the high of 1987, market averages roughly tripled. Common stocks outperformed bonds in the 1980s and in the long period since 1900.

11. A firm's balance sheet is a snapshot, at a given point of time, of its assets (what it owns) and its liabilities (what it owes). The amount by which assets exceed liabilities is the net worth of the firm: it is the owners' equity in the firm.

12. A firm's income statement details its receipts, expenses, and profits for a given period of time such as a quarter of a year.

KEY TERMS

(sole) proprietorship	dividend
partnership	capital gains
corporation	preferred stock
limited liability	corporate bond
double taxation	present value
common stock	balance sheet
tender offer	assets
hostile takeover	liabilities
economies of scale	net worth
greenmail	income statement
poison pill	depreciation
common stock	

STUDY QUESTIONS AND PROBLEMS

1. Assume that after you graduate from college you go into business and establish a prosperous computer software firm. After five years of growth you begin to consider the possibility of incorporating the firm. What considerations will influence your decision?

2. What are the advantages of a partnership over an individual proprietorship? What are the disadvantages?

3. What is the basis for the view that conflicting goals of corporate stockholders and management cause problems for stockholders as well as for society at large? What sort of mechanisms exist to inhibit these conflicting goals?

4. What is your position on the merits of the corporate takeover movement of the past decade? Defend your position analytically.
5. Assume you inherit $100,000 and are considering the purchase of common stocks, preferred stocks, and corporation bonds. How would you allocate the $100,000 among these three forms of investment? Defend the answer in the context of your personal investment objectives.
6. Why do you suppose that common stocks outperformed corporate bonds in the 1980s? In the period since 1900? In what kind of an environment would you expect bonds to outperform stocks?
7. Write down an expression (formula) that allows you to calculate the present value or price of the following:
   a. a bond that pays $80 per year (per $1000 denomination) each year until maturity (four years from now), if going interest rates are currently 9 percent.
   b. a zero coupon bond that makes a single payment of $1,000 in 1999, if interest rates are currently 11 percent.
   c. a promise to receive $100 in one year, if interest rates are currently 10 percent.
8. Look in *The Wall Street Journal,* Standard and Poor's *The Outlook* (or other financial publication) and examine the overall behavior of stock market prices during the past year. In terms of the present value formula presented in this chapter, explain the cause of this fluctuation in stock prices.
9. Using rough estimates or even guesses, prepare a balance sheet of your *family.* Based on your family's assets and liabilities, what is the size of the family's net worth? How has this net worth changed in the past year?

ANSWER TO YOUR TURN

(a) Stock prices of oil companies are likely to rise. Higher oil prices will sharply expand the revenues of oil companies in the future. This upward revision of future Rs (in the minds of investors) is immediately reflected in the higher stock prices of oil companies—as soon as OPEC makes its announcement. (b) In spite of higher stock prices for oil companies, the overall stock market is likely to drop for at least two reasons. First, the increase in oil prices will increase production costs for millions of firms. Energy prices, fertilizer prices, and other prices will increase, putting pressure on profits of nonoil-producing firms. Second, the inflationary effect of the oil price increase is likely to lead to restrictive policies implemented by the government in an attempt to limit inflation. Both these factors will lead market participants to revise downward the future returns expected from stocks (i.e., the Rs of Equation 6-1). The stock market is likely to plunge the moment the announcement is made by OPEC.

SELECTED REFERENCES

Demsetz, Harold, Mark Hirschey, and Michael Jensen, "The Market for Corporate Control," *American Economic Review*, May 1986, pp. 313–329. These three articles analyze the economic aspects of the corporate takeover movement.

Rohatyn, Felix G., "Takeover Mania," *Challenge*, May/June 1986, pp. 30–34. This article presents the case against a government laissez-faire policy toward corporate takeovers.

Symposium on Takeovers, *The Journal of Economic Perspectives*, Winter 1988, pp. 3–82. A series of excellent articles on the corporate takeover movement by leading experts in the field.

CHAPTER 7

GOVERNMENT IN THE ECONOMY— SPENDING AND TAXATION

Read my lips—no new taxes.[1]

We live in a mixed economy. The private markets and the government share in answering such fundamental questions as what *will be produced and* for whom *it will be produced. One cannot assess the role of government by means of a simple number. However, a crude indicator of the scope of government activity is that approximately 80 percent of U.S. goods and services is provided by private markets, whereas 20 percent is provided collectively by federal, state, and local governments.*

---

[1] Vice President George Bush, 1988 presidential campaign.

RATIONALE FOR GOVERNMENTAL PARTICIPATION IN THE ECONOMY

There are several reasons why societies deem it appropriate for governments to intervene in the economy. First, people benefit when markets are highly competitive. Governments seek to promote competition by enacting and enforcing antitrust laws, by prohibiting discrimination, and by other measures. Where competition is inherently impractical for technical reasons, governments impose regulations on producers in order to protect the public. Examples include regulations placed on utilities and local telephone services. Second, governments implement stabilization policies in an attempt to avoid the extremes of rampant inflation and economic depression. These stabilization policies, known as fiscal policy and monetary policy, are analyzed in detail in Parts II and III of this text. Third, governments deliberately intervene to modify the distribution of national income and wealth. This intervention is intended to moderate the extremes of poverty and affluence in society. Other important reasons for governmental economic activity include correcting for misallocation of the nation's resources resulting from external (or spillover) effects and stepping in to provide public goods.

Correcting for Misallocation of Resources Due to Externalities (or Spillover Effects)

The production of private goods and services often leads to *externalities,* or *spillover effects,* in which the costs incurred by producers or the benefits received by consumers differ significantly from the total costs of producing or total benefits of consuming when the whole of society is considered. External effects arise when the actions of producers and consumers affect *third parties*—people other than producers and consumers involved in the transactions. Spillover or external effects may be either positive or negative—they may be beneficial or detrimental.

Negative Externalities
Uncompensated costs imposed on third parties as a result of consumption or production by other individuals or firms.

Negative Externalities **Negative externalities** occur when producers or consumers impose costs on third parties not involved in the production or consumption of a good. For example, a firm burning coal to produce electricity may effectively ignore spillover costs (acid rain, air pollution, greenhouse effects) in a free, unfettered market. In this case, the cost of producing electricity from society's viewpoint exceeds the costs shouldered by the producer. When negative externalities exist, *market failure* occurs in the sense that signals are given to produce a socially excessive output of goods whose production yields such external effects.

Recall from Chapter 4 that the costs of producing a good influence the position of the supply curve for the good. An increase in the cost of producing a good—higher material prices, higher wages—shifts the supply curve to the left. When external costs are ignored, supply curves of goods whose production results in negative externalities lie farther to the right than when firms pay the *full* cost of production. Therefore market price is lower, and the quantity produced and exchanged is larger than is socially desirable. This principle is illustrated in Figure 7-1.

In the absence of government intervention, the supply curve of the product (electricity, steel, plutonium) whose production yields negative external effects is S_1. Given the demand curve (D), the market price is P_1 and the quantity produced and exchanged is Q_1. If a government forces a firm to pay the full costs by imposing a per-unit tax on a product equal to the per-unit spillover costs to society, the supply curve shifts leftward to S_2. This drives up the price to P_2 and reduces the quantity exchanged to Q_2. Because the cost of production in this scenario reflects spillover costs as well as private costs of production, the reduced output (Q_2) is optimal from

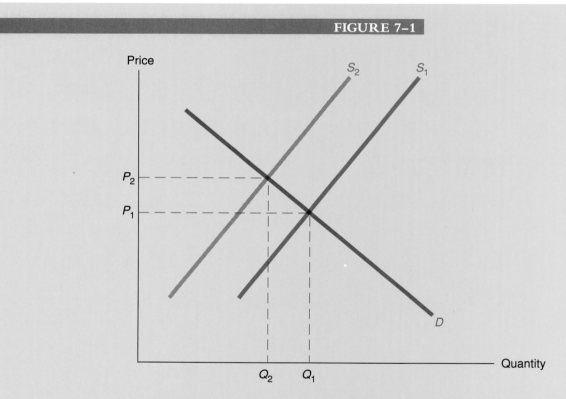

FIGURE 7–1

NEGATIVE EXTERNAL EFFECTS AND THE CASE FOR GOVERNMENT INTERVENTION

When polluting firms are allowed to ignore the negative externalities they impose on society, the supply curve of the product (S_1) reflects only the private costs of producing. Given the demand curve for the product (D), the market price is P_1 and the quantity exchanged is Q_1. If the firms were fully charged for these spillover costs, the supply curve would shift leftward to S_2, reflecting the true cost of production from society's viewpoint. As a result of the higher cost of production, market price would rise to P_2 and quantity of output produced and exchanged would fall to Q_2. This represents the optimum output from society's viewpoint.

society's viewpoint. The moral: free markets fail by giving us too many goods whose production involves negative externalities and therefore too few of everything else.[2]

There are several ways that governments can deal with the problem of negative externalities. As suggested, governments can impose a tax on production in order to drive up the price and reduce output. Also, governments can require firms to install pollution abatement equipment, regulate their output or shut them down, subsidize them to reduce pollution, or sell pollution rights. As to selling rights, polluting firms would be required to purchase the right to pollute, and the proceeds could, in principle, be used to reimburse those harmed by the pollution. (See Chapter 34 for further discussion.)

Positive Externalities
Benefits received but not paid for by third parties as a result of production or consumption by others.

Positive Externalities   **Positive externalities** occur when positive third-party effects occur—when production and consumption of a good confer benefits on society in excess of the benefits reaped by the aggregate of its consumers. Examples include medical research, other research on the cutting edge of technology, and education.

A substantially positive externality accompanied development of the polio vaccine when the millions who were not vaccinated were spared the disease. Similarly, development of an effective AIDS vaccination would benefit society far in excess of the benefits enjoyed by those who were vaccinated. Millions of persons (including those yet to be born) who would not be vaccinated but who otherwise would contract AIDS would be spared because of the effect of the vaccine in slowing the spread of the disease. In addition, all current and future medical insurance premiums would be lower if a successful vaccine were developed. Thus, the share of the nation's resources devoted to health care costs would be reduced.

In the case of education, positive external effects occur because an informed citizenry results in reduced crime rates and other social problems, and yields other benefits that exceed the purely economic benefits enjoyed by those who obtain the education.

In cases where positive external effects prevail, free markets allocate suboptimal amounts of resources. Because demand curves for such products ignore positive external effects, they are not far enough to the right when viewed from society's perspective. Therefore, unfettered markets would result in a lower quantity of such goods produced and exchanged than is socially desirable. Consequently, governments might justifiably intervene through subsidies for medical and scientific research, provision of public schools, and other mechanisms for stimulating output of goods with positive external effects.

Providing Public Goods

Public Good
A good or service that cannot be provided for one person without being made available to others, and once provided for one person can be provided for others at no additional cost.

A second example of market failure that necessitates government intervention in the economy involves a unique product known as a public good. A **public good** has two special characteristics. First, it cannot be withheld from those who do not pay for it (it lacks the *excludability* characteristic possessed by a private good). Second, once

---

[2]A less obvious application of market failure resulting from negative externalities is that of oil-tanker spills. Although such *spills* are described as "accidents," their frequency may be attributed to the fact that only a portion of the costs involved are borne by those responsible for the spills. Hence, from society's viewpoint, inadequate precautions are taken. If the oil companies were charged the full cost of such spills, their occurrence would be extremely rare. (Oil companies would ensure that tanker captains are not intoxicated while on duty.)

produced, the cost of providing the good or service to an extra user is negligible or zero. Examples of a public good include national defense, lighthouses, the national weather bureau. Because of its unique characteristics, a public good is provided collectively to society rather than privately to individuals.

Consider national defense. A defense system benefits me whether I help pay for it or not. It is inherently impossible to deny me the benefits of the system once it is in place. In contrast, if I refuse to pay for a Big Mac or a haircut (private goods), I am effectively barred from obtaining the good or service. Further in contrast to the hamburger or haircut, it costs nothing to provide the services of national defense, lighthouses, and the weather bureau to an extra user.

Public goods must be provided collectively via governments or they are unlikely to be available—or will be available in inadequate quantity. Assume a large river valley has been plagued by periodic flooding and a private contractor is considering building a dam at a cost of $100 million. The contractor attempts to sell *subscriptions* to each of the several thousand inhabitants of the valley. Because each inhabitant knows that he or she will benefit from the dam irrespective of whether a subscription is purchased, there is an incentive to hold back and depend on the generosity of neighbors. This *free-rider* problem makes it unlikely that the project will ever get off the ground. Thus a government steps in, builds the dam, and uses its taxing authority to pay for the project.

YOUR TURN	In order to hold down growth of the national debt, assume the government decides to market the SDI system ("Star Wars") privately by using a private firm to sell subscriptions to the American people. Estimated cost of the project over the next decade is $900 billion (approximately $3600 per American, or $12,000 per household). Analyze the viability of the proposal.

Note that many goods and services provided by governments do not strictly meet the criteria for public goods. For example, education is not a public good in the sense we have defined the concept; in principle, it can be withheld from nonpayers. Also, the cost of educating an additional person is certainly not zero. A system of private education coexists with our public system. The public education concept is usually defended on the basis of positive external effects and other grounds—not because it is a public good in the technical sense. Police protection comes very close to being a pure public good. It is extremely difficult to exclude me from the benefits of police protection (lower crime rates) if I refuse to help pay for it. In addition, the cost of protecting an additional individual is small. And what about snow removal from public streets provided by local governments?

Many goods and services provided by governments are **quasi-public goods,** having some (but not all) of the characteristics of pure public goods as we have defined them. Consider public libraries, tennis courts, golf courses, swimming pools, and roads.

THE GROWTH, SIZE, AND ALLOCATION OF GOVERNMENT SPENDING

Growth in Government

Although we live in a predominantly capitalistic economy in which the bulk of our needs are satisfied by private enterprise, government has grown enormously in size and scope during the past 100 years. This growth has occurred in virtually all industrial nations. At the beginning of the twentieth century in the United States, combined government expenditures (federal, state, and local) amounted to roughly eight percent of our gross national product. No federal income tax existed before 1913. Revenues from taxes on tobacco and liquor, and tariffs on imports sufficed to balance the federal budget. By 1990, combined government expenditures amounted to approximately 35 percent of our GNP. How can we explain this enormous expansion of government? Several factors have contributed.

The Urbanization Movement Demand for goods and services (schools, roads, parks, and so forth) provided by governments has grown faster than the nation's collective income. The movement from a predominantly rural society in which people are relatively self-sufficient to an urban society in which people are highly specialized and interdependent has myriad crucial implications. For example, such a transformation greatly impacts the need for public facilities: streets, transportation, police and fire protection, sanitation.

> A farmer in the last century may have drawn his water from his well, fed his garbage to his pigs, and protected his family with his rifle. His grandson in the city would be ill-advised to try to provide these services for himself.[3]

War and Defense Prior to World War II, we did not maintain a huge and expensive military operation in times of peace. We did not maintain military bases and armed forces throughout the world. Nor did we maintain a great and permanent arsenal of enormously expensive weapons. The escalation of the Cold War (1945–1950) increased the share of government expenditures on defense, though this share has declined somewhat since the 1960s. Yet today more than one-fourth of the federal budget (six percent of the nation's total income) is spent on national defense.

Egalitarianism and the Welfare State Government has increasingly provided for those adversely affected by the force of economic events as well as for those unable to provide for themselves due to infirmities. In earlier times, each family cared for its aged, infirm, and handicapped. Those without families lived on small pittances in a state of squalor. As life expectancy lengthened, family ties weakened, and average living standards increased, public support programs proliferated—including, but not limited to, welfare payments, disability income, unemployment benefits, social security, and agricultural subsidies. Increasingly, the masses of middle-class Americans have voted themselves more generous medical, retirement, and income support programs. Expanded spending on such **welfare-state** programs is the primary source of increase in the share of GNP spent by government in the past 30 years.

Government Purchases
Federal, state, and local government spending on final goods and services, including costs of hiring government employees but excluding government transfer payments.

Government Expenditures—Purchases and Transfers

Government expenditures consist of two principal categories: *government purchases of goods and services* and *government transfer payments.* Government purchases involve the costs of such finished goods as computers, tanks, and desks as well as the costs of such government employees as supreme court justices, highway patrol officers, high-school teachers, postal workers, and ground keepers. These **government purchases** are *exhaustive* in that they consume or preempt economic resources—such

---

[3]Otto Eckstein, *Public Finance,* (Englewood Cliffs, NJ: Prentice-Hall, 1964) p. 4.

resources are thus diverted from private use for use in providing public goods and services.

Government Transfer Payments

Government payments to individuals, but not in return for goods and services currently supplied.

Government transfer payments involve government payments to individuals or firms for which no concurrent good or service is provided to the government in exchange. Examples include social security costs, welfare payments, unemployment compensation, veterans benefits, and interest paid on federal debt. Government transfer payments differ from government purchases in that transfers are *nonexhaustive*. Transfers do not consume economic resources or reallocate them away from private use. The system of taxes and transfer payments merely transfers income—and claims to real resources—within the private sector of the economy.

Figure 7-2 indicates the pattern of total federal, state, and local government expenditures—government purchases and transfer payments—relative to GNP since 1955.

Note that although the ratio of total government spending to GNP has risen, this is accounted for almost entirely by the growth of transfer payments. Government purchases have continued to absorb approximately 20 percent of GNP since 1960.[4] Transfer payments have risen from roughly 6 percent to 15 percent of GNP in the same period.

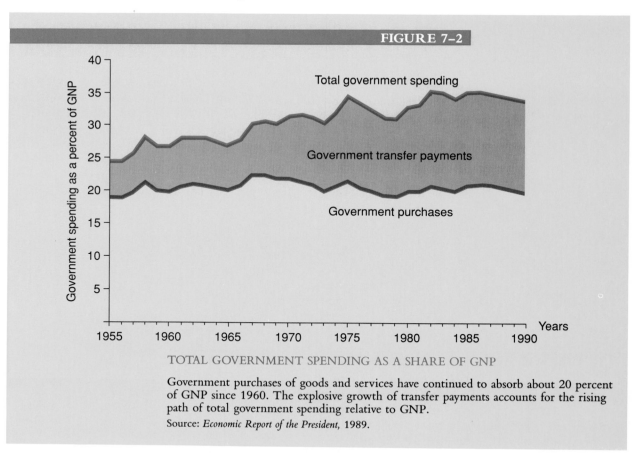

FIGURE 7–2

TOTAL GOVERNMENT SPENDING AS A SHARE OF GNP

Government purchases of goods and services have continued to absorb about 20 percent of GNP since 1960. The explosive growth of transfer payments accounts for the rising path of total government spending relative to GNP.

Source: *Economic Report of the President*, 1989.

[4]The ratio of government purchases/GNP increased sharply from 1900–1960. This increase was due chiefly to greater urbanization and resulting growth in demand for public goods, and the emergence of the American defense establishment following World War II.

Measuring the Relative Size of Government

Which is the better measure of the size of government, total spending (including transfer payments) or government purchases only? The answer depends on one's reason for asking the question. If one is trying to measure the portion of GNP absorbed or consumed by government, one looks at government purchases, which indicate the amount of economic resources removed from the private sector in order to satisfy the desire for goods provided by government. In this case government transfers are omitted because such funds are collected from the private sector and are paid back to the private sector, thus remaining available to satisfy private wants.

Nevertheless, total government spending (purchases plus transfers) is in some ways the superior measure of the magnitude of government. It is true that transfer payments do not consume real resources. However, the government determines to whom these resources are available via its system of taxes and transfers. Total expenditures (including transfers) indicate the share of the economy for which government decision making replaces private-market decision making. Assuming the norm of balanced budgets in the long run, total expenditures also indicate the fraction of the nation's GNP that must be paid in taxes to operate the government. By these standards, government has continued to expand steadily relative to GNP.

Although government spending in the United States has grown relative to GNP, in many nations government spending is considerably larger than in the United States. Figure 7-3 indicates the ratio of government expenditures to GNP in a sample of nations. A clear pattern exists for countries that are highly developed economically: they exhibit relatively large government sectors.

Government Spending—Where Does It Go?

Figure 7-4 (page 144) illustrates the allocation of federal expenditures and combined state- and local-government expenditures among alternative uses.

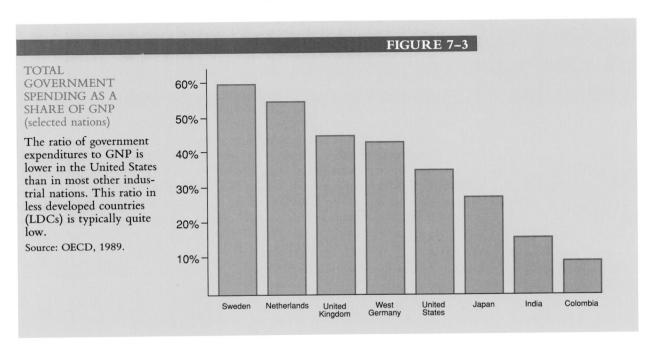

FIGURE 7–3

TOTAL GOVERNMENT SPENDING AS A SHARE OF GNP (selected nations)

The ratio of government expenditures to GNP is lower in the United States than in most other industrial nations. This ratio in less developed countries (LDCs) is typically quite low.

Source: OECD, 1989.

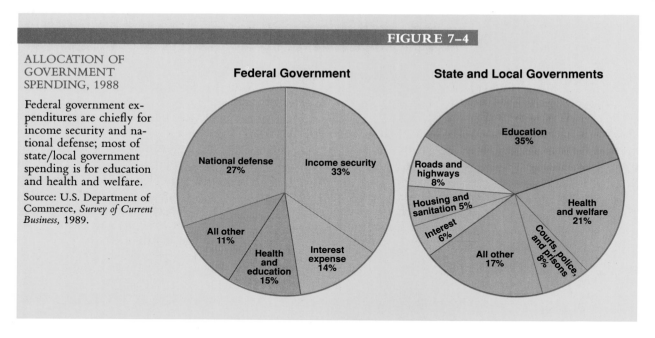

FIGURE 7–4

ALLOCATION OF
GOVERNMENT
SPENDING, 1988

Federal government expenditures are chiefly for income security and national defense; most of state/local government spending is for education and health and welfare.

Source: U.S. Department of Commerce, *Survey of Current Business*, 1989.

The largest components of federal expenditures are economic security (social security, farm subsidies), national defense, and health and education programs. However, interest expense (debt service) has been the fastest-growing expenditure during the past decade. This growth is attributable to the string of huge federal budget deficits that has tripled our national debt since 1980. A larger stock of debt (given the level of interest rates) necessitates larger annual interest expense for the debtor (the federal government).

The largest single expenditure for state and local governments is education. Other uses of state/local funds, in order of magnitude, include health and welfare, roads and highways, and courts, police, and prisons.

PAYING FOR GOVERNMENT EXPENDITURES—TAXATION

In principle, governments have access to three potential sources of funds to pay for their expenditures: printing money, borrowing from private individuals and firms, and levying taxes. Because only the federal government has the authority to print money, the first source is not open to state and local governments. Furthermore, national governments that have resorted to printing money to finance major expenditures have unleashed enormous inflationary forces.[5] Hence, the first source is not really a viable or responsible means for financing government. The second source—borrowing—is prohibited by statute for most state and local governments, except in the case of financing such capital expenditures as schools and roads. The heavy resort to borrowing by the federal government has serious adverse consequences, which are analyzed in Chapter 20.

---

[5]Severe inflation, known as hyperinflation, was experienced by several European nations in the early 1920s and again in the late 1940s as a result of printing money to finance war. In 1923, several trillion German marks were required to purchase what one mark purchased in 1913. On this, see Exhibit 13-1.

That leaves taxation as the most viable source of revenues for all levels of government. In the balance of this chapter, we analyze the various aspects of taxation, including each major type of taxes utilized to finance federal, state, and local government in the United States. We also analyze the most significant piece of federal income-tax legislation enacted in recent decades: The Tax Reform Act of 1986.

The Function of Taxes

One might view the purpose of taxes in two ways. The obvious function is to provide revenues with which to pay for goods and services provided by government. An alternative and more sophisticated way of viewing taxes is to regard them as a vehicle for releasing such real resources as steel, lumber, and workers from the production of private goods so they may be used to produce such government goods and services as schools, highways, missiles, and postal services. Taxes serve this function by depressing demand for (and therefore output of) private goods and services. For example, income taxes depress private consumption expenditures and output. Sales taxes perform a similar role. Property taxes motivate the building of less elaborate houses; they also reduce spendable income, thereby restraining consumption.

Natural instincts lead one to think in terms of the first (obvious) function of taxes as accommodating the release of economic resources from private goods and services for use in the provision of goods and services by the government.

Direct and Indirect Taxes

Taxes are sometimes classified on the basis of whether they are levied directly upon individuals and their financial resources or levied indirectly upon them through their expenditure. A **direct tax** is levied directly upon individuals. Examples include personal and corporate income taxes (the corporate entity being composed of individuals), payroll taxes, and inheritance and gift taxes. **Indirect taxes** are not levied directly on individuals but are incurred indirectly when individuals engage in certain activities, such as purchasing various types of goods and services. Examples of indirect taxes include sales taxes, excise taxes, and property taxes. The federal government relies predominantly upon direct taxes for its revenues; state and local governments rely more heavily on indirect taxes.

Progressive, Proportional, and Regressive Taxes

Various types of taxes may be classified by how total tax liability varies with level of income.

Progressive Tax
The fraction of income paid in tax rises as income rises.

Proportional Tax
The fraction of income paid in tax remains constant at all income levels.

1. A **progressive tax** is one in which the percentage of income paid in taxes rises with the level of income. A person who earns twice as much income pays more than twice as much tax. A familiar example is the federal income tax (as well as state income taxes), with its pattern of percentage tax brackets rising with income.

2. A **proportional tax** is one in which the percentage of income paid in taxes is the same for all income levels. A person who earns twice as much income pays exactly twice as much tax. Although examples are not easy to find, certain taxes come

close to being proportional within fairly broad ranges of income (though not for *all* ranges of income).

3. A **regressive tax** is one in which the percentage of income paid in taxes declines as income rises. Those with high incomes yield a smaller fraction of their income to the government than those with lower incomes. A classic example is the *poll tax,* in which each individual is charged a flat fee (perhaps $2), in order to vote. This tax was outlawed in 1973 by the 24th Amendment to the U.S. Constitution.

The concepts of progressive, proportional, and regressive taxes are illustrated schematically in Figure 7-5.

Shifting and Incidence of Taxes

As you think of various types of taxes, ask yourself whether each type appears to be progressive, proportional, or regressive. In certain cases the answer is more complex than meets the eye; this is because the tax is not always borne by the entity that actually remits the tax to the government. The **incidence** of a tax refers to the resting place of the tax—the entity that actually absorbs or bears the burden of the tax. In many cases taxes are *shifted* to second parties through higher prices, increased rents, lower wages, and the like. For example, apartment owners may shift all or part of an increase in property taxes to tenants by raising rents. Excise taxes levied on the sale of cigarettes may be partially shifted to consumers through higher prices. Although economists agree that the burden of the corporation income tax is shared by the public (via higher prices), by the owners of the corporation (via lower after-tax profits), and by the employees of the corporation (via lower wages and fringe benefits), they disagree on how this burden is allocated among the three.

Regressive Tax
The fraction of income paid in tax declines as income rises.

Tax Incidence
The distribution of the tax burden—that is, who ultimately pays the tax.

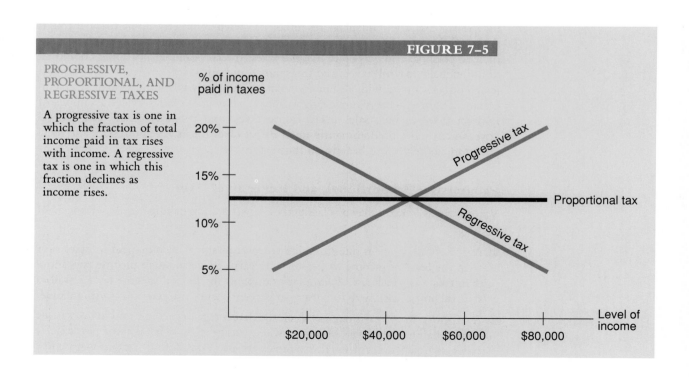

FIGURE 7–5

PROGRESSIVE, PROPORTIONAL, AND REGRESSIVE TAXES

A progressive tax is one in which the fraction of total income paid in tax rises with income. A regressive tax is one in which this fraction declines as income rises.

Concepts of Equity or Fairness

Issues of equity fall into the domain of *normative economics*. Reasonable individuals often differ in their interpretation of what is equitable or fair. Nevertheless, in the area of taxation there are two generally accepted norms of equity. It is widely agreed that our system of taxation should conform to the norms of horizontal and vertical equity. **Horizontal equity** means that those with equal ability to pay taxes should be treated equally (i.e., they should pay the same amount of taxes). **Vertical equity** refers to the principle that those of unequal ability should be treated unequally. Specifically, those with greater ability to pay should pay a larger absolute (and perhaps relative) amount of taxes.

When society perceives that widespread violations of the principles of horizontal and vertical equity exist in the tax code, taxpayer morale and compliance is likely to deteriorate. Certain federal tax reforms in recent years were implemented to remedy perceived gross violations of these principles.

THE FEDERAL TAX SYSTEM

The sources of funds utilized to finance the federal government are illustrated in Figure 7-6.

Unlike earlier decades, the 1980s became the era of huge federal budget deficits, when roughly one-sixth of the funds expended by the federal government were obtained through borrowing. Of the remaining funds expended, roughly 90 percent were obtained through three taxes—the individual income tax, the payroll tax, and the corporation income tax.

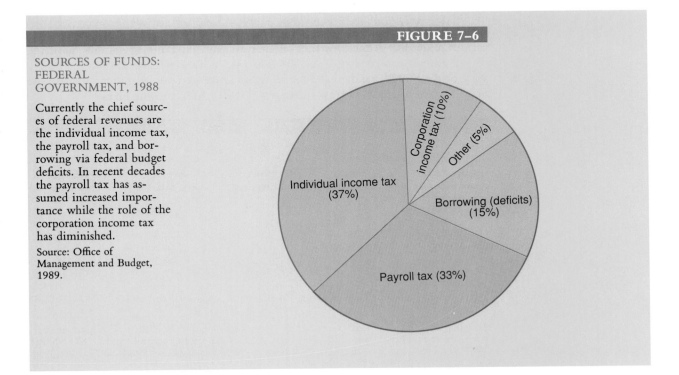

FIGURE 7–6

SOURCES OF FUNDS: FEDERAL GOVERNMENT, 1988

Currently the chief sources of federal revenues are the individual income tax, the payroll tax, and borrowing via federal budget deficits. In recent decades the payroll tax has assumed increased importance while the role of the corporation income tax has diminished.

Source: Office of Management and Budget, 1989.

Corporation income tax (10%)

Other (5%)

Individual income tax (37%)

Borrowing (deficits) (15%)

Payroll tax (33%)

Individual Income Tax

The federal individual income tax is familiar to everyone; it is the chief source of revenue for the U.S. Treasury. Given the perspective of U.S. history, however, it is a fairly recent source of revenue. The federal income tax was established in 1913 by the 16th Amendment to the U.S. Constitution, but was a minor source of federal revenue until the 1940s. Income tax rates were raised to extremely high levels during World War II, the top rate set at 91 percent. Tax rates have been lowered several times since then, including two major cuts in the 1980s. Today the top rate is 28 percent.

Each year April 15 is a day of reckoning, as more than 100 million taxpaying units are required to file a tax return and to settle up with the Internal Revenue Service. However, April 15 is fairly painless for most taxpayers because most have paid the bulk of their income taxes through regular *withholding* from paychecks during the calendar year. Employers are required to withhold funds from paychecks and to forward the proceeds, together with payroll tax receipts, to the IRS. Millions of taxpayers deliberately arrange to have their employer *overwithhold,* thus assuring a rebate from the IRS after the annual tax return is filed.

To illustrate the nature of the individual income tax, consider Table 7-1, which applies to a married couple with two children filing a joint income tax return in 1989.

In figuring tax liability, individuals and couples first calculate adjusted gross income. This is computed by adding total wage or salary income, dividends and interest earned, and other forms of income and subtracting certain allowable *adjustments* including alimony paid, moving expenses, and contributions to retirement plans. Taxable income is then calculated by subtracting exemptions and deductions from adjusted gross income. The allowance for *personal exemptions* was $2000 per person in 1989. Thus a family of four would have had $8000 in exemptions. In specifying total *deductions,* taxpayers have the option of *itemizing* various allowable deductions such as interest paid on a mortgage and charitable contributions, or accepting a *standard deduction.* In Table 7-1 we assume the family opts for the $5000 standard deduction. Because of exemptions and deductions, the first $13,000 of adjusted gross income is shielded from income taxes.[6]

TABLE 7-1				
FEDERAL INCOME TAX FOR FAMILY OF FOUR, 1989*				
Adjusted gross income	Taxable income	Personal income tax	Average tax rate (%)	Marginal tax rate (%)
10,000	0	0	0	0
20,000	7,000	1,050	5.2	15
30,000	17,000	2,550	8.5	15
40,000	27,000	4,050	10.1	15
100,000	87,000	20,460	20.5	28
1,000,000	987,000	272,460	27.2	28

*Assumes family uses standard deduction ($5000) rather than itemizing deductions.

[6]Actually, Table 7-1 and the discussion are somewhat oversimplified and technically slightly in error, though the basic conclusions are unaffected. A surcharge of 5 percent for incomes between $71,900 and $149,250 is levied, and personal exemptions are phased out for incomes in excess of $149,250 by applying a surcharge of 5 percent until all the benefits of personal exemptions have been totally offset. These thresholds are for 1988 and are indexed to increase over time with the price level.

Average Tax Rate
The percentage of total income paid in taxes.

We observe first that the personal income tax is progressive. This is indicated by the fact that the **average tax rate**—the fraction of income paid in taxes—rises with income.

$$\text{average tax rate (ATR)} = \frac{\text{tax paid}}{\text{income}}$$

According to the fourth column of Table 7-1, a family earning $20,000 pays 5.2 percent of this to the IRS, whereas a family earning $40,000 pays 10.1 percent and a family earning $100,000 pays 20.5 percent. A doubling of income more than doubles tax liability, implying that the tax is progressive.

Marginal Tax Rate
The percentage of an *additional* dollar of income paid in taxes.

The last column of Table 7-1 indicates the **marginal tax rate**—the percentage of any *increment* of income that must be paid in taxes.

$$\text{marginal tax rate (MTR)} = \frac{\text{increment in taxes paid}}{\text{increment of income}}$$

For taxable income, the personal income tax code currently has two marginal tax brackets. Roughly the first $30,000 of taxable income is subject to a marginal tax rate of 15 percent. All income above this threshold is subject to a marginal tax rate of 28 percent.[7] This tax rate structure was simplified considerably by the Tax Reform Act of 1986. Prior to that legislation there were 14 different marginal tax brackets, ranging from a low of 11 percent to a high of 50 percent.

The marginal tax rate is an important concept in economic analysis. Because it indicates the percentage of any *addition* to income that must be given up in taxes, the marginal tax rate is believed to influence incentives to work, invest, and take risks in order to earn extra income. One of the cornerstones of the Reagan Administration's policies in the 1980s was to reduce marginal tax rates in order to stimulate such incentives, thereby seeking to ignite an expansion in the nation's output and standard of living.

Progressivity of the Personal Income Tax   Two factors account for the progressive nature of the federal income tax (as illustrated in Table 7-1). The first several thousand dollars of adjusted gross income is not subject to any tax at all because of exemptions and deductions. A family of four taking the standard deduction owes no tax on the first $13,000 of income.[8] This is true whether the family earned a total of $20,000 or $100,000. Hence, a smaller percentage of a lower-income family's earnings are subject to the income tax. Moreover, the marginal tax rate is higher for upper-income families. These factors explain the progressive nature of the tax and the fact that the average tax rate converges toward, but never reaches, the marginal rate as income rises.

In reality the individual income tax is not as progressive as Table 7-1 suggests. Although the table assumes taxpayers choose the $5000 standard deduction, most higher-income individuals itemize deductions (many of which are called "loopholes" by critics), taking advantage of a myriad of features that open a large gap between total income earned and taxable income.

---

[7]This threshold ($30,000) income level, after which one jumps from a 15-percent to a 28-percent marginal tax rate, is indexed to the consumer price index. Hence, if by 1995 the CPI has risen by 20 percent (relative to 1989), the threshold will be $36,000. Also, the allowance for the personal exemption ($2000 in 1989) is indexed to rise with the CPI. Similarly the standard deduction will increase in line with the CPI.

[8]Each member receives a $2000 exemption and the standard deduction is $5000 for the family. Hence, exemptions and deductions total $13,000 in 1989 (more in later years).

In addition, the degree of progressivity of the income tax has been significantly reduced in recent decades. A series of tax reductions since the 1950s has reduced rates for all income levels, but especially for the upper brackets.[9] Upper-income bracket individuals increasingly have arranged their financial affairs so as to avoid taxes legally by utilizing more of the generous array of deductions and credits.

As a result of the decline in progressivity of the individual income tax and the sharply expanded role of the payroll tax, the overall American tax system today (including all types of taxes) is roughly proportional or perhaps slightly progressive. A 1985 study, which employed relatively progressive assumptions about the incidence of various taxes, indicated that the richest 10 percent of Americans yielded 25.3 percent of their income in taxes, whereas the poorest 10 percent paid 21.9 percent.[10] The corresponding ratios for 1966 were estimated at 30.1 percent and 16.8 percent, respectively.

Tax Loopholes   What are these **loopholes** that reduce the progressivity of the income tax and also produce numerous violations of the principles of horizontal and vertical equity? Although the Tax Reform Act of 1986 reduced the length of the list somewhat, many loopholes remain firmly entrenched in the law.

1. *Nontaxability of Interest on Municipal Bonds*   Income received in the form of interest on bonds issued by municipalities and other political subdivisions (for example, water districts) is not taxable by the federal government. By the same token, state governments do not tax interest earned on U.S. government securities. If an individual invests $1 million in municipal bonds yielding 7 percent, the $70,000 annual stream of interest income is not subject to federal income taxation. This special treatment is defended on the basis of encouraging local communities to issue bonds to finance schools, roads, sewers, and the like. The tax-free nature of the bonds makes it possible for communities to borrow at lower interest rates, and thus enjoy lower local taxes. Critics charge that this subsidy creates inequities and is inefficient, costing the government much more in lost revenues than is saved by cities. The difference is a windfall tax break for affluent Americans.

2. *Preferential Treatment of Homeowners*   Homeowners have access to two major deductions not available to renters: property taxes and interest on home mortgages. Consider two families with identical incomes and circumstances, except that one rents and the other owns. The renter pays considerably more income taxes, a violation of the principle of horizontal equity. Also, because homeowners have higher incomes on average than renters, this circumstance reduces the progressivity of the income tax.

3. *Other Loopholes*   Many fringe benefits are not taxable by the IRS. Suppose California pays its new English professors $25,000 per year and throws in $5000 worth of insurance premiums covering medical, dental, and life insurance. Suppose Colorado pays its new English professors $30,000 but provides no such

---

[9]The top bracket, for example, dropped from 91 percent in the early 1950s to 28 percent today. Middle- and lower-income bracket rates have not dropped as much, absolutely or relatively.

[10]See Joseph Pechman, *Who Paid the Taxes, 1966–85?* (Washington, DC: The Brookings Institution, 1985). Results such as these depend upon certain assumptions regarding tax incidence and are therefore somewhat controversial. When Pechman uses less-progressive assumptions about tax incidence, the overall tax system actually appears slightly regressive.

fringe benefits. Although the two teachers are compensated equally, the Colorado teacher pays tax on $5000 of additional income. Some argue that fringe benefits are a form of income and should be treated as such.

Another loophole deals with tax treatment of funds contributed to certain retirement programs. Many professionals and self-employed individuals establish retirement accounts and contribute large chunks of current income to the accounts each year. Income contributed to such accounts is not subject to taxation until it is withdrawn at retirement. Meanwhile, income otherwise taxable is compounding over the years in the retirement account of the contributor. Typically, upper-bracket individuals avail themselves of these attractive retirement programs; lower-bracket taxpayers find it difficult to do so.[11] This circumstance diminishes the progressivity of the individual income tax.

One could go on at length detailing the inequities and loopholes in the income tax. Yet in spite of loopholes, the general perception seems to prevail that the income tax is the *best* or *fairest* form of tax. Perhaps for this reason the personal income tax is becoming an increasingly important source of state tax revenue. Only six states currently have no income tax: Florida, Nevada, South Dakota, Texas, Washington, and Wyoming.

Payroll Tax

In 1935, in the depths of the Great Depression, Congress enacted the Social Security Act—thus creating a compulsory social insurance system for workers and self-employed persons. Employees are entitled to receive retirement benefits (up to a ceiling level) based on previous earnings and independent of need. The payroll tax may be viewed as the compulsory premium paid to cover this *old-age* insurance, as well as disability insurance and Medicare benefits.

In 1989, each individual *contributed* 7.51 percent of the first $48,000 of wage and salary income to cover these benefits, and the employer matched this payment. The base ($48,000 in 1989) is indexed to rise with the price level over time and the tax rate will rise to 7.65 percent in 1990. The payroll tax is easily the most rapidly growing source of federal government revenue: the share of federal revenues provided by the payroll tax has doubled since 1960. The maximum annual contribution (employee plus employer) has increased from $348 in 1965 to more than $7000 today, and continues to increase each year. Today the payroll tax generates almost as much revenue as the individual income tax.

The payroll tax is regressive. This is partly due to the fact that only the first $48,000 (in 1989) of wage, salary, and self-employment income is subject to the tax. An individual earning $90,000 pays the same amount of payroll tax as an individual earning $48,000. In addition, such other forms of income as dividends, rental income, interest, and capital gains are not subject to the tax. Because higher-income individuals receive a larger portion of their income from these non-wage sources than do lower-income individuals, they give up a smaller fraction of total income to the government via the payroll tax.

---

[11]The Economic Recovery Tax Act of 1981 (ERTA) authorized establishment of individual retirement accounts (IRAs) for virtually all workers. Contributions are deductible from federal income taxes, but the maximum annual contribution is rather low relative to some of the programs utilized by upper-bracket taxpayers. The Tax Reform Act of 1986 restricted deductibility of IRA contributions to those earning less than $50,000 annually. This Act also reduced the maximum deductible contributions allowable for other retirement programs.

EXHIBIT 7–1

THE SOCIAL SECURITY SYSTEM—WILL YOU EVER RECEIVE BENEFITS?

In 1983, the social security system was essentially transformed from a pay-as-you-go system to one that is funded. Prior to 1983, the contributions for social insurance were directly transferred from workers to retirees. The monthly social security check your grandparents received came *not* from funds they paid in earlier but from the payroll taxes your parents were paying each month. The trust fund picked up any annual surplus of payroll taxes in excess of benefits paid out, and it made good on any deficit. But the size of the social security trust fund was relatively small, amounting typically to less than one year's outlays.

This system worked fine as long as we had stable population, wage, and salary growth without major demographic changes. Given these favorable conditions, an expanding volume of payroll tax receipts can adequately fund an expanding pool of retirees. However, departure from these conditions may impair the actuarial soundness of the system and precipitate a crisis of confidence in its long-term viability. The soundness of the social security system was called into question in the late 1970s because of a slowdown in population growth, important emerging changes in the age structure of the population, and a slowdown of real wage and salary growth.

For many years the average expected life of Americans has been rising. In addition, the U.S. birth rate increased sharply during the baby-boom years of 1946–1964. Given the typical retirement age of roughly 65 years, these factors assure a surge of retirees coming on stream after 2010. Moreover, the percentage of the population above age 65 is expected to double between 1990 and 2030. Because the birth rate declined significantly after 1964, the number of young workers entering the labor force began declining in the early 1980s. In earlier years there were approximately five current workers paying into the system for each retiree drawing benefits. That ratio is now slightly above 3:1, and is projected to decline to 2:1 by the year 2030.

Viewed from the perspective of the late 1970s,

Corporate Income Tax

A generation ago the corporation income tax was second only to the individual income tax as a source of revenue for the federal government, accounting for about one-fourth of federal revenues. Because of liberalized depreciation allowances, expanded deductions, and tax credits—and especially because of the rapidly increasing roll of payroll taxes—its relative importance declined sharply between the 1950s and late 1980s. By 1986, the corporation income tax contributed less than 10 percent of federal revenues. However, the Tax Reform Act of 1986 put a stop to this declining trend by eliminating certain deductions and tax credits and slowing depreciation allowances. On balance, the Tax Reform Act shifted roughly $120 billion in taxes from individuals to corporations over a five-year period ending in 1992.

The **corporation income tax** is levied on profits, not on gross corporate income. All costs—such as wages and interest expense—are deductible from gross income before arriving at taxable income (i.e., profits). The corporation income-tax code applies a progressive or graduated tax-rate scale on profits of each corporation up to $100,000 and a flat ceiling of 34 percent against all profits above $100,000.[12] The tax therefore *appears* to be progressive overall, though basically proportional for

---

[12]The existing top rate is reduced from 46 percent to 34 percent by the Tax Reform Act of 1986. However, the Act also sharply reduces deductions and credits available to corporations. The net effect of the legislation is to significantly raise the taxes corporations actually pay.

other factors also contributed to an impending social security crisis. Real wages, which had grown steadily for generations, expanded more slowly after the 1960s. Congress liberalized benefits and expanded coverage to include a larger percentage of the population. This confluence of events made it readily apparent by the late 1970s that the system was in trouble.

In 1983, President Ronald Reagan appointed a bipartisan commission headed by Alan Greenspan (now chief of the Federal Reserve System). After studying the problem, the commission recommended a series of measures designed to increase revenues and reduce benefits. Congress immediately enacted these reforms into law.

As a result of these changes and the fact that the baby boomers are moving into their years of maximum earnings, today the trust fund is increasing rapidly and government actuaries expect it to reach the enormous sum of $12 trillion ($12,000 billion) by 2020. This means the fund would expand from about 3 percent of GNP in 1990 to about 30 percent of GNP in 2020. However, the fund is then expected to decline rapidly—as the masses of baby boomers retire—and be in the red by the year 2050.

The problem social security faces in the next decade or two is keeping Congress' hands off the nest egg. The surplus in social security is mixed in with general government revenues and expenditures in calculating the reported federal budget deficit. Due to the buildup of the trust fund, the reported budget deficit will be significantly reduced or eliminated in the next decade. This circumstance will surely tempt politicians to reduce taxes or expand programs. Such action would be utterly irresponsible because all the surplus funds (and possibly more) will be needed to keep the social security system afloat in the second quarter of the next century. To protect the system, social security should be taken totally off budget as soon as possible.

large corporations earning more than $100,000. However, some economists believe that the corporation income tax is largely shifted forward onto consumers in the form of higher prices. This issue is controversial among economists, and extremely difficult to resolve. To the extent that the tax is shifted onto consumers, it may be somewhat regressive like a sales tax.

Quite a few economists oppose the corporation income tax on the ground that it represents **double taxation** of corporate profits. Taxes are first levied on corporate profits and then levied, via the individual income tax, on dividends paid to stockholders. This double taxation is alleged to impair investment spending, long-term growth of productivity, and growth of living standards. Such critics advocate abolishing the corporation income tax and collecting the revenues via the individual income tax at the time profits are paid to the owners (i.e., the shareholders).

Advocates of the corporation income tax argue that its abolition would reduce federal revenues and necessitate increases in other taxes. Further, they believe the tax is progressive. If so, its elimination would further reduce the progressivity of the overall tax system.

STATE AND LOCAL GOVERNMENT FINANCE

State and local governments rely heavily on sales and property taxes and on grants from the federal government. However, state and local government tax receipts traditionally have been insufficient to cover expenditures. A major portion of the shortfall has been covered by federal transfers or grants to state and local governments. Typically, the federal government allocates grants to the states and the states award grants to local governments. These grants may be restricted, *earmarked* for specific uses, or may be unrestricted, *block* grants. Since the late 1960s, an increasing portion of these transfers has been unrestricted. In the 1980s, the total amount of federal grants decreased significantly. Lower levels of government increasingly have been required to call upon their own financial resources.

The sources of funds for all state and local governments combined are given in Figure 7-7.

Sales Tax and Excise Tax

The **sales tax** is a key source of revenue for most states, accounting for about one-third of the aggregate revenue of the 50 state governments. States typically levy a 4–7 percent charge on the value of sales, collectable from the merchants. Some states exempt food from the sales tax. A few states exempt certain other items, such as medical supplies. The sales tax is attractive to states because of its high yield and relatively low collection costs. Although the tax is levied on the seller, much of it is frequently shifted to the consumer.

The sales tax is regressive because it applies to expenditures but not to saving. On average, people with high incomes save a larger fraction of their incomes than do people with low incomes. Because a larger fraction of the low-income individual's income is spent, it is therefore subject to the sales tax. This principle is illustrated in Table 7-2.

TABLE 7-2			
REGRESSIVITY OF A 4-PERCENT GENERAL SALES TAX			
Income	**Spending**	**Tax paid**	**Tax paid ÷ income (%)**
$ 10,000	$10,000	$ 400	4.0
20,000	18,000	720	3.6
40,000	30,000	1,200	3.0
100,000	50,000	2,000	2.0

The table assumes a 4-percent sales tax, and also assumes that expenditures rise less than proportionally with income. A family with $10,000 income is assumed to spend the entire income. Hence, the family pays $400 in sales taxes, or 4 percent of its income. A family with $20,000 income saves $2000 and spends $18,000; it therefore pays $720 of sales taxes, or 3.6 percent of its income. As income rises, the percent of income spent declines. Hence, if a $100,000 income earner spends $50,000 annually, she pays $2000 in sales taxes, or only 2 percent of income. The sales tax is made less regressive by exempting food, since low-income families spend a relatively large portion of their income on food.

The **excise tax** is quite similar to the sales tax, except that it applies to a much narrower range of items. The federal government levies an excise tax on tobacco, liquor, gasoline, and long-distance telephone calls. States also levy excise taxes—typically on liquor, gasoline, cigarettes, and certain luxury items. The excise tax tends to be regressive for the same reason that the sales tax is regressive—the poor spend a larger fraction of their income on items subject to the tax than do the rich.

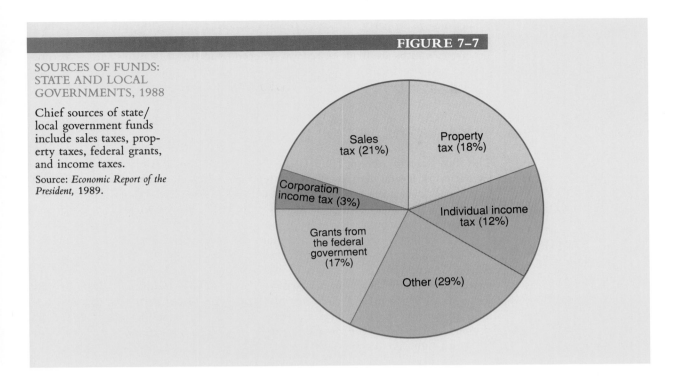

FIGURE 7–7

SOURCES OF FUNDS: STATE AND LOCAL GOVERNMENTS, 1988

Chief sources of state/local government funds include sales taxes, property taxes, federal grants, and income taxes.

Source: *Economic Report of the President*, 1989.

Sales tax (21%)

Property tax (18%)

Corporation income tax (3%)

Individual income tax (12%)

Grants from the federal government (17%)

Other (29%)

Property Tax

The chief source of revenue for local governments is the property tax, which is levied on the assessed value of homes, office buildings, and such other business and personal property as cars, boats, and land. Nonprofit organizations, such as colleges and churches, usually are exempt from the tax. Local governments calculate the appropriate tax *rate* on property by first establishing the *assessed value* on each piece of property. The tax rate is then set at a level that, given the aggregate assessed value of the community, yields the desired amount of tax receipts.

The property tax is controversial. Most economists believe it is regressive for the same basic reason that the sales tax and excise tax are regressive: poor families pay a larger fraction of their income for housing than do the affluent. Given that the property tax is proportional to the assessed value of the property, the fraction of income paid in the form of property taxes typically declines as income rises.

There are additional shortcomings associated with the property tax. Because it is an expensive undertaking, local communities do not have the resources to reassess values frequently. Because of rising property values caused by the inflation of recent decades, an older home may be assessed at 30 percent of current market value whereas a new home may be assessed at full value. Two homes of equal market value may therefore be subject to grossly different property taxes.

With the decay and declining property values of parts of America's inner cities, property tax *rates* may have to be raised to offset the decline in assessed valuation. Yet such measures can be self-defeating, as businesses and individuals are driven to relocate elsewhere. Meanwhile, in the burgeoning suburbs, rising home values and new home construction provide abundant tax receipts, and sometimes even permit reductions in property tax rates. Because school financing by local communities traditionally has been accomplished predominantly via property tax revenues, inner-city youths are likely to receive reduced educational facilities and opportunities. For this reason, the constitutionality of financing public education primarily through the property tax has been questioned in several states.

TAX REFORM ACT OF 1986

The Tax Reform Act of 1986 is the most fundamental revision of federal tax legislation in several decades. This Act represents the culmination of years of effort by our political system to come to grips with widely perceived shortcomings in our federal income-tax system, deficiencies especially apparent in two areas—equity (fairness) and economic efficiency (resource allocation).

It is believed that taxpayer morale and voluntary compliance had been deteriorating for years because of perceived inequities in the income tax system. This decline in morale and compliance was fueled by widely circulated stories of millionaires legally avoiding taxes, of a U.S. president claiming a six-figure tax write-off for donating his presidential papers, and of firms earning hundreds of millions in profits paying no taxes or actually receiving rebates (negative taxes). Such obvious violations of the principles of horizontal and vertical equity inevitably stimulate cynicism and hostility.

In addition, as hundreds of new deductions and tax credits were added piecemeal over the years, the federal income-tax system had become incredibly complex by the 1980s. Increasing numbers of Americans have had to hire accountants or tax lawyers to provide counsel and assistance in filing tax returns. Millions of people have been forced to spend 10, 20, perhaps 40 hours in the first half of April each year attempting to calculate their obligation to Uncle Sam. In addition, time must be spent throughout the year collecting receipts, keeping records, and arranging financial affairs in order to minimize the tax bite. All of such activities, although beneficial to the individuals involved, are wasteful and inefficient from society's viewpoint: they constitute a substantial misallocation of resources. Moreover, a substantial misallocation of resources occurs when millions of decisions are made on the basis of signals given by the tax code rather than on the basis of real economic returns. For example, large tax breaks for investing in apartment buildings tend to cause the construction of an above-optimal number of apartments with higher vacancy rates than are experienced in the absence of the subsidy.

The major impetus for tax reform was the desire to reduce inequities and inefficiencies in the federal tax code. The key principle involved is the notion of sharply increasing the **tax base**—income subject to taxes—by tightening deductions and loopholes, and using the potential additional revenues to finance a sharp cut in tax *rates*. By doing away with deductions and loopholes, perceptions of fairness (equity) would improve. Efficiency would increase through enhanced simplicity of the system. Further, time and resources required to deal with tax matters would be saved. Finally, elimination of false economic signals would enhance economic efficiency.

Idealists (dreamers) envisioned a system in which absolutely no deductions would be allowed and a *flat tax* rate of perhaps 20 percent would be applied against total income. Every American could then calculate annual tax liability in less than five minutes—"on the back of an envelope." However, realists quickly recognized

FLAT TAX

ACCOUNTANTS

I.R.S. BUREAUCRACY

LAWYERS

"Don't worry. The big dough will never let it happen."
By permission of Bill Mauldin and Wil-Joe Associates.

that many deductions were politically untouchable. Consequently, most of the major "sacred cows" were retained, including mortgage interest expenses, charitable contributions, property taxes, and state income taxes.

Nevertheless, the Tax Reform Act does significantly broaden the tax base, and the proceeds are used to finance a sharp cut in rates. Certain former deductions abolished by the Act include interest expenses on consumer loans, and state and local sales taxes actually paid. The Act also restricts medical and miscellaneous deductions, eliminates a $3000 deduction for working couples, makes long-term capital gains fully taxable (previously only 40 percent of such gains were subject to tax), restricts IRAs for high-income taxpayers, slows depreciation allowances, and eliminates certain passive tax shelters. Although it is too early to ascertain all the consequences of the Tax Reform Act of 1986, a preliminary report card is provided in Exhibit 7-2 (page 158). Of course, these grades, like many, are somewhat subjective.

Because the report card on the Tax Reform Act of 1986 does not reflect all As, we may expect continuing efforts at improving the federal tax law in the years ahead. Especially because of the poor grade on economic growth, new proposals to promote saving and investment are likely as Congress attempts to deal with the poor growth performance of the U.S. economy vis-à-vis Japan, West Germany, and other emerging economic powers.

EXHIBIT 7–2

TAX REFORM ACT OF 1986—BOON OR BANE?

The Act is graded on the basis of its consequences for three crucial considerations—fairness, economic efficiency, and long-term economic growth. The grades are *not* based on the norm of an ideal tax system, but rather on a comparison to previous tax law.

1. *Equity*   By sharply increasing the personal exemption (from $1080 in 1986 to $2000 in 1989) and by generously raising the standard deduction, five million low-income families were taken off the tax roles. Certain of the flagrant tax shelters that permitted high-income earners to avoid taxes were abolished. Special treatment of long-term capital gains was abolished—such income henceforth to be treated the same as ordinary income. Marginal tax rates were reduced for all income levels (although the largest cuts were in the upper income brackets). Many loopholes were closed, though hundreds remain.

    This grade is tough to determine, as issues of equity are normative issues. Using the norms of horizontal and vertical equity, the tax bill probably earns a B—a substantial improvement over the old tax law.

2. *Economic Efficiency*   By cutting tax *rates* and broadening the tax *base* (via reducing deductions), incentives to hire lawyers and accountants and to spend personal time arranging financial affairs in order to minimize tax exposure are reduced. These changes improve the nation's resource allocation. Moreover, abolition of certain tax shelters removes a signal to invest in areas that are economical only because of tax incentives. Thus the tax law moves us in the correct direction, although in the view of critics, not nearly far enough. On the other hand, the new tax law is not really any simpler than the old one. For procrastinators who figure their own taxes, April 15 remains a long day.

    Overall, we propose a grade of B+ on efficiency criteria—a solid improvement over previous law.

3. *Economic Growth*   To promote long-term economic growth, we must allocate a larger portion of current output to investment goods (tools, machinery, factories) at the expense of consumer goods. That is, we must encourage saving and stimulate investment in plant, equipment, and technology. However, the Tax Reform Act of 1986—perhaps because of its emphasis on equity and efficiency—moves in the wrong direction on long-term growth. The Act shifts some $120 billion of taxes from persons (low savers) to corporations (high savers and high investors) over a five-year period, thus tending to reduce aggregate saving. Also, because it is *revenue neutral* (i.e., has no effect on aggregate tax receipts), the bill skirts the chance to close the federal deficit. Reducing the deficit would have stimulated aggregate national saving (public plus private), thus reducing interest rates and stimulating investment spending. Finally, the bill features several specific changes that will probably inhibit investment spending, such as removing the tax credit for investment, stretching out depreciation schedules, and taxing capital gains as regular income.

    Overall, the bill earns a D on economic growth criteria.

SUMMARY

1. Government intervenes in the economy in order to promote competition, to implement policies that stabilize the macroeconomy, and to modify the distribution of income and wealth. In addition, the government steps in to provide public goods and sometimes intervenes to correct misallocations of resources associated with positive and negative externalities.

2. Government has become more pervasive in the sense that the ratio of government spending (and taxes) to our gross national product has gradually increased over the years. Among the sources of this government growth are the urbanization movement (especially 1900–1950) and the growth of the defense establishment (especially 1940–1965). Also contributing to the expanded role of government since the 1950s is the growth of the welfare state, the dominant source of government growth during the past 30 years.

3. Government purchases of goods and services are exhaustive—they consume scarce economic resources. Government transfer payments are nonexhaustive—they transfer income within the private sector of the economy but do not consume resources or divert them to the production of government goods and services. In the past 30 years, government purchases have expanded in line with GNP; government transfers have expanded much faster than GNP.

4. Federal government expenditures are primarily for economic security, national defense, health and education, and interest on federal debt. State-and-local government expenditures are mainly for education, health and welfare, police and fire protection, and roads and highways.

5. The real function of taxes is to limit the utilization of economic resources—lumber, labor, steel—in the production of private goods and services so that the resources may be used for public goods and services.

6. Taxes are classified as progressive, proportional, or regressive—depending on whether the percentage of income paid in taxes rises, remains constant, or declines as the level of income rises. Examples of progressive taxes are income and inheritance taxes. Examples of regressive taxes are payroll, sales, and excise taxes.

7. The federal government relies chiefly upon direct taxes—those levied directly on people or their resources. Examples include individual income taxes, corporation income taxes, and payroll taxes. State-and-local governments rely more heavily upon indirect taxes—those levied indirectly on people via their expenditures. Examples of indirect taxes include sales taxes, excise taxes, and property taxes.

8. In terms of the volume of tax receipts, the most significant tax is the individual income tax. Individuals compute their annual tax liability by first calculating adjusted gross income (adding all forms of income and adjusting the total for certain allowances). They then compute taxable income by subtracting from adjusted gross income their exemptions and deductions. The individual income tax is progressive chiefly because the ratio of taxable income to total income tends to rise as income rises (i.e., high-income earners find that exemptions and deductions shield a smaller percentage of their total income than is true for low-income earners). Also, the marginal tax rate is higher for taxable income above $30,000 than for income below. Notwithstanding, the degree of progressivity of the individual income tax has decreased in recent decades.

9. Certain loopholes exist that allow many taxpayers to legally reduce their tax liability. Examples include the nontaxability of interest income earned on municipal bonds, availability of deductible retirement contributions, and deductibility of property taxes and mortgage interest payments.

10. These loopholes sometimes create gross violations of the norms of horizontal and vertical equity. Horizontal equity is the notion that those of equal financial means should contribute equally to the financing of government. Vertical equity is the notion that those of greater financial resources should contribute more in taxes than those of lesser financial means.

11. Major federal tax legislation was enacted in the Tax Reform Act of 1986. This Act broadens the tax base and uses the proceeds to finance a considerable reduction in marginal tax rates. The tax base is broadened by significantly restricting the availability of deductions.

KEY TERMS

negative externalities
positive externalities
public good
quasi-public good
welfare state
government purchases
government transfer payments

direct tax
indirect tax
progressive tax
proportional tax
regressive tax
tax incidence
horizontal equity

vertical equity   payroll tax
federal individual income tax   corporation income tax
adjusted gross income   double taxation
taxable income   sales tax
average tax rate   excise tax
marginal tax rate   property tax
loophole   tax base

STUDY QUESTIONS AND PROBLEMS

1. Explain carefully why it is true that even a conservative economist—who seeks to minimize governmental intervention in economic affairs—might support a large tax on the production of electricity via nuclear power.
2. What is the economic rationale for a large government subsidy for research on the AIDS virus?
3. Explain the meaning of a pure public good. Discuss why each of the following can or cannot be classified as a pure public good:
   a. the public library in your hometown
   b. the national weather bureau
   c. the federal interstate highway system
   d. a municipal airport
   e. a municipal rose garden
   f. computer software, such as Wordperfect™
   g. municipal street snow removal
4. Today the ratio of total government expenditures (federal, state, and local) to GNP is roughly 35 percent. What do you project this ratio to be 30 years hence? Defend your projection.
5. Explain whether the following government expenditures are exhaustive or nonexhaustive:
   a. police protection
   b. veterans benefits
   c. salaries for high-school teachers
   d. food stamps
   e. national defense
   f. postal service
   g. interest on federal debt
6. Explain whether the following taxes or license fees are progressive or regressive:
   a. a $1 per barrel federal excise tax on beer
   b. a $25 hunting license
   c. the federal individual income tax
   d. the federal payroll tax
7. What might be done (via tax law) to make the federal income tax more progressive? Less progressive?
8. Some economists believe the corporation income tax is regressive. How can this be true? Explain.
9. Assume the U.S. birthrate rises dramatically in the 1990s. What implications does this have for a potential crisis in the social security system circa 2030? Explain.
10. Analyze the strengths and weaknesses of the Tax Reform Act of 1986.
11. Discuss the real economic function of a tax.
12. An industrial firm in your town routinely dumps toxic waste into the river instead of disposing of it in a manner that causes no negative externality. Relative to proper disposal, how does this practice affect the firm's cost of production? The price of its product? The output it produces? What sort of regulations, if any, do you favor imposing on the firm?

13. Concerning the individual income tax:
    a. explain the difference between average and marginal tax rates.
    b. if the marginal tax rate is higher than the average tax rate, is the tax progressive?
    c. if a constant tax rate of 20 percent is applied to all taxable income, and all deductions are eliminated but personal exemptions are continued, is the tax progressive? Explain.

ANSWERS TO YOUR TURN

Clearly, the project will stall because of the *free-rider* problem. No individual can be excluded from the benefits of the SDI system once it is operational. Few individuals would purchase subscriptions, especially in view of the exorbitant cost. This is a pure public good, and must be provided collectively or not at all.

SELECTED REFERENCES

Aaron, Henry J., and Harvey Galper, *Assessing Tax Reform* (Washington, DC: The Brookings Institution, 1985). This book analyzes various tax reform proposals in the light of basic principles of public finance.

Browning, Edgar K., and Jacqueline Browning, *Public Finance and the Price System* (New York: Macmillan, 1985). This government finance textbook includes a discussion of social security and the 1983 reforms.

Musgrave, Richard A., and Peggy B. Musgrave, *Public Finance in Theory and Practice,* 4th edition (New York: McGraw-Hill, 1984). A comprehensive textbook on government finance.

Pechman, Joseph A., *Who Paid the Taxes, 1966–85?* (Washington, DC: The Brookings Institution, 1985). A work that analyzes the distribution of the burden of taxes by income class.

PART II

MACROECONOMY, NATIONAL INCOME DETERMINATION, AND FISCAL POLICY

CHAPTER 8

INTRODUCTION TO MACROECONOMICS— OVERVIEW

> You can make even a parrot into a learned economist—all it must learn are the two words "supply" and "demand."
>
> ANONYMOUS

In recent years you have frequently encountered such terms as "inflation," "unemployment," "recession," "stagflation," "Federal Reserve policy," and "budget deficits." To understand the nature, role, and importance of such terms, we need a basic framework with which to analyze the macroeconomic performance of the U.S. economy. The basic model of aggregate demand and aggregate supply provides important insight into many key macroeconomic developments. The framework of aggregate demand and aggregate supply is sketched in this chapter and developed more thoroughly in the next several chapters. Once the framework is mastered, it is much easier to understand the causes of such crucial phenomena as inflation, business cycles, and changes in output and employment. In Chapter 8 we outline several key macroeconomic events of the past 30 years in the context of the model.

THE BASIC AGGREGATE SUPPLY–AGGREGATE DEMAND MODEL

The basic aggregate supply–aggregate demand framework is illustrated in Figure 8-1.

Aggregate Demand Curve

Recall from Chapter 4 the definition of a demand curve for a specific good or service. The demand curve for good *A* is the relationship between the price of good *A* and the quantity consumers wish to purchase—*other factors remaining constant.* If other factors relevant to demand for good *A* do not remain constant, the entire position of the demand curve for good *A* shifts rightward or leftward. For example, if income rises, the demand curve for steak shifts rightward.

Aggregate Demand Curve
The aggregate demand curve shows the quantity of the nation's output demanded at each possible price level.

In a somewhat analogous fashion, the nation's **aggregate demand curve** is defined as the relationship between the nation's price level and the amount of **real output** (goods and services) demanded—*other factors remaining constant.* If factors relevant to demand for real output other than the price level do not remain constant,

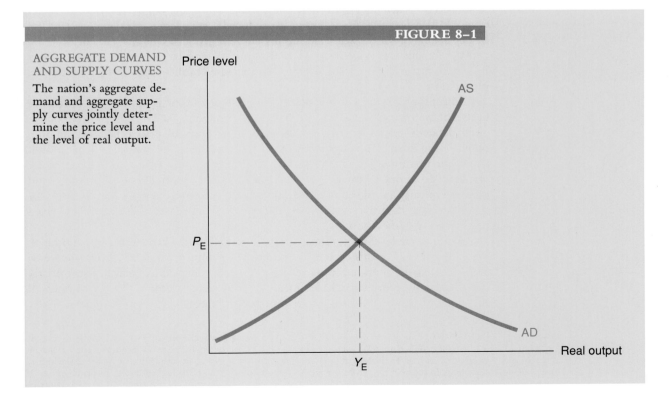

FIGURE 8–1

AGGREGATE DEMAND AND SUPPLY CURVES

The nation's aggregate demand and aggregate supply curves jointly determine the price level and the level of real output.

the entire position of the aggregate demand curve shifts. For example, if the stock market rises sharply, people feel wealthier and increase major purchases, shifting the aggregate demand curve rightward.

The fundamental explanation of the downward slope of the aggregate demand curve differs from the explanation of the shape of the demand curve for a specific product. If the price of steak falls, people substitute steak for hamburger and chicken, increasing the quantity of steak demanded. In the aggregate demand-curve formulation, the nation's **price level**—the average price of all goods and services— occupies the vertical axis. A decline in the price level indicates that prices of goods and services *on average or in general* are reduced. Hence, there is no substitution effect.

Several factors account for the downward slope of the aggregate demand curve. If the price level falls while the amount of personal money balances (checking accounts and currency holdings), stocks, bonds, and other financial assets remains constant, the real purchasing power of this financial wealth increases. This condition stimulates buying of goods and services. Moreover, a decline in American prices makes domestic goods more attractive to foreigners, and demand for American exports rises. Similarly, some American demand for imported goods is redirected toward domestically produced goods because of the decline in domestic prices. For these reasons, the aggregate demand (AD) curve in Figure 8-1 is downward sloping.

Aggregate Supply Curve

Aggregate Supply Curve
The aggregate supply curve shows the quantity of the nation's output supplied at each possible price level.

The **aggregate supply curve** is defined as the relationship between the nation's price level and the amount of output firms desire to produce—*other factors remaining constant.* As shown in Figure 8-1, the typical aggregate supply (AS) curve slopes upward. As prices rise, more output is produced—*other factors remaining constant.* An in-depth analysis of the aggregate supply curve is given in Chapter 12. For now, we explain the positive slope by the fact that profits tend to rise when prices rise—at least in the short run—and by the fact that increased profits motivate firms to step up production.

The profit earned by producing one unit of output is simply the difference between the price of the good and the cost of producing it. The cost of producing a good depends on input costs—wage rates, raw material prices, factory/building rents, and so forth. These input costs tend to remain fixed for considerable periods of time, but not indefinitely. Workers and firms often enter into contracts that fix wages for from one to three years. Even in the absence of such contracts, wages and salaries typically are adjusted once each year. The same scenario frequently holds for raw materials, as firms contract with suppliers to purchase the materials at fixed prices for a specified period.

As the price level rises, prices of at least some inputs remain fixed for significant periods of time. For this reason, *profit margins*—profits per unit of output—increase and firms expand output. Similarly, when the price level falls, certain costs initially fail to decline, profit margins decline, and firms reduce output. The sluggishness of input prices accounts for the positive slope of the aggregate supply curve.[1]

---

[1]It is useful to distinguish between a short-run and a long-run aggregate supply curve. In the short run, many input costs remain fixed as the price level rises. Firms respond to increased profit margins by sharply stepping up output. In the long run, wages and other input prices have ample time to adjust to the higher price level. In the long run, profit margins are not greatly stimulated by higher output prices and output is therefore less responsive to changes in the price level. The long-run aggregate supply curve is steeper than the short-run curve.

As is the case with the supply curve for an individual product, changes in factors that influence production (other than price) shift the entire position of the aggregate supply curve. An example is growth of *productivity,* which is defined as output per unit of input (such as one hour of work). Technological progress stimulates productivity, shifts the aggregate supply schedule rightward, and allows more output to be produced at each price level.

Equilibrium

In Figure 8-1, the aggregate demand (AD) and aggregate supply (AS) curves intersect to determine the nation's equilibrium price level (P_E) and real output—the level of real goods and services produced and exchanged (Y_E). In Figure 8-1, any price level above P_E causes an excess of aggregate production over aggregate sales (AS > AD), which leads to an undesired buildup of inventories and induces firms to reduce prices. A decline in prices discourages production and encourages buying—a process that continues until the price level returns to P_E.

If the price level is less than P_E, aggregate demand exceeds aggregate supply. This condition leads to an unintended decrease in the nation's inventories, and many buyers cannot obtain the goods and services they desire. Accordingly, the signal is given to raise prices, which encourages production and inhibits purchases—a process that continues until equilibrium returns at the price level of P_E and the output level of Y_E.

Changes in the Nation's Price Level and Real Output

In any economy, real output and the price level constantly undergo change. These changes are attributable to frequent shifts in the aggregate supply and aggregate demand curves illustrated in Figure 8-1. Certain of these changes are at least partially predictable, others are not. In Figure 8-1, we see that factors that raise aggregate demand (shifting the aggregate demand curve rightward) tend to raise the price level and the amount of real output produced and exchanged. A decrease in aggregate demand tends to reduce the level of prices and real output. Factors that increase aggregate supply (shifting AS rightward) reduce the price level and raise real output. A decrease in aggregate supply raises the price level and reduces real output.

Inflation
A persistent and sustained increase in the general price level.

Inflation is defined as a sustained or persistent increase in the level of prices. We see from the framework of Figure 8-1 that inflation may be caused by persistent increases in the aggregate demand curve, persistent decreases in the aggregate supply curve, or some combination of the two. Historically, the predominant source of inflation in all nations has been persistent increases in aggregate demand, fueled by government budget deficits and excessive growth in the nation's money supply.

Factors Shifting Aggregate Demand and Aggregate Supply

Components of aggregate demand include consumer spending, investment expenditures, government purchases, and net foreign demand for domestic products (i.e., foreign demand for U.S. exports minus American demand for imports). The components of aggregate demand shift for various reasons. Consumption may increase because of an improved economic outlook, higher wealth owing to higher stock and bond prices, or an income-tax reduction that increases take-home pay. Investment expenditures for new plant and equipment and housing may increase because of a decline in interest rates, an increase in the utilization rate of existing plant capacity, or an improved economic outlook. Government spending rises when federal, state, or local governments authorize higher outlays. Export demand may rise when foreign nations become more affluent, when trade barriers are removed, or when exchange-rate movements make prices of American goods and services (measured in yen, marks, francs, and so forth) lower to foreign buyers.

Several considerations influence the position of the aggregate supply curve. For example, the growth of American technology gradually shifts the aggregate supply curve rightward (increases aggregate supply) over time, as do growth in the labor force and increases in the amount of capital goods per worker. On the other hand, increases in input costs in the production process—such as higher wages, higher raw-material prices, higher oil and energy prices—shift the curve leftward.

Stabilization Policies—Monetary and Fiscal Policies

U.S. officials attempt to stabilize output at levels corresponding to reasonably low unemployment rates without triggering inflationary pressures. Such measures are known as **stabilization policies,** which consist of monetary and fiscal policy. **Monetary policy**—conducted by the Federal Reserve System—aims at bringing about deliberate changes in interest rates, credit availability, and the supply of money (checking accounts and currency) in order to influence aggregate expenditures. (We analyze this process in Part III.) **Fiscal policy** involves deliberate changes in the federal government's flow of expenditures and tax receipts in order to influence aggregate spending and overall performance of the economy. (Chapters 11, 12, and 20 address issues of fiscal policy.)

Both monetary and fiscal policies influence key macroeconomic variables, primarily by influencing the position of the aggregate demand curve.[2] For example, when output is low and unemployment is high, stimulative policies may be necessary. In this case, the Federal Reserve works to push down interest rates and increase the supply of money and credit, thereby increasing investment and consumption spending, and shifting the aggregate demand curve rightward. This results in higher real output, and the price level tends to rise. The federal government may also implement stimulative fiscal policy by reducing taxes (thus increasing consumption) or by increasing federal expenditures, which shifts the aggregate demand curve rightward.

To illustrate the general task of stabilization policy, consider the situation depicted in Figure 8-2, which depicts aggregate supply and aggregate demand curves with price level on the vertical axis and real output on the horizontal axis. Assume initially that the economy is at A, the intersection of AD_1 and AS_1. The price level is P_1 and real output is Y_1.

Corresponding to each level of real output is a specific magnitude of employment and unemployment. In Figure 8-2, the level of output Y_1 is far below capacity. Hence, employment is rather low and the unemployment rate is high—9

Stabilization Policies
Government programs designed to prevent serious economic downturns and rapid inflation by influencing the nation's aggregate demand curve.

Monetary Policy
The use of certain economic tools by the Federal Reserve System to alter availability of credit, level of interest rates, and supply of money in order to influence economic activity.

Fiscal Policy
The deliberate manipulation of federal expenditures and taxes for the purpose of influencing economic activity.

---

[2]Fiscal policy—such as investment tax credits and other tax devices—may provide incentives to install capital goods, thus enhancing production capability and ultimately shifting the aggregate supply curve rightward. Monetary policy—by influencing interest rates and investment spending for new plant and equipment—affects the position of the aggregate supply curve in the long run. Also, the *mix* of monetary and fiscal policies likely influences the composition of current output between consumption goods and investment goods, thereby influencing aggregate supply. Although we ignore these considerations here, we return to them in Part V.

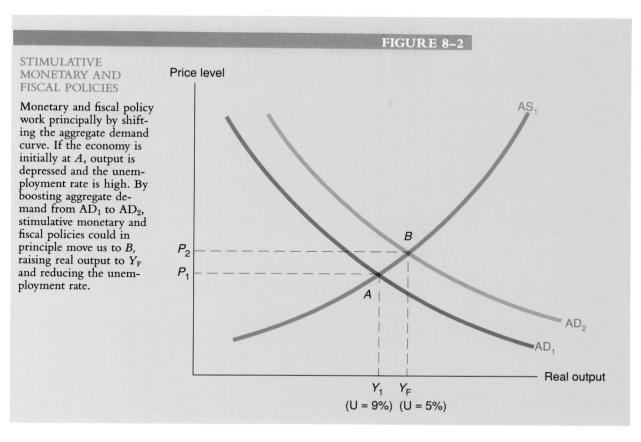

FIGURE 8-2

STIMULATIVE MONETARY AND FISCAL POLICIES

Monetary and fiscal policy work principally by shifting the aggregate demand curve. If the economy is initially at A, output is depressed and the unemployment rate is high. By boosting aggregate demand from AD_1 to AD_2, stimulative monetary and fiscal policies could in principle move us to B, raising real output to Y_F and reducing the unemployment rate.

Full Employment
Situation in which economy operates at lowest unemployment rate possible without setting off a boost in inflation; probably corresponds to an unemployment rate of 5 or 5.5 percent.

percent in this example. Figure 8-2 indicates that the level of output associated with **full employment** is Y_F. In other words, real output must be considerably larger than the current production level of Y_1 in order to generate enough jobs so everyone qualified and desirous of finding employment could do so within a reasonable time period. Although economists disagree on the actual unemployment rate under such conditions, for illustrative purposes assume *full employment* here is an unemployment rate of 5 percent.

In this situation, officials in charge of monetary and fiscal policies may in principle attempt to stimulate economic activity by shifting the aggregate demand curve rightward from AD_1 to AD_2. Ideally the output target (Y_F) would be hit and unemployment reduced to the desired level of 5 percent. However, because the price level would rise from P_1 to P_2, stabilization authorities may be reluctant to implement such stimulative policies.

Alternatively, picture an aggregate demand curve (AD_3) rightward of AD_2 in Figure 8-2 that intersects AS_1 at a point northeast of point B, yielding a real output level in excess of our full-employment output level Y_F. Such a situation is undesirable in the sense that the economy is attempting to produce an output level in excess of that which would obtain when unemployment is 5 percent. Severe inflation would ensue, and restrictive monetary and fiscal policies would be called for in order to return the aggregate demand curve to AD_2.

Although this may seem straightforward, policymakers face fundamental difficulties in the real world. For example, there is uncertainty about the position and slope of the aggregate demand and aggregate supply curves. Also, policymakers cannot know the precise nature of the nonpolicy factors currently shifting the AS and AD curves. Finally, there is disagreement about the level of real output that yields *full employment.* Hence, it is much more difficult to hit point B with real output at Y_F than one might assume from an analysis of Figure 8-2; real output may end up significantly below (or above) the Y_F magnitude because of the uncertainties involved. In fact, many economists believe the task so formidable and the potential errors so large that policymakers should not even make the attempt. In Parts III and IV we discuss in greater detail how monetary and fiscal policies are conducted in the U.S. and address the issue of whether deliberate efforts to conduct active stabilization policies are beneficial to the nation's economic health.

The principal measure of a nation's output is its **gross national product (GNP).** GNP is the dollar value of the nation's annual production of final goods and services. As a measure of the variable on the horizontal axes in Figures 8-1 and 8-2, GNP is flawed. When the prices of all goods and services together with wages and salaries increase by 10 percent, the nation's GNP rises by 10 percent—even though the actual quantity of final goods and services produced and exchanged remains constant. To resolve this measurement problem, economists construct a measure termed "real GNP" by adjusting reported GNP by the magnitude of the increase in the price level relative to some reference period, known as the *base year.* **Real GNP** is a measure of the value of the nation's real output expressed in dollars of constant purchasing power. Real GNP thus provides an effective yardstick for comparing output performance of the economy from year to year.

POST-1960 U.S. MACROECONOMIC HISTORY

Figure 8-3 illustrates real GNP for the period 1960–1988, along with a measure called **potential GNP.** The latter concept refers to the amount of real output the economy hypothetically produces under conditions of full employment—when the economy steams along at near-capacity production levels and unemployment exhibits a relatively low rate of perhaps 5 percent. Potential GNP rises over time as the work force expands and as productivity (output per worker) increases. The gap between actual GNP and potential GNP is an indicator of the output performance of the economy. The larger the gap, the greater the loss of output due to an underutilized or slack economy. And the nation's unemployment rate varies directly with the magnitude of this gap.

In Figure 8-3, the shaded areas indicate periods of **recession**—periods in which real GNP is declining.[3] For the period 1960–1988, the nation experienced five recessions. Unshaded areas represent periods of economic expansion—periods of uninterrupted growth of real GNP. Much of the post-1960 U.S. macroeconomic history is told by this figure, together with the simple macroeconomic framework presented in Figures 8-1 and 8-2. The following outline highlights certain key developments of the 1960s, 1970s, and 1980s.

Gross National Product
The value of the output of all final goods and services produced during a specific period (usually one year).

Real GNP
GNP adjusted for inflation; the value of gross national product in constant prices.

Potential Gross National Product
The real GNP the economy produces under conditions of full employment of labor and other resources.

Recession
A period of time in which a nation's real output declines.

[3]A *recession* is conventionally defined as a period in which real output declines at least two consecutive quarters (six months). There have been occasional periods in U.S. history in which real output fell only one quarter before resuming its advance. Such periods are not recessions.

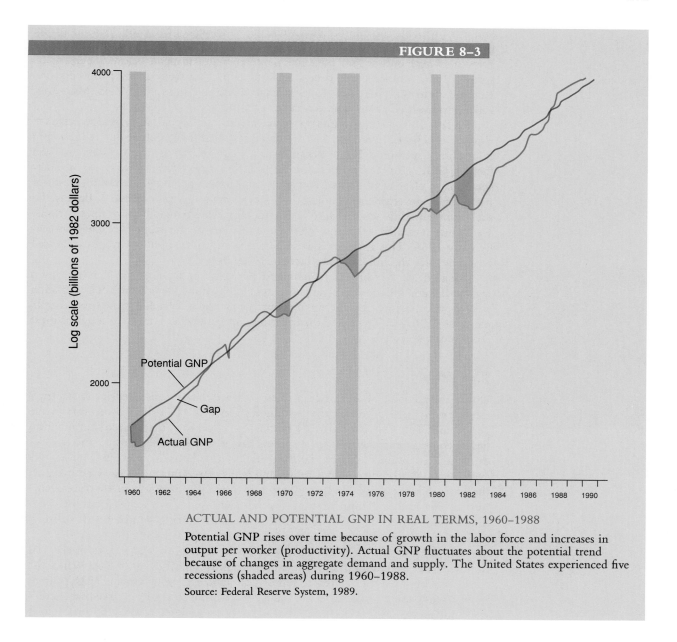

FIGURE 8-3

ACTUAL AND POTENTIAL GNP IN REAL TERMS, 1960–1988

Potential GNP rises over time because of growth in the labor force and increases in output per worker (productivity). Actual GNP fluctuates about the potential trend because of changes in aggregate demand and supply. The United States experienced five recessions (shaded areas) during 1960–1988.

Source: Federal Reserve System, 1989.

The 1960s

When John F. Kennedy was inaugurated president in January 1961, the U.S. economy was in a recession. As shown in Figure 8-3, a significant gap existed between actual and potential output. Furthermore, the Soviet Union had recently launched the satellite Sputnik, and fears abounded that Russia might be overtaking the United States technologically and gaining on us economically. Inflation in the United States had been rather subdued for several years, and the new administration felt the time was right to pursue policies designed to stimulate expansion of output and employment. Income-tax cuts were implemented in the early 1960s, shifting the aggregate demand curve rightward. The U.S. economy responded with rapid growth of real output and the unemployment rate dropped below 5 percent by spring 1965. At that point things looked good. The stock market moved to an all-time high, with the Dow-Jones average reaching 1000 in late 1965. Moreover, inflation remained at low and tolerable levels.

In late 1965, U.S. politicians made an ill-fated decision to sharply escalate expenditures for the Vietnam War without providing for a tax hike or a reduction in nonmilitary spending. The economy was already operating near capacity in 1965 (actual GNP close to potential GNP). Given the intention to raise military spending, a clear need existed to depress consumer spending (via tax increase) or nonmilitary government spending to avoid excessive aggregate demand. Because no such compensating actions were taken, the aggregate demand curve shifted rightward, output escalated sharply, and the unemployment rate dropped below 4 percent by early 1966. This excessively stimulative fiscal policy resulted in an overheated economy, and the inflation rate increased sharply.[4]

Richard M. Nixon was inaugurated president in January 1969, inheriting a legacy of high inflation and very low unemployment (3.4 percent). The inflation rate, approximately 5 percent, seemed outrageous and intolerable at the time. A mild recession (1969–1970) slowed the inflation rate somewhat, but not as much as most economists expected.

The 1970s

Unlike the record of most earlier business cycles, inflation continued at a rather high rate even in the first year of the ensuing *recovery* (1971). Although recovery is the period in which inflation normally reaches a cyclical low, it appeared that inflation had become so entrenched in the system that it was sustained not on the basis of exuberant economic activity, but merely on the basis of powerful *inflationary expectations.* Workers were demanding and firms were granting large wage hikes on the basis that the price level was expected to rise significantly in the foreseeable future. The Nixon Administration—which had previously espoused nonintervention by the government in marketplace decision making—turned 180 degrees, opting for a comprehensive **wage–price freeze.**

On August 15, 1971 an across-the-board freeze on wages and prices was imposed. The economics of this measure are illustrated in Figure 8-4. When the freeze was imposed, the aggregate supply (AS_1) and aggregate demand (AD_1) curves intersected to yield a price level of P_1 and a real output level of Y_1. Note that there is no tendency for the price level to rise above P_1 as long as AD_1 does not shift rightward or AS_1 shift leftward. Unfortunately, in the year following imposition of the freeze (1972), the aggregate demand curve shifted sharply rightward (AD_2 in Figure 8-4). In 1972, the money supply increased by more than 9 percent and fiscal policy also became more stimulative. Cynics suggest this occurred because the

---

[4]This policy error was attributable to political factors, not to any poor state of economic art or faulty economic advice. President Lyndon B. Johnson was warned in the fall of 1965 by his economic advisors that a tax increase was needed to compensate for expanded military spending and to avoid an overheated and inflationary economy. With Congressional elections on the horizon (November 1966), LBJ decided to wait until January 1967 to request the income-tax hike. Congress delayed action until July 1968, when a temporary 10-percent surtax was imposed. This measure proved too little too late! Furthermore, Federal Reserve monetary policy was relatively stimulative in 1967 and 1968, serving to negate the effects of the temporary tax hike.

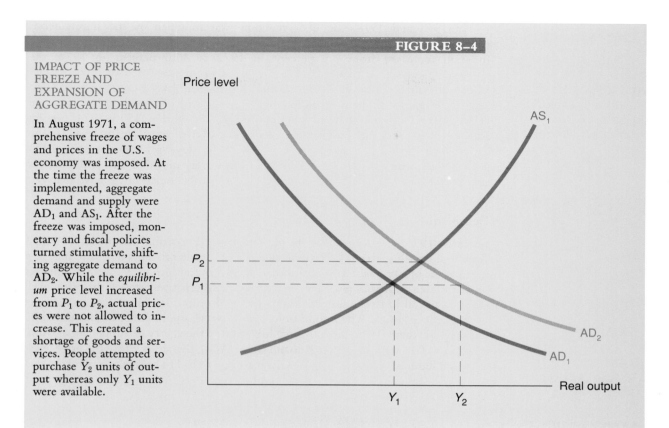

FIGURE 8–4

IMPACT OF PRICE FREEZE AND EXPANSION OF AGGREGATE DEMAND

In August 1971, a comprehensive freeze of wages and prices in the U.S. economy was imposed. At the time the freeze was implemented, aggregate demand and supply were AD_1 and AS_1. After the freeze was imposed, monetary and fiscal policies turned stimulative, shifting aggregate demand to AD_2. While the *equilibrium* price level increased from P_1 to P_2, actual prices were not allowed to increase. This created a shortage of goods and services. People attempted to purchase Y_2 units of output whereas only Y_1 units were available.

Nixon Administration desired to stimulate the economy and push the unemployment rate down before the November 1972 election.[5] Economic policy is sometimes intertwined with politics.

In any event, with the price level frozen at P_1, aggregate demand for goods and services (Y_2) exceeded aggregate supply (Y_1), inventories began to disappear from merchants' shelves, and buyers became frustrated. Even though reported inflation was dead in the water because of controls, the equilibrium price level P_2 was significantly higher than the actual level P_1 and prices rose quickly as soon as the controls were dismantled in 1973. The controls merely disguised and postponed inflation![6]

---

[5]Nixon lost the 1960 election to Kennedy by a mere 150,000 votes. As President Dwight Eisenhower's vice president for the period 1953–1960, he had the bad fortune to preside over a recession during the 1960 election. Some one million voters lost their jobs in the months preceding the 1960 election, and it is likely that this cost Nixon the election. Voters thrown out of work rarely vote for the incumbent party. Thus Nixon had every reason to desire a strong economy as the November 1972 election approached.

[6]One can make a case in favor of such controls when a psychological shock is needed to bring down inflationary expectations honed by years of high inflation. Entrenched inflationary expectations can lead to large wage hikes even in the absence of high demand. If so, the aggregate supply curve persistently shifts leftward even in the face of a slack economy, leading to higher prices and lower output. By announcing controls, the government attempts to provide the shock that eliminates inflationary expectations and halts the leftward shift of the aggregate supply curve. This was the major rationale for the imposition of controls in 1971.

In 1973 and 1974, the U.S. economy was humbled by the simultaneous existence of double-digit inflation and the severe contraction of economic activity. Inflation increased from 3.5 percent in 1972 to 12.3 percent in 1974; the unemployment rate escalated from 4.8 percent in August 1973 to more than 8 percent throughout 1975. A new term, **stagflation** (stagnation plus inflation) appeared in the economics jargon to describe this *worst-of-all-worlds* macroeconomic debacle. Part of the inflationary jump during the period 1973–1974 can be attributed to the rapid, predictable movement of the actual price level to the equilibrium price level upon the termination of wage–price controls in 1973 (movement from P_1 to P_2 in Figure 8-4). However, much of the problem was attributable to a series of adverse supply shocks—a phenomenon we now analyze.

Stagflation
A situation in which sluggish or declining output is accompanied by strong inflation.

Economics of Supply Shocks

In early 1973, the Organization of Petroleum Exporting Countries (OPEC) announced a 400-percent increase in the price of crude oil. This dramatic increase in the price of a crucial input meant that the real output producers were willing to supply at each and every price level was reduced. Alternatively stated, the price level required to call forth the supply of any given real-output level increased in the face of this **supply shock.** The implications of an adverse supply shock are illustrated in Figure 8-5, where the OPEC oil-price hike shifted the aggregate supply curve from AS_1 to AS_2. Given the aggregate demand curve (AD_1), this shock drove the price level to P_2 and reduced real output to Y_2. Given that more had to be spent to purchase the

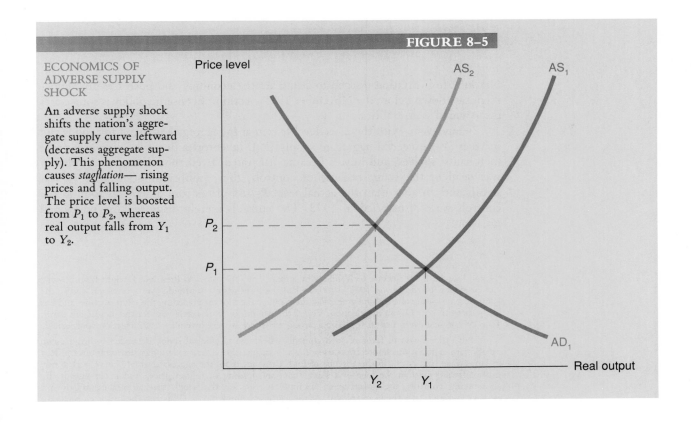

FIGURE 8–5

ECONOMICS OF ADVERSE SUPPLY SHOCK

An adverse supply shock shifts the nation's aggregate supply curve leftward (decreases aggregate supply). This phenomenon causes *stagflation*— rising prices and falling output. The price level is boosted from P_1 to P_2, whereas real output falls from Y_1 to Y_2.

higher-priced oil and related products, purchases of nonoil goods and services fell and real output declined.[7]

In addition to the enormous oil-price increase during 1973–1974, adverse worldwide weather in 1974 caused a severe shortfall in the production of basic agricultural foodstuffs. As a result, the price of corn, wheat, and soybeans doubled during one year. This phenomenon may also be viewed as contributing to the leftward shift of the aggregate supply curve, breathing additional life into the stagflation curse.

The delayed response of two *devaluations* of the U.S. dollar (late 1971 and early 1973) also may be viewed as an adverse supply shock. The markdown of the value of the dollar vis-à-vis other currencies meant that the dollar was worth fewer yen, marks, francs, and so forth.[8] Therefore, the dollar price of goods imported by the United States tended to rise in proportion to the magnitude of the devaluations (approximately 16 percent). To the extent that such higher-priced imports consisted of raw materials and other inputs in the production process, the aggregate supply curve shifted leftward in response to the devaluations.

Because inflation and unemployment are both undesirable, monetary and fiscal policymakers are placed in a *no-win* situation when adverse supply shocks occur. The dilemma is illustrated in Figure 8-6 (page 176).

Assume we begin at A, the intersection of AS_1 and AD_1, and the price level is P_1 while output is Y_1. The series of supply shocks shifts aggregate supply from AS_1 to AS_2, moving us from A to B, and the price level rises to P_2 while real output falls to Y_2. Assume further that U.S. officials declare inflation *public enemy number one*. By pursuing highly restrictive monetary and fiscal policies, aggregate demand can be reduced from AD_1 to AD_2, moving us to intersection C—the price level at the pre-shock level P_1. Thus inflation is prevented. Note, however, that now the real output level is Y_3, a low level corresponding to a very high unemployment rate. Inflation is prevented—but at the cost of a significant contraction in output and employment.

At the other extreme, assume the monetary and fiscal authorities are determined to prevent the supply shocks from reducing output below the initial level Y_1. They could implement highly stimulative measures, thereby shifting aggregate demand from AD_1 to AD_3. Given the aggregate supply curve AS_2, we move to D (in Figure 8-6), where output level remains at Y_1 but the price level balloons to P_3—inflation jumps to extremely high rates for a couple of years as the equilibrium price level increases from P_1 to P_3.

Monetary and fiscal policies that leave the aggregate demand curve anywhere between AD_2 and AD_3 inevitably lead to higher prices and lower output (higher unemployment) than existed prior to the adverse supply shocks. And monetary and fiscal authorities almost always are accused of *causing* inflation, unemployment—or perhaps both! Nevertheless, as we plainly see from Figure 8-6, the source of the problems are the supply shocks that produced the leftward shift in the aggregate

---

[7]In this analysis we assume that the aggregate demand curve remained unchanged in the face of the oil shock (i.e., that monetary and fiscal policymakers did not respond to the shock by aggressively tightening or easing their policies).

[8]Until March 1973, exchange rates were fixed from day-to-day and month-to-month—changing very infrequently. The U.S. dollar was devalued in 1934, 1971, and 1973. Such devaluations involved significant, one-shot markdowns of the value of the dollar in terms of the number of units of foreign currency per dollar. Since 1973, exchange rates have been allowed to float—changing each day in response to the market forces of supply and demand.

FIGURE 8–6

POLICY RESPONSES TO ADVERSE SUPPLY SHOCKS

An adverse supply shock that shifts aggregate supply from AS_1 to AS_2 simultaneously raises the price level and reduces output. If those responsible for monetary and fiscal policy attempt to prevent output from falling, they must boost aggregate demand, exacerbating the increase in prices. If they are determined to prevent inflation, they must reduce aggregate demand. But this causes a larger reduction in output and employment. In either case, monetary and fiscal policy makers are likely to be criticized. However, the real culprit is the supply shock itself, which necessarily increases prices, unemployment, or both.

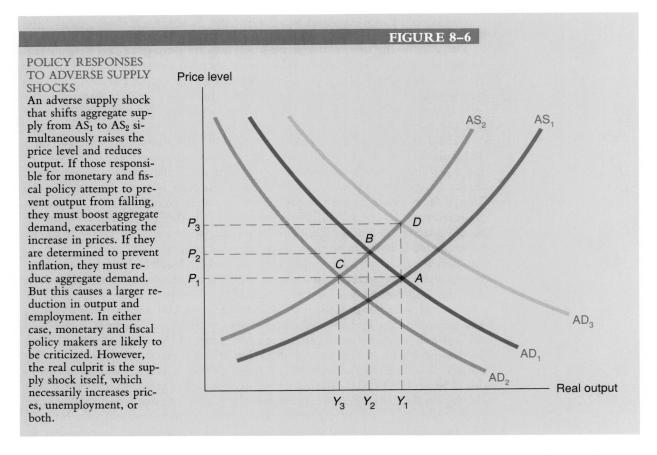

supply curve. The lesson in this analysis is that monetary and fiscal policies, no matter how competently implemented, cannot bring forth happiness from an adverse supply shock!

The U.S. responded to the supply shocks by pursuing an intermediate policy—allowing aggregate demand to be sufficiently high to permit a sharp increase in prices, but not high enough to prevent the severe recession of 1974–1975. Real output declined by some 5 percent and the unemployment rate reached 9 percent in May 1975, as the economy entered the recovery phase. Meanwhile, the inflation rate averaged 11 percent per year throughout a recession that was then the most severe since the Great Depression of the 1930s.

As the oil shock of 1973–1974 began to wear off, U.S. inflation slowed from the double-digit rates of 1973 and 1974 to around 6 percent in 1976. The economy emerged from recession in early 1975 and entered a recovery that would last almost five years.

The 1980s

The 1980s opened with the shortest recession followed by the briefest recovery on record. The recession lasted only the first six months of 1980; the ensuing recovery lasted only one year. A second OPEC oil-price hike in 1979 again doubled the price of crude oil. This shock, coupled with a very strong increase in aggregate demand in the late 1970s, boosted inflation back to double-digit levels in 1979 and 1980.

The election of 1980—which elevated Ronald Reagan to the presidency—may be regarded partly as a mandate for a return to better economic times—especially a mandate to tame the inflation dragon. An average inflation rate of 7 percent per year in the 1970s doubled the U.S. price level within a single decade. In addition, the growth of real output and living standards slowed to a trickle in the 1970s.

The monetary authorities, under the leadership of Paul Volcker (chairman of the Federal Reserve Board), cracked down on inflation with a vengeance in the early 1980s. Aggregate demand was reduced through a policy of restricted credit availability and extremely high interest rates. The brief recovery from mid-1980 to mid-1981 ended, and the economy descended into the most severe recession since the 1930s. The economists' long-absent term **depression** returned to network news as the unemployment rate soared to 10.8 percent in late 1982 and business bankruptcies, automobile repossessions, and home and farm foreclosures increased dramatically. The nation paid a large price for a successful battle against inflation.

Depression
A very severe and prolonged economic downturn.

The inflation rate decreased much faster than even the Reagan Administration had hoped, declining from an annual rate of more than 14 percent in the first half of 1980 to less than 4 percent by the end of 1982. Moreover, the inflation rate remained below 4 percent through 1986, before escalating somewhat during the remainder of the decade.

During the period 1983–1989, the unemployment rate descended slowly to around 5 percent as the economy staged a prolonged expansion phase following the 1981–1982 recession. To the surprise of many, the inflation rate continued to decline for several years during this recovery, reaching roughly one percent in 1986. This atypical phenomenon—declining inflation several years into economic recovery—can be explained using our aggregate demand-aggregate supply framework.

The 1980s witnessed an interesting reversal of certain adverse supply shocks of the 1970s. First, the U.S. dollar rose strongly on foreign-exchange markets during 1980–1985. This powerful appreciation of the dollar reduced the cost of goods imported into the United States and imposed great wage–price discipline on American industries exposed to foreign competition—especially the manufacturing sector. Second, shortly after the point at which the dollar stopped rising (early 1985), the price of crude oil collapsed, falling by more than 50 percent in less than one year. And bumper agricultural output helped hold down the price of such basic foodstuffs as wheat and corn.

In short, many observers believe the Reagan Administration had the *good fortune* to preside over a series of favorable supply shocks that reversed the *bad luck* of the Nixon, Ford, and Carter Administrations of the 1970s. The aggregate supply curve shifted rightward, conferring the benefits of higher output and lower prices.

To a significant extent, however, the strong dollar can be attributed to the policies implemented in the 1980s by the Reagan Administration. Any *consequences* of the strong dollar—such as lowering the price of imports and thereby lowering the rate of inflation—are thus attributable to the Administration's policies.[9] But the drop in oil prices in the mid-1980s was primarily attributable to the severe worldwide slump of 1981–1983, together with energy conservation measures

---

[9]Likewise, the enormous U.S. international trade deficits of the 1980s are also largely attributable to the strong dollar. When the U.S. dollar is expensive to foreigners, so are our export products. On the other hand, foreign products look cheap to Americans as the dollar buys more yen, marks, francs, and so forth. Hence, as a result of the strong dollar, U.S. imports soared and exports stagnated during 1983–1987. Because the dollar declined for several years beginning in early 1985, our trade deficit began to decline in the late 1980s.

EXHIBIT 8–1

THE ECONOMICS OF PRESIDENTIAL ELECTIONS

Conventional wisdom has it that the state of the economy at presidential election time is of crucial importance in determining the outcome of the election. Whether the incumbent party is returned to presidential office seems to a large extent a pocketbook issue. Incumbent presidential candidates are almost always reelected when the economy is *on their side* on election day. Pollster George Gallup once claimed that there is no way an incumbent president can lose if both peace and prosperity prevail. When an incumbent president does not seek reelection, the prospects of the incumbent party's candidate are believed strongly influenced by prevailing economic conditions. Especially important indicators of voter sentiment are thought to be the unemployment rate, the inflation rate, and the level of interest rates— especially the home mortgage rate. The recent growth rate of the economy also seems important, presumably because it yields insight into the economic outlook for the near-term.

Table 8-1 provides indicators of economic conditions at the time of the eleven presidential elections dating back to 1948.

Note that incumbent presidents (indicated by asterisk) sought reelection seven times during the 40-year interval. On the five occasions that an incumbent was successful the economy was solid. On the two occasions that an incumbent lost

(Gerald Ford in 1976 and Jimmy Carter in 1980) economic conditions were poor. For example, both inflation and unemployment rates were higher in 1976 than in the six previous election years. In 1980, inflation was out of control and interest rates were high; 1980 was a recession year in which real output was on the decline. Ronald Reagan defeated incumbent President Jimmy Carter in a landslide.

Economists have turned the intuition that Americans vote their pocketbooks into equations used to predict the winners of presidential elections. Perhaps the best-known prognosticator is Ray Fair of Yale University. Professor Fair uses a very simple model to explain voter behavior. The model includes the inflation rate for the two years before the election and the growth rate of real per-capita income for the six months before the election. The model also spots an incumbent-party candidate four percentage points. Arguably simplistic and naive, Fair's model correctly predicted 15 of the 18 presidential elections before the 1988 Bush-Dukakis campaign, and predicted the Bush victory in 1988. Before you use Fair's model as the basis for a wager, however, it is wise to acknowledge an alternative formula that also has proved amazingly accurate: If the American League wins the World Series in October of an election year, the Republicans win the White House.

---

implemented in the 1970s in response to the first oil shock. In addition, the favorable worldwide crop production was clearly a fortuitous event.

Critics of the Reagan Administration's policies tend to use terms such as "luck" to describe the coexistence of economic expansion and declining inflation. However, supporters point out that one cannot quarrel with success and, furthermore, that a good bit of the so-called "luck" can be accounted for by the new policies implemented by the Reagan Administration. We now turn to these new policies, known as *supply-side economics.*

REAGANOMICS—THE *SUPPLY-SIDE REVOLUTION*

The anemic growth of U.S. productivity and living standards in the 1970s, coupled with unacceptably high rates of inflation, created an intellectual environment

		TABLE 8-1			

ELECTION-YEAR ECONOMIES, 1948–1988

Election year	Candidate/(party) (winner listed first)	Economic indicator**			
		Unemployment rate (%)	Inflation rate (%)	Interest rate (%)	Growth rate (%)
1988	George Bush (R) Michael Dukakis (D)	5.6	4.1	10.0	2.7
1984	Ronald Reagan* (R) Walter Mondale (D)	7.5	4.3	13.0	4.0
1980	Ronald Reagan (R) Jimmy Carter* (D)	7.7	12.9	11.1	−4.6
1976	Jimmy Carter (D) Gerald Ford* (R)	7.8	5.7	7.0	1.7
1972	Richard Nixon* (R) George McGovern (D)	5.6	2.9	5.3	6.0
1968	Richard Nixon (R) Hubert Humphrey (D)	3.5	4.5	6.5	5.0
1964	Lyndon Johnson* (D) Barry Goldwater (R)	5.0	1.0	4.5	3.7
1960	John Kennedy (D) Richard Nixon (R)	5.6	1.4	4.8	−0.4
1956	Dwight Eisenhower* (R) Adlai Stevenson (D)	4.1	2.2	3.8	1.1
1952	Dwight Eisenhower (R) Adlai Stevenson (D)	3.4	3.1	3.0	1.3
1948	Harry Truman* (D) Thomas Dewey (R)	3.9	8.9	2.0	5.4

*Incumbent candidate.

**Variables are defined as follows: unemployment rate is for August of election year; inflation is rate of increase in consumer price index for 12-month period ending August of election year; interest rate is prime loan rate for August of election year; growth rate is annual growth rate in real GNP for 6-month period ending third quarter of election year.

Source: Adapted and updated from *Citibank Economic Database,* 1989.

conducive to new ideas in macroeconomic theory and innovations in macroeconomic policy. The thesis of *supply-side economics*—the catchphrase of Reagan economic philosophy—was that the supply side of the economy had for too long been neglected. Future policy should focus on expanding productive capacity and incentives to work and produce rather than focusing on measures that merely expand aggregate demand for goods and services. Government policy should be more concerned with the aggregate supply curve and less concerned with manipulating the aggregate demand curve.

Figure 8-7 (page 180) indicates the intended rationale of **supply-side economics**—to implement measures that shift the aggregate supply curve rightward. If successful, supply-side measures shift the aggregate supply curve from AS₁ to AS₂, moving the economy from *A* to *B*. This move involves an increase in real output, thus raising employment and lowering the unemployment rate. Moreover,

Supply-Side Economics Measures designed to shift the nation's aggregate supply curve rightward, thereby stimulating economic activity without raising prices.

the price level declines from P_1 to P_2, thus providing additional leeway for monetary and fiscal authorities to stimulate aggregate demand without igniting inflation. No person of sound mind can quarrel with the *objective* of supply-side economics!

Recall from the discussion of production-possibilities curves in Chapter 2 that nations which devote a larger share of current output to investment in plant, equipment, and technology experience a more rapid outward shift in the curve over time. Because saving and investment promote economic growth, a fundamental objective of supply-side economics must be to stimulate the share of income saved and the share of output allocated to investment goods. This farsighted objective requires reducing the public's consumption propensities and enhancing saving habits. It requires reducing the share of output sold to consumers and to the government and increasing the share devoted to productive investment in plant, equipment, and technology.

In the early 1980s, the Reagan Administration implemented federal tax legislation intended to promote investment incentives. By reducing the corporate income-tax rate, the Administration intended to free up funds with which to finance investment in new plant and equipment. Inasmuch as severe inflation is itself a likely detriment to long-range planning and investment, the Administration's success in bringing down inflation in the 1980s must be counted a positive factor in the investment and aggregate supply equations. Moreover, the Administration's contin-uation of a movement—initiated in the Carter Administration—toward less govern-

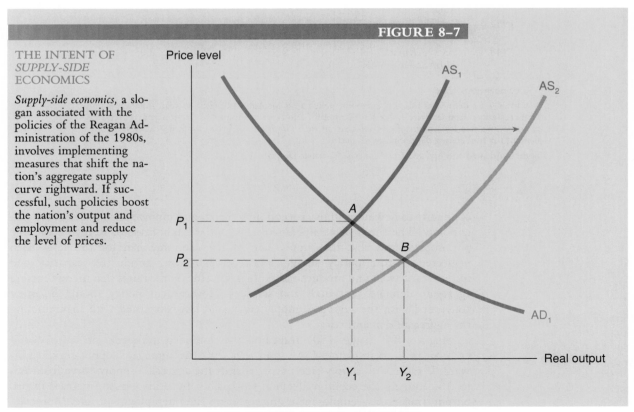

FIGURE 8–7

THE INTENT OF
SUPPLY-SIDE
ECONOMICS

Supply-side economics, a slo-gan associated with the policies of the Reagan Ad-ministration of the 1980s, involves implementing measures that shift the na-tion's aggregate supply curve rightward. If suc-cessful, such policies boost the nation's output and employment and reduce the level of prices.

Fig. 8-7   Title: Ragan Economics   3 of 3 S/S Black
Studio: Hans & Cassady, Inc.   (614) 276-5116

mental involvement in regulating private enterprise may have contributed to increased efficiency and growth.

On the saving front, individual taxpayers who established IRAs (Individual Retirement Accounts) were given a major tax break that encouraged them to save more in order to set aside funds for establishing and maintaining an IRA. By reducing marginal income-tax rates for millions of individuals and firms, the Administration hoped to stimulate incentives to work and produce as well as to save and invest.

Unfortunately, a major negative consequence of the tax cuts of the early 1980s was a string of annual budget deficits of unprecedented size—some $150–$200 billion per year. This huge increase in government dissaving more than offset any increase in private saving available, and the domestic pool of funds for investment spending dwindled. For this and other reasons, interest rates were exceptionally high during the first one-half of the 1980s, and America became dependent on foreign funds to finance domestic investment and budget deficits.

Critics of the Reagan Administration's supply-side policies point out that productivity growth was not substantially higher during the period 1981–1988 than during the dismal performance of the 1970s. Nor did the saving and investment rates respond positively to the policies implemented in the early 1980s. In fact, most measures of the private saving rates of Americans declined significantly in the 1980s. Supporters of the supply-side policies rely on two defenses: it's too early to tell or supply-side economics was never really tried. We analyze these issues in greater depth in Chapter 12.

SUMMARY

1. The intersection of the nation's aggregate demand and aggregate supply curves determines the price level and level of output of real goods and services.
2. An increase in aggregate demand causes higher real output and a higher price level. An increase in aggregate supply raises real output and reduces the price level.
3. Aggregate demand consists of four components: consumer demand, investment demand, government purchases of goods and services, and net foreign demand for U.S. goods and services. These components of demand shift in ways not always predictable, causing fluctuations in the nation's output and price level.
4. Government stabilization policies seek to maintain real output at levels high enough to keep unemployment reasonably low, but not so high as to cause severe inflation. Stabilization policies include monetary and fiscal policies. Monetary policy involves Federal Reserve management of the availability of credit, the level of interest rates, and the supply of money (currency and checking accounts). Fiscal policy involves government efforts to influence the nation's flow of expenditures by altering taxes or federal expenditures. Monetary and fiscal policies influence the economy principally by shifting the aggregate demand curve.
5. Gross National Product measures the value of a nation's output of final goods and services for a given year. One can deflate measured GNP to allow for price-level changes and obtain a measure of real GNP—GNP measured in dollars of constant purchasing power. This allows one to compare the performance of the economy from year to year.
6. Potential GNP is the (hypothetical) level of GNP the nation would produce if the economy were operating at a high utilization rate of capital and labor, with unemployment at some minimal and sustainable magnitude of perhaps five percent. The gap between actual GNP and potential GNP measures the loss of output due to a less-than-fully employed economy. This gap widens during periods of recession and typically declines during the recovery phase of a business cycle.

7. The U.S. economy of the 1960s can be divided into two periods. The 1961–1965 era witnessed rapid growth without inflation, the stock market moving to all time highs in late 1965. The 1966–1969 period witnessed an economy overstimulated with expenditures associated with escalation of U.S. involvement in Vietnam. Inflation increased and unemployment declined to unsustainably low levels. The decade ended in recession.

8. The U.S. economy of the 1970s was plagued by a series of supply shocks that shifted the aggregate supply curve leftward. These supply shocks included dramatic increases in the price of oil, adverse weather conditions in 1974, and two devaluations of the U.S. dollar. Largely because of the supply shocks, the 1970s was a decade of stagflation—persistent coexistence of inflation and economic stagnation with accompanying heavy unemployment and poor growth in productivity.

9. At the beginning of the 1980s, inflation was running at double-digit rates. A very severe recession (1981–1982) drove down inflation to approximately the 4-percent range.

10. A series of favorable supply shocks aided the economy during the period 1982–1986. The phenomenal appreciation in the U.S. dollar during 1982–1985 and the collapse of oil prices in 1986 shifted the aggregate supply curve rightward, partially reversing the bad fortune of the 1970s. These favorable supply shocks explain why the U.S. inflation rate continued to drift down from approximately 4 percent at the end of 1982 to approximately zero in mid-1986—even though the economy was in a period of economic expansion.

11. *Supply-side economics,* the economic slogan of the Reagan Administration of the 1980s, involves implementation of policies intended to shift the nation's aggregate supply curve rightward. Although no one disputes the merits of this intent, there is considerable doubt whether this maneuver was effectively carried out in the 1980s.

KEY TERMS

aggregate demand curve	gross national product (GNP)
real output	real GNP
price level	potential GNP
aggregate supply curve	recession
inflation	wage–price freeze
stabilization policy	stagflation
monetary policy	supply shock
fiscal policy	depression
full employment	supply-side economics

STUDY QUESTIONS AND PROBLEMS

1. Explain the fundamental difference between a demand curve for a specific good and an aggregate demand curve.

2. Why does a decrease in the nation's price level result in an increase in quantity of output demanded? A decrease in quantity supplied?

3. Explain the influence of the following upon the *position* of the nation's aggregate demand curve:
   a. a sharp decline in the stock market
   b. a 20-percent decline in the value of the U.S. dollar in foreign-exchange markets
   c. a decrease in income tax rates
   d. a sharp increase in interest rates
   e. an increase in the supply of money (currency holdings and checking accounts)

4. Explain the impact of the following upon the *position* of the aggregate supply curve:
   a. the price of oil falls by 50 percent
   b. workers accept a 10-percent wage cut
   c. the price level rises 20 percent

d. the amount of capital per worker declines

e. technological breakthroughs boost labor productivity

5. Using the aggregate supply-aggregate demand diagram, explain the forces that prevail when the economy is temporarily out of equilibrium.

6. What do we mean by the terms "monetary policy" and "fiscal policy"? Why are these policies sometimes called "stabilization policies"?

7. Assume the equilibrium real-output level is currently above the output level needed to generate full employment. What are the consequences, and what monetary and fiscal policies are called for to correct the situation?

8. Assume the government raises income tax rates sharply. Explain, using the aggregate demand-aggregate supply framework, what happens to the size of the gap between actual GNP and potential GNP.

9. Using the aggregate supply-aggregate demand framework, analyze the events of the 1970s that caused stagflation.

10. Explain what happens when aggregate demand is stimulated while rigid wage–price controls are in place.

11. Explain the dilemma in which those in charge of monetary and fiscal policies are placed when a major adverse supply shock occurs.

12. Utilizing the basic macroeconomic framework of this chapter, explain how it was possible for aggregate demand to increase significantly during 1983–1986 while the inflation rate continued to decline.

13. Analyze the rationale underlying *supply-side* economics. What supply-side policies were implemented in the 1980s? What policies, if any, were counterproductive? Explain.

SELECTED REFERENCES

Blinder, Alan S., *Economic Policy and the Great Stagflation* (New York: Academic Press, 1981). This work outlines the supply shocks of the 1970s.

Economic Report of the President (Washington, D.C., published annually). This annual report discusses contemporary macroeconomic events and conditions.

CHAPTER 9

MEASURING THE MACROECONOMY

In order to gauge the overall performance of the economy, we need measures of its aggregate output and income. In the absence of such measures, it would be impossible to ascertain, for example, the approximate level of income of the nation in 1990 relative to 1960 or some other year. It would also be impossible to judge the size or growth performance of the United States economy relative to Japan, Italy, or the Soviet Union.[1]

Businesses require valid measures of the economy's output performance as well as forecasts of expected performance in order to formulate crucial decisions regarding production, employment, inventories, and expenditures on new plant and equipment and on research and development.

Economists have a special need for reliable data on national output and income, and on the various elements contributing to output and income. To study the effects of macroeconomic policies and the influence of a myriad other events on national performance, reasonably accurate data on the overall economy's production and its major components are essential.

In the next several chapters, many new terms are introduced and new concepts developed. Your comprehension of macroeconomic principles is closely related to how well you master the new terms and concepts. Before turning to the nuts and bolts of measuring the nation's macroeconomy, let us sketch the nature of two essential categories of economic variables—stocks and flows.

Get your facts first, then you can distort them as you please.

—MARK TWAIN

---

[1]Even if each country has perfect data indicating the aggregate value of its output, it is difficult to compare the size of the various national economies because each country has its own currency. How many U.S. dollars are equivalent to one West German mark or one British pound? One is tempted to use the current exchange rate. Suppose the U.S.–British exchange rate is two dollars to the pound, with U.S. output measured at $5,000 billion per year and British output at £500 billion per year. Since one pound is twice as valuable as the dollar (via the exchange rate), one is tempted to state that the value of U.S. output is five times greater than the value of British output. However, such a calculation is subject to a wide margin of error because there is no assurance that the purchasing power of two dollars in the United States conforms to the purchasing power of one pound in England. Exchange rates often fail to accurately reflect differences in the domestic purchasing power of the two currencies.

ECONOMIC VARIABLES—STOCKS AND FLOWS

Most of the key variables in macroeconomics are *stock* variables or *flow* variables. A **stock variable** is one that is measured as an amount *at a given point of time.* Hence, one might state that on January 1, 1990, the U.S. population consisted of a stock of 250 million people. A lake is a stock of water; a shoe store's inventories consist of a stock of shoes or their dollar value. The U.S. capital stock consists of all its capital goods—plants, equipment, structures—at a given point of time. The U.S. money stock (the total of checking accounts and currency in the country, known as M-1) amounted to $796 billion on April 10, 1989.

Net worth or wealth is a stock variable because it is derived by subtracting the value of the stock of liabilities (debts) from the value of the stock of assets. If your family currently has total assets (home, cars, furniture, savings) of $100,000 and total liabilities (mortgage, consumer loans) of $60,000, your family's net worth is currently $40,000. The magnitude of your family's net worth changes every month as the value of assets and liabilities fluctuates, and as the monthly flow of saving (dissaving) adds to (subtracts from) family wealth.

Flow variables are measured as rates *per unit of time.* Hence, investment spending is expressed as the rate of spending on new plant and equipment per year. Population growth is the rate of change of the stock of population—the annual flow of births and net immigration minus deaths in the nation. Exports are the annual flow of products sold abroad. Expenditures are a flow of purchases per year. Family income is a flow of earnings expressed as a monthly rate or annual rate.

In economics, as in nature, stocks and flows interact and influence each other. Rainfall and the rate of evaporation (flows) influence the stock of water in a lake. Likewise, the flow of investment spending influences the nation's stock of capital. The stock of money in the economy influences the flow of expenditures on goods and services. Your family's stock of wealth or net worth influences its annual flow of expenditures. The nation's *birthrate* (flow) influences the population (stock), and the size of the population influences the flow of births as well as the birthrate. For example, because of China's enormous population, the government has imposed rigid sanctions limiting the number of children each woman is allowed to bear.

Whenever you come across a new variable or new concept in economics, it is an excellent idea to instinctively ask yourself: Is this a flow variable? A stock variable? Neither one? If you do this and also add the new terms to your list of economics terms (in your notebook), you will be a step ahead of the game!

NATIONAL INCOME ACCOUNTING

National income accounting is the study of the procedures for measuring the aggregate output and income of a nation, together with the components of this output and income. It is concerned with such *flow* variables as gross national product (GNP), investment, government purchases, net exports, wages and salaries, and profits. Although very crude attempts to measure the national output of England

National Income Accounting
The set of rules and procedures used to measure the total flow of output produced by a nation, together with the income generated by this production.

were initiated some 300 years ago, only in the post-World War II era have economists and international organizations implemented relatively serious attempts to systematically measure an economy's total output together with its components.

The acknowledged pioneer in the development of national income accounting is Simon Kuznets, recipient of the 1971 Nobel Prize in Economics. Kuznets developed many of the concepts for measuring the macroeconomy that have been used by industrial nations in the past 50 years. In 1984, British economist Sir Richard Stone was awarded the Nobel prize for his leadership in a United Nations program in which standardized procedures for national income accounting were developed and instituted. Today, more than 100 nations utilize these standardized procedures.

Gross National Product (GNP)
The aggregate money value of all final goods and services produced by the economy in a given period, typically one year.

In this chapter we sketch the elements of national income accounting and examine alternative methods of estimating **gross national product (GNP)**—the dollar value of a nation's production of final goods and services in a given year. GNP is the most popular measure of a nation's annual output; per capita GNP—that is, GNP divided by the population—is a commonly used indicator of the standard of living of the people of a nation. We survey the components of GNP and discuss the corrections that must be made to reported GNP in order to assess the changes in a nation's material progress over time. We also explore the shortcomings of GNP as a measure of the well being of a nation and discuss an experimental alternative measure.

GNP AND THE CIRCULAR FLOW OF INCOME

To understand the basic relationships among the flows of output, income, and expenditures in the macroeconomy, consider first a simplified economy with no government sector and no foreign trade. In other words, assume initially there are no taxes, there is no government spending, and the nation is totally isolated from all other nations. Figure 9-1 indicates the flow of income and output in such an idealized economy.

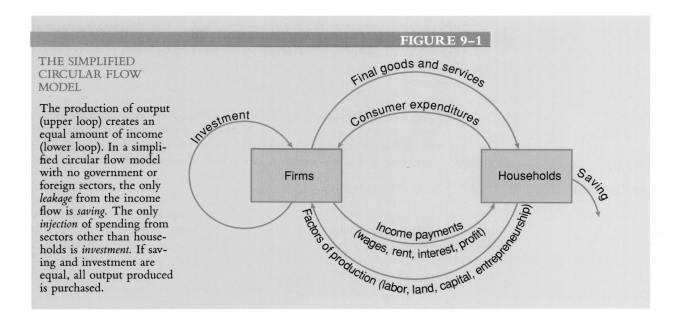

FIGURE 9–1

THE SIMPLIFIED CIRCULAR FLOW MODEL

The production of output (upper loop) creates an equal amount of income (lower loop). In a simplified circular flow model with no government or foreign sectors, the only *leakage* from the income flow is *saving*. The only *injection* of spending from sectors other than households is *investment*. If saving and investment are equal, all output produced is purchased.

In this scheme we lump all producing units into the category "Firms" and the spending units into the category "Households." Most members of society play a dual role in this system. In their role as "Firms," they are employed, produce goods and services, and earn income. In their role as "Households," they spend the bulk of their incomes on the same goods and services they collectively produce at the "Firms."

Firms purchase inputs in the form of labor, land, capital, and entrepreneurship (entrepreneurs)—known as *factors of production*—from the households, paying out wages, rent, interest, and profits in return. The firms then utilize these resources, along with other materials and intermediate goods they purchase from each other, to produce final goods and services. **Intermediate goods** and services are those used in the production of other goods and services. For example, leather is an intermediate good used in the production of shoes and baseball gloves. Steel is an intermediate good used in the production of buildings and cars. These final goods and services (gross national product) are then sold back to the households via the top loop of Figure 9-1.

A fundamental lesson of the **circular flow model** is that the production by firms of a certain value of goods and services (upper loop) creates a precisely equivalent flow of income for the factors of production (lower loop). Every dollar of output produced creates one dollar of income earned by the factors of production.

Another fundamental lesson of the circular flow model is that the income earned by the households (lower loop) provides the means by which households finance the purchases of the goods and services (upper loop) they collectively produce by supplying the factors of production to the firms.

Any event that causes a reduction in the production of goods and services produces an equivalent reduction of the income of the populace. Any factor that causes a reduction of expenditures leads to a reduction of output and income. Figure 9-1 illustrates the interdependence between production decisions and expenditure decisions in a market economy.

The model depicted in Figure 9-1 ignores the government sector and foreign trade. There are no taxes, government services, exports or imports. If the only goods produced were **consumer goods** and if the households spent their entire income on these consumer items, the upper flow of expenditures would always be precisely equal to the upper flow of output (GNP). Since the production of GNP always produces an equivalent flow of income, a zero-saving society would return 100 percent of its income to the spending stream. Whatever output firms collectively produce would always be sold to the households. There would never be any problems associated with insufficient or excessive spending relative to the volume of goods and services available.

However, even in the context of the simplified circular flow model of Figure 9-1, not all final output is in the form of consumer goods. A portion of output consists of **investment goods**—tools and machines that firms produce to facilitate production of goods and services. Also, households save part of their income. Therefore, not all the income paid to the households (lower loop) is returned to the spending stream by households (upper loop). Some of the income *leaks* from the circular flow in the form of saving. On the other hand, not all the expenditures of this simple model originate in the household sector. Firms purchase some of the final goods and services they produce; these are the investment goods noted in Figure 9-1.

In this two-sector model (consumption goods and investment goods), there is no assurance that output and expenditures will always balance. When—given current levels of output—the withdrawal of funds by households from the flow of spending (saving) exceeds the injection of spending on final goods by firms (investment), firms will not sell all their current output. The nation's inventories rise, signaling firms to cut the level of output and to lay off workers. When—given current levels of output—investment spending added to the expenditure flow by firms exceeds the withdrawal from the flow in the form of saving, firms will sell more than their current output. In this case inventories decline, signaling firms to expand production and employment. In this simple model *and in the real world,* fluctuations in saving and investment decisions result in fluctuations in national output and employment.

APPROACHES TO MEASURING GNP

In the simplified circular flow model illustrated in Figure 9-1, we assumed there was no government or foreign sector. We now move to a more realistic depiction, in which we acknowledge the existence of government spending and taxes, together with exports and imports. This more realistic circular flow model is presented in Figure 9-2.

Firms produce output (GNP), thereby creating an equal amount of income paid out to households in the process. There are now three *leakages* from this income stream that limit the amount of household spending on GNP. First, part of the income is saved. Second, part of it is taxed away. Third, part of the income is spent on imported goods. These three *leakages* from the flow signal that perhaps only

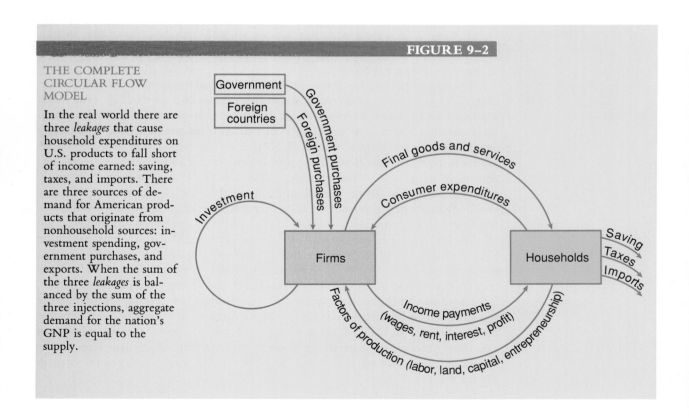

FIGURE 9–2

THE COMPLETE CIRCULAR FLOW MODEL

In the real world there are three *leakages* that cause household expenditures on U.S. products to fall short of income earned: saving, taxes, and imports. There are three sources of demand for American products that originate from nonhousehold sources: investment spending, government purchases, and exports. When the sum of the three *leakages* is balanced by the sum of the three injections, aggregate demand for the nation's GNP is equal to the supply.

two-thirds of the income generated in the production of GNP is returned to the stream by households. On the other hand, there are three sources of demand for American output coming from sources other than American households. Firms purchase part of the output in the form of new plants and equipment (investment). The government (federal, state, local) purchases part of it. And foreigners purchase part (exports). All output is sold when the three leakages from the income flow (saving, taxes, imports) are precisely balanced by the three nonhousehold sources of spending (investment, government purchases, exports).

There are two basic approaches to measuring a nation's output of goods and services (GNP): the **flow-of-output approach** (measuring the top loop of Figure 9-2) and the **flow-of-income approach** (measuring the bottom loop). Barring measurement error, the two approaches yield identical results. This follows from the previously mentioned principle that every dollar of output produced creates one dollar of income earned.

Flow-of-Output Approach

The flow-of-output approach seeks to sum the output of all newly produced final goods and services in a given year. **Final goods and services** are those not used in the production of other goods and services. In computing GNP, sales of new autos and new houses are included, but the steel sold to the automaker and to the building contractor are *not* included. To do so would mean *double counting* (i.e., counting the production of steel once as it rolls out of the steel mill and once again as it becomes part of the value of the auto or house).

Since the objective is to measure output in the *current* year, transactions involving used items are not counted. Hence, purchases of used houses or used cars have no impact on GNP. Similarly, sales of such assets as land, stocks, and bonds are not included because they do not represent current production.

In the flow-of-output approach to GNP accounting, four categories of goods and services are included: consumption expenditures (*C*), investment spending (*I*), government purchases (*G*), and net exports or exports minus imports ($X - M$). The various subcategories of these major components, along with their 1988 magnitudes, are given in Table 9-1(page 190). Consumption is the largest expenditure category, constituting two-thirds of the nation's GNP. The second largest category is government purchases of goods and services (20 percent of GNP), followed closely by gross private domestic investment (16 percent of GNP). Typically, exports and imports are approximately equal in size, thereby cancelling each other's impact on GNP. In the late 1980s, however, the U.S. trade deficit implied that net exports contributed negatively to our GNP—we purchased more of foreign nations' GNP than they did of ours. We turn now to a more detailed look at each component of GNP.

Consumption Expenditures (*C*)
Household expenditures on all goods and services except housing; consists of household expenditures on durable goods, nondurables, and services.

Consumption (C)   Consumption—variously known as "consumer expenditures" and "personal consumption expenditures"—includes such durable goods as automobiles, refrigerators, and VCRs; such nondurables as food, clothing, and tennis balls; and such services as medical care, haircuts, and educational expenditures. Consumer services are both the largest and fastest growing component of personal consumption expenditures. This is due to the fact that in an affluent nation such as the United States, most individuals have satisfied their rudimentary needs for basic food, shelter, and clothing. As income rises, an increasing portion of expenditures tends to be

TABLE 9-1

GROSS NATIONAL PRODUCT VIA SUM OF OUTPUT PRODUCED, 1988 ($ billions)

		Amount	% of GNP
I	*Consumption*	$3227	(66)
	Durable goods	451	
	Nondurable goods	1047	
	Services	1729	
II	*Gross private domestic investment*	$ 766	(16)
	Fixed investment		
	Nonresidential structures	143	
	Producers' durable equipment	345	
	Residential structures	230	
	Change in inventories	48	
III	*Government purchases of goods and services*	964	(20)
	Federal	380	
	State and local	584	
IV	*Net exports of goods and services*	−$ 94	*(−2)*
	Exports	520	
	Imports	614	
	Gross National Product =	$4863	(100)

Source: Department of Commerce, *Survey of Current Business,* 1989.

allocated to such consumer services as entertainment, travel, health services, and education.[2]

Consumer goods and services are not used to produce other goods and services but are directly used by households either immediately (food, entertainment) or gradually (clothing, ballpoint pens). Consumption spending is closely linked to national **disposable income**—household income available after taxes.

Gross Private Domestic Investment (I)   In an earlier chapter we defined investment as expenditures on capital goods—goods utilized to produce other goods and services. Investment involves expenditures that replace or add to the nation's stock of capital. **Gross investment** refers to *total* expenditures on investment goods, including those that replace worn out or obsolete machinery and other capital. **Net investment** refers to the *net addition* to the nation's total stock of capital in a given period of time.

Gross Investment (*I*)
The total value of all investment goods produced in the economy during a specific time period, normally one year.

Net Investment
The net addition to the nation's capital stock in a given period; gross investment minus depreciation.

---

[2]Economists use the concept of *income elasticity of demand* to measure the responsiveness of demand for various goods and services to a change in income. Income elasticity of demand is the percentage change in purchases of a product divided by the percentage change in income that initiated the change in purchases. A 10-percent increase in income may result in a 15-percent increase in expenditures on travel but only a 2-percent increase in spending on food. In this case the income elasticity of demand for travel and food are 1.5 and 0.2, respectively. In general, income elasticity of demand for consumer services is higher than for other components of consumer expenditures.

The difference between gross investment and net investment is known as depreciation, capital consumption, or replacement investment. In any given year, a large portion of gross investment involves replacing worn out and obsolete capital goods. Net investment is nearly always positive (gross investment > depreciation) in the United States. However, on rare occasions gross investment is insufficient to offset depreciation, the total capital stock declines, and net investment is negative. An example of this rarity occurred in 1933. Table 9-2 reflects the magnitude of the components of gross and net investment in 1929 and in several subsequent years. As indicated in Table 9-1, gross investment may be divided into fixed investment and inventory investment. *Fixed investment* includes spending on nonresidential structures, producers' durable equipment, and residential structures. (The relative magnitudes of these components for 1988 are shown in Table 9-1.)

The classification of new homes as investment rather than consumption is one of many rather arbitrary close calls that must be made in national income accounting. A home is a very long-lived asset that provides a flow of benefits to its occupants. However, the same could be said of a new set of encyclopedias or a new stereo receiver, both of which are classified as consumer goods in the national income accounts.

Inventory investment, which can be either positive or negative, is defined as the net change in national aggregate business inventories in a given year. The change in inventories serves as a balancing item in the national income accounts. GNP is intended to measure *output,* but does so by summing final *sales,* which are more accessible. When inventories rise in a given year, output necessarily exceeds sales; tallying up sales results in an understatement of output unless we add the increase in inventories to total sales. When inventories fall in a given year, the implication is that sales exceed output. Adding the (negative) change in inventories to sales provides an accurate measure of current output or GNP.

Government Purchases of Goods and Services (G)   Our measure of GNP must come to grips with the huge amount of goods and services the nation *collectively* provides via government.

Government output, unlike the other components of GNP, is not sold in private markets. Therefore, national income accountants are faced with a conceptual problem in placing a dollar value on government output. What is the value of the annual services provided by upgrading the interstate highway system? The services provided by a public high school algebra teacher? A highway patrolman? The

TABLE 9-2

GROSS AND NET INVESTMENT EXPENDITURES FOR SELECTED YEARS ($ billions)

Component of investment	1929	1933	1965	1988
Producers' durable equipment	$ 5.6	$ 1.5	$46.4	$334.8
New construction	8.9	1.5	57.2	372.7
Change in inventories	1.7	− 1.6	9.9	48.6
Gross private domestic investments	16.2	1.4	113.5	766.1
Depreciation	7.9	7.0	56.0	506.4
Net private domestic investment	8.3	− 5.6	57.5	259.7

accountants simply assume that the value of government goods and services is measured by their cost (e.g., the salary of the teacher or the expenditures on the interstate highways).

Government Purchases (G)
The value of goods and services purchased by all levels of government—federal, state, and local—in a given period; total government expenditures minus government transfer payments.

Government Transfer Payments
Expenditures by government for which no goods or services are concurrently received by the government.

The most straightforward way to estimate **government purchases** is to add the total expenditures of all three levels of government (federal, state, local) on goods and services and salaries of government employees. For example, the federal government spends on aircraft carriers, and on salaries of postal workers, the federal judiciary, and members of Congress. State governments spend on roads, bridges, and salaries of university football coaches and professors. Local governments spend on libraries, fire engines, and salaries for police officers and high school teachers.

It is important to understand that government purchases as measured in the national income accounts are considerably less than total government spending. As indicated in Chapter 7, a sizable portion of government's budget is in the form of transfer payments, which are not included in the GNP computation. **Government transfer payments** are government payments for which no concurrent goods or services are rendered. Coupled with taxes, they rearrange purchasing power in the private sector of the economy. Examples of transfer payments include unemployment benefits, social security payments, interest on the national debt, subsidies to agriculture, and veterans benefits. These payments do not represent expenditures for goods and services, which is what GNP attempts to measure. Adding transfer payments to GNP computation would make the national income accounts guilty of double counting, since most of the income received by recipients of transfer payments shows up in purchases of consumer goods.

A significant part of government purchases that shows up in GNP is investment expenditures. Federal spending on new airport safety equipment, state spending on new prison facilities or new university libraries, and local spending on new elementary schools all are forms of investment expenditures—spending on goods that increase the productivity of society and yield a long-lasting flow of benefits to the constituents of the nation. Since the national income accounts designate *investment* (gross private domestic investment) to include only *private* forms of investment spending, government investment expenditures are included with other forms of government purchases. If the federal government were to count separately its consumption and investment expenditures, total investment in the United States would appear higher.

Net Exports of Goods and Services (X − M)   If we attempt to tally American GNP by summing consumption, investment, and government expenditures, we would be off the mark. GNP is a measure of *output* produced in this country, and a significant amount of our *purchases* are produced abroad (Japanese automobiles, French wine). We must subtract such expenditures on imports to arrive at domestic output (GNP). On the other hand, some of what we produce is sold beyond our borders (exports), and the value of these transactions must be added to domestic sales (C, I, G). This reasoning indicates that we should add net exports (X − M) to C, I, and G in order to arrive at U.S. GNP.

Table 9-1 indicates that for 1988 net exports amounted to a negative $94 billion, or about 2 percent of our GNP. That is, the total flow of U.S. purchases exceeded production of GNP by $94 billion. By running substantial trade deficits in the late 1980s, we have in a sense been living *beyond our means,* enjoying more goods and services each year than we produce domestically, and financing the difference (the trade deficit) by borrowing from other nations. Prior to the 1980s, the United

States was a persistent net exporter, selling more goods and services to the rest of the world than we purchased from them. In those years our total output of GNP exceeded the sum of consumption, investment, and government purchases.

Behavior of the Four Shares of GNP ($C, I, G, X - M$)

Figure 9-3 illustrates the behavior since the 1940s of each of the four shares of GNP ($C, I, G, X - M$) expressed as a percentage of the total GNP. One is struck by the relatively high degree of stability of each of the four shares.[3] For example,

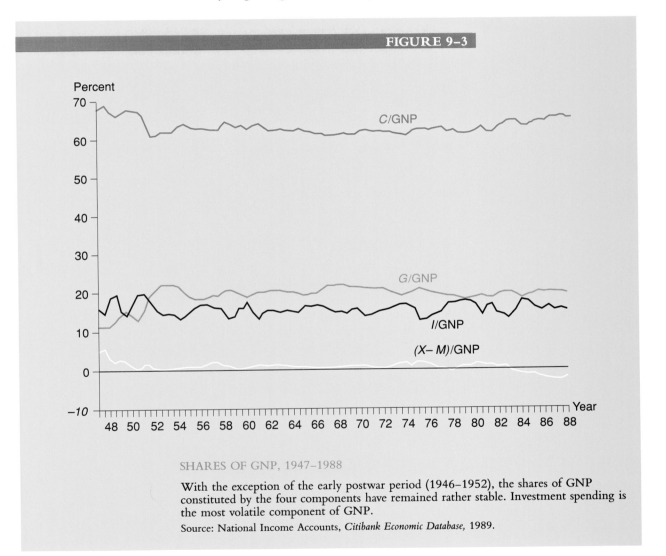

FIGURE 9–3

SHARES OF GNP, 1947–1988

With the exception of the early postwar period (1946–1952), the shares of GNP constituted by the four components have remained rather stable. Investment spending is the most volatile component of GNP.

Source: National Income Accounts, *Citibank Economic Database*, 1989.

---

[3]Note in Figure 9-3 that much of the instability in these ratios occurred in the first five years depicted (1947–1952). World War II had recently ended (1945). During that war many consumer goods were not available. Therefore, immediately after the war a temporary surge of spending on such items as refrigerators and washing machines occurred. By 1951 or so, this splurge was over. Similarly, the abnormally large net export surplus in the early postwar years resulted from a surge of American supplies ordered by war-ravaged European nations.

consumption has hovered round 65 percent of GNP and government purchases around 20 percent of GNP.[4] Investment expenditures exhibit the most short-range variability of the components, but the long-term trend in the ratio of the share of investment to GNP has been flat. Note that the U.S. trade balance has been negative since 1983. This swing from a positive to a negative trade balance reversed a long history of American trade surpluses.

Flow-of-Income Approach

Concerning Figure 9-2, we stated that the production by firms of any given magnitude of GNP (top loop) creates a precisely equivalent flow of income (bottom loop). Therefore, another way to tally the nation's GNP is to sum all the incomes earned in the economy. Consider the income earned in the production of a new Buick that sells for $20,000. Assume the following incomes are generated:

Wages of General Motors' employees	$10,000
Interest paid to GM bondholders	1,000
Rent paid on buildings	1,000
Profits of GM stockholders	2,000

However, this totals only $14,000. The remaining $6000 consists of materials that General Motors purchased from its suppliers (e.g., glass, steel, tires, engines, and so on). These materials are intermediate goods.

General Motors, in purchasing $6000 of materials and fashioning them into a final good worth $20,000, has contributed $14,000 of value to the product. This is known as **value added** —the difference between the sales price of a good and the cost of intermediate goods used to produce it.

Tracing this $6000 back to the producers of these materials, we find that the $6000 is accounted for by wages, interest, rent, profits *and* the purchases of materials from other firms.

The following accounting identity applies to each firm in the U.S. economy:

$$\text{revenues from sales} = \begin{array}{c} \text{wages paid} \\ + \\ \text{interest paid} \\ + \\ \text{rent paid} \\ + \\ \text{profits earned} \\ + \\ \text{purchases from other firms} \end{array}$$

This accounting identity follows from the definition of profits as a residual item—sales revenues minus all costs of production. If we apply this identity to all firms in the nation and subtract "purchases from other firms" from both sides of the equation, we obtain

---

[4] How does one square this little-known fact with the well-known fact that government budgets have outpaced GNP? The answer lies in the fact that government transfer payments, which are not included in GNP or in our G of Figure 9-3, have been the source of the growth of government budgets relative to GNP. Government purchases of goods and services have *not* grown faster than GNP since the early 1950s.

$$\text{revenues from sales} \atop \text{minus} \atop \text{purchases from other firms} \quad = \quad {\text{wages paid} \atop +} \atop {\text{interest paid} \atop +} \atop {\text{rent paid} \atop +} \atop \text{profit earned}$$

The left-hand side of the equation is total sales minus sales of intermediate goods. For the aggregate economy, this is equivalent to the sum of *values added* and also is the definition of GNP. Hence, the accounting identity for the entire U.S. economy is

$$\text{GNP = wages + interest + rent + profits}$$

which provides accountants a second method for computing GNP.

Table 9-3 provides the steps involved in calculating GNP via the flow-of-income approach. The components are discussed in turn.

Compensation of Employees This item, which constitutes about 60 percent of GNP, includes wages and salaries paid by firms and government to employees. It also includes such fringe benefits paid by employers as pension contributions, health insurance, and social security contributions. Since these supplementary payments are part of the cost to firms of employing labor, they are treated as wage and salary payments.

Net Interest This item includes interest payments paid by businesses to lenders. When you purchase a bond issued by a utility company, the interest payments you

TABLE 9-3

GROSS NATIONAL PRODUCT VIA SUM OF INCOME GENERATED, 1988

Item	Amount ($ billions)
Compensation of employees	$2,905.2
+	
Net interest	391.9
+	
Rental income	19.5
+	
Proprietor's income	324.7
+	
Corporate profits	323.8
equals	
National income (NI)	3,965.1
+	
Indirect business taxes and miscellaneous items	391.7
equals	
Net national product (NNP)	4,356.8
+	
Depreciation	506.3
equals	
Gross National Product (GNP)	$4,863.1

Source: Department of Commerce, *Survey of Current Business,* 1989.

receive are included. Interest paid by government is a government transfer payment, and is not included.

Rental Income   This item is the payment to property owners for the use of their resources. For example, house and apartment rents received by landlords are included.

Proprietor's Income   Proprietor's income consists of net income earned by businesses that are not incorporated—the net income of partnerships and proprietorships.

Corporate Profits   This item refers to the net income of corporations. It can be divided into three components: dividends paid to stockholders, retained earnings, and corporate income taxes.

All five items—compensation of employees, net interest, rental income, proprietor's income, corporate profits—are forms of income. Do these items add up to GNP? Unfortunately, no—economic life is not quite so simple. Two nonincome items must be added to the five forms of income in order to arrive at GNP: depreciation and indirect business taxes.

Depreciation
The value of the nation's capital equipment that is used up in a given period, normally one year; indicates how much investment is needed to keep the nation's capital stock intact.

Depreciation   Most machines and equipment survive well beyond the accounting period in which they are purchased. If all the cost of buying machines and equipment is allocated to the year in which a machine is purchased, profits for that period are severely understated. And profits of future years would be overstated. To avoid this, firms allocate the cost of equipment over a period of several years. The annual estimate of the amount of capital used up or consumed in each year is known as **depreciation**. Depreciation is an accounting mechanism that provides a more stable and accurate statement of profits in a given year. Table 9-3 reflects that in 1988 a huge charge of $506 billion was made against GNP for depreciation. This may be regarded as a portion of business receipts not available to pay out as income.

Indirect Business Taxes   The government imposes taxes on certain products, which firms treat as costs of production and add to the prices of their products. These **indirect business taxes** include license fees, customs duties, federal excise taxes, business property taxes, and sales taxes. This flow of indirect taxes does not create income for the nation, and must therefore be added to the five forms of income, along with depreciation, in order to arrive at GNP.

OTHER NATIONAL ACCOUNTS

In addition to GNP, there are several other measures of the nation's output and income that are essential to our study of macroeconomics. The output and income measures that separate GNP and disposable income—the income available to households after taxes—are briefly outlined.

Net National Product (NNP)
Gross national product minus a depreciation allowance for the value of capital goods wearing out during the period.

Net National Product (NNP)   Although gross national product (GNP) is predominately utilized to indicate the size of a nation's economy, **net national product (NNP)** is actually a better measure. GNP includes the production of output required to replace worn out equipment. If we subtract this depreciation or replacement investment from GNP, we obtain a measure of the net output available to society. If GNP in 1990 is $5500 billion and if $500 billion of that output represents production of capital goods to replace those worn out, the actual amount of new goods and services available is $5000 billion. This concept—gross national product minus depreciation or capital consumption—is known as net national product (NNP). NNP represents the value of new goods and services available to an economy in a given year.

If NNP is conceptually a more appropriate measure of an economy's performance, why is GNP the more popular concept? The answer lies in the difficulty in estimating depreciation or capital consumption. It is much easier to compute GNP than NNP. The two concepts are closely related, with NNP typically amounting to 90 percent of GNP.

National Income (NY)
The aggregate income received by the resource owners of land, labor, capital, and entrepreneurship; equal to GNP minus the sum of depreciation and indirect business taxes.

National Income (NY) When computing GNP and NNP, the prices paid by buyers of final goods and services are used. Encompassed in these prices are a variety of indirect taxes (as noted earlier). For example, a new automobile costing $15,000 may include in its price a $300 federal excise tax and a $600 state sales tax. These taxes are known as indirect taxes because they are not levied directly on incomes. We pay them indirectly by purchasing products on which such taxes are levied. These taxes produce revenues for governments but do not generate income for individuals. If we deduct these indirect taxes from NNP, we obtain the total payment of income to the factors of production—land, labor, capital, entrepreneurs. These payments are known as **national income (NY)**.

Personal Income (PY) A portion of national income is not received as income by persons. For example, only part of corporate profits are paid out (as dividends) to persons; some are paid to the U.S. Treasury (via corporation income tax), some are retained by the firm. Also, corporations pay contributions to the social security system for their workers. On the other hand, recall that government transfer payments are not included in GNP. However, they do lead to personal income. Given these considerations, to get from national income (NY) to **personal income** (PY) we subtract retained corporate profits, corporate income taxes, and social insurance contributions made by firms, and add government transfer payments.

Personal Disposable Income (Y_d)
Income in the hands of individuals after deducting income taxes; income available to households to spend and save.

Personal Disposable Income (Y_d) Not all of personal income is available to households for spending and saving. Individuals face federal, state, and sometimes local income taxes. Deducting these items from personal income yields **personal disposable income (Y_d)**—personal income available after income taxes. This is commonly referred to simply as *disposable income.*

Figure 9-4 (page 198) illustrates the relationship among the five alternative measures of the nation's income. Among these measures, the two that we frequently single out in macroeconomic models are gross national product and disposable income.

MEASURING GNP IN REAL TERMS

If you are the typical college student of 18–22 years of age, the U.S. gross national product has more than quadrupled during your lifetime. Table 9-4 (page 199) indicates that between 1970 and 1988, **nominal GNP** increased from a little more than $1 trillion ($1000 billion) to around $4.8 trillion. However, this by no means indicates that the real output and real income of the nation increased by a similar factor. When the prices of goods and services double over a period of years, nominal GNP doubles even when the actual amount of goods and services produced and sold

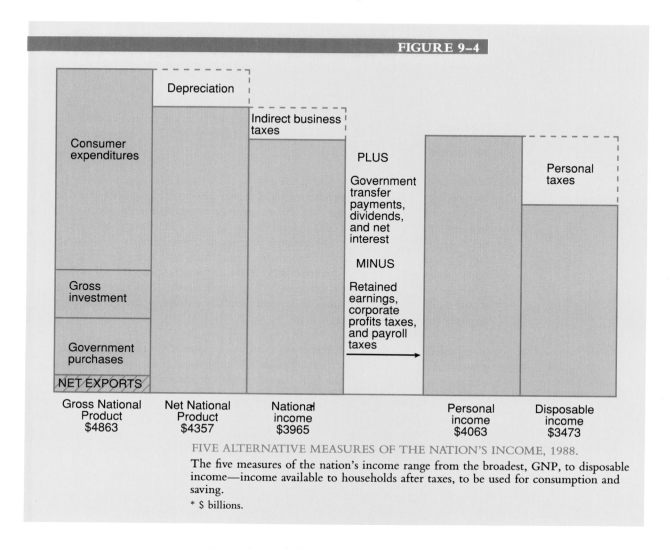

FIGURE 9–4

FIVE ALTERNATIVE MEASURES OF THE NATION'S INCOME, 1988.
The five measures of the nation's income range from the broadest, GNP, to disposable income—income available to households after taxes, to be used for consumption and saving.
* $ billions.

remains unchanged. Nominal GNP in any given year is reported in prices prevailing in that year. Since the price level typically rises over time, nominal GNP increases more rapidly than real GNP. This is illustrated in Figure 9-5, (page 200) which shows the behavior of nominal and real GNP since 1947.

Table 9-4 shows that while nominal GNP increased by more than 300 percent during 1970–1988, real GNP increased by approximately 60 percent. The price level increased by approximately 200 percent, i.e., it roughly tripled. Thus, in this particular period, most of the reported increase in GNP was merely due to higher prices, not to greater real output of goods and services.

To determine what actually happened to real output of goods and services over a period of years, we must adjust the nominal GNP to compensate for changes in the price level. Constructed for this purpose, the **GNP deflator,** a price index, is a weighted average of the prices of all final goods and services that enter into GNP.[6]

GNP Deflator
A price index constructed by taking a weighted average of prices of all goods and services that enter into the nation's gross national product; it reveals the change since the base year in the cost of purchasing the items that constitute the nation's GNP.

---

[5]By *a weighted average* we mean that all the prices that enter into the GNP deflator are not counted equally in calculating the index. If consumers spend 10 times as much on hamburger as they spend on butter, the price of hamburger is given 10 times the importance (*weight*) as the price of butter.

	TABLE 9-4		
	NOMINAL GNP, REAL GNP, AND THE GNP DEFLATOR, 1929 AND 1970–1988 ($ billions)		
Year	**Nominal GNP**	**GNP Deflator**	**Real GNP**
1929	103.9	14.6	709.6
. . .	. . .	. . .	. . .
. . .	. . .	. . .	. . .
. . .	. . .	. . .	. . .
1970	1015.5	42.0	2416.2
1971	1102.7	44.4	2484.8
1972	1212.8	46.5	2608.5
1973	1359.3	49.5	2744.1
1974	1472.8	54.0	2729.3
1975	1598.4	59.3	2695.0
1976	1782.8	63.1	2826.7
1977	1990.7	67.3	2958.7
1978	2249.7	72.2	3115.2
1979	2508.2	78.6	3192.4
1980	2732.0	85.7	3187.1
1981	3052.6	94.0	3248.8
1982	3166.0	100.0	3166.0
1983	3405.7	103.9	3279.1
1984	3772.2	107.7	3501.4
1985	4010.3	111.2	3607.5
1986	4235.0	114.1	3711.6
1987	4526.7	117.7	3847.0
1988	4863.1	121.7	3995.0

Source: Data from *Citibank Economic Database,* 1989.

The index is set relative to the prices that existed in a base year, when its starting value is taken as 100. Currently the GNP deflator is based on the reference year 1982 = 100.[6] If, in the current year, the GNP deflator is 135, the implication is that the average price of goods and services in the nation's GNP has risen 35 percent since 1982. 1989 real GNP is calculated using the following expression:

$$1989 \text{ real GNP} = \frac{1989 \text{ nominal GNP}}{\text{GNP deflator for } 1989} \times 100$$

Real GNP is sometimes called GNP in "constant" dollars as opposed to GNP in "current" dollars (nominal GNP).

YOUR TURN   Assume the (nominal) GNP for 1990 is $5580 billion and the GNP deflator is 138 (1982 = 100). Calculate real GNP for 1990.

LIMITATIONS OF GNP ACCOUNTING

Economists who work with macroeconomic data make no pretense that GNP provides an accurate indicator of the overall well-being of American society. There is no claim that GNP, income, or wealth reflects in any way a nation's collective

---

[6]Note in Figure 9-5 that nominal and real GNP are equal in 1982. This indicates that 1982 is the base year.

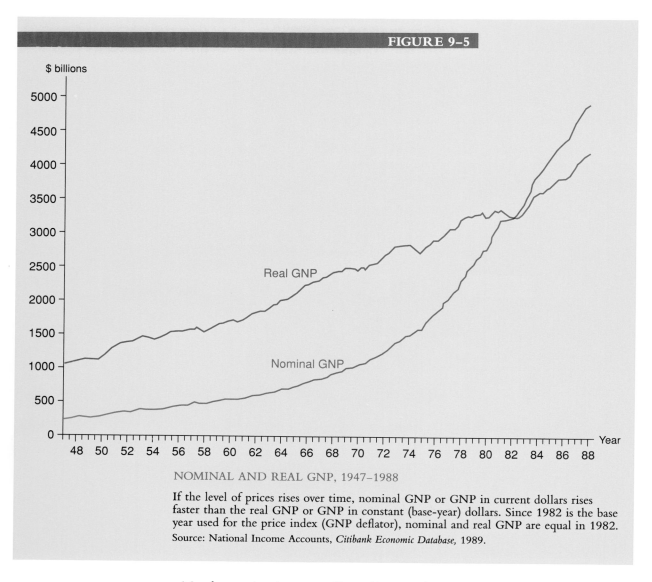

FIGURE 9–5

NOMINAL AND REAL GNP, 1947–1988

If the level of prices rises over time, nominal GNP or GNP in current dollars rises faster than the real GNP or GNP in constant (base-year) dollars. Since 1982 is the base year used for the price index (GNP deflator), nominal and real GNP are equal in 1982. Source: National Income Accounts, *Citibank Economic Database,* 1989.

spiritual, emotional, or overall condition. What GNP attempts to measure is the state of the nation's material well-being. However, even this narrower economic measure of the nation's pulse is very difficult to capture.

Why GNP Is a Flawed Measure of Actual Output

There are two major reasons why GNP is an imperfect measure of the nation's output and income.

Neglect of Nonmarket Activity   The valuable services of the spouse who chauffeurs the children, cleans the home, prepares the meals, and so on, is *not* included in the nation's GNP. If the spouse tires of this role, take a "real" job, and hires someone to perform the domestic services, not only is his or her income included in GNP, but so is the income paid to the hired domestic help. If two spouses are bored cleaning their own homes and hire each other to clean each other's home at $5000 apiece annually, the nation's GNP rises $10,000 per year! Clearly this points to a problem in national income accounting—in general, *only market transactions are counted.* If no dollars are actually paid out, the activity is not included in GNP.

If you repair your own plumbing, rake your own leaves, construct an addition to your home by the sweat of your brow, this productive activity is neglected in national income accounting. Because do-it-yourself activities are not counted, the measured GNP tends to understate the nation's true output. The only nonmarket activities included in GNP are the estimated value of food produced and consumed on the farm, the estimated fair market rental value of homes occupied by owners, and the estimated value of goods and services produced by government.

Since nations differ radically in the proportion of total economic activity conducted in the marketplace, official GNP data distort the true differences in output, income, and living standards among nations. Underdeveloped nations in Africa, for example, rely to a much lesser extent on organized markets than do industrialized nations. A larger portion of life's necessities are obtained via barter and family production (food, clothing) in underdeveloped nations, and therefore do not show up in GNP. The pitifully low per-capita incomes reported for such nations cannot meaningfully be compared to the reported figures for the United States. This is not to deny the enormous difference that exists between per-capita income in Nigeria and the United States, but keep in mind that the reported data overstate the true difference (more on this in Chapter 38).

The Underground Economy   Economists are convinced that a large portion of output of final goods and services is conducted in the "subterranean economy," and therefore never shows up in the GNP figures. Part of this output consists of such illegal activities as the cocaine trade, prostitution, and loan-sharking. For obvious reasons such transactions go unreported. Perhaps an even larger portion of the **underground economy** emanates from unreported legal activity, unreported so that income may be hidden from the Internal Revenue Service. Hence, some waiters and cab drivers fail to report all income earned. Some merchants do not enter all sales into the cash register. And some plumbers have been known to quote two prices for their services—$40/hour if you pay by check, $35/hour if you pay in cash.

Over the years a gradual increase in marginal tax rates faced by Americans increased the incentive to hide income (these rates were reduced in the 1980s). Some economists believe the steady increase in the amount of currency relative to checking accounts since 1960 indicates a relative growth of the underground economy.[7] The size of this underground economy is variously estimated at 5–20 percent of GNP. There seems to be disagreement over the issues of how fast the underground economy is growing and how fast the American ethic of voluntary income-tax compliance is eroding. But there is agreement that measured GNP would be at least $250 billion greater than the currently stated figure if all output of final goods and services were reported.

Why GNP Is a Flawed Measure of Well-Being

We have indicated that GNP understates actual output of the United States because it fails to include output not sold in markets and omits output sold in the

---

[7]In 1960 the ratio of currency to checking accounts in banks was about 25 percent. The ratio has steadily increased to about 40 percent today.

underground economy. Several additional considerations suggest that GNP is a poor measure of the *well-being* or welfare of the nation. Even if GNP were corrected to measure output accurately, it would be a flawed *measure of economic welfare.*

Neglect of Leisure Time   As citizens of a nation become wealthier, they often increase their leisure time; they opt for more *psychic income* from recreation, entertainment, and travel. For a family earning $60,000 annually, an extra thousand dollars of income may appear less inviting than a week in the mountains. As evidence of this, the length of the average American workweek has gradually declined from more than 50 hours in 1900 to around 35 hours in 1990. Hence, measured GNP has grown more slowly than would have been the case if we had maintained the 50-hour work ethic. Since the populace voluntarily opted for the additional leisure, we are clearly better off—but the increased well-being is not included in the GNP figures. This factor tends to make the growth of reported GNP understate the growth in well-being of the nation.

"Bads" as well as "Goods" are Counted in GNP   The 1986 Chernobyl nuclear disaster in the Soviet Union clearly made that nation worse off. Hundreds of people were immediately killed or incapacitated. The longevity of thousands more was threatened by extensive exposure to radiation. A considerable geographic area was rendered uninhabitable for generations. Yet the reported Soviet GNP was probably stimulated because of the accident, as major expenditures were required to clean up the area and to provide medical care and housing for those impaired by the accident.[8]

Similar analyses apply to such American natural disasters as the Chicago Fire of 1871, the San Francisco Earthquake of 1906, the Mount Saint Helens volcanic eruption of 1980, and numerous less-massive natural disasters. Wars are a powerful example of the principle. Clearly, World War II imposed great economic hardship on the nation's people as breadwinners were killed and wounded, income taxes were raised sharply, and production of such major durable goods as cars and refrigerators were suspended in order to devote massive resources to production of military goods. Yet American involvement in the war stimulated a major boost in reported GNP. Suppose, today, we could reach agreement with all nations to cut armaments production by 50 percent. Clearly we would be better off. The federal deficit would decline, taxes could be reduced, and we could enjoy more "goods" in place of the "bads" (bombs and missiles). Nevertheless, the reported GNP would decline temporarily.

Neglects Environmental Damages and Other Adverse Effects of Production   The output of the steel and chemical industries is counted in GNP in the form of final sales of cars and fertilizer. However, in producing steel and chemicals, *negative externalities* occur. Air and water in the vicinity of the steel and chemical plants may become contaminated. Since this pollution is undeniably detrimental to the country's well-being, its negative value should in principle be added to gross national product, thus reducing the reported GNP. However, no such correction is made, and therefore reported GNP overstates true GNP. Other similar shortcomings of reported GNP are commonplace. GNP counts output of services in the form of air

---

[8]Of course, the shut-down of the plant resulted in reduced output of electric power, no doubt temporarily offsetting some of the induced output created by the disaster. But part of the plant was reopened after a surprisingly brief shutdown.

transportation but not the *noise pollution* imposed upon residential areas surrounding airports, the market value of cigarettes produced but not the agony suffered by those who contract lung cancer, the value of liquor sold but not the enormous losses suffered by families of individuals killed by drunken drivers, the value of output produced in Los Angeles but not the inconveniences of urban congestion endured by those who reside there.

Correcting GNP—A Measure of Net Economic Welfare (NEW)

Professors William Nordhaus and James Tobin of Yale University have attempted to construct an improved measure of the nation's well-being that reflects the disenchantment with mere material goods and services. They have adjusted the reported GNP figures to deal with some of the shortcomings just discussed. For example, Nordhaus and Tobin add to the Commerce Department's GNP figures their estimated value of increased leisure time and of goods and services not transacted in formal markets. They deduct expenditures on bombs and missiles and the estimated value of the costs associated with commuting, urban congestion, and environmental degradation.

The result of their efforts is the measure of **Net Economic Welfare (NEW)**, which has increased more slowly over the past 50 years than has GNP. American society may choose, via the political process, to implement policies that reduce GNP in order to increase NEW. Government prohibition of strip-mining coal and careful limitation of timber cutting and oil drilling on government-owned land are examples. Similarly, the government imposes emission standards on new automobiles and coal-fired energy generating plants. Can you think of additional examples?

SUMMARY

1. National income accounting encompasses the procedures for measuring the nation's aggregate output and income, along with its components. Such data are needed to analyze and describe the economy's performance and to study the influence of various economic events and macroeconomic policies on the nation's economic activity.
2. Macroeconomic variables may be classified as stock variables and flow variables. Stock variables are measured at a given point of time and are expressed in units of quantity or dollar value. Examples include the population, the money supply, and the capital stock. Flow variables are measured as a rate per unit of time. Examples include investment, exports, consumption, profits, and income.
3. Gross national product (GNP), the most popular measure of the nation's output, is defined as the dollar value of a nation's production of final goods and services in a given year. A closely related concept, net national product (NNP), is constructed by deducting the amount of capital consumed or worn out from GNP. NNP is thus a measure of the net output available to society. Although NNP is conceptually a superior indicator, GNP is predominantly used because it is difficult to estimate the amount of capital worn out in a given year.
4. The circular flow model illustrates the interdependent nature of production decisions and expenditure decisions. Firms hire factors of production from households and produce final goods and services (GNP). In producing this GNP, firms pay out incomes to the households, allowing them to purchase the output they collectively helped to produce.
5. Two methods of measuring the nation's GNP are the flow-of-output approach and the flow-of-income approach. The former approach sums the sales of consumer goods, gross private domestic investment, government purchases of goods and services, and net exports. Since GNP seeks to measure *output,* and since *sales* do not always coincide with output in

any given accounting period, the change in business inventories is added and counted as a component of gross private domestic investment. The flow-of-income approach to computing GNP totals the wages and salaries, rents, interest, and profits to arrive at national income. GNP is then obtained by adding indirect business taxes, miscellaneous items, and depreciation to national income.

6. GNP is reported each year in current dollars. Because the price level typically rises over time, the growth of this reported or *nominal GNP* overstates the growth of actual output or *real GNP.* To compute real GNP, we use a special index of prices known as the *GNP deflator* to adjust the nominal GNP for changes in the price level. Real GNP is the appropriate variable to consider when seeking to determine the change in the nation's output or standard of living.

7. There are several imperfections in national income accounting that render reported measures of the nation's output somewhat flawed indicators of our well-being. GNP ignores the growth of leisure time and fails to record output not sold in organized markets, thus understating our well-being. On the other hand, GNP neglects environmental damage and other adverse side effects associated with producing the nation's GNP. Moreover, GNP counts the production of such "bads" as deadly nuclear missiles and expenditures to repair damages associated with nuclear and natural disasters on the same basis as the production of "goods." An experimental measure that seeks to correct these flaws is known as Net Economic Welfare (NEW).

KEY TERMS

stock variable	government purchases
flow variable	government transfer payments
national income accounting	value added
gross national product (GNP)	depreciation
intermediate good	indirect business taxes
circular flow model	net national product (NNP)
consumer goods	national income (NY)
investment goods	personal income (NY)
flow-of-output approach	personal disposable income (Y_d)
flow-of-income approach	nominal GNP
final goods and services	GNP deflator
consumption expenditures	real GNP
disposable income	underground economy
gross investment	net economic welfare (NEW)
net investment	

STUDY QUESTIONS AND PROBLEMS

1. Explain why measures of aggregate output and income are essential to businesses and economists.

2. At the beginning of the year, Joe Jogger buys 10 pairs of red sneakers on sale. Joe wears out and throws away a new pair approximately every four months. The number of pairs of red sneakers Joe has in his closet on any given day is what sort of variable? What sort of variable is the rate at which Joe wears out his sneakers? Is there a relationship between the variables?

3. Explain the difference between stock variables and flow variables. Give one example of a flow variable and one example of a stock variable in nature and in economics that is not mentioned in this chapter.

4. Imagine you are starting a business that makes a special kind of T-shirt. What are the *factors of production* you would need? What *intermediate goods*? Describe what your *final goods* might look like.

5. Why are intermediate goods not included in calculating GNP?
6. Which of the following are included in GNP?
   a. raw steel
   b. purchase of a new washing machine
   c. purchase of a used house
   d. sale of Ford automobiles to Japan
   e. purchase of 100 shares of Ford Motor stock
   f. social security payments
   g. salary of a university professor
   h. interest payments on the national debt
7. In 1985 nominal GNP was $3998 billion, the GNP deflator was 111.5, and the base year for the deflator was 1982 (1982 = 100). If both real and nominal GNP in 1982 were $3166 billion, how much had real GNP grown by 1985?
8. Analyze the basic principles illustrated in the circular flow-of-income model.
9. In the flow-of-output approach to GNP, we attempt to measure *output* by totaling *sales* of consumption, investment, government, and net export goods. Explain why the adjustment for the change in the nation's inventories makes this procedure a conceptually valid one.
10. In the flow-of-income approach to GNP, why do we add indirect business taxes and depreciation on top of employee compensation, interest, rents, and profits to arrive at GNP?
11. Discuss the shortcomings of U.S. reported GNP as an indicator of the nation's economic performance. In view of these shortcomings, do you believe that reported GNP overstates or understates the conceptually ideal measure of GNP as a measure of the well-being of the nation.

ANSWER TO YOUR TURN

$$\text{real GNP in 1990} = \frac{\$5580 \text{ billion}}{138} \times 100 = \$4043.5 \text{ billion}$$

SELECTED REFERENCES

Challenge Magazine, November/December 1979 contains two excellent articles on the underground economy: Edgar L. Feige, "How Big Is the Irregular Economy?" and Peter M. Gutmann, "Statistical Illusions, Mistaken Policies."

Kuznets, Simon, *Modern Economic Growth* (New Haven, CT: Yale University Press, 1966). Chapter 1 is devoted to national income accounting.

Nordhaus, William and James Tobin, "Is Growth Obsolete?" *Fiftieth Anniversary Colloquium V* (National Bureau of Economic Research, Columbia Press, 1972). Discusses the construction of the measure of Net Economic Welfare (NEW).

Sommers, Albert T., *The U.S. Economy Demystified* (Lexington, MA: Lexington Books, 1988, revised edition). Chapter 2 presents a clear discussion of national income accounting.

U.S. Department of Commerce, *Survey of Current Business.* Reports the national income data. See especially the July issue.

CHAPTER 10

AGGREGATE DEMAND— KEYNESIAN ECONOMICS

My problem lies in reconciling my gross habits with my net income.

—ERROLL FLYNN

As discussed in Chapter 8, the nation's price level and level of real output are jointly determined by aggregate supply and aggregate demand (illustrated in Figure 10-1). These aggregate supply and demand schedules frequently shift about, initiating changes in output and employment on the one hand and changes in the price level on the other.

In the past 50 years, the typical macroeconomic pattern has been one of rising output combined with rising prices over time. In terms of Figure 10-1, this implies that a rightward-shifting aggregate demand curve has directly initiated changes in real output and in the price level. In the long run, the aggregate supply curve gradually shifts rightward as the population, labor force, and output per worker all increase over time. The growth of productivity, which gradually shifts the aggregate supply curve rightward, is the predominant source of growth in living standards over the long run. But the fact that the U.S. price level has more than quadrupled since the end of World War II implies that the rightward shift of aggregate demand over the years has outpaced the rightward shift of the nation's aggregate supply curve.

Changes in aggregate demand account predominantly for short-run business-cycle phenomena. In the expansion phase of the business cycle the aggregate demand curve shifts rightward, which leads to expanding real output, declining unemployment, and a rising level of prices. A contraction in aggregate demand typically leads to recession, in which output declines and the price level falls or at least increases at a slower-than-normal pace.

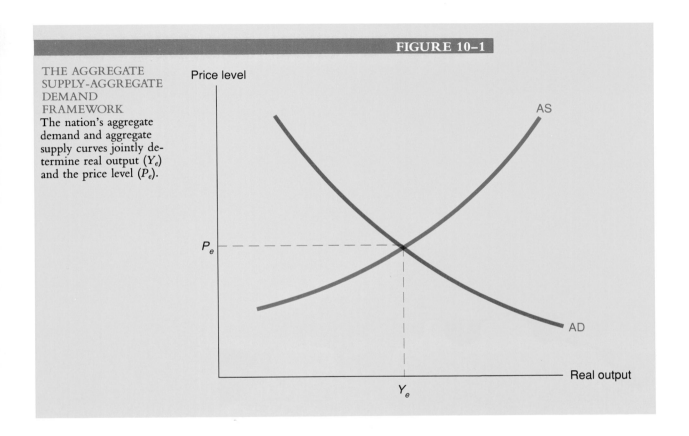

FIGURE 10–1

THE AGGREGATE SUPPLY-AGGREGATE DEMAND FRAMEWORK
The nation's aggregate demand and aggregate supply curves jointly determine real output (Y_e) and the price level (P_e).

AGGREGATE DEMAND—THE COMPONENTS

In this chapter we ignore the aggregate supply curve of Figure 10-1 and focus on the elements underlying the aggregate demand curve. In essence we are assuming that the aggregate supply curve is horizontal, so that increases in aggregate demand lead to comparable increases in real output with no increase in the price level. By the end of this chapter you will clearly understand the forces that shift the AD curve rightward or leftward.

As discussed in Chapter 9, aggregate demand consists of four components: **consumer demand (C), investment demand (I), government purchases (G),** and **net exports (X − M)** of U.S. goods and services. An increase in any of these factors results in a rightward shift of the aggregate demand curve, leading to greater real output. A contraction in any of these four components leads to a downward shift in aggregate demand, resulting in lower levels of output and employment.

The relative shares of our nation's aggregate demand (and gross national product) contributed by the four components of demand are illustrated in Figure

10-2. Consumption spending (*C*) makes up about two-thirds of total expenditures (aggregate demand) and consists of spending on durable goods, nondurables, and services. Government purchases of goods and services by all levels of government (*G*) accounts for about one-fifth of total spending.[1] Investment spending (*I*), which is comprised chiefly of expenditures for producers' durable goods and structures (residential and nonresidential), accounts for slightly less than government purchases. The final component of aggregate demand is net exports (*X* − *M*). Foreign purchases of American goods and services (*X*) is a direct source of demand for U.S. output. On the other hand, American demand for foreign goods and services (*M*) represents income earned by Americans that is siphoned off from the domestic expenditure scene. Since U.S. imports have exceeded exports in recent years, the *open economy* or international sector has been a net *negative* source of demand for American goods and services. In other words, we spend more on foreign goods than foreigners spend on ours. Hence, in Figure 10-2, *C* + *I* + *G* accounts for 102 percent of aggregate demand for U.S. goods and services. The trade deficit accounts for a negative 2 percent.

CONSUMER DEMAND (*C*)

Inasmuch as consumer spending constitutes the major portion of aggregate demand, economists have devoted an enormous amount of research effort toward understanding consumer behavior. The relationship between consumption and disposable income (personal income after taxes) is one of the cornerstones of macroeconomic analysis. This relationship forms the basis of a multiplier effect by which changes in

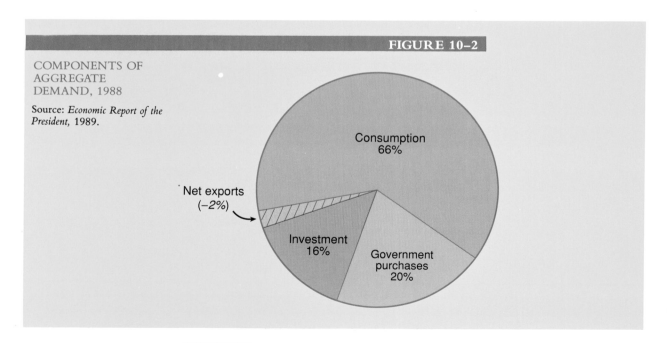

COMPONENTS OF AGGREGATE DEMAND, 1988

Source: *Economic Report of the President,* 1989.

FIGURE 10–2

[1]Remember that government purchases do not include all government expenditures. Some government expenditures are in the form of transfer payments such as unemployment compensation, social security benefits, and interest on the federal debt. Such transfer payments do not of themselves constitute demand for goods and services. However, such transfers directly place incomes into people's pockets and this leads to private expenditures, mainly in the form of consumption.

investment spending and other components of aggregate spending lead to amplified changes in the nation's level of output and income.

The Consumption Function

Intuition and plain common sense tell you that a major factor influencing your spending is your income, or more specifically, your **disposable income (Y_d)**— personal income available to spend after taxes. The same is true for the nation's aggregate consumption expenditures, which depend importantly on aggregate disposable income. The historical relationship between aggregate disposable income and aggregate consumption expenditures in the United States is illustrated in Figure 10-3. Note the extremely strong correlation between consumer spending and disposable income. But remember that correlation does not necessarily imply causation. From Figure 10-3, we can infer that at least one of the following is true:

a. disposable income strongly influences consumption
b. consumption strongly influences disposable income
c. some third factor simultaneously accounts for the behavior of both disposable income and consumption; their high correlation therefore does not indicate any causal association between the two

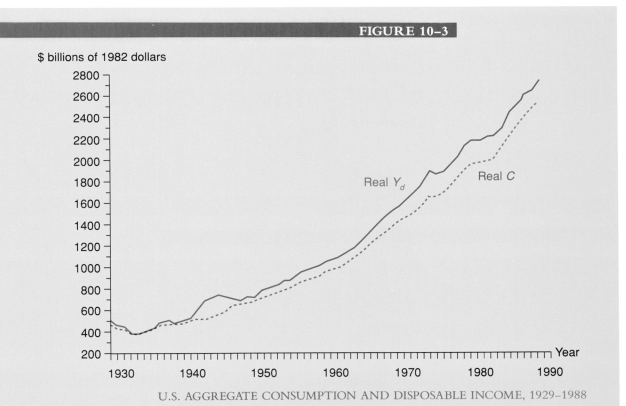

FIGURE 10–3

U.S. AGGREGATE CONSUMPTION AND DISPOSABLE INCOME, 1929–1988

Aggregate consumption expenditures and aggregate disposable income are highly correlated over time. Economists believe that much of this correlation reflects the influence of disposable income upon consumption spending.

Source: U.S. Department of Commerce, 1989.

John Maynard Keynes, the great British economist of the first half of this century, believed that the first explanation is correct. Keynes argued that a "fundamental psychological law" exists whereby consumers consistently respond to any increase in disposable income by spending a major portion of the extra income. This relationship between disposable income and consumption expenditures is known as the **consumption function** or the *propensity-to-consume relationship.* Keynes integrated the consumption function into macroeconomic analysis. His framework implies that shifts in any of the components of aggregate demand lead to an amplified change in the nation's output and income (i.e., a *multiplier effect*).

Assume the consumption-income relationship indicated in Table 10-1 applies to a typical American family.

Consumption Function
The relationship between consumer expenditures and disposable income, holding all other determinants of consumer spending constant.

TABLE 10-1				
RELATIONSHIP BETWEEN FAMILY DISPOSABLE INCOME AND FAMILY CONSUMPTION				
Y_d	C	S	MPC	MPS
0	4,000	−4,000	—	—
10,000	12,000	−2,000	.80	.20
20,000	20,000	0	.80	.20
30,000	28,000	+2,000	.80	.20
40,000	36,000	+4,000	.80	.20
50,000	44,000	+6,000	.80	.20

In relating the information in Table 10-1, consider the following equation:

$$S \equiv Y_d - C \qquad (10\text{-}1)$$

Saving is defined as disposable income (Y_d) minus expenditures on goods and services (C). This is simply the commonplace definition of saving (i.e., income not spent). From Equation 10-1 it follows by simple rearrangement that

$$C + S \equiv Y_d \qquad (10\text{-}2)$$

Autonomous Consumption
The portion of consumption that is independent of disposable income; consumer expenditures that would occur in the event that disposable income were zero.

Marginal Propensity to Consume (MPC)
The ratio of the change in consumption to the change in disposable income that induces the change in consumption; the slope of the consumption function.

That is, consumption and saving add up to total income after taxes.

Table 10-1 indicates that if the family earns no income in a given year, it still has certain unavoidable consumption needs ($4000), which can only be met by borrowing or drawing on the family's past savings. This factor is referred to as **autonomous consumption** or the portion of consumption that depends on factors other than income.

Note that if family income were $10,000 the family's expenditures would be $12,000. In addition to its autonomous consumption of $4000, the family spends 80 percent of additional income as income rises from zero. This factor is referred to as **induced consumption** or additional consumption triggered by the rise in disposable income. Keynes labeled this crucial concept the **marginal propensity to consume (MPC).** In Table 10-1:

$$\text{MPC} = \frac{\text{change in consumption}}{\text{change in disposable income}} \text{ or } \frac{\Delta C}{\Delta Y_d} = \frac{\$\,8000}{\$10,000} = 0.80$$

According to Keynes' *fundamental psychological law,* the size of the MPC is somewhere between 0 and 1. We have adopted this assumption in our example:

$$0 < \text{MPC} < 1$$

When disposable income changes, people change expenditures in the same direction—but not by the full change in income.

In Table 10-1 we observe that as income rises in increments of $10,000, expenditures respond in increments of $8000. In our example the family responds to increases in its income by spending 80 percent of the increase. That is, the MPC is 0.80.

Since the family responds to rising income by spending 80 percent of any increase, they are by definition saving the remaining 20 percent of the increase. The fraction of additional income saved is known as the **marginal propensity to save** (MPS). In Table 10-1

Marginal Propensity to Save (MPS)
The ratio of the change in saving to the change in disposable income that induces the change in saving; the slope of the saving function.

$$\text{MPS} = \frac{\text{change in saving}}{\text{change in disposable income}} \quad \text{or} \quad \frac{\Delta S}{\Delta Y_d} = \frac{\$\ 2000}{\$10,000} = 0.20$$

Saving rises $2000 each time disposable income rises $10,000. Given Equation 10-2, it follows that

$$\Delta C + \Delta S \equiv \Delta Y_d \tag{10-3}$$

and

$$\frac{\Delta C}{\Delta Y_d} + \frac{\Delta S}{\Delta Y_d} \equiv 1 \tag{10-4}$$

That is, MPC + MPS ≡ 1.

Equation 10-3 states that by definition any change in disposable income is allocated to a change in spending (ΔC) and to a change in saving (ΔS). If in Equation 10-4 we then divide Equation 10-3 by ΔY_d, we obtain the proposition that the marginal propensity to consume and the marginal propensity to save must total exactly 1. Hence, if you know the MPC you can immediately calculate the MPS. If you know the MPS you can immediately calculate the MPC.

The information provided in Table 10-1 can be expressed algebraically by the following equations:

$$C = \$4000 + .80\ Y_d$$

$$S = -\$4000 + .20\ Y_d$$

That is, the family depicted in Table 10-1 spends $4000 plus 80 percent of disposable income; it saves a negative *$4000* plus 20 percent of disposable income. The same information is conveyed graphically in Figure 10-4 (page 212).

The family consumption function (C–C) and **saving function** (S–S) are plotted directly from the information given in Table 10-1, and from the consumption and saving equations. When disposable income (Y_d) is zero, consumption is $4000 and saving is minus *$4000.* The family is forced to borrow or withdraw $4000 from past savings to finance this subsistence level of consumption.

Break-even Income Level
Income level at which consumption equals income; income level at which saving is zero.

As income rises to $20,000, expenditures also reach $20,000 and saving rises to zero (from a negative amount). The income level at which saving is zero is known as the **break-even level,** indicated in Figure 10-4 by the income at which the

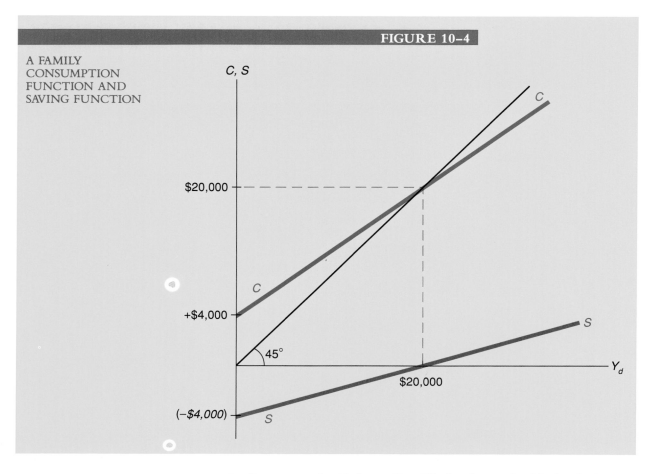

FIGURE 10–4

A FAMILY CONSUMPTION FUNCTION AND SAVING FUNCTION

consumption line crosses the 45-degree line. The break-even level is also the income level at which the saving line crosses the horizontal axis, indicating a zero level of saving. At income levels above $20,000, consumption falls short of income (the C–C line lies below the 45-degree line) and saving breaks into positive territory.

What meaning can we attach to the slopes of the consumption and saving schedules? Regarding the consumption schedule:

$$\text{slope} = \frac{\text{rise}}{\text{run}} = \frac{\Delta C}{\Delta Y_d} = \frac{+\$16,000}{+\$20,000} = 0.80.$$

Regarding the saving schedule:

$$\text{slope} = \frac{\text{rise}}{\text{run}} = \frac{\Delta S}{\Delta Y_d} = \frac{+\$\ 4000}{+\$20,000} = 0.20.$$

The slope of the consumption function is the MPC (0.80 in our example). The slope of the saving function is the MPS (0.20 in our example). Clearly, 0.80 + 0.20 = 1. This confirms Equation 10-4.[2]

---

[2]Question: What do you obtain when you geometrically add together the consumption line (C–C) and the saving line (S–S) of Figure 10-4? You obtain the 45-degree line that begins at the origin of the figure. Can you explain why? Since a 45-degree line bisects the right angle at which the vertical axis meets the horizontal axis, it delineates all points of equality of the variables on the two axes. Because C + S must total Y_d by definition, C–C plus S–S must add up to the 45-degree line.

At this point you should recognize the key implication of this analysis for aggregate demand: Any factor that changes disposable income also induces a change in consumption in the same direction. For example, an income-tax cut that raises Y_d also leads to a rightward movement along the consumption function, such as that in Figure 10-4. This movement, in turn, produces a rightward shift of the AD schedule of Figure 10-1. A tax hike, by reducing disposable income and inducing a contraction of consumption along the consumption function, shifts the AD schedule leftward. This shift also leads to a decline in economic activity. The consumption function provides the intellectual basis for the use of discretionary fiscal policy to influence economic activity.

YOUR TURN

Assume that your personal consumption function can be described by the equation $C = \$2000 + .90\ Y_d$:

a. Construct a table (like Table 10-1) that indicates your C, S, MPC, and MPS at various Y_d levels from 0 to $50,000.
b. What is your break-even level of disposable income?
c. What is your autonomous consumption?
d. If your disposable income were $100,000, how much would you save?

Other Factors that Influence Consumer Spending

We have discussed two general categories of consumption: an *autonomous* portion that occurs independently of disposable income and an *induced* portion that responds to changes in Y_d. Analytically, we may treat changes in Y_d as moving us *along* a given consumption schedule (e.g., line C–C in Figure 10-4). Changes in other factors influencing consumption are treated as *shifting the entire position* of the consumption schedule.[3] Several factors other than Y_d influence consumer spending and therefore shift the C–C line of Figure 10-4.

Wealth Consumers spend not only on the basis of current income (Y_d), but also on the basis of their stock of wealth or net worth (i.e., the net value of their assets minus their liabilities). Consider two families each earning $40,000 annually. Assume one family owns a home and $400,000 worth of stocks, bonds, and savings accounts. Assume the second family rents a home and owns $20,000 worth of financial assets. Quite likely the first family annually spends more on consumer goods than does the second family. In terms of Figure 10-5 (page 214), the wealthy family's consumption schedule (C_w–C_w) lies vertically above that of the poorer family (C_p–C_p).

In the context of the overall economy, changes in stock-market prices, prices of other financial assets, and real estate values can initiate important changes in wealth, thereby shifting the nation's consumption schedule. When the U.S. stock market crashed in October 1987, more than $1000 billion of financial wealth dissolved. Many economists anticipated a resulting downward shift in the nation's consumption schedule and a decline in aggregate demand for goods and services (see Exhibit 10-1; page 219).

---

[3]Recall the concept of a demand curve from Chapter 4. Now consider the demand curve for Coca-Cola. A change in the price of Coke moves you along the demand curve for Coke; a change in other factors relevant to the demand for Coke (price of Pepsi, income, population, and so on) shifts the entire position of the demand curve for Coke. Similarly with the consumption function. A change in disposable income moves us along the consumption function; a change in other factors influencing consumption shifts the entire position of the consumption function.

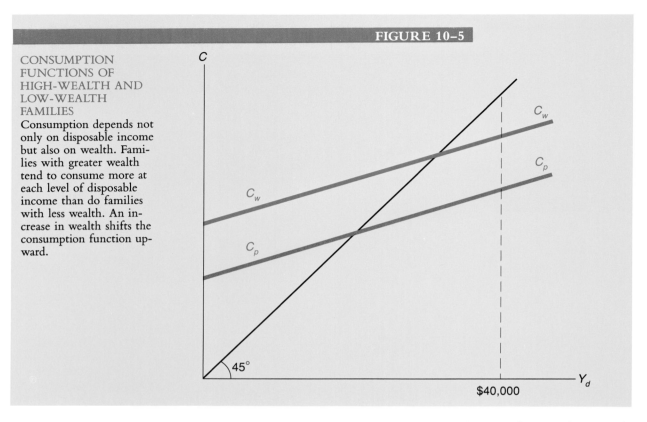

FIGURE 10-5

CONSUMPTION FUNCTIONS OF HIGH-WEALTH AND LOW-WEALTH FAMILIES
Consumption depends not only on disposable income but also on wealth. Families with greater wealth tend to consume more at each level of disposable income than do families with less wealth. An increase in wealth shifts the consumption function upward.

Recent Past Y_d Spending patterns move with an element of inertia (i.e., people become accustomed to a certain life-style and resist changes). For this reason, consumption spending depends not only on income in the current year but also on income in recent years. If income suddenly falls sharply in recession, consumers may at first draw down savings and perhaps even borrow in order to maintain certain accustomed buying habits. If the low income persists, consumers eventually are confronted with no choice but to reduce consumption in line with income.

Expected Future Y_d Spending patterns are influenced not only by current and recent disposable income but also by disposable income expected in the future. A just-graduated physician and a veteran college English professor may each earn $30,000 annually. Very likely, however, the physician will spend more than the professor because the physician's expected future income is much higher than the professor's. This insight has important macroeconomic implications. Suppose a recession emerges. Consumers may not cut back spending in line with the decline in disposable income because the setback is expected to be temporary. Moreover, federal tax changes implemented to influence aggregate consumption and aggregate demand must be perceived as permanent in order to be fully effective.[4] Hence, a

---

[4]Economist Milton Friedman was awarded the 1976 Nobel Prize in Economics for several path-breaking studies. One of the most significant was *A Theory of the Consumption Function.* In this work Friedman formalized the relationship between consumption and *permanent income,* a measure of average expected future income. Because Friedman believes that consumers spend on the basis of permanent income instead of current income, income-tax changes do not appreciably influence consumer spending if they are perceived as temporary. Friedman's work represents an important refinement of Keynes' theory, which treats consumption simply as a function of *current income.*

temporary tax hike in 1968 for the purpose of slowing consumption and aggregate demand had little effect on consumers. The tax increase was announced as a temporary, one-shot affair; consumers simply paid the taxes out of savings instead of restraining consumption.

The General Price Level   When the price level declines, the real value of such financial assets as money and government bonds rises. Consumers are thus better off, and the consumption function shifts upward. On the other hand, if the price level were to double, the real value of these financial assets would be cut in half. Consumers would feel poorer and the consumption function would shift downward. This phenomenon is known as the **wealth** or **real-balance effect.**

Wealth or Real-Balance Effect
The effect that a change in the nation's price level exerts on consumption, aggregate demand, and equilibrium output by changing the real value of such financial assets as money, savings accounts, and government bonds held by individuals.

The Expected Future Inflation Rate   Consumer behavior may be influenced by changes in the outlook for inflation. Suppose people expect the inflation rate to rise to 8 percent next year from a current rate of 5 percent. Some consumers may step up buying to beat the anticipated price hikes. If so, the consumption function may shift upward.[5] On the other hand, other consumers may feel more insecure about the future because of higher expected inflation. Such consumers are likely to step up their saving rates (i.e., their consumption functions shift downward). Because different consumers react differently to changes in expected future inflation, it is difficult to predict the effect of changes in expected inflation upon the consumption function. In this area, as in other areas of economics, human behavior is connected with psychology.

Stock of Durable Goods Owned by Households   When consumers are well stocked with state-of-the-art automobiles, VCRs, refrigerators, and vacuum cleaners, there is clearly little need to purchase durable goods. On the other hand, if the bulk of these durable goods owned by consumers are obsolete or in a run-down state, there is great scope for massive purchases of such items. This factor helps explain the enormous consumption boom immediately following the end of World War II. Automobiles, refrigerators, and many other durable goods were not produced during the war (1942–1945). Consumption simply exploded after the war as people rushed out to purchase newly available cars, washing machines, and other durables.

INVESTMENT EXPENDITURES

Investment demand—expenditures on producers' durable equipment and various types of building structures—is the most volatile component of aggregate demand. The categories of investment are reviewed in Table 10-2 (page 216). Gross investment or total spending on investment goods is predominantly made up of producers' durable equipment such as machines and tools, nonresidential structures such as factories and commercial buildings, and residential structures such as houses and apartment buildings.

---

[5]Is it rational in general to buy goods now in order to beat expected price hikes? This depends on whether the real interest rate you can earn on your savings is positive. Suppose a new Ford costs $15,000 this year and you expect next year's model to increase 6 percent to $15,900. If you can earn more than 6 percent on a savings account or 1-year certificate of deposit, you will accumulate sufficient funds to afford the higher price a year from now. Hence, there is no reason to run out and buy the car just to beat the price hike. During the 1980s, the interest rate available to consumers has exceeded the inflation rate by a significant margin.

TABLE 10-2	
GROSS INVESTMENT SPENDING BY COMPONENT, 1988 (in billions)	
Producers' durable equipment	$345
Nonresidential structures	143
Residential structures	230
Change in inventories	48
Gross investment	$766 billion

Source: U.S. Department of Commerce, *Survey of Current Business*, 1989.

Conceptually, it is useful to distinguish between *gross* investment and *net* investment. *Gross investment* is total spending on investment goods, including expenditures required to replace worn-out and obsolete equipment and structures. *Net investment* is the *net addition* to the nation's stock of capital goods in a given period, such as one year. Net investment is therefore the difference between gross investment and depreciation. Over time, as output grows, the capital stock required to produce this larger output increases. Hence, net investment is almost always positive (i.e., gross investment almost always exceeds depreciation).

net investment   = gross investment minus depreciation

gross investment = net investment plus depreciation or replacement investment

Investment Spending—The Role of Interest Rates

Investment goods are those produced for the purpose of facilitating production of other goods and services. Investment goods normally have a relatively long lifetime: a new lathe may last 30 years, a tractor 20 years, an apartment building 60 years. The bulk of investment expenditures are financed with borrowed money. Firms with substantial internal funds on hand have alternatives to using the funds for investment projects. For example, they can place the funds in such financial assets as bonds and earn the going interest rate. The opportunity cost of investing in new plant and equipment is the current interest rate. Entrepreneurs invest only in those potential projects for which the expected rate of return on the investment exceeds the interest rate by a margin sufficient to compensate for the risk involved. Given the array of returns expected from various potential investment projects in the nation, this implies that a decline in the level of interest rates brings more investment projects into the realm of feasibility—that is, more investment projects appear profitable and are undertaken. The relationship between the interest rate and total investment spending is illustrated in Figure 10-6.

The investment demand curve indicates an inverse relationship between the interest rate and investment spending, *all other factors remaining constant.* A new investment project expected to yield 7.5 percent annually (on the funds invested) will be built if interest rates are 6 percent, but not if they are 8 percent. Federal Reserve monetary policy, by influencing the level of U.S. interest rates, is capable of moving us along this demand curve, thereby altering the level of investment spending.

However, there are many other factors besides interest rates that strongly influence investment spending. Changes in these factors may be viewed as *shifting the*

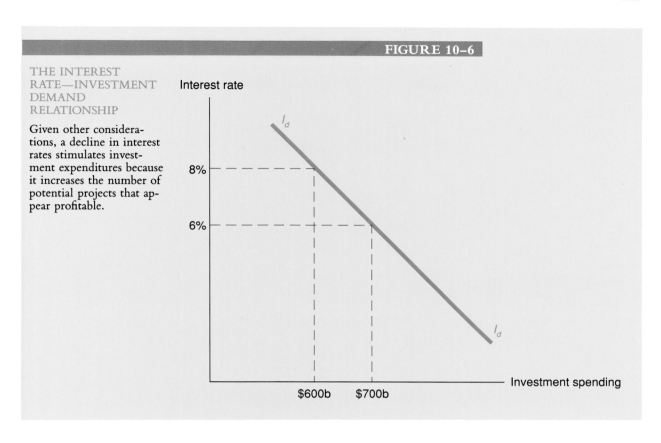

FIGURE 10–6

THE INTEREST
RATE—INVESTMENT
DEMAND
RELATIONSHIP

Given other considera-
tions, a decline in interest
rates stimulates invest-
ment expenditures because
it increases the number of
potential projects that appear profitable.

position of the investment demand curve of Figure 10-6. The position of the curve is believed to be quite volatile.

Other Factors that Influence Investment Spending

Among the factors that affect investment decisions and shift the investment demand curve are changes in business confidence, changes in the capacity utilization rate of existing plant and equipment and expected future growth of aggregate demand, changes in income-tax provisions, and changes in stock market prices.

Business Confidence   Investment spending is inherently a forward-looking activity. It is risky to borrow large sums of money to build a new factory or install new equipment. In doing so, one is *betting the business* on the future. When the outlook for the future of the economy worsens, returns expected from investment projects are revised downward. The investment demand curve illustrated in Figure 10-6 shifts leftward, and less investment spending is forthcoming at each and every interest rate. When the economic outlook improves, businesses revise expected returns upward, the investment demand schedule shifts rightward, and a larger magnitude of investment occurs at each and every interest rate. Keynes argued that investment depends upon the "animal spirits" of businesses. Translated, this suggests that business confidence is volatile, and returns expected from potential investment projects can be revised considerably and in a relatively brief time period. That is, the investment demand schedule shifts about, bringing sharp fluctuations in actual investment spending (review Figure 9-3).

Capacity Utilization Rate and Expected Future Growth of Demand   When firms are currently operating their existing plant at 80 or 90 percent of capacity and are anticipating healthy future demand growth for their product, they must expand or modernize their production facilities to meet the expected future market. Here the investment demand curve lies far to the right. On the other hand, when the existing plant is producing only at 60 percent of capacity because of limited sales and when the outlook for sales growth is modest or bleak, the investment demand curve is low or far to the left. Thus we can state that, *given other factors,* the higher the economy's current capacity utilization rate, the farther to the right is the investment demand schedule. The greater the expected future sales growth, *given other factors,* the farther to the right is the investment demand schedule. In the Great Depression of the 1930s, many firms were operating at less than 50 percent of capacity and the outlook was dismal. As a result, the investment demand schedule shifted far to the left. In spite of fairly low interest rates, investment spending was anemic; many firms did not spend enough to even replace worn-out capital equipment.

Income-Tax Provisions   Investment decisions are typically made on a rational basis. A potential builder of a new factory or apartment building calculates the expected returns from the project and evaluates the findings in view of the risk and the cost of borrowing money. A decision is then made. Government tax policy is sometimes capable of tilting this investment decision. From time to time the U.S. government allows a *tax credit* for new investment. A 10-percent *investment tax credit* means that if IBM decides to invest $10 million in new equipment, the corporation would owe $1 million less in taxes to the IRS. Because the government is essentially paying for 10 percent of the project, this is likely to have a positive influence on the investment decision.

The nature of *depreciation tax allowances* also has an important impact on investment decisions. Purchases of investment goods are a cost of doing business and the IRS provides a tax deduction (depreciation allowance) for such expenditures. A firm that installs new equipment is allowed to write off the cost of the equipment against taxable income *over a period of years.* When this depreciation policy is liberal—firms are allowed to write off investment expenditures quickly—potential projects are more attractive. The Economic Recovery Tax Act of 1981 (ERTA) generally liberalized depreciation allowances, thus tending to stimulate investment. However, more recent legislation removed some of the incentives supplied by ERTA by slowing down depreciation allowances.

The Level of Stock Market Prices   Firms may finance new investment projects by issuing debt (selling bonds or borrowing from banks) or by issuing equity shares (i.e., shares of stock). When stock prices are high, firms find it attractive to obtain funds by issuing new shares of stock. When stock prices are depressed, firms are reluctant to issue new shares. To do so dilutes the portion of the company owned by existing shareholders without obtaining a price commensurate with management's perception of the true worth of the company. Hence, when the stock market is depressed, the investment demand curve of Figure 10-6 is farther to the left than when stock prices are booming.

EXHIBIT 10–1

THE GREAT CRASH OF 1987—WHAT WERE THE CONSEQUENCES?

On Black Monday, October 19, 1987, the stock market crashed. The Dow-Jones Industrials lost 508 points, or 23 percent of its total value in a single day! Descriptions of the atmosphere on Wall Street ranged from "hysteria" to "panic." A few days later, a crazed Miami speculator walked into a Merrill-Lynch office and gunned down his broker and everyone else in sight. Several suicides were linked to the collapse. Stock market crashes are the stuff of personal tragedy.

What are the consequences of a stock market crash for the macroeconomy? Most economists agree that the net effect is contractionary (i.e., aggregate demand and economic activity are induced to fall). Following the *crash of '87,* economic prognosticators immediately revised their forecasts downward. However, no one can confidently predict how powerfully a stock market crash spills over to pull down the real economy, because the responses of people that produce the real economic effects are intimately connected with psychology.

Thomas Juster, an economist with the University of Michigan's highly regarded *Survey of Consumer Confidence,* believes that a stock market crash has two effects on consumers. First, there is a direct wealth effect. Roughly 20 percent of Americans own shares of stock directly, via their personal portfolio of common stock and mutual funds. For many more individuals, stocks are an important component of retirement or pension programs. On Black Monday, Americans lost $500 billion of this paper wealth. It simply evaporated in the stock market *meltdown of '87.* Since consumer spending—especially on expensive durable goods—depends on wealth or net worth as well as on disposable income, aggregate consumption is likely to decline when the stock market drops. A rule of thumb derived from empirical research on consumer behavior is that the drop in consumption is likely to amount to two or three percent of the contraction in paper wealth. Inasmuch as stock values declined roughly $1200 billion in the last five months of 1987, this wealth effect suggested a downward shift of the consumption function of perhaps $24–$36 billion for 1988.

Second, according to Juster, even the majority of Americans who do not own stock are likely to become more conservative in their spending propensities. A stock market crash, which they (and everyone else) fail to comprehend, tends to create anxiety about job stability and prospects for future income and living standards. An instinctive reaction is to postpone purchases of such big-ticket items as cars, houses, and furniture until the outlook clears.

Similarly, business firms that invest in plant and equipment and research and development are likely to become more cautious after a stock market crash. Investment spending is closely related to the outlook for the future. Historically, the stock market has been a leading indicator of economic activity. Thus, a crash in stock values is likely to be interpreted by business executives as a signal that less prosperous times may well lie ahead. Investment and research expenditures tend to be scaled back or postponed. For these reasons, most economists recognized that the *Great Crash of 1987* significantly raised the prospects for a contraction in aggregate demand and a recession in 1988.

As it turned out, a recession did *not* occur in 1988. A possible explanation lies in compensating measures implemented by the Federal Reserve to bolster the economy. Sensing that the stock market crash might spill over and pull down the real economy, the Fed quickly put into place policies to boost aggregate demand. Also, American exports began to increase strongly in 1988 in response to the decline in the international value of the dollar that began in 1985. These two considerations may have offset the effects of the crash in stock prices and prevented an economic downturn.

EQUILIBRIUM OUTPUT IN A SIMPLE ECONOMY WITH NO GOVERNMENT OR INTERNATIONAL TRADE

Imagine a primitive nation with no government sector (no taxes or government spending) and no foreign trade. Let this simple, closed economy be known as Primitavia. Remember the two types of goods produced—consumer goods and investment goods. Although this two-sector economy is in an infant stage of development, its people are like modern-day Americans in that they obey Keynes' "fundamental psychological law." Further, they have a marginal propensity to consume of 0.60, so that each dollar increase in income leads to an increase in consumer spending of 60 cents. Investment spending depends on such factors as business confidence and interest rates, and is assumed to be independent of the level of output and income.

Before analyzing equilibrium output in Primitavia, consider the circular flow of income and expenditures in this two-sector economy illustrated in Figure 10-7. Remember that every dollar's worth of output produced (upper flow) creates a dollar of income earned (lower flow). In Primitavia, since there are no taxes, every dollar of output creates a dollar of disposable income—income available to spend. Of course, a portion of this flow of income is withdrawn from the flow by households. This is saving, and is the only *leakage* from the circular flow. The larger portion of income is returned to the spending stream by households in the form of consumer spending. Investment is shown as an injection of spending into the flow by firms, although households actually also contribute to investment by spending on housing. You should observe that only when the withdrawal from the flow in the form of saving is precisely matched by investment do aggregate expenditures ($C + I$) precisely match aggregate output.

The expenditure schedule for Primitavia (i.e., the relationship between output and income on the one hand and consumption and investment spending on the other hand) is given in Table 10-3.

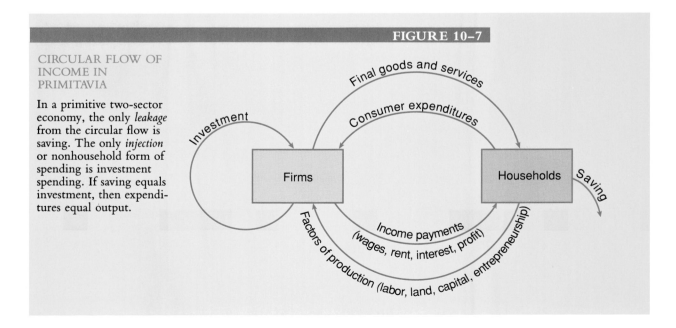

FIGURE 10–7

CIRCULAR FLOW OF INCOME IN PRIMITAVIA

In a primitive two-sector economy, the only *leakage* from the circular flow is saving. The only *injection* or nonhousehold form of spending is investment spending. If saving equals investment, then expenditures equal output.

TABLE 10-3

EXPENDITURE SCHEDULE FOR PRIMITAVIA

Output and income (Y)	Consumption (C)	Saving (S)	Investment (I)	Aggregate expenditures (C + I)	Relationship of sales to output	Involuntary change in inventories	Output decision
1200	920	280	400	1320	Sales > output	—	Increase
1300	980	320	400	1380	Sales > output	—	Increase
1400	1040	360	400	1440	Sales > output	—	Increase
1500	1100	400	400	1500	Sales = output	0	Maintain
1600	1160	440	400	1560	Sales < output	+	Decrease
1700	1220	480	400	1620	Sales < output	+	Decrease

Table 10-3 indicates that when output of $1200 per year is produced, consumers spend $920 per year. Since investment spending is $400, aggregate expenditures $(C + I)$ total $1320; firms sell more than current output and the nation's aggregate inventories decline involuntarily. This gives a clear signal to firms to step up their level of production.

Suppose firms respond by increasing output to $1700 per year. Consumers now spend $1220 and firms spend $400 on investment goods. Aggregate expenditures (total sales) are thus $1620 per year. In this instance firms are producing more than they can sell; the nation's inventories rise involuntarily and firms are given the signal to curtail production. Output accordingly falls to a lower level.

Note in Table 10-3 that only when output of $1500 per year is produced does aggregate spending $(C + I)$ precisely equal aggregate output. The overall economy is in a state of balance, or equilibrium, only when output is $1500 per year.

Conditions for Macroequilibrium in the Two-Sector Model

Equilibrium Output
The unique level of GNP at which aggregate demand equals output; the economy gropes toward equilibrium output because it is the only output level at which there is no involuntary change in inventories, hence no signal to change production.

There are three conditions for **equilibrium output** in Primitavia's simple, two-sector economy, and the three conditions are equivalent (i.e., they are three different ways of saying the same thing). If any one condition is met, all three are met. If any one condition is not met, no condition is met.

1. $Y = C + I$. Aggregate expenditures or sales $(C + I)$ equals aggregate output (Y).
2. $S = I$. The withdrawal of funds from the circular flow (saving) is precisely matched by the injection of funds (investment).
3. Involuntary change in inventories = 0. There is no involuntary change in the economy's aggregate stock of inventories.

Note in Table 10-3 that all three conditions are met when Primitavia produces an annual output of $1500. All three conditions are violated at all other levels of output. Thus Primitavia adopts an output level of $1500 per year.

Graphic Illustration of Equilibrium Output

Figure 10-8 (page 222) illustrates in diagrammatic form the same information given in Table 10-3. Aggregate output and income is indicated on the horizontal axis and aggregate expenditures $(C + I)$ on the vertical axis. This framework is called the **income-expenditure diagram** or the *45-degree diagram*. The aggregate expendi-

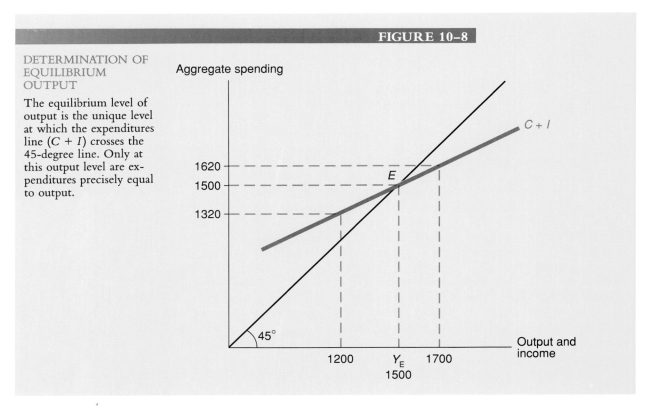

FIGURE 10–8

DETERMINATION OF
EQUILIBRIUM
OUTPUT

The equilibrium level of
output is the unique level
at which the expenditures
line ($C + I$) crosses the
45-degree line. Only at
this output level are ex-
penditures precisely equal
to output.

tures line ($C + I$) is an upward-sloping function of output and income because the
marginal propensity to consume is positive. Any increase in output pulls up
consumption and, hence, aggregate spending ($C + I$).

A 45-degree line starting from the origin of Figure 10-8 is drawn to serve as a
guideline that delineates equal magnitudes on the two axes. Since equilibrium
requires that aggregate spending (measured on the vertical axis) just precisely equals
aggregate output (measured on the horizontal axis), equilibrium must occur at the
point where the aggregate expenditures line intersects the 45-degree line. This
occurs in Figure 10-8 when Primitavia produces $1500 of output per year. If its
firms produce less than $1500, note that the aggregate spending line lies above the
45-degree guideline. In this event sales exceed output, the nation's inventories
decline, and firms step up output. If output exceeds $1500 per year, the aggregate
spending line lies below the 45-degree line. In this event output exceeds aggregate
sales, the nation's inventories rise, and firms curtail output. Only at point E, with
output at $1500, are output and sales in perfect harmony, with no signal given to
change the level of production. This is equilibrium.[6]

---

[6]To keep Figure 10-8 as simple as possible, the consumption, investment, and saving lines are not in the
figure. Were they, the upward-sloping saving schedule would intersect the horizontal investment line at
the output level of $1500. At output levels above $1500, saving exceeds investment (withdrawal from the
flow of income exceeds the injection of investment). At output levels below $1500, investment exceeds
saving. In a two-sector model, $C + I$ always intersects the 45-degree line at the same output level where
the saving and investment schedules intersect.

THE MULTIPLIER—BLACK MAGIC OR SIMPLE LOGIC?

Assume Primitavia is an agrarian society—the bulk of its people are dependent on agriculture and fishing for their livelihood. Further assume that breakthroughs in agricultural and fishing technology occur. Ladders are invented to assist in picking fruit from the trees and fishing nets are developed to increase the take from the seas. The producers in Primitavia—the farmers and fishermen—decide to take advantage of these new inventions, and increase their annual investment spending from $400 to $440. Assuming Primitavia initially has some idle resources—labor and materials—the expansion of investment expenditures causes equilibrium output to increase by some multiple (larger than one) of the initial shift in spending (investment) that touches off the expansion process. This expansion of equilibrium output in Primitavia is illustrated in Figure 10-9.

Initially the economy is in equilibrium at Y_{E_1}, with output running at $1500 per year. The intersection of the aggregate expenditures line ($C + I_1$) and the 45-degree guideline is at point *a* in Figure 10-9. The expansion of investment spending means that the aggregate spending line shifts upward to $C + I_2$, a vertical shift of $40. Starting at point *a* with output of $1500, demand and sales expand by $40 to $1540. This is shown in the figure as the move from *a* to *b*. The expansion of sales initially causes inventories to decline by $40, and thus induces firms to step up output by $40 to $1540 per year. This is indicated by the move from *b* to *c* in the figure. If this were the end of the process, the **multiplier** would be exactly one because the expansion

Multiplier
The ratio of the change in equilibrium output to the original change in spending (C, I, G, or net exports) that caused the change in output.

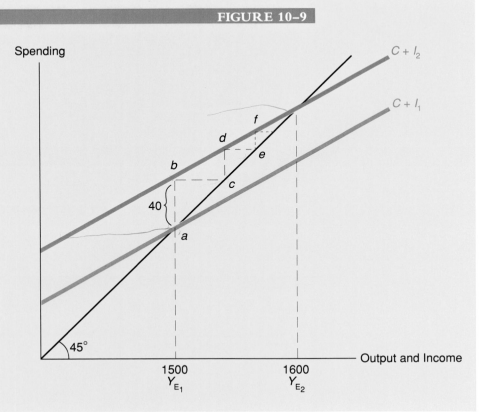

FIGURE 10–9

THE MULTIPLIER PROCESS—IMPACT OF AN INCREASE IN INVESTMENT SPENDING ON EQUILIBRIUM OUTPUT

An increase in investment expenditures, by inducing additional output and therefore placing added income in people's pockets, pulls up consumption. The result is that the increase in equilibrium output ($Y_{E_2} - Y_{E_1}$) is a *multiple* of the initial increase in investment spending.

of output would be precisely equal to the initial shift in spending that touched off the expansion of output.

However, the consumption function and the marginal propensity to consume now enter the picture. The expansion of output from $1500 to $1540 places an additional $40 of income into the pockets of the workers and the owners of firms. Given the MPC of 0.60, these individuals respond by increasing expenditures on consumer goods by $24. This is indicated in Figure 10-9 by the movement from c to d. The expansion of consumer spending causes output of consumer goods to expand by $24 ($d$ to e in the figure). This, in turn, puts additional income into people's pockets and induces a further rise of consumer spending of MPC $\times \Delta Y = 0.60 \times$ $24 = $14.40 ($e$ to f in the figure).

This two-way interactional process of additional consumer spending calling forth extra output that induces added consumer spending continues, theoretically, through an infinite number of steps. In the limit, as indicated in Figure 10-9, output reaches the new equilibrium level of $1600 per year. An expansion of investment expenditures of $40 per year pulls up equilibrium output by $100, which is 2.5 times the magnitude of the increase of investment spending. Hence, we know the multiplier is 2.5.

$$\text{multiplier} = \frac{\text{change in equilibrium output}}{\text{initial shift in spending that initiates change in output}}$$

$$\text{multiplier} = \frac{\$100 \text{ per year}}{\$ 40 \text{ per year}} = 2.5$$

Table 10-4 traces the multiplier process through a period of *rounds*. In the first round investment spending rises by $40 per year and firms respond by raising GNP by $40 per year. The income created by this additional GNP feeds back in the second round to pull up consumer spending by $24 per year. Firms react by stepping up production of consumer goods by $24 per year and the cumulative increase in GNP at this point is $64 per year. The two-way interaction between output growth and consumer spending continues until output has ultimately expanded by $100. Of this total, $60 is in the form of consumer goods and $40 is in the form of investment goods—ladders and fishing nets. This multiplier process is illustrated in Figure 10-10.

Note in Figure 10-10 that nothing is said about the amount of time that elapses in a given *round*. This depends on the time lag involved in output responding to

TABLE 10-4				
EXPANSION OF OUTPUT ASSOCIATED WITH SUSTAINED INCREASE IN INVESTMENT SPENDING OF 40 UNITS PER YEAR				
Round	ΔI	ΔC	$\Delta \text{GNP} \equiv \Delta Y_d$	Cumulative ΔGNP
1	+40		+40.0	+ 40.0
2		+24.0	+24.0	+ 64.0
3		+14.4	+14.4	+ 78.4
4		+ 8.64	+ 8.64	+ 87.04
5		+ 5.18	+ 5.18	+ 92.22
.		.	.	.
.		.	.	.
.		.	.	+100.00
		$\Sigma = +60$	$\Sigma = +100$	

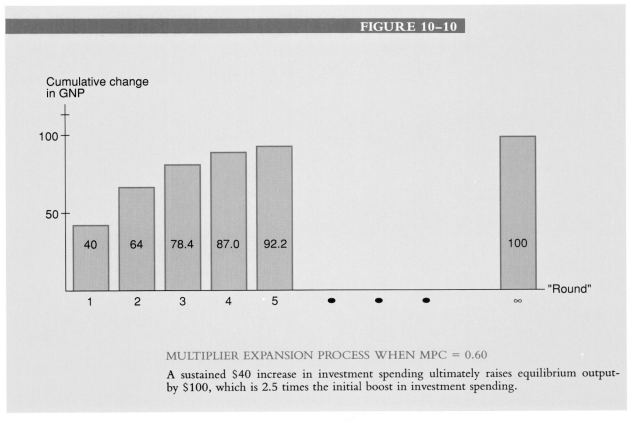

MULTIPLIER EXPANSION PROCESS WHEN MPC = 0.60

A sustained $40 increase in investment spending ultimately raises equilibrium output by $100, which is 2.5 times the initial boost in investment spending.

increased expenditures and the lag involved in consumers responding to income growth. However, the figure does indicate that more than 90 percent of the multiplier process has been completed after five (of the infinite number of) *rounds.*

The Multiplier as the Sum of an Infinite Geometric Series

In Table 10-4, the ΔC and ΔGNP columns contain a series of numbers related to each other by a common factor, 0.6, which is the MPC. You may recall from high-school algebra that such a series of numbers is known as an *infinite geometric progression.* The formula for the sum of such a series of numbers is the initial number in the series times $1/(1 - r)$, where r is the ratio that relates the numbers (0.6 in Table 10-4). Hence, the sum of the ΔC column is $24 \times 1/(1 - .60) = 60$ and the sum of the ΔGNP column is $40 \times 1/(1 - .60) = 100$. Because this ratio that relates the consecutive numbers in the column is in fact the MPC, the multiplier for the GNP column is $1 \div (1 - MPC)$:

$$\text{multiplier} = \frac{1}{1 - MPC}$$

Since MPC + MPS ≡ 1 and 1 − MPC ≡ MPS, we can also write the expression for the multiplier as follows:

$$\text{multiplier} = \frac{1}{MPS}$$

The size of this simple multiplier depends strictly on the size of the MPC and its close relative, the MPS. The larger the MPC (smaller the MPS) the larger the multiplier, as indicated in Table 10-5.

TABLE 10-5		
RELATIONSHIP BETWEEN MPC, MPS, AND THE SIMPLE MULTIPLIER		
MPC	**MPS**	**Simple multiplier**
0	1.0	1.0
.4	.6	1.67
.5	.5	2.0
.6	.4	2.50
.7	.3	3.33
.8	.2	5.0
.9	.1	10.0
.99	.01	100.0

The intuitive explanation underlying the positive relationship between the magnitude of the MPC and the magnitude of the multiplier is quite straightforward. A large MPC indicates that any initial shift in spending, by pulling up output and income, induces a large expansion in consumer spending. Total spending and output are therefore pulled up quite substantially after a series of *rounds*. At the other extreme, an MPC of zero indicates that any initial shift in spending, by pulling up output and income, induces no expansion in consumer spending. In this event the change in equilibrium output is identical to the initial shift in spending, and the multiplier equals one.

Why the Real-World Multiplier Is Smaller Than the Simple Multiplier

Economic studies estimate that the MPC in the United States is in the 0.8 to 0.9 range. Table 10-5 indicates that this puts the simple multiplier in the range of 5 to 10. An increase in investment spending of $10 billion—caused by lower interest rates or favorable tax changes toward business—is thus predicted to lead to an expansion in GNP of some $50 to $100 billion. In reality the true multiplier is only about 2, even though the MPC is in the 0.8 to 0.9 range. Three factors *water down* the actual expansion in the nation's real GNP associated with any given increase in spending.

Income Taxes   All modern societies have income taxes. As GNP begins to expand because of a shift in spending, part of the extra GNP is skimmed off in the form of taxes. Hence, an increase in GNP does not lead to an equivalent increase in disposable income. If the typical American is in a 25-percent marginal tax bracket (federal, state, and local income taxes combined), a one-dollar increase in gross income yields only a 75-cent increase in disposable income. Given an MPC of 0.8, the individual returns only 60 cents of the extra dollar in gross income to the spending stream (0.8 × 75 cents). The effective MPC out of GNP is reduced by the existence of income taxes, and the true multiplier is reduced considerably relative to a society with no income taxes. By reducing the swings in GNP associated with shifts in spending, income taxes act as an **automatic stabilizer** or *built-in-stabilizer.*[7] As GNP rises, so do taxes paid (the government budget deficit declines)—which holds back expenditures and limits the expansion. As GNP declines in recession, taxes paid drop off—which prevents disposable income from declining as much as GNP and thereby supports aggregate spending—and the government budget deficit expands, providing spending support to a depressed economy.

Effects on Investment Spending   Assume consumer spending or government spending shifts upward, touching off an expansion in GNP. The rising GNP is likely to induce an increase in the desire to borrow. Given the amount of funds available in the economy, this means that interest rates will go up. The interest rate-investment demand relationship of Figure 10-6 indicates that higher interest rates lead to lower investment expenditures, a phenomenon known as **crowding out.** The initial expansion of consumption or government spending, by driving up GNP and interest rates, may crowd out some investment spending. If so, part of the extra GNP (in the form of government goods and consumer goods) is offset by the reduced output of investment goods. In this event the true multiplier is not as large as the simple multiplier.

In reality, however, things are not quite so simple. Figure 10-6 indicates the relationship between interest rates and investment spending when *all other factors that influence investment are held constant.* As GNP increases in response to the initial increase in spending, the business outlook tends to improve and the utilization rate of existing plant capacity increases. These factors shift the investment demand curve of Figure 10-6 to the right. It is possible, therefore, that investment spending may increase *in spite of* higher interest rates. Instead of crowding out, we may get **crowding in**—a favorable response of investment spending to the initial shift in spending. The actual outcome produced by an initial shift in spending depends on the state of the economy at the time the economic stimulus occurs and the steepness of the investment demand curve of Figure 10-6. At any rate, the true multiplier is likely to differ from the simple multiplier as a result of induced effects on investment spending.

Price Level Effects   Equilibrium output in the income-expenditure or 45°-diagram framework is related to the aggregate supply-aggregate demand model in Figure 10-11 (page 228). The income-expenditure framework in the top portion of the figure neglects price-level considerations. Instead, the framework assumes that the relevant portion of the nation's aggregate supply curve is horizontal, so that the increased demand for goods and services is fully reflected in additional real output

---

Automatic Stabilizer or Built-in Stabilizer
A feature of the economy that acts automatically to inhibit economic fluctuations without discretionary policy changes being implemented.

Crowding-out Effect
The tendency for an expansionary fiscal policy to induce an offsetting reduction in investment expenditures by raising interest rates.

Crowding-in Effect
The tendency for an expansionary fiscal policy to induce an *increase* in investment spending by stimulating sales growth and utilization rate of existing plant and equipment.

---

[7]Adding income taxes (assume a marginal tax rate of t) into the model changes the multiplier expression to $m = \dfrac{1}{1 - MPC(1 - t)}$. When MPC is 0.8 and t is .25, the multiplier is $\dfrac{1}{1 - .8(.75)} = \dfrac{1}{.40} = 2.5$. By assuming a marginal income-tax rate of 25 percent in this instance, the multiplier is halved (from 5 to 2.5). The higher the marginal tax rate, the smaller the multiplier. One beneficial side effect of the increase in U.S. marginal income-tax rates during this century has been the reduction in the size of the multiplier. Shifts in expenditures now give rise to less volatile changes in output because the multiplier is smaller than in earlier times.

FIGURE 10–11

MULTIPLIER ANALYSIS IN INCOME-EXPENDITURE MODEL AND AGGREGATE SUPPLY-AGGREGATE DEMAND MODEL

An upward shift of the expenditures line $(C + I)$ in the top portion of Figure 10-11 raises equilibrium output from Y_{E_1} to Y_{E_2} and shifts the aggregate demand curve in the bottom portion of Figure 10-11 by the same horizontal distance $(Y_{E_2} - Y_{E_1})$. When the nation's aggregate supply curve is not horizontal, some portion of the added expenditures is manifested in higher prices rather than higher real output. Given the upward-sloping aggregate supply schedule in the bottom figure, real output increases only to Y_{E_3}, not to Y_{E_2} as the simple multiplier predicts.

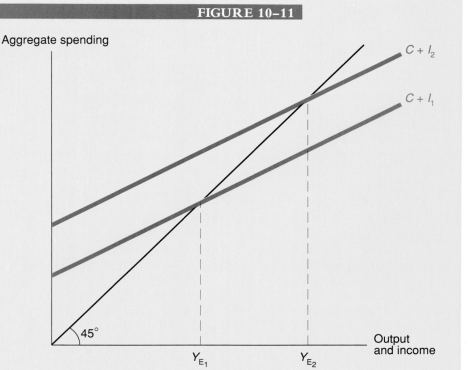

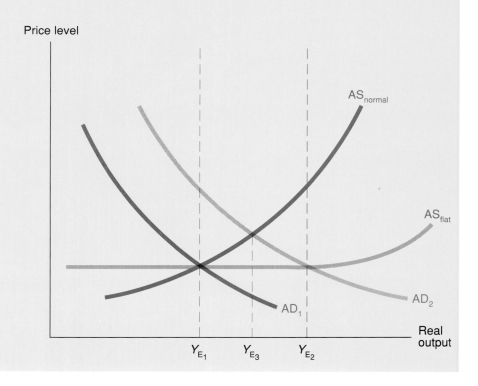

rather than partially reflected in higher prices. In Figure 10-11, when investment spending increases, the expenditure line shifts upward, touching off a multiple expansion of output and income from Y_{E_1} to Y_{E_2}. In the bottom portion of the figure, the aggregate demand curve shifts horizontally by the same magnitude, $Y_{E_2} - Y_{E_1}$. Thus, if the nation's aggregate supply curve were horizontal or flat (AS_{flat}), equilibrium output would increase from Y_{E_1} to Y_{E_2} in the lower portion of Figure 10-11. However, the aggregate supply curve normally slopes upward, as indicated by AS_{normal}. In the figure, equilibrium output actually rises only from Y_{E_1} to Y_{E_3}. Part of the increase in expenditures is manifested in higher prices rather than in higher real output.

The extent to which the initial increase in spending is dissipated in higher prices instead of greater real output depends on the state of the economy at the time the stimulus occurs. When the economy is initially operating far below capacity with considerable unemployment, the aggregate supply curve is quite flat and almost all the increased spending results in increased real output. When the economy is initially operating fairly close to full capacity, the aggregate supply curve is quite steep. In this event much of the increase in spending is reflected in higher prices.

SUMMARY

1. In the context of the aggregate supply-aggregate demand framework, business cycle phenomena are accounted for largely by a shifting aggregate demand curve. Aggregate demand shifts upward to account for cyclical upswings and downward to account for periods of declining economic activity. The chief long-run source of increasing living standards is a rightward-shifting aggregate supply curve stemming from growth in productivity. However, over the long term the aggregate demand curve has shifted rightward at a faster rate than the aggregate supply curve. As a result, the U.S. price level has persistently risen along with real output.

2. Aggregate demand for U.S. goods and services consists of four components: consumption, investment, government purchases, and net U.S. exports. The largest component is consumption expenditures; the smallest is net exports, which has been negative in recent years.

3. Factors that influence consumption spending include disposable income, wealth, recent income, expected future income, the general price level, expected future inflation, and the nation's stock of durable goods owned by households and firms.

4. A cornerstone of macroeconomics is the consumption function or the propensity-to-consume relationship—the relationship between disposable income and consumer spending when all other factors are held constant. Keynes postulated the existence of a "fundamental psychological law," whereby consumers consistently respond to any change in income by changing expenditures by a stable fraction of the change in income. This fraction is known as the marginal propensity to consume. Keynes' hypothesis has been borne out by extensive statistical analysis over the years.

5. Conceptually there are two components of consumer spending: autonomous consumption and induced consumption. Induced consumption is the portion dependent upon disposable income, depicted as a movement along the consumption function. Autonomous consumption is the portion of consumption attributable to factors other than income, depicted as the intercept of the consumption function on the vertical axis. Changes in autonomous consumption are caused by changes in wealth, expected future income, expected inflation, and other factors. These factors shift the entire position of the consumption function.

6. Saving, which is income not consumed, is also depicted graphically as a function of disposable income. The amount of saving at any income level is depicted as the vertical distance between the 45-degree line and the consumption schedule. The *break-even* level

of income is that level at which saving is zero and the consumption line intersects the 45-degree line. At income levels below the break-even level, saving is negative. At higher income levels, saving is positive.

7. The slope of the consumption function is $\Delta C/\Delta Y_d$, the marginal propensity to consume (MPC). The slope of the saving schedule is $\Delta S/\Delta Y_d$, the marginal propensity to save (MPS). The MPC and the MPS must add up to one. When one geometrically adds the consumption function and the saving function, one always obtains a 45-degree line starting from the origin.

8. Investment spending consists almost entirely of expenditures on producers' durable goods and structures—both residential and nonresidential. Since investment goods are typically long-lived and quite expensive, the bulk of investment is financed by borrowing. Therefore, the interest rate is a key determinant of the magnitude of investment spending. The investment demand schedule relates the volume of investment spending to the interest rate, all other factors (being) held constant.

9. Several other factors influence investment spending, and changes in these factors may be viewed as shifting the position of the investment demand curve. Factors that shift the investment demand curve include changes in business confidence, changes in the utilization rate of existing plant capacity, changes in expected future sales growth, changes in income-tax provisions, and changes in the level of stock market prices.

10. Equilibrium output occurs at the output level where aggregate spending equals output and income. In a simple two-sector economy (consumption and investment) with no government and no foreign trade, this is also the output level at which saving and investment are equal and where no involuntary change in inventories occurs. At equilibrium output the aggregate expenditures schedule $(C + I)$ intersects the 45-degree guideline.

11. The multiplier is defined as the ratio of the change in the nation's equilibrium output to the initial shift in spending that initiates the change in the nation's output. The magnitude of this multiplier depends on the magnitude of the MPC. If the MPC is zero, the multiplier is one because the initial shift in spending induces no additional response on the part of consumers. If the MPC is positive, the multiplier is larger than one. The larger the MPC, the larger the multiplier.

12. The actual, real-world multiplier is considerably smaller than the simple multiplier because income taxes reduce the effective MPC out of GNP and because part of the expenditure increase typically shows up in higher prices instead of higher real output. In addition, the initial increase in spending—by raising GNP and interest rates—may crowd out some investment spending.

KEY TERMS

consumer demand (C)
investment demand (I)
government purchases (G)
net exports (X − M)
disposable income (Y_d)
consumption function
saving
autonomous consumption
induced consumption
marginal propensity to consume
   (MPC)

marginal propensity to save
   (MPS)
saving function
break-even level
wealth or real-balance effect
equilibrium output
income-expenditure diagram
multiplier
automatic stabilizer
crowding-out effect
crowding-in effect

STUDY QUESTIONS AND PROBLEMS

1. Name the four components of aggregate demand and list them in descending order of magnitude (largest to smallest).
2. Explain why part of total government expenditures is not included as a component of aggregate demand under the *government* category (G).
3. Define the consumption function. Construct a table and a graph that illustrates your probable income-consumption relationship under various hypothetical incomes ranging from zero to $20,000. What sorts of factors would cause this consumption function to shift upward?
4. Define the marginal propensity to consume and the marginal propensity to save. In your consumption function (question 3), calculate your MPC and MPS in the income range $10,000–$20,000.
5. Explain why the MPC and the MPS must always add up to precisely one.
6. Draw a diagram illustrating the investment demand curve. Label the axes. Explain why the curve is downward sloping. What factors would shift this investment demand curve leftward? Explain.
7. Given other factors, explain the consequences of the following events for the position of the nation's investment demand curve:
   a. depreciation tables are lengthened (i.e., annual deductions are reduced)
   b. the nation's capacity utilization rate declines sharply
   c. expected future sales growth is revised upward
   d. the interest rate rises sharply
   e. the stock market crashes
8. In a two-sector economy (consumption and investment), explain the conditions for macroequilibrium. Why are these conditions equivalent?
9. Assume a simple two-sector economy with autonomous consumption spending of $1000 billion, an MPC of 0.80, and investment spending of $400 billion. Construct an expenditure table (such as Table 10-3) and indicate the equilibrium level of output. Construct a 45-degree diagram or income-expenditure diagram (see Figure 10-8) and indicate the equilibrium output level.
10. Assuming an MPC of 0.75 and an expansion in investment spending of $100 billion per year, trace the multiplier process on equilibrium output. What percent of the increase in equilibrium output occurs in the first five *rounds?*
11. Explain why a smaller MPS implies a larger multiplier.
12. Explain why our simple multiplier—that is, $\frac{1}{\text{MPS}}$ or $1/(1 - \text{MPC})$ is considerably larger than the true multiplier in the United States economy today.

a.

Y_d	C	S	MPC	MPS
0	2,000	−2,000	.90	.10
10,000	11,000	−1,000	.90	.10
20,000	20,000	0	.90	.10
30,000	29,000	+1,000	.90	.10
40,000	38,000	+2,000	.90	.10
50,000	47,000	+3,000	.90	.10

b. $20,000.
c. $2000.
d. $8000 because C = $2000 + .90 ($100,000) = $92,000.
   Alternatively, S = −$2000 + .10 ($100,000) = $8000.

SELECTED REFERENCES

Dillard, Dudley, *The Economics of John Maynard Keynes* (Englewood Cliffs, NJ: Prentice-Hall, 1948). This is a clear *translation* of the framework presented in Keynes' 1936 book, *The General Theory of Employment, Interest, and Money.*

Hall, Robert E., and John B. Taylor, *Macroeconomics: Theory, Performance, and Policy* (New York: Norton, 1988). Chapter 4 gives a clear discussion of consumption behavior and the multiplier.

Keynes, John Maynard, *The General Theory of Employment, Interest and Money* (New York: Harcourt Brace, 1936). This is Keynes' classic work, but is very heavy reading. Dillard's *translation* is recommended.

CHAPTER 11

MACROECONOMIC EQUILIBRIUM IN MODEL WITH GOVERNMENT SECTOR

I believe myself to be writing a book on economic theory which will largely revolutionize—not, I suppose, at once but in the course of the next ten years—the way the world thinks about economic problems.

—JOHN MAYNARD KEYNES (1935)

In Chapter 10 you studied the factors that drive consumption and investment spending. You learned that the nation's output gravitates to the level at which aggregate expenditures and output are in a state of balance. In the simplified two-sector (consumption and investment) world of Chapter 10, this occurs at the unique output level at which C + I spending equals GNP, or S equals I. You also learned that any shift in spending initiates a change in equilibrium output that is some multiple of the initial shift in spending. The size of this multiplier varies directly with the magnitude of the marginal propensity to consume (MPC).

In this chapter we bring government spending and taxation as well as international trade into the model and consider equilibrium output in the context of this more realistic framework. We then look at the connection between equilibrium output and the nation's employment level, and demonstrate that the economy may settle at an equilibrium output level either above or below the unique output level that just leads to full employment. Potential measures designed to move equilibrium output to the full-employment level are also analyzed. Further, in the absence of such discretionary policy actions, we assess the effectiveness of the economy's self-corrective mechanisms, which may operate eventually to move the nation's equilibrium output toward the full-employment output level.

233

OUTPUT DETERMINATION IN THE MODEL WITH GOVERNMENT SECTOR

To move closer to reality we introduce the government sector—expenditures and taxation—into our model. Consider the circular flow of income in the three-sector economy depicted in Figure 11-1. Firms produce the nation's GNP (top flow), which creates an equal amount of income (lower loop). This income is paid out to the households, which return most of the income to the spending stream via consumption expenditures (upper flow). However, taxes as well as saving represent withdrawals of income from the flow, which limit consumption spending out of gross income. These *leakages* are shown as S and T in the right-hand portion of the figure. Clearly, consumption expenditures are not sufficient to buy back all the output (GNP) produced. However, injections to the expenditure stream from the nonhousehold sector come from government purchases of goods and services (federal, state, local) as well as investment spending by firms.[1]

In this three-sector model, output gravitates to an equilibrium level at which aggregate spending $(C + I + G)$ just precisely exhausts aggregate output (GNP).

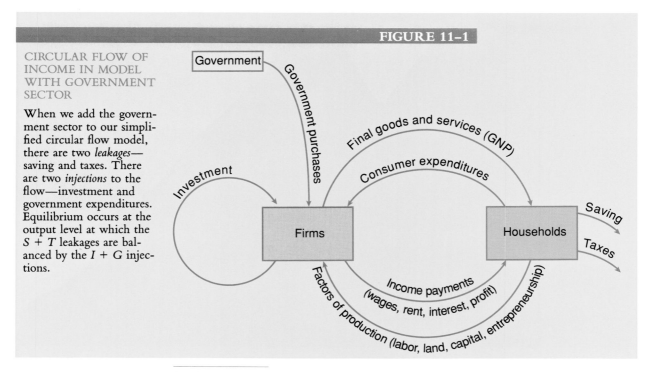

FIGURE 11–1

CIRCULAR FLOW OF INCOME IN MODEL WITH GOVERNMENT SECTOR

When we add the government sector to our simplified circular flow model, there are two *leakages*—saving and taxes. There are two *injections* to the flow—investment and government expenditures. Equilibrium occurs at the output level at which the $S + T$ leakages are balanced by the $I + G$ injections.

[1]Technically, since housing is counted as investment in the national income accounts, part of investment spending is provided by households. We ignore this consideration in Figure 11-1 by making the simplifying assumption that investment spending is initiated strictly by *firms*.

Another way to define this equilibrium condition is to state that the withdrawal of income by households from the circular flow $(S + T)$ is counterbalanced by the injections of spending into the flow by entities other than households $(I + G)$. In either case the nation's inventories do not change involuntarily and firms continue to produce the same GNP until equilibrium is disturbed by some change in spending (i.e., C, I, or G).

The nation's aggregate stock of inventories does not change *involuntarily*. This does not mean that firms may not *deliberately* alter inventories. For example, if aggregate demand and sales are expected to rise strongly, firms are likely to *voluntarily* increase inventories in order to accommodate the expected demand. In equilibrium, there can be no *involuntary* change in inventories stemming from an unexpected discrepancy between output and sales.

Conditions for Equilibrium in Three-Sector Model

Viewed from the perspective of the demand side of the economy (ignoring aggregate supply considerations), there are three equivalent conditions that must hold if output is to be in equilibrium.

$$\text{GNP or } Y = C + I + G \tag{1}$$

This statement indicates that aggregate expenditures must equal output.

$$S + T = I + G \tag{2}$$

Leakages from the circular income flow must equal injections into the flow from nonhousehold sectors.

$$\text{Involuntary change in inventories} = 0 \tag{3}$$

The nation's aggregate stock of inventories do not change involuntarily. Hence, there is no signal to change the level of output.

These three statements are alternative ways of saying the same thing. In equilibrium, all three conditions are satisfied. When the economy is out of equilibrium, none of the conditions is satisfied.

Table 11-1 indicates a hypothetical schedule of output and expenditures in a country with consumption, investment, and government expenditures.

With government purchases of goods and services (G) included in the model, equilibrium occurs at the output level at which aggregate spending $(C + I + G)$ precisely equals output. In Table 11-1, this occurs when output is $5000 billion. At

TABLE 11-1

OUTPUT AND EXPENDITURE SCHEDULE IN MODEL WITH GOVERNMENT SECTOR ($ billions per year)

Output (Y)	C	I	G	Aggregate expenditures	Involuntary change in inventories	Output
3000	2200	600	1000	3800	−	rises
4000	2800	600	1000	4400	−	rises
Y_E 5000	3400	600	1000	5000	0	remains unchanged
6000	4000	600	1000	5600	+	falls
7000	4600	600	1000	6200	+	falls

output levels below $5000 billion, aggregate spending exceeds output, inventories decline involuntarily, and firms are signaled to raise output. At output levels above $5000 billion, aggregate expenditures and sales ($C + I + G$) fall short of output, the nation's inventories rise involuntarily as long as output exceeds $5000 billion, and firms are signaled to cut back production. Hence, output of $5000 billion is **equilibrium output** for this economy—the output level at which aggregate production and sales are in a state of balance.

The information in Table 11-1 is illustrated in the context of our 45-degree diagram (income–expenditure diagram) by Figure 11-2, in which equilibrium output occurs where the $C + I + G$ line intersects the 45-degree line. This is the output level at which aggregate expenditures precisely equal output. Inventories remain at the current, desired level and no signal is given to deviate from current output of $5000 billion. At output levels above $5000 billion, note that the ($C + I + G$) line is below the 45-degree line, implying sales fall short of output and inventories rise involuntarily. This output is unsustainable; firms will cut back. At output levels below $5000 billion, the ($C + I + G$) line lies above the 45-degree line. Sales ($C + I + G$) exceed output, causing an undesired reduction of aggregate inventories. Firms are signaled to step up output. As in the simple two-sector model of Chapter 10, equilibrium output occurs at the output level at which aggregate expenditures equal output. The only difference is that we now include government purchases (G) as one of the components of aggregate expenditures. Our aggregate spending schedule now includes G, as well as C and I.

Equilibrium Output
The level of GNP at which aggregate demand is equal to GNP; the level of output toward which the economy tends to settle.

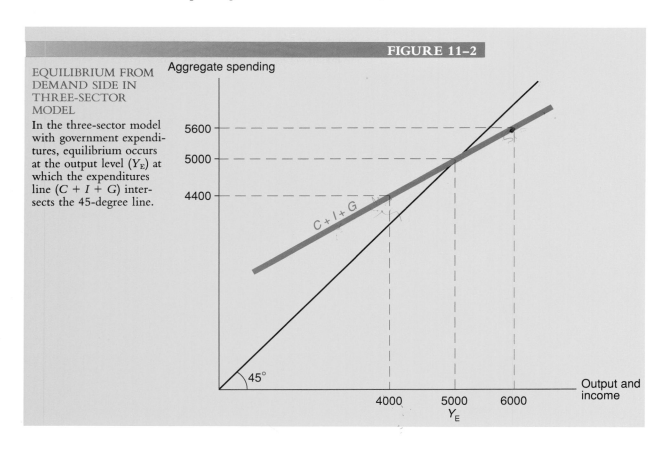

FIGURE 11–2

EQUILIBRIUM FROM DEMAND SIDE IN THREE-SECTOR MODEL

In the three-sector model with government expenditures, equilibrium occurs at the output level (Y_E) at which the expenditures line ($C + I + G$) intersects the 45-degree line.

The International Sector and Equilibrium in Complete Model

Thus far we have purposely neglected the role of international considerations in our analyses. American exports (X) constitute a source of expenditures or demand for U.S. goods and services. On the other hand, American expenditures for imports (M) represent a leakage from the circular flow of income. This suggests that net U.S. exports ($X - M$) should be included—along with C, I, and G—in our expenditures schedule. In our complete model, therefore, expenditures consist of $C + I + G + (X - M)$. For example, a $10-billion expansion in U.S. exports exerts the same effect on U.S. gross national product as a $10-billion increase in investment or government purchases.

International trade has become increasingly important in recent decades as the value of imports and exports have increased relative to our gross national product. The economic plight of nations has become increasingly intertwined. An expansion of income in Europe, for example, boosts American exports (X), thus increasing GNP in the United States. An increase in America's prosperity stimulates the Mexican, Japanese, and many other economies as we purchase more of their products.

Our equilibrium conditions must be modified somewhat when international trade is admitted into the income–expenditures model. First, the condition that output equals expenditures must be modified to indicate that GNP = $C + I + G + (X - M)$. Second, because imports and exports are leakages and injections, respectively, our leakages-equal-injections formulation for equilibrium becomes $S + T + M = I + G + X$. Finally, the third equilibrium condition is unaffected by adding international trade to the model: there can be no involuntary change in the nation's stock of inventories.

If exports and imports are equal, the ($X - M$) term may be dropped and equilibrium output may be analyzed without reference to international conditions. In much of the remainder of this chapter, we drop the ($X - M$) term for purposes of simplification so that we may focus on the role of fiscal policy (changes in government spending and taxing) in altering equilibrium output. Keep in mind, however, that a declining trade deficit fueled by expanding exports has been an important source of stimulus to U.S. economic activity in recent years.

The Multiplier Again

A shift in any of the components of aggregate spending (C, I, G, or $X - M$) shifts the aggregate expenditure line ($C + I + G + X - M$) and results in a change in equilibrium output that is a multiple of the shift in spending. If we abstract from international considerations by assuming $X = M$, the magnitude of this multiplier depends on the slope of the consumption function (MPC) and, hence, on the slope of the ($C + I + G$) schedule. The ($C + I + G$) schedule has the same slope as the consumption function in our model. This follows from the assumption that investment and government purchases depend *not* on output and income but on other factors. If shown separately in Figure 11-2, both the I and G lines would be horizontal lines, not varying with output and income. Thus, when we add $I + G$ spending to the consumption spending line, our aggregate spending line ($C + I + G$) is parallel to the consumption line and vertically above it by the amount of $I + G$ spending. Given the data of Table 11-1 and the construction of Figure 11-2, the MPC is 0.60. Accordingly, the slope of the ($C + I + G$) line is 0.60 and the multiplier is 2.5—that is, $1/(1 - .60)$. An increase in government expenditures of $400 billion, for example, raises equilibrium output by $1000 billion.

Note that we have not yet mentioned taxes in the context of this income–expenditures model. Analytically we may consider two types of taxes: lump-sum taxes, which are levied independently of income, and income taxes. Income taxes complicate matters somewhat by driving a wedge between gross income (Y) and disposable income (Y_d). A one-dollar increase in gross income raises disposable income by less than a dollar. This reduces the size of the multiplier because it reduces the magnitude of the effective MPC out of GNP. The model with an income tax present is treated in the appendix to this chapter. Here we deal with the simpler concept of lump-sum taxes.

Assume lump-sum taxes are reduced by $100 billion—that is, government reduces taxes by $100 billion via means other than reducing income tax *rates*. What is the effect on equilibrium output? Return to your multiplier intuition.

$$\text{shift in expenditures} \times \text{multiplier} = \text{change in } Y_e$$

Since the MPC is 0.60, the lump-sum tax cut of $100 billion shifts the consumption and total spending schedules upward by $60 billion. As a result, we compute the change in Y_e to be $60 billion $\times$ 2.5 = $150 billion. Equilibrium output rises by $150 billion as a result of the tax cut.

Alternatively, suppose government raises *transfer payments* (unemployment benefits, social security payments, and the like) by $100 billion. The analysis is quite similar. These transfers represent a dollar-for-dollar increase in disposable income. People increase consumption expenditures by the MPC times the change in transfers. Hence, the aggregate expenditures line shifts up by $60 billion and equilibrium output increases by $150 billion. A transfer payment is simply a negative lump-sum tax. An increase in transfer payments has the same effect as an identical cut in taxes.

EQUILIBRIUM OUTPUT VERSUS FULL EMPLOYMENT OUTPUT—RECESSIONARY GAPS AND INFLATIONARY GAPS

Each level of output (and income) is associated with a specific magnitude of employment—and a specific unemployment rate. An upward shift in aggregate expenditures raises the nation's output and employment levels and reduces its unemployment rate. A downward shift in aggregate spending initiates a contraction in the nation's output and employment and leads to an increase in its unemployment rate.

Full-Employment Level of Output
The level of GNP the economy would produce if its labor and other resources were fully employed.

Given the size of the nation's labor force, it follows that there is some output level that just suffices to generate full employment. We call this Y_f, the **full-employment level of output.** Output levels below Y_f result in a loss of output, income, and job opportunities for individuals seeking employment. Output levels above Y_f result in labor shortages in specific markets, bottlenecks and shortages in some product markets, and substantial inflationary pressures in labor and product markets.

Recessionary Gap

Keynes, writing in the 1930s, departed company with mainstream economists of his day. He asserted that the economy is likely at times to settle and remain at an equilibrium output level below the level required to yield full employment. In the

1930s, with the world economy mired in the Great Depression, Keynes understandably neglected the case in which equilibrium output exceeds the full-employment output level, Y_f. Instead, he focused attention on the issue of *underemployment equilibrium*—the prospect of an economy stuck in an equilibrium in which substantial involuntary unemployment persists. This case, known as a **recessionary gap,** is illustrated in Figure 11-3 (page 240).

The economy gravitates toward an output level of $5200 billion per year, the equilibrium level of output (Y_e) in Figure 11-3. However, an output level of $5400 billion is needed to generate full employment of the nation's labor force. The *recessionary gap* is the amount by which equilibrium (actual) output falls short of full-employment output. When a recessionary gap prevails in the economy, the unemployment rate is higher than the rate associated with full employment.[2]

If the nation's firms were to produce an output level of Y_f in the presence of a recessionary gap, aggregate spending ($C + I + G$) would be insufficient to purchase the output. Note in the top portion of Figure 11-3 that at output level Y_f, expenditures ($C + I + G$) fall short of the 45-degree line. Expenditures fall short of output, inventories rise involuntarily, and firms reduce output. There is not enough demand in the economy to justify producing a full-employment output level. The economy settles in at an *underemployment equilibrium.* In Figure 11-3, the magnitude of this recessionary gap is $200 billion.

Most of the time the U.S. economy operates with some recessionary gap. This is illustrated in Figure 11-4 (page 241), which shows actual and potential GNP for the period since 1960.

Potential GNP is defined as the hypothetical output level that would be produced if the economy were maintained at full employment. Potential GNP rises over time because the labor force and output per worker (productivity) increase over time. The distance between potential GNP and actual GNP when potential GNP exceeds actual GNP may be viewed as the magnitude of the recessionary gap. This gap reached its largest level in the recession year 1982, when it stood at roughly $300 billion.

The Self-Correcting Mechanism—Does a Recessionary Gap Automatically Self-Destruct?

Economists of Keynes' era argued that Y_e in Figure 11-3 could not really be considered an *equilibrium state,* because forces that would push Y_e rightward until it coincided with Y_f would automatically be unleashed. This alleged mechanism involved falling wages and prices and their influence via the **wealth effect** on spending and output. In particular, with output below Y_f, involuntary unemployment exists. Given competitive markets, this excess supply of labor should lead to declining wages and prices. Now recall our discussion in Chapter 10 about the role of changes in wealth shifting the consumption function and aggregate demand for goods and services. Keynes' contemporaries argued that falling prices—by raising the real value of people's checking accounts, savings accounts, and government bonds—would induce an upward shift in the consumption function. Therefore, the expenditures line ($C + I + G$) would shift upward. This mechanism is illustrated in Figure 11-5 (page 242).

Recessionary Gap
The amount by which equilibrium GNP falls short of the full-employment GNP level; the amount of additional output required to generate full employment.

Potential GNP
The level of GNP the nation would produce under conditions of full employment. Potential GNP rises over time because of growth in the labor force and productivity.

Wealth Effect
The effect that a change in the nation's price level exerts on consumption, aggregate demand, and equilibrium output by changing the real value of such financial assets as money, savings accounts, and government bonds held by individuals.

[2]Note that the existence of a recessionary gap does not imply that the economy is in recession—a period of falling real output. It merely implies that the output is below the full employment level. Output may be rising in the recovery phase of the business cycle and a large recessionary gap may exist because output is still a long way below the Y_f level.

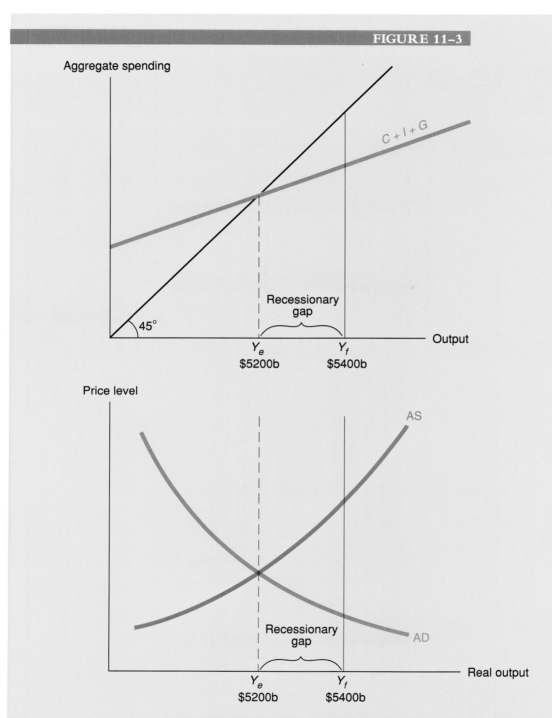

FIGURE 11–3

A RECESSIONARY GAP—EQUILIBRIUM BELOW FULL EMPLOYMENT

A recessionary gap occurs when equilibrium output (Y_e) is less than the full-employment output level (Y_f). This gap is defined as the amount of additional output required to generate full employment—$200 billion per year in this example.

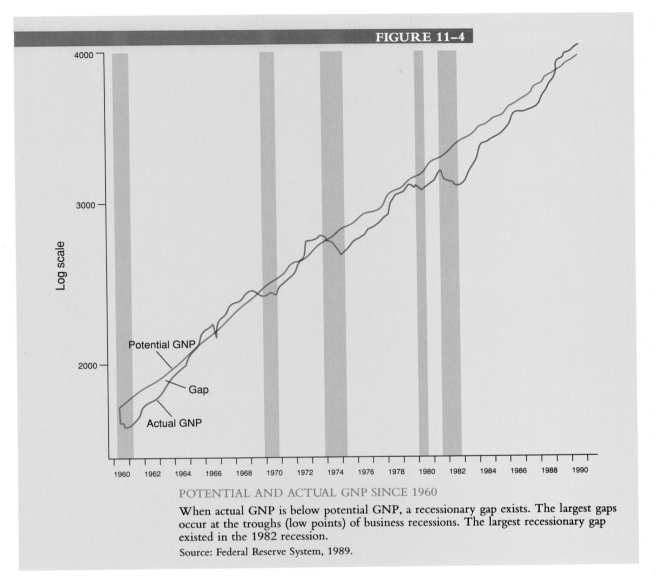

FIGURE 11-4

POTENTIAL AND ACTUAL GNP SINCE 1960

When actual GNP is below potential GNP, a recessionary gap exists. The largest gaps occur at the troughs (low points) of business recessions. The largest recessionary gap existed in the 1982 recession.

Source: Federal Reserve System, 1989.

In Figure 11-5, aggregate spending is initially $(C_1 + I + G)$ and output is in equilibrium at Y_{E_1}. Because wages and prices in competitive markets should decline when involuntary unemployment prevails, the initial output of Y_{E_1} is associated with falling prices. This leads, via the wealth effect, to an upward shift in consumption spending. Hence, aggregate expenditures shift upward to $(C_2 + I + G)$ and output is boosted to Y_{E_2}. However, since Y_{E_2} is also below Y_f, the price level continues to decline. The wealth effect continues to boost consumption spending and aggregate demand until output reaches Y_{E_4}, the state of full employment. In this view the only true equilibrium output is Y_{E_4}, the full-employment level.[3] In this view there is no

[3]An equilibrium is a state of balance in which there is no tendency toward change. At any output level below Y_f there *is* a tendency for output to change, *in this view,* because falling wages and prices, via wealth effects on consumption, shift up the aggregate expenditures schedule. In this event, Y_{E_1}, Y_{E_2}, and Y_{E_3} are not true equilibrium states. The only true equilibrium is Y_{E_4} or Y_f.

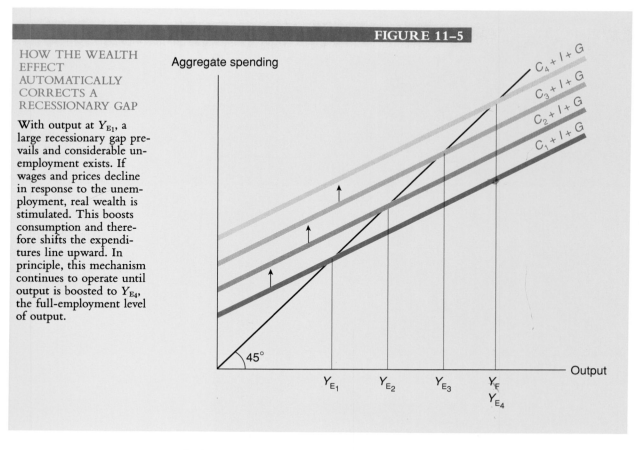

FIGURE 11–5

HOW THE WEALTH
EFFECT
AUTOMATICALLY
CORRECTS A
RECESSIONARY GAP

With output at Y_{E_1}, a
large recessionary gap prevails and considerable unemployment exists. If
wages and prices decline
in response to the unem-
ployment, real wealth is
stimulated. This boosts
consumption and there-
fore shifts the expendi-
tures line upward. In
principle, this mechanism
continues to operate until
output is boosted to Y_{E_4},
the full-employment level
of output.

**Self-Correcting
Mechanism**
The forces in the economy
that tend to push
equilibrium output toward
the full-employment output
level in the absence of
government implementation
of monetary and fiscal
policies.

such thing as an underemployment equilibrium, and no need for government to
intervene with its stabilization tools of monetary and fiscal policy to boost aggregate
spending. The economy contains a neat **self-correcting mechanism** and a
laissez-faire philosophy on the part of government is appropriate.

One did not have to possess an intellect as brilliant as Keynes' to observe in the
1930s that something was wrong with this analysis. Although output and employment remained at unusually low levels during the 1930s in nations throughout the
world, the system did not self-correct. It was only boosted out of its doldrums at the
end of the decade by the stimulus of government expenditures associated with the
onset of World War II.

Certainly in today's economy a major problem with the self-correcting
mechanism hypothesis lies in the assumption that the level of wages and prices
always declines when output is below the full-employment level. It is not unusual in
depressed times to find specific examples of declining commodity prices. Prices of
certain manufactured goods sometimes decline in periods of steep recession. Wages
and salaries in isolated sectors have been known to take a hit. However, the overall
level of wages and prices exhibits considerable resistance to downward pressure.
Even in 1982, when the U.S. unemployment rate pushed above 10 percent—the
highest level since the 1930s—the general level of wages and prices continued to
increase. There have been at least eight American recessions since World War II
ended in 1945. Contrary to earlier times, in none of these postwar recessions did the
overall level of wages or prices decrease. Resistance to downward wage and price

movements stems from written contracts, labor unions, minimum-wage laws, federal price supports, and noncompetitive economic behavior by firms. Also, some economists believe that an *implicit contract* (or *understanding*) exists between firms and workers that prevents wages and salaries from being cut in periods of temporarily depressed economic activity.[4]

If one assumes that wages and prices do not decline when output is below Y_f, the initial aggregate demand schedule of Figure 11-5 ($C_1 + I + G$) is not induced to shift upward—because the wealth effect via falling prices is nonexistent. Left to its own devices, the economy is stuck at output Y_{E_1} indefinitely. For this reason, Keynes called for active intervention on the part of government to boost aggregate demand and help the economy out of its stagnation. This can be done, in principle, by implementing stimulative monetary and fiscal policies. Although Keynes felt in the 1930s that stimulative fiscal policies were more effective, today most economists believe that stimulative monetary policy is equally effective (see Exhibit 11-1).

Removing Recessionary Gap Via Stimulative Macropolicies

Assume output (Y_e) is currently $5200 billion and Y_f is $5400 billion. A recessionary gap of $200 billion initially exists, as illustrated in Figure 11-6 (page 246). To boost equilibrium output from $5200 billion to $5400 billion and to remove the recessionary gap, we must consider the basic multiplier intuition.

$$\text{initial shift in spending} \times \text{multiplier} = \text{change in } Y_e$$

Assume the MPC is 0.75, so the multiplier is 4. The desired change in Y_e is $200 billion—the magnitude of the recessionary gap. Hence, we can write

$$\text{necessary shift in spending} \times 4 = \$200 \text{ billion}$$
$$\text{necessary shift in spending} = \$50 \text{ billion}$$

To totally remove the recessionary gap and bring the economy to full employment, macroeconomic policy must shift the aggregate expenditures line ($C + I + G$), upward (vertically) by $50 billion. By pulling up consumer expenditures, this touches off a multiplier effect and raises equilibrium output by $200 billion.

To shift the aggregate expenditures schedule upward by $50 billion, stimulative monetary and fiscal policies can be employed. Stimulative monetary policies, by bringing down interest rates and increasing the supply of money, boost investment spending and (perhaps) also consumption spending. Stimulative fiscal policy involves an increase in government purchases, a cut in taxes, an increase in government transfer payments—or some combination of these measures.

YOUR TURN

Assume a recessionary gap of $270 billion exists and the economy's marginal propensity to consume is 0.90. To eliminate the gap via three alternative procedures, calculate the

a. necessary increase in G
b. necessary cut in lump-sum taxes, T
c. necessary increase in transfer payments

---

[4]Arthur M. Okun has outlined this latter hypothesis in depth in *Prices and Quantities: A Macroeconomic Analysis* (Washington, DC: The Brookings Institution, 1981). In Okun's analysis, the implicit contract is based on long-term considerations and loyalty between employers and employees. In the implicit contract, firms forgo cutting wages in hard times in return for an understanding that workers stay with the firm in good times when new job opportunities develop.

EXHIBIT 11-1

WHAT IS
KEYNESIAN
ECONOMICS?

You have perhaps encountered the term "Keynesian" (pronounced "cān-esian") in connection with readings or discussions about economics. John Maynard Keynes, an Englishman, was probably the world's most eminent and influential economist in the period spanning the two great world wars (roughly 1915–1945). Keynes focused his analytical mind and brilliant pen on the crucial macroeconomic issues of his time.

Keynes' early writings were often polemical in nature, attacking contemporary politicians, important economic policy decisions, and conventional modes of thinking. For example, his *Economic Consequences of the Peace* (1919) exposed the folly of attempting to extract massive reparations payments from (the vanquished) Germany after World War I. *The Economic Consequences of Mr. Churchill* (1925) attacked Winston Churchill's decision to return England to the gold standard in 1925 at the exchange rate that existed prior to World War I. Since the level of prices in England had increased more rapidly than in most other countries, this decision mandated that England would have to sharply deflate her domestic price level in order to be competitive in international markets. To deflate domestic prices, the British government imposed an era of tight money and austere budgetary policies. While the United States and other industrial nations prospered during 1925–1929, the unemployment rate in England never fell below ten percent.

Keynes' most influential work was *The General Theory of Employment, Interest, and Money*, published in 1936. For years Keynes had been deeply bothered by the failure of the conventional economic analysis of the times to explain adequately the events of The Great Depression of the 1930s. The prevailing view held that economic downturns were self-correcting and did not require macroeconomic intervention on the part of government. Indeed, such efforts by the government were viewed as detrimental and inappropriate. Hence, a philosophy of *laissez-faire* ("let do" or "leave it alone") described the contemporary view of the proper role of government in macroeconomic life.

Keynes believed that changes in aggregate demand precipitated by private agents (principally consumption and investment spending) could lead to excessive or inadequate aggregate expenditures in the economy. In particular, such behavior could lead to a downward shift in aggregate spending (in both the 45-degree and aggregate demand-aggregate supply frameworks). This would result in depressed economic activity and distress for workers and firms. In the absence of government intervention, the AD curve could intersect the AS curve at a level of real output far below the level required to generate full employment of the work force. Further, the economy could remain stuck at such a suboptimal output level for an indefinite or at least intolerable period of time.

Keynes therefore advocated aggressive action by the central government to attempt to stabilize output at a level sufficient to generate high levels of employment and prosperity. In particular, he advocated fiscal policy measures to shift the expenditures line and AD curve upward in the 1930s. Keynes felt this could be done most effectively by increasing government expenditures or by reducing taxes to boost consumption spending. He published an *open letter* to

President Franklin D. Roosevelt in the New York Times in 1934. In this letter Keynes proposed ways the government could shift the AD schedule upward, thus lifting the economy out of the Great Depression.

During the 1950s and 1960s, a debate took place between Keynesians (followers of Keynes) and monetarists (Milton Friedman and his disciples) over the relative strength of fiscal policy and monetary policy. Keynesians typically argued that changes in taxes and government expenditures exert a more powerful and predictable effect on economic activity than do changes in the supply of money. Monetarists typically argued that changes in money are more powerfully and predictably linked to subsequent changes in economic activity than are fiscal policy measures. It is worth noting that Keynes (who died in 1946) believed that both monetary and fiscal policy were potent weapons in normal economic times. However, in a period of depression such as the 1930s, Keynes believed that monetary policy was ineffective and that stimulative fiscal actions were required to boost aggregate spending and economic activity.

By the 1970s, an element of consensus that both monetary and fiscal policy were powerful instruments of macroeconomic policy prevailed in the economics profession. The debate turned to the propriety of efforts to *actively employ* monetary and fiscal policies to stabilize economic activity. **Keynesian economics** has come to signify a philosophy of *activism* on the part of government in the macroeconomy. Keynesian economists generally advocate active implementation of both monetary and fiscal policy to attempt to stabilize the level of real output at levels sufficient to generate reactively high levels of output and employment but not so high as to lead to severe inflationary pressure.

Monetarists and other critics of Keynesians are very skeptical of the use of active implementation of monetary and fiscal policy to *fine tune* the economy. This skepticism is based on both technical factors and the belief that political considerations are likely to influence macroeconomic policy-making. These critics of Keynesian economics typically prefer a steady policy of modest growth in the money supply irrespective of the contemporary economic situation. They believe, in the long run, such a modest policy will outperform the activist prescription advocated by Keynesian economists. We analyze this debate in some depth in Chapter 19.

Some writers have depicted Keynes as anticapitalistic, perhaps even socialist. This portrayal is inaccurate. Keynes believed that the capitalistic system is the most desirable form of economic organization. In order for capitalism to operate properly, however, Keynes believed that occasional active intervention by government in the macroeconomy is necessary. On a personal level, Keynes benefitted considerably from the capitalistic system. He was never a man lacking in self-assurance. In the prime of his life, Keynes spent the first 20 minutes each morning in bed planning his day's speculations in the foreign-exchange and commodities markets. Though he suffered an early, severe setback in the post-World War I deflation, Keynes recovered his losses and ultimately amassed a fortune for his own portfolio and that of his academic affiliation—King's College, Cambridge.

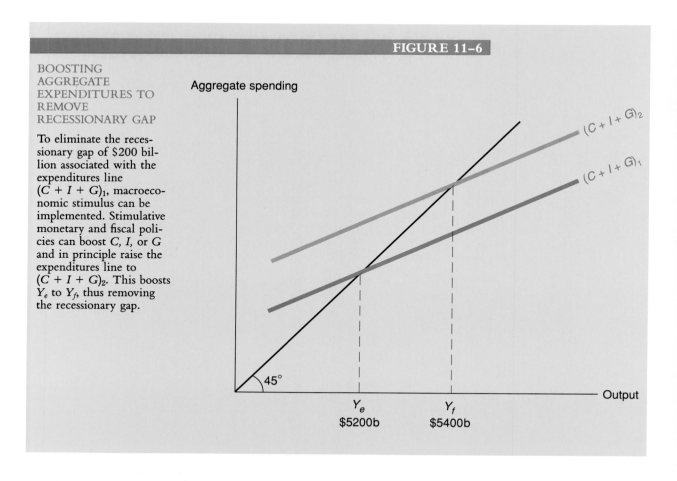

FIGURE 11-6

BOOSTING AGGREGATE EXPENDITURES TO REMOVE RECESSIONARY GAP

To eliminate the recessionary gap of $200 billion associated with the expenditures line $(C + I + G)_1$, macroeconomic stimulus can be implemented. Stimulative monetary and fiscal policies can boost C, I, or G and in principle raise the expenditures line to $(C + I + G)_2$. This boosts Y_e to Y_f, thus removing the recessionary gap.

Inflationary Gap

Inflationary Gap
The amount by which equilibrium GNP exceeds the full-employment GNP level; occurs when aggregate expenditures are excessive relative to the capacity to produce goods and services.

An **inflationary gap** occurs when there is excessive aggregate expenditures for goods and services. Firms, individuals, and government are collectively attempting to purchase more goods and services than the economy can produce. This situation is illustrated in Figure 11-7. In the event firms produce full-employment output, aggregate spending $(C + I + G)$ exceeds output. In other words, equilibrium output exceeds the full-employment output level, and the difference is known as the inflationary gap.

Historically, inflationary gaps are the typical state of affairs in time of war. However, they also occur in peacetime. In wartime, government expenditures on the military effort are rapidly increased without commensurate increases in taxes to force down consumption spending. As a result, aggregate spending becomes excessive and a period of inflation ensues. Examples in the American experience include World Wars I and II and the Korean and Vietnam Wars. In addition, inflationary gaps tend to occur in peacetime when the economy is near the peak of the business cycle. Review Figure 11-4. Those periods in which actual GNP exceeds potential GNP (1967–1969, 1973 and 1988–1989) are periods in which an inflationary gap prevails.

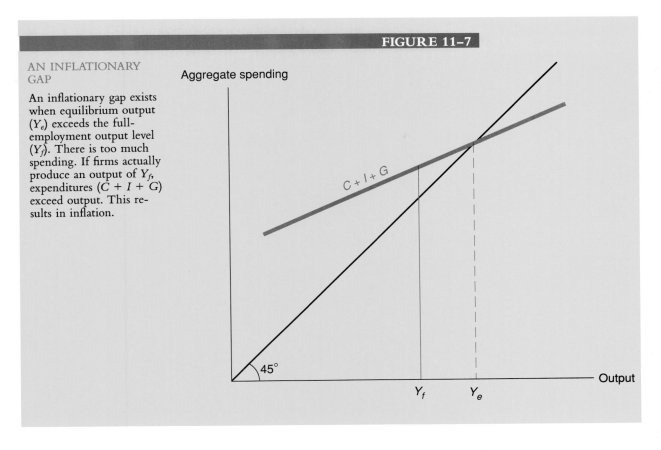

FIGURE 11–7

AN INFLATIONARY GAP

An inflationary gap exists when equilibrium output (Y_e) exceeds the full-employment output level (Y_f). There is too much spending. If firms actually produce an output of Y_f, expenditures $(C + I + G)$ exceed output. This results in inflation.

Inflationary Gap—The Self-Correcting Mechanism

In Figure 11-8 (page 248) we illustrate the automatic *self-correcting mechanism* that tends to remove an inflationary gap without any policy actions taken by government. In the figure, the economy is initially operating with aggregate expenditures of $(C_1 + I + G)$ and output at Y_{E_1}. The magnitude of the inflationary gap is initially $Y_{E_1} - Y_f$. This inflationary gap will self-destruct or automatically eliminate itself. As prices rise, the real value of the money, government bonds, and savings accounts held by individuals is reduced. Hence, the *real wealth* of individuals is reduced, resulting in a downward shift of the aggregate consumption function. In Figure 11-8, suppose the aggregate expenditures line initially shifts downward to $(C_2 + I + G)$, reducing equilibrium output to Y_{E_2}. Because a (smaller) inflationary gap of $Y_{E_2} - Y_f$ still exists, inflationary pressure continues, further reducing real wealth in the hands of private individuals. Accordingly, consumption spending and aggregate spending continue to shift downward in real terms, further reducing equilibrium output and lessening the inflationary pressures. Finally, when aggregate demand has shifted downward to $(C_3 + I + G)$, equilibrium output is reduced to Y_{E_3}. At that point the inflationary gap is eliminated via the automatic correcting force of the wealth effect. Barring outside factors that would continue to shift aggregate demand upward (such as rapidly increasing government spending or money supply), inflation experiences a natural death.

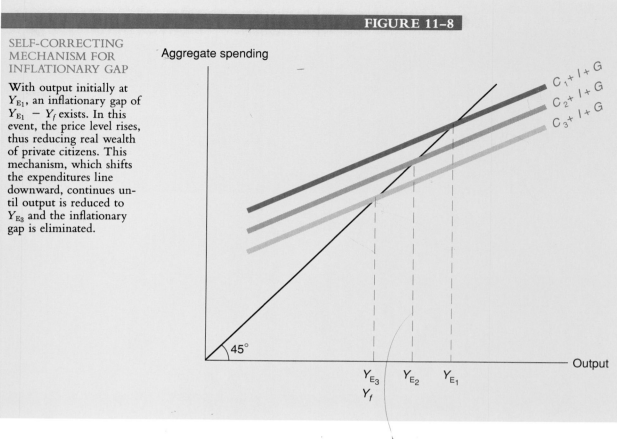

FIGURE 11–8

SELF-CORRECTING
MECHANISM FOR
INFLATIONARY GAP

With output initially at Y_{E_1}, an inflationary gap of $Y_{E_1} - Y_f$ exists. In this event, the price level rises, thus reducing real wealth of private citizens. This mechanism, which shifts the expenditures line downward, continues until output is reduced to Y_{E_3} and the inflationary gap is eliminated.

Asymmetry in the Self-Correcting Mechanisms

There is a fundamental asymmetry in the way our economy handles inflationary and deflationary gaps. An inflationary gap inevitably results in inflation, thereby reducing real aggregate expenditures via the wealth effect and thus self-destructing. A recessionary gap also corrects itself when it results in a falling level of prices. However, modern economies have strong institutional features that prevent the general price level from declining during normal periods of recession. Therefore, the recessionary gaps are not self-correcting in contemporary macroeconomic circumstances. Keynesian economists believe in such instances government should move in aggressively with stimulative monetary and fiscal policies to boost the economy to a higher level of activity.

Nipping an Inflationary Gap Via Monetary and Fiscal Restraint

The fact that an inflationary gap eventually disappears of its own accord does not mean that macroeconomic policy should ignore the opportunity to fight existing inflation or offset incipient inflationary pressures via monetary and fiscal restraint. As we document in Chapter 18, inflation is highly undesirable: it arbitrarily redistributes the nation's income and wealth, and thereby creates tension and distrust in society. In addition, inflation impairs the economy's long-term growth and induces various activities that are inefficient from society's viewpoint. Every effort should be made by those in charge of monetary and fiscal policy to keep inflation in check. Consider the situation illustrated in Figure 11-9.

In Figure 11-9, assume the marginal propensity to consume (MPC) and the slope of the initial aggregate expenditures line $(C + I + G)_1$ are both 0.80. Equilibrium output is $5300 billion and Y_f is $5200 billion. An inflationary gap of $100 billion prevails. To remove the inflationary gap, the aggregate expenditures line must be shifted downward from $(C + I + G)_1$ to $(C + I + G)_2$. This can be done by reducing any of the three components of demand—C, I, or G. Because we know that the MPC is 0.80, the multiplier is 5. Hence:

needed shift in spending × multiplier = needed change in Y_e

needed shift in spending × 5 = −*$100 billion*

needed shift in spending = −*$20 billion*

A downward shift of the aggregate expenditures schedule of $20 billion is required to eliminate the inflationary gap. This can be done via reducing government purchases by $20 billion, raising taxes or reducing transfer payments sufficiently to shift consumption downward by $20 billion, tightening monetary policy and raising interest rates sufficiently to snuff out $20 billion of investment spending—or some combination of these measures.

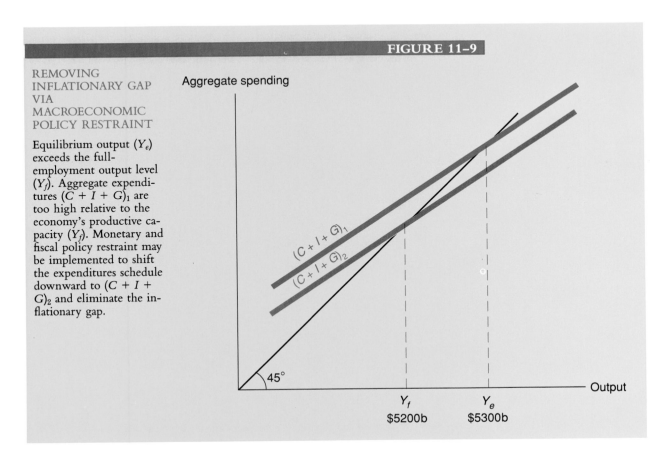

FIGURE 11–9

REMOVING INFLATIONARY GAP VIA MACROECONOMIC POLICY RESTRAINT

Equilibrium output (Y_e) exceeds the full-employment output level (Y_f). Aggregate expenditures $(C + I + G)_1$ are too high relative to the economy's productive capacity (Y_f). Monetary and fiscal policy restraint may be implemented to shift the expenditures schedule downward to $(C + I + G)_2$ and eliminate the inflationary gap.

Aggregate spending

$(C + I + G)_1$

$(C + I + G)_2$

45°

Output

Y_f
$5200b

Y_e
$5300b

SUMMARY

1. In a three-sector economy with government spending and taxes, macroeconomic equilibrium from the demand side occurs at the unique output level where $C + I + G$ spending equals output. Alternatively stated, equilibrium occurs where $S + T$ leakages from the circular income flow are precisely balanced by $I + G$ expenditures. When international trade is integrated into the model, equilibrium occurs where $C + I + G + (X - M)$ spending equals output or where $S + T + M$ leakages are balanced by $I + G + X$ expenditures.

2. Each output level in the economy is associated with a specific magnitude of employment and unemployment. Producing a larger output level induces an expansion of employment and a drop in the nation's unemployment rate. There is a unique output level (Y_f) that just suffices to create full employment.

3. If output settles below the level needed to generate full employment, a recessionary gap exists. If wages and prices are downwardly flexible in response to involuntary unemployment and excess plant capacity, the recessionary gap automatically corrects itself. The mechanism involved is that wages and prices decline in response to the involuntary unemployment, triggering a positive wealth effect on consumer demand that raises aggregate expenditures and output until Y_f is reached. If wages and prices are downwardly inflexible, the recessionary gap may persist unless aggregate spending is boosted by stimulative monetary and/or fiscal measures.

4. If equilibrium output exceeds the full-employment level, an inflationary gap exists. In this situation the levels of wages and prices rise persistently. This reduces the real wealth of households, thus shifting the consumption function and the aggregate expenditures schedule downward. This process continues until the inflationary gap is eliminated.

5. Since wages and prices exhibit greater upward than downward flexibility, inflationary gaps and recessionary gaps are asymmetrical in their self-correcting mechanisms. Left to its own devices, an inflationary gap will self-destruct. This need not be the case with a recessionary gap.

6. Macroeconomic policies to combat a recessionary gap include stimulative monetary policy to reduce interest rates and boost investment spending and stimulative fiscal policy in the form of tax cuts to boost consumption spending or increases in government expenditures. Policies designed to eliminate an inflationary gap include restrictive monetary policy to drive up interest rates and reduce investment spending and contractionary fiscal policy in the form of higher taxes to cut consumption spending and cuts in government expenditures.

7. Keynesian economists typically advocate active implementation of monetary and fiscal policies to attempt to stabilize output at a level near Y_f. For both political and technical reasons, critics of Keynesians are skeptical of this activist philosophy. These critics tend to advocate a more modest approach on the part of macroeconomic policymakers that calls for stable policies which are not substantially altered in an effort to influence macroeconomic activity.

KEY TERMS

equilibrium output

full-employment level of output

recessionary gap

potential GNP

wealth effect

self-correcting mechanism

Keynesian economics

inflationary gap

STUDY QUESTIONS AND PROBLEMS

1. Analyze the three conditions for equilibrium output in the three-sector economy. Explain why these three conditions are equivalent.

2. Assume actual output initially exceeds equilibrium output. Explain the mechanism by which output is induced to return to equilibrium. Illustrate via a 45-degree diagram.
3. Assume the MPC is 0.80 and equilibrium output is currently $4800 billion. Assume government purchases rise by $40 billion. Using a simple 45-degree diagram, analyze the impact on equilibrium output. Conduct the same analysis for the case in which lump-sum taxes are increased by $40 billion. In this analysis, what is the net effect of a combined increase in government purchases and lump-sum taxes of $40 billion each?
4. Explain the meaning of an *inflationary gap* and a *recessionary gap*. Analyze the mechanism by which these gaps are alleged to be *self-correcting*. Why might it be true that an inflationary gap may have a more effective automatic self-correction mechanism than a recessionary gap?
5. Assume a recessionary gap of $100 billion currently prevails and the economy's MPC is 0.75. How large an increase in government purchases would eliminate the gap? How large a cut in lump-sum taxes? How large an increase in government transfer payments?
6. What is the general attitude of Keynesian economists regarding the government's responsibility for the level of output and employment in the economy? On what bases can one oppose this Keynesian viewpoint? Analyze.
7. Assume the government wishes to eliminate an inflationary gap of $100 billion via fiscal policy measures. If the multiplier is 2, how much must the government cut its purchases? By how much must it raise (lump-sum) taxes to eliminate the gap? By how much must the government reduce transfer payments to eliminate the gap?

ANSWERS TO YOUR TURN

Since the MPC is given to be 0.90, the simple multiplier is 10. Hence, the expenditures line $(C + I + G)$ must be shifted upward by $27 billion in order to increase equilibrium output by $270 billion. This can be done by:

a. increasing G by $27 billion
b. reducing lump-sum taxes by $30 billion, which increases disposable income by $30 billion and shifts the consumption and aggregate expenditures schedules upward by $27 billion
c. raising government transfers by $30 billion, which operates in the identical fashion of a lump-sum tax cut of $30 billion, shifting the expenditures line $(C + I + G)$ upward by $27 billion.

SELECTED REFERENCES

Economic Report of the President (Washington, DC: published annually). Discusses contemporary macroeconomic events and policies.

Glahe, Fred R., *Macroeconomics: Theory and Policy,* 4th ed. (San Diego: Harcourt Brace Jovanovich, 1989). An intermediate macroeconomics text that analyzes these issues in depth.

Miller, Roger L., *The Economics of Macro Issues* (St. Paul: West Publishing Company, 1983). Discusses certain issues presented in this chapter.

ELEMENTARY MATHEMATICS OF INCOME DETERMINATION IN MODEL WITH GOVERNMENT SECTOR

With just a little elementary algebra we can learn a lot of elementary macroeconomics in a few pages. We begin with the condition for macroequilibrium in the economy with a government sector:

$$Y = C + I + G \qquad (11A\text{-}1)$$

In equilibrium, aggregate spending $(C + I + G)$ equals output or GNP (Y). We write general equations for consumption, investment, and government purchases as follows:

$$C = a + bY_d \qquad (11A\text{-}2)$$

$$I = I_0 \qquad (11A\text{-}3)$$

$$G = G_0 \qquad (11A\text{-}4)$$

Equation 11A-2, the consumption function, states that consumer spending has two components: an exogenous or autonomous portion (a) that depends on factors other than disposable income and a portion induced by disposable income. In the equation, b is the marginal propensity to consume (MPC) and bY_d indicates the magnitude of induced consumption (i.e., the consumption that depends on the level of Y_d).

Equations 11A-3 and 11A-4 indicate that investment and government purchases are *exogenous* (i.e., they are not dependent on income or output but are determined by factors outside the model). Such exogenous factors may include interest rates, business confidence, or political considerations. Diagrammati-

cally, we may depict the three equations in terms of our income-expenditure or 45-degree diagram (see Figure 11A-1).

In an economy with no taxes, output and gross income and disposable income are identical. However, in an economy with taxes, disposable income differs from output and gross income as follows:

$$Y_d = Y - T \qquad (11A\text{-}5)$$

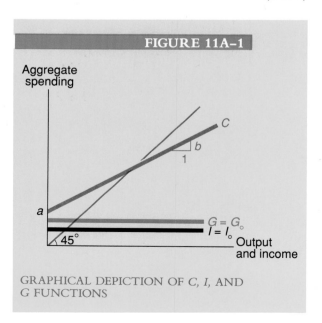

FIGURE 11A–1

GRAPHICAL DEPICTION OF C, I, AND G FUNCTIONS

In Equation 11A-5, T represents the dollar amount of taxes collected, Y is gross output and income, and Y_d is disposable income. Assuming we have an income tax that skims off a fixed proportion (t) of gross income, the taxes collected (T) are tY and

$$Y_d = Y - tY = Y(1 - t) \qquad (11A\text{-}6)$$

We can now restate the consumption function equation (11A-2) as follows:

$$C = a + bY(1 - t) \qquad (11A\text{-}7)$$

We are now in a position to solve for equilibrium output by substituting into Equation 11A-1:

$$Y = a + bY(1 - t) + I_0 + G_0$$

Solving, we obtain

$$Y - bY(1 - t) = a + I_0 + G_0 \qquad (11A\text{-}8)$$

$$Y = \frac{a + I_0 + G_0}{1 - b(1 - t)} \qquad (11A\text{-}9)$$

$$= \frac{1}{1 - b(1 - t)} \, (a + I_0 + G_0) \qquad (11A\text{-}10)$$

The expenditure shifts that can touch off the multiplier process in Equation 11A-10 are changes in autonomous consumption (Δa), changes in investment (ΔI), and changes in government purchases (ΔG). The multiplier is now $\dfrac{1}{1 - b(1 - t)}$. Note that for the special case in which there is no income tax (i.e., $t = 0$) the multiplier reduces to the simple multiplier employed in Chapters 10 and 11 $\left(\dfrac{1}{1 - \text{MPC}}\right)$, that is, $\dfrac{1}{1 - b}$.

Equation 11A-10 tells us that equilibrium output depends on five factors: autonomous consumption (a), autonomous investment (I_0), autonomous government expenditures (G_0), the MPC (b), and the existing income-tax rate (t). Now let's breathe life into the model by making some reasonable assumptions about the magnitudes of these key parameters. Solving for the nation's equilibrium level of output, assume

$$a = \$400 \text{ billion}$$

$$I_0 = \$600 \text{ billion}$$

$$G_0 = \$1000 \text{ billion}$$

$$b = 0.75$$

$$t = 0.20$$

Given these assumptions, Equation 11A-9 tells us that

$$Y = \frac{\$400b + \$600b + \$1000b}{1 - .75(.80)} = \$5000 \text{ billion}$$

Equilibrium output in these conditions is $5000 billion per year. The graphical depiction of aggregate expenditures and equilibrium output in this example is given by Figure 11A-2. In this model with income taxes, the multiplier differs from our simple multiplier:

$$\text{multiplier} = \frac{\text{change in } Y}{\text{initial shift in spending}}$$

$$= \frac{1}{1 - \text{MPC}(1 - t)}$$

In our simple model with no income tax ($t = 0$), the multiplier depended only on the MPC. In the presence of an income tax, the multiplier depends on the level of the tax rate (t) as well as the magnitude of the MPC (b). The income tax, by creating a wedge between Y and Y_d, reduces the effective MPC out of GNP. As GNP rises, Y_d rises by a lesser amount. Hence, income taxes restrain consumption out of GNP and reduce the size of the multiplier. The higher the level of the income-tax rate the larger the wedge, and given the MPC out of disposable income, the smaller the magnitude of the multiplier. This is

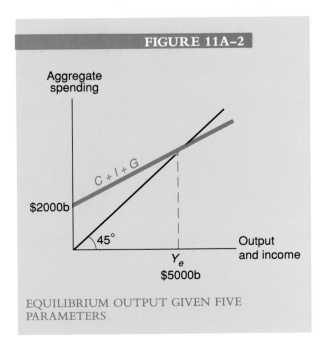

FIGURE 11A-2

EQUILIBRIUM OUTPUT GIVEN FIVE PARAMETERS

EXHIBIT 11A–1

INCOME-TAX RATES AND THE STABILITY OF ECONOMIC ACTIVITY

Economists have noted that economic fluctuations in the United States have been milder in the post-1945 period than in the prewar era. This condition is illustrated in Figure 11A-3, which indicates the annual percentage change in real output in the pre- and post-1945 eras.

Several factors may have contributed to the comparatively stable economy of modern times. Monetary and fiscal policymakers may have become more adept at implementing countercyclical policies to stabilize the economy. Such institutional changes as bank deposit insurance and unemployment insurance have surely contributed to economic stability by smoothing the *ripple effects* associated with economic downturns. Because of such changes, economic agents that precipitate shifts in consumption and investment spending may behave in a less volatile manner in the modern era. However, many economists would emphasize

an alternative explanation: income-tax rates were much lower in the earlier period. Following World War II, the income-tax system emerged as a powerful automatic stabilizer. No one likes high income-tax rates. They may have adverse incentive effects or supply-side effects that slow the long-term growth trend of potential GNP, a consideration we ignore in this model. However, on the demand side of the economy, high income-tax rates do have at least one favorable side effect. They serve as a shock absorber by acting to inhibit changes in economic activity initiated by shifts in C, I, or G spending. Given the fact that higher income-tax rates reduce the size of the economy's multiplier and given that income taxes were higher in the post-World War II era, one would expect to observe a more stable economic environment in the latter period.

Question: What are the implications of the income-tax cuts associated with the 1981 Economic Recovery Tax Act and the 1986 Tax Reform Act for future economic stability?

FIGURE 11A–3

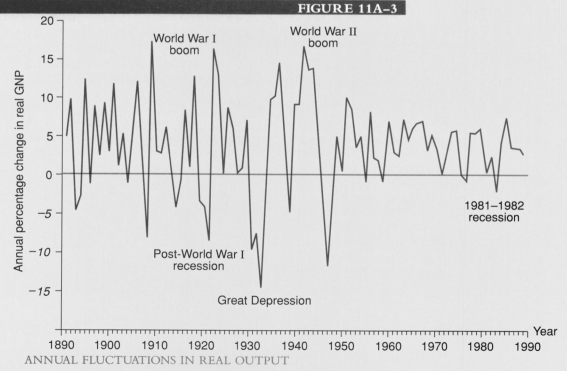

ANNUAL FLUCTUATIONS IN REAL OUTPUT

Fluctuations in economic activity have been milder in the post-World War II era than in earlier times.

Sources: *Historical Statistics of the United States* and *Economic Report of the President*, 1989.

illustrated in Table 11A-1, which utilizes this multiplier formula under alternative income-tax rates to compute the size of the multiplier.

TABLE 11A-1

THE MPC, INCOME-TAX RATE, AND THE MULTIPLIER

MPC	Simple multiplier $t = 0$	Multiplier when $t = 0.20$	Multiplier when $t = 0.50$
.5	2	1.67	1.33
.6	2.5	1.92	1.43
.75	4	2.50	1.60
.8	5	2.78	1.67
.9	10	3.57	1.82

Note that for any given MPC, an increase in the income-tax rate reduces the size of the multiplier. In the U.S. economy, with the MPC believed to be in the 0.80–0.90 range, the existence of an income tax brings down the multiplier by a very substantial amount. For this reason our tax system serves as an *automatic stabilizer* or *built-in-stabilizer*. Any swings in Y_e caused by shifts in C, I, or G spending are reduced or moderated in the presence of an income tax. In fact, the higher the income tax rate the greater the power of this stabilizing effect.

In our model, when the MPC is given, the multiplier process can be touched off by any one of four factors: a change in autonomous consumption (shift in consumption function), a change in investment spending, a change in government expenditures, or a change in t (the income-tax rate). A change in autonomous consumption, investment spending, or government spending shifts the $C + I + G$ line of Figure 11A-2, changing equilibrium output by the multiplier effect. A change in the income-tax rate (t) alters the *slope* of the $C + I + G$ line and changes the size of the multiplier, thereby changing equilibrium output. We examine these factors in turn.

Beginning with our initial assumed parameters and Y_e of $5000 billion, assume that the stock market crashes, shifting the consumption function downward by $40 billion. In terms of equation 11A-10, a has decreased by $40 billion. Our multiplier formulation indicates that

$$\Delta Y_e = \text{shift in spending} \times \text{multiplier}$$

$$\Delta Y_e = -\$40 \text{ billion} \times 2.5 = -\$100 \text{ billion}$$

Equilibrium output falls by $100 billion. Using similar analysis, if government spending rises by $80 billion, equilibrium output expands by $200 billion. If investment spending rises by $20 billion, equilibrium output expands by $50 billion.

Finally, beginning with an equilibrium output of $5000 billion, assume the income-tax rate (t) increases from 20 percent to 25 percent. We calculate from Equation 11A-10 that the multiplier is reduced from 2.50 to 2.285. If we multiply this by total autonomous expenditures ($a + I_0 + G_0$) of $2000 billion, the new equilibrium output is calculated to be $4570 billion.

THE MODEL OF AGGREGATE SUPPLY AND AGGREGATE DEMAND

I do believe in supply-side economics.

—RONALD REAGAN, 1981

Waiting for supply-side economics to work is like leaving the landing lights on for Amelia Earhart.

—WALTER HELLER, 1982

Chapter 8 introduced the simple aggregate supply-aggregate demand model and surveyed the U.S. economic history of recent decades using that model as a basic framework. Chapter 12 examines this simple model in greater detail, focusing especially on the nature of the aggregate supply and aggregate demand curves. As we shall discover, the shapes of these curves have important implications for many macroeconomic issues.

We indicated in Chapter 8 that the aggregate supply curve relates the output that the nation's firms collectively produce (horizontal axis) to the price level of the nation (vertical axis). The aggregate supply curve normally is positively sloped because, as the price level rises, certain production costs remain fixed in the short run. As output prices rise, profitability increases and firms step up output. In the long run, when all production costs have time to adjust to the higher level of output prices, higher prices result in little or no increased profitability and therefore in little or no incentive to increase production. Hence, the nation's aggregate supply curve is quite steep or even vertical in the long run.

ASPECTS OF AGGREGATE SUPPLY AND AGGREGATE DEMAND

The Level of Output and the Slope of the Aggregate Supply Curve

A more complete analysis of the **aggregate supply curve** indicates that its slope varies with the level of economic activity. This is illustrated in Figure 12-1, which divides the aggregate supply curve into three distinct ranges—the depression range, the normal range, and the classical range.

In the **depression range,** when output is quite low relative to the economy's potential output, the aggregate supply curve is horizontal. There are lots of well-qualified idle workers available, firms are operating their plants at a low rate of utilization, and materials are plentiful. Firms are glad to step up output from any low level to the level Y_a in Figure 12-1 without requiring an inducement in the form of higher prices of their products. Therefore, the aggregate supply curve is horizontal in the output range of zero to Y_a. This is the *depression range* of the aggregate supply curve because it represents a situation of substantial unemployment of workers and idle plant capacity.

Depression Range
The flat portion of the aggregate supply curve. More output can be called forth at the existing price level because substantial idle plant capacity exists and qualified workers are available to firms at existing wages.

FIGURE 12–1

THE THREE RANGES OF THE AGGREGATE SUPPLY CURVE

The aggregate supply curve may be divided into three ranges. In the depression range, the curve is flat. In the normal range, it is upward sloping. In the classical range, it is vertical, indicating that firms cannot respond to higher prices by increasing output.

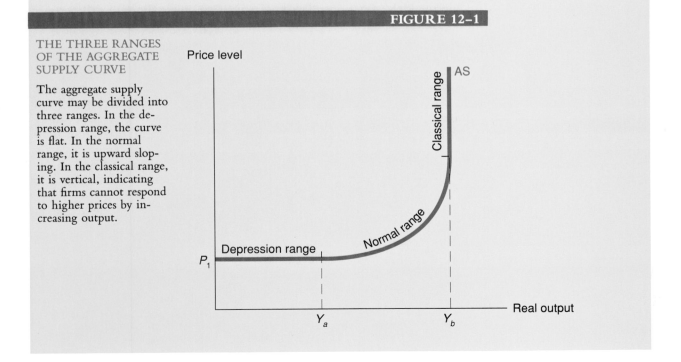

Normal Range
The upward-sloping
portion of the aggregate
supply curve; to induce
more production, higher
prices are required.

At output levels between Y_a and Y_b the economy is in the **normal** or **intermediate range** of the aggregate supply curve, and this curve is upward sloping. To induce firms to expand output in this region, higher prices are necessary. Costs of production begin to rise with expanded output because firms may have to hire somewhat less-productive workers as the pool of unemployed workers declines. As firms add to their payrolls, the ratio of capital to labor declines. The additional output provided by an additional worker begins to decline. Also, firms may have to bring on line less-efficient plant and equipment. Some firms may have to add shifts or pay an overtime wage premium. The extra cost of producing an extra unit of output begins to rise once output reaches Y_a, and higher output prices are therefore required to induce firms to step up output beyond that point. The aggregate supply schedule slopes upward and becomes increasingly steep as the economy approaches output of Y_b because these forces become more severe.

At output level Y_b firms are operating at full capacity with added production shifts in place. Actual GNP exceeds potential GNP and the unemployment rate is below the rate associated with full employment. In many sectors there are shortages of appropriately qualified workers. The economy is bursting at its seams, producing maximum output. No matter how high the price level goes, firms cannot respond by increasing production. The economy is at full capacity and the aggregate supply curve becomes vertical at that point. No further output can be squeezed out of the economy. The vertical portion of the aggregate supply curve is known as the **classical range**.

Classical Range
The vertical portion of the
aggregate supply curve.
Firms are incapable of
expanding output because
the economy is operating at
maximum capacity.

Effects of Changes in Aggregate Demand in the Three Regions

Assume aggregate demand increases (aggregate demand curve shifts rightward) because of increased government expenditures, a tax cut, or increased investment spending resulting from investment tax credits. The implications of the increased demand for the nation's output and price level depend critically upon where the economy is operating on its aggregate supply curve. This principle is illustrated in Figure 12-2.

Assume the nation's aggregate demand curve shifts rightward by $40 billion, from AD_1 to AD_2 in Figure 12-2. The nation's aggregate supply curve is horizontal in the relevant range, indicating the existence of substantial idle capacity and unemployment. Output is boosted by the full $40 billion, moving from Y_1 to Y_2, and the nation's price level remains constant at P_1. This depression case is sometimes referred to as the "Keynesian" region because Keynes' analysis emphasized the depression scenario. The simple Keynesian multiplier comes closest to being valid in this instance.[1] All the increased spending is reflected in output gains, none of it spilling over into higher prices.

In the normal, positively sloped region of the aggregate supply curve, assume again that the aggregate demand curve shifts rightward by $40 billion, from AD_3 to AD_4. The increase in output from Y_3 to Y_4 is less than $40 billion in this instance

---

[1]Note, however, that the simple multiplier formulation of $1 \div (1 - MPC)$ still overstates the real-world multiplier because it neglects the role of income taxes and financial market reverberations. As the initial shift in spending begins to be reflected in expanding output and income, the presence of income taxes prevents disposable income from expanding in line with gross output and income. This slows the consumption response to rising income and limits the multiplier. In addition, the expanding income may result in higher interest rates and possibly crowd out some investment spending. For these reasons, the aggregate demand curve does not shift rightward by the full shift in spending times the simple multiplier.

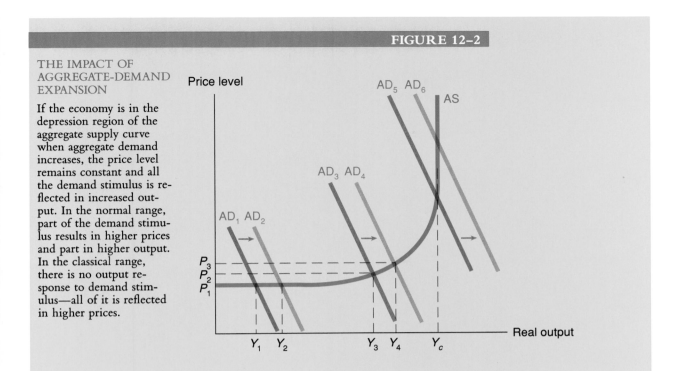

FIGURE 12-2

THE IMPACT OF AGGREGATE-DEMAND EXPANSION

If the economy is in the depression region of the aggregate supply curve when aggregate demand increases, the price level remains constant and all the demand stimulus is reflected in increased output. In the normal range, part of the demand stimulus results in higher prices and part in higher output. In the classical range, there is no output response to demand stimulus—all of it is reflected in higher prices.

because a portion of the added spending goes into higher prices as the nation's price level is boosted from P_2 to P_3. The closer the economy is to capacity output when aggregate demand increases, the greater the portion of the added demand that finds its way into higher prices rather than greater real output of goods and services. The simple Keynesian multiplier of Chapters 10 and 11 overstates the response of equilibrium output to a shift in expenditures when the economy is in the normal range of the aggregate supply curve.

Finally, assume the aggregate demand curve shifts rightward by $40 billion, from AD_5 to AD_6, when the economy is in the classical (vertical) range of the aggregate supply schedule. Since the economy is already cranking out goods and services at 100 percent of capacity (Y_c), output is unable to respond to the increased expenditures. All the increased spending is dissipated in higher prices, none of it being reflected in greater output. The real-world multiplier is zero, because no matter how much expenditures increase, the increase in equilibrium real output is zero.

Explanation of the Nature of the Aggregate Demand Curve

It is important to understand the relationship between the income–expenditures model (or 45-degree diagram model) of Chapter 11 and the aggregate demand curve of the aggregate demand-aggregate supply model. Figure 12-3 (page 260) helps explain this relationship. The figure indicates that although the horizontal axes of both models measure the nation's real output, the vertical axes differ. The income–expenditures model places aggregate real spending on the vertical axis and the aggregate demand-aggregate supply model utilizes the price level on the vertical axis.

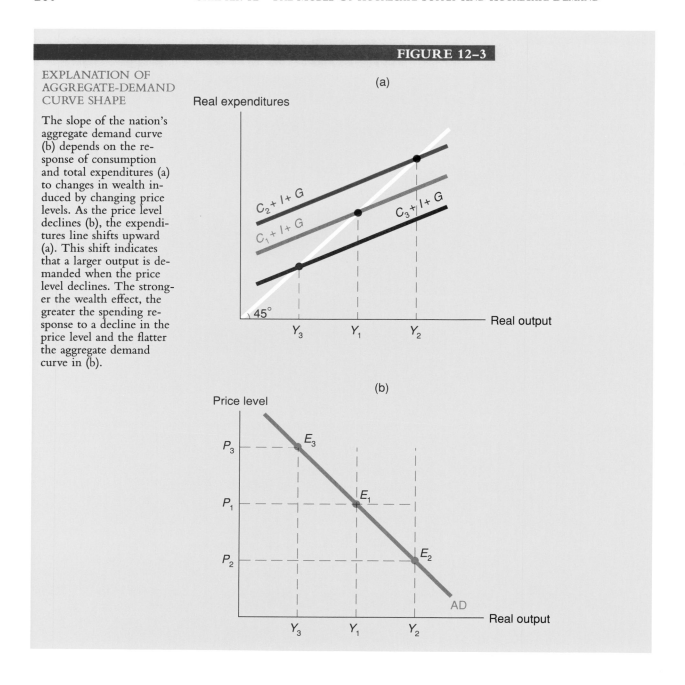

FIGURE 12-3

EXPLANATION OF AGGREGATE-DEMAND CURVE SHAPE

The slope of the nation's aggregate demand curve (b) depends on the response of consumption and total expenditures (a) to changes in wealth induced by changing price levels. As the price level declines (b), the expenditures line shifts upward (a). This shift indicates that a larger output is demanded when the price level declines. The stronger the wealth effect, the greater the spending response to a decline in the price level and the flatter the aggregate demand curve in (b).

Assume that aggregate expenditures are $(C_1 + I + G)$ in (a) of Figure 12-3, with the economy in equilibrium at E_1. The nation's output is Y_1, with the price level at P_1 in (b). To understand the linkage, suppose the nation's price level is lower—say P_2. What happens to the aggregate expenditures line (a) and, hence, to real output? Since the real value of money, savings accounts, and bonds held by private citizens and firms is greater, this positive *wealth effect* stimulates real consumption spending, thereby boosting the expenditures schedule to $(C_2 + I + G)$. The new equilibrium is

E_2 in (a), with output at Y_2. Accordingly, in (b), we indicate that the lower price level of P_2 is consistent with real output demanded of Y_2.

On the other hand, suppose the nation's price level is much higher—say P_3. The decline in private wealth shifts real consumption downward, reducing the nation's expenditure schedule (a) to $(C_3 + I + G)$. Output declines to Y_3, and (b) indicates that a price level of P_3 is consistent with output of Y_3 from the demand-side point of view.

The impact of the wealth effect on consumer spending associated with changes in the price level thus explains the downward slope of the nation's aggregate demand curve. If the wealth effect is quite strong, the aggregate demand curve is relatively flat. Small declines in the price level would trigger relatively strong wealth effects and thereby considerably increase output demanded. On the other hand, if these wealth effects are weak, a relatively large decline in the price level is required to bring about a significant boost in expenditures and output. The aggregate demand curve would be relatively steep. In the extreme case, suppose the wealth effect is nonexistent because people do not change consumption expenditures at all in response to changes in wealth. In this case, neither the consumption function nor the expenditure line (a) shifts in response to changing price levels. The same output level (Y_1) would prevail at all price levels. The aggregate demand schedule (b) would be a vertical line through E_1 and output level Y_1.

As a general proposition, **Keynesians** tend to be skeptical of the strength of the wealth effect; they believe that the aggregate demand curve is quite steep. In addition, they tend to believe in *sticky wages and prices*; Keynesians are wary of the proposition that prices are flexible on the downside. **Monetarists** typically believe that the wealth effect is powerful and therefore the aggregate demand curve is relatively flat. In addition, monetarists have more faith in the existence of downward price flexibility. These issues have important implications for the efficiency of the economy's **self-correcting mechanism** and, hence, the need for active implementation of monetary and fiscal policies by the government to stabilize economic activity at output levels near full employment.

Keynesians
School of economics characterized by advocacy of active use of monetary and fiscal policies to combat cyclical fluctuations. Keynesians are skeptical of the effectiveness of the economy's self-correcting mechanism.

Monetarists
School of economics characterized by skepticism of government ability to conduct effective countercyclical stabilization policies. Monetarists prefer to strengthen and place more emphasis on the economy's self-correcting mechanism.

The Economy's Self-Correcting Mechanism Once Again

In Chapter 11 we illustrated the economy's self-correcting mechanism via the income–expenditures framework. A decline in the nation's price level in response to a large **recessionary gap** boosts real consumption and aggregate expenditures, thus pushing the economy back in the direction of full employment. An **inflationary gap,** in which equilibrium output exceeds the full-employment output level, unleashes the opposite forces. Rising prices, by reducing real wealth, continue to exert a contractionary influence on real spending and output until the inflationary gap is eliminated. We illustrate these principles in the context of the more complete aggregate demand-aggregate supply framework in Figure 12-4 (page 262).

In Figure 12-4(a), assume the economy is initially at *A,* the intersection of AD and AS_1. The recessionary gap is equal to $Y_F - Y_1$. If wages and materials' prices decline in response to the unemployment and idle capacity, the aggregate supply curve shifts rightward. Why? Recall from Chapter 8 that reduced prices of inputs to the production process (oil, land, lumber, labor, and so forth) shift the aggregate supply curve rightward. As the aggregate supply curve shifts to AS_2, the economy moves to *B,* with output boosted to Y_2. Since a (smaller) gap still exists, the process continues until the aggregate supply curve shifts to AS_3. The economy moves to *C*

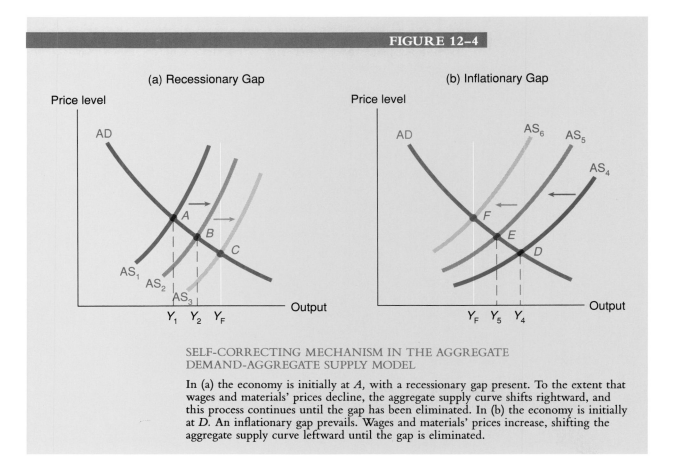

SELF-CORRECTING MECHANISM IN THE AGGREGATE
DEMAND-AGGREGATE SUPPLY MODEL

In (a) the economy is initially at A, with a recessionary gap present. To the extent that wages and materials' prices decline, the aggregate supply curve shifts rightward, and this process continues until the gap has been eliminated. In (b) the economy is initially at D. An inflationary gap prevails. Wages and materials' prices increase, shifting the aggregate supply curve leftward until the gap is eliminated.

and full employment is automatically restored, assuming wages and prices decline whenever excessive unemployment exists and assuming declining prices trigger a positive wealth effect on consumer spending.

In Figure 12-4(b), the economy is initially at D, the intersection of AD and AS_4. Output is at Y_4, and an inflationary gap of $Y_4 - Y_F$ prevails. Equilibrium output exceeds the full-employment output level; the economy is overheated. Wages and prices are rising rapidly. As wages and materials' prices escalate, the nation's aggregate supply curve shifts leftward (decrease in aggregate supply). The economy initially moves to point E in (b), with output at Y_5. However, since some inflationary gap still exists, the mechanism of increasing wages and materials' prices continues until the aggregate supply schedule shifts to AS_6. At this point (F), actual output has been reduced to the full-employment output level (Y_F) and the inflationary gap has self-destructed.

During the period in which the inflationary gap is being eliminated, the economy experiences *stagflation*—the unhappy combination of rising prices and falling or stagnant output. However, this stagflation is not as painful as some episodes of the disease because, in this case, the nation's output and employment are already at unsustainably high levels.

Keynesians, Monetarists, and the Self-Correcting Mechanisms

Keynesian and monetarist views on the reliability of the self-correcting mechanism, and therefore on the need for active stabilization policies, depend on the perceived nature of the nation's aggregate demand schedule as well as on the extent of price level flexibility in the economy. Consider the economy's self-correcting mechanism for a recessionary gap in the presence of two alternative aggregate demand schedules. Figure 12-5 illustrates the mechanism for the correction of the gap given Keynesian and monetarist perceptions of the nature of the nation's aggregate demand curve.

The Keynesian view of the aggregate demand curve (AD_k) is given in Figure 12-5(a). Since Keynesians believe the wealth effect is weak, they view the aggregate demand curve as quite steep. With the economy initially at the intersection of the aggregate demand curve and AS_1, a recessionary gap exists $(Y_F - Y_1)$. As falling prices and wages shift the AS curve rightward, the demand and output responses are relatively meager. In the figure, the price level must fall all the way to P_4 to boost the economy to full employment. Such a steep decline in prices might be unsettling to

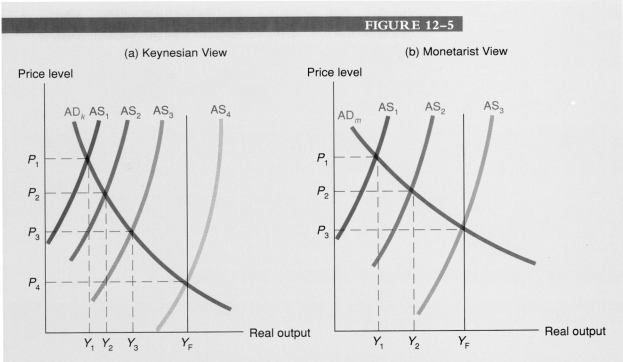

FIGURE 12-5

(a) Keynesian View

(b) Monetarist View

SELF-CORRECTING MECHANISM UNDER KEYNESIAN AND MONETARIST PERCEPTIONS OF THE AGGREGATE DEMAND CURVE

As indicated in (a), Keynesians view the aggregate demand curve as steep because the wealth effect is weak. In this case a major decline in the price level is required to shift the aggregate supply curve sufficiently rightward to return the economy to full employment. Monetarists believe the wealth effect is strong and the aggregate demand curve is relatively flat (b). A relatively modest decline in prices suffices to bring the economy to full employment.

normal economic relationships. For example, debtors would suffer considerable stress in paying off debts fixed in nominal dollars. Since Keynesians are also skeptical of the actual flexibility of wages and prices on the downside, they reject reliance upon the self-correcting mechanism. In the words of Nobel Laureate James Tobin, the wealth effect "is a pretty weak reed on which to pin hopes for self-adjustment of the economy."[2]

Because Keynesians are skeptical both of the power of wealth effects and of the existence of downward price flexibility, they advocate active use of government's monetary and fiscal policy tools to boost aggregate demand when large recessionary gaps prevail.

Monetarists view the aggregate demand curve as relatively flat, as indicated by AD_m in Figure 12-5(b). A decline in the price level from P_1 to P_3 would suffice to boost the economy to full employment, because the wealth effect is viewed as powerful. Coupled with the view that wages and prices are highly responsive to market forces of supply and demand, this leads monetarists to reject the Keynesian prescription for active government intervention in the macroeconomy. They believe that the natural forces of the market suffice to eliminate recessionary gaps and return the economy to full-employment levels of output. Rather than calling for active stabilization policies, monetarists advocate measures to assure competitive markets in the economy so that prices and wages maintain a high degree of flexibility.

SUPPLY-SIDE ECONOMICS

When Ronald Reagan became U.S. President in early 1981, the American economy was not healthy. Successful restriction of oil output by the OPEC cartel had driven the price of oil to $35 per barrel in 1980, some 14 times the price that had prevailed a decade earlier. Inflation was running at an annual rate of 12 percent and interest rates were sky high. The economy of the 1970s had been plagued by *stagflation*—the combination of stagnant output and rising prices. Productivity growth was slow, raising concerns about long-term increases in living standards. The time was ripe for innovations in economic ideas and policies.

Supply-side economics became the catchphrase of the Reagan Administration in the early 1980s, as several supply siders were appointed to high-level positions in the Administration. The idea was to deemphasize policies intended to boost aggregate demand and instead to concentrate on measures intended to shift the aggregate supply curve rightward by stimulating the desire to work, produce, save, and invest. Figure 12-6 illustrates the case for supply-side policies rather than traditional demand-side policies in order to boost output.

Ever since Keynes' pathbreaking analysis of the 1930s, macroeconomic policy had concentrated on aggregate demand. With the economy initially at A in Figure 12-6(a) and a recessionary gap present, stimulative monetary and fiscal policies are capable of boosting aggregate demand from AD_1 to AD_2. This raises output from Y_1 to Y_2, but unfortunately also pushes up the price level unless the economy is in the depression (horizontal) region of the aggregate supply curve. Supply-side economics (b) concentrates on the aggregate supply curve. If this curve can be shifted rightward from AS_1 to AS_2 via government policies, we can achieve higher output without

Supply-Side Economics
School of economics that emphasizes the importance of promoting policies to shift the aggregate supply curve rightward by implementing measures that boost the incentive to work, produce, save, and invest.

---

[2]James Tobin, "Keynesian Economics and Its Renaissance," in David A. Reese (ed.), *The Legacy of Keynes* (San Francisco: Harper and Row, 1987), page 116.

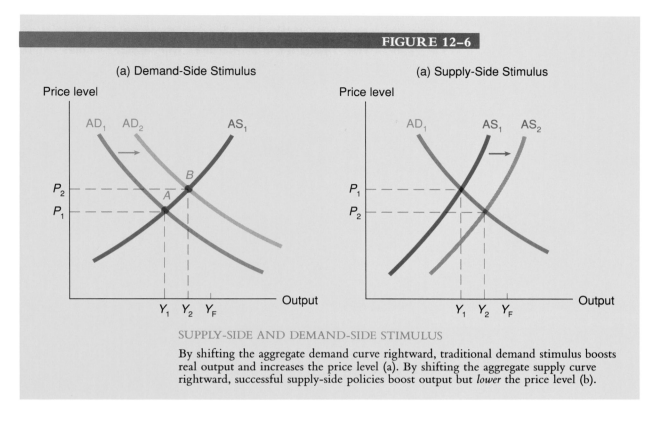

FIGURE 12–6

(a) Demand-Side Stimulus

(a) Supply-Side Stimulus

SUPPLY-SIDE AND DEMAND-SIDE STIMULUS

By shifting the aggregate demand curve rightward, traditional demand stimulus boosts real output and increases the price level (a). By shifting the aggregate supply curve rightward, successful supply-side policies boost output but *lower* the price level (b).

higher prices. In fact, as indicated in (b), the price level would decline from P_1 to P_2. Such a decline would allow room for some expansion in aggregate demand, thus yielding even more output without pushing prices above the original P_1 level—in principle.

Clearly, there is much to be gained from a successful supply-side program. In this sense we are all supply siders. Thoughtful liberals and conservatives, democrats and republicans alike, favor supply-side economics. The main point of contention is whether the Reagan Administration's policies of the 1980s in fact represented an efficient and effective set of supply-side measures. What measures does an ideal supply-side program include?

What Shifts the Aggregate Supply Curve Rightward?

Recall the sorts of factors that shift the nation's aggregate supply curve rightward, increasing the total output that firms willingly produce at each and every price level:

1. a decrease in wages and salaries
2. a decrease in the prices of other inputs—land, capital, materials
3. an increase in the nation's labor supply and work effort
4. an increase in the nation's capital stock
5. an increase in technology, which raises productivity

Supply-side economics, to be successful, must involve policies that implement changes in some of these five measures in order to promote a sustained and persistent rightward shifting of the nation's aggregate supply curve. Other than by promoting free international trade and competitive labor and product markets, there is little government potential for bringing about items 1 and 2. Supply-side economics must therefore focus on increasing the nation's labor force and work effort, boosting the stock of capital by promoting investment spending, and fostering technological change by boosting research and development efforts in private corporations and university and government laboratories. These are the arenas in which supply-side economics must work—stimulating the search for new technologies and increasing the incentives to work, produce, save, and invest.

To a large extent supply-side economics has two components: increasing the incentive to work and increasing the share of output allocated to investment in new plant, equipment, and technology. The latter objective is illustrated in Figure 12-7.

When supply-side measures successfully increase the share of the nation's output devoted to investment goods at the expense of consumption goods and government goods, we move from *A* to *B* on the production possibilities curve. This boosts the speed with which the curve shifts outward over time (i.e., it increases the rate of economic growth).[3] Also, when the incentive to work is stimulated, thus

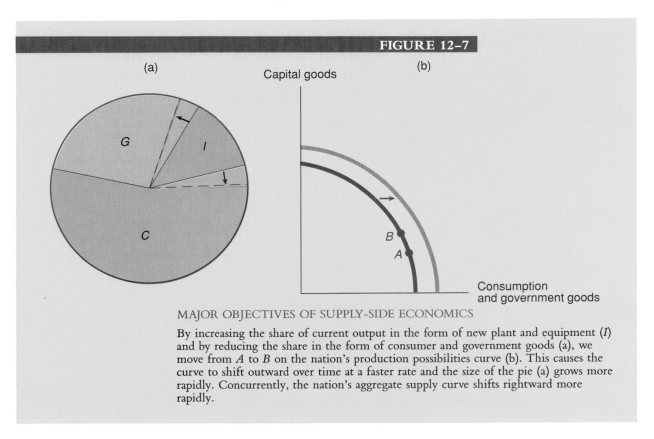

FIGURE 12–7

(a)   Capital goods   (b)

G

I

C

B

A

Consumption and government goods

MAJOR OBJECTIVES OF SUPPLY-SIDE ECONOMICS

By increasing the share of current output in the form of new plant and equipment (*I*) and by reducing the share in the form of consumer and government goods (a), we move from *A* to *B* on the nation's production possibilities curve (b). This causes the curve to shift outward over time at a faster rate and the size of the pie (a) grows more rapidly. Concurrently, the nation's aggregate supply curve shifts rightward more rapidly.

---

[3]In Chapter 9 we noted that some government purchases are actually investment goods such as bridges, university buildings, laboratories, and computers. From a supply-side viewpoint, little or nothing is to be gained by curtailing these investment-type government purchases in favor of more private investment spending. The benefits are yielded by reallocating from government noncapital-type expenditures and consumption expenditures to investment expenditures.

increasing the size of the nation's labor force and the effort expended per worker, the nation's production possibilities curve shifts rightward more rapidly. Given that these are the fundamental objectives of any viable supply-side economics program, was the Reagan Administration program efficiently designed to promote these objectives? What measures might the Bush Administration or future administrations implement to yield a more effective supply-side program?

The Reagan Program of the 1980s

The Reagan game plan at the beginning of 1981 consisted of the following planks:

1. knock out inflation
2. promote free trade
3. eliminate costly government regulations
4. reduce marginal tax rates on individuals
5. index federal income taxes to prevent *bracket creep*
6. provide a tax exemption for two-earner families
7. decrease taxes on income from savings
8. decrease taxes on capital gains
9. decrease corporate income-tax rates
10. provide more rapid depreciation allowances for investment
11. give tax credits for research and development expenditures

The first two planks were considered prerequisites for preparing the playing field for the supply-side program. Rapid inflation is believed to be detrimental to investment and research and development spending, and hence, to be incompatible with any supply-side program. (The inflation rate was brought down much more rapidly than anyone expected, thanks largely to restrictive Federal Reserve monetary policy during 1981–1982.) Free trade is required to promote competitive markets, hold down prices, insure an efficient worldwide allocation of resources, and maximize living standards. Almost all economists support the first two planks, even if supply-side considerations are not foremost in mind.

The core of the Reagan Administration's supply-side program consisted of planks 3–11. Government regulations and red tape were seen as diverting resources from productive activities and limiting the flexibility of firms to use resources efficiently. Wherever feasible, the Reagan Administration sought to reduce regulations. Most of the other measures were implemented in the major tax legislation of the first Reagan Administration, the Economic Recovery Tax Act of 1981 (ERTA).

ERTA reduced individual income-tax rates by a total of 25 percent in three stages from 1981 to 1983. When one includes federal and state income taxes and the social security payroll tax, the marginal tax rate faced by most individuals— especially those with high incomes—had increased considerably between the 1930s and 1980. The rationale in the 1981 legislation for the large reduction in these rates was the desire to boost incentives to work and earn income. High marginal tax rates had particularly impaired work incentives for affluent two-earner households. By 1980, marginal tax rates of such households had frequently reached 50 percent or higher. By providing an additional exemption for such households and sharply lowering marginal rates, ERTA sought to induce *both* members of potential two-earner families to enter the work force rather than for one to remain home and pursue household activities.

Bracket Creep
The tendency for inflation to automatically push individuals into higher marginal- and average-tax rates in an unindexed income-tax system.

Also, the individual income tax was indexed to prevent inflation from gradually kicking people into higher and higher marginal income-tax brackets. The 1970s was a decade of significant bracket creep, as rising wages and salaries—even when they merely kept pace with inflation—moved individuals into higher brackets in the progressive federal tax table. This meant that taxpayers whose gross earnings just kept pace with inflation found that their take-home pay (disposable income) did not. Tens of millions of Americans suffered a decline in their real disposable income during the 1970s because of the effects of *bracket creep* in an era of high inflation. Indexation of income taxes put an end to this mechanism by automatically triggering a reduction in marginal income-tax rates each year by an amount sufficient to prevent bracket creep.

Individual Retirement Account (IRA)
Voluntary, tax-deductible, self-managed retirement savings program authorized by legislation in the early 1980s to promote the incentive to save.

In an effort to boost the incentive to save and thereby reduce the share of output allocated to consumption and free up funds to finance the needed increase in the investment share of output, ERTA established a new voluntary retirement program featuring tax-deductible contributions by individuals. Individual Retirement Accounts (IRAs) were established. Every individual earning $2000 or more annually in wage or salary income was allowed to make a tax-deductible contribution to a self-managed retirement plan of up to $2000 per year. For an individual in a 25-percent marginal income-tax bracket, the current tax liability is reduced $500 annually if the individual makes the contribution. The idea is to reward people for

---

EXHIBIT 12–1

THE COUNCIL OF ECONOMIC ADVISORS

After World War II, Congress passed the Employment Act of 1946. This Act provided for the creation of a President's Council of Economic Advisors (CEA). In addition, the Act established the Joint Economic Committee of Congress and required that the President of the United States submit an annual *Economic Report.* This annual document, prepared by the Council of Economic Advisors, analyzes and defends the administration's economic policies. It also provides a gold mine of statistical information on the economy.

The stated purpose of the CEA is to gather data and make economic forecasts; educate the president, congress, and the public on economics matters; and formulate an economic program to achieve the goals set forth in the Employment Act of 1946. These goals call for policies to promote employment and price-level stability. The Employment Act charged the executive branch with responsibility for fulfilling the goals of the Act. In providing for the creation of the Council of Economic Advisors, Congress acknowledged the link between economic analysis and the nation's economic policy. The chairmanship of the CEA is a cabinet-level position.

The head of the CEA typically reflects the economic philosophy and political viewpoints of the President. Heads of the CEA in Democratic administrations (Kennedy, Johnson, Carter) in recent decades typically have been Keynesian, favoring active use of government's monetary and fiscal policy tools to maintain high levels of output and employment. Heads of the CEA in Republican administrations tend to be more conservative, favoring less intervention by government. Murray Weidenbaum, Martin Feldstein, and Beryl Sprinkle served as CEA heads during Ronald Reagan's presidency (1981–1988). Weidenbaum and Feldstein were important architects of the Administration's supply-side program. When large deficits emerged, Feldstein clashed publicly with Administration officials and returned to his teaching position at Harvard in 1984. He was

saving more (consuming less), thus raising the fraction of income saved by Americans. Also, by reducing marginal income-tax rates and bringing down inflation dramatically, the Reagan Administration raised the effective after-tax rate of return accruing to those who save.

To promote advances in technology, tax credits for research and development expenditures were granted. In an effort to stimulate investment spending, the corporation income tax was reduced, depreciation allowances were speeded up, and the capital gains tax was reduced. The latter measure was defended on the grounds of stimulating venture capital in risky areas in which the frontiers of technology are being challenged. When such companies hit paydirt, their stockholders' gains were to be accorded preferential tax treatment in that their capital gains would be taxed at lower rates than such other forms of income as wages and salaries. Supply-siders believe that favorable capital gains treatment helps direct funds into areas of high risk that have considerable promise for yielding technological advances.[4]

Most mainstream economists see considerable merit in the concept of supply-side economics. Reduction of marginal tax rates is likely to exert a positive effect on

[4]Preferential tax treatment of capital gains existed far before the 1981 ERTA, although that legislation further reduced the capital gains tax. The Tax Reform Act of 1986 terminated this preferential treatment, at least temporarily. In the 1988 presidential campaign, George Bush pledged to reestablish favorable treatment of capital gains.

replaced by Sprinkle, a University of Chicago-trained economist noted for his monetarist views.

When President George Bush assumed office in 1989, he appointed Michael Boskin of Stanford University to be head (chairman) of the CEA. The son of a self-employed contractor, Boskin grew up in Los Angeles. He attended the University of California at Berkeley, where his senior thesis explored the effects of taxes on work incentives of low-income residents of Oakland, a community adjacent to Berkeley. Boskin's study was published in the *National Tax Journal* and the Berkeley economics department awarded him the Chancellor's Cup as the most outstanding graduate of the class of 1967. Boskin stayed on at Berkeley for his Ph.D. His dissertation examined the effects of income maintenance programs (welfare) on the size of the labor force.

Boskin is considered a *mainstream conservative*. He is an eclectic economist, accepting portions of various schools of thought. Boskin regards the nation's budget deficit as a serious problem, and favors a *flexible freeze* on government spending rather than a tax hike as the preferred solution. In the flexible freeze, real (inflation-adjusted) government spending is not allowed to increase, though some government programs may increase at the expense of others. Over time, the real growth of economic activity gradually increases real revenues and eliminates the deficit.

Boskin considers himself a moderate supply-sider. He believes that incentives are very important and accepts the general philosophy of supply-side economics outlined in this chapter. For example, Boskin favors keeping marginal income-tax rates low and advocates favorable tax treatment of capital gains. However, he rejects some of the more extreme supply-side positions discussed later in this chapter. In fact, Boskin once wrote a book critical of some aspects of the Reagan Administration's supply-side program.

work incentives, particularly in two-earner households. Efforts to boost the share of output allocated to investment are widely commended as necessary to speed the growth of capital per worker and thereby boost productivity of labor. Economists believe that technological change is a key element yielding a rightward-shifting aggregate supply curve and economic growth. Mainstream economists who count themselves as moderate supply-siders include the head of President George Bush's Council of Economic Advisors (CEA), Michael Boskin, and former CEA head Martin Feldstein, who was an important architect of the supply-side legislation of the early 1980s.

Controversial Propositions of Extreme Supply-Siders

In their zeal to promote supply-side economics, however, some supply-siders took extreme positions that undermined the credibility of the overall program. While perhaps no individual simultaneously espoused all these controversial viewpoints, all of them were put forward at various times in the effort to move the major tax cuts proposed by supply-siders into legislation, which culminated in the enactment of ERTA in 1981.

Viewed from the perspective of a moderate supply-sider, three extreme propositions stand out.[5] (1) Large tax cuts do *not* lead to enlarged budget deficits. (2) Larger deficits *do* result, but their potential adverse consequences are neutralized by an offsetting increase in saving in the private sector of the economy. (3) Because of additional supply-side stimulus, restrictive monetary policy can knock out the ongoing inflation without reducing output or increasing unemployment.

ERTA and Budget Deficits   The proposed supply-side tax cuts of the early 1980s were quite large. Most economists were wary because they thought such cuts would cause unprecedented budget deficits. Some, nevertheless, defended the tax cuts as a mechanism for pressuring government to reduce expenditures or at least to hold the line on new programs. They saw the consequences of deficits as a reasonable price to pay for slowing the growth in government spending relative to GNP. But a radical fringe of the supply-side movement denied that the deficit would increase even if government failed to cut back expenditures. They argued that the incentive effects stimulated by the reduced tax rates would unleash such a torrent of economic activity that the federal government would collect as much or more revenue in spite of significantly lower tax rates. Arthur B. Laffer was the leader of this movement, and the **Laffer Curve** in Figure 12-8 illustrates the idea.

Laffer correctly reasoned that with zero- and 100-percent income-tax rates the government would reap no income-tax receipts. With a zero tax rate, lots of income would be earned but it would not be taxed. With a 100-percent tax rate, there would be no reason to work and earn income, at least in the *above-ground* economy. Hence, no income-tax receipts would accrue to the Treasury. Since the actual income-tax rate is between zero and 100 percent and since a large amount of income-tax receipts are actually received by the Internal Revenue Service, the curve in Figure 12-8 must begin at the origin, rise to a certain point (*M*), and then decline to meet the horizontal axis at the 100-percent tax rate. All of this seems agreeable enough.

---

[5]This discussion draws on the evaluation of supply-side economics by Martin Feldstein, head of the first Reagan Administration's Council of Economic Advisors. See Feldstein, "Supply-Side Economics: Old Truths and New Claims," *American Economic Review*, May 1986, pp. 26–30.

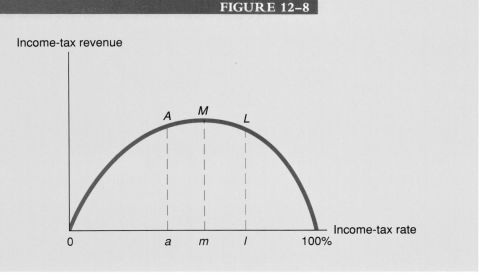

FIGURE 12–8

THE LAFFER CURVE

As income-tax rates increase from zero to 100 percent, tax revenues increase to point M, and then decline. Laffer argued that the economy was at L in 1981, at tax rate l above tax rate m, which maximizes tax revenue. If this were true, a tax cut would increase revenue. In reality, the economy was at A with income-tax rate a. The tax cut reduced revenue and ushered in large deficits—as most economists believed it would.

The controversial issue is: At what point on the Laffer Curve is the economy operating? Laffer asserted that the U.S. economy was by 1981 at some point (L) to the right of the point of maximum revenue (M). In Laffer's view, the income tax rate by 1981 (l) exceeded the rate (m) that would maximize federal tax revenue. It follows, in this view, that a cut in income-tax rates would stimulate revenues and therefore actually *reduce* the deficit. Very few economists agreed with this proposition.[6] Most felt the economy was at a point like A, to the left of the revenue-maximizing income-tax rate. Most economists correctly predicted that a tax cut would reduce federal tax revenues and enlarge the deficit.

Budget Deficits and Private Saving   The economy's total saving consists of private saving (by individuals and firms) and government saving or dissaving (budget surplus or deficit). A large pool of total saving is essential if a nation is to finance a healthy level of investment spending without borrowing from other nations. Opponents of the 1981 ERTA feared that the resulting budget deficit would result in a decline in the nation's gross pool of saving, produce an increase in interest rates, and result in either an increase in borrowing from the rest of the world or a contraction in domestic investment expenditures. Both increased foreign indebtedness and reduced investment are viewed as undesirable. The latter result—the *crowding out* of investment—is diametrically opposed to the goal of supply-side economics.

To refute the proposition that larger deficits would reduce the gross pool of domestic saving, a group of bright young economists trotted out an old doctrine

[6]Note that this issue hinges on the concept of elasticity. It is true that $R = B \times r$, where R represents income-tax revenue, B represents the tax base (income subject to the tax), and r represents the income-tax rate. If a 25-percent reduction in r leads to an increase in B of 25 percent or more, R does not decline and the deficit does not increase. Economists believe that a reduction in r boosts B somewhat by inducing people to work longer and harder and by providing less incentives to seek tax deductions and hide income in the underground economy. In the U.S. economy of the 1980s, however, few economists expected the relative increase in B to be as large as the relative cut in r. If they were correct, a reduction in r would lead to less R. This is what happened when income-tax rates were reduced in the early 1980s.

Ricardian-Equivalence Theorem
Hypothesis that increased federal budget deficits induce an equivalent increase in private saving, thus leaving the gross pool of saving (government plus private) unaltered. If valid, most of the alleged adverse consequences of budget deficits are nonexistent.

known as the **Ricardian-equivalence theorem.** This theorem postulates that under certain highly restrictive conditions, an increase in government budget deficits induces an offsetting boost in private saving, thus leaving gross saving unaltered. Individuals—aware of the increased burdens that deficits may place on their descendants—increase their saving rates so as to leave a larger inheritance with which their heirs can cover this future burden.

While Ricardo acknowledged that real-world people do not really behave that way, it seems that some of today's economists believe otherwise. Hence, the proposition is seriously advanced that larger deficits do not raise interest rates, crowd out investment, or lead to increased borrowing from abroad.[7] Contrary to the predictions of this remarkable viewpoint, the increased federal deficits of the 1980s were not accompanied by an increase in private saving rates. Instead, saving rates decreased to alarmingly low levels. Moreover, an enormous increase in American borrowing from abroad took place in the 1980s. The investment share of GNP failed to increase in spite of a series of investment incentives implemented in ERTA.

Supply-Side Economics and Cost-Free Disinflation   In early 1981, the new Reagan Administration inherited an intolerably high rate of inflation. The first order of business was to disinflate—to reduce inflation from double-digit rates to much lower, acceptable levels. Clearly, in the short run, this would require restrictive monetary policies to slow down aggregate demand. In the conventional view of economists, such restrictive measures inevitably lead to a transition period of at least a year or two of higher unemployment and financial distress for many individuals and firms.

A few extreme supply-siders denied that any hardship would be involved. True, the aggregate demand curve would shift downward as monetary policy became more restrictive. But the supply-side tax cuts would quickly shift the aggregate supply curve rightward, neutralizing the contractionary effects on output exerted by the decline in aggregate demand. Hence, in this view, inflation could be knocked out of the system without accompanying hardship in the form of reduced output and higher unemployment.

Moderate supply-siders and other mainstream economists doubted this proposition because supply-side measures require considerable time to develop. It takes time to plan new investment projects in response to new investment incentives, for example. And it takes time to build the investment projects after the plans are completed. It seems reasonable to assume that the nation's aggregate supply curve would slowly shift rightward in response to new incentives, taking years to reach maximum effect. On the other hand, restrictive monetary policy operates quickly to shift the aggregate demand curve downward. The overwhelming consensus among economists is that there is no way to knock out a powerfully entrenched inflation without paying for it with a transition period of hard times. This consensus view turned out to be correct. The 1981–1982 recession turned out to be the most severe since the 1930s. Output declined sharply and the unemployment rate soared above ten percent in 1982. Not until the second half of 1985 did the unemployment rate fall to seven percent.

---

[7]On this issue, key papers include Robert Barro, "Are Government Bonds Net Wealth?" *Journal of Political Economy,* November/December 1974, pp. 1095–1117 and Paul Evans, "Do Large Deficits Produce High Interest Rates?" *American Economic Review,* March 1985, pp. 68–87. For a critical view of the proposition, see Robert J. Gordon, *Macroeconomics* (Boston: Little, Brown Co., 1987) 4th ed., pp. 460–61.

A Critique of the 1980's Supply-Side Program

Looking back, it seems clear that the Reagan Administration's supply-side program was not as successful as many supply-siders predicted. Certainly many good things happened in the 1980s. Inflation was reduced dramatically. The stock market more than doubled from its depressed values of 1982. One of the longest cyclical expansions in history commenced at the end of 1982 and was still going strong in early 1989. However, other indicators reveal little reason for cheer. Budget deficits soared and the national debt tripled in eight years. The United States went from the world's largest international creditor nation in 1980 to the largest debtor nation by 1988. The nation's private saving rate declined to an all-time low. The bottom line is that productivity growth failed to recover strongly from its lethargic performance of the 1970s. The real wage of the average worker was virtually unchanged during the 1980s. With the aid of several years' hindsight, it is not difficult to pinpoint shortcomings in the Reagan Administration's supply-side program. Many of these shortcomings were immediately anticipated by mainstream economists when the proposed program was unveiled at the beginning of 1981.

The Supply-Side Effects Were Exaggerated   A consensus has developed that the likely supply-side responses were overstated. Research by Michael Boskin suggested that a 10-percent increase in the real after-tax yield from saving would boost actual saving by 2–4 percent. The Reagan program, by sharply reducing inflation, reducing marginal income-tax rates, and authorizing IRAs, did significantly boost the real after-tax returns from saving. However, aggregate private saving did not respond. While this by no means constitutes sufficient proof, it suggests that Boskin's estimates may have been too optimistic. Also, the labor force response to the reduction in marginal rates was muted. According to Charles Schultze, CEA head in the Carter Administration, "There's nothing wrong with supply-side economics that division by 10 couldn't cure." Schultze was suggesting that some supply-siders were grossly overstating the likely response of saving and work effort to the supply-side incentives. Clearly, the passage of ERTA was well timed to cushion the severe recession of the early 1980s. However, many economists believe the boost to the economy came principally from simple old Keynesian forces. That is, they believe that the demand-side effects of ERTA were stronger than its supply-side effects.

Large Deficits Negated the Favorable Aspects of the Program   The consensus view of economists is that both monetary and fiscal policies strongly influence aggregate demand. The enlarged deficits resulting from the 1981 ERTA represent powerful demand stimulus from fiscal policy. To prevent excessive aggregate demand in the face of this large increase in deficits, monetary policy had to be maintained in a relatively restrictive posture. This *mix of policies*—a stimulative fiscal policy accompanied by a restrictive monetary policy—is precisely the opposite prescription of the mix that one would propose if the objective is to increase the share of output devoted to investment goods and thereby shift the aggregate supply curve rightward. This perverse mix means that interest rates will be higher than would be the case if the mix were tilted toward more restrictive fiscal and more stimulative monetary policies. Since investment spending is more sensitive to interest rates than is consumption, the Reagan Administration's mix of policies was a prescription for a high-consumption, low-investment economy. Many economists regard the perverse mix of monetary and fiscal policies associated with the enlarged deficits of the 1980s as the *fly in the ointment* that neutralized the many favorable aspects of the supply-side program.

Supply-Side Programs Increase Inequality of Income Distribution Cynics have sometimes labeled supply-side economic programs "trickle-down" economics. This term suggests that if a lot of money is thrown at the rich, some of it will "trickle down" to the poor. This criticism is perhaps unfair, given the objective of the supply-side program. Supply-side policies almost inevitably increase the inequality of the nation's income distribution because such policies are designed to promote incentives by rewarding those who work hard and are successful. Furthermore, on balance, wealthy people receive the capital gains and dividends, own the corporations, and make the decisions to invest. And wealthier individuals tend to have higher marginal propensities to save than the less affluent. For these reasons the supply-side tax breaks are necessarily targeted toward those in the upper-income brackets if they are to achieve the goals of supply-side economics.

This is a good example of trade-offs in economics. To promote more rapid economic growth, one might have to pursue measures that sacrifice other objectives—in this case a more equal distribution of the nation's income. Those who place higher priority on the goal of reduced inequality than on economic growth naturally tend to view supply-side economics in a negative light.

SUMMARY

1. The nation's aggregate supply curve may be divided into three regions: a flat region in which firms are willing to supply any output at the existing price level, an upward-sloping region in which higher prices are required to call forth additional production, and a vertical region in which no more output can be produced—no matter how high the price level.

2. The horizontal region of the aggregate supply curve is known as the "Keynesian" or "depression" region. In this region, a shift in the aggregate demand curve exerts a full effect on real output. The price level remains unchanged.

3. The upward-sloping portion of the aggregate supply curve is the "normal" region. A shift in aggregate demand changes both output and the price level when the economy is operating in the normal region of the aggregate supply curve.

4. The vertical portion of the aggregate supply curve is the "classical" region. An increase in aggregate demand raises the price level but has no effect on output in this region. Hence, the multiplier is actually zero in this region.

5. The nation's aggregate demand curve depicts a negative relationship between the price level (vertical axis) and real output demanded (horizontal axis). The curve has a negative slope because a decline in the price level produces a positive wealth effect and shifts consumption spending and the total expenditures line $(C + I + G)$ upward.

6. Keynesians believe these wealth effects are weak. Therefore, they believe it takes a major decline in the price level to yield a large enough wealth effect to boost aggregate demand appreciably. This implies that the aggregate demand curve is quite steep. Monetarists view the aggregate demand curve as being relatively flat because they think wealth effects are strong.

7. In the context of the aggregate supply-aggregate demand model, one can view the economy's self-correcting mechanism as operating by shifting the aggregate supply curve. Assuming perfectly flexible prices, existence of a recessionary gap implies falling wages and prices of other inputs. This shifts the aggregate supply curve rightward and the process continues until the full-employment output is restored. An inflationary gap also tends to self destruct because rising prices shift the aggregate supply curve leftward until output is lowered to the full-employment output level.

8. Since Keynesians are skeptical of the strength of wealth effects and the existence of downward wage and price flexibility in today's economy, they are unwilling to rely upon the self-correcting mechanism to alleviate recessionary gaps. Instead, they prescribe stimulative monetary and fiscal policies. Monetarists, believing more strongly in the wealth effect and downward flexibility of prices and wages, prefer a government policy of nonintervention in the economy.

9. A viable supply-side economics program consists of a set of measures to boost the nation's aggregate supply schedule by stimulating incentives to work and produce, to speed the rate of technological innovation, and to boost the share of the nation's output allocated to investment goods.

10. The Reagan Administration supply-side program of the 1980s consisted of steep cuts in marginal income-tax rates to promote incentives to work and earn income and a series of measures to boost saving and investment. Many such measures were implemented with the enactment of the Economic Recovery Tax Act (ERTA) in 1981.

11. Some zealous supply-siders overstated the case for the supply-side tax cuts. Dubious propositions advanced by supporters of the tax cuts included the arguments that revenues would not decline and the deficit would not increase with the tax cut, that the deficit would increase but would be benign because it would stimulate a comparable increase in private saving, and that the favorable supply-side effect of the tax cut would permit a restrictive monetary policy to bring down inflation without adverse effects on output and employment.

12. Critics of the Reagan supply-side program charge that the effects of lower tax rates on incentives to work and save were overstated by supply-siders, that the ensuing large budget deficits counteracted the favorable effects of the program, and that the supply-side program caused an increase in income inequality in America.

KEY TERMS

aggregate supply curve
depression range
normal range
classical range
Keynesians
monetarists
self-correcting mechanism
recessionary gap

inflationary gap
supply-side economics
bracket creep
indexation of income taxes
Individual Retirement Account
    (IRA)
Laffer Curve
Ricardian-equivalence theorem

STUDY QUESTIONS AND PROBLEMS

1. What determines the slope of the nation's aggregate supply curve? Exlain the slope of the curve in the three distinct regions.

2. In which region of the aggregate supply curve is the real-world multiplier that relates initial shifts in spending to changes in equilibrium real output the smallest? The largest? Explain the reason for your answers.

3. Explain the reason that the aggregate demand curve is downward sloping. Do you think it is fairly steep or relatively flat? Why?

4. Explain the mechanism by which the aggregate supply curve is induced to shift in such a manner that an inflationary gap is automatically eliminated.

5. Analyze the different viewpoints of monetarists and Keynesians toward reliance on the economy's self-correcting mechanism when output is significantly below full-employment levels.

6. Explain the basic goals and appeal of supply-side economics.

7. Why is it almost inevitable that any successful supply-side program increases income inequality?

8. Why is a policy of promoting saving an integral part of any successful supply-side program? What actually happened to the nation's saving rate in the 1980s?

9. Explain the connection, if any, between the *mix* of monetary and fiscal policies and the shares of the nation's output allocated to consumption and investment goods.

10. Draw a Laffer Curve and label the axes. Do you think the nation's average income-tax rate today is above or below the rate that maximizes total income tax revenue? Defend your answer.

11. Suppose you could rewrite the Reagan Administration's supply-side program with the aid of hindsight. How would your program differ from the one implemented in the Economic Recovery Tax Act of 1981 (ERTA)? Rationalize your program.

SELECTED REFERENCES

Boskin, Michael J., "Tax Policy and Economic Growth: Lessons from the 1980s," *The Journal of Economic Perspectives,* Fall 1988, pp. 71–97. An evaluation of major tax legislation of the 1980s by the head of President George Bush's Council of Economic Advisors.

Bosworth, Barry P., *Tax Incentives and Economic Growth* (Washington, DC: The Brookings Institution, 1984). A critical review of the Reagan supply-side program.

Feldstein, Martin, "Supply-Side Economics: Old Truths and New Claims," *American Economic Review,* May 1986, pp. 26–30. A critique by a *moderate* supply-side economist.

Gordon, Robert J., *Macroeconomics,* 4th ed. (Boston: Little, Brown Co., 1987). Chapter 6, 7, and 15 provide in-depth analyses of aggregate supply and aggregate demand curves, the self-correcting mechanism, the Laffer Curve, and the Ricardian-equivalence theorem.

Hailstones, Thomas J., *Viewpoints on Supply-Side Economics* (Reston, VA: Reston Publishing Co., 1982). A discussion of all aspects of supply-side economics by economists of all persuasions.

Reese, David A., *The Legacy of Keynes* (San Francisco: Harper and Row, 1987). A retrospective on Keynesian economics by supporters and critics, including Nobel Laureates James Tobin and James Buchanan.

PART III

BANKING, MONETARY POLICY, INTEREST RATES, AND ECONOMIC ACTIVITY

CHAPTER 13

MONEY, BANKING, AND THE CREATION OF BANK DEPOSITS

A bank is a place that will lend you money if you can prove you don't need it.

—BOB HOPE

The subject of money is inherently interesting to most people. As the old adage states, "Money makes the world go 'round." Although philosophical types may be critical of the motive, the principal driving force propelling the majority of students to enroll in college (and to take this course) is intimately connected with money. Money is what we use to buy the goods and services we desire. The college education provides the job that yields the income that puts money in the bank and allows us to purchase the things we desire.

Actually, the term "money" is used loosely and often incorrectly in everyday conversation. Hence, we hear that engineers and accountants earn "good money" upon graduation and that 1988 World-Series baseball star Orel Hershiser has a "lot of money." Correct terminology would state that engineers and accountants earn a substantial income and that Hershiser has amassed considerable wealth as a result of years of very high income and wise investing.

In economics it is essential to avoid the imprecise use of such key terms as income, wealth, and money. **Income** is a flow of dollars per unit of time. A recent college graduate, for example, may earn income of $25,000 per year. **Wealth** is a stock concept, measured in dollars at a point in time. The wealth of an individual includes the stock of such financial assets as checking accounts, savings accounts, and bonds owned by the individual as well as such other assets as houses, cars, and jewelry. Money is also a stock concept, but one that is much narrower in scope than is wealth.

In this chapter we study the nature of money and role of financial institutions in the creation of money. Chapter 14 *analyzes the nature of our central bank—the Federal Reserve System—and the tools "the Fed" utilizes to conduct monetary policy and control the supply of money. Chapter 15 analyzes the link between money and the economy and outlines alternative views about the role that the supply of money plays in the economy.*

DEFINITION OF MONEY

Money
Anything widely accepted as payment for goods and services; any generally accepted medium of exchange.

Money is usually defined as the stock of those items that have a unique characteristic—widespread acceptability for the purpose of making payment. Such items as tobacco, gold, and woodpecker scalps served this function in more primitive times. Today, currency and coins are widely used to make payment. In fact, the government has designated these items to be *legal tender,* which simply means that no seller can refuse to accept currency and coins as payment for goods and services. However, a substance does not have to be legal tender to be money. Checking accounts in various financial institutions are widely used to make payment and are therefore considered money. Indeed, these checking accounts make up the bulk of our money supply even though they are not classified as legal tender.

Hence, our most widely quoted and popular measure of the supply of money consists of demand deposits and other checkable deposits in financial institutions and currency and coins in the hands of the public. This is known as **M-1,** or the *narrow* measure of money.

$$\text{M-1} = DDO + C^P$$

M-1
Demand deposits and other checkable accounts plus currency and coins in the hands of the public; the narrow medium of exchange or *transactions* measure of money.

C^P designates currency and coins available for immediate spending, held by the public—individuals and nonfinancial firms. C^P does not include currency and coin currently residing in financial institutions, the U.S. Treasury, or the Federal Reserve System. The *DDO* component of M-1 consists of demand deposits and other checkable accounts, including NOW (negotiable order of withdrawal) accounts and ATS (automatic transfer service) accounts. NOW and ATS are essentially interest-bearing checking accounts in financial institutions (commercial banks, savings and loan associations, mutual savings banks, and credit unions).

FUNCTIONS OF MONEY

Money serves several crucial functions in a society, and the importance of these functions becomes quite apparent when one considers the alternative to a monetary economy (i.e., a barter economy). A barter economy is one in which market participants exchange goods and services for other goods and services rather than for money. In a monetary economy, money serves three functions—a medium of exchange, a unit of account, and a store of value.

Medium of Exchange   Money serves as a **medium of exchange** or a physical means of payment. One gives up a $10 bill for a box-seat ticket to a major-league baseball game. Consider the complexity of life without money—a farmer would have to trade perhaps three bushels of wheat for the baseball ticket. If the baseball club was not interested in wheat, the farmer would have to first find a third party wishing to buy wheat who offered a product acceptable to the baseball club. For exchange to take place in a barter economy a *coincidence of wants* must exist—both parties to the transaction must desire the goods offered by the other party. One does not have to be especially imaginative to see the inefficient state of affairs today if we were to revert to a barter system.

Indeed, it is difficult to imagine a society ever achieving a level of prosperity comparable to that enjoyed by modern industrial countries in the presence of a barter system. Vast amounts of time would be expended in the process of exchange, leaving less time for productive work and the enjoyment of leisure. Introduce money in the form of the $5 bill, the $20 gold piece, or the woodpecker scalp, and you eliminate the exchange prerequisite of a coincidence of wants. In a money economy, each person exchanges his or her product or labor for dollars and directly utilizes these dollars to purchase goods and services.

Unit of Account   The American dollar, Italian lira, and German mark (and other currencies) serve as measuring sticks or standards of value by which we judge the material worth of apples, shoes, or a ticket to a symphony orchestra performance. In the United States, the dollar serves as a yardstick or common denominator by which we compare the relative value of thousands of goods and services. Most of us have a firm impression of the approximate value in dollars of the hundreds of items we frequently purchase—hamburgers, movie tickets, telephone services, haircuts, and many others. In a barter economy, without money serving as the **unit of account,** no common denominator or yardstick would exist. Each product would be potentially exchangeable for every other product, and we would therefore have to become acquainted with a vastly larger number of rates of exchange or prices in order to survive the rigors of economic life.[1] Instead of apples having one price (e.g., 49 cents per pound) as is the case in a money economy, apples would have a different price for each of the thousands of other goods and services (e.g., one haircut per five pounds of apples, one gallon of gas per two pounds of apples, and so forth). One can see that economic life is greatly simplified when money is introduced to serve the function of the unit of account.

Store of Value   All of us make expenditures that do not synchronize precisely with our receipt of income. We may deposit a paycheck or other source of funds on the first of the month, but gradually spend the funds throughout the month. Similarly, we may hold back some funds earned earlier in the year to be spent at Christmas or during a vacation. By holding money (primarily in checking accounts), we store

---

[1] The formula in statistics for the number of different combinations of n items taken 2 at a time is $n(n-1)/2$. In a barter economy with 1000 items, because each good can be potentially traded for each other good, there would exist $1000(999)/2 = 499,500$ different prices. In a money economy, there would exist only 1000 prices, each one expressed in dollars—the unit of account or standard of value.

EXHIBIT 13–1

HYPERINFLATION

In approximately a dozen episodes in documented history, inflation became so severe that the store-of-value and medium-of-exchange functions of money totally broke down. In these episodes, known as *hyperinflation,* the monetary system collapsed. People refused to accept the currency and ultimately a new currency had to be issued.

In each instance of hyperinflation, an enormous increase in the quantity of money in circulation accompanied the acceleration of inflation. All of these episodes occurred in periods of great political upheaval—revolution or all-out war—in which the survival of the existing government was in jeopardy. These governments were either unable or unwilling to finance themselves via taxation or by borrowing from private firms and individuals. Instead, they simply printed currency.

When the inflationary process becomes sufficiently extreme that people rush to spend the currency quickly, hyperinflation may ensue. The desire to get rid of money before it loses its value shifts the nation's aggregate demand curve rightward and only accelerates the speed of the inflation. One hears stories of German children in the early 1920s waiting outside the factory gates on payday. When their parents handed them their pay, the children raced to the store as quickly as possible to spend the money before prices doubled again. Ultimately, merchants and others refused to accept the currency.

Hyperinflation creates grotesque examples of income redistribution. Note in Table 13-1 the German inflation of the 1920s. Suppose a German worker took out a valuable life insurance policy on himself, equivalent to ten years of current income, in November 1922. Suppose the worker died one year later. The policy would be worthless. His family would not bother to collect the proceeds because they would not suffice to even pay for a postage stamp.

Could hyperinflation happen in the United States? The evidence indicates that it is extremely unlikely, barring a civil war or overthrow of the U.S. government. Many countries have experienced inflation at rates of 50 or 100 percent per year for many years without crossing the threshold that touches off the mad scramble of hyperinflation. Alternatively stated, no country's monetary system has ever collapsed without prolonged abuse as witnessed by years of inflation at rates in excess of 100 percent per annum. Nevertheless, these episodes serve as a reminder of what can happen if a government abandons all semblance of responsibility in its conduct of government finance.

TABLE 13-1

FOUR EPISODES OF HYPERINFLATION

Country	Approximate period	Ratio of price level (ending month to beginning month)
Germany	August 1922–November 1923	1.02×10^{10}
Greece	November 1943–November 1944	4.70×10^{8}
Hungary	August 1945–July 1946	3.81×10^{27}
Russia	December 1921–January 1924	1.24×10^{5}

Source: Adapted from Phillip Cagan, "The Monetary Dynamics of Hyperinflation," in Milton Friedman (ed.), *Studies in the Quantity Theory of Money* (Chicago: University of Chicago Press, 1956), page 26.

purchasing power through time. This **store of value** allows us to finance a flow of expenditures not synchronized with the receipt of funds. But money is not the only medium in which wealth may be stored. One may hold common stocks, gold, bonds, real property, and the like. Money, however, has the advantage that it is perfectly liquid—that is, it is immediately available to spend. Various assets differ in

Liquidity

The ease and willingness with which one may convert an asset into money when one needs cash. Savings accounts are highly liquid, land is not.

their liquidity, or ease with which they may be converted to money. Savings accounts are very liquid because it is easy and almost costless to convert these accounts to checking accounts (M-1). On the other hand, real estate and common stocks are relatively *illiquid*—significant costs are incurred when these assets are sold.

If the price level is stable over time, money serves as a satisfactory vehicle for storing value. If prices are rising rapidly, money functions poorly and people attempt to reduce the use of money as a means of storing value. In those historical instances when inflation has become extremely severe, the breakdown of the store-of-value function of money has also led to a collapse of its medium-of-exchange function. People simply refused to accept money because they had lost confidence in its store-of-value function. Accordingly, the process of exchange degenerated into a system of barter (see Exhibit 13-1, page 281).

Broader Measures of Money (M-2, M-3, L)

The definition of money is arbitrary. Moreover, the boundary that separates a specific measure of money and its close substitutes is not perfectly distinct. Economists who emphasize the medium-of-exchange function of money prefer the narrow (M-1) measure of money. M-1 includes only those items used to finance transactions—hence, it is sometimes referred to as the *transactions* measure of money. However, other economists prefer alternative, broader measures of money— measures that include other highly liquid financial assets besides the ones actually used to make payment. Such economists sometimes emphasize the store-of-value function of money. More importantly, they stress that the purpose of defining and controlling the money supply is to allow monetary policy the opportunity to contribute to the stability of economic activity by controlling the quantity of money. Therefore, the *best* measure of money is the one most closely connected with economic activity.

The preceding discussion suggests that selecting the assets to be included in our definition of money becomes an empirical issue. After all, there exists a multitude of highly liquid instruments that, though not directly usable to finance transactions, are easily converted to transactions money (M-1). Of all the potential candidates for our measure of the money supply, we should focus on the one most intimately associated with aggregate spending and economic activity. Although there is currently no consensus on which measure is the *best,* the Federal Reserve regularly reports four separate measures of money: M-1, M-2, M-3, and L. The items included in each measure are given in Table 13-2.

It is beyond the scope of this economics course to define all the various items (in the table) that go into the various broader measures of money (i.e., M-2, M-3, and L). The main point is that these items consist of highly liquid *near-monies* that are close substitutes for M-1 because of the ease with which they may be converted to the medium-of-exchange form of money, M-1. These various measures of the money supply are frequently referred to as the **monetary aggregates.** Their growth and relative magnitudes are illustrated in Figure 13-1 (page 284). The chief measure of money is M-1, and that is the measure we use throughout this book.

Monetary Aggregates

The various measures of the nation's money supply, including M-1, M-2, M-3, and L.

THE EVOLUTION OF MONEY

In ancient civilizations, certain substances that were esteemed and available in convenient sizes emerged naturally as money and became widely acceptable as a means of payment. Because of their ornamental qualities and divisibility into

TABLE 13-2

MONETARY AGGREGATES AND COMPONENTS

M-1

Currency
Demand deposits
Other checkable deposits*

M-2

M-1
Overnight RPs issued by commercial banks
    plus overnight Eurodollar deposits
Money market mutual fund shares (general purpose)
Savings deposits at all depositary institutions
Small time deposits at all depository institutions**
Money market deposit accounts (MMDAs)

M-3

M-2
Large time deposits at all depository institutions***
Term RPs
Term Eurodollar deposits
Money market mutual fund shares (institutions)

L

M-3
Banker's acceptances
Commercial paper
Savings bonds
Short-term Treasury securities

---

*Includes NOW, ATS, and credit-union share-draft balances and demand deposits at thrift
   institutions.

**Time deposits issued in denominations of less than $100,000.

***Time deposits issued in denominations of $100,000 or more.

Source: *Federal Reserve Bulletin,* 1989.

convenient sizes, such metallic substances as bronze, silver, and gold became common forms of money thousands of years ago.

Full-Bodied Money
A form of money whose value in exchange (as money) is equivalent to its value as a commodity.

Early monies were **full-bodied** or **commodity monies.** Their value was the same whether used in exchange for goods and services (as money) or for nonmoney purposes (as a commodity). Natural economic forces of supply and demand ensured this equality of value. If a gold coin were worth more in its money use than in its commodity use, industrial users would discontinue using metallic gold and sell the metal for use as coins. This reduced the industrial supply of gold, driving up its price for nonmoney uses. At the same time, the quantity of gold used as money increased, driving down the purchasing power of each coin. If gold was worth more as a commodity than its monetary value, gold was withdrawn from circulation, melted down, and utilized for industrial purposes. This mechanism ensured that the value of gold as money never deviated markedly from its value as a commodity.

Fiat Money
Money that attains its value by government decree; it has little value as a commodity. All U.S. currency and coins today are fiat money.

Today, all our monies are **fiat** or **fiduciary monies.** They derive their value from government decree rather than from the material of which they are composed. Their value in exchange considerably exceeds their value as a commodity. A $20 bill contains only about two cents worth of paper, printing inks, and other materials. A quarter contains perhaps five cents worth of nickel and copper. An advantage of fiat money over full-bodied money is that it costs the government much less to

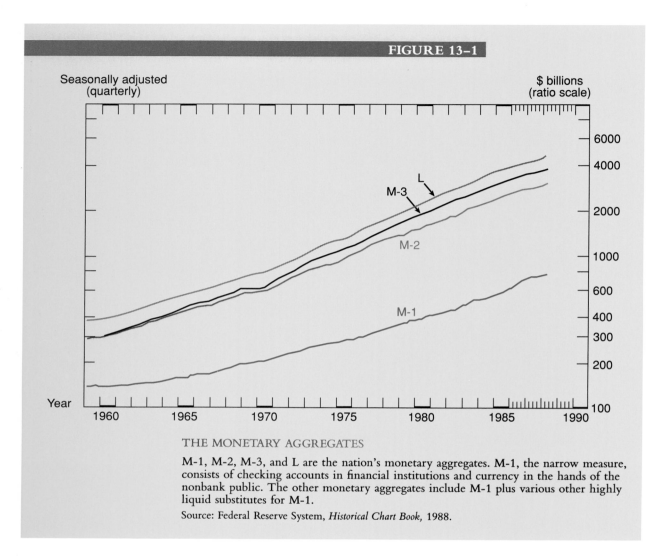

FIGURE 13-1

THE MONETARY AGGREGATES

M-1, M-2, M-3, and L are the nation's monetary aggregates. M-1, the narrow measure, consists of checking accounts in financial institutions and currency in the hands of the nonbank public. The other monetary aggregates include M-1 plus various other highly liquid substitutes for M-1.

Source: Federal Reserve System, *Historical Chart Book*, 1988.

produce—fewer of the nation's resources are used to produce the money, freeing the resources for other uses. Our 1990 money supply (M-1) of approximately $800 billion would cost roughly $800 billion to produce if it were a full-bodied or commodity money. It actually costs a tiny fraction of that to produce our fiat money.

The disadvantage of fiat money is the tendency for those in control (the government) to sometimes issue too much. When this happens, we get inflation—the persistent decline in the value of the dollar. Some politicians and a few economists are so concerned about the prospects for the potential overissue of money that they advocate a return to the *gold standard*—an old-fashioned system of full-bodied money.

Goldsmiths—A Forerunner of Modern Fractional Reserve Banking

Our modern fractional-reserve banking system has its roots in the *goldsmiths* who operated hundreds of years ago. These craftsmen, who were in the business of molding gold into fine ornamental objects for merchants and aristocrats, possessed secure storage facilities for their gold. Wealthy individuals and merchants in possession of gold coins and bullion therefore were attracted to the goldsmiths as a safe means of storing gold. The goldsmiths provided these storage services for a modest fee, issuing a receipt to the owner in exchange for the gold. These receipts, or *gold certificates,* were *as good as gold* because they entitled the bearer to a specific amount of gold on demand. Inevitably, the receipts became widely acceptable as a medium of exchange and began to circulate as money. What seller would refuse payment in gold certificates if these certificates were redeemable in gold upon demand?

At first this system involved the creation of no new money. The goldsmiths were mere warehouses for gold, issuing receipts for gold deposits and maintaining the metal as 100-percent backing behind the receipts. Soon, however, the goldsmiths noted that withdrawals of gold on a given day were only a small fraction of total gold deposits. Furthermore, on a typical day new gold deposits were roughly equivalent to withdrawals. The goldsmiths saw an opportunity for earning handsome profits without undue risk. Why not make loans to local merchants or other reputable borrowers and earn interest income by doing so? Soon the goldsmiths were granting loans by issuing new gold certificates or by loaning out some of the gold deposited by other individuals.

Although this procedure was probably illegal, the goldsmiths were engaging in money creation! Whenever they granted new loans, the volume of the medium of exchange increased—the currency component (C^P) of the money supply increased. Of course, the goldsmiths no longer maintained 100-percent gold backing behind the paper currency in circulation. You will soon note the analogy to our modern banking system, the main difference being that the process is now perfectly legal!

COMMERCIAL BANKING AND THE SUPPLY OF MONEY

The largest portion of our money (M-1) today consists of *checking accounts*—demand deposits and other accounts in *banks* on which checks may be written in order to make payments. We use the term "banks" broadly, to include not only commercial banks but also savings and loan associations, mutual savings banks, and credit unions.[2] These latter three institutions are sometimes known as *thrift institutions.* Changes in the volume of these checking accounts (hence, the money supply) in the nation are intimately connected with activities of these banks. Therefore, it is essential that we learn about the nature of banks and their role in the money-creation process.

The Bank Balance Sheet

Bank Balance Sheet
A statement of a bank's assets, liabilities, and capital accounts (or net worth).

The most efficient way to begin our analysis of banking is to study the **bank balance sheet**—the statement of the bank's assets and liabilities at a given point in

---

[2]Because of deregulation of the financial system in the 1980s, these various institutions have become more homogeneous in nature—more similar in the activities they are allowed to pursue. Earlier regulations limited the banking activities of the nonbank financial institutions (savings and loan associations, mutual savings banks, and credit unions) and ensured the uniqueness of commercial banks in various traditional activities. Although many specific regulations still exist constraining the activities of banks and nonbank financial institutions alike, these institutions today compete against each other on a much more level playing field.

time. The hypothetical balance sheet of a representative American bank illustrated lists only the major categories; some details are deliberately omitted so that we can focus on the *big picture*.

A balance sheet is a statement of assets and liabilities of a corporation, individual, or other entity *at a given point in time*. **Bank assets** are indications of what the bank *owns* or of claims that the bank has on outside entities. **Bank liabilities** are indications of what the bank *owes* or of claims that outsiders have on the bank. Fundamental accounting identities that always hold true include:

$$\text{net worth} = \text{assets} - \text{liabilities} \tag{13-1}$$

or

$$\text{assets} = \text{liabilities} + \text{net worth} \tag{13-2}$$

Because net worth at any point in time is defined as the difference between assets and liabilities (Equation 13-1), it follows that assets are identically equal to liabilities plus net worth (Equation 13-2). In banking, the term "capital" or **capital accounts** is usually employed in place of "net worth." In other words, *capital accounts* is synonymous with the *net worth* of the bank.

Bank Assets   Bank assets include cash, deposits maintained at the Federal Reserve System, earning assets (loans and securities), and such other assets as data processing equipment, typewriters, and buildings. All banks are required to hold **reserves,** defined as cash on hand and deposits at the Federal Reserve. The dollar amount of reserves that each bank must maintain is known as **required reserves.** Required reserves are calculated by utilizing the Fed's **reserve requirement** or required-reserve ratio, a percentage figure applicable to the volume of the bank's demand deposits and other checkable accounts.[3]

Assume the reserve requirement applicable to demand deposits and other checkable accounts is 10 percent. In the case of our Representative Bank, the dollar magnitude of required reserves is calculated as 10% × $50 million = $5 million. Note that the $50 million total to which the 10-percent reserve requirement applies is the sum of the bank's demand deposits, NOW, and ATS accounts.

Bank Assets
Items a bank owns.

Bank Liabilities
Items a bank owes; the debts of the bank.

Capital Accounts
The difference between a bank's assets and its liabilities; indicates owners' equity stake in the bank.

Reserves
Cash holdings of a financial institution plus its deposit at the Federal Reserve.

Required Reserves
The minimum amount of reserves a financial institution is required to hold based on the institution's deposit liabilities and the percentage reserve requirement set by the Fed.

Reserve Requirement
The percentage of a bank's deposit liabilities that by law it must hold in reserves—in cash or deposits with the Federal Reserve.

REPRESENTATIVE BANK

Assets		Liabilities	
Cash	$1 million	Demand deposits and NOW and ATS accounts	$50 million
Deposits at Federal Reserve	4.1 m		
Loans	80 m	Time and savings accounts	75 m
Securities	50 m		
		Other liabilities	10 m
Other assets	8.9 m	Total liabilities	135 m
		Capital accounts	9 m
Total assets	$144 m	Total liabilities and capital	$144 m

[3]Actually a second set of reserve requirements (much lower) applies to certain types of bank time deposits. In the interest of simplicity, we ignore this consideration here.

Excess Reserves
The amount by which the reserves of a financial institution exceed its required reserves.

Actual reserves, indicated on the bank's balance sheet, are $5.1 million ($1 million cash plus $4.1 million in deposits at the Fed). The bank therefore has **excess reserves**—reserves in excess of the required amount—of $0.1 million.

Since banks are in business to earn profits, and since reserves yield no return in the form of interest, banks typically keep only a minimal amount of excess reserves. The great bulk of bank assets are interest-earning assets (i.e., loans and securities).[4] Banks would carry an even larger portion of assets in the form of interest-earning assets were it not for the constraints on bank activities posed by the existence of reserve requirements.

Reserve requirements may be regarded as a form of tax levied on banks, which forces them to maintain a larger percentage of their assets in the form of idle, noninterest-earning assets (reserves) than they would voluntarily maintain. As we shall discover, the existence of reserve requirements enhances the Federal Reserve's ability to achieve broad control over the banking system's lending and investing activities and the nation's supply of money. These reserve requirements may therefore be viewed as socially desirable, inasmuch as they facilitate the government's constitutional mandate of regulating the creation of money.

Bank Liabilities and Capital Accounts   A crucial category of bank liabilities involves checking or *transactions accounts*—demand deposits and other checkable deposits. These accounts are important because they constitute the major portion of our money supply (M-1) and exert an important influence upon economic activity. Time and saving deposits consist of various types of interest-bearing noncheckable bank deposits, including passbook savings accounts, small certificates of deposits (CDs), and large-denomination CDs (negotiable CDs). Some of these deposits— though not included in the nation's narrow (M-1) measure of money—are included in the broader measures (M-2 and M-3 and L), as reflected in Table 13-2. Other liabilities consist of other claims by outsiders upon the bank—for example, debts incurred by the bank in borrowing funds from the Federal Reserve and alternative sources—and bills payable.

The capital account or the net worth of the Representative Bank is $9 million, or 6.25 percent of the value of its total assets (or total liabilities plus capital). This capital account may be viewed as the bank owners' equity in the business and derives from personal funds invested in the bank by its owners plus profits plowed back into the bank over the years. The capital account may be regarded as a *cushion* that protects the bank owners and large depositors from the possibility of **insolvency** (most depositors are protected by federal insurance of $100,000 maximum per depositor in each bank).

Banks need this cushion of protection. Given a bank's deposits and other liabilities, the value of its assets fluctuates continuously as security prices change and some borrowers default on loans. If the value of assets drops below the value of liabilities at any point in time, the bank is technically insolvent and may be closed or merged with another bank. This involves a change of ownership and management together with a total loss of investment and equity to the original owners. Given other factors, the larger the bank's *capital accounts ratio* (capital accounts/total assets), the lower its exposure to risk of insolvency.

---

[4]These loans are diversified and include business, real-estate, consumer, and agricultural loans. The securities banks purchase are predominantly bonds issued by municipalities and bonds and short-term obligations issued by the U.S. government.

The Trade-Off Between Bank Safety and Profitability

In view of the preceding considerations, bank management is torn between conflicting objectives. On the one hand, management must prudently limit the risk of insolvency by maintaining a reasonably healthy capital accounts cushion and by allocating its assets prudently.[5] On the other hand, management strives to earn a high rate of return on the owners' investment dollar. To earn higher rates of return, management must seek higher-yielding (hence often riskier) securities and loans. Moreover, the bank must not maintain an excessive ratio of capital accounts to total assets. Given the rate of return earned on the bank's assets, the rate of return on the owner's equity (or capital) declines as the capital accounts ratio rises.[6] Balancing this inherent trade-off between safety and profitability is a constant challenge to bank management. With the aid of hindsight, it is clear that many banks were not sufficiently prudent in the 1980s. Bank failures soared.

Why Do Banks Fail?

Banks become insolvent when assets decline sharply in value, dissolving the net worth or capital accounts—the residual that remains when liabilities are subtracted from assets. This almost always occurs when loans become *bad loans* as a result of changes in market conditions. In the 1980s, for example, a classic squeeze on farm income imposed by rising costs and falling agricultural prices made it impossible for many farmers to meet interest payments on their loans. Even though the banks may have been able to repossess farmers' property (pledged as loan collateral), plummeting farm-land values frequently meant that the collateral was worth less than the amount owed the bank.

Similarly, the sharp decline of oil prices in the 1980s caused widespread defaults on loans in the oil patch. In addition, many of our larger banks had huge outstanding loans to such developing nations as Brazil, Argentina, and Mexico. Raw materials prices of products produced and exported by these nations plummeted during the severe 1981–1982 worldwide recession, and remained depressed for several years thereafter. This made it quite difficult for these nations to generate revenues with which to meet their debt-service payments. The viability of many of these loans remains fragile even today.

Figure 13-2 (page 290) illustrates the number of bank failures each year since 1960, clearly indicating the severe deterioration during the 1980s. Largely because of the depressed conditions in the agriculture and energy sectors, more U.S. banks failed each year during 1982–1989 than in any year since the 1930s. In the late 1980s, the American banking system reported a less-than-robust state of financial health. The Federal Deposit Insurance Corporation's (FDIC's) list of "problem banks"—those whose financial condition warrants concern and rather close surveillance by the regulatory authorities—remained lengthy. The number of banks

---

[5]In the latter regard, extensive regulations prohibit banks from investing in such risky securities as common stocks, gold, real estate, and corporation bonds. Banks are basically confined to purchasing municipal and U.S. government securities and making loans.

[6]Assume our Representative Bank typically earns annual profits equal to one percent of its total assets (1% × $144 million = $1.44 million). If it maintains a capital account cushion of 10 percent of total assets ($14.4 million), its rate of return on equity for the owners is 10% per year (i.e., $1.44 million/$14.4 million). If it operates on a 5 percent capital/total assets ratio ($7.2 million of capital), the bank owners reap a return of 20 percent per annum (i.e., $1.44 million/$7.2 million). In reducing its capital accounts ratio, bank management earns a greater rate of return but increases the risk of insolvency.

EXHIBIT 13–2

THE COLLAPSE OF THE CONTINENTAL ILLINOIS BANK

A vivid example of bank failure involves the 1984 collapse of the nation's eighth-largest bank, the Continental Illinois Bank of Chicago. The demise of the huge, $40 billion bank may be traced to a combination of imprudent decisions by the management of the bank coupled with some bad luck wrought by the powerful forces of the market.

In the 1970s, top management of Continental Illinois Bank decided to shoot for a very rapid rate of growth. However, since Illinois law prohibited a bank from establishing more than three branches, the Bank was effectively barred from achieving rapid growth via tapping the masses of Illinois depositors. To obtain funds with which to finance the desired rapid growth of loans (and total assets), the Bank elected to issue huge blocks of large-denomination certificates of deposits known as *negotiable CDs*. These short-term IOUs issued by large banks to firms and other large lenders are often in blocks of $1 million and up. By 1981, Continental Illinois owed about $13 billion to foreign investors in the form of large negotiable CDs and other forms of short-term borrowings. Since only the first $100,000 of each customer's deposit is insured by the FDIC, one can imagine the potential stampede by the large depositors to withdraw funds in the event the bank came under suspicion.

By early 1984 it was becoming apparent that Continental Illinois had problem loans of large magnitude in the areas of energy and agriculture, two sectors depressed by market conditions in the early 1980s. In addition, it had large loans out-standing to some of the increasingly troubled Latin American nations. The beginning of the stampede may be traced to early 1984, when the banking regulatory authorities forced Continental Illinois to absorb large losses on energy sector loans it had purchased from the failed Penn Square Bank of Oklahoma City. Only about $4 billion out of Continental Illinois' April 1984 deposits of $29 billion were covered by FDIC insurance. As rumors concerning other bad loans on Continental's books circulated, large depositors withdrew huge blocks of funds from the bank. Since an imprudent portion (79 percent) of the Bank's assets were tied up in nonmarketable loans, the bank quickly ran out of funds with which to pay the depositors.

By August 1984 the Bank had lost about $9 billion of deposits. Without government intervention, the Bank would have failed immediately, possibly triggering a run on other large banks. The Federal Reserve and FDIC moved in aggressively, pumping in billions of dollars in the form of loans from a consortium of large U.S. banks and the Federal Reserve System. Top management was replaced and stockholders lost their investment in the bank.

However, unlike the 1930s-style panics, no depositor lost a penny in the fiasco. Unable to find a merger partner, the FDIC was forced to temporarily nationalize the huge bank. The objective was to restore its financial stability and eventually sell it to private owners. The rescued bank is currently a downscale version of the bank that in the 1970s was regarded as a model of success.

gaining notoriety by making the list increased from less than 400 in the mid-1970s to approximately 1600 by 1989.

HOW FINANCIAL INSTITUTIONS CREATE MONEY

One of the most unfathomable topics in economics for those who have not formally studied the subject is the question of how money comes into existence and what makes the quantity of money fluctuate. Who controls the money supply? What role do banks play in this process? Why was M-1 in the early 1990s approximately five times larger than it had been two decades earlier? As we learn in this chapter and in Chapter 14, the keys to these questions are locked up in the fact that the bulk of our money supply consists *not* of physical substances like paper currency and metallic

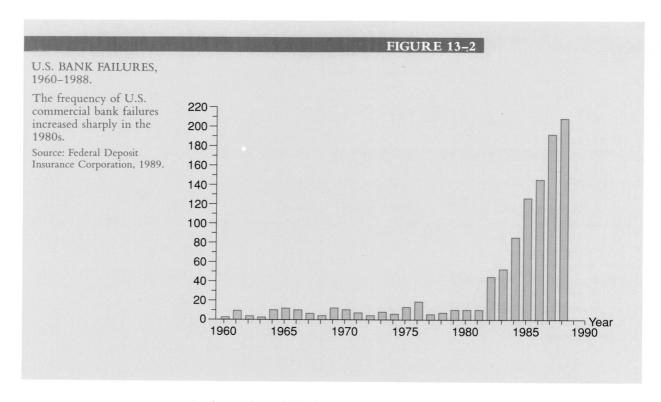

FIGURE 13-2

U.S. BANK FAILURES, 1960–1988.

The frequency of U.S. commercial bank failures increased sharply in the 1980s.

Source: Federal Deposit Insurance Corporation, 1989.

coins but rather of checking accounts, which are simply entries on the ledgers of banks. We also learn that, while banks collectively create money via their lending and investing activities, the Federal Reserve System maintains a rather firm grip on the ability of banks to engage in these money-creating activities. Clearly, the Fed is responsible for the *trend* behavior in the supply of money, though perhaps not for the weekly gyrations.

As you know from personal experience, checking accounts—demand deposits and other checkable accounts—serve as our primary means of payment. You probably pay your apartment rent or dorm fee and most other large payments by transferring funds from your checking account to that of the payee. Checks are the instruments used to bring about these transfers of funds. However, the actual payments consist of the transfer of deposit accounts—the bookkeeping entries. Although numerous smaller purchases are conducted by the payment of currency and coins, well over 90 percent of the *total dollar value* of transactions in the United States are financed via the transfer of demand deposits in financial intermediaries.

Within our holdings of money ($DDO + C^P$) and other liquid assets, the public determines the portion held as currency (C^P). If you have $600 in your checking account or passbook savings account, you are free to withdraw whatever portion of the $600 you desire to hold as currency. Hence, the currency portion (C^P) of the money supply is determined by the public within the constraints of its deposit balances. Banks respond passively to the wishes of the public in granting currency.

Paradoxically, however, even though C^P passively adapts to the public's needs, the total money supply ($DDO + C^P$) does not. Although short-run variations in M-1 are influenced by actions of banks and the public, the basic trend behavior of the money supply is determined by the Federal Reserve System. A goal of Chapter 14 is to outline the tools used by the Fed to achieve this control over the money supply. In the remainder of this chapter, we analyze the important role of banks in creating money in a system of **fractional reserve banking**—a system in which banks maintain only a rather small proportion of deposit liabilities in the form of reserves (cash and deposits at the Federal Reserve).

The Simple Mechanics of Money Creation

Whenever banks make new loans or purchase securities, new money is created. We illustrate via the device of the *T-account,* which is simply a statement of the *change in the balance sheet* associated with a given event.

Bank Lending and Deposit Creation   Suppose your Hometown Bank loans a local hardware store $100,000 to expand its inventories of products. The bank's T-account indicates the following:

HOMETOWN BANK

Assets	Liabilities
loans + $100,000	Demand deposits + $100,000

The bank makes the funds available to the hardware store by increasing the store's demand deposit account.[7] No exchange of physical currency or coins takes place. The bank has created new money (*DDO*) by simply adding an entry to its books stating that the checking account of the borrower is being increased by $100,000. The compensating item on the asset side (balance sheets must always balance!) is the increase in loans.

Of course, the local merchant who borrowed the $100,000 is not going to leave the funds sitting in a checking account. Instead, assume the funds are for use in purchasing inventories from firms that do not bank at Hometown Bank. In that event, the final state of the T-accounts associated with the loan is as follows:

HOMETOWN BANK   VARIOUS OTHER BANKS

Assets	Liabilities	Assets	Liabilities
Loans + $100,000		Deposits at Fed + $100,000	DDO + $100,000
Deposits at Fed − *$100,000*			

The hardware store owner wrote checks amounting to $100,000 to suppliers for the purchase of hardware items. These checks were deposited in various other banks, which sent the checks to the Federal Reserve. Why the Fed? Because the Fed serves as a clearing agent for checks involving banks in different cities. Remember that each bank maintains accounts, known as reserves, at the Fed. In this example, the Fed

---

[7]Of course, the borrower may demand the funds in currency. This would be highly unusual but would not alter our conclusion that new loans create new money. Remember that M-1 = DDO + C^P. If the loan is requested in currency, C^P rises by $100,000 but DDO does not change. While sitting in the bank, the currency does not count as part of C^P or M-1. When outside the bank in the hands of the public, it does.

clears the checks by marking down the reserve account of Hometown Bank and marking up the reserve account of the various other Banks. The Fed then returns the checks to Hometown Bank so that it becomes aware they were written. The transactions are completed when Hometown Bank reduces the hardware store's checking account by $100,000. This negates the initial demand deposit entry created on Hometown Bank's balance sheet when the loan was granted.

Note in the preceding T-account that Hometown Bank ends up with the same amount of deposits it had before the $100,000 loan was granted. So is the money supply back to its initial pre-loan level? NO—the money supply remains higher by $100,000 as long as the loan remains outstanding. The $100,000 increase in money, initially created by Hometown Bank, remains in the banking system in accounts at various other banks. The basic principle is simple: Whenever bank lending rises, bank deposits and the supply of money increase. On the other hand: When bank lending is reduced, deposits are extinguished and the supply of money falls. People write checks to banks, reducing the amount of *DDO* and the supply of money.

Bank Security Purchases and Deposit Creation   Money also is created whenever banks purchase securities. Assume Metro Bank buys $400,000 worth of U.S. Government securities from various securities dealers. The relevant T-accounts are as follows:

METRO BANK		VARIOUS SECURITIES DEALERS' BANKS	
Assets	**Liabilities**	**Assets**	**Liabilities**
U.S. securities + $400,000		Deposits at Fed + $400,000	*DDO* + $400,000 (of securities dealers)
Deposits at Fed − *$400,000*			

As in the Hometown Bank example, bank deposits at the Fed are involved when Metro Bank pays for its securities by writing checks on its Federal Reserve account in the amount of $400,000. These checks, when deposited by the various securities dealers in commercial banks, result in $400,000 of new demand deposits (and money) in the United States. The dealers' banks increase the dealers' checking accounts and send the checks to the Federal Reserve. The Fed completes the transaction by reducing Metro Bank's reserve account and increasing the securities dealers' banks' reserve accounts by $400,000. The money supply is increased for as long as the securities held by banks are increased.

The key to understanding why the money supply rises when banks buy securities from the public (or dealers) is that banks use their Federal Reserve accounts (which are not part of the money supply) to pay for the securities. As soon as these checks are deposited into checking accounts by the public (or dealers), *DDO* and the money supply immediately increase. On the other hand, when banks sell securities to the public (or dealers), the money supply declines as checks are written to the banks by the public (or dealers) to pay for these securities. The public utilizes checking accounts to pay for these securities, and the supply of money falls.

At this point you may view this system of money creation as potentially chaotic and uncontrollable. Inasmuch as banks can always increase profits by expanding loans and purchasing securities, aren't they likely to engage in more of such activities than is consistent with the national interest? Aren't they likely to tend toward creating *too much* money? The answer is NO—at least not as long as the Federal Reserve has its eye on the situation and its hands on the wheel.

Recall—both in the loan and security examples—that the initial bank involved lost reserves when it acquired earning assets. Hometown Bank, in expanding loans by $100,000, lost deposits at the Fed (reserves) of $100,000. Metro Bank, in buying $400,000 of securities, paid for them by giving up $400,000 of reserves. Whenever individual banks acquire loans and securities, they lose reserves on a dollar-for-dollar basis. Therefore, such acquisition by any given bank can occur only if the bank has reserves it can afford to lose (i.e., excess reserves).[8] Once banks use up their excess reserves, expansion of bank lending and investing activities comes to a screeching halt. Since the Fed exerts a firm grip over the amount of reserves and excess reserves in the American banking system via techniques discussed in Chapter 14, it has ultimate control over aggregate bank lending and investing, and hence, the money-creation process.

Multiple Expansion of Bank Deposits

A *fractional-reserve banking system* is one in which banks are required to maintain reserves that are only a fraction of deposit liabilities. The amount of bank deposits is a rather sizable multiple of the amount of reserves (cash and deposits at the Federal Reserve System) maintained by the banks. Each additional dollar of reserves that enters the banking system results in an expansion of several dollars in the amount of deposits in the system (and in M-1, M-2, and the other monetary aggregates). Although any one bank can contribute to the deposit expansion process only by the amount of its excess reserves, the *banking system* (all banks combined) can create an amount of new deposits that is a *multiple* of any initial excess reserves in the banking system.

New reserves come into the banking system from several sources. We learn in Chapter 14 that the Federal Reserve System, via deliberate measures, is easily capable of dominating the aggregate amount of reserves. The public, by withdrawing or depositing currency in banks, also initiates fluctuations in reserves. Regardless of the source of the change in reserves in the banking system, the deposit expansion process is fundamentally the same.

Assume the reserve requirement applicable to all demand deposits is ten percent and that initially the banking system has no excess reserves (i.e., it is fully *loaned up*). Now assume a customer of Bank A deposits $1 million of currency in a checking account. The immediate effect on Bank A's T-account is as follows:

BANK A

Cash + $1 million	DDO + $1 million

The bank gains $1 million of liabilities in the form of demand deposits and $1 million of assets in the form of cash. Since the bank is only required to maintain ten percent reserve backing on demand deposits, its required reserves increase by

---

[8]If the Metro Bank had only $100,000 in excess reserves prior to purchasing $400,000 in securities, it would have become deficient in reserves by $300,000. Banks have no choice but to abide by the Fed's reserve requirements since the regulatory authorities have the ultimate power to deny FDIC insurance. Such denial would inflict a severe, if not fatal, wound upon the bank.

$0.1 million (or $100,000). However, because its reserves increased by a full $1 million, it initially finds itself with $0.9 million ($900,000) of excess reserves. To earn additional profits, Bank A has an incentive to trade its excess reserves for earning assets (remember, reserves pay no interest). Suppose the bank uses its excess reserves to expand its loans by $0.9 million.

BANK A (steps)			BANK A (net final effect)		
1. Cash	+ $1 m	DDO + $1 m	Cash	+ $1 m	DDO + $1 m
			Deposits at Fed	− *$0.9m*	
2. Loans	+ $0.9m	DDO + $0.9m	**Addendum: reserves**	**+ $0.1m**	
			Loans	+ $0.9m	
3. Deposits at Fed	− *$0.9m*	DDO − *$0.9m*			

In the left-hand T-account, Bank A receives the original $1 million cash deposit in step 1. In step 2 the Bank creates new deposits of $0.9 million in making a loan to a local farmer to purchase equipment. In step 3 the farmer writes checks for the equipment totalling $0.9 million and the funds are cleared out of Bank A. The net effect on Bank A of all three steps is indicated in the right-hand net T-account. Deposits in the Bank are increased by $1 million (the original cash deposit). Reserves are increased by $100,000, which is sufficient to support the additional deposits—given the ten-percent reserve requirement. The remaining $900,000 of reserves initially deposited in Bank A were loaned out, and thus have left Bank A.

Now suppose the farm implement dealers bank with Bank B. After the farmer presents his checks to the implement dealers and the checks clear, Bank B's T-account is indicated in step 1.

BANK B (steps)		BANK B (net final effect)	
1. Deposits at Fed + $0.9m	DDO + $0.9m (implement dealers)	Deposit at Fed + $0.09m	DDO + $0.9m
2. U.S. Securities + $810,000 Deposits at Fed − *$810,000*		U.S. Securities + $.81m	

In step 1 the implement dealers deposit the checks and the bank increases the checking accounts accordingly. The Fed also increases (credits) Bank B's reserve account. Bank B is now in a position quite similar to that initially experienced by Bank A. Bank B's reserves have increased by $900,000, but its required reserves have increased by only $90,000 (i.e., 10% × $900,000). Bank B finds itself with $810,000 of excess reserves. Suppose Bank B trades those excess reserves for earning assets by purchasing $810,000 of securities from various dealers.

Step 2 indicates the acquisition of securities by Bank B. The bank pays for the securities by writing a check on its Federal Reserve account and the Fed *collects* from Bank B by decreasing its Federal Reserve checking account. The net final effect on Bank B, shown in the right-hand T-account, indicates that its demand deposit liabilities increased by $0.9 million ($900,000), its reserves increased by $0.09 million ($90,000), and its earning assets in the form of securities increased by $0.81 million ($810,000).

Bank B, in purchasing government securities, wrote checks on its Fed account and gave the checks to various securities dealers who bank with Bank C. When the checks are deposited and cleared, Bank C's T-account is as follows:

BANK C

1. Deposits at Fed + $810,000	DDO + $810,000 (securities dealers)

Bank C increases the checking accounts of the securities dealers by $810,000 and sends the checks to the Fed, which credits Bank C's reserve account by $810,000. Bank C is now in the same position in which Bank A and Bank B earlier found themselves—with excess reserves. Since Bank C's actual reserves increased by $810,000 while required reserves expanded only by $81,000, its excess reserves have increased by $729,000. Bank C therefore trades these excess reserves for earning assets (loans and/or securities), and a fourth bank (Bank D) enters the picture.

Assuming each bank trades all its excess reserves for earning assets, the final disposition of the original reserves of $1 million injected into the banks via the deposit of currency is illustrated in Table 13-3. Also illustrated is the expansion of demand deposits in each bank in the chain.

TABLE 13-3

FINAL DISPOSITION OF RESERVES AND DEPOSITS RESULTING FROM $1,000,000 CASH DEPOSIT

Bank	Reserves*	Deposits
A	+ $ 100,000	+ $ 1,000,000
B	+ 90,000	+ 900,000
C	+ 81,000	+ 810,000
D	+ 72,900	+ 729,000
.	.	.
.	.	.
.	.	.
Banking System	+ $1,000,000	+ $10,000,000

*Reserve requirement is assumed to be ten percent.

The $1 million of new reserves, initially deposited in Bank A in the form of currency, is now scattered throughout the banking system. Each bank maintains just enough additional reserves to support its increased deposits. Given the reserve requirement of ten percent, each bank maintains reserves in the amount of one-tenth its increased deposits. Each bank, in the process of ridding itself of excess reserves by adding to its holdings of loans and/or securities, creates new deposits that eventually reside elsewhere in the chain of banks.

Note that the final, total expansion of deposits in the banking system amounts to $10 million, or ten times the initial deposit of $1 million of reserves. This follows from the fact that the **simple deposit expansion multiplier** is the reciprocal of the reserve-requirement percentage:

$$\text{simple deposit expansion multiplier} = \frac{1}{\%RR_{DDO}} = \frac{1}{10\%} = 10$$

Actually, we may view the expansion of deposits as consisting of two parts: the $1-million deposit directly established by the original deposit of cash and the additional $9 million of *derived deposits* induced by bank lending and investing activities. This critical, induced portion is indicated by the following formula:

$$\text{induced change in deposits} = \text{initial change in excess reserves} \times$$
$$\text{simple deposit expansion multiplier}$$

$$\text{induced change in deposits} = \$0.9 \text{ million} \times 10$$

$$\text{induced change in deposits} = \$9 \text{ million}$$

In the example, the initial change in excess reserves induced by the $1-million cash deposit is $900,000. The simple deposit expansion multiplier, the reciprocal of the reserve-requirement percentage, is ten. Hence, the induced expansion of deposits is $9 million.[9]

The key to understanding the deposit expansion process lies in grasping that although each *individual bank* loses reserves on a dollar-for-dollar basis when it grants loans or purchases securities, these reserves are not lost to the *banking system*—they remain in the banks. Bank A, in lending or investing, loses reserves that flow into Bank B. An *individual bank* may easily rid itself of excess reserves of $1 million by lending or investing $1 million. But the only way the entire *banking system* can rid itself of $1 million of excess reserves is to create enough new deposits so that all excess reserves become required reserves. If the reserve requirement is 20 percent, demand deposits must expand by $5 million before required reserves can rise by $1 million and all excess reserves can be exhausted. If the reserve requirement is 10 percent, excess reserves are exhausted when deposits have expanded by $10 million.

Real-World Deposit Multiplier Versus Simple Deposit Multiplier

In the real world, the expansion of deposits in response to new reserves in the banking system is not as large as predicted by the simple deposit expansion multiplier. The simple multiplier overstates the true expansion multiplier. For one thing, banks do not actually attempt to maintain zero excess reserves. For precautionary reasons banks hold some excess reserves and as the deposit expansion process unfolds, banks deliberately add to their excess reserves. Since they do not really rid themselves of all excess reserves, the banking system does not create as many deposits as the simple multiplier formula predicts. Also, as the expansion of deposits takes place, the public is likely to hold some of this added financial wealth in the form of currency. To the extent that currency is withdrawn from banks during the deposit expansion process, bank reserves decline somewhat. This decline means that fewer deposits can be supported than is the case if the public failed to increase currency holdings during the deposit expansion process (as the simple deposit expansion multiplier assumes).

A Look Ahead

You now have the tools with which to understand how banks create money as a side-effect of their efforts to earn profits by purchasing securities and making loans.

---

[9]The total change in M-1 induced by the $1-million cash deposit is $9 million. Demand deposits increased by $10 million ($1 million direct and $9 million induced). However, C^P decreased by $1 million when the cash was deposited in the bank. Hence, M-1 increased by $9 million.

In Chapter 14 you learn how the Fed maintains control over these banking activities and, hence, over the nation's supply of money. In Chapter 15 we analyze the link between money and economic activity (i.e., how changes in the supply of money influence the economy).

SUMMARY

1. Money is commonly defined as the stock of those items widely used to make payment. In the United States the most prevalent measure is M-1, the *transactions* or *narrow* measure of the money supply. M-1 consists of checking accounts in financial institutions plus currency and coins held by individuals and firms.

2. The supply of money is an important concept because its magnitude influences such key macroeconomic variables as GNP, employment, and the level of prices. The Federal Reserve is capable of controlling the money supply within reasonable bounds.

3. Money serves the functions of medium of exchange, unit of account, and store of value.

4. As primitive societies evolved from barter to money economies, early monies were full bodied. This meant that the substance was worth roughly the same amount whether used as a material or as money. Gold coins at the turn of the century were full bodied. Today all of our money is fiduciary or fiat money. The value of money as a substance is considerably less than its value as money (i.e., its value in purchasing goods and services).

5. Today the bulk of our money supply consists of checking accounts in depository institutions or *banks*. The lending and investing activities of these banks create deposits and therefore intimately influence the nation's supply of money.

6. Bank assets include reserves (cash and deposits at the Fed), earning assets (loans and securities), and such other assets as equipment and buildings. Bank liabilities include transactions accounts (demand deposits and other checkable deposits), time deposits (savings accounts, CDs, negotiable CDs), and other liabilities (borrowings and bills payable).

7. Capital accounts are simply a residual item equivalent to total assets minus total liabilities. Capital accounts are the bank owners' equity in the bank. The capital account may be regarded as a cushion that protects the bank from possible insolvency owing to a potential contraction in the value of assets. A bank is technically insolvent at any time the value of its assets drops below the value of liabilities (i.e., when its capital accounts or net worth becomes negative).

8. More banks failed in the 1980s than in any period since the Great Depression of the 1930s. The causes may be found in the depressed agriculture and energy sectors and in the problem loans to LDCs. Banks were forced to write off bad loans, formally acknowledging that they would not be repaid. Hence, the value of bank assets declined without a corresponding decline in bank liabilities.

9. Banks create new money when they grant new loans and purchase additional securities (i.e., when they expand their earning assets). Such acquisition of earning assets is constrained by the existence of reserve requirements. Reserve requirements mandate that banks maintain at least some minimum percentage of their transactions-accounts liabilities in the form of reserves. Reserves consist of cash in banks and deposits at the Fed. Since reserves pay no interest, banks have an incentive to maintain few, if any, excess reserves (i.e., reserves in excess of required reserves).

10. When new reserves enter the banking system, the amount of demand deposits in the system ultimately expands by a multiple of the new reserves. This happens because, in order for all the new reserves to become required reserves, deposits must expand by a multiple $(1/\%RR_{DDO})$ of the new reserves. Banks have an incentive to keep expanding loans and investments (thus creating deposits) until they use up excess reserves. Given a ten-percent reserve requirement, demand deposits must expand by $50 million in order to exhaust $5 million of new reserves.

KEY TERMS

income
wealth
money
M-1
DDO
medium of exchange
unit of account
store of value
liquidity
monetary aggregates
full-bodied/commodity money
fiat/fiduciary money
bank balance sheet
bank assets
bank liabilities

capital accounts
reserves
required reserves
reserve requirement
excess reserves
insolvency
fractional reserve banking
simple deposit expansion
    multiplier

STUDY QUESTIONS AND PROBLEMS

1. Distinguish among the terms "money," "income," and "wealth." Is money a form of income? Is money a form of wealth?
2. Explain the contribution to society that money makes by analyzing the major problems that would exist if we were to revert suddenly to a system of barter.
3. What are the advantages and disadvantages of replacing our fiduciary money system with one of full-bodied money?
4. Explain the meaning of a bank's capital accounts. What is meant by bank insolvency? Why have so many banks become insolvent in recent years?
5. Define the following terms: "reserves," "required reserves," "excess reserves." Assuming a 15-percent reserve requirement and a $6-million deposit of coins by Scrooge McDuck into his checking account, calculate the initial change in his bank's:
   a. reserves
   b. required reserves
   c. excess reserves
6. Is money created directly when you
   a. deposit $10,000 cash in your checking account?
   b. borrow $10,000 from your bank?
   Explain each answer.
7. If additional loans and securities owned by banks mean more profits for banks, and if banks create money when they make loans and buy securities, why don't banks engage in much more lending and investing than they do?
8. Explain why the U.S. money supply falls when Hometown Bank sells $600,000 in securities to dealers.
9. "Even though any individual bank can lend or invest only the amount of initial excess reserves it possesses, the aggregate banking system can lend or invest a rather large *multiple* of its initial excess reserves." Is this statement true? If so, can you resolve the apparent paradox?
10. Assume the reserve requirement is 20 percent and that $10 million of currency found in a cave is deposited into a Bank A checking account. Compute:
    a. the maximum expansion of loans and securities by Bank A.
    b. the maximum expansion of the amount of demand deposits in the banking system.

SELECTED REFERENCES

Hutchinson, Harry D., *Money, Banking, and the United States Economy,* 6th ed. (Englewood Cliffs, NJ: Prentice-Hall, 1988). Excellent treatment of commercial banking and money creation.

Mishkin, Frederic, *Money, Banking, and Financial Markets,* 2nd ed. (Boston: Little, Brown Co., 1989). Discusses bank creation of money.

Thomas, Lloyd B., *Money, Banking, and Economic Activity,* 4th ed. (Englewood Cliffs, NJ: Prentice-Hall, 1986). A clear discussion of the nature and functions of money in Chapters 1 and 2.

CHAPTER 14

THE FEDERAL RESERVE SYSTEM AND ITS CONDUCT OF MONETARY POLICY

> There have been three great inventions since the beginning of time: fire, the wheel, and central banking.
>
> —WILL ROGERS

Every major nation has a **central bank**—*an organization whose chief function is to set the tone for the nation's financial policies, interest rates, and availability of money and credit. The U.S. central bank is the Federal Reserve System, popularly known as* **the Fed.** *The Fed was established when President Woodrow Wilson signed the Federal Reserve Act into law in 1913. However, central banks have existed in other nations for hundreds of years. The Bank of England, for example, was established in 1694. Other prominent central banks include the Bank of Japan, the Banque de France, and the Deutsche Bundesbank. The central bank of the Soviet Union is known as the Gosbank.*

The Federal Reserve System was established as an independent agency of government in response to a series of banking panics in the late nineteenth and early twentieth centuries. Recall from Chapter 13 that banks maintain on hand a rather small fraction of their assets in the form of cash. Such a system is inherently unstable in the event of panic. In the early banking panics, the rush by depositors to withdraw currency forced thousands of banks to suspend payments. What was severely needed was an agency to provide liquidity (i.e., cash) to the banking system in the event of distress. This was the major motivating force underlying the establishment of a central bank in this country. As we document in this chapter, however, the contemporary role of a central bank goes far beyond this important original function.

FUNCTIONS OF THE FEDERAL RESERVE SYSTEM

Overview

Federal Reserve System (the Fed)
The central bank of the United States; the organization responsible for conducting monetary policy by influencing the supply of money and credit and the level of interest rates.

Today the Federal Reserve System performs several important functions, the most interesting of which is to conduct monetary policy—a subject that we carefully survey in this chapter.

Supervising and Regulating Banks   The Fed is one of three federal agencies that sets regulations governing banks and oversees their operations. As discussed in Chapter 13, the Fed sets reserve requirements for banks and establishes guidelines for banks' capital accounts. The Fed also enforces liquidity standards that require banks to keep at least some minimal portion of their assets above and beyond their required reserves in highly liquid form (i.e., in assets easily and quickly convertible to cash). Other agencies participating in bank supervision and regulatory functions are the Comptroller of the Currency, the Federal Deposit Insurance Corporation, and individual state banking agencies.

Operating a Check-Collection System   Many out-of-town checks are processed by the Fed. Processing is facilitated by the fact that all banks and thrift institutions maintain deposit accounts at the Fed. The Fed clears checks by making simple bookkeeping entries. Banks in which checks are deposited have their Fed accounts credited; banks on which checks are written have their accounts reduced (debited) by the amount in question.

Issuing Currency   Today all the paper currency is placed into circulation by the Fed. Look at a $1 bill (or any other denomination bill) and note the inscription "Federal Reserve Note." All coins are issued by the Treasury. The Fed and the Treasury put currency and coins into circulation in response to the amount requested by the public, as manifested by deposits and withdrawals of currency and coins from banks and other financial institutions.

Serving as Banker's Bank and Fiscal Agent for the U.S. Treasury   The Fed provides banking services to private banks and thrift institutions. These private financial institutions maintain accounts at the Fed just as people have checking accounts at private banks. The U.S. Treasury also maintains a checking account at the Fed, conducting enormous daily transactions via that account.

Conducting the Nation's Monetary Policy   This is perhaps the most important and most challenging function of the Fed. In this function the Fed attempts to influence such key variables as GNP growth, the unemployment rate, and the nation's inflation rate by utilizing certain tools of monetary policy.

STRUCTURE OF THE FEDERAL RESERVE SYSTEM

The rather complex structure of the Federal Reserve System is outlined in Figure 14-1. Major players in this scheme include the Board of Governors, the Federal Open Market Committee, the Federal Reserve Banks, and the member banks.[1]

The U.S. central banking system is unique in the world in that we have 12 separate Federal Reserve Districts, each district having a Federal Reserve Bank. There are also 25 branches associated with these 12 Fed banks. This system was conceived as a political compromise between populists who voiced strong distrust of "big bankers" and concentration of financial power in the hands of a few, and those

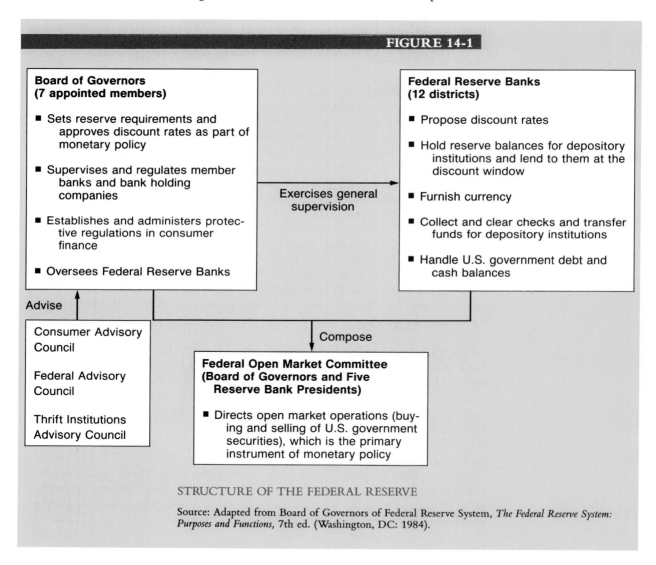

FIGURE 14-1

Board of Governors (7 appointed members)

- Sets reserve requirements and approves discount rates as part of monetary policy
- Supervises and regulates member banks and bank holding companies
- Establishes and administers protective regulations in consumer finance
- Oversees Federal Reserve Banks

Exercises general supervision

Federal Reserve Banks (12 districts)

- Propose discount rates
- Hold reserve balances for depository institutions and lend to them at the discount window
- Furnish currency
- Collect and clear checks and transfer funds for depository institutions
- Handle U.S. government debt and cash balances

Advise

Consumer Advisory Council

Federal Advisory Council

Thrift Institutions Advisory Council

Compose

Federal Open Market Committee (Board of Governors and Five Reserve Bank Presidents)

- Directs open market operations (buying and selling of U.S. government securities), which is the primary instrument of monetary policy

STRUCTURE OF THE FEDERAL RESERVE

Source: Adapted from Board of Governors of Federal Reserve System, *The Federal Reserve System: Purposes and Functions,* 7th ed. (Washington, DC: 1984).

---

[1]The three Advisory Councils are much less important players. For example, the Federal Advisory Council consists of one banker from each of the 12 Federal Reserve Districts. The function of this council is to receive advisory input from the banking community. The consumer and thrift institutions' advisory councils provide similar functions.

who favored the traditional model of a single central bank. The populists favored as many as 50 separate central banks, each with autonomy to conduct policies deemed appropriate for its geographical region. The compromise resulted in twelve regional banks that initially had considerable autonomy over setting policies. However, the decision-making power has since shifted to the central unit—the *Board of Governors* in Washington. Today the twelve regional (district) banks are little more than branches, with the power residing in Washington.

Board of Governors

Board of Governors (of the Federal Reserve System)
Key seven-person board that dominates the decision-making process in conducting monetary policy.

This crucial seven-person **Board of Governors** is the nucleus of the Federal Reserve System. Each member is appointed by the President of the United States for a 14-year term. The terms are staggered so that one appointment expires every two years. This staggering was intentionally arranged to prevent a president from *stacking* the board with individuals sympathetic to the incumbent party's political interests. Normally a president makes two appointments in one term of office and four appointments in a two-term presidency.[2]

One member of the Board of Governors is designated by the President to serve as Chairperson for a four-year term. This appointment is renewable within the 14-year term on the Board of Governors. The Chairperson of the Board of Governors—via public statements, international diplomacy, and ability to influence views and votes of other Board members—holds a position of considerable power. In fact, it is often asserted that the Chairperson of the Federal Reserve Board is the second most powerful individual in America!

Discount Rate
The interest rate charged on loans to financial institutions made by the Federal Reserve.

The Board of Governors dominates the conduct of U.S. monetary policy. It sets the level of reserve requirements and the **discount rate**—the interest rate charged by the Fed on loans it makes to banks and thrift institutions. Also, the Board constitutes the majority of the **Federal Open Market Committee (FOMC)**, which establishes the overall tone of monetary policy and wields the most important instrument of policy—*open market operations.*

Federal Open Market Committee (FOMC)

Federal Open Market Committee (FOMC)
The committee responsible for determining the basic thrust of monetary policy and conducting open market operations; consists of the seven members of the Board of Governors and five of the twelve Federal Reserve Bank presidents.

The Federal Open Market Committee meets in Washington, DC, approximately every six weeks to formulate the nation's monetary policy. The FOMC consists of the seven members of the Board of Governors and five of the twelve district Federal Reserve Bank presidents. Actually, each of the twelve Fed Bank presidents, accompanied by a key research staff member, attends the FOMC meetings and voices opinions on the appropriate thrust of policy. However, only five are permitted to vote on policy decisions. The New York Fed Bank president is a permanent voting member of the FOMC. The remaining eleven presidents serve on an alternating basis, four at a time.

In the FOMC meetings, current trends in inflation, unemployment, exchange rates, and other key data are reviewed. In the light of current and expected developments, members of the FOMC express their opinions concerning implementation of appropriate policies. After extended discussion, and when a near consensus

---

[2]Exceptions occur in the case of death or resignation from the Board. Such resignations have become frequent in recent years. When Alan Greenspan joined the Board in August 1987, he became the seventh member of the existing Board to have been appointed by then President Ronald Reagan.

Alan Greenspan, chairman
of the Federal Reserve
Board of Governors,
1987-

appears imminent, a policy statement known as a FOMC directive is written. Members of the FOMC then formally vote on whether to implement the directive. This directive—usually stated in terms of the desired thrust of interest rates, credit availability, and behavior of the monetary aggregates (M-1, M-2, and so forth)— forms the operational basis of policy. That is, the FOMC directive establishes the degree of monetary stimulus or restraint to be implemented.

The District Federal Reserve Banks

Nominally, each of the twelve district Federal Reserve Banks is *owned* by the member banks within the district. Each member bank buys shares of stock in the district Fed and receives a modest annual dividend on those shares. However, this *ownership* of the Fed by private commercial banks does not carry implications of *control* in any meaningful sense. Indeed, if it did, the potential conflict of interest could easily result in implementation of policies contrary to the public interest.

Each of the twelve district Federal Reserve Banks is governed by a nine-person board of directors. The directors consist of three bankers, three individuals from the nonbank business community, and three individuals from other occupations. The district boards elect the presidents of the individual Federal Reserve Banks. As mentioned, the presidents sit on the important FOMC. One can visualize the potential influence of private bankers on Fed policy via their presence on the board of directors of the Federal Reserve Banks. This potential conflict of interest has resulted in occasional proposals to disenfranchise the Fed Bank presidents from voting privileges on the FOMC. Supporters of the status quo argue that the three-tier background requirement of the composition of the board of directors provides a sufficient safeguard.

Figure 14-2 illustrates the boundaries of the twelve Federal Reserve districts, together with the cities in which the twelve district banks and their branches are located.

Member Banks

Of some 15,000 commercial banks in the United States, fewer than 6000 are currently members of the Federal Reserve System. All national banks—those chartered by the U.S. Comptroller of the Currency—are required to be members. Banks chartered by the individual states (state banks) are *not* required to be members, and less than 20 percent have chosen to join. The member banks technically own the Fed, as noted, and share certain of the costs and benefits that come with membership. However, both the costs and benefits of membership were reduced significantly in the 1980s when federal legislation subjected all banks (and thrift institutions) to a uniform set of *reserve requirements* and simultaneously gave them all access to borrowing privileges at the Fed.[3]

---

[3]Recall from our discussion in Chapter 13 the notion that reserve requirements are essentially a *tax* that forces banks to hold more noninterest-bearing funds than they would otherwise prefer. Prior to the 1980s, nonmember banks were subject to more lenient reserve requirements (set by their state banking authority) than member banks. This was the major cost of membership—forgoing a chance to earn bigger profits. The benefits included access to the Fed's discount window, check-clearing services, other services, and perhaps a slight prestige factor. The Depository Institutions Deregulation and Monetary Control Act of 1980 (DIDMCA) imposed a uniform set of reserve requirements on *all* depository institutions (member and nonmember) and gave borrowing privileges to all institutions.

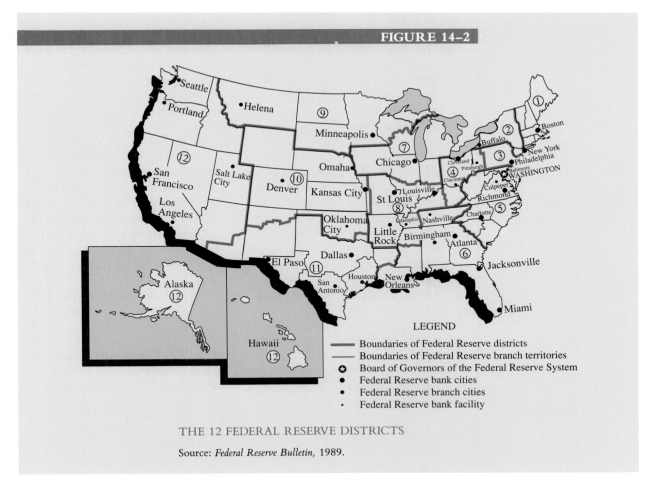

FIGURE 14–2

LEGEND

― Boundaries of Federal Reserve districts
― Boundaries of Federal Reserve branch territories
◉ Board of Governors of the Federal Reserve System
● Federal Reserve bank cities
● Federal Reserve branch cities
· Federal Reserve bank facility

THE 12 FEDERAL RESERVE DISTRICTS

Source: *Federal Reserve Bulletin,* 1989.

The Independent Status of the Fed

When the Fed was established, there was a deliberate intent to minimize exposure of the organization to political pressures from both the executive and legislative branches of government. The fear that the conduct of monetary policy might be swayed by politically motivated desires of incumbents is responsible for the long and staggered appointments of members of the Board of Governors, and for prohibition of reappointment to the Board for more than one full term. Even more critical in maintaining the political independence of the Fed, in the view of many observers, is the fact that it is set up to be independent of the purse strings of Congress. Unlike other government agencies, the Fed does not receive funding from Congress. By virtue of its huge portfolio of securities, the Fed earns revenues of nearly $20 billion annually. Operating expenses in 1989 were less than $2 billion. The Fed simply uses whatever funds it needs to run its operations appropriately and turns the remainder of its revenues over to the U.S. Treasury.

There are pros and cons to the independent status of the Fed—a status that is unique among central banks around the world. The major advantage is that the Fed can potentially ignore short-term political needs of incumbent politicians seeking reelection. It can afford to take the *long view,* which is essential to prudent economic management and to a stable macroeconomic and financial environment. In particular, the existing arrangement reduces the prospects for a *political business cycle,* in which the economy is alternately subjected to monetary stimulus in the year prior to elections and monetary restraint to control inflation immediately thereafter.

A potential serious disadvantage of the Fed's independence is that monetary policy can sometimes operate at cross purposes with other aspects of economic policy. Coordination of monetary and fiscal policies is essential to a smooth-running economy. Critics of the existing system charge that the Fed is not subject to appropriate constraints. Some suggest that the Fed should be made part of the Treasury Department, thus coming under the purview of the executive branch and the President of the United States. The voters would then evaluate the conduct of monetary policy via the political process. In the event of monetary policy negligence, voters could "throw the rascals out." Opponents of this viewpoint believe that monetary policy is too arcane a subject to be comprehended by the electorate and therefore the democratic mechanism would fail to function properly. Furthermore, such individuals are fearful of entrusting the monetary reins to politicians. As evidence of the abdication of responsibility by politicians, they point to the huge budget deficits of the 1980s.

Notwithstanding, we must be careful not to overstate the extent of the Fed's independence from the political mechanism. Its independence is fragile—the freedom to conduct short-range monetary policy, not the freedom to pursue actions deemed by objective observers to be contrary to the interests of the nation. The Congress originally created the Federal Reserve System and could potentially modify, emasculate, or even abolish the Fed. The Fed, acutely aware of the fragility of its independence, is eager to preserve it. Toward that end the Fed is in frequent communication with both the White House and Congress in order to assure a smooth coordination between monetary policy and other facets of national economic policy.

Balance Sheet of the Federal Reserve System

Consider briefly a simplified balance sheet of the Federal Reserve Banks (all twelve District Banks combined). Understanding the Fed's balance sheet is essential to a clear understanding of the Fed's functions, how it finances itself, and how it conducts monetary policy. The Fed's assets and liabilities as of January 31, 1989, are shown in Table 14-1; some lesser details of the balance sheet are intentionally omitted, however, so we are not overwhelmed.

Federal Reserve Assets   The Fed's asset holdings include coins, loans to banks and other financial institutions, holdings of U.S. government securities, and such other assets as buildings, furniture, automobiles, and computers. Coins are Treasury-minted metallic currency held at Federal Reserve banks for the purpose of supplying the public's coin needs on request. When individuals and firms need coins, they withdraw them from their accounts in banks and thrift institutions. When these institutions run low, they request a shipment of coins from the Fed and pay for them by having their balances at the Fed marked down (reduced). When the Fed itself runs low on coins it contacts the Treasury, which sends a shipment to the Fed. The Fed pays the Treasury by marking up (increasing) the Treasury's account at the Fed (liability side of Fed's balance sheet).

Loans to financial institutions by the Fed—known in the financial market jargon as **discounts and advances**—are made in response to requests by the banks

TABLE 14-1			

FEDERAL RESERVE SYSTEM BALANCE SHEET, JANUARY 31, 1989 ($ billions)

Assets		**Liabilities**	
Coins	$ 0.48	Federal Reserve Notes	$221.62
Loans to financial institutions	.86	Deposits of financial institutions	35.81
Government securities	232.93	Deposits of U.S. Treasury	11.77
Other assets	52.50	Other liabilities	12.90
		Capital accounts	4.67
Total assets	$286.77	*Total liabilities and capital accounts*	$286.77

Source: *Federal Reserve Bulletin,* April 1989.

and other financial institutions. These loan requests are initiated in order to meet unanticipated reserve deficiencies. Suppose a bank, at the end of the day, calculates its reserves to be $18 million and its required reserves to be $18.2 million. It can avoid the potential reserve deficiency by calling the Fed and requesting a short-term loan of $200,000. The change in the Fed's balance sheet associated with this transaction is simply:

FED

Assets	**Liabilities**
Loans + $200,000	Deposits of banks + $200,000

For our purposes, the most crucial Federal Reserve asset is also its largest—holdings of U.S. government securities. The Fed—unlike any individual, firm, or government agency—has *unlimited* capacity to purchase securities at its own discretion. The Fed pays for such purchases by simply marking up (increasing) the deposit account of the seller's bank at the Fed. In other words, *the Fed pays for its security purchases by creating new reserves in the banking system.* Suppose the Fed purchases $750 million of U.S. government bonds from private citizens. The T-account (Fed's balance sheet change) is simply:

FED

Assets	**Liabilities**
U.S. government securities + $750 million	Deposits of banks + $750 million

The $750 million of reserves created by the transaction show up on the liability side of the Fed's balance sheet. The Fed does not buy securities for the same reason that private citizens, banks, and others do (i.e., to earn interest or profits). The Fed buys (or sells) securities solely with the intent of providing the amount of reserves in the U.S. banking system deemed appropriate to provide the desired financial climate in the nation. However, a pleasant side effect of the Fed's huge security portfolio is that it provides it with handsome annual revenues of some $15–$20 billion.

Federal Reserve Liabilities   Liabilities of the Fed include the paper currency outstanding that it has issued (Federal Reserve Notes); deposits of banks, other financial institutions, and the U.S. Treasury at the Fed; and other liabilities such as bills payable.

All paper currency is presently issued in the form of Federal Reserve Notes (formerly the Treasury issued paper currency as well). Federal Reserve Notes make up the bulk of the C^P portion of the money supply (remember that M-1 = DDO + C^P). Treasury coins constitute only a tiny portion of C^P. The Fed issues new currency passively in response to public demand. As the public demands additional currency from banks, the banks wire the Fed and request currency. The Fed issues new paper currency, sends it to the banks via armored truck service, and the liability item *Federal Reserve Notes* increases accordingly.

The other chief liabilities of the Fed are the deposits they maintain for depository institutions (banks and thrift institutions) and the U.S. Treasury. The Fed serves as a *bank* for private banks and the Treasury in the same sense as private commercial banks serve as banks for citizens and firms. Banks and the Treasury maintain checking accounts at the Fed, and these accounts are actively used to make payments.

The Fed's capital accounts represent *shares* in the Federal Reserve owned by banks, together with certain other accounts. In a real sense, however, the Fed is owned by all the people, not just by the banks.

TOOLS OF FEDERAL RESERVE POLICY

The ultimate goal of monetary policy is to provide a stable financial environment and to move the economy closer to such macroeconomic objectives as price level stability, low unemployment, and perhaps a stable exchange rate in international markets. To achieve these goals the Fed employs certain instruments or tools of policy. These tools include open market operations, discount rate policy, and changes in reserve requirements. We now sketch the mechanism by which each of these tools influences interest rates, credit availability, and the nation's money supply.

Open Market Operations

Whenever the Fed purchases *anything* from private individuals, firms, or banks, it creates new reserves in the banking system on a dollar-for-dollar basis. To illustrate, assume the Fed purchases a new fleet of cars for official business purposes. Assume the Fed issues a check drawn on itself to General Motors Corporation for $900,000. General Motors deposits the check in its commercial bank account in Detroit. The U.S. money supply immediately rises by $900,000. More important, however, is the impact on *reserves*. The Detroit bank sends the check to the Fed, which pays off the bank by marking up its deposit account at the Fed by $900,000. This is a pure bookkeeping entry, with no exchange of physical units of money involved. Since these bank deposit accounts at the Fed count as reserves, total reserves in the banking system have expanded by $900,000.

A similar result would occur if the Fed purchased ballpoint pens, candy bars, common stocks, corporation bonds, or pork-bellies futures. No matter what the Fed buys, it pays for its purchase by creating new reserves (i.e., deposits of private banks at the Federal Reserve). For purposes of controlling total reserves in the banking system, the Fed has chosen to focus its activities on the market for U.S. government securities. The market in which existing government securities are traded is sometimes referred to as the "open market." Hence the term **open market operations** The government securities market is an extremely active and well-developed financial market. Thousands of banks and thrift institutions are in the market regularly, along with such other institutions as money market mutual funds, pension funds, nonfinancial corporations, and wealthy individuals. Approximately 40 dealers make markets in government securities; the dealers have been chosen by the Fed to do business with the Fed based on their size and quality. These dealers hold inventories of government securities and stand ready to buy or sell upon request. Since the government securities market is so highly developed and efficient, it makes sense that the Fed conducts its policy almost exclusively by buying and selling in this market.

Open Market Operations
Buying and selling of U.S. government securities by the Fed with a view toward influencing monetary and credit conditions.

Suppose total reserves in the banking system are $50 billion and the Fed desires an expansion to $51 billion in order to increase the availability of money and credit and drive down interest rates. The Fed simply contacts the 40 dealers and arranges to purchase $1 billion from the dealer offering the most competitive quotation (lowest price and highest yield). The Fed then issues a check to the dealer for $1 billion and the relevant T-accounts are as follows:

FED		DEALER'S BANK	
Assets	**Liabilities**	**Assets**	**Liabilities**
U.S. securities + $1 billion	Deposit of dealer's bank + $1 billion	Deposit at Fed + $1 billion	DDO (dealer) + $1 billion

As soon as the dealer deposits the check, the money supply (M-1) increases by $1 billion. The dealer's bank then forwards the check to the Fed, which pays the dealer's bank by adding $1 billion to the bank's account at the Fed. Bank reserves in the system have thus increased by $1 billion. Since the bulk of these new reserves are *excess reserves,* a multiple expansion of deposits (and money) is touched off as banks expand their holdings of securities and loans.

When the Fed wishes to implement a restrictive monetary policy, it contacts the dealers and arranges to sell securities. The dealers write checks to the Fed. Demand deposits and the money supply fall. The Fed collects on the checks by deducting (reducing) the reserve accounts of the dealers' banks. Hence, bank reserves decline dollar-for-dollar with the magnitude of the Fed's portfolio of securities.

The open market operations tool gives the Federal Reserve fingertip control over aggregate reserves in the banking system.[4] This ability to fine-tune reserves is the

---

[4] A major part of the Fed's open market operations are conducted for *defensive purposes*—to defend bank reserves from undesired short-term changes emanating from a horde of factors. When private citizens withdraw currency from banks to finance vacations, reserves fall (remember that a bank's reserves include cash on hand as well as deposits at the Fed). The Fed purchases securities to replenish the reserves. When the U.S. Treasury writes checks on its Fed account to pay government employees, this action pumps reserves into banks. The Fed sells securities in the open market to offset this factor and to maintain its grip over total reserves. Each year the Fed buys and sells hundreds of billions of dollars worth of government securities to defend total reserves—to maintain the status quo.

chief advantage of this tool, which is the bread-and-butter instrument of Fed policy. Although the Fed can accurately control aggregate bank reserves, its control over the supply of money is much less precise. This imprecision is due to the fact that the multiplier linking reserves to the money stock fluctuates in a way that is not easily predictable.

Discount Policy

All banks and other depository institutions are granted the privilege of occasionally borrowing at the Federal Reserve for the purpose of covering short-run reserve deficiencies. In financial jargon, this facility is known as the **discount window**. The Federal Reserve establishes the *rules of the game* or criteria for legitimate use of the discount window and sets its interest rate, known as the *discount rate*. Although the Fed changes the discount rate periodically, the criteria for borrowing remain fixed. Financial institutions are permitted to borrow to meet unanticipated reserve deficiencies resulting from unexpected losses of reserves. However, it is not considered legitimate to borrow for *profit*—to turn around and use the proceeds from the discount window to make new loans or to purchase securities.

For analytical purposes we can separate the consequences of a change in the Federal Reserve discount rate into two effects—a mechanical effect and a psychological or announcement effect.

Mechanical Effect of Discount Rate Change   Assume the Fed raises its discount rate. All banks currently borrowing at the Fed experience an immediate increase in their cost of funds. Some of these banks decide to quickly pay off their loans from the Fed, and some sell off certain short-term securities to obtain funds to do so. Some banks also raise the loan rates they charge their customers, encouraging them to repay the loans. These actions suggest that interest rates tend to rise. As banks repay the discount window, bank reserves and the money supply tend to decline. Hence, an increase in the Fed's discount rate leads to monetary restriction—higher interest rates and a lower money supply. By the same token, a reduction in the Federal Reserve discount rate tends to lead to monetary expansion and to a decline in interest rates.

The association between the discount rate and other short-term interest rates is fairly strong, as illustrated in Figure 14-3. Part of this strong statistical relationship between the discount rate and other interest rates is due to the fact that a change in the discount rate precipitates a sympathetic move in other rates, as just indicated. However, a good part of the association is explained by the fact that the Fed often changes its discount rate to keep it in line with other rates in the economy. Hence, if short-term interest rates rise sharply, the Fed is likely to raise its discount rate.

Announcement Effect of Discount Rate Change   If a change in the Fed's discount rate catches the financial markets by surprise, a fairly strong *announcement effect* occurs. Suppose the Fed unexpectedly jumps its discount rate from seven percent to eight percent. Economic agents are almost sure to interpret this discount-rate hike as a signal that the Fed is moving toward a more restrictive monetary policy. One can expect the Fed to follow up the discount-rate hike with restrictive open market operations—sales of securities by the Fed to drain reserves from the system. Hence, bankers and others are given the signal that interest rates will soon move higher and credit availability will become more restrictive in the weeks ahead.

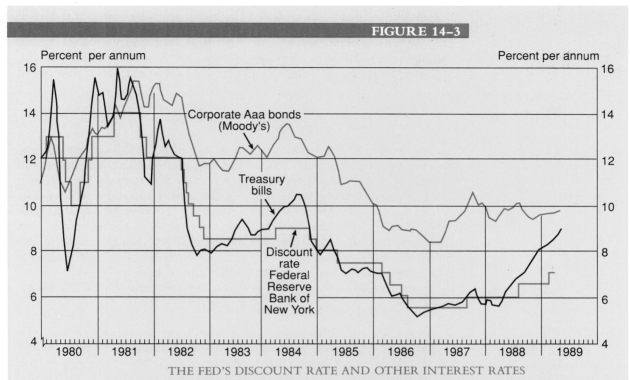

FIGURE 14–3

THE FED'S DISCOUNT RATE AND OTHER INTEREST RATES

The Federal Reserve discount rate is closely correlated with other interest rates in the
economy. This is due partly to the influence that the discount rate has on other interest
rates. Also, it reflects the fact that the Fed tends to change the discount rate to keep it in
reasonably close alignment with other interest rates.

Source: Council of Economic Advisors, 1989.

To prepare for this more stringent financial climate, bank management is likely
to become more conservative in its lending and investing policies. Bankers may
examine loan applications more carefully and raise loan rates across the board.
Hence, if the Fed has reason to believe the banks are becoming too expansionary in
their lending practices, a good way to rein them in is to post a sharp increase in the
discount rate. Since financial markets dislike monetary restriction, the announcement of the discount-rate hike is likely to set off an immediate drop in stock and
bond prices.

If the Fed fears an undesired recession is imminent and believes that commer-
cial-bank lending policies should be loosened, it might shock the markets with a
sharp drop in the discount rate. Bankers and others would immediately infer that
monetary stimulus is on the way. This move would create anticipation of lower
interest rates and more liberal provision of reserves by the Fed to the banking system.
Hence, bankers are likely to become more accommodative of loan requests. Loan
rates and yields in the market are likely to decline. The money supply will increase
as banks expand loans. Stock and bond prices may rise when the discount-rate cut is
announced.

Frequently, however, a change in the Fed's discount rate has little or no
announcement effect because bankers and other financial market participants often

see the discount-rate change coming. As noted, the discount rate is usually kept in fairly close alignment with certain short-term yields, such as those on government securities. When this differential becomes fairly large, it is a pretty good bet that the Fed will restore the normal relationship by changing its discount rate. The majority of the changes in the Fed's discount rate therefore fail to catch agents in financial markets by surprise.

Changes in Reserve Requirements

Reserve Requirements
The percentage of deposits that financial institutions are required by the Fed to hold in the form of reserves—cash and deposits at the Fed.

Within broad ranges set by law, the Fed is authorized to change the **reserve requirements** applicable to all banks and thrift institutions. This is potentially an extremely powerful tool of policy; however, it is not used frequently. Furthermore, the tool is redundant in the sense that the open market operations tool provides sufficient ammunition for the Fed to achieve its policy objectives. Unlike other tools of policy, a change in reserve requirements does not operate by changing reserves in the banking system. Instead, it alters the multiplier linking reserves to the money supply.

Recall from the analysis in Chapter 13 that the relationship between reserves and aggregate deposits in the banking system is given by the following formula:

$$\text{demand deposits} = \text{reserves} \times \text{deposit multiplier}$$

Whereas open market operations and changes in the discount rate derive their impact principally by altering reserves in the system, a change in reserve requirements leaves reserves unchanged but alters the deposit multiplier linking reserves to deposits. A cut in reserve requirements, by initially freeing up excess reserves and causing an expansion of bank lending and security purchases, increases the deposit multiplier. An increase in reserve requirements forces banks to reduce loans and security holdings, thus reducing deposits and the supply of money. The amount of deposits that can be supported by the existing stock of reserves decreases. In other words, the deposit multiplier decreases when reserve requirements are raised.

We illustrate the potential power of the reserve requirement tool by examining its effect on the aggregate balance sheet of *all* banks. Assume initially the reserve requirement is ten percent, applicable to *DDO*—demand deposits and other checkable deposits. The initial balance sheet of the aggregate banking system is as follows:

ALL BANKS ($ billions)

Assets		Liabilities	
Reserves (cash and deposits at Fed)	$ 40	*DDO*	$400
Loans and securities	$360	Other liabilities and capital	$200
Other assets	$200		

Given the ten-percent reserve requirement, the banking system is fully extended: there are just enough reserves ($40 billion) to support existing deposits ($400 billion). In other words, there are no excess reserves in the aggregate banking system.

Now assume the Fed reduces the reserve requirement for *DDO* to eight percent. Required reserves in the banking system immediately drop from $40 billion to $32 billion. Actual reserves are unaffected, remaining at $40 billion. The system suddenly finds itself with $8 billion of excess reserves.

Individual banks, in order to increase profits, use their excess reserves to expand loans and security holdings. This, in turn, creates new deposits (and money) in the banking system. This process of deposit expansion continues until the system runs out of excess reserves. Given the eight-percent reserve requirement, excess reserves are exhausted when banks have collectively expanded their loans and investments by $100 billion, driving *DDO* up by $100 billion to a level of $500 billion. At the end of the expansion process the aggregate balance sheet is as follows:

ALL BANKS ($ billions)

Assets		Liabilities	
Reserves (cash and deposits at Fed)	$ 40	*DDO*	$500
Loans and securities	$460	Other liabilities and capital	$200
Other assets	$200		

This result can be confirmed by a calculation using our simple deposit formulation:

initial change in excess reserves × deposit multiplier =
ultimate change in deposits
$8 billion × (1/.08) = $100 billion

The reduction in reserve requirements releases $8 billion of excess reserves. The deposit multiplier, which is the reciprocal of the percentage reserve requirement (.08), is now 12.5. We confirm that *DDO* (and M-1) ultimately expands by $100 billion as a result of the reduction in reserve requirements.

As you can see, this tool is quite powerful. In fact, it is too blunt to be used as a day-to-day tool of policy. Instead, the Fed conducts its monetary policy primarily via the other two instruments and leaves reserve requirements unaltered for years at a time. In the severe 1974–1975 recession, however, the Fed reduced reserve requirements three times in an effort to provide a strong dose of monetary stimulus.

INTERMEDIATE TARGETS OF MONETARY POLICY

The Fed manipulates its instruments—open market operations, the discount rate, and reserve requirements—in order to influence the unemployment rate or the rate of inflation. For example, the Fed purchases securities in the open market when it seeks to drive down the unemployment rate. In order for the Fed security purchases to reduce unemployment, they must first expand bank reserves, touch off an expansion of bank lending and investing activities, reduce interest rates and increase the supply of money, and lead to an expansion of aggregate demand for goods and services. All this causes firms to step up production and hire more workers. This chain of influence of Federal Reserve policy is illustrated schematically in Figure 14-4 (page 316).

Although the Fed's ultimate goal is to influence output, employment, and prices, the Fed cannot use these variables to guide its day-to-day and week-to-week decisions. The reason is that moving through the sequence illustrated in Figure 14-4 takes time. For example, it may take six to twelve months for Federal Reserve open

EXHIBIT 14–1

DISASTER IN THE SAVINGS AND LOAN INDUSTRY

The plight of America's savings and loan (S and L) industry today represents the nation's biggest financial disaster in at least 50 years. Hundreds of S and Ls, though insolvent by conventional accounting standards, were allowed to continue to operate in the late 1980s. The government agency that traditionally insured the deposits issued by S and Ls, the Federal Savings and Loan Insurance Agency (FSLIC), effectively went bankrupt, having nowhere near the financial resources necessary to make good on the liabilities of the insolvent S and Ls to their depositors in the event that the insolvent institutions were to be shut down. A huge federal bailout has been put in place, a bailout that is likely to cost American taxpayers some $100 billion and possibly even more.

Who's to blame? There are plenty of culprits. Congress, the regulatory authorities, the accounting firms that audit the S and Ls, and the S and L industry itself have contributed to the mess that burst into the national spotlight in the late 1980s.

Born in the Great Depression as a mechanism for encouraging home ownership for the masses of Americans, the S and L concept was flawed from the beginning. These institutions were to issue short-term savings deposits and use the funds to provide 15-, 20-, and 30-year home mortgages at interest rates fixed over the life of the loans. This system was a disaster waiting to happen. If interest rates were ever to increase sharply, the cost of obtaining funds would rise above the average yield earned on an institution's portfolio of fixed-rate mortgages, which changes only slowly over time. That, of course, is a prescription for losing money. If sustained for a long period it is a ticket to insolvency for the S and Ls—including those that are managed quite prudently.

For 45 years the S and L industry was stable and prosperous. Interest rates did trend gradually upward from the 1940s through the mid-1970s, but remained at tolerable levels. In order to protect the S and Ls and other thrift institutions, legal limits were placed on the interest rates these institutions were allowed to pay depositors. Because financial markets remained relatively stable, crises of disaster proportion were avoided until the late 1970s. Then all hell broke loose.

In the late 1970s, U.S. inflation escalated into the double-digit range. In a successful effort to bring down inflation, the Federal Reserve pushed interest rates to extremely high levels. Because the regulated yields paid to S and L customers became quite unattractive relative to other yields in the economy, the institutions faced the prospect of massive *disintermediation*—withdrawal of funds by depositors. This would have forced the S and Ls to sell off bundles of mortgages and other assets at prices significantly below their original cost. This, in turn, might have quickly bankrupted a large percentage of the nation's S and Ls.

To avoid this, the S and Ls got Congress to pass legislation. The Depository Institutions Deregulation Act of 1980 phased out the ceilings on interest rates payable to depositors. This measure slowed the demise of the S and Ls but did not solve the basic problem. As long as their average cost of obtaining funds exceeded the average interest earned on their portfolio of mortgages, the S and Ls operated in the red. The net worth of the nation's 3200 S and Ls declined from about $32 billion in 1980 to approximately $20 billion in 1982. 1981 and 1982 were especially bad years for the industry: industry losses after taxes totaled $8 billion, and some 500 S and Ls became insolvent by conventional accounting standards.

In 1981, S and Ls were first permitted to issue adjustable-rate mortgages (ARMs). ARMs were designed to protect the S and Ls by shifting the risk of rising interest rates onto the homebuyer. ARMs trigger automatic increases in the interest rate on outstanding mortgages in periods of increasing interest rates. While increasing reliance on ARMs figured eventually to help stabilize the S and L industry, the instrument provided little short-term relief. The chief problem was that the S and Ls were locked into previously issued long-term fixed-rate mortgages for years to come.

In an additional effort to allow S and Ls to compete on a level playing field, Congress passed the Garn-St. Germain Depository Institutions Act of 1982. This Act permitted S and Ls to enter new activities such as making loans to businesses and consumers. The idea was sensible—allowing the S and Ls to diversify their assets in order to provide more long-term stability to the industry.

Although these laws designed to help the S and Ls augured well for the long term, they came a bit late. Like drought-stricken farmers praying for rain, the S and Ls were praying for a decline in interest rates. Unfortunately, these rates remained abnormally high throughout the first half of the decade of the 1980s, partially because of federal budget deficits. Finally, when interest rates came down sharply, the other shoe fell. The price of oil collapsed. Oil-producing states were hard hit. The problem in Texas is illustrative. Plummeting oil prices hammered the Texas economy and brought down the real estate industry to which the S and Ls had loaned heavily. In Houston and other Texas cities, prices of homes and commercial real estate collapsed.

As more and more S and Ls became insolvent by conventional accounting standards, the FSLIC became aware of the enormity of the crisis. Moreover, they did not have nearly enough resources to cover the losses of the insolvent S and Ls. The regulatory authorities then made an ill-fated decision to liberalize accounting procedures to disguise the insolvencies, hoping to buy time for an industry recovery that might return many bankrupt institutions to solvency.

While the 1982 Garn-St. Germain Act sensibly allowed the S and Ls to diversify assets somewhat, several states became swept up in the deregulation mania and implemented foolish provisions. Texas, California, and Florida, for example, authorized state-chartered S and Ls to engage in almost any lending practices they desired. These institutions began committing funds to windmill farms, racetracks, fish farms, and large real estate ventures of dubious merit. The deregulation of both interest rates payable by S and Ls and their allowable activities greatly increased the opportunities for risky business. These opportunities, coupled with the weakened condition of the FSLIC, provided a signal for risk-prone wheeler-dealers to enter the industry. Speculative behavior increased and fraudulent activity became prevalent. In more than one-half of the insolvent institutions, fraud has been cited as a contributing factor.

Common sense dictates that if the S and Ls are to be authorized to take more risk with their depositors' money while the government insures the depositors, more surveillance over S and L activities is required. Unfortunately, the regulatory authorities did not have the resources. The Federal Home Loan Bank Board, the organization charged with policing the S and L industry, was pitifully staffed during the period in which the crisis was developing. Budgets have been tight in the era of huge federal budget deficits. Especially foolhardy is the policy of permitting *insolvent* S and Ls to continue operations in a laissez-faire environment. These institutions have a powerful incentive to take more risk in a desperate effort to increase their returns and pull themselves out of insolvency. Because no individual owner's wealth is at stake (the firm being insolvent), the firm faces essentially a "heads I win, tails the government loses" proposition. The insolvent S and Ls went further and further into the red, at the taxpayers' eventual expense, as speculative activity became increasingly rampant. The FSLIC is left holding the bag. The insolvent S and Ls should have been shut down immediately.

In early 1989, President George Bush unveiled a plan designed to resolve, in time, the S and L disaster. Bush proposes that the federal government spend $157 billion over the next decade to close or merge some 500–700 insolvent or nearly insolvent S and Ls. Much of the cost is to be borne by taxpayers, although some is to be paid by the industry. In addition, the program calls for higher capital requirements for S and Ls to cushion against recurrence of such crises. Further, the powers of the FDIC are to be expanded, including the absorption of the devastated FSLIC. The FDIC is mandated to take over the insolvent S and Ls until it can arrange for liquidation or merger of these institutions. By summer 1989, the FDIC was operating more than 250 insolvent S and Ls in more than 30 states.

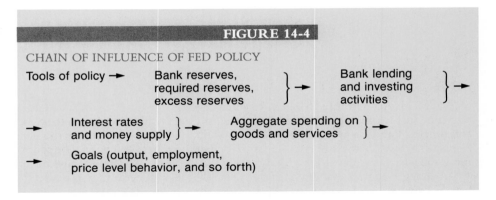

FIGURE 14-4

CHAIN OF INFLUENCE OF FED POLICY

market security purchases to be reflected in a decline in the nation's unemployment rate. Furthermore, there is no hard-and-fast linkage between Fed security holdings and the unemployment rate. This absence of a rigid link is due to the fact that many other factors besides the Fed security portfolio influence reserves, interest rates, the money stock, aggregate demand, and unemployment.

For these reasons the Fed conducts monetary policy by setting shorter-term objectives known as **intermediate targets.** An intermediate target variable is one that is closely connected with the ultimate goal (e.g., the unemployment rate) but that the Fed can influence more quickly and accurately than the ultimate goal. Any of the variables of Figure 14-4 positioned between the tools of policy and the goals are potential intermediate targets of monetary policy. For example, the Fed might set target levels for M-1 or corporation bond yields that it feels are consistent with achieving the desired unemployment-rate goal. The Fed then aggressively uses its tools in an effort to hit the intermediate targets. If, as the year progresses, new information becomes available indicating that the initial target magnitude is inconsistent with the goal, the Fed revises the target level. Also, in light of ongoing developments in the economy, the Fed may modify its goals and hence its intermediate target values.

Intermediate Target
A variable (such as the money supply or interest rates) the Fed attempts to control in the short run in order to influence such ultimate objectives as unemployment and inflation rates.

Criteria for an Ideal Intermediate Target

To be a viable intermediate target of monetary policy, a variable must have a powerful effect on the economy. In addition, it must be strongly linked to aggregate spending and the nation's GNP. If it is not, the Fed is wasting its time in controlling the variable. Further, to be a useful target the Fed must be capable of *dominating,* or at least strongly *influencing,* the behavior of the variable. Finally, a reasonably frequent and accurate measurement of the variable must be possible. If, for example, a variable is measured only once per month, it is not an ideal target. The Fed would be unable to judge its own progress in using its instruments to achieve the goals on a daily or weekly basis.

Disagreement exists among professional economists and among individual members of the Federal Open Market Committee regarding which variable is the *best* monetary policy target. This is primarily attributable to differences of opinion about which monetary variables are most closely linked to aggregate demand and GNP. Some economists, known as **monetarists,** believe that the money supply measures (M-1, M-2, and so on) should be utilized as targets. Such economists believe that the link between the money supply and GNP is very strong. **Keynesian**

economists believe that interest rates exert stronger influence on spending decisions and GNP than do M-1 and M-2. Such individuals prefer an interest-rate target. If the goal of policy is to slow down aggregate spending and reduce the inflation rate, monetarists might recommend slowing the annual growth of M-1 from, say, six percent to four percent. Keynesians might advocate raising short-term interest rates, for example, from seven percent to nine percent.

Evolution of the Fed's Targeting Policy

During World War II and for several years thereafter, the Fed adopted a strategy of strict targeting of interest rates. To help hold down interest expense for the U.S. Treasury in a period of extremely rapid growth of government debt, the Fed agreed to hold interest rates at very low levels. This agreement between the Treasury and the Fed required that the Fed directly intervene in the open market to prevent long-term bond yields from exceeding two and one-half percent. Treasury bill yields were to be kept at or below three-eighths of one percent! This agreement implied that whenever yields threatened to move above these targets, the Fed was obligated to aggressively purchase securities in the open market. This pumped reserves into the banking system, expanded bank lending and investing activities, and held down the level of interest rates. This single-minded effort to prevent interest rates from rising is referred to as **pegging interest rates.**

The Fed policy of rigidly pegging yields—which was conducted during 1942–1951—is today regarded by most economists as unwise and counterproductive. The implications of the policy are illustrated in Figure 14-5 (page 318), where the supply and demand for loanable funds interact to determine the interest rate. For example, the Fed can influence the supply curve of funds available, shifting it rightward when it purchases securities in the open market. The demand for funds shifts about in response to changes in economic activity and other phenomena. As an example, the demand curve shifts rightward (increases) when GNP rises sharply.

When the demand curve is quite stable, the Fed can peg interest rates without causing great volatility in the quantity of funds and the supply of money. Unfortunately, this is not always the case. When the economy picks up steam, the demand for funds shifts rightward as people seek to borrow more funds and to hold more transactions accounts to finance purchases of the enlarged output. With the economy initially at point A in Figure 14-5—with the interest rate on target— suppose the economy strengthens. Then demand for funds shifts to D_{f2}. To prevent the economy from moving to point B—with interest rates exceeding the target—the Fed must shift the supply curve of funds to S_{f2}. We end up at point C—with the interest rate remaining on target but the quantity of funds expanding to Q_3.

This illustrates an important principle: A policy of strict interest-rate pegging is a **procyclical policy**—stimulating the economy when it is already strong and restricting the economy when it is weak. This is precisely what happened during World War II. Although the economy was already booming because of sharply escalated military spending, the Fed's successful efforts to hold down interest rates resulted in M-1 growth that averaged more than 20 percent per year during 1942–1945. When price controls were lifted in 1945, a period of severe inflation ensued.

After the inflationary implications of the policy became clear, the Fed reached an *accord* with the Treasury in 1951, freeing itself to abandon its strict interest-rate pegging regime. Nevertheless, Fed policy in the 1950s, 1960s, and much of the

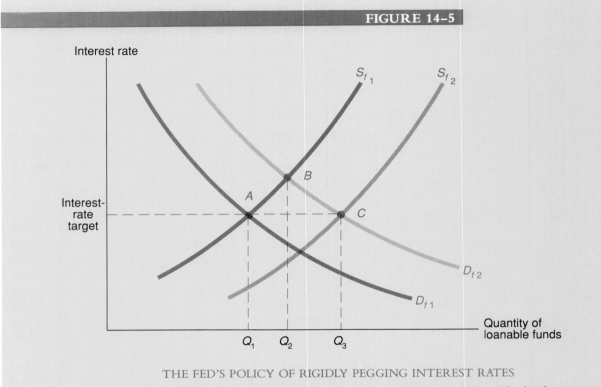

FIGURE 14–5

THE FED'S POLICY OF RIGIDLY PEGGING INTEREST RATES

A Federal Reserve target regime of pegging interest rates is a procyclical policy—it destabilizes the economy. When economic activity is expanding, the demand for funds rises, tending to increase interest rates. To prevent this and remain on its interest-rate target, the Fed must increase the supply of funds (and money) at a time when the economy is already gaining momentum. In periods of economic weakness, demand for funds declines, tending to pull down interest rates. To stay on its interest-rate target, the Fed must tighten its policy and reduce the supply of funds available.

1970s, though not going to the extreme of *pegging* interest rates, may be accurately characterized as *smoothing* the fluctuations in interest rates. Increases in demand for funds in this period were typically met by accommodative Fed actions to increase the supply and resist the upward pressure on yields. Money supply growth in periods of strong economic activity typically exceeded money growth during recessions.

By the early 1970s, many academic economists and financial market practitioners had become convinced that the growth rate of the money supply was a crucial determinant of economic activity in general and inflation in particular. For the first time in peacetime American history, inflation reached double-digit levels in 1973 and 1974. Largely because of these developments, Congress passed legislation in 1975 requiring the Fed to adopt and publicly announce target ranges each year for money growth (M-1, M-2, and so on) for the forthcoming year.

In actuality, the money supply has frequently departed from its specified range. This is partially attributable to the difficulty of controlling the short-run movements in the money supply. But mostly it is due to the fact that, as a particular year unfolds, unforeseen developments occur that convince the Fed that the original target is not appropriate. The experience of 1986 is a good example. As the year unfolded, the economy weakened and interest rates came down significantly. In many quarters talk of *deflation* replaced fears of inflation. To avert recession, the Fed implemented a stimulative policy of open market security purchases and pushed money supply growth sharply above the target range it had announced at the beginning of the year.

The Money Supply Targeting Experiment, 1979–1982

Although the Fed began announcing money growth targets in 1975, it also specified certain interest-rate targets. When the interest-rate and money-growth targets came into conflict, the Fed typically opted for interest rates, allowing money growth to deviate from the target range. This priority ended in late 1979, when the Fed elevated money growth to its number one priority. This became known as the "monetarist experiment."[5]

In the late 1970s, the U.S. economy experienced a sustained recovery from the 1973–1975 recession. Output expanded rapidly and the inflation rate escalated from less than six percent in 1976 to more than ten percent in 1979. The U.S. dollar fell sharply in foreign-exchange markets in 1979 as speculators pointed to rapid U.S. money growth as evidence of our lack of resolve to contain inflation.

In October 1979, only two months after Paul Volcker was appointed Chairman of the Fed's Board of Governors, a new policy was announced. Targets would no longer be set for interest rates. Instead, interest rates would be permitted to rise to whatever level was consistent with the Fed's (reduced) money growth targets. No longer would the Fed provide funds to the market via open market security purchases to hold down the upward pressure on interest rates when the demand for funds was rising. The Fed stuck religiously to this policy for almost three years. Interest rates reached unprecedented levels. For example, the prime loan rate went above 20 percent in 1980 and again in 1981.

This *monetarist regime* had both good and bad consequences. On the positive side, inflation was rather quickly brought under control. Also, the long and dramatic foreign-exchange market slide of the dollar was halted and replaced with a five-and-one-half-year rally that continued until 1985. On the negative side, the nation sustained two back-to-back recessions during 1980–1982, separated by the briefest recovery phase on record. The magnitude of financial distress—as indicated by farm foreclosures, business failures, and loan defaults in general—reached extremely high levels. And the unemployment rate was unusually high in the early 1980s.

Partly because of these adverse events of the early 1980s and partly because there was reason to expect that the link between money and economic activity would remain rather uncertain for several years as the American financial system was deregulated, the Fed abandoned strict monetary targeting in August 1982. In the late 1980s, the Fed even refused to specify a target range for the growth of M-1, although it did continue indicating target ranges for M-2 and M-3. It remains to be seen whether or when the Fed will return to a policy of rigid adherence to money supply growth targets.

---

[5]Many monetarists do not consider this episode a "monetarist experiment" because a crucial tenet of monetarism was violated—that the growth rate of money should be quite modest and stable.

SUMMARY

1. A central bank is an agency or organization that establishes the overall financial policy in the nation. This agency influences the nation's interest rates, availability of credit, and supply of money. The American central bank, in existence less than 80 years, is known as the Federal Reserve System (or the Fed).

2. Functions of the Federal Reserve System—in addition to conducting monetary policy—include supervision and regulation of banks and thrift institutions, issuing paper currency, processing checks, serving as a banker's bank, and serving as a bank for the U.S. Treasury.

3. The Fed is unique among central banks in the world in that it is deliberately set up to be independent of both the executive and legislative branches of government. It also is unique in that it entails twelve separate banks. At an earlier time these individual Fed banks possessed considerable autonomy over decision making. Today the power is centralized in the Board of Governors in Washington, DC.

4. The Board of Governors consists of a seven-person committee, each member appointed by the President of the United States for a 14-year term. The terms are staggered so that one appointment expires every two years. One member of the Board is designated by the President to serve as Chair. The Board sets reserve requirements, determines the discount rate, and comprises the majority of the voting members of the Federal Open Market Committee (FOMC).

5. The FOMC consists of the seven members of the Board of Governors and the twelve presidents of the individual Federal Reserve Banks. Only five of these presidents are voting members of the FOMC at any given time. The FOMC meets in Washington about eight times annually and also meets on short notice via special telephonic hookup. The FOMC decides upon the thrust of monetary policy in the light of contemporary economic developments and policy goals.

6. The chief Federal Reserve assets are its holdings of U.S. government securities and loans to financial institutions. Important liabilities include paper currency it issues (Federal Reserve Notes) and deposits held by banks and thrift institutions at the Fed. The U.S. Treasury also keeps a checking account at the Fed and utilizes this account to pay for government purchases and for salaries of government employees.

7. Whenever the Fed purchases goods, services, or securities from nongovernment entities it makes payment by marking up (increasing) some depository institution's deposit account at the Fed (i.e., it makes payment by creating new reserves).

8. Reserves play a crucial role in determining the availability of credit and the supply of money in the economy. The Fed has fingertip control over the total amount of reserves in the banking system because it has *total* control over its portfolio of government securities. Each dollar of securities the Fed purchases from private entities creates one dollar of new reserves in the banks. Each dollar of securities the Fed sells extinguishes one dollar of reserves. Changes in aggregate reserves touch off a multiple expansion or contraction of deposits (and money) in the U.S. economy. The size of the deposit expansion multiplier varies considerably over time. Therefore, the Fed's control over total deposits and the money supply is much less precise than its control over reserves.

9. To implement an expansionary monetary policy, the Fed may purchase securities in the open market, reduce the discount rate, and reduce the level of reserve requirements. To pursue monetary restriction the Fed may sell securities from its portfolio, raise the discount rate, and raise the reserve requirement.

10. Because it takes considerable time for the Fed's tools to impinge upon the goals of policy and because the relationship between the tools and the goals is rather uncertain, the Fed employs a system of intermediate targets. An intermediate target is a variable that strongly influences aggregate spending and policy goals and that the Fed can control more sensitively in a given week or month than such goals as unemployment or inflation. Prominent candidates for intermediate targets include the level of interest rates and the growth rate of the money supply.

11. Monetarists advocate selection of the money supply as the Fed's intermediate target. Monetarists believe the Fed can accurately control the money supply and that it is closely linked to aggregate spending. Keynesians typically prefer an interest-rate target because they believe expenditures are more closely linked to interest rates than to the money supply.

KEY TERMS

central bank

Federal Reserve System (the Fed)

Board of Governors (of the
    Federal Reserve System)

discount rate

Federal Open Market Committee
    (FOMC)

FOMC directive

member banks

national banks

state banks

discounts and advances

open market operations

discount window

reserve requirements

intermediate targets

monetarists

Keynesian economists

pegging interest rates

procyclical policy

STUDY QUESTIONS AND PROBLEMS

1. What are the chief functions of our central bank—the Federal Reserve System?
2. What features give the Federal Reserve *independence* from the executive and legislative branches of government? Is this independence desirable? Analyze.
3. What is the largest asset holding of the Federal Reserve? Why is this an asset?
4. List the two largest liabilities of the Fed. Explain why these items are liabilities of the Fed.
5. Suppose the Federal Reserve System were to sell off $600,000 worth of used office equipment to private citizens. Explain why both the money supply and bank reserves would decline by $600,000.
6. Explain how the Fed tool of open market operations gives the Fed *fingertip control* over aggregate bank reserves in the United States.
7. Suppose the Fed were to reduce sharply its discount rate from seven percent to five percent, catching the financial community by surprise. Explain the consequences of this measure for:
   a. reserves
   b. the money supply
   c. interest rates
8. Two alternative means of providing stimulus to a depressed economy are for the Fed to purchase securities in the open market and for the Fed to reduce reserve requirements applicable to banks and thrift institutions. Analyze the differences in how these two instruments derive their monetary stimulus.
9. Outline the three monetary policy instruments the Fed can implement if its objective is to cool off an economy suffering from excessive demand for goods and services.
10. Define the meaning of an intermediate target of monetary policy. What characteristics should a particular variable possess to be considered a potential intermediate target of monetary policy?
11. Suppose the Fed is rigidly targeting short-term interest rates and the economy unexpectedly slides into a severe recession. What would the Fed be forced to do to remain on its target? How would you characterize this policy? Explain.
12. What is the basis for disagreement between monetarists and Keynesians regarding the appropriate variable for the Fed to select as its intermediate monetary policy target?

SELECTED REFERENCES

Board of Governors of the Federal Reserve System, *The Federal Reserve System: Purposes and Functions,* 7th ed. (Washington, DC: Board of Governors, 1984). This primer, free from your district Fed bank, surveys the structure and functions of the Fed. See especially Chapters 1, 2, 7.

Klein, John J., *Money and the Economy,* 6th ed. (New York: Harcourt Brace Jovanovich, 1986). This money and banking textbook discusses the details of monetary policy.

Thomas, Lloyd B., *Money, Banking, and Economic Activity,* 4th ed. (Englewood Cliffs, NJ: Prentice-Hall, 1986). Gives in-depth coverage of Federal Reserve policy.

Wilcox, James A., *Current Readings on Money, Banking, and Financial Markets* (Boston: Little, Brown and Co., published annually). This reader contains a series of timely articles on financial markets, banking, and monetary policy.

THE IMPACT OF MONEY ON ECONOMIC ACTIVITY

The Great Depression in the United States, far from being a sign of inherent instability of the private enterprise system, is a testament to how much harm can be done by the mistakes of a few men when they wield vast power over the monetary system of a country.

—MILTON FRIEDMAN

In Chapter 14 we demonstrated that the Federal Reserve System, via its instruments of monetary policy, is capable of exerting appreciable influence upon the supply of money and the level of interest rates. In Chapter 15 we explore the transmission mechanism of monetary policy—the channels through which monetary policy influences economic activity. We also explore different viewpoints about the impact of changes in the money supply upon economic activity. We note that although there exist differences of opinion among economists about the transmission mechanism and other aspects of monetary policy, there is a clear consensus that monetary policy is a potent tool. Almost all economists agree that Federal Reserve actions have an important impact upon economic activity via the effect upon aggregate demand for goods and services.

MONETARY POLICY

How Does Monetary Policy Influence the Economy?

There are three alternative channels through which Federal Reserve monetary policy can influence the economy: the interest-rate, portfolio-adjustment, and wealth channels.

Interest-Rate Channel　Federal Reserve monetary policy can influence economic activity through its impact on interest rates and thereby through its effects upon interest-sensitive components of aggregate expenditures. Investment expenditures on plant, equipment, inventories, and housing are thought to be sensitive to the level of interest rates. In addition, such other components of spending as consumption and local government expenditures can be influenced somewhat by interest rates. When the Fed is pursuing a stimulative monetary policy, it purchases securities in the open market. This action pumps reserves into the banking system, increases the money supply, and lowers the level of interest rates. The decrease in interest rates, after some elapse of time, results in increased homebuilding activity; increased expenditures by firms on plant, equipment, and inventories; and perhaps some stimulus to consumption and local government spending. Hence, economic activity is boosted by the decrease in interest rates. This is the channel emphasized by Keynesians.

Portfolio-Adjustment Channel　A second avenue through which Fed policy and the money supply can influence economic activity is by upsetting the *portfolio equilibrium* of the public. In this mechanism people hold a balanced portfolio of money, financial assets such as bonds and stocks, and real assets such as houses and cars. When the Fed increases the supply of money, a disequilibrium is created in which people are holding more money than desired relative to bonds, stocks, cars, and houses. To restore equilibrium, the public spends these excess money balances. This spending stimulates the bond and stock markets as well as the automobile and housing industries. When holdings of such nonmoney assets as bonds and durable goods reach the desired relationship to the enhanced supply of money, the adjustment process is complete and the economy reaches a new equilibrium. In this channel an increased supply of money directly stimulates spending, independently of any effect on interest rates.

Wealth Channel　A third way in which Federal Reserve monetary policy may influence economic activity is by altering the net worth or wealth of the private sector of the economy, thereby stimulating consumption spending, the largest component of aggregate demand. In this mechanism an increase in the supply of money reduces interest rates and elevates stock and bond prices. Tens of millions of Americans own stocks, either directly or through retirement fund holdings. Hence the net worth of millions of individuals rises, resulting in an increase in expenditures on new cars and other durable consumer goods.

The Link Between Money and Economic Activity—The Equation of Exchange

An efficient means of analyzing the influence of the supply of money (hence the Federal Reserve System) on the economy is by the famous **equation of exchange,** expressed in Equation 15-1.

$$MV = \Sigma P_i Y_i \tag{15-1}$$

In the equation, M represents the supply of money (most commonly the M-1 version) and V represents the **velocity** of money or the turnover rate of money in purchasing newly produced goods and services (i.e., GNP). On the right-hand side, P_i represents the price of individual good or service i and Y_i represents the annual number of units of good or service i purchased. Clearly then, $P_i Y_i$ indicates annual expenditures on item i (say, eggs). If we sum such expenditures on all of the goods and services that enter in to the nation's gross national product, we arrive at spending on GNP (i.e., $\Sigma P_i Y_i$).

Frequently the equation of exchange is presented in slightly altered form

$$MV = PY \tag{15-2}$$

where Y represents the quantity of the nation's output of goods and services or an index of such output and P represents the average price at which the output is purchased or an index of such prices.

The right-hand side of Equations 15-1 and 15-2 thus indicates the annual expenditures on newly produced goods and services (GNP) and is sometimes termed the "goods side" of the equation of exchange. The left-hand side of the equations, known as the "money side," states that the supply of money times its velocity is also a way of defining expenditures on newly produced goods and services (i.e., GNP). This is true by virtue of the fact that velocity is defined as the ratio of GNP to the stock of money:

$$V = \frac{\Sigma P_i Y_i}{M} = \frac{PY}{M} = \frac{\text{GNP}}{M}$$

Since V is defined strictly in terms of the other three variables in the equation of exchange, the equation is an *identity* or *tautology*—true by definition. Everyone agrees with the equation of exchange. It must be true; it cannot be falsified. If M is $900 billion and GNP is $5400 billion per year, then V is 6/year. If M is $900 billion and GNP is $6300 billion per year, then V is 7/year. The equation of exchange is a simple identity that states that GNP expenditures viewed from the *money side* precisely equal GNP expenditures viewed from the *goods side.*

Because the equation of exchange is an identity or tautology, one is tempted to ask, "How can it be of any use?" Its value lies in illuminating the key role played by the velocity of money. Look again at Equations 15-1 and 15-2. Note that velocity can be viewed as a multiplier that links the stock of money to the premier measure of the nation's economic activity—GNP. Suppose the money supply rises. Then one of two things (or a little of each) *must* happen: velocity must decline or GNP ($\Sigma P_i Y_i$ or PY) must rise.

If velocity remains constant in the face of an increase in M engineered by the Fed, GNP spending must increase in proportion to M—a seven-percent increase in M causes a seven-percent increase in GNP spending. On the other hand, if velocity fluctuates in a wild and unpredictable manner, one cannot predict with any confidence the effect that a seven-percent increase in M would have on the nation's

Velocity
The number of times annually that an *average dollar* is spent on final goods and services; the ratio of the nominal GNP to the money supply.

GNP. Hence, the equation throws into clear relief the crucial role of the velocity of money.

Also, one can analyze the role of *fiscal policy* (changes in government taxation, expenditures, and transfers) upon GNP expenditures in the context of the equation. A stimulative fiscal policy involves increased government spending or transfer payments or a reduction in taxes in the context of a situation in which the money supply remains constant. Since M is held constant, a stimulative fiscal policy must boost velocity if it is to successfully stimulate GNP expenditures. Likewise, a restrictive fiscal policy must reduce velocity in order to reduce GNP expenditures. Again, the crucial importance of understanding the nature of velocity is evident.

Monetarist and Keynesian Views of Velocity

As a general principle, economists of monetarist persuasion (Milton Friedman, Allan Meltzer, Karl Brunner, William Poole, Beryl Sprinkle) believe that velocity is a stable and well-behaved variable that tends to move in steady, rather predictable trends, and is independent of the supply of money. Changes in the supply of money therefore have a predictable and powerful impact on aggregate spending and GNP. Monetarists believe that fiscal policy measures exert little impact on velocity and therefore are incapable of having much impact on aggregate spending and GNP. Monetarists simply believe that monetary policy is a substantially more powerful tool than fiscal policy.

Keynesian economists (Paul Samuelson, James Tobin, Franco Modigliani, Robert Eisner, and Alan Blinder) believe that the money supply exerts an important impact on aggregate spending, but tend to be quite skeptical about the alleged stability and predictability of velocity. Therefore, if the supply of money increases by seven percent, the impact on aggregate spending and GNP is thought to be uncertain. Aggregate spending and GNP may rise twelve percent or perhaps only two percent. Stimulative fiscal measures, in the view of Keynesians, boost the velocity of money and produce a strong increase in expenditures and GNP, even when the supply of money is held constant. In short, Keynesians view the velocity of money as rather unstable, elastic in response to fiscal policy measures, and extremely difficult to predict. To Keynesians, fiscal policy is at least as powerful as monetary policy.

For you to draw your own conclusions about velocity and find your own position along the Keynesian-monetarist spectrum of viewpoints, we must explore the nature of the velocity beast and its close relative—money demand—in some depth.

THE NATURE OF VELOCITY AND MONEY DEMAND

There are several alternative measures of velocity—one for each measure of the supply of money. Hence we can designate $V_1 = \dfrac{GNP}{M\text{-}1}$, $V_2 = \dfrac{GNP}{M\text{-}2}$, $V_3 = \dfrac{GNP}{M\text{-}3}$, and so on. Each measure of velocity is a multiplier that links a particular measure of money to GNP expenditures.

The velocity of M-1 and M-2 over a long span of years preceding 1960 is illustrated in Figure 15-1. In Figure 15-2 (page 328) we illustrate the velocity of M-1 in the past 30 years.

Velocity is intimately tied to the amount of money people find it desirable to hold relative to expenditures. Most individuals and firms have *several* forms in which

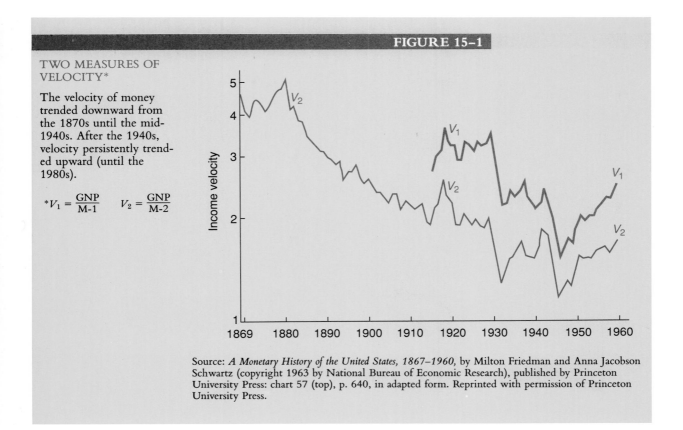

FIGURE 15–1

TWO MEASURES OF VELOCITY*

The velocity of money trended downward from the 1870s until the mid-1940s. After the 1940s, velocity persistently trended upward (until the 1980s).

$$*V_1 = \frac{GNP}{M\text{-}1} \qquad V_2 = \frac{GNP}{M\text{-}2}$$

Source: *A Monetary History of the United States, 1867–1960,* by Milton Friedman and Anna Jacobson Schwartz (copyright 1963 by National Bureau of Economic Research), published by Princeton University Press: chart 57 (top), p. 640, in adapted form. Reprinted with permission of Princeton University Press.

their wealth is held. They may hold wealth in money, bonds, stocks, real estate, works of art, certificates of deposits, gold coins, and in many other media. Individuals, within the limits of their own wealth, have the discretion to determine how they allocate this wealth among the various forms, including money balances (demand deposits and currency).

Holding wealth in the form of money has both advantages and disadvantages. The primary advantage is convenience and **liquidity**—wealth held in money form is immediately available to spend.[1] The disadvantage of holding money involves the forfeiture of the return one might have obtained via interest on bonds, dividends from stocks, or appreciation from real estate or gold. In other words, the cost of holding money is an *opportunity cost*—the return one forgoes by holding wealth in the form of money, which traditionally has paid no interest.[2]

---

[1]A related point is that money has perfect stability of nominal (though not real) value. If one holds $1000 in money, it will still be $1000 a year from now. If one holds $1000 in common stock or real estate, it is likely to amount to less or more than $1000 a year from now. This absence of fluctuation of nominal value contributes to the desirability of holding money, at least in noninflationary times.

[2]In the past, money paid no interest. Currency obviously does not pay interest and legislation enacted in the 1930s prohibited payment of interest on checking accounts. Since 1980, federal legislation has allowed banks nationwide to pay interest not on regular checking accounts but on NOW accounts and ATS accounts, classified as "other checkable deposits." These accounts constitute a growing portion (about 25 percent in 1989) of M-1.

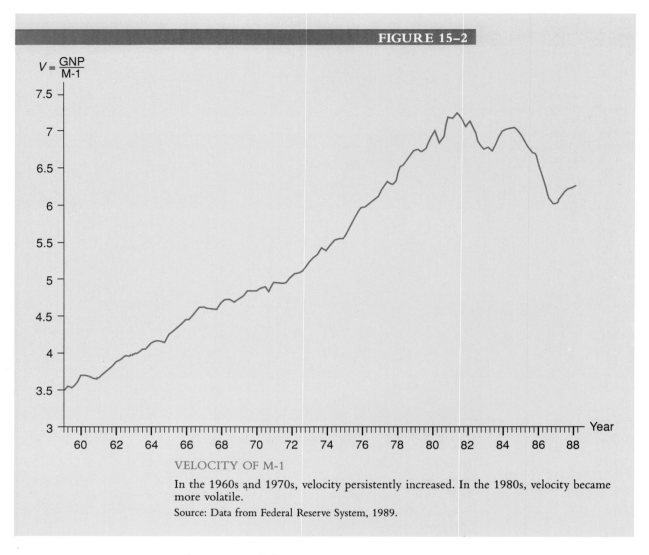

FIGURE 15–2

$$V = \frac{GNP}{M\text{-}1}$$

VELOCITY OF M-1

In the 1960s and 1970s, velocity persistently increased. In the 1980s, velocity became more volatile.

Source: Data from Federal Reserve System, 1989.

The Demand for Money

Transactions Demand for Money
Money held to finance a stream of expenditures that does not coincide precisely in time with the receipt of funds such as paychecks.

The motives for holding money (**demand for money**) may be divided into three categories: the **transactions motive,** the **precautionary motive,** and the **speculative motive.** People and firms hold money to finance anticipated expenditures (transactions motive), to provide a prudent safety net to protect against unforeseen expenses or loss of income (precautionary motive), and to take advantage of a good investment opportunity in the event it should arise (speculative motive).

Economists concur that the predominant reason for holding money is the transactions motive—the motive we emphasize in our analysis. Money balances (demand deposits and currency) must be maintained in order to finance a pattern of expenditures that is not synchronized precisely over time with the receipt of income. People are typically paid on a monthly, biweekly, or weekly basis but spend funds almost daily. Money must be held to finance expenditures that come later in the week or month. In Figure 15-3 we illustrate the behavior of a typical worker's money balances over time.

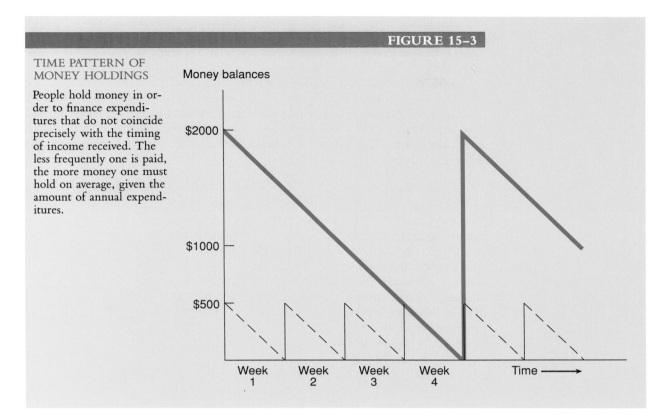

FIGURE 15–3

TIME PATTERN OF MONEY HOLDINGS

People hold money in order to finance expenditures that do not coincide precisely with the timing of income received. The less frequently one is paid, the more money one must hold on average, given the amount of annual expenditures.

Assume the worker earns $2000 (take-home pay) at the beginning of each month and spends the entire income each month. Assume for simplicity that the worker holds no precautionary or speculative money balances and thus ends each month with zero holdings of money. The worker deposits $2000 in the bank on the first of the month and spends the funds at a constant rate until the money balances are exhausted on the last day of the month. Then another paycheck of $2000 is received and the cycle repeats itself.

We can compute this worker's average demand for money and velocity of money. Money demand, or the average stock of money maintained, is approximately $1000 because the worker starts the month with $2000, ends with zero, and spends the funds at a constant rate. The velocity of this worker's money may be computed as follows:

$$\text{velocity} = \frac{\text{annual expenditures}}{\text{average money holdings}} = \frac{\$24,000/\text{year}}{\$1000} = 24/\text{year}$$

The transactions velocity of this worker's money balances is 24 times per year.[3] In other words, if average money holdings of $1000 must finance annual expenditures

---

[3]Note that our measure of velocity in this example differs slightly from that employed in Equations 15-1 and 15-2 and Figures 15-1 and 15-2. In the numerator of this example we utilize *total expenditures* or *transactions,* not just expenditures for newly produced goods and services (*GNP*). GNP does not include purchases of used items or financial transactions in stocks, bonds, and the like. Our measure of velocity (known as *transactions velocity*) of the typical worker is therefore considerably larger than *V* (GNP velocity) of Equations 15-1 and 15-2 because total transactions are considerably larger than GNP. However, the basic principles governing the behavior of the two measures of velocity are the same.

of $24,000, the turnover rate or number of times the average dollar must be spent is 24 times per year. Another way to state the same proposition is to say that the worker holds sufficient money on average to finance 1/24 of a year's expenditures or a little more than 15 days worth of expenditures.

Suppose the worker's employer switches to a weekly pay period, paying out $500 the first of each week (assume a 28-day month with precisely four weeks for simplicity). This money balance pattern is also shown in Figure 15-3 (broken lines). The worker begins each week with $500 and spends the funds at a constant rate, exhausting the funds at the end of each week. Average money balances are now only $250 and velocity increases to 96/year.

$$\text{velocity} = \frac{\text{annual expenditures}}{\text{average money holdings}} = \frac{\$24,000/\text{year}}{\$250} = 96/\text{year}$$

The move to a weekly pay period increases the efficiency of the payments system by increasing the degree of synchronization between receipt and expenditure of funds, thus reducing money demand. This raises the velocity of money. Anything that improves this synchronization and reduces money demand pulls up the velocity of money. Anything that permits the financing of annual expenditures without holding as much money on average results in an increase in the velocity of money. Hence, increasing use of charge accounts and credit cards and a movement toward more frequent pay periods have worked to increase the nation's velocity of money since the 1940s, as indicated in Figures 15-1 and 15-2.

Determinants of Money Demand and Velocity

In our analysis of the typical worker we have emphasized the transactions motive for money demand and the role of institutional factors such as frequency of pay periods. A more complete analysis of the determinants of money demand and velocity includes the following factors: institutional factors underlying the payments process, *financial technology* and the availability of substitutes for money, the level of interest rates, and the degree of economic uncertainty.

Institutional Factors and the Payments Process   As indicated in the preceding analysis, more frequent pay periods reduces the average money balances one needs to maintain throughout the month, thus raising velocity. Increasing usage of charge accounts and credit cards has a similar impact because it increases the degree of synchronization between receipt and expenditures of funds. If one is paid on the first of the month and uses a credit card to finance most expenditures, one needs to hold very little M-1 except on the date when the credit card bill comes due. If the credit card bill comes due around payday, one holds very little money on average and velocity is quite high. The increasing use of credit cards since World War II has contributed to the rising trend of velocity illustrated in Figure 15-2.

Financial Technology and Substitutes for Money   The emergence of a large array of satisfactory substitutes for demand deposits has also contributed to the uptrend in velocity. Passbook savings accounts, bank certificates of deposit (CDs), U.S. government securities, money market mutual fund shares (MMMFs), and other instruments designed for firms and other large-deposit customers allow firms and individuals to economize on relatively unattractive demand deposits as a means of storing wealth over time.[4] We characterize these various money-economizing devices under the rubric *financial technology*.

Interest Rates Interest rates clearly influence money demand and velocity. When interest rates are high, the opportunity cost of holding money is high and individuals and firms scramble to convert demand deposits into such interest-yielding alternatives as CDs, MMMF shares, and securities. When interest rates are low, the incentive to economize on money is reduced and people hold more money balances relative to expenditures—velocity falls. Interest rates exhibit a pronounced *procyclical* pattern, rising during the expansion phase of the business cycle and declining in recessions. Since velocity is directly influenced by interest rates, velocity also exhibits a procyclical pattern—rising during business expansions and declining (or at least rising more slowly than its long-term trend) in periods of recession.

EXHIBIT 15–1

MONEY MARKET MUTUAL FUNDS AND THE VELOCITY OF M-1

An excellent example of the way that financial innovations influence money demand and velocity is the emergence of **money market mutual funds (MMMFs)** in the U.S. economy in the late 1970s.

MMMFs issue *shares* that are actually interest-bearing deposits with limited check-writing privileges. Most MMMFs authorize checks to be written in amounts of not less than $250 or $500. A minimum initial deposit of anywhere from $1000 to $20,000 is normally required to open a MMMF account. MMMFs pool the savings of thousands of individuals and invest the funds in large blocks of safe, short-term securities issued by the U.S. government, large banks, and nonfinancial corporations of high credit standing. The MMMFs pay interest on the shares at a rate that floats daily in line with the yield earned on the portfolio of short-term securities.

These MMMFs are attractive to individual savers because of their competitive yield and check-writing features. Unlike savings accounts in banks and thrift institutions, MMMF shares are not insured. However, they are considered quite safe because the MMMF portfolio of assets consists of relatively safe investments.

In the late 1970s—when interest rates soared at a time that banks and thrift institutions were subject to ceilings on rates payable on savings and time deposits—MMMFs became extremely popular. Total assets of MMMFs soared from $4 billion at the beginning of 1978 to $230 billion by the end of 1982. A significant portion of these funds were transferred from bank demand deposits to MMMF shares. This reduced the propensity to hold bank demand deposits and rapidly pulled up the velocity of M-1—GNP/(M-1)—during the late 1970s (review Figure 15-2). MMMF shares are included in M-2 but not in M-1.

By the mid-1980s, ceiling interest rates payable by banks and thrift institutions were phased out. These institutions are now allowed to pay competitive interest rates. Recently, therefore, there is less tendency to switch funds from banks and savings and loan institutions to MMMFs in times of soaring interest rates. Nevertheless, MMMF shares remain as a very attractive, liquid saving instrument for millions of individuals in our deregulated financial environment. In mid-1989, Americans held more than $300 billion in some 600 MMMFs. The current yields payable, along with total assets and average maturity of assets, are quoted regularly in the financial pages of major American newspapers.

---

[4]Two recently developed techniques that allow firms and other entities with substantial funds to hold less money on average are *sweep accounts* and *repurchase agreements*. In a sweep arrangement, the bank's computer automatically *sweeps* checking account funds into interest-bearing savings accounts each day. A repurchase agreement specifies that the bank sell securities to a customer in exchange for checking account funds at the close of business each day. The next morning when the bank opens, it *repurchases* these securities by replenishing the funds (with interest) in the checking account.

Economic Uncertainty   The degree of economic uncertainty or the extent of confidence in the economic future influences the amount of wealth individuals and firms seek to hold in liquid form, thus influencing velocity. When there is great uncertainty or lack of confidence in the future, people seek to hold fewer common stocks, bonds, and other nonmoney assets; they prefer to hold the most conservative of assets—money. As one perceives the future more clearly and confidence improves, one is willing to take more risks—getting out of money in favor of the stock market, bonds, and real estate. Velocity of money thus rises. This uncertainty factor helps to explain why velocity is often low in periods of economic depression and war. In this connection, note in Figure 15-1 the sharp drop in velocity during the early 1930s and again during World War II (1941–1945.)

Accounting for the Major Changes in Velocity

Given our analysis thus far, we can broadly account for the long-term swings in velocity illustrated in Figures 15-1 and 15-2. On balance, velocity trended downward during 1880–1945 and increased afterward until the 1980s. In the quarter century following the American Civil War, the U.S. price level declined and interest rates remained relatively low. In such an environment, money is the favored medium for storing wealth. Banking flourished without significant inroads from such nonbank competitors as savings associations and credit unions. Few substitutes for money were available. Velocity drifted downward. During the 1930s and 1940s, velocity was given an additional powerful downward thrust by the uncertainties of depression and war and by the prevalence of extremely low and falling interest rates.[5]

In the period following World War II, a horde of events conspired to account for the prolonged upward movement in velocity. Savings and loan associations and credit unions spread rapidly throughout the nation, giving millions of individuals an alternative to holding funds in bank demand deposits. New financial instruments (treasury bills, money market mutual fund shares, sweep accounts, repurchase agreements, and others) came on stream to give individuals and firms viable alternatives to holding deposits. These developments, coupled with the fact that interest rates trended upward from the 1940s until the early 1980s, resulted in steady increases in the opportunity cost of holding money. Hence, the demand for money steadily declined relative to income. Velocity increased. Charge accounts and credit cards became increasingly prevalent, improving the synchronization process just outlined. The early postwar successes in confining recessions to mild downturns and avoiding depression-magnitude catastrophes gradually raised confidence that a repeat of the experience of the 1930s was not in the cards. The growth of velocity from 1945–1981 was remarkably persistent (Figures 15-1 and 15-2).

Since 1981, velocity has deviated from its sustained post-World War II uptrend (review Figure 15-2). Significant declines in velocity occurred in the 1981–1982 recession and again in 1986. The first decline might be attributed to the severe 1981–1982 recession (the deepest since the 1930s). This recession produced a decline in interest rates and an increase in economic uncertainty. The unprecedented nine-percent 1986 contraction in velocity is largely attributable to the sharp decline in interest rates in that year. Individuals apparently decided to park lots of

---

[5]Primarily because of aggressive efforts by the Federal Reserve to minimize borrowing costs for the U.S. Treasury, short-term yields were maintained at less than one percent during the 1940s. Clearly, in those years, people weren't sacrificing much income by stashing large amounts of wealth in checking accounts.

funds in bank checking deposits, especially in interest-bearing *other checkable deposits* (included in M-1). This decision was apparently made as a result of the sharp decline in the yield advantage of securities, CDs, and other instruments relative to the yields on NOW and ATS accounts.[6]

THE CRUDE QUANTITY THEORY OF MONEY AND MODERN MONETARISM

Monetarists emphasize the dominant role of the transactions demand for money; they are dubious about the relative importance (or even the existence) of other motives for holding money. Therefore, monetarists stress the first two factors on our list of determinants of money demand and velocity. Because these institutional factors underlying the payments process and the state of financial technology evolve only slowly and smoothly over time, monetarists believe velocity is stable in the short run and is not influenced by the supply of money.

The Old-Fashioned Quantity Theory of Money

Early forerunners of today's monetarists took the preceding notions to an extreme, arguing that one could regard velocity as constant in the short run—it being determined by the slowly evolving factors underlying the synchronization between receipts and expenditures. These *crude quantity theorists* also believed that the normal level of output was the full-employment level. Any deviations from a full-employment output were thought to set up a powerful corrective mechanism returning output to the full-employment level, as we outlined in Chapters 11 and 12. These beliefs are summarized in Equation 15-3, in which bars (overbars) above variables indicates the variables are fixed or constant in the short run.

$$M\overline{V} = P\overline{Y} \qquad (15\text{-}3)$$

If one takes velocity (V) and real output (Y) as constant in Equation 15-3, as early forerunners of today's monetarists did, it is clear that the level of prices (P) varies in exact proportion to the supply of money (M): a 12-percent increase in M causes precisely a 12-percent increase in P. In this framework a necessary and sufficient cause of inflation is growth in the stock of money. This proposition, known as the **crude quantity theory of money**, denies any role for such nonmonetary factors as oil prices or wage behavior in the inflation process. The proposition also denies a role for excessively stimulative fiscal policies—government spending hikes and tax cuts—in the inflation process.

Crude Quantity Theory
The proposition that velocity is constant in the short run and that aggregate demand (PY) and the price level vary proportionally with the money supply.

A simple test of the crude quantity theory is provided in Figure 15-4 (page 334), which illustrates the relationship between money growth and inflation in recent years in a cross section of nations. The crude quantity theory implies that the points should fall along the 45-degree line, the inflation rate being equal to the growth rate of money. Although this prediction cannot be confirmed, it is true that countries with high money growth (Italy, France) experienced rapid inflation, whereas the

---

[6]These interest-bearing *other checkable accounts* first became available nationwide with the 1980 passage of the Depository Institutions Deregulation and Monetary Control Act. Since they are included in M-1, one would expect some initial increase in demand for M-1 and decline in velocity as the public became accustomed to these deposits in the 1980s. Since the interest rates payable on these insured NOW and ATS accounts are more sluggish than those in the financial markets, these accounts become more attractive in a period of sharply declining yields (1986).

FIGURE 15-4

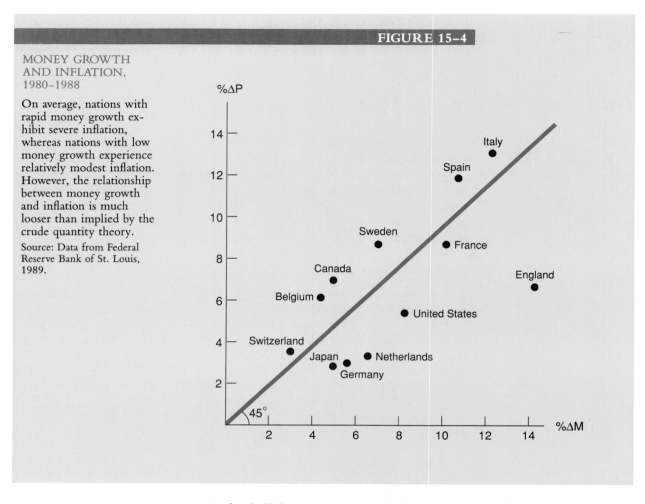

MONEY GROWTH
AND INFLATION,
1980–1988

On average, nations with
rapid money growth ex-
hibit severe inflation,
whereas nations with low
money growth experience
relatively modest inflation.
However, the relationship
between money growth
and inflation is much
looser than implied by the
crude quantity theory.

Source: Data from Federal
Reserve Bank of St. Louis,
1989.

countries that held down money growth (Japan, Switzerland) experienced relatively
modest inflation.

In Figure 15-5, we further test the crude quantity theory by examining the
relationship between U.S. money growth and inflation in various decades. Again, a
positive relationship exists between money growth and inflation, but it is a loose one.
Money growth averaged around 6.5 percent in both the 1970s and 1980s. However,
the average annual inflation rate in the 1970s was 7.4 percent but less than 5 percent
in the 1980s. The inflation rate in the 1940s and 1980s was only approximately
one-half the growth rate of the money supply, whereas the inflation rate exceeded
the money growth rate in the 1970s. Clearly, money growth fails to tell the whole
story in accounting for inflation. (Note that many points in Figures 15-4 and 15-5
fall significantly off of the 45-degree line, in contrast to the predictions of the crude
quantity theory.)

There is little dispute that runaway money growth is the dominant culprit in
accounting for the instances of extreme inflation in the past—such as the episodes
experienced by eastern European nations immediately following World Wars I and
II (see Exhibit 13-1). However, many economists tend to be eclectic in their
approach to inflation, arguing that such phenomena as higher oil prices, wage hikes,
increases in import costs, and other factors on the cost side often initiate inflation.

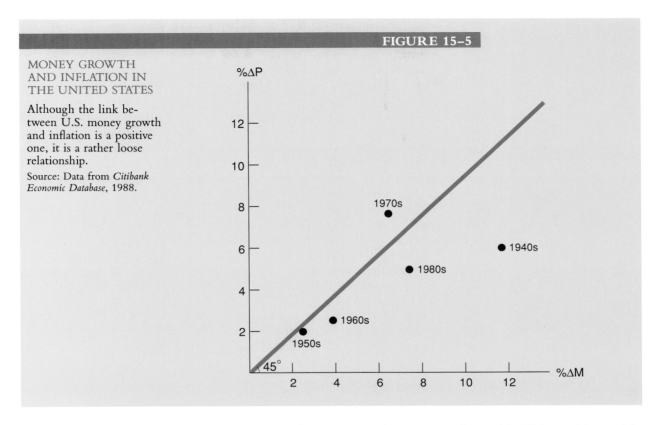

FIGURE 15–5

MONEY GROWTH AND INFLATION IN THE UNITED STATES

Although the link between U.S. money growth and inflation is a positive one, it is a rather loose relationship.

Source: Data from *Citibank Economic Database*, 1988.

Furthermore, such critics argue that aggregate demand (MV) is not driven solely by the money supply. Stimulative fiscal policy, as well as monetary policy, may give rise to excessive aggregate demand for goods and services, which is the fundamental cause of inflation. Critics of the crude quantity theory (and critics of modern monetarism) believe that velocity is highly elastic, capable of stretching significantly when nonmoney factors favor an expansion of economic activity. Suppose firms are bullish and wish to expand spending on inventories or plant while the Fed is holding back on the money supply. These firms may approach financial institutions for loans. The banks may have no excess funds on hand because of tight Fed policies. However, the institutions can normally obtain the funds by either liquidating securities or issuing large blocks of negotiable CDs to corporate lenders. In utilizing these channels, the banks are tapping idle money balances and transferring the funds to active spenders. Alternatively, the firms may bypass the financial institutions and issue bonds or short-term IOUs known as *commercial paper* directly to the public. Although such actions do not change the supply of money, they do stimulate the velocity of money by transferring money balances from inactive money holders to active money holders—those who wish to spend on goods and services. Hence, aggregate spending (MV) rises in spite of a constant money supply.[7] Velocity of money is boosted.

---

[7]This analysis helps explain why velocity exhibits a distinct procyclical pattern. In a period of strong economic expansion, banks sell securities and certificates of deposit to obtain funds with which to meet burgeoning loan demand. Velocity rises as funds are transferred (via the banks) from savers to active spenders. In periods of recession, such activities cease as loan demand drops off. Velocity falls or returns to its long-term trend dictated by the evolution of the payments process and the state of financial technology.

Many economists are critical of the assumption that the normal state of affairs is one of full employment. The impact of an increase in the money supply upon the price level surely depends on the state of the economy at the time the monetary stimulus is applied. These ideas are illustrated in Figure 15-6.

In Figure 15-6(a), the stimulative monetary policy occurs when the economy has a significant pool of unemployment and unused plant capacity. The aggregate supply curve is relatively flat in the relevant region, indicating that extra output can be called forth without necessitating sharply higher prices. The stimulative policy shifts the aggregate demand curve from AD_1 to AD_2, causing a slight increase in the nation's price level (P_1 to P_2) and a significant expansion in real output (Y_1 to Y_2). In terms of the *equation of exchange,* a ten-percent increase in M gives rise to perhaps an eight-percent increase in Y and a two-percent increase in P.

In Figure 15-6(b), the stimulus occurs in the context of an economy already functioning at close to full capacity. The relevant portion of the aggregate supply curve is steeply rising, indicating that additional output is forthcoming only at sharply higher levels of prices. The stimulative monetary policy shifts the aggregate demand curve from AD_3 to AD_4, causing a sharp increase in the price level and only a modest increase in real output. A ten-percent increase in M results in perhaps a two-percent increase in Y and an eight-percent increase in P.

The illustrations in Figure 15-6(a) and (b) indicate that stimulative monetary policies, by increasing aggregate demand for goods and services, normally increase *both* real output *and* the level of prices. The distribution of this mix of output growth

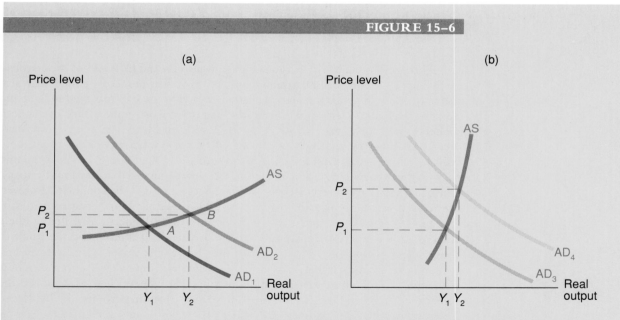

FIGURE 15–6

EFFECT OF MONETARY STIMULUS ON REAL OUTPUT AND PRICE LEVEL

The manner in which money growth is divided between inflation and output growth depends on the steepness of the nation's aggregate supply curve. If the aggregate supply curve is relatively flat, money growth is reflected mainly in output growth. If the aggregate supply curve is quite steep, most of the money growth is reflected in higher prices.

EXHIBIT 15-2

MILTON
FRIEDMAN
(1912–   )

Ask any economist who the world's foremost monetarist is and the response is almost surely to be Milton Friedman. The recipient of the 1976 Nobel Prize in Economics, Friedman is clearly one of the most influential economists of this century.

Friedman is well known to the public for his tenacious defense of free markets. His best-selling book, *Free to Choose* (coauthored with his wife, Rose Director Friedman), was developed into a television series with the same title. The theme of the book and TV series concerns the merits of a free-market economy with minimal government regulation and intervention in promoting individual initiative, prosperity, and economic growth. For many years Friedman delved into major contemporary issues in his regular column in *Newsweek*. Unlike many famous economists, his writings have had a significant effect on laymen, as well as on students and professional economists.

Friedman has made major contributions to the economics literature in many areas. One of his most outstanding contributions is his monumental book, *A Monetary History of the United States (1867–1960)*, coauthored with Anna J. Schwartz in 1963. This book contains a treasure of data and information for students of monetary economics. Covering almost a century of history, it traces the relationship between the rate of change in the supply of money and changes in economic activity. The thesis of the book is that many major U.S. economic fluctuations—periods of severe inflation and deep recession—were caused by prior changes in the nation's money supply. Especially provocative is the chapter titled "The Great Contraction, 1929–33." In this chapter Friedman marshals evidence in support of his hypothesis that America's Great Depression was caused primarily by a series of mistakes made by the Federal Reserve System.

One of Friedman's more contested positions is his view that the Federal Reserve should give up efforts to stabilize the economy by discretionary monetary policy measures and instead simply increase the money supply at a slow, constant rate each year. He advocated this position in his book, *A Program for Monetary Stability*, written more than 40 years ago—and has never wavered in this position over the years.

Although undoubtedly a controversial figure, Friedman is enormously respected by economists of all ideological stripes. Many consider him to be the most creative economist of their lifetime. Friedman retired from the University of Chicago more than a decade ago, following nearly thirty years of service to that institution. He continues to encourage and stimulate the younger generation of economists from his current base at Stanford University's Hoover Institution.

and inflation depends upon the state of the economy when the stimulus is applied. Only when the aggregate supply curve is vertical is *all* the demand stimulus reflected in higher prices.

The Modern Quantity Theory—Monetarism

The problems with the crude quantity theory lie in the assumptions that V and Y may be regarded as constant in the short run. Figures 15-1 and 15-2 illustrate clearly that velocity has exhibited considerable variability over time. Therefore, aggregate spending (MV) does not move in proportion to M. Furthermore, output (Y) is not always pumping at full capacity. When the economy is operating at less than full capacity, a ten-percent increase in spending (MV) does not result in a ten-percent rise in prices—some of the increased spending is reflected in larger output (Y).

Hence, modern monetarists as well as nonmonetarists reject the crude quantity theory of money because its assumptions caricature the true nature of velocity and real output. But again, it is acknowledged that the theory is not far off the mark in explaining the role of money in the extreme pathological episodes of runaway inflation.

Monetarism
The viewpoint that monetary instability is the dominant cause of output fluctuations and that money supply growth is the dominant cause of inflation.

The Monetarist View of Velocity   Modern **monetarists** reject the notion that velocity is constant; however, they argue that it is stable and predictable. The hypothesis of stable velocity follows from the monetarist view that people hold money only to finance expenditures. The timing of these expenditures does not mesh perfectly with the receipt of income. The amount of money people must hold relative to expenditures, in the monetarist view, evolves only slowly over time as the state of financial technology and other institutional factors underlying the synchronization between receipts and expenditures slowly change. Modern monetarists acknowledge that major changes in interest rates and uncertainty can alter money demand and velocity, but they tend to de-emphasize these factors.

Hence, monetarists argue that the multiplier linking money and GNP—velocity—is more stable and predictable than our expenditures multiplier of Chapter 11, the multiplier linking changes in government or investment expenditures to the change in GNP. Monetarists therefore believe that monetary policy is a more reliable and powerful instrument than fiscal policy.

In contrast to monetarists, nonmonetarists emphasize the sensitivity of money demand and velocity to interest rates and economic uncertainty. Since it is difficult to forecast interest rates, nonmonetarists believe that changes in velocity seldom can be predicted accurately. Keynesian economists believe that the expenditures multiplier is more stable than the velocity of money. It follows then that Keynesians place more faith in the power of fiscal policy than in monetary policy.

The Monetarist View of Inflation   Monetarists typically argue that the root cause of inflation can always be found in excessive growth of the nation's supply of money. The strong statistical association between money growth and inflation, such as that illustrated in Figures 15-4 and 15-5, is often presented by monetarists as evidence that inflation is a monetary phenomenon. Critics charge that the strong positive correlation between money growth and inflation, while undeniable, is sometimes misleading and is misinterpreted by monetarists. Correlation does not imply causation.

Utilizing our aggregate demand-aggregate supply framework, assume prices of imported raw materials rise, or oil prices increase, or Congress raises the level of the minimum wage. Any such event gives rise to a leftward shift (decrease) in the nation's aggregate supply curve. In Figure 15-7, AS_1 shifts to AS_2. If the Fed does not respond, the aggregate demand curve remains at AD_1 and we move from point A to point B. Real output declines from Y_1 to Y_2 and the price level rises from P_1 to P_2. If the Fed is concerned about the decline in output and employment, it may pursue a stimulative policy of increasing the money supply to counteract the decline in economic activity. If so, the aggregate demand curve shifts from AD_1 to AD_2. Real output is returned to its original Y_1 level, but the price level is boosted to P_3 as we move to point C in the illustration. During this event, inflation occurs as the level of prices rises from P_1 to P_3.

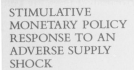

FIGURE 15-7

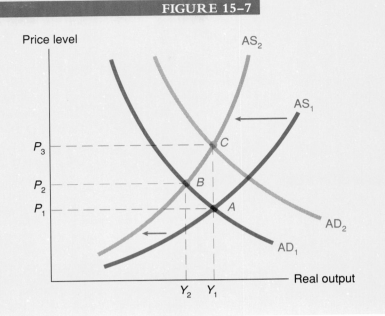

STIMULATIVE MONETARY POLICY RESPONSE TO AN ADVERSE SUPPLY SHOCK

An aggregate supply shock such as an oil price hike shifts the nation's aggregate supply curve leftward. This raises the price level and reduces output. If the Fed wishes to prevent a decline in output, it must increase the money supply to boost the aggregate demand curve. In this situation, what then is the cause of the inflation? Economists differ in their interpretation of the causes of inflation.

After the fact, we note in Figure 15-7 that both the money supply and the price level increased. But was the money growth the *root cause* of the inflation? Monetarists, since they believe that the fundamental responsibility of the Federal Reserve is to ensure price level stability, would respond in the affirmative. But many economists would disagree, citing factors that shifted the aggregate supply curve as the fundamental sources of the inflation. If the aggregate supply curve had not shifted in the first place—due to higher import prices, higher oil prices, or higher wages—no inflation would have occurred. Those who place high priority on high output and employment performance argue that the adverse supply shock is what forced the Fed to increase the supply of money to avert recession. Critics of monetarism argue that monetarists tend to forget the complex interaction between aggregate supply forces and monetary policy that contributes to the powerful correlation between money growth and inflation we observe when we analyze graphs such as Figures 15-4 and 15-5.

The Monetarist View of Discretionary Monetary Policy   Partly because they believe that monetary policy is an extremely potent tool, monetarists favor removing the Federal Reserve's power to conduct discretionary stabilization policies. Many monetarists are convinced the political and technical obstacles that confront the Fed's objective of conducting policies designed to successfully smooth the swings in economic activity are very formidable. These monetarists advocate that the Fed abandon its discretionary monetary policy and adopt a *monetary growth rule*. In this rule the money supply grows at some specific slow and steady rate, *irrespective of contemporary economic conditions.*

Inasmuch as they believe that velocity moves in a stable and consistent pattern, monetarists are confident that slow and stable money growth leads to a rather steady expansion of aggregate spending (*MV*) and GNP. Although the money growth rule may not lead to the elimination of the business cycle, monetarists believe that it would lead to the elimination of future episodes of double-digit inflation and severe recession. And that, they point out, is a better economic performance than the Fed has been able to deliver in the past.

The majority of economists today do *not* favor implementation of the constant money growth proposal; they favor continuation of discretionary monetary policy. These critics of monetarism admit that the Fed has made many serious mistakes in the past. However, they believe that the Fed has learned from these mistakes. In the current state of the art, they believe the Fed is today capable of outperforming a constant money growth rule. We analyze the *rules-versus-discretion debate* in some depth in Chapter 19.

SUMMARY

1. Monetary policy and the supply of money can influence economic activity by altering the level of interest rates, by creating a disequilibrium in portfolio holdings of money relative to other financial and nonfinancial assets, and by altering stock and bond prices and the wealth of private citizens and firms. Economists disagree about the relative importance of these three channels of influence.

2. An effective mechanism for highlighting the role of money is the *equation of exchange.* This equation, an identity, states that the money supply times velocity is precisely equal to aggregate demand for GNP, which is also equivalent to the number of units of final output purchased times the average price of these final goods and services. The *equation of exchange* states that if aggregate demand is to rise, either the money supply or its velocity (or both) must rise.

3. Old-fashioned or *crude* quantity theorists asserted that both velocity (V) and real output (Y) are constant in the short run and therefore the price level (P) varies exactly in proportion to the supply of money (M). A 15-percent increase in M causes a 15-percent increase in P. In this theory the one and only cause of inflation is excessive money supply growth.

4. Modern monetarists as well as nonmonetarists reject the crude quantity theory as too rigid. They believe that money growth can influence real output as well as prices in the short run. Furthermore, monetarists reject the notion of a constant velocity in favor of a stable and predictable velocity. They believe that velocity, which is the multiplier linking the money supply to GNP spending, is more stable and predictable than the Keynesian multiplier, which links changes in government and investment spending to GNP spending.

5. Nonmonetarists regard velocity as a flexible and elastic variable whose behavior is extremely difficult to predict in advance. Hence, the link between the money supply and the economy is alleged to be weak and highly uncertain. Fiscal policy is thought to be just as powerful as monetary policy.

6. Real-world data indicate a positive statistical association between money growth and inflation, both for a cross section of nations in a uniform time interval and for the United States in different decades. Monetarists and nonmonetarists disagree over the underlying causal role of money in this statistical association.

7. Money growth is more likely to result in inflation if it occurs while the economy is close to full employment than if the economy contains considerable *slack.* This is because the nation's aggregate supply curve becomes increasingly steep as output approaches the full-employment level.

8. Monetarists believe that fiscal policy has little effect on aggregate demand and output, since it allegedly does not affect velocity. Keynesians believe fiscal policy alters velocity, thereby strongly influencing aggregate demand and output.

9. Monetarists tend to place a higher priority on containing inflation than on minimizing unemployment in the short run, and they believe the economy has built-in features that

tend to maintain output and employment at high levels. Nonmonetarists believe these automatic corrective measures are quite weak and tend to favor a *high-pressure* or stimulated economy to hold down unemployment. They are willing to run more risks of inflation to keep unemployment low than are monetarists.

10. Monetarists favor the abdication of monetary policy discretion. They believe that a rule in which money growth is fixed at a modest, constant rate of increase provides a more stable, healthy economic environment than the Fed can deliver via efforts to stabilize the economy through discretionary policies. Keynesians disagree, asserting that monetary discretion can surely outperform any predetermined constant money growth rule.

KEY TERMS

equation of exchange

velocity (*V*)

liquidity

demand for money

transactions motive

transactions demand for money

precautionary motive

speculative motive

money market mutual funds (MMMFs)

crude quantity theory

monetarism

STUDY QUESTIONS AND PROBLEMS

1. Assume the Fed decides to implement a restrictive monetary policy and conducts a policy of open market sales of securities, thereby reducing the supply of money. Analyze three different channels through which this restrictive policy might successfully achieve its objective of restraining aggregate demand for goods and services.

2. Utilizing a rough estimate of your annual expenditures and your average M-1 holdings, compute the transactions velocity of your money. Why is this so much higher than the recent level of income velocity in the United States illustrated in Figure 15-2 (between 6.0 and 7.0)?

3. In your own words explain why the *equation of exchange* is an identity rather than a theory that one could potentially test in order to ascertain its truth or falsity.

4. Assume GNP is currently $5600 billion per year and the supply of money is $800 billion. What is the velocity of money? The nation collectively holds enough money to finance how many days worth of GNP expenditures?

5. What is the chief advantage of holding money as a means of storing wealth over time? What is the chief disadvantage?

6. Analyze as many factors as you can think of that would make the velocity of money decline.

7. Explain why velocity systematically tends to increase in periods of robust economic expansion.

8. Outline the differences of opinion between monetarists and Keynesians regarding the nature and behavior of velocity.

9. What is the effect on velocity if the following occurs?
   a. Congress outlaws the use of credit cards.
   b. Banks begin to pay interest on regular demand deposits.
   c. Great uncertainty is created as the chairman of the Federal Reserve Board resigns.

10. Suppose *M* increases 8 percent in the next year while *V* remains constant. Outline the consequences for inflation and real output growth if the economy were initially operating with
   a. 11-percent unemployment
   b. 5-percent unemployment

11. What differences in views distinguish modern monetarists from their forerunners, the crude quantity theorists?

SELECTED REFERENCES

Friedman, Milton, "Money: Quantity Theory," *International Encyclopedia of the Social Sciences* (New York: Macmillan Company and Free Press, 1968), pp. 432–447. A lucid exposition by the world's most eminent monetarist.

Mayer, Thomas, *The Structure of Monetarism* (New York: Norton, 1978). Delves into some of the broader, philosophical aspects of monetarism.

Modigliani, Franco and Thomas Mayer, "The Monetarist Controversy Revisited" and "Response," *Contemporary Policy Issues,* October 1988, pp. 3–24. A critique of modern monetarism (by Modigliani) and a rebuttal by a monetarist (Mayer).

Thomas, Lloyd B., *Money, Banking, and Economic Activity,* 3rd ed. (Englewood Cliffs, NJ: Prentice-Hall, 1986). Chapters 15–17 provide in-depth coverage of demand for money and velocity.

CHAPTER 16

INTEREST RATES

The truth is that the rate of interest is not a narrow phenomenon applying only to a few business contracts, but permeates all economic relations. It is a link which binds man to the future and by which he makes all his far reaching decisions.

IRVING FISHER, 1907

Few variables have a greater bearing on the state of your material well-being than interest rates. The income you earn from savings accounts, the mortgage payment on your home, your automobile loan payments, and credit card charges all affect your standard of living. In a less direct sense, by influencing foreign exchange rates, interest rates even exert a major impact on the cost of imported VCRs and automobiles and on the cost of trips to Europe.

For many businesses, interest costs represent an important component of total costs. Examples include airlines (new aircraft are purchased with borrowed funds), agriculture (spring planting is financed via bank loans), retailing (inventories are financed by borrowing), and construction (new homes and commercial buildings are financed through construction loans). Many businesses are affected by the influence of interest rates on the demand for their products. For example, rising interest rates reduce the demand for new homes by raising monthly mortgage payments for prospective buyers. Rising interest rates also reduce the demand for new capital goods such as tractors and factories as well as consumer durable goods such as cars and television sets. Industries negatively affected by rising interest rates are known as interest-sensitive industries.

Interest rates also perform important functions from the perspective of society at large. Interest rates influence decisions to save and to invest in plant and equipment, thereby helping determine the growth in the nation's standard of living over time. Moreover, interest rates (or yields on various assets) provide signals that direct the flow of capital both internationally and domestically to the areas of greatest need. For example, when interest rates (properly adjusted for risk) are higher in the U.S. than in Japan, funds tend to flow from Japan to the U.S., thus helping finance profitable U.S. ventures. When interest rates (adjusted for risk) are higher for farm loans than for business loans, this indicates a greater need for the direction of funds to agriculture. By providing

343

signals that indicate where the usefulness of funds is greatest, interest rates help allocate credit in a socially desirable way.

In Chapter 16 we consider the meaning of interest rates and study the distinction between nominal (actual) and real (inflation-adjusted) interest rates. We develop a simple but useful framework that allows you to understand the forces that cause interest rates to fluctuate considerably over time. For example, the framework enables you to understand why interest rates almost always rise in inflationary times and fall during periods of declining inflation. The analytical framework also gives you an intuitive feel for the role played by other important factors—such as large federal budget deficits, the Federal Reserve System, and the natural influence of the business cycle—in interest-rate determination.

THE MEANING OF INTEREST RATES

Interest Rate
The price paid per dollar borrowed per year, expressed as a percentage (e.g., 8 percent).

The **interest rate** may be defined as the price for the use of credit or the price for the use of loanable funds. It is sometimes referred to as the time value of money. Even in a world of zero inflation, you can expect to receive a positive interest rate for the temporary use of your funds. This is due to the human trait of *time preference*. Both you and the borrower prefer present consumption over future consumption. By utilizing your funds, the borrower can advance consumption from the future to the present; the borrower can enjoy the goods and services *now*. This is worth something, and the borrower is willing to pay (interest) for it. In other words, you charge interest to compensate for postponing your consumption.

In addition, capital is productive. Society can step up its total output and standard of living in the future by abstaining from current consumption—by currently producing more capital goods and fewer consumption goods. The act of saving (refraining from consuming) is the essential economic mechanism for freeing up resources for the production of capital goods. For example, an entrepreneur is willing to pay you a positive interest rate for the use of your funds because capital is productive. The entrepreneur uses your funds to purchase capital goods and to earn a positive rate of return by doing so.

Hence, because of time preference and productivity of capital, interest rates would be positive even in a hypothetical world of zero inflation. Such an interest rate would fluctuate over time and normally would be rather low—perhaps in the two-to-three percent range. In the real world of positive inflation rates, interest rates are significantly higher and fluctuate in a broader range.

Which Interest Rate?

In the U.S. economy there are literally thousands of different interest rates or yields. Securities, loans, savings accounts, and other interest-bearing instruments differ in safety, tax considerations, maturity, marketability, and other characteristics that create a difference in the supply–demand environment and hence, in the yield. However, all these various interest rates typically move in tandem, driven by similar supply and demand considerations. Many of these yields are essentially determined in auction markets and, like the price of wheat, fluctuate every hour of the trading day. A few, such as the interest rates charged by banks to borrowers, are set at a fixed level for weeks or months at a time and are changed only periodically. Even these interest rates, however, are ultimately governed by underlying market forces. A few of the more visible and commonly quoted interest rates are singled out for special mention.

Prime Loan Rate
A benchmark bank loan rate that is widely publicized and used as a standard by which other bank loan rates are set.

Prime Loan Rate   The **prime loan rate** (the prime) is a benchmark interest rate that major banks use to set their loan rates for various customers. A well-established small business borrowing $40,000 might be charged two percentage points above the prime rate, whereas a middle-income household seeking a home improvement loan may have to pay four percentage points above the prime. The prime rate is sometimes defined as the rate banks charge their biggest and best corporate customers. However, this is not strictly correct, since some large corporations frequently obtain multimillion dollar loans *below* the prime loan rate (i.e., at a discount from the prime rate). The prime loan rate is adjusted periodically by banks in response to changes in the cost of funds to banks—that is, to movements in short-term interest rates in the U.S. economy. The behavior of the prime rate in recent years is illustrated in Figure 16-1.

Treasury Bill Yield
The yield on safe, short-term government securities known as Treasury bills.

Treasury Bill Yield   This is the interest rate or yield available on short-term U.S. government securities. These securities are perhaps the safest of any in the U.S. economy. This follows from the fact that the U.S. government has constitutional authority to raise taxes or print money, if need be, to honor its obligations. There is virtually no chance that the U.S. government will default on its debt obligations. The **Treasury bill yield** is therefore often quoted as a sort of standard, minimal yield among securities. Recent behavior of the Treasury bill yield is illustrated in Figure 16-2, (page 346), alongside other yields or interest rates.

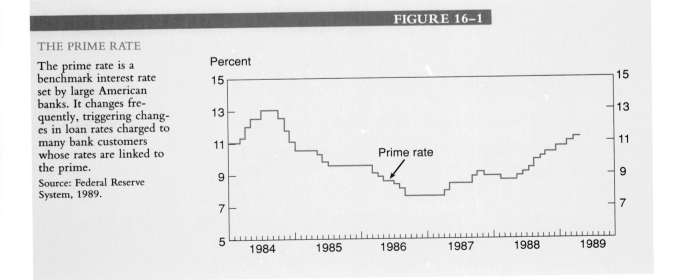

FIGURE 16-1

THE PRIME RATE

The prime rate is a benchmark interest rate set by large American banks. It changes frequently, triggering changes in loan rates charged to many bank customers whose rates are linked to the prime.
Source: Federal Reserve System, 1989.

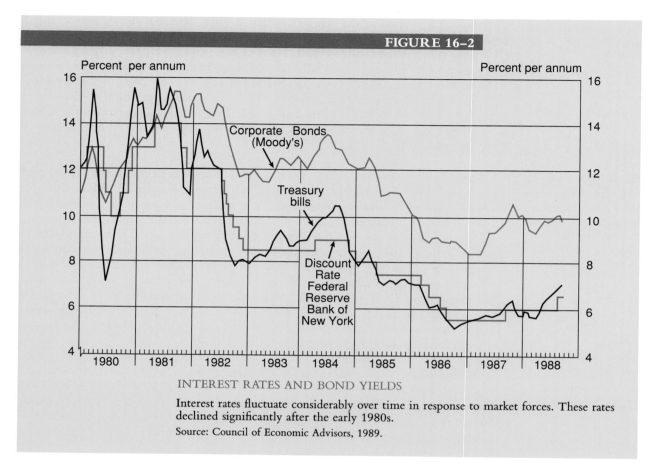

FIGURE 16–2

INTEREST RATES AND BOND YIELDS

Interest rates fluctuate considerably over time in response to market forces. These rates declined significantly after the early 1980s.

Source: Council of Economic Advisors, 1989.

Discount Rate
The interest rate charged by the Fed on loans to banks and other depository institutions.

Discount Rate   This is the interest rate charged by the Federal Reserve System to financial institutions that borrow on a very short-term basis from the Fed. This rate typically remains fixed at a given level for several weeks or months before being changed. The Fed periodically adjusts the **discount rate** in order to implement a change in monetary policy or to simply keep its loan rate in line with other changing rates in the economy. The discount rate is frequently lower than many other interest rates and yields in the economy. Its recent pattern is illustrated in Figure 16-2.

Federal Funds Market
Market in which banks trade their excess reserve deposits (with the Fed) on a one-day basis.

Federal Funds Rate
The interest rate on loans made among financial institutions in the federal funds market.

Federal Funds Rate   This is the interest rate involved in the trading of short-term funds between depository institutions such as commercial banks. Such institutions are required to maintain reserve deposits at the Federal Reserve, as noted in Chapter 14. The dollar amount of required reserves is calculated by multiplying the percentage reserve requirement times the checking account liabilities of the bank or thrift institution. The **federal funds market** is the market in which institutions with excess reserves loan these Federal Reserve deposits to institutions that are deficient, usually on a one-day basis. The **federal funds rate,** a sensitive barometer of conditions in financial markets, is commonly cited in the financial press.

Corporate Bond Yield   Businesses that need funds for such long-term projects as building factories or purchasing capital equipment often issue long-term bonds. A *bond* is a debt instrument or IOU that makes a series of annual interest payments and returns the principal to the lender at maturity, which is often 10–30 years after the bond is issued. There are hundreds of thousands of corporate bonds outstanding. **Corporate bond yields** differ because of differing maturities and because of perceived differences in the financial condition of various corporations. These bond yields are quoted daily in *The Wall Street Journal* and on the financial pages of many newspapers. The yield on high-quality corporate bonds is illustrated in Figure 16-2.

Mortgage Rate   A mortgage is a long-term loan secured by a lien on the real property being financed. The great majority of American homes are financed by mortgages, either at fixed-interest rates or at rates that vary over time. During 1975–1985, an increasing portion of mortgages were ARMs—adjustable rate mortgages. The interest rate payable on ARMs is linked by formula to certain interest rates and changes periodically. However, fixed-rate mortgages have returned to favor in recent years as households have been willing to pay a premium to eliminate the risk of higher monthly mortgage payments. The **mortgage rate** is crucial to millions of Americans, since the mortgage payment is typically the dominant expenditure item in the family budget.

THE LOANABLE FUNDS MODEL OF INTEREST RATES

As we stated, an interest rate is a price—the price for the use of funds. Interest rates, much like the price of wheat and lemons, are determined in the marketplace by the impersonal forces of supply and demand. The model we use to understand the forces governing interest rates employs the **supply of loanable funds** and the **demand for loanable funds**—hence its name, the **loanable funds model** of interest rates. This model is illustrated in Figure 16-3.

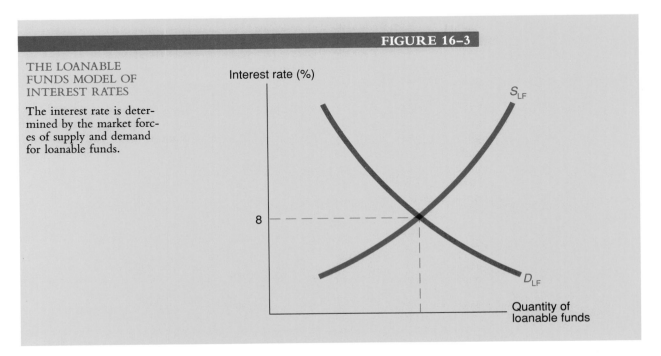

FIGURE 16–3

THE LOANABLE FUNDS MODEL OF INTEREST RATES

The interest rate is determined by the market forces of supply and demand for loanable funds.

The Supply of Loanable Funds

Lenders are willing to make their funds available at a price—the rate of interest. The supply of loanable funds originates from millions of individual savers, thousands of firms, and other entities that find themselves in a *surplus position.* These surplus units have more funds available than their current expenditures. They serve their own needs, as well as society's, by loaning out their funds at interest. Note that this supply curve (like most) is upward sloping. This slope indicates that potential lenders must be compensated via a higher interest rate in order to coax from them a larger supply of funds. Potential lenders have other options besides lending. They may purchase real estate, play the stock market, or blow the funds on consumer goods or vacations. The level of the interest rate influences the attractiveness of lending relative to using the funds for these alternative activities. A higher interest rate makes lending more attractive, thus inducing an increase in the quantity of loanable funds supplied in the market.

Of course, a horde of other factors besides the interest rate influences the willingness of potential lenders to supply funds to the market. Attitudes toward thrift, the need to acquire a nestegg to finance retirement or a college education, the perceived risk involved in the loan, tax considerations, and a hundred other factors influence the supply of loanable funds. These factors, as they change over time, shift the entire position of the supply curve of Figure 16-3. For example, the introduction of special tax incentives for establishing *Individual Retirement Accounts* (IRAs) in the 1980s may have stimulated the willingness of Americans to save and thereby may have shifted the supply of loanable funds to the right (remember, this is an *increase* in the supply of loanable funds). Also, because different age groups in society exhibit different saving patterns, a change in the age structure of the population normally shifts the supply curve.[1] The Federal Reserve System, via its tools of monetary policy discussed in Chapter 14, can also shift the supply curve rightward or leftward. That is, the Fed can increase or decrease the supply of loanable funds available in the market.

The Demand for Loanable Funds

The demand for loanable funds originates from *deficit-spending units* in society—individuals, firms, or governments that spend more than current income and that finance the difference by borrowing. Typically included in this group are millions of individuals, the majority of business firms, the federal government, and many local units of government.[2] The demand curve for loanable funds is downward sloping since a lower interest rate makes it more attractive (or less painful) to borrow. However, potential borrowers often have alternatives to borrowing. Usually, these alternatives involve liquidating other assets such as securities or savings accounts to

---

[1]On balance, older people in their retirement years are dissavers. They tend to spend more than current income, drawing on past savings earned during their working years. When the proportion of the population in retirement rises, this tends to pull down the saving rate and shift the supply of loanable funds leftward.

[2]Most households, firms, and units of government simultaneously engage in lending *and* borrowing. If you have a mortgage on your house and a savings account, you are a borrower (via your mortgage) and a lender (via your savings account) simultaneously. In the aggregate, on balance, households are net-surplus units or lenders. Firms and governments on balance are net-deficit-spending units or borrowers.

obtain funds or postponing the purchase of the new house, automobile, or TV. An increase in interest rates makes these alternatives more attractive and eliminates some of the potential borrowers from the loanable funds market.

Like the supply curve, the demand curve for loanable funds is constructed under the assumption that all other factors affecting borrowing except the interest rate are held constant. That is, the demand curve for loanable funds is a hypothetical concept that isolates the relationship between the interest rate and the quantity of loanable funds demanded. In reality, as these other factors change over time, the entire position of the demand curve shifts. For example, an increase in federal budget deficits or an increase in the general willingness of Americans to incur debt due to a change in attitudes increases borrowing at each and every rate of interest. This shows up as a rightward shift in the demand for loanable funds (an *increase* in demand). The Tax Reform Act of 1986 eliminated the federal income-tax deductibility of interest expense incurred from consumer borrowing. This Act, by making borrowing less attractive, shifted the demand curve leftward (*decrease* in demand).

HOW CHANGES IN SUPPLY AND DEMAND AFFECT INTEREST RATES

The equilibrium rate of interest is determined by the intersection of the supply and demand curves for loanable funds. In Figure 16-3 this intersection occurs at an interest rate of eight percent. In financial markets, actual interest rates adjust rapidly toward equilibrium. The supply and demand curves for loanable funds shift frequently in response to a multitude of different events, thus bringing about frequent changes in the interest rates observed. Review Figures 16-1 and 16-2, and note the considerable fluctuation in the level of interest rates over time.

Note further that each of the four interest-rate series depicted in Figures 16-1 and 16-2 shows considerable variability over time. Any event that increases the demand for loanable funds (shifts D_{LF} rightward) or reduces the supply of loanable funds (shifts S_{LF} leftward) results in higher interest rates. Any factor that decreases the demand for loanable funds or increases the supply of loanable funds results in lower interest rates. The underlying analysis for interest-rate changes is illustrated in Figure 16-4 (page 350).

In Figure 16-4(a), suppose we begin initially with S_{LF}^1, D_{LF}^1, the equilibrium at A, and an interest rate of eight percent. When individuals become less thrifty and go on a consumption binge, the supply curve shifts leftward to S_{LF}^2. The new supply-demand intersection occurs at B, and the interest rate rises to ten percent.

In Figure 16-4(b), suppose we begin initially at C, with a supply and demand for loanable funds of S_{LF}^1 and D_{LF}^1, and an initial interest rate of eight percent. Suppose further that businesses become more pessimistic about the outlook for future sales and reduce borrowing to finance inventories and expansion of facilities. This shifts down the demand for loanable funds from D_{LF}^1 to D_{LF}^2. As indicated in (b), the intersection of supply and demand moves from C to D, and the interest rate declines to six percent.

Another example or two may help reinforce your understanding of the mechanics of interest-rate determination. Suppose that the federal budget deficit rises sharply because of increased government expenditures. Because the government must finance this deficit, the demand curve for loanable funds shifts rightward, pulling up the level of interest rates. Suppose further that the public becomes concerned about the financial condition of the social security system and increases

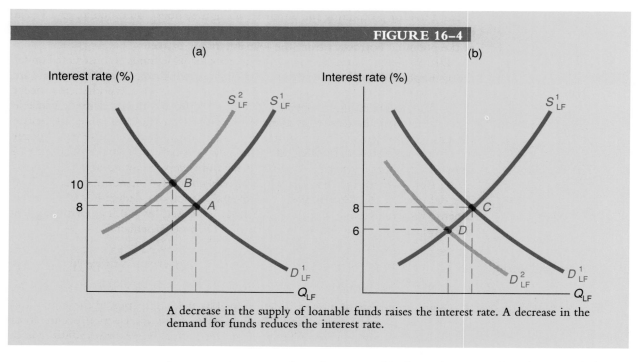

FIGURE 16–4

A decrease in the supply of loanable funds raises the interest rate. A decrease in the demand for funds reduces the interest rate.

its propensity to save in order to provide for retirement. This change in behavior shifts the supply curve for funds rightward (increase in supply), resulting in a reduction of interest rates.

YOUR TURN   Suppose XYZ Corporation, a highly respected and previously stable manufacturing firm, stuns financial markets by announcing a huge operating loss in the current year. Analyze, via supply and demand analysis, the effect of this announcement on the yield of XYZ corporate bonds currently being issued.

THE ROLE OF EXPECTED INFLATION IN INTEREST-RATE BEHAVIOR

The rate of inflation that the public expects to prevail in the future exerts an important effect on the current level of interest rates. The public's expectation of inflation tends to be strongly influenced by recent inflation and by other factors that affect the outlook. When inflation has been high during recent times, people tend to expect it to remain high. As a result, interest rates are usually very high in periods of severe and sustained inflation and relatively low in periods of subdued inflation. Our simple loanable funds model in Figure 16-5 may be used to demonstrate why interest rates tend to vary with the rate of inflation expected to prevail.

Suppose initially we are in a period of relatively low inflation. Expected inflation is currently quite low, and the supply and demand curves for loanable funds are represented by S_{LF}^1 and D_{LF}^1. The equilibrium is at A and the interest rate is i_1 (relatively low). Suppose further that some event occurs that causes the public to raise its perception of the inflation rate likely to prevail during the next several years.

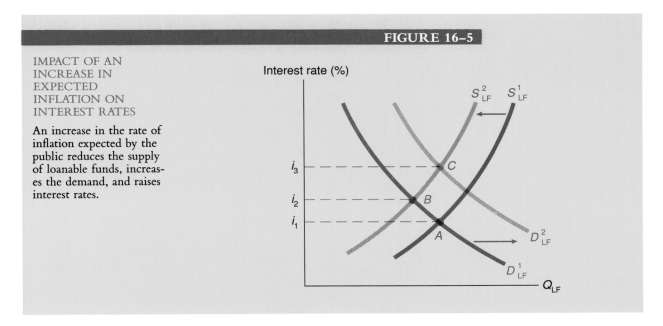

FIGURE 16–5

IMPACT OF AN INCREASE IN EXPECTED INFLATION ON INTEREST RATES

An increase in the rate of inflation expected by the public reduces the supply of loanable funds, increases the demand, and raises interest rates.

This event might be a major hike in oil prices, initiation of military hostilities, a large increase in the money supply, a sharp fall in the foreign-exchange market value of the dollar, or any of several other events. Whatever the cause, when expected inflation rises, both the supply and demand for loanable funds shift, bringing about a new and higher level of interest rates.

Because people believe inflation will be higher, they are less willing than before to loan funds at any given interest rate. This follows directly from the fact that the real value of the principal loaned out will diminish more rapidly if inflation is severe. Lenders will be repaid in dollars with lower purchasing power. Lending is therefore less profitable. In terms of Figure 16-5, this implies that the supply curve shifts leftward (a *decrease* in supply) to S_{LF}^2. In the figure, this decrease in the supply of funds moves the equilibrium to B and raises the interest rate to i_2.

However, the story is not over. For the same reason that the supply of loanable funds shrinks, the demand for loanable funds increases. Potential borrowers—encouraged by the fact that higher inflation reduces the real burden of their debt (principal incurred)—want to borrow *more* at each and every interest rate. The demand for funds shifts rightward (*increase* in demand) to D_{LF}^2.

The increased demand for funds, in conjunction with the decreased supply, moves the equilibrium to C in Figure 16-5. Hence, the increase in expected inflation pulls up the interest rate from i_1 to i_3.

This tendency of expected inflation—via the forces of the marketplace—to strongly influence interest rates is known as the **Fisher Effect**. Irving Fisher, the great American economist of the early twentieth century, analyzed in depth the role of inflation in financial markets. Fisher hypothesized that the level of interest rates should move approximately on a one-for-one basis with the magnitude of expected inflation. As a result, if correctly anticipated, actual inflation should have a neutral impact on the distribution of wealth between borrowers and lenders. That is, the interest rate should rise just enough to compensate the lender for the damage done to the real value of the principal by inflation. Inflation would be *neutralized* by the

Fisher Effect
The effect that higher expected inflation has in inducing higher interest rates.

increase in interest rates. Fisher's efforts were acknowledged by later students of the subject who dubbed his theory the "Fisher Hypothesis."

Does the principle illustrated in Figure 16-5 really work in practice? Yes, provided that interest rates are allowed to be determined by market forces rather than being set by administrative decree or by regulation or law. We offer two pieces of evidence that the Fisher Effect works in practice: evidence from the U.S. economy and evidence from a cross section of nations.

U.S. Evidence on the Fisher Effect

Figure 16-2 indicates that U.S. interest rates were very high during 1980–1982 and were considerably lower during 1983–1989. The 1980–1982 period was one of rampant inflation and therefore *expected* inflation was also very high. As the public increased its perception of expected inflation in the late 1970s and early 1980s in response to a dramatic increase in world oil prices and rapidly escalating wage and price level increases, the supply curve of loanable funds shifted leftward, the demand curve shifted rightward, and interest rates escalated dramatically. The Treasury bill yield (Figure 16-2) reached 16 percent in 1981.

As inflation subsided after 1981, the public gradually became convinced that the days of severe inflation were over—at least for awhile. Because of this decline in expected inflation, the willingness to lend increased (S_{LF} shifted rightward), the desire to borrow decreased (D_{LF} shifted leftward), and interest rates came down.

Studies indicate that financial markets have become more sensitive to inflation in recent decades. Prior to World War II, interest rates often failed to rise during periods of inflation. After World War II and especially in the late 1960s, expected inflation began to exert a strong influence on the behavior of borrowers and lenders. Following some 15 years of very subdued inflation, prices began to increase rapidly after the mid-1960s. With some time lag, interest rates began to rise in response. The 1965–1982 period, an era of rather volatile inflation behavior, witnessed a high degree of interest-rate responsiveness to the state of expected inflation.

Although interest rates have been responsive to inflation in the past 30 or 40 years, interest rates have not increased sufficiently on average to fully preserve neutrality between debtors and creditors in periods of high inflation. That is, on average debtors have benefitted during periods of severe inflation.[3]

International Evidence on the Fisher Effect

A second way to conduct a crude test of the Fisher Hypothesis that interest rates are strongly influenced by expected inflation is to compare interest rates in nations experiencing considerably different rates of inflation. If the Fisher Effect is working, countries experiencing high rates of inflation should exhibit high interest rates. Note the evidence in Figure 16-6.

The pattern illustrated in Figure 16-6 is consistent with Fisher's Hypothesis. Nations that have experienced relatively severe inflation (Italy, France) typically have exhibited relatively high interest rates. Such nations as Japan, Switzerland, and

---

[3]Much sophisticated research has been conducted on measuring the strength of the Fisher Effect. The consensus in the literature seems to be that although interest rates definitely rise with expected inflation, they do not rise sufficiently to preserve neutrality. Typical estimates for the period since 1960 suggest that changes in interest rates usually amount to 60–80 percent of changes in expected inflation. The Fisher Hypothesis suggests that the response should be a full 100 percent.

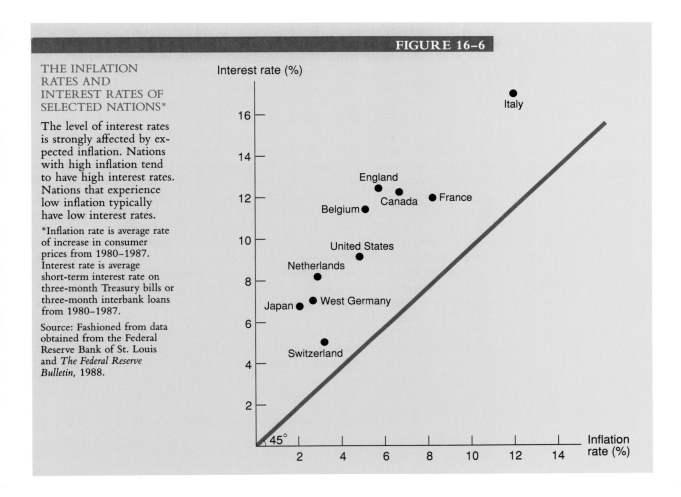

FIGURE 16–6

THE INFLATION RATES AND INTEREST RATES OF SELECTED NATIONS*

The level of interest rates is strongly affected by expected inflation. Nations with high inflation tend to have high interest rates. Nations that experience low inflation typically have low interest rates.

*Inflation rate is average rate of increase in consumer prices from 1980–1987. Interest rate is average short-term interest rate on three-month Treasury bills or three-month interbank loans from 1980–1987.

Source: Fashioned from data obtained from the Federal Reserve Bank of St. Louis and *The Federal Reserve Bulletin,* 1988.

Germany—which have been able to keep inflation in check—have experienced relatively low interest rates. This strong positive association between inflation rates and interest rates among a cross section of nations is no coincidence. The forces of supply and demand really work!

OTHER FACTORS THAT INFLUENCE INTEREST RATES

In addition to expected inflation, many other factors influence the level of interest rates by influencing the supply and/or demand for loanable funds. Among the most important factors thought to influence interest rates are the business cycle, the size of the federal budget deficit, and the Federal Reserve System.

The Role of the Business Cycle

Interest rates typically exhibit a pronounced cyclical pattern, rising during the expansion phase of the business cycle and falling in recessions. This pattern is primarily attributable to the behavior of private credit demands over the course of the business cycle.

In the expansion phase of the business cycle, unemployment declines and job stability and consumer confidence improve. Consumers are more inclined to purchase such *big-ticket* items as cars and stereo equipment, which tend to be financed largely by borrowing. Moreover, businesses become more optimistic as sales and profits rise. These firms expand borrowing to finance purchases of additional plant and equipment and to build up inventories to meet the expected increase in sales. Thus the demand for funds shifts rightward, tending to pull up interest rates.

As the economy gains strength, two other factors often contribute to additional upward pressure on interest rates. The actual inflation rate and therefore expected inflation are usually rising as the economy approaches the peak of the cycle. This increase in expected inflation boosts interest rates via the Fisher Effect. In addition, the Federal Reserve, fearing an acceleration of inflation, is likely to tighten credit and reduce the supply of funds in this phase of the business cycle.

In periods of recession, firms cut output and lay off workers. Unemployment rises and profits fall. Both consumer and business confidence tend to deteriorate in this environment. Demand for funds to finance consumer durable goods and business investment declines. This downward shift in the demand curve for loanable funds during recession pulls down interest rates. Once the Federal Reserve becomes aware of the seriousness of the recession, it is likely to implement a stimulative monetary policy. The Fed is likely to purchase securities in the open market and reduce its discount rate. These actions by the Fed shift the supply curve of loanable funds rightward, giving the interest rate an additional downward thrust. Finally, as the trough of the recession approaches, the rate of inflation typically declines. The decline in actual and expected inflation reinforces the downward pressure on interest rates by way of the Fisher Effect.

In Figure 16-7 we illustrate the cyclical pattern of interest rates during the past 20 years. Note that interest rates declined in each of the periods of recession (shaded areas). Interest rates tended to rise during economic expansion, particularly in the later phases of the cyclical upswing. It is clear that in order to accurately forecast interest rates, one must be able to forecast the business cycle. This has proven a difficult task.

The Role of Federal Budget Deficits

Intuitively it may seem apparent that an increase in federal budget deficits should raise interest rates. Indeed, we have indicated that an increase in borrowing by deficit spenders directly shifts the demand curve for loanable funds rightward. This tends to raise the interest rate. Moreover, larger budget deficits might arouse fears of higher inflation, thus pulling up interest rates via the Fisher Effect.

Most economists agree that budget deficits do raise interest rates. However, we must point out that there is disagreement in the profession on this issue. There is surprisingly little empirical evidence, at least prior to the 1980s, that past U.S. budget deficits increased interest rates. Economists who do not believe that budget deficits significantly raise interest rates have advanced two reasons to support their conclusion. One concerns the worldwide scope of the *capital market* or market for loanable funds. The other concerns the alleged tendency of larger budget deficits to stimulate the propensity of individuals to save.

The first reason for doubting that U.S. budget deficits substantially affect interest rates is that the size of these deficits, though enormous in an absolute sense,

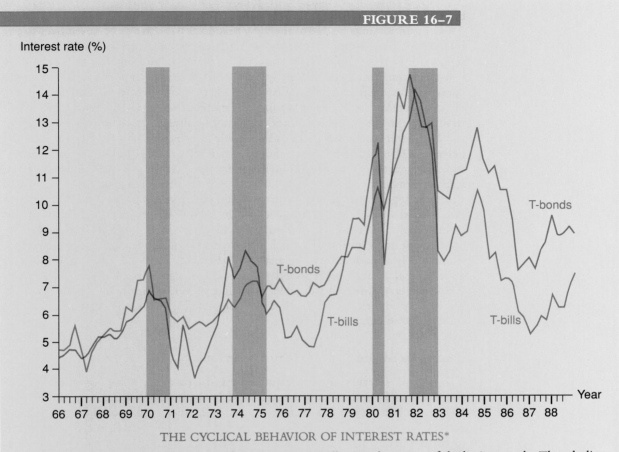

FIGURE 16–7

THE CYCLICAL BEHAVIOR OF INTEREST RATES*

Interest rates fluctuate systematically over the course of the business cycle. They decline during recessions (shaded areas) and increase during the expansion phase of the cycle, especially in the late stages.

*Shaded areas are periods of recession; unshaded areas are periods of cyclical expansion.
Source: Data obtained from the Federal Reserve System, 1989.

is rather small relative to the total pool of available funds in the world. Financial markets in various nations have become increasingly integrated in recent decades so that these markets are now almost worldwide in scope. As interest rates in the United States begin to rise in response to large federal borrowing demands, the quantity of funds available to meet the demands increases sharply as institutions in foreign nations lend their money in the United States. This sensitive supply response tends to limit the upward pressure on American interest rates.[4]

The second reason that some economists deny that large deficits affect U.S. interest rates involves the alleged relationship between larger deficits and saving

[4]Note that this is really a hypothesis about the elasticity or responsiveness of the supply curve for loanable funds. Specifically, the hypothesis is that this supply curve is very flat—the quantity of funds supplied is highly responsive to the interest rate. A small increase in the U.S. interest rate allegedly induces a large increase in the quantity of funds supplied since funds are drawn to the United States from all around the world. If this is true, larger deficits would have a modest (though positive) effect on interest rates.

behavior of individuals. Suppose the public is *future oriented* and perceives that larger budget deficits today imply higher taxes or a lower standard of living in the future. This perception may be due to the view that taxes will have to be raised later to pay interest on the enlarged debt or due to the view that the deficits hinder the future prosperity of the economy. To protect themselves (or their heirs) from the future belt-tightening, the public allegedly steps up its current saving rate. If so, the supply curve of loanable funds shifts rightward, perhaps sufficiently to neutralize the direct effect on interest rates of the government's increase in demand for funds with which to finance the deficit. Interest rates might not be affected by deficits in this analysis.

Supporters of the second position point out that it is consistent with rational behavior. That is, since larger deficits today imply greater future interest expenditures by government to finance the larger debt and therefore higher future tax rates, it makes sense for perceptive individuals to increase their saving rate today. Critics of this view regard it as a bit unrealistic. Have any of your friends raised their saving rate because of the increased deficits of the 1980s? Those who are dubious of this position point out that almost all measures of private saving rates have *declined* in the 1980s—the same period in which the large federal deficits emerged in the U.S. economy. Professional financial market participants believe almost uniformly that larger actual deficits or expected future deficits significantly raise interest rates. Academic economists are divided in their opinion. Ultimately the issue will be resolved by empirical investigation. As we enter the 1990s, the empirical evidence on the role of deficits is mixed.[5]

The Role of the Federal Reserve System

The Federal Reserve System is capable of exerting a major impact upon the level of interest rates by influencing the supply of loanable funds available in the market. When the Fed desires lower interest rates and easier credit conditions, it pursues actions to provide an increase in the funds available in financial institutions (primarily banks) for loans to the public. The supply curve for loanable funds shifts rightward and interest rates decline. When the Fed is in a restrictive mood, it takes actions which reduce the amount of funds that financial institutions have available to loan out. The supply curve of loanable funds decreases (shifts leftward), and interest rates rise.

During the 1940s, the Fed overwhelmed the other forces influencing interest rates and forced these rates down to abnormally low levels in order to assist the Treasury in financing the War. However, such a herculean effort by the Fed to dictate interest rates may have adverse side effects on the economy and may not be in the nation's interest. For example, if the Fed attempts to hold down interest rates during a period of rising inflation, the Fed is likely to exacerbate the inflation.

The Federal Reserve has the tools with which to bring about major changes in interest rates if it desires to do so. However, there is probably a tendency among the lay public and the financial press to attribute to the Fed changes in interest rates that are actually caused principally by such other factors as changes in inflationary expectations and changes in cyclical conditions in the economy. Note the dramatic upswing in interest rates during 1978–1981 (Figure 16-7). This episode may best be

---

[5]Paul Evans, in a series of papers, has advanced the view that larger deficits and expected future deficits are neutralized by an induced increase in saving, and therefore do not affect interest rates. See, for example, "Do Large Deficits Produce Higher Interest Rates?" *American Economic Review,* March 1985, pp. 68–87. For a contrary view, see Lloyd B. Thomas and Ali Abderrezak, "Anticipated Future Budget Deficits and the Term Structure of Interest Rates," *Southern Economic Journal,* July 1988, pp. 150–161.

described *not* as resulting from aggressive efforts by the Fed to reduce the supply of funds and push up interest rates but rather by the Fed passively allowing interest rates to rise in response to escalating inflationary expectations. The Fed could perhaps have prevented this increase in interest rates by aggressively pumping funds into banks. The Fed chose not to do so because it wanted to choke off the inflation that had been escalating in the 1970s.

By the same token, the major decline in interest rates after 1981 was not principally due to more stimulative policies implemented by the Federal Reserve. Rather, this decline in interest rates is best viewed as the response of financial markets first to the severe recession of the early 1980s and somewhat later to the gradual decline in expected inflation. Certainly the Fed was quite willing to see interest rates come down after the early 1980s. But it would *not* be correct to suppose that the big drop in yields during these years was caused by the Fed aggressively increasing the supply of funds available.

When the economic environment is one of substantial inflation and the public is highly sensitized to the inflation, the Fed may find it difficult or impossible to use stimulative monetary actions to bring down long-term interest rates such as those on mortgages and bonds. Suppose that the Fed aggressively pumps funds into the banks in a period in which inflation is relatively high. If the public is convinced that rapid expansion of the supply of loanable funds and the supply of money will result in higher inflation, the announcement that the Fed is stepping up the growth of loanable funds may itself alter the expected rate of inflation. In that event, the announcement of the move to a more stimulative policy by the Fed may, via the Fisher Effect, actually *boost* long-term interest rates. Thus, the role of the Fed in interest-rate behavior is a complex one in an era in which people are highly sensitized to inflation.

REAL VERSUS NOMINAL INTEREST RATES

Real Interest Rate
The nominal (actual) interest rate minus the expected rate of inflation; indicates the real cost to the borrower (and return to the lender) in terms of goods and services.

In economic analysis it is crucial to distinguish between the *real* interest rate and the *nominal* (actual) interest rate. The **real interest rate** is the rate that would prevail in a hypothetical world of zero permanent inflation. But the world we live in is a world of varying and almost always positive rates of inflation. To calculate the real interest rate, we subtract the expected rate of inflation from the **nominal (actual) interest rate.** If a student loan is granted at eight percent and expected inflation is five percent per annum, the real interest rate on the loan is three percent. If the 30-year mortgage on your home is at ten-percent interest and you expect inflation to average six percent per year during the next 30 years, the real mortgage rate is four percent. By engaging in this transaction, the lender earns and the borrower pays four percent per year after allowing for inflation.

The real interest rate is difficult to calculate in many instances because of the problem in estimating the expected rate of inflation. Most of us are fairly confident that inflation in the next six months or a year will not differ radically from its recent behavior. In addition, there are survey opinion polls of professional economists and the general public regarding short-run inflation expectations. However, no one can feel confident about forecasting the average inflation rate over a long period such as a decade.[6] There are simply too many factors that can influence inflation in future

---

[6]Inflation during the 1970s was much higher than anyone would have predicted at the beginning of the decade. And the Federal Reserve's policy of disinflation implemented in 1980 brought down the inflation rate in the early 1980s much faster than even the most ardent supporters of the policy had hoped or predicted.

years that cannot be anticipated. Such factors include future oil prices, agricultural conditions, military and political developments, economic policies, and many others. Therefore, long-term real interest rates are inherently difficult to measure.

The fundamental forces underlying the level of the real rate of interest are the thriftiness of the populace and the productivity of capital—although other factors temporarily influence real rates. When people become more thrifty, the supply of loanable funds increases and the real interest rate falls. When the rate of return expected on real economic investment (productivity of capital) rises, the demand for funds rises and the real rate of interest rises. It is the level of the *real* interest rate, not the actual or nominal interest rate, that governs many important economic decisions. The flow of financial capital (loanable funds) among nations, the decision to invest in new plant and equipment, and the redistributive effects of inflation between borrowers and lenders are strongly influenced by the real rate of interest (see Exhibit 16-1).

As an indication of the general behavior of real interest rates in the past 25 years, we have computed the real prime-loan rate and the real yield on U.S. Treasury bills. These real interest rates are illustrated in Figure 16-8, which indicates that real yields were generally positive (although low) until around 1973, swung into negative territory during the remainder of the 1970s, and moved up sharply to very high levels in the 1980s. These high real interest rates had important consequences for the U.S. economy in the 1980s. Lenders benefitted handsomely from the situation, whereas debtors were burned—sometimes to the point of insolvency. A massive flow of foreign funds poured into the U.S. financial markets, attracted by the high real yields on bonds and other assets. The great demand for the U.S. dollar (to finance acquisition of these assets) drove up the foreign-exchange market value of the dollar to the point that many American industries became subject to intense foreign competition.[7] A record-magnitude U.S. international trade deficit was experienced in the 1985–1989 period, partly in response to high American real interest rates and associated inflows of loanable funds from abroad.

Explanation for the High Real Interest Rates in the 1980s

There are several alternative hypotheses seeking to explain the remarkably high real interest rates that prevailed in the 1980s. Some analysts emphasize the improved U.S. business climate resulting from major tax reductions for the corporate sector in the early 1980s, the general movement toward dismantling government regulations, and perhaps a perceived pro-business attitude on the part of the Reagan and Bush Administrations. Such developments tend to increase the returns expected from investment in plant and equipment—increase the expected productivity of capital. This stimulates the demand for loanable funds and raises real interest rates. The strong stock-market performance of the 1980s is consistent with this view.

A less assuring explanation for the high real interest rates of the 1980s is that huge actual and prospective federal budget deficits forced up actual and real rates to abnormal levels.[8] Another explanation, applicable only to the *early* 1980s, is that the

---

[7]Suppose the dollar rises from 120 yen to 150 yen because of the increased demand for high-yielding American financial assets. The cost of the dollar, and therefore the cost of U.S. goods and services, rises some 25 percent as viewed by the Japanese. Correspondingly, the cost to Americans of the yen and Japanese products falls sharply. This places the American manufacturing sector under increased competitive pressures.

[8]Some seat-of-the-pants support for this view comes from the observation that interest rates fell sharply on the announcement in late 1985 that the Gramm-Rudman-Hollings Act (deficit-reduction legislation) became law.

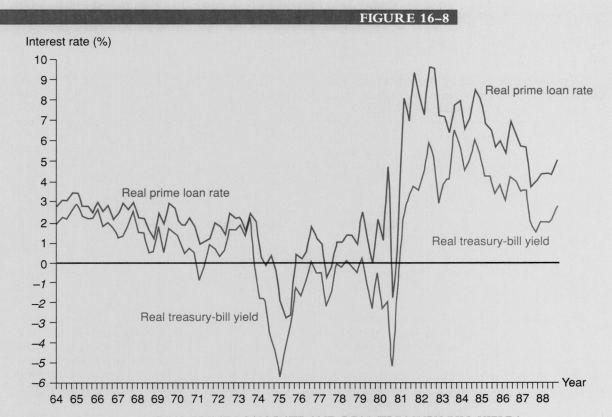

FIGURE 16–8

Interest rate (%)

Real prime loan rate

Real prime loan rate

Real treasury-bill yield

Real treasury-bill yield

Year

64 65 66 67 68 69 70 71 72 73 74 75 76 77 78 79 80 81 82 83 84 85 86 87 88

REAL PRIME LOAN RATE AND REAL TREASURY-BILL YIELD*

Real (inflation-adjusted) interest rates declined (and often became negative) in the 1970s but then increased to unusually high levels in the early 1980s.

*Real rates are calculated using Federal Reserve data for prime loan rate and Treasury-bill yield, and assumes expected inflation for each period is equal to the actual inflation rate in the most recent six months.

Federal Reserve System overreacted to the severe inflation of the 1979–1981 period and pursued a highly restrictive monetary policy. This policy allegedly maintained actual and real interest rates at abnormally high levels in the early 1980s. It seems plausible that more than one factor contributed to the unreal level of real interest rates in the 1980s.

An interesting alternative explanation is that, on deeper analysis, real interest rates actually were not high at all. If one allows for the fact that interest paid is often tax deductible and interest earned is taxable, interest rates in the 1980s do not seem unreasonable. Suppose you pay 10 percent for your bank loan while inflation is running at 4 percent and your combined federal-state-local income-tax bracket is 40 percent. If we ignore taxes, we compute the real interest rate as 6 percent—historically a very high rate. However, your *after-tax* real rate is only 2 percent.[9] If

---

[9]Because you are in a 40-percent income-tax bracket and because interest expense is tax deductible, you are paying only 60 percent of the interest. The government pays the rest. Hence, your after-tax *nominal* interest rate is 6 percent (.60 × 10 percent). Deducting the 4-percent inflation from this figure, we obtain an after-tax *real* interest rate of 2 percent.

EXHIBIT 16–1

REAL INTEREST RATES—THE CONSEQUENCES FOR INCOME
REDISTRIBUTION

The extent to which the Fisher Effect is operable—the extent to which interest rates adjust to the ongoing rate of inflation—has a powerful effect on the distribution of income in the nation and on the well-being of various sectors of the economy. Consider the following three scenarios involving the relationship between inflation and the interest rate.

occurs when financial markets are free, expectations are accurately formed, and the Fisher Effect is fully working. The interest rate is roughly three percentage points above the inflation rate, so the real interest rate is positive but rather low. There are no major redistributive effects between borrowers and lenders in this scenario in which the Fisher Effect is working to perfection.

	Scenario A(%)	Scenario B(%)	Scenario C(%)
Interest rate	10	8	12
Inflation rate	13	5	4
Real interest rate	−3	+3	+8

In Scenario A, interest rates are not sufficiently high to compensate for inflation. The real interest rate is *negative*. Debtors benefit at the expense of lenders, as inflation rapidly reduces the real value of the principal and the interest rate fails to compensate for this. Debtor groups in society generally include the government, business firms, farmers, and middle-aged people. Lenders generally include the household sector and elderly individuals. Many individuals, however, are net debtors. In fact, the classic beneficiary of Scenario A is the family of the 40-year-old breadwinner with a home financed by a $100,000 mortgage. The value of the home rises each year by an amount in excess of the interest payable on the mortgage (which is tax deductible). The real net worth of the family rises at the expense of the individuals (lenders) who placed funds in the savings institution that granted the mortgage. This scenario occurred in the 1970s as the U.S. inflation rate kept ratcheting higher, and as interest-rate ceilings and the Federal Reserve tended to inhibit rising interest rates.

Scenario B is the normal state of affairs. It

In Scenario C, the interest rate is exceptionally high in relation to the ongoing inflation rate. Real interest rates are very high. This situation occurred in the 1980–1985 period (see Figure 16-8). It also occurred in the 1930s, when interest rates were fairly low but the inflation rate was *negative*. This scenario reverses the consequences of Scenario A. Income is redistributed from debtors to lenders. The government loses and bondholders benefit. The business sector in general comes under pressure, as this sector is a net debtor on balance. Many small businesses fail. Farm foreclosures soar as the burdens of debt become overwhelming. Bank failures increase as a rising percentage of bank loans become *bad loans*. Elderly individuals as a group fare well in this scenario, as do others who lend money.

If Scenario B always prevailed, the financial markets would neutralize many damaging consequences of changes in the price level. Unfortunately, this is not always the case. The economy often takes the shape of Scenario A or C.

one adds tax considerations to the analysis, real interest rates in the 1980s seem reasonable. The actual mystery in this view is not why real rates were so high in the 1980s, but rather why they were so low in earlier years.

SUMMARY

1. An interest rate is the price of loanable funds. There are many different interest rates or yields in the economy because of differences in the characteristics of various types of loans.
2. Interest rates are determined in competitive markets by the impersonal forces of supply and demand. An increase in demand for or a decrease in supply of loanable funds raises interest rates. An increase in supply of or a decrease in demand for loanable funds reduces interest rates. The demand and supply curves for loanable funds are continually shifting about, causing frequent changes in interest rates.
3. When actual and expected inflation escalate, the supply of loanable funds decreases and the demand increases, thus raising interest rates. Hence, when inflation is rampant, interest rates are typically high. This serves to compensate lenders for depreciation of the real principal loaned due to inflation. The Fisher Effect in its strong form asserts that interest rates should rise sufficiently during inflation to preserve neutrality between lenders and borrowers. However, studies indicate that in most episodes of severe inflation borrowers benefit because interest rates fail to increase sufficiently to fully protect lenders.
4. Interest rates exhibit a strong procyclical tendency, rising in business expansions to a peak in the boom phase of the cycle and declining in recessions. This procyclical behavior of interest rates can be attributed primarily to fluctuations in the demand for loanable funds by households and businesses over the course of the business cycle.
5. The Federal Reserve System, by manipulating the supply of loanable funds, is capable of exerting a major impact on the level of interest rates. However, most major swings in interest rates historically were not initiated by deliberate Fed actions, but were attributable to cyclical factors and major swings in expected inflation.
6. Large federal budget deficits increase the demand for loanable funds and therefore raise interest rates unless the supply of loanable funds also increases. Some economists believe that the general populace responds to budget deficits by raising their current saving rate, thereby shifting the supply of loanable funds rightward and neutralizing the impact of the deficits on interest rates. Also, world financial markets have become more integrated in recent years. As U.S. interest rates begin to rise, foreign funds are attracted to the United States. Since the size of U.S. budget deficits is rather small relative to this world-wide pool of funds, the impact of deficits on U.S. interest rates may not be as large as is commonly believed.
7. Because many important economic decisions are governed by *real* interest rates, it is important to distinguish between *real* and *nominal* (actual) interest rates. The real interest rate is the rate computed after deducting the expected inflation rate from the actual interest rate. Real interest rates swung from very low levels in the 1970s to high levels in the 1980s. This major swing may be attributable to an increase in the expected productivity of capital, increased federal budget deficits, or more restrictive Federal Reserve policy. Alternatively, one could argue that real interest rates were not very high in the 1980s considering the income-tax treatment of interest income and interest expense. In this view, the real question is why real rates were so low prior to the 1980s.

KEY TERMS

interest rate	mortgage rate
prime loan rate	supply of loanable funds
Treasury bill yield	demand for loanable funds
discount rate	loanable funds model
federal funds market	Fisher Effect
federal funds rate	real interest rate
corporate bond yield	nominal (actual) interest rate

STUDY QUESTIONS AND PROBLEMS

1. Assume interest rates rise sharply next year. What impact would this have on you personally? What are the implications for the U.S. economy?
2. Distinguish between the real interest rate and the nominal interest rate. How do the concepts of time preference and productivity of capital enter into the determination of the real interest rate?
3. Note from Figure 16-2 that the Treasury bill yield is typically lower than the corporate bond yield. Can you explain why?
4. Explain why the supply curve of Figure 16-3 is upward sloping. What factors shift the supply curve leftward? If Americans change from an *enjoy-now* to a *plan-for-the-future* society, what happens to the supply curve? To interest rates?
5. Explain why the demand curve of Figure 16-3 is downward sloping. List three factors that would shift this demand curve rightward.
6. Explain the reasoning that lies behind the Fisher Effect. Using the tools of supply and demand, explain how a sharp decline in expected inflation would bring about a decline in interest rates.
7. Assume the economy slides into a period of severe recession. Explain via supply and demand analysis what would happen to interest rates.
8. Why do you suppose interest rates were so high in 1981? Why did they drop so much in 1982 (see Figures 16-1 and 16-2)?
9. Analyze the impact of increased budget deficits on the level of interest rates.
10. Obtain data from the most recent *Federal Reserve Bulletin* on the recent prime-loan rate, Treasury bill yield, and the recent trend rate of inflation. From this data compute the real prime-loan rate and the real Treasury-bill yield. How do your figures compare to the real prime rate in the mid-1980s (see Figure 16-8)? What do you think accounts for the change in these real rates since the mid-1980s?
11. How might it be that the announcement of a large increase in the U.S. money supply would lead to an *increase* in actual interest rates on long-term bonds and mortgages?

ANSWER TO YOUR TURN

The announcement makes lenders less willing to purchase bonds of XYZ Corporation. The supply curve of loanable funds to this firm shifts leftward, raising the yield on XYZ bonds. An increase in the perceived default risk on a particular bond always raises the yield on the bond (reduces the bond's price) by reducing willingness of lenders to purchase it. The yield rises sufficiently to compensate lenders for the risk involved in holding the bond.

SELECTED REFERENCES

Fisher, Irving, *The Theory of Interest* (New York: Macmillan, 1930). This is the classic treatment of the role of expected inflation in interest-rate determination.

Summers, Lawrence H., "The Nonadjustment of Nominal Interest Rates: A Study of the Fisher Effect," in James Tobin, ed., *Macroeconomics, Prices, and Quantities* (Washington: The Brookings Institution, 1983), pp. 201–241. This is a comprehensive and technical study of the Fisher Effect during the past 100 years.

Thomas, Lloyd B., *Money, Banking, and Economic Activity,* 3rd ed. (Englewood Cliffs, NJ: Prentice-Hall, 1986). Chapters 5 and 6 cover interest rates in depth.

Van Horne, James C., *Financial Markets: Rates and Flows,* 2nd ed. (Englewood Cliffs, NJ: Prentice-Hall, 1984). This work is the most comprehensive analysis of all aspects of interest rates available today. Chapter 4 summarizes much of the empirical literature on the Fisher Effect.

PART IV

INFLATION, UNEMPLOYMENT, AND ECONOMIC POLICIES

CHAPTER 17

UNEMPLOYMENT AND THE PHILLIPS CURVE

Employment is
nature's physician, and
is essential to human
happiness.

—GALEN, circa A.D. 170

When more and more
people are thrown out
of work,
unemployment results.

—CALVIN COOLIDGE,
1916

High employment of workers is one of the nation's paramount macroeconomic objectives. Jobs provide individuals and families with incomes. Moreover, jobs give people a sense of fulfillment—a sense of importance, well-being, and solidarity with society. Involuntary unemployment breeds alienation. Since the Great Depression of the 1930s, a major objective of U.S. macroeconomic policy has been to establish and maintain a high level of employment. This is perhaps the most important single function of government in the area of economics—to provide maximum opportunity for all Americans to enjoy a reasonably prosperous and fulfilling life.

As illustrated in Figure 17-1, unemployment is a worldwide problem. Some countries (Japan, Sweden) have had more success than the United States in achieving low unemployment. Other nations (France, England) have had considerably less success recently than the United States.

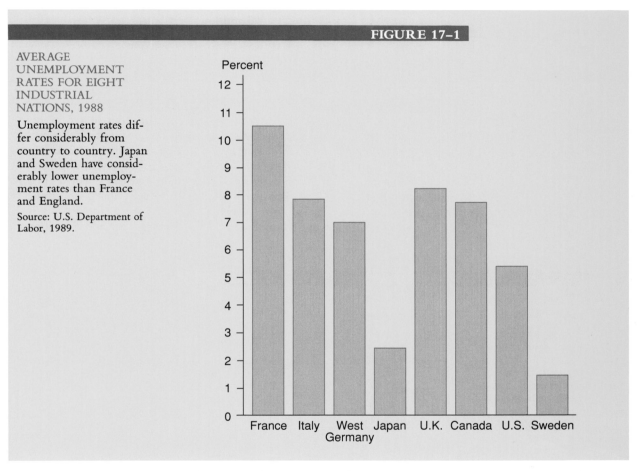

FIGURE 17–1

AVERAGE UNEMPLOYMENT RATES FOR EIGHT INDUSTRIAL NATIONS, 1988

Unemployment rates differ considerably from country to country. Japan and Sweden have considerably lower unemployment rates than France and England.

Source: U.S. Department of Labor, 1989.

MEASURING UNEMPLOYMENT IN THE UNITED STATES

To estimate the nation's unemployment rate, the Bureau of Labor Statistics (BLS) of the Department of Labor samples 56,000 U.S. households each month. Each member of the family age 16 or older is first asked whether he or she is employed. If so, the person is counted by the government as *employed.* If not employed, the person is then asked whether he or she looked for work in the last month. If the person did, then he or she is counted as *unemployed.* If not, the person is considered *not in the labor force.* The **labor force** is made up of all those who have been classified as employed plus those who have been classified as unemployed. The labor force excludes those persons who are neither working nor looking for work.

Labor Force
Those individuals 16 years of age and over who are counted as either employed or unemployed.

$$\text{labor force} = \text{those classified as employed} +$$
$$\text{those classified as unemployed}$$

The findings of the BLS 56,000 household survey are then extrapolated in order to estimate the overall U.S. unemployment rate. If the estimates for the labor force and the number unemployed are 125,000,000 and 7,500,000, respectively, the nation's **unemployment rate** is estimated to be

Unemployment Rate
The percentage of people in the labor force who are unemployed—that is, who are not working but are looking for work.

$$\text{unemployment rate} = \frac{\text{number unemployed}}{\text{number in labor force}} \times 100$$

$$U = \frac{7.5 \text{ million}}{125 \text{ million}} \times 100 = 6.0 \text{ percent}$$

The historical pattern of the U.S. unemployment rate since 1900 is depicted in Figure 17-2.

The preceding equation for measuring the unemployment rate, however, tends to understate the severity of the unemployment problem for two reasons.[1] First, anyone who is employed even for a few hours each week is counted as being employed. Many such people may be **underemployed** in the sense that they would prefer full-time work but are unable to find it. At the bottom of the 1982 recession, when 10.7 million Americans were officially listed as unemployed, another 5.9 million were reported as working part time "for economic reasons" (involuntarily working part time). Second, workers may become discouraged about job prospects after a period of unsuccessful job search and stop looking for work. Such **discouraged workers** are not counted as part of the labor force and therefore do

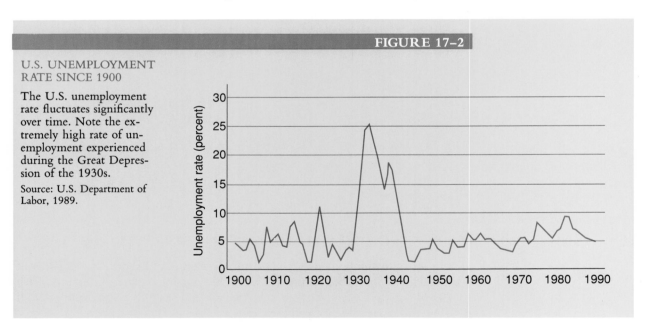

| FIGURE 17–2 |

U.S. UNEMPLOYMENT RATE SINCE 1900

The U.S. unemployment rate fluctuates significantly over time. Note the extremely high rate of unemployment experienced during the Great Depression of the 1930s.

Source: U.S. Department of Labor, 1989.

---

[1]Partially offsetting this bias, however, is the fact that the following *are* counted as unemployed: people who register for work in order to qualify for welfare but who really do not want work and persons who do not find work because they have set unrealistic demands in terms of salary or other aspects of the job (such as hours of work).

not show up in the unemployment statistics. The understatement of unemployment because of discouraged workers is especially significant in periods of economic recession when unemployment is high and job prospects are bleak. In such circumstances, millions of people may stop actively searching for work. These discouraged workers, who are not counted as being officially unemployed, are known as the **hidden unemployed.** Hidden unemployment increases significantly when the economy weakens and the reported unemployment rate rises. At the bottom of the 1982 recession it was estimated that 1.8 million workers wanted jobs but were not looking because they thought none were available.

Hidden Unemployed
Discouraged workers who stop seeking work and are not counted as unemployed.

This line of argument suggests that when unemployment is rising during an economic downturn, the increase in the reported unemployment rate *understates* the additional hardship felt by individuals and families. However, there is a mitigating consideration. Many of those who become officially (or hidden) unemployed during hard times are **secondary workers** in a family—workers in households in which two or more members are labor force participants. If the primary family breadwinner remains fully employed but a spouse or teenage son or daughter becomes unemployed (officially or hidden), one could argue that things are not as bad as they sound.

Labor Force Participation Rate
The percentage of the working-age population that is in the labor force.

An important labor-market concept is the **labor force participation rate (LFPR)**—the fraction of the population age 16 and above officially in the labor force. Among approximately 187 million working-age (16 and older) civilians in 1989, roughly 124 million were in the labor force. Hence, the LEPR of 16-and-over civilians was roughly 66 percent. This is the primary measure of the LFPR. One could compute the labor force participation rate for such other subsets of the population as teenagers, blacks, women, men over age 60, and so forth. A demographic phenomenon with important economic implications is the fact that the LFPR of women in the United States has trended strongly upward from 20 percent in 1900 to more than 55 percent today.

$$\text{labor force participation rate (LFPR)} = \frac{\text{labor force}}{\text{population}} \times 100$$

CATEGORIES OF UNEMPLOYMENT

For conceptual purposes it is useful to classify unemployment into three categories: frictional, structural, and cyclical or deficient-demand unemployment.

Frictional Unemployment

Frictional Unemployment
Unemployment due to normal job search by individuals who have quit their jobs, are initially entering the labor force, or are reentering the labor force.

Given the method for measuring the U.S. unemployment rate, it is inevitable that a significant number of normally employed people happen to be between jobs for a brief period at the time of the survey. One worker may have quit a job to look for another. Another worker may have been fired one week before the survey and may end up finding a new job three weeks later. Another individual may be seeking initial employment one month after graduating from high school or college. In a dynamic and free labor market, it is inevitable on any given day that a substantial number of viable workers are gainfully involved in the labor-market search process. Such individuals who are temporarily *in the pipeline* are considered to be **frictionally unemployed.** While the volume of frictional unemployment fluctuates with the state of the economy, demographic factors, and other considerations, perhaps two to four percent of the labor force are frictionally unemployed at a given point of time.

Workers differ in background, skill, and other characteristics. Jobs differ in terms of working conditions, required skills, concentration and effort required, and the like. It therefore takes time to line up the right workers in the right jobs. It is often rational for a worker to remain unemployed for several weeks, even though jobs are being offered, in order to find a better job. Only in a totalitarian society or one in which workers are never willing to leave a job to seek a better alternative would one observe little or no frictional unemployment. Frictional unemployment is a normal manifestation of a healthy, vibrant labor market.

Structural Unemployment

Structural Unemployment
Unemployment due to structural changes in the economy; the portion of unemployment accounted for by those out of work for long periods because their skills do not match those required for available jobs.

Structural unemployment results from important changes in the structure of the economy and other factors that create a mismatch between job skills sought by employers and job skills possessed by unemployed individuals. Unlike frictional unemployment, structural unemployment constitutes a serious national problem. In the case of structural unemployment, lots of job vacancies coexist for long periods of time with lots of unemployed workers. The vacancies perhaps call for skills in accounting, engineering, or the use of computers and other high-tech equipment. The unemployed workers may be trained in areas of low demand or, more likely, possess few skills because they never attended college or perhaps even dropped out of high school. The latter individuals frequently do not possess the technical skills required by employers in a modern society. In general, the level of skills sought by employers with vacant jobs significantly exceeds the skills possessed by the structurally unemployed.

A continuing pool of structural unemployment persists because of continuing changes in technology, the structure of government and private expenditures, and other factors. The supply of workers with particular skills adapts to an increase in demand with a significant time lag. In the 1950s the coal mining industry introduced automated mining equipment at the same time that millions of American households converted their home heating systems from coal to natural gas or oil. Demand for coal miners dropped sharply and large pockets of structural unemployment cropped up in Appalachia and other U.S. coal mining regions. Many of these workers were 40–60 years of age and found it quite difficult to retool, move to a new region or city, and find alternative work. In the mid-1980s, while the U.S. service sector was booming, special circumstances created problems in many portions of the agriculture and manufacturing sectors. In particular, an unusually strong dollar in foreign-exchange markets during 1983–1985 put American industries subject to foreign competition at a disadvantage. Thousands of blue-collar workers in the steel, textile, automobile (and other) industries lost their jobs. More recently, workers in industries serving national defense were hurt by cuts in defense spending triggered by heightened budget-deficit awareness.

Even in a booming economy, a residue of structural unemployment persists. To attack this problem, incentive programs and microeconomic policies to improve job training and labor mobility have been tried from time to time. In general, a massive upgrading of the education and job-skill levels of the bottom one-third of youngsters coming through our school systems would be required to substantially reduce structural unemployment. Barring such a Herculean achievement, it is difficult to be optimistic about solving the problem of structural unemployment. Stimulative monetary and fiscal policies are relatively inefficient means of attacking the problem, though a vibrant and strong economy is essential if the massive uplifting of education, job skills, and training are to have a chance to succeed in sharply reducing the magnitude of structural unemployment.

Cyclical Unemployment

Cyclical Unemployment
Unemployment attributable to inadequate aggregate demand; the difference between the actual unemployment rate and the unemployment rate associated with full employment.

Cyclical unemployment—the component of unemployment most sensitive to the business cycle—occurs when the economy is operating at an output level below its potential. Cyclical unemployment is sometimes called "deficient-demand" unemployment because it typically is associated with levels of aggregate spending (aggregate demand) too low to call forth a high level of output and employment. When economic activity is far below capacity levels, demand for labor is low and millions of normally employed and productive individuals are involuntarily out of work for a sustained period. As the economy picks up strength, these people are put back to work. At the peak of the business cycle we typically approach *full employment,* a condition in which cyclical unemployment is eliminated. In today's economy, *full employment* is probably consistent with a reported unemployment rate of 5 to 5.5 percent. Cyclical unemployment is the type of unemployment most potentially amenable to eradication via stimulative monetary and fiscal policy measures.

The Fuzzy Line Separating the Three Types of Unemployment

Care should be taken not to overstate the distinction among frictional, structural, and cyclical unemployment. All three types of unemployment may respond to the overall state of the economy. When aggregate demand and output strengthen materially, cyclical unemployment declines as firms step up output and hire workers. But frictional and structural unemployment are also likely to decline somewhat. The number and quality of job vacancies increase, thereby reducing average search time required by many individuals to find the desired job. This reduces the amount of frictional unemployment. A stronger economy is also likely to reduce structural unemployment, as firms are more likely to hire workers with marginal skills and train them for productive work. During the economic booms associated with World War II and the Korean War of the early 1950s, the U.S. unemployment rate fell below three percent. At the end of the long economic expansion of the 1960s, when the U.S. economy was clearly in a state of excessively stimulated activity, the unemployment rate remained somewhat above three percent. Most economists believe that, under similar conditions today, this minimal unemployment rate would be at least one percentage point higher than in the late 1960s.

Figure 17-3 (page 370) indicates certain characteristics of unemployment that provide insight into its nature. Figure 17-3(a) shows the distribution of the unemployed by duration of unemployment. More than 40 percent of total unemployment involves people out of work for less than 5 weeks; less than 20 percent of the unemployed typically remain out of work for more than 27 weeks. In recessions, the incidence of long-term unemployment always increases. As economic expansion occurred following the 1981–1982 recession, the proportion of the unemployed who were out of work for short periods increased while the proportion out of work for long periods declined.

Figure 17-3(b) shows the proportion of the unemployed that lost jobs (were fired or laid off), voluntarily left jobs, were reentrants to the labor force after a period of absence, or were entrants to the labor force for the first time. Approximately one-half of the unemployed lost work, 10 percent quit, and 40 percent reentered

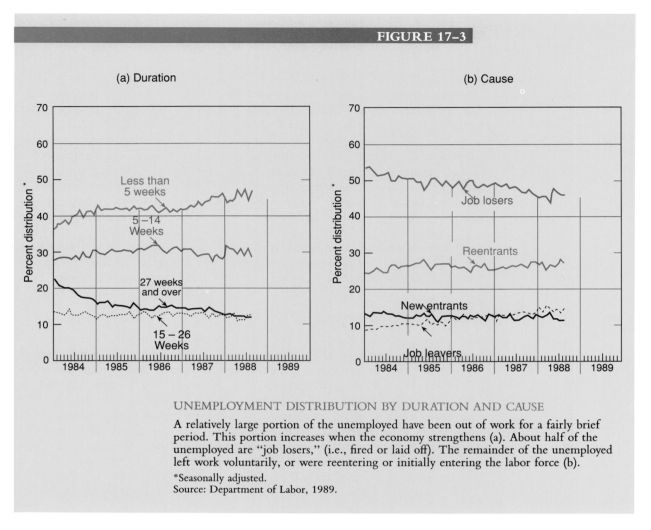

FIGURE 17–3

UNEMPLOYMENT DISTRIBUTION BY DURATION AND CAUSE

A relatively large portion of the unemployed have been out of work for a fairly brief period. This portion increases when the economy strengthens (a). About half of the unemployed are "job losers," (i.e., fired or laid off). The remainder of the unemployed left work voluntarily, or were reentering or initially entering the labor force (b).

*Seasonally adjusted.
Source: Department of Labor, 1989.

or initially entered the labor force. The proportion of the unemployed who are job losers rises when an economic downturn occurs. Conversely, as (b) shows, the proportion of job losers in the total pool of unemployment declines during business cycle expansions (1984–1989).

THE *FULL-EMPLOYMENT* UNEMPLOYMENT RATE—THE NATURAL RATE OF UNEMPLOYMENT

Full employment does not imply zero unemployment. In fact, the lowest U.S. unemployment rate for any single year in the past 35 years is 3.5 percent (1969). In the four most-recent business cycles, the low point on the unemployment rate cycle—which occurs near the peak of the business cycle—has produced an average unemployment rate of 5.3 percent. Most economists today believe that efforts to push the reported unemployment rate below 5 percent via stimulative macroeconomic policies would unleash powerful forces that would accelerate the inflation rate in labor and product markets.

Natural Rate of Unemployment
The minimum sustainable unemployment rate below which inflation tends to accelerate; the percentage of the labor force either frictionally or structurally unemployed.

The unemployment rate that would prevail if actual GNP were precisely equal to potential GNP has been dubbed the **natural rate of unemployment.** We might regard it as the unemployment rate existing when cyclical unemployment is eliminated, leaving only the core of frictional and structural unemployment. Some economists dislike the connotation of the term since the natural rate of unemployment fluctuates over time and since there is nothing *natural* or *good* about a situation in which millions of people remain involuntarily out of work because of structural unemployment. Some economists have suggested an alternative, though cumbersome term—**NAIRU** (nonaccelerating inflation rate of unemployment)—since the natural unemployment rate is defined as the lowest unemployment rate that could be sustained without touching off an acceleration in the existing rate of inflation. At NAIRU or the natural unemployment rate, wages and prices may be rising but the inflation rates are *stable*—they are neither accelerating nor decelerating. Labor markets are in a state of balance, with expectations of inflation adapted fully to the ongoing rate of inflation. There is neither excessive nor deficient demand for labor. Inasmuch as the term "natural unemployment rate" has been accepted in the economics literature, we use it in this book.

Fluctuations in the Natural Unemployment Rate

The natural unemployment rate fluctuates over time, and there is a strong consensus that it increased significantly between the early 1960s and the early 1980s. Several factors contributed to this phenomenon. Most importantly, the percentage of the U.S. labor force made up of young workers (under age 25) increased steadily in this period because of the *baby boom* of 1946–1964. The baby boom produced a sustained increase in the number of 18-year-olds coming into the labor force after 1963. Young workers on average exhibit weaker job attachment and higher labor-market turnover rates than older workers. Hence, frictional unemployment rates are higher for younger workers. Structural unemployment also is relatively high among young workers because of their lack of job skills. The influx of young workers into the labor force from the mid-1960s to the early 1980s pulled up the nation's frictional and structural unemployment rates. The natural unemployment rate increased.

In the same period a major and sustained increase in the labor force participation rate of women took place. Like youthful workers, women on average have exhibited higher turnover rates and higher frictional unemployment rates than adult males. The increasing proportion of the labor force comprised of women contributed to the increase in frictional and natural unemployment rates. In addition, the nation generally liberalized its provision of benefits for unemployed workers. This reduced the personal financial hardship of being unemployed and allowed individuals to be more selective and deliberate in their job search. The lengthening of average search time raises the frictional and the natural unemployment rate.

Since the early 1980s, at least one of these factors has worked in reverse—*lowering* the natural unemployment rate. Because the American birthrate dropped after 1964, the number of youths graduating from high school and entering the labor force began to decline around 1982. This factor and the gradual aging of the *baby boomers* worked to pull down the natural unemployment rate. Although the labor force participation rate of women may continue to increase in the future, it seems unlikely to increase faster than in the past 25 years. Furthermore, the skill levels of women in the labor force are increasing and female turnover rates are declining. It therefore seems likely that the natural unemployment rate in the early 1990s will be lower than it was a decade earlier.

Government Policies to Reduce the Natural Rate of Unemployment

If output could be boosted above *potential GNP* by reducing unemployment below the natural unemployment rate, gains would accrue to society in terms of higher incomes and living standards. Offsetting this gain, however, would be an unacceptable acceleration of inflation and other problems. No one, therefore, advocates deliberate use of monetary and fiscal policy to push the unemployment rate below the natural rate. However, if the *natural unemployment rate itself* could be reduced via policy measures, we could aim for higher living standards and lower unemployment rates without experiencing the scourge of accelerating inflation.

Microeconomic programs with incentives to improve the functioning of labor markets have been suggested. Labor-market information services with computerized job lists and training opportunities might reduce frictional and structural unemployment. Some have advocated public service employment—the government serving as an *employer of last resort.* A less radical proposal would have the government simply remove some of the obstacles that its own institutions and laws have created. For example, the social security, welfare, and disability insurance programs could be altered to increase incentives to work and earn income. The system of unemployment insurance could be redesigned along the same lines. Finally, a reduction in the level of the minimum wage or establishment of a subminimum wage for youths could remove an obstacle that blocks employment prospects for many unskilled young individuals. Experience and labor market research, however, suggest that the potential for policy-induced reductions in the natural unemployment rate is not dramatic.

CONSEQUENCES OF UNEMPLOYMENT

Several adverse effects occur when unemployment increases significantly. The most straightforward economic consequence of unemployment is the resulting sacrifice of aggregate output and income in the nation. In addition, the *distribution of the impact* of unemployment is highly uneven—it falls disproportionately on such disadvantaged groups as ethnic minorities, unskilled workers, youth, and the lower-economic classes. Moreover, a rise in unemployment induces social problems such as delinquency, alcoholism, and mental debilitation; reduces government tax revenues and thereby impairs the provision of public goods such as streets and roads and other infrastructure; and probably impairs the economy's longer-term growth prospects. In Exhibit 17-1 we sketch certain of the noneconomic consequences of unemployment.

Loss of Output and Income

An increase in unemployment above the natural rate moves us further below society's production possibilities curve. An increase in unemployment shrinks the nation's output and income, thereby reducing the standard of living of the nation as a whole. There is simply less income to be distributed in the nation. The relationship between the U.S. unemployment rate and this loss of output at any time is quantified

EXHIBIT 17–1

THE HUMAN TRAGEDY OF UNEMPLOYMENT

In discussing unemployment it is essential to keep in mind that the consequences go far beyond the purely economic effects. In our culture, an individual's perception of personal worth and self-esteem is tied to working—maintaining a job. Social scientists believe that next to the death of one's spouse or being sent to jail, involuntary loss of one's job is among the most traumatic and stressful experiences of life. If society cares about the individuals that constitute the society, then full employment is a desirable goal for social as well as economic reasons.

A leading U.S. student of the personal consequences of unemployment has estimated that a one-percentage point increase in the nation's unemployment rate sustained over a six-year period leads to an additional*

    920 suicides

    648 homicides

    495 deaths from cirrhosis of the liver

20,240 fatal heart attacks or strokes

37,000 total premature deaths

  3340 admissions to state prisons

  4227 admissions to mental hospitals

The dimensions of the personal consequences of unemployment may be glimpsed through the following personal recollection from the 1930s and the photograph from the 1980s.

Hell yes. Everybody was a criminal. You stole, you cheated through. You were getting by, survival. Stole clothes off lines, stole milk off back porches, you stole bread. I remember going through Tucumcari, New Mexico, on a freight. We made a brief stop. There was a grocery store, a supermarket kind of thing for those days. I beat it off the train and came back with rolls and crackers. This guy is standing in the window shaking his fist at you.

It wasn't a big thing, but it created a coyote mentality. You were a predator. You had to be. The coyote is crafty. He can be fantastically courageous and a coward at the same time. He'll run, but when he's cornered, he'll fight. I grew up where they were hated, 'cause they'd kill sheep. They'll kill a calf, get in the chicken pen. They're mean. But how else does a coyote stay alive? He's not as powerful as a wolf. He has a small body. He's in such bad condition, a dog can run him down. He's not like a fox. A coyote is nature's victim as well as man's. We were coyotes in the Thirties, the jobless.**

*Harvey Brenner, "Estimating the Social Costs of National Economic Policy: Implications for Mental and Physical Health, and Criminal Aggression," study prepared for the Joint Economic Committee, U.S. Congress (Washington, DC, October 1976).

**Studs Terkel, *Hard Times* (New York: Pantheon Books, 1970), page 34.

EATING FROM A MCDONALD'S DUMPSTER—THE 1980s

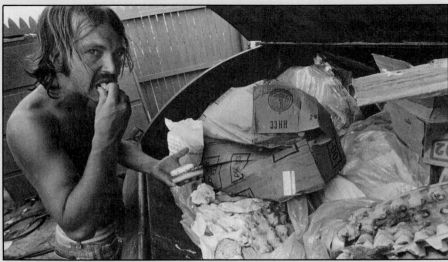

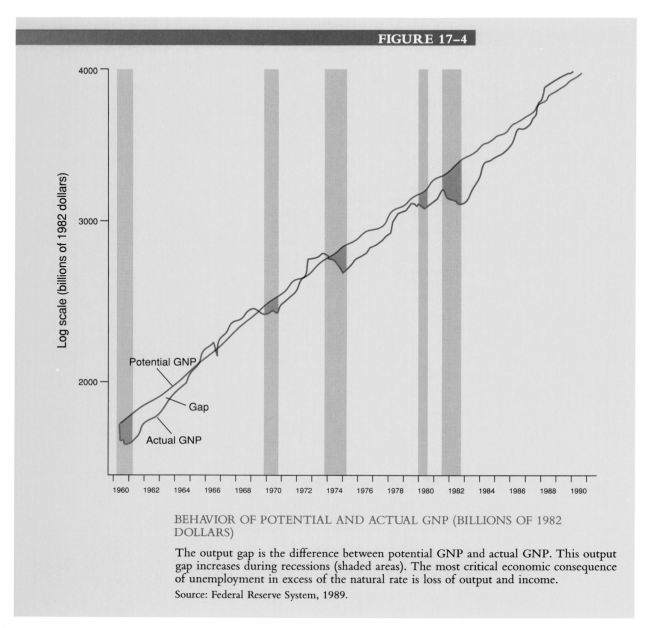

FIGURE 17-4

BEHAVIOR OF POTENTIAL AND ACTUAL GNP (BILLIONS OF 1982 DOLLARS)

The output gap is the difference between potential GNP and actual GNP. This output gap increases during recessions (shaded areas). The most critical economic consequence of unemployment in excess of the natural rate is loss of output and income.

Source: Federal Reserve System, 1989.

in what has become known as *Okun's Law*. Arthur Okun, member and Chairman of the President's Council of Economic Advisors in the 1960s, was concerned about the national sacrifice or waste associated with the operation of the economy at an output level significantly below the full-employment level. To understand this cost, consider Figure 17-4, which illustrates actual and potential GNP since the early 1960s.

Potential GNP may be defined as the hypothetical level of output that would be produced if there were no cyclical unemployment. Alternatively, we could define it as the magnitude of GNP that would be produced if the actual unemployment rate were precisely equal to the economy's natural unemployment rate. Potential GNP rises over time because of growth of the labor force and expansion of labor productivity—output per worker. At any point in time, actual GNP may deviate from potential GNP because the unemployment rate deviates from the natural rate of unemployment. Occasionally, when the economy exhibits extreme exuberance, the unemployment rate falls below the natural rate and actual GNP rises above potential (1967–1969, 1973, and 1989 in Figure 17-4). Much more commonly, the nation's unemployment rate exceeds the natural rate and actual GNP falls short of potential GNP. In this case an **output gap** or recessionary gap exists.

In Figure 17-4, shaded areas indicate periods of recession—periods when real output is declining. Unshaded areas indicate periods of expanding economic activity. Most of the time an output gap has existed as output has remained below potential. **Okun's Law,** which estimates the relationship between the nation's unemployment rate and this loss of output, may be expressed in equation form:

$$\frac{\text{potential GNP} - \text{actual GNP}}{\text{actual GNP}} = 2.5(U - 5.5\%) \qquad (17\text{-}1)$$

The left side of the equation expresses the dollar magnitude of the GNP gap—the gap between actual and potential GNP at any point in time—as a percentage of actual GNP. Hence, if potential and actual GNP are running at rates of $5200 billion per year and $5000 billion per year, respectively, the output gap is four percent of actual GNP. If actual and potential GNP are each $5200 billion per year, there is no output gap.

On the right side of the equation, U represents the unemployment rate. The expression states that each one percentage point of unemployment above the *full-employment* or *natural* unemployment rate (assumed to be 5.5 percent) is associated with a 2.5-percent output gap. Hence, if the unemployment rate is 7.5 percent currently, the output gap is 5 percent—the gap is running at 5 percent of actual GNP. If (in a severe recession year like 1982) unemployment averages 9.5 percent, the economy is operating with a 10-percent output gap. In the $3000 billion (GNP) 1982 U.S. economy, the output gap was running at approximately $300 billion per year, or a loss of income averaging roughly $1200 per year for each man, woman, and child.[2]

Output Gap
The magnitude by which actual GNP falls short of potential GNP.

Okun's Law
Estimated relationship between the unemployment rate and the national loss of output; each one percent of unemployment above the natural unemployment rate is associated with a 2.5 percent gap between actual and potential GNP.

YOUR TURN

Assume the economy turns weak in 1991 and the unemployment rate increases to eight percent. Using Okun's Law as expressed in Equation 17-1, calculate the 1991 loss of output if actual GNP is $5500 billion in 1991.

Distribution of the Impact of Increased Unemployment

If (when the unemployment rate rises from 5.5 percent to 7.5 percent) each American loses five percent of annual income, the financial burden of the unemployment is shared equally. But this is hardly what happens. Instead, the burden falls predominately upon a small segment of society—those thrown out of

[2]Since demographic factors and other important aspects of the economy change over time, the precise magnitude of the parameters of Equation 17-1 also change over time. Unlike the laws of physics or astronomy, economics laws are not constant over the years. In the 1970s, a large influx of women and teenagers into the labor force occurred. This temporarily raised the natural unemployment rate above the 5.5 percent level presumed in Equation 17-1. In the 1990s, it is likely that the aging of the post-World War II *baby boomers* will reduce the natural unemployment rate. Hence, the 5.5-percent estimate of the natural unemployment rate in Equation 17-1 may soon be replaced by perhaps 5.0 percent.

	TABLE 17-1	
UNEMPLOYMENT RATES (%) FOR VARIOUS GROUPS		
Group	**November 1982**	**April 1989**
White workers, total	9.6	4.6
Black workers, total	18.7	10.8
White teenagers	21.3	12.3
Black teenagers	46.0	30.8
White males over age 20	9.0	4.0
Black males over age 20	17.6	10.0
Overall unemployment rate	10.7	5.3

Source: Bureau of Labor Statistics, *Monthly Labor Review,* 1982 and 1989.

work and their families. A large portion of the unemployed are low-income, unskilled workers heavily composed of minority groups and youthful workers. A crude rule of thumb is that the unemployment rate of blacks is double that of whites. Hence, a one-percentage point increase in the white unemployment rate in an economic downturn is likely to be accompanied by a two-percentage point rise in unemployment of black workers. Unemployment rates of teenagers are several times that of white workers over age 20. Unemployment rates of black teenagers fluctuate within a range of roughly 25–50 percent, depending on the state of the economy.

Table 17-1 gives the unemployment rate of selected groups at two points in time: November 1982 and April 1989. The first date represents a point of very weak economic activity, the trough of the most severe recession of the past 50 years. The second date represents a time of very strong economic activity, when the U.S. economy was near the peak of the business cycle. Note the differential impact of increased unemployment across groups in 1982 relative to the prosperous year 1989: the unemployment rate of white workers in 1982 was 5-percentage points higher; the unemployment rates of blacks, black teenagers, and white teenagers were roughly 8-percentage points, 15-percentage points, and 9-percentage points higher, respectively. Another indicator of the uneven impact of unemployment across groups is illustrated in Figure 17-5, which shows unemployment rates of college graduates and high-school (only) graduates over a recent two-decade period.

As expected, Figure 17-5 confirms that unemployment rates of college graduates are always lower than for those who have only a high-school education (the unemployment rate for high-school dropouts, though not illustrated, is much higher). Note that while unemployment rates of both high-school and college graduates increase in recessions (shaded areas), the gap widens significantly. The burden of increased unemployment falls more heavily on those with less education. Note that the gap between the two unemployment rates has widened since the early 1970s. A college diploma seems to be an even better insurance policy against unemployment today than in earlier times.

Other Consequences of Unemployment

Sociologists have established that crime rates, juvenile delinquency, and alcoholism are linked to the unemployment rate (see Exhibit 17-1; page 373). So are the

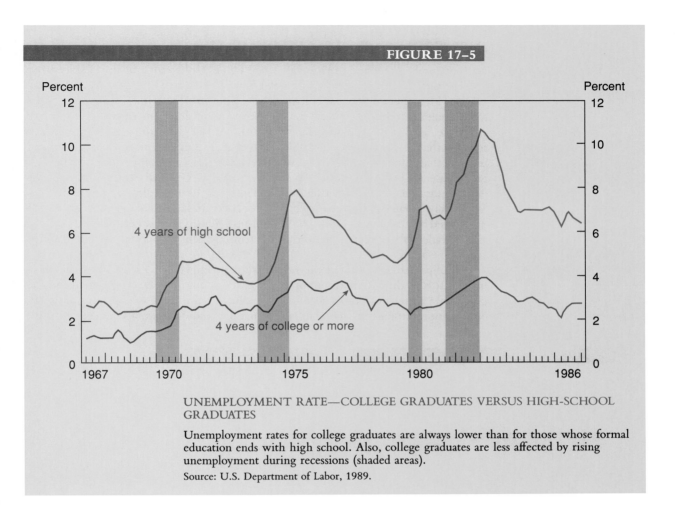

FIGURE 17–5

UNEMPLOYMENT RATE—COLLEGE GRADUATES VERSUS HIGH-SCHOOL GRADUATES

Unemployment rates for college graduates are always lower than for those whose formal education ends with high school. Also, college graduates are less affected by rising unemployment during recessions (shaded areas).

Source: U.S. Department of Labor, 1989.

incidence of mental health problems, suicide, and other social maladies. Also (returning to economic considerations), when unemployment is high and output is depressed, fewer revenues flow into state and local government treasuries. After some time lag, one is therefore likely to observe a deterioration in the quality of such public services as streets, parks, libraries, and university educational facilities as a result of lower levels of economic activity.[3] Finally, in addition to shrinking the nation's *current* standard of living, severe unemployment may have longer-run effects on the economy's productive capacity. By depriving young individuals of an early opportunity to gain jobs skills and a viable livelihood, attitudes and motivation levels may be adversely affected. This factor—coupled with impairment of business profits, government support of scientific research, and investment spending during economic downturns—may mean that the *future level of potential GNP* may be adversely affected by a high current level of unemployment.

---

[3]The federal government also suffers a reduction of revenues during economic downturns. Unlike the federal government, however, state and local governments typically are required to balance their budgets. Hence, they have no choice but to slash budgets and cut back provisions of services.

THE PHILLIPS CURVE—THE TRADE-OFF BETWEEN INFLATION AND UNEMPLOYMENT

Both unemployment and inflation are undesirable. Unhappily, much evidence from the past indicates the existence of a short-run conflict between the goal of creating full employment and the goal of maintaining price-level stability. Ideally, one hopes that monetary and fiscal policies can be adjusted to push the unemployment rate to a very low level without touching off any inflation. Unfortunately, the evidence suggests that this may not be possible. Early studies provided evidence that seems to indicate that inflationary forces begin to set in when the economy is well short of full employment—before actual GNP reaches potential GNP. Furthermore, this evidence indicated that the inflation rate accelerates as the unemployment rate declines. Statistical evidence of this *trade-off* conflict between inflation and unemployment was discovered by British economist A. W. Phillips. The hypothesis of the existence of a stable trade-off between inflation and unemployment is known as the **Phillips Curve.**

Phillips Curve
A graph illustrating the relationship between the unemployment rate and the rate of inflation.

Phillips actually studied the relationship in England between the unemployment rate and the inflation rate of *wages.* Over a long period of British history he observed a pattern of points such as those illustrated in Figure 17-6. In the figure, each point represents the actual unemployment rate and the average percentage wage

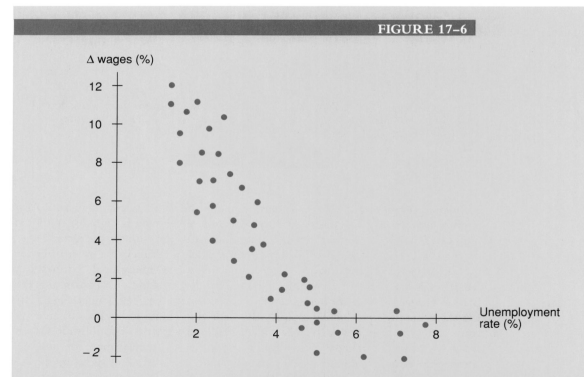

FIGURE 17–6

RATE OF CHANGE IN WAGES AND UNEMPLOYMENT RATES IN ENGLAND FOR VARIOUS YEARS

A. W. Phillips discovered that, in England, wages increased rapidly in years when the nation's unemployment rate was low. Wages increased more slowly or even declined in years when the unemployment rate was high. This statistical relationship formed the basis of what came to be called the "Phillips Curve."

hike in England for a particular year. Phillips was struck by the powerful tendency for wages to rise rapidly in years of low unemployment and for wages to rise more slowly in years of high unemployment. In years of extremely high unemployment, the rate of change in wages was typically *negative*—the *level* of wages actually *declined.*

Phillips did not offer any explanation or hypothesis to account for the powerful statistical relationship. However, subsequent economists did so, and we turn to the theoretical underpinnings of the Phillips Curve momentarily.

Since wages make up the major portion of production costs, the rate of wage increase and the rate of inflation are highly correlated. Large wage hikes lead to large price hikes; modest wage increases are typically associated with modest inflation. Because the rate of inflation is of more interest to economists than the rate of wage increase, the Phillips Curve was reestimated with the inflation rate on the vertical axis. Such a Phillips Curve, as conventionally drawn, is shown in Figure 17-7.

In Figure 17-7, note again that the rate of *inflation* is indicated along the vertical axis. This conventional Phillips Curve indicates the terms of the hypothesized trade-off between inflation and unemployment. Low unemployment is alleged to be associated with relatively high inflation; high unemployment tends on average to be associated with low inflation.

The terms of the trade-off are indicated by the *slope* of the Phillips Curve. The slope in Figure 17-7 shows the extra inflation incurred when the unemployment rate is reduced by one percentage point. Alternatively stated, the slope indicates the reduction in inflation obtained when the unemployment rate rises by one percentage point. As traditionally drawn, the Phillips Curve is relatively flat at high unemployment rates and becomes steeper as unemployment declines. As unemployment declines, the terms of the trade-off *worsen* as larger increases in inflation are required to obtain equal successive reductions in unemployment.

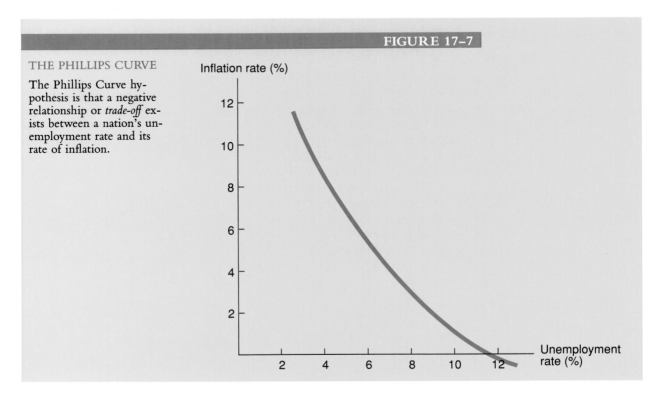

FIGURE 17–7

THE PHILLIPS CURVE

The Phillips Curve hypothesis is that a negative relationship or *trade-off* exists between a nation's unemployment rate and its rate of inflation.

THEORETICAL INTUITION UNDERLYING THE PHILLIPS CURVE

How can we rationalize the alleged existence of a Phillips Curve—the existence of a trade-off between inflation and unemployment—as depicted in Figure 17-7? There are several potential explanations that appear intuitively plausible: a theory of wage behavior based on labor-management bargaining, a structural explanation, and an aggregate demand-aggregate supply explanation.

Bargaining Hypothesis

Suppose average wage hikes in the nation are determined via a bargaining process between representatives of labor and management. When the economy is booming and unemployment is low, one expects large wage hikes to be forthcoming on average. The bargaining advantage goes to labor in this situation because sales are very strong, profits are doing nicely, and there is little in the way of alternative labor available to firms because unemployment is quite low. The cost to firms of a strike is extremely high in this scenario. Large wage hikes tend to emerge in such circumstances. Workers demand big pay hikes and firms are willing to grant such wage increases because market conditions are such that firms can shift the increased costs onto consumers via higher prices. On the other hand, when unemployment is high, the tables are turned and management has the upper hand in the negotiations. Sales and profits are down, alternative workers may be available to firms, and the cost of a strike is relatively low. Firms know that significant price hikes cannot be made to stick in a sluggish economic environment, so they adopt a hard-nosed approach in negotiations and tend to grant very meager wage hikes. Because average price-level inflation is closely connected to average wage increases in the nation, this reasoning implies that inflation and unemployment rates are inversely related.

Structural Explanation

Assume initially we are far to the right on the Phillips Curve of Figure 17-7. Unemployment is high and almost all sectors of the economy exhibit excess productive capacity. There is very little pressure for price increases in any of the industries, and the nation's inflation rate is therefore low. As the economy expands and unemployment declines, the pace of expansion is not uniform across all sectors of the economy. A few sectors hit full capacity and begin to experience rapid price increases even when the nation's unemployment rate is still at, say, seven or eight percent. As the expansion proceeds and unemployment declines below seven percent, more and more sectors reach full capacity. They run into *production bottlenecks,* or inability to expand output, and sharp price increases occur. Finally, when unemployment is reduced to approximately five percent, prices are rising in almost all sectors of the economy. Since the proportion of the nation's industries or sectors experiencing these inflationary pressures increases as the unemployment rate falls, this reasoning indicates the existence of a Phillips Curve—a negative relationship between inflation and unemployment.

A General Aggregate Supply-Aggregate Demand Explanation

Over time, both the nation's aggregate demand curve and its aggregate supply curve shift outward (rightward). The aggregate supply curve drifts rightward over time because of increases in such resources as labor and capital and increases in productivity. The amount of output that firms collectively produce at each and every price level expands with labor force, capital stock, and productivity growth. Aggregate demand also rises over time because of such factors as increases in household and government expenditures and growth of the nation's money supply. Furthermore, the aggregate demand curve typically shifts rightward faster than the aggregate supply curve. Consider the analysis depicted in Figure 17-8.

From an initial equilibrium at A, suppose aggregate supply increases from AS_1 to AS_2 in a one-year period. This moves us to B in Figure 17-8. However, suppose aggregate demand also increases (shifts rightward) by a relatively large amount, to AD_2, moving the equilibrium to C. The move from A to C implies higher equilibrium levels of prices and real output. As the price level moves from P_1 to P_2, we experience inflation. The *rate* of inflation is positively related to the magnitude of the change in the equilibrium price level—to the difference between P_2 and P_1.

Now, to demonstrate how this framework can generate a trade-off between inflation and unemployment (a Phillips Curve), suppose further that aggregate demand had shifted by a different amount than from AD_1 to AD_2. First, suppose the aggregate demand schedule had shifted farther to the right than to AD_2. Then the new equilibrium price level and output level would have exceeded P_2 and Y_2, respectively. This implies that inflation would have been more severe and unemployment would have been lower (since real output would have increased by a larger amount) than was the case when aggregate demand shifted from AD_1 to AD_2. We would have moved up and to the left along a Phillips Curve. Alternatively, suppose aggregate demand had shifted up by a *lesser* amount than indicated by the move from AD_1 to AD_2. Then both output growth and price-level inflation would have proceeded more slowly. The slower output growth (accompanied by lower inflation) would have resulted in a higher unemployment rate. We would have moved downward and rightward along a Phillips Curve. We can see that a world in which

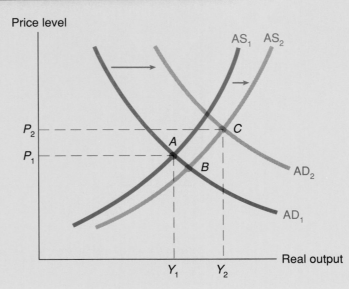

FIGURE 17–8

AGGREGATE SUPPLY-AND-DEMAND BEHAVIOR AND THE PHILLIPS CURVE

The greater the rightward shift of the aggregate demand curve, the more rapid the increase in price level and the greater the new level of output (lower the unemployment rate). A downward-sloping Phillips Curve is generated when shifts in the nation's aggregate supply curve are dominated by shifts in the aggregate demand curve.

aggregate demand consistently shifts outward by a larger (though varying) magnitude than does aggregate supply generates a series of unemployment rate and inflation rate observations that would trace out a negative relationship between inflation and unemployment—a Phillips Curve of the nature illustrated in Figure 17-7.[4]

THE SHIFTING PHILLIPS CURVE

The conception of the Phillips Curve as a stable and predictable inverse relationship between inflation and unemployment reached its high point in the late 1960s. After that, it collapsed. Figure 17-9 depicts the *actual combinations* of inflation and unemployment prevailing each year since 1963. In the 1960s, inflation and unemployment rates clustered along a well-defined Phillips Curve (shown in the lower left segment of the figure). However, since the 1960s, the points no longer fall

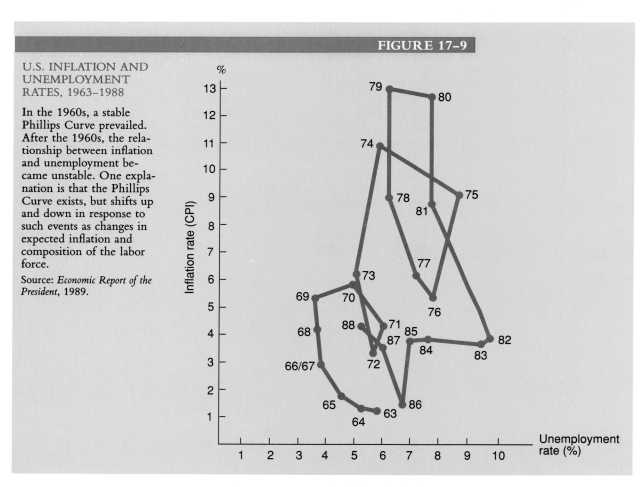

FIGURE 17–9

U.S. INFLATION AND UNEMPLOYMENT RATES, 1963–1988

In the 1960s, a stable Phillips Curve prevailed. After the 1960s, the relationship between inflation and unemployment became unstable. One explanation is that the Phillips Curve exists, but shifts up and down in response to such events as changes in expected inflation and composition of the labor force.

Source: *Economic Report of the President*, 1989.

---

[4]On the other hand, if the aggregate supply curve shifts by a larger amount than the aggregate demand curve, we would derive a *positively* sloped Phillips Curve. Can you demonstrate this? In the *supply-shock* inflation of 1974–1975, we experienced rising unemployment and increasing inflation at the same time. This is the phenomenon of *stagflation* discussed in Part II of this text.

along a single, stable Phillips Curve. Rather, there appear to be a *family* of Phillips Curves, each pertaining to a rather brief interval of time. In this family of Phillips Curves one observes separate, negatively sloped segments for the 1960s, 1976–1979, 1980–1982, and 1986–1988.

One way to interpret the pattern of points in Figure 17-9 is to think of the Phillips Curve being based on "other things equal," just like a demand curve. As we change the amount of demand stimulus in the economy—*holding constant all other factors that influence inflation and unemployment*—we trace out a Phillips Curve. But there are many factors in the economic environment besides the magnitude of macroeconomic stimulus that influence unemployment and inflation. Examples include demographic factors, technological change, supply shocks, and changes in expected inflation. As these factors change over time, the *entire position* of the trade-off changes—the Phillips Curve shifts. A trade-off between inflation and unemployment still exists, in this view, but its position is unstable and shifts up or down periodically. Although few economists recognized in the 1950s or 1960s that it might happen, the Phillips Curve shifted sharply rightward in the 1970s and early 1980s. Since the early 1980s, happily, it has shifted back to the left.

Rightward-Shifting Phillips Curve—Late 1960s to Early 1980s

At least three factors combined during the period from roughly 1969–1982 to worsen the position of the Phillips Curve—to shift it rightward. As a result, the nation's **discomfort index**—the sum of the unemployment rate and the inflation rate—increased in this period.[5]

Demographic Changes   We have already outlined the consequences of the substantial influx into the labor force of women and teenagers for the nation's frictional and overall unemployment rates. From the perspective of the Phillips Curve, these demographic changes imply that the unemployment rate associated with each and every magnitude of economic stimulus (and hence, inflation) increased between the 1960s and the early 1980s. Stated alternatively, given the increase in frictional unemployment associated with the change in labor force composition, the amount of economic stimulus (hence inflation) required to achieve any given unemployment rate increased. This means the Phillips Curve shifted rightward.

Liberalization of Unemployment Benefits   On average, unemployment benefits were made more generous after the 1960s. This generosity increases frictional unemployment by increasing the incentive to quit an unsatisfactory job and to take more time in the job-search process. This implies, again, that achieving any given unemployment rate requires a more stimulated economy and, hence, more inflation. Thus, the move toward more liberal unemployment benefits predictably shifted the Phillips Curve rightward. The magnitude of the shift was probably relatively modest, however.

---

[5]This term was popularized by the Reagan Administration in the mid-1980s to illuminate the improvement in U.S. macroeconomic conditions during President Reagan's tenure. In 1980, the year before the Reagan Administration took office, the unemployment and inflation rates stood at 7.1 percent and 12.4 percent, respectively. This yielded a discomfort index of 19.5 percent. In 1988, the unemployment and inflation rates were 5.5 percent and 4.1 percent, respectively, yielding a discomfort index of 9.6 percent. What was it last year? Check your *Federal Reserve Bulletin* or most recent *Economic Report of the President.*

Rising Inflationary Expectations   For any given amount of macroeconomic stimulus (hence, unemployment rate), wage and salary hikes are likely to be closely related to the outlook for inflation. If inflation is expected to be severe, average wage and salary increases are large. If inflation is expected to be subdued, these increases are modest. All this implies that an increase in expected inflation shifts the Phillips Curve rightward. Without question this happened in the 1970s and the early 1980s. Years of rising inflation commencing in the mid-1960s convinced people by the beginning of the 1970s that inflation was going to be around for awhile—that we would not soon see the low inflation rates of the early 1960s. Note in Figure 17-9 that the cluster of unemployment-inflation points for the 1970s lies rightward of the points for the 1960s. In the late 1970s, inflation again accelerated, this time reaching double-digit levels. This further ratcheted inflationary expectations upward. This ratcheting shifted the Phillips Curve rightward again in the early 1980s, as indicated by the points for 1980–1982. Many economists agree that the chief factor accounting for the rightward shift of the Phillips Curve from the 1960s to the early 1980s was the significant increase in inflationary expectations.

The 1980s—A Leftward-Shifting Phillips Curve

Two of the three factors that conspired to shift the Phillips Curve rightward during the 1970s worked in reverse to shift the Phillips Curve leftward in the 1980s. As a result, we enjoyed a more favorable combination of unemployment and inflation in the 1984–1989 period than we had experienced in almost 20 years. The factors responsible for the leftward-shifting Phillips Curve were the changing-age composition of the labor force and the reduction of inflationary expectations resulting from the successful disinflation of the early 1980s.

Because the U.S. birthrate declined significantly after the early 1960s, the number of youths coming into the labor force declined in the 1980s. Also, the *baby boomers* were aging in the 1980s—many were entering middle age. These factors reduced frictional unemployment and pulled down the overall unemployment rate associated with any given amount of economic stimulus and inflation. The surprisingly rapid reduction of inflation during 1981–1983, coupled with the maintenance of very modest inflation for several years thereafter, convinced people that severe inflation was gone for the foreseeable future. The gradual winding down of inflationary expectations in the 1980s resulted in a leftward-shifting Phillips Curve. Hence, the long business cycle expansion of 1982–1989 resulted in a sustained reduction of unemployment without reigniting inflation because the Phillips Curve was gradually shifting leftward.

IS THE PHILLIPS CURVE REALLY A MENU OF POLICY CHOICES?

As noted earlier, both theoretical intuition and observation from history suggest that a stimulated economy tends to exhibit relatively low unemployment and high inflation, whereas a *soft* economy typically results in higher unemployment and lower inflation. That is, both history and intuition suggest the existence of a Phillips Curve. Within broad limits, government can manipulate its monetary and fiscal policy tools to provide any desired magnitude of macroeconomic stimulus. Hence, one's first instinct might be to regard the Phillips Curve as a menu of policy choices—that is, that the government may choose to operate at any point along the

Curve. Most economists today believe that such a conception of the Phillips Curve is incorrect. The reasoning is subtle, and involves the effect of changes in actual inflation upon expected inflation and, hence, on the *position* of the Phillips Curve. Consider the analysis in Figure 17-10.

If one regards the Phillips Curve as a long-run menu of the various attainable combinations of unemployment and inflation, the government might attempt to move us from *A* to *B* in Figure 17-10. That is, government could attempt to trade off an increase in inflation as the price for achieving a reduction in unemployment. To bring about this change, the government would implement stimulative monetary and fiscal policies. At first—as inflation begins to rise—workers are fooled by the inflation and real wages decline. Business profits expand and firms step up output and employment.[6] Therefore, unemployment declines and the move from *A* to *B* in Figure 17-10 is achieved successfully in the short run.

However, in the long run, expectations of inflation adjust to the ongoing rate of inflation. As soon as workers become aware that their wages have fallen relative to the price level, they demand *catch-up* compensation. When this happens firms' profits, output, and employment revert to the normal levels and the unemployment rate returns to the normal level, U_N. Hence, we would move from *B* to *C* in Figure 17-10.

When the government notes that its attempts to reduce unemployment have been frustrated, it could further boost economic activity in an attempt to push the unemployment rate below U_N. As inflation again accelerates (to perhaps nine percent), workers are fooled again. Output, profits, and employment rise and unemployment declines again—temporarily. We move from *C* to *D,* again experiencing a *short-run* trade-off between inflation and unemployment. Once the inflation

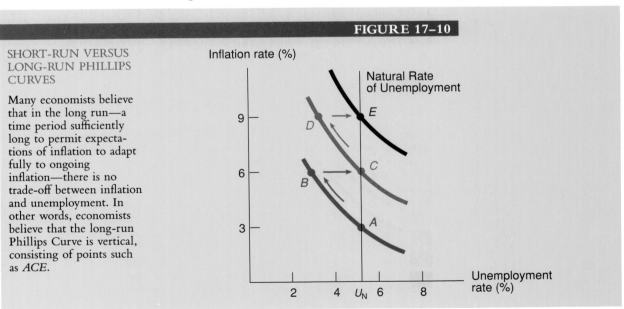

FIGURE 17–10

SHORT-RUN VERSUS LONG-RUN PHILLIPS CURVES

Many economists believe that in the long run—a time period sufficiently long to permit expectations of inflation to adapt fully to ongoing inflation—there is no trade-off between inflation and unemployment. In other words, economists believe that the long-run Phillips Curve is vertical, consisting of points such as *ACE.*

[6]Those frictionally unemployed workers in the process of job search might mistake the new higher *nominal* wage and salary offers as being higher *real* offers. If so, they would tend to terminate job search and accept employment. Frictional (and total) unemployment therefore declines when inflation exceeds expected inflation.

becomes fully anticipated, however, profits, output, and employment return to normal levels and we move to point E in Figure 17-10. Hence, the long-run Phillips Curve consists of points such as *ACE* in the figure. That is, the long-run Phillips Curve is a vertical line at the economy's natural or NAIRU unemployment rate.

In the long run, expectations of inflation catch up with actual inflation. There is no *labor fooling* in the long run. Since efforts to move along a perceived short-run Phillips Curve to reduce unemployment raise inflation and thereby raise *expected* inflation, the position of the Phillips Curve shifts rightward as we move from A to B. Policy efforts to exploit a short-run Phillips Curve systematically produce a shift in the Phillips Curve. In this analysis, the only way to keep the unemployment rate below U_N is to attempt to fool workers permanently by always keeping actual inflation above expected inflation. But this requires a disastrous policy of continual escalation of the inflation rate. We would soon have runaway inflation. In terms of Figure 17-10, point A is clearly preferable to point E. Hence, the clear implication is that government should not attempt to reduce the unemployment rate below the natural rate via stimulative macroeconomic policies.

The problem, of course, is that the precise level of the natural unemployment rate is not known. Furthermore, it fluctuates over time. Economists disagree about the level of the natural rate, liberals tending to believe it is relatively low and conservatives estimating it to be higher. Clearly, however, the farther the nation's unemployment rate declines below six percent the greater the chances of running into accelerating inflation. For this reason, as unemployment drifted down from six percent toward five percent during 1987–1989, the Federal Reserve moved toward a more restrictive policy posture—it implemented a slowdown in the growth rate of bank reserves and the nation's supply of money.

Although economists disagree about the level of the natural unemployment rate, they agree unanimously that efforts to reduce the natural rate itself would be beneficial. Such measures would shift the Phillips Curve leftward, conferring benefits in the form of a lower inflation rate associated with each unemployment rate.

SUMMARY

1. The nation's labor force officially consists of those who are employed plus those not working but searching for employment. The U.S. Department of Labor counts as unemployed those who are out of work but seeking employment. The nation's official unemployment rate is the ratio of the number unemployed to the number in the labor force (times 100).

2. The labor force participation rate is the percentage of the population above age 16 in the labor force. The overall U.S. labor force participation rate has steadily increased in the past 30 years because of increasing labor force participation rates of women.

3. Unemployment may be categorized as frictional, structural, and cyclical. Frictional unemployment consists of those temporarily in the job-search process on the day the unemployment survey is taken. Much of the frictional unemployment is voluntary. Structural unemployment is a more serious situation in which millions of job vacancies coexist with millions of involuntarily unemployed workers because the skills sought by the employers differ from the skills possessed by the unemployed. Cyclical unemployment occurs when the nation's output is below potential GNP and normally employed workers are thrown out of work.

4. The natural unemployment rate is the minimum unemployment rate that could be sustained without inducing an increase in the nation's inflation rate. It is considered to be the unemployment rate prevailing when actual and potential GNP are equal and when

only frictional and structural unemployment exist. The natural unemployment rate fluctuates over time because of fluctuations in the percentage of the labor force frictionally and structurally unemployed. The natural unemployment rate increased from the mid-1960s until the early 1980s and has declined somewhat since.

5. When the nation's unemployment rate rises significantly, several adverse consequences occur. Output and income are sacrificed, reducing the standard of living of the nation. Minorities, youth, and unskilled workers absorb a disproportionate share of the burden of increased unemployment. Human costs are large, as family problems, divorce rates, alcoholism, drug abuse, and mental debilitation rise with the unemployment rate. Public goods such as infrastructure, parks, and schools deteriorate when unemployment rises because revenues flowing into state and local treasuries decrease. Finally, unemployment may have longer-range adverse consequences for the nation's production capacity or potential GNP.

6. The Phillips Curve hypothesis refers to the alleged existence of a stable trade-off between inflation and unemployment. High unemployment is depicted as being compatible with low inflation; lower unemployment leads to higher inflation in the view of the Phillips Curve. Contrary to the viewpoint widely accepted before the 1970s, the Phillips Curve has been unstable in the past 20 years, shifting about in response to such factors as changes in expected inflation and changes in the age makeup of the labor force.

7. The fact that historical experience has generated a series of points that might suggest a Phillips Curve trade-off between inflation and unemployment does not necessarily imply that government can regard the Phillips Curve as a menu of policy choices. The government may be unable to *exploit* a perceived Phillips Curve. For example, if the government attempts to move up and to the left on a perceived Phillips Curve by applying stimulative monetary and fiscal policies, the increase in inflation elevates inflation expectations and shifts the entire position of the Phillips Curve outward. The net outcome might be to leave the original unemployment rate unchanged but result in a higher inflation rate.

KEY TERMS

labor force
unemployment rate
underemployment
discouraged workers
hidden unemployed
secondary workers
labor force participation rate
  (LFPR)
frictional unemployment

structural unemployment
cyclical unemployment
natural rate of unemployment
NAIRU
output gap
Okun's Law
Phillips Curve
discomfort index

STUDY QUESTIONS AND PROBLEMS

1. Explain how the U.S. unemployment rate is measured. What shortcomings do you see in this procedure? Can you think of a better method for measuring the unemployment rate?
2. Define the following terms:
   a. underemployment
   b. discouraged worker
   c. hidden unemployment
   d. secondary worker
   e. labor force participation rate
3. Why do most economists believe that in today's economy it is virtually impossible to push the unemployment rate below 3–4 percent via stimulative macroeconomic policies?
4. Assume you have been appointed chair of the President's Council of Economic Advisors.

What programs would you recommend to the President to attack the problem of structural unemployment?

5. Define the concept of the natural rate of unemployment. Why does it fluctuate over time?

6. Suppose the unemployment rate is currently 9 percent and actual GNP is $6000 billion per year. Using Okun's Law (Equation 17-1), compute the loss of output for the current year. Given a U.S. population of 250 million people, compute the per capita output loss.

7. Analyze the distribution of the impact of increased cyclical unemployment in economic downturns between black and white, skilled and unskilled, and young and middle-aged workers.

8. Define a Phillips Curve and analyze two intuitively plausible explanations for its existence.

9. If data from history seem to confirm the existence of a Phillips Curve, why do many economists believe that government policy is unable to exploit the trade-off in buying less unemployment by accepting more inflation?

10. List and define the three types of unemployment. Which is the most amenable to change by monetary and fiscal policies?

11. What factors have caused the natural unemployment rate to decline since the early 1980s? Explain.

12. How would the following events alter the position of the nation's short-run Phillips Curve?

    a. The labor force participation rate of women declines.

    b. Eligibility requirements for unemployment benefits are severely restricted.

ANSWER TO YOUR TURN

Given the information provided, the only *unknown* in Equation 17-1 is potential GNP. If we multiply both sides of the equation by actual GNP to clear fractions we obtain:

$$\text{potential GNP} - \text{actual GNP} = 2.5 \, (U - 5.5\%)(\text{actual GNP})$$

If we plug in the data given, we obtain

$$\text{potential GNP} - \$5500 \text{ billion} = 2.5(8\% - 5.5\%)(\$5500 \text{ billion})$$

$$\text{potential GNP} = 6.25\% \, (\$5500 \text{ billion}) + \$5500 \text{ billion}$$

$$\text{potential GNP} = \$5843.75 \text{ billion}$$

The loss of output is the difference between potential GNP and actual GNP. $5843.75 billion − $5500 billion = $343.75 billion.

SELECTED REFERENCES

Baily, Martin N. and Arthur M. Okun (eds.) *The Battle Against Unemployment and Inflation,* 3rd ed. (New York: Norton, 1982). This series of articles analyzes the relationship of monetary and fiscal policies to unemployment.

Ehrenberg, Ronald G. and Robert S. Smith, *Modern Labor Economics,* 3rd ed. (Glenview, IL: Scott, Foresman, 1988). This popular labor economics textbook goes into greater depth on the issues surveyed in this chapter.

Friedman, Milton, "The Role of Monetary Policy," *American Economic Review,* March 1968, pp. 1–17. This article presents the natural unemployment rate hypothesis and foresees the demise of the notion of a stable Phillips Curve.

INFLATION— MEASUREMENT, NATURE, AND CONSEQUENCES

Inflation has gone up over a dollar a quart.

—W. C. FIELDS

One of the most serious and stubborn economic problems facing both developing nations and industrialized societies since World War II has been **inflation**—the persistent upward movement in the general level of prices. Leaders of industrial nations in which domestic prosperity and economic freedom are accorded high priority have been unable to devise a successful cure for inflation. And developing nations seem to have an even higher propensity toward the disease of inflation. In Chapter 18, we present a broad perspective on the problem of inflation. We discuss the measurement and nature of inflation, sketch the history of inflation in the United States (focusing especially on the post–World War II experience), and analyze its consequences.

You are undoubtedly aware of some of the ways in which inflation influences your own pattern of life. After studying this chapter, you will emerge with a much clearer view of the impact that inflation exerts on you, your family, and the U.S. economy.

INTRODUCTION

Inflation has been a major nemesis, periodically afflicting all market economies throughout time. During periods of war and political instability, inflation has been almost universally prevalent. However, prior to World War II (1940–1945), temporary periods of inflation were often followed by deflation—periods of falling prices. As a result there was little or no upward trend in the general level of prices. In the post-World War II period the problem of inflation has become more persistent, and the average inflation rate experienced by industrial nations has been considerably higher than in the pre-World War II era.

In the 1970s, many industrial nations experienced an unprecedented phenomenon—double-digit inflation during peacetime conditions. In the first half of the 1980s, widespread popular backlash against inflation resulted in implementation of governmental policies that produced a substantial easing of inflationary pressures in most industrial nations. Nevertheless, inflation rates experienced during this period exceeded the rates considered tolerable a couple of decades earlier.

The average-annual inflation rates experienced by a sample of 13 countries during 1980–1987 are indicated in Table 18-1. A glance at the table reveals the

TABLE 18-1		
AVERAGE ANNUAL INFLATION RATE, SELECTED COUNTRIES, 1980–1987		
Country	**Inflation rate (% per year)**	**Time required to double the price level (in years)**
Argentina	346.0	0.46
Israel	238.5	0.57
Brazil	158.6	0.73
Mexico	72.9	1.3
Italy	11.5	6.4
Spain	10.7	6.8
France	7.7	9.4
Canada	6.5	11.0
United Kingdom	6.2	11.5
United States	4.7	15.1
Switzerland	3.4	20.8
Germany	3.0	23.5
Japan	2.1	33.3
Industrial countries	8.6	8.4
Developing countries	37.1	2.2
World	15.5	4.8

Sources: Calculated from data in International Monetary Fund, *International Financial Statistics,* various issues, and Federal Reserve Bank of St. Louis, *International Economic Conditions,* June 1988.

extreme diversity of inflation rates experienced by different countries. In Argentina the inflation rate exceeded 300 percent per year in the 1980–1987 period, indicating that prices doubled approximately every six months. Israel, a highly industrialized nation, averaged more than 200 percent annual inflation during 1980–1987 and witnessed an annual inflation rate as high as 900 percent during certain briefer intervals. On the other hand, Japan managed to hold inflation to approximately 2 percent per year. The United States averaged 4.7 percent inflation, a rate significantly below the average for all industrial countries. The average *world* inflation rate was 15.5 percent, a rate that doubles the level of prices in less than five years.

MEANING AND MEASUREMENT OF INFLATION

Inflation
A sustained increase in the aggregate price level; a persistent decline in the value of the monetary unit (e.g., the dollar).

Inflation refers to a sustained, continuing increase in the general level of prices or a sustained, continuing decrease in the purchasing power of the domestic monetary unit of account—for example, the dollar, mark, or yen. When there is inflation, the value of a currency in terms of the goods and services it buys persistently declines.

Measuring Inflation

Price Index
A weighted average of the prices of goods and services expressed in relation to a base year value of 100.

To measure inflation, economists use a **price index**. A price index is a measure of the average level of prices in a given year *relative* to the average level of prices in a particular year, called the **base year.** The price index is therefore designed to show the *change* in the general level of prices since the base year. The current price index is *calculated* by comparing the cost of buying a particular bundle of goods in the current year with the cost of buying exactly that same bundle of goods in the base year. For example, the price index for 1990, using 1982 as the base year, is calculated as follows:

$$P_{1990} = \frac{\Sigma P_i^{1990} \times Q_i^{1982}}{\Sigma P_i^{1982} \times Q_i^{1982}} \times 100 \qquad (18\text{-}1)$$

In Equation 18-1, P_i indicates the price of good i and Q_i indicates the quantity purchased of good i in the year indicated in the superscript. P_i times Q_i indicates expenditures on good i. Hence, the denominator of the equation represents the sum of expenditures on the items in the market basket in 1982, the base year. The numerator indicates what it costs in 1990 to purchase the same market basket of goods that was purchased in 1982. Both the numerator and denominator are expressed as a flow of expenditures per year. Therefore, the ratio of the two expressions is a pure number, devoid of units. This ratio is multiplied by 100 to create an index number of convenient magnitude. Thus, if the flow of expenditures on the basket of goods in 1982 was $8000 and the expenditures required in 1990 to purchase that same basket is $16,000, our price index for 1990 is 200. This is shown as follows:

$$P_{1990} = \frac{\$16,000/\text{year}}{\$8000/\text{year}} \times 100 = 200$$

This index number of 200 implies that the cost of purchasing the market basket has doubled since the base year of 1982, when the index value was established at 100. Alternatively, we may say that the level of prices has increased by 100 percent since the year 1982. If this price index were a precise measure of purchasing power change, one would need $200 in 1990 to be as well off as one would have been in

1982 with $100. Note that a price index does *not* indicate the absolute *level* of prices; it indicates the *change* in the price level since the base year.

In the United States there are three major indexes of prices: the **consumer price index (CPI)**, the **producer price index (PPI)**, and the **GNP deflator**.

Consumer Price Index
The most widely quoted index of U.S. prices; based on the market basket of goods and services purchased by a typical household.

Consumer Price Index (CPI) This index number is possibly the most widely quoted economic statistic in the world. The consumer price index, sometimes called the "cost-of-living" index, seeks to measure the change in the cost of the basket of goods and services purchased by the typical American consumer. To construct the CPI, the Bureau of Labor Statistics employs about 250 agents to collect price information from 24,000 retail stores, 18,000 homeowners, and 18,000 tenants in 85 cities. Approximately 125,000 individual price quotations are obtained each month. The CPI is based on prices of food, clothing, housing, transportation, fuel, medical expenses, and other items purchased for day-to-day living. The base year of the CPI is the average of 1982–1984 (1982–1984 = 100).

Producer Price Index
A price index based on a large sample of materials and goods purchased by firms; formerly known as the wholesale price index.

Producer Price Index (PPI) This index, also computed by the Bureau of Labor Statistics, differs fundamentally from the CPI. It does not include services. The PPI focuses on prices paid by firms for their inputs, rather than on prices paid by households. The PPI, which replaced the old Wholesale Price Index in 1978, measures prices at an early stage of the distribution system. The sample of goods involves 2800 items, including raw materials and intermediate products such as glass and steel. Both published price data and data obtained via questionnaires sent to producers are utilized. The PPI is a relatively sensitive price index, moving rapidly in response to changes in the nation's aggregate supply and aggregate demand curves. The PPI often signals changes in inflationary pressures before the CPI. This follows from the fact that higher costs to producers (as measured by the PPI) often lead to higher prices paid by households (as measured by the CPI). The base year for the PPI is 1982 (1982 = 100).

GNP Deflator
A weighted average of the prices of all final goods and services produced in the economy; the ratio of nominal GNP to real GNP (times 100).

GNP Deflator Although it receives less publicity than the CPI and PPI, this index is often preferred by professional economists. The U.S. Department of Commerce computes the GNP deflator in order to ascertain changes in the price level of those goods and services entering into our nation's GNP. This index differs from the CPI in that it excludes import prices and interest rates and encompasses a broader group of goods and services. While the CPI and PPI are published monthly, the GNP deflator is available only on a quarterly basis. A subindex of the GNP deflator, the

YOUR TURN

Assume you entered college three years ago and that selected items in your annual budget have increased in price as follows since you matriculated:

a. apartment rent: $250 to $275
b. soft drinks: $0.50 to $0.75
c. tuition: $4000 to $5000
d. gas for car: $0.90 to $1.20

Assume further that in your first year of college you paid rent 12 times annually, consumed 600 soft drinks, paid tuition once annually, and purchased 1000 gallons of gas. Using only these four items as your *market basket,* calculate your current price index relative to the base year (your first year of college). What is the percentage increase in your price index since the base year?

personal consumption expenditures (PCE) deflator, is sometimes considered superior to the CPI by professional economists because of its method of construction.

Shortcomings in Our Price Indexes

The price indexes (particularly the CPI) are of more than casual interest to millions of Americans. In fact, a significant portion of the population is directly affected by the price indexes via the widespread use of escalator clauses. Approximately 9 million American workers have contracts calling for wage hikes tied explicitly to the CPI. About 2.5 million military and civil-service retirees and some 30 million social-security recipients receive benefits indexed to the CPI. Even the fate of 20 million school children who eat subsidized hot lunches is dependent on the reported CPI because of escalator clauses in funding provisions.

It is therefore clearly important that our price indexes be valid indicators of changes in the level of prices. However, for several reasons our price indexes tend to *overstate* the true rate of inflation. That is, it is widely believed that our price indexes exhibit *upward bias*. Given the number of people with a strong vested interest in the reported price indexes, it is not surprising that political considerations have sometimes delayed implementation of measures required to correct obvious flaws in these measures of inflation.[1]

There are two major sources of bias in the popular price indexes. The first concerns the evolving *quality* of goods and services produced. The price indexes are intended to measure the change over time in the cost of purchasing a given market basket of goods and services. However, the quality of those goods changes over time and, for the most part, is gradually improving. Think back some 15–20 years ago to items that your family presently purchases—cars, tires, and shirts, for example. Cars in those days got about 15 miles per gallon and tires lasted about 25,000 miles. Today you can get 30–50 miles per gallon on many automobiles and tires are typically good for 40,000–50,000 miles. Twenty years ago one had to spend 20 minutes ironing a shirt. Today we have no-iron shirts. And although today we have to spend considerably more for cars, tires, and shirts than we did in the past, we generally get a more desirable product. Part of what shows up as an increase in price then is actually payment for the increase in quality of the product. The price indexes, by inadequately addressing this consideration, tend to overstate the true price increases.[2]

The second major source of bias springs from the use of a *prior year's* consumption pattern in determining the *weights* of various products in the current price index. Note in Equation 18-1 that the price index for 1990 is built on the assumption that consumers still purchase the same quantities of each item they purchased in 1982. The index shows the change in the flow of expenditures required

---

[1]It has been estimated that in the extreme instance of the first half of 1980—when the CPI was overstating true inflation of consumer goods by some five-percentage points—indexing clauses artificially inflated government spending (primarily on social security benefits) and increased the budget deficit by some $8 billion. See Robert J. Gordon, "The Consumer Price Index: Measuring Inflation and Causing It," *The Public Interest*, Spring 1981, pp. 112–134. Certain of the flaws pointed out by Gordon have been corrected.

[2]Only in the case of automobiles does the BLS adequately allow for quality change. Each year the BLS sends a team of analysts to Detroit. As innovative and quality-improving features are added to new models, the BLS adjusts the price accordingly before entering it into the CPI. Hence, if a new car costs an additional $500 to produce this year due to installation of air bags, $500 is deducted from the final price before entering it into the CPI. To use this procedure on thousands of individual products would be prohibitively expensive.

in 1990 to purchase the same quantities of each item purchased in 1982. In reality—since we know that demand curves are almost universally downward sloping—consumers change the relative quantities of the various goods and services purchased in response to price changes. In 1990, consumers will expand purchases of items whose prices have fallen since 1982—such as PCs, VCRs, and CD players—and restrict purchases of items whose prices have risen sharply. The index therefore puts too much weight on items that have risen in price and too little weight on items that have declined in price. Hence, the reported price index overstates the increase in the *cost of living.* Anyone whose disposable income keeps pace with the reported CPI is actually coming out ahead, even if the quality of goods and services is constant over time.[3] Both the CPI and PPI employ prior-year weights and therefore are subject to this **substitution bias.**

Other biases have sometimes entered into our price indexes. For a long time our CPI placed disproportionate weight on housing. Both the full purchase price *and* the mortgage rate were entered. That is, the BLS constructed the index as if the homebuyer laid out the full cost of the house *and also* took out a mortgage on the house—an obvious flaw. In the 1970s, when house prices and mortgage rates soared, the CPI was significantly overstating inflation. In the early 1980s, an adjustment was made to correct this problem.

The upshot of these shortcomings in our price indexes is that perhaps the first percentage point or so of inflation reported each year may be written off as merely reflecting upward bias in the price index. Reported inflation above that amount is probably the real stuff.

THE NATURE AND HISTORY OF U.S. INFLATION

Figure 18-1 illustrates the history of the U.S. price level. The figure depicts the behavior of the wholesale price index, the forerunner of our producer price index, from the beginning days of the republic to the present. The CPI has exhibited a very similar pattern.

The most striking aspect of Figure 18-1 is the difference in price-level behavior in the post–World War II era relative to that in the nation's first 170 years. Although the early period was subject to periodic bursts of inflation, these episodes were followed by falling prices—deflation. The price level kept returning to its *normal* or standard level. In the post–World War II era, these episodes of deflation—like the massive herds of buffaloes—have disappeared from the American scene.[4] The level of prices has followed a one-way street—upward.

Price-Level Behavior Before World War II

The basic early pattern was one of severe wartime inflation followed by a major postwar contraction of economic activity and deflation of prices. Hence the general

---

[3]The reported CPI accurately reports changes in the cost of living in this regard only for the individual who never changes his buying patterns in response to changes in relative prices among goods and services. That is, it is only accurate for those individuals whose demand curves for all items in the market basket are perfectly inelastic.

[4]One need not look with regret at this departure of deflation from the American scene. These periods of falling prices were typically hard times, with heavy unemployment, financial distress, and widespread foreclosures on farms and other debts. A primary concern in the U.S. presidential election of 1896 was the issue of halting the 20-year deflation of prices that was bankrupting thousands of enterprises. Though it may sound strange, *deflation* is in many ways a much more damaging phenomenon than *inflation.*

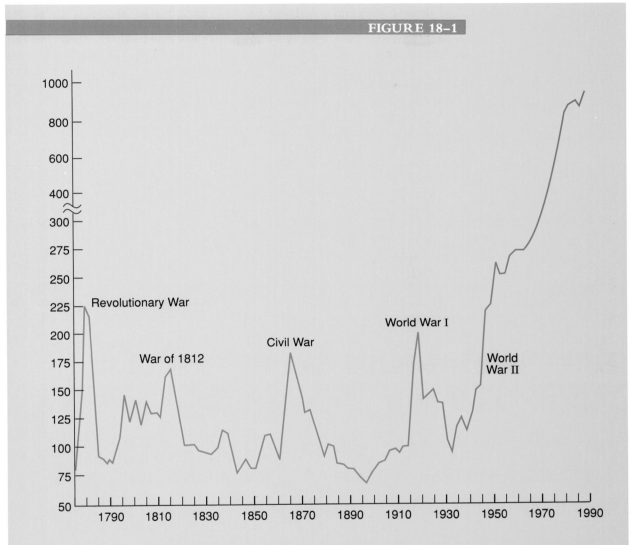

FIGURE 18–1

AMERICAN PRICE-LEVEL HISTORY, 1775–1988 (wholesale price index, 1910–1914 = 100)*

Prior to 1940, periods of rising prices (inflation) were followed by episodes of falling prices (deflation). Hence, there was no long-term upward trend in the American price level during the period 1775–1940. Since 1940, the U.S. economy has developed a bias toward inflation; periods of deflation have disappeared from the American experience.

*Wholesale price index, 1910–1914 = 100; note change of scale at 300.
Sources: Data from *Historical Statistics of the United States* and *Economic Report of the President*, 1988.

level of prices was approximately the same in 1800, 1875, 1925, and 1945. Emerging prominently in Figure 18-1 are the sharp price-level increases during the Revolutionary War, the War of 1812, the Civil War, and the two World Wars. These are classic examples of **demand-pull inflation,** when aggregate demand increases faster than the nation's capacity to produce goods and services.

Typically what happens in time of war is that increased government expenditures on military hardware and services raise aggregate demand for goods and services. This situation coincides with reduced supply capability resulting from the reallocation of a significant portion of the civilian labor force into the armed services. The urgency of war and political considerations are such that major conflicts are seldom fully financed by tax increases. The resulting government deficit is financed by issuing bonds to the public and to the central bank (Federal Reserve System). Central bank purchasing of government debt is essentially equivalent to government printing of currency to finance war. Governments fail to force down other forms of expenditures sufficiently to compensate for the expansion of military expenditures. Aggregate demand becomes excessive, as illustrated in the aggregate supply-aggregate demand framework of Figure 18-2.

In Figure 18-2 the prewar situation is depicted by aggregate supply curve AS_0 and aggregate demand curve AD_0, yielding an equilibrium price level P_0 and real output level Y_0. This output level is assumed initially to be somewhat below the level required to create full employment (Y_F). The wartime fiscal and monetary stimuli shift the aggregate demand curve rightward to AD_1 and AD_2, creating an inflationary gap of $Y_2 - Y_F$ and pulling up the price level to P_1 and P_2. As long as the aggregate demand curve keeps shifting rightward, we get demand-pull inflation.

At the end of each war prior to World War II, a sharp cutback in government expenditures on military procurement occurred while large numbers of men

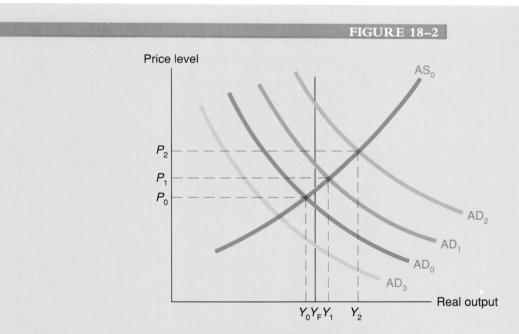

FIGURE 18-2

WARTIME EXCESS-DEMAND INFLATION

In time of war, rising government military expenditures typically boost aggregate demand for goods and services. This results in a burst of inflation. At the conclusion of American wars prior to 1940, aggregate demand declined sharply with cessation of hostilities. Both output and the price level declined. These periods of deflation were times of great economic and personal hardship.

released from the armed forces entered the civilian labor force. The sharp reduction in aggregate demand resulted in severe cuts in output and employment. Hence, the wartime boom was inevitably followed by a postwar bust in which profits declined precipitously, unemployment increased, and widespread financial distress prevailed. In Figure 18-2, the bloated wartime aggregate demand curve AD_2 was reduced to AD_3 following the termination of hostilities, thus lowering real GNP and the general level of prices.

One should remember that activist monetary and fiscal policies to combat heavy unemployment are a phenomenon of the past 50 years or less. In the earlier period, one may characterize the government's role in the macroeconomy as one of *laissez-faire*. There was no attempt to use monetary and fiscal policies to boost economic activity during the postwar contractions that occurred before World War II. Furthermore, there was limited *scope* for doing so since the Federal Reserve System was not established until 1913. And many institutional features of the economy that today limit downward flexibility of wages and prices did not come on stream until during or after the depression of the 1930s. The severe business-cycle contractions that prevailed before World War II were thus characterized by sharp declines in wages and prices.

Post-World War II Price-Level Behavior

Before the Second World War, the American price level exhibited a symmetrical pattern. Price-level increases and decreases occurred with equal frequency. (You may be surprised to learn that the price level was higher in 1780 and 1810 than in 1935.) Inflation was always followed by deflation, leaving the long-term trend of prices roughly unchanged. This symmetry has given way in recent decades to considerable *downward inflexibility* of wages and prices. A glance at Figure 18-1 confirms the one-way nature of price-level changes in the past 40 or 50 years. The last year in which the consumer price index declined for the year as a whole was 1955.[5]

In Figure 18-3 (page 398) we examine the most recent 35-year period in more detail by illustrating two measures of inflation—the rates of change in the consumer price index and in the producer price index. Clearly evident in the figure are the experience of relatively stable prices (low inflation) during 1955–1965, the acceleration of inflation during 1965–1970 (the Vietnam War years), the two episodes of double-digit inflation (peaking in 1974 and 1980), and the successful period of disinflation during 1981–1983.

Causes of the Change in Price-Level Behavior Since the 1930s

In Figure 18-3, shaded areas represent periods of business recession and unshaded areas periods of economic expansion. An important point to note is that post-World War II recessions have been successful in stemming inflation only in the sense that the *inflation rate* was induced to fall. The price *level* continued to rise but at a slower rate. This contrasts with the pre-1940 experience, in which inflation rates became

---

[5]The powerful upward momentum of the price level is indicated by the fact that during some 200 consecutive months from 1965 until 1982, the CPI failed to decline for even a *single month,* even though the 17-year interval encompassed four recessions. During the 1950–1990 period, the CPI exhibited a decline in less than two percent of the months. The PPI tells a similar though somewhat less severe story.

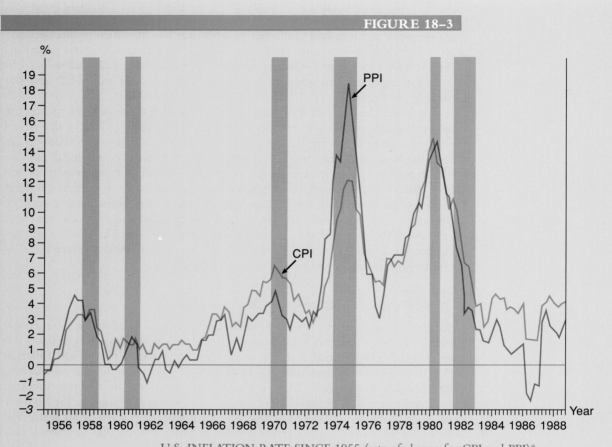

U.S. INFLATION RATE SINCE 1955 (rate of change for CPI and PPI)*

Two measures of inflation are the annual rate of increase in the consumer price index (CPI) and in the producers price index (PPI). Inflation was subdued in the early 1960s, accelerated during the Vietnam War (1965–1970), and reached rates in excess of 10 percent per year in both 1974 and 1980 following major increases in oil prices. Inflation came down dramatically in the early 1980s, and remained below 5 percent through 1988.

*Points plotted are 12-month moving average rates of inflation. Shaded areas depict business recessions.
Source: Data from *Citibank Economic Database*, 1989.

negative (price level *fell*) during severe recessions. Note in the figure that even at the low ebb of the inflation cycle following the two most severe postwar recessions (1973–1975 and 1981–1982), the CPI inflation rate was proceeding at more than two percent per year. Some economists believe that several factors have increased the inertia in the inflation process, making the price level less downwardly flexible since the 1930s.

Role of Government in the Economy   As a result of the severe economic hardship experienced during the 1930s, the philosophy toward government responsibility for the overall performance of the economy underwent a major transformation.

Instrumental in this change in thinking was the development by Keynes of a new framework of macroeconomic analysis. This framework was generally interpreted as implying that deliberate use of monetary and fiscal policies for purposes of contributing to economic stability was both feasible and appropriate. A *laissez-faire* philosophy toward the macroeconomy was alleged to be passé. This emerging belief that government should take responsibility for the state of economic prosperity was embodied in the Employment Act of 1946. The Act mandates that the federal government implement its monetary and fiscal policies in such a manner as to contribute toward "maximum production, employment, and purchasing power."

The *technical feasibility* of achieving greater economic stability improved dramatically in the first two or three decades after the Great Depression of the 1930s. This was partially the result of the government's new activist philosophy toward minimizing the severity of economic setbacks via implementation of stimulative monetary and fiscal policies.[6]

However, even more important was the increasing strength of the **automatic** (or built-in) **stabilizers** associated with the federal budget. The ratios of taxes to GNP and of government expenditures to GNP increased from less than 10 percent in the 1920s to more than 25 percent by the 1960s. As GNP falls in recession, tax receipts automatically decline and transfer payments rise. This provides stimulus to aggregate demand and output, thus cushioning the economic contraction. With the growth of the government budget relative to GNP, these automatic stabilizers became more powerful—absorbed a larger portion of any potential decline in GNP during recessions.[7]

Because of the increased power of the automatic stabilizers, the willingness to implement monetary and fiscal policies to stabilize the economy, and the reduced volatility on the part of individuals and firms that these factors induced, the stability of aggregate demand for goods and services has increased significantly since World War II. The average duration of recessions has been cut in half and periods of expansion have lasted twice as long. The economy has operated much closer to capacity on average. Fluctuations of output about the long-term growth trend have diminished. (Review Figure 11-A3, page 254.)

The relative mildness of the first few postwar recessions, coupled with increasing public awareness of the government's commitment to high employment, strengthened the emerging perception that severe economic downturns like the 1930s could be avoided in the future. A potent side effect of this growing perception was an increase in the inflationary tendency of the economic system. The growing awareness that future depressions could be avoided increased the resolve of workers toward resisting wage cuts and reduced the vigor with which firms pursued wage cuts in recessions. Hence, the post-World War II American economy has exhibited increasingly *sticky wages and prices*—a reduction in the extent to which wages and prices fall in response to excess capacity and unemployment.

---

[6]Prior to World War I, the United States was on the gold standard. This prevented implementation of stimulative monetary policy measures, even if they were deemed to be desirable, because the money supply was rigidly tied to the U.S. gold stock. Even though the gold standard was abandoned in 1914, the Federal Reserve's modern philosophy of implementing discretionary monetary policies to combat cyclical instability did not evolve until the 1950s.

[7]It has been estimated that the portion of any potential decline in GNP during recessions absorbed by the automatic stabilizers increased from about 6 percent in 1932 to more than 35 percent by the mid-1970s. See Robert J. Gordon, "Postwar Macroeconomics: The Evolution of Events and Ideas," in Martin Feldstein (ed.), *The American Economy in Transition* (Chicago: University of Chicago Press, 1980).

These tendencies have probably been reinforced by implementation of measures to reduce the financial hardship of the unemployed. Increased availability of unemployment benefits and other government transfer payments may have caused workers to become less willing to accept pay cuts and more willing to become unemployed. As a result, a much more severe economic contraction would be needed to bring about a reduction in the price level today than would have been required in the 1870s or 1930s, for example.

The Labor Movement and Institutional Changes   The great hardship suffered by workers in the 1930s stimulated the American unionization movement. The Wagner Act of 1935 guaranteed the right of workers to organize, and the proportion of the U.S. labor force belonging to unions increased from 6 percent in 1933 to more than 30 percent in the 1950s (though it has declined considerably in recent decades). Because union wages are less likely to decline in time of weak economic activity than are nonunion wages, greater unionization has probably contributed to increased wage rigidity in the post-1930s era.

Other institutional changes, many of which were initiated in the 1930s, have contributed to the decreased downward flexibility of prices and have increased the inflation tendency of the system. Federal insurance of bank deposits—implemented in 1934 with the creation of the Federal Deposit Insurance Corporation—was without question a socially beneficial change. However, an important side effect of FDIC insurance has been the virtual elimination of the bank runs and contraction of deposits that contributed to falling prices in pre-1934 cyclical downturns. Minimum-wage laws, first implemented in the Fair Labor Standards Act of 1938, produce an obvious obstacle to downward wage and price flexibility. Also, as noted earlier, unemployment insurance and other measures that reduce the personal cost of being unemployed probably have reduced the willingness of workers to accept lower wages, which previously contributed to downward wage and price flexibility.

Supply Shocks and Productivity Behavior   The decade of the 1970s has been called the "era of supply shocks." A series of events shifted the aggregate supply curve leftward—reduced the aggregate output firms were willing to produce at any price level. The most notorious supply shocks were the quadrupling of oil prices by the OPEC cartel in 1973–1974 followed by an additional 140 percent hike during 1979–1980. In 1974, adverse worldwide weather conditions resulted in an unusually low production of basic foodstuffs. This shortfall resulted in dramatic price increases of corn, wheat, soybeans, and other basic sources of food.

Beginning in the early 1970s, the U.S. suffered a sharp slowdown in productivity growth. Given any pattern of wage increases, slower productivity growth implies increased production costs. Hence, a slowdown in productivity shifts the aggregate supply curve leftward or at least slows its tendency to shift rightward gradually. The causes of the productivity slowdown are complex and controversial (see Chapter 21). Of course, one major factor was the dramatic increase in energy prices. This increase creates incentives to substitute labor for energy-intensive capital, thus reducing capital/labor ratios and impairing productivity growth of labor. Another important factor was the high inflation rate of the 1970s. High inflation inhibits investment and productivity via channels discussed later in this chapter. Also, demographic factors contributed to the productivity slowdown. During the 1970s, the proportion of the labor force comprised of females and youthful workers increased significantly. Since experience and productivity *levels* of these groups were lower on average than those of adult males, this shift in the composition of the labor force probably contributed to the slowdown in productivity growth.

The Inflation Process in the Context of Supply Shocks and a Government Commitment to High Employment

Figure 18-4 illustrates the inflation mechanism in the context of aggregate supply shocks given a government committed to high levels of output and employment. Assume initially that aggregate demand (AD_0) and aggregate supply (AS_0) intersect at point A with price level P_0 and real output level Y_0, slightly below the full-employment output level Y_F. Assume further that OPEC raises the price of oil, or unions obtain a large wage hike, or Congress raises the level of the minimum wage. Any such supply shock shifts the aggregate supply curve leftward to AS_1. This raises the price level to P_1 and reduces real output to Y_1. The supply shock moves us from A to B, simultaneously causing a recession and a higher level of prices. This is the phenomenon of *stagflation* discussed in Part II of this text.

If the government is committed to maintaining a high level of output (say Y_0 or more) and employment, it must introduce monetary and/or fiscal stimulus. This stimulus shifts the aggregate demand curve to AD_1, raising output toward Y_0 and further boosting the price level to P_2. We are now at point C. Additional wage hikes in response to higher prices or other adverse supply forces may shift AS_1 to AS_2, thus inducing the government to again stimulate the economy and shift the aggregate demand curve to AD_2. The pattern of points traced in this scenario of continuing supply-demand interaction is *ABCDE*. The result is continuing upward pressure on wages and prices—a wage–price spiral.

To address this wage–price spiral, it is clear that we must either attack the forces that produce the leftward shifts in the aggregate supply curve or abandon the

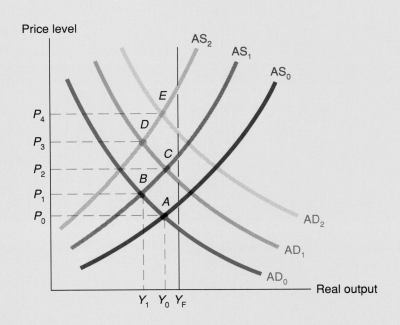

FIGURE 18-4

INFLATION PROCESS WITH SUPPLY SHOCKS AND COMMITMENT TO HIGH EMPLOYMENT

Aggregate supply shocks such as major oil price hikes shift the nation's aggregate supply curve leftward. Given the level of aggregate demand, this raises prices and reduces output. If the government wishes to prevent a decline in output, it must implement stimulative monetary and/or fiscal measures to boost aggregate demand. A period of inflation is inevitable if the government actively uses stabilization policy to prevent economic downturns in the face of negative aggregate supply shocks.

government's commitment to high levels of output and employment. If the government is committed to high employment and output while the aggregate supply curve is shifting leftward, the wage–price spiral is inevitable.

CONSEQUENCES OF INFLATION

Economists believe that inflation influences the distribution of the nation's income and wealth, the long-run growth of the economy, the efficiency with which our resources are utilized, and the stability of the economy. For several reasons, these consequences are quite difficult to establish definitively. To begin with, the consequences of inflation depend heavily upon the extent to which inflation is *anticipated accurately.* Unanticipated inflation—the kind that fools people—is generally considered more harmful than inflation that is accurately anticipated. When inflation is correctly anticipated, certain adjustments are made that mitigate some of inflation's effects. Further, the consequences of inflation depend upon the extent to which individuals and firms can incorporate their expectations into contracts governing wage agreements and other financial matters. Finally, our institutions are induced to adapt over time to ongoing inflation. The consequences of inflation in the 1990s are therefore likely to be quite different than those in the first half of the twentieth century.

The great English economist John Maynard Keynes used to argue that a little inflation was good medicine for the economy—it redistributed income and wealth from the idle classes (retired) to the active groups (currently employed) and ensured a healthy level of profits. The stimulus to profits was believed to aid investment in plant and equipment and, hence, long-run economic growth. Today there is a strong consensus among economists that inflation is harmful in its consequences. Yet this does not necessarily imply that Keynes was wrong. The consequences of inflation in recent decades are probably quite different than in Keynes' era.

Pure and *Impure* Inflation

In recent decades we have experienced two potentially distinguishable phenomena. First, the general price level has been rising. Second, we have experienced changes in *relative* prices of goods and services as some prices rise rapidly, some slowly, and some actually decline. This change in *relative* prices is due primarily to market forces of supply and demand. The phenomenon of *general* price increases is due primarily to the fact that the growth of aggregate expenditures outpaces the capacity of real output of goods and services to expand. The nation's aggregate demand curve shifts rightward faster than its aggregate supply curve. This situation occurs in part because it is less painful politically for those in charge of the nation's monetary and fiscal policies to accommodate market-induced changes in relative prices within an environment of a rising general price level. To accommodate changes in relative prices in a zero-inflation environment, prices of many goods and services must decline to offset those that rise. But *declining prices imply declining incomes* for those who produce those goods. The scenario of millions of Americans experiencing declining incomes is not a happy one for politicians seeking to remain in office.[8] This outcome is avoided in an environment where the price level persistently rises, thereby minimizing the number of goods whose prices must decline.

---

[8]Of course, in *real terms,* changes in relative prices imply that many people (those who supply the goods whose relative prices have decreased) must suffer a decline in their *real* income or standard of living. But this process is more obscure and less obvious if it occurs while the overall price level is rising. People are apparently less cognizant of a declining standard of living when their income rises more slowly than the general price level than when their income actually *declines* in the context of a stable general price level.

Pure Inflation
A hypothetical type of inflation in which all prices increase at exactly the same rate so there is no change in *relative* prices among goods and services.

Impure Inflation
The *real-world* type of inflation in which *relative* prices of goods and services are changing while the general level of prices increases.

A pure inflation is a *hypothetical* type in which all prices are rising at the same rate, so that there is no change in relative prices. An impure inflation is the type we actually experience—widespread changes in relative prices in the context of a rising overall price level. The distinction is useful in refuting the fallacy that inflation, *per se,* directly reduces the standard of living of the masses of Americans.

In 1980, when the CPI increased 12 percent, the average American was robbed of 12 percent of his/her income.

The statement is fallacious because increases in the prices of goods or services systematically increase incomes of those who own the resources with which the goods or services are produced. Increases in corn prices raise farm income. Increases in haircut prices raise income of barbers. Increases in legal fees raise lawyers' income. If the price of the good or service (including wages and salaries) supplied by each of us increased by 20 percent in a hypothetical pure inflation, none of us would be any better or worse off. Yet it is a sure bet that there would be much grumbling about higher doctor's fees, movie prices, food prices, and so on.[9]

In the preceding statement, the same forces that drove up prices by 12 percent in 1980 also drove up incomes by the same amount. It is clearly impossible, therefore, for the "average American" to be "robbed of 12 percent of his/her income." The "average American" is not robbed of anything by inflation—at least in the short run—since there is no reduction in aggregate output and real income.[10] However, inflation does involve significant consequences for the *distribution* of income and wealth. Although the "average" person may be unharmed by inflation, millions of Americans benefit and millions suffer because of inflation. Inflation thus sets up a social tension, creating a decline in morale and pitting one group in society against another. Moreover, economists believe that inflation unleashes a series of forces likely to adversely affect the long-term development of the economy. Hence, our standard of living is likely to be lower a generation from now if we acquiesce to rapid inflation than if we hold it to some minimal level.

Impact on Distribution of Income and Wealth

In the past, inflation has resulted in a rather arbitrary redistribution of income and wealth. To a great extent the redistributive effects of inflation depend on whether or not inflation is accurately anticipated by the people and whether various institutions are adapted to deal with the phenomenon of inflation.

For example, the impact of inflation upon debtor–creditor relationships depends on the behavior of real interest rates during inflation. If the nominal interest rate adjusts sufficiently to maintain the real interest rate unchanged during inflation, the debtor–creditor relationship is unaltered by the inflation. There will be no

[9]This dissension can be explained by the existence of myopia, in which each of us tends to believe our own increase in income is due to "merit" whereas everyone else's increase is due to "greed," "luck," and the like. In truth, the great bulk of the increases in income stem from the same basic force—general inflationary pressure. Many of us seem to forget that if we take away inflation, we take away the primary source of the increase in our income.

[10]There are several ways in which inflation of any genre, even the hypothetical case of pure inflation, imposes short-run costs on society. In inflationary times more hours are devoted to the task of marking up prices. These hours could be spent more usefully. Also—since inflation implies elevated interest rates—the opportunity cost of holding cash and noninterest-bearing checking accounts rises with inflation. It pays people to hold less of such assets, which implies more time spent managing one's financial affairs. What is prudent for an individual is a waste of resources from society's viewpoint. These costs are likely to be rather modest at least for the type of inflation we have experienced in the U.S. since World War II.

redistributive effects between borrowers and lenders. Let us illustrate this consideration via examination of three potential scenarios in which inflation escalates from two percent to seven percent.

| | Scenario A | | Scenario B | | Scenario C | |
	Period 1	Period 2	Period 1	Period 2	Period 1	Period 2
Inflation rate	2%	7%	2%	7%	2%	7%
Nominal interest rate	5%	6%	5%	10%	5%	13%
Real interest rate	+3%	−1%	+3%	+3%	+3%	+6%

In each scenario, inflation accelerates from 2 percent to 7 percent. In Scenario A the interest rate rises only from 5 percent to 6 percent, so the *real* or *inflation-adjusted* interest rate declines from 3 percent to −1 percent. This could happen if the public was surprised by the acceleration of inflation. It could also happen if the Federal Reserve deliberately held down interest rates or if various legal barriers such as statutory interest rate ceilings or usury laws prevented interest rates from rising in line with inflation.[11]

Because the real interest rate declines as inflation accelerates in Scenario A, income and wealth are redistributed from creditors to debtors. Debtors reap a windfall in this case. Inflation erodes the burden of the debt (the real value of the principal) and the interest rate is not high enough to compensate for this, let alone provide a *positive* real return to the lender for the use of the funds.

Who are the debtors and who are the creditors? In the aggregate, households are net creditors, saving a small portion of income and lending it out to deficit-spending units. Firms and the federal government are debtors on balance, spending more than current income and financing the deficits by selling bonds and other claims to the households. In the late 1980s, the total amount of debt owed in the U.S. was some $8 trillion or $8000 billion. When intra-sector debts are netted out, businesses and governments owed some $2000 billion to households. For each one percentage point that the real interest rate declines because of inflation (as in Scenario A), approximately $80 billion is redistributed from debtors to creditors, including a net redistribution of $20 billion from households to firms and the government.

Scenario A tends to occur when inflation is on the upswing. Expectations do not adjust instantaneously to current information and interest rates may fail to rise point-for-point with inflation. Thus the 1965–1980 period, when the inflation rate ratcheted higher and higher, was a period of low and often negative real or inflation-adjusted interest rates (review Figure 16-8). In this period the elderly, being major creditors, were adversely affected by inflation. People of age 25–50, being debtors on balance, came out ahead.

In Scenario B inflation is neutral as far as debtor–creditor relationships are concerned. The real interest rate remains unchanged while inflation accelerates. This scenario tends to occur if three conditions exist: inflation is accurately anticipated so that people are not fooled, the Fed permits interest rates to rise freely in the marketplace, and statutory interest ceilings and other impediments that prevent interest rates from rising do not come into play.

---

[11]In the 1970s, scenario A prevailed at least partially because regulations prevented financial institutions from paying more than certain stipulated interest rates on various types of savings and time deposits. The abolishment of these ceilings in the 1980s is a good example of the way in which inflation induces changes in society's institutions. Inflation rendered these ceilings obsolete and counterproductive, so they were removed.

In Scenario C real interest rates are very high. This scenario tends to happen when inflation is running at a lower rate than the general populace has been expecting or when the rate of inflation is dramatically reduced. This occurred in the U.S. during 1981–1985 as the inflation rate dropped from more than 10 percent to less than 4 percent. High real interest rates can also occur during periods in which the Federal Reserve is conducting a highly restrictive monetary policy. In this scenario, creditors benefit at the expense of debtors from the abnormally high real yields available. Households—particularly elderly individuals living off the proceeds of past savings—benefit at the expense of firms and the federal government. Business bankruptcies, farm foreclosures, and home repossessions increase in Scenario C as high real interest rates place debtors in a position of increased stress.

If inflation is accurately predicted in advance and if society's institutions have been adapted to the phenomenon of inflation, its redistributive consequences will be diminished. When widespread escalator clauses exist to protect workers, retirees, and owners of financial assets from the potential consequences of inflation, then clearly fewer people are adversely affected. That is why many industrial nations have moved toward implementation of more comprehensive **indexation** in the past two decades.

Indexation
Widespread use of escalator clauses that tie wages, rents, and other prices directly to the nation's price index in order to reduce the redistributive effects of inflation.

Impact on Long-Term Economic Growth

Keynes thought inflation stimulated economic growth. Implicitly, he assumed Scenario A always prevailed during inflation. Firms, being debtors, benefit in this scenario. Since people are fooled by inflation in this case, real interest rates decline and wages rise more slowly than prices. Profit margins of firms expand because of reduced real wages and real interest rates. This healthy expansion of business profits, by stimulating business optimism and corporate cash flow, makes for strong growth in investment in plant and equipment. Economic growth is stimulated.

Most economists believe that although Keynes' thinking may have been valid in the first half of this century, it is certainly not valid today. The overwhelming consensus today is that inflation is damaging to long-term economic growth. The first fallacy in Keynes' reasoning is to assume that inflation necessarily reduces real interest rates and real wages, thereby raising the share of corporate profits in national income. In the inflationary era since World War II, the profit share in national income has *declined* somewhat. Once inflation becomes entrenched, and once society's laws and institutions have been adapted to it, Scenarios B and C are as likely to prevail as Scenario A. Scenario B is basically neutral in its implications for the share of profits in national income; Scenario C has negative implications.

In addition, several other negative implications of inflation for economic growth exist. First, higher inflation rates tend to be associated with *more variable* inflation and, hence, *less predictable* inflation. This is illustrated in Figure 18-5 (page 406), which shows the relationship between the *average* rate of inflation and a measure of its *variability* (the standard deviation of inflation) among 10 major industrial nations during 1980–1988. Note the clear positive relationship between the inflation rate and its variability. This implies inflation is harder to predict in such high-inflation countries as Italy and France than in nations that have contained inflation, such as Germany and Japan. A potential investment project may be highly profitable when an entrepreneur projects 10 percent inflation but unprofitable in a 4-percent inflation scenario. Investment decisions in a high-inflation economy thus become more of a gamble. The increased uncertainty about future price levels tends to shrink the planning horizon of risk-averse firms and creates a bias against projects

FIGURE 18–5

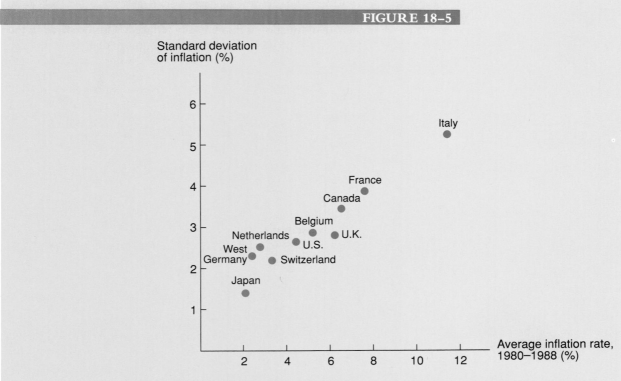

RELATIONSHIP BETWEEN INFLATION RATE AND ITS VARIABILITY

As the *rate* of inflation increases, its *variability* increases. This means that it becomes more difficult to predict or accurately anticipate inflation. Because many of the costs of inflation stem from *unanticipated* inflation, such costs escalate significantly with the rate of inflation. Investment spending is likely to decline in a high-inflation environment because of the great uncertainty about future prices.

Source: Calculated from data published by the Federal Reserve Bank of St. Louis, *International Economic Conditions*, 1989.

with long-term payoffs. Such long-term investment projects often introduce technological change and are thus favorable for long-term economic growth.

Until the 1980s, the tax system, in conjunction with inflation, probably created a bias against investment and economic growth. Depreciation allowances, which provide tax write-offs for expenses associated with plant and equipment expenditures, were based on *historic* or *actual* costs rather than *replacement* costs. With replacement costs rapidly escalating over time, firms did not recoup sufficient tax savings to finance a major portion of replacement costs. Moreover, the tax code forced firms to value inventories of goods at current prices at the end of each accounting period. The cost of acquiring this inventory at an earlier date was lower than at the end of the current accounting period and at the beginning of the next period. Unless firms were willing to change to (otherwise) less-desirable accounting procedures, this resulted in an overstatement of true profits for income-tax purposes. Firms were paying taxes on fictitious profits. Because changes in tax laws in the 1980s reduced these biases against corporations, future inflation may not affect investment as severely as was the case in the 1965–1980 era. This move to *index* our tax system is a major example of the way in which society's institutions are induced to adapt to the phenomenon of inflation.[12]

In addition, inflation probably impairs economic growth in other ways. Inflation drives funds away from stocks and bonds in favor of such inflation hedges as gold, silver, real estate, and works of art. As a result, an inadequate supply of funds may be available for productive investment in plant and equipment. Economic growth therefore suffers. The same result may occur when inflation reduces the savings rate in a country. Further, a country experiencing high inflation is likely to become trapped into applying inconsistent monetary and fiscal policies, a syndrome known as *stop–go macroeconomic policy.* The economy is alternatively restricted by *stop* policies as the inflation rate exceeds acceptable thresholds and stimulated by *go* policies after the restraint results in excessive unemployment. Such swings of policy add to the environment of instability that inhibits investment and economic growth.

Other Adverse Effects of Inflation

In times of relatively high inflation, individuals are induced to behave in ways that though advantageous from their personal vantage point, are highly inefficient from *society's* point of view. As a result, real output declines and the nation's standard of living is reduced.

Inflation imposes a tax on money balances. Such balances depreciate each year in *real* value at a rate equal to the inflation rate. Thus, in periods of high inflation it pays people to hold less wealth in the form of money balances. But this requires more financial transactions, more trips to the bank, and more time generally spent on personal finance. Time available for productive activities is reduced. This has been dubbed the **shoe-leather cost** of inflation. In a similar vein, inflation diverts managerial efforts of business enterprise away from the task of producing goods and services to the socially nonproductive task of coping with the uncertainties of inflation. Time spent on hedging activities in futures markets and foreign-exchange markets are examples of socially wasteful efforts to protect against major price changes.

Other examples of socially wasteful behavior come from financial markets and labor markets. Long-term contracts become too risky for all parties. In financial markets, bonds are risky to both borrowers and lenders. If inflation turns out to be higher than expected, bondholders (lenders) lose. If inflation is less severe than expected, bond issuers (borrowers) lose. Firms have difficulty servicing their debt because interest rates reflect expected inflation that failed to materialize. As a result of these perceived risks to both parties, activity in long-term financial markets dries up. An increasing portion of the flow of funds from savers to deficit-spending units derives from short-term loans. This implies more time devoted to financial affairs since more frequent refinancing decisions by firms and more frequent personal investment decisions by individuals are required. The same principle applies to labor markets. Shorter contracts induced by the uncertainties of inflation implies more

---

[12]An interesting side effect of this adaptation to inflation (via indexation) is that it may erode the will to fight inflation. The less harmful inflation's consequences are perceived, the less vigorously the war against inflation is prosecuted. In Israel, where widespread escalator clauses protect almost everyone from the direct redistributive effects of inflation, there seems to be little popular resistance to inflation. The average annual inflation rate in the past decade in Israel has exceeded 100 percent (see Table 18-1).

human resources devoted to negotiating wages and less resources available for producing goods and services.

These efficiency losses depend on the magnitude of inflation. When the inflation rate is held to a low level, such losses are probably very modest. In times of double-digit inflation, such losses may become quite significant.

SUMMARY

1. All market-oriented economies have been plagued periodically by inflation. Inflation has become more persistent and severe after World War II and was especially virulent in the 1970s.
2. To measure inflation we use a price index—an index of the cost of purchasing a market basket of goods relative to the cost of buying that basket in some base year. In the United States the three main price indexes are the consumer price index (CPI), the producer price index (PPI), and the GNP deflator.
3. These price indexes are of importance to Americans because of considerable use of escalator clauses in wage, salary, and retirement benefits. It is believed that the indexes are subject to a slight upward bias—they tend to overstate the true magnitude of inflation.
4. Prior to World War II, inflation and deflation occurred with equal frequency. Wartime inflation was followed by postwar deflation. As a result, the price level was approximately the same in 1800 and 1945. Since World War II, we have no longer experienced episodes of deflation. The U.S. price level today is more than five times higher than it was in 1945.
5. Several factors have contributed to the increased inflation inertia and the decreased downward wage and price level flexibility in the post-World War II era. These factors include the increased power of automatic stabilizers associated with the federal budget, the more active role of the government toward stabilization policy, the perception on the part of the populace that the government is committed to avoiding severe economic downturns, the increased strength of labor unions, and such institutional changes as federal insurance of bank deposits, minimum wage legislation, and introduction of unemployment insurance. Supply shocks contributed to the inflationary environment of the 1970s.
6. If the government is committed to high levels of output and employment and if a continuing flow of events occurs to produce leftward shifts in the aggregate supply curve, a wage–price spiral of continuing inflation occurs.
7. A *pure* inflation is a hypothetical type in which there are no changes in *relative* prices—all prices rise at the same time. An *impure* inflation is the type we get in the real world. Relative prices are fluctuating while the overall price level is rising. In the hypothetical *pure* inflation, the only adverse consequences are loss of efficiency due to increased time spent marking up prices and managing personal financial affairs.
8. In the *impure* inflations experienced in the real world, inflation has many consequences. Inflation redistributes the nation's income and wealth. The direction and extent of this redistribution depends on the extent to which the inflation is accurately anticipated, the extent to which society's institutions are adapted to inflation, and the behavior of the real (inflation-adjusted) interest rate.
9. Inflation has negative consequences for the long-term growth of the economy and the efficiency with which a nation utilizes its resources. Adverse growth considerations include increased economic uncertainty that reduces investment in plant and equipment and in research and development. Efficiency losses stem from increased time spent on financial affairs due to preference by both lenders and borrowers for shorter-term financial instruments. Similarly, inflation causes both labor and management to prefer shorter-term wage contracts. This requires devoting more time and effort to the bargaining process, a socially nonproductive endeavor.

KEY TERMS

inflation	substitution bias
deflation	demand-pull inflation
price index	automatic stabilizers
base year	pure inflation
consumer price index	impure inflation
producer price index	indexation
GNP deflator	shoe-leather cost

STUDY QUESTIONS AND PROBLEMS

1. By utilizing the current prices of a half dozen major items in your personal budget, together with the prices of these items five years ago (if you aren't sure, estimate them), compute your personal price index today relative to the base year of five years ago.
2. Explain why the CPI is said to overstate the true increase in the cost of living.
3. Explain why the changing role of government in macroeconomic life may have imparted a predisposition toward inflation in the economy in recent decades, as compared to the pre–World War II era.
4. Using the analytical tools of aggregate supply and aggregate demand curves, explain how continuing supply shocks lead to a wage–price spiral if the government is committed to high levels of output and employment. What do you believe is the best way to combat this inflation mechanism? Explain.
5. What do we mean by *pure inflation?* Would such an inflation, if it actually occurred, have any adverse consequences? Explain.
6. "In 1988, when the CPI rose by 4.1 percent, the average American's standard of living declined by 4.1 percent." Analyze this statement.
7. Why might *real* interest rates decline during a period of accelerating inflation? What are the consequences of a decline in real interest rates for the distribution of income and wealth?
8. From your *personal* vantage point, do you prefer a very high or a very low real interest rate over the next decade? Explain.
9. Aside from the effects upon the distribution of income and wealth, explain what you believe are the main adverse consequences of inflation.
10. Why do economists claim that the consequences of inflation depend on the extent to which the inflation is accurately anticipated by the people?

ANSWER TO YOUR TURN

The current price index is calculated as follows. Take the expenditures needed today to purchase the market basket consumed in the base year, divide by the expenditures required in the base year to buy the same basket, and multiply the answer by 100. Expenditures in the *base year* to purchase the four items were $250 (12) + $0.50 (600) + $4000 (1) + $0.90 (1000) = $8200. The current cost of buying the same basket is $275 (12) + $0.75 (600) + $5000 (1) + $1.20 (1000) = $9950. Hence

$$\text{price index} = \frac{\$9950}{\$8200} \times 100 = 121.3$$

The percentage increase in the price level since matriculation is estimated to be 21.3 percent.

SELECTED REFERENCES

Eckstein, Otto, *Core Inflation* (Englewood Cliffs, NJ: Prentice-Hall, 1981). This provocative book presents the hypothesis that inflation develops great momentum and is very difficult to eradicate via restrictive monetary and fiscal policies.

Feldstein, Martin S., "Inflation and the American Economy," *The Public Interest,* March 1982, pp. 63–76. A lucid analysis of inflation's consequences.

Fischer, Stanley and Franco Modigliani, "Towards an Understanding of the Real Effects and Costs of Inflation," *Weltwirtschaftliches Archiv,* 1978, pp. 810–833, Examines the economic effects of inflation.

Gordon, Robert J., "The Consumer Price Index: Measuring Inflation and Causing It," *The Public Interest,* Spring 1981, pp. 112–134. This article points out flaws in our chief measure of prices (some of which have now been corrected).

Hall, Robert E. (ed.), *Inflation: Causes and Effects* (Chicago: University of Chicago Press, 1982). These twelve articles by eminent economists explore various aspects of inflation.

Solow, Robert, "The Intelligent Citizen's Guide to Inflation," *The Public Interest,* Winter 1975, pp. 30–66. Excellent analysis of the effects of inflation, written for the layperson, in which Solow distinguishes between pure and impure inflation.

Triplett, Jack E., "The Measurement of Inflation: A Survey of Research on the Accuracy of Price Indexes," in Paul H. Earl (ed.), *Analysis of Inflation* (Lexington, MA: Lexington Books, 1975). Chapter 2 summarizes economists' studies of our price indexes.

CHAPTER 19

ALTERNATIVE VIEWPOINTS ON THE CONDUCT OF STABILIZATION POLICIES

Unfortunately, policymakers cannot act as if the economy is an automobile that can quickly be steered back and forth. Rather, the procedure of changing aggregate demand is much closer to that of a captain navigating a giant super-tanker. Even if he gives a signal for a hard turn, it takes a mile before he can see a change, and ten miles before the ship makes the turn.

—ROBERT J. GORDON

One of the most controversial issues in contemporary macroeconomics concerns the question of how monetary and fiscal policies should be conducted to best contribute to a healthy and prosperous economy. Macroeconomic issues of this kind tend to be extremely difficult to resolve via scientific inquiry. It is relatively easy to specify the necessary conditions for monetary or fiscal policy to exert a powerful and predictable effect on the economy. But whether these conditions actually prevail in the real world is amazingly difficult to disentangle, even in a world of massive data bases, high-speed computers, and large macroeconomic models. Furthermore, the structure of the economy changes over time. Unlike physics and chemistry, fundamental relationships in economics change. For example, the relationship between the money supply and economic activity was altered by the deregulation of the financial system in the 1980s.

Viewpoints of economists on the appropriate role of government in conducting policies to stabilize the economy have changed significantly in the past century. To understand and appreciate the development of macroeconomic policy, one must go back about one hundred years.

In the nineteenth century and the first third of the twentieth century, classical economics held sway. Classical doctrine espoused a laissez-faire philosophy toward macroeconomic intervention on the part of government, stressing the automatic correction mechanism *outlined in Chapters 11 and 12.*

411

The Great Depression of the 1930s resulted in the demise of classical economics. Because of the depression and a new theoretical framework supplied in Keynes' 1936 The General Theory of Employment, Interest, and Money, *a new consensus prevailed from roughly the 1940s through the 1960s. This consensus held that Keynesian economics—the active use of monetary policy and fiscal policy to keep economic activity at robust but noninflationary levels—was fundamentally appropriate.*

This Keynesian viewpoint was challenged modestly in the 1950s and 1960s and severely in the 1970s by the monetarists, led by Milton Friedman and other economists at the University of Chicago. Monetarists believe that monetary policy is much more powerful than fiscal policy but cannot be implemented successfully to stabilize economic activity. Monetarists believe that it is inappropriate for the Federal Reserve to attempt to use discretionary monetary policy. They believe the Fed should simply increase the money supply at some modest, fixed rate each year, irrespective of current economic conditions.

A fourth framework, which emerged in the 1970s, is rational expectations macroeconomics (REM) or the new classical macroeconomics. Developed by Robert Lucas (University of Chicago), Robert Barro (University of Rochester), and Thomas Sargent and Neil Wallace (University of Minnesota), this school mounts an even stronger rejection of Keynesian economics. Emphasizing the role of expectations and the efficient, market-clearing mechanisms of classical economics, REM proponents argue that systematic, discretionary monetary and fiscal policies are likely to have little or no impact on such key variables as output, employment, and unemployment.

In Chapter 19 we survey the four basic schools of thinking about the appropriate strategy for implementation of monetary and fiscal policies. It would be an exaggeration to say that orthodox thinking has come full circle from classical economics to Keynesianism to monetarism to new classical economics during this century. Nevertheless, the predominant mode of thinking has evolved dramatically since the 1920s. Most economists today remain Keynesian in the sense that they favor active use of monetary and fiscal policies to combat major economic fluctuations. However, both monetarists and proponents of REM have posed serious challenges to this viewpoint in the past 25 years.

CLASSICAL ECONOMICS AND MACROECONOMIC POLICY

Classical Economics
Viewpoint that dominated economic thinking before Keynes. It held that market prices would quickly adjust to boost the economy out of recession, and therefore government intervention in the macroeconomy was unnecessary.

Classical economists (the generations that preceded Keynes' analyses in the 1930s) emphasized the natural tendency of the economy to reach equilibrium at a full-employment level of output. When aggregate demand is insufficient initially to buy back a full-employment level of output, interest rates, wages, and prices decline. These changes boost aggregate demand and raise output. As long as output is below capacity levels, these mechanisms continue in operation, thus boosting economic activity. Hence, there is no such thing as an equilibrium (resting place) below full-employment output levels, in the classical view. The only true equilibrium is said to be at full employment.

Say's Law

Say's Law
The view that production creates its own demand because it generates an equivalent amount of income with which the output may be purchased.

The cornerstone of classical economics was **Say's Law,** which states that the production of goods and services creates the necessary and sufficient means with which to purchase everything produced. In simplified language, "Supply creates its own demand." The implication is that when a full-employment level of output is produced, all of it is purchased. In a barter economy one cannot quarrel with Say's Law. A farmer exchanges wheat for lumber and clothing. The production (supply) of wheat is the direct source of the demand for lumber and clothing. Supply of goods and services in general gives rise to an equivalent demand for other goods and services.

In a money economy it is not so obvious that Say's Law is necessarily valid. The farmer's wheat is exchanged for *money,* but not all receipts are necessarily exchanged for goods and services. The act of saving—the withdrawal of income from the expenditure stream—potentially causes complications in the analysis. Unless the saving is counterbalanced by an equivalent amount of investment spending when output is at full employment, aggregate spending may be insufficient to buy back all the output produced.

The Classical Adjustment Mechanism

In the classical view, the interest rate adjusts sensitively to equate saving and investment intentions, as illustrated in Figure 19-1 (page 414).

In classical economics the interest rate is viewed as the reward for saving, or the opportunity cost of consuming. People make choices regarding *present* consumption versus *future* consumption. Individuals have a positive *time preference*—they prefer to consume *now* rather than later. The higher the rate of interest, the more wealth one accumulates for future consumption by abstaining from consumption now (i.e., by saving).[1] In this view, an increase in interest rates—by increasing the opportunity cost of current consumption—stimulates saving. Hence, our saving schedule in Figure 19-1 is an upward-sloping function of the interest rate. Classical economists believed (as do modern economists—see Chapter 10) that investment spending is

---

[1]Suppose a rational individual is deciding whether to spend $1000 now on a vacation or save the funds for retirement in 40 years. At a two-percent real interest rate, the $1000 would grow to $2208 in inflation-adjusted terms in 40 years. At a five-percent rate, the funds would grow to $7040 in real terms in 40 years. You can see intuitively how an increase in real interest rates raises the opportunity cost of current consumption and therefore works to overcome the natural preference to *enjoy now.* Each dollar set aside today in *depriving yourself* buys more goods and services in the future. As interest rates increase, this margin of future buying power over present buying power escalates dramatically.

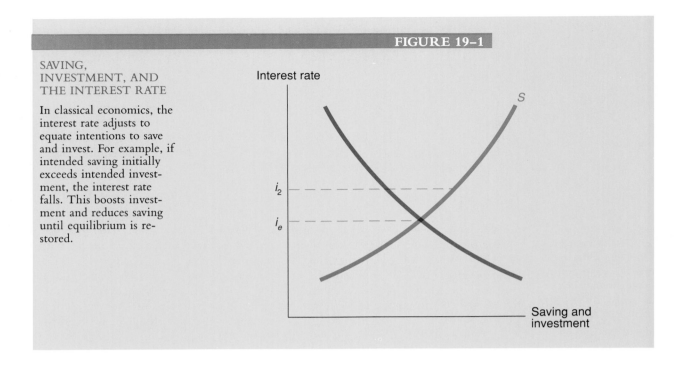

FIGURE 19-1

SAVING, INVESTMENT, AND THE INTEREST RATE

In classical economics, the interest rate adjusts to equate intentions to save and invest. For example, if intended saving initially exceeds intended investment, the interest rate falls. This boosts investment and reduces saving until equilibrium is restored.

also related to the interest rate in the manner illustrated in Figure 19-1. Hence, in the classical scheme of things, the interest rate adjusts to bring saving and investment decisions into equilibrium. In classical thinking, when aggregate demand is insufficient to buy back all the full-employment output, intended saving exceeds intended investment. In terms of Figure 19-1, this implies that the interest rate (i_2) exceeds the equilibrium interest rate (i_e) and must therefore decline. The decline in interest rates, by stimulating investment and retarding saving (boosting consumption), works to remedy the shortfall of aggregate demand.

Also, in the classical view, free and competitive market forces ensure that wages and prices fall when output is initially below full-employment levels. Involuntary unemployment implies that the quantity of labor supplied exceeds the quantity demanded at the existing wage rate. Wages (and therefore prices) allegedly decline whenever less than full employment prevails. Declining prices trigger an increase in the real value of money balances, savings accounts, and government bonds held by individuals and firms. This boost in real wealth induces an increase in expenditures on goods and services. Given flexible prices, this *wealth effect* (as outlined in Chapters 11 and 12) works to stimulate economic activity until full employment is reached.

This classical view implies that there is no need for active government intervention in the macroeconomy. Free and competitive markets suffice to keep the economy hovering near full employment and always give the economy a corrective boost when it temporarily drops below full employment. The appropriate role of government in the economy is a very limited one, in this view, and does not include active attempts to use monetary and fiscal policy to attempt to influence economic activity. A philosophy of *laissez-faire* permeated the thinking of the classical economists: government should keep its hands off the macroeconomy.

THE KEYNESIAN REVOLUTION

It is no coincidence that the seeds of the Keynesian revolution were planted in the 1930s with the publication of Keynes' pathbreaking *General Theory* in 1936. The decade was not kind to classical economics. Real GNP fell by 30 percent from 1929 to 1933 and did not return to 1929 levels until 1939. Unemployment soared to 25 percent and remained above 10 percent throughout the decade. The classical self-correcting mechanism did not appear to be working. In the *General Theory*, Keynes presented an alternative set of analytical tools for understanding the macroeconomy.

Keynes emphasized that saving and investment decisions are made by different sets of people. Furthermore, he believed that these decisions were not effectively brought into balance by changes in the interest rate. In Keynes' framework the crucial determinant of saving is *not* the interest rate, but rather the level of disposable income (recall the consumption function and saving function of Chapter 10). Also, Keynes felt that investment spending was relatively insensitive to changes in the interest rate and depended largely on the highly variable "animal spirits" of businesses. Finally, Keynes argued that technical factors at times might prevent the interest rate from falling enough to bring saving and investment into equilibrium. For all these reasons, Keynes rejected the classical view of the interest rate as the equilibrator of saving and investment decisions, as portrayed in Figure 19-1. When, at current output levels, saving exceeds investment, these variables are brought into equilibrium via a contraction in output and income instead of a decline in interest rates.

Furthermore, Keynes questioned the classical assumption of highly flexible wages and prices. He did not quarrel with the proposition that wages and prices rise in periods of excess demand for labor, goods, and services. But he believed that certain impediments inhibited the downward flexibility of wages and prices in periods of weak demand or excess supply. He believed that the structure of the economy could not be described adequately by the idealized supply and demand model of perfectly competitive markets. Unions, monopolistic and oligopolistic industries, minimum wage laws, government price supports, and other institutional factors render the classical assumption of downwardly flexible wages and prices unrealistic. When wages and prices are inflexible in the downward direction, the classical self-correcting mechanism fails to lift the economy out of depression. Keynes attacked those who advocated reliance on the economy's self-corrective mechanism through his famous dictum: "In the long run, we're all dead."

Inasmuch as Keynes believed the self-correcting mechanism does not work on the downside, he called for aggressive government intervention to boost aggregate demand when the economy is weak.[2] Given the disastrous experience of the 1930s, economists throughout the free world became convinced that Keynes was fundamentally correct. To maintain prosperity, the capitalistic system required occasional intervention by government to give the economy a "shot in the arm."

---

[2]Keynes' framework of analysis is symmetrical in that it applies equally to the reverse case in which an inflationary gap exists—the case in which aggregate demand is excessive at full-employment output. Such a situation calls for implementation of contractionary or restrictive monetary and fiscal policies. Since Keynes developed his framework in the midst of the Great Depression, he naturally emphasized the recessionary gap situation.

Keynesians
Economists who, like Keynes, believe that a capitalistic economy does not tend automatically toward a full-employment equilibrium; hence, activist monetary and fiscal policies are advocated.

In the Employment Act of 1946, the U.S. government officially acknowledged a commitment to promote a prosperous and strong economy—implicitly by utilizing its tools of monetary and fiscal policy when needed. The Keynesian prescription was adopted not only by Keynes' homeland (England) and the United States, but by all industrialized nations. By the late 1940s, classical economics had been thoroughly overturned by the new Keynesian orthodoxy. This Keynesian prescription for active implementation of monetary and fiscal policies to stabilize economic activity went relatively unchallenged for almost three decades after Keynes' book appeared in the 1930s.

Today, however, the economics profession is divided, with many economists unwilling to be labeled "Keynesian." Keynesian economics reached its high tide of popularity in the mid-1960s. A picture of Keynes appeared on the cover of Time Magazine in 1965, a year that represents a sort of watershed in macroeconomic thinking. It came *after* the Keynesian-inspired tax cuts of the early 1960s gave a much-needed boost to economic activity and *before* the escalation of the Vietnam War (1966–1968) ushered in a 15-year era of economic nightmares in the United States.

The Monetarist Critique of Keynesian Economics

In the early days of their debates (1950s and 1960s), Keynesians and monetarists clashed over the issue of whether monetary policy or fiscal policy was the more powerful and effective instrument of policy. Keynesians—armed with the consumption function, multiplier, and other analytical tools introduced in Keynes' 1936 work—argued that fiscal policy was the more powerful. Monetarists—emphasizing the stability of money demand and velocity as well as the crowding-out hypothesis—were convinced that monetary policy was the more powerful. In fact, some monetarists claimed that fiscal policy was *totally* ineffective. By the 1970s, a consensus had been reached in the profession that both monetary and fiscal policy were quite potent.

Monetarists
Economists who share the view that money exerts a dominant effect on economic activity and that a capitalistic economy has an effective self-regulating mechanism. Activist policies are thought to hinder these corrective mechanisms and to destabilize economic activity, and are therefore rejected.

More recently the debate turned to the issue of whether policy makers are capable of implementing these powerful tools to contribute to a more stable business cycle. Keynesians argue in the affirmative, advocating policy activism to attempt to stabilize the economy at a high level of output and employment. Monetarists dissent from this view, arguing that efforts to implement discretionary policies to stabilize economic activity are likely to make things worse.

In the unqualified simple diagrams used in introductory economics (Figure 19-2), the case for active government intervention to stabilize economic activity at high output levels appears to be unassailable and noncontroversial at first glance.

Given the aggregate supply and aggregate demand schedules, the economy settles to an output level of Y_E, well short of full-employment output (Y_F). A recessionary gap ($Y_F - Y_E$) exists. The natural inclination of Keynesian-trained economists is for the government to "go for it"—to use monetary and fiscal policy measures to boost aggregate demand and move the equilibrium output toward Y_F.

In the real world, however, things are not nearly so simple. Critics of policy activism point out that such diagrams are quite nice for pedagogical purposes in the classroom, but in the real world we really *don't know* the positions of the aggregate demand and aggregate supply schedules—these positions are subject to considerable

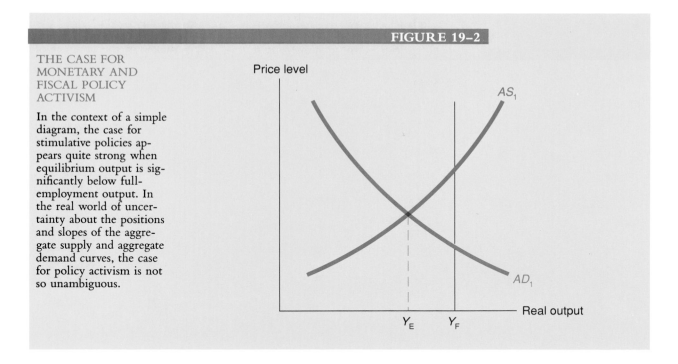

FIGURE 19–2

THE CASE FOR MONETARY AND FISCAL POLICY ACTIVISM

In the context of a simple diagram, the case for stimulative policies appears quite strong when equilibrium output is significantly below full-employment output. In the real world of uncertainty about the positions and slopes of the aggregate supply and aggregate demand curves, the case for policy activism is not so unambiguous.

uncertainty. Also, there is disagreement about the *slopes* of these schedules. If the aggregate supply curve is relatively steep, as monetarists tend to believe, stimulus to aggregate demand results in considerable inflation. Furthermore, there is much uncertainty about the *dynamics* of the system—how rapidly the aggregate demand and aggregate supply schedules shift over time and how fast output and the price level change in response to such shifts. Many economists believe that monetary and fiscal policies influence the economy with a rather significant and variable time lag. This simply means that economists are not sure exactly when monetary and fiscal policy measures are reflected in changes in output, employment, and inflation.

Finally, there is even disagreement among economists as to what output level constitutes *full employment*. As noted in Chapter 17, the natural unemployment rate fluctuates over time and is subject to uncertainty.[3] This is another way of saying that the full-employment output level of the economy is not known.

Given these uncertainties about the positions, slopes, and dynamics of the aggregate supply and demand schedules and the uncertainty about the full-employment output level, monetarists stress the fact that mistakes are inevitable when using discretionary policies. The larger and more frequent such mistakes are, the less attractive is the case for utilizing discretionary policies. This is particularly true if the economy's self-correcting mechanism is operable. Why employ uncertain

---

[3]In the spring of 1989, the U.S. unemployment rate dropped to 5.0 percent, its lowest level in 15 years. Some economists proclaimed that full employment was at hand. Others argued that we should aim for a 4.5 percent rate.

policy measures if the economy inherently stabilizes at output levels near full employment when left to its own devices?

Monetarists can point to numerous serious past mistakes in the conduct of Federal Reserve monetary policy. Numerous gross errors were made in the 1930s. The Fed sharply raised its discount rate in 1931 while output, income, and the price level were declining and the unemployment rate was above ten percent. The Fed sat back and passively watched the collapse of the banking system as the public panicked and withdrew currency from banks, thereby precipitating a multiple contraction of bank deposits and money. Moreover, the Fed raised reserve requirements in 1937 and 1938 while the economy was still mired in depression.

In the 1940s, the Fed became an engine of inflation as it held interest rates at artificially low levels. In the late 1960s and again in the late 1970s, the Fed was too stimulative, thus paving the way for episodes of severe inflation. In retrospect, it seems clear that the Fed hit the brake too hard in 1981–1982, helping to account for a severe recession and the first instance since the 1930s in which the unemployment rate went above ten percent.

Advocates of activist monetary and fiscal policies cannot deny that errors have frequently been made in the past. But they point out that this does *not* imply that discretionary policies have done more harm than good. In numerous instances, policy measures have been beneficial. Some point to the increase in economic stability in the post-World War II era as evidence of superior macroeconomic policies in the past 40 years. However, other factors may account for this improvement in economic stability.[4] Furthermore, the Fed has surely learned from its past mistakes. No one today can imagine the Fed repeating its gross mistakes of the 1930s. The improvement in economic information and economic analysis as well as the experience gained from past mistakes convince activists that discretionary policies on balance will contribute to economic stability in the future.

Nevertheless, the monetarist critics of activist policies have, at the least, done the world a favor by emphasizing how complicated the economy is and by outlining the obstacles to conducting successful discretionary stabilization policies. Lags are a serious problem. There is considerable uncertainty in the various links through which changes in policy ultimately influence economic activity. Things are not at all simple. Policymakers have every reason to be humble in view of their past record.

THE MONETARIST POSITION

Monetarists usually assert that the Federal Reserve, on balance, has actually contributed to the *instability* of the economy in the past. Furthermore, monetarists believe that discretionary monetary policy is likely to continue to destabilize economic activity in the future. This is thought to be true partly because of political forces and partly because the Fed has demonstrated an annoying propensity to

---

[4]Because income-tax rates have been much higher in the postwar period, the size of the effective marginal propensity to consume out of GNP and the size of the income multiplier have decreased sharply (see Chapter 11, p. 254). Therefore, exogenous shifts in investment, net exports, and other components of aggregate demand give rise to smaller fluctuations in economic activity. The *automatic stability* or *built-in stability* of the economy has increased. This factor, rather than implementation of successful monetary and fiscal policy, probably accounts for most of the improvement in economic stability in the second half of the twentieth century. See Robert J. Gordon, "Evolution in Postwar Macroeconomics," in Martin S. Feldstein (ed.), *The American Economy in Transition* (University of Chicago Press, 1980).

become sidetracked from its true objective by various *pseudo objectives* such as attempting to hold down nominal interest rates to assist the government in financing its debt or attempting to influence foreign-exchange rates or stock market fluctuations.

Monetarists also believe that the Fed is incapable of contributing to economic stability even if it casts aside all political considerations and focuses all attention on the one valid objective of monetary policy—stabilizing aggregate demand for goods and services. This skeptical viewpoint is based on forecasting inadequacies and the uncertainties about the positions, slopes, and dynamics of the aggregate supply and demand schedules (as noted earlier). In the current state of the art, in the view of monetarists, the Fed is simply incapable of consistently putting in place policies that contribute to economic stability.

To obtain an understanding of the procedures recommended by monetarists, we return to the equation of exchange, $MV \equiv PY$. Recall that M represents the money supply and V (velocity) indicates the turnover rate of the money supply in purchasing newly produced goods and services (GNP). MV thus represents spending on final goods and services (GNP). On the right side, P is the average price of the individual goods and services entering into GNP and Y is the real quantity of GNP produced. Hence, PY is a measure of nominal GNP. The equation of exchange states that spending on GNP from the *money* side (MV) is identically equal to GNP spending viewed from the *goods* side (PY).

The equation of exchange describes the relationship among the money supply, velocity, and GNP expenditures at a given point in time, such as 1990. If we convert the equation to its dynamic form to relate the *growth rates over time* of these variables, we obtain the following:

$$\%\Delta M + \%\Delta V = \%\Delta P + \%\Delta Y \qquad (19\text{--}1)$$

In this expression, the growth rate of money plus the growth rate of velocity is the growth rate of GNP expenditures, which in turn is equivalent to the growth rate of the price level (the inflation rate) plus the growth rate of real output. If the supply of money grows eight percent in one year and velocity increases two percent, nominal GNP rises at a ten-percent annual rate. The inflation rate ($\%\Delta P$) and the real-output growth rate ($\%\Delta Y$) must therefore sum to ten percent. If $\%\Delta P$ is 5%, $\%\Delta Y$ is also 5%. If $\%\Delta P$ is 8%, $\%\Delta Y$ must be 2%.

The Constant Money-Growth Rule

The goal of monetary policy, in principle, should be to ensure that aggregate expenditures ($\%\Delta M + \%\Delta V$) expand at a rate that allows real output to grow over time at a rate comparable to the growth of potential real GNP without igniting inflationary pressures. Most monetarist economists are convinced that the political and technical obstacles confronting the Fed's efforts to conduct policies that successfully smooth the swings in economic activity are very severe. These economists advocate that the Fed abandon its discretionary monetary policy and adopt a rule in which the money supply grows at some slow and steady rate *irrespective of contemporary economic conditions.* But how fast should the supply of money grow in this automatic scheme? We can shed some light on that issue by examining the variables in Equation 19-1.

Ideally, a worthy goal is to aim for zero inflation in the long run ($\%\Delta P = 0$). Real output growth ($\%\Delta Y$) can expand in the long run only as fast as the sum of labor-force growth and productivity growth—roughly three percent per year. Hence, the desired growth rate of nominal GNP expenditures is approximately three percent per year. To arrive at the appropriate rule for constant money growth ($\%\Delta M$), one must forecast (or guess) the trend growth rate of velocity ($\%\Delta V$). If the best forecast for velocity is zero growth, the appropriate money growth rule is three percent per year. If one expects a rising trend for velocity, the money growth rule is established at a somewhat slower rate.

The Lags of Policy   The existence of monetary policy lags is instrumental in the monetarist view that the fixed money-growth rule is superior to the conventional activist or discretionary policy. The monetarist viewpoint is illustrated through the hypothetical cyclical output behavior indicated in Figure 19-3. With the aid of hindsight in this hypothetical scheme, we note that output peaked at time t_0 and that the economy then began to slide into recession. Ideally, a stimulative monetary policy is immediately implemented at that point (if not earlier) to cushion the downturn. However, given the lags in publication of data and the imperfections of and conflicting stories told by business cycle indicators, those in charge of policy are

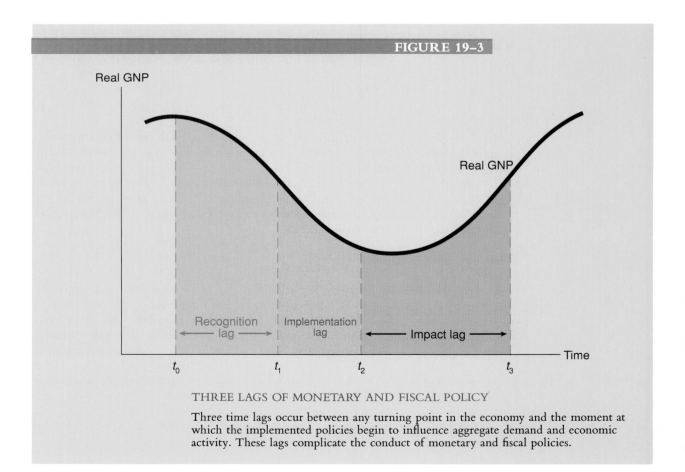

FIGURE 19–3

THREE LAGS OF MONETARY AND FISCAL POLICY

Three time lags occur between any turning point in the economy and the moment at which the implemented policies begin to influence aggregate demand and economic activity. These lags complicate the conduct of monetary and fiscal policies.

Recognition Lag
The time period that elapses between the point at which a change in policy is needed and when the need is recognized by policymakers.

Implementation Lag
The time period that elapses between the point at which a need for policy change is recognized and when the change in policy is implemented.

Impact Lag
The time period that elapses between the point at which a new policy is implemented and when the policy begins to influence economic activity.

not aware of the economic downturn until t_1. This passage of time $(t_0 - t_1)$ is known as the **recognition lag.**

In any bureaucratic organization, further time elapses between the recognition of need for action and the implementation of corrective action. This period $(t_1 - t_2)$ is known as the **implementation lag.** In the case of discretionary *fiscal policy*, the implementation lag can be long and frustrating because legislated changes in tax rates and expenditures require congressional action. Such action is heavily influenced by the prevailing political winds and other impediments. In the case of monetary policy, the implementation lag tends to be brief because the FOMC conducts regularly scheduled meetings every six weeks in Washington and is equipped (via special telephonic hookup) to conduct emergency meetings if necessary. The FOMC has authority to order immediate changes in monetary policy.

Finally, at time t_2, stimulative policies are put in place. The Fed may reduce its discount rate and pump reserves into the banking system via open market purchases of securities. However, considerable time passes $(t_2 - t_3)$ before the stimulative measures begin to strongly influence spending, GNP, and employment. This **impact lag** of monetary policy is believed to be rather long and variable.[5] The economic stimulus—which ideally would have occurred at time t_0—does not occur until time t_3, at a time when the economy has already bottomed out and is recovering strongly on its own. The emerging stimulus, by contributing to an overheated economy and its associated inflationary pressures, can do more harm than good.

Monetarists argue, in terms of the dynamic equation of exchange, that velocity growth behaves in a smooth, predictable pattern. Hence, slow and steady growth in M yields slow and steady growth in aggregate spending ($\%\Delta M + \%\Delta V$), the desired norm. By doing this, the **constant (fixed) money-growth rule** avoids the extremes of severe inflation (such as the 1970s) and depressions (such as 1929–1933). No one claims that the money growth rule is Utopian—that it prevents periods of inflation and recession.[6] Monetarists admit that unexpected movements in velocity are bound to give rise to occasional bouts of mild inflation and recession. Allegedly, however, we would experience a more satisfactory economic performance than the Fed has delivered in the 75 years of its existence.

The Activist Critique of the Monetarist Position

Advocates of activist monetary and fiscal policies believe that the monetarists overstate both the power of the automatic corrective mechanisms in the economy and the stability and predictability of velocity. Such economists view velocity as a flexible variable, increasing in cyclical recoveries, declining in recessions, and fluctuating sharply in response to changes in institutional factors, expectations, interest rates, and uncertainty. Therefore, the link between the money supply and economic activity is believed to be a loose and uncertain one. If one cannot predict the future behavior of velocity within reasonable bounds, one cannot specify in

---

[5]Milton Friedman once estimated the impact lag of monetary policy to be anywhere from 6 to 18 months. More recently, Robert Gordon has estimated the mean lag to be 9 months.

[6]Monetarists frequently assert that the Fed has a natural tendency to be too stimulative. Political forces may dictate this bias, since stimulative policies tend to influence output and employment more quickly than they influence inflation. Congress often pressures the Fed to pursue stimulative policies to get the economy moving in election years (every other year). A constant money-growth rule would tend to make the Fed immune to such pressures, as suggested in Exhibit 19-1 (page 422).

EXHIBIT 19–1

FED POLITICS AND THE CASE FOR A CONSTANT MONEY-GROWTH RULE

When the Federal Reserve System was founded many decades ago, its framers were wary of the possibility of political considerations creeping in to influence Fed policy. Numerous safeguards were implemented with a view toward minimizing the exposure of the institution to political pressures. Governors were to have one nonrenewable 14-year term. Appointment dates were staggered so that one governor's term expired every two years. Hence, a one-term U.S. president normally would appoint only two of the seven members of the Board of Governors, and thus be unable to *stack* the Board for political purposes. Most importantly, the Fed has its own financial resources—mainly in the form of large annual interest income from its huge portfolio of securities. Unlike government agencies that must request operating budgets from Congress each year, the Fed is financially independent. This enables the Fed to be objective in its decision making, because it reduces the feasibility of retribution by Congress for unpopular policy actions the Fed believes are needed for the nation's long-term economic health.

In spite of the safeguards, the Fed is by no means immune to outside political considerations. Some economists speak of a "political business cycle" in which the Fed is alleged to have a propensity for stimulating economic activity in (especially presidential) election years and then moving to compensate by tightening credit once the election is past. The evidence seems mixed. President Nixon sought reelection in 1972. As the election approached, with wage and price controls in place, Fed policy turned quite stimulative. This, coupled with a severe oil-price shock a few months later, boosted U.S. inflation into the double-digit range in 1973. In 1980, however, as President Jimmy Carter ran for reelection against Ronald Reagan, the Fed clamped down in an effort to contain inflation that was already rampant. Interest rates increased dramatically.

An excellent test of the Federal Reserve's political independence was presented in the 1988 election year as George Bush opposed Michael Dukakis in the presidential campaign. Because of certain premature retirements from the Board of Governors, President Reagan had appointed all six members of the Board, with the seventh seat on the Board temporarily vacant. The entire Board was Republican, appointed by the Reagan-Bush Administrations of 1980–1988, and a natural suspicion developed in 1988 that the Fed might be sympathetic to a Bush victory in November. Bush stood to benefit from a booming economic environment accompanied by reasonably low interest rates. Some observers were skeptical that the Fed had the objectivity to apply the restrictive monetary medicine normally prescribed for an economy entering the boom phase of the business cycle. If the skepticism were well founded, we would pay for it later with higher inflation and a post-election recession to bring the inflation back down.

An advantage of a constant money-growth rule is that the Fed is unable to play politics with the U.S. economy as hostage. If such a rule had been in place in 1988, Fed critics argue, the money supply would not have been allowed to increase as fast as it did (seven-percent annual rate in the first half of 1988). Interest rates would have been allowed to rise more rapidly in response to the expanding economic activity and rising inflationary expectations as the U.S. economic boom of 1988 progressed. The Fed would have been powerless to attempt to hold down interest rates. The Fed could face down any politician by simply observing that it had no choice—it was following the constant money-growth rule. To the extent that the *political business cycle* really exists and is damaging to the U.S. economy in the long run, the case for the constant money-growth rule emerges quite strongly. However, the evidence on the existence of a *political business cycle* is inconclusive.

advance the appropriate growth rate of money for the constant money-growth rule. Critics of monetarism charge that the strong historical correlation between money and GNP has misled the monetarists into overstating the true influence of money (see Exhibit 19-2).

These policy activists (including most Keynesians) believe the Fed should maintain a discretionary policy so that it can respond to these surprise changes in

ROBERT J. BARRO, University of Rochester—a leading proponent of Rational Expectations Macroeconomics

velocity by aggressively altering the growth rate of money. In 1986, for example, the velocity of money (GNP/M-1) declined by about nine percent. The Fed, by rapidly expanding the supply of money (M-1 increased 16 percent in 1986), prevented a potential contraction in aggregate demand (*MV*), thus saving the nation from a recession. In a constant money-growth rule regime, the Fed is handcuffed and unable to respond to such swings in money demand and velocity.

On average, a philosophical difference exists between monetarists and nonmonetarists concerning the relative magnitude of the costs of inflation and unemployment. Monetarists tend to be politically conservative and regard inflation as *public enemy number one.* Keynesians (the activists) are on the liberal side of the spectrum, typically regarding unemployment as a more serious social disease than inflation. Activists typically prefer a high-pressure economy, and are willing to accept the risk of higher inflation as a price for maintaining low rates of unemployment.

Critics of the constant money-growth rule cannot deny that the Fed has made some major policy mistakes in the past. However, they believe that the Fed has learned from these errors. The state of the art of central banking has surely improved. Advocates of activist Federal Reserve monetary policy are convinced that the Fed of the 1990s can significantly outperform a rigid constant money-growth rule.

RATIONAL EXPECTATIONS MACROECONOMICS (REM)—THE NEW CLASSICAL MACROECONOMICS

Rational Expectations Macroeconomics (REM) or New Classical Macroeconomics
Modern school of economists that emphasizes the effectiveness of market forces pushing the economy toward full employment and views discretionary stabilization policies as being ineffective.

By combining the flexible price, market clearing tenets of classical economics with some fairly strong assumptions about the way people form future expectations, the new classical macroeconomics school arrives at some rather startling conclusions about macroeconomic policy.

Like monetarists, proponents of **Rational Expectations Macroeconomics (REM)** believe the economy contains an inherent, powerful self-correcting mechanism. This mechanism is thought to bring equilibrium output back to the natural level—the level corresponding to the natural unemployment rate. Like monetarists, proponents of REM stress the possibility of instability created by efforts to conduct active monetary and fiscal policies in an attempt to smooth economic fluctuations. Unlike monetarism, REM implies that *systematic* and *predictable* changes in the money supply have *no impact* on real output and unemployment. Hence, proponents of REM arrive at the same conclusion as monetarists—government should not attempt to implement countercyclical monetary and fiscal policies—via a totally different route.

Let us examine the assumptions underlying REM so we understand the basis for the startling conclusion that discretionary monetary and fiscal policies are useless—even harmful—and should be abandoned.

Assumptions of REM

As the term implies, the key ingredient in REM is the assumption that individuals and firms form expectations *rationally.* Expectations are said to be rational if economic agents take into account all *relevant, available* information and utilize this information *efficiently* in formulating expectations about the future. This by no means implies that economic agents have perfect foresight, anticipating the future with perfect accuracy. Forecasts are frequently incorrect. But REM assumes that

---

EXHIBIT 19–2

INTERPRETING THE CORRELATION BETWEEN MONEY SUPPLY AND GNP

The strong historical correlation between the supply of money and nominal GNP is well known—although the correlation diminished somewhat in the 1980s. This relationship is demonstrated in Figure 19-4. Some analysts have pointed to the strong statistical association illustrated as evidence that money has a powerful effect on the economy. There is undeniably a strong correlation between money and GNP. But remember that correlation does not imply causation. The change in money supply might be causing the change in GNP, the change in GNP might be causing the change in the money supply, or some third factor might be inducing both GNP and the money supply to move in tandem.

Given their framework of analysis, monetarists interpret the causal nexus as running from money to GNP. People are said to hold money to finance transactions, and the amount they hold is alleged to be a stable proportion of such transactions. An increase in the actual money supply therefore upsets the equilibrium between actual money holdings and desired holdings. People spend these excess money balances on goods and services as well as on financial assets and other things. GNP rises until the normal relationship between the existing money stock and output is restored. Hence, changes in the money supply cause an approximately proportional change in GNP. Money drives spending and GNP, in the monetarist view.

Nonmonetarists have a different explanation of the forces accounting for the powerful statistical association between M-1 and GNP. Keynesians, for example, believe that autonomous shifts in consumption, investment spending, government purchases, and net exports—independent of changes in the money supply—are the principal factors causing changes in aggregate demand and GNP. Given the Federal Reserve's historic propensity for stabilizing interest rates in the short run, an upward shift in aggregate demand places upward pressure on interest rates and induces the Fed to pump reserves into the banking system and increase the money supply. By the same token, a slump in aggregate spending exerts downward pressure on interest rates. To remain on its interest rate target, the Fed must drain reserves from the banking system and reduce the supply of money. One could argue that changes in GNP are causing changes in M-1, given the Federal Reserve's policy process.

This nonmonetarist viewpoint implies that if the Fed were to deemphasize or abandon its policy of attempting to stabilize interest rates, the correlation between M-1 and GNP would diminish or disappear. In fact, the correlation did decrease significantly in the 1970s and 1980s as the Fed moved toward placing more emphasis on money supply targets. Monetarists assert that this decrease in the stability of velocity was a temporary phenomenon induced first by the rash of financial

---

economic agents do not make *systematic* mistakes in forecasting future economic phenomena. For example, people do not consistently overestimate or underestimate future inflation. Forecast errors are *random*—sometimes too high, sometimes too low—because people quickly learn from past mistakes and try not to repeat them.

This assumption is in contrast with much earlier work in economics, which held that expectations are *adaptive*—change gradually over time in response to recent phenomena. Given adaptive expectations, economic agents tend to persistently underestimate inflation while it is accelerating and overestimate it while it is slowing down.

Proponents of REM believe that individuals and firms are quite sophisticated in economic matters, that they understand the fundamental workings of the economy. For example, individuals and firms are well aware of the linkage between money supply growth, inflation, and interest rates. They are aware of the tendency for a *political business cycle*—the tendency for the economy to be well stimulated in election years. And they are aware of the threshold unemployment and inflation rates

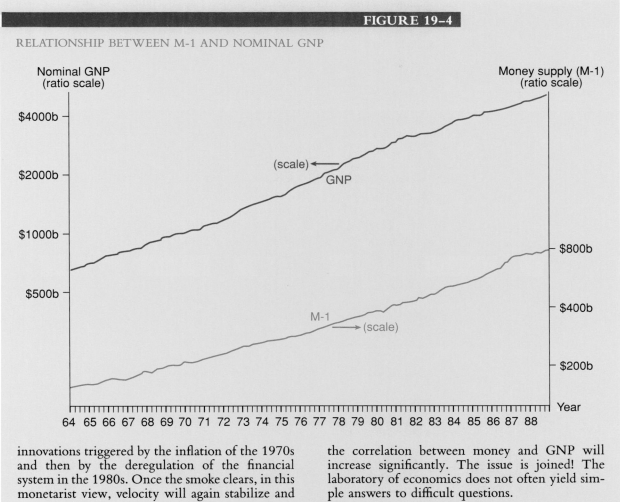

FIGURE 19–4

RELATIONSHIP BETWEEN M-1 AND NOMINAL GNP

Nominal GNP
(ratio scale)

Money supply (M-1)
(ratio scale)

$4000b

$2000b

(scale) ←

GNP

$1000b

$800b

$500b

$400b

M-1

(scale)

$200b

Year

64 65 66 67 68 69 70 71 72 73 74 75 76 77 78 79 80 81 82 83 84 85 86 87 88

innovations triggered by the inflation of the 1970s and then by the deregulation of the financial system in the 1980s. Once the smoke clears, in this monetarist view, velocity will again stabilize and the correlation between money and GNP will increase significantly. The issue is joined! The laboratory of economics does not often yield simple answers to difficult questions.

that trigger corrective efforts by the Federal Reserve System. Basically, these economic agents are as smart and perceptive as the best economic analysts.

Suppose the inflation rate has been declining in recent years from eight percent to six percent to four percent currently. In adaptive expectations, agents sluggishly revise their forecasts of future inflation downward in response to the recent decline in actual inflation. If rational expectations prevail, economic agents focus attention on the behavior of the factors that state-of-the-art economic models include as determinants of future inflation—changes in oil prices, the money supply, the U.S. exchange rate with other nations, and so forth. If these factors on balance indicate that inflation will accelerate, agents revise their inflationary expectations upward in spite of the fact that the recent trend of inflation has been downward.

In addition, rational expectationists believe that the competitive model of supply and demand accurately describes most of our product and resource markets. Prices of goods, services, and labor (wages) change quickly in response to shifts in supply and demand schedules. Economic agents quickly process new information into supply and demand schedules and prices and wages respond quickly to the information. Markets continuously clear and are in equilibrium.

Implications of REM for Macroeconomic Policy

As indicated, REM has crucial implications for the effectiveness of countercyclical monetary and fiscal policies. We illustrate this point in Figure 19-5.

Given the aggregate supply (AS_1) and aggregate demand (AD_1) curves of Figure 19-5, assume the economy currently is at A, with equilibrium output (Y_{E1}) significantly below Y_F. A recessionary gap prevails. The natural inclination of a Keynesian is to implement stimulative monetary and fiscal policies to shift the aggregate demand curve rightward from AD_1 to AD_2, thereby raising output toward the full-employment level. A monetarist—skeptical of the motives of government officials and cognizant of uncertainty, forecasting difficulties, and policy lags—counsels the Fed and Congress to restrain themselves and leave the macroeconomy to its own devices. An advocate of REM argues that stimulative monetary and fiscal policies are ineffective and inappropriate for an entirely different reason. Actions of the public taken in response to the (correct) anticipation of implementation of stimulative policies nullify the real effects of the policies, rendering them ineffective in boosting output and employment.

Based on past experience, the public comes to expect the government to implement stimulative macroeconomic measures to boost the economy whenever a large output gap develops. As soon as such policy is announced via a tax cut, boost in money supply growth, or whatever, firms raise prices and workers push for larger wage hikes. Firms generally grant the wage increases, both firms and workers believing that these price and wage hikes will be *ratified* or *validated* by the stimulative

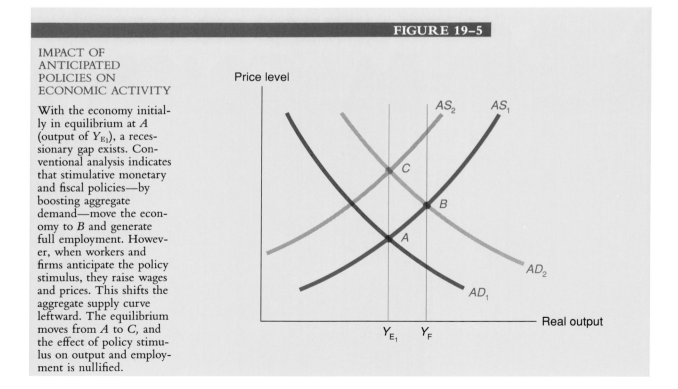

FIGURE 19–5

IMPACT OF ANTICIPATED POLICIES ON ECONOMIC ACTIVITY

With the economy initially in equilibrium at A (output of Y_{E1}), a recessionary gap exists. Conventional analysis indicates that stimulative monetary and fiscal policies—by boosting aggregate demand—move the economy to B and generate full employment. However, when workers and firms anticipate the policy stimulus, they raise wages and prices. This shifts the aggregate supply curve leftward. The equilibrium moves from A to C, and the effect of policy stimulus on output and employment is nullified.

macropolicies. These price and wage hikes shift the nation's aggregate supply schedule leftward to AS_2, nullifying all or much of the potential impact of the stimulative policy upon real output and employment. Instead of moving from A to B in Figure 19-5, we move from A to C. Since the aggregate supply schedule shifted leftward, much of the additional demand imparted by monetary and/or fiscal stimulus is simply dissipated in higher prices.[7]

If workers and firms formulate expectations rationally, and if wages and prices adapt immediately to changes in expectations, predictable monetary and fiscal policies are totally ineffective in stimulating output and employment. Only *unanticipated* or *surprise* policies have an impact.

> *Policy Ineffectiveness Theorem*   *Anticipated* changes in the money supply and/or fiscal policy have no effect on real variables such as output, income, and employment; they only affect the price level. In the REM framework, only *unanticipated* or *surprise* policies influence output and employment.

Policy Ineffectiveness Theorem
Proposition advocated by proponents of REM or new classical macroeconomics that only *surprise* or *unanticipated* policies have an effect on such real economic variables as output and employment.

The **policy ineffectiveness theorem,** if valid, yields both good news and bad news. The bad news is that discretionary monetary and fiscal policies are useless for purposes of assisting the economy out of a recession. The only effective discretionary policies are the unexpected ones, and the public quickly catches on to the government's game of trying to stimulate the economy whenever it is down. Since government policy is incapable of fooling the people consistently for constructive purposes, government should give up the game. Besides, in the view of REM proponents, the economy *self-corrects* on its own, the unemployment rate gravitating powerfully toward its natural level. An implication of REM is that the government should rescind the Employment Act of 1946, the Humphrey-Hawkins Full-Employment Act of 1978, and abandon use of discretionary monetary and fiscal policies.

The good news implied by REM is that a *credible,* preannounced anti-inflationary macropolicy can lead us out of inflation without any accompanying loss of output or increase in unemployment. Suppose, while inflation has been running at an annual ten-percent rate, the Fed announces its intention to slow annual money growth from ten percent to two percent. To the extent that economic agents are convinced that the Fed means business, wage hikes are severely curtailed because of the anticipated severely restricted economic environment. The aggregate supply curve shifts rightward, or at least dramatically slows its leftward movement. This means that the output loss associated with eliminating inflation is reduced. Under strong assumptions about totally credible anti-inflation measures, rational expectations, and instantaneous market clearing in labor and product markets, inflation may be eliminated without any cost in the form of a temporary rise in unemployment.

Phillips Curve Implications of REM

The preceding analysis is explained in the context of a Phillips Curve framework in Figure 19-6 (page 428). Recall from Chapter 17 that most economists believe stimulative macropolicies can boost us from A to B in the *short run,* buying at least a temporary reduction in unemployment by accepting a higher rate of inflation. The

---

[7]It has been suggested that well-intentioned countercyclical policies might even serve to systematically *destabilize* economic activity. Suppose the government systematically grants large investment tax credits in recessions to boost investment and later removes the credits when the economy is strong. As the economy starts into recession, firms postpone investment projects as they wait for the credits to be granted. This slows investment spending in the recession, causing the downturn to be deeper than it would otherwise be.

FIGURE 19–6

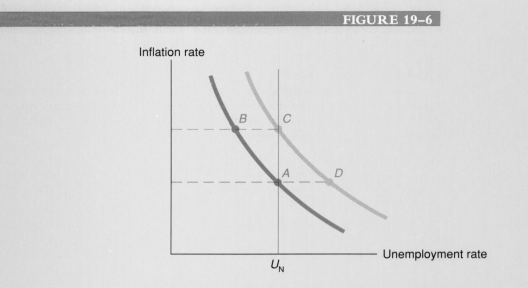

REM AND THE VERTICAL SHORT-RUN PHILLIPS CURVE

Conventional analysis indicates that a short-run trade-off between inflation and unemployment exists. By boosting aggregate demand, monetary and fiscal policy can fool workers, reduce real wages (by boosting inflation), and reduce unemployment for a time. In a rational-expectations world, people learn to anticipate such stimulative policies whenever the economy is depressed. Workers are not fooled, the boost in inflation does not reduce real wages, and unemployment does not decline. In a REM world, the short-run Phillips curve is vertical. Policy is ineffective.

boost in inflation tends initially to fool workers, depress real wages, and boost profits, output, and employment. Hence, the stimulative macropolicies reduce unemployment in the short run—until people's expectations adjust to the new level of inflation.

Not true in a world of rational expectations! Agents observe the stimulative macropolicies as they are implemented and immediately revise their inflation expectations upward. Wage inflation is boosted immediately—as soon as the policy is announced. Because the workers are not fooled by the stimulative policies, real wages fail to decline, profits do not increase, and neither do output and employment. Unemployment remains at the same level (U_N in Figure 19-6), and we move from A to C rather than from A to B. The stimulative policy, since it was immediately diagnosed and acted upon by firms and individuals, had no effect on such real variables as output, employment, and unemployment, *even in the short run*. Only when individuals and firms are *surprised* by monetary and fiscal policies do these policies generate real effects.

By the same token, conventional analysis indicates that to get out of an entrenched inflation environment we must endure a transition period of higher unemployment. As macropolicies become highly restrictive, inflation slows down, wage deceleration lags behind, and real wages initially rise. Hence, profits decline and firms reduce output and employment. Unemployment rises at first, and we move from C to D in Figure 19-6. Inflation comes down, but at a cost of a transition period of higher unemployment.

EXHIBIT 19-3

RATIONAL EXPECTATIONS THEORY AND THE DISINFLATION OF 1981–1983

Some economists touted the Fed's efforts to bring down U.S. inflation in the early 1980s as constituting a good laboratory experiment for testing the validity of *REM*. By the time President Jimmy Carter appointed Paul Volcker to Chair the Board of Governors in August 1979, inflation was running at double-digit rates. This inflation (based on the CPI) had escalated from less than 7 percent in 1977 to more than 13 percent by early fall 1979. This acceleration in U.S. inflation, coupled with an apparent lack of confidence around the world in the U.S. government's resolve to fight it, resulted in a persistent decline in the value of the dollar in foreign-exchange markets. In October 1979, under the leadership of Volcker, the Fed announced a dramatic change in the manner it would conduct monetary policy in the future.

Instead of attempting to hit established targets for short-term interest rates, the Fed announced it would instead seek to hit money-growth targets, which would be set at much more modest growth rates than actual recent money-growth rates. This implied that the Fed would no longer purchase securities and pump reserves into the banking system to hold down interest rates during periods in which the rates were under upward pressure. Interest rates would be permitted to rise dramatically, if need be, in order to equilibrate surging credit demands with the modest growth in funds available, as consistent with the Fed's modest money-supply target.

The Fed was in essence telling the world of its new resolve to conquer inflation irrespective of the short-range consequences for financial markets and economic activity. The Fed was announcing a *change of regime* from one of short-run accommodation of credit demands to one of strict monetarism—strict adherence to modest money growth.

This change of regime was deliberately implemented with a view toward bringing down the public's expectations of inflation in order to allow the Fed to fight inflation with minimum damage to U.S. output and employment. The Fed's implementation of this policy is itself testimony to the increased influence of REM. According to critics of REM, this episode clearly constitutes an *anticipated* tightening of monetary policy since it was announced publicly and had a major impact on the outlook for inflation. The strong form of REM predicts that *expected* changes in policy only influence price level behavior, not such real economic variables as output and employment. According to REM, the short-run Phillips Curve is vertical and inflation should have come down without an increase in unemployment. REM states that the unemployment rate is not influenced by *anticipated* changes in policy.

As predicted by REM, inflation came down sharply—much more sharply in fact than most economists or the Reagan Administration thought possible. But output went into a slump and the unemployment rate surged above ten percent in 1982, reaching its highest level since the 1930s. Critics of REM claim this episode shows the folly of the theory. A severe tightening of monetary policy announced clearly in advance, contrary to the predictions of REM, threw some six million people out of work. Clearly, the short-run Phillips Curve is hardly vertical!

Supporters of REM believe this episode does not tarnish the credibility of their theory. After decades of Federal Reserve deceit and unreliability, the institution's credibility was said to be at a low ebb by 1979. The public simply did not believe the Fed when it announced its commitment to sharply reduce money growth. In order for the Fed to make its commitment to eradicate inflation truly credible to the American populace, according to many advocates of REM, the Fed would probably have to abandon discretionary monetary policy. This could only be accomplished by returning to a gold standard or yielding to a constant money-growth rule, as advocated by Milton Friedman and other monetarists.

In the extreme REM view, we can get out of the inflation without cost. The announcement of the credible restrictive policy itself reduces expected inflation and immediately slows wage inflation in line with actual inflation. Therefore, real wages do not rise during the period of disinflation. Hence there is no reduction in profits, output, and employment. Unemployment does not rise, and we move from C to A

in Figure 19-6, rather than from *C* to *D*. Presto! The inflation is reduced without cost.

In the REM world, even the short-run Phillips Curve is vertical. There exists no trade-off between inflation and unemployment, even in the short run. Both the long-run and short-run Phillips Curves are vertical lines.

Like the monetarist world, the rational expectations world tends to paint the government as the villain—the cause of most of the economy's problems. Since the economy allegedly has powerful, inherent correction mechanisms and since *anticipated policy change* is nullified by actions of the public, the government should not intervene in the macroeconomy. Indeed, any failure of the economy to adjust its output to the natural level is attributable to government measures that have created rigidities. These measures include minimum wage legislation, farm price supports, and other measures that provide barriers to competition, and failure to use antitrust statutes to break up monopolies. In the view of REM, government policies should be aimed at promoting competitive markets instead of meddling in the macroeconomy.

While Keynesians tend to paint the government as the *good guy*—riding in to eradicate recessions caused by the inherent instabilities of a capitalistic, free-market economy—REM proponents tend to view government as the *villain* that interferes with the natural tendency of a market economy's *invisible hand* to yield optimal results. Hence REM, or the new classical macroeconomics, turns Keynesian economics on its head!

Critique of REM or New Classical Macroeconomics

REM has made a considerable impact on the economics profession in the relatively short period of the past 15 years. Nevertheless, only a small minority of economists believe the doctrine is valid in its strong form that implies macropolicy is *totally* ineffective. Many believe that REM overstates the economics acumen and awareness of individual firms, workers, and consumers. Do they really comprehend the workings of the economy? Do they really understand monetary and fiscal policy and pay close attention to those who implement such policies?

It seems unlikely that individuals and firms are rational in the sense defined by REM. Although it is true that the assumption that expectations are strictly *adaptive* seems naive, given the uncertainty about future events it seems likely that past events do play a significant role. Our expectation about inflation next year is conditioned by current and recent inflation as well as by new developments that macroeconomic models indicate are important determinants of inflation. Studies demonstrate that inflation expectations are sluggish. They exhibit considerable inertia, not changing radically in response to current swings in oil prices, money growth, and other factors that a sophisticated macroeconomic model might predict would bring about a change in the inflation rate. When inflation was ratcheting upward during 1965–1980, inflation expectations consistently lagged behind actual inflation. As the actual inflation rate came down in the early 1980s, expectations again lagged behind.[8]

Moreover, contracts and other impediments prevent wages from adapting quickly to changes in expected inflation. Three-year labor contracts for workers

---

[8]See M. A. Akhtar, A. Stephen Englander, and Cornelis A. Los, "Surveys of Expectations: Forward or Backward Looking?" *Quarterly Review* (Federal Reserve Bank of New York, Winter 1983–1984), pp. 63–66.

written in 1980 and 1981 prevented wage hikes from slowing down in the next two or three years in line with the reduction in actual and expected inflation. What *appeared* to be rational when the contracts were written no longer appeared rational a year or two later. Numerous studies of the nature of expectations have been conducted. Only a few demonstrate rationality on the part of economic agents. Some studies of the policy ineffectiveness hypothesis demonstrate that anticipated as well as unanticipated changes in aggregate demand exert a powerful impact on output and employment. The prediction of REM that actual unemployment rates should cluster closely around the natural unemployment rate with random departures from the natural rate is not supported by the facts.

Nevertheless, rational expectations theory is probably here to stay as an integral element of macroeconomic analysis. The unsatisfactory performance of the U.S. economy since the mid-1960s, the disenchantment with Keynesian economics, and the reduced appeal of monetarism in the 1980s have opened the door for alternative approaches to macroeconomics. Though few economists take REM seriously in its extreme policy ineffectiveness version, most agree that it contains a very important kernel of truth. As people systematically come to expect a policy change, they take actions that significantly diminish the policy's impact on such real economic variables as output and employment. At the very least, REM has provided an alternative mode of analysis that has stimulated thinking among economists about aggregate supply as well as aggregate demand. REM has elevated the role of expectations to center stage in the analysis of macroeconomic policy. (See Exhibit 19-4 on pages 432–33.)

SUMMARY

1. Economists strongly disagree over the issue of the propriety of government efforts to intervene actively in the macroeconomy to attempt to reduce the fluctuations of output and income inherent in a free-market economy. Keynesians favor such efforts; monetarists and rational expectationists do not.

2. The classical economists who preceded Keynes' pathbreaking *General Theory* of 1936 emphasized the tendency of the economy to gravitate strongly toward a full-employment level of output. Key elements in the framework of classical economics were the role of the interest rate in equilibrating saving and investment decisions and the role of wage and price level flexibility in generating an automatic corrective mechanism in the macroeconomy.

3. In his attack on classical thinking, Keynes introduced a whole new kit of analytical tools. Keynes was especially critical of the assumption of downward wage and price flexibility and the assumption that the interest rate would adjust to bring saving and investment into equilibrium at full employment. In Keynes' view, the economy could settle at an equilibrium far short of full employment. Therefore, Keynes felt that government should intervene actively with stimulative policy measures when the economy was depressed. In Keynes' view, a laissez-faire philosophy was inappropriate.

4. Keynesian economics held center stage from the late 1930s through the late 1960s. Monetarism gradually made some inroads in the 1950s and 1960s, and became a powerful force in the 1970s as inflation accelerated throughout the world. Its influence diminished somewhat in the 1980s, as the link between the various money supply measures and GNP loosened.

5. Monetarists emphasize the political and technical obstacles that make it difficult to conduct successful discretionary macroeconomic policies. Technical obstacles include uncertainty about the nature of the aggregate supply and aggregate demand schedules, the natural unemployment rate, and the lags of policy. Monetarists believe that well-intentioned Fed policies have actually done more harm than good in the past and are likely to continue to do harm in the future. Monetarists recommend that the Fed abandon discretionary policies

EXHIBIT 19–4

RATIONAL EXPECTATIONS AND THE CHANGE IN PRICE-LEVEL
BEHAVIOR AFTER WORLD WAR II

Prior to World War II, periods of deflation (falling prices) alternated with periods of inflation, with the result that prices were no higher on average in the 1900–1930 era than in the 1770–1800 era. There was no net inflation in America over the sweep of history until World War II. Today, however, the price level is at least four times higher than it was in 1950 (note the discontinuity in the vertical scale of Figure 19-7). Downward price-level flexibility has disappeared from the American scene. Why?

There are plenty of potential explanations. Some economists claim that the economy has become less competitive—that unions have become stronger and industries more concentrated. Others attribute the disappearance of downward price flexibility to the increasing strength of the nation's built-in stabilizers. As the size of the government sector (and the level of tax rates) has increased relative to the economy, this has imparted a high degree of inertia to aggregate demand. For this reason, we no longer experience the severe cyclical contractions that formerly led to deflation. The increased stability of the U.S. economy allegedly accounts for the radical change in price-level behavior.

While certain of the preceding hypotheses may in fact contribute to the explanation, proponents of REM emphasize another consideration that seems highly plausible—the commitment of the U.S. government to the maintenance of a high level of prosperity in general and output and employment in particular. In acknowledgement of the Keynesian revolution, Congress passed into law the Employment Act of 1946. This law mandated that the government implement stimulative monetary and fiscal policies, if necessary, to keep the economy strong. As time progressed, workers and firms learned to anticipate stimulative policies being implemented whenever the economy weakened significantly. In earlier times, macroeconomic weakness in the economy often portended great personal hardship for workers and financial disaster for firms. As the economy weakened, wages and prices declined abruptly as workers and firms scrambled to survive.

If allowing the economy to remain depressed is against the law, workers and firms are basically insured against widespread unemployment and widespread loss of sales. The downside risk is largely eliminated, or at least severely reduced. In that event, there is no reason for workers to accept wage cuts and firms to reduce prices in periods in which the economy is temporarily weak. Macroeconomic stimulus can be counted on to bring the economy back up to snuff.

A side effect of the Keynesian revolution is the elimination of the symmetrical price-level behavior that existed before World War II. In the view of REM, only the abandonment of discretionary macroeconomic policies would bring back the noninflationary long-term environment of the olden days. If valid, this analysis implies that we should abolish the Employment Act and the Humphrey-Hawkins Act, and leave the economy to its own internal self-correcting devices.

and implement a constant money-growth rule. In such a regime, the Fed simply increases the money supply at some modest but constant rate, irrespective of contemporary economic conditions.

6. Rational expectations macroeconomics (REM) or the new classical macroeconomics is critical of policy activism for different reasons. Once it becomes understood that the government systematically implements stimulative policies whenever the economy weakens, workers and firms take actions that serve to nullify partially or totally the effects of the policies on output and employment. In the view of REM, only unanticipated or surprise policies have real effects. Since the government cannot systematically fool the people for

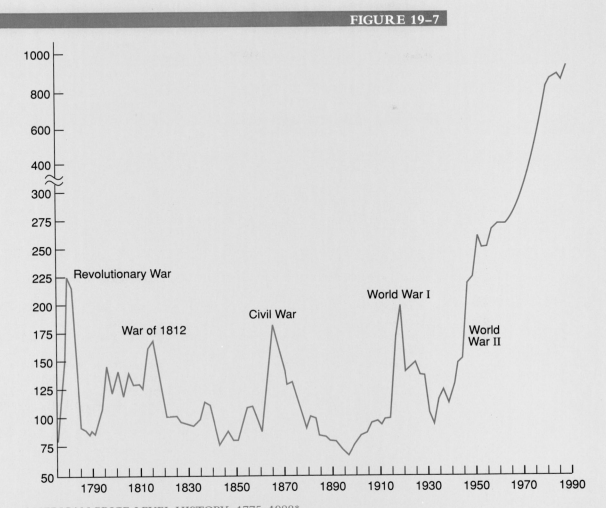

FIGURE 19–7

AMERICAN PRICE-LEVEL HISTORY, 1775–1988*

Prior to 1940, periods of rising prices (inflation) were followed by episodes of falling prices (deflation). Hence, there was no long-term upward trend in the American price level during the period 1775–1940. Since 1940, the U.S. economy has developed a bias toward inflation; periods of deflation have disappeared from the American experience.

*Wholesale price index, 1910–1914 = 100; note change of scale at 300.
Sources: Data from *Historical Statistics of the United States* and *Economic Report of the President*, 1988.

socially beneficial purposes, it should abandon discretionary monetary and fiscal policies.

7. Today the economics profession is splintered on the issue of macroeconomic policy. While some economists fit squarely in the Keynesian, monetarist, or REM camp, many economists are eclectic in these matters. Bits and pieces of each of the three camps' viewpoints seem sensible to many economists. Most economists still favor policy activism, but there seems to be a consensus that *fine tuning* is inappropriate. The powerful instruments of monetary and fiscal policy should be adjusted only in response to *major* swings in aggregate demand, aggregate supply, output growth, and inflation.

KEY TERMS

classical economics
Say's Law
Keynesian
monetarists
rational expectations
    macroeconomics (REM) or
    new classical macroeconomics

recognition lag
implementation lag
impact lag
constant (fixed) money-growth
    rule
policy ineffectiveness theorem

STUDY QUESTIONS AND PROBLEMS

1. Explain the logic of the classical view that the only true equilibrium output is a full-employment output.
2. Assume you are debating *against* the proposition that government should adopt a laissez-faire philosophy toward the macroeconomy. What elements of the classical model would you attack? Explain why.
3. Analyze the factors that make the successful conduct of activist monetary and fiscal policies more difficult than appears at first glance.
4. Assume the Federal Reserve decides to abandon discretionary policies in favor of a constant money-growth rule. You are hired by the Fed as a consultant to determine how fast the money supply should grow in this new regime. How would you go about arriving at an appropriate decision?
5. Do you think a constant money-growth rule would outperform monetary discretion over the next five years? Defend your answer.
6. "The Keynesian prescription for activist macroeconomic policies to stabilize output at high levels, while effective at first, has met with inevitable failure and should now be abandoned." What is the intellectual basis for this statement?
7. In what ways are monetarism and rational expectations macroeconomics (REM) similar? In what ways do they differ?
8. "Policymakers cannot even exploit a *short-run* Phillips Curve, much less a *long-run* trade-off." What is the logic of this argument? Do you agree or disagree?

SELECTED REFERENCES

Barro, Robert J., *Macroeconomics* (New York: Wiley and Sons, 1984). An intermediate macroeconomic text by a leading proponent of rational expectations macroeconomics.

Begg, David, *The Rational Expectations Revolution in Macroeconomics* (Baltimore: The Johns Hopkins University Press, 1982). A complete and somewhat technical exposition of rational expectations macroeconomics.

Forman, Leonard, "Rational Expectations and the Real World," *Challenge Magazine,* November/December 1980. A critique of rational expectations macroeconomics.

Gordon, Robert J., "Evolution in Postwar Macroeconomics," in Martin S. Feldstein (ed.), *The American Economy in Transition* (Chicago: University of Chicago Press, 1980). An excellent review of the recent history of macroeconomic thinking.

Maddock, Rodney and Michael Carter, "A Child's Guide to Rational Expectations," *The Journal of Economic Literature,* March 1982, pp. 39–51. A worthwhile survey of the issues involved in rational expectations macroeconomics.

PART V

THE
NATIONAL
DEBT,
ECONOMIC
GROWTH,
AND
PRODUCTIVITY

CHAPTER 20

THE ECONOMICS OF FEDERAL BUDGET DEFICITS AND THE NATIONAL DEBT

Large budget deficits will bleed the country slowly.

—ROBERT M. SOLOW
Nobel Laureate in Economics

Perhaps the most crucial macroeconomic issue facing the United States in the past decade involves the economic consequences of large federal budget deficits and the burgeoning stock of government debt. Following the extensive income-tax reductions and national defense buildup of the early 1980s, annual budget deficits of unprecedented magnitude became part of the national economic landscape. The annual federal budget deficit is the amount by which annual federal government expenditures exceed tax receipts. The pattern of federal government outlays, receipts, and deficits during the 1970s and 1980s is illustrated in Figure 20-1.

The figure indicates that budget deficits occurred in every year since 1970. In fact, since 1960 a deficit has occurred in every year except 1969. The magnitude of the deficits increased sharply during Ronald Reagan's presidency in the 1980s. The national debt—the cumulative sum of past deficits—roughly tripled during President Reagan's two terms in office (January 1981 to January 1989). In other words, the national debt increased twice as much in this recent 8-year period as it did in the previous 200-plus-year history of this nation!

Growing awareness of the adverse consequences of large budget deficits resulted in congressional legislation in the 1980s that mandated a scheduled phaseout of the deficit over a period of several years. For a variety of reasons, however, it seems unlikely that the 1990s will be an era devoid of federal budget deficits.

Everyone has heard acquaintances speak of the federal government's fiscal management in dire terms of gloom and doom. And aspiring politicians seeking to unseat incumbents rail against

436

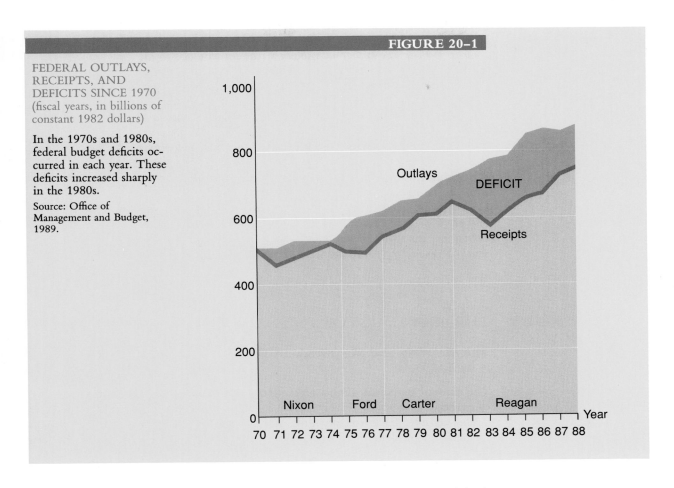

FIGURE 20-1

FEDERAL OUTLAYS, RECEIPTS, AND DEFICITS SINCE 1970 (fiscal years, in billions of constant 1982 dollars)

In the 1970s and 1980s, federal budget deficits occurred in each year. These deficits increased sharply in the 1980s.

Source: Office of Management and Budget, 1989.

deficit spending by invoking images of a bankrupt federal Treasury or unconscionable burdens placed upon the backs of our grandchildren. As we shall learn in Chapter 20, the issues are far more complex than indicated by the everyday discussion of politicians and the public.

Large budget deficits have both short-term and long-run consequences. And these deficits have private consequences (to you personally) and social consequences (to the nation as a whole). Some of the short-term consequences probably have affected you personally, though you may not have been aware that these effects are attributable to budget deficits. The payments on an auto loan, the cost of an imported stereo or VCR, and the cost of a summer vacation in Europe are all influenced by federal budget policy. If you live in an urban area in which manufacturing firms are subject to serious foreign competition, your summer-job prospects may even be influenced in subtle ways by large budget deficits. However, not all of these short-run consequences are adverse. You may have benefited in certain ways from the large deficits.

In this chapter we explore the facts and principles concerning federal budget deficits and the national debt. Perspectives on the magnitude of deficits and the national debt are obtained by comparing their size and growth to other relevant variables in the economy. We put to rest some commonly expressed fallacious or bogus views about the national debt frequently expressed by the person on the street. *Legitimate concerns about the potential adverse effects of large deficits are carefully analyzed. Conceptual measurement problems associated with deficits and the debt are discussed so that one may achieve a realistic view of the magnitude of deficits and the stock of debt. The existing federal budget deficit is divided into a* cyclical *portion and a* structural *portion, and the economic meaning and significance of each is outlined. Finally, we explore some issues associated with the* mix of monetary and budgetary or fiscal policies. In particular, the consequences of *combining stimulative fiscal policy (large budget deficits) and restrictive monetary policy are scrutinized.*

THE ECONOMICS OF THE NATIONAL DEBT

The Meaning and Magnitude of Federal Budget Deficits and the National Debt

Budget Deficit
The shortfall of federal receipts relative to expenditures, measured at an annual rate.

National Debt
The total stock of bonds and other federal government IOUs outstanding; the sum of past federal budget deficits minus the sum of past surpluses.

The amount by which annual federal tax receipts exceed annual federal expenditures is the **budget surplus** or **budget deficit** (if negative). This surplus or deficit is a *flow* variable, measured per unit of time (usually one year). The government finances budget deficits by selling bonds and shorter-term securities to American individuals and firms, foreigners, U.S. government agencies, and the Federal Reserve System. The sum total of these bonds and other securities outstanding at a given point of time is the government debt or **national debt.** This is a *stock* of financial claims against the federal government. When the government exhibits a surplus in its budget, some debt is retired—the national debt decreases. When budget deficits are experienced, the federal government issues new securities—the national debt increases.

Because the federal budget has been in surplus only one year since 1960, the national debt has increased persistently in recent decades. The growth of the total federal debt—the *gross national debt*—including that portion held by government agencies (about 20 percent of the gross debt) is illustrated in Figure 20-2 for the period 1900–1988. For many purposes the *net* debt is a superior measure. The *net national debt* excludes that portion held by government agencies, thereby measuring the net indebtedness of the federal government to private American firms and individuals, foreigners, and the Federal Reserve System. The gross debt and the net debt exhibit the same general pattern of growth.

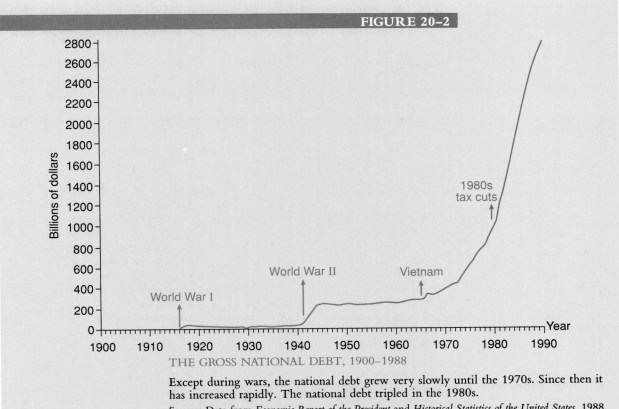

FIGURE 20-2

THE GROSS NATIONAL DEBT, 1900–1988

Except during wars, the national debt grew very slowly until the 1970s. Since then it has increased rapidly. The national debt tripled in the 1980s.

Source: Data from *Economic Report of the President* and *Historical Statistics of the United States,* 1988.

The most striking aspect of Figure 20-2 is the dramatic increase in the national debt since the mid-1970s, especially during the 1980s. Prior to the 1980s, it is clear that the great bulk of the debt was incurred during wars and periods of depression or recession. Note the increases in the debt during World War I and World War II. All nations have typically found it impractical to raise taxes precipitously enough in wartime to match increased military expenditures. Hence, they experienced large budget deficits and an escalation of the national debt. In cyclical downturns like the 1930s, 1974–1975, and 1981–1982, the debt almost inevitably increases rapidly because the depressed economic activity automatically increases the budget deficit. This is primarily due to the induced slowdown in tax receipts of the U.S. Treasury, although expenditures for unemployment benefits and other assistance programs are also stimulated in recessions.

In 1989 the gross national debt passed the $2800 billion or $2.8 trillion mark. The *net* debt came to about $2200 billion or $2.2 trillion. These figures may seem more meaningful when we calculate that in 1989 the gross debt and net debt amounted to approximately $11,000 and $9000, respectively, for every man, woman, and child in the United States. These magnitudes approximately tripled in the decade of the 1980s. As we discuss later in the chapter, this recent unprecedented rate of growth of the national debt, together with the prospect of further rapid growth to come, is cause for serious concern to most professional economists.

EXHIBIT 20-1

OWNERSHIP OF THE GOVERNMENT DEBT

Figure 20-3 illustrates who owns the national debt—the bonds and other securities issued to finance budget deficits over the years. The debt is distributed among the American private sector (banks, other corporations, and individuals), the government sector (federal agencies, state and local governments, and the Federal Reserve), and foreign holders.

One of the largest holders of government debt is the U.S. government itself; the Federal Reserve System and federal agencies hold almost one-third of the total debt. As indicated in our discussion of monetary policy (Chapter 14), the Fed buys and sells government securities (components of the national debt) in order to implement open market operations, its chief policy tool. In mid-1989 the Fed's total portfolio of government debt amounted to almost $250 billion, or about 9 percent of the total national debt. Since the Fed turns back some 90 percent of its total revenues (predominantly interest earned on government bonds) to the U.S. Treasury, the portion of the debt sold to the Fed is almost without interest cost to the Treasury.

Other government agencies also purchase government bonds. The Social Security Administration, for example, maintains a trust fund to cover any monthly shortfall between current payroll tax receipts and current retirement benefits. This trust fund consists primarily of government bonds. Altogether, government agencies besides the Federal Reserve own about one-fifth of the national debt.

More than 10 percent of the federal debt is owned by state and local government units. State and local governments exhibit budget surpluses and invest those funds predominantly in safe U.S. government bonds.

American individuals *directly* own some 7 percent of the federal debt in the form of U.S. Savings Bonds and other types of government securities. Figure 20-3 indicates that almost 40 percent of the national debt is held by banks and such other financial and nonfinancial firms as money market mutual funds, insurance companies, and other entities with idle funds to invest. Because this wealth is ultimately owned by the individual Americans who have invested in money market mutual funds, purchased insurance, and own stock in American firms, U.S. households directly or indirectly own a large share of the debt.

Foreign investors including individuals, banks, corporations, and governments own about 13 percent of the U.S. national debt. These foreign buyers are attracted to our government debt because of its attractive yield, perceived safety, and

A Fallacious View of the National Debt

At this point we pause to examine a fallacious argument sometimes expressed by observers of American budgetary policy. Consider the following hypothetical quotation:

> Like all debts, the national debt must eventually be paid off. We are placing an unfair burden on future generations by forcing them to tighten their belts and sacrifice in order to pay off debts incurred by the present generation.

The fallacy lies in the assumption that the national debt must be paid off at some future date. *The national debt never will be paid off—any more than debt incurred by General Motors, AT&T, or the aggregate of American consumers or mortgagors (home buyers) will ever be extinguished.*

Although the federal government pays off each individual holder of government debt when the securities mature, it does so on balance by *rolling over* or *refinancing* the debt—by issuing new securities.[1]

---

[1]The U.S. Treasury is heavily involved in financing activities every· week. This process involves refinancing debt currently maturing as well as issuing additional debt to finance current budget deficits. About one-half the marketable debt matures every 18 months. Treasury issue of new debt frequently amounts to $10–$15 billion each week.

OWNERSHIP OF THE NATIONAL DEBT

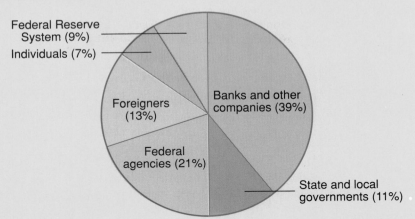

Because of its safety and marketability, American banks and other corporations hold large quantities of U.S. government debt. Other important owners of government bonds include federal agencies, state and municipal governments, The Federal Reserve, American individuals, and foreigners.

Source: U.S. Treasury Department, 1989.

because of the widespread acceptability of dollar-denominated assets in international commerce. The portion of our national debt that is *externally* held has increased from less than 3 percent in the 1950s to around 13 percent today. The external portion increased sharply in the 1970s but has declined somewhat from peak levels in the late 1970s.

The process is precisely the same as that followed by the aggregate of American corporations and individuals. Each debt is honored as it comes due at maturity. However, on balance, the funds that pay off maturing debt come from issuing new debt. Hence, the total debt of GM, AT&T, and most other stable American corporations shows a sustained uptrend over time. Likewise, while each individual consumer debt and home mortgage are eventually repaid or extinguished (barring personal bankruptcy), the total magnitude of consumer debt and mortgage debt expands over time in any prosperous, growing economy. Willingness to incur debt, if done in a conservative and prudent manner, is an essential element in the economic process. Modern industrial societies would never have reached their current state of affluence in the absence of the willingness of firms and individuals to borrow.

U.S. government debt is a highly safe and desirable investment outlet for thousands of banks and other financial and nonfinancial firms, and for millions of individual savers. Since the U.S. Treasury has the constitutional authority to tax or even print money to honor its debt obligations, there is a perception on the part of the public that securities issued by the U.S. Government are the safest investments in the world. The Treasury has no difficulty finding lenders—buyers of its securities—though one cannot deny that at times the cost to the Treasury of doing so (interest rate offered) is quite high.

When one acknowledges that the national debt need not and will not ever be repaid or extinguished, a totally different perception of the *burden* of this debt emerges. Our grandchildren (or theirs) need not tighten their belts to the tune of $11,000 or more per person and pay off the debt resulting from our *extravagance.* Any *intergenerational burden* of the debt—burden imposed by one generation upon a future generation—is not attributable to the necessity of paying off or even reducing the magnitude of the national debt.

Measures of the Relative Growth of the National Debt

It seems reasonable to assume that just as a growing economy is capable of supporting prudent growth in such private forms of debt as consumer debt and mortgage debt, it is also capable of supporting a moderate or reasonable rate of growth in the stock of government debt. To place some perspective on the growth of U.S. government debt relative to other forms of debt, Figure 20-4 illustrates the ratios of U.S. government debt to mortgage debt, consumer debt, and business loans made by American banks in the past four decades. The figure clearly indicates a sustained decline in the relative magnitude of the national debt from 1950 to the mid-1970s, followed by a leveling off and a slight uptrend in the 1980s. The stock of government debt has grown much more slowly than major categories of private debt over the interval since World War II.[2] Especially during the first 20 years after the end of the War, the diminishing relative role of the U.S. government in the debt markets made available a more than adequate supply of funds with which to finance the postwar boom in construction activity as well as the strong expansion in consumer spending and corporate investment spending.

During the major portion of the postwar period, government debt expanded at less than one-half the growth rate of private forms of debt. In this period most economists found it difficult to get excited about any alleged deleterious effects of deficit spending or arguments about imposing a *burden* on future generations. Note, however, that government debt has expanded more rapidly than private debt during the 1980s. The comforting downtrend in the ratios depicted in Figure 20-4 has been reversed in the past decade.

Intergenerational Burden
The costs imposed by the current generation upon future generations by bequeathing an inadequate capital stock.

Economists believe that any **intergenerational burdens**—burdens imposed by one generation upon another are attributable to the quality and quantity of the physical and human capital stock passed on to the next generation. A legitimate concern of informed observers of the American economic scene of the past decade is that large budget deficits and the escalating national debt may ultimately *crowd out* or displace private investment in plant, equipment, and technology. Unless the deficits are attributable to growth of government *capital expenditures*—projects such as schools and infrastructure—these deficits may lead to a reduced rate of growth of the national's capital stock. We return to this argument later in the chapter.

It is incorrect to start with the assumption that future generations will have to tighten their belts, reduce consumption, and use the proceeds to extinguish the debt they have inherited. However, interest must be paid to those who lend to the government—those bondholders and other owners of the stock of government debt. To obtain funds with which to pay this interest, the government must either issue additional debt or obtain funds via tax receipts. As we shall establish in this chapter,

---

[2]The average annual growth rate of U.S. government debt during 1950–1988 was 6.2 percent. The average annual growth rates of mortgage debt and consumer debt during the same interval were 10.3 percent and 9.5 percent, respectively. However, the growth rate of the government debt during the more recent end of the interval, 1975–1988, accelerated to 12.7 percent per annum!

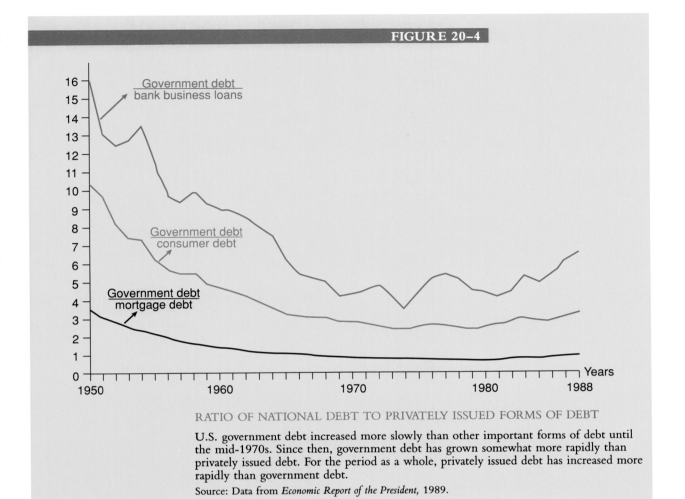

FIGURE 20-4

RATIO OF NATIONAL DEBT TO PRIVATELY ISSUED FORMS OF DEBT

U.S. government debt increased more slowly than other important forms of debt until the mid-1970s. Since then, government debt has grown somewhat more rapidly than privately issued debt. For the period as a whole, privately issued debt has increased more rapidly than government debt.

Source: Data from *Economic Report of the President,* 1989.

when the government pursues a passive attitude of habitually stepping up its borrowing to meet growing interest expense on a rapidly expanding debt, severe inflation may ultimately occur. Hence, to be prudent, the government must meet growing interest costs on the national debt via increased tax revenues.

Source: Calvin & Hobbes ©1988 Universal Press Syndicate. Reprinted with permission. All rights reserved.

A Second Fallacy: Interest Payments Are a Drain of Resources

This brings us to a second bogus argument associated with the national debt, expressed in the following hypothetical plea:

> Interest payments on the national debt represent a drain on the nation's limited economic resources. It is a pure waste of our resources to use them just to pay interest on the debt.

This argument is fallacious because interest payments on the debt—to the extent that the debt is domestically held—do not represent a use of economic resources at all. It is true that if our debt is held by foreigners, we *will* suffer a loss of resources. That is, we *will* have to give up American goods and services as they exchange their interest coupons, either now or later, for American computers, wheat, and high-tech equipment. In other words, less of America's resources would be available for domestic use. However, only about 13 percent of the total U.S. government debt is owned by foreigners.

In the case of domestically held debt, interest payments on the debt involve a *transfer of income* from American taxpayers to American bondholders of the same generation. Hypothetically, if each individual in the U.S. holds an equal share of the bonds and also is in the same tax bracket, one could view this process as one in which each individual is simply taking dollars out of one pocket and putting them back into another pocket. However, taxpayers and bondholders are different entities. A large national debt therefore inevitably involves income redistribution effects. But domestically held debt does not involve any using up of the nation's real economic resources.

Indicators of the Magnitude of the Debt Burden

If funds to service the debt are to be obtained via tax revenues, it is true, given other factors, that *the larger the debt the higher the tax rates required to service the debt.* And if the increased tax rates required to service the debt (fund the interest payments) produce a reduction in the incentive to work, save, or invest, then economic growth and the future standard of living will be reduced relative to that which would prevail if the debt were lower. Also, given the political realities that place a limitation on government spending, more dollars spent on interest payments means fewer government dollars spent on national defense, education, health care, and social security benefits. Increased interest expenditures are likely to result in a reduction in other forms of government spending.

Some perspective into the probable quantitative importance of these considerations may be obtained by observing the trends of the ratios of government debt/GNP and interest payments/GNP. In Figure 20-5, we illustrate the ratio of the national debt to GNP since 1939. Given a set of tax *rates,* federal tax *receipts* rise at least proportionally with the growth of GNP. Therefore, unless interest rates increase, *tax rates* do not have to be raised over time to meet interest payments on the national debt as long as the debt grows no more rapidly than GNP. Figure 20-5 indicates that, after reaching a peak of more than 100 percent at the end of World War II, the ratio of the debt to GNP persistently declined until the mid-1970s. The government debt was growing much more slowly than economic activity in general. Any *burdens* or economic consequences of the debt were declining during this era, and economists often were impatient with those who spent time worrying about the

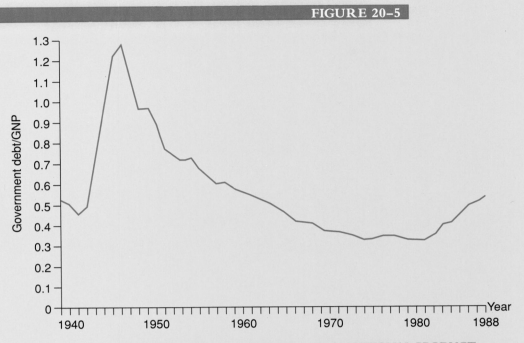

RATIO OF NATIONAL DEBT TO GROSS NATIONAL PRODUCT

The size of the national debt relative to a nation's gross national product may be viewed as an indicator of the nation's capacity to handle the debt. The ratio of the national debt to GNP continually declined from the end of World War II (1945) until the mid-1970s. In the past 15 years, the ratio has been increasing.

Source: Data from *Economic Report of the President, 1989.*

debt. Note, however, that the debt/GNP ratio has begun to increase in recent years. The debt has been growing considerably faster than GNP since 1980.

An even better indicator of potential problems associated with the national debt is the ratio of the cost of *servicing* the debt to GNP. This ratio of government interest expenditures to GNP for the 1940–1988 period is illustrated in Figure 20-6 (page 446).

The percentage of GNP that must be taken in taxes to meet the interest payments on the national debt declined steadily from almost 2 percent in 1946 to about 1.2 percent during the 1960s. That is, the transfer of income from taxpayers to bondholders amounted to only about 1 percent of the nation's GNP during the 1960s. This ratio increased dramatically after the mid-1970s to more than 3 percent in the mid-1980s, and has been higher in recent years than at any time since the World War I era.[3] The portion of the federal government budget spent on debt service—interest—has increased sharply, as indicated in Figure 20-7 (page 447).

---

[3]The discrepancy between the behavior of debt/GNP (Figure 20-5) and interest/GNP (Figure 20-6) after the mid-1970s is explained by the escalation of interest rates in the more recent period. In the 1980s, the increase in interest rates (especially *real* interest rates) resulted in a significant redistribution of income in favor of owners of government debt. The most rapidly growing component of government spending in the 1980s was interest payments on the national debt.

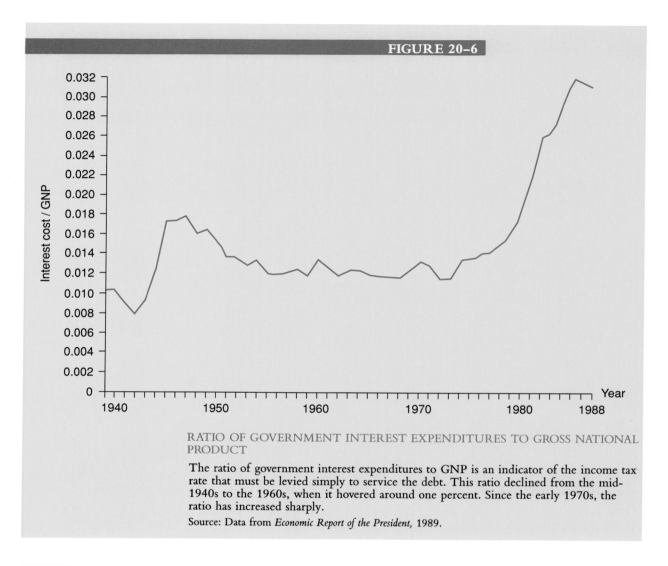

FIGURE 20–6

RATIO OF GOVERNMENT INTEREST EXPENDITURES TO GROSS NATIONAL PRODUCT

The ratio of government interest expenditures to GNP is an indicator of the income tax rate that must be levied simply to service the debt. This ratio declined from the mid-1940s to the 1960s, when it hovered around one percent. Since the early 1970s, the ratio has increased sharply.

Source: Data from *Economic Report of the President*, 1989.

THE ECONOMICS OF BUDGET DEFICITS

Actual, Structural, and Cyclical Budget Deficits

The existing budget deficit may be divided into a cyclical or induced portion and a structural or high-employment portion. It is quite useful to distinguish between the cyclical and structural portions of the existing deficit.

total budget deficit = cyclical deficit + structural deficit

Cyclical Deficit
The portion of the actual deficit attributable to a shortfall of actual GNP relative to full-employment GNP.

The **cyclical deficit** is the portion of the deficit attributable to the shortfall of actual GNP from potential GNP. That is, the cyclical deficit is due to the effect of economic slack (depressed economic activity) upon federal expenditures and receipts. It has been estimated that for each $100 billion that actual GNP falls short of potential GNP, the budget is induced to swing into the direction of deficit (or increased deficit) by about $30 billion. Hence, if our $6000 billion (GNP) economy

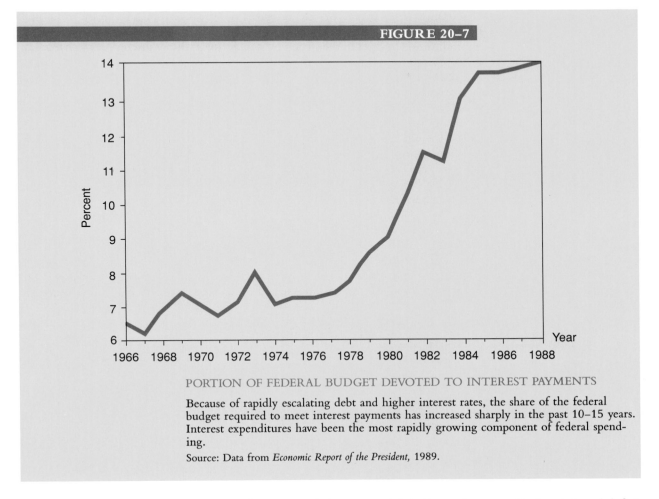

FIGURE 20–7

PORTION OF FEDERAL BUDGET DEVOTED TO INTEREST PAYMENTS

Because of rapidly escalating debt and higher interest rates, the share of the federal budget required to meet interest payments has increased sharply in the past 10–15 years. Interest expenditures have been the most rapidly growing component of federal spending.

Source: Data from *Economic Report of the President,* 1989.

is operating five percent below potential GNP, we have a cyclical or induced deficit of approximately $90 billion.[4] Economic recessions thus automatically lead to significantly larger budget deficits even in the absence of any changes in tax rates or spending decisions. Budget deficits are reduced automatically during periods of economic recovery unless legislated tax cuts are implemented or government programs are expanded.

Structural Deficit or High-Employment Deficit
The deficit that would prevail under conditions of full employment; depends on legislated programs and tax rates, not on economic activity.

The **structural deficit** (or surplus), sometimes referred to as the **high-employment deficit** (or surplus), indicates the size of the deficit or surplus that would *hypothetically* exist if the economy were operating at a high level of output and employment. This high level of output and employment is commonly taken to be that which would prevail if the unemployment rate were at the economy's *natural unemployment rate,* an unemployment rate of perhaps 5 or 5.5 percent. The structural deficit (or surplus) is attributable to the level and structure of taxes and government expenditures and is not altered, for example, as aggregate demand and GNP increase during the expansion phase of the business cycle. Since the cyclical effect of

[4]Five percent of $6000 billion indicates an output shortfall of $300 billion. Since each $100 billion of output loss raises the budget deficit by $30 billion, we compute a cyclical or induced deficit of $90 billion.

economic activity on the federal budget is removed, any changes in the structural budget deficit or surplus reflect changes in tax legislation or changes in government expenditures. Changes in the structural deficit thus indicate discretionary changes in fiscal policy—changes in tax and expenditure decisions.

In Figure 20-8 the horizontal axis measures the economy's current utilization rate—the ratio of actual GNP to potential GNP—which increases as we move right to left. The vertical axis measures the budget deficit or surplus. For any given legislated budget—legislated government expenditures and existing federal tax code—the figure indicates the responsiveness of the federal deficit to the state of the economy. For example, if Budget *A* is in place and actual GNP is 95 percent of potential, the budget deficit is $60 billion. If the economy were at full employment (actual GNP/potential GNP being 100 percent) with Budget *A* in place, a surplus of $30 billion would exist. The structural deficit associated with Budget *A* is a negative $30 billion—a structural budget *surplus* of $30 billion. In this circumstance, with the economy operating at point *E* in the figure, the actual budget deficit of $60 billion can be decomposed into a cyclical deficit of $90 billion and a structural surplus of $30 billion.

Note that, for any given legislated budget, the intersection of the budget line with the vertical axis indicates the size of the structural deficit or surplus. Hence, in

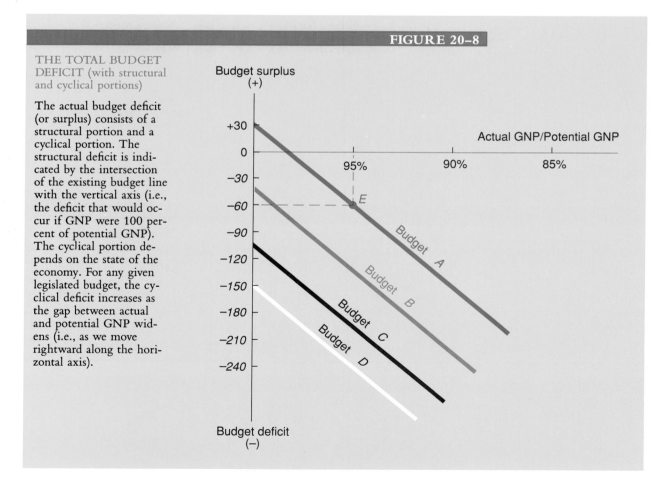

FIGURE 20–8

THE TOTAL BUDGET DEFICIT (with structural and cyclical portions)

The actual budget deficit (or surplus) consists of a structural portion and a cyclical portion. The structural deficit is indicated by the intersection of the existing budget line with the vertical axis (i.e., the deficit that would occur if GNP were 100 percent of potential GNP). The cyclical portion depends on the state of the economy. For any given legislated budget, the cyclical deficit increases as the gap between actual and potential GNP widens (i.e., as we move rightward along the horizontal axis).

Figure 20-8, Budget *A* exhibits a structural budget *surplus* of $30 billion and Budget *B* a structural *deficit* of approximately $40 billion. Budget *D* exhibits a structural deficit of $150 billion.

The slope of the budget line in Figure 20-8 indicates the magnitude of the **automatic stabilizing effect** of the federal budget. As actual GNP moves farther below potential GNP (left to right on the horizontal axis), the budget moves in the direction of increasingly large deficits. This is entirely due to the cyclical component of the budget deficit. A decrease in GNP induces a contraction of federal tax receipts and an increase in federal transfer payments in the form of income-support programs.

The concept of the structural deficit or surplus allows us to compare the magnitude of fiscal stimulus among alternative budgets. The actual budget deficit does not permit such comparisons, since the actual budget deficit or surplus depends on both the existing tax and expenditure structure *and* the current state of the economy. Budget *B* in Figure 20-8 is more stimulative than Budget *A*, since Budget *B* involves a larger deficit at each and every level of economic activity. By the same token, Budget *D* is more stimulative than Budgets *A, B,* and *C.* A convenient benchmark for gauging the macroeconomic posture of federal budget policy from year-to-year is the change in the structural deficit. When the structural deficit is reduced in a given year, budgetary policy is becoming more contractionary or restrictive. Clearly, if Budgets *A, B, C,* and *D* occur in chronological order, federal budget policy or fiscal policy is becoming increasingly stimulative.

Economists are more concerned about possible adverse effects of long-lasting structural budget deficits than cyclical deficits. In fact, cyclical deficits are almost uniformly viewed as being beneficial, since they provide support to a depressed economy. When, for example, the economy moves into a period of recession due to a decrease in consumer and business confidence, the deficit increases as federal tax receipts automatically decline and transfer payments increase in the form of unemployment and public-assistance benefits. All this puts more cash into the hands of private citizens and firms, thereby providing support to aggregate demand and economic activity. When the economy is booming, the deficit shrinks as tax receipts surge and transfers decline somewhat, thus inhibiting aggregate demand for goods and services. Some economic studies suggest that this automatic stabilizing effect of the budget prevents perhaps 35–40 percent of the fluctuations in GNP that would occur if the budget were not structured to serve this stabilizing function.[5]

If one were to attempt to prevent cyclical deficits from occurring, one would have to raise tax rates and reduce government expenditures during periods of depressed economic activity. This would further depress the economy. In a booming economy, if the actual budget were in surplus, a policy of insisting on an annually balanced budget would require a tax cut or expenditure increase, thus creating

---

YOUR TURN   The presidential campaign of 1932 between Herbert Hoover and Franklin D. Roosevelt was waged during the depths of the Great Depression. Both candidates advocated fiscal measures to attempt to reduce the budget deficit—tax hikes and/or expenditure reductions. Evaluate the soundness of these proposals.

---

[5]See Robert J. Gordon, *Macroeconomics* (Boston: Little, Brown, 1978), p. 494.

excessive economic stimulus and exacerbating inflationary pressures. Rigid adherence to a philosophy of annually balancing the budget would necessitate implementation of perverse fiscal policies that would lead to an amplification of economic fluctuations. Thus, no economist would advocate a philosophy calling for a rigid policy of balancing the budget each year.

Large Structural Deficits of the 1980s

As the U.S. economy recovered from the severe 1981–1982 recession during 1983–1987, the overall budget deficit failed to decrease appreciably (although it did decline somewhat in the late 1980s). Even though the cyclical deficit was reduced sharply during the economic expansion, a steadily expanding structural component of the deficit prevented the overall deficit from coming down. This is illustrated in Figure 20-9.

In Figure 20-9, the budget line shifted downward over time as a result of discretionary increases in government expenditures and decreases in tax rates. Although the economy staged a strong economic recovery after 1982, the actual deficit failed to decrease. Instead of moving from *A* to *B* to *C*, as would have occurred if tax rates and expenditure authorizations had remained unaltered, the economy actually moved from *A* to *D* to *E*. The structural deficit expanded enough to roughly counteract the decline in the cyclical element of the deficit. Fiscal policy was becoming increasingly stimulative in this period.

The correct measure of the general posture or thrust of fiscal policy is the structural deficit, not the cyclical deficit or the total deficit.

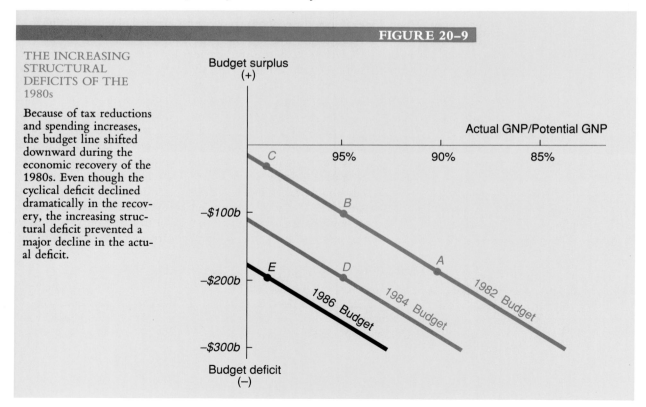

FIGURE 20–9

THE INCREASING STRUCTURAL DEFICITS OF THE 1980s

Because of tax reductions and spending increases, the budget line shifted downward during the economic recovery of the 1980s. Even though the cyclical deficit declined dramatically in the recovery, the increasing structural deficit prevented a major decline in the actual deficit.

To illustrate changes in U.S. government budgetary posture since the mid-1950s, we show the actual quarterly behavior of the structural budget deficit or surplus relative to GNP in Figure 20-10. A cursory glance at the figure indicates several key facts. First, the structural budget exhibited a surplus, on balance, during 1955–1962. In the next decade the structural budget was in deficit by an average magnitude of perhaps one percent of GNP. This swing toward fiscal stimulus was initiated by tax cuts in the early 1960s and by escalation of both domestic social programs and military spending associated with Vietnam during 1965–1968. Deescalation of the Vietnam War and a tax hike in the late 1960s reduced the

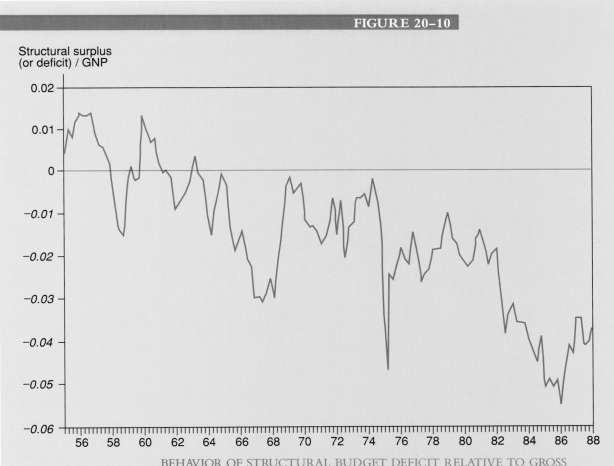

FIGURE 20–10

Structural surplus (or deficit) / GNP

BEHAVIOR OF STRUCTURAL BUDGET DEFICIT RELATIVE TO GROSS NATIONAL PRODUCT

A structural budget *surplus* typically prevailed before the 1960s; structural deficits have consistently prevailed since then. These structural deficits increased sharply in the 1980s, reaching more than four percent of GNP by the mid-1980s. The structural deficits have declined somewhat in recent years.

*These figures are actually deficits cyclically adjusted to the *midpoint* of cyclical expansions and not to the *peaks* of expansions. They therefore overstate somewhat the high-employment deficit magnitudes.

Source: Data from *Survey of Current Business*, 1989.

relative size of the structural deficit somewhat for a few years. However, the structural deficit increased after 1974 to about two percent of GNP during 1975–1980 and ballooned to as much as five percent of GNP during the mid-1980s. It has declined somewhat in recent years.

The unprecedented peacetime structural budget deficits of the 1980s are attributable largely to the generous income-tax cuts of the first Reagan Administration, along with the escalation of defense expenditures unaccompanied by significant cuts in nondefense spending. Unlike large structural deficits of the past—which occurred *temporarily* under the emergency conditions of wartime finance—the deficits of the 1980s occurred in time of peace and proved to be more intractable in nature. This is why interest on the part of economists, news commentators, and the general public in the venerable issues of deficit finance and debt burdens has staged a resurgence in the past decade.

Measurement and Conceptual Problems in Interpreting Budget Deficits

In addition to the need to adjust the deficit to allow for cyclical conditions, several other considerations complicate any analysis of budget deficits and debt burdens. The net result of these considerations is to reduce somewhat the perceived size and adverse consequences of large budget deficits.

Off-Budget Activities   Borrowings of certain government agencies to finance services provided to the public are listed as **off-budget activities** and are not included in official budget deficits. One could argue that such off-budget deficits, amounting to perhaps $20 billion annually, should be reported as budget deficits. This consideration suggests that reported deficits *understate* the true deficits.

State and Local Government Surpluses   In recent years, state and local governments have collectively exhibited net surpluses of some $30–$50 billion per annum. At the same time, federal grants to state and local governments have typically amounted to about $60–$80 billion per year. One could view part of the federal deficit as the source of state/local surpluses. The net deficit of *all* levels of government—federal, state, and local—is smaller than the federal deficit.

Absence of Federal Government Capital Budget   American business firms and most state and local governments compile a separate **capital budget** and **operating budget** to emphasize the distinct difference between borrowing to fund such capital projects as schools and bridges that yield a flow of benefits far into the future and borrowing to meet current operating costs. The federal government does not do this. One could argue that federal expenditures on buildings, dams, highways, education facilities, and so forth should be included in a separate capital budget, thus making the reported budget deficit considerably smaller.

Inflation Accounting for Interest Payments   Assume the net government debt is $2000 billion, the average interest rate paid for debt service is currently nine percent, and inflation is five percent. Nine percent interest on a $2000 billion debt implies annual interest expense of $180 billion. All this interest is reported as current government spending and thus contributes, dollar-for-dollar, to the reported budget deficit. However, since five-percent inflation implies that the real value of the stock of debt decreases $100 billion during the year, one may conceptually regard $100 billion of the interest paid as simply compensation paid to the lender for the reduction in the real value of the debt. The government gains $100 billion in real terms because of the reduction in real value of its debt liability. In other words, one could argue that only the *real* interest expense—$80 billion—should be included in the reported budget deficit. The net cost to the government is $80 billion, not $180 billion. The other $100 billion is compensation paid by the government for the $100 billion *balance sheet* gain shifted from private individuals and firms to the government. If inflation is relatively severe, this consideration suggests that the actual deficit considerably exceeds the **real deficit**—which is calculated by subtracting from the reported deficit this balance-sheet gain experienced by the government.[6]

Real Deficit
The actual deficit adjusted for the net balance sheet gain experienced by government because of inflation; actual deficit minus the inflation rate times the net federal debt outstanding.

The Mix of Monetary and Fiscal Policy

Because both monetary and fiscal policy strongly affect aggregate demand and GNP, any desired level of nominal GNP can in principle be attained through various combinations of monetary and fiscal stimuli. That is, a given level of GNP can be achieved by powerful fiscal stimulus coupled with rigid monetary restraint, by powerful monetary stimulus coupled with severe fiscal restraint, and by various other combinations of monetary and fiscal policies. Although the *level* of GNP can in principle be achieved with various combinations of monetary and fiscal policies, the *composition* of that output is likely to depend on the *mix* of monetary and fiscal policies.

Many economists believe that in the first half of the 1980s a combination of strong fiscal stimulus coupled with monetary restraint produced economic distortions that impaired several sectors of the U.S. economy. One might describe the situation via the analogy of driving a car with one foot on the accelerator (fiscal stimulus) coupled with one foot on the brake (monetary restraint). The car (economy) may continue to lurch forward, but the process is hard on the engine (economic growth and certain sectors of the economy).

Large structural budget deficits coupled with monetary restraint in the early 1980s placed upward pressure on real (inflation-adjusted) interest rates in the United States. This created a large demand on the part of foreigners for high-yielding U.S. financial assets. This *capital inflow* drove up the value of the U.S. dollar in foreign-exchange markets to levels that made it difficult for American industries exposed to foreign competition to compete in world markets. U.S. exports stagnated and imports increased dramatically. Our international trade deficit increased from about $30 billion in 1981 to $140 billion in 1985, and remained above $100 billion throughout the 1980s. Many economists believe that the dollar was significantly overvalued (in the sense of putting American firms at a competitive disadvantage) during much of this period, causing considerable hardship for such U.S. industries as textiles, agriculture, lumber, electronics, automobiles, and shoes.[7]

---

[6]See Robert Eisner, *How Real Is The Deficit?* (New York: The Free Press, 1986). Eisner emphasizes the distinction between the reported deficit and the real deficit. The real deficit may be defined as the difference between the reported deficit and the reduction in the real value of the existing stock of government debt in a given year owing to inflation. Eisner marshalls support for the hypothesis that the real deficit is the superior measure.

[7]Martin Feldstein, head of President Ronald Reagan's Council of Economic Advisors during 1982–1984, frequently espoused this viewpoint.

A combination of less fiscal stimulus (smaller budget deficits) and more monetary stimulus may have resulted in the same level of aggregate demand and GNP but in a stronger performance by American export- and import-competing industries. The U.S. manufacturing sector would have been stronger and perhaps the service sector would have been weaker in this scenario.

Moreover, the fiscal/monetary imbalance in the early 1980s, by driving up real interest rates, reduced the fortunes of interest-sensitive industries relative to other sectors. Hence, construction activity and investment in plant and equipment may have been stronger had the mix of policy included less fiscal stimulus and more stimulative monetary policy. In other words, the mix of policy may have tilted the mix of output toward less investment and more consumption than would have prevailed in the presence of a more balanced mix of policies. This view is difficult to test empirically because, at the same time that the mix of policies tilted toward fiscal expansion/monetary restraint in the early 1980s, a horde of measures were implemented to stimulate the flow of saving and investment. However, the mix of monetary/fiscal policies pursued in the 1980s seems to have been counterproductive to the stated Reagan Administration objectives of stimulating investment and economic growth.

LEGITIMATE CONCERNS ABOUT THE SPIRALING DEBT

There are two potential long-range consequences of the federal budget policy conducted during the past decade that are a continuing source of concern to thoughtful observers of the American economic and political scene. Both of these potential consequences—impaired investment spending and severe inflation—have been discussed earlier and are now addressed in greater depth.

The Issue of Crowding Out

As mentioned, because the stock of government debt grew much more slowly than privately issued debt in the first 20 years after World War II, there was room for vast expansion of construction activity and healthy expansion of private investment in plant and equipment. The federal government was not competing in the capital markets against private firms and individuals for the limited pool of funds available, and interest rates were relatively low.

Beginning with the growth of social programs and the escalation of the U.S. involvement in the Vietnam War in the 1960s, federal deficit spending increased in magnitude. These deficits escalated dramatically in the early 1980s. Real interest rates rose to unusually high levels in the 1980s. Those who believe in the **crowding-out hypothesis** would assert that these high real-interest rates were attributable in large part to the massive budget deficits that tended to displace private borrowers in the marketplace and impair expenditures on the crucial category of plant, equipment, and research and development. If valid, this hypothesis implies that large budget deficits impose a burden on future generations in the form of a reduced capital stock inherited by them.[8]

Crowding Out
The adverse effect of increased deficits on investment spending owing to the negative effect of higher interest rates associated with the larger deficits.

---

[8]Again, it is important to specify the types of government expenditures leading to rapid growth in the debt. If the debt grows to finance expansion of transfer payments and military spending, the capital stock bequeathed to future generations will likely be reduced. If the public debt is incurred to build highways, dams, universities, and high-tech facilities, the expanding debt may actually be increasing the stock of capital available to future generations.

Intuitively there is reason to believe that larger budget deficits and the resulting rapid escalation of the stock of government debt should exert upward pressure on the level of interest rates. Increased budget deficits mean increased demand for loanable funds, which unless offset by an equivalent increase in the supply of funds available, must pull up interest rates.[9] If investment spending is sensitive to the interest rate, budget deficits may result in a lower capital stock passed on to future generations, and hence a reduced future standard of living. This is the sense in which our *extravagance* today may come at the expense of our grandchildren.

However, it is not clear that deficit spending inevitably reduces current investment spending and the future capital stock. In assessing this issue, one should take into account the circumstances in which the budget deficits are incurred. One should also distinguish between structural deficits—those due to changes in tax rates or planned expenditures—and cyclical deficits. If increasing deficits are due to the automatic influence of depressed economic activity upon the federal budget, it is unlikely that crowding out of investment will occur. In fact, since the budget deficit in this case tends to cushion the drop in economic activity, the increased deficit may have a favorable effect on investment.

Crowding In
The favorable effect of increased deficits upon investment spending owing to the stimulative effect upon aggregate demand, output, and the utilization rate of capital equipment.

Even if the larger deficit is *structural* in nature, one must be cautious in advancing the crowding-out hypothesis. If such stimulative budgetary policy is conducted at a time of depressed economic activity, we may get **crowding in**—a *positive* response of investment spending to increased structural deficits. The stimulative fiscal policy may encourage investment spending. Investment in plant and equipment may be stimulated because of the beneficial effect of the increased deficit upon output, employment, and the utilization rate of plant and equipment. Though interest rates are probably higher than they would otherwise be as a result of the larger deficit, the expected rate of return from investment spending is also higher because of the beneficial effect of the deficit upon economic activity. Hence, firms may step up investment spending in spite of higher interest rates.

When the government exhibits large deficits in years of very strong economic activity, conditions are most conducive to crowding out. In this instance, sustained federal-government pressures on credit markets and interest rates are likely to tilt the mix of output away from private investment in plant and equipment. Only when the government deficit spending is used primarily to fund scientific research or highly productive public capital projects can we be optimistic in this instance about the impact of deficit spending upon the total capital stock and standards of living in the future.

Because the large structural deficits of the 1980s persisted as the economy hovered around full employment during the 1986–1989 period, the possibility of significant crowding out of investment increased relative to conditions in the first half of the decade when substantial excess capacity prevailed. The huge structural

---

[9]Actually, economic studies frequently have been unable to discern any positive relationship between budget deficits and interest rates in the American data prior to the 1980s. This seems rather surprising. Two explanations have been advanced. The first is that there *is* a causal relationship, but the magnitude of federal deficits prior to the 1980s was so small relative to the economy that the statistical studies were unable to uncover the relationship. The second explanation—known as the *Ricardo Equivalence Theorem*—asserts that budget deficits trigger an increase in the supply of savings, which neutralizes the impact of government deficits on interest rates. The alleged mechanism is that the budget deficits trigger a perception on the part of the public that future tax rates must rise and the standard of living must fall. To cushion this expected effect, the public steps up its current rate of saving. The increase in supply of funds owing to the increase in saving offsets the increase in demand for funds owing to the enlarged deficit, and the increase in budget deficits is alleged to have no impact on interest rates.

EXHIBIT 20–2

CONTROLLING BUDGET DEFICITS BY LEGISLATION

Because of increasing public pressure to control budget deficits and growing frustration with its own ability to hold down spending, Congress passed legislation in December 1985 designed to ensure the automatic elimination of the deficit over a six-year period. Congress enacted the Balanced Budget and Emergency Deficit Control Act, better known as the Gramm-Rudman-Hollings Act (*Gramm-Rudman* for short).

The immediate impetus for its enactment was a stalemate between President Reagan and Congress over the budget in 1985. The President ruled out defense cuts and tax hikes to deal with the deficit, insisting that nondefense and nonentitlement expenditures—those not already locked in by prior legislation—absorb the entire cuts. Congress favored a broader attack on the deficit, including cuts in the defense budget and perhaps some increase in taxes.

Gramm-Rudman mandated a phaseout of deficits by implementing a declining schedule of deficit ceilings from 1986 to 1991, as indicated in Table 20-1. The legislation requires that the president submit a budget proposal to Congress each year that meets the stipulated deficit limits for that year. If the proposed budget is not enacted into legislation, or if Congress fails to enact an alternative deficit reduction program acceptable to the President, *automatic spending reductions* are imposed. These spending cuts are across the board with the exception of interest on the debt, social security benefits, and certain other entitlements. The main point is that the spending cuts encompass both defense and social programs.

By a 7–2 vote, the Supreme Court ruled Gramm-Rudman unconstitutional on a technicality in July 1986. Congress amended the Act in 1987, buying time for deficit-reduction strategy by postponing the elimination of the deficit until 1993.

Many economists are critical of economic analysis that calls for an explicit reduction of the deficit each year irrespective of contemporary economic conditions. Suppose the economy weakens, automatically increasing the (cyclical) deficit because of lower-than-expected tax revenues. If the automatic cut in government spending is triggered, aggregate demand is reduced and the economic

deficits of the 1980s may in fact produce a lower standard of living for future generations than would occur with smaller structural deficits.[10]

The Possibility of Debt Explosion and Ultimate Inflation

The abrupt shift in federal budget posture in the 1980s to one of structural deficits of unprecedented magnitudes created visions of a nightmarish scenario in which the deficits feed upon themselves, thus degenerating into a vicious circle of escalating growth. In this case, the ratio of debt/GNP and interest payments/GNP follow a continuously increasing path. If such a path becomes established, the ultimate outcome is likely one of severe inflation created by the government as a means of alleviating the pressures caused by the debt explosion.

To illustrate the mechanism proposed in the preceding discussion, assume the stock of the national debt held by the public is currently $1500 billion. Assume further that the budget deficit is currently running at a rate of $200 billion annually and the average interest rate the government is paying to service the debt is ten percent. This means that in the current year, $150 billion is being paid to bondholders in the form of interest by the U.S. Treasury. Since the current deficit is

---

[10]A large inflow of foreign capital to purchase American securities during the 1980s helped hold down U.S. interest rates and release funds for domestic investment *here.* Proponents of the crowding-out hypothesis worry that we cannot count on indefinite continuation of this capital inflow. When it tapers off because foreigners become cautious about lending additional funds *here,* some fear that crowding out may arrive with a vengeance.

TABLE 20–1		
THE GRAMM-RUDMAN-HOLLINGS (GRH) DEFICIT TARGETS		
Fiscal year	Original GRH	Revised GRH
1986	176	*
1987	144	*
1988	108	144
1989	72	136
1990	36	100
1991	0	64
1992		28
1993		0

*A revised Gramm-Rudman bill was enacted in 1987.

downturn is exacerbated. Gramm-Rudman would require reductions in the structural deficit—*fiscal restraint*—during periods of economic weakness. Furthermore, many economists dispute the view that there is magic in a zero-deficit figure. The debt-burden indicators—debt/GNP, interest payments/GNP, and so forth—can be placed on a downward trajectory by judicious, well-timed reductions in the structural deficit without going all the way to a balanced budget.

It seems likely that even if the Gramm-Rudman targets are not met, the legislation has served to increase the visibility of the choices that must be made in budget decisions. New programs must be financed by cutting other government programs, by raising taxes, or by increasing the deficit. If Congress is forced to describe how new programs are to be financed, fewer new programs are likely to be proposed. Hence, for those who would like to see a slowdown in the growth of the government sector, the deficit-reduction legislation serves a real purpose. In this sense Gramm-Rudman may be a "bad idea whose time has come."

$200 billion, the debt a year hence will be $1700 billion and interest costs will expand to $170 billion if the interest rate remains at ten percent. This means that, given no change in taxes or expenditures, the deficit will expand next year to $220 billion. The debt will therefore expand the following year to $1920 billion and interest costs will balloon to $192 billion annually.

Note in the preceding scenario that the interest-service portion of government expenditures grows from $150 billion to $192 billion in two years, a growth rate of about 13 percent per year. Unless GNP grows at an exceptionally rapid rate or interest rates fall, the ratio of interest expense to GNP will continue to rise. Because interest payments on the accumulated stock of government debt are a significant component of government spending, a high level of deficits incurred *now* builds in high future interest costs and makes it more difficult for future budget makers to control deficits.

During the 1980s, interest payments on the national debt were the most rapidly growing portion of the federal budget.

Large budget deficits, once established, become increasingly difficult to control because of the escalating locked-in component of interest expenditures.[11]

[11]To avoid this debt explosion path, it is not necessary to balance the budget. Given reasonable assumptions about real GNP growth and the level of interest rates, deficits amounting to two or three percent of GNP avoid this disastrous path. However, deficits of the magnitude experienced during 1982–1986 (four and five percent of GNP) leave the issue very much alive. In the late 1980s, the deficit was reduced to about 3 percent of GNP.

Figures 20-6 and 20-7 illustrate the nature of the increasing role of interest expenditures in the past decade.

In this scenario, the longer the political process delays taking measures to halt the explosion of deficits, debt, and interest payments, the greater will be the magnitude of tax hikes and austerity programs required to reverse the process. At some point, responsible judgement will likely give way to expediency and the government may give in to the temptation to extricate itself from the vicious circle of increasing debt and interest payments via inflation. That is, the government may, in effect, repudiate its interest payments obligation by paying in depreciated dollars.

This process commences when the Federal Reserve System purchases large amounts of government debt rather than insisting that it be predominantly absorbed in the private marketplace. This method of government finance is virtually identical in its effects to a procedure of simply printing currency to finance government expenditures. Either procedure results in rapid growth of the money supply and aggregate demand and the resulting diminution in the value of the currency—inflation.[12]

Not only is the procedure of repudiation highly irresponsible in that it violates the trust of those who voluntarily loaned money to their government, but it also unleashes all the adverse effects associated with inflation that we studied in Chapter 18. The history of nations that have abandoned all semblance of budgetary prudence is a history of inflation.

SUMMARY

1. The national debt is the cumulative sum of past deficits. It consists of a stock of long-term and short-term securities held by American firms and individuals, foreigners, government agencies, and the Federal Reserve System. Since budget deficits have been exceptionally large in the 1980s, the debt has increased at a very rapid rate. Its magnitude tripled during the 1980s.

2. Over the entire period since the end of World War II, the national debt has grown more slowly than GNP and also more slowly than such private forms of debt as mortgage debt, consumer debt, and business indebtedness at banks. However, since the mid-1970s the government debt has increased more rapidly than these other variables. This has stimulated renewed interest in the economic consequences of deficits and the national debt.

3. It is a fallacy to assume that our debt places a burden on future generations because it ultimately must be paid off. While individual components of the debt are repaid at maturity, the government is continually involved in refinancing the debt. A growing economy is capable of supporting a growing volume of debt, both public and private. The national debt will never be retired or paid off. The same is true of business debt, consumer debt, and mortgage debt.

4. It is a fallacy to assume that interest payments on a domestically held debt represent a use of American resources. Such payments do not use up resources but do have effects upon the distribution of U.S. income and wealth. However, given other factors such as the level of

---

[12]When the Treasury finances expenditures by selling bonds to the *public,* the reduced checking accounts (money balances) of the bond buyers neutralizes the increased money balances placed into the hands of the recipients of government expenditures. The money supply does not change. When the Treasury finances expenditures by selling bonds to the Federal Reserve System, no funds are withdrawn from the checking accounts of private citizens to offset the funds pumped in when the Treasury issues checks to pay for its expenditures. The money supply rises. Regulations prohibit the Fed from purchasing *newly issued* government debt. However, the Fed could circumvent the intent of this regulation by purchasing large quantities of already outstanding bonds at the same time that the government issues a large amount of new debt.

GNP, a larger debt implies that tax rates must be higher in order to service the debt without displacing other forms of government spending. These higher tax rates could reduce incentives to work, save, or invest, thus possibly reducing future standards of living. Also, if the debt is held by foreigners, American resources are given up when foreigners cash in their interest checks for American-made merchandise.

5. The actual budget deficit conceptually may be divided into a cyclical component and a structural component. The cyclical component is due to the feedback of economic activity on federal tax receipts and expenditures. The structural component is the portion that would exist in the event the economy were operating at a high level of output and employment. Discretionary changes in fiscal policy—changes in tax rates or expenditures—produce shifts in the structural deficit.

6. Interpretation of federal budget deficits is clouded because of failure to include off-budget activities and state and local government surpluses, and because of absence of capital budgeting and inflation accounting for interest payments.

7. Economists are more concerned about large, long-lasting structural deficits than about cyclical deficits because structural deficits are more likely to crowd out investment and result in a lower future capital stock. The magnitude of structural deficits increased during the 1980s because of large tax cuts and defense expenditure growth.

8. The *mix* of monetary and fiscal policies has important implications for the composition of current output as it pertains to the consumption–investment mix and the prosperity of industries exposed to foreign competition relative to purely domestic sectors.

9. There are two important potential adverse consequences of large budget deficits and burgeoning stock of debt. First, business spending on plant and equipment may be reduced. If so, the capital stock inherited by future generations is reduced, thus lowering their standard of living. This is the sense in which our deficit spending may impose an *intergenerational burden.* Whether or not crowding out of private investment occurs is a complicated issue, hinging on the circumstances in which budget deficits occur. The second potential consequence of large deficits and increasing debt is the development of a vicious circle of expanding interest payments, deficits, and debt. If deficits exceed a certain threshold relative to GNP, this debt explosion may occur. If so, the only feasible way for the government to relieve the burden of the exploding interest expense is via inflation. In practice, this occurs when the Federal Reserve heavily *monetizes* the debt—the Treasury borrows heavily from the Fed rather than from the public. If this happens, inflation arrives with a vengeance.

KEY TERMS

budget surplus

budget deficit

national debt

intergenerational burden

cyclical deficit

structural deficit or
     high-employment deficit

automatic stabilizing effect

off-budget activities

capital budget

operating budget

real deficit

crowding out

crowding in

STUDY QUESTIONS AND PROBLEMS

1. Explain the relationship between budget deficits and the national debt.
2. Explain the effects of large budget deficits on firms that rely heavily on exporting for business.
3. Itemize several *short-term* consequences for America of the large budget deficits of the 1980s.

4. What causes the federal deficit to respond to changes in economic activity? Which part of the deficit acts as an automatic stabilizer? Explain.
5. Should we set a timetable to pay off the national debt by a certain year—for example, by the year 2010? Explain why or why not.
6. Discuss the various indicators of the relative size or *burden* of our national debt. Which do you believe is the most important? Explain.
7. Why is it sometimes asserted that large budget deficits lead to a situation in which federal interest expenditures displace other forms of government expenditures?
8. Differentiate between the actual budget deficit and the structural deficit. Under what conditions are the two measures identical?
9. Evaluate the hypothesis that federal budget deficits crowd out private investment expenditures. Why is the hypothesis highly debatable? Under what circumstances is the hypothesis most likely to be valid?
10. Why might increased deficits *crowd in* investment during a severe recession?
11. Explain three considerations that suggest our reported deficits may understate or overstate the deficit.
12. Why might a very complacent attitude on the part of Congress and the president ultimately result in severe inflation?

ANSWER TO YOUR TURN

Any efforts to balance the budget during a depression would only exacerbate the state of the economy. To balance the budget or reduce the deficit, tax hikes and expenditure cuts are necessary. But both these measures reduce aggregate demand and the level of economic activity. In other words, the structural deficit is being reduced (fiscal policy becomes more restrictive) when economic activity is weak. Structural budget deficits should be reduced during periods of robust economic activity, not during periods of weakness.

SELECTED REFERENCES

Congressional Budget Office, *The Economic and Budget Outlook: Fiscal Years 1990–1994*, (Washington: 1989). This annual document details the budget and project future outlays, receipts, and deficits.

Courant, Paul N., and Edward M. Gramlich, *Federal Budget Deficits: America's Great Consumption Binge* (Englewood Cliffs, NJ: Prentice-Hall, 1986). This concise book provides balanced coverage of major issues associated with the U.S. budget deficits of the 1980s.

Eisner, Robert, *How Real Is the Federal Deficit?* (New York: The Free Press, 1986). In this provocative work, Eisner presents the case for a new measure of federal deficits—one that takes account of inflation and other economic phenomena.

Mills, Gregory B., and John L. Palmer, *The Deficit Dilemma: Budget Policy in the Reagan Years* (Washington, DC: The Urban Institute Press, 1983). This work examines the political and economic predicament posed by the large federal deficits of the early 1980s.

U.S. Treasury, *Treasury Bulletin*. This quarterly publication provides a wealth of data on all aspects of the national debt and government financing activities.

CHAPTER 21

ECONOMIC GROWTH AND PRODUCTIVITY BEHAVIOR IN INDUSTRIAL NATIONS

The capitalist achievement does not typically consist in providing more silk stockings for queens but in bringing them within reach of factory girls in return for steadily decreasing amounts of effort.

JOSEPH A. SCHUMPETER, 1942

On average, members of your generation are considerably richer in terms of material possessions and living standards than your grandparents were when they were the same age. Furthermore, your grandchildren are likely to be considerably more affluent than you. Real output and income per person in the United States today is at least six times the level of one hundred years ago. Moreover, growth in per-capita income is not unique to the United States. It has occurred in all of the industrialized nations during the past 150–200 years.

In Chapter 21 we focus on the long-run growth in output, income, and living standards in industrial nations. Chapter 38 analyzes the growth challenges of less developed countries (LDCs)—nations in which some three-fourths of the earth's inhabitants dwell. Per-capita income in LDCs is typically less than one-tenth that of such industrial nations as France, Japan, and the United States.

THE MEANING AND IMPORTANCE OF ECONOMIC GROWTH

Economic Growth

Long-run expansion in an economy's capacity to produce goods and services. Implies a sustained rightward shifting of a nation's production possibilities curve and aggregate supply curve.

To an economist, **economic growth** indicates the gradual long-run expansion of a nation's capacity to produce goods and services. Economic growth concerns the slope of the *potential* GNP line—the growth of GNP under conditions in which the unemployment rate is maintained at the natural rate of unemployment. Economic growth means that the nation's production possibilities curve and aggregate supply curve are shifting rightward over time. Economic growth extracts from short-run business cycle conditions and looks at the longer-term trend of economic progress.

Analysts sometimes use the term "economic growth" rather loosely to describe expansion of actual output and income in a short-run context. For example, a newspaper might state that "economic growth is expected to be three percent next year," indicating that real GNP is expected to rise three percent in the next year. Such "growth" can occur even in the absence of a rightward shift of the production possibilities curve or aggregate supply curve as the economy advances in the recovery phase of the business cycle. In this instance, we might be simply increasing output within the context of a given capacity because the aggregate demand curve shifts upward during economic recovery.

In Parts II and III of this text, we discussed the use of government's monetary and fiscal policy tools to boost economic activity when it is sluggish and when the unemployment rate significantly exceeds the economy's natural rate of unemployment. Such stabilization policies essentially increase short-run output and income within the context of a given capacity to produce goods and services. These stabilization policies, when successful, clearly benefit society by stimulating output and income in the short run. However, they do not constitute an important source of rising living standards from one generation to the next. In that sense, they pale in significance when compared to the true source of economic progress—the long-run expansion of the average worker's capacity to produce goods and services.

Measures of Economic Growth

Two measures of economic growth are commonly used. The first is the rate of growth of *real GNP*—the output of goods and services of the nation—over a period of years. The second measure is the growth rate of **per-capita real GNP.** Recall that production of output creates an equal amount of income in the nation as a whole. This is the central importance of output or GNP—it is our collective source of income.

Depending on the nature of one's interest in economic growth, one might prefer to focus on the growth rate of real GNP or on the growth rate of per-capita real GNP. If one is interested in a nation's potential *economic power* and the growth thereof, real GNP and its growth are the relevant variables. China's real GNP clearly exceeds that of Switzerland. Furthermore, China's real GNP is growing faster than Switzerland's. Hence, China probably has more economic power than Switzerland.

On the other hand, if one's interest is to examine the *well-being of the average inhabitant* of a country and its rate of change, real output per capita and its growth rate are the relevant indicators. Real output (or income) per capita is known as the standard of living. Even though China is potentially more powerful than Switzerland (the Chinese economy is larger), Switzerland has a much higher standard of living. Switzerland produces roughly one-fourth as much output as China with less than one percent of China's population. The average Swiss citizen has far more material possessions than her Chinese counterpart. In this chapter our primary focus is on growth of living standards—output per capita.

Table 21-1 indicates the growth of real output and per-capita real output for the United States over the past 60 years. Over the 60-year period, real output increased at an average annual rate of 2.9 percent. Since the population increased at an average rate of 1.2 percent per year, the standard of living (per-capita output) grew at an average annual rate of 1.7 percent. This performance implies that living standards double in 41 years.

The growth rate of per-capita real income is not a perfect measure of the rate of improvement in welfare. It ignores such important considerations as changes in leisure time and other indicators of change in quality of life (e.g., changes in environmental pollution) and also ignores the distribution of income across the population. Clearly, it makes a difference whether the fruits of economic progress are widely shared by the people or are captured by a tiny minority of the population. Nevertheless, the growth rate of real output (and income) per capita provides a reasonable approximation of the improvement in living standards. Economists place considerable stock in this variable.

In this chapter we concentrate on the principles of long-term economic growth—the gradual rightward shifting of production possibilities curves and aggregate supply curves over time. We especially emphasize productivity growth of labor—the expansion of output per hour of work. Productivity growth is the predominant source of rising living standards that commenced roughly 200 years ago and has continued to the present. After surveying productivity growth in various

Standard of Living
The average output or real income per person; annual output divided by the population.

Productivity Growth
Expansion of output and real income per hour of work; the main source of rising living standards.

TABLE 21-1

U.S. REAL GNP AND PER-CAPITA REAL GNP, 1929–1988

Year	GNP (billions of 1982 dollars)	Population (millions)	Per-capita GNP (1982 dollars)
1929	710	122	5,820
1933	499	126	3,960
1940	773	132	5,553
1950	1,204	152	7,921
1960	1,665	181	9,199
1970	2,416	205	11,785
1980	3,187	228	13,978
1988	3,996	246	16,244

Source: *Economic Report of the President,* 1989.

countries, we explore the fundamental determinants of productivity growth and assess the probable causes of the slowdown of American productivity growth in the past 20 years. The chapter concludes by analyzing certain proposals designed to boost America's sagging productivity growth.

Productivity Growth and Growth in Living Standards

Technically, one must distinguish between growth in productivity (output per *hour of work*) and growth in living standards (output per *capita*). If the length of the workweek and the fraction of the total population employed were to remain constant over time, growth in living standards would proceed at precisely the same rate as the growth of productivity. Since the length of the workweek and the fraction of the total population working both fluctuate over time, the growth rate of output per worker (per-capita income) typically differs somewhat from the growth rate of productivity.

Over relatively brief intervals of time, it is not unusual for growth of per-capita income to outpace productivity growth. This occurs when the percentage of the population employed rises, as in the 1970s when the baby boomers (born in 1946–1963) flooded into the work force and as the labor force participation rate of women increased.

In the United States the length of the workweek has been gradually declining for decades. This decline has been offset by the increasing labor force participation rate. But there are obvious limits to the growth of the labor force participation rate attributable to changes in the age structure of the population and other factors that influence the fraction of the population working or seeking employment. For all intents and purposes, these factors tend to wash out in the long run and the growth rate of productivity is the overwhelmingly predominant source of growth in living standards. The growth rate of productivity is one of the most crucial variables in economic analysis.

Importance of Economic Growth

In the short-run context of a single year, economic growth means relatively little to the material well-being of the average individual. In the long run—say over a 25-, 50-, or 100-year period—the rate of growth makes a tremendous difference. Relatively small annual increases in output per capita, when compounded for 50 or 100 years, add up to surprisingly large increases in living standards. The immense difference in living standards that exists today between LDCs such as Nigeria and Ethiopia and developed nations such as France and Germany can be explained by the two-percent annual growth differential in favor of Germany and France sustained over 150 years. If Nigeria and Germany start with identical per-capita incomes and Germany grows two percent per year for 150 years while Nigeria remains stagnant, the standard of living in Germany at the end of the period is 19.5 times that of Nigeria!

Per-capita U.S. GNP in 1990, measured in 1985 dollars, was roughly $18,000. Suppose you plan to retire in the year 2040. If per-capita output growth averages two percent per year over the 1990–2040 period, GNP per capita in 2040 will be somewhat more than $48,000 (in dollars of 1985 purchasing power). If three-percent annual growth could be achieved, GNP per capita would exceed $78,000 when you retire (in 1985 dollars). Clearly, small differences in growth rates make big differences in living standards over the long haul.

YOUR TURN   Assume, hypothetically, that per-capita output in Modernia grows steadily at 1.5 percent annually while that in Laggardia remains constant. If the countries initially had identical living standards, how much richer would Modernians be (than Laggardians) after 50 years? 100 years? 200 years? *Hint:* Use a calculator with a y^x key, where $y = 1.015$ and x is the number of years.

Fostering productivity growth is crucial to America for many reasons. Obviously, more rapid growth means more material possessions for Americans. But there are more important, substantive considerations. America's international position of economic superiority is dwindling and the vast gulf that once separated our living standards from our nearest competitors' is gone. More rapid growth would help fortify our position of world leadership. Economic growth can provide the basis for freeing up more leisure time, a healthier workplace, a safer environment, and a more adequate provision of education and medical services to all Americans. As Nobel Laureate Robert Solow observed, "redistributing income is *not* something Americans are very good at." Realistically, strong economic growth is essential if we are to come to grips with the compelling problems of poverty and adequate health care for our people as we enter the twenty-first century.

Economic Growth in Historical Perspective

Given the long scope of human history, economic growth is a recent phenomenon. Until some 200 years ago, the human condition was characterized by almost universal poverty, hunger, disease, and periodic plagues—an existence of misery and brief life expectancy. Living standards in Europe at the time European settlers began to arrive on American soil were roughly the same as those that prevailed some 1500 years earlier. Century after century went by without any significant change in living standards. The experience of low and basically unchanging living standards endured in the twentieth century by such LDCs as Ethiopia and Nigeria are much closer to the norm of historical experience than are the modern growth miracles of the United States, Japan, and western European nations.

Significant, sustained increases in living standards commenced with the industrial revolution in England at the beginning of the eighteenth century and spread to Europe and the United States somewhat later. Modern economic growth is attributable to **industrialization**—the application of machinery and technology to the production process. The increasing reliance upon automation in place of animal sources of power and unskilled labor-intensive processes steadily pulled up output per worker and living standards in the past 150–200 years.

INTERNATIONAL LEVEL AND GROWTH OF LIVING STANDARDS SINCE 1870

Productivity growth in nations that today are industrialized has resulted in an enormous increase in the standard of living over the past one or two centuries. In the sample of 16 nations for which reliable output and income data going back more than a century are available, the average standard of living increased by a factor of more than eight between 1870 and 1990.

In the United States the level of affluence has expanded somewhat faster than this average. American productivity (output per work hour) increased thirteen-fold

EXHIBIT 21-1

ECONOMIC GROWTH AND THE FUTURE INTERNATIONAL POWER STRUCTURE

Although we should not take the results very seriously, let us conduct a provocative experiment in the hypothetical economics of growth. Given the 1985 actual GNP size (gross national product in 1985 American dollars) or various nations and given the actual growth rate of real GNP experienced by each nation over the 20-year period ending in 1987, what will be the magnitudes of these economics roughly 10 and 40 years from now if these growth rates continue? The information is provided in Table 21-2.

In the unlikely event that the growth rates of the past 20 years continued for several decades, some interesting changes in the international power structure would emerge in the next 40 years. Japan—with roughly one-half the population and one-third the output of the United States in 1985—would overtake us before the year 2030. China (the People's Republic)—last on our short list in 1985 with an output less than 10 percent of America's—would reach parity with the stronger

European economies within a decade, surpass them shortly thereafter, and begin to seriously challenge the United States and Japan in the battle for economic supremacy by the year 2030. England—the predominant world power of the nineteenth century and roughly at parity with Italy and France in 1985—would continue her long pattern of decline and slide to last place on the list by the year 2030.

Before you lose any sleep over these projections, read the section on the convergence of living standards. It is quite unlikely that past growth rates generated by Japan and China can continue for a long period. Indeed, Japan's growth rate in the 1980s has slowed to approximately four percent per year. China's growth rate shows no sign of slowing down yet. In fact, it accelerated to about nine percent per year during 1981–1988. Given the enormous gulf between China's living standard and ours, her rapid growth is consistent with the past experience of emerging economic powers.

TABLE 21-2

ACTUAL REAL OUTPUT IN 1985 AND PROJECTED OUTPUT FOR THE YEARS 2000 AND 2030

Country	1985 GNP	Growth rate (%) 1968–1987	Projected real GNP (in 1985 U.S. dollars) Year 2000	Year 2030
U.S.	3947	2.6	5800	12,528
France	631	3.3	1027	2,720
Italy	619	3.0	964	2,340
Great Britain	618	1.9	820	1,442
Germany	743	2.6	1092	2,358
Canada	386	3.9	685	2,159
Japan	1425	5.0	2962	12,804
China	345	7.4	1007	8,570

Sources: 1985 GNP from *Statistical Abstract of the United States, 1988.* 1968–1987 growth rates of real GNP from Federal Reserve Bank of St. Louis, *International Economic Conditions,* 1988, except for China's, which is from *Economic Report of the President,* 1988. Last two columns are calculated by extrapolating 1985 GNP in U.S. dollars at 1968–1987 growth rates ahead to the years 2000 and 2030.

between 1870 and 1990 (slightly more than two percent per year). Given the significant reduction in the average length of the workweek, the standard of living of the average American increased somewhat more slowly. In 1990 it was roughly nine times higher than that of our 1870 counterpart.[1]

Tendency for Living Standards to Converge

All industrial countries have experienced sustained growth in productivity and income per capita. In addition, both productivity levels and living standards have clearly tended to *converge*. Today's industrial nations that exhibited relatively low productivity levels and living standards in the nineteenth century have systematically tended to grow faster than nations that were relatively affluent. In Table 21-3 we list the 16 nations for which output per capita data are available for 1870 and 1979. These countries are ranked according to the 1870 level of output per capita, from low (Japan) to high (Australia).

The data in Table 21-3 reveal the existence of a strong negative relationship between the *level* of the early (1870) standard of living and the subsequent *rate of growth*. Countries relatively poor in 1870 have consistently grown faster than those

TABLE 21-3			
PER-CAPITA OUTPUT LEVELS AND GROWTH RATES IN INDUSTRIAL NATIONS, 1870–1979			

Country	1870 GDP/Capita*	1979 GDP/Capita*	Ratio 1979 to 1870	Average growth per year (%) (per-capita output)
Japan	251	4419	17.6	2.66
Finland	384	4287	11.2	2.24
Sweden	415	4908	11.8	2.29
Norway	489	4760	9.7	2.11
Germany	535	4946	9.2	2.06
Denmark	572	4483	7.8	1.91
Austria	573	4255	7.4	1.86
Italy	593	3577	6.0	1.66
Canada	619	5361	8.6	2.00
France	627	4981	7.9	1.92
U.S.	764	6055	7.9	1.92
Switzerland	786	4491	5.7	1.61
Netherlands	831	4396	5.3	1.54
Belgium	925	4986	5.4	1.56
Great Britain	972	3981	4.1	1.30
Australia	1393	4466	3.2	1.07
Mean	671	4647	6.9	1.79

*Figures are in 1970 U.S. dollars. For our purposes, GDP (gross domestic product) may be regarded as equivalent to GNP.

Source: Angus Maddison, *Phases of Capitalist Development* (Oxford: Oxford University Press, 1982), p. 8. Reprinted by permission of the publisher.

[1]These observations are based on data on pages 8 and 212 of Angus Maddison, *Phases of Capitalist Development* (Oxford: Oxford University Press, 1982), updated by authors.

that were relatively rich. In other words, there is a powerful tendency for living standards to converge. Japan, Finland, and Sweden, the poorest countries in 1870, have exhibited the fastest growth rates. Australia and Great Britain, the two richest in 1870, have experienced the lowest rates of advance.

The American standard of living in 1870 was more than three times that of Japan. By 1979, the U.S. margin of superiority over Japan was only 37 percent. The range between the richest and poorest of the 16 countries has narrowed dramatically. In 1870 the richest nation (Australia) had a standard of living roughly 5.5 times that of the poorest (Japan). By 1979 the ratio of the richest standard of living (the United States) to the poorest (Italy) was less than two-to-one.

The **convergence principle** is illustrated in Figure 21-1. Clearly, the figure indicates that countries that were rich in 1870 have grown more slowly than countries that were relatively poor.[2] Why is this true? What explanation lies behind the convergence phenomenon?

Convergence Principle
Tendency of industrial nations with relatively low living standards to grow more rapidly than more affluent nations, thereby reducing the gap in living standards.

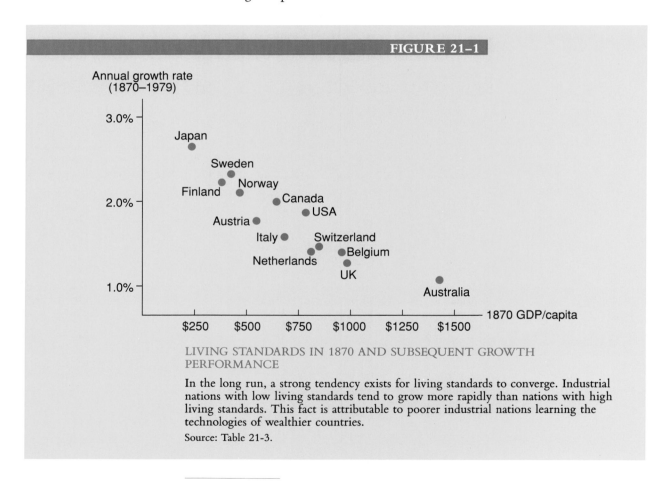

FIGURE 21–1

LIVING STANDARDS IN 1870 AND SUBSEQUENT GROWTH PERFORMANCE

In the long run, a strong tendency exists for living standards to converge. Industrial nations with low living standards tend to grow more rapidly than nations with high living standards. This fact is attributable to poorer industrial nations learning the technologies of wealthier countries.

Source: Table 21-3.

---

[2]Modern evidence supporting the convergence hypothesis is yielded by the recent growth performance of the newly industrialized nations of the Pacific Rim, such as Korea, Singapore, Taiwan, and Malaysia. In the past two decades these emerging economies have been experiencing growth rates of per-capita output at least *twice* those exhibited by the United States and European countries. Japan dramatically narrowed its gap with the United States in the 1950s and 1960s with phenomenal growth rates in excess of ten percent per year.

What Explains the Tendency of Living Standards to Converge?

All reasonably developed nations stand to benefit from shared information. European nations benefit from advances in American computer technology; America benefits from advances in Japanese robotic technology. Although economists have not pinpointed all the factors that account for the tendency of living standards of industrialized nations to converge, there is a consensus that the international diffusion of technological advances is at the heart of the phenomenon.[3] Today these technological improvements spread from country to country much more rapidly than in the past.

Improved communications among countries enable new technology to spread across borders more rapidly. Widespread and technically rigorous education levels permit nations to obtain technological knowhow and train the work force to implement new production procedures. Although the technologically poor nations have much to learn and benefit handsomely from the technologically advanced nations, the reverse flow of information and corresponding benefits are meager. This fundamental asymmetry in the spread of technology across nations does much to explain the convergence of living standards. The relatively poor among the industrial nations tend to close the gap on the rich by learning and implementing their technologies.

One implication of the convergence phenomenon is that one nation need not perceive other countries as rivals in technological innovation. In the long run, each nation benefits from the scientific achievements of other countries. Factors encouraging innovation in one nation ultimately pull up living standards in many other countries. Competitiveness among countries is a short-run phenomenon. Each individual in the advanced nations eventually benefits from technological breakthroughs—whether they occur at home or abroad.

One should not conclude that convergence of living standards among industrialized nations is an inevitable, preordained phenomenon. At one time people believed that Argentina was destined to be a great economic power. Moreover, nations can fall from a position of preeminence. Spain was the richest nation in the world in the sixteenth century. England was a great power in the nineteenth century, but note her position in the rankings today (Table 21-2). And don't forget the decline of the Roman Empire in the fifth century. It is foolish to assume that America will *necessarily* be one of the great economic powers of the world 100 years from now, irrespective of how we manage our economic affairs in the interim.

The Convergence Phenomenon and Less Developed Nations (LDCs)

In Chapter 38 we analyze the problems of less developed nations (LDCs) in some depth. A huge chasm exists between the affluence level of the industrial nations just discussed and the LDCs. Furthermore, in many cases the convergence phenomenon is nonexistent. The chasm has been widening instead of narrowing.

In LDCs the education level of the population is quite low. A severe shortage of engineers, scientists, and technicians prevails. Advanced technological developments benefitting the industrial nations are often not feasible to implement in the LDCs. Even more fundamental, most LDCs concentrate production in the areas of

---

[3]See William J. Baumol, "Productivity Growth, Convergence, and Welfare," *American Economic Review,* December 1986, pp. 1072–1085.

agriculture and raw materials. The absence of a substantial manufacturing base reduces the feasibility of imitating the sophisticated technological breakthroughs that have lifted living standards in industrial nations. However, LDCs do benefit from the technology of advanced nations, especially in the area of agriculture. But the scope for widespread diffusion of the technological breakthroughs of the advanced nations to the LDCs is inherently limited.

THE SOURCES OF ECONOMIC GROWTH

Societies increase their output and income in two fundamental ways—by increasing their inputs of such resources as labor, capital, and land and by increasing the productivity of these inputs. It is useful to focus on the following expression:

$$\text{total output} = \text{worker hours} \times \text{labor productivity}$$

The nation's aggregate output (GNP) is viewed as the product of labor input (expressed in hours of work) and the productivity of labor (measured as output per worker per hour).

In a hypothetical economy with one million workers, each working 2000 hours per year (a 50-week, 40-hour per week pattern), total hours worked per year are 2 billion. If average productivity (average real output per hour of work) is $10, the real output or GNP of this society is $20 billion per year.

In this framework it is clear that output can be increased only by an increase in hours worked, an increase in labor productivity, or some combination of the two. What determines the number of hours worked? This depends upon the working-age population, the labor force participation rate (the fraction of the working-age population actually in the labor force), and the average length of the workweek. Productivity of labor depends chiefly upon the level of technology; the amount of capital available for each worker; and the level of education, training, and skills of the work force. These factors that determine real output of a nation are summarized in Figure 21-2.

In the United States, real output has grown over the years partly because of an increase in labor input but chiefly because of growth of productivity of labor. Total hours worked have increased markedly over the long haul as the massive increase in employment has overwhelmed the effect of a declining workweek. One of the most respected students of economic growth is Edward F. Denison. In a careful empirical study, Denison found that for the 1929–1982 period in the United States, an increase in the quantity of labor accounted for about one-third of the increase in real output and income whereas the increase in labor productivity accounted for about two-thirds of the growth. Denison further analyzed the sources of the increase in labor productivity during the period. His findings are reported in Table 21-4.

Technological Change

Invention
The discovery of new knowledge.
Innovation
The application of new technical knowledge to such economic processes as production and distribution.

At a given point of time, a society has a certain stock of knowledge pertaining to the production of goods and services. Discovery of new knowledge leads to technological change. Development of this technical knowledge consists of **invention** and **innovation.** Invention is the discovery of new knowledge. Innovation is the development of methods for applying this knowledge to economic processes. The development and implementation of technical knowledge are the leading sources of

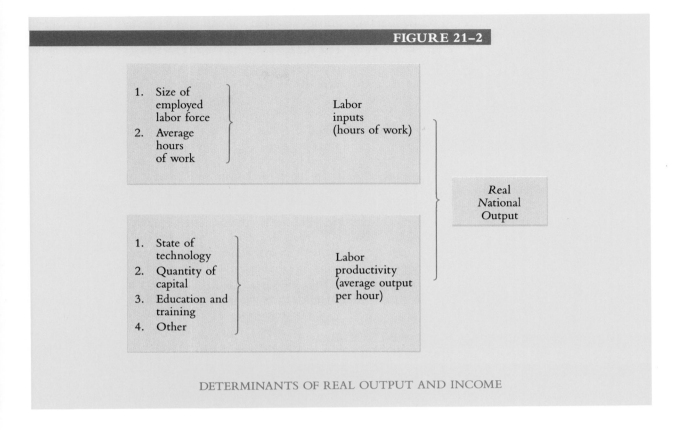

FIGURE 21–2

DETERMINANTS OF REAL OUTPUT AND INCOME

TABLE 21-4

ACCOUNTING FOR U.S. PRODUCTIVITY GROWTH, 1929–1982

1. Technological advance	40%
2. Quantity of capital	28
3. Education and training	21
4. Other factors	11
	100%

Source: Edward F. Denison, *Trends in American Economic Growth,* 1929–1982 (Washington, DC: The Brookings Institution, 1985), p. 30.

productivity growth. Denison estimated that these factors accounted for 40 percent of productivity growth during 1929–1982.

In American economic history, numerous examples remind us of the powerful role of technological change in lifting our productivity and living standards. In the field of agriculture, animal sources of power were replaced by machines powered by fossil fuels. Development of fertilizers, hybrid seeds, and irrigation technology have also contributed to the tremendous increase in agricultural productivity. This productivity growth is reflected in the fact that the percentage of the American population engaged in agriculture has declined from 70 percent in 1840 to 2 percent today. In transportation, railroads replaced animals, sailing vessels were rendered obsolete by steamships, and then automobiles, trucks, and airplanes largely superseded the railroads. In the field of communications, the pony express was replaced by the telegraph, which in turn yielded to the telephone, radio, and television.

Research and development (R and D) expenditures are an indicator of the resources devoted by a nation to the growth of technology. In recent decades, the United States has allocated between two and three percent of its annual GNP to research and development. The U.S. effort in this area, along with that of several other nations, is illustrated in Figure 21-3.

Of the countries illustrated in Figure 21-3, only the Soviet Union clearly dominates the United States in its research and development effort. Economists believe that the returns to investment in nonmilitary research and development are quite high, both to society and to the firm making the investment. Such returns to society have been estimated to be in the neighborhood of 30 percent. So why don't we spend more on R and D? There are two reasons. First, the expected returns, though large, are highly *uncertain*. Risk-averse firms therefore tend to shy away from heavy R and D spending. Second, great uncertainty exists about the feasibility of the inventor preventing imitation by rivals. Hence, returns to society may be significantly higher than returns to individual firms making the breakthroughs.

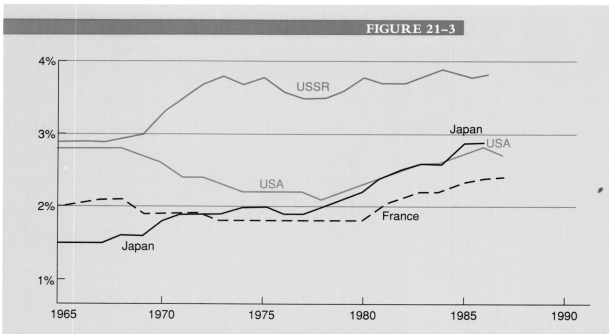

FIGURE 21-3

RESEARCH AND DEVELOPMENT SPENDING AS A FRACTION OF GNP, 1965–1988

In recent years the United States, Japan, and France have allocated two or three percent of GNP to research and development (R and D) efforts. The Soviet Union allocates a significantly larger portion of GNP to R and D. However, a much larger share of the Soviet effort involves military—not civilian—research and development.

Source: *Statistical Abstract of the United States, 1989.*

Research and development expenditures have large positive externalities or spillover effects—they ultimately provide benefits to society far in excess of the benefits captured by the individuals consuming goods directly resulting from R and D efforts. Recall our discussion in Chapter 7 in which we noted that free markets do not allocate adequate resources to endeavors in which positive spillovers exist. For this reason government intervention is appropriate. Accordingly, government laboratories conduct R and D activities, and the government sometimes subsidizes private research and development spending.

The Capital Stock

Capital Deepening
Expansion in the average amount of capital goods per worker. An important source of productivity growth.

Workers become more productive when equipped with a larger capital stock—more plant, machinery, and tools. Net investment results in growth of the nation's capital stock. Over the long run America's capital stock has grown faster than its labor force, resulting in an increase in capital per worker. This process, known as **capital deepening,** is a prime source of rising labor productivity and living standards. In the past 100 years the American ratio of capital stock to labor has increased by a factor of about three. Denison estimates that this growth of real capital accounts for 28 percent of the increase in labor productivity in America during 1929–1982.

The saving-investment process is the mechanism that provides for growth of the capital stock over time. If our objective is to boost the growth rate of labor productivity, we must save and invest a larger portion of our current incomes. That is, we must produce *fewer* sports cars, shirts, and TV sets and *more* machine tools, tractors, and blast furnaces.

The fraction of U.S. gross national product allocated to investment goods has been lower than that of most other industrial nations. Partly for this reason and partly because of the demographically induced spurt of labor-force growth during 1965–1982, the U.S. capital/labor ratio slowed its rate of growth significantly and even declined for several years after 1965. At the same time, our productivity growth also slowed appreciably. It is unlikely that this timing reflects mere coincidence.

Figure 21-4 (page 474) illustrates the fraction of output allocated to investment goods and the growth rate of productivity in the manufacturing sector for a sample of eight industrial nations during the 1960–1983 period. Note that the positive relationship, while leaving room for other factors to influence productivity growth, is fairly strong. Japan, which devoted the largest share of output to capital goods, also experienced the most rapid productivity growth rate. The United States and England, which had the weakest investment performance, ranked poorly in terms of productivity growth.

Human Capital—The Education, Training, and Skills of the Work Force

Human Capital
The stock of knowledge and skills possessed by the population.

Human capital refers to the collection of skills and knowledge embodied in the hands and minds of workers. A nation's growth rate is influenced significantly by the rate at which it invests in this human capital via formal education, vocational education, and on-the-job training. In the United States, our stock of human capital has increased over the years. In 1870, 2 percent of our 18-year-olds were high-school graduates; today more than 75 percent are. In 1950, 8 percent of the work force were college graduates; today more than 20 percent have completed

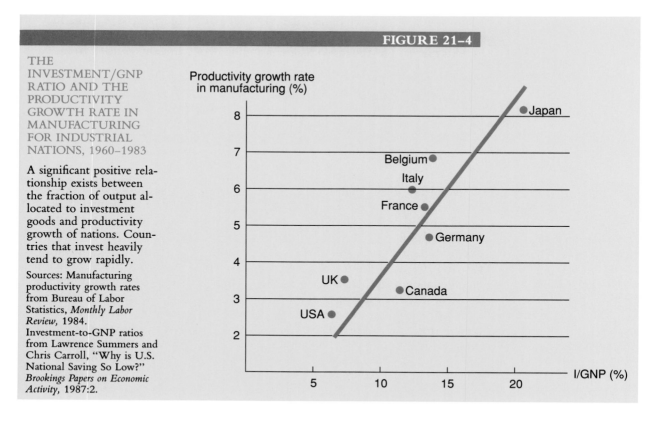

FIGURE 21-4

THE INVESTMENT/GNP RATIO AND THE PRODUCTIVITY GROWTH RATE IN MANUFACTURING FOR INDUSTRIAL NATIONS, 1960–1983

A significant positive relationship exists between the fraction of output allocated to investment goods and productivity growth of nations. Countries that invest heavily tend to grow rapidly.

Sources: Manufacturing productivity growth rates from Bureau of Labor Statistics, *Monthly Labor Review,* 1984. Investment-to-GNP ratios from Lawrence Summers and Chris Carroll, "Why is U.S. National Saving So Low?" *Brookings Papers on Economic Activity,* 1987:2.

college. Denison estimated that one-fifth of the productivity growth in the 1929–1982 period was attributable to improvements in human capital.

The United States has plenty of room for improvement in the area of human capital. The American school system falls woefully short of the Japanese system in the crucial areas of mathematics and science. Scholastic Aptitude Test (SAT) scores of American high-school students declined for 20 consecutive years before hitting bottom in the mid-1980s. Millions of American high-school graduates are ill-equipped to perform work other than menial chores. To assure continuance of our position of economic and political superiority, major changes are needed in this area now and in the future.

Other Factors Influencing Productivity

Productivity is also influenced by a multitude of additional factors that are difficult to quantify. Attitudes and motivation of workers play a role. Improved resource allocation has helped boost productivity over the years, and has come from several sources. A major source was the large transfer of workers out of agriculture into the manufacturing sector. Because productivity levels are higher in manufacturing, this transfer pulled up the overall productivity of the labor force. Other positive factors were the movement over the years since 1930 toward freer international trade, which stimulated efficiency, and the decline in discrimination in hiring practices. Negative factors influencing productivity include work stoppages, expenditures necessitated to combat dishonesty and crime, and government regulations that inhibit production.

THE SLOWDOWN IN PRODUCTIVITY GROWTH SINCE THE LATE 1960s

In recent decades American productivity growth has lagged behind that of many of our competitors. The productivity performance relative to 1960 of the manufacturing sector in a sample of industrial nations is illustrated in Figure 21-5. This figure indicates only the *change* in productivity since 1960, not the *level* of productivity of each nation. By latest count the U.S. economy is still the most productive in the world. We produce about ten percent more output per worker than Germany and roughly 33 percent more than Japan.

Since 1960, Japan's manufacturing sector productivity growth has averaged more than 7.5 percent per year; the corresponding growth rates for France and Germany have been 5.0 percent and 4.4 percent, respectively. Even England's 3.6 percent rate topped the U.S. performance of 2.8 percent per year. Part of this experience may be simply a manifestation of the convergence principle already discussed.

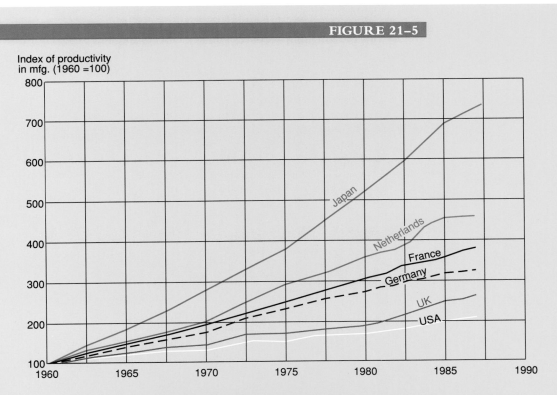

FIGURE 21–5

INTERNATIONAL TRENDS IN LABOR PRODUCTIVITY GROWTH IN MANUFACTURING (index number, 1960 = 100)

Japan has experienced phenomenal productivity growth since 1960, whereas the United States has lagged behind other nations in this regard. Note, however, that this condition may be primarily a manifestation of the convergence principle. Although the *growth rate* of U.S. productivity is quite low, our *level* of productivity (not shown) is the highest in the world.

Source: U.S. Department of Labor, *Monthly Labor Review,* 1989.

Nevertheless, there is reason for concern. The United States has experienced a severe slowdown in productivity growth since the mid-1960s. Although the slowdown has hit all industrial nations, it has hit the United States harder. In certain sectors, such as steel and automobile manufacturing, our productivity *levels* have been surpassed by other countries. To the extent that productivity growth is influenced by government policy measures of all stripes and colors, it seems essential to bear in mind these productivity implications in designing such government policies.

Table 21-5 details the U.S. productivity performance since World War II. Two measures of productivity growth are given: the total business sector (the broader measure) and the nonfarm business sector. The key points may be summarized briefly. The 1947–1965 period was a *golden age* of productivity growth, with productivity growth in the total business sector proceeding at rates that would double living standards in less than 22 years. Productivity growth slowed moderately during 1965–1973, and plunged dramatically in the 1973–1988 period.

Additional detail is provided in the last three rows of Table 21-5. We focus here on the productivity growth experience by decades but have adjusted slightly the period starting-and-ending points to capture cyclical peak-to-peak results in order to minimize the potentially distorting effects of cyclical fluctuations on longer-term productivity growth comparisons.[4] The key observation here is that both measures of productivity indicate that productivity growth plunged in the 1970s and remained depressed in the 1980s.

The post-World War II performance of productivity in the total business sector (the broadest productivity measure) is illustrated in Figure 21-6. The figure reveals that productivity growth slowed dramatically in the 1970s. The performance of the 1980s records only a marginal improvement over the dismal experience of the 1970s. Reactions to this severe slowdown have been highly variable. Some have recoiled with alarm, experiencing visions of America as a second-rate power 50 or 100 years from now. These pessimists fear that for the first time in American history our living standards could begin declining so that future generations will be poorer

TABLE 21-5

TRENDS IN AMERICAN PRODUCTIVITY GROWTH
(average annual growth rates)

Period	Sector	
	All business (%)	**Nonfarm business (%)**
1947–1965	3.29	2.73
1965–1973	2.44	2.17
1973–1988	0.91	0.74
1960:1–1969:3	2.71	2.36
1969:3–1979:4	1.14	1.00
1979:4–1988:4	1.35	1.26
1947–1988	2.25	1.89

Source: U.S. Department of Labor, Bureau of Labor Statistics, 1989.

[4]On the cyclical behavior of productivity growth, see Exhibit 21-2.

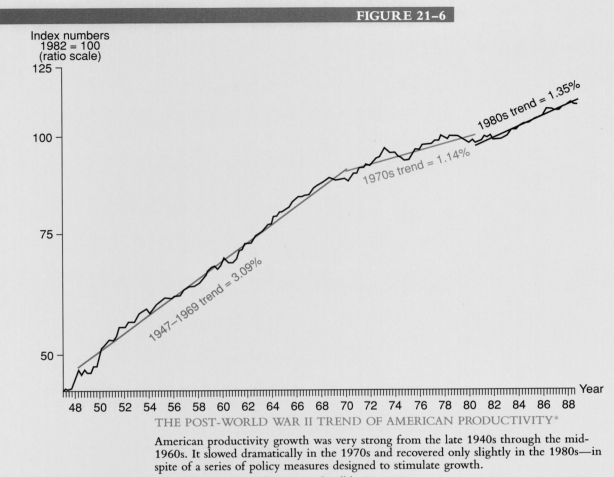

FIGURE 21-6

THE POST-WORLD WAR II TREND OF AMERICAN PRODUCTIVITY*

American productivity growth was very strong from the late 1940s through the mid-1960s. It slowed dramatically in the 1970s and recovered only slightly in the 1980s—in spite of a series of policy measures designed to stimulate growth.

*Series illustrated is productivity in the all-business sector.
Source: U.S. Department of Labor, *Monthly Labor Review*, 1989.

than we are today. Others express little concern about the recent slowdown. When viewed from the vantage point of a longer period of history, they point out, things don't look so bleak. For one thing, the growth of productivity from the late 1940s through the mid-1960s was far above the long-term norm. The post-1965 trend doesn't look quite as bad when compared to the pre-World War II trend. Moreover, many factors ganged up to cause the recent slowdown—several of which are reversible and are already changing with implications for a better productivity performance in the 1990s. These optimists, therefore, see an imminent reversal of the sluggish productivity performance of the past two decades.

Part of the explanation for the differing reactions to the post-1965 slowdown in productivity growth lies in the fact that there is no consensus in the economics profession as to its cause. A host of factors that might reasonably be linked with the slowdown have occurred, but economists disagree upon the weights to be assigned these factors.

Causes of the Productivity Slowdown

As mentioned, there is disagreement about the causes of the American productivity slowdown. Productivity is difficult to measure and students of the subject use different methodologies. Some economists might delete some of the factors on our list and add others. However, most of the following considerations would appear on any list compiled by leading scholars in the field. The factors are *not* intended to be ranked in order of importance.

Changes in the Composition of the Labor Force   Because of the U.S. baby boom of 1946–1963, a large influx of young workers into the labor force occurred during the period from the mid-1960s until the early 1980s. In addition, a steady increase in the labor force participation rate of women took place. Having had less experience on the job, these youthful workers and newly working women exhibited lower productivity *levels* than the work force as a whole. Hence, the gradual increase in the proportion of the labor force comprised of youthful workers and women tended to slow the trend growth of productivity. In addition, the rapid growth in the sheer number of workers coming on stream served to hold down the growth of capital per worker, thus inhibiting productivity growth of labor.

Increasing Government Regulations   During the 1970s, an increase of governmental regulation of American business occurred. Firms were required to invest substantial sums in safety and pollution-abatement equipment. The speed limit on highways was reduced to 55 miles per hour. Resources were spent in order to comply with affirmative action guidelines. While many of these regulations undoubtedly contributed to an improved quality of life, they diverted time and effort from other productive activities and diverted corporation funds from investment in plant and equipment and research and development. The regulations therefore contributed to the productivity slowdown.

A Poor Investment and Saving Performance   As noted earlier, net investment results in growth in the nation's capital stock. Over the long run America's capital stock has grown faster than its labor force, thus resulting in more capital per worker. This capital deepening has been a prime source of rising labor productivity and living standards. Investment spending tends to embody new technology. Obsolete equipment is replaced, raising output per worker. A worker using a jackhammer can remove old pavement faster than one with a pick. A worker using a backhoe can move more dirt than one using a shovel. A secretary using a word processor can type a manuscript more efficiently than one using a typewriter. Included among the many factors that have contributed to the relatively poor investment performance of recent years are a declining saving rate of the American people, an unstable macroeconomic environment, the adverse effect of inflation on the financial condition of firms, and the large structural budget deficits of the 1980s.

Macroeconomic Conditions   The 1965–1982 period was one of considerable instability in the American economy. The 17-year period included two separate bouts with double-digit inflation, the two most severe recessions since the Great Depression of the 1930s, the Vietnam War, and an experiment with wage–price controls. No one can be certain of the precise effect of the macroeconomic environment on long-term economic growth, but it seems likely that it plays a significant role. Recessions impair productivity growth by reducing corporate profits and investment spending. Inflation reduces productivity growth in the long run by shortening the planning horizons of firms and by diverting funds from research and development and projects with long-term payoffs embodying technological change to speculative hedges and investment projects with quick payoff periods. During most of this period (until the tax-law changes of the early 1980s), economists believe that inflation created a negative bias against investment spending via the tax system.

A Slowdown in Research and Development Spending   Technological change has been the most important factor contributing to rising productivity and living standards over the long run. New technology leads to innovation, which raises output produced per worker. Research and development expenditures lead to technical change, innovation, and economic growth. The share of U.S. gross national product allocated to research and development expenditures fell by some 25 percent during 1965–1978, from 2.8 percent to 2.1 percent of GNP. This decline in R and D spending was attributable partly to a cutback in federal support and partly to a decline in spending by business in response to the economic instability of the 1970s. In the 1980s, research and development spending returned to its earlier and larger share of GNP. Given the lags between R and D spending and productivity growth, we were probably still feeling the adverse effects of the 1965–1978 slowdown in the 1980s.

Supply Shocks of the 1970s   In 1974 and again in 1979–1980, the Organization of Petroleum Exporting Countries (OPEC) posted dramatic increases in the price of oil. Energy prices soared. Capital goods are energy-intensive; they use a lot of energy. The sharp increase in the cost of energy rendered a significant portion of the nation's capital stock obsolete. Many older and relatively inefficient capital goods such as generators, furnaces, and gas-guzzling trucks were retired from service. The oil shocks exerted an effect almost like a nuclear exchange, immobilizing a portion of our capital stock. The decline in the capital/labor ratio induced by the energy shocks naturally exerted a contractionary influence on productivity. An increase in energy prices induces firms to use more workers per unit of capital in production processes because labor is less energy-intensive. This signal slows down the capital deepening process and exerts a drag on labor productivity.

Shift to a Service Economy   In recent decades a significant shift in the composition of American output has occurred toward services and away from manufacturing and agriculture. Americans are spending a smaller fraction of their incomes on food and manufactured items. They are spending an increasing portion on services— education, medical care, legal services, entertainment, financial advice, beauty salon services, and restaurant meals. In general, productivity levels in services have significantly lagged behind those in manufacturing and agriculture. Services, on average, tend to be labor-intensive; they cannot be put on an assembly line and standardized. For this reason, productivity in services is inherently lower than that of manufacturing. Some economists argue that the United States and other industrial economies are becoming increasingly service oriented and that productivity growth must therefore inevitably slow down.[5]

---

[5]However, development of the service sector may raise productivity in manufacturing and agriculture. Computer consultants may lead to more efficient inventory management of firms. Accounting firms may free up time for taxpaying firms and individuals, leading to productive effort. If the growth of the service sector reflects primarily a decision by agricultural and manufacturing firms to hire services formally accomplished internally, it is not clear that the rise of the service sector inevitably leads to a decline in the nation's overall productivity.

The Outlook for Productivity Growth in the 1990s

To the extent that the preceding factors predominantly account for the slowdown in productivity growth in the 1970s and 1980s, there is reason to be optimistic about productivity growth assuming a more robust path in the 1990s. Most of the negative factors are reversible and in fact have been changing since the early 1980s in a manner conducive to an improved productivity performance. For example, the baby boomers that flooded into the labor force after the mid-1960s are entering middle age. The average woman in today's labor force has more longevity and higher productivity than her counterpart of 20 years ago. Fewer youths are entering the labor force. All these demographic considerations work in a direction conducive to raising the level of productivity.

EXHIBIT 21-2

THE CYCLICAL PATTERN OF PRODUCTIVITY

If we remove the growth trend from the labor productivity data, we find that productivity exhibits a regular and largely predictable pattern over the course of the business cycle. Productivity rises during the expansion phase of the business cycle and declines during recessions.

In looking at productivity growth over time intervals such as a five- or ten-year period, it is essential to be aware of the cyclical characteristics of productivity. Otherwise one is likely to miscalculate the *trend growth* of productivity, which is the item of crucial importance. Suppose one is interested in the rate of growth of productivity in the decade of the 1980s. One can simply look at the productivity *level* at the beginning and end of the decade and compute its annual *growth rate.* But this procedure yields an incorrect estimate of the trend growth of productivity. January 1980 happened to be a business cycle peak; December 1989 was not. By mixing cyclical effects with the growth trend, one *underestimates* the trend growth of productivity in the 1980s. To accurately calculate trend productivity growth, it is essential to begin and end the sample period at comparable points of the business cycle.

Labor productivity typically rises strongly in the early phases of the business cycle expansion and increases more slowly in the second half of the expansion. In the early phases of business downturns (recessions), productivity growth becomes negative as the *level* of productivity declines. In the second half of the downturn, the productivity level tends to flatten before expanding rapidly again when recovery ensues.

In recessions, as declining aggregate demand induces firms to reduce output, firms are reluctant initially to reduce employment in proportion to the contraction in output. Uncertain of the eventual depth and duration of the downturn and mindful of the costs of rehiring and retraining workers when prosperity returns, firms react cautiously. Since firms reduce employment by a relatively lesser amount than they reduce output, labor productivity (output per worker hour) declines as a matter of arithmetic. As the recession continues and deepens, firms are forced by financial pressures to lay off more workers. In this latter phase of the downturn, employment declines roughly in step with output. This yields a flat pattern for productivity—approximately zero productivity growth.

As the recession gives way to economic recovery, firms again proceed with caution. As output starts to pick up, firms are conservative about taking on new workers. Instead, existing employees are utilized more fully. Output is boosted much faster than employment, and productivity increases at a rapid pace. As the recovery continues and economic activity becomes more robust, firms begin adding aggressively to their payrolls. This slows the growth of productivity after the first year or two of recovery. Nevertheless, productivity still expands nicely during the middle portion of recovery. In the latter stages of the expansion phase of the cycle, productivity growth tapers off. Firms may hire workers of lower quality as the pool of unemployed workers approaches depletion. In addition, utilization rates of the economy's productive capacity may rise above optimal levels, reducing efficiency of workers.

A host of other factors point in the same direction. Government regulations were eased during the Reagan Administrations of the 1980s and there is no strong sentiment to move back toward a heavily regulated economy. The macroeconomic climate improved after the 1981–1982 recession. Research and development spending regained its 1965 share of GNP—rebounding sharply from its lows of the 1970s—though much of the resurgence was in *military* R and D expenditures. Civilian R and D expenditures are more beneficial to productivity growth. Oil prices fell sharply after the mid-1980s and remained at less than 50 percent of their peak levels in real terms throughout the remainder of the decade. The only factors failing to shift in a direction conducive to improved productivity growth are the investment- and saving-to-GNP ratios and the share of services in the economy.

POLICIES TO BOOST ECONOMIC GROWTH

The unsatisfactory performance of American productivity growth during the past quarter century naturally has stimulated interest in measures that might boost the rate of growth of American living standards. Indeed, to a significant extent, the *Reagan Revolution* of the 1980s involved this issue. As is commonly the case, economists disagree about the most fruitful measures for stimulating productivity and long-term economic growth.

A widely accepted viewpoint held by economists of all persuasions is that, other things equal, a larger capital stock implies more output per worker and higher living standards. If we currently produce more investment goods and fewer consumption and government goods, the nation's capital stock will grow more rapidly and so will productivity and living standards. In other words, a movement from A to B along America's production possibilities curve in Figure 21-7 increases the speed with which the curve shifts outward over time.

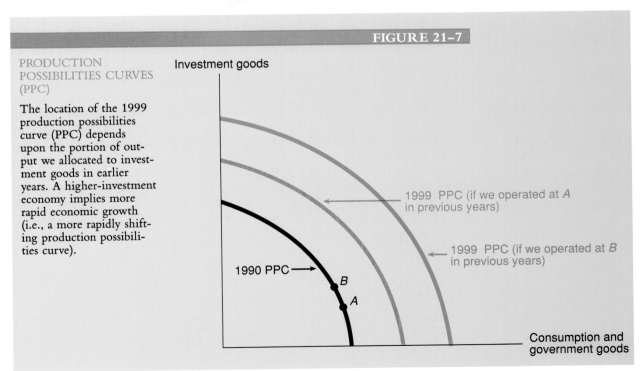

FIGURE 21–7

PRODUCTION POSSIBILITIES CURVES (PPC)

The location of the 1999 production possibilities curve (PPC) depends upon the portion of output we allocated to investment goods in earlier years. A higher-investment economy implies more rapid economic growth (i.e., a more rapidly shifting production possibilities curve).

Investment goods

1999 PPC (if we operated at A in previous years)

1999 PPC (if we operated at B in previous years)

1990 PPC →

B

A

Consumption and government goods

Economists disagree about the appropriate mechanisms for bringing about the movement from *A* to *B* in Figure 21-7, as well as about other measures for enhancing economic growth.

Keynesian Views

Keynesians advocate the active use of both monetary and fiscal policies to keep the economy strong, with actual GNP hovering close to potential GNP—to keep the unemployment rate close to the natural rate. During recessions, investment declines by a relatively larger amount than do other components of output. As a result, we experience a significant slowdown in the growth of the nation's capital stock. After the recession ends, the capital stock per worker is lower than would have been the case in the event the recession had been avoided. Furthermore, research and development expenditures tend to be scaled back during severe economic downturns. Keynesians support the aggressive use of both monetary and fiscal policies to minimize the frequency, duration, and depth of economic downturns.

Keynesians are quite critical of the *mix* of monetary and fiscal policies in the 1980s. In principle, a given level of aggregate demand and output can be obtained with various mixes of monetary and fiscal stimuli. A stimulative monetary policy (rapid money supply growth) could be combined with restrictive fiscal policy (a budget surplus or high-employment surplus) to produce a desired level of output. The same current output could be obtained via a tighter monetary policy combined with a more stimulative fiscal policy.

The mix of monetary and fiscal policies is likely to influence the *composition* of current output—the share of output consisting of investment goods versus consumption and government goods. With the defense buildup and the tax cuts of the early 1980s, the Reagan Administration implemented a stimulative fiscal policy (large budget deficits) and the Federal Reserve responded with tight money. Keynesians argue that this tight money/stimulative fiscal policy mix is precisely the *opposite* of the correct prescription if the objective of policy is to boost the share of output allocated to investment goods.

Keynesian economists James Tobin of Yale University (top) and Robert Solow of the Massachusetts Institute of Technology, both Nobel Laureates in economics, were critical of the mix of policies implemented in the 1980s.

The large budget deficits and the restrictive monetary policies of the early 1980s pushed interest rates (and real interest rates) to very high levels. An increase in interest rates moves us upward and leftward along our investment demand schedule of Chapter 10 (Figure 10-6), reducing investment spending. Although other measures to stimulate investment spending were implemented under the Reagan economic program, Keynesians regard the perverse mix of monetary and fiscal policies as the major factor that prevented the desired increase in the share of output going to investment (the move from *A* to *B* in Figure 21-7).

Some Keynesians favor a national sales tax or some other form of consumption tax as a means of discouraging consumption spending and reducing the federal budget deficit. To the extent that the resulting increase in the nation's aggregate saving rate (private plus government) resulted in lower interest rates and greater investment spending, the enactment of a consumption tax would tend to promote the desired reallocation of current output from consumer goods to capital goods.

The Supply-Side Position

Supply-siders emphasize the disincentive effects of high tax rates. In this view, taxes were too high in America prior to the 1980s. The high tax rates stifled the incentive to save, invest, and work. Progressive income taxes, higher social security taxes, and inflation combined to boost millions of middle-income Americans into high tax brackets. When one includes federal income taxes, payroll taxes, and state income taxes, the typical American worker earning $28,000 annually was yielding 30–40 cents of each additional dollar of income to the government by 1980. Higher-bracket individuals were yielding even more. Such rates, in the view of supply-siders, create serious adverse supply-side effects.

In the inflationary environment of the 1970s, taxes on capital gains and interest income depressed the effective rate of return on investment. Inflation and the existing income-tax code combined to impair the financial condition of many firms and to create a bias against investment in plant and equipment. Furthermore, existing tax loopholes encouraged socially wasteful diversion of funds into luxury condominiums, hobby farms, and purebred horses—diverting these funds from more socially useful investment.

The centerpiece of supply-side economics was the substantial reduction in income-tax rates implemented under the Economic Recovery Tax Act of 1981. This law, by reducing the tax due on each extra dollar of income earned, stimulated the incentive to earn income—hence to work and invest.

Supply-siders advocated removing the bias against saving and investment by reforming capital gains taxes and depreciation allowances, by eliminating the tax deductibility of consumer interest expense, and by indexing the income tax to prevent inflation from pushing taxpayers into higher brackets. Except for the capital gains tax proposal, all these proposals were implemented under the new tax law. However, the Tax Reform Act of 1986 took back some of the investment incentives implemented in the Economic Recovery Tax Act of 1981. In addition to these fiscal measures, supply-siders successfully pushed for a streamlining of environmental restrictions and an easing of other forms of government regulation thought to inhibit productivity.

But what was the supply-siders' response to the charge made by contemporary critics that the large income-tax cut would increase the federal budget deficit and interest rates and therefore interfere with the goal of boosting investment? Some supply-siders believed that the tax cut would force government to reduce expenditures, thereby averting significantly larger deficits. Most were aware that the deficit would increase but felt that the beneficial effects of lower tax rates would outweigh any detrimental effects of larger deficits. A few extreme supply-siders took refuge in the Laffer Curve proposition that the deficit would not increase because the reduction in income-tax rates would unleash a substantial increase in effort, output, and taxable income. This proposition, held by few economists, was rejected by events of the 1980s—the emergence of the huge budget deficits.

Some say that supply-side economics in general has been discredited by the events of the 1980s. Others argue that it was not really given a chance—that tax rates were not significantly reduced on balance or that tight Federal Reserve policy counteracted the beneficial effects of the supply-side measures. At any rate, the fact remains that American productivity growth improved only slightly in the 1980s over its dismal performance in the 1970s. Productivity growth remains a major challenge for policymakers in the early 1990s.

SUMMARY

1. The two primary measures of economic growth are the rates of increase in real output (real GNP) and per-capita real output. Real output of a nation is an indicator of the economic power of the nation; per-capita output indicates the well-being or standard of living of the people.

2. Economic growth involves increases in the economy's productive capacity over time. Economic growth implies that the nation's production possibilities curve and its aggregate supply curve are shifting outward over time.

3. The standard of living is measured by output per capita. Labor productivity refers to output per hour of work. If the length of the average workweek and the fraction of the population working both remain constant over time, the growth rates of productivity and living standards are identical. In recent decades, output per capita (the average standard of living) has grown somewhat faster than productivity because the fraction of the population working has trended upward. In the long run, the overwhelming source of rising living standards is growth in productivity.

4. The enormous chasm between living standards of affluent nations such as the United States and Japan and impoverished countries such as Ethiopia and Nigeria can be explained by the miracle of compound interest over a period of a century or two. If two countries start with identical living standards and one experiences two-percent annual growth in per-capita output for 150 years and the other stagnates (zero growth), the country experiencing growth achieves a standard of living some 20 times as high as the stagnant country.

5. Economic growth is a comparatively recent phenomenon, encompassing only the last two or three centuries. Prior to the Industrial Revolution, living standards were relatively unchanged for thousands of years.

6. Living standards of industrial nations have a tendency to converge over time. That is, industrial nations with low levels of per-capita output and income tend to grow faster than those with high levels. This phenomenon is chiefly due to the international diffusion of technological change. Less-affluent industrialized nations adopt the sophisticated technologies developed by the most advanced of the industrial nations. In general, however, less developed nations find it quite difficult to benefit from this international diffusion of technology. The immense gulf between living standards in LDCs and industrial nations has been *widening* over time.

7. Growth of total output can be decomposed into a portion attributable to growth of labor inputs and a portion due to growth of productivity of labor. Over a period encompassing most of this century, roughly one-third of the increase in output has been attributable to increases in labor inputs. About two-thirds of the growth is accounted for by rising labor productivity. The three most critical factors accounting for increases in labor productivity have been technological advances, increases in the quantity of capital goods, and improved education and skills embodied in the work force.

8. The period from the end of World War II until the mid-1960s was one of rapid growth in productivity and living standards. The industrialized nations experienced a slowdown in productivity growth after the mid-1960s, and the U.S. slowdown was especially severe. Some of the factors contributing to this productivity slowdown have been a rather anemic saving and investment pattern, government regulations that diverted resources from investment in new plant and equipment, unstable macroeconomic conditions, a slowdown in research and development efforts, the supply shocks of the 1970s, and changes in the composition of the labor force. Moreover, the trend toward a service economy has worked to slow productivity growth because productivity in the service sector tends to be lower than that in manufacturing and agriculture.

9. With the exception of the increasing role of services, the forces that have slowed American productivity growth appear to be potentially reversible. In fact, several of the forces that reduced productivity growth during 1965–1982 are now working to boost productivity growth. These include a more stable macroeconomic environment, some improvement in research and development spending, a significant decline in real oil and energy prices, a decrease in government regulations, and favorable changes in the composition of the labor force. The continuing weakness in private saving and investment patterns together with the large federal budget deficits remain as negative forces working to inhibit productivity growth.

10. Policies designed to stimulate productivity growth must recognize the fundamental importance of technological change, capital deepening, and human capital in the growth process. In this vein, measures that encourage research and development spending, stimulate saving and investment, and encourage investment in education and training (human capital) are appropriate.

KEY TERMS

economic growth   convergence principle
per-capita real GNP   invention
standard of living   innovation
productivity growth   capital deepening
industrialization   human capital

STUDY QUESTIONS AND PROBLEMS

1. In what sense is the growth rate of a nation's real GNP a good measure of the nation's economic progress? Per-capita real GNP?
2. Define the term *productivity growth.* Define the term *standard-of-living growth.* Is it possible for growth in productivity to exceed growth in living standards? For growth in living standards to exceed growth in productivity? Explain.
3. Explain why the process of industrialization results in a major increase in living standards.
4. Explain the meaning of the convergence principle in living standards. What accounts for its existence? If the principle is valid, what does it imply about the relative growth rates to be experienced by England and the United States in the next decade?
5. Explain carefully why the current *mix* of monetary and fiscal policies may have important implications for the long-term growth in living standards.
6. Suppose, after graduation, that your income rises in line with the growth in living standards during the ensuing 30 years. How much more affluent will you be after 30 years if living standards grow at three percent annually than if they remain constant? *Hint:* Using the calculator's y^x key, y is 1.03 and x is 30.
7. What are the three chief factors accounting for growth in labor productivity? Explain in your own words why each of these factors lifts productivity and living standards.
8. Do you feel that we should be concerned about the American productivity slowdown of the past 25 years? Why?
9. Assume you are chairperson of the President's Council of Economic Advisors and the president charges you with developing a plan to significantly boost America's productivity growth. What would be the key ingredients of your plan? Explain and defend.
10. Explain why productivity of labor fluctuates over the course of the business cycle.

ANSWER TO YOUR TURN

After 50 years, Modernians would be 2.10 times as affluent as Laggardians. After 100 years, Modernians would be 4.43 times richer. After 200 years they would be 19.64 times richer than Laggardians.

SELECTED REFERENCES

Baumol, William J., "Productivity Growth, Convergence, and Welfare," *American Economic Review,* December 1986, pp. 1072–1085. This article outlines the basis for the convergence hypothesis and presents evidence in support of the hypothesis. For an exchange of views on this issue, see the December 1988 issue of the *American Economic Review.*

Dension, Edward F., *Trends in American Economic Growth, 1929–82* (Washington, DC: The Brookings Institution, 1985). This quantitative study details the determinants of economic growth and analyzes the slowdown since 1973.

Kendrick, John (ed.), *International Comparisons of Productivity and Causes of the Slowdown* (Cambridge, MA: Ballinger Publishing Company, 1984). Several economists analyze causes of productivity growth and its slowdown in the United States and in other nations.

Maddison, Angus, *Phases of Capitalist Development* (Oxford, England: Oxford University Press, 1982). This work contains a wealth of information on the history of growth in living standards over many countries.

"Symposium on the Slowdown in Productivity Growth," *The Journal of Economic Perspectives,* Fall 1988, pp. 3–97. This is an excellent and timely collection of articles by such outstanding economists as Stanley Fischer, Zvi Griliches, Dale Jorgenson, Mancur Olson, and Michael Boskin.

PART VI

CONSUMER
AND
BUSINESS
BEHAVIOR

CHAPTER 22

DEMAND AND UTILITY

Why, asked Adam Smith, is the price of water low, the price of diamonds high? Should not water, which is necessary for life, be valued more highly than diamonds, which we could easily survive without? This **paradox of value** can be resolved with marginal utility theory, *the focus of this chapter.*

We would not devote almost a chapter to marginal utility theory if that were its sole contribution. It is not. The theory provides a deeper understanding of demand, including added insight into the law of demand. It presents a method for allocating income so as to maximize a consumer's level of satisfaction. It explains why a community concerned about crime may nonetheless refuse to hire additional police.

Chapter 22 also shows how to derive a market demand curve from the demand curves of individual consumers, how to value the benefits to consumers of being able to purchase a good, and how research using rats supports demand theory.

Nothing is more useful than water: but it will purchase scarce any thing; scarce any thing can be had in exchange for it. A diamond, on the contrary, has scarce any value in use; but a very great quantity of other goods may frequently be had in exchange for it.[1]

---

[1]Adam Smith, *The Wealth of Nations* (New York: Random House, 1937), p. 28. (Originally published in 1776.)

488

MARGINAL UTILITY THEORY

Measuring Utility

The theory of marginal utility rests upon certain assumptions. The first is that consumers maximize their well-being, what economists call **utility.** A second and less defensible assumption is that utility can be measured. Not only must a person be able to indicate which of two goods is preferred, but the intensity of preference must also be quantifiable. It is not enough that a person prefers Pepsi to Coke, but that person must also indicate by how much—for example, a glass of Pepsi yields ten units of utility, a glass of Coke eight.

The founders of marginal utility theory believed that a utility-measuring device would be developed one day. Perhaps it will. Imagine being plugged into a machine that senses the pleasures you experience. A needle swings farther to the right the greater the pleasure. Mom's homemade apple pie kicks the needle well to the right of center; dorm food barely budges the needle. Such a device could open up a whole new world of advertising. Pepsi might adopt the slogan "more utility per glass." But, while such developments may lie ahead, utility meters remain, at present, only a dream.

If the assumption that utility can be measured is currently unrealistic, then why not abandon marginal utility theory? Quite simply because marginal utility provides some important insights. After sketching this theory, we consider some of its applications.

Two Measures of Utility—Total and Marginal

Total Utility
The total amount of satisfaction received from all the units consumed of a good.

Marginal Utility
The extra satisfaction (change in total utility) from consuming one more unit of a good.

Consumption of a good generates utility. If more than one unit is consumed, it is important to distinguish between total utility and marginal utility. **Total utility** measures the cumulative satisfaction received from *all* units of a good that are consumed. It is obtained by summing the utilities generated by each unit of the good. That is, you add the utility of the first unit consumed, the utility of the second unit, and so on. In contrast, **marginal utility** of a good simply measures the satisfaction provided by the *last* unit consumed.

Which concept is more appropriate? That depends on the question being asked. If the question is whether a pizza or a dish of ice cream is more satisfying, the issue revolves around which provides more *total* utility. If you choose ice cream, you may then face the decision of whether you want two scoops or three. Now the emphasis is on *marginal* utility. How much extra utility would a third scoop of ice cream provide?

Marginal utility and total utility schedules are related, as the following example illustrates. Suppose you spend an afternoon at the student union. While there you consider drinking some Coke. Columns (a) and (b) of Table 22-1 (page 490) present a hypothetical total utility schedule that measures the satisfaction you derive from

(a) Quantity	(b) Total utility	(c) Marginal utility
0	0	
1	20	20
2	32	12
3	37	5
4	40	3

Table 22-1

TOTAL AND MARGINAL UTILITY OF COKES

Although drinking additional Cokes increases total utility, the marginal utility of successive Cokes diminishes.

various quantities of Coke. A single Coke provides 20 units of utility, two Cokes provide 32 units, and so on. From the total utility schedule, you can compute the marginal utility of any given Coke. For example, the marginal utility of the third Coke is 5—drinking three Cokes rather than two increases total utility by 5 units (from 32 to 37). The marginal utility numbers are given in column (c) of Table 22-1 and presented graphically in Figure 22-1. Observe that these numbers become smaller as the quantity of Cokes consumed increases. That first Coke tastes great. But additional Cokes are less satisfying. As you drink more and more, your thirst subsides and you start to fill up. You may even tire of the taste. Thus, while *total* utility increases with consumption, *marginal* utility declines.

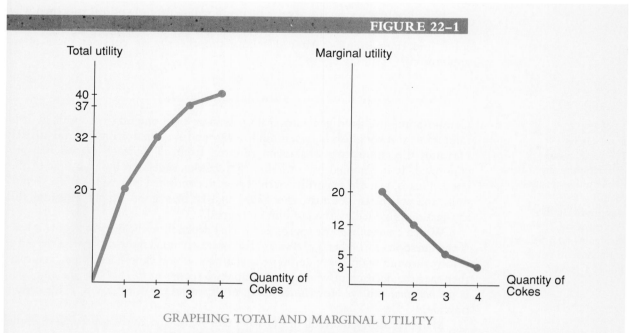

FIGURE 22-1

GRAPHING TOTAL AND MARGINAL UTILITY

These figures (drawn from Table 22-1) demonstrate that the marginal utility of successive Cokes diminishes.

Law of Diminishing Marginal Utility
The proposition that marginal utility of a good eventually declines as consumption of the good increases.

Declining marginal utility is not something unique to Coke; it is so common that economists have developed a name for it: **the law of diminishing marginal utility**. Formally, the law of diminishing marginal utility can be stated as follows: Beyond some point, the more units of a good consumed the less utility an additional unit provides.[2] This law or hypothesis is the centerpiece of marginal utility theory.

Although the numbers in Table 22-1 are all positive, it is possible that marginal utility could eventually become zero—further consumption would not alter total utility. For example, if the student union provides unlimited free Coke refills on "student appreciation day," there is still a limit to how many glasses you want to drink. You can be expected to stop at the point at which further consumption provides no further utility. The fact that some students walk away from cups still half full indicates they have reached the point where marginal utility is zero.

Negative marginal utilities may also occur—when consumption is pushed too far. Take dinner at grandma's. She does something special to cauliflower that only she can do. As you say to yourself, "If I eat another bite of this I'll get sick," Grandma empties the bowl on your plate. "I made this cauliflower just for you," she says; so you choke it down despite its negative marginal utility.

Consumer Equilibrium

Marginal utility theory can also be used to solve allocation problems. Because of scarcity you must choose among competing bundles of goods, but which bundle should you choose? That is, how should you spend your income?

To keep matters simple, we initially consider two goods and assume the law of diminishing marginal utility holds for each. Later we extend the analysis to include additional goods. The model assumes that the consumer has a fixed income or budget to spend on these goods. Furthermore, this income is not large enough to satisfy all wants.[3] The consumer also faces fixed prices. Under these conditions, how should the income be spent in order to maximize utility? *Total utility is maximized when the marginal utility per dollar of each good is equal and all income is spent.* When these requirements are satisfied, the consumer is said to be in *equilibrium.*

Consumer Equilibrium
A situation in which the consumer is obtaining the maximum total utility consistent with a given income (budget); a consumer is in equilibrium when marginal utility per dollar is the same for each good and all income is spent.

To illustrate **consumer equilibrium**, consider the following example. You arrive at the student union with $4 in your pocket, planning to spend this money on drink and song. Cokes are $1.00 each and the jukebox is $.50 per selection. Table 22-2 (page 492) presents utility schedules for Cokes and records—total utility, marginal utility, and marginal utility per dollar—which is simply the ratio of the marginal utility of a good to the price of the good. From these schedules it is clear that both goods satisfy the law of diminishing marginal utility. Assuming these utility schedules reflect your preferences, how should you spend your money?

The first purchase should be a Coke. It provides more utility per dollar, more bang per buck, than does a record. After that, head for the jukebox (as Table 22-3, page 492, demonstrates). The marginal utility per dollar of the first record (18)

---

[2]The law of diminishing marginal utility does not rule out the possibility that marginal utility might initially increase before starting its decline, but only the declining segment of the marginal utility schedule is relevant. As long as marginal utility is increasing, it is always worthwhile to consume the next unit of the good. That is, consumption will continue until after marginal utility has started to decline.

[3]Without this budget constraint, the solution to our problem would be trivial: consume as much as you want—that is, consume each good up to the point where marginal utility is zero.

Table 22-2

UTILITY SCHEDULES FOR COKES AND RECORDS

COKES

Quantity	Total utility (TU)	Marginal utility (MU)	MU/P*
1	20	20	20
2	32	12	12
3	37	5	5
4	40	3	3

RECORDS

Quantity	Total utility (TU)	Marginal utility (MU)	MU/P**
1	9	9	18
2	17	8	16
3	24	7	14
4	30	6	12
5	35	5	10
6	39	4	8

*The price per Coke is assumed to be $1.00.
**The price per record is assumed to be $.50.

Table 22-3

ALLOCATION OF INCOME BETWEEN COKES AND RECORDS

Sequence of purchases	Reason for purchase	
First purchase: Coke	MU/P of first Coke MU/P of first record	(20) > (18)
Second purchase: Record	MU/P of first record MU/P of second Coke	(18) > (12)
Third purchase: Record	MU/P of second record MU/P of second Coke	(16) > (12)
Fourth purchase: Record	MU/P of third record MU/P of second Coke	(14) > (12)
Fifth purchase: Either*	MU/P of fourth record MU/P of second Coke	(12) = (12)

Based on information in Table 22-2, Table 22-3 indicates how you should spend your income in order to maximize total utility. Consumer equilibrium is reached with the purchase of two Cokes and the playing of four records.

*If you buy a Coke here, your sixth and final purchase will be a record. If you play a record, your final purchase will be a Coke.

exceeds the marginal utility per dollar of the second Coke (12). Note that the emphasis is on marginal utility *per dollar*. To be sure, the second Coke has a higher marginal utility than the first record. But, while the Coke costs twice as much, it fails to deliver twice the satisfaction. It is not presently a *good buy*. In making purchases, consumers consider price as well as utility. We recognize this by dividing marginal utility of a good by its price to obtain marginal utility per dollar.

After playing the first record, you play a second and a third—marginal utility per dollar is higher for these records than for the second Coke. At this point you have $1.50 left. How should you spend it? Marginal utility per dollar of the second Coke is identical to that of the fourth record, so you are indifferent to which good you buy. In fact, you have just enough money to buy both. Which is purchased first does not matter.

This situation corresponds to consumer equilibrium. You have spent your entire budget, and the marginal utility per dollar of the last Coke is identical to the marginal utility per dollar of the last record. To further convince yourself that utility is maximized by purchasing two Cokes and playing four records, consider any other combination of purchases costing $4 or less. All have lower total utility.

For example, if you were to buy three Cokes, you could afford to play only two records. Although the extra Coke would provide 5 more units of utility, foregoing the third and fourth records would reduce total utility by a greater amount—by 13 units (7 + 6). Drinking three Cokes would therefore reduce total utility by 8 units (13 − 5). Nor would you maximize utility if you were to drink only one Coke. Although you could now afford to play records five and six, the extra utility derived from hearing them (9 units) is less than the utility you would lose by foregoing the second Coke (12 units).

Given the utility schedules of Table 22-2, total utility is maximized only with two Cokes and four records, the combination for which the marginal utility of the last dollar spent on each is equal.[4] This condition can be restated algebraically as

$$\frac{MU_{Coke}}{P_{Coke}} = \frac{MU_{record}}{P_{record}}$$

where P denotes price.

What if we consider more than two goods? In that case our condition for consumer equilibrium generalizes. When a consumer purchases n goods, the following equality must hold:

$$\frac{MU_1}{P_1} = \frac{MU_2}{P_2} = \cdots = \frac{MU_n}{P_n}$$

From Marginal Utility to Demand

Demand curves can be derived directly from a consumer's marginal utility schedules. To illustrate, we return to the student union and consider the effects of a

---

[4]The astute reader may observe that in some cases strict equality of ratios may not be possible. For instance, what if you had decided to spend one more dollar at the student union? Regardless of whether you purchase an extra Coke or play two more records, the marginal utility of the last dollar spent on Coke will not equal the marginal utility of the last dollar spent on records. What should you do? In this case play two more records, since marginal utility of those two records (9) exceeds marginal utility of another Coke (5). More generally, total utility is maximized if (1) buying one more unit of a good (e.g., Coke) does not increase total utility, (2) buying one less unit of the good does not increase total utility, and (3) the entire income is spent. Given $5, these three requirements are satisfied with the purchase of 2 Cokes and 6 records.

price change. Suppose the price of Coke is reduced to $.50. At this price buying two Cokes and playing four records no longer maximizes your total utility. The marginal utility per dollar of the second Coke does not equal the marginal utility per dollar of the fourth record. Nor is the budget being fully spent. To achieve consumer equilibrium, you must buy three Cokes and play five records. When you do this, your budget is fully spent, and the marginal utility per dollar is the same for the last Coke and the last record.[5] Total utility is therefore maximized.

We have just plotted two points on your demand curve. At a price of $1.00 you demand two Cokes; at a price of $.50 you demand three Cokes. In a similar fashion, by considering other prices we could finish tracing your demand curve (see Figure 22-2).

The link between marginal utility and demand can also be thought of in less technical terms. Because the marginal utility of the first Coke is high, you are prepared to buy it even at a relatively high price. But successive Cokes provide less and less additional utility. Therefore, you are willing to buy them only at lower prices. The lower the marginal utility of an additional Coke, the less you are willing to pay for it. Because of diminishing marginal utility, consumers are willing to buy more of a good only if its price is reduced—demand curves are downward sloping.

Irrational Behavior

Consumers are not always rational; sometimes they react impulsively, failing to consider the consequences of their actions. For example, they may buy certain eye-appealing food while shopping because they are tired or hungry, even though it is not a good buy. Is this sufficient reason to reject marginal utility theory? No, the theory can still be useful despite an occasional irrational act.

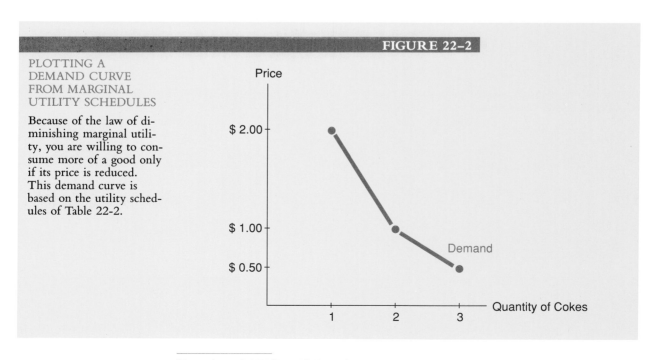

FIGURE 22–2

PLOTTING A DEMAND CURVE FROM MARGINAL UTILITY SCHEDULES

Because of the law of diminishing marginal utility, you are willing to consume more of a good only if its price is reduced. This demand curve is based on the utility schedules of Table 22-2.

[5]For each good, MU/P = 5/.50 = 10.

EXHIBIT 22-1[6]

CONSUMER SURPLUS

Consumer Surplus
The difference between the maximum amount a consumer is willing to pay for a given quantity of a good and the amount actually paid.

Another implication of diminishing marginal utility is that the total benefit a consumer derives from consuming a good generally exceeds the amount the consumer spends on that good. That is, the consumer reaps a surplus or net benefit from the purchase of the good. Formally, this added value is known as **consumer surplus**

To illustrate, assume the price of a Coke is $.50. If you are willing to pay a maximum of $2.00 for the first Coke, up to $1.00 for the second, and up to $.50 for the third, the total value to you of three Cokes is $3.50 ($2.00 + $1.00 + $.50). Yet, at a price of $.50, the cost of three Cokes is only $1.50. You enjoy a consumer surplus of $2.00 ($3.50 − $1.50).

Consumer surplus can also be depicted diagramatically, as in the following figure:

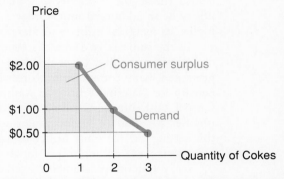

Because the demand curve indicates a consumer's willingness to pay, consumer surplus is represented by the shaded area beneath the demand curve and above the market price. At a price of $.50, consumer surplus is $2.00, consisting of $1.50 from the first Coke and $.50 from the second.

Under certain circumstances consumer surplus can be used to evaluate various projects or goods. For example, suppose the university, as a show of appreciation, wants to either give a free concert or provide five-cent Cokes during finals week. Which gesture would have a greater value to students? Consumer surplus provides one possible framework for answering this question. Suppose each student's consumer surplus can be estimated for both the free concert and the five-cent Cokes. By adding the consumer surplus of each student, we can estimate the aggregate consumer surplus of the free concert and the five-cent Cokes. Whichever option has the higher consumer surplus can be taken to be the one the students value more highly.

First, the model indicates the optimal choice, providing a standard with which to judge the actual choice. Second, because most people act rationally most of the time, the model predicts which combination of goods a consumer will actually purchase. Finally, at the aggregate level the model predicts consumption patterns of the general population. Although a few people may act irrationally at any point in time, their actions are outweighed by the majority of people who are rational. For example, even when a few people violate the law of demand, as long as most people behave rationally the aggregate demand curve for a good slopes downward.

[6]This exhibit can be omitted without loss of continuity to the chapter.

Resolving the Paradox of Value

Early economists puzzled over the relationship between price and value. Why should the price of diamonds exceed the price of water? Isn't water more valuable? Shouldn't it therefore command a higher price? Equipped with an understanding of marginal utility theory, we can explain why diamonds have a higher price than water and why early economists were confused about the matter. (You have an opportunity to understand something that Adam Smith, one of the greatest economists of all time, did not fully comprehend!)

The key to the puzzle is scarcity and how it affects marginal utility. Water is cheap because it is so abundant. Another gallon provides little additional utility. Therefore, consumers are willing to pay very little for the extra water. In contrast to water, the supply of diamonds is extremely limited. Because the value or utility of an additional diamond is high, consumers are prepared to pay a high price for it. Of course, the degree of scarcity may change over time and, as it does, so will marginal utility of an additional unit. Other things equal, the scarcer a good becomes, the higher its marginal utility and therefore its market price.

In the summer of 1986, the southeastern United States experienced its worst drought in a century. Lakes dried up; crops withered and died. The lack of water prompted many communities to restrict water use. In Brentwood, Tennessee, the penalty for watering a lawn or washing a car was having your water shut off. In Chapel Hill, North Carolina, "wasting water" could land you in jail. Atlanta imposed a ban on all outdoor water use, and other communities rationed water. In this setting the marginal utility of additional water soared, and so did the price consumers were willing to pay for it.

Early economists stumbled over the concept of value because they failed to distinguish marginal utility from total utility. Yes, water is essential to life. Yes, it has a high total value or total utility. But, contrary to their thinking, this does not imply that water should have a high market value. *Price depends on marginal utility, not on total utility.* Because water is so plentiful it has a low marginal utility, and consequently a low price, even though its total utility is high. Although the solution to the puzzle may appear obvious today, early economists can hardly be faulted for not thinking in terms of marginal utility. Marginal utility theory was not developed until the nineteenth century (see Exhibit 22-2).

Other Applications of Marginal Utility Theory

Marginal utility theory helped reformulate economic thinking. Its centerpiece, marginal analysis, has been extended to other areas of economics, including production and labor markets. Although we cover these topics later, before leaving marginal utility theory we consider a few of its other applications.

Marginal utility theory can explain what might appear to be the irrational voting behavior of a community. Suppose a community is very concerned about crime. Does this imply that it will want to expand its police department? Are voters likely to pass a proposal to hire additional police officers? Not necessarily. Although the total utility of police protection may be high, the marginal utility of a little more protection may be low. Citizens may feel that the money to hire additional police could be better spent filling pot holes or providing new parks. Or they may prefer lower taxes, accepting less police protection in the process. There is nothing inconsistent about thinking that police protection is the most important service the government can provide and yet voting not to spend more on this service. When

EXHIBIT 22–2

THE FOUNDERS OF MARGINAL UTILITY THEORY

Although Adam Smith posed the water–diamond paradox, neither he nor his contemporaries satisfactorily resolved this paradox. Not until the *marginal revolution* of the late nineteenth century did economists have a model able to explain why luxuries could command a higher price than necessities. Although the seeds of marginal utility theory can be found in earlier writings, credit for developing this theory is attributed to three economists—William Stanley Jevons, Carl Menger, and Lèon Walras. Working independently of one another—Jevons in England, Menger in Austria, and Walras in Switzerland—the three economists published separate books between 1871–1874 that laid out the elements of marginal utility theory.

In a sharp break from the prevailing line of thought, the three economists argued that value and price depend on marginal utility to the consumer, not on the cost of producing a good or on the amount of labor.[7] This argument was used, especially by Menger's followers, to attack the works of Karl Marx, which are based on a labor theory of value. Despite the importance to economics of marginal analysis and utility, economists did not generally recognize the significance of marginal utility theory until the twentieth century.

[7]Were the marginalists right or were their contemporaries? For a resolution of this debate, return to Chapter 4, Exhibit 2.

citizens vote on a proposal, they are voting on its marginal utility, not its total utility.

The same logic applies to various organizations. A zoo may consider its big cat exhibit to be its prize attraction, yet there is nothing inconsistent about trading one of its cats for monkeys or exotic birds. The marginal utility of an improved monkey exhibit may be high; the loss of a big cat may be low.

Marginal utility theory was even behind Mayor Edward Koch's plan to conserve water in New York City. The city's houses and apartment buildings do not have water meters. Therefore the price that a homeowner pays for additional water—to water a lawn or fill a swimming pool—is zero. Because additional water is free to the consumer, the consumer uses water up to the point where its marginal utility is zero. As long as the marginal utility of an additional gallon is positive, it is used. But while additional water is free to the consumer, it costs the city money.

The mayor proposed requiring owners of all residences to install water meters by 1996. Once water usage can be measured, it will be possible to charge customers directly on the basis of their usage. When forced to pay for extra water, consumers will refrain from using water that has low marginal utility. Studies suggested that installing and using meters would curtail water consumption by at least 15 percent.[8]

YOUR TURN

According to a California physicist, high temperatures and high atmospheric pressure on Uranus and Neptune may have transformed their indigenous carbon into diamonds. Suppose he is correct. If these diamonds are mined and transported to earth, then (for residents of earth): (a) How will the total utility of diamonds change? (b) Will the marginal utility of diamonds rise, fall, or remain unchanged? (c) How will the price of diamonds be affected?

[8]See *New York Times,* "Mayor Koch Says Meters in Homes Will Save Water," January 12, 1986, p. 6E.

THE LAW OF DEMAND—AN ALTERNATIVE EXPLANATION[9]

Some students are uneasy about using marginal utility to explain the law of demand. Although a theory should be judged primarily in terms of its ability to predict and explain, the assumption that utility can be measured is admittedly unrealistic. For those troubled by this assumption, an alternative explanation of the inverse relationship between price and quantity demanded involves using income and substitution effects.

The Income and Substitution Effects of a Price Change

A price change is likely to affect quantity demanded for two reasons: it alters consumers' purchasing power and it changes the attractiveness of this good relative to its substitutes. For example, assume the price of a good is reduced and the prices of all other goods are unchanged. Due to the lower price of this good, you can now buy a given bundle of goods with less income than before. With the income that remains you can make additional purchases of various goods including, if you wish, the good whose price has been reduced. For example, if the price of Pepsi-Cola falls, you may spend part of the additional income to buy another quart or six-pack of Pepsi. This change in quantity demanded resulting from a higher effective income (or purchasing power) is called the income effect.

A price change may also affect quantity demanded by changing *relative prices*—that is, the price of one good compared to another. If the price of Pepsi falls and the prices of other beverages remain unchanged, Pepsi becomes a better buy than it was before the price cut. This induces many consumers to change their spending patterns—to buy more Pepsi and less of other beverages. This is exactly what happened several years ago. In an effort to increase sales volume in supermarkets, Pepsi aggressively reduced its price. As a result, it won a bigger share of soft-drink sales, overtaking Coke in many stores. The increased quantity demanded resulting from a lower relative price is termed the substitution effect.

Income Effect
The change in quantity demanded of a good that results from a change in purchasing power (when the price of the good changes).

Substitution Effect
The change in quantity demanded of a good due to a change in the price of that good relative to its substitutes.

From Income and Substitution Effects to a Demand Curve

As you may recall from earlier chapters, consumers respond to higher incomes by increasing purchases of normal goods and by decreasing purchases of inferior goods. This means that the income effect is positive for normal goods but negative for inferior goods. These income effects have implications for the shape of demand curves.

For normal goods the income effect reinforces the substitution effect. Suppose the price of a good falls. Consumers buy more of the good while cutting back on substitute products (the substitution effect). In addition, the lower price results in greater purchasing power, which again increases quantity demanded (the income effect). In other words, both substitution and income effects lead to an inverse relationship between price and quantity demanded. Therefore, demand curves for normal goods must slope downward.

For inferior goods matters are more complicated, because income and substitution effects tug in opposite directions. A lower price still induces a consumer to buy

[9]Some instructors may wish to delete this section, which contains technical material.

relatively more of a good (the substitution effect) and it still increases the consumer's effective income. But a consumer reacts to an increase in income by demanding *less* of an inferior good. Thus, while the substitution effect leads to an increase in the quantity demanded, the income effect leads to a reduction in the quantity demanded.

As long as the substitution effect is stronger than the income effect, the demand curve of an inferior good slopes downward. If the income effect outweighs the substitution effect, however, a lower price leads to a *lower* quantity demanded—the demand curve of the inferior good slopes upward! Although this theoretical possibility cannot be dismissed, empirical research has failed to uncover a convincing, real-world example of an upward-sloping demand curve. Therefore, demand curves apparently slope downward—even for inferior goods.[10] Although most research on demand curves has dealt with human consumption, some innovative studies find that demand curves slope downward even for animal consumers (see Exhibit 22-3, page 500).

FROM INDIVIDUAL DEMAND TO MARKET DEMAND

Market Demand Curve
A curve showing the relationship between the price of a good and the total quantity demanded by all consumers in the market (per period of time); obtained by summing the demand curves of individual consumers.

Both marginal utility theory and income and substitution effects explain why the quantity demanded by an individual consumer can be expected to be inversely related to price. In turn, when individual demand curves slope downward, so does the **market demand curve**. To obtain aggregate or market demand for a good, we simply add the demand of all individuals in the market. This procedure is illustrated in Table 22-4 and the accompanying Figure 22-3 (page 501). For simplicity we assume the market contains only two consumers, you and a friend. But the same technique can be applied to any market, regardless of the number of consumers.

Market demand for a good is obtained by adding, at each price, the quantity demanded by all consumers in the market. For example, if the price is $2 you want to buy one unit, your friend none; total quantity demanded is therefore one unit. If price falls to $1, your quantity demanded rises to two, your friend's to one;

Table 22-4			
DERIVING MARKET DEMAND FOR A TWO-CONSUMER MARKET			
(1) Price	(2) Quantity demanded by consumer 1 (you)	(3) Quantity demanded by consumer 2 (a friend)	(4) Quantity demanded by all consumers (you and your friend)
$2.00	1	0	1
1.00	2	1	3
.50	3	3	6

The market demand schedule indicates the total quantity demanded at each price (column 4). Total quantity demanded is obtained by adding, at each price, the quantities demanded by all consumers in the market (columns 2 and 3).

---

[10]Economists have looked far and wide for an exception to the law of demand—that is, for a good whose demand curve slopes upward. Some claim that potatoes in nineteenth century Ireland may have been such a good, but most economists find this argument unconvincing. See Gerald Dwyer, Jr., and Cotton Lindsay, "Robert Giffen and the Irish Potato," *American Economic Review* (March 1984), pp. 188–192.

EXHIBIT 22–3

OH RATS! TESTING CONSUMER DEMAND THEORY INSIDE A CAGE

Scientists study animals to determine whether their behavior is consistent with that of humans. Often behavioral patterns are found to apply across species. Is this true for economic behavior? In a rather unusual experiment, this question was addressed by economists working in collaboration with psychologists and biologists. At issue: Is the behavior of animals consistent with consumer demand theory?

Male rats were placed in experimental chambers, each containing two levers.[11] Depressing the first lever would release one liquid (e.g., root beer); depressing the second lever would release a different liquid (e.g., cherry cola). Food and water were always available, so the rats did not need to consume either flavored beverage to satisfy their hunger or thirst. Experiments were conducted to answer two questions: (1) Is the rats' behavior consistent with the substitution effect? (2) Are demand curves of rats downward sloping?

Each rat was given an "income" of so many lever presses per day (e.g., 300). Once the income was used up, the lights above the levers were turned off for the remainder of the day. The next morning the lights were turned back on, signaling that additional income (lever presses) had been provided. The amount of fluid released by a lever could be adjusted, which corresponded to a change in price. For example, doubling the amount of root beer released by a lever would be equivalent to a 50 percent reduction in the price of root beer. By changing the amount of a fluid released, the researchers could determine the response of the animals to a change in price.

In the first experiment, the price of, say, root beer was lowered while the price of cherry cola was raised. At the same time, income was adjusted to guarantee that our animal consumer could still purchase the original combination of beverages. For example, if a rat initially purchased 12 milliliters of root beer per day and 3 milliliters of cherry cola, he would be given sufficient income to still be able to purchase these quantities. Of course, eco-

nomic theory predicts that the consumption pattern will change. According to the substitution effect, a lower relative price for root beer should lead consumers to purchase more root beer and less cherry cola. In fact, for all rats the predicted response prevailed.

Confirmation of the substitution effect does not, however, guarantee that demand curves will slope downward. If a particular beverage is an inferior good and if the income effect is stronger than the substitution effect, then the demand curve will slope upward. To determine the actual shape of rats' demand curves, a second experiment was conducted. The price of one beverage was changed while holding constant income and the price of the other good. By repeating this experiment, researchers were able to plot a rat's demand curve. For every rat considered and every beverage, the quantity consumed was inversely related to price. As predicted by the law of demand, the demand curves were downward sloping.

Source: Adapted from John Kagel, Raymond Battalio, Howard Rachlin, and Leonard Green, "Demand Curves for Animal Consumers," *Quarterly Journal of Economics* (February 1981), pp. 1–15.

[11]Rats are not the only animals used in such experiments. See, for example, Raymond Battalio, John Kagel, Howard Rachlin, and Leonard Green, "Commodity-Choice Behavior with Pigeons as Subjects," *Journal of Political Economy* (February 1981), pp. 67–91.

altogether three units are demanded. At a price of $.50, you each want three units; so the aggregate quantity demanded is six units.

Although marginal utility theory provides information about individual and market demand, it focuses exclusively on the buying side of the market. Because

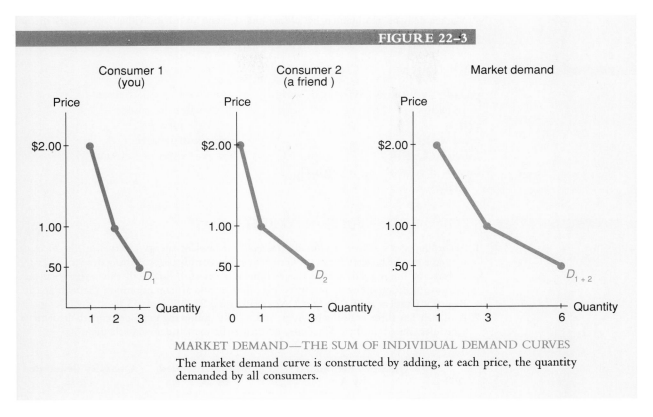

FIGURE 22-3

MARKET DEMAND—THE SUM OF INDIVIDUAL DEMAND CURVES
The market demand curve is constructed by adding, at each price, the quantity demanded by all consumers.

supply is as important as demand in determining price and quantity, we present a detailed analysis of production in Chapter 23.

SUMMARY

1. Total utility denotes a consumer's total level of satisfaction. Marginal utility refers to the change in total utility associated with a one-unit change in consumption.
2. According to the law of diminishing marginal utility, as consumption increases, marginal utility eventually declines. Because of the law of diminishing marginal utility, demand curves slope downward.
3. Consumer equilibrium occurs when the consumer spends the entire budget and the marginal utility per dollar is the same for each good consumed. At consumer equilibrium total utility is maximized.
4. Price depends on marginal utility of a good, not on total utility. This explains why many goods necessary for survival (e.g., water) have lower prices than many nonessential goods (e.g., diamonds). Although the total utility of water is high, its marginal utility is low.
5. A price change for a good triggers both substitution and income effects. According to the substitution effect, consumers want to buy more of a good when its relative price is reduced. A lower price also increases effective income. The change in quantity demanded due to this change in effective income is called the income effect.
6. For normal goods demand curves must be downward sloping. For inferior goods demand curves slope downward when the substitution effect outweighs the income effect. Available evidence indicates that for all known inferior goods the substitution effect is more powerful than the income effect. Therefore, demand curves evidently slope downward even for inferior goods.

7. Market demand is obtained by adding the demand of all individual consumers in the market. Market demand indicates the total quantity demanded by consumers at each price.

KEY TERMS

paradox of value (diamond/water paradox)
utility
total utility
marginal utility
law of diminishing marginal utility

consumer equilibrium
consumer surplus
income effect
substitution effect
market demand curve

STUDY QUESTIONS AND PROBLEMS

1. According to a scientist at Cornell University, abundant energy reserves, in the form of methane gas, lie beneath the earth's crust. Sweden recently began drilling deep into a crater in hope of finding this gas. If the drilling is successful, how will this affect total and marginal utilities of energy products (e.g., heating and air conditioning)? (Source: Sharon Begley, "Gushers at 30,000 Feet," *Newsweek,* June 27, 1988, p. 53.)

2. A market has three consumers: A, B, and C. The following table presents their demand schedules. Based on these schedules, construct the market demand schedule.

Price	Quantity demanded by A	Quantity demanded by B	Quantity demanded by C
$4	1	0	1
3	2	1	3
2	3	2	5
1	4	3	7

3. Jennifer enjoys bowling and miniature golf. The extent of her enjoyment is revealed by the following utility schedules.
Compute Jennifer's marginal utility schedule for each activity.

Games of bowling	Total utility	Games of miniature golf	Total utility
1	8	1	12
2	12	2	20
3	15	3	24
4	17	4	26

4. Refer to the utility schedules of question 3. (a) Assume initially that the price for both bowling and miniature golf is $2 per game. Given a budget of $6, how many games of each should Jennifer play? (b) Now suppose the price per game of bowling is $1, half the price of miniature golf. With a $6 budget, how many games of each would maximize Jennifer's utility? Justify your answers. (c) Based on the above information, plot Jennifer's demand for bowling.

5. (This problem is based on Exhibit 22-1.) (a) From your answer to question 4, compute Jennifer's consumer surplus from bowling when the price is $1 per game. (b) Which has a higher consumer surplus, water or diamonds? (c) How would the consumer surplus of water change if water were a free good?

6. Suppose the price of movie tickets rises. (a) According to the substitution effect, how are consumers likely to respond? (b) How will the income effect influence quantity demanded? On what does your answer depend?

(a) An increase in the quantity of diamonds should increase the total utility of diamonds. (b) Because diamonds would be less scarce, the marginal utility of an additional diamond would be lower. (c) Accordingly, the price consumers would be willing to pay would also fall.

INDIFFERENCE CURVE ANALYSIS

As noted in the foregoing chapter, marginal utility theory rests on the assumption that utility (or satisfaction) can be quantified. For example, in Table 22-2 it was assumed that one Coke provides 20 units of utility, two Cokes 32 units of utility. The theory developed in this appendix is based on a more realistic assumption—that an individual can indicate which of two bundles, if either, is preferred. The level of utility need not be quantified. Because this assumption is less restrictive, many prefer this theory to that of marginal utility. As was true for marginal utility theory, the theory presented can be used to indicate which combination of goods maximizes a consumer's utility and to explain why demand curves slope downward. We demonstrate both points immediately after introducing the key components of the theory—indifference curves and budget lines.

Indifference Curves

Consider two bundles of goods, A and B. Given your preferences, there are three distinct possibilities: bundle A is preferred, bundle B is preferred, or bundles A and B are valued equally (you are indifferent to the two bundles). An **indifference curve** consists of all combinations of goods to which you are indifferent.

Indifference Curve
A curve depicting all combinations of two goods to which an individual is indifferent—that is, all combinations that have the same total utility.

As an example of an indifference curve, consider Figure 22A-1, which we will assume depicts your preferences toward pizza and ice cream. Each point on the indifference curve represents the same value or utility. Although bundle A contains more pizza, bundle B contains more ice cream. The extra ice cream in bundle B just compensates for the loss of three slices of pizza. In other words, four slices of pizza and two scoops of ice cream generate the same utility as seven slices of pizza and one scoop of ice cream.

Characteristics of Indifference Curves

Downward Slope   As long as both goods generate utility, indifference curves must have a negative slope. An increase in the amount of one good must be offset by a decrease in the amount of the second good in order to keep the level of satisfaction the same. If you receive more pizza without foregoing any ice cream your utility increases, implying that you are no longer on the same indifference curve.

Convex Shape   The indifference curve in Figure 22A-1 is drawn with a *convex* shape, meaning that it bows toward the origin. In other words, the slope of the indifference curve becomes flatter as you move down the curve.[12] Your willingness to substitute pizza for ice cream depends on how much of each you currently have. Another scoop of ice cream has greater value the less ice cream you already have.

---

[12]The slope of the indifference curve is called the *marginal rate of substitution* because it indicates the rate at which the consumer is willing to substitute one good (e.g., pizza) for the other (e.g., ice cream). The fact that the indifference curve becomes flatter as you move down the curve implies that there is a diminishing marginal rate of substitution between the two goods.

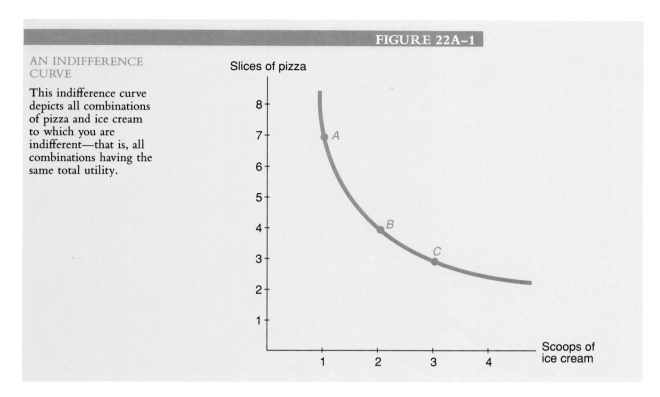

FIGURE 22A–1

AN INDIFFERENCE CURVE

This indifference curve depicts all combinations of pizza and ice cream to which you are indifferent—that is, all combinations having the same total utility.

Likewise, another piece of pizza has less value the more pizza you have. If you are at point *A* on the indifference curve, you are willing to trade three pieces of pizza for another scoop of ice cream. But if you are at point *B*, with less pizza and more ice cream, you are willing to give up only one piece of pizza for another scoop. It is because of this diminished willingness to part with pizza that the indifference curve is convex.

Bigger Bundles Mean More Utility   Using a different combination of goods we can now trace a new indifference curve. Suppose you begin with five pieces of pizza and three scoops of ice cream, and list all other combinations that you consider equally attractive. All these points must lie on another indifference curve. This indifference curve (along with two others) appears in Figure 22A-2 (page 506). A graph containing multiple indifference curves is called an **indifference map**.

Indifference Map
A set of indifference curves.

Note that indifference curves with larger bundles of goods lie farther up and to the right than do indifference curves with smaller bundles. What does

this say about the utility of the respective indifference curves? Assuming that you place a positive value on additional units of each good, bigger bundles of goods generate higher levels of utility. Five pieces of pizza and three scoops of ice cream (point *D* on indifference curve I_3) provide more satisfaction than four pieces of pizza and two scoops of ice cream (point *B* on indifference curve I_2). This implies that points on indifference curve I_3 are associated with higher utility than points on I_2. More generally, movements to the northeast on the indifference map correspond to increases in utility.

Indifference Curves Do Not Intersect   Assuming that more of a good is preferred to less, indifference curves cannot cross. Thus, the situation portrayed in Figure 22A-3 (page 506) cannot exist. According to this figure, the consumer is indifferent to points *A* and *B* (since they lie on the same indifference curve) and also indifferent to points *A* and *C*. It therefore follows that the consumer must be indifferent to points *B* and *C*. But this cannot be. Point *B* is associated with the same amount of ice cream and more pizza. Therefore, point *B* is preferred to point *C*. Allowing indifference curves to intersect violates the assumption that the consumer wants more of each good.

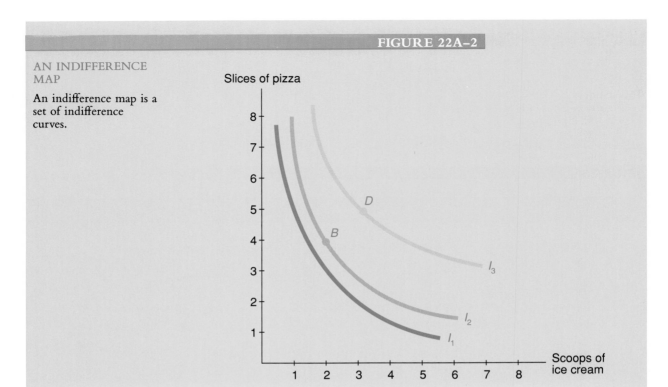

AN INDIFFERENCE
MAP

An indifference map is a
set of indifference
curves.

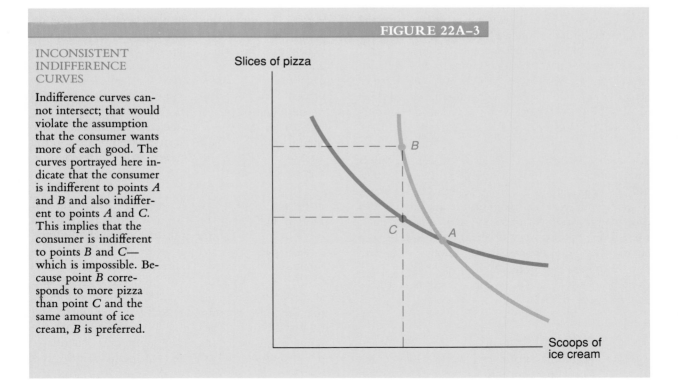

INCONSISTENT
INDIFFERENCE
CURVES

Indifference curves can-
not intersect; that would
violate the assumption
that the consumer wants
more of each good. The
curves portrayed here in-
dicate that the consumer
is indifferent to points A
and B and also indifferent to points A and C.
This implies that the
consumer is indifferent
to points B and C—
which is impossible. Be-
cause point B corre-
sponds to more pizza
than point C and the
same amount of ice
cream, B is preferred.

The Budget Line

In the quest for higher utility, the consumer faces a constraint—a limited budget or income. The consumer does not have sufficient funds to purchase all combinations of the two goods. The limits imposed by the budget are revealed through the consumer's **budget line.** A budget line incorporates information on both the available funds to spend and the price of each good. We illustrate this by continuing our example.

Budget Line
A line indicating all combinations of two goods that can be purchased with an income, given the price of each good.

Suppose you have $4 to spend on pizza and ice cream. Further suppose that you must pay $.50 for each slice of pizza and $1.00 for each scoop of ice cream. Figure 22A-4 illustrates your budget line. If you devote your entire budget to pizza, you can purchase eight pieces (point X). At the other extreme, by foregoing pizza entirely, you can purchase four scoops of ice cream (point Y). Alternatively, you could purchase various combinations of both pizza and ice cream. For example, if you buy four slices of pizza, you still have enough income to buy two scoops of ice cream (point Z).

Because a budget line is derived from a given income and given prices, any change in income or prices leads to a new budget line. For example, a

YOUR TURN

(a) Assume you have $4 in income. If pizza is priced at $.50 per slice and ice cream at $.50 per scoop, draw your budget line. To your diagram add the budget line of Figure 22A-4. What can you conclude about the effect of a price reduction on the budget line, other things equal? How would a price increase affect the budget line? (b) Assume pizza is priced at $.50 per slice and ice cream at $1.00 per scoop. What will the budget line look like if your income is $3? Now draw budget lines associated with incomes of $4 and $5. What can you conclude about the effect of a higher income, assuming that prices do not change?

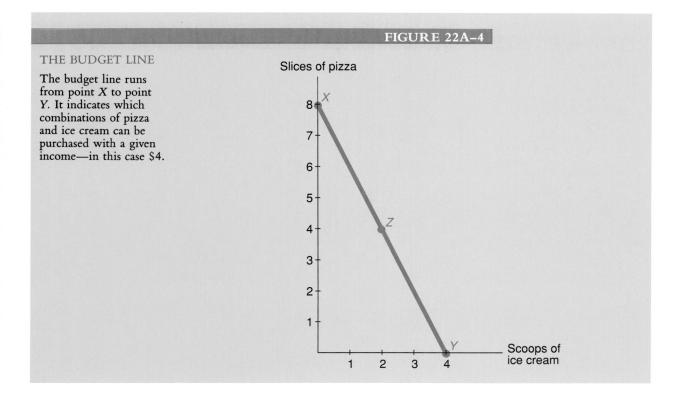

FIGURE 22A–4

THE BUDGET LINE

The budget line runs from point X to point Y. It indicates which combinations of pizza and ice cream can be purchased with a given income—in this case $4.

Slices of pizza

Scoops of ice cream

reduction in the price of ice cream increases the amount of ice cream that can be bought with a given income.

Consumer Equilibrium

Bringing together the indifference map and the budget line, we have yet another example of scarcity and choice. In this case the issue is: Given a limited income, what combination of goods should you buy to maximize total utility? This can be visualized in terms of Figure 22A-5, which plots Figures 22A-2 and 22A-4 on the same graph.

As noted earlier, higher indifference curves correspond to higher levels of utility. As such, you prefer points on I_3 to points on I_2, which in turn are preferred to points on I_1. Unfortunately, every combination of goods shown on I_3 costs more than \$4; therefore, they are unattainable. Only points on or below the budget line satisfy the requirement that you spend no more than \$4.

Given this budget constraint, utility is maximized at point B, where indifference curve I_2 is tangent to (just touches) the budget line. Any other combination

of goods that satisfies the budget constraint (e.g., point E) lies on a lower indifference curve, indicating a lower level of utility. Therefore, **consumer equilibrium** occurs at point B. To maximize your utility, you should buy four slices of pizza and two scoops of ice cream.

Consumer Equilibrium

A situation in which the consumer obtains the maximum total utility consistent with the consumer's budget; occurs where the consumer's indifference curve is tangent to the budget line.

Deriving Demand from Indifference Curves

Indifference curve analysis can also be used to derive a consumer's demand curve. To illustrate, consider the effect of changing the price of ice cream. Assuming income and the price of pizza remain unchanged, how will a change in the price of ice cream alter consumer equilibrium? Answer this question and you have your demand curve for ice cream.

Assume the price of ice cream falls to \$.50 per scoop. This rotates the budget line—as Figure 22A-6

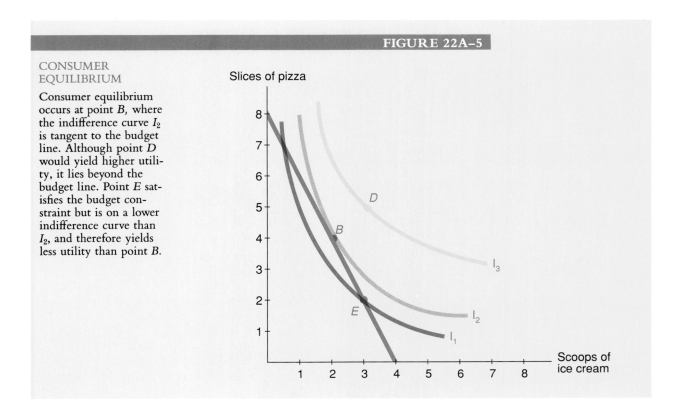

FIGURE 22A–5

CONSUMER EQUILIBRIUM

Consumer equilibrium occurs at point B, where the indifference curve I_2 is tangent to the budget line. Although point D would yield higher utility, it lies beyond the budget line. Point E satisfies the budget constraint but is on a lower indifference curve than I_2, and therefore yields less utility than point B.

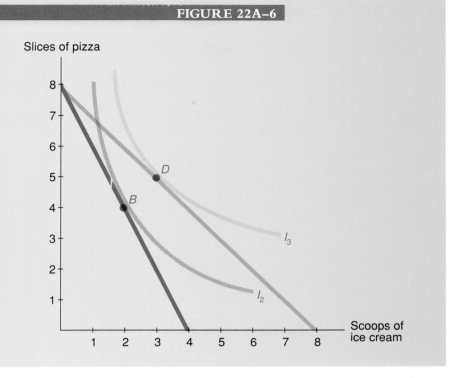

FIGURE 22A-6

THE EFFECT OF A CHANGE IN PRICE

When the price of ice cream falls, the budget constraint rotates outward—enabling you to reach a higher indifference curve. Point *D* represents the new consumer equilibrium.

illustrates—so that consumer equilibrium no longer occurs at point *B*. Given the lower price of ice cream, it is now possible to reach a higher indifference curve, I_3. In particular, the new consumer equilibrium occurs at point *D*, where I_3 is tangent to the new budget line. You now maximize utility by buying five slices of pizza and three scoops of ice cream.

This experiment provides us with a second point on your demand curve (Figure 22A-7; page 510). When ice cream is $1.00 a scoop you demand two scoops. But at a price of $.50 you demand three scoops. Your demand curve slopes downward. By repeating this experiment (utilizing other budget lines and other indifference curves), you can obtain other points on your demand curve.

SUMMARY

1. Indifference curve analysis can be used in place of marginal utility theory. Both indicate the combination of goods that maximize a consumer's utility, and both can be used to derive demand curves. An advantage of indifference curve analysis is that it is applicable even when utility cannot be measured.

2. An indifference curve comprises all combinations of two goods to which an individual is indifferent. Assuming that the consumer wants more of each good, indifference curves slope downward and are convex—become flatter as you move down the curve. Higher indifference curves mean a higher utility level. Indifference curves do not intersect.

3. A budget line consists of all combinations of the two goods that can be purchased with a specified income. The budget line is determined by the level of income and the prices of the two goods.

4. Consumer equilibrium occurs where the budget line is tangent to an indifference curve. It indicates the combination of goods that maximizes utility subject to the budget constraint. Any other combination of goods satisfying the budget constraint provides less utility; any combination providing more utility violates the budget constraint.

5. A consumer's demand curve can be obtained by varying the price of the good while holding constant income and the price of the other good. A change in the price leads to a new budget line and therefore to a new consumer equilibrium. By finding the quantity demanded at each price, we can construct the consumer's demand curve.

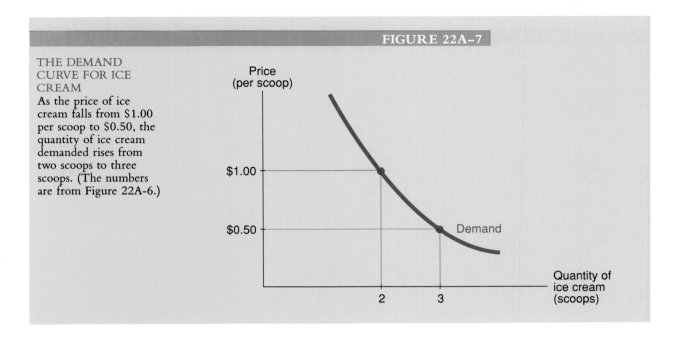

FIGURE 22A–7

THE DEMAND CURVE FOR ICE CREAM
As the price of ice cream falls from $1.00 per scoop to $0.50, the quantity of ice cream demanded rises from two scoops to three scoops. (The numbers are from Figure 22A-6.)

KEY TERMS

indifference curve   budget line
indifference map   consumer equilibrium

STUDY QUESTIONS AND PROBLEMS

1. You have $100 to spend on movies and compact disks. Movies are priced at $5, compact disks at $20.
   (a) Draw your budget line, labeling the axes of your diagram.

(b) The price of compact disks falls to $10. On the same diagram draw your new budget line. Be sure to indicate which is the new budget line.
(c) Not only does the price of compact disks fall to $10, but the price of movies is reduced to $2.50. Draw and label this third budget line.

2. In Figure 22A-6 a lower price for ice cream led to an increase in the desired quantity of *pizza*. Why would you buy more pizza when its price was not reduced?

ANSWERS TO YOUR TURN

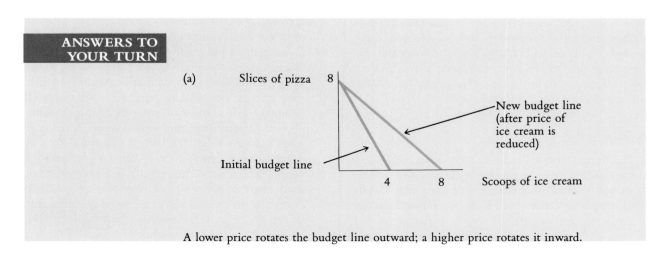

A lower price rotates the budget line outward; a higher price rotates it inward.

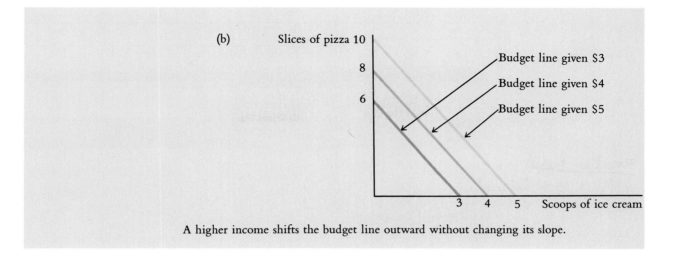

A higher income shifts the budget line outward without changing its slope.

CHAPTER 23

COSTS AND PRODUCTION

We are not interested in size for size's sake. What is important is the size of the profits.[1]

Scott Olson, the owner of a Wisconsin dairy farm, and IBM are both in business to make money. The giant computer maker has been somewhat more successful of late, with annual profits running in the billions of dollars.[2] Scott has never earned more than $30,000 from his dairy operations, and last year he lost money. Still, there are similarities between Scott's company and IBM. Both make production decisions, both are concerned about costs, and both are weighing the consequences of expanding operations.

Chapter 23 studies these kinds of general business decisions and concerns. As such it focuses on the production side of the market, unlike Chapter 22, which dealt with the buying side. Obviously, consumers are important. IBM would not produce computers and Olson would not produce dairy products unless there was sufficient demand for their products. In subsequent chapters demand reemerges as a major force, influencing price, production, and profits. But first a detailed understanding of production is essential.

---

[1]Frank Lorenzo, chairman of Texas Air, commenting on his company's acquisition of Eastern Airlines and People Express; *New York Times,* September 21, 1986, p. 20F.

[2]According to accountants, IBM's 1988 profits amounted to $5.5 billion.

PROFIT, COST, AND REVENUE

Maximizing Profits

To understand and predict the production decisions of a firm, we first must agree on what motivates the firm. What is the target a business aims at when making decisions? We assume that the goal of business firms, from Olson's dairy to IBM, is to maximize profits.

Admittedly, there are exceptions to this rule. The owner of a company may hire her incompetent son as vice president, knowing that profits will suffer as a consequence. Because of prejudice, white workers may be hired even though equally qualified blacks are willing to work at lower wages. In such cases the owner sacrifices profits for other considerations.

Why then do we assume profit-maximizing behavior? First of all, for most firms this is a reasonable assumption. Companies are in business primarily to make money, and generally they pursue policies designed to make as much as possible. Second, profit maximization is a simple assumption on which powerful models can be built. More complex behavior could be assumed, but that would lead to more complicated, less manageable models. Models are judged primarily in terms of how well they explain and predict. On that score, models based on the profit-maximization assumption perform well. They do a good job of explaining business behavior; their hypotheses generally are supported by available evidence. In essence, the assumption of profit maximization simplifies without detracting from models' ability to explain economic decisions and relationships.

Profit for a firm is defined as follows:

$$\text{profit} = \text{total revenue} - \text{total cost}$$

Profit may be either positive or negative. A positive profit indicates that the total revenue accruing to the firm from production exceeds the total cost of production. A negative profit, known as a *loss,* occurs when revenues fall short of production costs. If total revenue and total cost are equal, profit is zero.

Measuring revenue is usually straightforward. Total revenue is simply the average price per unit times the number of units sold:

$$\text{total revenue} = \text{price} \times \text{quantity}$$

To measure total cost requires an added step: we must first determine what constitute costs of production.

Economic Costs and Economic Profit

Explicit Costs
Direct payments made to others for the resources they own.

Economists define the total cost of production as the sum of explicit and implicit costs. **Explicit costs** arise when a firm makes payments to others. Examples are the wages paid to workers, the cost of electricity purchased from a utility, and the rental charges on equipment leased from an office supply store. The firm receives resources

Implicit Costs
The opportunity costs of using resources already owned by the firm.

Economic Profit
Total revenue minus the total cost of production (implicit as well as explicit).

accounting Profit
total revenue - total cost

from others and, in return, makes a direct or explicit payment for those resources. **Implicit costs** are the opportunity costs of using resources the firm already owns. Even though no payment is made to others, there is a cost to using your own resources: you sacrifice the income that could have been earned from alternative uses of these resources.

Economic profit is the difference between total revenue and total cost, as defined by economists. It is obtained by subtracting all costs, explicit and implicit, from a company's total revenue.

To illustrate the concept of economic profit, and the importance of implicit costs, consider the dairy barn that Scott Olson could rent to others for $10,000 per year. If he decides instead to use the barn himself, he must forgo that $10,000. Although no money actually changes hands, using his own barn implicitly costs Olson $10,000. (If you like, think of Olson as renting the building to himself.) Suppose Olson uses this building to generate $100,000 in total revenue. In addition to the implicit rent, he incurs $90,000 in explicit costs. Has Olson earned any economic profit from his dairy operations? Clearly not. Once implicit costs are included, total cost equals total revenue (see Table 23-1a). Even though total revenue exceeds payments to others, Olson is no better off producing than had he decided not to produce and, instead, rented the barn to someone else. Production has added nothing to profit.

As important as implicit rents are to Olson, other implicit costs are just as relevant to other producers, including salaries forgone by the owner and depreciation of company equipment. Consider Sam, the owner/manager of a local grocery store. Because he owns the business, Sam decided not to pay himself a salary, despite the fact that he could earn $30,000 per year at Winn-Dixie. Last year the store generated $150,000 in total revenue and $125,000 in explicit costs. Sam claims that his store earned $25,000 in profits. Do you agree?

The $25,000 figure is inflated because Sam has ignored the implicit cost of managing his store. By working for himself, Sam sacrificed the $30,000 he could have earned elsewhere. Rather than working for free, Sam has an imputed salary of $30,000. Once we add this to the explicit costs of operating the store, we see that the total cost amounted to $155,000. The store actually lost $5000 (see Table 23-1b). Financially, Sam would have been better off working for Winn-Dixie.

Depreciation refers to the decline in an asset's value due to wear and tear or to obsolescence. Suppose a company owns a machine whose market value at the start of

TABLE 23-1		
TWO EXAMPLES OF ECONOMIC PROFIT		
(a) Olson's Dairy Farm		
Total revenue		$100,000
Total cost		100,000
Explicit (payments to others)	$90,000	
Implicit (rent on barn)	10,000	
Profit (total revenue − total cost)		$0
(b) Sam's Grocery Store		
Total revenue		$150,000
Total cost		155,000
Explicit	$125,000	
Implicit (forgone salary)	30,000	
Profit		−$5,000

the year is $1000. After the firm operates the machine for a year, its value falls to $700. The machine has depreciated by $300. This is the cost of using the machine, even though the company already owns it.

To compute economic profit it is necessary to consider all costs of production, implicit as well as explicit. Not only must we count direct payments made to others, we must also include implicit rent, imputed salary, depreciation, and any other costs of using a firm's own resources.

Economic Versus Accounting Profits

Accountants have their own definition of profit. Whereas the economist includes all costs of production, both explicit and implicit, the accountant either ignores implicit costs or measures them differently. For example, an accountant does not include Sam's forgone salary of $30,000 as a cost. Because no money was ever paid, the value of Sam's services does not appear in the accountant's ledger. As a result, **accounting profit** differs from economic profit.

Depreciation is another area of disagreement. Accountants use generally accepted accounting practices to compute depreciation. One such practice is *straight-line depreciation,* which assumes that an asset declines in value by a constant amount each year. Suppose a machine is purchased for $1000, lasts five years, and has no scrap value at the end of the period. Then straight-line depreciation is $1000/5 or $200 per year. In contrast, the economist emphasizes the change in market value. If the machine has a market value of $700 after one year, the economist measures depreciation in the first year as $1000 − $700 = $300.

That accountants treat implicit costs differently than economists is no indictment of the accounting profession. It merely underscores the fact that economic profits and accounting profits are different concepts with different roles to play. The accountant is concerned with keeping an accurate record of transactions to satisfy the demands of investors and to comply with government regulations, including the payment of taxes. Such records are also used to spot embezzlement and other missappropriations.

Accounting costs are often less subjective and easier to measure than economic costs. Take depreciation. The accountant merely plugs information on historical costs and asset life into a formula. The economist must estimate the market value of a machine after it has been in use—not always an easy task.

Despite such problems, economic profit remains the appropriate concept for measuring the economic success of a firm. To the extent that accounting profit ignores implicit costs, it may overstate true profitability—recall Sam the grocer. Economic profit tells the owners of a firm whether they could benefit from reallocating their resources—working for others or renting out the company's property. A negative economic profit (economic loss) indicates that a firm is not earning enough to cover its opportunity costs—the firm's resources would receive a higher return if employed elsewhere. Unless conditions are expected to improve sufficiently, the owners would be better off discontinuing production and selling assets or reemploying them in alternative, more profitable lines of business.

In contrast, a positive or **pure economic profit** is a sign of success. It tells the firm not to take its resources out of the industry. Even a zero economic profit—what economists call **normal profit**—is acceptable, being just enough to keep the firm in business. It signifies that the firm could not benefit from reallocating resources. Total revenue is high enough to reimburse the owners for all explicit costs and to fully compensate them for use of their own resources. Although a pure economic profit

Accounting Profit
Total revenue minus accounting costs. (Because accountants and economists measure costs differently, accounting profit differs from economic profit.)

obviously is preferred, a firm earning a zero economic profit has no incentive to discontinue production. Because production decisions are based on economic profit rather than accounting profit, unless otherwise stated "profit" in this book means economic profit.

When total revenue exceeds total cost (explicit plus implicit), a firm is said to earn pure economic profit.

When total revenue equals total cost, a firm is earning a normal profit.

When total revenue is less than total cost, a firm is suffering an economic loss.

The Allocative Function of Profits

Why did the U.S. oil industry grow so rapidly in the 1970s? Why did the automotive industry expand early this century while the horse and buggy industry contracted? Why have so many farmers left agriculture? The answers lie in the high economic profits of the former industries (oil and automobiles) and the losses of the latter industries.

In addition to measuring the economic success of an individual firm, economic profits allocate resources throughout the economy. Resources flow out of sectors suffering losses and into sectors earning profits. If firms in an industry are losing money, this is a signal that the resources owned by these firms are not employed in the activity where they are valued most highly. The fact that returns to these resources fall shy of their opportunity costs indicates that higher returns are available in other industries. To take advantage of these higher returns, owners pull their resources out of the unprofitable industry. As a consequence, production in the industry shrinks. Some firms scale back operations; others leave the industry altogether.

In contrast, pure economic profits pull resources into an industry. With the added resources, output expands as new firms enter the industry and existing firms increase production. Only when firms in an industry are earning normal or zero economic profits is there no incentive to reallocate resources. With normal profits there is no reason for additional resources to flow into the industry nor for existing resources to leave.

TWO TIME PERIODS: THE SHORT RUN AND THE LONG RUN

Business has been so poor lately that Sam contemplates leaving the grocery business. In the mean time he faces a more pressing issue: should he lay off some of his employees? Down the road, the owners of Stephenson's Orchards are weighing whether to apply more fertilizer and fungicides to the trees this year and whether to plant additional orchards (even though the trees would not bear fruit for at least several years). The Hues Paint Company is deciding how many workers to hire this month and whether building a larger factory makes economic sense.

Decisions, decisions. Businesses make them every day. Some pertain to current operations—the volume of grocery business this period, the number of apples grown, the quantity of paint produced. Other decisions center on the future ability of a company to produce. Should the company remain in business and, if so, what scale of operations is most appropriate?

Based on the time dimension, economists partition business decisions into two categories: the short run and the long run. The distinction is based on the ability to vary quantities of *inputs*—the resources used in production. The **short run** is

Short Run
A period of time so short that the quantities of some inputs cannot be changed.

Long Run
A period of time long
enough to change the
quantities of all inputs.

defined as a period of time so short that the quantities of some inputs cannot be changed (e.g., the size of a building or the number of fruit-bearing trees). In the **long run,** in contrast, a firm has sufficient time to vary the quantities of all inputs. New factories can be built, new orchards can be planted, stores can change size or even go out of business.

In the following sections we examine the firm's operations, first in the short run and then in the long run. To keep matters simple, we assume the firm uses only two inputs in production—capital and labor.[3] The amount of capital is assumed to be fixed in the short run—only labor can be varied. In the long run, however, the amounts of both inputs can be changed.

PRODUCTION IN THE SHORT RUN

The Production Function

Production Function
A relationship indicating
the maximum amount of
output that can be
produced per period with
various quantities of inputs
and a given technology.

With additional quantities of inputs, the firm can alter the level of output or *total product* it produces. The technical relationship between the amount of inputs a firm uses and the maximum producible output is known as the firm's **production function.**

A production function is simply a device for converting information about input usage into information about potential output. You might think of it as a computer that has been programmed by a production engineer. You ask the computer to determine the maximum output that can be produced with a given quantity of inputs, and the computer flashes the answer on the screen. An assumption underlying production functions is that the level of technology is fixed. If technological advances make it possible to squeeze more output from a given quantity of inputs, the result is a new production function—the computer must be reprogrammed.

A short-run production function for the Hues Paint Company is presented in Table 23-2 (a) and (b). In the short run, labor is the only variable input. Therefore, the short-run production function is simply the relationship between labor and total product, given a fixed amount of capital.

TABLE 23-2

THE SHORT-RUN PRODUCTION FUNCTION OF THE HUES PAINT COMPANY

(a) Labor	(b) Total product*	(c) Marginal product*	(d) Average product*
0	0		
1	100	100	100
2	220	120	110
3	330	110	110
4	420	90	105
5	480	60	96
6	510	30	85

*Gallons per week.

The production function shows the relationship between units of labor and total product. Based on the production function, marginal product and average product can be calculated.

---

[3]The case where a firm uses more than two inputs is examined in Chapter 30.

Average Product and Marginal Product

Average Product of Labor
Total product divided by the quantity of labor, holding capital constant.

Marginal Product of Labor
The increase in output associated with a one-unit increase in labor, holding capital constant.

At the Hues Company labor is essential for production—without labor paint cannot be produced. With a single worker, 100 gallons can be produced per week. With two workers, output rises to 220 gallons per week. Thus with two workers **average product of labor,** the average output per worker, is 220/2 = 110 gallons.

Another concept, even more important than average product, is the **marginal product of labor.** Defined as the change in total product divided by the change in labor, marginal product measures the increase in output attributable to the hiring of an additional unit of labor. When the firm increases labor from one worker to two, total product rises from 100 to 220 gallons, an increase of 120. Therefore, marginal product of the second worker is 120 gallons. For each worker Table 23-2 reveals total product, marginal product, and average product. Total product and marginal product are also graphed in Figure 23-1.

The Law of Diminishing Returns

How does marginal product change as the amount of labor increases? According to the <u>law of diminishing returns,</u> marginal product of labor ultimately declines. Eventually, each extra unit of labor increases total product by less than the preceding unit. Formally, the law of diminishing returns can be stated as follows:

> When at least one input is fixed, increases in the variable input beyond some point lead to increasingly smaller additions to output.

Note that the law of diminishing returns assumes that some input is fixed. In our discussion we are assuming that the amount of capital cannot be changed. Accordingly, the law of diminishing returns is a short-run proposition; it does not apply to the long run.

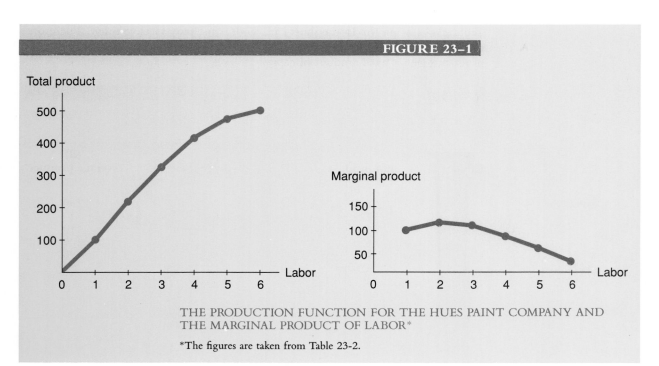

FIGURE 23–1

THE PRODUCTION FUNCTION FOR THE HUES PAINT COMPANY AND THE MARGINAL PRODUCT OF LABOR*

*The figures are taken from Table 23-2.

The notion of diminishing returns is intuitive. Assume you have a fixed plant size and a fixed number of machines. If you keep adding workers, the number of machines per worker declines. Workers must share machines to a greater extent and eventually may have to wait for an available machine. In addition, because the most important jobs are completed first, as more and more workers are hired they are assigned to less-important work. In this environment, employing additional labor increases output by relatively smaller and smaller amounts. Marginal product declines. Eventually, marginal product may even turn negative. (At some point, given the fixed plant size, workers start to get in each other's way.)

Or consider the case of agriculture, where land can be considered fixed. Does output double every time a farmer doubles the labor input? Certainly not. When labor doubles, the amount of land per worker is cut in half. Ultimately, working on smaller plots of land takes its toll. At some stage total product increases more slowly than labor. The same reasoning applies to other variable inputs. Farmers can increase their crop yields through irrigation, but as additional water is applied, the gains from further application of water decline (see Exhibit 23-1).

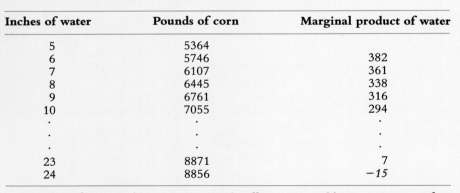

EXHIBIT 23-1

WATER IN THE FIELDS—A PRODUCTION FUNCTION FOR COLBY, KANSAS

Those who have witnessed parched fields realize the importance of water to farming. Even today states battle over water rights. But precisely how do yields respond to applications of water? How much additional corn (or wheat or cotton) can a farmer anticipate from additional irrigation? This is an issue of no small importance to farmers.

To learn the answer, economists, working with agronomists, have estimated production functions. Because weather conditions vary across and even within states, separate production functions must be estimated for different regions. The following is a segment of a production function for Colby, Kansas, based on data for 1971. It shows the relationship between irrigation water, measured in inches per acre, and corn yield, measured in pounds per acre.[4]

Inches of water	Pounds of corn	Marginal product of water
5	5364	
6	5746	382
7	6107	361
8	6445	338
9	6761	316
10	7055	294
.	.	.
.	.	.
.	.	.
23	8871	7
24	8856	−15

As these figures indicate, water greatly affects corn yields. An irrigation of 23 inches of water maximizes the yield per acre. Until that point is reached, additional water increases the output of corn. Notice that over this range each additional inch of water has a smaller impact than prior doses. In other words, water is important, but there are diminishing returns to irrigation.

[4]The yield per acre also depends on the amount of fertilizer. The production function presented here is based on an application of 180 pounds of nitrogen per acre.

Source: Adapted from Roger W. Hexem and Earl O. Heady, *Water Production Functions for Irrigated Agriculture* (Ames, IA: Iowa State University Press, 1978), p. 79, equation 6.1.

EXHIBIT 23–2

ADAM SMITH ON THE DIVISION OF LABOR

Adam Smith considered the division of labor so important that this was the first topic addressed in *The Wealth of Nations*. In a classic passage, Smith recounts the manufacture of pins in eighteenth-century England:

One man draws out the wire, another straights it, a third cuts it, a fourth points it, a fifth grinds it at the top for receiving the head; to make the head requires two or three distinct operations; to put it on, is a peculiar business, to whiten the pins is another; it is even a trade by itself to put them into the paper; and the important business of making a pin is, in this manner, divided into about eighteen distinct operations, which, in some manufactories, are all per-

formed by distinct hands, though in others the same man will sometimes perform two or three of them.

According to Smith, one pin factory employing ten workers in distinct jobs produced 48,000 pins per day, an average of 4800 pins per worker. In contrast, Smith claims that a single worker forced to perform each and every task in that factory could produce no more than 20 pins per day. Because of increased specialization of labor, an increase in the number of workers initially leads to a more than commensurate increase in output.

Source: Adam Smith, *The Wealth of Nations.* New York: Random House, 1937 (originally published in 1776), pp. 3–5.

The law of diminishing returns does not rule out the possibility that marginal product may initially rise before turning downward. In fact, this is what occurs in Table 23-2. Marginal product of the second worker exceeds that of the first worker. Diminishing returns do not set in until after two workers are employed.

Why the delay? Why doesn't marginal product decline at the outset? Some machines or operations run more smoothly with two workers than with one. Consider a large factory with a single worker. That worker must run back and forth across the floor to operate all machines and perform all jobs. The factory was not designed for such an arrangement. With one worker, labor is *spread too thin.* When a second worker is added, output more than doubles. The additional worker permits division of labor, with each worker specializing in certain tasks (see Exhibit 23-2). The workers can devote a larger share of their time to production and waste less time moving from one job to another.

Marginal product may continue to increase for awhile but ultimately, as more and more labor pours into the factory, the gains from further division of labor evaporate. The plant becomes crowded, the amount of equipment per worker shrinks, and as a consequence marginal product falls. The law of diminishing returns does not predict exactly when marginal product will peak, only that marginal product will turn lower at some point and thereafter continue its descent.

COSTS IN THE SHORT RUN

Fixed Costs and Variable Costs

Higher levels of output require greater amounts of inputs. Therefore, as production expands, total costs increase. In the short run these costs can be divided into two categories—fixed costs and variable costs.

Fixed Costs
Costs that are independent of the level of production.

Fixed costs do not fluctuate with the level of output. They reflect payments to fixed inputs and must be paid regardless of how much, if anything, is produced.

Property taxes and fire insurance are examples. So is the salary of a security guard hired to keep people out of a building at night. If the company president draws a fixed salary, independent of the company's operations, this too is a fixed cost.

Variable Costs
Costs that increase as the level of production rises.

Variable costs depend on the level of production. If production is to increase, companies must use additional variable inputs—for example, additional electricity, raw materials, and hourly production workers. Therefore, spending on variable inputs must rise.[5]

The **total cost** of production is the sum of total fixed cost plus total variable cost:

$$\text{total cost} = \text{total fixed cost} + \text{total variable cost}$$
$$(\text{TC} = \text{TFC} + \text{TVC})$$

Figure 23-2 illustrates the relationship among these three terms. Because total variable cost depends on the level of production, so does total cost.

Per-Unit Costs

Costs of production can alternatively be presented on an average or per-unit basis. Because most of the analysis in subsequent chapters relies on an understanding of unit costs, it is necessary to introduce the following terms.

Average fixed cost is total fixed cost divided by the quantity of output produced:

$$\text{AFC} = \frac{\text{TFC}}{q}$$

Average variable cost is total variable cost divided by the quantity of output:

$$\text{AVC} = \frac{\text{TVC}}{q}$$

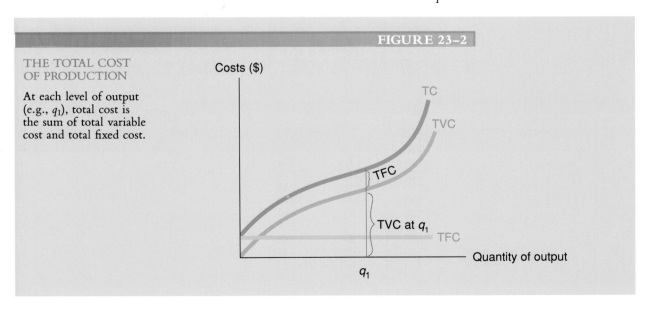

FIGURE 23–2

THE TOTAL COST OF PRODUCTION

At each level of output (e.g., q_1), total cost is the sum of total variable cost and total fixed cost.

Costs ($)

TC

TVC

TFC

TVC at q_1

TFC

Quantity of output

q_1

[5]We assume that the firm faces a fixed price for each input. The possibility that an input price depends on the quantity of inputs used is explored in Chapter 30.

Average total cost is total cost divided by the quantity of output:

$$ATC = \frac{TC}{q}$$

Equivalently, average total cost can be rewritten as ATC = AFC + AVC.

Marginal Cost

Our analysis requires one final measure of cost, in many ways the most important.

Marginal cost is the change in total cost divided by the change in output:

$$MC = \frac{\Delta TC}{\Delta q}$$

Marginal cost is generally computed by considering a one-unit change in output ($\Delta q = 1$). That is, *marginal cost measures the increase in total cost associated with the production of an additional unit of output.* Because only variable costs change with output (remember, fixed costs are fixed), marginal cost can be expressed alternatively as the change in total variable cost divided by the change in output:

$$MC = \frac{\Delta TVC}{\Delta q}$$

Tying Costs Together

Table 23-3 presents the cost schedules for a hypothetical firm. Note that average fixed cost declines as the quantity of output increases. This reflects the fact that total fixed cost does not vary with output. Thus, for the firm in question, average fixed cost can be expressed as: AFC = $120/q$. As total fixed cost is *spread* over a larger quantity of output, the fixed cost per unit declines.

			TABLE 23-3				
		COST SCHEDULES FOR A HYPOTHETICAL FIRM					
q	TFC	TVC	TC	AFC*	AVC*	ATC*	MC
0	$120	$ 0	$120				
1	120	50	170	$120	$50	$170	$ 50
2	120	84	204	60	42	102	34
3	120	108	228	40	36	76	24
4	120	127	247	30	32	62	19
5	120	150	270	24	30	54	23
6	120	180	300	20	30	50	30
7	120	218	338	17	31	48	38
8	120	266	386	15	33	48	48
9	120	325	445	13	36	49	59
10	120	400	520	12	40	52	75
11	120	495	615	11	45	56	95
12	120	612	732	10	51	61	117

*Amounts are rounded to the nearest dollar.

In contrast, Table 23-3 reveals that average variable cost, average total cost, and marginal cost initially decline but then turn higher. This reflects the fact that marginal productivity of labor initially rises and then, when diminishing returns set in, marginal product falls. Productivity and costs are inversely related, as Figure 23-3 illustrates. *Whenever marginal product of labor rises, the marginal cost of output falls. Whenever marginal product falls, marginal cost rises.*

To understand why this is so, consider what happens when the marginal product of labor is rising. When this occurs, output is increasing more rapidly than labor. As output per worker expands, the amount of labor required to produce an additional unit of output falls. Therefore, the cost of producing an additional unit of output (marginal cost) must also fall.

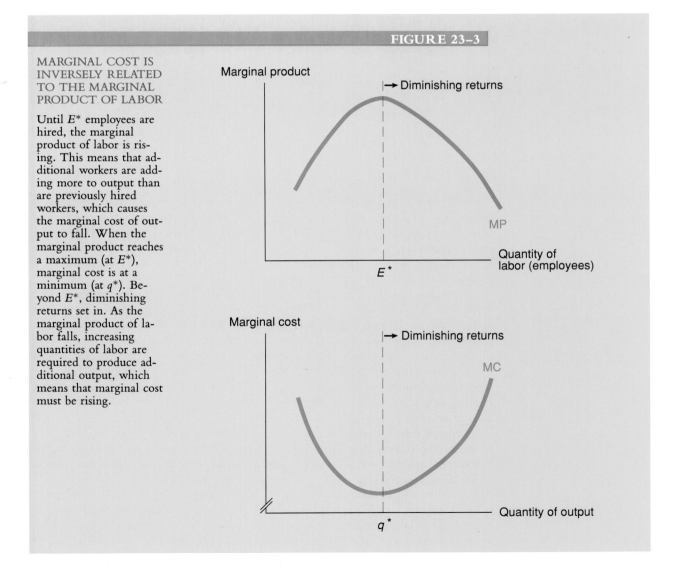

FIGURE 23–3

MARGINAL COST IS INVERSELY RELATED TO THE MARGINAL PRODUCT OF LABOR

Until E^* employees are hired, the marginal product of labor is rising. This means that additional workers are adding more to output than are previously hired workers, which causes the marginal cost of output to fall. When the marginal product reaches a maximum (at E^*), marginal cost is at a minimum (at q^*). Beyond E^*, diminishing returns set in. As the marginal product of labor falls, increasing quantities of labor are required to produce additional output, which means that marginal cost must be rising.

On the other hand, falling marginal productivity implies that each additional unit of labor is adding less to output than previous units. Because the contributions of labor are becoming smaller and smaller, the firm requires an ever-increasing amount of labor to produce a given increase in output. These growing labor requirements mean that the marginal cost of output is rising. For example, when the marginal product of labor is cut in half, a firm needs twice as much labor as before to produce one more unit of output—marginal cost doubles.

YOUR TURN

The cost terms introduced in this chapter are related to one another. Once you know certain costs, you can solve for others. Verify this by computing the missing values in the following table.

q	TFC	TVC	TC	AFC	AVC	ATC	MC
1	$60	$110	$___	$___	$___	$___	$___
2	___	200	___	___	___	___	___
3	___	___	360	___	___	___	___
4	___	___	___	___	___	120	___
5	___	___	___	___	___	___	155

Short-Run Cost Curves

Figure 23-4 presents graphically information taken from the last four columns of Table 23-3. As previously noted, average fixed cost declines as output increases. The other curves decline at first but then turn higher. Note that the marginal cost curve intersects average variable cost and average total cost at their lowest points. This is no accident. It reflects a mathematical property. Marginal and average values are related, as the following example shows.

Consider a basketball star who scores 20 points in the first game of the season. Assuming the player nets an additional 10 points in the second game, the player's average falls to 15 points per game (see Table 23-4). If fewer than 15 points are scored in the third game, the average falls again; if more than 15 points are scored, the average rises. More generally, whenever the marginal value (in this case, points scored in the most recent game) is below the previous average, the average must fall; whenever the marginal value is above the previous average, the average must rise. Finally, whenever the marginal value coincides with the previous average, the average remains unchanged.

Because this marginal/average relationship is universal, it also applies to costs. Consider the relationship between marginal cost and average cost (that is, ATC). Whenever marginal cost is below average cost, average cost must be falling. Whenever marginal cost is above average cost, average cost must be rising. Finally, whenever marginal cost equals average cost, average cost is neither rising nor falling—average cost has reached its minimum value but has not yet started to rise. Graphically, this means that *the marginal cost curve intersects the average cost curve at its minimum value* (see Figure 23-4). The same logic applies to average variable cost. The marginal cost curve intersects the AVC curve where AVC is at its minimum.

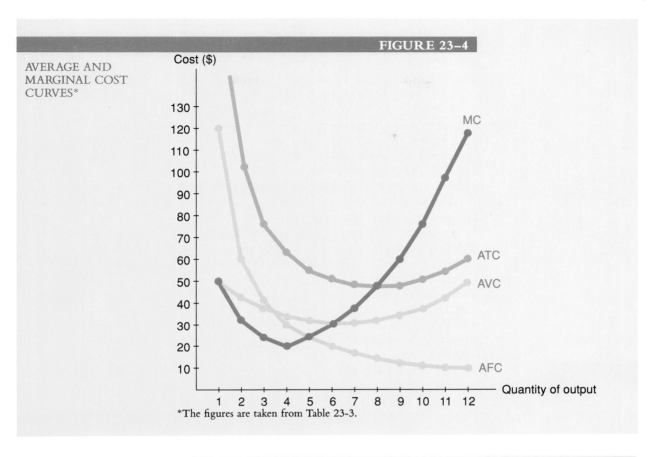

FIGURE 23–4

AVERAGE AND
MARGINAL COST
CURVES*

*The figures are taken from Table 23-3.

TABLE 23-4

THE RELATIONSHIP BETWEEN MARGINAL VALUE AND
AVERAGE—AN EXAMPLE

Game	Marginal value*	Average	Comment
1	20	20	
2	10	15	
3	(a) < 15	< 15	Marginal value less than average pulls down average.
	(b) > 15	> 15	Marginal value greater than average pulls up average.
	(c) 15	15	Marginal value equal to average keeps average unchanged.

*Marginal value refers to points scored in the most recent game—that is, the increase in total points for the season resulting from the play of one more game.

COSTS IN THE LONG RUN

The short run is characterized by fixed costs: at least one input—for example, plant size—is fixed. In the long run, however, the firm has sufficient time to change the quantities of all inputs. It can build a different plant, either larger or smaller. *In the long run there are no fixed costs; all costs are variable.*

A firm's short-run cost curves are based on its fixed inputs. With a different amount of fixed inputs—for example, a larger plant—the firm would have a different set of cost curves. By taking advantage of different cost structures associated with different plant sizes, a firm can switch in the long run to a plant that is more suited to a given level of output. That is, in the long run a firm can move to a plant that produces a given level of output at the lowest possible cost.

Assume that in the long run a firm has a choice of three plant sizes: small, medium, and large. The short-run average total cost curves associated with these three plants are depicted in Figure 23-5, where they are labeled $SRAC_s$, $SRAC_m$, $SRAC_l$, respectively. For low levels of production the small plant is appropriate. For example, q_1 output can be produced more economically with the small plant than with the medium plant—at q_1 the $SRAC_s$ curve is below $SRAC_m$. For output levels between q_2 and q_3, average (total) cost is lower with the medium plant than with either the small or the large plant. Therefore, over this range the company must use the medium plant if it is to minimize its production costs. If business continues to grow, at some stage even the medium plant will become uneconomical. For output beyond q_3, costs are lowest with the large plant.

Each plant size is appropriate over a different range of production. Which plant the firm should select in the long run therefore depends on the expected level of

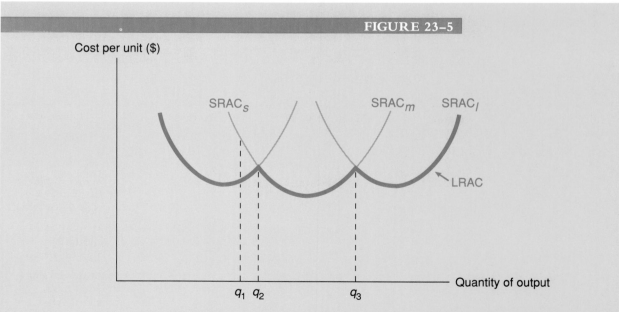

FIGURE 23–5

DERIVING LONG-RUN AVERAGE COST FROM SHORT-RUN COST CURVES

The long-run average cost curve consists of segments from short-run average cost curves, each corresponding to a different plant size.

Long-Run Average Cost Curve
A curve revealing the lowest cost per unit at which a firm can produce each level of output, given sufficient time to change all inputs.

production. Based on the three short-run average cost curves in Figure 23-5, it is possible to construct the firm's **long-run average cost curve.** The long-run average cost curve (LRAC) indicates the least costly way to produce a given level of output, once the firm has time to alter all inputs, including plant size. In Figure 23-5, the long-run average cost curve is represented by the heavy color line. Why don't we distinguish between average total cost and average variable cost in the long run? There is no need—all costs are variable in the long run.

Generally, a firm has available more than three plant sizes in the long run. When it does, the LRAC curve contains segments from more than three short-run average total cost curves. In the limit, a different plant size—and therefore a different short-run cost curve—may exist for each level of output. Figure 23-6 depicts a long-run average cost curve comprised of an infinite number of short-run cost curves, each tangent to the long-run cost curve at a single point.

The long-run average cost curve in Figure 23-6 is smoother than the corresponding curve in Figure 23-5, reflecting the fact that minor adjustments in plant size are possible. Still, the shapes are broadly similar. In both cases LRAC initially declines but ultimately, as the level of production increases, the curve turns higher. Are other shapes possible? What determines the particular shape?

The Scale of Operations

The shape of a firm's long-run average cost curve depends on how average costs change as production is expanded. As the level of production increases, average costs may decrease, remain constant, or increase.

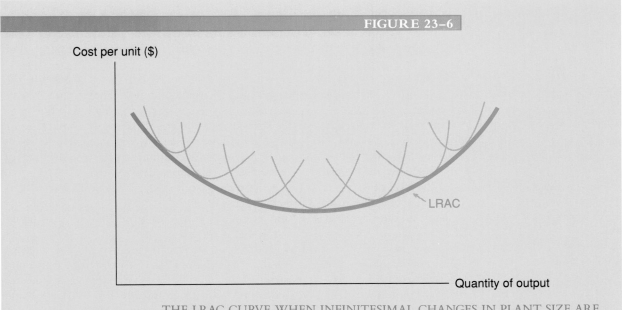

FIGURE 23–6

THE LRAC CURVE WHEN INFINITESIMAL CHANGES IN PLANT SIZE ARE POSSIBLE

This smooth long-run average cost curve consists of points from an infinite number of short-run average cost curves, some of which are illustrated.

Economies of Scale
A situation in which long-run average cost declines as the firm increases its level of output.

Economies of Scale   With economies of scale, long-run average cost falls as output rises—the firm's long-run average cost curve slopes downward. Economies of scale arise for a number of reasons. First, a greater scale of operations allows for greater specialization. As additional workers are hired, work can be divided into smaller, more narrowly defined jobs. This division of labor allows workers to master one job, rather than attempting to perform many. This is the idea behind Henry Ford's assembly line, which greatly reduced the cost of producing automobiles.

Specialization extends to nonlabor inputs as well. A precision metal-cutting machine or an advanced computer system may not be worth the cost to a company producing low levels of output because the machines cannot be fully utilized—they will stand idle much of the time. Therefore, at low levels of output the company may settle for machines that are less suited to the tasks at hand. But as production expands, companies can take advantage of the more specialized equipment. Moreover, machines that can handle twice the load typically cost less than twice as much as the smaller machines. So by moving to larger, more sophisticated machines a company may be able to cut costs per unit.

Average cost may fall for other reasons. The costs of designing a car are independent of the number produced. Design costs per vehicle therefore decline as more vehicles are produced. This gives General Motors a cost advantage over smaller automakers. Likewise, any given level of advertising costs General Motors less per vehicle. For such reasons, one might anticipate that the automotive industry is characterized by economies of scale. Available evidence supports this contention. General Motors and Chrysler have been found to enjoy significant economies of scale and, with a different product mix, so would Ford.[6]

Constant Returns to Scale
A situation in which long-run average cost does not change with the level of output.

Constant Returns to Scale   Beyond some point, further reductions in long-run average cost may not be possible. Economies of scale may ultimately give way to constant returns to scale. Constant returns to scale are characterized by a flat LRAC curve. If output doubles, total cost also doubles. Therefore, cost per unit of output remains unchanged.

For example, a study of the electricity industry found that, as of 1970, the average cost of producing electricity declined until 20 billion kilowatt hours per year of electricity were produced. Beyond that point, the average cost was the same whether a company produced 20 billion kilowatt hours, 30 billion, or more. Despite differing firm sizes, most electricity in the United States is generated by companies experiencing constant returns to scale.[7] Thus, with constant returns to scale, firms of different sizes can coexist, each experiencing similar unit costs.

Minimum Efficient Scale
The level of output at which economies of scale end.

The level of output at which economies of scale disappear is called minimum efficient scale. Figure 23-7 depicts the case of a firm that experiences economies of scale until output reaches q_1 and constant returns to scale beyond that point. Accordingly, q_1 is the firm's minimum efficient scale.

The prevalence of economies of scale differs by industry. Consequently, minimum efficient scale also differs. Table 23-5 reports estimates of minimum efficient scale for selected industries. According to these estimates, economies of scale are more important in the cigarette and paint industries than in the shoe and

[6]Ann Friedlaender, Clifford Winston, and Kung Wang, "Costs, Technology, and Productivity in the U.S. Automobile Industry," *Bell Journal of Economics* (Spring 1986), pp. 1–20.

[7]Laurits Christensen and William Greene, "Economics of Scale in U.S. Electric Power Generation," *Journal of Political Economy* (August 1976), pp. 655–676.

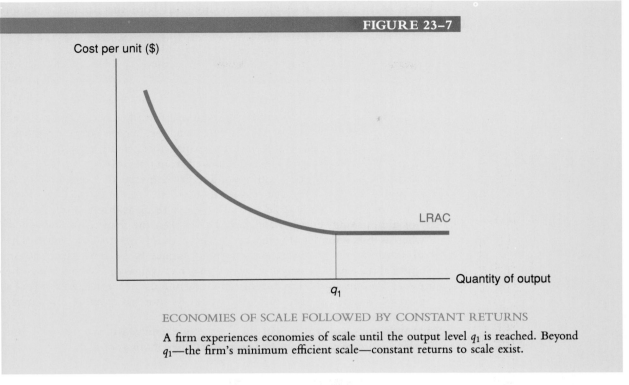

FIGURE 23–7

ECONOMIES OF SCALE FOLLOWED BY CONSTANT RETURNS

A firm experiences economies of scale until the output level q_1 is reached. Beyond q_1—the firm's minimum efficient scale—constant returns to scale exist.

fabric industries. Therefore, technological considerations suggest that the cigarette and paint industries will have fewer firms.

Diseconomies of Scale A firm may become too big, too unwieldy. Long-run average cost may rise as production expands. In that event, a firm is experiencing

TABLE 23-5

MINIMUM EFFICIENT SCALE AS A PERCENT
OF INDUSTRY OUTPUT

Industry	Firm output as a percent of industry output*
Shoes	1
Fabrics	1
Cement	2
Ordinary steel	3
Petroleum refining	4–6
Glass bottles	4–6
Cigarettes	6–12
Paints	14

*For firm operating at minimum efficient scale.

Source: Adapted from William G. Shepherd, *The Economics of Industrial Organization,* 2nd ed. (Englewood Cliffs, NJ: Prentice-Hall, 1985), p. 189.

Diseconomies of Scale
A situation in which long-run average cost rises with the level of output.

diseconomies of scale. Steven Jobs, who founded both the Apple Computer Company and NeXT, is familiar with this concept:[8]

> When you start growing [too big], you start adding middle management like crazy. . . . People in the middle have no understanding of the business, and because of that, they screw up communications. To them, it's just a job. The corporation ends up with mediocre people that form a layer of concrete.

Large companies may find it difficult to motivate workers or to control and coordinate operations. They may become too bureaucratic, bogged down in red tape. As a company grows, it may add extra layers of management that contribute little to output. Those at the top may become so insulated from operations that they find it difficult to assimilate information and respond to problems. As the company grows, total costs outpace output—average cost rises.

Note that diseconomies of scale are not the same thing as diminishing returns. The law of diminishing returns was invoked to explain the shape of *short-run* cost curves, whereas diseconomies of scale refer to the shape of *long-run* cost curves. The law of diminishing returns requires at least one input to be fixed. In contrast, diseconomies of scale explain why average cost may rise even as the firm increases the quantities of all inputs. Although diminishing returns must occur in the short run, a firm may never experience diseconomies of scale. Its short-run average cost curves must turn up; its long-run average cost curve need not.

Some industries have LRAC curves like the one depicted in Figure 23-7. But even here one must be careful not to assume that diseconomies of scale could never

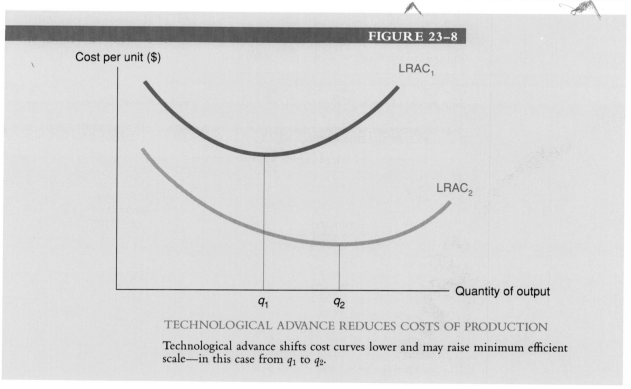

FIGURE 23–8

Cost per unit ($)

LRAC₁

LRAC₂

Quantity of output

q₁   q₂

TECHNOLOGICAL ADVANCE REDUCES COSTS OF PRODUCTION

Technological advance shifts cost curves lower and may raise minimum efficient scale—in this case from q_1 to q_2.

---

[8]Deborah Wise and Catherine Harris, "Apple's New Crusade," *Business Week,* November 26, 1984, p. 156.

arise. It is possible that, if firms push production to higher levels than they have yet experienced, LRAC might eventually turn up. Without evidence on what happens to costs at production levels not yet experienced, one cannot know whether or not diseconomies will ultimately appear.

In more competitive industries, characterized by a large number of small producers, the data indicate that diseconomies of scale do arise. This is why no firm grows large enough to take a big share of the market. This is also why the model of perfect competition (the focus of Chapter 24) is based on U-shaped long-run average cost curves.

Shifting the Cost Curves

The cost curves of this chapter are drawn on a number of assumptions. The most important of these is that input prices and the state of technology are constant. For different input prices or a different technology, the result would be a different set of short-run, and therefore long-run, cost curves.

Lower input prices drive down the cost of producing any given level of output, thereby shifting down the cost curves. Conversely, higher input prices, by raising the cost of production, shift cost curves higher. As with lower input prices, technological advances also reduce the cost of production. In addition, technological advances may alter the shape of the LRAC curve, prolonging the range over which economies of scale exist (see Figure 23-8). As a result, optimal firm size may increase—as it has in the beer industry (see Exhibit 23-3).

EXHIBIT 23–3

GROWING ECONOMIES OF SCALE—THE CASE OF BEER

The number of independent breweries in the United States declined from 369 in 1950 to just over 30 today. At the same time, average output per brewery skyrocketed. Why has the industry moved to fewer but larger companies? One of the main reasons has been technological advancement, which has increased the range over which economies of scale hold. As a consequence, brewers that expanded have been able to drive down their cost per unit. Those that did not grow faced higher unit costs, which ultimately drove them from the industry.

Economies of scale grew for several reasons. First, more advanced equipment was developed, with subsequent cost savings. For example, high-speed canning lines handle 2000 cans per minute, more than six times the volume handled by older equipment. To keep these modern lines running, a plant must produce at least 2.2 million barrels per year. Other innovations reduced the cost of build-ing large plants and allowed breweries to take advantage of greater automation. Another breakthrough came in the area of water treatment. Because water quality and taste vary by region, breweries initially could not produce the same, homogeneous beer in different parts of the country. But with advances in water treatment, breweries were able to operate multiple plants. Because beer is a heavy, high-cost product to ship, the opening of additional plants closer to major markets reduced shipping costs. Large brewers also have been able to take advantage of national advertising campaigns, which can reduce the cost per consumer of delivering a message.

For such reasons, economies of scale in the beer industry have grown over time. According to one study, minimum efficient scale increased from 4 million barrels in 1960 to 8 million barrels in 1970 and 18 million barrels in 1978.

Sources: Adapted from Victor J. Tremblay, "Scale Economies, Technological Change, and Firm Cost Asymmetries in the U.S. Brewing Industry," *Quarterly Review of Economics and Business* (Summer 1987), pp. 71–86; Charles Keithahan, "The Brewing Industry," Staff Report of the Bureau of Economics, Washington, U.S. Federal Trade Commission, December 1978.

WHEN THE PAST DOES NOT MATTER—THE CASE OF SUNK COSTS

Sunk Cost
A cost that has already been incurred and cannot be recovered.

As you will learn in Chapter 24, all costs are not equally important. At any point in time, the only costs relevant for current decisions are costs not yet incurred—that is, costs over which a person has some control. The rational person should ignore **sunk costs,** costs incurred in the past that are not affected by what happens now or in the future.

Suppose you paid $20 apiece for some Christmas trees, planning to sell them for $40. 'Twas the night before Christmas and all through the lot stood many a tree not yet bought. A bearded gentleman approaches, offering $5 for a tree. Should you refuse to sell on the grounds that you will lose $15 on the transaction? No, the cost of the tree is a *sunk* cost; it is no longer relevant. In retrospect, you wish you had not bought so many trees, but you cannot roll back time. In a couple hours the trees will have no value. Take whatever you can get for the tree.

Or consider another example. Suppose you paid $5000 for a machine that will last two years. It has no resale value—perhaps it would cost more to move and reassemble than it is worth. After you purchased the machine the business climate worsened. The machine no longer looks like a good buy. If used it will contribute $6000 to revenues over the next two years and $4000 to variable costs. But the total cost of buying and using the machine ($5000 + $4000) will exceed total revenue.

Does it make sense to operate the machine in the short run? The decision is not whether or not to buy the machine—it already has been purchased. At issue is whether or not to operate the machine. Because the machine will contribute more to revenue than to variable costs, it should be used. In the short run the cost of acquiring the machine is a sunk cost and therefore can be ignored. This is not the case, however, in the long run. The cost of buying and using a yet unpurchased machine would exceed the revenues generated by that machine. Therefore, the current machine will not be replaced once it wears out.

SUMMARY

1. Economic models generally assume that the goal of firms is to maximize profit. Economic profit is the difference between total revenue and the explicit and implicit costs of production.
2. Explicit costs refer to actual payments to resource owners outside the firm. Implicit costs are the opportunity costs of using the firm's own resources.
3. Positive or pure economic profits pull resources into an industry; economic losses cause resource owners to move resources out of the industry. An economic loss indicates that the firm is better off selling its resources or employing them in another business. If total revenue equals total cost, the firm is receiving a normal profit; it is earning enough to cover all explicit and implicit costs but nothing extra.
4. In the short run at least one input is fixed; therefore, the firm incurs fixed costs. In the long run all inputs and therefore all costs are variable.
5. A production function shows the relationship between a firm's inputs and the maximum producible output. Marginal product refers to the change in output associated with a one-unit increase in the variable input. According to the law of diminishing returns, when at least one input is fixed, increasing the variable input ultimately causes its marginal product to fall.
6. Because of declining marginal productivity, average and marginal cost curves must eventually rise in the short run. Marginal cost intersects the average variable cost and average total cost curves at their minimum value.

7. Each plant size has associated with it a different set of short-run cost curves. By changing plant size, a company can alter average cost in the long run. The long-run average cost curve, which consists of segments of short-run cost curves, indicates the least costly way to produce a given level of output once the firm has had time to alter all inputs, including plant size.

8. When a firm enjoys economies of scale, its long-run average cost curve slopes downward. Over any output range for which the firm experiences constant returns to scale, its long-run average cost curve is flat—average cost is constant. If the firm encounters diseconomies of scale, its long-run average cost curve rises.

9. In different industries, firms have different-shaped long-run average cost curves. In competitive industries, characterized by a large number of small firms, long-run average cost curves are U-shaped. They decline at first, but beyond some level of output they turn higher.

10. Higher input prices shift cost curves higher. Lower input prices or technological advances shift cost curves lower.

11. Costs incurred in the past that cannot be recovered are called sunk costs. The only costs relevant for current decisions are costs not yet incurred. Sunk costs should be ignored.

KEY TERMS

explicit costs
implicit costs
economic profit
accounting profit
pure economic profit
normal profit
short run
long run
production function
average product of labor
marginal product of labor
law of diminishing returns
fixed costs
variable costs
total cost
average fixed cost
average variable cost
average total cost
marginal cost

long-run average cost curve
economies of scale
constant returns to scale
minimum efficient scale
diseconomies of scale
sunk costs

STUDY QUESTIONS AND PROBLEMS

1. Indicate whether each of the following is an implicit cost or an explicit cost:
   a. payments to AT&T for long-distance telephone service
   b. depreciation on company-owned machinery
   c. interest payments a company does not have to make because the owner loans money to the company *interest free*
   d. the secretaries' salaries
   e. the lease payments forgone by a service station that decides to operate its tow truck instead of renting it out
   f. insurance payments on the company car

2. a. Construct the marginal product schedule for the following production function:

Labor	Total product	
0	0	
1	3	3
2	8	5
3	15	7
4	21	6
5	25	4
6	26	1
7	24	-2

  b. Graph the total product and marginal product curves.
  c. When does the firm first experience diminishing returns to labor?
3. a. Because of IBM's policy of lifetime employment, workers draw salaries regardless of current production schedules. Do these salaries constitute a fixed cost or a variable cost?
  b. In the textile industry many employees are paid on the *piece-work* system. If workers receive $2 per garment and no further compensation, are their labor costs classified as fixed or variable?
4. Suppose a company experiences economies of scale for the first 100 units produced each period and constant returns to scale thereafter. (a) Draw its long-run average cost curve. (b) If the average cost of producing 101 units of output is $3, what is the total cost of producing 101 units? The total cost of producing 102 units? The marginal cost of increasing production to 102 units? (c) Over the range of constant returns to scale, how do marginal cost and average cost compare?
5. The Little Red Wagon Company has the following cost schedule:

Wagons produced	Total cost
0	$ 30
1	60
2	80
3	90
4	110
5	150

  a. Construct the schedules for total fixed cost, total variable cost, average fixed cost, average variable cost, average total cost, and marginal cost.
  b. Graph the average variable cost, average total cost, and marginal cost curves.
6. "If the law of diminishing returns did not hold, the world's entire food supply could be grown in a single flower pot." Explain this argument. (The amount of land can be considered fixed. Analyze what happens as more and more labor is applied.)
7. The price of oil fell by more than 50 percent in 1986, causing many oil companies to incur losses. These companies had to decide which wells, if any, to shut down. (a) In making their decisions, should the oil companies consider the past costs of drilling for oil? (b) Should drilling costs be considered when deciding whether or not to drill new oil wells?
8. Only medium-size companies in a given industry are earning pure economic profit. Both small and large companies are losing money. (a) What does this say about the long-run average cost curves of firms in this industry? (b) What long-run response is appropriate for firms that wish to remain in the industry?

	q	TFC	TVC	TC	AFC	AVC	ATC	MC
ANSWERS TO YOUR TURN	1	$60	$110	170	60	110	170	110
	2	60	200	260	30	100	130	90
	3	60	300	360	20	100	120	100
	4	60	420	480	15	105	120	120
	5	60	575	635	12	115	127	155

THE OPTIMAL COMBINATION OF VARIABLE INPUTS

Companies often hire more than one input. In the long run the firm hires both labor and capital. Even in the short run a firm may hire multiple inputs—for example, skilled labor and unskilled labor. Appendix 23A presents a method for determining the optimal input mix when the firm buys two separate inputs and input prices are fixed—that is, independent of the amount the firm buys. A more general approach is presented in Chapter 30, which allows for both the possibility that the firm hires more than two inputs and the possibility that the price of an input changes as the firm purchases additional quantities of the input.

ISOQUANTS

Assume that a firm uses two inputs. To be specific, let us call these inputs capital and labor (but the analysis is the same no matter what name we give the inputs). Generally, a given level of output can be produced in a number of different ways. For example, a company may be able to substitute computers or robots (capital) for workers. By using more capital, the firm can produce the same output with fewer hours of labor. Alternatively, by expanding labor the company can cut back on capital.

The relationship between output and potential combinations of inputs can be depicted graphically by an **isoquant.** An isoquant shows all possible combinations of labor and capital that can produce a given level of output, assuming the inputs are used efficiently. (Efficiency, in this context, means that the firm is operating on its production function—that is, obtaining the maximum output from its inputs.)

Isoquant
A curve depicting the various input combinations that are capable of producing a given level of output when used efficiently.

In Figure 23A-1, isoquant $q_1 = 10$ illustrates the various methods of producing 10 units of output. Isoquant $q_2 = 20$ shows how 20 units of output can be produced. Note that q_2 lies beyond q_1, indicating that the firm needs a larger quantity of inputs to produce 20 units of output than to produce 10. In turn, 30 units of output require an even greater amount of inputs, which is why q_3 is the highest of the three isoquants.

As was true with indifference curves, isoquants generally have a convex shape—the slope flattens as you move down the curve. This reflects a diminishing ability to substitute labor for capital. When a firm is producing output with a relatively high mix of capital, it is easy to substitute labor for capital. But as the amount of capital is reduced, substitution of labor for capital becomes more difficult—the amount of labor required to replace a unit of capital increases.[9]

THE ISOCOST LINE

In producing any given level of output, a firm has a choice of options. Which combination of inputs

[9]On a technical note, the slope of the isoquant reflects the marginal product of labor divided by the marginal product of capital (slope $= -\text{MP}_l/\text{MP}_k$). Because movements down the isoquant signify an increase in labor and a decrease in capital, they imply that the marginal product of labor is falling relative to the marginal product of capital. That is, the slope of the isoquant becomes flatter as the firm moves down the curve.

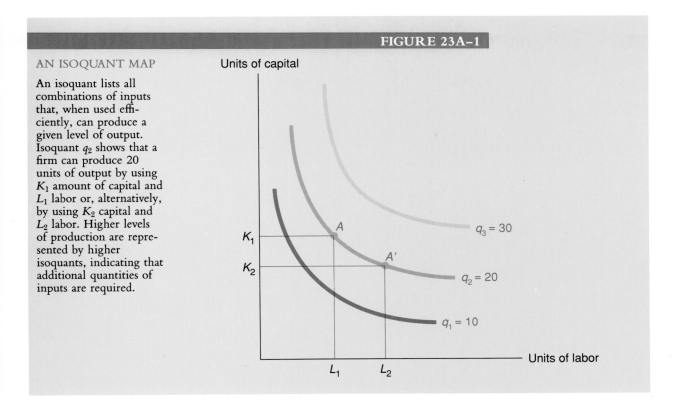

AN ISOQUANT MAP

An isoquant lists all combinations of inputs that, when used efficiently, can produce a given level of output. Isoquant q_2 shows that a firm can produce 20 units of output by using K_1 amount of capital and L_1 labor or, alternatively, by using K_2 capital and L_2 labor. Higher levels of production are represented by higher isoquants, indicating that additional quantities of inputs are required.

should it select? The answer depends on the price of capital and the price of labor. To see this, we introduce the **isocost line.** An isocost line shows the various input combinations that can be purchased with a given sum of money. The equation for an isocost line is as follows:

$$(P_l \times L) + (P_k \times K) = \text{total cost}$$

Isocost Line

A line showing all the combinations of capital and labor that can be purchased with a given amount of money.

Suppose a company contemplates spending $100 on inputs. If the price of labor is $5 per unit and the price of capital is $10, the company's isocost line is:

$$(\$5 \times L) + (\$10 \times K) = \$100$$

This line is illustrated in Figure 23A-2 (page 538). As this figure shows, with $100 the company can buy 20 units of labor and no capital, or 10 units of capital and no labor, or various combinations of both labor and capital (e.g., 10 units of labor and 5 units of capital). Also illustrated in Figure 23A-2 are the isocost lines associated with expenditures of $80 and $120.

The Least-Cost Combination of Inputs

Let us return to the question posed earlier: Which combination of inputs should the firm use to produce a given level of output? For example, suppose the company plans to produce 20 units of output. Which combination of labor and capital allows the firm to produce this output at the lowest possible cost? The answer is found in Figure 23A-3 (page 538), which presents the isoquant and isocost lines on the same diagram.

Total cost is minimized at point A, where the isoquant is tangent to the $100 isocost line. This corresponds to the purchase of 6 units of capital and 8 units of labor. Note that this is the lowest isocost line to reach the isoquant. The firm cannot produce 20 units of output if it spends less than $100 on inputs. Other input combinations (e.g., B and C) also allow the firm to produce 20 units of output, but such combinations lie on a higher isocost line—that is, they cost more than $100. *To minimize the cost of producing a given level of output, the firm must operate on the lowest isocost line consistent with that level of production.*

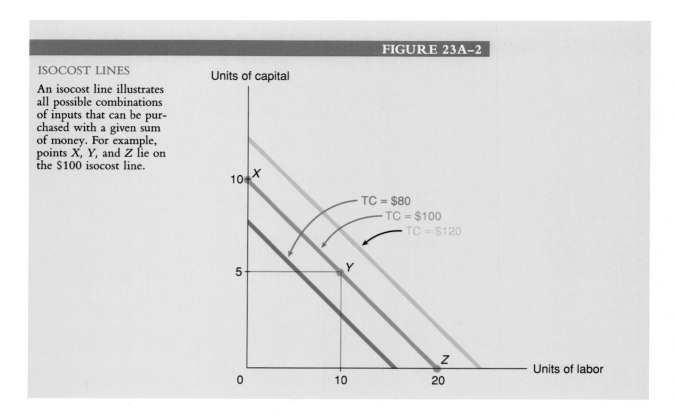

FIGURE 23A–2

ISOCOST LINES

An isocost line illustrates all possible combinations of inputs that can be purchased with a given sum of money. For example, points X, Y, and Z lie on the $100 isocost line.

Units of capital

TC = $80
TC = $100
TC = $120

Units of labor

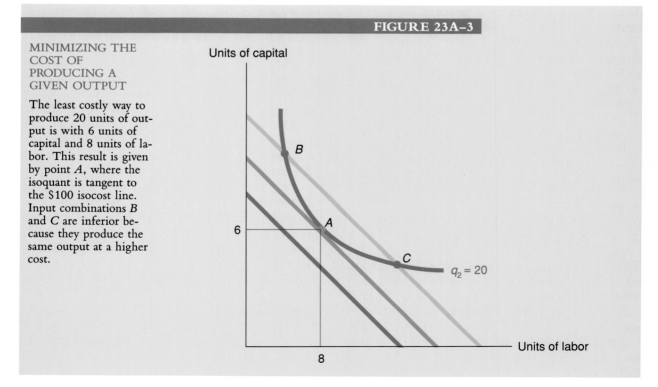

FIGURE 23A–3

MINIMIZING THE COST OF PRODUCING A GIVEN OUTPUT

The least costly way to produce 20 units of output is with 6 units of capital and 8 units of labor. This result is given by point A, where the isoquant is tangent to the $100 isocost line. Input combinations B and C are inferior because they produce the same output at a higher cost.

Units of capital

$q_2 = 20$

Units of labor

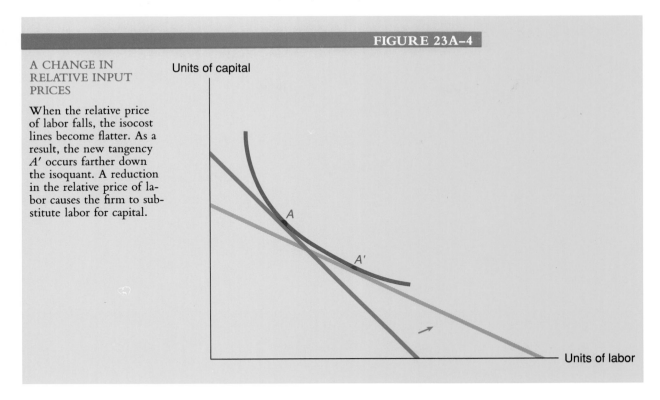

FIGURE 23A–4

A CHANGE IN RELATIVE INPUT PRICES

When the relative price of labor falls, the isocost lines become flatter. As a result, the new tangency A' occurs farther down the isoquant. A reduction in the relative price of labor causes the firm to substitute labor for capital.

Units of capital

A

A'

Units of labor

When relative input prices change, so does the optimal combination of inputs. A decline in the price of labor relative to capital induces the firm to substitute labor for capital; this is illustrated in Figure 23A-4. As the relative price of labor falls, the isocost line becomes flatter. This leads to a new tangency, at point A'. In other words, firms change their technique of production in response to changing input prices. When the relative price of labor falls, the firm substitutes labor for capital; when the relative price of capital falls, capital is substituted for labor.

SUMMARY

1. An isoquant indicates the alternative methods of producing a given level of output. Assuming that inputs are used efficiently, it shows all input combinations capable of producing a particular level of output. Higher levels of output can be represented by higher isoquants.
2. Isoquants generally have a convex shape, reflecting the fact that the less you have of one input the more difficult it is to substitute that input for a second input.
3. An isocost line shows the various input combinations that can be purchased with a given amount of money.

4. The optimal input combination is given by the tangency of the isoquant with an isocost line. This represents the least costly way to produce the given level of output.
5. A change in relative input prices shifts the slope of the isocost lines. This leads to a new tangency with the isoquant and therefore a new least-cost combination of inputs. The company uses more of the input whose relative price has fallen and less of the input whose relative price has risen.

KEY TERMS

isoquant   **isocost line**

STUDY QUESTION

Assume a company faces a price of $10 per hour for both capital and labor. (a) Draw an isocost line corresponding to expenditures of $200. (b) Draw an isoquant that is tangent to this line. (c) Now assume the price of labor rises to $20 per hour. Draw the new isocost line associated with expenditures of $200. (d) Can the company still reach the isoquant drawn in part (b)?

PART VII

MARKET STRUCTURE AND GOVERNMENT INTERVENTION

CHAPTER 24

PERFECT COMPETITION

Does the number of producers in a market matter? Does it make any difference whether a town is served by one grocery store or by many? Adam Smith argued that competition benefits society and that competition is greater where there are many producers. Most economists agree with Smith that competition generally lowers price, and they cite other potential advantages, including the way resources are distributed across industries. Yet, under certain conditions, unbridled competition may be undesirable.

How do markets differ, and why are these differences important to society? Should we promote a certain type of market? After an overview of the different market structures, Chapter 24 focuses on Adam Smith's ideal—perfect competition. Alternative types of markets are examined in subsequent chapters.

If [production] is divided between two different grocers, their competition will tend to make both of them sell cheaper, than if it were in the hands of one only; and if it were divided among twenty, their competition would be just so much the greater, and the chance of their combining together, in order to raise the price, just so much the less.[1]

---

[1]Adam Smith, *The Wealth of Nations* (New York: Random House, 1937), p. 342. [Originally published in 1776.]

THE STRUCTURE OF MARKETS

Although all firms sell a product, they do not all sell in similar types of markets. Agricultural markets, for example, differ from apparel markets. Buyers of wheat pay the same price for a given grade of wheat, no matter who produced it. Wheat from Gormely's farm is indistinguishable from wheat grown by thousands of other farmers. In contrast, different brands of jeans are not viewed as identical. Consumers are willing to pay more for designer jeans than for basic jeans. Therefore, while Gormely cannot influence the price of his wheat, Calvin Klein has some control over the price of his jeans.

Different yet is the market for electricity. In most communities the market contains only one seller of electricity: you either buy electricity from the local utility or you do without. Unlike producers of wheat or jeans, the utility company does not face competition from other firms in the market—there are no other firms. Some barrier, in this case a government license, prevents competing firms from entering the market.

Given such differences in the structure of markets, no single model can be expected to explain adequately the outcomes in all markets. Instead, different models are appropriate for different types of markets. Although real-world markets sometimes defy easy classification, economists recognize four basic **market structures:** perfect competition, monopoly, monopolistic competition, and oligopoly. Markets are categorized on the basis of various characteristics, the most important of which are now discussed (and summarized in Table 24-1).

Market Structure
The distinguishing characteristics of a market, including number of firms, the similarity of the products they sell, and the ease with which new firms can enter the market.

	TABLE 24-1				
A COMPARISON OF THE FOUR MARKET STRUCTURES					
Market structure	**Number of firms**	**Type of product**	**Entry into industry**	**Firm's influence over price**	**Examples**
Perfect competition	Many	Homogeneous (identical)	Easy	None	Many agricultural markets*
Monopolistic competition	Many	Differentiated	Easy	Moderate	Clothing, restaurants, dry cleaners
Oligopoly	Few	Homogeneous or differentiated	Difficult	Moderate or substantial	Autos, steel, oil
Monopoly	One	Unique	Difficult or impossible	Substantial*	Local utilities

*In the absence of government regulation.

Number of Sellers

Perfect competition and monopolistic competition are each characterized by a large number of sellers. In contrast, oligopoly has a small number of sellers; monopoly has but one.

Type of Product

In perfectly competitive markets all firms produce a homogeneous (identical) product. Monopolistic competition, on the other hand, is noted for product differentiation—consumers view each firm's product as distinct. Although other firms in the monopolistically competitive market produce close substitutes, none produces the exact same product. In the case of oligopoly, products may be either homogeneous (e.g., steel) or differentiated (e.g., autos). Steel is steel, no matter who produces it, but a Chevrolet is not the same as a Ford. Finally, because the monopolist is the only producer in the market, its product is unique.

Entry into the Industry

Producers find some markets easier to enter than others. Almost anyone can grow vegetables. The main requirements are soil and seeds. By comparison, the auto industry is much harder to crack. To start an auto company requires technical knowledge and perhaps billions of dollars. Even then it is a risky proposition, as John DeLorean discovered. In addition to financial and technical barriers, entry may be limited by government policy, including patents, or by inaccessible resources. If potential companies can be denied access to the raw materials needed for production, they can be kept out of a market.

Both perfect competition and monopolistic competition are characterized by **free entry**; new firms find it easy to set up shop and start producing. This is not the case with oligopoly or monopoly. There, considerable barriers to entry greet would-be producers. In fact, it is because of these barriers that oligopoly has only a few producers and monopoly has only one.

Although much is made of barriers to entry, it should be observed that barriers to exit sometimes occur. This means that firms attempting to leave an industry face obstacles—for example, laws restricting plant closings. Another example comes from the state of Rhode Island. Beginning in 1982, Rhode Island adopted a plan designed to slow the exodus of land from agriculture. Farmers signing up for this program promised that their land would never be developed. These agreements restricted land use not only for those signing the contract but for all future owners of the land. Perfect competition requires complete mobility of resources and thus **free exit** as well as free entry.

Firm's Influence over Price

A perfectly competitive firm has no control over the price of its product. Because the market contains many other producers of the same product, the individual firm has no market power. In all other market structures, producers have the potential to influence price.

Unless restricted by the government, a monopolist can set any price it wishes. Its only constraint is the demand for its product—a higher price reduces the amount consumers want to buy. Even a monopolistically competitive firm has some limited market power, despite the fact that it must compete with numerous other firms in its market. Because each firm produces a product slightly different from that of its competitors, a firm can raise price without losing all its customers.

The extent to which an oligopolist can influence price depends on whether or not the oligopolist *combines together* with other oligopolists in the industry. Sometimes oligopolists form a *cartel,* an organization designed to raise price and profits for members of the cartel. Perhaps the most famous cartel is OPEC, which in its first ten years succeeded in raising the price of oil from less than $3 per barrel to about $34 per barrel. In other oligopolistic industries, such as steel, producers do not band together. Instead, they actively compete against one another. This limits the ability of steel companies to influence price.

Examples

The preceding theoretical considerations provide a basis for categorizing markets. Sometimes a particular designation is arbitrary—real-world markets do not always neatly fit into a given category. Nonetheless, economists generally agree on most classifications.

Most public utilities are monopolies—the government usually allows only one natural gas company to serve a community, only one electric company, and only one sewage treatment company. Polaroid is an example of a monopoly that is not a utility. Because of the patents it holds, Polaroid is the only company that sells a camera with self-developing film. Examples of oligopolistic industries are aluminum, tires, and autos. Much of the manufacturing sector is oligopolistic. Most retail markets are characterized by monopolistic competition, including grocery stores, florist shops, and restaurants. Many agricultural markets come closest to the perfectly competitive framework. This is not always the case though. For many years the state of New York limited entry into the dairy market, permitting the emergence of an oligopolistic milk cartel (see Exhibit 24-1).

EXHIBIT 24-1

RESTRICTING ENTRY AND THE PRICE OF MILK IN NEW YORK CITY

With almost eight million people, New York City has a lot of milk drinkers, but until recently only five dairies were licensed to distribute milk in the city. A 1937 state law authorized entry restrictions "to prevent destructive competition"—a euphemism for maintaining high prices and guaranteeing profits for existing producers. The five dairies took full advantage of the law. Repeatedly, they were found guilty of price fixing and dividing up markets (agreeing not to compete for each other's customers). Milk prices in New York were among the highest in the country and dramatically higher than in neighboring New Jersey.

In 1985, barriers to entry were eased in Staten Island. Then in 1987, a federal judge ruled the state licensing law unconstitutional. This opened the milk spigots of other dairies. With additional milk flowing to the market, the price of milk in New York City fell by about $.50 per gallon. Do barriers to entry affect price? Clearly they do.

Sources: Adapted from William Greer, "Is Albany Helping Maintain the Sellers' Market in Milk," *New York Times,* February 23, 1986, p. 7E; Mark Uhlig, "Milk Regulations Are a Hot Potato," *New York Times,* January 18, 1987, p. 6E.

Implications of Market Structure

Economists have developed theories for each market structure. These theories indicate that different market structures have different implications concerning industry output, price, and profit potential. Market structure also influences the flow of resources into an industry, the level of advertising, and perhaps other factors as well. Some economists argue, for example, that the rate of technological innovation depends on market structure.

The remainder of this chapter is devoted to perfect competition. Monopoly (in Chapter 25) and monopolistic competition and oligopoly (in Chapter 26) follow. Although Chapters 24, 25, and 26 analyze markets in the absence of government intervention, subsequent chapters introduce government regulation and antitrust policy.

PERFECT COMPETITION

Competition has many meanings. You and other students compete for parking spaces; workers compete for jobs; companies compete for customers. **Perfect competition** has a more specific meaning. It refers to a particular market arrangement in which individual firms have no control over the price of the product they sell. For a market to be perfectly competitive, the following conditions must hold:

1. The product market contains *a large number of buyers and sellers,* none of whom has a significant share of the market. Each of the market participants is too small to appreciably affect market supply or demand.
2. The firms all sell an *identical (homogeneous) product.*
3. The industry is characterized by *free entry* and *free exit.* No barriers prevent firms or resources from entering the industry or from leaving it.
4. Buyers and sellers have *perfect information* about price and other conditions in the market.

Price Taker
An economic unit that has no control over price. The perfectly competitive firm is a price taker in the product market.

Together, these four conditions imply that the perfectly competitive firm is a **price taker**—it has no control over output price. The firm can sell as much as it wants at the market price, but if it attempts to charge a higher price it will find no buyers. There are a large number of other producers selling the identical product. Moreover, buyers know the price each seller is asking. In this environment, no buyer is willing to pay a firm more than the lowest price available elsewhere. Any firm attempting to charge more than its competitors will find no takers. At the same time, the perfectly competitive firm has no reason to offer its product for less than the prevailing market price. It can sell as much as it chooses at this price; to sell for less would mean forgoing profits. Graphically, the demand curve facing a perfectly competitive firm is perfectly elastic (see Figure 24-1).

The model of perfect competition rests on a number of rigorous assumptions. Doesn't this limit the usefulness of the model? Why study it? First of all, some markets closely approximate perfect competition. This is certainly true for many agricultural products (see Exhibit 24-2). Some economists go further, arguing that the predictions of this model are widely confirmed, even in markets that are not perfectly competitive. For example, Milton Friedman writes:

> [A]s I have studied economic activities in the United States, I have become increasingly impressed with how wide is the range of problems and industries for which it is appropriate to treat the economy as if it were competitive.[2]

---

[2]Milton Friedman, *Capitalism and Freedom* (Chicago: University of Chicago Press, 1962), p. 120.

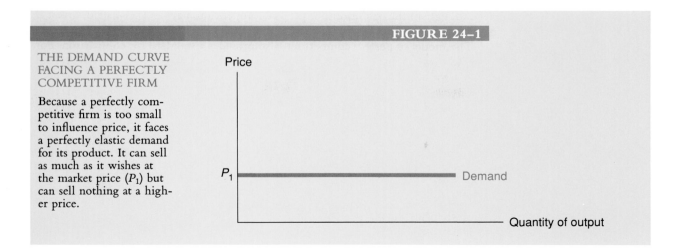

FIGURE 24–1

THE DEMAND CURVE
FACING A PERFECTLY
COMPETITIVE FIRM

Because a perfectly competitive firm is too small
to influence price, it faces
a perfectly elastic demand
for its product. It can sell
as much as it wishes at
the market price (P_1) but
can sell nothing at a higher price.

EXHIBIT 24–2

THE INDIVIDUAL FARMER AS A PRICE TAKER

According to the 1982 Census of Agriculture, 436,000 U.S. farms raised wheat. Harvesting 77.9 million acres, they produced 2.8 billion bushels. Worldwide, wheat production totaled 17.7 billion bushels. An even larger number of farms produced corn and soybeans (see Table 24-2). The number of farms has shrunk slightly since the census but remains high.

Admittedly, the large farms produce much of the output, but even they account for a small share of the market. In 1982, the largest 65,000 U.S. farms harvested only 20 percent of U.S. cropland. Even the largest farm was too small to appreciably affect supply.

A second requirement of perfect competition is that firms produce a homogeneous output. Again, this condition is satisfied. For each grade

and variety of wheat, each farm's output is identical. Buyers do not care where the wheat comes from.

The assumptions about entry/exit and perfect information also hold, at least approximately. Every year new farmers start growing wheat, while others reemploy the land in other crops or leave farming altogether. No significant barriers obstruct movement into or out of this industry. Finally, information about markets is widely available. Buyers and sellers know crop estimates, level of sales, and related facts. At any time, farmers know what they can sell their wheat for.

The end result is that individual wheat farmers are price takers. None is large enough or powerful enough to influence the price of wheat.

TABLE 24-2

NUMBER OF U.S. FARMS AND PRODUCTION BY CROP, 1982

Crop	Number of farms selling (in thousands)	Acres harvested (in millions)	Units of output (in millions)
Corn for grain	505	72.7	8235 bushels
Wheat	436	77.9	2765 bushels
Soybeans	508	69.4	2190 bushels
Hay	300	59.8	149 tons

Source: U.S. Department of Commerce, *Statistical Abstract of the United States, 1985,* Tables 1122, 1166.

Even though all the conditions for perfect competition may not be satisfied, this still may be the most appropriate framework for analysis.

The model of perfect competition also provides a standard for comparison. For example, monopolists often are accused of charging high prices. But what does "high" mean? A relevant interpretation is given by comparing price under monopoly with price under perfect competition. Because perfect competition is in some sense *ideal,* it is the logical basis for comparison. It may even serve as a target for government policy.

PRODUCTION IN THE SHORT RUN

How much output should a perfectly competitive firm produce? We tackle this issue first in the short run and then in the long run. In the short run at least one input (e.g., plant size) is fixed. The production decision therefore centers on the most profitable level of output given the constraint of the fixed inputs. In the long run the firm has greater flexibility; since no inputs are fixed, it can switch to a larger plant or a smaller plant. This gives the firm a greater opportunity to affect its average costs. Long-run adjustments in output are also greater at the industry level. An industry can expand in the long run as new firms enter or shrink as existing firms leave.

Although long-run adjustments are addressed shortly, the present section focuses on the short run. We begin by examining the conditions for profit maximization. What level of output maximizes short-run profits for a perfectly competitive firm? Two equivalent approaches are presented. The first focuses on total revenue and total costs; the second centers on price and marginal cost.

Profit Maximization—Comparing Total Revenue and Total Cost

Because profit is defined as total revenue minus total cost, a straightforward approach to profit maximization is to (1) compute total revenue and total cost for each potential level of output; (2) subtract total cost from total revenue, yielding the profit possible at the various levels of output; and (3) select that level of output for which profit is greatest.

To illustrate this approach we use the cost schedules from Table 23-3. The total variable cost and total cost schedules are reproduced in Table 24-3. Total fixed cost for the firm is $120, the difference between total cost and total variable cost. To save space the schedule for total fixed cost is omitted from Table 24-3.

Total revenue is the product of price times quantity. Therefore, the total revenue that this firm can earn from production depends on the output price. Column 4 presents the total revenue schedule for a price of $60. If the firm sells one unit of output it receives $60; if it sells two units it receives $120, and so on. Column 5 indicates the profit (or loss) that can be earned at various levels of output. It is simply the difference between total revenue (column 4) and total cost (column 3). For example, if the firm produces two units of output it receives $120 in total revenue but incurs $204 in costs. The result is a loss of $84.

Given a price of $60, how much output should the firm produce? From column 5, we see that the maximum profit possible is $95. This is the amount that is earned if the firm produces nine units of output. For any other level of output, profit is less than $95. Figure 24-2 (page 550) illustrates the situation diagramatically. The difference between total revenue and total cost is greatest for nine units of output; therefore, to maximize profit the firm must produce nine units of output.

	TABLE 24-3							

THE PROFIT-MAXIMIZING LEVEL OF OUTPUT FOR (a) P = $60, (b) P = $40, (c) P = $20

Costs			Price = $60		Price = $40		Price = $20	
(1) q	(2) TVC	(3) TC	(4) TR	(5) Profit	(6) TR	(7) Profit	(8) TR	(9) Profit
0	$ 0	$120	$ 0	−$120	$ 0	−$120	$ 0	−$120
1	50	170	60	− 110	40	− 130	20	− 150
2	84	204	120	− 84	80	− 124	40	− 164
3	108	228	180	− 48	120	− 108	60	− 168
4	127	247	240	− 7	160	− 87	80	− 167
5	150	270	300	30	200	− 70	100	− 170
6	180	300	360	60	240	− 60	120	− 180
7	218	338	420	82	280	− 58	140	− 198
8	266	386	480	94	320	− 66	160	− 226
9	325	445	540	95	360	− 85	180	− 265
10	400	520	600	80	400	− 120	200	− 320
11	495	615	660	45	440	− 175	220	− 395
12	612	732	720	− 12	480	− 252	240	− 492

If a firm produces, it should choose that level of output for which TR − TC is greatest. This corresponds to 9 units when P = $60 and 7 units when P = $40. If P = $20, the firm shuts down, since TR < TVC for all output.

The preceding analysis is based on a price of $60. With a different price, total revenue for the firm also differs. Column 6 presents the firm's total revenue schedule when the price is $40 (TR = $40 × q). An examination of column 7, listing profits, reveals that all the numbers are negative. At a price of $40 the firm cannot earn a profit, no matter how much it produces.

Shutting Down
Temporarily halting operations; producing no output in the current period. This limits the firm's loss to its fixed costs.

Does this mean that the firm should produce nothing? That is, should the firm **shut down?** Clearly not. If it ceases operations in the current period, it loses $120, the fixed costs of production. If, instead, it produces seven units of output, it can cut its loss to $58. No one is in business to lose money, but sometimes there is no alternative. In such cases the best option is to minimize loss. Given a price of $40, losses are minimized at an output level of seven units.

Suppose the price falls to $20. The total revenue and profit schedules based on a price of $20 are given in columns 8 and 9. Once again the firm is destined to lose money. This should come as no surprise. If the firm cannot make a profit when the price is $40, it cannot do so at a price of $20. What is different about these two cases is that, given a price of $20, production simply exacerbates the firm's loss. The minimum possible loss, $120, occurs when the firm produces nothing. Given a price of $20, the firm should shut down.

YOUR TURN

MINIMIZING LOSSES—A GRAPHICAL ACCOUNT
(a) On the same diagram, graph the total cost curve of Table 24-3 and the total revenue curve when price = $40. For which level of output is the vertical distance between the two curves minimized? (b) On another diagram, graph the total cost curve and the total revenue curve when price = $20. For which level of output are the two curves closest?

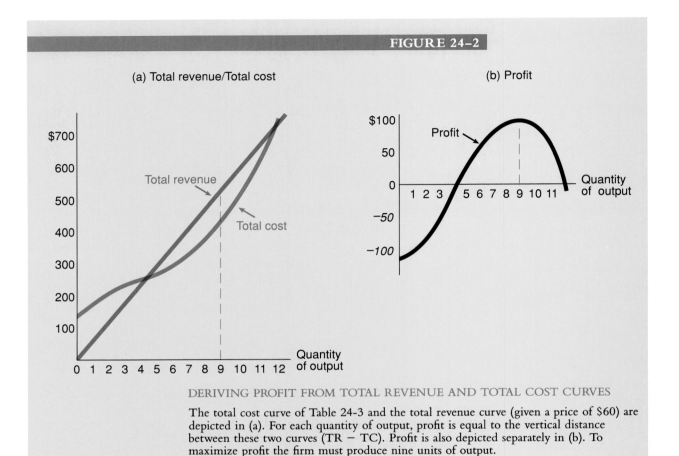

FIGURE 24–2

DERIVING PROFIT FROM TOTAL REVENUE AND TOTAL COST CURVES

The total cost curve of Table 24-3 and the total revenue curve (given a price of $60) are depicted in (a). For each quantity of output, profit is equal to the vertical distance between these two curves (TR − TC). Profit is also depicted separately in (b). To maximize profit the firm must produce nine units of output.

Shutting Down—the General Rule   The preceding example demonstrates two points. (1) Sometimes a firm should produce in the short run even though it loses money. (2) At some sufficiently low price the firm is better off shutting down. But exactly when should a firm produce, and under what conditions does it make sense to halt operations? *The firm should produce in the short run if total revenue from production exceeds total variable cost. If total revenue is below total variable cost at all levels of output, the firm should shut down.*

In the short run, fixed costs are sunk costs: regardless of whether or not the firm produces, they cannot be avoided. As such they are irrelevant for decisions in the short run. The firm has control only over its variable costs. Therefore, in deciding whether or not to produce in the short run, the firm compares total revenue with total variable cost (not total cost).

If the firm does not produce it loses an amount equal to its fixed costs. If production can trim these losses, or eliminate them, it should be undertaken. This occurs when production contributes more to revenues than it adds to costs—that is, when total revenue exceeds total variable cost. On the other hand, production makes no sense if it adds to a firm's losses—which is what happens when total revenue is less than total variable cost. Therefore, a necessary condition for production is:

$$TR \geq TVC$$

[handwritten notes in left margin:]
TR ≥ TVC
TR ≤ TVC
firm should
shut down

In our foregoing example, this condition was satisfied given a price of $60 or $40. It was not satisfied for a price of $20, which is why the firm shut down in the final case.

The preceding analysis explains why businesses sometimes operate despite losing money. It is not that those running a company are unaware of the losses, which in some instances may be quite heavy (see Exhibit 24-3). Rather, they have reached the conclusion that, regardless of the level of output, their company will lose money in the current period. They continue to produce because they believe losses would be even greater if they shut down.

A Restatement　　The preceding analysis can be summarized as follows. Firms make two types of production decisions. The first concerns whether or not to produce. The second centers on the level of output once the decision has been made to produce. The profit-maximizing firm is guided by two principles: (1) *produce only if TR ≥ TVC* and (2) *if production is to occur, choose that level of output for which TR − TC is greatest.*

Profit Maximization—Comparing Marginal Revenue and Marginal Cost

Rather than implement the preceding approach, economists generally rely on a second, equivalent method for determining the profit-maximizing level of output. Whereas the previous approach emphasized total cost and total revenue, the alternative focuses on marginal cost and marginal revenue.

Marginal Revenue
The increase in total revenue associated with a one-unit increase in output.

Marginal Revenue　　**Marginal revenue** measures the increase in total revenue that the firm receives from selling one more unit of output. In the model of perfect competition (and only in perfect competition), marginal revenue coincides with price. Because the perfectly competitive firm is a price taker, each additional unit sold adds to total revenue an amount equal to its price. This is illustrated in Figure 24-3(a) (page 552). Given a perfectly elastic demand curve at price P_1, the

---

EXHIBIT 24-3

DESPITE LOSSES, TWA KEEPS FLYING

Trans World Airlines lost $170 million in the first three months of 1986 and another $87 million in the next three months.[3] A weaker U.S. dollar was partially to blame. This raised the cost of visiting foreign countries, thereby reducing international travel. Increased terrorist activity in early 1986 also cost the company ticket sales overseas. Finally, a strike by flight attendants contributed more than $100 million to losses.

Given this unfavorable climate, did it make sense to keep the planes flying? Definitely. Airline analysts agree that, because of the tremendous fixed costs of operating a major airline, TWA would have incurred substantially greater losses had it shut down.

Business later improved as concern over terrorism abated, the strike ended, and fuel costs declined. But TWA wisely decided to keep flying and not to wait for this upturn. Even during the lean months, ticket revenues exceeded the variable costs of operating the airline.

---

[3]These are estimates of accounting profits provided by the company. But economic profits, properly defined, were also negative during this period.

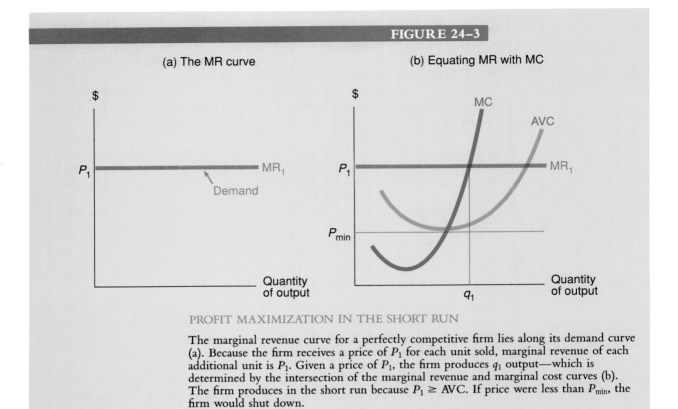

FIGURE 24–3

(a) The MR curve

(b) Equating MR with MC

PROFIT MAXIMIZATION IN THE SHORT RUN

The marginal revenue curve for a perfectly competitive firm lies along its demand curve (a). Because the firm receives a price of P_1 for each unit sold, marginal revenue of each additional unit is P_1. Given a price of P_1, the firm produces q_1 output—which is determined by the intersection of the marginal revenue and marginal cost curves (b). The firm produces in the short run because $P_1 \geq AVC$. If price were less than P_{min}, the firm would shut down.

firm receives an additional P_1 in revenue for each additional unit of output it sells ($MR = P_1$). Thus, the firm's marginal revenue curve (MR_1) is a horizontal line drawn at the price P_1.

MR = MC If the firm produces, it maximizes profit by producing up to the point where marginal revenue equals marginal cost (MR = MC). This is given by the intersection of the marginal revenue and marginal cost curves. In Figure 24-3(b) this occurs at output level q_1. At output levels below q_1, marginal revenue is greater than marginal cost. This means that another unit of output contributes more to revenue than to cost—it adds to a firm's profit or decreases its loss. As long as marginal revenue exceeds marginal cost, the firm continues to expand its output. Therefore, production continues until point q_1.[4]

    Why doesn't the firm produce more than q_1 output? If it did, the additional output would cost more to produce than it generated in revenue (MC > MR). Because this would reduce the firm's profits or increase its losses, the firm does not produce beyond q_1. The profit-maximizing firm produces only to the point where MR = MC.

---

[4]When dealing with whole units of output, there is often no level of output for which marginal revenue equals marginal cost. In such a case, the firm should produce the highest level of output for which marginal revenue exceeds marginal cost. For example, in Figure 24-3(b), if $q_1 = 10\ 1/2$ machines, the firm should produce 10 machines.

THE BORN LOSER ®by Art Sansom

Source: Reprinted by permission of NEA, Inc.

P ≥ AVC   The preceding was based on the assumption that the firm does in fact choose to produce in the current period. But as you recall, unless the firm receives a sufficiently high price for its output it shuts down. Therefore, before deciding how much to produce, the firm must first decide whether or not to produce. That decision is based on the relationship between price and average variable cost.

We previously showed that the firm will produce only when:

$$\text{TR} \geq \text{TVC}$$

Because $\text{TR} = P \times q$ and $\text{TVC} = \text{AVC} \times q$, this requirement can be restated as:

$$P \times q \geq \text{AVC} \times q$$

Dividing both sides by q yields the following equivalent expression:

$$P \geq \text{AVC}$$

The profit-maximizing firm produces only when $P \geq \text{AVC}$. If for all levels of output $P < \text{AVC}$, the firm shuts down.

In terms of Figure 24-3(b), the firm produces only when it receives a price of $P_{\min}$ or higher, where $P_{\min}$ is given by the minimum value of the average variable cost curve. For $P \geq P_{\min}$ there is some level of output for which $P \geq \text{AVC}$. But for $P < P_{\min}$ price is less than average variable cost for all levels of output, so the firm shuts down. Because $P_1 > P_{\min}$, the firm in Figure 24-3(b) produces in the short run.

Short-Run Profit or Loss   Profit for the firm can be computed with the aid of the ATC curve. Total profit is profit per unit times the number of units sold: $(P - \text{ATC}) \times q$.[5] When price is greater than average total cost, the firm earns an economic profit; when price is less than average total cost, the firm incurs a loss. Both possibilities are depicted in Figure 24-4 (page 554). The firm in (a) produces q_1 output, earning a profit of $P_1 - \text{ATC}_1$ on each unit sold. Total profit is $(P_1 - \text{ATC}_1) \times q_1$, which is represented by the shaded area in Figure 24-4 (a).

---

[5]To see that this is equivalent to our definition, note that:

$$\begin{aligned} \text{profit} &= \text{TR} - \text{TC} \\ &= P \times q - \text{ATC} \times q \\ &= (P - \text{ATC}) \times q \end{aligned}$$

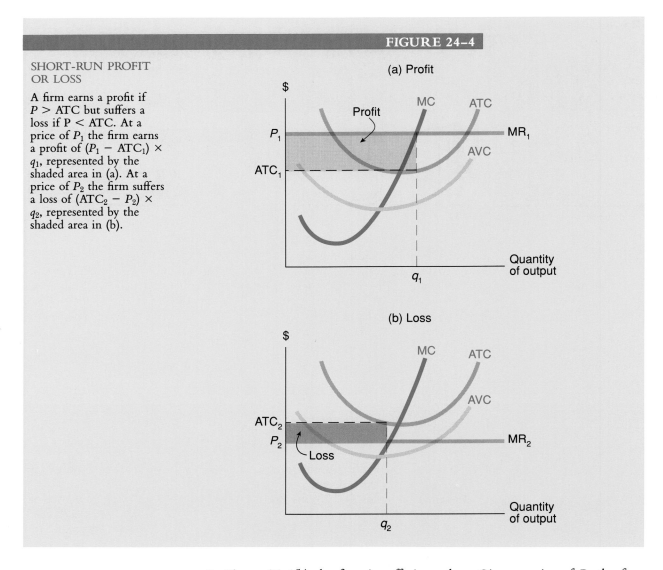

FIGURE 24-4

SHORT-RUN PROFIT
OR LOSS

A firm earns a profit if
$P > ATC$ but suffers a
loss if $P < ATC$. At a
price of P_1 the firm earns
a profit of $(P_1 - ATC_1) \times q_1$, represented by the
shaded area in (a). At a
price of P_2 the firm suffers
a loss of $(ATC_2 - P_2) \times q_2$, represented by the
shaded area in (b).

(a) Profit

(b) Loss

In Figure 24-4(b) the firm is suffering a loss. Given a price of P_2 the firm
produces q_2 amount of output (where $MR_2 = MC$). At this level of output, price is
less than average total cost ($P_2 < ATC_2$). Nonetheless, the firm produces because
price exceeds average variable cost. Although the firm is not recovering all its costs,
the price is high enough to more than cover variable costs.

YOUR TURN

NORMAL PROFIT
Illustrate diagrammatically the situation where a profit-maximizing firm earns a normal
profit (i.e., economic profit equals zero). At the profit-maximizing level of output, how do
the values of average total cost and price compare?

Summary To maximize profit the firm must satisfy two requirements: (1) *produce only if* P ≥ *AVC and* (2) *if production occurs, produce up to the point where MR = MC.* When the firm does produce, it earns a profit when *P* > ATC but suffers a loss when *P* < ATC.

Our Example Revisited

Our earlier example helped illustrate the first approach to profit maximization (comparing total revenue and total cost). Let us return to that example, but this time applying the rules of the second approach (MR = MC, *P* ≥ AVC). Instead of examining the firm's TVC and TC schedules (as we did in Table 24-3), we look at the firm's cost data from a different perspective. Table 24-4 presents three cost schedules: average variable cost, average total cost, and marginal cost—all consistent with the cost schedules of Table 24-3.

Let us determine the profit-maximizing level of output for each of three prices. Assume initially that the price is $60. Then marginal revenue for each level of output is $60 (see column 5). Marginal revenue exceeds marginal cost for the ninth unit of output ($60 > $59) but not for the tenth unit ($60 < $75). Therefore, if the firm produces it should produce nine units of output. But is the firm better off shutting down? Because price exceeds average variable cost at nine units of output ($60 > $36.11), the firm determines that production should proceed. Given a price of $60, the firm produces nine units of output in order to maximize profit.

The actual level of profits can be computed by plugging the appropriate value of ATC into the formula: profit = (*P* − ATC) × *q*. For example, if six units are sold, ATC = $50; therefore, total profit equals ($60 − $50) × 6 = $60. Column 6 of

TABLE 24-4

FINDING THE PROFIT-MAXIMIZING LEVEL OF OUTPUT BY COMPARING MR AND MC

	Costs			Price = $60		Price = $40		Price = $20	
(1) q	(2) AVC*	(3) ATC*	(4) MC	(5) MR	(6) Profit	(7) MR	(8) Profit	(9) MR	(10) Profit
0					−$120		−$120		−$120
1	$50.00	$170.00	$ 50	$60	− 110	$40	− 130	$20	− 150
2	42.00	102.00	34	60	− 84	40	− 124	20	− 164
3	36.00	76.00	24	60	− 48	40	− 108	20	− 168
4	31.75	61.75	19	60	− 7	40	− 87	20	− 167
5	30.00	54.00	23	60	30	40	− 70	20	− 170
6	30.00	50.00	30	60	60	40	− 60	20	− 180
7	31.14	48.29	38	60	82	40	− 58	20	− 198
8	33.25	48.25	48	60	94	40	− 66	20	− 226
9	36.11	49.44	59	60	95	40	− 85	20	− 265
10	40.00	52.00	75	60	80	40	− 120	20	− 320
11	45.00	55.91	95	60	45	40	− 175	20	− 395
12	51.00	61.00	117	60	− 12	40	− 252	20	− 492

*Numbers are rounded to nearest cent.

To maximize profit, the firm should produce when *P* = $60 or *P* = $40 (since *P* > AVC) but not when *P* = $20 (since *P* < AVC). Once it decides to produce, the firm compares MR and MC. The profit-maximizing level of output is 9 when *P* = $60 and 7 when *P* = $40.

Table 24-4 presents the profit schedule for different levels of output given a price of $60. It confirms that profits are maximized at an output of nine units. Given $P = $60, the firm can earn $95 in profit.

When the price falls to $40, the firm reduces output to seven units. This is the last level of output for which marginal revenue ($40) exceeds marginal cost. Moreover, at seven units of output, price ($40) exceeds average variable cost ($31.14), indicating that production should occur. Even though the firm is losing money (see column 8), this is better than shutting down—in which case losses would swell to $120.

Finally, consider a price of $20. Although marginal revenue is greater than marginal cost for the fourth unit of output, the firm should not produce. If it does, price is less than average variable cost. This tells the firm that its best option is to shut down, thereby limiting its loss to $120.

An examination of Tables 24-3 and 24-4 reveals that, as advertised, the two approaches to profit maximization yield identical answers. Whether you rely on the total approach (comparing TR and TC) or the marginal approach (comparing MR and MC), you reach the same conclusion concerning the amount of output a firm should produce and the amount of profit it earns.

The Short-Run Supply Curve of a Perfectly Competitive Firm

Thus far the discussion has focused on the production decisions of a perfectly competitive firm, where price plays a central role in the analysis. Price for the individual firm is given—the firm is a price taker. But how is that price determined? To obtain the answer it is necessary to derive the short-run supply curve, first for the individual firm and then for the industry in which the firm is selling.

The firm's short-run supply curve is derived from its marginal cost curve. To be explicit: *the firm's short-run supply curve is given by the segment of its marginal cost curve that lies above average variable cost.* This is illustrated in Figure 24-5.

As previously indicated, production occurs only when $P \geq P_{min}$, where P_{min} equals the minimum value of average variable cost. At P_{min} the firm is indifferent

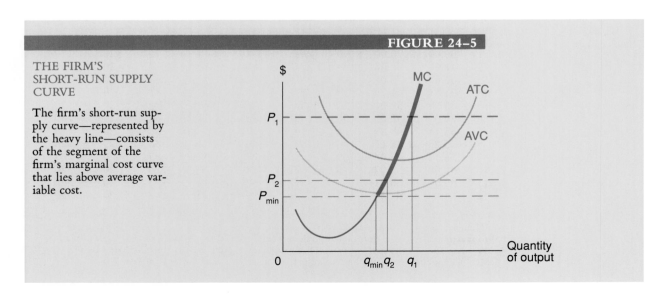

FIGURE 24-5

THE FIRM'S SHORT-RUN SUPPLY CURVE

The firm's short-run supply curve—represented by the heavy line—consists of the segment of the firm's marginal cost curve that lies above average variable cost.

between producing q_{min} and shutting down. In either case, its loss equals its fixed costs. For prices above P_{min} the firm supplies output, and the marginal cost curve indicates how much (since the firm produces to the point where $P = MC$). For example, when $P = P_1$ the firm supplies q_1 output. When $P = P_2$, output falls to q_2. In other words, the marginal cost curve above minimum average variable cost reveals the relationship between price and quantity supplied. Therefore, this segment of the marginal cost curve must be the firm's short-run supply curve.

The Industry's Short-Run Supply Curve

The Industry's Short-Run Supply Curve
A curve indicating the relationship between the price of a good and the amount supplied by the industry in the short run. (In the short run the number of firms in the industry is fixed.)

The industry's short-run supply curve is derived from the short-run supply curves of firms currently in the industry. Because the number of firms is fixed in the short run, industry output can be increased only by increasing the output of existing firms. The industry supply curve indicates the aggregate quantity supplied, at each price, by all firms in the industry. When input prices do not change as the industry expands, the short-run supply curve for the industry is obtained by adding (horizontally) the short-run supply curves of each firm in the industry. This is illustrated in Figure 24-6.

Even though competitive industries have many firms, for simplicity we demonstrate this technique for an industry with two firms. The same process

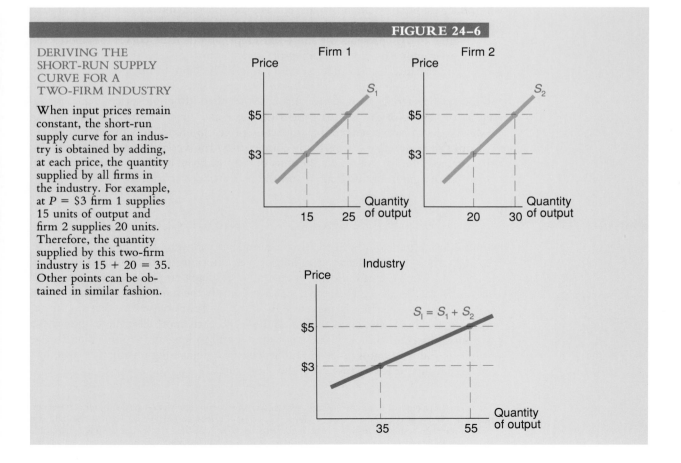

FIGURE 24–6

DERIVING THE SHORT-RUN SUPPLY CURVE FOR A TWO-FIRM INDUSTRY

When input prices remain constant, the short-run supply curve for an industry is obtained by adding, at each price, the quantity supplied by all firms in the industry. For example, at $P = \$3$ firm 1 supplies 15 units of output and firm 2 supplies 20 units. Therefore, the quantity supplied by this two-firm industry is $15 + 20 = 35$. Other points can be obtained in similar fashion.

applies, however, regardless of the number of firms in the industry. At a price of $3 firm 1 supplies 15 units of output and firm 2 supplies 20 units. The total amount supplied by this industry for $P = \$3$ is $15 + 20 = 35$ units of output. When price rises to $5 the two firms supply, respectively, 25 and 30 units of output. Altogether, 55 units are supplied by the industry.

In the event that all firms in the industry have identical cost curves, deriving the industry's short-run supply curve is even simpler. For example, if the industry contained 1000 firms all similar to firm 1, each would supply 25 units when the price was $5. Therefore, the quantity supplied by the industry at this price would be $1000 \times 25 = 25,000$. More generally, the amount supplied by the industry at any price would simply be 1000 times the amount supplied by firm 1.

The aggregation procedure just discussed is based on the assumption that input prices remain constant as the industry expands. Later in the chapter we explain why input prices might change. When input prices do change, derivation of the supply curve becomes more complicated.[6]

Short-Run Equilibrium for the Industry

Given the industry's supply curve, we are now in a position to describe short-run equilibrium for the industry and, in the process, explain how price is determined for the perfectly competitive firm. In addition to industry supply, it is necessary to introduce industry demand. This consists of the demand by all buyers of the industry's product.

Figure 24-7(b) presents the short-run supply and demand curves for a perfectly competitive industry. Equilibrium price and quantity for the industry are determined by the intersection of these two curves. The equilibrium price, $5, is then taken as given by all firms in the industry. Figure 24-7(a) depicts the situation for an individual perfectly competitive firm. Note that although price depends on aggregate supply of the industry, the firm represents such a minuscule part of the industry that it has no perceptible impact on price, no matter how much it supplies. It is for this reason that the perfectly competitive firm is considered a price taker. In this example the firm produces 25 units of output, given by the intersection of the price (or marginal revenue) curve and the marginal cost curve.

LONG-RUN EQUILIBRIUM IN PERFECT COMPETITION

Short-run equilibrium, both for the firm and the industry, are depicted in Figure 24-7. But how can we characterize long-run equilibrium? In the long run all inputs are variable. Firms can build larger plants, in response to profit opportunities, or switch to smaller plants. Even the number of firms in the industry may change in the long run. Profits lure new firms to the industry and losses cause some existing firms to leave the industry, since their resources can earn more elsewhere. For these reasons short-run equilibrium may not correspond to long-run equilibrium. In the long run, industry output may expand or contract, depending on whether firms are earning profits or losing money in the short run.

---

[6]When input prices increase as the industry expands, the short-run supply curve of the industry is steeper than when input prices remain constant. With higher input prices, cost curves for firms in the industry shift upward. In response, firms scale back the amount of output they are willing to sell. Therefore, although higher output prices still induce firms to increase the quantity supplied, firms increase quantity by a lesser amount when input prices also rise.

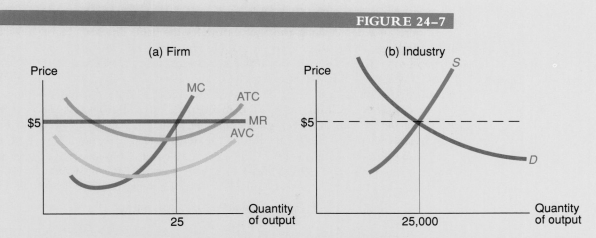

FIGURE 24–7

SHORT-RUN EQUILIBRIUM FOR A PERFECTLY COMPETITIVE INDUSTRY AND ONE OF ITS FIRMS

The equilibrium price and quantity are determined by the intersection of industry supply and demand curves. The equilibrium price, $5, is taken as given by the individual firm. To maximize profits, the firm produces 25 units of output.

Equilibrium refers to a state of balance. In long-run equilibrium the firm has no incentive to change its operations: it is producing the desired amount of output and its plant is just the right size. The desired amount of output, of course, is the amount that maximizes profits. In the long run, profits are maximized when marginal revenue or, equivalently, price equals long-run marginal cost. The logic is similar to that applied in our short-run analysis. The only difference is that, in the long run, all inputs are variable. Therefore, when the firm increases its output it also increases its plant size. In the short run, of course, plant size is fixed.

Long-run equilibrium requires that the firm produce its output at the lowest possible long-run cost. The firm must not be able to produce the same level of output more cheaply by switching to a different plant size. This means that the firm must be operating on its long-run average cost curve. Thus, in long-run equilibrium firms produce the profit-maximizing level of output with the optimal plant size.

Another condition for long-run equilibrium is that firms earn zero economic profits (i.e., normal profits). In other words, price must equal average total cost. To see why, suppose instead that firms in the industry were earning positive economic profits. Because entry into a perfectly competitive industry is easy, new firms would be moving into the industry to take advantage of profits there. Alternatively, if firms were suffering losses, some would be leaving the industry and reemploying their resources elsewhere, in order to earn higher returns.

An industry cannot be in a state of balance if firms are still in the process of moving into or out of the industry. Long-run equilibrium requires that all adjustments be completed, that the industry be at rest. As long as economic profits are positive or negative, the industry is not at rest. Firms are either entering the industry (when profits are positive) or leaving the industry (when profits are negative). Only when economic profits equal zero is there no incentive for additional entry or exit. Therefore, only when economic profits equal zero can an industry be in long-run equilibrium.

Long-run equilibrium requires that (1) firms maximize profits ($P = \text{LRMC}$) and (2) firms earn normal profits ($P = \text{LRAC}$).

Figure 24-8 depicts long-run equilibrium for the firm. The firm, facing a price of P_1, produces q_1 output. The firm is maximizing profits ($P = \text{LRMC}$) and earning normal profits ($P = \text{LRAC}$). These two conditions, in turn, imply that LRMC = LRAC. (When $P = \text{LRMC}$ and $P = \text{LRAC}$ then LRMC = LRAC.) As Chapter 23 explained, marginal cost and average cost are equal at only one point—where average cost is at a minimum (point E in Figure 24-8). Thus *long-run equilibrium implies that the firm must be producing at the minimum point of its long-run average cost curve.*

Because the firm is producing q_1 with the optimal plant size, point E is also the minimum point on the firm's short-run average cost curve. Consequently, at point E short-run marginal cost equals short-run average cost (SRMC = SRAC). Putting everything together, in long-run equilibrium the following equality holds:

$$P = \text{LRMC} = \text{LRAC} = \text{SRAC} = \text{SRMC}$$

An implication of the preceding analysis is that perfect competition forces firms to produce at the lowest possible average cost in the long run. Firms that do not have the optimal plant size cannot survive in the long run. Nor can firms that operate their plants at the wrong level, producing either too much or too little. To remain in business in the long run, a firm must earn at least normal profits. In perfect competition this occurs only when the firm produces efficiently—that is, at the lowest possible average cost. Firms that are not efficient cannot compete with those that are, and ultimately are driven from the industry.

Long-Run Supply for the Industry

Long-run equilibrium for the firm is represented in Figure 24-8, but how can we illustrate long-run equilibrium at the industry level? Equilibrium, whether short-run or long-run, requires that industry demand equal industry supply. The only

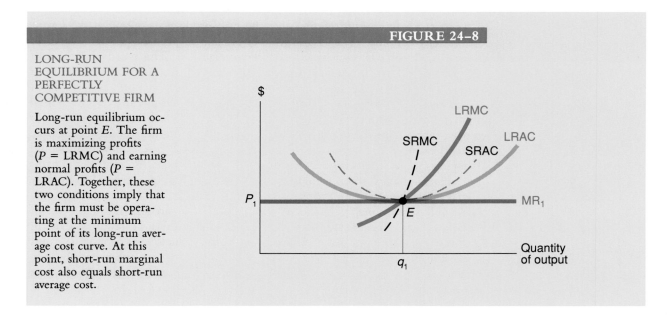

FIGURE 24-8

LONG-RUN EQUILIBRIUM FOR A PERFECTLY COMPETITIVE FIRM

Long-run equilibrium occurs at point E. The firm is maximizing profits ($P = \text{LRMC}$) and earning normal profits ($P = \text{LRAC}$). Together, these two conditions imply that the firm must be operating at the minimum point of its long-run average cost curve. At this point, short-run marginal cost also equals short-run average cost.

difference between the short run and the long run is that entry and exit of firms affects industry supply in the long run.

Different perfectly competitive industries have different **industry long-run supply curves.** The shape depends on what happens to input prices (and therefore cost curves) as new firms enter the industry. In **constant-cost industries,** input prices remain constant as the industry expands; in **increasing-cost industries,** input prices increase; and in **decreasing-cost industries,** input prices decrease. The following sections derive the long-run supply curve and describe long-run equilibrium for all three cases.

Constant-Cost Industries   Assume an industry is initially in long-run equilibrium (illustrated at point A in Figure 24-9). At the equilibrium price (P_1) the firm produces q_1 output and the industry produces Q_1. Now assume further that demand for the industry's product increases, perhaps because of an increase in population or a change in tastes. Let us work through what happens, first in the short run and then in the long run. Let S_1 denote the initial short-run supply curve, based on the number of firms in the industry prior to the increase in demand. Once demand increases, the industry moves from point A on the short-run supply curve to point B. Price rises from P_1 to P_2, and industry output expands to Q_2. At the higher price, existing firms increase production in the short run to q_2 in order to maximize profits.

The situation just outlined corresponds to short-run equilibrium, but does it represent long-run equilibrium? Obviously not. At q_2, firms in the industry are

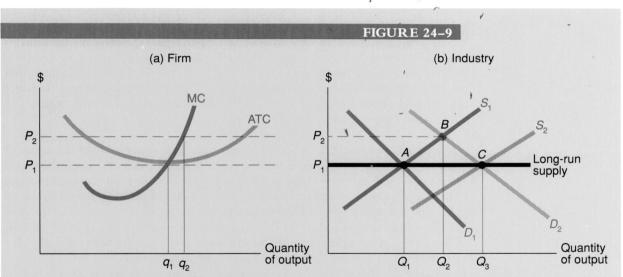

FIGURE 24-9

(a) Firm

(b) Industry

LONG-RUN EQUILIBRIUM IN A CONSTANT-COST INDUSTRY

Initially the industry is in equilibrium at point A, producing Q_1 output and selling it at price P_1. At this price the firm sells q_1 output, earning normal profits. If industry demand increases to D_2, price rises to P_2 in the short run and industry output rises to Q_2, as individual firms increase output to q_2. Firms are now earning economic profits ($P > $ ATC), which attracts additional firms to the industry. Their entry leads to a new short-run supply curve, S_2, and a new long run equilibrium, point C. At P_1 the firm once again produces q_1 output; however, because of the additional firms, industry output rises to Q_3.

earning economic profits, since $P_2 >$ ATC. In response, new firms are drawn into the industry. With additional firms, industry output expands. This expansion is represented by a rightward shift in the short-run supply curve. Firms continue to enter the industry, and the supply curve continues to shift rightward, until profits are eliminated. This occurs at point C, where the short-run supply curve is S_2.

Because of the entry of new firms, the initial equilibrium price, P_1, is restored in the long run. Firms once again produce q_1 output, earning normal profits. There is no incentive for additional firms to enter the industry or for existing firms to leave. Point C therefore corresponds to long-run equilibrium.

The line running through point A (the initial equilibrium) and point C (the final equilibrium) is the industry's long-run supply curve. *For a perfectly competitive constant-cost industry, long-run supply is perfectly elastic.* An increase in demand leads to an increase in output but in the long run has no effect on price. P_1 is the only price consistent with long-run equilibrium, since it is the only price for which firms earn a normal profit.

What if, instead of increasing, demand shifts to the left? If demand falls, long-run equilibrium is once again established through a change in the number of firms in the industry, only now it is the exodus of firms that brings the industry back into equilibrium. Suppose the industry is initially at point C in Figure 24-9. If demand falls from D_2 to D_1, price initially falls below P_1, leading to short-run losses. Some firms leave the industry and, as they do, the short-run supply curve shifts leftward, raising price. This process continues until price returns to P_1. The new long-run equilibrium corresponds to a smaller number of firms, each producing q_1 output. As with an increase in demand, quantity changes in the long run but not price.

A key assumption of this analysis is that the firm's cost structure remains constant as the industry expands or contracts. Whether an industry contains 1000 firms or 10,000, the firm's cost curves are the same. It is because of this assumption that the industry is labeled a constant-cost industry. This assumption does not always hold, however, and in such cases the story has a different ending. To understand this, read on.

Increasing-Cost Industries   As an industry expands it requires larger quantities of inputs—additional labor, raw materials, machinery, and so forth. In constant-cost industries input prices remain fixed even as the industry purchases increasing amounts of inputs. Generally, however, an expansion of industry output drives up input prices. For example, an increase in the demand for wheat may raise the price of land, as wheat farmers bid away land from competing uses, or may increase the cost of irrigation, as farmers are forced to use more arid land. In such cases, the cost curves of wheat farmers shift upward as the industry expands.

Figure 24-10 illustrates long-run equilibrium for an increasing-cost industry. Initially the industry is in equilibrium at point A. Once again assume that demand for the industry's product increases, raising price in the short run to P_2. Because firms earn profits at this price new firms enter the industry, shifting the industry supply curve rightward. This is where the similarity with constant-cost industries ends. As the increasing-cost industry expands, its firms' cost curves shift upward. Profits are squeezed from two directions: price falls (as industry supply increases) and average cost rises (due to higher input prices).

This process continues until once again price equals average cost ($P_3 =$ ATC$_2$ in Figure 24-10a). Note that the price associated with the final equilibrium (P_3) exceeds the price at the initial equilibrium (P_1). This implies that an increased

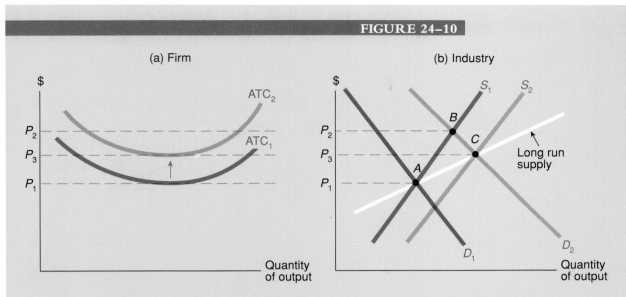

FIGURE 24–10

(a) Firm   (b) Industry

LONG-RUN EQUILIBRIUM IN AN INCREASING-COST INDUSTRY

An increase in industry demand raises price in the short run from P_1 to P_2. As new firms enter the industry, supply increases from S_1 to S_2. The expansion of industry output shifts the firm's average cost curve from ATC_1 to ATC_2. Because of higher unit costs, additional output will be supplied in the long run only at a price above the initial equilibrium price (i.e., $P_3 > P_1$). The long-run supply curve in an increasing-cost industry is upward sloping.

quantity is available in the long run only at a higher price. *The long-run supply curve of an increasing-cost industry slopes upward.* Available evidence indicates that most industries fall into the increasing-cost category—that is, most industries have upward-sloping supply curves in the long run as well as the short run.

Decreasing-Cost Industries   A third possibility exists, although it is rare in practice. As an industry expands, its firms may face *lower* input prices. For example, as the personal computer industry expands, its firms buy more and more microchips. This could lead to lower chip prices, perhaps due to economies of scale in the microchip industry. In such event, firms in the personal computer industry find that their cost curves shift lower as their industry expands. If average cost falls, the only way economic profits can be eliminated is if price falls below its initial level (see Figure 24-11, page 564). In that case, an increase in demand for the industry's product leads not only to increased output in the long run but also to a lower price. *The long-run supply curve of a decreasing-cost industry is downward sloping.*

AN EVALUATION OF PERFECT COMPETITION

Now that the mechanics of perfect competition have been studied, it is time to assess this market structure. In what ways is perfect competition the best of all possible worlds? In what ways does it fall short of the ideal? Certain government policies (e.g., antitrust laws) are predicated on the belief that society benefits when markets are made more competitive. What is the basis of this contention?

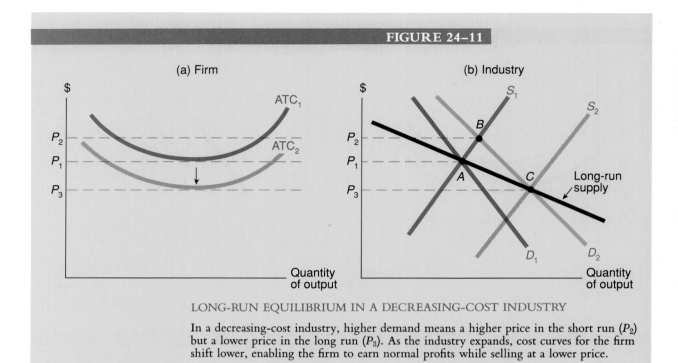

FIGURE 24-11

(a) Firm

(b) Industry

LONG-RUN EQUILIBRIUM IN A DECREASING-COST INDUSTRY

In a decreasing-cost industry, higher demand means a higher price in the short run (P_2) but a lower price in the long run (P_3). As the industry expands, cost curves for the firm shift lower, enabling the firm to earn normal profits while selling at a lower price.

In Praise of Perfect Competition

Productive Efficiency   One virtue of perfect competition is that it leads to output being produced in the long run at the lowest possible cost. Resources are being used efficiently. Firms cannot lower average cost of production by building a different plant size or operating their plant at a different level of output. To survive in the long run, firms must produce at the minimum point of their long-run average cost curves. This condition, known as **productive efficiency,** guarantees that an industry's output cannot be produced at a lower cost.

Productive Efficiency
An industry's output is produced at the lowest cost possible.

Not only is production efficient under perfect competition, but consumers pay a price just high enough to cover those costs. The requirement that firms earn only normal profits in the long run means that the market price is the minimum price producers require to supply that level of output. Price is inflated by neither unnecessary costs nor by excess profits. It is in this sense that price is kept to a minimum.

Efficient Allocation of Resources   Production may be efficient in the sense that average costs are minimized, but that by itself does not assure maximum consumer satisfaction. Firms may be producing the wrong mix of goods. For example, a country may be producing both barley and corn at their minimum average cost, but if it produces more barley than desired and not enough corn, then the economy is in some sense inefficient. In particular, it is inefficient in the way it allocates resources among its industries. It is overallocating resources to the production of barley—that is, funneling too many resources into this industry—and underallocating resources to the production of corn.

The price consumers are willing to pay for another unit of a good measures the value consumers place on that unit. Stated differently, price reflects the marginal benefit derived from a good. Marginal cost, on the other hand, measures the cost of producing another unit of the good. Think of it as the opportunity cost of the resources used to produce the additional output.

When price exceeds marginal cost, the value consumers place on an additional unit exceeds the cost of producing it. Therefore, consumers benefit from its production. But when price is less than marginal cost, the extra output should not be produced. The value consumers place on this additional output falls short of the costs of producing it. In other words, the resources required to produce the additional output are valued more highly in another industry. Thus, consumers benefit from additional production of a good when $P > MC$ and are made worse off when $P < MC$.

The ideal situation is for production to proceed up to the point where $P = MC$. The last unit produced would have a value that just matched the cost of producing it. When this occurs resources are said to be allocated efficiently. Resources cannot be redistributed among industries without reducing consumer satisfaction. Because price equals marginal cost under perfect competition, resources are allocated efficiently when all industries are perfectly competitive.

Efficient allocation of resources occurs when $P = MC$ in each industry.

Other Considerations   Apart from reasons of efficiency, some individuals favor perfect competition because it is consistent with maximum individual freedom. Decisions are made by individual consumers and producers, not dictated by some third party. There is no need for outside intervention. Individuals acting in their self-interest promote the public interest. For those who distrust government bureaucrats and dictators, this is an appealing arrangement. To quote Adam Smith:

> The statesman who should attempt to direct private people in what manner they ought to employ their capitals, would not only load himself with a most unnecessary attention, but assume an authority which could safely be trusted to no one and would be dangerous in the hands of a man who had folly and presumption enough to fancy himself fit to exercise it.[7]

There are no economic power brokers in the world of perfect competition. No individual consumer or business is powerful enough to rig the market, to pursue policies that economically harm other parties. Not only are resources allocated efficiently, some people consider the way they are allocated to be a virtue itself. Be that as it may, conditions exist in the real world that make perfect competition less than perfect.

Some Possible Drawbacks to Perfect Competition

Although perfect competition has some advantages, it may be impossible or undesirable for several reasons.

Economies of Scale   Perfect competition requires a particular technology, one in which economies of scale disappear when firm size is small. Costs of production are

---

[7]Same as 1, p. 423.

minimized when there are a large number of small firms each operating at the minimum point of its long-run average cost curve. Suppose, however, that an industry is characterized by extensive economies of scale. We cited several examples of such industries in Chapter 23 (e.g., automobiles, utilities, and breweries). In such industries costs of production are minimized when an industry contains very few firms, each operating a large plant. We return to this issue in Chapters 25 and 26. The point of the present discussion is this: when extensive economies of scale exist, it is neither efficient nor desirable for an industry to have a large number of small firms, as perfect competition requires.

Externalities   A stated advantage of perfect competition is that it leads to efficient allocation of resources. This is true, however, only when private producers pay the full cost of their production. When there are externalities—for example, pollution—resources are not allocated efficiently under perfect competition.

It is useful to distinguish between the private cost of production and the social cost. The *private cost* includes only those costs paid by the producer; the *social cost* adds to this figure any additional costs borne by society. Assume that production in an industry creates pollution that causes $1 billion worth of damage to the environment. This $1 billion is included in the social cost of production but excluded from the private cost, since firms do not actually pay these pollution costs.

For resources to be allocated efficiently from the perspective of society, price should equal social marginal cost—that is, the relevant marginal cost concept includes the added cost to society of the additional pollution. Under perfect competition, however, producers consider only the costs that they themselves must pay. Therefore, production occurs at the point where price equals private marginal cost. When private and social marginal cost diverge, perfect competition leads to an allocation of resources that is inefficient from the perspective of society. This issue is addressed in Chapter 34, along with ways to correct this misallocation.

Other Considerations   Some individuals criticize perfect competition on other grounds, including equity, innovation, and variety of products. Even if perfect competition would lead to efficient production and efficient allocation of resources among industries, some would not embrace it.

Perfect competition maximizes satisfaction of consumers subject to a given distribution of resources among members of society. Some individuals are wealthy, others are poor. If you do not like the initial distribution of resources, you will not like the distribution of products under perfect competition. Some critics are willing to sacrifice a certain amount of efficiency for greater equity—that is, for a more equal distribution of output among the populace. They consider perfect competition less than perfect because it does not conform to their notion of the ideal distribution of output.

Others contend that perfect competition may not be the optimal market structure for innovation. Why should a perfectly competitive firm invest in research and development if other firms, which do not bear these costs, can quickly adopt any new technology? Unless a firm can gain an edge over its competitors, it has little incentive to develop a new technology. Concentrated industries (i.e., those dominated by a few large firms) may prove more conducive to innovation because barriers to entry deny new firms access to the company's technology. Moreover, large noncompetitive firms may have more money to invest in research and development than small competitive firms. Therefore, some economists suggest that technological progress is likely to occur more rapidly when product markets are not perfectly competitive. We return to this argument in Chapter 26.

Finally, some believe that a world of perfect competition would be rather bland. Perfect competition does not allow for product differentiation among producers. Do we really want a world where all department stores stock the same merchandise, where clothing of one manufacturer is indistinguishable from clothing of other manufacturers, where all colas taste the same? Some would be willing to trade a little efficiency for product variety and greater consumer choice.

Before perfect competition can be fully evaluated vis-à-vis other market structures, we must examine these other market structures in more detail. That is the goal of the next two chapters.

SUMMARY

1. Markets differ from one another in terms of number of firms, ease of entry, type of product (homogeneous or differentiated), and ability of the firm to influence price. Economists recognize four market structures: perfect competition, monopoly, monopolistic competition, and oligopoly. An industry's price, level of output, potential for profits, and related matters all depend on its market structure.

2. Perfect competition requires a large number of buyers and sellers of a homogeneous product, free entry and exit, and perfect information. Under these conditions the firm is a price taker—that is, demand for the firm's product is perfectly elastic. Because of this, the marginal revenue from selling an additional unit of output equals the price.

3. To maximize profits in the short run a perfectly competitive firm must satisfy two conditions. (1) Produce only when TR $\geq$ TVC or, equivalently, $P \geq$ AVC. If this condition is not satisfied, the firm should shut down. (2) Produce that level of output for which TR $-$ TC is greatest. This means producing to the point where MR = MC.

4. The short-run supply curve of a perfectly competitive firm consists of that segment of its marginal cost curve that lies above average variable cost. For any given price, the marginal cost curve above average variable cost indicates the quantity of output the firm supplies to maximize profits. The industry's short-run supply curve is obtained by adding (horizontally) the short-run supply curves of all firms in the industry.

5. Short-run equilibrium for the industry requires that demand for the industry's product equal industry supply. Once the industry's price is determined, it is taken as given by individual firms in the industry.

6. Long-run equilibrium in perfect competition requires that firms maximize profits ($P =$ LRMC) and that firms earn only normal profits ($P =$ LRAC). These conditions are satisfied only when the firm produces at the minimum point of its long-run average cost curve. To survive in the long run, a perfectly competitive firm must produce efficiently—it must have the optimal plant size and operate this plant at the level that minimizes average cost.

7. The number of firms in an industry is fixed in the short run but may change in the long run. New firms enter an industry if it is profitable; some existing firms leave if the industry is losing money. Because of this, supply in the long run differs from supply in the short run.

8. The shape of the long-run supply curve depends on what happens to input prices as the industry expands. In constant-cost industries, long-run supply is perfectly elastic. Because input prices (and therefore cost curves) remain constant, there is no pressure in the long run for the output price to rise or fall. In increasing-cost industries, higher input prices lead to a higher output price and therefore to an upward-sloping supply curve in the long run. In decreasing-cost industries, lower input prices result in a downward-sloping supply curve.

9. Perfect competition has several appealing characteristics. Because of productive efficiency, an industry's output is produced at the lowest possible cost. Assuming that there are no

externalities, resources are also allocated efficiently across industries. Under these conditions, consumer satisfaction is maximized. Perfect competition is also consistent with maximum freedom of individuals.

10. Perfect competition is neither possible nor desirable when an industry has extensive economies of scale. In such a situation efficient production requires that an industry have a small number of firms, large in size, rather than many small firms. When private costs of production differ from social costs, resources are not allocated efficiently under perfect competition. Some people believe that perfect competition has other shortcomings: the distribution of output may be highly unequal, technological advances may not be as rapid as possible, and the choice of products may be limited.

KEY TERMS

market structure
free entry
free exit
perfect competition
price taker
shutting down
marginal revenue
the firm's short-run supply curve

the industry's short-run supply curve
the industry's long-run supply curve
constant-cost industry
increasing-cost industry
decreasing-cost industry
productive efficiency
efficient allocation of resources

STUDY QUESTIONS AND PROBLEMS

1. (a) Some industries produce a homogeneous product, others a differentiated product. Explain the difference between these two types of products.
(b) A large city may have hundreds of gasoline stations. Are they perfect substitutes for one another? What type of market structure best describes the retail gasoline market in Los Angeles? Why?
2. If no industry fully satisfies the assumptions of perfect competition, is there any reason to study this market structure? Defend your answer.
3. A perfectly competitive firm has fixed costs of $60 and the variable costs given in the following table:

q	1	2	3	4	5
TVC	$110	$200	$300	$420	$575

(These numbers come from the Your Turn section of Chapter 23.) How many units of output should the firm produce in the short run if (a) $P = \$95$, (b) $P = \$105$, (c) $P = \$115$, (d) $P = \$125$? How much profit would be earned in *each* case?
4. (a) Draw the short-run supply curve for the firm described in question 3. (b) Assume the industry contains 10,000 firms all identical to this firm. Draw the short-run supply curve for the industry.
5. Assume a firm is producing ten units of output. The marginal cost of the tenth unit is $50; the price is $40. If the firm wishes to maximize profit, should it increase production, decrease production, or leave production unchanged? Why?
6. Why does long-run equilibrium for a perfectly competitive firm occur at the minimum point of its LRAC curve?
7. As the trucking industry expands, it requires additional motor fuel. More fuel can be supplied only when the petroleum industry operates high-cost oil wells, which drives up the price of fuel. (a) Under these conditions would the trucking industry be characterized

as a constant-cost, an increasing-cost, or a decreasing-cost industry? (b) Suppose demand for trucking increases. How does this affect the price of trucking services in the long run?

8. Assume the price of shirts is $20 and the price of pants is $30. The marginal cost of producing each is $25. Are resources being allocated efficiently? Which industry, if either, should receive additional resources? (Assume there are no externalities.)

9. For many industries Congress has erected barriers that restrict access of foreign producers to U.S. markets, thereby limiting foreign competition. How are such restrictions on the supply of foreign producers likely to affect the prices paid by U.S. consumers?

ANSWERS TO YOUR TURN

(a) Minimum loss (TC − TR) is at $q = 7$.
(b) Minimum loss is at $q = 0$.

MINIMIZING LOSSES, A GRAPHICAL ACCOUNT

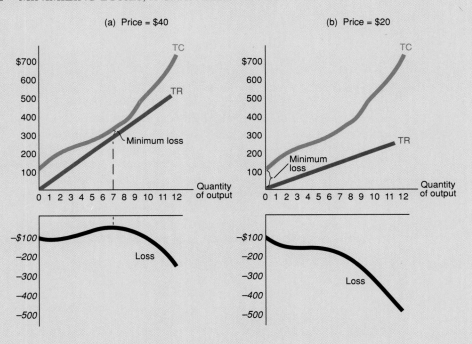

(a) Price = $40

(b) Price = $20

ANSWER TO YOUR TURN

Profit maximization requires $P = MC$; normal profit requires $P = ATC$. Both conditions are satisfied only when price intersects the ATC curve at its minimum value.

NORMAL PROFIT

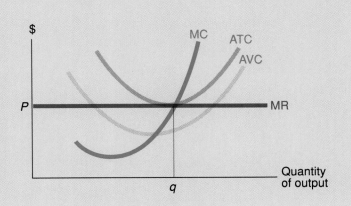

MONOPOLY

Monopoly and perfect competition are polar extremes. Under perfect competition there are a large number of producers, none powerful enough to influence price. With monopoly there is but one seller of a product. You either buy from that seller or do without. As the exclusive seller of a product, the monopolist has the potential to dictate price. Although this potential is sometimes constrained by the government (see Chapter 28), the unregulated monopolist can charge any price it chooses.

Chapter 25 analyzes monopoly in the absence of government regulation. How do monopolists determine which price to charge? Does monopoly guarantee profits? Why do monopolists have a bad image? To what extent is it deserved?

The monopolists, by keeping the market constantly understocked, by never fully supplying the effectual demand, sell their commodities much above the natural price, and raise their emoluments [profits].[1]

---

[1]Adam Smith, *The Wealth of Nations* (New York: Random House, 1937), p. 61. [Originally published in 1776.]

THE MEANING OF MONOPOLY

Monopoly
An industry with only one seller. There are no good substitutes for the product of the monopolist.

Monopoly is derived from two Greek words: *mono* (single) and *polein* (to sell). A monopolist then is the only seller of a product that has no close substitutes. Because no other firm sells a similar product, the industry is comprised of a single producer, the monopolist. Unlike the case of perfect competition, there is no need to distinguish between the firm and the industry. With monopoly, the firm *is* the industry!

Given this definition, monopoly might appear easy to identify. In reality, the issue of what constitutes monopoly is more complex. Whether a market contains more than one seller depends on how you define the market. If only one bus company carries passengers between St. Louis and Chicago, is it a monopolist? In the narrow sense it is—it is the only company providing bus service over this route. On the other hand, if the market is defined more broadly as the market for transportation, the bus company ceases to be a monopolist. It competes with airlines, automobiles, and the railroad.

The issue is whether other forms of transportation are a good substitute for bus travel. Substitutability is a matter of degree. Because of this, some prefer to also think of monopoly as a matter of degree. Any firm that faces a downward-sloping demand curve has some **monopoly power.** The greater the firm's influence over price, the greater its monopoly power.

Monopoly Power
The ability of a firm to influence output price by changing the amount it sells. Any firm facing a downward-sloping demand curve has some monopoly power.

The preceding discussion suggests a certain arbitrariness in classifying a company as a monopolist. Despite this, such classifications are important because monopoly is often prohibited by law (see Chapter 27). Although no clear-cut procedures exist to identify monopoly, economic tools are available to make the government's job more manageable. Certain of these tools are discussed later, but you are already familiar with one—the cross elasticity of demand. Evidence that two goods have high, positive cross elasticities has been accepted by courts as proof that two goods are close substitutes (Exhibit 5-4). If a good has a close substitute, its producer is not a monopolist.

MAINTAINING MONOPOLY THROUGH BARRIERS TO ENTRY

The economic behavior of a monopolist is examined shortly, but first a preliminary question must be addressed. How can a firm maintain its monopoly position? In other words, why don't competing firms enter the industry? Although various reasons can be offered, depending on the particular industry, the major explanations are control of strategic raw materials, economies of scale, and assorted government restrictions.

Control of an Essential Raw Material

One way to assure monopoly status is to deny other producers access to a resource essential for the production of a good. It is difficult to produce polished diamonds unless you first possess raw diamonds. By controlling an estimated 80 percent of the world's raw diamonds, the DeBeers Company of South Africa has gone a long way toward establishing a diamond monopoly. And until the U.S. government intervened in the 1940s, Alcoa was able to maintain a virtual monopoly in the aluminum industry. Alcoa accomplished this by controlling almost all the known bauxite, an ore necessary for the production of aluminum.

Economies of Scale

Assume an industry experiences economies of scale over the entire range of production. Under these circumstances, a monopoly is likely to evolve. As a company becomes larger, its average cost of production falls. The largest company in the industry can produce output at a lower average cost than all other firms. Because of this cost advantage, it can profitably sell its output at a price below what other companies require to stay in business. As these other companies experience losses year after year, they ultimately leave the industry. Unable to duplicate the low costs of the monopolist, new firms are unlikely to enter. Under these circumstances, the monopoly may be maintained indefinitely.

Patents and Copyrights

Patent
An exclusive right, granted by the government, to market a product or process for 17 years.

Government protection provides an additional source of monopoly. When the government issues a **patent,** it grants its holder the exclusive right to market a product or process for 17 years (longer if the patent is renewed). The purpose of a patent is to encourage research and development, which ultimately may benefit millions in society. The Burroughs-Wellcome Company spent tens of millions of dollars developing a drug (AZT) to impede the AIDS virus and to prolong the lives of its victims. The Upjohn Company made a similar investment developing Minoxidil, which promotes hair growth in some balding men. Without the prospect of being able to recoup investment costs—which the patent provides—drug companies would have little incentive to undertake costly research.

Patents helped launch Xerox and other high-tech companies. Today patents motivate companies to design new computer hardware and software. Of course, some research would be undertaken even without this form of monopoly protection. Dan Bricklin invented VisiCalc, the computer spreadsheet, without bothering to file for a patent. Today he regrets his inaction. With a patent he would have earned not only the admiration of computer users but also millions of dollars.

As Bricklin's achievements demonstrate, technological progress occurs even in the absence of patents. But advances would come at a much slower pace. Without patents, competitors could copy a company's product at will. The rewards for innovation would quickly disappear, as other firms began selling similar products. Realizing this, a company would have less incentive to invest in research and development—let someone else make the heavy investment. The present system was created to dispel this attitude and, instead, to promote innovation by granting the inventor exclusive rights to a product over the life of the patent. Of course, patent rights must be enforced if they are to have any value. As Exhibit 25-1 demonstrates, those who violate patents do so at their own peril.

EXHIBIT 25–1

PATENTS—HEED THEM OR WEEP

Companies are sometimes tempted to copy a patented product or process, hoping to tap into a monopolist's profits. The penalty for those that succumb can be stiff. In 1986, a judge ruled that Smith International had infringed on a patent granted the Hughes Tool Company. The patented product was a rubber seal used in drilling for oil. Smith International was ordered to pay Hughes $227 million, thereby wiping out one-half of Smith's net worth.

Bentley Laboratories and Kodak were other losers. The former company was required to pay

Shiley Inc. $45 million for violating a blood-oxygenator patent. Kodak was forced out of the instant-camera business and ultimately may have to pay Polaroid $1 billion for infringing on its patents. Although obtaining a patent may take years and may cost thousands of dollars, such companies as Shiley and Polaroid consider the investment well worth the cost.

Sources: Adapted from Clemens P. Work, "Inventors' Just Rewards," *U.S. News & World Report,* March 3, 1986, p. 43; Bob Davis, "Computer Firms Turn to Patents," *The Wall Street Journal,* January 28, 1986.

Copyright

An exclusive right, granted by the government, to publish, copy, or sell a piece of music, art, or literature.

A **copyright** grants the holder exclusive rights to literary and artistic works. Composers copyright songs, authors copyright books, studios copyright movies. Similar to patents, the purpose is to protect the property of authors and artists and, in so doing, to encourage creativity.

Licensing and Other Government Restrictions

Government sponsorship of monopolies is not limited to patents and copyrights. Congress has given exclusive rights to deliver first-class mail to the U.S. Post Office, thereby creating a postal monopoly. Other activities, from selling drugs to operating a television station, require the approval of federal agencies. When only one company is granted permission to engage in an activity, at least in a certain region of the country, a monopoly is born. State and local governments also create monopolies. For example, a city may grant a company exclusive rights to sell cable television service or to operate a race track.

THE BASIC MODEL OF MONOPOLY

Price and Marginal Revenue for the Monopolist

Because of barriers such as those just described, a monopolist is the sole source of a product, the only producer in an industry. Therefore, demand for the monopolist's product coincides with demand for the industry's product. Industry demand curves are downward sloping and, accordingly, the monopolist must lower price if additional units are to be purchased. Later we consider the case where the monopolist can sell its good to different consumers at different prices. But for now, assume that all output is sold at the same price.

In order to sell additional output, a monopolist must lower price—not just on the last unit sold but on all preceding units as well. Because of this, for all output beyond the first unit *marginal revenue is less than price.* This is illustrated in Table 25-1 (page 574).

If the monopolist sets the price at $18, a single unit is purchased. To sell two units the monopolist must lower the price to $16. The marginal revenue of the

TABLE 25-1

DEMAND, MARGINAL REVENUE, AND TOTAL REVENUE FOR A MONOPOLIST

Price	Quantity	Total revenue	Marginal revenue
$20	0	$ 0	
18	1	18	$18
16	2	32	14
14	3	42	10
12	4	48	6
10	5	50	2
8	6	48	− 2
6	7	42	− 6
4	8	32	−10
2	9	18	−14

The monopolist must lower price in order to sell additional output. Because price must be reduced for all units, not just the last unit sold, marginal revenue is less than price for all output beyond the first unit.

second unit is $14 (i.e., $32 − $18). Thus, the marginal revenue from selling the second unit is $2 less than the price received. (The reason, of course, is that the monopolist must cut the price of the first unit by $2). As Table 25-1 shows, for all units after the first, marginal revenue is less than price.

The demand and marginal revenue schedules of Table 25-1 are portrayed graphically in Figure 25-1.[2] Because marginal revenue is less than price, the marginal revenue curve lies below the demand curve. The demand and marginal revenue curves of the monopolist lie in stark contrast to those of the perfectly competitive firm. Whereas the competitive firm faces perfectly elastic demand and marginal revenue curves, the demand and marginal revenue curves of the monopolist are downward sloping.

Marginal Revenue, Total Revenue, and Elasticity of Demand

Figure 25-1 also illustrates the relationship among marginal revenue, total revenue, and the elasticity of demand (E_d). As you may recall from Chapter 5, total revenue reaches a maximum where $E_d = 1$. (This occurs at the midpoint of a linear demand curve.) When $E_d > 1$, total revenue can be increased by reducing price. When $E_d < 1$, total revenue can be increased by raising price. Because marginal revenue is derived from total revenue, it is similarly linked to the elasticity of demand.

What does this tell us about the price a monopolist would like to charge? The answer is that a monopolist would not want to operate on the inelastic segment of its demand curve. For example, the firm in Figure 25-1 would not want to set a price of $6. Because demand is inelastic at $6, the firm could increase total revenue by raising price and reducing output. A lower output would also reduce any variable costs of production. Therefore, when a firm is on the inelastic range of its demand curve, it can increase profits simply by raising price.

The same conclusion can be reached by examining marginal revenue. When demand is inelastic marginal revenue is negative. The last unit sold *reduces* total

---

[2]Notice that the marginal revenue curve is twice as steep as the demand curve. This is true for all linear (straight-line) demand curves.

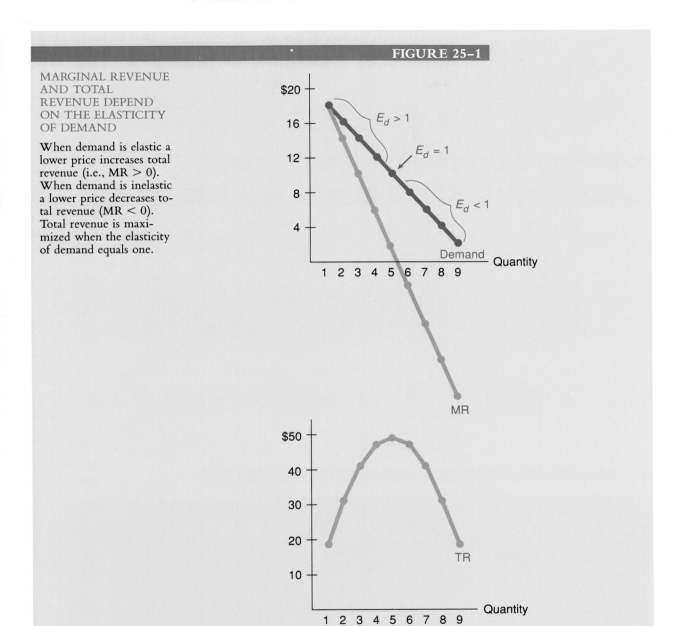

FIGURE 25-1

MARGINAL REVENUE AND TOTAL REVENUE DEPEND ON THE ELASTICITY OF DEMAND

When demand is elastic a lower price increases total revenue (i.e., MR > 0). When demand is inelastic a lower price decreases total revenue (MR < 0). Total revenue is maximized when the elasticity of demand equals one.

revenue. The firm can earn additional profits by restricting output and raising price. Exactly which price the monopolist should charge depends on the costs of production (as we see in the next section). But even without considering costs, we

YOUR TURN

If there were no costs of production, we could skip the next section. The firm would concentrate exclusively on total revenue. (If TC = 0, profit = TR − 0.) Assuming production is costless, how much output should the firm in Table 25-1 produce in order to maximize profits? What price should it charge? How much profit will the firm earn?

can conclude that the monopolist does not want to be on the inelastic segment of its demand curve.

Profit Maximization in the Short Run

The general rules for profit maximization are the same for all firms regardless of their market structure. *If a monopolist produces, it should produce to the point where marginal revenue equals marginal cost.* Until that point is reached, additional output adds more to revenue than to costs and thus increases profits.

Profit maximization for a monopolist is illustrated in Figure 25-2. The monopolist produces Q_1 output, given by the intersection of the marginal revenue and marginal cost curves. But what price does the monopolist charge? To maximize profit the monopolist chooses the highest price *consistent with the sale of Q_1 units.* This is given by point A on the demand curve, which lies directly above Q_1. Consumers are willing to pay P_1 for Q_1 output, but not a penny more. Thus price is equal to the vertical distance between Q_1 and the demand curve.

Observe that P_1 is not the highest possible price. The monopolist could have set a price of P_2 and sold Q_2 output. Why didn't the monopolist charge the higher price? Quite simply because a higher price in this case would have reduced profits. For all output between Q_2 and Q_1 marginal revenue exceeds marginal cost. Each of these units contributes to profits. Therefore, the firm should not stop producing until it reaches an output rate of Q_1. *The monopolist does not charge the highest price that anyone would be willing to pay.*

Also observe that, unlike perfect competition, price does not equal marginal cost at the profit-maximizing level of output. Because price is greater than marginal revenue for the monopolist, price is also greater than marginal cost. MR = MC is the general rule for profit maximization; P = MC is a special case that holds only in perfect competition.

Profit maximization can also be illustrated with a numerical example. Table 25-2 replicates the demand and revenue schedules of Table 25-1. Because a

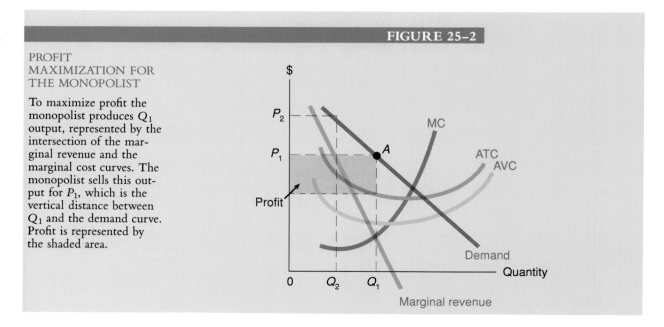

FIGURE 25–2

PROFIT MAXIMIZATION FOR THE MONOPOLIST

To maximize profit the monopolist produces Q_1 output, represented by the intersection of the marginal revenue and the marginal cost curves. The monopolist sells this output for P_1, which is the vertical distance between Q_1 and the demand curve. Profit is represented by the shaded area.

TABLE 25-2

PROFIT MAXIMIZATION FOR A MONOPOLIST

(1) Quantity	(2) Price	(3) Total revenue	(4) Marginal revenue	(5) Total cost	(6) Marginal cost	(7) Profit
1	$18	$18	$18	$20	$ 8	$− 2
2	16	32	14	24	4	8
3	14	42	10	32	8	10
4	12	48	6	44	12	4
5	10	50	2	60	16	−10

The monopolist maximizes profit by producing three units and selling each for $14.

profit-maximizing monopolist would not produce where MR < 0, the inelastic portion of the demand schedule is deleted. Also appearing in Table 25-2 are the total cost, marginal cost, and profit schedules of the monopolist. From the table we see that the third unit of output is the last unit for which MR > MC. Therefore, to maximize profit the monopolist produces three units of output, sets a price of $14 (from column 2), and earns a profit of $10.

Minimizing Short-Run Losses

Monopoly does not guarantee profits. If demand for a product is weak, total cost may exceed total revenue at all levels of output. A patented technique for turning gold into lead is unlikely to earn its inventor any profits. In a similar vein, although a bus company may have exclusive rights to transport passengers between two towns, if demand for bus service is sluggish the company may lose money.

When profits are unattainable, the short-run goal of the monopolist is to minimize losses. The same rules apply as in perfect competition. The monopolist produces in the short run provided that $P \geq AVC$. This is illustrated in Figure 25-3 (page 578), where losses are minimized at Q_1 output. Although price falls short of average total cost, price does exceed average variable cost. The monopolist loses less money than if it produced no output.

On the other hand, in situations where $P < AVC$, production only adds to losses. Accordingly, the monopolist's best option is to shut down. *If P < AVC the monopolist does not produce in the short run.*

Long Run for the Monopolist

The monopolist has greater flexibility in the long run. Given time the monopolist can alter plant size to take advantage of possible cost savings. But when losses persist—regardless of plant size—the monopolist leaves the industry in the long run. Like other firms, the monopolist seeks the maximum return on its resources. When higher returns are available elsewhere, the monopolist transfers its resources to other industries.

Although losses are not consistent with long-run equilibrium, profits are. In the case of perfect competition, the entry of new firms into the industry ultimately eliminates economic profits. With monopoly, however, barriers to entry shield the monopolist from competitors. As a result, the monopolist may be able to enjoy economic profits even in the long run.

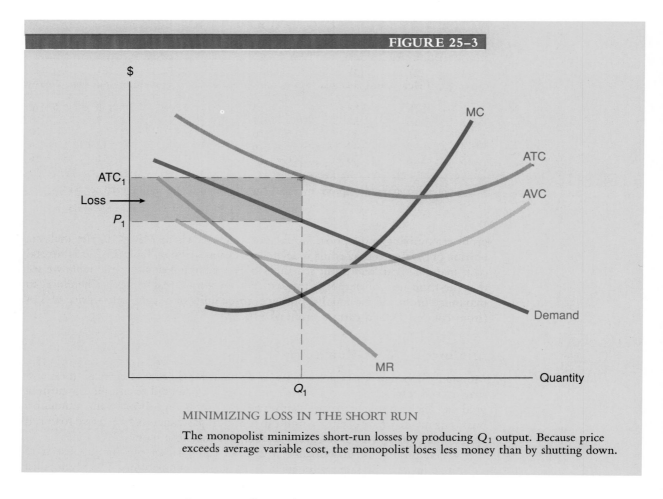

FIGURE 25-3

MINIMIZING LOSS IN THE SHORT RUN

The monopolist minimizes short-run losses by producing Q_1 output. Because price exceeds average variable cost, the monopolist loses less money than by shutting down.

Concern about the Long Run May Constrain the Monopolist in the Short Run

Although barriers to entry protect the monopolist, that protection is not always complete. In some cases barriers can be overcome. Firms may locate alternative sources of a crucial raw material or develop a new, competing technology. Often the government intervenes. For example, the government ended Alcoa's virtual monopoly of the aluminum industry by building integrated aluminum plants during World War II and then selling them to Reynolds Metals and Kaiser Aluminum. In addition, the government has split up some companies, such as Standard Oil and AT&T, while forcing others to sell plants to rival firms.

For such reasons a monopolist may worry that its industry will eventually evolve into a different market structure. Even if the monopolist can maintain its barriers to entry, it may fear other government action. For example, in the past the oil industry has been slapped with price controls and a *windfall* or *excess-profits* tax.

Such concerns may force the monopolist to alter its behavior. If its goal is to maximize profit over the long run, the monopolist may choose to sell more output to the public and charge a lower price than the model of short-run profit maximization suggests. Lower short-run profits have two advantages: (1) they reduce the incentive of other firms to attempt entry into the monopolist's industry and (2) they make government intervention less likely. In both cases the result may be to prolong the period over which economic profits are earned. In summary, when a monopolist feels threatened by potential rivals or by adverse government actions, it may sacrifice short-run profits in order to earn greater profits over the long run.

PRICE DISCRIMINATION

Price Discrimination
The practice of selling a good at different prices that are not attributable to differences in cost.

The basic model of monopoly must also be modified when the monopolist is able to charge different prices to different customers. Until now we have assumed that the monopolist sets a single price, but clearly this is not always the case. Universities typically charge students a lower price for football tickets than they charge the general public. They also reduce the price of education for certain students by offering scholarships. Some pharmacies and restaurants offer senior-citizen discounts. Movie theatres generally set lower ticket prices for children than for adults. Railroads charge different customers different rates depending on what is shipped. Producers sometimes sell their products for less in foreign markets than at home, a practice known as *dumping*.[3]

Price discrimination occurs when a company charges different prices to different buyers and when these price differences are not due to differences in cost. Note the second requirement. A person lodging at the San Francisco Hilton pays more than someone staying at the Hilton in Little Rock, Arkansas, but this is not price discrimination. The San Francisco Hilton cost more per room to build. In addition, wages, taxes, and other operating costs are higher in San Francisco. Nor does AT&T discriminate against citizens of Los Angeles when it charges them more to call New York than it charges residents of Philadelphia. Transmission costs increase with distance. In contrast, the practice of charging young moviegoers less than adults does constitute price discrimination, since it costs no more to show a movie to adults.

The primary motive for price discrimination is to increase profits. Consider an orthodontist whose services are demanded by two new patients. Suppose one patient is prepared to pay $3000 to have his teeth straightened but the other will go no higher than $2000. If the orthodontist sets a common price of $3000, she earns $3000 in fees from the first patient and nothing from the second. If she charges both $2000, she earns a total of $4000. But she can do better than that. By charging the first patient $3000 and the second $2000, she earns a total of $5000. The orthodontist may not know exactly what each patient is prepared to pay but, by gathering information on where the patients (or their parents) are employed, where they live, whether they are covered by dental insurance, and so forth, she can usually differentiate among clients on the basis of ability to pay.[4]

Not all businesses charge different prices. Before a company can engage in price discrimination, three conditions must hold:

---

[3]Dumping is discussed in Chapter 36.

[4]This practice is by no means limited to orthodontists. A noted psychologist acknowledged charging patients anywhere from $5 per hour to $100. "Everybody should pay, but nobody can pay more than he can afford." [Cited in James Koch, *Industrial Organization and Prices,* 2nd ed. (Englewood Cliffs, NJ: Prentice-Hall, 1980), p. 394.] Even unions discriminate. Construction unions often charge lower rates for residential work than for industrial projects. When Chrysler was experiencing financial difficulties, the United Automobile Workers Union charged it less (in wage rates) than General Motors and Ford.

1. The company must have some monopoly power and therefore face a downward-sloping demand curve.
2. The company must be able to segment buyers into different markets having different elasticities of demand.
3. The company must be able to prevent the resale of its product.

The first condition is obvious. Only companies with a downward-sloping demand curve have the ability to influence price. The second condition is more subtle. To maximize profit the firm must equate marginal revenue and marginal cost in each market. When elasticity of demand differs across markets, the price at which MR = MC also differs. This is illustrated in Figure 25-4 where, for simplicity, marginal cost is assumed to be constant. The company charges a higher price in the market where demand is less elastic because consumers there are less responsive to higher prices.

Not only must a company be able to sell in two or more markets, it must be able to prevent the resale of its product across markets. Why doesn't Sony charge men more than women (or bankers more than clerks)? If it attempted to do so, men would ask their wives or girlfriends to make the purchase for them, thereby avoiding the high-price market. More generally, secondary markets would crop up—low-price buyers would purchase a good from the company and then resell that good in the high-price market for less than the company was asking. Some companies have considered drastic measures to prevent the resale of their product. Rohm & Haas provides a classic example (see Exhibit 25-2).

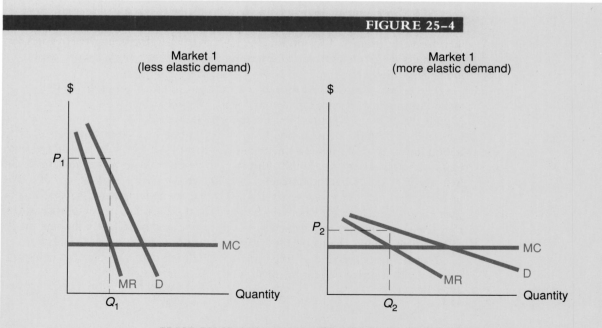

FIGURE 25–4

Market 1
(less elastic demand)

Market 1
(more elastic demand)

PRICE DISCRIMINATION—THE EFFECT OF ELASTICITY OF DEMAND

To maximize profit the price-discriminating firm equates marginal revenue and marginal cost in each market, which leads to a price of P_1 in market 1 and a price of P_2 in market 2.

EXHIBIT 25–2

NO ARSENIC PLEASE

The Rohm & Haas Company sold a plastic, methyl metacrylate, which was a key ingredient in the manufacture of dentures. Dental laboratories were charged $45 per pound. This compound also had a less glamorous use as an industrial plastic. Because other industrial materials were close substitutes, Rohm & Haas set a price of only $.85 per pound for its industrial users.

When dental labs learned of the price differential, some began purchasing the material from industrial buyers. Determined to halt this practice, Rohm & Haas contemplated ways to keep the markets separate. One proposal was to add poison to the industrial plastic. The company reasoned that the Food and Drug Administration (FDA) would never allow dental labs to manufacture

dentures with tainted materials. This plan was detailed in company correspondence:

> A millionth of one percent of arsenic or lead might cause them [the FDA] to confiscate every bootleg unit in the country. There ought to be a trace of something that would make them rear up.

Although Rohm & Haas rejected this proposal, it did leak stories that the industrial plastic had been contaminated.

Sources: Adapted from Corwin D. Edwards, *Economic and Political Aspects of International Cartels*, U.S. Senate, Subcommittee on War Mobilization of the Committee on Military Affairs, 78th Congress, Second Session (1944), p. 19, cited in Douglas F. Greer, *Industrial Organization and Public Policy*, 2nd ed. (New York: Macmillan, 1984), p. 311.

Unlike Rohm & Haas, the orthodontist does not have to worry about the resale of her product—orthodontic services cannot be transferred from one patient to another. Nor do movie theatres need to be concerned about children selling their tickets to adults. Adults are admitted only if they have an adult ticket, which is distinguishable from a child's ticket.

Although price discrimination increases profits for producers, it has a mixed effect on consumers. Some buyers are forced to pay more as a result of price discrimination. On the other hand, many buyers in the low-price market would be forced to forgo consumption if the producer sold to everyone at the same price. Without price discrimination, fewer children would attend the movies and fewer low-income individuals could afford orthodontic treatment.

AN EVALUATION OF MONOPOLY

Let's face it: monopolists have a bad image. Consumers complain of shabby treatment at the hands of monopolies, and governments are often eager to break up monopolies (as we learn in Chapter 27). These negative connotations are sometimes deserved but they are not the entire story. Let's assess monopoly, first dwelling on its vices and then considering possible redeeming features. To keep things simple, we consider a monopolist not engaged in price discrimination.

The Evils of Monopoly

Restricting Output and Raising Price   A major criticism of monopoly is that it leads to a higher price than does perfect competition and to a lower output. Thus consumers are harmed on two fronts. To illustrate this argument, consider an industry that is initially perfectly competitive. Now assume that someone buys all existing plants in the process becoming a monopolist. For the moment, assume that the cost of producing a given level of output is the same under monopoly as it was under perfect competition, so that the marginal cost curve of the monopolist is identical to the industry supply curve under perfect competition. (The monopolist's marginal cost curve and the supply curve under perfect competition are both obtained by summing the marginal cost curves of all plants in the industry.)

The consequences of transforming the industry from perfect competition to monopoly are illustrated in Figure 25-5. Under perfect competition Q_c output is produced and sold at a price of P_c, given by the intersection of the industry supply and demand curves. In contrast, the monopolist equates marginal revenue and marginal cost. Thus, the monopolist restricts output to Q_m while raising price to P_m.

On theoretical grounds then, monopolists can be expected to inflate price in order to increase profits. But do monopolists really behave in this fashion? As Exhibit 25-3 indicates, available evidence supports the theory of monopoly. Indeed, the effect of monopoly on price and profits is sometimes dramatic.

Inefficient Allocation of Resources   In the absence of externalities, perfect competition leads to efficient allocation of resources. Resources flow into an industry until the value to consumers of another unit of output (price) equals the cost of producing another unit (marginal cost). In contrast, *monopoly is characterized by an underallocation of resources to the industry.*

This situation is illustrated in Figure 25-5. At Q_m price exceeds marginal cost—the value of another unit is greater than the cost of producing it. Society would like additional resources to flow into this industry. But the monopolist restricts the flow of resources into the industry in order to limit output. These resources are diverted instead to other industries for the production of output that has a lower value to consumers.

This misallocation of resources reduces the welfare of society. But by how much is society harmed? Economic studies place this welfare loss at roughly one

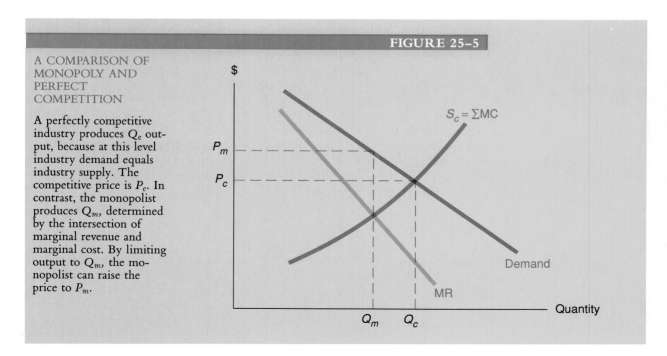

FIGURE 25–5

A COMPARISON OF MONOPOLY AND PERFECT COMPETITION

A perfectly competitive industry produces Q_c output, because at this level industry demand equals industry supply. The competitive price is P_c. In contrast, the monopolist produces Q_m, determined by the intersection of marginal revenue and marginal cost. By limiting output to Q_m, the monopolist can raise price to P_m.

EXHIBIT 25-3

EXAMPLES OF MONOPOLY PRICING

Tungsten carbide is a hard metal with important industrial applications. It was available in the 1920s for about $50 per pound until General Electric and the Krupp Company of Germany established a world monopoly giving General Electric exclusive rights to the U.S. market. During the time that General Electric monopolized the U.S. market, the price of tungsten carbide fluctuated between $225 and $453 per pound. In 1942 the U.S. government, relying on antitrust laws, broke up this monopoly. With other producers in the market, the price of tungsten carbide fell below $45 per pound and remained there. Thus, the price under monopoly was approximately five to ten times greater than the price charged in the face of competition.

In the early 1970s, when Bausch & Lomb possessed monopoly power in the soft contact-lens market, it produced these contact lenses at a cost of roughly $1 each and sold them for more than $60. When competitors eventually broke into the market, the price fell sharply.

Burroughs-Wellcome spent $80 million researching and developing a drug (AZT) to treat the AIDS virus. In 1987, the Food and Drug Administration approved the drug for distribution in the United States. This gave Burroughs-Wellcome exclusive rights to the only drug known to help victims of AIDS. For a one-year supply of the drug, the company set a rather healthy price of $8300 wholesale ($10,000 retail). At that price, revenues in the first year alone were estimated to be $250 million—more than triple the research and development costs. When asked why such a high price was chosen, the company president responded that "the efficacy and speed of introduction of competitive products are unknown." In other words, convinced that competition ultimately would drive down the price, the company wanted to earn as much as possible before those competitive pressures materialized.

Sources: Adapted from Walter Adams, "Public Policy in a Free Enterprise Economy," in Walter Adams, ed., *The Structure of American Industry,* 5th ed. (New York: Macmillan, 1977), p. 485 [cited in Edwin Mansfield, 6th ed., *Economics* (New York: Norton, 1989), p. 503]; William G. Shepherd, *The Economics of Industrial Organization* (New York: Prentice-Hall, 1985), p. 126; Marilyn Chase, "AIDS Drug Comes to a Worried Market," *The Wall Street Journal,* March 23, 1987, p. 6.

percent of the nation's output.[5] These low estimates have led some observers to suggest that monopoly may not be so bad after all. Some have even questioned the value of regulating monopoly and enforcing antitrust (antimonopoly) laws. Might these resources be better employed elsewhere?[6]

Before giving up the fight against monopoly, we must be confident that we are measuring the full costs of monopoly. Today most economists believe that monopoly imposes other costs on society in addition to the direct costs stemming from output restrictions.

Monopoly Rent Seeking and Regulation   To the extent that a monopoly generates profits—or what are often called "monopoly rents"—it is a valuable asset to its owner.[7] Companies are therefore willing to devote resources in an attempt to secure this asset. For example, companies competing for a cable television franchise may

[5]The initial study was by Arnold Harberger, "Monopoly and Resource Allocation," *American Economic Review* (May 1954), pp. 77–87. See also F. M. Scherer, *Industrial Market Structure and Economic Performance,* 2nd ed. (Chicago: Rand-McNally, 1980), p. 464; Paul D. Scanlon, "FTC and Phase II: The McGovern Papers," *Antitrust Law and Economics Review* (Spring 1972), pp. 33–36.

[6]George Stigler quipped that if the cost of monopoly were as low as some suggest, "economists might serve a more useful purpose if they fought fires or termites instead of monopoly." See G. Stigler, "The Statistics of Monopoly and Merger," *Journal of Political Economy* (February 1956), p. 34.

[7]See Gordon Tullock, "The Welfare Costs of Tariffs, Monopolies, and Theft," *Western Economic Journal* (June 1967), pp. 224–232.

hire lawyers and lobbyists in an effort to win the franchise or even bribe public officials. From the perspective of society, resources used in the pursuit of monopoly power are wasted—they produce no socially valuable output. The social cost of **rent-seeking** activities is the value of the output these resources could have created had they been used in other activities.

Rent Seeking
The use of scarce resources in an attempt to secure a monopoly and therefore earn monopoly profits.

The value of monopoly rents appears to be high. One study estimated that they amounted to more than 7 percent of national output in India and about 15 percent in Turkey.[8] Given rents of this magnitude, one would expect rent seeking to attract considerable resources (although reliable estimates are not yet available).

The social costs of monopoly also include the costs of preventing and controlling monopolies. Resources used in fighting monopoly are being diverted from the production of goods and services. Thus, in assessing monopoly the costs of rent seeking and regulation must be added to the costs of restricting output.

Technological Progress   Some economists argue that monopolists may be slow to innovate, denying society the benefits of new technologies and slowing economic growth. Rather than push hard to introduce new technologies, monopolists may pursue a more leisurely pace. In the view of Sir John Hicks, "The best of all monopoly profits is a quiet life."[9] Such tendencies may be offset by other forces, however, as we see shortly.

Income Distribution   At the same time that monopolists reduce the size of the economic pie through inefficiency, they take a large slice for themselves. That is, monopolists increase their share of income at the expense of others. Surely some monopolists are noble; some may be sweet, loving grandmothers. But it is difficult to argue that monopolists as a class are more deserving than nonmonopolists. Accordingly, some attack monopoly for contributing to an "unfair distribution of income."

Although fairness is in the eyes of the beholder, we can say something objective about the distribution of income. Because monopoly creates wealth for those who hold it, there is a tendency for monopoly to make the distribution of income more unequal. According to one study, the wealthiest 0.27 percent of families in the United States own 18.5 percent of the country's assets. If all monopoly power were eliminated, the wealth of these super-rich would fall to approximately 13 percent of assets.[10] To those who value an egalitarian distribution of income, monopoly is moving us in the wrong direction.

Potential Advantages of Monopoly

The case against monopoly having been presented, can anything be said in defense of monopoly? Monopoly has two potential advantages, both related to costs. Under certain circumstances monopoly may (a) reduce current costs of production and (b) promote more rapid technological progress, thereby reducing costs in the future.

[8]Anne O. Krueger, "The Political Economy of the Rent-Seeking Sector," *American Economic Review* (June 1974), pp. 291–303.

[9]John Hicks, "Annual Survey of Economic Theory: The Theory of Monopoly," *Econometrica* (January 1935), p. 8.

[10]William S. Comanor and Robert H. Smiley, "Monopoly and the Distribution of Wealth," *Quarterly Journal of Economics* (May 1975), pp. 177–194.

Natural Monopolies   Earlier we examined the consequences of transforming a competitive industry into a monopoly. We showed that *if the total cost of producing a given level of output is the same under perfect competition and monopoly,* price is higher under monopoly and output is lower. We now relax this assumption and consider the case where the cost of production is lower with monopoly

Natural Monopoly
An industry characterized by extensive economies of scale. The total cost of producing a given output is minimized when only one firm is in the industry.

Certain monopolies arise because of economies of scale; these are called **natural monopolies.** In a natural monopoly the average cost of production declines throughout the relevant range of production. Therefore, a given level of output can be produced at the least cost when there is only one producer in the industry. This is illustrated in Figure 25-6. A single firm can produce 100 units at an average cost of $10, leading to a total cost of $1000. With two firms each producing 50 units, total cost rises to $1500. With four firms producing 25 units apiece, total cost climbs to $2000. Other options are similarly inferior to monopoly. If output is to be produced with the fewest resources, there can be only one firm in the industry.

Although costs are minimized with one producer, restricting output to a single firm has an ambiguous effect on price. To remain in business, a company must charge a price that covers costs. If the industry were comprised of two or more smaller firms, they would have higher average costs than the monopolist and therefore require a higher price to stay in business. In other words, the monopolist's lower costs permit it to charge a lower price. On the other hand, there is no guarantee that the monopolist will actually charge less—at least voluntarily. This is why governments often regulate natural monopolies. The government may attempt to take advantage of economies of scale by allowing only one producer while, at the same time, trying to protect the public by restricting the ability of the monopolist to raise price. The reasons for regulating natural monopolies, and their potential problems, are analyzed in Chapter 28.

Technological Innovation   Monopoly power may promote investment in research and development, thereby spurring technological advances. As previously mentioned, this is the rationale for patents. The incentive to innovate depends on the expected financial returns. When these returns must be shared with other producers, the incentive to innovate is blunted.

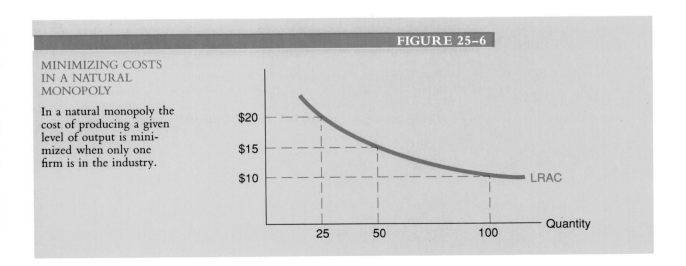

FIGURE 25–6

MINIMIZING COSTS
IN A NATURAL
MONOPOLY

In a natural monopoly the cost of producing a given level of output is minimized when only one firm is in the industry.

There may be a second, related reason for protecting the monopolist.[11] If other producers were allowed to enter the market once they "stole" a monopolist's invention, they would have an incentive to devote resources to the theft of this invention. At the same time, the monopolist would invest resources to protect its invention. The resources devoted both to theft and to its prevention are socially unproductive, adding nothing to output. Patents and other forms of monopoly protection free up resources to produce output valued by society.

Has monopoly had the predicted effect? Do innovations occur more rapidly in the presence of monopoly power? We examine the evidence in Chapter 26 after presenting the models of monopolistic competition and oligopoly.

SUMMARY

1. A monopolist is the only seller of a product that has no close substitutes. Other firms are kept out of the industry through barriers to entry. The major barriers are control of an essential raw material, economies of scale, and government protection, including patents, copyrights, and licenses.
2. As the only producer in the industry, the monopolist faces a downward-sloping demand curve. To sell additional output, the monopolist must lower price on each unit sold. Because of this, the marginal revenue from additional output is less than price.
3. The monopolist does not want to operate on the inelastic segment of the demand curve, since marginal revenue is negative there. When demand is inelastic, the monopolist can increase profit by restricting output and raising price.
4. To maximize profits in the short run the monopolist produces where marginal revenue equals marginal cost, provided that price is at least as high as average variable cost. If price is less than average variable cost the monopolist shuts down to minimize losses.
5. Once the level of output is determined, the monopolist sets the highest price consistent with the sale of this output. Although higher prices could be charged, the monopolist would not be able to sell the profit-maximizing level of output at these higher prices.
6. Because of barriers to entry, a monopolist may be able to earn positive economic profits in the long run. Unless the monopolist can earn at least normal profits it will leave the industry.
7. Price discrimination occurs when different buyers are charged different prices not resulting from differences in cost. This practice allows the monopolist to increase profits. Price discrimination is possible only if the monopolist can segment buyers into different markets and prevent the resale of its product.
8. Compared to perfect competition, monopoly leads to a higher price and reduced output in the industry. Because the monopolist restricts the flow of resources into the industry, monopoly leads to an inefficient allocation of resources. Other social costs of monopoly include the costs of monopoly rent seeking and regulation. Monopoly has also been criticized for making the distribution of income more unequal.
9. In certain circumstances monopoly may have beneficial effects. In a natural monopoly the costs of producing a given output are minimized when only one firm is in the industry. Monopoly protection (e.g., patents) may also accelerate technological innovation.

KEY TERMS

monopoly	price discrimination
monopoly power	rent seeking
patent	natural monopoly
copyright	

---

[11]This argument comes from Richard A. Posner, "The Social Costs of Monopoly and Regulation," *Journal of Political Economy* (August 1975), p. 825.

STUDY QUESTIONS AND PROBLEMS

1. Explain why you agree or disagree with the following statements:
   a. "The price of monopoly is upon every occasion the highest which can be got."—Adam Smith
   b. To maximize profit, the monopolist should equate price with marginal cost.
   c. The monopolist may be able to earn positive profit in the long run.
   d. Even a monopolist may lose money.
   e. If marginal revenue declines as output increases, total revenue must also decline.
2. In what sense is the New York Yankees ballclub a monopoly? The ability of the ballclub to raise ticket prices is tempered by the availability of alternative activities. In the broad sense, there are substitutes for Yankees ballgames. List some of these substitutes.
3. Why does the marginal revenue curve of the monopolist slope downward?
4. Consider the monopolist whose demand schedule is:

P	$9	$8	$7	$6	$5	$4	$3
Q	0	1	2	3	4	5	6

   Assume each and every unit costs $5 to produce—the total cost of one unit is $5, the total cost of two units is $10, and so on.
   a. Construct the monopolist's marginal revenue schedule.
   b. Compute its marginal cost schedule.
   c. Assuming that the goal of the monopolist is to maximize profits, how much output should it produce?
   d. What price should it charge?
   e. How much profit will it earn?
5. In each case indicate whether the monopolist should increase or decrease production in order to maximize profits. Explain your reasoning.
   a. The elasticity of demand is 0.50.
   b. Marginal revenue of an additional unit exceeds marginal cost.
   c. The monopolist is producing at the point where its demand curve intersects its marginal cost curve.
6. In *Welfare and Competition*, Tibor Scitovsky claims that the monopolist "may regard his immunity from competition as precarious or be afraid of unfavorable publicity and public censure." What does Scitovsky mean? Isn't a monopolist immune from competition and therefore free to do anything it pleases?
7. Which of the following constitute price discrimination?
   a. selling lobsters at a lower price in Maine than in Colorado
   b. giving employees a 25-percent discount on all items purchased from the store
   c. charging children less than adults for a luncheon buffet
   d. charging business executives more to fly on an airplane than vacationers
   e. selling a Japanese good at a higher price in Japan than in the United States
   f. selling a Japanese good for less in Japan than in the United States
8. Economists argue that monopoly causes misallocation of resources. Explain this argument.
9. Sometimes governments create monopoly—for example, allowing only one electric company to serve a community. What is the economic justification for this?

ANSWERS TO YOUR TURN

To maximize profits the firm should produce five units of output, selling each for $10, and earning $50 in profits.

MONOPOLISTIC COMPETITION AND OLIGOPOLY

Both monopolistic and competitive forces combine in the determination of most prices, and therefore a hybrid theory affords a more illuminating approach to the study of the price system than does a theory of perfected competition, supplemented by a theory of monopoly.[1]

The world is filled with companies like McDonald's. Facing stiff competition from Burger King, Wendy's, and other fast-food restaurants, McDonald's can hardly be characterized as a monopolist. Yet it is not a perfectly competitive firm either; it sells a product that differs slightly from that of its competitors. This gives McDonald's some influence over the price of its burgers and fries. As with most firms in the real world, McDonald's falls somewhere between perfect competition and monopoly.

Until about 60 years ago most economists were content with just two models of market structure: perfect competition and monopoly. Even today some economists argue that other models are incomplete, less powerful, or even unnecessary. For example, they concede that the fast-food industry does not satisfy all the requirements of perfect competition but argue that this model nonetheless does a good job of explaining price and output in this market.

Most economists, however, believe that models of intermediate market structures help us better understand how real-world markets operate. They point out that certain facts are inconsistent with the model of perfect competition. For example, the perfectly competitive firm would never advertise, since it cannot influence the price of its product. Yet McDonald's spends more than $300 million a year on television commercials, trying to convince consumers to frequent its restaurants.

Chapter 26 considers models that fall in between perfect competition and monopoly, focusing on the market structures

---

[1]Edward H. Chamberlin, *The Theory of Monopolistic Competition* (Cambridge, MA: Harvard University Press, 1933), preface.

known as monopolistic competition *and* oligopoly. *Similar to monopolies, both oligopolistic and monopolistically competitive firms have some control over the price of their product. But unlike monopolies, they must share the market with other firms. Monopolistically competitive industries consist of a large number of small firms; oligopolistic markets are dominated by a few large firms. We begin with a discussion of monopolistic competition.*

MONOPOLISTIC COMPETITION

The theory of monopolistic competition is credited to independent work by Edward Chamberlin of Harvard University and to influential British economist Joan Robinson (see Exhibit 26-1, page 590).[2] This theory, argues Robinson, is an attempt at greater realism. Traditionally, when economists observed some real-world phenomenon that was

> inconsistent with the assumptions of perfect competition, they were inclined to look for some complicated explanation of it, before the simple explanation occurred to them that the real world did not fulfill the assumptions of perfect competition.[3]

To Robinson and Chamberlin a more reasonable approach was to formulate a new theory, which was consistent with the facts.

The theory of **monopolistic competition** rests upon three assumptions: product differentiation, a large number of sellers, and free entry and exit.

Product Differentiation   In monopolistically competitive markets each firm produces a product that, while highly similar to those of other firms, is viewed by consumers as distinct. That is, the products of the various firms are close but not perfect substitutes. The Nashville phone directory lists more than 70 different new car dealers. All sell cars, but all dealers are not the same. They differ in location, size, reputation, quality of service, friendliness, and makes of automobiles. Their products are therefore distinct.

Product differences may be real or imagined. What is important is that consumers believe that such differences exist. Even when two goods are identical, as long as a consumer views one as superior, he or she is willing to pay a higher price for that good. Accordingly, producers have an incentive to distinguish their product, to make it appear more attractive than others on the market.

The aspirin industry provides a classic example of **product differentiation**. Inherently all brands of aspirin are indistinguishable: they all contain the same chemical compound. Yet the price of aspirin varies widely, with Bayer aspirin

Monopolistic Competition
A market structure characterized by a large number of firms selling distinct (differentiated) products and in which entry into and exit from the industry is easy.

---

[2]Chamberlin, *The Theory of Monopolistic Competition;* Joan Robinson, *The Economics of Imperfect Competition* (London: Macmillan, 1933).

[3]Robinson, same as 2, p. 4.

EXHIBIT 26–1

JOAN V. ROBINSON
(1903–1983)

The accomplishments of Joan V. Robinson extended well beyond the theory of monopolistic competition. A gifted and prolific writer, Robinson made important contributions in such diverse fields as growth theory, international trade, economic philosophy, and Keynesian macroeconomics. Indeed, she is credited with helping Keynes formulate the ideas behind his *General Theory.*

Robinson was critical of laissez-faire economics, lambasting the marginal productivity theory of distribution. At the same time, she defended Marxian economics. Although much of her work was outside of mainstream economics, she was widely respected by economists of all persuasions. One economist, writing before Robinson's death, claimed:

> She is the only great economist that has ever lived who is not a man. She is also the only great living economist who has not been awarded the Nobel prize. These two are the great scandals of the economics profession.[4]

Except for a spell in India, Joan Robinson spent most of her career on the faculty of Cambridge University in England. She continued writing after her retirement in 1971, publishing an introductory economics text at the age of 70.

[4]Thanos Skouras, "The Economics of Joan Robinson," in J. R. Shackleton and Gareth Locksley, *Twelve Contemporary Economists* (London: Macmillan, 1981), pp. 216–17.

typically selling for several times as much as lesser-known brands. Much of this is due to advertising. Bayer has convinced many consumers that it is the Cadillac of the aspirin industry, somehow more effective than other brands. A positive image can be worth more than any real difference.

Admittedly, all brands of aspirin are not identical in every dimension. Subtle differences exist in terms of freshness, child-proof containers, tamper-proof packaging, liquid or tablet or capsule form, flavoring, and buffering. But actual differences are less than commonly perceived. Aspirin makers have been extremely effective in differentiating their products. Sometimes this differentiation has bordered on the deceptive. For a long time Anacin advertised that it contained the ingredient most recommended by doctors without revealing the ingredient: aspirin. In its commercials Excedrin boasted that it contained two ingredients, failing to name either: aspirin and caffeine. Whatever it takes, aspirin makers want you to believe that what they are selling is superior to other products on the market.

Number of Sellers   A monopolistically competitive market contains enough sellers so that the actions of each can be considered independent. Not only are there too many firms to collude (to coordinate their decisions), but each firm constitutes such a small share of the market that its behavior has only a negligible effect on others in the market. Consequently, each firm can assume that rivals will ignore its actions. This means, for example, that monopolistically competitive firms set their prices in isolation, without fear that others will follow their lead.

Not all industries satisfy this requirement. As one of this country's *big-three* automobile producers, General Motors is aware that its competitors are watching closely. Any price change it announces is likely to influence Ford and Chrysler. If it offers rebates or discount financing, its rivals are likely to follow suit. The automobile manufacturing industry simply does not have enough sellers to be monopolistically competitive. Instead it is oligopolistic.

In contrast, there are sufficient retail car dealers in Nashville for the assumption of independence to be defensible. A dealer can discount its car prices or improve service without worrying how its competitors will respond. Likewise, there are so many shoe stores, dry cleaners, and video shops in urban areas that such markets are considered monopolistically competitive.

Free Entry and Exit   The final requirement is that producers must be free to move resources into or out of the industry. Unlike the monopolist, firms in a monopolistically competitive market are not sheltered from competition. When the market is profitable, new firms enter; when conditions sour, firms pull out. For example, when car sales plummeted nearly 30 percent in the early 1980s, more than 4400 U.S. dealerships went out of business. When car sales later improved, thousands of new dealerships were formed.

Monopoly and Competition—A Bit of Each

The similarities to perfect competition are obvious. Both monopolistically and perfectly competitive industries are characterized by a large number of firms and by easy entry and exit. But unlike perfect competition, each monopolistically competitive firm sells a distinct product. This is where the monopoly element appears. Because no other firm sells exactly the same product, a monopolistically competitive firm has some control over its price—its demand curve slopes downward.

A monopolistically competitive firm can raise its price without losing all its customers. Some shoppers will continue to buy from the firm—despite its higher price—because they believe it offers a superior product, or they trust the manager, or they find the store conveniently located. Brand loyalty often plays a role. Whatever the reason, some customers will stick with a company even if it raises its price relative to its competitors. In contrast, a perfectly competitive firm attempting to charge more than competitors ends up with no customers.

Although product differentiation gives the firm some discretion over price, the presence of close substitutes limits the firm's ability to raise price. With similar products on the market, consumers are highly sensitive to price. A car dealer that raises its prices by ten percent can expect to lose more than ten percent of its customers. In other words, the firm's demand curve, even though not perfectly elastic, is highly elastic.

The demand curve of a monopolistically competitive firm is illustrated in Figure 26-1 (page 592). Note that, similar to a monopolist, the firm also has a downward-sloping marginal revenue curve. As you learned in Chapter 25, a downward-sloping demand curve implies that the firm must lower price to sell additional output, meaning that marginal revenue declines with output.

Equilibrium in the Short Run

The rules for short-run profit maximization are the same for the monopolistically competitive firm as for the monopolist. Production continues to the point where marginal revenue equals marginal cost. The firm then sells this level of output for the highest price possible given its demand curve. If price exceeds average total cost, the firm earns a profit; if price falls short of average total cost, the firm suffers a loss;

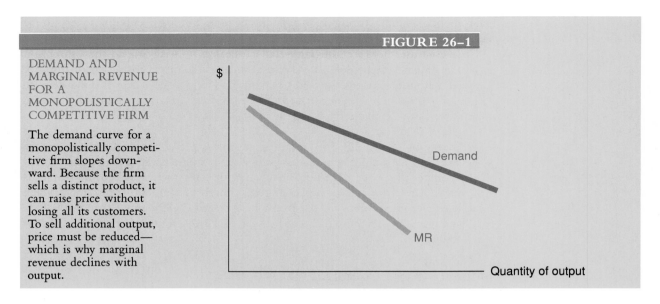

FIGURE 26–1

DEMAND AND MARGINAL REVENUE FOR A MONOPOLISTICALLY COMPETITIVE FIRM

The demand curve for a monopolistically competitive firm slopes downward. Because the firm sells a distinct product, it can raise price without losing all its customers. To sell additional output, price must be reduced—which is why marginal revenue declines with output.

if price equals average cost, the firm earns a normal profit. All three cases are illustrated in Figure 26-2. For simplicity, the average variable cost curve has been omitted from the diagram, but $P \geq$ AVC remains a condition for production.

Long-Run Equilibrium

The monopolistically competitive firm does not accept losses in the long run and, unlike the monopolist, cannot earn long-run profits either. Only normal profits are

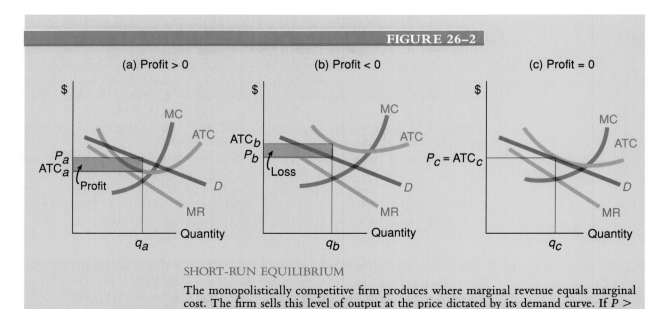

FIGURE 26–2

SHORT-RUN EQUILIBRIUM

The monopolistically competitive firm produces where marginal revenue equals marginal cost. The firm sells this level of output at the price dictated by its demand curve. If $P >$ ATC the firm earns a profit in the short run (a). If $P <$ ATC the firm suffers a loss (b). If $P =$ ATC the firm breaks even (c).

possible in the long run. To understand why this must be true, assume that firms are enjoying short-run profits. Because entry is easy, new firms will be drawn into the industry. As the number of competitors increases, each firm's share of the market dwindles: new firms take away some of the existing firms' customers. For example, with more car dealers in a city, existing dealers can expect to sell fewer cars, other things equal. This is represented by a leftward shift in the firm's demand curve.

Entry into the industry continues and demand continues to fall until profits are eliminated. Thus, long-run equilibrium is characterized by two conditions: profit maximization (MR = MC) and normal profit (P = LRAC). The second condition occurs when the demand curve is tangent to the long-run average cost curve (point X in Figure 26-3).

Alternatively, if the industry is characterized by short-run losses, equilibrium is achieved by the departure of firms from the industry. As some firms pull out, remaining firms gain customers—their demand curves shift rightward. This process continues until normal profits are established. Only then is the industry in long-run equilibrium.

Evaluating Monopolistic Competition

Perfect competition was praised for efficiently allocating resources to those sectors where they are valued most highly and for producing an industry's output at the lowest possible cost. Monopolistic competition falls short of the perfectly competi-

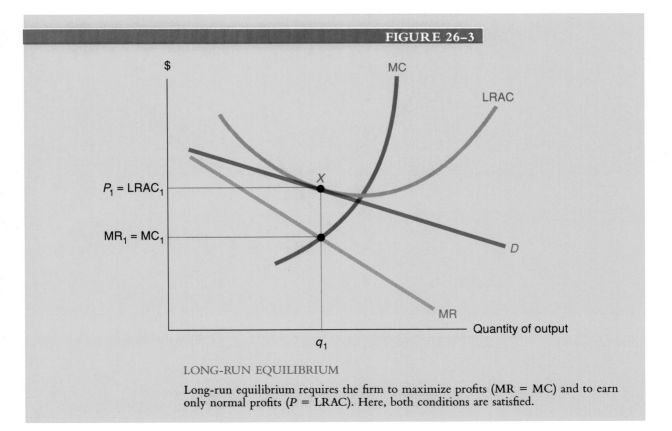

FIGURE 26-3

LONG-RUN EQUILIBRIUM

Long-run equilibrium requires the firm to maximize profits (MR = MC) and to earn only normal profits (P = LRAC). Here, both conditions are satisfied.

tive ideal, yet few economists are alarmed by this. In fact, in some industries the advantages of monopolistic competition may outweigh the disadvantages. At issue are the costs and benefits of product differentiation. We begin first with the costs.

Resources are not allocated efficiently under monopolistic competition. As illustrated in Figure 26-3, price exceeds marginal cost—the value to consumers of another unit of output is greater than the marginal cost of producing it. From the perspective of society, not enough output is being produced.

Nor is industry output being produced efficiently—that is, at the minimum possible cost. Long-run equilibrium for the firm occurs where demand is tangent to the long-run average cost curve. Because the firm's demand curve is downward sloping, this tangency can occur only on the declining segment of the average cost curve, not where average cost is at a minimum. This is illustrated in Figure 26-4. The firm produces q_1 output at an average cost of $LRAC_1$. Had the firm produced q_2 output instead, the average cost would have been only $LRAC_2$.

Another way to describe the situation is to say that monopolistically competitive firms have *excess capacity*—they are underutilizing their resources. By producing more output, monopolistically competitive firms could drive down unit costs. In a sense, the monopolistically competitive industry is being populated with too many firms. With fewer firms, each producing a greater output, average cost could be reduced and with it price.

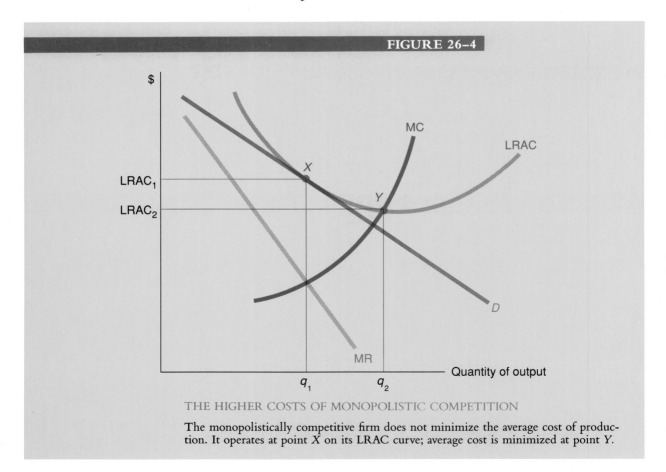

FIGURE 26–4

THE HIGHER COSTS OF MONOPOLISTIC COMPETITION

The monopolistically competitive firm does not minimize the average cost of production. It operates at point X on its LRAC curve; average cost is minimized at point Y.

But do we really want fewer firms? A large number of restaurants provides greater variety of food and atmosphere. Having many brands of clothing permits consumers to satisfy their individual tastes. Remember too that monopolistically competitive firms differ in quality and service. With fewer dry cleaners you may be forced to accept shirts that are too starchy or poorly pressed. With fewer car dealers you may be unable to find one that gives you the level of service you desire.

The existence of extra firms also saves consumers time. If a community has fewer grocery stores, each serving more people, consumers on average must travel farther to do their shopping. Average travel time to restaurants, dry cleaners, and similar establishments also increases. Given the value of consumers' time, as well as the value they place on choice and variety, monopolistic competition does not appear so bad after all. Whether it is as desirable as perfect competition, with its lower prices but homogeneous output, depends on how the benefits of product differentiation stack up against the costs. On this issue, opinions vary.

Nonprice Competition

Monopolistically competitive firms are always introducing "new and improved" products in an effort to win additional customers. The debate over the benefits of product differentiation deals largely with the extent to which "new and improved" is really better.

Although the monopolistically competitive firm earns only normal profits in the long run, the short run is another story. By increasing demand for its products, a firm may be able to create short-run profits. These profits ultimately disappear as competitors imitate successful products; by then, however, the firm may have another new product to dazzle the public.

Monopolistically competitive firms can increase demand for their products through various forms of **nonprice competition,** including product development, packaging, and advertising. Product development refers to the creation and introduction of a distinct product, either totally new or in a different form. Examples include liquid soap, chicken nuggets, soft and chewy cookies, and disposable diapers. Such products are often the outgrowth of research and development. Product development can also take the form of a new or improved service (see Exhibit 26-2, page 596).

Even if the basic product remains unchanged, companies can often increase market share by repackaging an item. Cosmetic companies discovered that the same lipstick they had been selling for years became a big hit once it was placed in see-through tubes. Heinz boosted its sales by introducing ketchup in a squeezable bottle and Motts scored big when it brought out applesauce in single-serving containers. So strong was the demand for convenience that consumers gobbled up the newly packaged applesauce even though a six-pack of single-serving containers was priced 35-percent higher than a jar containing the same volume of applesauce.

Companies can sometimes boost demand without changing either the basic product or the way it is packaged. A successful advertising campaign may convince consumers that a product is better, or at least more alluring. Often ads do little more than create an image or make better use of an established image. The Morris-the-Cat commercials were so successful for 9-Lives that the brand became the leading seller of canned cat food. Sales of dry and semimoist 9-Lives, which consumers did not associate with Morris the Cat, remained sluggish. The company, however, found an

---

EXHIBIT 26–2

WIPE YOUR FEET, PLEASE

John Grubb wanted to distinguish his San Francisco construction company, Clearwood Building Inc., from a host of competitors. So, in early 1983, he and his brother Robert started talking to Clearwood's customers: the architects and designers who hired their services.

What, the brothers asked their customers, were the worst features of Clearwood's competitors? The answer: Bad manners, workers who tracked dirt across carpets, and beat-up construction trucks, which high-class clients objected to having parked in their driveways.

Those seemingly small points were the signal for a repositioning. The brothers decided to make

Clearwood the contractor of choice among the Bay Area's upper crust. The company bought a new truck and kept it spotless. Its estimators donned jackets and ties. And its work crews, now impeccably polite, began rolling protective runners over carpets before they set foot in clients' homes. In less than two years, Clearwood's annual revenue jumped to $1 million from $200,000.

Source: Steven Galante, "More Firms Quiz Customers for Clues about Competition," *The Wall Street Journal*, March 3, 1986, p. 17. Reprinted by permission of *The Wall Street Journal.* © Dow Jones & Company, Inc. 1986. All rights reserved.

---

easy way to change that. It added a picture of finicky Morris to its packages of dry and semimoist cat food. Within four months, sales of these two items doubled.[5,6]

The Effects of Advertising

The goal of advertising is to increase demand, thereby boosting revenue for the firm. By creating a favorable image or name (face) recognition, advertising can sell anything from cat food to designer jeans. But advertising is also an expense. As illustrated in Figure 26-5, advertising shifts the firm's cost curves upward.

This does *not* mean, however, that the average cost of the firm's product is higher if it advertises. Because advertising increases the amount the firm can sell, it causes the firm to move down its average cost curve. To the extent the firm enjoys economies of scale, advertising could boost sales sufficiently so that average cost is actually lower in the presence of advertising. In Figure 26-5, if advertising increases output from q_1 to q_3, average cost falls from ATC_1 to ATC_3. Of course, if output rises only to q_2, average cost climbs to ATC_2. The effect of advertising on the firm's average cost is therefore ambiguous. In summary, advertising generates benefits for the firm, including increased product demand and possibly a lower average cost. When the benefits of advertising exceed the costs, the firm finds it profitable to advertise.

Even when the firm benefits from advertising, it is not clear that society does. Do the millions of dollars spent on 9-Lives commercials really benefit consumers? They do not improve the product, and it is questionable whether they provide any useful information. To take a more dramatic case, consider advertisements for

---

[5]Some economists prefer to classify the pet-food industry as oligopolistic rather than as monopolistically competitive. Chapter 27 looks at certain procedures used by economists in an effort to categorize industries.

[6]The previous two paragraphs incorporate examples from Philip Gutis, "What's New in Food Packaging," *New York Times*, June 8, 1986.

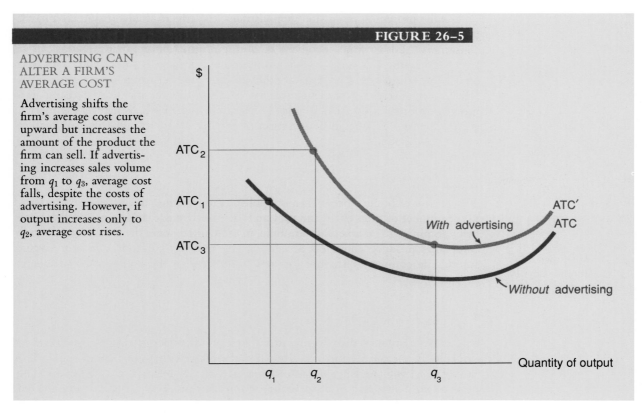

FIGURE 26-5

ADVERTISING CAN
ALTER A FIRM'S
AVERAGE COST

Advertising shifts the
firm's average cost curve
upward but increases the
amount of the product the
firm can sell. If advertising increases sales volume
from q_1 to q_3, average cost
falls, despite the costs of
advertising. However, if
output increases only to
q_2, average cost rises.

cigarettes. They were considered so harmful to society that in 1971 the U.S.
government banned cigarette ads on television and imposed restrictions on printed
ads. Other advertisements have been criticized as misleading. For such reasons, some
individuals want the government to place further restrictions on advertisements and,
in the process, to lessen firms' ability to differentiate their products.

Advertising also has its defenders. At its best, advertising informs. Consumers
learn of competing products and the advantages of each. Advertising can also convey
valuable information about price—for example, letting consumers know that a
discount store sells the same drug as a pharmacy but at half the price. This
information saves consumers time and money.

A much-cited study compared the price of eyeglasses in states that permitted
advertising and states where advertising was restricted. The study found that the
price of eyeglasses was at least 25-percent higher in states that restricted advertising.
Prohibition on advertising increased the monopoly power of established companies,
making it harder for new firms to break into the market.[7]

Sometimes professional groups condemn advertising as unethical or demeaning.
The real reason may be economic. State bar associations prohibited advertising by
lawyers until 1977, when the United States Supreme Court ruled these bans
unconstitutional. Taking advantage of the opportunity to advertise, lawyers began
aggressively competing for clients and, as they did, the price of many legal services
fell by 50 percent or more.

---

[7]Lee Benham, "The Effect of Advertising on the Price of Eyeglasses," *Journal of Law and Economics*
(October 1972), pp. 337–352.

As the preceding discussion demonstrates, the effects of advertising are mixed. Sometimes advertising leads to lower prices and more-informed decisions by consumers. At other times it conveys no useful information and may even mislead. It is for this reason that an overall assessment of advertising is so difficult. This also underscores the controversy over whether product differentiation, which often relies heavily on advertising, benefits society. Perhaps the merits of advertising and product differentiation are best judged on a case-by-case basis. Whatever the merits, advertising and product differentiation often play a key role in the final market structure—oligopoly.

OLIGOPOLY

Oligopoly
A market structure in which a small number of firms dominates the industry; other firms are kept out through barriers to entry.

The central difference between monopolistic competition and **oligopoly** pertains to the number of firms in the industry and their relative size. In oligopoly a few large firms dominate the market. For example, in the United States the four largest aircraft companies produce about 66 percent of the industry's output; the four largest automobile companies account for over 90 percent of the domestically produced automobiles.

Barriers to Entry

In contrast to monopolistic competition, firms find entry into oligopolistic markets difficult. Barriers exist for basically the same reasons they do in monopoly. The number of companies having access to a critical raw material may be small. The government may permit only a limited number of producers in a community. For example, it may grant only two cable television franchises or may license only a handful of radio stations. Alternatively, economies of scale may provide cost advantages for large, established firms. It has been estimated, for example, that to minimize the average cost of production the locomotive industry can have no more than four producers, the cigarette industry no more than seven.[8]

Mutual Interdependence

Mutual Interdependence
An interrelationship among producers. Firms, aware that their actions affect others in the industry, make decisions only after taking into account how rivals are likely to respond.

Because an oligopolistic industry has relatively few firms, the assumption of the monopolistically competitive model—that rivals ignore a firm's decisions—is no longer tenable. A firm realizes that once it accounts for a significant share of the market, its actions are likely to influence others in the market. Accordingly, each firm takes into account the anticipated response of rivals when formulating its own strategy. This relationship among firms in the industry is known as **mutual interdependence.**

To the giant steelmaker USX, mutual interdependence means looking beyond its own factory gates. If it accepts a strike, rather than accede to union demands, it may be unable to meet customer orders. In that event, other steel companies will increase production in order to sell to present USX customers. USX is aware of this and knows that some of these lost customers may never come back. It also realizes that price cutting after the strike ends may be an ineffective way to rebuild business. Other steel companies, wanting to hold on to their customers, are likely to cut their

---

[8]Louis Esposito, Norman Noel, and Francis Esposito, "Dissolution and Scale Economies: Additional Estimates and Analysis," *Antitrust and Law Review* (Fall 1971), Table 1.

prices as well. Therefore, before taking any action USX must carefully consider how its decisions will affect rival steel producers and, in turn, how their responses will affect USX.

Similarly, General Motors is aware that any increase in Ford's share of the U.S. automotive market comes partially at GM's expense. Therefore, General Motors closely monitors activity at Ford. When the aerodynamic styling of Ford's Taurus and other cars became a big hit, General Motors accelerated plans to redesign its own cars.

Type of Product

Firms in an oligopolistic industry may produce either homogeneous or differentiated products. The output of the steel and the aluminum industries is usually considered homogeneous—uniform across producers. Differentiated oligopolies include the automobile, aircraft, and mainframe computer industries.

Nonprice Competition

When the products of different firms are distinct, an oligopolistic firm has an incentive to make its product stand out. Therefore, as with monopolistic competition, advertising is common. For example, in a recent year Proctor & Gamble, Philip Morris, and RJR Nabisco each spent close to $1 billion on advertising.

Nonprice competition is generally viewed by companies as preferable to price cutting. If Proctor & Gamble lowers the price on Tide, other detergent makers can quickly match the decrease, thereby maintaining their share of the market. The end result may be lower not higher profits at Proctor & Gamble. But if Proctor & Gamble can run an effective advertising campaign—convincing consumers that Tide really is better than other detergents—the competitors may be unable to prevent Tide from taking away customers.

Product development has a similar advantage over price cutting. Even when a successful new product is ultimately imitated by competitors, it may take years before they can bring their versions to market. In the mean time, the oligopolist introducing the new product may be able to earn substantial profits.

This is what Apple Computer did when it introduced its Macintosh personal computer with desktop publishing capability. The product enjoyed enviable success and was largely responsible for Apple's rebound. While earnings at IBM fell, earnings at Apple soared 150 percent in 1986. Apple's stock, which was selling at $14 per share in mid-1985, vaulted to $82 in less than two years.

As might be expected, competitors took notice. To quote one publication:

> The Macintosh won't be unique for long. Graphics options for the IBM PC are improving fast, and dozens of companies are finding ways to adapt PCs for desktop publishing. . . . The competition has its eye on other Macintosh features too.[9]

In summary, although competitors can quickly and easily match a price reduction, responding to a successful advertising campaign or to a new product is more difficult and takes longer. Therefore, where products are distinct, oligopolists typically rely on nonprice competition as a means to improve their position in the market.

---

[9]Katherine Hafner and Geoff Lewis, "Apple's Comeback," *Business Week,* January 19, 1987, p. 86.

Price Stability

If oligopolistic firms compete primarily through nonprice competition, rather than by adjusting price, one would predict that such industries will be characterized by considerable price stability. There is evidence that in many oligopolistic industries prices are stable over long periods of time. One study found that prices in the steel and chemicals industries remain unchanged on average for more than twelve months at a time.[10] Even more dramatic is the case of sulphur. From 1926–1938 its price was frozen at $18 per ton. Compared to more competitive markets, oligopolistic prices tend to be sticky.

FORMAL MODELS OF OLIGOPOLY

Fifty years ago the economist Paul Sweezy observed that:

> Oligopoly is probably the typical case throughout a large part of the modern economy, and yet the theory of oligopoly can scarcely be said to be in a very advanced state, consisting as it does of special cases which allow of little generalization.[11]

Despite the emergence since then of new theories of oligopoly, this view remains largely true today.

Unlike other market structures, there is no universal theory of oligopoly. Instead, the theory of oligopoly consists of a large number of different models, each a special case that holds only under certain restrictive conditions. Before a model can be formulated, various assumptions must be made. In the case of oligopoly, the number of potential assumptions is enormous. How do other firms in the industry react when one firm adjusts its price? Do they maintain their present prices, match the first firm's price change, or adopt some different strategy? Do firms cooperate with each other—that is, collude—or do they regard each other as adversaries? Is there one firm that is the first to change prices, a price leader?

Different assumptions lead to different models. While one model may appear most appropriate for a particular oligopolistic industry, a different model may be superior for a second industry. No model is consistent with the behavior of every oligopolistic industry. Time constraints prevent a discussion of all models of oligopoly, but the present section discusses some of the most famous models, starting with Sweezy's kinked demand curve.

The Kinked Demand Curve Model

Kinked Demand Curve
The demand curve facing an oligopolist if rivals in the industry match the firm's price reductions but ignore its price increases.

The **kinked demand curve** model was posed as a potential explanation of price stability under oligopoly. Its central premise is that "rivals react differently according to whether a price change is upward or downward."[12]

Consider an industry in which firms sell differentiated products and do not collude. Assume one of the oligopolists is currently selling q_1 output at a price of P_1. How much, it wonders, can it sell if it adopts a new price? In other words, what does its demand curve look like? The answer clearly depends on how its rivals react.

---

[10]Dennis W. Carlton, "The Rigidity of Prices," *American Economic Review* (September 1986). pp. 637–58.

[11]Paul Sweezy, "Demand Under Conditions of Oligopoly," *Journal of Political Economy* (August 1939), p. 568.

[12]Same as 11, p. 568.

If rivals ignore the price change, the firm's demand curve will be highly elastic. Because products in the industry are close substitutes, the firm stands to win many new customers if it lowers its price and lose many customers if it raises price. On the other hand, if rivals match any price change demand will be much less elastic. A lower price will increase sales somewhat as consumers buy more of the industry's product, but the firm cannot expect to take customers away from its competitors since they are similarly reducing their prices. Thus the firm faces two potential demand curves, which are labeled D_{ignore} and D_{match} in Figure 26-6(a).

Which demand curve is relevant? According to this model, the firm's demand curve consists of segments of each. If the firm lowers its price it expects others to follow suit, in order to retain their customers. Thus for prices below P_1, D_{match} is the appropriate demand curve. But if the firm raises its price it expects rivals to do nothing since, by keeping their prices unchanged, they pick up many of the firm's customers. Accordingly, for prices above P_1, D_{ignore} is relevant. The firm's complete demand curve is represented by the heavy color line in Figure 26-6(a), with a kink at P_1.

Corresponding to the demand curves D_{ignore} and D_{match}, respectively, are the marginal revenue curves MR_{ignore} and MR_{match}. These are added to the model in Figure 26-6(b). Each marginal revenue curve is applicable over the price range where

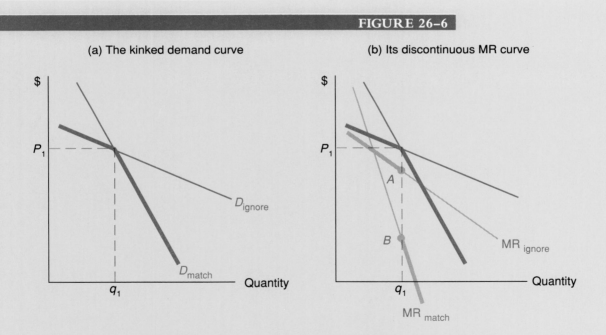

FIGURE 26–6

(a) The kinked demand curve

(b) Its discontinuous MR curve

DERIVATION OF THE KINKED DEMAND CURVE AND THE CORRESPONDING MARGINAL REVENUE CURVE

According to the kinked demand curve model, a firm assumes that rivals ignore a price increase but match a price cut. The result is a kinked demand curve (depicted by the heavy line), which consists of segments of D_{ignore} (for $P > P_1$) and D_{match} (for $P < P_1$). The marginal revenue curve associated with the kinked demand curve is discontinuous, jumping from point A to point B.

its demand curve is applicable. Thus, MR_{ignore} comes into play for prices above P_1, and MR_{match} comes into play for prices below P_1. The relevant section of each marginal revenue curve is depicted by a heavy color line. Notice that at q_1, where the kink occurs, marginal revenue jumps from point A to point B. That is, the marginal revenue curve associated with a kinked demand curve has a gap or vertical break in it. This has important implications.

The kinked demand curve and its corresponding marginal revenue curve are reproduced in Figure 26-7. Assume the firm initially faces the marginal cost curve MC_1. To maximize profit, it produces q_1 output and charges a price of P_1. (The firm would not produce less than q_1 since $MR > MC$ here nor more than q_1 since that would lead to $MC > MR$.) Now assume that the marginal cost curve shifts upward to MC_2. Profits are still maximized at an output of q_1 and a price of P_1. In fact, for any marginal cost curve that intersects the marginal revenue curve at its vertical break, P_1 remains the optimal price for the firm. This model thus explains why prices of oligopolistic firms are so inflexible. Given a kinked demand curve, prices remain rigid for a wide range of costs.

Despite the insights of this model, the kinked demand curve has been highly criticized. First, it is not a complete model. It explains why a price, once established, is likely to persist over time. But it does not explain how that price was initially obtained. Second, some empirical work suggests that prices are frequently no more rigid in oligopolistic industries than in monopolistic industries, despite the fact that

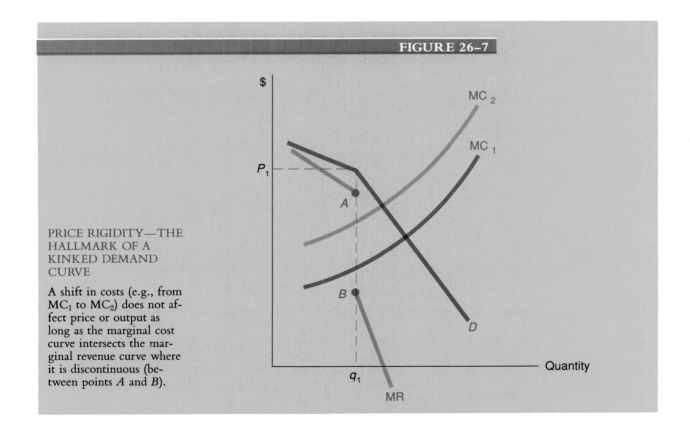

FIGURE 26-7

PRICE RIGIDITY—THE HALLMARK OF A KINKED DEMAND CURVE

A shift in costs (e.g., from MC_1 to MC_2) does not affect price or output as long as the marginal cost curve intersects the marginal revenue curve where it is discontinuous (between points A and B).

monopolists do not have kinked demand curves.[13] This suggests that price rigidity is often due to some factor other than a kinked demand curve. Most economists conclude that the kinked demand curve model remains a special case, relevant for no more than a small number of oligopolistic industries.

The limited applicability of the kinked demand curve is actually not surprising once you realize that there are other, equally defensible ways to model the behavior of rival firms. For example, *game theory* provides an alternative approach (see Exhibit 26-3). In addition, the kinked demand curve is limited to those cases where firms in

---

EXHIBIT 26-3

GAME THEORY

Although **game theory** can be highly mathematical—depending on the number of *players* in the game and on their strategies—we illustrate this theory with a simple two-player game. The players are two oligopolists—Jones and Johnson. The strategy in this game concerns price.

Suppose production costs have just increased. Each company must decide whether to maintain its price at $10 or to raise it to $12. If both companies raise price, each will earn $1000 in profits (see Table 26-1). If one company raises price to $12 and the other keeps price at $10, the low-price company will see its profits rise to $1200 while the high-price company—losing many of its customers—will see its profits fall to $400. Finally, if both companies keep the price at $10, each will earn $600.

What should Jones do? Assuming that Jones and Johnson do not communicate with one anoth-

er, the solution is for Jones to charge a price of $10. No matter which price Johnson sets, Jones will earn $200 more by charging $10 rather than $12. Johnson has a similar payoff table and, for the same reason, can also be expected to charge $10.

From the perspective of the individual firm it is rational to maintain the price at $10. Yet Jones and Johnson would each be better off if they *both* raised the price to $12. In that event, profits of each would climb from $600 to $1000. The problem is that neither believes the other will charge $12. Each firm, aware of the other's situation, expects its rival to charge $10. If only Jones and Johnson could coordinate their activities—could work together for a common end—they would each agree to charge $12. This example underscores the incentive that firms have to collude and provides another perspective on price stability in the absence of collusion.

TABLE 26-1

PAYOFF TABLE (profits) FOR JONES

		Johnson	
		$P = \$12$	$P = \$10$
Jones	$P = \$12$	$1000	$400
	$P = \$10$	$1200	$600

The profit that Jones earns depends on the price each firm charges. If Johnson sets a price of $12, Jones can earn $1000 by also charging $12 or $1200 by charging $10. If Johnson's price is $10, Jones can earn $400 by charging $12 or $600 by charging $10.

---

[13]George Stigler, "The Kinky Oligopoly Demand Curve and Rigid Prices," *Journal of Political Economy* (October 1947), pp. 432–449; "The Literature of Economics: The Case of the Kinked Oligopoly Demand Curve," *Economic Inquiry* (April 1978), pp. 185–204.

an industry are adversaries. In many industries firms work together as partners, rather than as rivals. In such instances the appropriate model must be built upon the assumption of collusion.

Collusion

The preceding discussion was based on the assumption that firms do not coordinate their activities—that they do not collude. Collusion is tempting, however, because it offers firms an opportunity to increase their prices and profits.

Collusion may be secret or public, formal or implied. Sometimes producers band together to form a **cartel**—an organization that determines how much output each firm will produce and either explicitly or implicitly determines price. The goal of the cartel is to increase profits in the industry and to apportion these profits among the individual firms.

Collusion is generally illegal in the United States, but that does not prevent its occurrence. Each year the Justice Department prosecutes companies for conspiring to fix prices or restrict output. One of the most famous cases involved the electric equipment industry. In the 1950s, the major suppliers of electrical equipment devised a number of ingenious schemes for rigging the market. For government contracts, bids were coordinated to assure each company a specified share of the market. For example, it was agreed ahead of time that General Electric would submit the winning bid 40.3 percent of the time. Other firms would intentionally quote the government higher prices, assuring General Electric the work no matter what price it charged. Other approaches were also adopted:

> A "phases of the moon" system was used to allocate low-bidding privileges in the high voltage switchgear field, with a new seller assuming low-bidding priority every two weeks. The designated bidder subtracted a specified percentage margin from the book price to capture orders during its phase, while others added various margins to the book price. The result was an ostensibly random pattern of quotations, conveying the impression of independent behavior.[14]

Although this conspiracy was uncovered, and the guilty parties punished, other conspiracies go undetected.

It must also be remembered that collusive arrangements are legal in many countries; sometimes they even enjoy government protection. When a few countries are the major suppliers of a commodity, they often band together to form *international commodity agreements* whose purpose is to maintain high prices for the commodity and high revenues for the producing countries. Among the commodities that have been covered by such agreements are bauxite, tin, rubber, and tea. Because such commodities are traded in international markets, consumers cannot escape the effects of collusion even when firms in their own country do not participate.

Some collusion is more subtle than cartels or agreements to fix market share. Often companies are aware of common goals (e.g., high prices) and informally work together to achieve these goals. They may refrain from such competitive practices as advertising and posting prices, and each may agree not to precipitate a price war. Executives who violate the implicit code of behavior may be brought back in line

Cartel
An organization of producers that is designed to set price and output for its members.

---

[14]F. M. Scherer, *Industrial Market Structure and Economic Performance,* 2nd ed. (Chicago: Rand-McNally College Publishing Co., 1980), p. 171.

through arm twisting or intimidation by other members of the industry. Sometimes companies have an understanding that they will not *raid* each other for customers, in essence making customers captives of their present supplier. Informal agreements such as these are often referred to as **gentlemen's agreements**

Gentlemen's Agreement
An informal understanding among members of a group to pursue practices that are in the best interests of the group.

Although less structured than cartels and the like, informal agreements may nonetheless be effective. A case in point is the famous "Gary dinners," hosted by Judge Elbert Gary, chairman of the board at U.S. Steel, and attended by executives of all major steel companies:

> Judge Gary once explained that the "close communication and contact" developed at these dinners generated such mutual "respect and affectionate regard" among steel industry leaders that all considered the obligation to cooperate and avoid destructive competition "more binding . . . than any written or verbal contract."[15]

Whatever its form, collusion is designed to increase industry profits. In fact, in the limiting case the colluding partners act as a monopolist operating more than one plant.[16] The industry marginal cost curve is obtained by summing the marginal cost curves of the individual firms. The group then decides to produce that level of output for which industry marginal revenue equals industry marginal cost and to charge that price given by the industry demand curve. The difficult part in this arrangement is agreeing on how to distribute industry profits. For example, if individual firms are to be assigned a certain share of the market, each firm will lobby for a large share. Ultimately however, the firms must reach a consensus if the cartel is to survive.

Survival is by no means assured. The success and longevity of a collusive agreement hinges on a variety of factors, including number of firms, heterogeneity of products, and antitrust laws.

Number of Firms   The more firms in the industry the more likely it is that at least one of them will not go along with the agreement. By operating outside a cartel—undercutting its price—a rogue firm stands to pick up much of the cartel's business, perhaps causing the cartel to unravel. Even when all firms agree to collude, cheating may still occur. The more firms there are in an industry, the more difficult it is to spot cheating and identify the guilty party.

An individual firm has an incentive to secretly shave its price since, by so doing, it can increase greatly the amount of output it sells. It will gain customers at the expense of firms adhering to the cartel price. Once secret discounting begins, it has the potential to spread throughout the industry, undermining the agreement among producers. For example, cheating threatened to rip OPEC apart, as the following passage indicates:

> Ali Khalifa al Sabah, oil minister of Kuwait, warned that a "significant drop" in oil prices would inevitably result if other OPEC members continued hidden discounting and other violations of OPEC agreements. Without naming any countries, but obviously with Iran, Libya, Nigeria, and Venezuela in mind, Sheik Ali said that "individual interests have dominated collective interests inside OPEC. . . . We cannot continue to sacrifice if other members continue to violate the resolutions."[17]

---

[15]Same as 14, p. 170.
[16]This case was discussed in Chapter 25, pp. 581–82.
[17]Youssef Ibrahim, "OPEC Confronts Deep Split in Ranks," *The Wall Street Journal,* October 21, 1982, p. 37.

Product Heterogeneity Collusion is more difficult when products in the industry are distinct, rather than identical. With identical products, firms decide on a single common price. But when products are distinct, firms must agree on an entire set of prices. For example, if Ford and General Motors were to collude, they would have to come to terms on the prices each charges. They might agree that General Motors should charge more for its Cadillac Allante than Ford charges for its Lincoln Continental, but settling on the size of that premium would be difficult. Ford would favor a large premium, in order to make the Continental a better buy; General Motors would push for a more modest premium.

Legal Barriers Collusion in the United States is also hindered by antitrust laws. Ford and General Motors cannot legally coordinate pricing decisions or otherwise conspire to raise their collective profits. As the electric equipment conspiracy demonstrates, laws are sometimes broken; but legal restrictions and the penalties imposed on guilty parties raise the cost of colluding and reduce its occurrence.

Other Concerns Even where legal, collusive arrangements typically have been short lived. Problems mount over time. To the extent collusion succeeds in raising price and profits, it increases the incentive of new firms to enter the industry. Although entry into oligopolistic markets is not easy, barriers can sometimes be overcome. When new firms gain access to the market, existing firms lose customers and see profits fall. If the new firms do not participate in the collusion, they can force existing firms to abandon their arrangements, or at least modify them.

In addition, demand for an industry's product is more elastic in the long run than in the short run. Consumers' ability to substitute increases with time. Therefore, other things equal, if firms maintain an artificially high price they can anticipate losing more and more business as time passes. For such reasons, even successful cartels generally see their power erode over time (see Exhibit 26-4).

Price Leadership

Price Leadership

A practice in certain oligopolistic industries whereby one firm initiates price changes and other firms in the industry follow its lead.

Although collusion is generally illegal in the United States, companies have been able to skirt antitrust laws through the practice of **price leadership**—firms in an industry follow the lead of a particular company, the price leader. When it raises price, so do they; when it lowers price, they quickly follow suit. Even though representatives of the individual companies may never make contact with one another, the end result is common prices.

Sometimes companies follow the lead of the largest firm in the industry, especially when that firm dominates the market (as does IBM in the mainframe computer market). At other times companies follow the low-cost firm, realizing that it is in their best interests to avoid a price war. If they attempted to charge less than the firm with the lowest average cost, it could retaliate by driving the price down to a level where only it enjoyed profits. To avoid this situation, other firms let the low-cost firm set the price and they follow suit. Finally, the price leader may be a *barometric firm*—that is, the first to realize that industry demand or costs have changed. If other firms recognize the barometric firm's ability to quickly detect changing market conditions, they may follow any price change it initiates.

Among the price leaders in U.S. industries have been Alcoa (aluminum), duPont (nylon), American Can and Continental Can (tin cans), and American Tobacco and R. J. Reynolds (cigarettes). As the latter two industries indicate, price

EXHIBIT 26–4

THE DECLINE OF OPEC?

The Organization of Petroleum Exporting Countries, OPEC, is considered one of the most successful cartels in history, yet not even it is immune to economic forces. Members of OPEC realized that, as a united front, they wielded tremendous economic power; they were producing most of the world's oil, and beneath their soil lay most of the known oil reserves. In 1973, they shocked the world by raising the price of oil from approximately $2.50 per barrel to $10, and making this price stick. Within ten years oil was selling for $34 per barrel, and OPEC had created hundreds of billions of dollars in new wealth for its members.

History teaches us that the very success of cartels often leads to their own undoing. A high price deters consumption while, at the same time, encouraging greater production. Between 1979 and 1985, oil consumption in the United States fell from 37 quads (quadrillion British thermal units) to 30 quads. Worldwide, oil consumption declined by about 20 percent. Meanwhile, spurred by the high price of oil, non-OPEC countries increased drilling and exploration. Major discoveries in the North Sea, Alaska, and Mexico provided new sources of oil. In this environment, OPEC was forced to cut back its own production in order to prop up prices. Daily production by OPEC nations fell from 31 million barrels in 1979 to 16 million in 1985. With the cutback, OPEC's share of the market fell to 30 percent and oil revenues sagged. Saudi Arabia, which had absorbed much of the decline in production, watched its oil revenues plunge from $113 billion in 1981 to $16 billion five years later.

OPEC realized that under a strategy of enforcing high prices its share of the market would continue to decline. Therefore, in late 1985 it adopted a new approach—it would maintain its "fair share" of the market. Unfortunately for OPEC, that meant accepting a much lower price. It could have a high price or high output, but not both. Although OPEC is not through as a cartel, many oil analysts believe that its best days are history. It is unlikely to enjoy the high measure of success that it did in the late 1970s.

leadership sometimes rotates from one company to another. In the steel industry, USX (formerly U.S. Steel) has traditionally set prices, as the following passage demonstrates:

> Four of the nation's largest steelmakers said they will match a price increase by U.S. Steel Corp. The move by the No. 1 steelmaker will boost prices by about 3% on sheet steel. U.S. Steel led a similar pricing move January 1 that boosted flat-rolled steel prices as much as 10%.[18]

AN EVALUATION OF OLIGOPOLY

In many respects oligopoly possesses the same advantages and disadvantages as monopoly. Because of economies of scale, costs may be minimized when an industry contains only a few producers. On the negative side, consumers are likely to face a price in excess of average total cost inasmuch as barriers to entry permit economic profits even in the long run. In addition, oligopoly leads to an inefficient allocation of resources—the value of another unit of the oligopolist's product exceeds the marginal cost of producing it.[19]

---

[18]J. Ernest Beazley, "Four Large Steelmakers to Boost Prices About 3%, Matching U.S. Steel Move," *The Wall Street Journal,* March 11, 1986, p. 6.

[19]Because the oligopolist's demand curve is downward sloping, price exceeds marginal revenue. Given that marginal revenue equals marginal cost in equilibrium, price must therefore exceed marginal cost.

Oligopoly and Technological Change[20]

The assessment of oligopoly also hinges on the relationship between market structure and technological progress. Some economists have argued that, compared to more competitive markets, oligopoly facilitates the introduction of new technology, thereby fostering economic growth. According to John Kenneth Galbraith: "A benign Providence . . . has made the modern industry of a few large firms an almost perfect instrument for inducing technical change."[21] Prior to Galbraith, Joseph Schumpeter extolled the virtues of large firms and monopoly power.[22]

Schumpeter-Galbraith Hypothesis
The claim that innovation occurs more rapidly when firms are large in size and comprise a substantial share of the market.

According to the **Schumpeter-Galbraith Hypothesis,** innovation frequently requires massive investment and perhaps a large research and development staff. Xerox spent more than $16 million creating its 914 copy machine and RCA poured $65 million into the development of its color television. Individuals and small companies do not have the resources necessary to undertake such investments. Beyond that, companies operating in a competitive environment do not have as strong an incentive to undertake research and development since their rewards for innovation quickly disappear as competitors flood the market with imitations of the new product. In contrast, barriers to entry provide the oligopolist with some protection and may permit it to earn economic profits on the new product even in the long run. Thus, according to this scenario, large oligopolistic firms have a greater ability and a greater incentive to innovate than do small competitive firms.

Not everyone subscribes to the Schumpeter-Galbraith view that big is better. Some contend that the bureaucracies of large firms stifle creativity and that oligopolistic firms often become complacent. Consistent with this latter view, studies of the major inventions since 1880 reveal that most were attributable to individuals or small businesses.[23] Less than one-third were the outgrowth of research and development by corporate giants.

But inventions are only the first stage of creating a useful product. Typically, inventions must be developed and refined before they are marketable. Because this can be an expensive, time-consuming process, it is here that the corporate resources often prove valuable. For example, although Kodachrome film was invented outside of the Kodak laboratories, it required an additional ten years of research—financed by Kodak—before this invention was ready to market. Thus, while large oligopolies are not generally the *source* of new ideas, they often play a key role in turning these ideas into finished products.

Highlighting the importance of size, statistics reveal that large firms contribute disproportionately to research and development in the United States. Manufacturing companies with 5000 or more employees spend about seven times as much per employee on research and development as do smaller companies. Most small companies do not even engage in formal research and development. Thus size appears important for technological growth, but only to a point. In general, the very largest firms spend no more on research and development per employee than slightly smaller firms, nor do they receive a proportionately greater share of patents.

---

[20]This section draws heavily from Scherer, same as 14, pp. 407–438.

[21]J. K. Galbraith, *American Capitalism: The Concept of Countervailing Power* (Boston: Houghton Mifflin, 1952), p. 91.

[22]Joseph Schumpeter, *Capitalism, Socialism, and Democracy* (New York: Harper & Row, 1942).

[23]John Jewkes, David Sawers, and Richard Stillerman, *The Sources of Invention* (New York: St. Martin's Press, 1959); Daniel Hamberg, "Invention in the Industrial Research Laboratory," *Journal of Political Economy* (April 1963), pp. 95–115.

These results are broadly supportive of the Schumpeter-Galbraith view, as are findings that productivity growth tends to be greater in oligopolistic industries than in more competitive industries.[24] Even so, economists continue to debate the importance of market structure. A leading authority on the subject finds evidence that industries classified as oligopolies have been blessed with greater opportunities for advancement. He concludes that these industries would have experienced above-average technological growth regardless of market structure. In other words, he questions whether an oligopolistic market structure actually *causes* the more rapid rates of innovation that have been observed.[25]

Others concede that oligopoly facilitates technological progress in some industries but argue that the optimal amount of market power varies from industry to industry. In their view, a mix of competitive and oligopolistic industries is more conducive to technological growth than having all industries oligopolistic (or all industries competitive). In summary, there is no consensus over the extent to which oligopoly promotes technological growth. The Schumpeter-Galbraith view may have some merit, but how much is unclear.

LOOKING AHEAD

This completes our formal presentation of market structure. In Chapter 27, we examine how market structure in the United States has changed over time. Is the economy becoming less competitive, as some have suggested? What role has the government played in shaping American industry and, in turn, how has government policy changed over time? Drawing on the analysis common to recent chapters, we study the actual structure of American business.

SUMMARY

1. Most industries in the real world fall somewhere between perfect competition and monopoly. The theories of monopolistic competition and oligopoly were formulated in an attempt to help explain behavior in these intermediate market structures.
2. Monopolistically competitive markets contain many firms, acting independently of one another, selling differentiated products. Entry to and exit from the industry is relatively easy. Because no other firm sells exactly the same product, a monopolistically competitive firm has some discretion over the price it charges.
3. Assuming that price covers average variable cost, the monopolistically competitive firm maximizes profit in the short run by producing where marginal revenue equals marginal cost. For long-run equilibrium a second condition must also hold: price equals average total cost. That is, monopolistically competitive firms earn only normal profit in the long run.
4. A feature of monopolistic competition is nonprice competition, designed to increase demand for the firm's product. In addition to product development and packaging, nonprice competition includes advertising. Advertising increases a firm's total cost but, given economies of scale, it may boost sales sufficiently to reduce average cost. Although some advertising harms society—for example, by misleading consumers—studies show that where advertising increases competition it can lead to lower prices.

---

[24]Douglas Greer and Stephen Rhoades, "Concentration and Productivity Changes in the Long and Short Run," *Southern Economic Journal* (October 1976), pp. 1031–1044.

[25]F. M. Scherer, "Market Structure and the Employment of Scientists and Engineers," *American Economic Review* (June 1967), pp. 524–531.

5. Under monopolistic competition resources are not allocated efficiently (price does not equal marginal cost), nor is the average cost of production minimized. If the industry contained fewer firms, each producing a larger output, average cost would be lower. On the other hand, the wide range of products under monopolistic competition provides consumers greater choice, and the presence of numerous firms saves consumers time.

6. Oligopoly is characterized by mutual interdependence. Because a few large firms dominate the market, each is aware that its actions affect rivals.

7. Where oligopolistic products are distinct, competition is more likely to consist of product development or advertising than price cutting, since the former is more difficult to respond to. This preference for nonprice competition is one reason prices tend to be more stable under oligopoly than in more competitive market structures.

8. The kinked demand curve offers a second explanation for price stability. According to this model, rivals match a price cut but ignore a price increase. Since neither response is what the firm wants, it is reluctant to alter price in either direction.

9. Although the kinked demand curve model assumes that firms are adversaries, firms have a strong incentive to collude. By working together against consumers, rather than against each other, firms can increase their profits. Collusion is generally against the law in the United States but is condoned and even promoted in many countries. Even where illegal, it sometimes still occurs.

10. Collusion can take many forms, from price fixing to allocating market shares to gentlemen's agreements. An organization of producers that sets price or output is called a cartel. Collusive agreements are more likely to be successful when the industry contains very few firms and when they produce a homogeneous product.

11. Some oligopolies are characterized by price leadership. Whenever a particular firm raises or lowers price, other firms follow suit.

12. Resources are allocated inefficiently under oligopoly, and price may exceed average total cost even in the long run (due to barriers to entry). On the other hand, where economies of scale are important, oligopoly may be the market structure that minimizes the average cost of production.

13. Some economists, including Schumpeter and Galbraith, argue that oligopoly favors technological progress. According to this view, large oligopolistic firms have both a greater capacity to finance research and development and a greater incentive than do small competitive firms. The evidence is mixed. Although oligopoly does not lead to a greater number of inventions, in some industries it helps develop the inventions—turning others' ideas into finished products. Large firms do carry out a disproportionate amount of research and development. But while oligopolies typically invest heavily in research and development, thereby spurring technological progress, the exact contribution of market structure is unclear. Some economists believe that investment in research and development depends primarily on factors other than market structure.

KEY TERMS

monopolistic competition	game theory
product differentiation	cartel
nonprice competition	gentlemen's agreement
oligopoly	price leadership
mutual interdependence	Schumpeter-Galbraith Hypothesis
kinked demand curve	

STUDY QUESTIONS AND PROBLEMS

1. Describe the demand curve of a monopolistically competitive producer. Why does it assume this particular shape?

2. Does the monopolistically competitive firm operate at the minimum point of its average total cost curve? Defend your answer.

3. A monopolistically competitive firm produces 100 units of output per period, selling each for $75. Marginal revenue and marginal cost of the one-hundredth unit are each $50. Average total cost is $60. (a) Does this situation correspond to short-run equilibrium? Why or why not? (b) Does this situation correspond to long-run equilibrium? Why or why not?

4. (a) Advertising has been criticized as wasteful to society or even worse. Explain why. (b) Now discuss some of the ways society may benefit from advertising.

5. (a) In what ways is monopolistic competition similar to perfect competition? In what ways is it different? (b) In what ways is monopolistic competition similar to oligopoly? In what ways is it different?

6. (a) What gives the kinked demand curve its kink? (b) If oligopolists are reluctant to change price, as the kinked demand curve model implies, does this mean that they do not compete against one another? Explain.

7. What is a *gentlemen's agreement?* How does it differ from a cartel?

8. In 1987, IBM announced price cuts of up to 35 percent on its personal computers. Within days AT&T, Hewlett-Packard, Epson, and NCR announced similar price reductions on their personal computers. Is the reaction of these other computer makers consistent with (a) the kinked demand curve model and (b) price leadership? Which model do you feel is more appropriate for the personal computer industry? Why?

9. Although collusion in the United States is generally illegal, agricultural *marketing orders* allow Sunkist and other fruit growers to form cartels. For some crops, boards limit the amount of output each producer in the United States can legally sell. (a) Discuss two factors that are likely to determine the success of these cartels. (b) If successful, how are the cartels likely to affect price and output?

10. Evaluate the following argument:

> The design of a new, more advanced aircraft or a super train requires many tens of millions of dollars. Size is important. Therefore, if we want to spur technological growth in agriculture, we should replace small, family farms with large, corporate farms.

SELECTED REFERENCES

Kenneth Clarkson and Roger Miller, *Industrial Organization* (New York: McGraw-Hill, 1982).

J. K. Galbraith, *American Capitalism: The Concept of Countervailing Power* (Boston: Houghton Mifflin, 1952).

James V. Koch, *Industrial Organization and Prices,* 2nd ed. (Englewood Cliffs, NJ: Prentice-Hall, 1980).

F. M. Scherer, *Industrial Market Structure and Economic Performance,* 2nd ed. (Chicago: Rand-McNally College Publishing Co., 1980).

CHAPTER 27

INDUSTRIAL ORGANIZATION AND ANTITRUST POLICY

Antitrust enforcers have struggled for [100] years—since the Sherman Act was passed in 1890—to define what constitutes an "unacceptably few" number of competitors.[1]

In 1986, PepsiCo petitioned the Federal Trade Commission for permission to acquire Seven-Up. Shortly thereafter, the Coca-Cola Company attempted to purchase Dr. Pepper. The Federal Trade Commission rejected both requests on the ground that the acquisitions would seriously restrict competition in the soft-drink industry. A subsequent merger of Seven-Up and Dr. Pepper was allowed.

As Chapter 26 indicated, concentrating power in the hands of a few large companies may either benefit consumers or harm them. How do government agencies, including the Federal Trade Commission, determine which mergers to approve and which to oppose? Although some subjectivity is involved, government agencies rely heavily on the tools discussed in this chapter. These tools assess the extent of competition within an industry and measure the change in competition in the event of a merger.

They also enable us to track changes in the competitiveness of the overall economy. Some individuals worry that market power is becoming concentrated in the hands of a dwindling number of companies. Is there any merit to this argument?

A country's industrial structure depends on political as well as economic considerations. In the United States, government policy has evolved over time through legislation, judicial rulings, and enforcement activities of the executive branch. The second half of the chapter traces U.S. antitrust policy over the past century, highlighting major laws and court rulings, and discussing the more tolerant approach toward big business under the Reagan Administration.

---

[1]Robert Pitofsky, "Coke and Pepsi Were Going Too Far," *New York Times,* July 27, 1986, section 3, p. 2.

ASSESSING THE EXTENT OF COMPETITION

Monopoly power, or the ability to influence price, varies from industry to industry. At the one extreme (perfect competition), firms have no influence over price. At the other extreme, a firm is the only seller of the product and can dictate any price it chooses. Most industries fall somewhere between these two extremes: firms have slight to moderate control over price, depending on such factors as number of firms in the industry and their relative size. The market power of producers tends to be greater when an industry contains a few large firms rather than many small firms.

Based on these observations, economists have devised a number of measures of monopoly power. Although none is perfect, each reveals valuable information about specific markets. These gauges enable us to compare the degree of competition across industries and to determine whether a given industry is becoming more competitive or less competitive over time. When used in conjunction with other data, the measures generally paint a fairly reliable picture of market power within an industry. The two most commonly used measures of monopoly power are the *market concentration ratio* and the *Herfindahl Index*.

THE MARKET CONCENTRATION RATIO

A concentration ratio measures the share of the market accounted for by the largest firms in an industry. For example, the *four-firm concentration ratio* measures sales of the four largest firms in the industry as a percentage of total industry sales. Although one could just as easily compute concentration ratios for the largest five firms or eight firms in the industry, the four-firm concentration ratio is the one most widely used. Therefore, unless otherwise specified, **market concentration ratio** refers to the market share of the four largest firms.

Market Concentration Ratio
The percentage of industry sales attributable to the four largest firms in an industry.

Concentration ratios range in value from 0 to 100 percent. Highly competitive industries have very low concentration ratios, since the four largest firms produce only a small fraction of the industry's output. At the other extreme, industries containing no more than four firms have concentration ratios of 100 percent—four firms or fewer produce all the industry's output.

In general, the higher the concentration ratio the greater the monopoly power wielded by firms in the industry. Accordingly, concentration ratios provide evidence of market structure. Based on its concentration ratio of 66 percent, the U.S. tire industry is classified as oligopolistic—a few firms dominate the market. On the other hand, a concentration ratio of 6 percent reveals that the women's dress industry is highly competitive.

Defining the Product Market

Although concentration ratios are easy to compute, they must be used with care. The first consideration involves defining the relevant product market. If a market is defined too broadly or too narrowly, the concentration ratio may be misleading. A case in point is the soft-drink industry.

In defending their proposed acquisitions, the managements of Pepsi and Coke argued that their beverages compete directly with juices, powdered drinks, teas, milk, and other beverages. Had the market been defined broadly to include all these drinks, the concentration ratio would have been very low even after the mergers. The implication—that considerable competition exists—would make it difficult for the government to reject the mergers.

The Federal Trade Commission, however, argued that the relevant market included only carbonated soft drinks. Coke and Pepsi controlled 68 percent of this narrowly defined market, and their combined market share would have swelled to 82 percent had the mergers actually taken place. Seen in this light, the market was dominated by two giants, and allowing them to gobble up their rivals would have seriously diluted competition. Once the market was narrowly defined, the decision to deny the mergers was easy.[2]

Shortcomings of the Concentration Ratio

Even if the product market is properly defined, the market concentration ratio suffers from several weaknesses. (a) It overlooks competition from imports, other industries, and prospective producers. (b) It focuses on national output, even though many markets are local or regional. (c) It ignores the distribution of sales among the top four producers.

Other Sources of Competition   Concentration ratios measure producers' share of *domestically* produced output. By ignoring imports, they overstate the power of domestic producers. For example, even though the market concentration ratio in the U.S. automobile industry exceeds 90 percent, U.S. producers are severely limited in their ability to control price. With imports recently accounting for more than 25 percent of the market, U.S. automobile producers face stiff competition from foreign suppliers.

Concentration ratios also overstate the power of companies that face competition from other industries. Despite the high concentration ratio in the soft-drink industry, Coca-Cola and PepsiCo find their ability to raise price limited by the presence of beverages from other industries. Similarly, the advertising rates charged by the major television networks (ABC, CBS, and NBC) are constrained by other communications industries. Although these three networks dominate the national television industry, advertisers have alternative avenues for reaching consumers—local television, cable, radio, newspapers, magazines, billboards, mail, and telephone. Monopoly power is influenced not just by the market structure within an industry but also by the degree of competition across industries.

In addition to actual competition from producers in other countries or industries, firms may also experience pressure from *potential* new rivals in the industry. In the absence of effective entry barriers, profits attract new firms to the industry. As in perfectly competitive markets, the increased supply reduces price and, in the long run, eliminates profits. Thus, even though an industry may have few

[2]Although the issue of what constitutes the relevant market is not always clear-cut, another economic tool guides policymakers in this decision. The *cross elasticity of demand* indicates whether two goods are close substitutes. If they are, they are part of the same market. See Exhibit 5-4.

firms at present, the ability of new firms to break into the market may undermine the market power of current producers. According to a new theory, competitive pressures depend more on resource mobility than on the number of firms in the industry (see Exhibit 27-1).

Geographic Markets Although concentration ratios may overstate market power for the preceding reasons, at other times they understate market power. Typically, concentration ratios are computed for the country at large. For national markets, such as breakfast cereals and cigarettes, this is the correct procedure. But where markets are local or regional, national concentration ratios underestimate the market power of producers. Even though individual producers may each claim only a small

---

EXHIBIT 27-1

THE THEORY OF CONTESTABLE MARKETS

A **contestable market** is one where resources can be moved into and out of an industry at little or no cost. All resources, including capital, are highly mobile. As an example, some point to the market for air travel. Airplanes and flight crews can easily be transferred from one route to another. Therefore, regardless of the number of airlines currently serving a city, the market for air travel to and from the city may be viewed as contestable.

An implication of this theory is that competition is based not on the number of producers currently in an industry but instead on the number of actual plus *potential* producers. A market may have a concentration ratio of 100 percent yet, if it is contestable, its producers earn only normal profits in the long run. If they attempted to charge a price in excess of average total cost, new firms would quickly enter the industry, charge a lower price, and take business away from existing producers. The presence of potential competition prevents existing firms from earning economic profits.

Although this theory is largely untested, it has been used to defend mergers in markets that already have high concentration ratios. For example, in 1986, TWA was allowed to merge with Ozark Airlines, its main rival in the St. Louis market. After the merger, TWA controlled 82 percent of the market. Those favoring the merger claimed that other airlines would invade the St. Louis market if TWA set excessive air fares. They also observed that TWA competes with other cities for connecting flights. If travel through St. Louis became more expensive, an increased number of flights would be booked through Kansas City,

Chicago, or other cities (on other airlines). Accordingly, supporters of the merger argued that the St. Louis market would remain competitive despite TWA's high market share.

Opponents countered that although the theory of contestable markets is impeccable, it is not widely applicable to the real world and certainly not relevant in the airline industry.[3] They noted that TWA controls nearly three-fourths of the gates at St. Louis's Lambert Airport (other airlines have similar locks at other airports). Because this severely limits the number of flights other airlines can offer to and from St. Louis, many analysts believe that TWA is effectively shielded from competition—both from existing carriers and from potential rivals.

In conclusion, the theory of contestable markets awaits further scrutiny. But, to the extent it is relevant for certain markets, it provides another reason why concentration ratios should not be used blindly. If markets are contestable, current producers may have less influence over price than concentration ratios would suggest.

---

[3]See William G. Shepherd, " 'Contestability' vs. Competition," *American Economic Review* (September 1984), pp. 572–587.

Sources: Adapted from William J. Baumol, John C. Panzar, and Robert D. Willig, *Contestable Markets and the Theory of Industry Structure* (San Diego: Harcourt Brace Jovanovich, 1982); Scott Kilman, "Growing Giants," *The Wall Street Journal*, July 20, 1987, p. 1; *Kansas City Times*, "TWA Boosted '87 Fares in St. Louis by Twice U.S. Average, Report Says," September 21, 1988, p. D1.

share of national sales, within their respective local markets each may have few if any rivals.

A good example of this is newspaper publishing. Despite a relatively low concentration ratio of 22 percent for the country as a whole, most cities contain only one or two daily newspapers. The potential for monopoly power is therefore great. Similarly, the four largest producers of ready-mixed concrete capture a combined 6 percent of the national market. But, because of high transportation costs, cement tends to be purchased locally, and that often means doing business with the only cement company around.

Distribution of Market Share   A final criticism of concentration ratios is that they do not reveal how the market share is distributed among the four largest producers. Suppose industries X and Y have concentration ratios of 60 percent. The largest company in industry X controls 45 percent of the market and the next three companies each have a 5-percent share. In contrast, the four largest companies in industry Y each have a 15-percent share of the market. Are the two industries equally competitive?

Most economists would argue that industry X is less competitive. The largest firm sells nine times as much as its nearest rival, controlling almost one-half the market. As the dominant force in the industry, it is likely to wield considerable power. By way of comparison, the largest firm in industry Y must compete with three other firms just as large. Because market share is distributed more evenly, no firm has much influence over price.

Need for Supplemental Information   Because of the shortcomings just documented, the concentration ratio must be used with care. The implication is not that it has little value but that market power is multidimensional. No single instrument can adequately characterize the power of firms in an industry. Concentration ratios provide important insights into markets, but they must be supplemented with additional information. Industry analysts must also pay attention to imports, interindustry competition, barriers to entry, the geographic nature of markets, and the distribution of output among the largest producers. When used in conjunction with such data, the concentration ratio provides a good description of competitive pressures within an industry. It can help identify market structures and guide policymakers on the advisability of mergers.

THE HERFINDAHL INDEX

Herfindahl Index
A measure of market concentration obtained by squaring the market share of each firm in the industry and then summing these numbers.

A competing gauge of industrial concentration is the **Herfindahl Index** (or, as it is sometimes called, the Herfindahl-Hirschman Index). The Herfindahl Index (HI) sums the market share of all firms in the industry, but only after the market shares have been squared. Thus, assuming there are n firms in the industry, the Herfindahl Index is computed as

$$\text{HI} = \sum_{i=1}^{n} S_i^2$$

where S_i^2 is the market share squared of firm i.

Under monopoly, the Herfindahl Index achieves its maximum possible value of $100^2 = 10,000$. Although the Herfindahl Index could theoretically approach zero, its lowest observed value is approximately 11. As with concentration ratios, higher numbers indicate greater concentration of power. In general, industries with higher concentration ratios have higher Herfindahl Indexes, but there are exceptions, as Table 27-1 illustrates.

The Herfindahl Index is subject to many of the same criticisms as the concentration ratio. It does, however, overcome one shortcoming—the failure of the concentration ratio to distinguish between industries dominated by a single firm and industries where the largest firms are approximately equal in size (and therefore more effective rivals). By squaring market shares, the Herfindahl Index assigns disproportionately high values to dominant firms. For example, one firm with a 45-percent market share contributes substantially more to the Herfindahl Index than three firms with 15-percent market shares. [$45^2 = 2025 > 675 = 3 \times (15^2)$.] Thus, the Herfindahl Index effectively captures the market power of firms that dwarf their competitors.

In 1982, the Justice Department began emphasizing the Herfindahl Index rather than the concentration ratio. Under guidelines issued at that time, an industry

TABLE 27-1

CONCENTRATION IN MANUFACTURING, SELECTED INDUSTRIES, 1982

Industry	Number of firms	Concentration ratio	Herfindahl Index
Man-made fibers, cellulose	5	ND*	2970
Cigarettes	8	ND*	2623
Refrigerators and freezers	39	94	2745
Motor vehicles	284	92	ND*
Turbines	71	84	2602
Malt beverages	67	77	2089
Photographic equipment	723	74	2157
Aircraft engines	281	72	1778
Tires and innertubes	108	66	1591
Soap and detergents	642	60	1306
Farm machinery	1787	53	1468
Pet food	222	52	1167
Glass containers	41	50	966
Radio and TV sets	432	49	751
Electronic computing equipment	1520	43	793
Blast furnaces and steel mills	211	42	650
Petroleum refining	282	28	380
Newspapers	7520	22	193
Sporting and athletic goods	1453	17	140
Jewelry, precious metals	2159	16	91
Sheet-metal work	3579	7	29
Ready-mixed concrete	4161	6	18
Women's dresses	5489	6	24
Commercial printing, lithography	17,332	6	20
Wood pallets	1649	5	17

*ND = not disclosed.

Source: U.S. Bureau of the Census, *Census of Manufactures, 1982, Concentration Ratios in Manufacturing* (1986).

is considered to be "unconcentrated" if its Herfindahl Index is less than 1000, "moderately concentrated" if it has a value between 1000 and 1800, and "highly concentrated" if the Herfindahl Index exceeds 1800. Although the Justice Department considers other factors—including import competition and ease of entry into the industry—mergers are evaluated primarily in terms of their impact on the Herfindahl Index. In general, the Justice Department opposes mergers if they increase the Herfindahl Index by more than 100 points in moderately concentrated industries or by more than 50 points in highly concentrated industries. Mergers are usually approved if the Herfindahl Index rises by a lesser amount or if the industry remains unconcentrated despite the merger (see Table 27-2).

These Justice Department guidelines explain why certain mergers in the brewing industry were approved and others disallowed. Table 27-3 presents the market shares of the major brewers in 1981. At that time the Herfindahl Index was just above 1600, indicating a "moderately concentrated" industry. Heileman, the fourth largest brewer, wanted to merge with Schlitz, the third largest. Had the

TABLE 27-2

JUSTICE DEPARTMENT MERGER GUIDELINES

Value of Herfindahl Index after the proposed merger	Industry classification	Likely response of Justice Department
< 1000	Unconcentrated	Approve merger.
1000–1800	Moderately concentrated	Approve merger if Herfindahl Index increases by less than 100 points; oppose merger if Herfindahl Index increases by more than 100 points.
> 1800	Highly concentrated	Approve merger if Herfindahl Index increases by less than 50 points; oppose merger if Herfindahl Index increases by more than 50 points.

Source: U.S. Department of Justice, *1982 Merger Guidelines.*

TABLE 27-3

MARKET SHARE BY BREWERY, 1981

Company	Percent
Anheuser-Busch	30.4
Miller	22.5
Schlitz	8.0
Heileman	7.8
Pabst	7.5
Coors	7.4
Stroh	3.5
Others	12.9

merger been allowed, the market share at Heileman would have climbed to approximately 16 percent.

Defenders of the merger, while conceding that it would raise the concentration ratio and Herfindahl Index, argued that the merger would actually create greater competition in the industry. The two big brewers, Anheuser-Busch and Miller, shared 53 percent of the market, and their market share had been climbing over time. Some worried that the industry was evolving into a *duopoly* (two-firm industry) in which Anheuser-Busch and Miller, after squeezing out their competitors, would be free to inflate their prices. If a third large brewer could be created—for example, through the Heileman-Schlitz merger—it would slow the growth of these two giants. Furthermore, with a strong rival, Anheuser-Busch and Miller would have less discretion over price. In essence, supporters of the merger argued that an industry with three big companies is likely to be more competitive than an industry having just two.

Despite this argument, the Justice Department ruled against Heileman. The merger would have caused the Herfindahl Index to rise by 125 points in an industry that was moderately concentrated.[4] Because this exceeded the allowable increase of 100 points, the Justice Department considered the merger to be anticompetitive. Although some have criticized this decision, pointing out that the combined share of Anheuser-Busch and Miller has continued to grow, the Herfindahl numbers explain the rationale for rejecting the merger.

They also explain why, the following year, Stroh was allowed to acquire Schlitz. Because Stroh was smaller than Heileman, the Stroh-Schlitz merger satisfied the Justice Department's guidelines—it added only 56 points to the Herfindahl Index.

YOUR TURN

CONCENTRATION RATIOS AND THE HERFINDAHL INDEX
The following table depicts the market shares in industries A and B:

Firm	Industry A (%)	Industry B (%)
1	22	42
2	20	10
3	20	10
4	18	8
5	6	8
6	5	8
7	5	7
8	4	7
Total	100	100

(a) Compute the concentration ratio for each industry. (b) Compute the Herfindahl Index.
(c) According to the concentration ratio, is industry A or B more highly concentrated?
(d) Do you obtain similar results with the Herfindahl Index? Why or why not?

---

[4]The increase in the Herfindahl Index is given by the formula

$$\Delta HI = S_{a+b}^2 - S_a^2 - S_b^2$$

where S_a and S_b are the premerger market shares of firms a and b, and S_{a+b} is the combined postmerger share. In the case of Heileman and Schlitz, the increase would have been $15.8^2 - 8.0^2 - 7.8^2 = 124.8$.

OVERALL CONCENTRATION IN THE U.S. ECONOMY

The preceding discussion has focused on concentration within specific industries—but how concentrated is the overall economy? Has it become more or less concentrated over time? Some who worry about the evils of market power—high prices, reduced output, inefficiency—claim that market power is becoming concentrated in the hands of fewer and fewer companies. They argue that big firms are gobbling up their smaller rivals and, as a consequence, the economy is becoming less competitive. It is easy to cite specific instances. For example, the concentration ratio for the brewing industry has soared from about 18 percent 40 years ago to 80 percent today. But is this representative of the economy at large? What do aggregate data reveal?

Value Added in Manufacturing

Aggregate concentration can be measured in various ways. One approach is to measure the *value added* of the largest companies, where value added refers to a company's net contribution to output. (For example, if a company purchases materials for $300 and turns them into a product selling for $400, it has contributed $100 to output.) As measured by value added, concentration within manufacturing has increased over time (see Table 27-4). In 1947, the 50 largest manufacturing companies contributed 17 percent of the value added in manufacturing. By 1982, the percentage had risen to 24 percent. Similarly, the share of value added by the 100 and 200 largest manufacturing companies also rose.

Of course, many large companies are *conglomerates*—firms that sell unrelated product lines. For example, General Electric operates in more than two dozen industries, including light bulbs, refrigerators, brokerage services, medical equipment, defense, and television broadcasting (it owns NBC). Even though conglomerates may be large in terms of total value added, when their production is spread out across many industries, they may have small market shares within individual industries. Indeed, much of the period since World War II has been characterized by *diversification*—adding new product lines. For example, in 1950 only 5 percent of the 200 largest manufacturing companies sold products in 31 or more different industries. By 1968, the figure had quadrupled (see Table 27-5). To the extent companies diversify by transferring resources from traditional products to new lines

TABLE 27-4					

SHARE OF VALUE ADDED BY THE LARGEST MANUFACTURING COMPANIES*

	Year				
	1947	**1958**	**1967**	**1977**	**1982**
50 largest companies	17	23	25	24	24
100 largest companies	23	30	33	33	33
200 largest companies	30	38	42	44	43

*Percentage of total value added in U.S. manufacturing accounted for by the largest manufacturing companies.

Source: U.S. Bureau of the Census, *Census of Manufactures, 1982, Concentration Ratios in Manufacturing* (1986).

TABLE 27-5		
INCREASED DIVERSIFICATION IN MANUFACTURING*		
Number of industries in which company sells a product	**Percentage of companies**	
	1950	**1968**
1–10	55.5	27.0
11–30	39.5	53.5
31 or more	5.0	19.5
Total	100.0	100.0

*Diversification of the 200 largest U.S. manufacturing companies.

Source: Federal Trade Commission. *Conglomerate Merger Performance* (1972). Cited in F. M. Scherer, *Industrial Market Structure and Economic Performance,* 2nd ed., p. 76. Copyright © 1980 by Houghton Mifflin Company. Adapted with permission.

of business, their market shares in their traditional industries may actually shrink. Thus, the increase in value added by large companies is no indication that industries in general are becoming less competitive.

Concentration Ratios in Manufacturing

Most economists argue that concentration ratios provide a more accurate picture of market power than do data on aggregate value added. The distribution of concentration ratios reveals information about market structure at one point in time, and changes in that distribution indicate whether market power is increasing or decreasing.

There are different ways to extract information from concentration ratios. Perhaps the simplest is to look at the share of output (measured by value added) that is produced in concentrated industries. In 1947, 24 percent of manufacturing output was produced in industries having a concentration ratio of 50 percent or higher. By 1972, the figure had climbed to 29 percent, suggesting an increase in concentration in the period following World War II. But this is *not* indicative of a long-term trend. At the turn of the century almost 33 percent of output was produced in concentrated industries (see Table 27-6). Thus, the share of manufacturing output originating in

TABLE 27-6	
THE SHARE OF TOTAL VALUE ADDED PRODUCED BY CONCENTRATED INDUSTRIES (manufacturing only)*	
Period	**Percent of value added by concentrated industries**
1895–1904	32.9
1947	24.4
1958	30.2
1972	29.0

*Concentration ratio ≥ 50 percent.

Source: F. M. Scherer, *Industrial Market Structure and Economic Performance,* 2nd ed., p. 68. Copyright © 1980 by Houghton Mifflin Company. Adapted with permission.

concentrated industries has not trended upward this century; if anything, it has edged lower.

An alternative approach is to examine the change in concentration in industries identified as oligopolistic. Between 1947–1967, concentration ratios increased in eight oligopolistic industries but declined in ten.[5] By this measure, oligopolistic industries have not become more concentrated, even in the postwar period. Average concentration ratios also fail to detect any clear trend. Average concentration for manufacturing was almost the same in 1972 (38.5 percent) as it was in 1947 (38.0 percent).[6] Because of statistics such as these, many industrial economists still agree with an assessment made 40 years ago:

> The extent of concentration shows no tendency to grow, and it may possibly be declining. Any tendency either way, if it does exist, must be at the pace of a glacial drift.[7]

Concentration in the Aggregate Economy

The preceding discussion has centered on concentration in manufacturing. One reason for this focus is that manufacturing has traditionally been the largest sector of the U.S. economy. More important, statistics on concentration are more widely available for manufacturing industries than for nonmanufacturing industries.

Despite the shortcomings of nonmanufacturing data, William Shepherd has studied the market structure of the aggregate U.S. economy.[8] He concludes that: (a) most output is produced in "effectively competitive" industries (defined as those with concentration ratios below 40 percent, low entry barriers, and flexible pricing) and (b) the economy has become more competitive over time. Shepherd estimates that 77 percent of output was produced by effectively competitive industries in 1980, compared to 52 percent in 1939 (see Table 27-7). Among the explanations

TABLE 27-7
THE STRUCTURE OF THE U.S. ECONOMY

Type of industry	Percent of national output		
	1939	1958	1980
Monopoly	6.2	3.1	2.5
Oligopoly	41.4	40.6	20.8
Effectively competitive*	52.4	56.3	76.7
Total	100.0	100.0	100.0

*Concentration ratio < 40 percent, low entry barriers, and flexible pricing.

Source: Adapted from William G. Shepherd, "Causes of Increased Competition in the U.S. Economy," *Review of Economics and Statistics* (November 1982), Table 2. Reprinted by permission of Elsevier Science Publishers B. V. (Amsterdam).

[5]James V. Koch, *Industrial Organization and Prices,* 2nd ed. (Englewood Cliffs, NJ: Prentice-Hall, 1980), p. 187.

[6]Scherer, *Industrial Market Structure and Economic Performance,* 2nd ed. (Chicago: Rand-McNally College Publishing Co., 1980), p. 70.

[7]Morris Adelman, "The Measurement of Industrial Concentration," *Review of Economics and Statistics* (November 1951), p. 295.

[8]William G. Shepherd, "Causes of Increased Competition in the U.S. Economy, 1939–1980," *Review of Economics and Statistics* (November 1982), pp. 613–626.

given for this increased competition are imports, deregulation, and antitrust policy. To repeat an earlier caveat, confidence in this study must be tempered by data concerns. But at a minimum, this study reinforces the conclusion of the previously discussed manufacturing studies: *market concentration has not increased over time.*

ANTITRUST

In addition to economic factors, such as economies of scale, concentration depends on government policy toward big business. The government can encourage big business, halt its spread, break up large companies, or force them to leave certain markets. The government also establishes the rules of the game, spelling out which business practices are acceptable and which are not. Government actions aimed at influencing the structure and conduct of business are referred to as **antitrust policy**

Antitrust Policy
Government laws and procedures designed to shape market structure and influence the behavior of firms.

Antitrust policy is neither static nor consistent. Behavior considered legitimate at one point in time is sometimes deemed inappropriate at some other point in time. Nor is there consistency across all segments of the economy. Various lines of business—including agriculture, banking, baseball, and newspaper publishing—are exempt from at least some antitrust provisions. Nor do antitrust laws currently apply to export associations or labor unions.[9]

Although the stated objective of antitrust laws is to channel market structure and firm behavior in competitive directions, these laws do not always promote competition or protect consumers from the abuses of business. In some instances antitrust policy actually results in *higher* prices. This reflects the fact that policy is influenced by political as well as economic considerations. In this section we review antitrust policy, summarize important laws and court rulings, discuss the major issues, and examine how antitrust policy in the United States has evolved over time.

MAJOR ANTITRUST LEGISLATION

Antitrust laws were motivated by developments in the late nineteenth century. Advances in mass production, communication, and finance contributed to growing economies of scale. At the same time, the railroad linked diverse regions of the country, enabling companies to expand their markets. In many industries companies discovered that they must grow to survive. Often this meant merging with other companies. Mergers were frequently accomplished by forming a **trust**, in which a board of trustees coordinated the activities of the individual companies. That is, the trust acted along the lines of a cartel.

Trust
A combination of companies acting in concert in order to increase control of an industry.

Many trusts maintained monopoly or near-monopoly positions, doing whatever was necessary to eliminate competitors. For example, through its control of pipelines, Standard Oil was able to deny competitors access to crude oil. In addition, it required railroads to carry its oil at discount prices and even forced them to pay Standard Oil if they shipped competitors' oil. Through such practices, Standard Oil was able to capture 90 percent of the market.

Predatory Pricing
A practice whereby one or more firms temporarily reduce price in order to drive weaker firms from the industry and then raise price once these competitors have been eliminated.

Other trusts engaged in **predatory pricing**. They would sell a product below cost until weaker rivals, unable to withstand the mounting losses, were forced from the industry. Once the competitors were eliminated, the trust would then raise

---

[9]Initially the courts ruled that unions were covered by antitrust law. As a result, certain practices (e.g., the union boycott) were declared illegal. Congress later exempted unions.

prices, often to exorbitant levels. The public, questioning both the tactics employed by trusts and the results, petitioned Congress for relief. The result was a series of antitrust laws (see Table 27-8).

The Sherman Act

The first antitrust law was the *Sherman Act,* enacted by Congress in 1890. Its key provisions are:

> *Section 1*   Every contract, combination in the form of a trust or otherwise, or conspiracy, in restraint of trade or commerce among the several states, or with foreign nations, is hereby declared to be illegal. . . .

> *Section 2*   Every person who shall monopolize, or attempt to monopolize, or combine or conspire with any other person or persons to monopolize any part of the trade or commerce among the several states, or with foreign nations, shall be deemed guilty of a misdemeanor.[10]

Although setting the tone of government policy, this law proved less effective than supporters envisioned. The main problem was lack of clarity; the language was general and often ambiguous. What constitutes a monopoly? Must a firm control the entire market? Is monopoly *per se* illegal or only monopoly achieved through illegal practices? Which practices are legal, and which are illegal? In an attempt to be more specific, Congress enacted additional legislation.

The Clayton Act

The *Clayton Act* of 1914 prohibits certain clearly defined business practices. It bans some, though not all, forms of *price discrimination*—selling goods to different buyers

TABLE 27-8	
SUMMARY OF MAJOR ANTITRUST LAWS	
Law (date enacted)	**Key Provisions**
Sherman Act (1890)	Restricts interstate restraint of trade and attempts to monopolize.
Clayton Act (1914)	Outlaws tying contracts, interlocking directorates, and other specific business practices.
Federal Trade Commission Act (1914)	Created an agency (the FTC) to help enforce antitrust laws.
Robinson-Patman Act (1936)	Generally limits price concessions, especially to large buyers, if one or more competitors would be harmed.
Celler-Kefauver Act (1950)	Places restrictions on mergers (e.g., by prohibiting companies from buying the assets of a rival if this reduces competition).

---

[10]This was later changed to make violations felonies rather than misdemeanors.

at different prices not justified by cost differences. It also outlaws **tying contracts**, in which the sale of one good is conditional on the sale or purchase of a second good. This means, for instance, that General Motors (GM) could not require railroads hauling GM cars to purchase locomotives manufactured by GM.

The Clayton Act prevents companies from buying stock in other companies if the result is reduced competition. It also bans **interlocking directorates** between competing companies. If two companies compete in the same market, the same individual cannot serve on the board of directors of both companies.

The Federal Trade Commission Act

The *Federal Trade Commission Act* is a companion to the Clayton Act. Enacted in 1914, it prohibits "unfair methods of competition in commerce." Its central feature, however, was the creation of the Federal Trade Commission (FTC), an agency to enforce both the Clayton and FTC Acts. The Commission can initiate lawsuits and issue *cease-and-desist orders,* directing companies to halt practices deemed by the FTC as violating antitrust laws. The Commission also conducts economic research on market structure.

As amended in 1938 by the *Wheeler-Lea Act,* the FTC also has authority to halt false or deceptive business practices. For example, in the absence of evidence to support its claim, Listerine mouthwash was ordered to stop advertising that it killed the germs causing sore throats. A bread company, advertising that it contained 400 percent more fiber than whole wheat bread, was ordered to disclose the source of its fiber—wood pulp.

The Robinson-Patman Act

The most controversial antitrust law is probably the *Robinson-Patman Act.* Enacted in 1936, this law amends the Clayton Act by further restricting price discrimination. Unless justified by differences in cost, charging competing companies different prices for "goods of like grade and quality" is generally prohibited if at least one competitor would be harmed.

The intent of the Robinson-Patman Act is to protect small retailers from chain stores that, because of their high-volume purchasing, were often able to buy goods at a lower price than the smaller companies. By passing these cost savings on to consumers in the form of lower prices, the chains were able to gain business at the expense of the small retailers. This law attempts to halt volume discounts and other preferential treatment, thereby shielding small companies from the competitive pressures of large companies. Where small companies are less efficient, this has the effect of fostering inefficiency and promoting higher prices. For this reason, economists are generally critical of the Robinson-Patman Act.

The Celler-Kefauver Act

The Clayton Act was further strengthened through enactment of the *Celler-Kefauver Act* of 1950. This law adds several provisions designed to strengthen restrictions against mergers. Although the Clayton Act prohibits companies from acquiring stock in another company in order to reduce competition, companies discovered an alternative way to gain control of rival firms—buying their assets. The Celler-Kefauver Act closes this loophole.

KEY ANTITRUST RULINGS

Although Congress enacts the laws, it is the responsibility of the courts to interpret them. Given the vagueness of certain statutes, judicial rulings play a critical role in shaping antitrust policy. Certain of the major antitrust cases are presented in the following pages (and summarized in Table 27-9).

Price Fixing

The courts have strongly opposed *price fixing*—agreements among companies to set prices—arguing that such behavior is in and of itself illegal. In the *Addyston Pipe Case* (1899), six producers of iron pipes were convicted of rigging prices. Although they claimed that their prices were fair and reasonable, the Supreme Court rejected this defense, ruling that the level at which prices were set was irrelevant. Price fixing was a violation of the Sherman Act.

The *Socony-Vacuum Case* (1940) reinforced the *Addyston* ruling. The Supreme Court held: "Any combination which tampers with price structures is engaged in unlawful activity." Conspiracies to fix prices are "illegal *per se*." The *per se* doctrine makes conviction relatively easy. Prosecutors need not consider motives or reasonableness of behavior, but only show that price fixing actually occurred.

Standards for Monopoly

The policies of the courts toward monopoly have been less consistent than their policies toward price fixing. A controversy continues even today over the appropriate standard for monopoly. Is monopoly *per se* illegal, or must a monopoly first engage in unacceptable behavior? One of the first cases to address this issue involved *Standard Oil of New Jersey.*

TABLE 27-9

SUMMARY OF MAJOR ANTITRUST CASES

Ruling (date issued)	Key provision
Addyston Pipe (1899), *Socony-Vacuum* (1940)	Ruled that price fixing is always illegal.
Standard Oil of New Jersey (1911)	Established the rule of reason, allowing "reasonable" monopolies.
Alcoa (1945)	Overturned the rule of reason, arguing that the Sherman Act forbids all monopolies.
Berkey Photo versus Eastman Kodak (1979)	Retreated from the Alcoa decision—a monopoly may be defensible if achieved because of lower costs.
duPont (1957)	Restricted vertical mergers.
Bethlehem Steel (1958)	Restricted horizontal mergers that impair competition.
Von's Grocery (1966)	Restricted horizontal mergers that contribute to a trend toward concentration.

The Rule of Reason In 1911, the Supreme Court found Standard Oil in violation of the Sherman Act. The Court ruled that (a) Standard Oil, with a 90-percent share of the petroleum market, could be considered a monopoly and (b) Standard Oil had achieved its monopoly position illegally—through

> acts and dealings wholly inconsistent with . . . advancing the development of business power by usual methods, but which, on the contrary, necessarily involved the intent to drive others from the field and to exclude them from their right to trade.

Rule of Reason
The doctrine that all monopolies are not illegal, only monopolies that have engaged in unreasonable behavior.

This second finding was critical because, according to the decision, monopoly *per se* is not illegal, only monopoly achieved through unreasonable business practices. This doctrine became known as the **rule of reason**. Because the Standard Oil trust achieved its dominance through unreasonable behavior, it was dissolved, leading to competition among the many companies that had comprised the trust.

The rule of reason played a central role in the *U.S. Steel* ruling, issued in 1920. Although U.S. Steel controlled 52 percent of the market, the Supreme Court, noting that its market share had slipped, concluded that the company had not achieved monopoly status. Furthermore, even though the company may have enjoyed market power due to its large size, U.S. Steel had not abused that power. According to the Court: "The law does not make mere size an offense or the existence of unexerted power an offense. It . . . requires overt acts."

In the wake of the rule of reason, cases involving monopolizing markets dwindled. Although market dominance was often easy to establish, prosecutors had a more difficult time proving that a company had obtained its monopoly position as the result of particular overt acts. The burden of prosecution eased, however, as the result of the **Alcoa Case** (1945).

The Alcoa Case Alcoa held 90 percent of the market for aluminum ingots. In keeping with earlier court rulings, this was sufficient to classify the company as a monopoly under the Sherman Act. At issue was whether Alcoa violated section 2 of the Sherman Act. Had Alcoa attempted to monopolize the market? It had not engaged in price fixing, predatory pricing, or other unreasonable activities. Rather, its dominance stemmed primarily from its patents and its control over the key raw material, bauxite ore. Nonetheless, the New York Court of Appeals ruled against Alcoa.[11] In its decision, the Court declared:

> Having proved that Alcoa had a monopoly of the domestic ingot market the [government] had gone far enough. . . . Congress . . . did not condone "good trusts" and condemn "bad" ones; it forbade all.

With the *Alcoa* decision, the courts effectively overturned the rule of reason. No longer must a prosecutor show that a company is a bad monopoly, having engaged in unreasonable acts. All that is required is proof that it is a monopoly. Whereas the rule of reason required evidence on *conduct* (overt acts), the *Alcoa Case* established a much weaker standard for conviction: evidence on market *structure* (a monopoly or near-monopoly position). As a result of this decision, prosecution of monopolies intensified.

Reassessing the Alcoa Case Beginning in the mid-1970s, the courts appeared to retreat from the *Alcoa* decision and move closer to the rule of reason. For example, in

---

[11]The Supreme Court did not hear this case because four of its judges disqualified themselves on the ground they had been involved in earlier litigation of the case.

Berkey Photo versus Eastman Kodak (1979) an appellate court ruled that "[t]he mere possession of monopoly power does not ipso facto condemn a market participant"; behavior of the monopolist must also be considered.

In *Berkey* the court determined that Kodak's monopoly of the film and camera markets was defensible because it resulted from innovation, rather than improper behavior. The court ruled that the Sherman Act does not

> deprive the leading firm in an industry of the incentive to exert its best efforts. . . . If a firm that has engaged in the risks and expenses of research and development were required in all circumstances to share with its rivals the benefits of those endeavors, this incentive would very likely be vitiated.

Accordingly, the court's decision generally favored Kodak.

As the preceding discussion indicates, judicial standards are dynamic, evolving over time. Given changes in both public attitudes and composition of the courts, this is hardly surprising. Undoubtedly, the courts will continue to redefine standards. But such rulings, regardless of their nature, are unlikely to still the debate: Should antitrust policy be based on market conduct or on market structure?

Mergers

Horizontal Merger
A merger between companies in the same market.
Vertical Merger
A merger between a company supplying an input and a company buying it.
Conglomerate Merger
A merger between companies in unrelated markets.

A *merger,* or joining of two firms, can assume different forms. A **horizontal merger** occurs when the two firms are competitors, selling in the same market (e.g., when one brewery purchases a second brewery). A **vertical merger** occurs when the output of one company is an input of the other company. An example is the acquisition of an auto parts company by an automobile manufacturer. Finally, a **conglomerate merger** involves companies in unrelated markets. For example, an automobile company might purchase a brewery.

The Clayton and Celler-Kefauver Acts place restrictions on horizontal and vertical mergers but do little to block conglomerate mergers—which in recent decades have constituted roughly three-fourths of all merger activity. The full impact of these laws can be assessed only by studying judicial decisions involving mergers. Based on such decisions, it is clear that horizontal and vertical mergers have been curtailed.

In 1957, the Supreme Court ruled that duPont's acquisition of stock in General Motors constituted a vertical merger. Noting that General Motors purchased two-thirds of its finishes from duPont and over one-half of its fabrics, the Court concluded that the supplier/purchaser relationship between the two companies denied competitors access to a large part of the automotive market. Accordingly, duPont was ordered to sell its 23-percent interest in General Motors.

The following year a district court prevented a horizontal merger between *Bethlehem Steel* and Youngstown Steel. The merger would have created a company with a 21-percent share of the overall steel market and higher market shares for such product lines as cold-rolled steel. Even in the absence of the merger, the industry was highly concentrated. For such reasons the court concluded that the merger would have seriously impaired competition.

In 1966, the Supreme Court tightened the standards for horizontal mergers when it prevented the *Von's Grocery* Company from acquiring Shopping Bag Food Stores, even though the two companies had a combined market share of only 7.5 percent of the Los Angeles market. The Supreme Court, however, was concerned about the growing concentration in this market. Between 1948 and 1958, the 20 largest grocery companies in Los Angeles had increased their share of the market from 44 percent to 57 percent. The Court argued that if it permitted continued merger activity, the market

> would slowly but inevitably gravitate from a market of many small competitors to one dominated by one or a few giants, and competition would thereby be destroyed. Congress passed the Celler-Kefauver Act to prevent such a destruction of competition.

Accordingly, the merger was disallowed.

ENFORCEMENT

Antitrust policy does not end with judicial decisions; the final ingredient is enforcement. In the United States, enforcement is primarily the responsibility of two government agencies—the Federal Trade Commission (FTC) and the Antitrust Division of the Justice Department. The agencies can investigate the activities of firms, issue standards outlining acceptable and unacceptable behavior, and file suits to halt certain actions. In addition, the FTC can issue cease-and-desist orders if it believes a company is violating the law. The FTC's decisions, however, can be appealed through the courts. Finally, private parties can initiate suits seeking damages for antitrust violations by other firms, and for relief from further violations.

The aggressiveness of the antitrust agencies has varied over time depending, among other things, on the philosophy of the president and those serving on the agencies. Following a sluggish start, "trust busting" became a passion under Teddy Roosevelt. The passion soon cooled, only to be rekindled in the wake of the Great Depression, when public resentment toward big business intensified. The number of antitrust suits filed by the Justice Department soared, setting a record in the 1940s. After another lull, antitrust efforts picked up from 1968–1980. During this period the FTC and the Justice Department attacked numerous companies, including such giants as IBM, AT&T, Xerox, and the major cereal companies.

Under President Reagan (1980-88), antitrust activity again ebbed. Suits against IBM and the cereal companies were dropped (see Exhibit 27-2, page 630). Standards for mergers were relaxed. The Justice Department began emphasizing the "efficiency-enhancing potential" of mergers, "which can increase the competitiveness of firms and result in lower prices to consumers."[12] It also promised to pay more attention to foreign competition, arguing that concentration poses less of a threat when U.S. producers compete with imports.

Reagan appointees applauded the court's decision in *Berkey Photo versus Eastman Kodak* and argued for a return to the rule of reason. In outlining administration policy, the chief of the Justice Department's Antitrust Division stated that antitrust prosecution requires evidence of

> serious business improprieties, that are intended to interfere with competitors, other than by improving the situations of one's consumers. A company that is large and has a large market share is free and should be free to go on competing aggressively, keeping its prices down and capturing an even larger market share if it can.[13]

The Reagan policy called for opposing mergers that would harm the public and prosecuting such illegal acts as price fixing. But large companies would no longer automatically be viewed with suspicion. Instead, the Reagan Administration often

[12]Department of Justice, *1984 Merger Guidelines.* In *Federal Register* Vol. 49, No. 127, p. 26834.
[13]Robert Taylor, "Antitrust Enforcement Will Be More Selective," *The Wall Street Journal,* January 1, 1982, p. 6.

EXHIBIT 27–2

CONCENTRATION IN THE CEREAL INDUSTRY

In 1972, the FTC launched an antitrust case against Kellogg, General Mills, and General Foods, which together held an 80-percent share of the ready-to-eat cereal market. The cornerstone of this suit was the theory of **shared monopoly**— the firms were allegedly acting as a monopolist attempting to maximize joint industry profits. Even though the FTC had uncovered no evidence of price fixing or of any conspiracy to limit competition, it asserted that the companies must be acting in concert. How else could their dominance be explained? Because economies of scale were relatively unimportant, the agency claimed that the industry would not have evolved naturally into its present, highly concentrated state.

The FTC suggested that the companies used heavy advertising and product proliferation to deny rivals entry into the market. In essence, they were charged with introducing enough products to fill available shelf space in grocery stores. The cereal makers countered that these practices were evidence of competition, not collusion. Companies introduced new brands to satisfy consumer wants and in an effort to win customers from rival producers.

The FTC dropped the case in 1982, amid criticism from the Reagan Administration that a novel theory (shared monopoly) should not serve as the basis for breaking up the cereal companies. Many in Congress were also unimpressed with the FTC's case. A majority of Senators and over 100 Representatives sponsored a bill to prevent the

FTC from proceeding with the case. The FTC has now backed away from the theory of shared monopoly and, as a result of appointments to the FTC in the 1980s, has developed a more benign attitude toward big business.

Sources: Adapted from Margaret Warner, "Ruling to Drop Suit Against Cereal Firms Deals Blow to 'Shared Monopoly' Theory," *The Wall Street Journal*, September 11, 1981. "FTC Drops 10-Year-Old Antitrust Suit Against the 3 Largest U.S. Cereal Makers," *The Wall Street Journal*, January 18, 1982, p.4.

Superiority Hypothesis
The claim that large oligopolistic producers captured sizable market shares due to their superior efficiency (lower cost curves).

emphasized the **superiority hypothesis**: Companies with a large market share were successful, not because of monopoly power, but because of their superior performance.[14] That is, a favorable cost structure (lower cost curves) allowed high-efficiency companies to grow more rapidly than their competitors and thus obtain a large share of the market.

Antitrust enforcement remains an art. Although subject to the broad directives of Congress, antitrust agencies have considerable latitude over both the intensity and direction of their activities. From an economic perspective, these agencies should balance the benefits of concentration, including economies of scale, against the abuses of monopoly power. Because different people have different perceptions about the benefits and costs of big business, there is a range of opinion over what

---

[14]The source of the superiority hypothesis is Harold Demsetz, "Industry Structure, Market Rivalry, and Public Policy," *Journal of Law and Economics* (April 1973), pp. 1–9.

constitutes optimal policy. Although the Justice Department and the FTC adopted a generally more sympathetic view toward big business in the 1980s, it remains to be seen how policy will evolve over the current decade.

YOUR TURN   MARKET SHARE AND PROFITABILITY
There is evidence that large, oligopolistic firms earn a higher rate of profit than small, competitive firms. This may be due to monopoly power of the large firms or to their cost superiority. (a) Explain these alternative views. (b) Do both views predict that prices will rise as large firms increase their market share? (c) Which view is more critical of big business?

SUMMARY

1. Highly concentrated markets are difficult to evaluate. The domination by a few large firms may reflect favorable cost developments, either economies of scale or superior efficiency of the successful firms. Alternatively, concentration may result from the exploitation of monopoly power. In the latter case, the result is higher prices and reduced output. Concern over the abuse of monopoly power has led to antitrust policy— government actions aimed at influencing the structure and conduct of business.

2. There are various proxies for monopoly power, the two most popular being the market concentration ratio and the Herfindahl Index. The market concentration ratio measures the percentage of industry sales claimed by the four largest producers in the industry. The Herfindahl Index is obtained by summing the market share squared of each firm in the industry. For both measures, higher values indicate greater concentration of power.

3. Neither the market concentration ratio nor the Herfindahl Index provides a complete picture of monopoly power. Accordingly, each should be supplemented with information about competition from imports, other industries, and potential new rivals. In addition, markets must be properly defined if these measures are to provide reliable information.

4. Current antitrust policy emphasizes the Herfindahl Index. Mergers in concentrated industries are generally not allowed if they would increase the Herfindahl Index by more than a specified amount.

5. The share of value added by large manufacturing companies has increased over time. But because of diversification, the concentration of power within individual industries has not increased. That is, although the largest companies are producing a greater share of total manufacturing output, market concentration ratios have not trended upward. If anything, market concentration—both in manufacturing and for the overall economy—may be lower today than at the start of the century.

6. Concentration depends in part on government policy. This consists of antitrust legislation, court rulings, and enforcement by the two antitrust agencies—the Federal Trade Commission (FTC) and the Antitrust Division of the Justice Department.

7. National antitrust legislation began with the Sherman Act in 1890. Thereafter, laws were added to prohibit specific practices and make enforcement easier.

8. The courts are responsible for interpreting the legislation. Although the courts have consistently opposed certain practices (e.g., price fixing), their policy toward monopoly has changed over time. Initially the courts adopted the "rule of reason," condemning only those monopolies that engaged in unreasonable behavior. The *Alcoa* decision changed the standard from behavior to market structure—monopoly, even if achieved as a result of reasonable behavior, was declared illegal. More recently the courts appear to have retreated from the *Alcoa* decision, adopting a more tolerant attitude toward monopoly power.

9. The FTC and the Justice Department enforce the antitrust laws—investigating the practices of firms, attempting to halt violations, and establishing guidelines (e.g., for

mergers). In addition, the FTC investigates fraudulent advertising and issues cease-and-desist orders.

10. Enforcement has fluctuated over time. Under the Reagan Administration, merger guidelines were relaxed and, in general, antitrust agencies became more tolerant of big business.

KEY TERMS

market concentration ratio   rule of reason
contestable market   Alcoa Case
Herfindahl Index   horizontal merger
antitrust policy   vertical merger
trust   conglomerate merger
predatory pricing   shared monopoly
tying contract   superiority hypothesis
interlocking directorates

STUDY QUESTIONS AND PROBLEMS

1. Explain what effect, if any, the following actions have on the industry's market concentration ratio.
   a. In the face of falling demand for U.S. steel, the largest steel company in the United States purchases an oil company.
   b. A foreign automobile company starts manufacturing cars in the United States, rather than overseas, and becomes the fifth-largest automobile producer in the United States.
   c. Each of the aluminum companies loses ten percent of its sales, as soft-drink companies switch from aluminum cans to bottles.
   d. The fourth-largest brewery sells one of its plants to the second-largest brewery.
   e. The fourth-largest brewery sells one of its plants to the tenth-largest brewery.

2. (a) What is monopoly power? (b) Explain why market concentration is not a perfect measure of this power.

3. Assume an industry consists of six firms. Sales figures for each are as follows:

Firm number	Annual sales (millions of units)
1	100
2	80
3	80
4	60
5	40
6	40

   a. Compute the concentration ratio and the Herfindahl Index for this industry.
   b. How would a merger of the two smallest firms affect the concentration ratio and the Herfindahl Index?
   c. Would such a merger satisfy the guidelines of the Justice Department? Why or why not?

4. In 1987, Chrysler purchased American Motors Corporation (AMC). Prior to this purchase the market share of vehicles produced in the United States was as follows:

General Motors	55%
Ford	25%
Chrysler	14%
Honda	3%
American Motors	1%
Volkswagen	1%
Nissan	1%

a. According to Justice Department guidelines, was this industry unconcentrated, moderately concentrated, or highly concentrated?

b. Did the merger satisfy the Justice Department guidelines? Explain.

c. Do you think the merger will decrease competitive pressures within the automotive industry? Explain.

d. Would a merger of Chrysler and Honda have satisfied the merger guidelines?

5. We should rethink our attitude toward profitable giants such as the International Business Machines Corporation. . . . We ought to think about how to get more I.B.M.s, instead of attacking the one we have.[15]

Do you agree with the preceding quotation? Explain the pros and cons of having industry giants such as IBM. What do you think our antitrust policy should be toward such giants?

6. Indicate whether each of the following constitutes a horizontal, vertical, or conglomerate merger.

a. Trans World Airlines purchases Ozark Airlines.

b. The publisher Doubleday buys the New York Mets baseball club.

c. Harcourt Brace Jovanovich acquires another publishing company: Holt, Rinehart and Winston.

d. Nabisco, which makes cookies and crackers, buys a flour mill.

e. The tobacco company R. J. Reynolds acquires Nabisco.

f. IBM buys stock in Intel, which manufactures computer chips.

7. Identify the law prohibiting

a. tying contracts and interlocking directorates.

b. "conspiracy in restraint of trade or commerce . . ."

c. purchase of a competitor's assets in order to gain control of the company.

d. volume discounts on the purchase of "goods of like grade and quality."

8. Which court decision

a. established the "rule of reason"?

b. overturned the rule of reason, claiming that Congress outlawed even good monopolies?

c. declared price fixing "illegal *per se*"?

ANSWERS TO YOUR TURN

CONCENTRATION RATIOS AND THE HERFINDAHL INDEX

(a) The concentration ratio is 80 percent for industry *A* and 70 percent for industry *B*. (b) The respective values for the Herfindahl Index are 1710 and 2254. (c) Industry *A*. (d) No. In contrast to the concentration ratio, the Herfindahl Index indicates that industry *B* is more highly concentrated. This is because industry *B* contains a firm with a very large market share. The Herfindahl Index (because it squares market shares) weights the influence of large firms more heavily than does the concentration ratio.

ANSWERS TO YOUR TURN

MARKET SHARE AND PROFITABILITY

(a) According to the monopoly power view, a highly concentrated market gives firms the ability to raise price and earn economic profits in the long run. In contrast, the efficiency view (superiority hypothesis) argues that a company with a high market share can produce at a lower cost per unit than can smaller companies, enabling it to earn a higher rate of profit. (b) No. Only the monopoly power view predicts higher prices (due to increased monopoly power). A company with superior efficiency earns high profits because of its lower costs, not higher prices. An increase in its market share will not increase price. (c) The monopoly power view.

---

[15]Joseph Bower, "The Case for Building More I.B.M.s," *New York Times,* February 16, 1986, p. 2F.

d. prevented the merger of two companies with a combined 7 1/2 percent share of the market out of concern that mergers would eventually reduce the competitiveness of this market?

9. How would you characterize antitrust policy in the 1980s? How did it differ from antitrust policy in the prior ten years or so? Explain.

SELECTED REFERENCES

James V. Koch, *Industrial Organization and Prices,* 2nd ed. (Englewood Cliffs, NJ: Prentice-Hall, 1980).

F. M. Scherer, *Industrial Market Structure and Economic Performance,* 2nd ed. (Chicago: Rand-McNally College Publishing Co., 1980).

William G. Shepherd, *The Economics of Industrial Organization,* 2nd ed. (Englewood Cliffs, NJ: Prentice-Hall, 1985).

Irwin M. Stelzer, *Selected Antitrust Cases: Landmark Decisions,* 7th ed. (Homewood, IL: Irwin, 1986).

Don E. Waldman, *The Economics of Antitrust* (Boston: Little, Brown and Co., 1986).

CHAPTER 28

REGULATION

The essence of
regulation is the
explicit replacement
of competition with
government orders.[1]

Not only does government influence market structure through
antitrust policy, it oversees the operation of various markets. The
federal government decides which products AT&T may sell and
how much it may charge for long-distance calls. It determines who
may operate television and radio stations and what they may
broadcast. Financial regulations limit the investment activities of
banks, force companies to follow specific accounting rules, and
prohibit inside trading of stocks (trading based on confidential
information). Various government agencies limit the amount of
pollution companies may generate and require them to provide a
safe work environment. Still other agencies force the recall of
unsafe products, limit the use of food additives, and prevent the sale
of new drugs pending government approval.

According to the Center for the Study of American Business,
the federal government operates 51 separate regulatory agencies
with a combined staff of more than 100,000.[2] Beyond that,
individual states and cities have their own regulatory bodies that
determine how land shall be used (zoning regulations), who shall
be allowed to cut hair or sell eyeglasses (occupational licensing),
and how much utilities may charge for natural gas and electricity.
Some cities regulate local transportation, limiting the number of
taxis on city streets and setting their fares. Regulation affects
virtually every business and consumer in some form or another.

What are the reasons for regulation and what are its
consequences? Does society in general benefit or merely special
interest groups? Although governmental regulations remain
pervasive, they have eased in certain industries—notably
transportation, communication, and finance. Entry restrictions
have been relaxed, and firms have been given greater discretion over

---

[1]Alfred Kahn, The Economics of Regulation, Vol. 1 (New York: John Wiley &
Sons, 1970), p. 20.

[2]Melinda Warren and Kenneth Chilton, The Regulatory Legacy of the Reagan
Revolution: An Analysis of 1990 Federal Regulatory Budgets and Staffing (St. Louis:
Washington University Center for the Study of American Business, 1989).

price and service. Has this deregulation of industry been a success or a failure? Chapter 28 explores these issues, following a brief survey of regulation in the United States.

THE EVOLUTION OF FEDERAL REGULATION

The same distrust of big business that motivated antitrust laws also led to the creation of the Interstate Commerce Commission (ICC) in 1887. Consumers worried about the growing monopoly power of railroads and the effect on price. Competition by a large number of railroads was not practical. With duplicate trains, depots, and tracks, the costs of rail transportation would be unnecessarily high. Economic efficiency demanded that only a small number of railroads serve a region. But with little competition from other carriers, what was to prevent a railroad from charging exorbitant prices? The solution was to create a government agency (the ICC) that would control entry into the industry, thereby limiting the costs of transportation, and at the same time would cap the rates that railroads could charge their customers.

Unlike the railroad industry, trucking has the ingredients of a competitive industry. The market is capable of supporting a large number of trucking companies, and competition among these companies could be expected to keep trucking rates low. As the highway system developed, the trucking industry began taking business away from railroads. Even where railroads enjoyed a cost advantage, they were unable to match lower trucking rates, since rail charges were set by the ICC. For railroads to compete with trucking, either they had to be given the freedom to reduce their rates or truckers had to be prevented from undercutting the price of rail service. Congress chose the latter option, and in 1935 the trucking industry was brought under the jurisdiction of the ICC.

During the 1930s, regulation was similarly extended to other industries. The Civil Aeronautics Board (CAB) was created to regulate air travel and the Federal Communications Commission (FCC) to regulate the various means of communications—telephone, telegraph, and broadcasting. The Securities and Exchange Commission (SEC) was established to guarantee more accurate information on the value of stocks and other securities, to combat fraud and malpractice in the securities industry, and to regulate brokers and other securities dealers. The SEC was also empowered to set brokerage fees, although it has not done so since 1975. The number of federal regulatory agencies continued to grow through 1978, with the greatest growth occurring from 1969–1978.

In 1970, the Occupational Safety and Health Administration (OSHA) was created to reduce the incidence of death and injury in the workplace. This agency issues safety and health rules and inspects job sites for compliance. Employers are cited and fined for each violation, and ordered to take corrective action. These fines can be substantial. For example, in 1987, Chrysler was fined $1.6 million for exposing workers at its Newark, Delaware, plant to dangerous chemicals. The following year the Doe Run Company was assessed $1.25 million and forced to provide back pay and health benefits to workers injured at its lead smelting plant near St. Louis.

In 1972, the push for increased safety reached the product market. The Consumer Product Safety Commission (CPSC) was established "to protect the public from unreasonable risks of injury associated with consumer products." The commission requires companies to report defects in their products and to correct them. It can also ban the sale of hazardous products.

The Environmental Protection Agency (EPA) was formed in 1970 to coordinate environmental policy. The agency seeks abatement of air and water pollution and the control of solid waste, pesticides, radiation, and toxic substances. It monitors activities affecting the environment, sets standards and enforces them, and engages in research. The responsibilities of the EPA and various other regulatory bodies are summarized in Table 28-1.

TABLE 28-1

SELECTED FEDERAL REGULATORY AGENCIES

Agency	Year created	Principal function
Intersate Commerce Commission (ICC)	1887	To regulate interstate ground transportation, including the railroad, trucking, bus, and water carrier industries.
Federal Energy Regulatory Commission (FERC)*	1920	To regulate water power and the interstate sale of electricity and natural gas.
Federal Communications Commission (FCC)	1934	To regulate interstate and foreign communications by radio, television, telephone, telegraph, and the like.
Securities and Exchange Commission (SEC)	1934	To regulate the markets for stocks and other securities and to protect investors by seeking full disclosure of pertinent information.
Civil Aeronautics Board (CAB)**	1938	To regulate the airline industry.
Environmental Protection Agency (EPA)	1970	To coordinate environmental policy, set pollution standards, and otherwise enforce environmental legislation.
Occupational Safety and Health Administration (OSHA)	1970	To promote the health and safety of workers by issuing and enforcing rules covering the workplace.
Consumer Product Safety Commission (CPSC)	1972	To reduce injuries to consumers from unsafe products.

*Formerly known as the Federal Power Commission.

**Abolished in 1984.

Sources: Adapted from Ronald Penoyer, *Directory of Federal Regulatory Agencies* (St. Louis: Center for the Study of American Business, 1982); Office of the Federal Register, *The United States Government Manual, 1989/90* (Washington, DC: GPO, 1989).

The Changing Nature of Regulation

The focus of regulation has shifted over time. Early regulation tended to be industry specific—directed, for example, at the railroad industry, the airline industry, or the securities industry. It was concerned primarily with setting price, controlling entry into the industry, and establishing service standards. Because this type of regulation focused on economic outcomes in the industry, it became known as **economic regulation**. In contrast, the new regulation of recent decades has been primarily **social regulation**. Concerned with the general well-being of society, social regulation attempts to improve the quality of the environment and to promote greater health and safety throughout the economy, for both workers and consumers. Social regulation is broader in scope than economic regulation, with regulatory bodies generally having jurisdiction over all industries.

As social regulation expanded, so did the costs of regulation. Between 1970 and 1980, the administrative costs of regulatory agencies increased by 140 percent in real terms—that is, after netting out for the effects of inflation. Staffing of federal regulatory agencies also soared, from just over 73,000 employees in 1970 to 119,000 in 1980.

The growth in regulatory budgets slowed in the 1980s, and the staffing actually declined (see Table 28-2). Although partially attributable to President Reagan, who campaigned against "regulatory excesses," the turnaround actually began prior to the Reagan presidency. Both Presidents Ford and Carter pushed regulatory reform. Indeed, most of the laws **deregulating** industry were passed during the Carter Administration. Foremost was the Airline Deregulation Act of 1978, which relaxed entry restrictions, allowed airlines to reduce fares, and led to the eventual elimination of the CAB. Two years later Congress extended deregulation to the trucking, railroad, and financial industries.[3]

But whereas President Carter was committed to reducing *economic* regulation, President Reagan was equally intent on scaling back *social* regulation. Reagan sliced the budget at OSHA, arguing that many of the agency's regulations imposed costs on business without contributing to health or safety. By the end of his second term the number of OSHA inspectors had been cut by 30 percent. Similarly, the budget for

Economic Regulation
The regulation of specific industries, designed to influence such outcomes as price, service, and number of producers in an industry.
Social Regulation
Broad-based regulations designed to improve the environment and to enhance health and safety.

Deregulation
The removal of government regulations.

TABLE 28-2

STAFFING AND ADMINISTRATIVE COSTS OF FEDERAL REGULATORY AGENCIES

Year	Staffing (full-time positions)	Administrative costs (millions of 1989 dollars)
1970	73,375	$ 3828
1980	118,849	9254
1990	107,194*	10,619*

*Estimated.

Source: Melinda Warren and Kenneth Chilton, *The Regulatory Legacy of the Reagan Revolution: An Analysis of 1990 Federal Regulatory Budgets and Staffing* (St. Louis: Washington University Center for the Study of American Business, 1989), Tables 2 and 3. Adapted with permission.

---

[3]The specific laws achieving deregulation were the Motor Carrier Act, the Staggers Railway Act, and the Depository Institutions Deregulation and Monetary Control Act.

the Consumer Product Safety Commission was lower in Reagan's final year in office than in President Carter's final year. Although the budget of the EPA continued to grow, its rate of advance was more moderate during the Reagan Administration. In summary, President Reagan reined in the growth of social regulation. This, combined with the economic deregulation that was already under way, enabled the federal government to reduce the size of its regulatory staff.

THE COSTS AND BENEFITS OF REGULATION

Left to their own, private markets may fail to allocate resources efficiently. In such cases, government regulation can increase the well-being of society. Even the harshest critics of regulation acknowledge the legitimate role of government. At issue is not the need for government regulation, but its scope.

Those seeking to reduce government's role attack regulations on two grounds: (a) regulations are sometimes extended to markets that would operate more efficiently unregulated and (b) in markets where intervention is appropriate, regulation is often excessive. Regulations impose costs on society. These consist of both the administrative costs of regulatory agencies, including staff salaries and overhead, and the costs of complying with the regulations. In addition to the extra paperwork, regulations force firms to add product features they would not otherwise provide (e.g., catalytic converters on automobiles) and to alter production processes. For instance, coal-burning power plants built after 1979 must install stack scrubbers to reduce sulphur emissions from the coal. This raises the cost of electricity.

Costs rise even further because of the inefficient resource use mandated by various regulatory agencies. Prior to deregulation the ICC forced trucks to return empty on long hauls rather than picking up additional cargo. Moreover, by equalizing fares across competing modes of transportation (trucking, railroads, barges), the ICC removed the incentive to use the most efficient mode. For example, trucks are often more efficient than trains for transporting goods short distances while trains are more efficient for long hauls. Ideally, these cost differences would be reflected in rate schedules, so that shippers would choose the least costly mode of transportation. The ICC, however, frequently equalized rates to guarantee each industry a share of both long-distance and short-distance markets. In some cases the ICC even subsidized trucking companies making long hauls so they could compete on routes where railroads were more efficient. As a result, transportation resources best suited for long-distance travel were often used for short hauls while resources best suited for short-distance travel were used for long hauls.

For such reasons government regulations increase the costs of production. During the 1970s, compliance costs were estimated to be about 20 times greater than administrative costs.[4] If that ratio still holds, then based on administrative costs of roughly $10.6 billion (see Table 28-2), the total cost of federal regulations is currently in the neighborhood of $212 billion per year.

From an economic perspective, the costs of regulation should be compared with the benefits. Further regulation is advantageous to society when the benefits from additional regulation exceed the costs of additional regulation. But when the additional benefits fall short of the additional costs, then regulation is excessive. In

---

[4]Murray Weidenbaum and Robert DeFina, *The Cost of Federal Regulation of Economic Activity* (Washington, DC: The American Enterprise Institute, May 1978), p. 2.

that case society would benefit from transferring resources from regulation to other activities—for example, producing greater output for consumers.

Some regulations pass the cost/benefit test, others do not. For example, one study found that mandated safety features on automobiles provided benefits in excess of costs but that regulations dealing with automobile emissions and fuel economy had costs that exceeded benefits.[5] Before assessing the impact of various regulations, it is important to understand their rationale. This will help you understand why certain regulations are socially desirable and why others are not.

WHY REGULATE?

There are two principal theories of regulation: the **public interest theory** and the **special interest theory**. The former argues that regulations arise because of the failure of private markets to generate socially optimal outcomes (in terms of price, costs, and output). Where market failure exists, regulations can improve the well-being of society. The special interest theory paints a less favorable view of regulation. According to this theory, regulation is designed to protect special interest groups at the expense of the general public. For example, regulators may restrict competition and raise price, enabling a regulated firm to earn higher profits but harming consumers.

THE PUBLIC INTEREST THEORY OF REGULATION

Adam Smith extolled the virtues of private markets, arguing that consumers and producers "promote the public interest" more effectively than any government. If this were always true, then government intervention could only harm the public interest. Smith's argument holds, however, only when certain ideal conditions prevail. When these conditions are not satisfied, market outcomes are not optimal. In such cases government may serve the public interest. Among the reasons for market failure, and therefore government regulation, are natural monopoly, externalities, and imperfect information.

Natural Monopoly

In a natural monopoly the average cost of production falls as the scale of operations increases (see Figure 28-1). In this situation competition is not efficient. The average cost of producing a given output is minimized when only one firm is in the industry. Therefore, by limiting production to a single firm the government minimizes costs of production. Society does not necessarily benefit, however, if the firm granted monopoly status is allowed to charge any price it wishes. Therefore, in the case of natural monopoly, regulation has a second function—to protect consumers from high prices.

Externalities

Externalities arise when parties engaged in neither the production nor the consumption of a good are nonetheless affected by the good. For example, production may

[5]Robert W. Crandall, Howard Gruenspecht, Theodore Keeler, and Lester Lave, *Regulating the Automobile* (Washington, DC: The Brookings Institution, 1986).

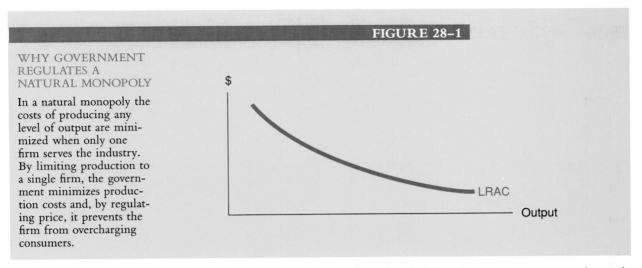

FIGURE 28-1

WHY GOVERNMENT
REGULATES A
NATURAL MONOPOLY

In a natural monopoly the
costs of producing any
level of output are mini-
mized when only one
firm serves the industry.
By limiting production to
a single firm, the government minimizes produc-
tion costs and, by regulating price, it prevents the
firm from overcharging
consumers.

entail a side effect—pollution. The individual firm has no incentive to voluntarily
reduce pollution. Expenditures on pollution control would put the firm at a
competitive disadvantage—it would face higher costs than firms that did not control
pollution. Therefore, if society wants less pollution, the government must step in
and regulate industry. Regulation may assume a variety of forms, from direct
controls requiring specific pollution-control equipment to taxation. These forms are
examined in Chapter 34. Regardless of its form, however, regulation is necessary if
society is to respond to externalities.

Imperfect Information

Consumers cannot choose wisely if they lack relevant information. Unaware of the
dangers, they may consume unsafe drugs, buy defective products, and work with
hazardous chemicals. Companies generally lack the incentive to voluntarily reveal
shortcomings in their products. Worse than that, they may be able to boost sales by
making false claims. Information is valuable and, accordingly, consumers are
prepared to spend income on services such as *Consumer Reports,* which evaluate
various products. But markets may fail to provide adequate information or to
adequately discipline unscrupulous producers. In that event, government can benefit
society by gathering and disseminating information pertinent to consumers and
workers and by preventing companies from making false or deceptive claims. This is
the rationale for warning labels on cigarettes, EPA mileage ratings on cars, and
posted weight limits and safety instructions on ladders.

Some individuals argue that the government should do more than assure
consumers of accurate information—that it should force unsafe products from the
market and mandate minimum safety standards in the workplace. According to this
argument, even when information is widely available, consumers lack the expertise
to evaluate it. If consumers are not sophisticated enough to make intelligent
decisions, the government should decide for them—for example, force them to buy
products with extensive safety features.

Others dismiss this view, contending that once consumers have sufficient
information they should be free to choose. By restricting consumer choice to safe
products and safe workplaces, the government may actually reduce the well-being of
its citizens. This argument is illustrated in Figure 28-2 (page 642).

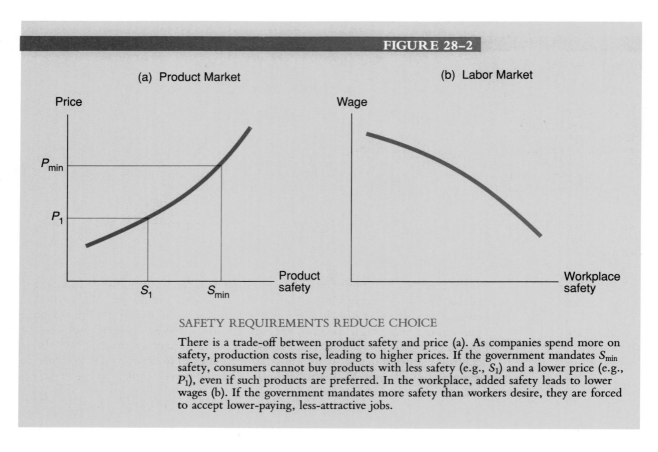

SAFETY REQUIREMENTS REDUCE CHOICE

There is a trade-off between product safety and price (a). As companies spend more on safety, production costs rise, leading to higher prices. If the government mandates S_{min} safety, consumers cannot buy products with less safety (e.g., S_1) and a lower price (e.g., P_1), even if such products are preferred. In the workplace, added safety leads to lower wages (b). If the government mandates more safety than workers desire, they are forced to accept lower-paying, less-attractive jobs.

Safety features are costly to provide, both in products and in the workplace. As products are made safer, production costs rise, pushing up price (Figure 28-2a). A product with S_1 safety sells for P_1, but with S_{min} safety, price rises to P_{min}. Similarly, wages depend on safety in the workplace. A competitive firm can afford to spend only so much per worker. The less it spends on safety, the more it has left for wages (Figure 28-2b). Consistent with this view, empirical studies find that, other things equal, riskier (less safe) jobs pay higher wages.[6]

Suppose the government imposes minimum product safety standards of S_{min} [see (a)]. Consumers must now pay at least P_{min} for this product. Consumers who do not feel the added safety is worth the higher price prefer a product with fewer safety features, but are denied the chance to buy it. Moreover, low-income consumers unable to pay P_{min} are squeezed from the market entirely. Likewise, minimum workplace standards keep workers from less-safe, higher-paying jobs even when workers believe the higher wage more than compensates for the added risk of injury. Therefore, according to this view, by restricting choice, safety regulations can reduce the satisfaction of workers and consumers.

To summarize, when markets fail to provide adequate information, government regulations can improve social well-being. There is a debate, however, over whether the government should merely provide information or whether it should force

---

[6]See Greg J. Duncan and Bertil Holmlund, "Was Adam Smith Right After All? Another Test of the Theory of Compensating Wage Differentials," *Journal of Labor Economics* (October 1983), pp. 366–379.

EXHIBIT 28-1

ALL-TERRAIN VEHICLES

The all-terrain vehicle (ATV) has a poor safety record. These three- and four-wheeled motorized bikes often overturn, leaving the driver vulnerable. From 1982–87, ATVs were responsible for an average of 15 deaths and 5000 injuries per month. Citing these statistics, various consumer groups and politicians argued that government intervention was necessary to protect consumers. Some wanted the Consumer Product Safety Commission to establish a minimum age for driving the ATV and to force manufacturers to refund the purchase price to previous buyers now concerned about the vehicle's safety. Others urged the CPSC to go further—to declare the ATV unsafe and ban its use.

At the other extreme, some objected to government intervention entirely. They noted that motorcycle accidents claim the lives of nearly 400 riders each month, yet the CPSC would not dream of banning their use. Why should ATVs be singled out? Besides, claimed supporters, ATVs are safe when operated properly; the fault lies with the rider. As evidence they cited statistics that many accidents occurred when riders were driving unfamiliar terrain at high speed, were riding double (contrary to manufacturers' directions), or were under the influence of alcohol. Almost one-third of the accidents involved people 14 years and younger, who often lack the experience to safely drive any vehicle. Even though the fault often lies with the rider, manufacturers were developing their own voluntary standards. For such reasons, many saw no need for government regulation.

After considering both sides of the debate, the government adopted an intermediate position. In 1988, the CPSC—working in conjunction with the Justice Department—reached a settlement

with ATV manufacturers in which they agreed to halt all sales of three-wheeled ATVs, to sponsor training programs for new customers, to spend $8.5 million advertising the potential hazards of ATVs, and to stop marketing the ATV as a vehicle suitable for children. Under the agreement, companies are allowed to continue selling four-wheeled ATVs and are under no obligation to make refunds.

Sources: Adapted from Jeanne Saddler, "Consumer Safety Agency's Role Is Questioned," *The Wall Street Journal*, September 23, 1987, p. 64; Jeanne Saddler, "Pact of All-Terrain Vehicle Makers with U.S. Revised," *The Wall Street Journal*, March 15, 1988, p. 22; *Kansas City Times*, "Plan Limiting Sales of ATVs Receives Final Approval," April 28, 1988, p. A3; U.S. Department of Commerce, *Statistical Abstract of the United States, 1988* (U.S. Government Printing Office), Table 999.

consumers to act according to what it perceives to be the consumers' best interests. Should individuals be free to accept known risks, or are some risks so great that the government should step in to protect individuals from their own voluntary decisions? Exhibit 28-1 provides a specific example around which to focus the debate: Should government regulate all-terrain vehicles?

THE SPECIAL INTEREST THEORY OF REGULATION

The public interest theory of regulation is grounded in the belief that regulation is an attempt to improve the general well-being of society. In contrast, the special interest theory holds that regulation is designed to benefit certain segments of the economy at the expense of others—without improving the general well-being of society. According to this view: "As a rule, regulation is acquired by the industry and is designed and operated primarily for its benefit."[7]

Industry may receive direct benefits from the government, including tax breaks and subsidies, or indirect benefits, including reduced competition. For example, prior to deregulation the CAB protected existing airlines by refusing to allow a single new carrier to fly any of the major routes. In trucking, the ICC actually reduced the number of licensed carriers, despite continued growth in the volume of freight transported by truck.

Regulatory agencies can also legitimize otherwise illegal activities. Price fixing among private producers violates antitrust statutes, yet regulatory agencies can legally fix prices. In many instances these prices exceed the levels that would prevail in the absence of regulation. When regulatory agencies restrict competition and raise price, they achieve the same results as an industry cartel. It is no wonder then that producers rather than consumers often petition for regulation. Nor is it any surprise that many producers bitterly fight deregulation. Without government protection from competitors, profits of existing companies are likely to fall and inefficient firms may be driven out of business.

Even if regulation is not initially for the benefit of industry, many economists believe that the regulators will soon be *captured* by industry. According to the **capture hypothesis**, regulators pursue policies to protect the industry's firms rather than to protect consumers. Regulators might advance the interests of industry for a variety of reasons. First, regulators may identify with and be sympathetic toward industry. Members of regulatory commissions often come from the industry they regulate. Furthermore, many return to that industry some time after leaving the commission (although federal regulators must wait one or more years before returning to the industry they regulated).

Even when regulators lack a pro-industry bias, they may find it difficult to restrain the firms they are charged with overseeing. Where they lack important information about a firm, they may mistakenly allow the firm to charge excessive rates. Alternatively, regulated firms may be able to sidestep any constraint. For instance, if price is capped, firms may reduce the quality and therefore the cost of providing their service. In other words, a commission may be outgunned or outflanked by firms in the industry.

Finally, regulatory commissions try to avoid driving firms out of business. By setting price high enough to allow inefficient firms to earn normal profits, they guarantee that firms with lower unit costs will earn economic profits. To protect its firms, a regulatory commission may even limit competition from other industries. Recall how the ICC acquired jurisdiction over trucking and water transportation, limiting the ability of these industries to undersell railroads. Thus, instead of promoting competition, regulatory commissions sometimes squash it for the benefit of regulated firms.

Unions may also have a vested interest in regulation. Where existing firms are unionized, regulatory barriers prevent low-wage nonunion firms from entering the industry, taking business away from union firms, and therefore jobs away from union members. By propping up price, regulation also limits competition among existing firms in the industry. Even if some other firm obtains a cost advantage through lower labor costs, it is not permitted to undercut the firm's price and take away its

Capture Hypothesis
The claim that regulators promote the interests of the industry they regulate rather than protecting the public.

---

[7]George Stigler, "The Theory of Economic Regulation," *Bell Journal of Economics and Management Science* (Spring 1971), p. 3.

customers. By protecting a firm from its more efficient rivals, regulation lessens the firm's opposition to higher union wages.

At the same time, regulation increases the union's incentive to negotiate higher wages. Because the firm will not lose market share to its rivals, the union need not fear that higher wages will lead to massive job loss. Interpreted in this light, trucking and airline unions did not oppose deregulation out of fear that the public would be harmed. Instead, they sought to preserve their own highly paid jobs.

Similarly, various consumer groups find regulation advantageous. Even if most consumers are harmed, certain segments may benefit. For example, regulators sometimes establish "lifeline" programs, forcing companies to provide electricity or telephone service at less than cost to those with an income below some threshold. The regulators then allow the companies to make up these losses by charging other consumers higher rates. In this case the subsidized low-income users rally behind regulation. The special interest theory of regulation also explains why small communities opposed deregulation of the airline industry. The CAB had forced airlines to retain unprofitable, low-traffic routes. The communities worried that they would lose air service if airlines were free to pull out.

Even the regulators have a vested interest in continued regulation. Not only are their jobs at stake, but their prestige, power, and chances for promotion depend on the size and growth of the regulatory agency. Regulatory growth is a form of empire building. In conclusion, according to the special interest theory of regulation, regulation exists not because it is in the public interest, but because various groups promote regulation as a means of serving their own personal interests.

THE EFFECTS OF REGULATION

With these insights into the *why* of regulation, it is now appropriate to examine the consequences. Regulation has led to cleaner air, a safer workplace, and more-informed consumers. It has also increased the costs of production. Beyond these obvious effects, regulation has altered the price of output, quality of service, profits, productivity, and wages.

Price

Consistent with the capture hypothesis, regulatory agencies often set prices above the levels that would prevail in the absence of regulation. An FTC study found that taxi fares were 13–16 percent higher in cities that regulate taxis. In industries where price restrictions have been eliminated, prices have tended to fall immediately. Deregulation has led to lower rates for rail and trucking transportation, brokerage services, and air travel. Lower air fares alone are estimated to save consumers $6 billion per year.[8]

In addition to directly raising price, regulation often inflates price by increasing costs of production. Economists at the Brookings Institution estimate that government-mandated safety features add more than $600 to the price of a new car and that regulations on automobile emissions raise the cost of owning and operating a car by an additional $1600.[9]

---

[8]Steven Morrison and Clifford Winston, *The Economic Effects of Airline Deregulation* (Washington, DC: The Brookings Institution, 1986), p. 33.

[9]Same as 5.

Where the industry is a natural monopoly, regulation may lower price, yet even this is unclear. A widely cited study of electrical utilities found no evidence that regulation had reduced the average price of electricity.[10] Either electric utilities have little long-run monopoly power or regulatory commissions have been ineffective in keeping down rates. Instances where regulation reduces price are rare; more commonly price rises.

Service

The effect of regulation on service is mixed. When regulation creates a monopoly, it may lessen the level of service. Certainly it lessens consumer choice. Consumers dissatisfied with the services of the monopolist cannot switch to another producer in the industry. Second, if regulation forces a firm to accept a lower price than desired, the firm may try to offset the lower price by reducing service. Consistent with these arguments, customers in the railroad and trucking industries reported that service improved greatly following deregulation: "A corporate traffic manager described negotiating for trucking service in the fall of 1981 as being 'like walking into a candy store.'"[11]

In other industries the situation is reversed: regulation leads to a greater level of service. For example, regulators sometimes force cable franchises to carry more television channels than the companies would like. Moreover, where regulation eliminates price competition, companies may switch to nonprice competition. This is what happened in the airline industry. When the CAB prevented airlines from reducing fares, they competed for passengers by spending more on meals, offering greater personal attention (more employees per passenger), allowing customers to cancel reservations without penalty, and maintaining flights with low-load factors (numerous empty seats).

In a very real sense, airlines provided too much service. Consumers placed a lower value on many services than it cost to provide them. That is, consumers preferred lower fares to the additional services. Accordingly, following deregulation consumers flocked to no-frills, low-fare airlines and booked seats on heavily discounted flights, despite numerous restrictions. The effect of deregulation on airline service is examined more fully in Exhibit 28-2. In summary, regulation may either increase or decrease service. Yet, to the extent that regulation prevents consumers from choosing the mix of services they desire, it is likely to reduce consumer well-being.

Profits

Regulation has an ambiguous effect on profits. Where regulation promotes a cartel by restricting entry and raising price, it may increase industry profits. On the other hand, regulation imposes costs on firms and limits their ability to adjust price. The regulated price may be set either too low or too high to maximize profits.

In the airline industry, regulation apparently had an adverse effect on profits. According to one study, profits increased by at least $2.5 billion per year once the

---

[10]George Stigler and Claire Friedland, "What Can Regulators Regulate? The Case of Electricity," *Journal of Law and Economics* (October 1962), pp. 1–16.

[11]Martha Derthick and Paul J. Quirk, *The Politics of Deregulation* (Washington, DC: The Brookings Institution, 1985), p. 1.

EXHIBIT 28-2

AIRLINE SERVICE AFTER DEREGULATION

Airline deregulation was opposed largely because of a concern that service would deteriorate. Some feared that service to small communities would be curtailed, while others worried that safety would suffer. Fortunately, neither of these predictions has come to pass.

With deregulation, airlines were free to add and drop routes. Where air traffic was low, major airlines did in fact halt service. But where major airlines pulled out, commuter airlines stepped in. The number of communities served actually increased under deregulation.

The other major concern was that airlines would skimp on safety. Critics of deregulation argued that high fares allowed airlines to devote more resources to safety and that, under deregulation, airlines would be forced to sacrifice safety in order to match competitors' lower fares. Although the Federal Aviation Administration (FAA) continued to monitor safety, airlines had traditionally exceeded FAA standards, meaning that they were legally free to reduce safety. Moreover, the FAA's budget was cut following deregulation, making it less likely that airlines violating FAA safety standards would be caught.

Despite such arguments, there is no evidence that airline safety has suffered following deregulation. Two separate studies of the issue find that regulation has had no effect on air safety. Indeed, both the overall accident rate and the accident rate involving fatalities have fallen since airlines were deregulated. According to these studies, market forces are sufficiently strong to prevent airlines from shortchanging safety. Airlines with subpar safety records face higher insurance rates and a loss in passengers. Manufacturers of aircraft (e.g., Boeing, McDonnell Douglas, and Lockheed) suffer large drops in the value of their stock whenever one of their planes is in an accident involving design flaws. In summary, a strong safety record is vital to the commercial success of airlines and aircraft manufacturers. Safety is good business, even in unregulated skies.

Even though deregulation has not eliminated air travel to small communities or reduced safety, it has affected service. Airlines have cut back on certain amenities, including meals. With greater traffic, flight delays have become more common. On the positive side, travelers have a greater number of flights from which to choose. They also have a greater variety of flights, ranging from no-frills to premium service. Finally, the percentage of passengers required to change airlines in order to complete a flight has declined, as has the percentage of passengers required to change planes.

Sources: Adapted from Richard McKenzie and William F. Shughart II, "Deregulation and Air Travel Safety," *Regulation* (No. 3/4, 1987), pp. 42–47; Andrew Chalk, "Market Outperforms FAA as Air-Safety Enforcer," *The Wall Street Journal*, September 1, 1987, p. 26; Steven Morrison and Clifford Winston, *The Economic Effects of Airline Deregulation* (Washington, DC: The Brookings Institution, 1986); *Economic Report of the President, 1986* (Washington, DC: Government Printing Office, 1986), Chapter 5.

industry was deregulated.[12] Freed of government constraints, airlines have been able to switch to the more efficient hub-and-spoke system, in which travelers are routed through major airports (hubs). With improved scheduling, special fares, and increased flexibility, airlines have also been able to increase both the number of flights and the number of passengers per flight. Because of heavy fixed costs, the result is a lower cost per passenger.

Similarly, deregulation has increased profits in the railroad industry. The Staggers Rail Act of 1980 eased government restrictions and gave railroads greater discretion over price. Although price has declined, so has average cost. Railroads have been able to reduce the fraction of time rail cars are empty and to otherwise

---

[12]Same as 8, p. 40.

improve efficiency. Labor productivity (ton-miles per employee) rose by 44 percent in the four years immediately following enactment of the Staggers Act.[13]

Labor Productivity

The adverse effects of regulation on labor productivity (output per worker) are not specific to the railroad industry. To the extent funds are used to meet government regulations rather than to acquire capital, workers have less equipment to work with. Moreover, workers may be forced to spend time complying with regulations rather than producing output. Finally, regulations sometimes impede the introduction of new technology. It has been estimated that nationwide regulations have reduced productivity growth by 0.4 percent per year.[14]

Union Wages

Where regulation limits competition from low-wage firms, unions may be able to negotiate higher wages. Conversely, deregulation, by increasing competition, may erode union wages. There is some evidence that it has. Following deregulation new airlines were created and existing airlines expanded into new markets. Competition led to lower fares, especially in markets served by low-cost, nonunion airlines. Once one airline cut fares, others serving the same route were forced to follow suit to avoid losing passengers.

When two recessions hit during the early 1980s, several airlines were in serious financial trouble. To keep their companies afloat, unions at Braniff, Western, and Pan Am agreed to wage cuts of approximately ten percent. To remain competitive, other airlines demanded similar concessions. Virtually every union contract negotiated between 1981 and 1983 mandated pay cuts for airline employees.[15] Some contracts further reduced wages by introducing a *two-tiered wage structure,* in which new employees are paid substantially lower wages than current employees.

Although the wage cuts were partially attributable to the recessions, many analysts believe they would not have been possible without deregulation. Not only had regulation sheltered inefficient airlines from competition, it had also encouraged unions to resist concessions. Their jobs would be secure even if the company faltered. The CAB would find a healthy airline to acquire their company and would even force the new airline to recognize their seniority rights. Therefore, when the industry was regulated, unions had little reason to be conciliatory. Deregulation changed the bargaining climate, paving the way for concessions. This is true not only for the airline industry but also for trucking and railroads.

REGULATING NATURAL MONOPOLY—A CLOSER LOOK

The analysis to this point has been rather broad in scope, discussing the various reasons for regulation and considering the consequences. In this final section, we take a more detailed look at the special case of natural monopoly, thereby gaining an

---

[13]*Economic Report of the President, 1986,* p. 164.

[14]Robert E. Litan and William D. Nordhaus, *Reforming Federal Regulation* (New Haven: Yale University Press, 1983), p. 33.

[15]Peter Cappelli, "Airlines," in David Lipsky and Clifford Donn, eds., *Collective Bargaining in American Industry* (Lexington, MA: Heath and Co., 1987), p. 160.

appreciation of how regulatory commissions operate under natural monopoly and what potential problems they face. We also consider an alternative to regulation—public ownership.

THE ROLE OF A REGULATORY COMMISSION

The government frequently grants monopoly status to companies providing local telephone service, electricity, water, or natural gas. This avoids duplication of costs (unnecessary wiring, pipelines, and so forth) and allows the output to be produced at a lower cost than possible with multiple producers. This situation, natural monopoly, is depicted in Figure 28-3. Because the demand curve intersects a declining average cost curve, the average cost of production is minimized when only one firm serves the market.

Typically, the government creates a regulatory commission to oversee the operation of natural monopolies. If left to itself, a monopolist would produce to the point where marginal revenue equals marginal cost, Q_m, and set a price of P_m. To protect the public interest, the regulatory commission limits the price that the monopolist may charge. But what price should the commission allow?

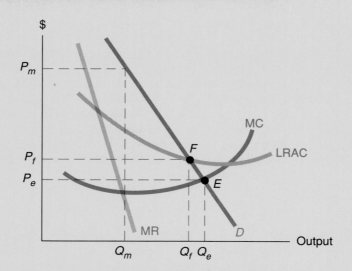

FIGURE 28–3

SETTING PRICE FOR A REGULATED MONOPOLY

An unregulated monopolist sells Q_m output at a price of P_m in order to maximize profit. This is less output than society desires and a higher price. Efficient allocation of resources occurs at E, where marginal cost intersects the demand curve (the marginal cost of producing Q_e output corresponds to the price consumers are willing to pay). However, if the regulatory commission sets price at P_e, the firm will not produce in the long run because price is less than long-run average cost. To ensure long-run production while limiting the firm to normal profit, the regulatory commission may choose to equate price with long-run average cost (F). Confronted with a price of P_f, the firm will produce Q_f output.

Marginal Cost Pricing

Marginal Cost Pricing
A regulatory procedure intended to equate price with marginal cost, and thereby promote efficient allocation of resources.

If resources are to be allocated efficiently, production should continue to the point where price equals marginal cost (**marginal cost pricing**). This is given by the intersection of the demand and marginal cost curves (point E). But whereas P_e is necessary for efficient allocation, it is also impractical. At a price of P_e the firm would lose money, since price is below average cost. Therefore, if the regulatory commission were to set a price of P_e, in an attempt to achieve efficient allocation of resources, it would drive the firm out of business.

Average Cost Pricing

Average Cost Pricing
A regulatory procedure intended to equate price with average cost, and thereby limit the firm to normal profits.

Rather than equate price with marginal cost, the commission may choose to set price equal to average cost (**average cost pricing**). This occurs where demand intersects the average cost curve (point F). By capping price at P_f, the commission limits the firm to normal profits. The firm earns enough to stay in business but nothing extra. Although P_f does not provide efficient allocation of resources, it is superior to the unregulated price of P_m. Consumers benefit from both a lower price and a higher level of output $(Q_f > Q_m)$.

Subsidies and Access Fees

There are ways to keep the firm in business at a price below P_f, but they involve supplemental funding. For instance, the government could subsidize the firm, paying it an amount equal to its production losses. If the firm loses $1 million from production, the government would pay the firm $1 million to keep it operating. Indeed, by setting a price of P_e and coupling that with a subsidy, the government could induce the firm to produce Q_e output, thereby achieving efficient allocation of resources.

Alternatively, funds could be raised by charging consumers an *access fee* independent of their usage. For instance, telephone users are charged a monthly access fee for the privilege of making long-distance calls. This fee is above and beyond the payment for any calls actually made. The access fee allows the commission to set a lower price on the service provided (e.g., long-distance calls). If price is set below average cost, the access fee can offset the loss the firm incurs in providing the service.

REGULATION IN PRACTICE

In theory, a regulatory commission may wish to equate price with marginal or average cost, but often the location of a firm's cost curves is unknown to the regulatory commission. How then does the commission set price? Two approaches are common: rate-of-return regulation and price-cap regulation.

Rate-of-Return Regulation

Rate-of-Return Regulation
A form of regulation limiting a firm to a prescribed rate of return on its capital (rate base).

Under **rate-of-return regulation**, the regulatory commission establishes (a) a **rate base** and (b) an allowable **rate of return**. The rate base measures the value of the firm's capital as determined by the regulatory commission. The rate of return is the percentage return the firm earns on its rate base. For example, a firm receiving $12 per year on each $100 of its rate base has a 12-percent rate of return.

The commission may not allow all of a company's capital to be included in its rate base. If the commission considers the cost of capital excessive, it may include

Rate Base
The value of a firm's capital, as determined by a regulatory commission.

Rate of Return
The annual return received on a firm's capital (or rate base), expressed as a percentage of the firm's capital.

only a fraction of the cost. If equipment is considered unnecessary, its cost may be excluded altogether. Once the commission establishes a rate base, it then calculates the price the firm must charge in order to earn the allowable rate of return. This is the price consumers pay. By adjusting the rate of return and therefore price, the commission determines how much profit the firm will be allowed to earn. Typically the commission seeks a "fair rate of return," designed to achieve normal profits.

The rate-of-return approach has been criticized for inflating costs. If the firm expects to earn normal profits, what incentive does it have to be efficient? If costs rise, the commission will increase price in order to maintain the allowable rate of return. Similarly, the firm has little incentive to introduce a new cost-saving technology. The commission will offset any reduction in costs by decreasing revenues.

Costs may be further inflated if the commission allows an excessive rate of return. If the rate of return includes an element of economic profit, then the firm has an incentive to acquire unnecessary capital. By increasing its rate base the firm can earn additional economic profits. As noted earlier, although the commission may not include all capital expenditures in the rate base, often a firm can rationalize unnecessary costs, especially if the commission has been *captured* by the firm. If regulated firms incur added costs, then the commission may be unable to effectively suppress the firm's price. This may explain why regulated utilities apparently charge as much for electricity as unregulated utilities.[16]

Price-Cap Regulation

Price-Cap Regulation
A form of regulation limiting the price a firm may charge (but not limiting allowable profits).

There is an alternative to rate-of-return regulation. Rather than adjust price to achieve a given rate of return, the commission could simply set a ceiling on the price a firm is allowed to charge. Such an approach—**price-cap regulation**—ends the firm's willingness to incur unnecessary costs. With a price cap, the more a firm reduces the costs of producing a given output the greater the firm's profits. The challenge of price-cap regulation is to choose an initial price cap and a formula for adjusting the cap over time. Exhibit 28-3 indicates the approach recently adopted by the FCC.

EXHIBIT 28-3

CAPPING THE PRICE OF LONG-DISTANCE TELEPHONE SERVICE

In 1989, the FCC voted to abandon rate-of-return regulation in favor of a price cap on long-distance telephone service. At the time, AT&T had an allowable rate of return of just over 12 percent on equipment used for interstate calls. Under the FCC ruling, prices of long-distance telephone calls are initially capped at their December 1988 levels but are allowed to rise thereafter by 3 percent less than the annual inflation rate. For example, if inflation is 5 percent in a particular year, AT&T can raise prices by 2 percent.

The FCC estimates that adoption of the price cap will save consumers $900 million in the first four years alone. AT&T, which supported the change, is also expected to benefit because of cost savings. As a spokesman for AT&T acknowledged, "We'll have the incentive to really try to be more efficient." Analysts expect major gains in efficiency and are predicting that profits at AT&T will increase as a result of the FCC ruling.

Sources: Adapted from Mary Lu Carnevale and Janet Guyon, "FCC Alters Long-Distance Regulation of AT&T," *The Wall Street Journal,* March 17, 1989, p. A3; Janet Guyon, "FCC Hopes New Regulations Will Cut Phone Rates," *The Wall Street Journal,* August 6, 1987, p. 23.

---

[16]Same as 10.

PUBLIC OWNERSHIP

Rather than regulate firms, sometimes governments own and operate a business themselves. Examples of public (government) ownership at the federal level include the Post Office, Tennessee Valley Authority, Amtrak, and the Government Printing Office. Locally, many governments provide water, trash collection, electricity, street repair, transportation, and a host of other services.

Through public ownership, the government can achieve the desired level of output and prevent private firms from inflating price. On the other hand, government ownership often leads to inefficiency. Because public firms are not in business to maximize profits, management has little incentive to minimize costs. Unlike the private sector, rewards to management are not based on its contribution to profits; political considerations may be more important than economics. For instance, where politicians determine the wages of public employees, they may be able to win the votes of public employees by paying high wages and preserving unnecessary jobs. Consistent with this view, a large body of evidence indicates that, on average, federal employees earn more than comparable employees in the private sector.[17]

Privatization
Transferring production of a good from the public sector to the private sector.

The Office of Management and Budget (OMB) estimates that the federal government could save more than $1 billion annually by contracting out services such as data processing. According to the Government Accounting Office (GAO), federally operated hydroelectric power plants cost 20 percent more to operate than comparable plants in the private sector.[18] Similarly, public trash collection is more costly than collection by private firms (see Exhibit 28-4). Such findings have sparked interest in **privatization**—turning selected government functions over to private firms. Where the result is lower costs, governments can ease budgetary pressures. In summary, even though regulation of private firms entails various difficulties, public ownership often fails to provide a superior alternative.

SUMMARY

1. Government regulates business by imposing various rules on producers. *Economic regulation* refers to rules imposed on a specific industry—designed, for example, to limit entry into the industry, set price, and mandate various services. By contrast, *social regulation* cuts across industries. Its goal is to achieve certain results throughout the economy—a cleaner environment, safer products, and a workplace free of hazards.

2. Regulation has tended to expand since the creation of the Interstate Commerce Commission more than 100 years ago. At first the growth consisted of additional economic regulation, but more recently the emphasis has shifted to social regulation. Among the new agencies charged with social regulation are the Consumer Product Safety Commission, the Occupational Safety and Health Administration, and the Environmental Protection Agency. The growth of regulatory budgets slowed in the 1980s and the number of federal regulators declined. This was due both to economic deregulation and to the slowdown in social regulation accompanying the Reagan presidency.

3. There are two competing explanations for regulation. According to the public interest theory of regulation, government intervention is a response to market failure and therefore

---

[17]See Sharon P. Smith, *Equal Pay in Public Sector: Fact or Fantasy* (Princeton: Princeton University Press, 1977); Alan B. Krueger, "Are Public Sector Workers Paid More Than Their Alternative Wage?" in Richard Freeman and Casey Ichniowski, eds., *Public Sector Unionism* (Chicago: University of Chicago Press, 1987).

[18]*Economic Report of the President, 1986,* p. 185.

EXHIBIT 28–4

A BETTER WAY TO COLLECT SOLID WASTE

Solid waste can be collected either directly by the government (e.g., through a city sanitation department) or by private refuse companies. In Canada the two approaches are equally common; in the United States the majority of municipalities rely on private firms. The presence of both arrangements in the same industry has provided economists an opportunity to assess the impact of public ownership. At least in this industry, public ownership is the inferior option.

A study of 132 Canadian municipalities found that, other things equal, the cost of collecting solid waste was 28-percent lower for private firms. A second study examined the consequences of privatization in Canada—replacing public trash collection with private trash collection in the same municipality. Both West Vancouver and Richmond converted from public collection of solid waste to private collection. The private firms served the same households and even used the same vehicles (purchased directly from the cities). The private firms improved service by removing restrictions on the number of cans allowed each household, yet still managed to reduce collection costs. Costs fell by 19 percent in West Vancouver and by 66 percent in Richmond.

Economists have reached similar conclusions in the United States. Public waste collection suffers from inferior management and lower labor productivity. One study of 1377 U.S. communities concluded:

> Compared to private firms with contracts in cities of over 50,000, municipal [public] refuse-collection agencies in such cities have higher employee absentee rates (12 percent vs. 6.5 percent); employ larger crews (3.26 men vs. 2.15); serve fewer households per shift (632 vs. 686); spend more time servicing each household (4.35 man-hours per year vs. 2.37); and are less likely to utilize labor-incentive systems (80 percent vs. 89 percent).[19]

When it comes to collecting solid waste, private firms are more efficient than public agencies.

[19]E. S. Savas (see Source below), p. 71.

Sources: Adapted from Glen Tickner and James C. McDavid, "Effects of Scale and Market Structure on the Costs of Residential Solid Waste Collection in Canadian Cities," *Public Finance Quarterly* (October 1986), pp. 371–393; J. C. McDavid, "The Canadian Experience with Privatizing Residential Solid Waste Collection Services," *Public Administration Review* (September 1985), pp. 602–608; E. S. Savas, "Policy Analysis for Local Government: Public Versus Private Refuse Collection," *Policy Analysis* (Winter 1977), pp. 49–74.

designed to benefit society. Reasons for market failure include natural monopoly, externalities, and imperfect information.

4. In contrast, the special interest theory of regulation holds that regulation is designed to protect special interest groups at the expense of the general public. For instance, regulation may shield existing producers from competition by restricting entry of new firms into an industry and by propping up price. Regulation may also benefit unions, certain consumer groups, and even the regulators themselves.

5. Regulation has achieved various benefits, from a cleaner environment to safer products. It has also imposed various costs on society. Resources must be transferred from production to administer regulations and to comply with them. Costs rise further when regulations prevent efficient allocation of resources—for example, when the ICC induced shippers to use high-cost modes of transportation. Regulations have also affected price, service, profits, labor productivity, and wages. To accurately assess regulations, one must compare their benefits with their costs.

6. Government commissions frequently regulate utilities and other natural monopolies. The objective is to minimize costs of production and to keep price low for consumers. Unless a regulated monopolist receives other funds (e.g., access fees or a government subsidy), it must be allowed to charge a price that covers average cost—otherwise it will not produce in the long run.

7. Under rate-of-return regulation, the commission sets a price that enables the company to earn an allowable rate of return on its rate base. Generally, the allowable rate of return is chosen with the intention of achieving normal profits. A drawback of rate-of-return regulation is that if the firm expects to receive normal profits, regardless of its production costs, it loses its incentive to minimize costs.

8. With price-cap regulation firms maintain their incentive to minimize costs, since lower costs mean higher profits. The difficulty here is choosing the initial price cap and setting a formula that will adjust it in the future.

9. Public ownership is an alternative to regulation of private firms. By directly producing a good, the government can determine price and output levels. A drawback to this approach is that government production is generally more costly than production by private firms.

KEY TERMS

economic regulation
social regulation
deregulation
public interest theory of
    regulation
special interest theory of
    regulation
capture hypothesis

marginal cost pricing
average cost pricing
rate-of-return regulation
rate base
rate of return
price-cap regulation
privatization

STUDY QUESTIONS AND PROBLEMS

1. What is the difference between economic regulation and social regulation? Provide an example of each.

2. Do you consider deregulation of the airline industry to be a success? Why or why not?

3. Under what circumstances does regulation benefit society?

4. Are there any industries where you think regulation is either excessive or inadequate? Support your view.

5. In 1987, the National Transportation Safety Board considered new regulations for the fishing industry. These included formal training for both captains and crews, new safety requirements for vessels, and periodic inspection of vessels.
   a. Cite at least one benefit of such proposals.
   b. Many in the fishing industry opposed added safety requirements. What could account for their opposition?

6. New drugs can be sold in the United States only if they win the approval of the Food and Drug Administration. To be approved, the drugs must be tested and found to be safe and effective. Noting that drugs are often available for sale in other countries prior to FDA approval, some have advocated a more lenient FDA policy. What is the major benefit of maintaining tough standards, based on extensive testing and compelling evidence that a drug is safe and effective? What is a drawback of such a policy?

7. Some economists argue that certain public utility commissions have set rates of return so low that their utilities are unable to earn a normal profit. What effect would such a practice have on the price of utility services in the short run? How would this affect the ability of utilities to meet consumer needs in the long run? Explain your reasoning.

8. What is the objective of marginal cost pricing? Why might a regulatory commission decide not to equate price with marginal cost?

9. Explain why rate-of-return regulation may promote inefficient production. Does price-cap regulation suffer from the same drawback? Explain.

10. First-class mail is delivered by a publicly owned monopoly—the U.S. Post Office. How might costs change if mail delivery were turned over to the private sector? Why?

SELECTED REFERENCES

Martha Derthick and Paul J. Quirk, *The Politics of Deregulation* (Washington, DC: The Brookings Institution, 1985).

George C. Eads and Michael Fix, *Relief or Reform* (Washington, DC: The Urban Institute Press, 1984).

Economic Report of the President, 1986 (Washington, DC: Government Printing Office, 1986).

Alfred Kahn, "I Would Do It Again," *Regulation* (No. 2, 1988), pp. 22–28.

James V. Koch, *Industrial Organization and Prices,* 2nd ed. (Englewood Cliffs, NJ: Prentice-Hall, 1980).

Kenneth J. Meier, *Regulation* (New York: St. Martin's Press, 1985).

Steven Morrison and Clifford Winston, *The Economic Effects of Airline Deregulation* (Washington, DC: The Brookings Institution, 1986).

F. M. Scherer, *Industrial Market Structure and Economic Performance,* 2nd ed. (Chicago: Rand-McNally College Publishing Co., 1980).

Robert S. Smith, "Compensating Wage Differentials and Public Policy," *Industrial & Labor Relations Review* (April 1979), pp. 340–41.

George Stigler, "The Theory of Economic Regulation," *Bell Journal of Economics and Management Science* (Spring 1971), pp. 3–21.

Murray L. Weidenbaum, *Business, Government, and the Public,* 3rd ed. (Englewood Cliffs, NJ: Prentice-Hall, 1986).

PART VIII

THE
DISTRIBUTION
OF
INCOME

CHAPTER 29

THE LABOR MARKET—WHY ARE MY WAGES SO LOW (HIGH)?

Human labor is not an *end* but a means.

—FRÉDÉRIC BASTIAT (1801–1850), *Sophismes Économiques*

In a recent year, airline pilots pulled down $91,000 from the friendly skies of United, plus an additional $34,000 in fringe benefits. Major league baseball players averaged $513,000 per year; top executives earned in excess of $1 million. In contrast, many college students toil for the minimum wage. Even for broadly defined occupations, major wage differences emerge. Managerial and professional workers earn almost four times as much as private household workers (see Table 29-1). How are wages determined? What accounts for the extreme variance in earnings?

Although these questions may be of interest in their own right, there are other reasons for studying the labor market. Labor is the most important factor of production and the primary source of income. Wages and salaries account for approximately three-fourths of national income in the United States. Without an appreciation of the labor market, one cannot fully understand the economy.

Labor markets differ from other factor markets in terms of the personal relationships involved. Another unique feature is the trade union. How do unions affect wages? What else do unions do? Do they benefit the country or impoverish it? These are some of the questions addressed in Chapter 29. After a discussion of wage determination in competitive labor markets, we consider reasons for wage differences across workers and then turn to the economic impacts of unions.

Chapters 30 and 31 extend our analysis of labor markets. In Chapter 30 we modify the competitive model of this chapter to consider the case of a company large enough to influence price, in either the product market or the labor market. We also address the situation in which a firm hires multiple inputs (e.g., both skilled and unskilled labor). In Chapter 31 we examine the labor market success of different groups (e.g., men versus women, blacks versus whites) and consider reasons for these differences.

TABLE 29-1

MEDIAN EARNINGS OF FULL-TIME WAGE AND SALARY WORKERS BY OCCUPATION, 1988

Occupation	Number of workers (in thousands)	Weekly earnings
Managerial and professional	21,770	$552
Technical, sales, and administrative support	24,931	347
Technicians	2,960	448
Administrative support (including clerical)	14,230	318
Service occupations	8,669	245
Private household	328	140
Protective service	1,747	417
Precision production, craft, and repair	11,175	430
Mechanics and repairers	3,850	439
Operators, fabricators, and laborers	14,763	313
Transportation and material movers	3,853	389
Handlers, equipment cleaners, helpers, and laborers	3,505	277
Farming, forestry, and fishing	1,383	229

Source: U.S. Bureau of Labor Statistics, *Employment and Earnings,* January 1989, p. 221.

THE MODEL OF PERFECT COMPETITION

According to the model of perfect competition, each firm buys too little labor to influence the price of labor (the wage rate). Nor can workers dictate how much they are paid. Instead, the price of labor is taken as given by individual firms and workers. The product market is likewise assumed to be competitive, which means the firm is a price taker there as well as in the labor market. Assuming the firm wishes to maximize profits, how much labor does it employ?

THE DEMAND FOR LABOR

The Firm's Demand for Labor

Suppose you operate a small clothing company while in school, perhaps employing needy students and professors. How many workers should you hire? To answer this question, you first need to know how much workers contribute to output—in this case, how many sweatshirts they produce. Such information is contained in the production function depicted in columns (i) and (ii) of Table 29-2. Based on this information, the first worker hired would produce 15 sweatshirts per day, the second 12 sweatshirts, and so forth. The additional output from hiring another unit of labor, which we previously defined as the *marginal product of labor,* is depicted in column (iii). Consistent with the law of diminishing returns, marginal product falls as additional labor is employed.[1]

Marginal Revenue Product of Labor
The increase in total revenue to a firm resulting from the hiring of an additional unit of labor.

To convert labor's contribution from physical output (sweatshirts) to dollars, we calculate the **marginal revenue product of labor**—the increase in revenue received by a firm as the result of hiring an additional unit of labor. When a firm sells its output in a competitive product market, marginal revenue product is simply equal to the marginal product of labor times output price.

Returning to our example, suppose each sweatshirt sells for $10. Then the first unit of labor contributes $150 per day to revenue, $10 for each of the 15 sweatshirts it produces. Accordingly, its marginal revenue product is $150. In turn, marginal revenue product of the second worker is $10 × 12 = $120. These and other values of marginal revenue product appear in column (iv) of Table 29-2.

Now that you know how much each additional unit of labor would generate in revenue, how many units should you hire? That depends on the price of labor. Assume you must pay each worker a wage of $80 per day. Then, to maximize profits

TABLE 29-2

DERIVING YOUR FIRM'S DEMAND FOR LABOR

(i) Units of labor (workers)	(ii) Total output per day (sweatshirts)	(iii) Marginal product of labor	(iv) Marginal revenue product
0	0	—	—
1	15	15	$150
2	27	12	120
3	36	9	90
4	43	7	70
5	48	5	50
6	51	3	30

Columns (i) and (ii) show the quantity of output that can be produced with various amounts of labor. Based on this information, the marginal product of labor, column (iii), can be computed. Marginal revenue product, column (iv), indicates how much additional revenue your company would receive from the hiring of an additional unit of labor. Given an output price of $10, marginal revenue product is equal to $10 times the marginal product of labor.

[1]The law of diminishing returns does not rule out the possibility that marginal product may initially increase before declining, but we can safely ignore the range of increasing marginal product. If it is profitable to hire a given amount of labor, and the marginal product of an additional unit of labor is still higher, then it is even more profitable to hire that additional labor. In other words, a profit-maximizing firm would not stop hiring in the range where marginal product of labor is rising. We lose nothing essential, and gain simplicity, by assuming marginal product of labor declines from the outset.

you should hire three workers. Each of the first three workers adds more to revenue than to costs, thereby bolstering profits. The same cannot be said for additional labor. Beyond the third worker additional labor would cost more than it contributed to revenue, which would eat into profits. This leads to the following hiring rule:

Hire additional labor as long as MRP > wage; do not hire when MRP < wage.

At a wage of $80, the third worker should be hired (MRP = $90 > wage) but not the fourth worker (MRP = $70 < wage).

What if you faced a wage of $50 per day? How many workers should you employ? Not only do the first three workers contribute to profits, but now so does the fourth (MRP = $70 > wage). Therefore, the fourth worker should also be hired. What about the fifth? Hiring the fifth worker would neither contribute to profits nor detract from them. The fifth worker would add the same amount to revenue as to costs—$50. For that reason, profits can be maximized by employing either four units of labor or five. The MRP numbers from Table 29-2 are duplicated in Figure 29-1(a).

Until now we have implicitly assumed that labor must be hired in whole units, but that is not always the case. Sometimes companies can hire fractional units of labor—for example, hire a worker for one-third or one-half of a day. When labor is perfectly divisible, MRP can be represented as a continuous line, as in Figure 29-1(b). Profits are maximized when the amount of labor hired is given by the

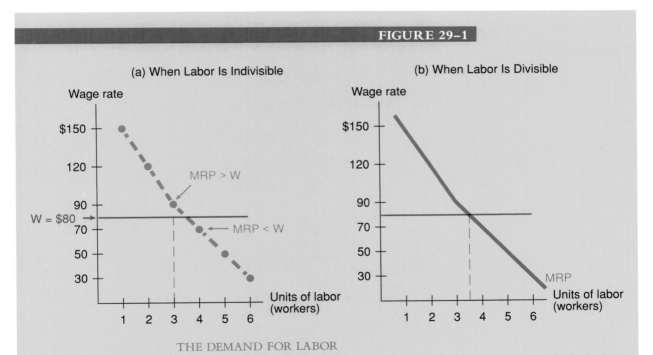

FIGURE 29-1

THE DEMAND FOR LABOR

When labor must be hired in whole (indivisible) units (a), a company should employ the largest amount of labor for which MRP > W. Given a wage rate of $80 per day, 3 units of labor should be hired (b). When labor is divisible (b), a company should employ the amount of labor for which MRP = W. The MRP curve in (b) is constructed to intersect the points in (a). Given this curve and a wage of $80 per day, 3 1/2 units of labor will maximize profits.

intersection of the MRP curve and the wage. Given a wage of $80 and divisible labor, you should hire 3 1/2 units.

The labor demand curve of a firm is based on the MRP of labor. For a given wage, the MRP curve indicates the amount of labor a company should employ in order to maximize profits. But what determines the wage that must be paid? To learn this, we must go beyond your (hopefully lucrative) enterprise and consider the market demand for labor and the market supply of labor.

The Market Demand for Labor

Market Demand for Labor
The relationship between the wage rate and the total amount of labor demanded by all firms in the labor market (other things equal).

Derived Demand
The demand for a resource; determined by (derived from) the demand for the product it produces.

Competitive labor markets are characterized by multiple buyers of labor. The **market demand for labor** is obtained by summing the labor demand (or MRP) curves of the individual firms in the market. The market demand curve indicates, for each wage, how much labor is demanded by all firms in a particular labor market. Because labor demand curves of individual firms are inversely related to wages, the market demand curve for labor must also slope downward.

Demand for labor is a **derived demand**—that is, it depends on the demand for the product it produces. Labor is employed not as an end, but as a means to produce something else. If demand for new housing increases, demand for construction workers likewise increases. If tax simplification reduces households' demand for tax assistance, demand for tax accountants falls.

YOUR TURN

The Bond Paper Company sells its paper for $20 per box. It has no influence over either the price of paper or the wage it must pay its workers. The following table shows the relationship between labor and output.

Employees	Boxes of paper per day
0	0
1	20
2	35
3	45
4	53
5	60
6	65

(a) What is the MRP of the second worker?
(b) How many employees should be hired if the wage is $225 per day? (Assume workers must be paid for a full day.)
(c) How many employees should be hired if the wage is $165 per day?
(d) Now suppose that due to increased demand for paper the price of paper rises to $30 per box. (i) How does this affect the firm's labor demand curve? Why? (ii) Facing a wage of $165 per day, how many workers should the company employ?

THE SUPPLY OF LABOR

Labor Supply of an Individual

Consider the wage you were paid on your most recent job (or your current job). If that wage were increased, would you want to work more hours or less? Your

Substitution Effect (for labor)
The change in the amount of labor supplied that can be attributed to a change in the opportunity cost of leisure. By increasing the opportunity cost of leisure, a higher wage rate induces an individual to substitute work for leisure.

Income Effect (for labor)
The change in the amount of labor supplied that can be attributed to a change in income. A higher income increases the demand for leisure, reducing the hours of work.

response may differ from that of your classmates. The reason is that an increase in the wage rate has offsetting effects: the **substitution effect** and the **income effect**. Whether you choose to increase or decrease hours of work depends on which of these two effects is stronger. At a higher wage the reward for working increases. Put another way, you now sacrifice more for each hour you do not work. As the opportunity cost of not working (leisure) rises, you have an incentive to substitute work for leisure—to spend more time working and less time in leisure.

Although a higher wage encourages additional hours of labor via the substitution effect, the income effect works in the opposite direction. A given amount of work generates more income at a high wage than at a low wage. With the additional income, a consumer can afford more leisure. Assuming that leisure is a normal good, the increase in income (stemming from the higher wage) increases the demand for leisure. To obtain additional leisure, the consumer reduces hours of work.

If the substitution effect dominates, the labor supply curve has the traditional upward slope of most supply curves [Figure 29-2(a)]. If the income effect dominates, labor supply has a negative slope [Figure 29-2(b)], indicating that a higher wage rate *reduces* the amount of labor supplied. Finally, it is possible for an individual's labor supply curve to be *backward bending* [Figure 29-2(c)]. In that event the individual responds differently to a wage change, depending on the level of the wage. Initially an increase in the wage rate brings forth additional labor, but beyond some point [W_0 in Figure 29-2(c)] a higher wage rate results in less labor being supplied. This occurs once the income effect outweighs the substitution effect.

Empirical studies have been performed separately for males and for females. They suggest that, overall, the substitution effect is stronger for females—higher

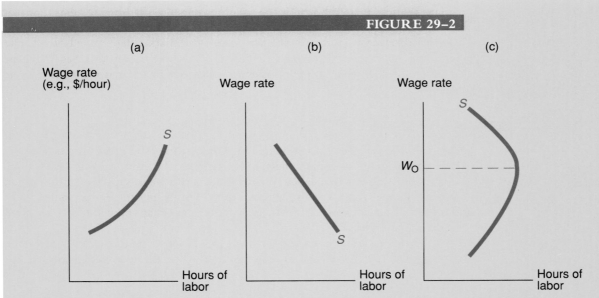

FIGURE 29–2

POTENTIAL LABOR SUPPLY CURVES FOR AN INDIVIDUAL

In (a) the substitution effect outweighs the income effect—a higher wage increases the amount of labor supplied. In (b) the income effect is stronger—a higher wage decreases the amount of labor supplied. In (c) the substitution effect dominates for wages below W_0, and the income effect dominates for all higher wages. The result is a backward-bending labor supply curve.

wages induce women to work additional hours. The evidence is less clear for men. Although males appear less responsive to wages, studies suggest that for many groups of males the income effect dominates.

The Market Supply of Labor

Market Supply of Labor
The relationship between the wage rate and the total amount of labor supplied to the market (other things equal).

Although the labor supply curve for individuals can take different shapes, the **market supply of labor** is upward sloping. A higher wage in a labor market brings forth additional labor for two reasons. First, a higher wage rate can be expected to attract individuals who were not previously working. Now that the reward for work has increased, some people formerly out of the labor force will decide to enter this labor market. Second, some people working in other labor markets (e.g., different occupations or industries) will want to switch to this labor market in response to the higher wage. In fact, empirical research indicates that workers are very responsive to wage differences across markets.[2]

WAGE DETERMINATION

Wage rates are determined in competitive markets by the interaction of labor supply and demand. In Figure 29-3(a) the equilibrium wage rate is $80 per day. At higher wages the quantity of labor supplied would exceed the quantity demanded, driving down wage rates. At lower wages labor shortages would develop, causing firms to bid up wage rates.

Although labor supply is upward sloping for the market, this is not the case for individual firms in the market. Remember that the theory of competitive labor markets assumes that each firm is too small to influence the price of labor. For that reason labor supply to a firm can be represented as a horizontal line [Figure 29-3(b)]. The interpretation is that each firm pays the market-determined wage rate ($80/day), regardless of the quantity of labor it employs. Given this wage rate, the firm then hires labor up to the point where the wage rate equals marginal revenue product.

WAGE DIFFERENTIALS

The theory of wage determination in competitive markets provides insight into why some workers earn more than others. Labor supply and demand vary across markets. Workers in markets where labor demand is high relative to supply earn more than workers facing less favorable market conditions. This helps explain why some groups of workers (e.g., aerospace engineers) earn more than others (e.g., fast-food workers). See Figure 29-4.

Why don't fast-food workers get jobs as aerospace engineers? Lacking the necessary skills, they do not directly compete with the engineers. They are in

---

[2]This responsiveness can be illustrated in terms of college decisions. Statistical analysis by Richard Freeman reveals that college enrollments can largely be explained by labor market conditions for college graduates:

> Over 95% of the variation in the fraction of young men in college over the 1951–74 period can be attributed to two simple measures of the economic incentive to enroll: the income of graduates relative to other workers and relative employment opportunities.

Freeman also finds students' choice of majors to be highly responsive to relative wages of occupations. See R. Freeman, *The Overeducated American* (New York: Academic Press, 1976), p. 53.

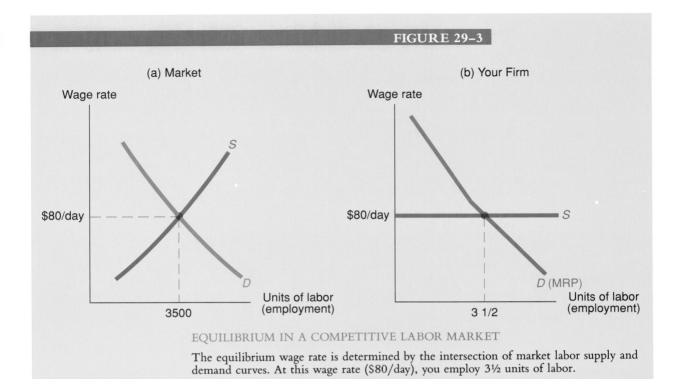

FIGURE 29-3

(a) Market

(b) Your Firm

EQUILIBRIUM IN A COMPETITIVE LABOR MARKET

The equilibrium wage rate is determined by the intersection of market labor supply and demand curves. At this wage rate ($80/day), you employ 3½ units of labor.

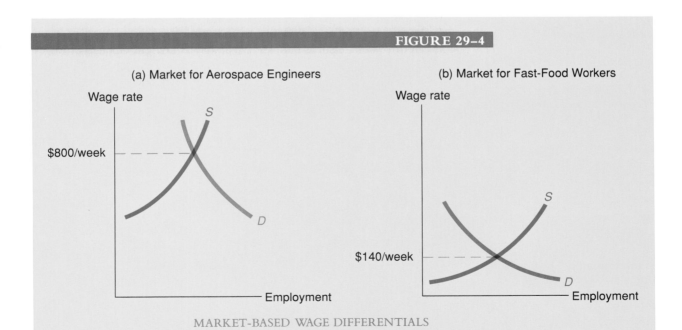

FIGURE 29-4

(a) Market for Aerospace Engineers

(b) Market for Fast-Food Workers

MARKET-BASED WAGE DIFFERENTIALS

A relatively strong demand for and low supply of aerospace engineers leads to a high rate of pay; the opposite is true for fast-food workers.

EXHIBIT 29–1

THE MARKET FOR PROFESSIONAL BASEBALL PLAYERS

Increased competition for major-league baseball players has led to a dramatic increase in average salaries, from about $45,000 in 1976 to $513,000 in 1989. The source of the competition? *Free agency.* Until 1977, professional baseball players were covered by the *reserve clause,* which gave the ball club exclusive rights to the player's services for as long as he stayed in baseball. A player either accepted the club's offer or found another line of work. In addition, the team owner could sell a player's contract, whether or not the player approved. This arrangement enabled the owner to suppress the player's salary.[4] Statistical analysis suggests that, under the reserve clause, salaries were no more than 20 percent of a player's contribution to team revenues.[5]

Beginning in 1977, ball players with at least six years of major league experience were allowed to become free agents after their contracts expired. As a free agent a player can sell his services to the highest bidder. Competition for the top athletes has made many players millionaires. In 1989, the Los Angeles Dodgers signed Orel Hershiser to a three-year contract for $7.9 million. Apparently the owner of the Dodgers was convinced the talented pitcher would contribute at least $7.9 million to team revenues over the three years.

[4]Formally, the owner has *monopsony* power. This model is developed in Chapter 30.
[5]Gerald Sculley, "Pay and Performance in Major League Baseball," *American Economic Review* (December 1974), pp. 915–930.

---

different labor markets. One should not conclude, however, that labor markets are completely independent. If the wage earned by aerospace engineers rises relative to wages in other occupations, one would predict that more people will enter this line of work—that is, acquire the skills necessary to become aerospace engineers.

One reason then for wage inequality is skill differences. Some differences are innate, others acquired. Differences in innate ability can lead to **economic rents**. Few people can throw a baseball as hard and accurately as Dwight Gooden or Roger Clemens. Few entertainers can generate the excitement of Michael Jackson and Madonna or Luciano Pavarotti. Those with scarce natural talents can command wages well in excess of what they could earn in other lines of work. Top baseball players contribute more than $1 million per year to their team in terms of added ticket sales, broadcast revenues, and concessions.[3] Although club owners yearn for the days of cheap talent, competition among owners for the services of star athletes has driven up salaries so that they are now more commensurate with players' values (MRP) than was formerly the case (see Exhibit 29-1).

Economic Rent of a Worker
The return to a scarce natural talent; the difference between the wage received (because of that talent) and the wage available in the best alternative line of work.

HUMAN CAPITAL

Those of us not blessed with extraordinary talents can enhance our earnings by investing in ourselves, incurring present costs in the expectation of higher wages in the future. Examples of self-investment or **human capital** are schooling and training. Economic studies clearly show that workers with more human capital tend to earn higher wages than those with less human capital. Less clear are the reasons for this difference.

Human Capital
The knowledge and skills acquired by workers, principally through education and training.

---

[3]See Charles Link, "The Economic Value of Major League Baseball Players," Working Paper, University of Delaware, 1989. Some of yesterday's stars were even more productive. Link estimates that if they were playing today, Babe Ruth and Sandy Koufax could each add more than *$5 million* to team revenues.

EXHIBIT 29-2

A MULTIMILLIONAIRE'S CLUB?

According to a recent survey of large corporations, chief executive officers (CEOs) were paid an average of $2.0 million in 1988, including salary, bonuses, and long-term compensation. Michael Eisner, chairman of Walt Disney Company, topped the list, earning $40.1 million. Although special one-time considerations inflated Eisner's salary in 1988, he has averaged close to $12 million per year in compensation since coming to Disney in 1984. Is any executive really worth that kind of money, or is this simply a situation of management rewarding itself to the detriment of stockholders?

Roy Disney, a major shareholder in the Walt Disney Company, argues that executives such as Eisner are "worth every penny of what we're paying them. . . . I would hate to think where we would be without them." The editors of *Business Week* are similarly impressed:

> [Eisner] may be the sharpest executive in Hollywood. He's turned Disney around in four years. With hits such as *Good Morning Vietnam* and *Roger Rabbit,* [the] studio may hit 20% [market] share in 1988, up from 3% in 1985. Expanding everywhere—parks, tourist attractions, broadcast.

Because of such success, the value of Disney stock has increased five-fold under Eisner's stewardship.

Analysts estimate that the most talented CEOs contribute millions of dollars to their companies, millions more than would be earned had their companies hired managers with only average skills. As in the case of baseball, the superstars in the field tend to pull their own weight. Companies could hire less talented personnel, but the lower labor costs would be offset by lower revenues.

Still, $12 million is a lot to pay an executive. Why couldn't Disney cut Eisner's pay from $12 million to $1 million, which is still a hefty sum? If it did that, the company would undoubtedly end up searching for a new CEO. Eisner has proven himself to be one of the best managers around. Other companies are interested in his talents and would be willing to compensate adequately for them, even if Disney were not. Actual or potential competition for Eisner forces Disney to pay him his lofty salary.

Admittedly, a manager's contributions cannot be measured perfectly. Sometimes companies make mistakes, paying executives more than they are worth. But managers who do not *earn* their high salaries are not likely to keep drawing these salaries.

Sources: Adapted from John Byrne, "Is the Boss Getting Paid Too Much?" *Business Week,* May 1, 1989, pp. 46–52; "Who Made the Most and Why," *Business Week,* May 2, 1988, pp. 50–56; *Business Week,* "The Corporate Elite," October 21, 1988, p. 147.

Human capital theory argues that these investments directly contribute to earnings by increasing a worker's skills. Workers with greater skills are worth more to a company (have a higher MRP) and consequently command higher wages. Critics of human capital theory offer alternative explanations for the positive association between education and earnings.

The **screening (credentialism) hypothesis** asserts that education opens doors for those receiving it but does not increase their productivity. Even if this were true, it would not follow that education has no value. Individuals differ in terms of characteristics that appear to be correlated with education—ability, motivation, capacity to learn, and so forth. Even if education did not increase a worker's

Screening Hypothesis
The claim that employers make hiring decisions on the basis of a person's education but that education does not make a worker more productive.

productivity, it could signal to employers that certain workers, by virtue of their higher education, are likely to have high ability and motivation. Thus, education could help sort employees, matching highly productive employees with companies that value high productivity the most. Such sorting would benefit society through a more efficient allocation of labor, as well as benefitting the individual through higher wages. Needless to say, the social benefits from education are higher if education does more than sort individuals. Human capital theorists claim that it does; supporters of the screening hypothesis are more skeptical.

Is education a good investment for an individual? As Figure 29-5 illustrates, at each age earnings tend to be higher the more education a person has. By age 47 college graduates on average are earning almost twice as much as those who have not

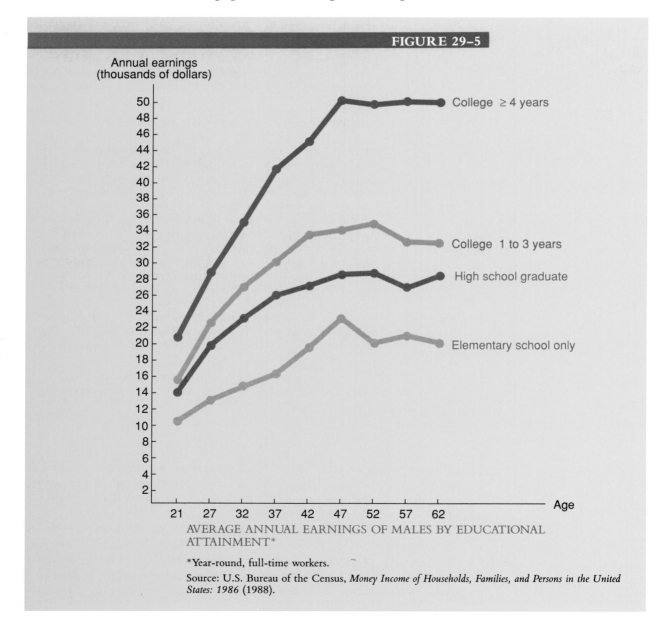

FIGURE 29–5

AVERAGE ANNUAL EARNINGS OF MALES BY EDUCATIONAL ATTAINMENT*

*Year-round, full-time workers.

Source: U.S. Bureau of the Census, *Money Income of Households, Families, and Persons in the United States: 1986* (1988).

attended college. But weighing against these higher earnings are the costs of education. Tuition alone typically runs several thousand dollars per year at public universities and exceeds $20,000 per year at some private colleges. In addition to direct costs—including tuition, fees, and books—education also entails the opportunity cost of forgone earnings. Suppose you earn $5000 this year, working either part-time during the school year or in the summer. Had you not committed yourself to college, you probably could have earned a higher salary, perhaps $15,000. In that event you are implicitly sacrificing $10,000 this year to attend college—the difference between the $15,000 you could have earned and the $5000 you did earn. This too is a cost of education.

There are other reasons for attending college besides higher earnings, but these nonfinancial considerations are difficult to measure. Therefore, we focus here on the financial benefits. Are the increased earnings you can expect to receive with a college degree sufficiently high to compensate you for the costs of your education? Although no guarantees are given, the available evidence indicates that for most individuals the expected returns from investing in college are high, at least as high as the returns from investing in stocks and other financial instruments. Education appears to be a good investment.

COMPENSATING WAGE DIFFERENTIALS

Compensating Wage Differential
The wage premium a worker receives for a job with undesirable characteristics, to compensate for those characteristics.

Differences in skills and education are not the only reasons for wage differentials; nonwage characteristics of the job can also be important. Jobs differ in various dimensions: safety, working conditions, job security, and the like. According to the **theory of compensating wage differentials,** a person requires extra compensation—a wage premium—to accept a job with unpleasant characteristics. In other words, jobs with undesirable features require higher wages to attract workers of a given skill level than do jobs with desirable features.

Empirical research provides some support for this theory. Industries with low job security (high layoff rates) pay more than industries offering greater security.[6] In addition, occupations with a high risk of death pay higher wages than *safe* occupations.[7] An example of a job with a compensating wage differential is provided by *The Wall Street Journal* (October 10, 1983):

> Each day when Tom Geer goes to work, it's with the satisfying thought that he will labor for only 10 minutes and be paid for 12 hours. . . . The catch—and of course there has to be one—is the job site. Mr. Geer does his work deep inside a nuclear power plant [where radiation increases his risk of cancer].

MARKET IMPERFECTIONS AND DISCRIMINATION

Although wage differentials would arise even in perfectly competitive markets, market imperfections also contribute to wage disparity across individuals. If certain

---

[6]See James Ragan and Sharon Smith, "The Impact of Differences in Turnover Rates on Male/Female Pay Differentials," *Journal of Human Resources* (Summer 1981), pp. 343–365.

[7]See Robert Smith, "Compensating Wage Differentials and Public Policy: A Review," *Industrial and Labor Relations Review* (April 1979), pp. 339–352; Stuart Dorsey, "Employment Hazards and Fringe Benefits: Further Tests for Compensating Differentials," in John Worrall, ed., *Safety and the Work Force* (Ithaca, NY: ILR Press, 1983). Empirically, the death rate is defined as work fatalities per 10,000 workers. Studies indicate that each additional death per 10,000 employees raises annual pay between $20 and $300 per worker. For a company with 10,000 employees this translates into an additional $200,000 to $3 million in wage costs.

EXHIBIT 29–3

MINIMUM WAGE LEGISLATION

The Fair Labor Standards Act of 1938 established a minimum wage of $.25/hour. This law has been amended numerous times, and in late 1989 the federal minimum wage stood at $3.35 per hour. The effects of a minimum wage depend on its level. If set below the market-determined wage, a minimum wage does not adversely affect employment (see Figure 29-6a). But if set above the competitive wage, employment falls (as illustrated in Figure 29-6b).

Because young workers are among the least skilled and experienced, one might predict that they would bear the brunt of any employment loss. Empirical research bears this out. After reviewing more than a dozen studies, a widely cited article concludes that each ten-percent increase in the minimum wage reduced teenage employment by between one and three percent.[8]

Workers losing their jobs obviously experience a reduction in income. On the other hand, low-productivity workers still employed after the minimum wage hike see their hourly wages raised from W_1 to MIN. Whether their wage *income* (wage per hour times hours worked) rises or falls depends on how hours worked are affected. One study finds

evidence that employers respond to a higher minimum wage by forcing teenagers out of full-time jobs and into part-time employment.[9] In some cases the result is lower income despite a higher hourly wage rate.

Even where income is raised, workers are not necessarily better off. Employers may respond to higher minimum wages by cutting other costs—for example, by reducing fringe benefits or providing less training. In the latter case, higher wages today may come at the expense of future wages. Because wages rise with human capital, any reduction in the acquisition of training can be expected to lead to slower wage growth in the future.[10]

[8]Charles Brown, Curtis Gilroy, and Andrew Kohen, "The Effect of the Minimum Wage on Employment and Unemployment," *Journal of Economic Literature* (June 1982), p. 508.
[9]Edward Gramlich, "Impact of Minimum Wages on Other Wages, Employment, and Family Incomes," *Brookings Papers on Economic Activity* (1976, 2), pp. 442–43.
[10]Support for this hypothesis is provided by Masanori Hashimoto, "Minimum Wage Effects on Training on the Job," *American Economic Review* (December 1982), pp. 1070–1087, and Linda Leighton and Jacob Mincer, "Effects of Minimum Wages on Human Capital Formation," in Simon Rottenberg, ed., *The Economics of Legal Minimum Wages* (Washington, DC: American Enterprise Institute, 1981), pp. 155–173.

FIGURE 29–6

(a) Market for Skilled Labor

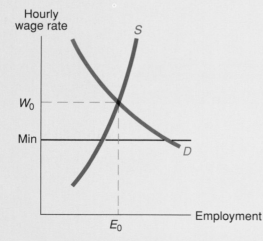

(b) Market for Unskilled Labor

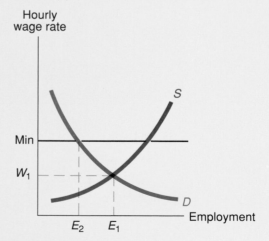

THE EFFECT OF A MINIMUM WAGE

Because the minimum wage is set below W_0, employment of skilled labor is unaffected (a). In contrast, the employment of unskilled workers falls (b). Because companies are forced to raise the hourly wage from W_1 to MIN, they reduce employment of unskilled labor from E_1 to E_2.

groups (e.g., women or minorities) are barred from high-paying jobs, they will tend to earn lower wages. Other forms of discrimination may also affect wages, as we will see in Chapter 31. To the extent unions contribute to higher wages, those denied access to unions earn less than their union counterparts. Relative wages are also influenced by legislation (e.g., minimum wage laws). See Exhibit 29-3.

LABOR UNIONS

> 4% of nothing is nothing. . . . We want 12%.
>
> —anonymous placard of union worker on strike

Union

An organization of workers that negotiates on a collective basis (as one body) in order to increase the bargaining power of the workers.

The model of perfect competition in labor markets is not applicable when either buyers or sellers of labor control the price of labor. Monopoly power on the part of companies (monopsony) is discussed in Chapter 30. The balance of this chapter considers the opposite situation, where sellers of labor form a monopoly—a **union**.

In 1988, 17 million U.S. workers—16 percent of all employees outside agriculture—were members of labor unions. Wages of these workers were directly affected by their unions. Unions can even influence wages of nonunion workers. In addition to wages, unions affect employment, labor productivity, fringe benefits, and the level of output. For such reasons, our discussion of labor markets cannot be complete until we consider the roles of unions.

EARLY LABOR UNIONS

The earliest unions in the United States were formed in the 1790s, and consisted of workers from a common craft or trade. Among the first unions were those representing shoemakers in Philadelphia, carpenters in Boston, and printers in New York. The major objectives of these unions included raising wages and reducing the workday, which at the time was commonly twelve hours or longer.

Beginning in Philadelphia in 1827, various unions began forming citywide federations or associations of labor unions. A few years later, national federations were organized. Many of the early unions and their federations were short-lived. They often folded in response to economic downturns, which reduced the bargaining power of unions, or as the result of government intervention, which was decidedly hostile.

In the early nineteenth century the courts considered unions "criminal conspiracies." Even after unions were declared legal in 1842, the courts regularly issued *injunctions*—restraining orders that prohibited unions from striking, picketing, and other activities. The courts ruled that such actions violated employers' rights. The Sherman Act of 1890, as interpreted by the courts, further limited union powers on the ground that efforts by unions to raise wages constituted "restraint of trade."

The courts even sanctioned *yellow-dog contracts*—agreements workers signed as a condition of employment whereby they promised not to join a union. Workers who then joined could be fired for breach of contract. More important, union organizers could be found guilty of inducing workers to violate their contracts. The yellow-dog contract enabled employers to obtain injunctions halting organization drives. Certainly the climate was not conducive to the growth of unionism.

MAJOR LABOR LEGISLATION

Political attitudes toward unions gradually changed, and by the early 1930s many in Congress had become convinced that government intervention was both excessive and biased. With the courts so heavily involved in labor-management relations, some complained of "government by injunction." Others argued that a government of, by, and for the people should welcome such democratic institutions as labor unions, rather than oppose them. Out of this new and more sympathetic environment came two important pieces of pro-union legislation.

The first was the *Norris-LaGuardia Act* of 1932, limiting the ability of courts to issue injunctions against unions and outlawing yellow-dog contracts (see Table 29-3). That was followed three years later by the *National Labor Relations Act (NLRA)*. Also known as the *Wagner Act,* the NLRA is considered so important to unions that it has been dubbed labor's Magna Carta. This law prohibits management from interfering with workers' rights to organize and forces management to bargain in "good faith" with unions representing a majority of their employees. The Wagner Act also created the *National Labor Relations Board (NLRB)*. This agency investigates unfair labor practices and, when deemed appropriate, issues cease-and-desist orders against management. The NLRB also has responsibility for *certifying* unions—that is, conducting elections to allow workers to choose which union, if any, they want to represent them.

The legislation of the 1930s marked a switch in government attitudes from one of obstructing unions to one of encouragement. Largely due to this legislation, union membership more than doubled between 1930 and 1940 (see Table 29-4). Sentiment toward unions later soured, however, in part because of the large number of strikes immediately following World War II. To balance the pro-union legislation of the 1930s and to protect the public, some parties advocated new legislation. In this environment, and despite intense lobbying by unions, Congress passed the *Taft-Hartley Act* of 1947 (formally entitled the Labor-Management Relations Act).

Among its provisions, the Taft-Hartley Act permits the president to seek an injunction ordering union workers back to work during an 80-day "cooling off" period if the strike threatens the public health or safety. These injunctions have not

TABLE 29-3		
MAJOR LABOR LEGISLATION		
Law	**Date enacted**	**Major provisions**
Norris LaGuardia Act	1932	Limited injunctions against unions; prohibited yellow-dog contracts.
National Labor Relations Act (Wagner Act)	1935	Established the National Labor Relations Board to halt unfair labor practices by management and to conduct union representation elections; required companies to bargain with unions chosen by their workers.
Taft-Hartley Act	1947	Restricted unfair labor practices by unions; allowed states to prohibit union shops.
Landrum-Griffin Act	1959	Increased democracy within unions; restricted potential abuse by union officers.

TABLE 29-4		
UNION MEMBERSHIP IN THE UNITED STATES, 1930–1988		
	Union Membership	
Year	**Number (in thousands)**	**As a percentage of nonagricultural employment**
1930	3,401	11.6
1935	3,584	13.2
1940	8,717	26.9
1945	14,322	35.5
1950	14,267	31.5
1955	16,802	33.2
1960	17,049	31.4
1965	17,299	28.4
1970	19,381	27.3
1975	19,611	25.5
1980	20,095	22.2
1985	16,996	17.4
1988	17,002	16.0

Sources: U.S. Bureau of Labor Statistics, *Handbook of Labor Statistics* (1980); *Earnings and Other Characteristics of Organized Workers* (1980); *Employment and Earnings,* January 1987 and 1989.

Closed Shop
A work arrangement that permits a company to hire only those workers who are currently members of a union.

Union Shop
A work arrangement that requires employees to join a union within a certain period of time after they are hired.

Open Shop
A work arrangement in which employees cannot be compelled to join a union, even if one has been chosen to represent the company's work force.

Right-to-Work Laws
Legislation enacted by certain states to require open shops (i.e., to outlaw compulsory union membership).

always succeeded in getting union members back to work, as President Carter discovered during the 1977 coal strike. Whereas the Wagner Act prohibits unfair labor practices on the part of management, the Taft-Hartley Act proscribes unfair labor practices by unions. Unions are required to bargain in good faith, and procedures were established to allow workers to *decertify* (vote out) unions.

The Taft-Hartley Act also affects work arrangements. In a **closed shop,** companies cannot hire workers who do not already belong to the union representing its employees. In a **union shop,** companies face no restriction on who is hired, but new employees must join the union or forfeit their jobs. In an **open shop,** companies have discretion over who is hired, and individual workers choose whether or not to join a union, if one exists. The Taft-Hartley Act outlaws most closed shops and permits states to ban union shops. To date, approximately 20 states have **right-to-work laws** requiring open shops.

Responding to charges of corruption among union leaders, Congress passed the *Landrum-Griffin Act* in 1959 (formally known as the Labor-Management Reporting and Disclosure Act). Although expanding the list of unfair labor practices by unions, it was designed primarily to protect individual union members and increase union democracy. The Landrum-Griffin Act requires election of union officials by secret ballot, limits union loans to its officers, and places restrictions on union office-holding by ex-convicts.

HARD TIMES FOR UNIONS

As Table 29-4 indicates, unionization rates have been declining since the mid-1950s. Unions have found it increasingly difficult to organize workers and in recent years have been winning less than one-half of all *representation elections,* in which workers decide whether or not to become affiliated with a union (see Table 29-5, page 674). At the same time, more and more workers are voting out (decertifying) their unions.

	TABLE 29-5			
REPRESENTATION ELECTIONS AND DECERTIFICATION VOTES				
Fiscal year	Representation elections	Percent won by union	Decertification votes	Percent lost by union
1955	4372	66.4	157	65.0
1960	6380	58.6	237	68.8
1965	7576	60.8	200	64.0
1970	8074	55.2	301	69.8
1975	8577	48.2	516	73.4
1980	8198	45.7	902	72.7
1985	4614	42.4	865	75.6

Sources: National Labor Relations Board, *Fiftieth Annual Report* (1989), pp. 12–15, and selected earlier annual reports.

Increasingly, management is taking on unions and winning, replacing strikers with new employees. This practice appears to have gained momentum in the wake of President Reagan's 1981 decision to fire air traffic controllers engaged in an illegal strike. Also tarnishing the image of unions have been the wage give backs in steel, copper, airlines, trucking, and other industries (see Exhibit 29-4).

What accounts for the hard fortune of unions in recent years? First of all, attitudes have changed. Some analysts contend that unions' views are no longer representative of the general public. Legislation in recent years has generally not been pro-union, and the elections of Presidents Reagan and Bush did not help the union cause. Union leaders are especially critical of President Reagan's appointments to the NLRB, arguing that this body has adopted a pro-management bias. Management, in turn, has become more sophisticated and militant, hiring lawyers and other specialists to combat unions. This is especially true in industries facing stiff competition. Deregulation in the airline and trucking industries and increased foreign competition in other sectors have put intense pressure on some companies to cut costs.

Shifts in the composition of employment have also hurt unions. Industries with high unionization (including manufacturing, construction, and transportation and public utilities) have experienced a decline in relative employment at the expense of industries having low unionization rates (including retail trade, finance, and services). Even if unionization rates had remained constant in each industry, aggregate unionization would have declined.

A related development has been women's increased share of employment. Women are less likely to join unions than are men. This appears to be due in part to the different distribution across jobs—women tend to hold occupations and work in industries characterized by low unionization. Moreover, as discussed in Chapter 31, women tend to have a more intermittent history of work and are more likely to work part time. Support for unions tends to be greater among full-time workers and among those with a strong, continuous commitment to work. Because unions have been less successful in organizing women, the increased share of women in the labor market has accentuated the decline in unionization.

Aware of the problem, unions are intensifying efforts to organize women and workers in traditionally nonunion industries. Whether their efforts will succeed remains to be seen, but unions have made gains in at least one area. The share of government workers represented by unions is much higher today than 30 years ago.

EXHIBIT 29–4

DO WAGE CONCESSIONS REALLY SAVE JOBS?

In difficult times unions occasionally accept wage cuts. Such "give backs" became increasingly common in the early 1980s, prompting unions to debate the wisdom of this practice. As one reporter observed:

Many [union members] believe that past concessions haven't saved jobs and that calls for such aid have become merely a new management tactic to lower workers' wages rather than a way to keep companies afloat. . . . The workers here [at General Tire] note that about two dozen rubber industry facilities have closed nationwide in the past five years despite numerous concessions by [union] workers. And they say the fortunes of auto, steel, trucking and airline companies haven't improved with the help of wage cuts.[11]

What about it? If employment falls despite wage cuts, can we conclude that lower wage rates do not affect union employment?

No. Given a downward-sloping labor demand curve, employment is higher with wage concessions than without. The problem faced by some unions is that labor demand has declined over time due to reduced product demand or, in some cases, to substitution of capital for labor. Given this decline in labor demand, employment may fall even if wage rates are reduced. This illustrated in Figure 29-7.

Assume labor demand falls from D_1 to D_2. If the wage rate remains at W_1, employment falls from E_1 to E_2. Wage concessions can limit, if not totally prevent, the loss of jobs. By accepting a cut in pay to W_2, the union can save $E_3 - E_2$ jobs. Wage rates do matter.

In some cases production remains unprofitable despite the concessions. But even here wage cuts reduce company losses. This may permit the company to stay in business longer (and workers to remain employed longer) even if the plant eventually closes. When it comes to employment, wage rates are important, although they are not the whole story.

---

[11]Robert Greenberger, "More Workers Resist Employers' Demands for Pay Concessions," *The Wall Street Journal,* October 13, 1982, pp. 1 and 16.

FIGURE 29–7

WAGE CUTS IN THE FACE OF DECLINING LABOR DEMAND

If labor demand falls from D_1 to D_2, employment may decline despite a wage cut (e.g., from E_1 to E_3). Even so, employment is higher than if the wage rate does not fall ($E_3 > E_2$). Given a downward-sloping demand curve, wage cuts have a positive effect on employment.

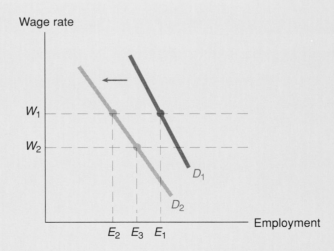

THE AFL-CIO

Most large unions are affiliated with the AFL-CIO, an organization formed in 1955 by the merger of the American Federation of Labor (AFL) and the Congress of

Industrial Organizations (CIO). The AFL, which dates back to 1886, was an association of national *craft* unions, representing workers with a common skill or craft. The CIO embodied an alternative approach to unionism—organizing workers along *industrial* lines, as when a single union represents all workers in the auto industry regardless of their skills or the nature of their jobs.

As separate entities, the AFL and CIO often engaged in representational fights, each side raiding the other for members. By merging, the two organizations ended their rivalry and created a unified front, which they hoped would be more effective in achieving common goals (e.g., the defeat of antiunion legislation). Despite such hopes, the merger was unable to rekindle growth in unionization or to increase labor's might. In the final analysis, the success of a union depends on its ability to affect conditions in the labor market or to induce employers to make concessions, not on the size of the federation with which it is affiliated.

HOW UNIONS RAISE WAGES OF THEIR MEMBERS

Unions have many goals, perhaps the foremost being higher wages for their members. Wages can be raised by (a) increasing the demand for union workers, (b) restricting labor supply, or (c) collective bargaining.

Increasing the Demand for Union Labor

Because the demand for labor is a derived demand, anything increasing demand for their employer's product raises demand for union workers. This, in turn, puts upward pressure on union wages and employment (see Figure 29-8). This is the rationale behind the *union-label* campaign. If a union can convince you to buy clothing manufactured by the International Ladies Garment Workers Union and to shop at grocery stores employing union cashiers, it is increasing demand for union garment workers and cashiers.[12]

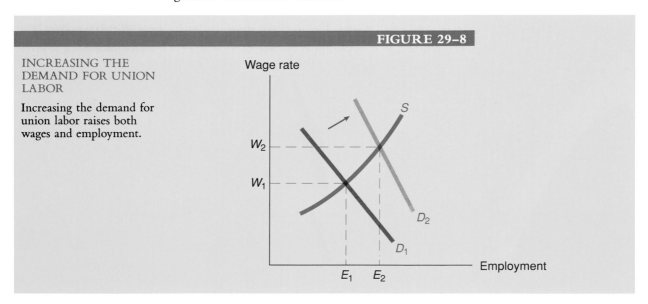

FIGURE 29–8

INCREASING THE DEMAND FOR UNION LABOR

Increasing the demand for union labor raises both wages and employment.

---

[12]This may be a good time to ask your instructor to sing the ILGWU theme song: "Look for the Union Label." Then again, it may not.

Legislation provides an alternative means for achieving union goals. Laws requiring that grain or oil be transported in U.S. ships and tankers benefit the U.S. maritime industry and its heavily unionized work force. The United Auto Workers Union has lobbied Congress to limit imports of automobiles into the United States. Because the overwhelming majority of U.S. autoworkers belong to the UAW, any shift of auto production from other countries to the United States offers the UAW the potential to expand union employment.

"We're from the Central Labor Union Council and we're doing a survey on union label purchases. Please unmake your bed for a sheet, blanket and pillowcase check, and remove your trousers for an underwear check."

Source: *St. Louis Post Dispatch,* 1985. Reprinted by permission; Tribune Media Services.

Featherbedding
Restrictive work practices of unions designed to force a company to hire more labor than desired at the union wage rate.

Featherbedding may also increase union wages and employment. Featherbedding is a practice whereby companies are forced to pay for more labor than is necessary to produce a given amount of output. For example, union rules require theatres to employ a minimum number of union musicians at Broadway musicals, regardless of the number of musicians actually needed or used. Although only 9 musicians performed at *The Best Little Whorehouse in Texas,* the union forced the producers to pay 25 musicians. Under featherbedding a union imposes a restriction on both the minimum wage paid (e.g., W_2 in Figure 29-8) and minimum employment (E_2). Thus, when successful, featherbedding can be viewed as increasing the demand for union labor. But sometimes featherbedding backfires. When the union constraints are too costly, the company may halt production, thereby eliminating union jobs. In addition, featherbedding induces substitution by employers. For example, broadway theatres may run more dramas and comedies, which may reduce employment of musicians rather than expand it.

Restricting the Supply of Labor

If a union can restrict the number of people trained or certified for an occupation, it can raise wages in that occupation (see Figure 29-9). For example, some states require workers in certain occupations (e.g., barbers and electricians) to obtain licenses before they may work in the state. Here, supply can be restricted by the licensing board, which may be influenced by the union. Alternatively, a craft union may be able to control supply by inducing employers to hire only workers who have completed an apprenticeship program operated by the union. Note that supply restrictions reduce employment, unlike programs that increase demand for union labor.

Collective Bargaining

Collective Bargaining
The process through which unions and management negotiate wages, fringe benefits, and nonmonetary terms of employment.

A third route to higher wages is **collective bargaining,** through which the union and management negotiate a contract. Management may agree to pay higher wages than it would like in order to avoid a strike. By withholding labor from the company, a union can generally impose costs on the company: lost sales and profits.[13] To avoid this and the ill will resulting from a strike, management may agree to pay higher wages than would prevail in the absence of the union (see Figure 29-10). Unlike the previous two cases, where unions achieved higher wages by shifting labor demand or labor supply, collective bargaining leads to an excess supply of labor for high-paying union jobs. For an example of how a union can create excess supply of

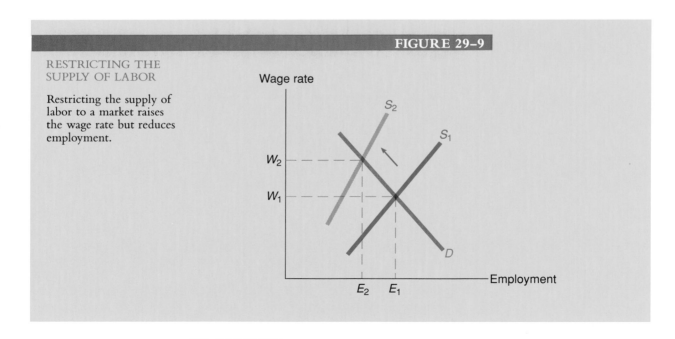

FIGURE 29–9

RESTRICTING THE SUPPLY OF LABOR

Restricting the supply of labor to a market raises the wage rate but reduces employment.

[13]Costs from a strike may extend to other parties as well. In some instances strikes can have a dramatic impact on the overall economy. Consider the 1984–85 strike by coal miners in Great Britain. Even though the miners' union ultimately backed down, analysts estimate that the strike reduced output by a full percentage point and added at least $3 billion to fuel and police costs. See *Business Week,* "The Strike Is Ended, but the Malady Lingers On," March 18, 1985, p. 42.

FIGURE 29–10

NEGOTIATING HIGHER WAGES

In the absence of a union, competitive pressures dictate the wage W_1. However, through collective bargaining, the union may negotiate a higher wage, W_2. At W_2 there is excess supply of labor ($E_3 - E_2$). The higher wage reduces the quantity of labor demanded while simultaneously increasing the quantity supplied.

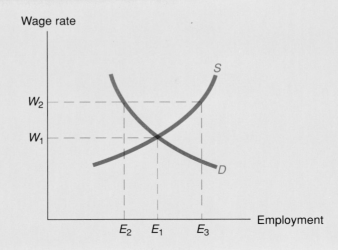

EXHIBIT 29–5

ARE STRIKES BECOMING LESS EFFECTIVE?

When 155,000 members of the Communications Workers of America walked off their jobs at AT&T in June [1986], the nation's long-distance telephone users were hit by a strike few even realized was going on. Though the walkout is the largest work stoppage against a single employer since the union's three-week strike against AT&T in 1983, it barely made a dent in service. Most of the 33 million calls that AT&T handles each day are put through automatically without operators. . . .

Like AT&T, companies throughout the country are discovering that they can survive a strike by using the new scabs of the '80s—their computers. And that is having a dramatic effect on labor-management relations. "Automation has shifted the whole balance of power in favor of management," says [UCSD] Professor Harley Shaiken, who has given the trend a name: telescabbing.

Shaiken and others cite many recent examples of strikes that had negligible effects because of automation. A strike against Consolidated Edison Co., which ended last week after more than two months, went unnoticed by most New Yorkers because the electric system is highly automated. A

major strike against several oil refineries had little impact because the pumps and valves are almost completely automated. And a strike at a jet-engine plant in Ohio didn't stop production because computers have simplified the work of highly skilled machinists so it now can be done by superiors and secretaries. Even in the steel industry, new processes make it possible to continue operating during a strike. A new study by the Wharton School at the University of Pennsylvania found that many capital-intensive companies achieve 90 percent of usual production levels during a strike; most other firms manage 50 to 80 percent.

Automation and computerization have other strike-breaking effects. Because of them, the ratio of workers to supervisors has dropped dramatically in the past 20 years: at AT&T, from 5 to 1 to 2 to 1, which is one reason why supervisors have been able to handle the system during the strike.

Sources: *U.S. News & World Report,* "An AT&T Strike? . . . What Strike?" June 16, 1986, p. 8; John Brecher and Alexander Stille, "'Telescabbing': The New Union Buster," *Newsweek,* August 29, 1983, p. 53. Reprinted by permission.

labor, consider the sanitation workers union of New York City. In response to 100 job openings in the early 1970s, 63,147 people applied.[14]

The success of a strike cannot be guaranteed. A strike is most effective when it shuts down production. If a company continues to produce, the strike's cost to the company is reduced. A company may be able to continue operations by (a) replacing strikers with new employees (called "scabs" by the workers on strike), (b) shifting current, nonstriking employees (e.g., supervisors) to the union jobs, or (c) substituting capital for labor. According to some analysts, companies are becoming better equipped to carry on production during a strike. For that reason, a strike puts less pressure on many companies today than it did in the past (see Exhibit 29-5, page 679).

The cost of a strike to a company also depends on what is being produced. If a good can be inventoried (e.g., steel and tires), the company can build up a large stockpile in anticipation of a strike. By drawing down inventories during a strike, the company may be able to maintain its revenues. In contrast, some goods and services (e.g., newspapers and airplane travel) cannot be inventoried. Accordingly, a strike is likely to prove more costly to companies producing such items than to companies producing goods that can be inventoried.

HOW UNIONS AFFECT WAGES OF NONUNION WORKERS

The effect of unions may spill over to the nonunion sector. Consider an industry with both union and nonunion companies. Suppose that managers of the nonunion companies wish to remain union-free. What can they do to lessen the likelihood that their employees will vote for union representation? They can reduce the incentive to unionize by paying wages higher than dictated by competitive labor markets. If union wages rise, nonunion companies may respond by raising wages of their employees too (although perhaps by a lesser amount). In that event, both union and nonunion employees in the industry benefit from higher union wages.

Other nonunion workers may not fare so well. In particular, the positive effect discussed in the preceding paragraph does not carry over to industries where employers do not feel threatened by potential unionization of their work forces. Collective bargaining raises wages in unionized companies (from W_1^u to W_2^u in Figure 29-11a), thus reducing union employment (from E_1^u to E_2^u). Some of the displaced workers ($E_1^u - E_2^u$) may flow over to nonunion markets—a low-paying nonunion job may be preferable to no job at all. This increase in labor supply to nonunion markets depresses wages there (from W_1^n to W_2^n). According to this scenario, higher union wages depress nonunion wages. In summary, some nonunion workers appear to have their wages raised because of unions (although not as high as union wages); others have their wages pulled down.

THE UNION WAGE PREMIUM

What is the relative wage premium associated with union membership—that is, how much more do union workers receive than comparable nonunion workers? That depends on the union and the time period. Some unions are more powerful than others; some time periods are more conducive to large union premiums than are other periods. If we consider the average premium in normal times, it appears that

---

[14]This example was cited in Robert I. Lerman, "The Public Employment Bandwagon Takes the Wrong Road," *Challenge* (January/February 1975).

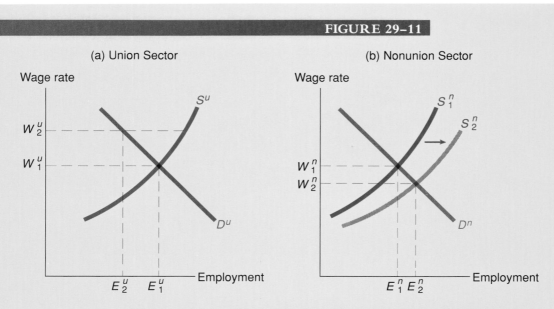

FIGURE 29-11

HOW UNIONS MAY LOWER THE WAGES OF NONUNION WORKERS

Higher wages in the union sector (a) reduce union employment (from E_1^u to E_2^u). When some workers unable to obtain union employment switch to the nonunion sector (b), labor supply in the nonunion sector increases. Assuming wages in the nonunion sector are determined by labor supply and demand, the result is lower wages for nonunion workers (W_2^n).

union employees receive wages approximately 15 percent higher than nonunion workers with similar skills and backgrounds.

As Table 29-6 illustrates, the net advantage of union membership varies by race and by gender. Because unions typically raise wages by a larger percentage for low-paid workers, blacks tend to benefit more from union membership than whites. For the same reason, one might also expect women to benefit more than men. But women are less likely to be members of powerful unions, so the effect of union membership by gender is mixed.

TABLE 29-6

ESTIMATED WAGE PREMIUM FROM UNION MEMBERSHIP
BY YEAR AND RACE/GENDER*

	1967	1973	1975
All workers	11.6	14.8	16.8
White men	9.6	15.5	16.3
Black men	21.5	22.5	22.5
White women	14.4	12.7	16.6
Black women	5.6	13.2	17.1

*The wage premium is an estimate of the percentage wage gain due to union membership.

Source: Orley Ashenfelter, "Union Relative Wage Effects," in Richard Stone and William Peterson, eds., *Econometric Contributions to Public Policy* (New York: St. Martin's Press, 1979), Table 6, p. 33. © 1979 by St. Martin's Press, Incorporated.

NONWAGE EFFECTS OF UNIONS

The impact of unions extends well beyond wages; among its nonwage effects are higher fringe benefits. One economist estimated that whereas union wages are approximately 14.8 percent higher than nonunion wages, when fringe benefits are included the net advantage rises to 17.3 percent.[15]

Through strikes and featherbedding, unions reduce output; but in other areas their effects are positive. By reducing sources of discontent, they may increase morale and, in turn, output per worker. By raising wages, unions may force management to run a tighter ship, to find ways to cut other costs. They may also foster a spirit of cooperation among workers. Under unionism, wages and job security depend more on seniority (i.e., job tenure) than on performance of the individual. In this environment, workers are less likely to see each other as rivals and more likely to work together, to train and assist those needing help. Unions can also be a source of information to management, pointing out ways to improve operations within a company.[16] Yet, do these positive effects outweigh the negative effects? On that issue the evidence is mixed. In some industries unions raise the output per worker; in other industries the reverse is true.

Unions also affect the distribution of income. Although one may not applaud the wage gains achieved by baseball or pilots' unions, unions appear especially concerned about workers at the bottom of the income distribution. One result is less racial inequality of wages. Blacks are more likely to belong to unions than whites; they also enjoy a union wage premium at least as large as that received by whites (see Table 29-6). Together these statements imply that unions narrow the difference in pay between blacks and whites—in the absence of unions, the pay of blacks would be even further behind that of whites.

In addition, unions protect the rights of individual workers, reducing the ability of management to engage in capricious or discriminatory behavior. Unions demand that employees be treated fairly, with dignity, rather than as some impersonal resource to be used at the will of management. For some workers this is the most important reason to join a union.

Unions have also been a major force behind the enactment of important pieces of legislation, from the Civil Rights Act to laws on child labor, worker safety, and plant closings. Because these laws affect the entire work force—not just union members—some consider unions a voice for all workers. For such reasons, unions enjoy support even in the nonunion community.

SUMMARY

1. According to the model of perfect competition, wages are determined by the intersection of market labor supply and demand. The firm's labor demand curve is based on the marginal revenue product of labor. A profit-maximizing firm should hire up to the point where the wage rate equals marginal revenue product.
2. Demand for labor is derived from product demand. When product demand increases (decreases), so does labor demand.
3. The number of hours an individual wants to work may vary positively or negatively with the wage rate, depending on whether the substitution effect or income effect dominates. But the amount of labor supplied to a market increases with the wage rate.

[15]Richard Freeman, "The Effect of Trade Unionism on Fringe Benefits," *Industrial and Labor Relations Review* (July 1981).

[16]These arguments on the positive effects of unions come from Richard Freeman and James Medoff, *What Do Unions Do?* (New York: Basic Books, 1984).

4. Wage rates vary greatly across individuals. One reason is because of differences in labor supply and demand. Wages tend to be higher for those with large amounts of human capital. Wage differences also arise because of economic rents, compensating wage differentials, labor market imperfections, and discrimination.

5. When set above the market rate of pay, a minimum wage reduces employment. Each ten-percent increase in the minimum wage reduces teenage employment by between one and three percent. Although minimum wages raise the income of some workers, others find their income reduced, because of either lost employment or a reduction in hours worked. To the extent employers respond to a higher minimum wage by providing less training to their employees, a minimum wage may result in slower wage growth.

6. About one in six U.S. workers belongs to a labor union. Unionization soared after the pro-union legislation of the 1930s but has been declining in recent years.

7. Unions can raise wages of their members by increasing demand for union workers, restricting labor supply, or engaging in collective bargaining.

8. Unions may increase or decrease wages of nonunion workers. Nonunion companies that worry about possible union organization may raise wages of their employees in an effort to keep them from voting for union representation. In contrast, when workers displaced by high union wages transfer to nonunion markets, increasing labor supply there, the result can be lower nonunion wages.

9. On average, union workers appear to earn approximately 15 percent more than comparable nonunion employees, but the size of this premium varies over time and across unions.

10. Unions raise fringe benefits, exert both positive and negative effects on output, and alter the distribution of income. Unions narrow differences in pay between black and white workers.

KEY TERMS

marginal revenue product of labor	screening hypothesis
market demand for labor	compensating wage differential
derived demand	union
substitution effect (for labor)	closed shop
income effect (for labor)	union shop
market supply of labor	open shop
economic rent of a worker	right-to-work laws
human capital	featherbedding
	collective bargaining

STUDY QUESTIONS AND PROBLEMS

1. Assume your firm faces the following production function:

Number of workers	Units of output
0	0
1	50
2	90
3	120
4	145
5	165

Each unit of output sells for $2 regardless of the number of units sold.

a. What is the marginal product of the third worker?

b. What is the third worker's marginal revenue product?

    c. Assuming that your goal is to maximize profit, how many workers should you hire if the wage is $65 per worker?

    d. How many workers should you hire if the wage is $45 per worker?

2. Why don't all workers receive the same wage rate? Provide several explanations.

3. What is a backward-bending labor supply curve? Why does it bend backwards?

4. How does additional education affect the rate of pay a worker can expect to receive? Provide two alternative explanations for the relationship between education and earnings.

5. Economists argue that a higher minimum wage harms many of the workers it was designed to help—those with low skills and low income. Explain this argument.

6. Explain how government policy toward unions has changed over time. Has this had any impact on the success of unions?

7. (a) What do you consider to be the major contributions of unions? (b) Do unions have any adverse effects on the economy? Explain.

8. What is the difference between a craft union and an industrial union? Which category best describes the earliest U.S. unions?

9. Explain why a strike may impose greater costs on some companies than on others.

10. How has the rate of unionization changed in the United States over the past 40 years? What accounts for this change?

11. Do unions raise or lower wages of nonunion workers? Explain.

ANSWERS TO YOUR TURN

(a) $300. (b) 2. (c) 3. (d) (i) The labor demand curve shifts rightward. Other things equal, a higher output price increases MRP. To prove this, first compute MRP when the price is $20 per box. Then construct the new MRP schedule for a price of $30 per box. (ii) 5.

SELECTED REFERENCES

Brown, Charles, Curtis Gilroy, and Andrew Kohen, "The Effect of the Minimum Wage on Employment and Unemployment," *Journal of Economic Literature* (June 1982), pp. 487–528. Surveys minimum wage research.

Ehrenberg, Ronald and Robert Smith, *Modern Labor Economics,* 3rd ed. (Glenview, IL: Scott, Foresman and Co., 1988). A popular labor economics text.

Estey, Marten, *The Union,* 3rd ed. (New York: Harcourt Brace Jovanovich, 1981). Provides history and background on organized labor.

Freeman, Richard and James Medoff, *What Do Unions Do?* (New York: Basic Books, 1984). Discusses the positive and negative effects of unions.

Hamermesh, Daniel and Albert Rees, *The Economics of Work and Pay,* 4th ed. (New York: Harper and Row, 1988). Another widely used text on labor economics.

Killingsworth, Mark, *Labor Supply* (Cambridge, England: Cambridge University Press, 1983). Reviews studies on labor supply.

Marshall, F. Ray and Vernon Briggs, Jr., *Labor Economics,* 6th ed. (Homewood, IL: Irwin, 1989). Discusses the history of the union movement and important labor legislation.

Rees, Albert, *The Economics of Trade Unions,* 3rd ed. (Chicago: University of Chicago Press, 1989). An extensive but nontechnical economic discussion of unions.

CHAPTER 30

ALTERNATIVE MODELS OF THE FACTOR MARKET[1]

Hospitals possess and exert monopsony power . . . wages are depressed to an artificially low level in the market for nurses because [of this power].

—RICHARD HURD, 1973

Firms participate in two types of markets: product markets, where they sell their output, and factor markets, where they buy their inputs. Chapter 29 sketched the theory of wage determination on the assumption that the firm was too small to influence either the price of its output or the price of its variable input, labor. In other words, the model assumed that the firm hired labor in a perfectly competitive labor market—paying the market wage—and sold its output in a perfectly competitive product market. But as you know, not all product markets are (perfectly) competitive. Where firms face downward-sloping demand curves, they can influence product price. Similarly, not all factor markets are competitive. In some labor markets the wage a company pays depends on the amount of labor it hires. In such markets the firm can obviously influence the wage it must pay.

Chapter 30 studies hiring decisions of firms that operate in product markets or factor markets that are not perfectly competitive. We consider first the case where firms influence wage rates and then the case where firms have control over their product price. Next, we extend the analysis to consider the situation where a company buys more than one variable input. If a company is hiring several different types of labor or, say, buying capital as well as labor, how should these inputs be combined? We tackle this issue first for the case where factor markets are competitive and then for the case where firms have some influence over the price they pay for their inputs.

---

[1]Chapter 30 is more technical than Chapter 29. Instructors who do not want to give their course a heavy theoretical emphasis can delete as much material as they choose from this chapter without creating gaps in later chapters.

685

The models of this chapter and the previous chapter are tied together by a common thread: demand for a factor is based on the marginal productivity of that factor. We wrap up our discussion by analyzing what marginal productivity theory does and does not say about the distribution of income.

MONOPSONY IN THE LABOR MARKET

Monopsonist
The only buyer of a particular input.

Marginal Factor Cost
The increase in the total cost of an input associated with using an additional unit of the input.

The model of perfect competition assumes that firms confront a given, market-determined wage—that is, firms are *wage takers*. This is not always true. When a company is the only one hiring a particular type of labor, it can influence the price of labor. It has monopoly power on the buying side of the market. Such a company is called a **monopsonist.**

With only one firm in the labor market, the supply of labor to the firm is synonymous with the supply of labor to the market. Thus, a monopsonist confronts an upward-sloping labor supply curve (Figure 30-1). **Marginal factor cost (MFC)** measures the incremental cost of hiring an additional unit of the factor of

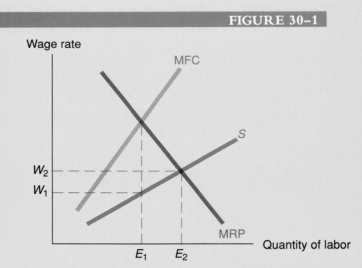

FIGURE 30–1

LABOR MARKET OUTCOMES UNDER MONOPSONY AND PERFECT COMPETITION

A monopsonist hires where MFC = MRP (E_1) and pays the lowest wage necessary (W_1) to obtain this amount of labor. In competitive labor markets, the intersection of market MRP and labor supply determines the wage rate (W_2) and employment (E_2). Compared to competitive labor markets, monopsony leads to a lower wage rate and lower employment.

production—in this case, labor. For example, suppose a company must pay each worker $90/day if it hires three workers but $100/day if it hires four. MFC of the fourth worker is $130 — the wage of the fourth worker ($100) *plus* an additional $10 for each of the first three workers.[2] Because MFC exceeds the wage (e.g., $130>$100), MFC lies above the labor supply curve.

Hiring Decisions Under Monopsony

As observed in the previous chapter, a worker's contribution to revenue is measured by the worker's marginal revenue product (MRP). To maximize profit the monopsonist hires labor up to the point where MRP = MFC. Until this point is reached additional labor adds more to revenue than to costs (MRP > MFC). Beyond this point the reverse is true (MRP < MFC). The monopsonist portrayed in Figure 30-1 hires E_1 workers and pays a wage of W_1. Note that the wage is not given by the height of the MFC curve at E_1. To maximize profits the monopsonist pays the lowest wage possible consistent with hiring E_1 workers. That wage, given by the point on the supply curve directly above E_1, is W_1.

YOUR TURN

MONOPSONY
The marginal revenue product for a monopsonist is given by the following schedule:

Number of workers	MRP
1	$8.00
2	7.50
3	7.00
4	6.50
5	6.00
6	5.50

The monopsonist faces the labor supply schedule presented below:

Number of workers	Wage
1	$5.00
2	5.50
3	6.00
4	6.50
5	7.00
6	7.50

a. Construct the MFC schedule of the monopsonist.
b. What level of employment satisfies the monopsonist's rule for profit maximization?
c. Given your answer to b, what wage will the monopsonist pay in order to maximize profit?

---

[2]Alternatively, MFC can be computed directly as the change in total labor cost associated with hiring the fourth unit of labor. When four workers are employed instead of three, total labor cost rises from 3 × $90 = $270 to 4 × $100 = $400, a change of $130.

In competitive labor markets, wages and employment are determined by the intersection of market MRP and market labor supply. In terms of Figure 30-1, the competitive outcome would be W_2 and E_2. This illustrates how the monopsonist uses its monopoly power to curtail wages and employment.

As an example of monopsony, consider an isolated community with a single mining company. By deciding how many miners to employ (E_1), the company determines the wage rate (W_1). Other markets may be approximated by the model of monopsony, even when they contain more than one employer. The majority of registered nurses work in hospitals. If the hospitals act in concert, they may be able to suppress wages of RNs.[3]

How Unions And Minimum Wages Alter Hiring Decisions

In the preceding discussion, we assumed that the monopsonist was free to choose the wage rate. However, unions or minimum wage legislation may place a lower limit on wages. If that limit is above the wage the monopsonist would have chosen, wage rates rise. Based on our discussion of competitive markets, you might predict that higher wage rates reduce employment. Surprising as it may seem, in monopsonistic markets the employment effect of a higher wage rate may be either positive or negative, depending on how much the wage is raised.

A minimum wage, whether imposed by the government or a union, precludes certain wages. Accordingly, it changes the shapes of the labor supply and MFC curves. To the left of E_2 in Figure 30-2, the supply and MFC curves become horizontal, with values equal to MIN. This reflects the fact that until the wage rate is raised above MIN, each additional unit of labor costs MIN. Beyond E_2 (where MIN intersects S), the original supply and MFC curves prevail.

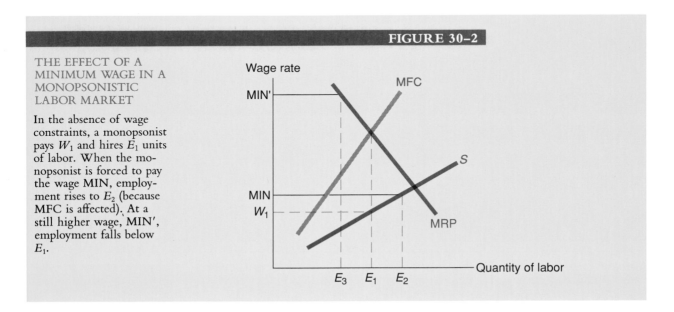

FIGURE 30–2

THE EFFECT OF A MINIMUM WAGE IN A MONOPSONISTIC LABOR MARKET

In the absence of wage constraints, a monopsonist pays W_1 and hires E_1 units of labor. When the monopsonist is forced to pay the wage MIN, employment rises to E_2 (because MFC is affected). At a still higher wage, MIN′, employment falls below E_1.

[3]For evidence of this, see Richard Hurd, "Equilibrium Vacancies in a Labor Market Dominated by Non-Profit Firms: The 'Shortage' of Nurses," *Review of Economics and Statistics* (May 1973), pp. 234–240; Charles Link and J. H. Landon, "Monopsony and Union Power in the Market for Nurses," *Southern Economic Journal* (April 1975), pp. 649–659.

Confronted with a wage rate of MIN, the monopsonist *increases* employment from E_1 to E_2. (The monopsonist would not hire less than E_2 since, for employment less than E_2, MRP > MFC.) Even under monopsony, if the minimum wage is set too high, employment falls. For example, a wage of MIN′ reduces employment to E_3.

Although the model of monopsony indicates that a minimum wage may increase employment, economists discount this possibility on the ground that monopsony is rare. As predicted by the competitive theory of labor markets, empirical studies invariably find that a higher minimum wage reduces employment of low-productivity workers.

YOUR TURN

WHEN A MONOPSONIST CONFRONTS A MINIMUM WAGE
The MRP and labor supply schedules of the preceding Your Turn are combined below:

Number of workers	MRP	Wage
1	$8.00	$5.00
2	7.50	5.50
3	7.00	6.00
4	6.50	6.50
5	6.00	7.00
6	5.50	7.50

An assumption of this labor supply schedule is that the monopsonist is free to set any wage it chooses. But suppose the monopsonist is now confronted with a minimum wage of $6.50.

a. Construct the monopsonist's new labor supply schedule, given the constraint that it must pay each worker a wage of at least $6.50.
b. Construct the MFC schedule associated with this new labor supply schedule.
c. Given a minimum wage of $6.50, what level of employment satisfies the monopsonist's rule for profit maximization?
d. Given your answer to c, what wage must the monopsonist pay in order to maximize profit?
e. Does the minimum wage cause the monopsonist to increase or decrease the level of employment? (How does your answer to c compare to your answer to b in the preceding Your Turn?)

FACTOR DEMAND IN NONCOMPETITIVE PRODUCT MARKETS

Let us drop the assumption that the firm is a monopsonist. Instead, assume that the firm is in a perfectly competitive labor market, paying a given wage regardless of the number of workers hired (i.e., it faces a perfectly elastic labor supply curve). Assume, however, that the firm is selling its output in a noncompetitive product market and therefore must lower price in order to sell additional output.

Recall that **marginal revenue product** is the increase in revenue attributable to the hiring of an additional unit of labor. Equivalently, it is equal to the marginal product of the additional labor times the marginal revenue of the output (MR):

$$MRP = MP_l \times MR$$

If product markets are competitive (as we assumed in the previous chapter), the marginal revenue from selling an additional unit of output is simply the price received. Therefore, in competitive product markets MRP can be rewritten as $MP_l \times P$.

In contrast, in noncompetitive product markets MR < P, as we observed in Chapters 25 and 26. Multiplying both sides of the inequality by MP_l, we have:

$$MP_l \times MR < MP_l \times P$$

This has important implications. It says that marginal revenue product is lower for a firm with monopoly power than for an otherwise similar firm that sells in a perfectly competitive product market. This is illustrated in Figure 30-3. For a given marginal product schedule, MRP_c depicts the MRP curve when the output market is competitive (MR = P) and MRP_m shows the corresponding MRP curve when the firm has monopoly power (MR < P).[4]

Not only does MRP_m lie leftward of MRP_c, it is also steeper (less elastic). For a firm selling in a competitive product market MRP slopes downward for only one reason—as additional labor is hired the marginal product of labor declines. But for a firm selling in a noncompetitive product market marginal revenue also declines—since the firm must lower price to sell the additional output. This further lessens labor's contribution to revenue, thereby causing MRP to fall more precipitously than if the product market had been competitive.

The shape and location of a firm's MRP curve become important when considering how much labor the firm must hire in order to maximize profit.

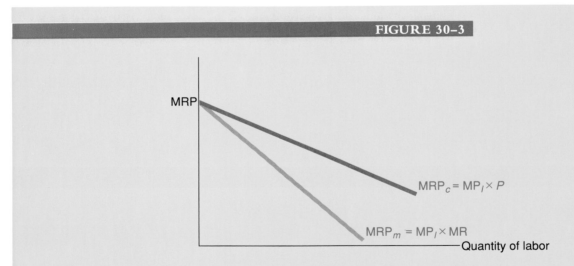

FIGURE 30-3

MONOPOLY POWER IN THE PRODUCT MARKET REDUCES MARGINAL REVENUE PRODUCT

MRP_c denotes the marginal revenue product curve of a competitive firm—one that faces a fixed output price. MRP_m depicts the marginal revenue product curve of an otherwise identical firm that sells its output in a noncompetitive product market. Because the noncompetitive firm must lower price to sell additional output, the firm's marginal revenue is less than price. For this reason, the firm's marginal revenue product curve is steeper and lies leftward of the competitive firm's marginal revenue product curve.

[4]The marginal revenue product of a firm in a competitive product market—what we have labeled MRP_c—is sometimes called the *value of marginal product*.

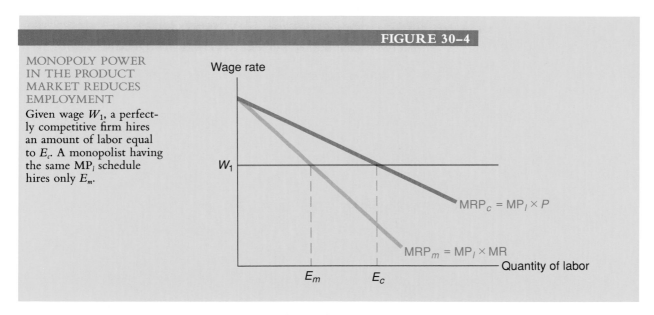

FIGURE 30–4

MONOPOLY POWER IN THE PRODUCT MARKET REDUCES EMPLOYMENT

Given wage W_1, a perfectly competitive firm hires an amount of labor equal to E_c. A monopolist having the same MP_l schedule hires only E_m.

Assuming the firm faces a fixed wage rate, the firm should hire labor up to the point where:

$$\text{MRP} = W$$

Because $\text{MRP}_m < \text{MRP}_c$, a monopolist (or any other firm able to influence product price) hires less labor than a perfectly competitive firm with the same marginal product schedule. This is illustrated in Figure 30-4. A monopolist hires up to the point where $\text{MRP}_m = W$; the competitive firm continues to hire until $\text{MRP}_c = W$. In other words, *monopoly power in the product market leads to lower employment in the labor market.* This should come as no surprise. In comparing monopoly with perfect competition, we previously observed that the monopolist restricts output in order to drive up price and profit. Because the monopolist produces less output it hires less labor.

THE GENERAL RULE FOR HIRING: MRP = MFC

We have addressed the firm's hiring decisions in different settings, based on whether product and labor markets are competitive or noncompetitive. As it turns out, there is a general rule that applies in each case—regardless of the type of market in which the firm operates: To maximize profit, a firm should hire up to the point where

$$\text{MRP} = \text{MFC}$$

The cost of hiring an additional unit of labor (marginal factor cost) should equal the revenue contributed by that unit (marginal revenue product). Even though this rule is perfectly general, the values of MRP and MFC depend on the nature of the product and labor markets.

The model of the preceding chapter was a special case in which both product and labor markets were competitive. Because the labor market was competitive, the wage rate did not change as the firm hired additional labor. Rather, the cost of another worker was simply the wage that must be paid to that worker:

$$\text{MFC} = W$$

TABLE 30-1		
HOW MONOPOLY POWER AFFECTS MRP, MFC, WAGE RATES, AND EMPLOYMENT		
	Perfectly competitive product market	**Noncompetitive product market**
Perfectly competitive labor market	$MRP = MP_l \times P$ $MFC = W$	$MRP < MP_l \times P^*$ $MFC = W$
Noncompetitive labor market (monopsony)	$MRP = MP_l \times P$ $MFC > W^{**}$	$MRP < MP_l \times P^*$ $MFC > W^{**}$

*Compared to perfect competition in the product market, $MRP < MP_l \times P$ leads to reduced employment.

**Compared to perfect competition in the labor market, $MFC > W$ leads to reduced employment and a lower wage rate.

Because the product market was competitive, the marginal revenue of additional output was equal to the output price and, consequently

$$MRP = MP_l \times P$$

As shown in this chapter, when a firm has monopoly power in the labor market

$$MFC > W$$

When monopoly power exists in the product market

$$MRP < MP_l \times P$$

In either case—whether monopoly arises in the labor market or the product market—the result is a lower level of employment (see Table 30-1). When monopoly power exists in the labor market, the wage rate is also reduced. In contrast, monopoly power in the product market has no effect on the wage a firm must pay.

SHIFTS IN LABOR DEMAND

A firm's labor demand curve is drawn on the basis of certain conditions. When these conditions change, so does the firm's labor demand curve.

Product Demand

As you learned in Chapter 29, demand for labor is a derived demand, based on demand for the product the firm is producing. When product demand increases, leading to higher levels of production, demand for labor also rises (shifts rightward). In technical terms: an increase in product demand increases marginal revenue and consequently MRP. Likewise, a decline in product demand lowers MRP.

Marginal Productivity of Labor

Companies respond to a change in labor productivity by buying either more or less labor, depending on whether marginal product rises or falls. Although workers can increase their productivity by investing in human capital, labor productivity also depends on factors over which the worker has no control. Workers generally interact with other inputs (e.g., capital). A change in the quantity or quality of capital is likely to change the marginal product schedule of labor and, with it, the demand for labor. Whether labor demand falls or rises depends on whether capital and labor are **substitute inputs** or **complementary inputs**.

Substitute Inputs
Inputs that are substitutes in production; an increase in the price of one increases demand for the other.

Complementary Inputs
Inputs that are complements in production; an increase in the price of one reduces demand for the other.

Assume a company increases its use of capital, perhaps because of technological advance raising the productivity of capital or perhaps because the price of capital has been reduced. If capital can be substituted for labor, the company may reduce its demand for labor. For example, increased use of industrial robots has reduced demand for welders and spray painters. Likewise, demand for farm labor has declined sharply in the United States as farmers substituted combines, mechanical cotton pickers, and other machinery for labor.

In other cases, capital and labor are complements. Here firms respond to increased capital usage by demanding more workers. For example, an increase in the number of computers can be expected to increase demand for computer programmers, data processors, and computer repair workers. An increase in commercial airplanes is likely to increase demand for pilots, flight attendants, and mechanics.

MULTIPLE INPUTS

We have been focusing on the demand for labor even though firms often hire other variable inputs. In the long run, when capital is variable, firms simultaneously adjust quantities of both capital and labor. Even in the short run a company may hire different types of labor (e.g., skilled and unskilled). We now consider input demand when a firm hires more than one variable input. We address two questions. (a) What combination of inputs enables the firm to produce a given level of output at the lowest cost? (b) How much of each input should the firm hire in order to maximize profit? We take up these questions first for competitive and then for noncompetitive factor markets.

MINIMIZING COSTS WHEN FACTOR MARKETS ARE COMPETITIVE

The total cost of producing a given output is minimized when the marginal product of the last unit of each input hired is proportional to the input's price. If capital (k) and labor (l) are the inputs, the cost-minimizing rule is to hire inputs until

$$\frac{MP_k}{P_k} = \frac{MP_l}{P_l}$$

In other words, the marginal product per dollar is the same for each input. Alternatively, this expression can be rewritten as

$$\frac{MP_k}{MP_l} = \frac{P_k}{P_l}$$

Costs are minimized when the ratio of marginal products equals the ratio of input prices.

To understand why this condition minimizes the costs of producing a given level of output, consider what happens when the condition does not hold. In particular, suppose the firm chooses a combination of capital and labor for which

$(MP_k/P_k) > (MP_l/P_l)$. This implies that the last dollar spent on capital contributes more to output than does the last dollar spent on labor. At the margin, capital has a bigger bang per buck than labor. This tells the firm that it should buy more capital and less labor. By substituting capital for labor, the firm can increase its output without spending any more on inputs. In a similar vein, if $(MP_l/P_l) > (MP_k/P_k)$, the firm can costlessly increase output by substituting labor for capital. Only when $(MP_k/P_k) = (MP_l/P_l)$ does the firm get the most output for its money. Only then is it purchasing the optimal mix of inputs.

The same logic applies when more than two inputs are used. Given inputs 1 through n, the firm should buy quantities of each so that

$$\frac{MP_1}{P_1} = \frac{MP_2}{P_2} = \cdots = \frac{MP_n}{P_n}$$

Cost Minimization—An Application[5]

As farmers know, fertilizer can increase corn yields. Two fertilizers often applied are nitrogen and phosphorous. Their exact contribution to corn yields depends on how much of each is used and on soil conditions. In an experiment on Ida Silt loam in western Iowa, different amounts of these fertilizers were applied to different plots of land. Corn yields were then estimated as a function of the amounts of nitrogen and phosphorous applied. Table 30-2 lists some of the combinations of nitrogen and phosphorous that resulted in a yield of 130 bushels per acre.[6] Also presented in Table 30-2 is the ratio of the marginal products for each combination of fertilizer.

Such information tells corn farmers in western Iowa how to achieve yields of 130 pounds per acre at the lowest possible cost. Cost minimization requires that marginal product ratios equal input price ratios. When nitrogen costs five times as much per pound as phosphorous, cost minimization requires that the marginal

TABLE 30-2

ALTERNATIVE WAYS TO PRODUCE CORN YIELDS OF 130 POUNDS PER ACRE

Pounds of nitrogen	Pounds of phosphorous	MP of nitrogen/ MP of phosphorous
186	228	5
190	211	2
195	207	13/9
207	195	1/2
215	193	1/5

Source: Earl Heady, John Pesek, William Brown, and John Doll, "Crop Response Surfaces and Economic Optima in Fertilizer Use," Chapter 14, in Earl Heady and John Dillon, *Agricultural Production Functions* (Ames, IA: Iowa State University Press, 1961), Table 14.11. Reprinted by permission. © 1961 by Iowa State University Press.

---

[5]This section is based on Earl Heady, John Pesek, William Brown, and John Doll, "Crop Response Surfaces and Economic Optima in Fertilizer Use," Chapter 14, in Earl Heady and John Dillon, *Agricultural Production Functions* (Ames, IA: Iowa State University Press, 1961).

[6]Nitrogen was applied in the form of ammonium nitrate and phosphorous in the form of triple superphosphate. Thus, the numbers in Table 30-2 measure the pounds of ammonium nitrate and triple superphosphate per acre.

product of nitrogen be five times as great as the marginal product of phosphorous. This condition is met when the farmer applies 186 pounds of nitrogen per acre and 228 pounds of phosphorous (line 1, Table 30-2). When nitrogen costs twice as much as phosphorous, the least-cost combination is 190 pounds of nitrogen and 211 pounds of phosphorous (line 2). More generally, information on marginal products tells a producer how to vary input ratios in response to changing input prices.

MAXIMIZING PROFIT WHEN FACTOR MARKETS ARE COMPETITIVE

Maximizing profit requires not just producing a given output at the lowest possible cost; the firm must also choose the appropriate level of output. When a company produces too much output or too little output it does not maximize profits, even if that output is produced using the optimal combination of inputs.

We previously showed that the firm should hire labor until its MRP equals the price of labor. More generally, profit maximization requires that the MRP of each input equals the price of that input. When capital and labor are the inputs, the conditions for profit maximization are

$$MP_l \times MR = P_l$$

$$MP_k \times MR = P_k$$

where MR denotes the marginal revenue of output. These conditions can be rewritten as

$$\frac{MP_l}{P_l} = \frac{1}{MR}$$

$$\frac{MP_k}{P_k} = \frac{1}{MR}$$

For more than two inputs, the rule can be stated as

$$\frac{MP_1}{P_1} = \frac{MP_2}{P_2} = \cdots = \frac{MP_n}{P_n} = \frac{1}{MR}$$

As the preceding equations indicate, the conditions for profit maximization are stronger than the conditions for minimizing the costs of producing a given output. Not only must the marginal product of each input be proportional to the input price, but for each input the ratio of marginal product to input price must equal the reciprocal of the marginal revenue of output.

To understand the significance of this latter condition, assume that $MP_l/P_l = MP_k/P_k > 1/MR$. Although the firm is producing its output at the lowest possible cost (since $MP_l/P_l = MP_k/P_k$), it is not maximizing profit. In particular, the firm is producing too little output. Additional labor would contribute more to revenue than to costs, and so would additional capital. Therefore, to maximize profits, the firm must hire more of both inputs and expand its production. As additional inputs are used, their marginal products will fall, driving down MP_l/P_l and MP_k/P_k. The firm should keep adding capital and labor until MP_l/P_l and MP_k/P_k each equal the reciprocal of marginal revenue. Conversely, if $MP_l/P_l = MP_k/P_k < 1/MR$ the firm is producing too much output and, consequently, must reduce its use of labor and capital.

Where product markets are competitive, the rule for profit maximization can be restated as

$$\frac{MP_1}{P_1} = \frac{MP_2}{P_2} = \cdots = \frac{MP_n}{P_n} = \frac{1}{P}$$

where P is the output price. Because marginal revenue equals price in competitive output markets, the reciprocal of marginal revenue equals the reciprocal of price.

YOUR TURN   MULTIPLE INPUTS
Assume you hire both skilled and unskilled labor. Their marginal products are three and two, respectively. Skilled labor costs $9 per unit; unskilled labor costs $6. Your output sells in a competitive product market for a price of $2 per unit. Are you hiring the profit-maximizing amounts of labor? If not, should you hire more or less skilled labor? Should you increase or decrease the amount of unskilled labor? Explain your answers.

Profit Maximization—An Application

Let us return to the Iowa corn farmers who must determine how much nitrogen and phosphorous to apply to their fields. Because the price of corn is fixed for individual farmers, the rule for profit maximization can be expressed as follows:

$$\frac{MP_{nit}}{P_{nit}} = \frac{MP_{phos}}{P_{phos}} = \frac{1}{P_{corn}}$$

Optimal input use depends on the prices of both inputs and output. Suppose nitrogen costs $.18 per pound and phosphorous costs $.12. If corn sells for $2.00 per bushel, the condition for profit maximization is

$$\frac{MP_{nit}}{\$.18} = \frac{MP_{phos}}{\$.12} = \frac{1}{\$2.00}$$

The farmer should continue applying fertilizer until the marginal product of the last pound of nitrogen is .09 bushel of corn and the marginal product of the last pound of phosphorous is .06 bushel of corn. (These are the numbers for which the preceding equalities hold.) Based on estimated marginal product schedules, these conditions are satisfied when the farmer applies 185 pounds of nitrogen per acre and 190 pounds of phosphorous.[7]

More generally, when marginal product schedules are known, producers can adjust input usage until the conditions for profit maximization are met. The theory of optimal input use is not some idle theory. As the preceding application indicates, it helps farmers and other producers make important economic decisions.

HIRING MULTIPLE INPUTS IN NONCOMPETITIVE FACTOR MARKETS

In the case of monopsony, the price of an input no longer coincides with marginal factor cost. Therefore, the conditions for combining inputs must be modified. For example, when labor and capital are the variable inputs, the condition for minimizing the cost of a given output is

---

[7]This example is taken from Heady, Pesek, Brown, and Doll, same as 5, Table 14.8.

$$\frac{\text{MP}_l}{\text{MFC}_l} = \frac{\text{MP}_k}{\text{MFC}_k}$$

The requirement for maximizing profit can be expressed as

$$\frac{\text{MP}_l}{\text{MFC}_l} = \frac{\text{MP}_k}{\text{MFC}_k} = \frac{1}{\text{MR}}$$

THE MARGINAL PRODUCTIVITY THEORY OF INCOME DISTRIBUTION

The theory of factor pricing in competitive markets is called marginal productivity theory—to emphasize that the demand for a factor is based on its marginal product. However, this title is misleading in the sense that it gives top billing to demand. As you are aware, in competitive factor markets an input's price is determined by supply as well as demand. Marginal productivity theory tells firms how much labor to hire in order to maximize profits. Beyond that, it predicts how income will be distributed.

In competitive factor markets, profit maximization requires companies to hire labor up to the point where wage equals marginal revenue product. Because marginal productivity theory applies equally to nonlabor inputs, this proposition can be generalized: Each factor receives a payment equal to its marginal revenue product. Thus, according to the **marginal productivity theory of income distribution**, income payments are based on the contribution to revenue of the last unit of a factor hired. Inputs whose marginal contribution to revenue is high receive high incomes; those that contribute less are paid less. Although some find this conclusion reassuring, the marginal productivity theory of income distribution has been widely attacked. Two criticisms frequently are raised.

Marginal Productivity Theory of Income Distribution
The theory that income is distributed to factors of production according to each factor's marginal revenue product. In particular, the theory predicts that each input will be paid an amount equal to its marginal revenue product.

"The Distribution of Income Is Not Just"

Is it fair that some people live regally, simply because they inherited property? Should others be condemned to poverty because they were born without wealth and have few labor market skills? What about people unable to work because of their age or some physical or mental disability? Doesn't fundamental justice dictate that all individuals receive at least some minimal income regardless of how much they contribute to output?

Posing questions such as these, some critics attack marginal productivity theory because they don't like its conclusion about how income will be distributed. Some go so far as to say that this theory was created to rationalize the actual distribution of income in capitalistic societies. Such criticisms are invalid. Marginal productivity theory falls within the realm of positive economics. It predicts how income will be distributed but makes no claim that this distribution is best. One can accept marginal productivity theory without denying that the government has the legitimate right to alter the distribution of income through a system of taxes and transfers.

"Labor Markets Are Not Competitive"

Marginal productivity theory predicts how factor payments will be determined in *competitive* factor markets. Some contend that, as elegant as it may be, this theory is irrelevant because factor markets frequently are not competitive. In monopsonistic markets, workers are paid a wage less than their marginal revenue product. At the same time, through policies such as featherbedding, some unions can force companies to pay their members a wage in excess of marginal revenue product. Clearly then, the prediction of marginal productivity theory—that wages equal marginal revenue product—is not always correct. Those who see abundant imperfections in the labor market will be more dubious about the applicability of this theory than those who see the labor market as basically competitive.

Granted that marginal productivity theory does not explain perfectly the distribution of income, most economists believe that it does a pretty fair job—especially in the long run, when competitive forces are at their strongest. Although some embrace alternative models (e.g., Marxian economics),[8] most economists contend that marginal productivity theory provides the best framework currently available for explaining how factor incomes are determined.

This does not mean that noncompetitive forces should be ignored. Where appropriate, the competitive model should be modified. For example, in Chapter 31 we introduce discrimination into otherwise competitive labor markets. We analyze the impact of discrimination on pay and productivity and assess the extent to which pay differentials reflect differences in productivity and the extent to which they reflect traits unrelated to productivity. Our argument is not that competitive forces completely determine the distribution of income. It is that, in the opinion of most economists, one cannot satisfactorily explain factor payments without accounting for a factor's marginal productivity.

SUMMARY

1. According to marginal productivity theory, demand for a factor is based on that factor's marginal product. If the marginal product schedule increases or if output demand rises, demand for the factor increases.
2. To maximize profit a firm should hire labor, or any other factor, up to the point where marginal revenue product equals marginal factor cost.
3. In the case of monopsony there is only one buyer of labor. Therefore, that buyer can influence the price of labor. Compared to the case of perfect competition, monopsony leads both to lower employment and to lower wage rates.
4. Monopoly power in the product market has no effect on wage rates but does reduce employment. Because monopolists restrict industry output, they demand less labor.
5. In competitive labor markets the condition for profit maximization simplifies to MRP = W. Because of this, the marginal productivity theory of income distribution predicts that each factor will receive a payment equal to marginal revenue product. This theory makes no claim, however, that this distribution is just or somehow superior to alternative distributions of income.
6. If a firm hires multiple inputs, the total cost of producing a given output is minimized when the ratio of marginal product to marginal factor cost is the same for each input.
7. For a firm to maximize profit, the ratio of marginal product to marginal factor cost for each input should equal the reciprocal of the marginal revenue of output.

[8]This is discussed in Chapter 39.

KEY TERMS

monopsonist
marginal factor cost (MFC)
marginal revenue product (MRP)
substitute inputs
complementary inputs
marginal productivity theory
    of income distribution

STUDY QUESTIONS AND PROBLEMS

1. Draw the labor supply curve for (a) a firm in a perfectly competitive labor market and (b) a monopsonist. Why are the shapes different?
2. Explain how each of the following would affect demand for coal miners. Indicate whether the labor demand curve would increase, decrease, or remain unchanged.
   a. an increase in the demand for coal
   b. an increase in capital, when capital and labor are substitute inputs
   c. an increase in capital, when capital and labor are complementary inputs
   d. a decrease in the wage rate of coal miners
3. Assume nitrogen costs $.05 per pound and phosphorous costs $.10 per pound. Based on information in Table 30-2, what is the least costly way to produce 130 pounds of corn per acre?
4. Assume a company has no control over wage rates: it must pay $12 per hour for skilled labor and $9 per hour for unskilled labor. The marginal product of skilled labor is six and the marginal product of unskilled labor is three. Indicate whether the company is using the optimal input mix, relatively too much skilled labor (and not enough unskilled), or relatively too much unskilled labor (and not enough skilled). Explain how you reached your conclusion.
5. The Ace Card Company operates in perfectly competitive product and labor markets. It hires two types of workers—craftsmen and operatives. Currently, the marginal product of craftsmen is four and the marginal product of operatives is two. Output sells for $4 per unit.
   a. If the company must pay a wage rate of $16 for craftsmen and $8 for operatives, is the company hiring the profit-maximizing amounts of labor? (If not, should the company hire more or less of each?)
   b. Suppose the wage rate for craftsmen falls to $12 and the wage rate for operatives falls to $6. How should the company change the amounts of labor it uses?
   c. What can you conclude about the effect of lower input prices?
6. (a) Does the marginal productivity theory of income distribution claim that factor payments should be based on a factor's contribution to revenue? (b) If we agree that income should be based in part on need, must we reject marginal productivity theory as an explanation of how income is actually determined? Defend your answer.
7. *Bilateral monopoly* refers to the situation where a monopsonist bargains with a union. Here, there is only one buyer of labor, the company, and only one seller of labor, the union. In this setting, the union may be able to limit the ability of the monopsonist to depress wages and employment. That is, employment and wages may more closely approximate the perfectly competitive equilibrium if a monopsonist is restrained by a union. Present this argument in diagrammatic form. First show the labor market outcome for a monopsonist when the firm is not forced to negotiate with a union. Then indicate the union wage rate that would cause employment to rise to the level of a perfectly competitive labor market.

ANSWERS TO YOUR TURN

MONOPSONY

a.

Number of workers	MFC
1	$ 5
2	6
3	7
4	8
5	9
6	10

b. MRP = MFC = $7 when 3 workers are hired.
c. Wage = $6.00 (from the labor supply schedule).

ANSWERS TO YOUR TURN

WHEN A MONOPSONIST CONFRONTS A MINIMUM WAGE

a.

Number of workers	Wage
1	$6.50
2	6.50
3	6.50
4	6.50
5	7.00
6	7.50

b.

Number of workers	MFC
1	$ 6.50
2	6.50
3	6.50
4	6.50
5	9.00
6	10.00

c. MRP = MFC = $6.50 when 4 workers are hired.
d. Wage = $6.50.
e. The minimum wage causes the monopsonist to *increase* the level employment from 3 workers (when there was no minimum wage) to 4 workers.

ANSWERS TO YOUR TURN

MULTIPLE INPUTS
No. You should cut back on skilled *and* unskilled labor. The MRP of each type of labor is less than its wage—each is contributing less to revenue than it costs. $MRP_s = MP_s \times P = 3 \times \$2 = \$6 < P_s = \$9$. $MRP_u = 2 \times \$2 = \$4 < P_u = \$6$. (Alternatively, $MP_s/P_s = MP_u/P_u = 1/3 < 1/P = 1/2$.)

Women's secondary status is at least as striking in the labor market as it is everywhere else. Every standard labor market statistic shows marked differentials on the average between men and women, in both the level of economic participation and the distribution of economic rewards.[1]

DISCRIMINATION AND DIFFERENCES IN LABOR MARKET OUTCOMES

Last year in the United States about two-thirds of all adults were either working or looking for work. Not all groups fared equally. The unemployment rate of blacks was more than double the unemployment rate of whites. Among full-time employees, women earned almost $10,000 less than men.

Chapter 31 highlights differences in labor market success by race, ethnicity, and gender, and analyzes possible reasons for these differences. After defining certain essential terms, we assess the divergent trends in male and female labor supply. We then examine differences in pay and unemployment across groups.

---

[1]Cynthia B. Lloyd and Beth Niemi, *The Economics of Sex Differentials* (New York: Columbia University Press, 1979), p. 1.

LABOR FORCE PARTICIPATION

Measuring Labor Force Participation

Labor Force
Those individuals who have a job or are looking for one; the number of people employed or unemployed.

The **labor force** is comprised of all individuals who either have a job or are actively searching for one. Those with jobs are classified as *employed*. Those without jobs but looking for work are counted as *unemployed*. Thus, the labor force consists of all individuals who are either employed or unemployed. Excluded from the labor force are individuals not interested in working as well as those who are interested but, convinced that suitable employment is presently unavailable, are not currently searching for work. A country's population is comprised of two mutually exclusive groups: those in the labor force and those not in the labor force.[2] The preceding relationships are illustrated in Figure 31-1 for the population 16 and older.

Labor Force Participation Rate
$$\frac{\text{labor force}}{\text{population}} \times 100$$

One measure of a country's labor supply is its **labor force participation rate**—the percentage of the population that is in the labor force. Based on the numbers in Figure 31-1, the 1988 labor force participation rate for the United States can be computed as follows:

$$\frac{121.669 \text{ million}}{184.613 \text{ million}} \times 100 = 65.9 \text{ percent}$$

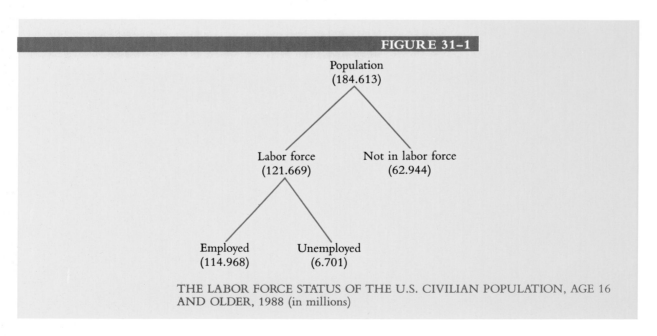

FIGURE 31–1

Population
(184.613)

Labor force
(121.669)

Not in labor force
(62.944)

Employed
(114.968)

Unemployed
(6.701)

THE LABOR FORCE STATUS OF THE U.S. CIVILIAN POPULATION, AGE 16 AND OLDER, 1988 (in millions)

---

[2]Actually, there are two population and labor force series—one limited to civilians, the other including members of the armed forces. The numbers presented here refer to the more widely used civilian series.

			TABLE 31-1		

LABOR FORCE PARTICIPATION RATES, 1900–1980*

Year	Males	Males, aged 65 and older	Females	Married females
1900	85.7	63.1	20.0	5.6
1920	84.6	55.6	22.7	9.0
1930	82.1	54.0	23.6	11.7
1940	79.1	41.8	25.8	15.6
1950	81.6	41.4	29.9	23.0
1960	80.4	30.5	35.7	31.7
1970	76.6	24.8	41.4	40.2
1980	75.1	19.3	49.9	49.3

*Data for 1950 and later refer to the population 16 and older; earlier figures refer to 14 and older.

Sources: U.S. Bureau of the Census, *Historical Statistics of the United States, Colonial Times to 1970* (1975); *1980 Census of the Population, General Social and Economic Characteristics, United States Summary* (1983).

Labor Force Participation by Gender

In addition to this country's aggregate labor force participation rate, the United States Department of Labor also publishes separate labor force participation series by gender. Females have a lower labor force participation rate than males, but this difference has been narrowing over time (see Table 31-1 and Figure 31-2). Labor force participation of males fell from 86 percent in 1900 to 75 percent in 1980. This primarily reflects the fact that men have been retiring earlier and living longer. Thus, the share of the male population 65 and older has risen over time and the labor force participation rate of this group, which was already low, has dropped sharply. Both effects have depressed the overall labor force participation rate of men.

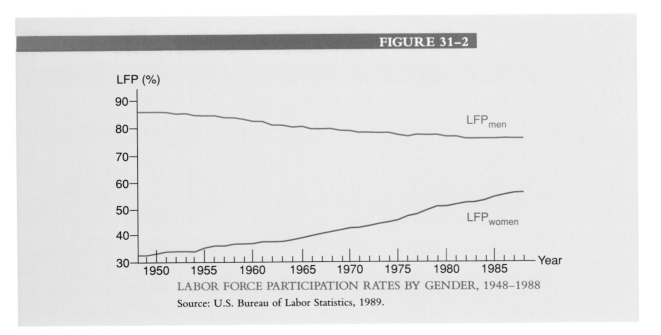

	FIGURE 31–2

LABOR FORCE PARTICIPATION RATES BY GENDER, 1948–1988

Source: U.S. Bureau of Labor Statistics, 1989.

Labor force participation of women has moved in the opposite direction. At the turn of the century, only one in five women was in the labor force. By 1980, the figure was one in two, and today a clear majority of women are either working or looking for work. Although labor force participation has increased for all groups of women, the fastest growth has been among married women.

This explosion in the labor supply of women has occurred worldwide, not just in the United States (see Table 31-2). It has accelerated economic growth and increased our standard of living. Many consider it to be "the most revolutionary change taking place in the labor market."[3]

Why Has Female Participation Increased?

Researchers have studied this phenomenon extensively and offered various explanations for it. Among the most frequently cited factors are lower birth rates, higher wages, the emergence of labor-saving devices, an improving job distribution, and a change in attitudes.[4]

The U.S. birthrate (births per population) has fallen throughout most of this century, especially over the past 40 years. According to a companion statistic, the *fertility rate,* the estimated births per female declined from 3.5 in the 1950s to 1.8 in the 1980s. Children, especially young children, inhibit labor force participation of women. Therefore, the reduction in number of children has opened the door for women to spend more time in the labor force.

The decision to work also depends on the compensation one receives. Research strongly indicates that higher wages attract additional women into the labor market.

	TABLE 31-2			
LABOR FORCE PARTICIPATION OF WOMEN BY COUNTRY				
	All women		**Married women**	
Country	**1960**	**1980**	**1960**	**1980**
Australia	29.5	55.4	19.2	50.8
Britain	43.4	62.3	33.7	57.2
France	44.5	57.0	35.6	52.6
Germany	46.5	56.2	36.5	54.4
Israel	29.0	39.2	25.7	43.5
Italy	35.2	39.9	18.5	35.4
Japan	47.7	52.7	36.0	41.9
Spain	22.7	33.2	N/A	26.0
Sweden	51.0	76.9	43.1	75.6
USSR	77.4	88.2	N/A	N/A

N/A = not available.

Source: Jacob Mincer, "Intercountry Comparison of Labor Force Trends and of Related Developments," *Journal of Labor Economics* (Chicago: University of Chicago Press, January 1985, Supplement), Table 1. Reprinted by permission.

[3]Ronald Ehrenberg and Robert Smith, *Modern Labor Economics,* 3rd ed. (Glenview, IL: Scott, Foresman, 1988), p. 168.
[4]These explanations are not totally independent. As wages of women have increased over time, the opportunity cost of withdrawing from the labor force to raise a family has increased. Therefore, higher wages have contributed to the decline in the birthrate.

Over the past 40 years wages of women have been rising an average of 1.5 percent per year above and beyond the inflation rate. Responding to this growing compensation, more and more women are entering the job market and staying. According to two experts, the increased wages of women combined with their reduced fertility explain nearly 60 percent of the growth in female labor force participation since 1950.[5]

Other factors are also important, but their contributions are difficult to quantify. Attitudes concerning women in the workplace have progressed and job opportunities have improved. Some researchers emphasize the emergence of a large clerical sector early this century and, more recently, the rapid growth in service, retail trade, and other traditionally female jobs. Part-time employment has increased relative to full-time employment, making it easier for women to both work and meet other commitments. Microwaves, dishwashers, and other modern appliances allow work at home to be accomplished more quickly. Families also save time by eating out more frequently and making greater use of dry cleaning, daycare, and other services. The result is more time available for market work.

In summary, a rising wage has increased the incentive to work, while factors such as reduced fertility, time-saving innovations, and increased availability of part-time work have provided women with greater opportunities to work. The result has been a tendency to substitute work in the labor market for work at home. Because work at home is not counted as labor force activity, the switch from home to market has corresponded to an increase in the labor force participation of women.

YOUR TURN

LABOR FORCE PARTICIPATION
How would each of the following affect labor force participation?
a. increasing the fertility rate
b. reducing the cost of working through subsidized daycare
c. postponing eligibility for social security retirement benefits (e.g., from age 62 to age 67)
d. increasing the wages of women
e. redefining the labor force to include unpaid homemakers

THE MALE/FEMALE PAY GAP

> The Lord spoke to Moses and said, Speak to the Israelites in these words: When a man makes a special vow to the Lord which requires your valuation of living persons, a male between twenty and sixty years old shall be valued at fifty silver shekels. . . . If it is a female, she shall be valued at thirty shekels.[6]
>
> —Leviticus 27:1–4

Pay Gap
The difference in pay between two groups, traditionally specified in percentage terms.

Since the time of Moses, the economic plight of women has been inferior to that of men. One reason women tend to earn less than men is that they are more likely to work part-time or part-year. But even if we restrict ourselves to full-time year-round workers, annual data indicate that women are paid roughly 60 percent as much as men. That is, they experience a 40 percent **pay gap**. According to data on weekly earnings, the pay gap is smaller but only slightly [see Table 31-3, page 706, columns

---

[5]James P. Smith and Michael P. Ward, "Time-Series Growth in the Female Labor Force," *Journal of Labor Economics* (January 1985, Supplement), p. 89.
[6]The full passage indicates that the higher "valuation" of males is based on their greater ability to pay (wages).

	TABLE 31-3		

FEMALE EARNINGS AS A PERCENTAGE OF MALE
EARNINGS, FULL-TIME EMPLOYEES

Year	(a) Annual earnings	(b) Weekly earnings	(c) Hourly earnings
1939	58.1	N/A	N/A
1960	60.8	N/A	N/A
1965	60.0	N/A	N/A
1967	57.8	62.4	68.8
1970	59.4	62.3	68.7
1975	58.8	62.0	67.7
1980	60.2	63.4	69.1
1981	59.2	64.6	70.4
1982	61.7	65.0	70.7
1983	63.6	65.6	71.3
1984	63.7	67.8	74.0
1985	64.6	68.2	74.2
1986	64.3	69.2	75.3
1987	65.0	70.0	76.3
1988	N/A	70.2	76.7

N/A = not available.

Sources: Median annual earnings of year-round full-time employees are from the U.S. Bureau of
Census; median weekly earnings of full-time employees are from the U.S. Bureau of Labor Statistics.
Hourly earnings are computed by dividing the weekly earnings of full-time workers by their average
weekly hours.

(a) and (b)]. The lower earnings of women depress their labor force participation,
increase poverty among female-headed families, and raise concerns about equity.
These pay differences demand an explanation.

After tackling the pay-gap issue, we analyze the data in Table 31-3, which
suggest that the relative earnings of women have improved since the mid-1970s. Is
this upturn transitory, or is it a sign of real progress by women?

Why Do Women Earn Less than Men?

Hours Worked   One reason women earn less than men is that they work fewer
hours. Within the class of full-time employees—defined by the U.S. Department of
Labor as those working 35 or more hours per week—men typically work an extra
3 1/2 to 4 hours per week. For example, in 1988, male full-time employees averaged
45.1 hours per week compared to 41.3 hours for female full-time employees. Part of
the higher weekly pay of men is compensation for extra hours of work. In particular,
for every additional $100 earned by a male, roughly $20 is payment for the extra
hours worked. When measured on an hourly basis, the earnings of women move
closer to the earnings of men [see Table 31-3, column (c)].

Human Capital   Because of their higher labor force participation, men tend to have
more years of experience than women. Not only do they have more total experience,
they generally have greater experience on their present job. The typical man has
spent five years with his current employer, the typical woman three years.
Furthermore, on average men have completed twice as much job training as

women.[7] Men also have slightly higher educational attainment. In 1987, 23.6 percent of men 25 and older had completed at least four years of college compared to 16.5 percent of women.

According to the theory of human capital, a worker's productivity and therefore earnings depend on the worker's human capital. Men, by virtue of their greater human capital, earn more than women. One commonly cited study found that differences in education, training, and other work history accounted for 40 percent of the pay gap between white men and women.[8] Other studies put the figure slightly lower. Altogether, differences in human capital and in hours worked appear to explain about 50 percent of the male/female pay gap.

Occupation and Level of Work   As Table 31-4 reflects, men and women are distributed unevenly across jobs. Women account for 98 percent of all dental hygienists but only 9 percent of all dentists. They comprise 85 percent of the elementary school teachers but less than 39 percent of college faculty. About 99 percent of secretaries are women, but only 1 percent of automobile mechanics. The uneven job distribution is important because women tend to be concentrated in low-paying jobs, men in high-paying jobs.

TABLE 31-4

PERCENTAGE OF FEMALE WORKERS, 1988
(selected occupations)

Occupation	Percent female
Secretaries	99.1
Dental hygienists	97.6
Childcare workers	97.3
Receptionists	97.1
Household cleaners and servants	95.6
Registered nurses	94.6
Dressmakers	94.4
Bank tellers	91.0
Telephone operators	89.8
Elementary school teachers	84.8
College and university teachers	38.5
Physicians	20.0
Dentists	9.3
Engineers	7.3
Airplane pilots and navigators	3.1
Tool and die makers	2.4
Heavy-truck drivers	2.3
Firefighters	2.1
Carpenters	1.5
Automobile mechanics	0.7
Loggers	0.5
Plumbers	0.4

Source: U.S. Bureau of Labor Statistics, *Employment and Earnings* (January 1989), pp. 183–88.

[7]Greg J. Duncan and Saul Hoffman, "On-the-Job Training and Earnings Differences by Race and Sex," *Review of Economics and Statistics* (November 1979), pp. 594–603.
[8]Mary Corcoran and Greg J. Duncan, "Work History, Labor Force Attachment, and Earnings Differences between Races and Sexes," *Journal of Human Resources* (Winter 1979), pp. 3–20.

Not only is this true for broad occupational categories, it also holds for detailed classifications within an occupation. When accounting work is broken down into five levels, data indicate that 46 percent of entry-level accountants are women but only 5 percent of senior accountants (see Table 31-5). Similarly, women are largely concentrated at the bottom rungs of the attorney, personnel, and drafting positions. Even though *at each level* women earn 90–103 percent as much as men, within the broader occupational categories they earn substantially less—due to their unfavorable distribution within each occupation. A good part of the lower earnings of women can be attributed to the fact that women are concentrated in the low-paying occupations and, within a given occupation, in the lower positions.

This *explanation* is incomplete, however, since it begs the question of why women generally hold inferior jobs. On that topic a debate rages: to what extent is the different job distribution of men and women due to discrimination, and to what extent does it reflect nondiscriminatory factors, such as differences in preferences?

Even in a world without labor market discrimination, the distribution of jobs would differ. To begin with, culture and socialization each play a role. Surveys indicate that women place less emphasis on monetary rewards than do men and are more interested in nurturing and helping others. Consistent with these preferences,

TABLE 31-5

THE DISTRIBUTION OF WOMEN WITHIN FOUR OCCUPATIONAL CATEGORIES, 1981

Occupation and level	Average monthly salary	Female pay as a percent of male pay	Female percent of workers
Accountant I	$1377	99	46
Accountant II	1679	98	34
Accountant III	1962	96	19
Accountant IV	2402	95	11
Accountant V	2928	90	5
All accountants		83	23
Attorney I	1873	103	28
Attorney II	2338	99	24
Attorney III	3031	95	13
Attorney IV	3738	94	9
All attorneys		78	15
Personnel I*	2321	101	21
Personnel II*	2933	94	10
Personnel III*	3574	90	7
All personnel		87	13
Drafter I	923	103	34
Drafter II	1075	101	26
Drafter III	1301	96	18
Drafter IV	1611	94	8
All drafters		82	13

*Director of personnel.

Source: Adapted from Mark S. Sieling, "Staffing Patterns Prominent in Female–Male Earnings Gap," *Monthly Labor Review* (June 1984), pp. 29–33.

women are more likely to be in such fields as health care, social work, and primary education.[9]

Job choice is also influenced by family responsibilities, which have been shouldered disproportionately by women. Because of such responsibilities, women are more likely than men to place restrictions on hours of work and to limit themselves to jobs that are close to home. They are also less likely to relocate. Such restrictions limit the choice of jobs.[10]

Finally, according to human capital theory, women choose different jobs than men because of differences in their expected work lives. Individuals expecting to work a relatively short time find it unprofitable to incur the heavy investments necessary to enter certain occupations (for example, medicine, law, higher education). Instead, they choose occupations requiring less human capital. Similarly, those expecting to withdraw temporarily from the labor force have an incentive to avoid areas (such as engineering and the physical sciences) where one's skills quickly deteriorate upon withdrawal from the labor force. Rather, they gravitate toward fields subject to less obsolescence (for example, the fine arts and humanities).

Because women, on average, have shorter work lives than men and a greater tendency to withdraw from the labor force,[11] they choose different occupations than men—generally those requring less human capital and having lower rates of obsolescence. Consistent with this view, studies show that occupational choice does depend on one's expected work life.[12] Taking this argument a step further, to the extent women have less human capital within a given occupation, they are more likely to be in the lower-level positions within that occupation. Thus, human capital theory offers an explanation for the inferior job distribution of women.

A competing school of thought argues that human capital is less important than discrimination in explaining occupational distribution. First of all, differences in human capital may themselves result from discrimination. For example, employers may train men for a certain position, but not women. Beyond that, doors are sometimes shut to women regardless of their human capital. Until 1967, when it was sued, Southern Bell Telephone Company had not permitted any woman to work as a switchman. Instead, women had been assigned to lower-paying occupations, such as telephone operator. Similarly, some banks have traditionally hired men and women for different jobs. A woman may be hired as a teller, whereas a man with similar education and experience is hired as a loan officer.

Other positions have requirements—often of questionable validity—that all applicants must be a certain minimum height or be able to lift a minimum weight. Because women are less likely to meet these requirements, many find their paths into

[9]Thomas N. Daymont and Paul J. Andrisani, "Why Women Earn Less Than Men: The Case of Recent College Graduates," *Industrial Relations Research Association, Proceedings of the Thirty-Fifth Annual Meeting* (1983), pp. 429–430.

[10]Beth Niemi, "Geographic Immobility and Labor Force Mobility: A Study of Female Unemployment," in Cynthia B. Lloyd, ed., *Sex, Discrimination, and the Division of Labor* (New York: Columbia University Press, 1975), pp. 61–89.

[11]In 1950, the expected work life (number of years in the labor force) was 15 years for young women and 41 years for young men. By 1980, the difference had narrowed, but young men still could be expected to work 10 more years than young women (37 years versus 27). See Shirley Smith, "Revised Worklife Tables," *Monthly Labor Review* (August 1985), Table 3.

[12]Solomon Polachek, "Occupational Self-Selection: A Human Capital Approach to Sex Differences in Occupational Structure," *Review of Economics and Statistics* (February 1981), pp. 60–69; Arthur E. Blakemore and Stuart A. Low, "Sex Differences in Occupational Self-Selection: The Case of College Majors," *Review of Economics and Statistics* (February 1984), pp. 157–163.

Theory of Occupational Crowding
A theory that the lower wages of women (or minority workers) result from their being denied entrance into certain high-paying occupations and, instead, their being crowded into other occupations, thereby depressing wages in those occupations.

Comparable Worth
A doctrine that each job has an intrinsic value, independent of labor supply and demand, and that jobs with similar intrinsic values have similar (comparable) worth.

these occupations blocked. To the extent women are denied access to certain higher-paying occupations, their job distribution is neither voluntary nor consistent with maximum earnings.

According to the **theory of occupational crowding,**[13] women are crowded into certain occupations, resulting in low wages there (see Figure 31-3a). In contrast, restricting the supply of labor into male-intensive occupations leads to high wages in those occupations (see Figure 31-3b). From an economic perspective, the optimal means of ending this type of discrimination is to break down barriers to entry, ensuring that women have the same access to jobs as do men. Some groups, however, advocate a different approach, **comparable worth,** which would force companies to raise wages in female-intensive occupations, regardless of labor supply and demand (see Exhibit 31-1).

In addition to the discrimination of employers, women may be underrepresented in certain jobs because of the prejudices of employees or customers. According to the theory of **employee discrimination,** if males prefer working with or being supervised by other males, they will demand additional compensation if females are hired. To avoid the added costs of men and women working together, employers will maintain work forces segregated by gender.[14] **Customer discrimination** arises when consumers are not indifferent about who supplies a service. If

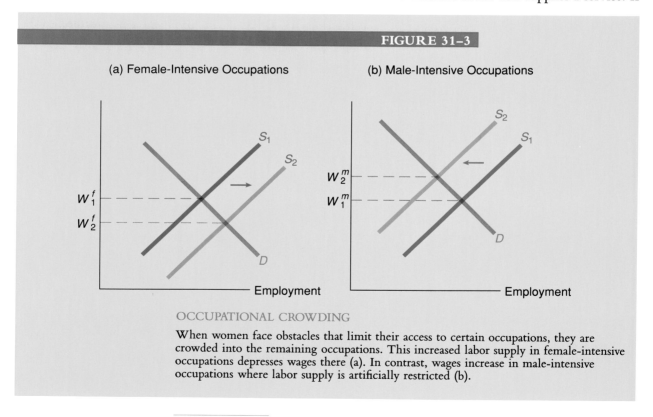

FIGURE 31-3

OCCUPATIONAL CROWDING

When women face obstacles that limit their access to certain occupations, they are crowded into the remaining occupations. This increased labor supply in female-intensive occupations depresses wages there (a). In contrast, wages increase in male-intensive occupations where labor supply is artificially restricted (b).

[13]Barbara Bergmann, "Occupational Segregation, Wages and Profits When Employers Discriminate by Race or Sex," *Eastern Economic Journal* (April/July 1974), pp. 103–110.
[14]See Gary Becker, *The Economics of Discrimination* (Chicago: University of Chicago Press, 1957). Although the evidence is limited, one study of young workers finds no sign of employee discrimination against women. See James Ragan and Carol Tremblay, "Testing for Employee Discrimination by Race and Sex," *Journal of Human Resources* (Winter 1988), pp. 123–137.

EXHIBIT 31-1

COMPARABLE WORTH

Jobs dominated by women pay less than jobs dominated by men. To some this is evidence that women's work is undervalued. The solution they propose is equal pay for *comparable worth*. Under such a system, jobs are evaluated in terms of such characteristics as skills, responsibility, mental demands, and working conditions. The number of points assigned to each category is then summed to determine a job's total score or evaluation. If librarians received the same score as electricians, their pay would be raised to equal that of electricians. Since most librarians are women and most electricians men, the net effect would be to narrow pay differences by gender. Recently, a number of city and state governments have switched to such point systems, and a major push is now under way to extend the comparable worth approach to other sectors of the economy, both government and private.

Opponents of comparable worth cite various criticisms. First, the approach is subjective. The characteristics chosen to evaluate jobs and the weights assigned to each are arbitrary. Beyond that, there is no objective way to compare these characteristics across jobs. Second, the comparable worth approach assumes there is an intrinsic value for each job, independent of market forces. The value of a librarian is assumed to be the same regardless of the number of librarians and regardless of society's demand for librarians. Because wages are set independently of labor supply and demand, the result will be too many people in some occupations and not enough in others. Having the wrong mix of workers will reduce the value of the country's output and lower the standard of living.

By changing the structure of wages across occupations, comparable worth sends the wrong signal to women. In recent years women have made great strides in penetrating many previously male-dominated fields. Between 1972 and 1988, the percentage of lawyers and judges who are women increased from 3.8 percent to 19.5 percent, the percentage of engineers from 0.8 percent to 7.3 percent, the percentage of police and detectives from 2.6 percent to 13.4 percent, and the percentage of pharmacists from 12.7 percent to 31.9 percent. If the relative pay of librarians, secretaries, and other female-intensive occupations increases, the incentive for women to enter traditionally male occupations will be blunted. Occupational segregation will persist.

Finally, an increase in the pay of female-intensive jobs will cause employers to reduce employment there. Because most of the workers in these jobs are female, the brunt of the disemployment will be borne by females. Thus, a policy designed to help women will make many worse off.

Taking a different view, supporters of comparable worth contend that market forces are already constrained by unions, minimum wage laws, and various institutional forces. Given existing market imperfections, they argue that the economy can accommodate the comparable worth system without drastic consequences. They also criticize market wages for failing to accurately measure a worker's value. Because of discrimination, workers (women) may be paid less than they contribute to output. Finally, some stress equity or fairness over efficiency. Even if comparable worth does create problems and reduce the value of output, they are willing to pay that price to create greater equality of pay by gender.

Ultimately, one's assessment of comparable worth depends on how much confidence one has in market forces and on how much weight one assigns to nonmarket considerations, such as equity. Most economists are critical of comparable worth, but many women's groups and unions embrace the concept.

YOUR TURN   OCCUPATIONAL DISTRIBUTION

Some states have enacted laws that "protect" women by keeping them out of jobs deemed "too strenuous" or "too dangerous." How are such laws likely to affect the earnings of women? Why?

Employee Discrimination
A preference of employees to work with members of the same group (e.g., other males) and to avoid contact with different workers (e.g., women).

Customer Discrimination
A preference of consumers to be served by members of a particular group (e.g., males).

consumers prefer male surgeons, male auto mechanics, and male pilots, women entering such occupations can expect less business and lower pay. In turn, women will be less likely to choose such lines of work.

To summarize, the occupational distribution of men and women is likely to differ both because of voluntary choice (e.g., due to differences in expected work lives) and because of discrimination. Unfortunately, research to date does not permit us to estimate with any confidence the relative importance of these competing explanations. Although occupational differences contribute substantially to male/female differences in pay, debate continues on why such differences exist.

Discrimination Within an Occupation   Not only may discrimination lead to an uneven distribution of jobs among men and women, it may also result in lower pay for women *within a given occupation*. On this issue, the evidence is mixed. Within a given company, women doing the same job as men almost invariably receive the same pay. Indeed, the **Equal Pay Act of 1963** requires a company to establish "equal pay for equal work."

On the other hand, there is evidence that compared to women in the same occupation, men are more likely to find employment in the higher-paying companies.[15] Again, the question is why. One view is that the higher-paying employers can have their pick of employees and, preferring men to women, they discriminate against women. Alternatively, it may be that men are disproportionately concentrated in higher-paying companies because they have more human capital than women and companies that pay the highest wages demand the most productive employees. There seems to be merit in both arguments.

Where does this leave us? Among full-time employees, women earn approximately 30 percent less per week than men. About one-half of this difference (15 percent of the 30 percent) apparently reflects differences in human capital and in hours worked. The other one-half is due largely to the fact that women are concentrated in low-paying occupations and, within an occupation, tend to work for low-paying companies. This inferior job distribution of women reflects both discrimination and differences in human capital, the contribution of each being difficult to measure.

Is the Pay Gap Narrowing?

Whether measured on an annual, weekly, or hourly basis, since the mid-1970s the pay of women has increased faster than the pay of men. For example, weekly earnings of women as a percentage of men's earnings increased from 62 percent to a record 70 percent. Will these gains be maintained or will they turn out to be transitory? Although only time will tell, three recent studies suggest that the higher relative pay of women is here to stay and that continued advances are likely in the future.[16]

These predictions are based on changes in the relative human capital of men and women. From 1950 through the early 1970s, educational attainment of female

---

[15]Francine D. Blau, *Equal Pay in the Office* (Lexington, MA: Heath and Co., 1977).
[16]James P. Smith and Michael P. Ward, *Women's Wages and Work in the Twentieth Century* (Santa Monica: The Rand Corporation, 1984); June O'Neill, "The Trend in the Male–Female Wage Gap in the United States," *Journal of Labor Economics* (January 1985, Supplement), pp. 91–116; Francine D. Blau, "Occupations and Earnings of Women Workers," in Karen S. Koziara, et al., eds., *Working Women: Past, Present, Future* (Washington, DC: Bureau of National Affairs, 1987), pp. 37–68.

workers relative to male workers declined. Moreover, most of the increased labor force participation of women resulted from the entry of young and inexperienced workers into the labor force. That is, the share of employed females with limited work experience increased. As a result, there was no increase in the average human capital of female workers relative to male workers.

More recently, the percentage of female employees with college degrees and the percentage with extensive experience have both increased. As differences in the human capital of men and women have narrowed, relative earnings of women have improved. The human capital gains of women are expected to continue and, if they do, further contraction of the male/female pay gap can be anticipated. According to one study:

> By the year 2000 a 40-year-old working woman will have 5.2 more years of work experience than her counterpart had in 1980. As a result . . . wages of working women will rise at least 15 percent faster than those of men [over this period.][17]

INCOME DIFFERENCES BY RACE

Earnings vary by race as well as gender. Among year-round full-time workers, black and other nonwhite males earn approximately 25 percent less than white males; nonwhite females earn nearly 10 percent less than white females.

Many of the explanations cited for the lower pay of females also apply to our discussion of racial differences. For example, nonwhites generally have less human capital than whites. Among blacks—the largest racial minority in the United States—only 11 percent of those 25 and older have college degrees compared to 21 percent of whites. Moreover, there is evidence, at least among older workers, that blacks have often received an inferior education. Since the returns to education depend on the quality of education as well as on the quantity, blacks have been at a double disadvantage.

Blacks are six years younger on average than whites, and black males have a considerably lower rate of labor force participation than white males. For such reasons, blacks have less job experience than whites. They also have less job training. According to numerous studies, the lower human capital of blacks (as measured by education, experience, and training) accounts for most of their lower earnings.

The inferior job distribution of blacks also plays a role—blacks are concentrated in low-paying jobs. As with women, this appears to reflect both lower levels of human capital and discrimination. Some researchers also stress

> the enormous prelabor market disadvantage of blacks—the burden of coming from families and neighborhoods of low socioeconomic conditions which fail to provide the background resources [such as reading materials] that facilitate economic success.[18]

Although nonwhites continue to earn less than whites, their relative position has generally improved, despite occasional backtracking (see Figure 31-4, page 714). From 1955 through 1965, nonwhite males (in year-round full-time jobs) earned between 58 and 66 percent as much as white males. Beginning in 1975, the income ratio of nonwhite to white males has ranged from 72 to 79 percent. The gains of nonwhite women have been even more dramatic. In 1955, they earned just over half

[17]Smith and Ward, same as 16.
[18]Richard Freeman, "Black Economic Progress after 1964: Who Has Gained and Why?" in Sherwin Rosen, ed., *Studies in Labor Markets* (Chicago: University of Chicago Press, 1981), p. 283.

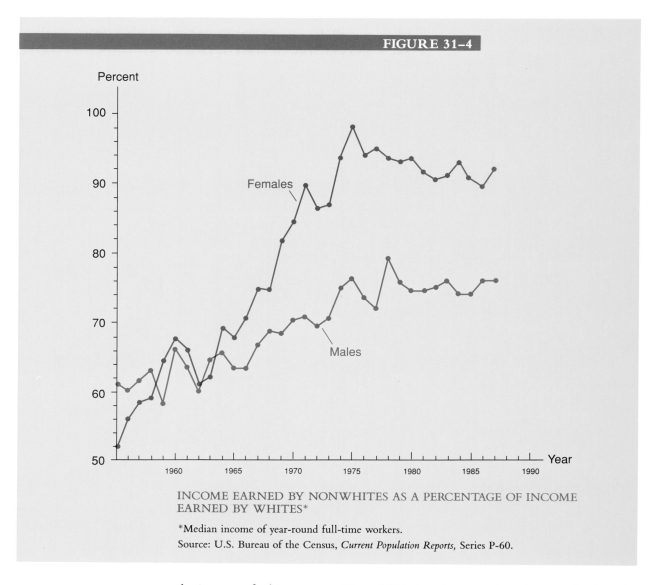

INCOME EARNED BY NONWHITES AS A PERCENTAGE OF INCOME EARNED BY WHITES*

*Median income of year-round full-time workers.

Source: U.S. Bureau of the Census, *Current Population Reports,* Series P-60.

the income of white women. Since 1974, they have consistently earned at least 90 percent as much as white women.

These advances have not occurred evenly across age groups. The relative income of older blacks has improved very little. The bulk of the gains have accrued to young blacks, especially those with substantial education. Since the late 1960s, the starting salaries of recent college graduates have been the same for blacks as for whites.[19] In other words, young blacks are getting off to a better start vis-à-vis whites than their parents did. If this success can be maintained, then as today's young blacks age and as their parents retire, the overall ratio of black income to white income is likely to climb even higher. However, before we can predict the future, we must first understand the past. Why has the income of black workers been rising faster than the income of white workers?

---

[19]Same as 18, p. 254.

Explaining the Increased Relative Income of Blacks

A major factor contributing to the income gains of blacks has been their overall increase in education. In 1960, median educational attainment of whites was three years greater than the educational attainment of blacks. Today whites enjoy an advantage of less than one year. As suggested earlier, advances have also been made in terms of quality of education. The practice of teaching blacks in segregated, largely underfunded schools is no longer as common.

Blacks have also benefited from increased government intervention in labor markets. In the 1960s, Congress enacted legislation outlawing racial discrimination and President Johnson signed an executive order calling for contractors to increase their hiring of minorities or risk losing government contracts (see Exhibit 31-2).

EXHIBIT 31-2

ANTIDISCRIMINATION LAWS AND AFFIRMATIVE ACTION

Three of the government's main weapons against discrimination are the *Equal Pay Act,* the *Civil Rights Act,* and *Executive Order 11246.* The Equal Pay Act of 1963 mandates "equal pay for equal work." While accepting pay differences based on skill, effort, responsibility, and working conditions, the law prohibits pay discrimination based on such factors as a worker's race or gender. Unfortunately, this law has not been especially effective. An employer can sidestep the equal-pay provisions by assigning blacks and whites to different jobs or by not hiring blacks at all. Unless blacks and whites perform the same job, the Equal Pay Act does not apply.

The **Civil Rights Act of 1964** is broader in scope and therefore more effective, banning discrimination in terms of both pay and employment. In particular, **title VII** makes it illegal

> to refuse to hire or to discharge any individual, or otherwise to discriminate against any individual with respect to his compensation, terms, conditions, or privileges of employment, because of such individual's race, color, religion, sex, or national origin.

Following a 1972 amendment—which strengthened the law and extended its coverage—the Civil Rights Act applies to private employers with 15 or more workers, unions with 15 or more members, employment agencies, nonreligious educational institutions, and state and local governments.

The *Equal Employment Opportunity Commission (EEOC)* administers both the Equal Pay Act and the Civil Rights Act. Although responsible for enforcement of these laws, its powers are limited. The Commission cannot issue cease-and-desist orders, fine employers, or require that workers

fired as the result of discrimination be reinstated. The EEOC typically seeks voluntary compliance and, if that fails, encourages individuals to file lawsuits. Until the Reagan presidency, it also emphasized class-action lawsuits against companies it believed to have exhibited a pattern of discrimination. Both AT&T and General Motors signed out-of-court settlements with the EEOC, each calling for the particular company to spend more than $40 million to hire, train, and promote women and minorities and, in the case of AT&T, to provide back pay for the injured parties.

In 1965, President Johnson signed Executive Order 11246, establishing the Office of Federal Contract Compliance Programs. This order requires all but the smallest companies doing business with the federal government to refrain from discrimination against women and minorities. Beyond that, these employers must statistically analyze their work forces and identify any areas where women or minorities are underrepresented. If significant underrepresentation does occur, the employer must file an **affirmative action** plan that sets forth specific goals and timetables for increasing the employment of women or minorities. Companies that do not file affirmative action plans or fail to meet their timetables can lose current government contracts and be barred from bidding on future contracts. At present, close to 30 million workers are covered by this executive order.

Affirmative Action
A policy designed to increase the representation of women or minorities (e.g., to increase their relative employment).

"We don't disciminate on the basis of age, sex, religion, color or national orgin—we just don't hire Scorpios."

Source: From *The Wall Street Journal*—permission, Cartoon Features Syndicate.

Several studies provide evidence that these actions had a direct bearing on the economic progress of blacks.[20]

Although progress has occurred, there is evidence that some of the reported advances are illusory. That is, blacks have not benefited nearly as much as statistics (such as those portrayed in Figure 31-4) suggest. During most of the period when the relative income of black workers was improving, labor force participation of blacks declined, both in absolute terms and relative to the labor force participation of whites. The blacks dropping out of the labor force were predominately those with low skills and therefore low earnings. Had they remained in the labor force, the average income among black workers would have been lower. In other words, part of the reported increase in relative income of black workers is artificial, reflecting the fact that fewer low-skilled blacks are now included in the income statistics. Accordingly, statistics on the average income of black workers overstate the economic progress of blacks. On the other hand, there is evidence that more than one-half of the reported gains are real.[21] Advances in education and a reduction in discrimination have led to an unambiguous improvement in the relative income of blacks.

PAY DIFFERENCES BY ETHNICITY

Recently, as more and better data have become available, economists have begun studying pay differences by ethnicity. A general theme of this research is that education explains a good portion of these differences in pay. On average, the lower a group's educational attainment the lower its earnings (see Table 31-6). This is true

---

[20]Same as 18, pp. 269–283; Jonathan Leonard, "The Impact of Affirmative Action on Employment," *Journal of Labor Economics* (October 1984), pp. 439–463.

[21]Charles Brown, "Black–White Earnings Ratios Since the Civil Rights Act of 1964: The Importance of Labor Market Dropouts," *Quarterly Journal of Economics* (February 1984), pp. 31–44.

TABLE 31-6

RELATIVE PAY AND EDUCATION OF VARIOUS
ETHNIC GROUPS (males only)

Ethnic group	Pay as a percent of pay received by whites	Years of education as a percent of education of whites
Hispanic		
Mexican	72	76
Puerto Rican	76	79
Cuban	89	91
Cental and South American	83	95
Other Hispanic	87	89
Asian origin		
Filipino	74	95
Chinese	108	110
Japanese	106	107

Sources: Adapted from Cordelia Reimers, "Labor Market Discrimination Against Hispanic and Black Men," *Review of Economics and Statistics* (November 1983), Table 1; Barry Chiswick, "An Analysis of the Earnings and Employment of Asian-American Men," *Journal of Labor Economics* (April 1983), Table 1.

not only for broadly defined ethnic groups, such as Hispanics, but also for various subgroups. For example, Mexican Americans generally have less education than Cuban Americans and earn correspondingly lower wages. Some groups—including Japanese, Chinese, and Jewish Americans—have more education than whites in general and earn higher salaries. This suggests that the inhibiting effects of discrimination can sometimes be offset through heavy investment in human capital.

Earnings also vary with fluency in English and, for immigrants, with length of time in the United States and place of education. The U.S. labor market places a lower value on foreign schooling, either because it is of a lower quality or because some of what is learned in other countries is not relevant in the United States. Similarly, those with language deficiencies are at a disadvantage compared to other immigrants and to native Americans.[22]

THE STRUCTURE OF UNEMPLOYMENT

Unemployment Rate
Percentage of the labor force unemployed:
$$\frac{\text{unemployment}}{\text{labor force}} \times 100$$

Another measure of labor market success, besides earnings, is the **unemployment rate**—the percentage of the labor force that is unemployed. As Table 31-7 indicates, unemployment is distributed unevenly across groups. The unemployment rate of blacks is more than double the unemployment rate of whites and about 40 percent higher than the unemployment rate of Hispanics. More subtle differences in unemployment exist by gender, with women usually but not always experiencing a higher unemployment rate than men.

Some of the same factors contributing to differences in earnings also influence the structure of unemployment. Unemployment varies inversely with human

[22]Geoffrey Carliner, "Wages, Earnings, and Hours of First, Second, and Third Generation American Males," *Economic Inquiry* (January 1980), pp. 87–102; Gilles Grenier, "The Effects of Language Characteristics on the Wages of Hispanic-American Males," *Journal of Human Resources* (Winter 1984), pp. 35–52; Walter McManus, William Gould, and Finis Welch, "Earnings of Hispanic Men: The Role of English Language Proficiency," *Journal of Labor Economics* (April 1983), pp. 101–130.

TABLE 31-7	
UNEMPLOYMENT RATES BY RACE, HISPANIC ORIGIN, AND GENDER, 1988	
White	4.7
Black	11.7
Hispanic origin	8.2
Male	5.5
Female	5.6

Source: U.S. Bureau of Labor Statistics, *Employment and Earnings,* January 1989.

capital. For instance, the unemployment rate for those with less than four years of high school is almost six times greater than the unemployment rate for college graduates. Unemployment is also a function of occupation and industry (see Table 31-8). In addition, discrimination can increase a group's unemployment rate. Because human capital, the distribution of employment, and extent of discrimination vary by race, ethnicity, and gender, these factors contribute to differences in group unemployment rates.

Added insight into unemployment can be gained by examining frequency of unemployment (how often members of a group become unemployed) and duration of unemployment (how long the unemployment lasts). Blacks have a higher frequency of unemployment than whites, in part because of higher layoff rates (job

TABLE 31-8	
UNEMPLOYMENT RATES BY OCCUPATION, INDUSTRY, AND EDUCATIONAL ATTAINMENT, 1988	
Occupation	
Managerial and professional	1.9
Technical, sales, clerical	4.0
Service	6.9
Precision production	5.4
Operators, fabricators, laborers	8.3
Industry	
Mining	7.9
Construction	10.6
Manufacturing	5.3
Transportation and utilities	3.9
Wholesale and retail trade	6.2
Finance, insurance, real estate	3.0
Service industries	4.9
Agriculture	10.6
Government and self-employed	2.4
Educational attainment	
Less than 4 years of high school	9.4
High school: 4 years only	5.4
College: 1 to 3 years	3.7
4 years or more	1.7

Sources: Adapted from U.S. Bureau of Labor Statistics, *Employment and Earnings,* January 1989; "Educational Level of U.S. Work Force Continues to Rise," *News Release,* August 29, 1988.

loss). In addition, once unemployed, they tend to remain unemployed longer than whites. Thus, both frequency and duration of unemployment are unfavorable for blacks.

In turn, women have a higher frequency of unemployment than men. One reason is that women are more likely than men to move into and out of the labor force, in part because of their typically greater family responsibilities. Because entry into the labor force is often accompanied by unemployment (it takes time to find a job), women are more likely to become unemployed than men. On the other hand, women have shorter spells of unemployment. This shorter duration of unemployment partially offsets their greater frequency of unemployment.

During the late 1960s, the unemployment rate of women was more than 50 percent higher than the unemployment rate of men. Since that time, the unemployment rates of men and women have moved closer together. Indeed, recently the unemployment rate of women dipped below the unemployment rate of men (see Figure 31-5).

Several factors appear responsible for the improvement in the relative unemployment rate of women. First, male–female differences in total experience and tenure on current job have narrowed over time. As women acquire additional human capital and greater job seniority, they become relatively less vulnerable to layoffs. In addition, the growing labor force attachment of women implies fewer bouts of unemployment associated with entry into the labor market. In other words, in terms of experience, length of time on current job, and labor force attachment, men and women are becoming more and more alike. Affirmative action may have also benefited women by increasing demand for female workers relative to male workers. Exhibit 31-3 (page 720) addresses this issue.

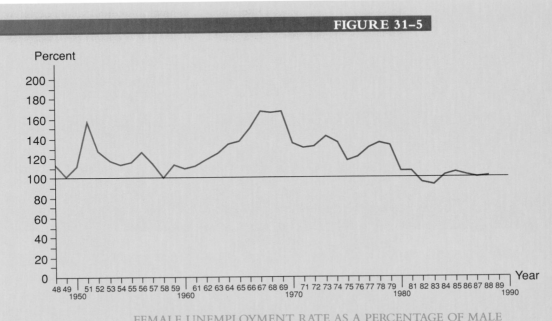

FIGURE 31-5

FEMALE UNEMPLOYMENT RATE AS A PERCENTAGE OF MALE UNEMPLOYMENT RATE

Source: U.S. Bureau of Labor Statistics, 1989.

EXHIBIT 31–3

THE IMPACT OF ANTIDISCRIMINATION POLICY

The government has adopted various measures to combat discrimination in the labor market (see Exhibit 31-2). For example, the Equal Pay Act requires that discriminating employers raise the pay of women to equal that of men performing the same work. By increasing the relative pay of women, this law induces employers to substitute male for female workers. The increased pay of women leads to lower female employment, as the following figure illustrates.

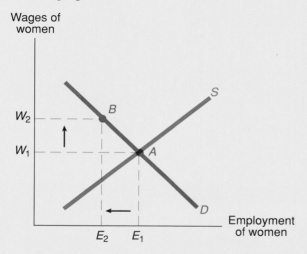

Some of those losing jobs ($E_1 - E_2$) wind up unemployed. (Others may withdraw from the labor force now that jobs are harder to find.) The net effect of higher pay for women is reduced employment and a higher rate of unemployment.

Other government policy is more benign toward women. For example, through affirmative action plans, the government forces contractors to increase the ratio of female employment. This can be represented as an increase in the demand for female workers. As indicated in the following figure, females benefit from both higher wages and higher employment.

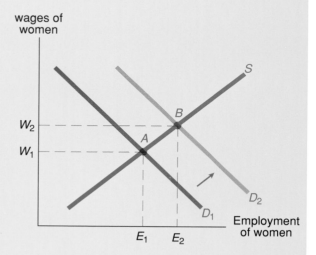

The impact on unemployment depends on what happens to female labor force participation. Higher wages coupled with increased job prospects are likely to draw additional women into the labor market. However, as long as labor force participation rises by a proportionately smaller amount than employment, the unemployment rate of women will fall.

In summary, government policies designed to raise wages of women adversely affect female employment unless the government simultaneously raises demand for female workers. Although the preceding analysis is presented in terms of female unemployment rates, it applies equally to the unemployment rates of minorities.

Fluctuations in the pattern of unemployment also reflect changes in the strength of the economy. As the economy weakens and the overall unemployment rate rises, the *relative* unemployment of women falls. There are two reasons for this. To begin with, men tend to be concentrated in those sectors of the economy most sensitive to changes in economic activity. When the unemployment rate rises, it rises most dramatically in male-intensive industries, such as construction and manufacturing. (During the economic downturn of 1982, more than one-third of all automobile workers were laid off, and the unemployment rate in construction topped 20 percent.) In contrast, employment is much less sensitive to economic downturns in female-intensive sectors, such as retail trade and services. As a consequence, when the economy weakens, male job loss exceeds female job loss.

Beyond that, women who become unemployed during a downturn are more likely than men to drop out of the labor force and therefore not be counted as unemployed. Women are more likely to time labor force participation, working when jobs are easy to find and wages good and withdrawing when conditions deteriorate. For these reasons, differences in the unemployment rates of men and women tend to narrow as the economy weakens and to widen as the economy improves.

Although this concludes the discussion of labor markets, much of the material in this chapter is relevant to our analysis of income inequality and poverty. Individuals with low labor force participation and low wages have a disproportionate chance of being poor. We return to this topic in Chapter 33, but first concentrate on other factor payments: interest, rent, and profits.

SUMMARY

1. Whether measured by labor force participation, wages, or unemployment, labor market outcomes vary by gender, race, and ethnicity. Chapter 31 helps explain the reasons behind these differences.

2. The labor force participation rate measures the percentage of the population either employed or looking for work. Although labor force participation remains higher for men, differences by gender have narrowed over time. Labor force participation of men has declined, due largely to lower labor market activity among elderly men. In contrast, labor force participation of women, especially married women, has climbed steadily throughout the century. Among the reasons are increased wages of women, lower fertility, labor-saving devices, and changes in attitudes.

3. Among year-round full-time workers, women have long earned approximately 60 percent as much as men. This reflects lower human capital among women, shorter workweeks, discrimination, and occupational distribution—women tend to be concentrated in low-paying occupations and, within an occupation, in low-paying companies.

4. Occupational differences reflect both discrimination and voluntary choice, the importance of each being hotly debated. According to human capital theory, differences in expected work lives lead women to choose different occupations than do men. But sometimes women settle for certain occupations not by choice but because they are denied entrance to other occupations. According to the theory of occupational crowding, women are channeled into traditionally female jobs, which drives down wages there.

5. Although the male/female pay gap remains wide, it has apparently narrowed over the past 15 years. During that time frame, the relative human capital of women has risen and women have increased their penetration of certain traditionally male occupations.

6. Blacks earn less than whites, in part because of their lower average age and education, an inferior job distribution, and discrimination. Differences in human capital appear responsible for over one-half of racial differences in pay.

7. Racial pay differences have narrowed over time, especially among women and young workers. Increases in the relative quantity and quality of education have played a role, as have antidiscrimination laws and affirmative action policies. Although real, the improvement in the average income of black workers has been overstated by the withdrawal from the labor force of many low-skilled blacks.

8. Ethnic differences in pay reflect many of the same factors that underlie pay differences by gender and race. In addition, language skills and, for immigrants, origin of education are relevant. Some groups with high education (Chinese, Japanese, and Jewish Americans) earn more than most white Americans; Hispanics earn less.

9. Differences in unemployment rates arise from such factors as human capital, sector of employment, and discrimination. The unemployment rate for blacks is more than double the unemployment rate for whites. The unemployment rate for women is generally higher than that of men, but unemployment differences by gender have narrowed greatly, in part because of the increase in relative experience and seniority of women. Because men are concentrated in cyclically sensitive industries, recessions raise the unemployment rate by a greater amount for men than for women.

KEY TERMS

labor force
labor force participation rate
(male/female) pay gap
theory of occupational crowding
comparable worth
employee discrimination
customer discrimination
Equal Pay Act of 1963
Civil Rights Act of 1964, title VII

affirmative action
unemployment rate

STUDY QUESTIONS AND PROBLEMS

1. Pleasantville has a (working-age) population of 1000. Currently, 540 residents are employed and 60 are unemployed.
   a. How large is the labor force in Pleasantville?
   b. Compute the town's labor force participation and unemployment rates.

2. It isn't right that a woman should get 59 cents on the dollar for the same work as a man.   —Geraldine Ferraro, 1984

   a. Do women earn only about 59 percent as much as men for the same work? Defend your answer.
   b. Why do women, on average, earn less than men?

3. If 45 percent of all workers are women, why aren't 45 percent of all plumbers, bankers, and corporate officers women?

4. (a) Why do blacks earn less than whites? (b) What forces might cause racial wage differentials to shrink in the future?

5. Why are blacks more likely to be unemployed than whites?

6. Differences between men and women in pay, labor force participation, and unemployment rates have all declined in recent years. How would you explain the narrowing of each?

7. In most universities, faculty in finance, computer science, and engineering earn substantially higher salaries than faculty in philosophy, modern languages, and education, even though faculty in the different fields have comparable amounts of education and comparable teaching responsibilities. Some universities, however, have adopted a policy of paying faculty in all departments the same salaries. Assess this policy. What are the economic consequences of eliminating pay differences by field? (*Hint:* see Exhibit 31-1.)

8. Michigan has a law that prohibits employers from discriminating on the basis of a person's weight. Arguing that obesity does not affect work performance, the Association to Aid Fat Americans has lobbied for national legislation banning weight discrimination.
   a. If Congress enacted legislation requiring equal pay regardless of weight, how might this affect employment and unemployment of overweight workers?
   b. Would the law's impact be any different if an affirmative-action clause were added? Explain your answers. (*Hint:* read Exhibit 31-3).

ANSWERS TO YOUR TURN

LABOR FORCE PARTICIPATION

(a) Decrease labor force participation; (b), (c), (d), (e) increase labor force participation.

ANSWERS TO YOUR TURN

OCCUPATIONAL DISTRIBUTION

The protected jobs tend to be highly paid. The high salaries may be to compensate workers for strenuous or dangerous work (the theory of compensating wage differentials) or they may result from the very restrictions that limit labor supply (the theory of occupational crowding). The *protective* laws may even be a screen to preserve highly paid jobs for men (to legalize discrimination). In any case, to the extent women are denied access to these high-paying jobs, the salaries of women are depressed.

CHAPTER 32

INTEREST, RENT, AND PROFIT

It is a socialist idea that making profits is a vice; I consider the real vice is making losses.

—SIR WINSTON CHURCHILL

The idea was simple—discount retailing. Starting with a single store in Arkansas, Sam Walton built one of the largest retailing empires in the United States—Wal-Mart. Fortune *magazine* estimated his wealth at $7.4 billion, making him the second richest person in America and fifth richest in the world.[1] *Although Walton worked hard, his wealth is not a testament to his raw labor. Others work equally hard but without Walton's financial success. Rather, Walton's wealth grew out of a different source of income—profit.*

Previous chapters focused on labor income, and rightly so since the bulk of all income consists of wages. But as Walton's success demonstrates, wages are not the only source of income. Chapter 32 examines three other types of income—interest, rent, and profit.

---

[1]*Fortune,* "The Billionaires," September 12, 1988, p. 71.

INTEREST

Each year millions of consumers borrow to finance purchases of automobiles, housing, clothes, and even college education. They are joined by various businesses that borrow funds to build new factories and purchase equipment. Even the federal government enters the credit market, borrowing to finance its budget deficit.

In each case, borrowers pay for the privilege of obtaining credit—that is, gaining access to lenders' funds. They agree not only to return the borrowed funds but also to pay interest on these funds. Their interest payments depend on both the volume of credit (amount borrowed) and the price of credit—the **interest rate**. For example, if you borrow $2000 for one year at an interest rate of 10 percent, your interest payments are 10 percent of $2000 (i.e., $200). Equivalently, your lender receives $200 in interest income. More generally, **interest income** refers to the interest payments received by lenders for the use of their funds. In 1988, net interest income of U.S. lenders exceeded $390 billion.

Interest Rate
The price paid for the use of lenders' funds (expressed in percentage terms).

Interest Income
The payments received by lenders for the use of their funds (expressed in dollars).

THE MARKET FOR LOANABLE FUNDS

According to the **loanable funds model**, interest rates are determined by the supply of and demand for credit. By saving part of their past income, millions of households accumulate surplus funds. Various businesses and state and local governments also acquire more funds than they presently need. These entities are willing to lend funds—at a price—to parties willing to pay for use of these **loanable funds**. The interest rate is the price borrowers pay for the use of lenders' funds. It is determined by the demand for and supply of loanable funds.

Loanable Funds Model
A model that explains interest rates in terms of the demand for and supply of lenders' funds. According to this model, the interest rate is the price paid for the use of these funds.

Demand for Loanable Funds

The demand for loanable funds is the cumulative demand by consumers, businesses, and government. Consumers generally seek funds because of a **positive time preference**—they prefer consumption in the present to consumption in the future. Rather than wait until they have saved enough to purchase a new car, many consumers want to drive that new car today. They place such a premium on present consumption that they are willing to borrow, at a positive interest rate, to make that consumption possible.

Positive Time Preference
A preference to consume now rather than wait.

The principal reason businesses borrow funds is because of the *productivity of capital*. Output could be produced with little or no capital. Crops could be grown without tractors; fish could be caught without nets; medicine could be practiced without hospitals. Why then do firms want capital? Simply put, capital permits higher levels of output. It increases the amount of corn produced, the number of fish caught, and the health of consumers.

Roundabout Production
The process of obtaining capital and using it to produce consumer goods rather than producing consumer goods directly, without capital.

Capital leads to **roundabout production**. Instead of producing consumer goods directly, resources are first used to create capital, which itself is a resource.

Capital is then combined with other resources to produce the consumer goods. Thus, roundabout production entails using the output of some earlier time period, capital, to increase production in the present period.

When a firm lacks the desired amount of capital, it seeks additional capital, and the funds necessary to purchase this capital. Even though the firm must pay interest on any funds it borrows, the capital it obtains with these funds increases output and therefore revenue to the firm. As long as additional capital contributes more to revenue than to costs, a firm has an incentive to acquire the additional capital.

The productivity of capital also contributes to consumers' demand for funds. Education and other forms of *human capital* may contribute sufficiently to a person's future earnings so that he or she can enjoy a higher standard of living by borrowing funds to attend college, even though the funds must be paid back with interest.

The final entity seeking loanable funds is the government. By borrowing funds the government finances expenditures in excess of the revenues it receives from taxes, fees, and other sources. These expenditures may be either to acquire capital (e.g., highways and bridges) or to increase present consumption by various citizens (e.g., to buy food and medicine for low-income families).

The aggregate demand for loanable funds consists of the total demand by consumers, businesses, and government. The demand for loanable funds is downward sloping (see Figure 32-1). An increase in the interest rate raises the price of borrowed funds and therefore reduces the quantity demanded, both for present consumption and for investment (acquiring capital). A higher interest rate means that consumers must sacrifice more consumption in the future for each dollar they borrow. As present consumption becomes more expensive, consumers scale back current spending and consequently reduce the amount of funds they wish to borrow. Similarly, a higher interest rate raises the cost of acquiring capital with loanable funds. Because of the increased cost, businesses, consumers, and (to a lesser extent) government all seek fewer funds with which to purchase capital.

FIGURE 32–1

THE MARKET FOR LOANABLE FUNDS

The equilibrium interest rate is determined by the supply of and demand for loanable funds. The demand for loanable funds slopes downward, reflecting the fact that borrowers want additional loanable funds when the price of these funds (the interest rate) falls. The supply of funds slopes upward, reflecting the fact that a higher interest rate induces lenders to part with a greater quantity of funds.

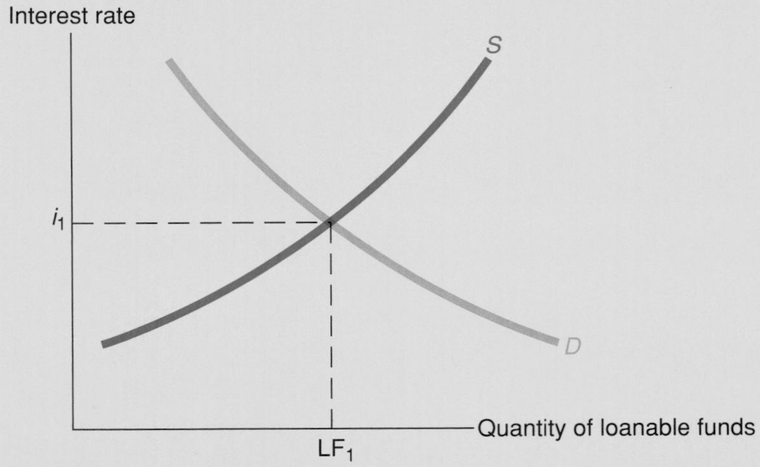

Supply of Loanable Funds

While some consumers, businesses, and governments seek to borrow loanable funds, other entities are willing to supply such funds. The amount of funds made available depends on the interest rate. Other things equal, lenders supply a greater quantity of loanable funds when the interest rate rises. That is, the supply of loanable funds is upward sloping.

Lenders have alternatives to loaning out their funds. Households with past savings can purchase more goods for themselves or can buy stocks, real estate, and other assets. Businesses with cash balances can acquire additional assets, or even other companies. State and local governments with surpluses can increase spending or reduce taxes. The willingness of those with surplus funds to make these funds available to other entities depends on the price they receive for loaning out their funds. That price is the interest rate.

The Equilibrium Interest Rate

As in other markets, the equilibrium price is determined by supply and demand. In the market for loanable funds, the equilibrium interest rate is given by the intersection of the demand for loanable funds and the supply of loanable funds. This is represented in Figure 32-1 by the interest rate i_1. Of course, if the demand for loanable funds shifts (e.g., due to a change in the productivity of capital), the equilibrium interest rate also changes. Similarly, a shift in the supply of loanable funds alters the interest rate. One factor that shifts both the supply and demand curves is a change in the expected rate of inflation—that is, the rate at which prices are expected to rise from one year to the next.

INFLATIONARY EXPECTATIONS AND REAL VERSUS NOMINAL INTEREST RATES

Assume that those in the market for loanable funds initially expect prices to be the same this year and next (i.e., they expect a zero inflation rate). Consider what will happen if expectations change. For example, suppose borrowers and lenders suddenly expect prices to rise by five percent over the coming year, perhaps due to a change in government policy. The expectation of higher inflation reduces lenders' willingness to supply funds—it shifts the supply of loanable funds leftward (see Figure 32-2, page 728). Equivalently stated, it raises the price (interest rate) lenders require to provide a given quantity of funds.

A higher expected inflation rate also increases the demand for loanable funds. For any given interest rate, borrowers seek more funds the greater the expected increase in prices. This reflects the fact that as prices rise borrowers can repay their loans with "cheaper" dollars. That is, a dollar received one year from now will buy less than a dollar buys today. The higher the inflation rate the greater the advantage from being able to buy now, before prices rise, and therefore the greater the incentive to obtain funds today. Because an increase in expected inflation reduces the supply of loanable funds while increasing demand for loanable funds, it raises the equilibrium interest rate. The new equilibrium interest rate in Figure 32-2 is i_2.

The actual interest rate borrowers pay lenders—the rate specified in the loan agreement—is called the **nominal interest rate**. The nominal interest rate

Nominal Interest Rate
The interest rate measured in actual dollars borrowers must pay.

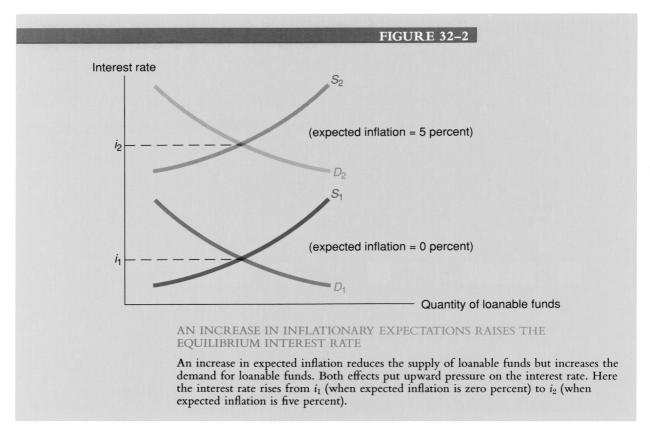

FIGURE 32-2

AN INCREASE IN INFLATIONARY EXPECTATIONS RAISES THE
EQUILIBRIUM INTEREST RATE

An increase in expected inflation reduces the supply of loanable funds but increases the
demand for loanable funds. Both effects put upward pressure on the interest rate. Here
the interest rate rises from i_1 (when expected inflation is zero percent) to i_2 (when
expected inflation is five percent).

Real Interest Rate
The nominal interest rate
minus the expected rate of
inflation.

indicates the number of dollars that must be paid in one year for every $100
borrowed today. As inflationary expectations rise, so does the nominal interest rate.

The nominal interest rate can be contrasted with the **real interest rate.** The
real interest rate is defined as the nominal interest rate minus the expected inflation
rate. It indicates how much borrowers must pay lenders above and beyond the
expected inflation rate in order to gain access to their funds. If each one-percent
increase in expected inflation raises the nominal interest rate by one percent, as some
economists believe, then the real rate of interest is independent of the expected rate
of inflation.

The real rate of interest is not constant over time, as Figure 32-3 indicates.
Changes in the supply of or demand for loanable funds can affect real as well as
nominal interest rates. For instance, real interest rates rise if the population becomes
less thrifty, reducing the supply of loanable funds, or if capital becomes more
productive, increasing the demand for loanable funds. Both reasons have been cited
for the unusually high real interest rates of the 1980s. An alternative explanation,
favored by some, is the increased demand for funds by the federal government,
which was forced to borrow large sums to finance the mammoth budget deficits of
the 1980s.

THE STRUCTURE OF INTEREST RATES

To this point our discussion has been in terms of a single interest rate (actually a
single real interest rate and, given expectations about inflation, a corresponding

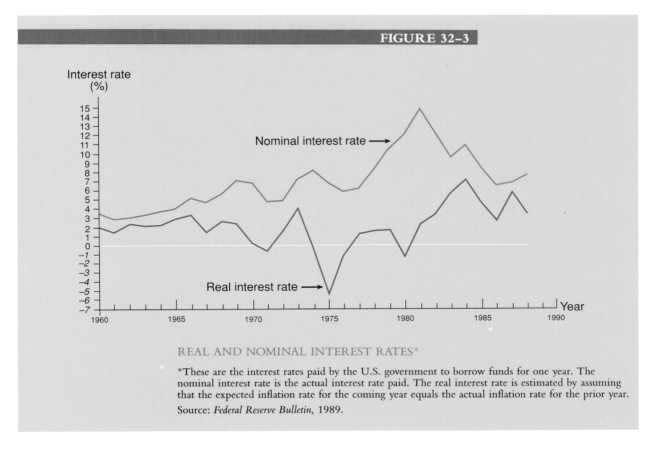

FIGURE 32–3

REAL AND NOMINAL INTEREST RATES*

*These are the interest rates paid by the U.S. government to borrow funds for one year. The nominal interest rate is the actual interest rate paid. The real interest rate is estimated by assuming that the expected inflation rate for the coming year equals the actual inflation rate for the prior year.
Source: *Federal Reserve Bulletin*, 1989.

nominal interest rate). In reality, there is an array of different interest rates at any given moment in time. All borrowers do not pay the same price for access to loanable funds. Interest rates vary with the length of loan, the risk of default, and the cost of administering the loan.

Length of Loan

Interest rates typically differ, depending on how soon a loan must be repaid. One reason is that borrowers and lenders may expect conditions to change from one period to the next. For example, the interest rate on one-year loans might be expected to rise from six percent this year to eight percent next year. Then, by making consecutive one-year loans, lenders could expect to earn an average of seven percent over the two-year period. For this reason, they will not agree to a two-year loan that pays less than seven percent. By the same token, because one-year loans are expected to become more expensive next year, borrowers are willing to pay a higher price to obtain funds for two years than for one year. More generally, expectations that short-term interest rates will rise in the future pull up long-term interest rates today.

Even when short-term interest rates are not expected to rise, long-term interest rates may exceed short-term rates. If lenders are reluctant to tie up their funds for an extended period of time, they will demand a premium (higher interest rate) on long-term loans. Consistent with this view, for almost 80 percent of the period since

1950 long-term rates have exceeded short-term rates.[2] For example, in 1988 the U.S. government was forced to pay an interest rate of 9.0 percent to borrow funds for 30 years, compared to a rate of 7.7 percent to borrow funds for one year. (In 1989, short-term and long-term rates moved closer together.)

Risk of Default

When a lender loans funds there is always a **risk of default**—the borrower may fail to pay interest or to repay the loan. In the 1980s, U.S. banks lost billions of dollars when Mexico and other debtor nations defaulted on their loans. Similarly, those who loaned funds to the Washington Public Power Supply System (aptly nicknamed "whoops") lost $2.25 billion plus interest when the utility halted construction of two nuclear power projects. Without revenues from the power plants, the utility was unable to meet its financial obligations.

Although lenders cannot eliminate the risk of default, they take this risk into account when making loans. Borrowers with a higher risk of default are charged higher interest rates to compensate lenders for the possible loss of their funds. For example, troubled Eastern Airlines recently paid an interest rate of 17 percent to borrow funds through 1997, almost double the rate paid by the U.S. government. This reflected lenders' convictions that Eastern Airlines was much more likely to default than the U.S. government.

Administrative Costs

Lenders incur various loan-processing costs (e.g., bookkeeping). These costs are often the same regardless of a loan's size. Consequently, administrative costs per dollar loaned tend to fall as size of the loan increases. Because of this cost advantage, large loans typically carry a lower interest rate, other things equal, than small loans. In turn, the fact that large companies tend to borrow greater sums of money helps explain why they generally pay lower interest rates (for a given risk of default) than small companies and households.

INTEREST RATES AND THE ALLOCATION OF CAPITAL

Although capital is productive, additional capital is not equally productive for every firm or project. An additional $100 million in capital may increase revenues by $15 million per year if used to open new Wal-Mart stores but by only $5 million per year if used to build another plant for Bethlehem Steel. Society benefits when resources, including capital, are allocated efficiently—when they are used in those sectors where they create the greatest value for society.

When interest rates are determined competitively—by the supply of and demand for funds—they allocate capital where it is most productive. If the market interest rate (adjusted for risk) is ten percent, projects that return at least $10 per year on each $100 borrowed will be undertaken; projects with lower rates of return will not. In our example, Wal-Mart will borrow funds because it can use them profitably, but Bethlehem Steel will not. In summary, competitively determined interest rates allocate loanable funds and therefore capital to those firms and projects where they are valued most highly. On the other hand, when interest rates are set artificially, capital is not allocated efficiently (see Exhibit 32-1).

---

[2]Lloyd B. Thomas, Jr., *Money, Banking, and Economic Activity,* 3rd ed. (Englewood Cliffs, NJ: Prentice-Hall, 1986), p. 118.

EXHIBIT 32–1

USURY LAWS

State governments sometimes attempt to *pro-tect* borrowers through **usury laws**, which impose a ceiling on legal interest rates. When that ceiling is below market rates, interest rates can no longer perform their rationing function. In the following figure, the amount of funds demanded at the maximum legal interest rate is Q_2, but lenders are willing to supply only Q_1 funds.

Usury Laws
Legislation that prohibits lenders from charging more than a specified interest rate on certain types of loans.

Because interest rates are not allowed to determine who obtains credit and who does not, banks and other lenders are forced to resort to various means of nonprice rationing. They make funds available only to their best customers and to those with the very best credit ratings—borrowers with the highest incomes (primarily white males) and the most collateral. These privileged borrowers benefit from usury laws because they are able to obtain funds at below-market interest rates. Other borrowers are squeezed from the market entirely, unable to obtain any funds at legal interest rates. Their only source of funds are *loan sharks,* who

charge exorbitant interest rates, in part to compensate for the risk of being jailed or fined for violating usury laws. An irony of usury laws is that the very people they were intended to help—the poor and powerless—are the ones victimized by these laws.

Another consequence of usury laws is that lower-valued projects may be funded at the expense of higher-valued projects. For example, suppose Rachel is willing to pay an interest rate of 20 percent to borrow funds but Joe, an equal credit risk, is prepared to pay only 15 percent. If the maximum legal interest rate is 15 percent, lenders have no reason to prefer loaning funds to Rachel, even though she values the funds more highly. Given excess demand for credit, Rachel is just as likely to be squeezed from the market as Joe (and perhaps more likely if the lender considers gender when rationing funds).

Finally, it is worth emphasizing that usury laws, when effective, not only distort the distribution of credit, they also reduce the *volume* of credit. In the absence of the interest rate ceiling, the quantity of loanable funds would be Q_{mkt} rather than Q_1.

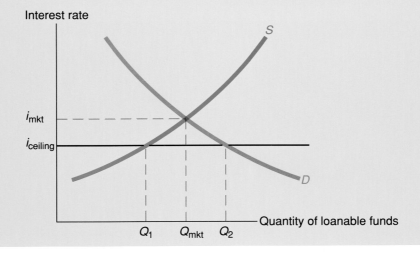

RENTS

Pure Economic Rent
The payment for using a resource that is fixed in supply.

Noneconomists use the term "rent" to describe payments for the use of various property—a car leased from Avis, an apartment, even space on a billboard. To the economist, rent means something different. **Pure economic rent** is the payment to a resource that is fixed in supply—that is, a resource whose supply curve is perfectly inelastic. The classic example is land. Indeed, economists first studied economic rent in the context of rent on land. Today the term economic rent is used more broadly to include certain income payments to resources other than land.

To understand the concept of economic rent, it is helpful to consider the controversy that initially prompted economic analysis of rents. The discussion is then extended to cover rents to inputs other than land.

LAND RENTS

The price of grain—what the British call "corn"—rose sharply in early nineteenth-century Britain. This led to widespread economic hardship and to public indignation. Who was responsible? Noting that high land rents accompanied high corn prices, some blamed the landowners. Claiming that high rents caused high corn prices, they proposed limiting the amount of rent landowners could charge. Economist David Ricardo, however, argued that causation ran in the opposite direction: "Corn is not high [in price] because a rent is paid, but a rent is paid because corn is high."

Ricardo's analysis is presented in Figure 32-4. Ricardo argued that the amount of land, or what he called "the original and indestructible powers of the soil," is fixed, determined by nature. As such, the supply of land is perfectly inelastic. Changes in rent (the price of using land) are therefore completely determined by changes in the demand for land. If demand increases from D_1 to D_2, rent rises from P_1 to P_2. Similarly, a reduction in the demand for land lowers rents. If demand falls to D_3, land is no longer scarce and therefore landowners receive no rent. Because landowners gain nothing by leaving land idle, they rent their land at the market price whether that price is high, low, or even zero.

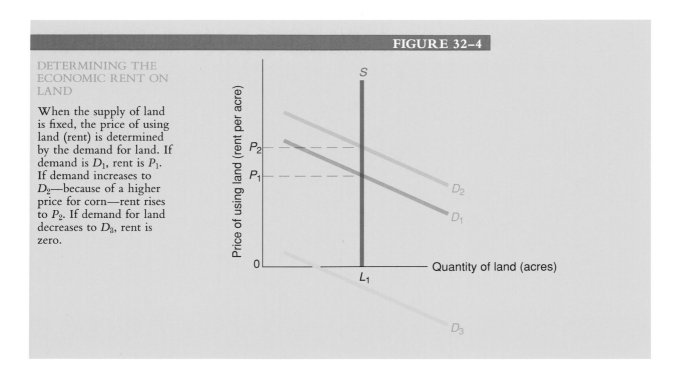

FIGURE 32–4

DETERMINING THE ECONOMIC RENT ON LAND

When the supply of land is fixed, the price of using land (rent) is determined by the demand for land. If demand is D_1, rent is P_1. If demand increases to D_2—because of a higher price for corn—rent rises to P_2. If demand for land decreases to D_3, rent is zero.

In modern terminology, the demand for land is a *derived demand,* determined by the demand for corn.[3] When the price of corn is high, demand for land is similarly high, leading to high rents. Although landowners benefit from high rents, they are in no way responsible for those high rents. High rents result from high corn prices.

Because high rents are the consequence of high corn prices, not the cause, forcing landowners to roll back rents would not reduce the price of corn. It would merely transfer income from landowners to tenants. The path to lower corn prices, claimed Ricardo, lay not in lower rents but in greater availability of corn. Accordingly, he and his followers fought to repeal the Corn Laws, which limited imports of food into Britain. In 1846, after a long struggle, the Corn Laws were rescinded. Corn imports increased, and the price of corn fell, as Ricardo had predicted.

Taxing Land Rents

Even though lower rents would not reduce the price of corn, they offered government an opportunity to raise tax revenues without reducing either the supply of land or the quantity of corn. When supply is upward sloping, a tax on any resource raises the price of that resource and reduces the quantity supplied (see Figure 32-5a). With fewer resources employed, the country's output falls.

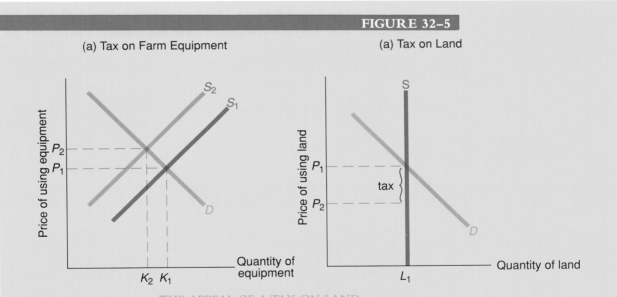

FIGURE 32–5

(a) Tax on Farm Equipment

(a) Tax on Land

THE APPEAL OF A TAX ON LAND

In general, a tax levied on a resource raises the price of that resource and lowers the amount used by producers (a). On the other hand, if the supply of a resource is fixed, the tax neither raises the price of the resource nor curtails its use. Because the supply of land is perfectly inelastic, landowners cannot pass on any of the tax to users (b). The after-tax payment received by landowners decreases by the full amount of the tax, from P_1 to P_2. Because the price and quantity of land used are unaffected by the tax, the price and quantity of the output produced with land are similarly unaffected.

---

[3]For a review of the concept "derived demand," see p. 662.

EXHIBIT 32–2

HENRY GEORGE AND THE SINGLE TAX

Henry George viewed land as a free gift of nature. He believed that society in general contributed to the value of land and therefore society in general should share the rewards. This could be accomplished by taxing away the pure economic rent of land and using these proceeds for the public good.

George's proposal was known as the *single tax* because he believed this tax would raise sufficient revenue for the government so that no other taxes would be needed. Under George's plan the government would not tax improvements to land (e.g., from draining swamps or irrigating arid farm land). Nor would George tax capital, such as the buildings on land. His tax would be based solely on the rents land would command in the absence of all such improvements.

George sketched his theory in *Our Land and Land Policy* and developed it more fully in *Progress and Poverty,* a highly successful book published in 1879. Critics attacked his single tax on the grounds that it would not raise sufficient revenue for the government, that it would be difficult to administer, and that it would be unfair to the many landowners who had purchased land at high prices in the expectation of receiving high rents. His views proved popular with many voters, however, and he twice ran for mayor of New York City. He finished second in 1886 and died during the 1897 campaign.

In contrast, when supply is perfectly inelastic, a tax affects neither price of the resource nor the quantity supplied. For example, in Figure 32-5b, the tax reduces the after-tax return to landowners from P_1 to P_2, but landowners still supply L_1 units of land. Tenants continue to pay P_1 rent (since demand for land is not affected by the tax), but landowners must now remit $P_1 - P_2$ of this rent to the government. That is, the tax is borne entirely by landowners. Because the price of land does not change to tenants, the tax does not distort the allocation of resources. Farmers continue to use the same amount of land and to produce the same level of output. Thus, the tax raises revenue for the government without harming economic efficiency.

This is one reason various economists have found land taxes to be so appealing. Land taxes have also been supported by those who view rent as an *unearned surplus.* If demand for land increases—as one would expect in a growing economy—landowners receive higher rents even though they have done nothing to make their land more productive.

Ricardo predicted that, over time, competition for land would raise the share of income going to landowners. This bothered some political thinkers, who viewed landowners as no more deserving of rising income than tenants. Economist John Stuart Mill suggested that future increases in rent be taxed away from landowners. Henry George went further, proposing that all rent be expropriated from landowners—present rents as well as future increases in rent (see Exhibit 32-2).

RENTS TO OTHER RESOURCES

Economic Rent
The premium received by a resource in excess of its opportunity cost.

Landowners are not alone in receiving a surplus—that is, a payment in excess of opportunity cost. George Brett, Don Mattingly, and other top sluggers receive $2 million per year to play baseball, considerably more than necessary to induce them to face opposing pitchers. This premium or additional income is as much a surplus as the payments to landowners. As such it can be considered an **economic rent.** More generally, any resource is said to receive an economic rent when it receives a payment in excess of its opportunity cost—that is, an income greater than required to keep the resource in its present employment.

The difference between economic rent and the previously defined pure economic rent is that opportunity cost is zero in the case of pure economic rent. When supply is perfectly inelastic, the entire payment to a resource owner constitutes economic rent. In contrast, when opportunity cost is positive, only a portion of the factor payment is economic rent. Thus, a pure economic rent is a special type of economic rent that arises when supply of a resource is perfectly inelastic.

Whenever input supply curves are upward sloping, all but the last unit supplied receive an economic rent. This is illustrated in Figure 32-6(b), which depicts supply and demand for librarians. If the wage is W_1, all librarians except the last receive a wage in excess of their opportunity cost—that is, all but the last librarian are willing to work for less than W_1. The aggregate economic rent received by all librarians can be represented by the area above the supply curve and below the market wage.

YOUR TURN

The town of Gulliesville has hired three deputy sheriffs—John, Sue, and Terry—at a market wage of $12,000 per year. Had John not received a $12,000 offer, he would have refused the job. Sue, on the other hand, was willing to accept the job provided that it paid at least $11,000 per year. Terry, who has always wanted to be a deputy sheriff, would have worked for a wage as low as $9000 per year. What is the economic rent of (a) John, (b) Sue, (c) Terry, and (d) the deputies as a group?

FIGURE 32–6

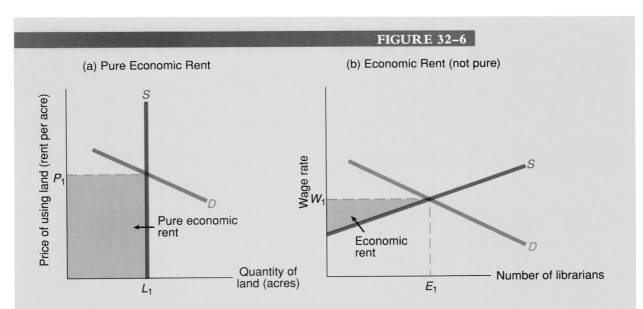

ECONOMIC RENT

Economic rent is the difference between the payment received by a resource and the opportunity cost of that resource. When supply is perfectly inelastic (a), the resource has a zero opportunity cost and the entire payment is pure economic rent (shaded rectangle). When supply is upward sloping (b), the opportunity cost is greater than zero. For an individual librarian, economic rent is the difference between the actual payment (W_1) and the minimum payment he or she requires to work as a librarian (given by the supply curve). Aggregate economic rent of all librarians is depicted by the shaded triangle in (b).

PROFIT

By selling a product, a firm generates revenue. Out of this revenue the firm must pay for any resources it uses. That is, costs, both explicit and implicit, must be subtracted from total revenue. (Remember that the economist, unlike the accountant, subtracts implicit costs as well as direct payments to others.) The *residual*—what remains after paying for the use of resources—is the firm's **economic profit**. For this reason, the firm is sometimes called the *residual claimant.* When the firm can sell its output for less than the cost of production, it is rewarded with a positive residual—a profit. But when resource costs exceed total revenue, the firm bears the consequences: the residual is negative, and the firm suffers a loss.

THE SOURCES OF PROFIT

Why does a residual exist? Why do costs and revenues sometimes differ? To understand the origin of profit it is helpful to first examine the opposite situation—a world in which all firms earn zero economic profits (normal profits).

Assume markets are perfectly competitive, the future is known, and innovation is nonexistent. In such an environment there is no potential for profit. Lacking entry barriers, firms cannot earn monopoly profits. Nor do firms have the opportunity to gamble on the future—for example, to try to anticipate a change in consumer demand before other firms do. All firms know in advance which products consumers want. Moreover, the lack of innovation prevents firms from creating successful new products or introducing new techniques for cutting costs. Under these conditions, the opportunity for profit is nonexistent.

Profits arise because the preceding conditions fail to hold. In particular, most economists recognize three sources of profit: monopoly power, uncertainty, and innovation.

Monopoly Power

Firms are not all price takers; many enjoy monopoly power—the ability to drive up price by restricting output. As we learned earlier, this may lead to economic profit. Although other firms are attracted to profitable industries, various barriers may prevent their entry into these industries. Among the barriers discussed in Chapter 25 were patents, government licenses, and control of crucial raw materials. Because of such barriers, firms are sheltered from competition and may be able to earn economic profits, even in the long run.

Uncertainty

Firms must make decisions in an uncertain world. As such, they assume risks. They make subjective assessments about future markets, costs, government policy, even the weather. When these assessments prove correct, or when the firm is plain lucky—as when an unanticipated event boosts product demand—the firm is rewarded with profit. On the other hand, when fate is unkind, the firm incurs a loss. Viewed in this light, profit and loss are the fruit of decision making under uncertainty. For those who succeed—the ones with foresight or good fortune—the fruit is sweet; for others the taste is bitter.

Consider the uncertainty faced by automakers. What type of cars will consumers want in five years? What types of styling will appeal to them? How important will be size, safety, comfort, and miles per gallon? The answers depend on income levels, the price of gasoline, and consumer tastes. Although these are all unknowable, the lead time required to plan and design a new car forces automobile producers to make judgments about the future.

Sometimes those judgments will be wrong. Automobile companies may produce too many large cars, as happened after the oil crisis in the mid-1970s. Or they may produce cars that are too boxy, as General Motors did during part of the 1980s. Ford did a better job of anticipating consumer preferences. Its reward was to earn greater profits than General Motors. In turn, the owners of Ford (the shareholders) saw their stock climb 31 percent during the period 1986–87, while stock in General Motors dropped 13 percent in price.[4]

Innovation

Even in the absence of innovation, uncertainty would lead to profit and loss. Firms would still be forced to make assessments about future demand, government policy, and a host of other developments. The fact that firms can introduce new products and new methods of production creates added uncertainty. Will the new products catch on? Will new methods of production really cut costs? Depending on the answer, innovations may create either profit or loss.

In some cases the success of an innovation is stunning, and so are the rewards. Consider Bill Gates and Estée Lauder. Sensing an opportunity to write and sell computer software, Gates dropped out of school at age 19 to start his own company. That company, Microsoft, proved so successful that in 1987, at age 31, Gates became a billionaire. Before Gates was even born, Estée Lauder was peddling her skin cream to the beauty salons of New York City. The cream was so popular that department stores added her line of products. By the time she was 79, the daughter of Jewish immigrants had built a sales staff of 7500 and a personal fortune of $1.6 billion.[5]

Not all new products are a success. To the contrary, losses are more common—as most small companies fold within a few years after beginning operations. Innovation carries with it considerable risk. But for those who accept the risk and succeed, the rewards can be substantial. Ask Bill Gates.

THE ROLE OF PROFIT

The role of profit is not always appreciated. Sometimes profit is attacked as undeserved, even harmful to the economy. Where profit results from entry restrictions, which shelter a firm from competition, the interests of society may indeed be harmed. But some criticize all profit. For instance, Karl Marx argued that profit results from the exploitation of labor. Such a view neglects the positive functions of profit. Most economists argue that profit, where it does not result from entry restrictions, serves three important functions: allocating resources, inducing efficient production, and encouraging innovation.

Resource Allocation

For the value of society's output to be maximized, resources must flow to those sectors where they are valued most highly. Profit and loss signal whether additional resources should enter an industry or present resources should leave. When firms in an industry are earning profit, this indicates that the value of resources employed

---

[4]These figures exclude dividend payments. If dividends are included, the value of Ford's stock increased by 41 percent while the value of GM's stock was virtually unchanged.
[5]*Fortune,* "The Billionaires," October 12, 1987, pp. 144–49.

there exceeds their opportunity cost. Society therefore benefits when additional resources are drawn into the industry. Conversely, when firms in an industry are losing money, the implication is that resources are valued more highly elsewhere and should therefore leave their present industry.

Efficient Production

If output is to be maximized, resources must also be used efficiently within an industry. Production that wastes resources reduces the amount of output available to society. Profit is the incentive for firms to use resources efficiently; loss is the penalty for wasting resources.

Innovation

Profit also spurs new ideas, new products, new production techniques. Without the opportunity for profit, entrepreneurs would have little reason to innovate and society would be the worse off, since innovation leads to faster economic growth and additional products for consumers. However, innovation does not guarantee perpetual profits. Harvard economist Joseph Schumpeter argued that competition would ultimately eliminate profit to the innovator, as other firms copied the new product or process. But one innovation would be followed by another and, where successful, the innovator would earn short-run profits. According to Schumpeter, it is the lure of profit, even temporary profit, that leads to innovation.[6]

THE FUNCTIONAL DISTRIBUTION OF INCOME

How is a country's income divided? What are the shares going to wages, interest, rent, and profit? Government statistics are available (see Table 32-1), but it is important to realize that they are not based on economic definitions. For instance, statistics on profit pertain to accounting profit. Recall that accounting profit ignores certain implicit costs—for example, forgone salary and implicit rent on land owned by the company. To the extent certain costs are excluded, accounting profit overstates economic profit.

Government statistics on rent include payments for the use of capital as well as for the use of land. On the other hand, they exclude economic rent to labor. Income received by proprietorships (noncorporate businesses) includes both profit and the imputed salary of the proprietor. Despite the fact that government statistics do not mesh precisely with economic definitions, these statistics still provide useful information. Among the major conclusions that can be drawn are the following.

1. The share of income going to profits is less than commonly perceived. At present, corporate profits amount to less than 10 percent of the income in the United States (see Table 32-1).
2. The bulk of income consists of payments to labor. Measured narrowly as employee compensation, labor income accounted for 73 percent of total income in 1988. If proprietors' income is included, the figure climbs to 81 percent.

---

[6]For further discussion of Schumpeter's theory, see Chapter 26 or refer directly to Joseph Schumpeter, *Capitalism, Socialism, and Democracy* (New York: Harper and Row, 1942).

	TABLE 32-1					

THE DISTRIBUTION OF INCOME IN THE UNITED STATES, 1900–1988*

Time period	Compensation of employees (%)	Proprietors' income (%)	Rental income of persons (%)	Corporate profits (%)	Net interest (%)	Total (%)
1900–1909	55.0	23.7	6.8	5.5	9.0	100.0
1910–1919	53.6	23.8	9.1	5.4	8.1	100.0
1920–1929	60.8	17.5	7.8	6.2	7.7	100.0
1930	63.8	15.2	5.7	8.6	6.7	100.0
1940	65.6	15.8	3.4	11.1	4.1	100.0
1950	64.8	16.2	3.2	14.5	1.3	100.0
1960	69.8	12.3	3.6	11.6	2.7	100.0
1970	74.3	9.6	2.2	9.0	4.9	100.0
1980	74.4	8.2	0.3	8.0	9.1	100.0
1988	73.2	8.2	0.5	8.3	9.8	100.0

*The top three lines are from Irving B. Kravis, "Income Distribution: Functional Share," from David L. Sills, ed., *International Encyclopedia of Social Sciences,* Vol. 7 (New York: Macmillan and Free Press, 1968), p. 134. Reprinted with permission of Macmillan Publishing Company. Copyright © 1968 by Crowell Collier and Macmillan, Inc. More recent data are from the U.S. Department of Commerce, *The National Income and Product Accounts of the United States, 1929–82* (1986) and *Survey of Current Business,* June 1989.

3. Contrary to the prediction of Ricardo, rent's share of income has not increased over time. Although rents have tended to rise in absolute dollars, as a percentage of income they have fallen.
4. When measured by employee compensation, labor's share has increased from 55 percent at the start of the century to 73 percent today. On the other hand, if proprietors' income is attributed to labor, labor's share has been fairly stable. These divergent findings reflect the fact that proprietors' share of income has trended downward, offsetting the increase in employee compensation. The decline in proprietors' relative income is due, in turn, to the changing nature of production. As economic activity has become increasingly organized by corporations, proprietorships have become less important.
5. Interest income rose during the 1980s. As previously discussed, interest rates were unusually high during this period.

SUMMARY

1. Interest income refers to the payments borrowers make to lenders for the use of their funds. Consumers are willing to pay interest because of a positive time preference—they prefer present consumption to future consumption. Firms are willing to pay for the use of funds because they can be used to acquire capital, which permits an expansion of output. Firms have an incentive to acquire additional capital as long as it contributes more to revenue than to costs.
2. Interest income depends on the price charged for using funds (the interest rate) and the volume of funds loaned. According to the loanable funds model, these are determined by the demand for and supply of loanable funds.
3. The actual interest rate that borrowers pay lenders is called the nominal interest rate. The nominal interest rate fluctuates with the expected rate of inflation. Other things equal, a

higher expected rate of inflation increases demand for loanable funds while reducing the supply. Both put upward pressure on the nominal interest rate.

4. The real interest rate is defined as the nominal interest rate minus the expected rate of inflation. Both nominal and real interest rates depend on length of the loan, risk of default, and cost of administering the loan.

5. When interest rates are determined competitively—by the supply of and demand for loanable funds—they allocate funds where they are valued most highly. But when interest rates are set artificially low, through usury laws, they are unable to allocate funds efficiently. Usury laws also reduce the volume of credit and the share received by those with low credit ratings.

6. Economic rent is the difference between the payment received by a resource and the opportunity cost of that resource. In the special case where supply of a resource is fixed, the entire payment constitutes rent. To signify this, the expression *pure economic rent* is used.

7. When supply is fixed, a tax on the resource is borne entirely by the resource owner. Because price does not rise to resource users, the quantity of the resource used does not change. As such, the tax has no adverse effect on the economy's output.

8. When resource supply is upward sloping, all but the last unit supplied receive a payment in excess of opportunity cost. Therefore, all but the last unit hired receive some economic rent.

9. Profit, as defined by economists, is the residual that accrues to a firm after all costs have been netted out (implicit as well as explicit). That residual may be either positive or negative. The opportunity for profit comes from several sources: monopoly power, uncertainty, and innovation.

10. Profit serves three important functions for the economy—it promotes efficient allocation of resources, efficient production, and innovation.

11. As measured by statistics of the U.S. government, employee compensation accounts for almost three-fourths of all income in the United States. If proprietors' income is included, labor's share exceeds 80 percent.

12. Employee compensation has been rising faster than income in general and, contrary to the predictions of Ricardo, rent's share of income has fallen.

KEY TERMS

interest rate	real interest rate
interest income	risk of default
loanable funds model	usury laws
loanable funds	pure economic rent
positive time preference	economic rent
roundabout production	economic profit
nominal interest rate	

STUDY QUESTIONS AND PROBLEMS

1. What happens to the equilibrium interest rate in each of the following cases and why?
   a. Consumers decide to save more of their income in order to support themselves better after they retire.
   b. Technological innovations increase the productivity of additional capital.
   c. Households decide that college education is no longer a good investment, and the percentage of the population wanting to attend college falls.
   d. States enact stricter usury laws, which reduce the rate of interest lenders may legally charge.

2. Why does the nominal interest rate differ from the real interest rate? Under what condition are the two interest rates the same?

3. Why do lenders charge different customers different interest rates? Is this practice justified?

4. Assume the government, concerned about a declining farm economy, induces lenders to make more funds available to agriculture than lenders would in the absence of government intervention. On what basis could this action be criticized?

5. The following table depicts the supply of mechanics to a community:

Annual wage	Quantity supplied
$20,000	1
21,000	2
22,000	3
23,000	4

a. If the market wage is $21,000 per year, how much economic rent does the first worker receive? How much does the second receive?

b. If the market wage rises to $23,000, how much economic rent do the first and second workers now receive?

c. What is the total economic rent of all four mechanics when the annual wage is $23,000?

6. Even though the opportunity cost of land *in the aggregate* is zero, individual parcels of land have alternative uses [e.g., agriculture, residential housing, or commercial development (including retail shopping and office use)].

a. Draw the supply curve of land available for commercial use. Is it perfectly inelastic?

b. Assume land is taxed only when used for commercial purposes. How will this tax affect the quantity of land used commercially? How will it affect the price tenants pay for use of this land? Explain your reasoning.

7. A seat on the New York Stock Exchange entitles its holder to earn income by buying and selling stocks for clients. The price of a seat fell from $1.1 million in mid-1987—before the stock market crash—to $700,000 one year later. The number of seats on the Stock Exchange is fixed, and therefore did not change during this period. What accounted for the lower price? Illustrate this situation using supply and demand curves.

8. What does it mean to say that a firm is the "residual claimant"?

9. Why do economic profits exist? If firms are willing to accept normal profits, why do some receive positive economic profits?

10. Suppose the government taxed away all profits and reimbursed firms for any losses they incurred in production. What effect would this have on the economy?

11. How has labor's share of income in the United States changed this century? Does your answer depend on how "labor's share" is defined? Explain.

ANSWER TO YOUR TURN

(a) $0, (b) $1000, (c) $3000, (d) $4000.

SELECTED REFERENCE

Mark Blaug, *Economic Theory in Retrospect,* 4th ed. (London: Cambridge University Press, 1985). Provides a historical discussion of roundabout production, the corn laws, and the single tax.

POVERTY AND THE DISTRIBUTION OF INCOME

You have the poor
among you always.

—John 12:8

The United States has one of the highest standards of living in the world. It also has over 30 million people living in poverty. Why does poverty exist in a nation as affluent as the United States? Who are the poor, and how have their numbers changed over time? Is the nation winning its self-proclaimed "war on poverty," or is it on the verge of surrender? Chapter 33 studies the distribution of income in the United States, paying special attention to those at the bottom. It also examines the major government programs designed to alleviate poverty.

THE DISTRIBUTION OF INCOME

Measuring Income Inequality

Although median family income in the United States is approximately $31,000,[1] that income is distributed unevenly. One family in four has an annual income of at least $50,000, but nearly 5 percent of all families have incomes below $5000 (see Table 33-1). Although these numbers are revealing, they do not readily lend themselves to analysis. As incomes have risen over time, have they risen more rapidly for those at the bottom of the income distribution or for those at the top? That is, has the distribution of income become more equal or less equal? To answer such questions, the distribution of income is generally presented in an alternative fashion.

One convention is to arrange families in order of income and then to divide them into five groups of equal size called *quintiles*. The first quintile consists of the 20 percent of families having the least amount of income in a year. The second quintile consists of the next 20 percent of families, arranged in order of income, and so forth. In 1987, families with incomes of $14,450 or less were assigned to the first quintile; families with incomes between $14,451 and $25,100 made it to the second quintile. The full distribution by quintile is presented in Table 33-2 (page 744).

Table 33-3 (page 744) presents the *cumulative* distribution of income for families. It contains the same information as Table 33-2, but in a different format.

TABLE 33-1

THE DISTRIBUTION OF FAMILY INCOME BY INCOME BRACKET, 1987*

Family income	Percent of families
Under $5000	4.4
$ 5,000 to $ 9,999	7.3
$10,000 to $14,999	9.1
$15,000 to $24,999	18.7
$25,000 to $34,999	17.4
$35,000 to $49,999	20.2
$50,000 and over	22.9
Total	100.0
Median income	$30,853

*Before taxes.

Source: U.S. Department of Commerce, *Current Population Reports*, Series P-60, No. 162 (1989), p. 34.

---

[1]"Median" means midpoint. Half of all families have an income below the median income; half of all families have a higher income.

TABLE 33-2			
THE DISTRIBUTION OF FAMILY INCOME BY QUINTILE, 1987*			
Quintile	**Income**	**Percent of families**	**Percent of income**
First (bottom)	$14,450 or less	20	4.6
Second	$14,451 to $25,100	20	10.8
Third	$25,101 to $36,600	20	16.9
Fourth	$36,601 to $52,910	20	24.0
Fifth (top)	$52,911 or more	20	43.7
	Total	100	100.0

*Before taxes.

Source: U.S. Department of Commerce, *Current Population Reports*, Series P-60, No. 162 (1989), p. 42.

TABLE 33-3			
THE CUMULATIVE DISTRIBUTION OF FAMILY INCOME BY QUINTILE, 1987*			
Quintile	**Income**	**Percent of families**	**Percent of income**
First	$14,450 or less	20	4.6
Second or lower	$25,100 or less	40	15.4
Third or lower	$36,600 or less	60	32.3
Fourth or lower	$52,910 or less	80	56.3
Fifth or lower	All levels	100	100.0

*Before taxes.

Source: Same as Table 33-2.

The cumulative distribution indicates the percentage of income received by a given quintile or a lower quintile. For example, the first quintile received 4.6 percent of total income in 1987; the second quintile received 10.8 percent. Together they received 15.4 percent. Therefore, the cumulative percentage of income received by the bottom two quintiles was 15.4 percent. Similar calculations reveal the cumulative distribution of the bottom three and bottom four quintiles (32.3 percent and 56.3 percent, respectively).

Information about the cumulative distribution of income can be presented diagramatically with a **Lorenz curve.** A Lorenz curve shows the relationship between percentage of families and percentage of income. For example, the Lorenz curve of Figure 33-1 shows that in 1987 the bottom 40 percent of families, when arranged by income, received 15.4 percent of the nation's total income.

All Lorenz curves share a common feature. They start at the bottom left corner of the box (zero percent of families receive zero percent of income) and they end at the top right corner (100 percent of families receive 100 percent of income). What is revealing is the path of the Lorenz curve between these two points. If the distribution of income were perfectly equal, the first 20 percent of families would receive 20 percent of income, the first 40 percent of families would receive 40 percent of income, and so on. Therefore, the Lorenz curve would be a diagonal line.

A comparison of the actual Lorenz curve with this hypothetical Lorenz curve reveals how much inequality exists within a country. The more evenly income is

Lorenz Curve

A diagram illustrating the cumulative distribution of income by families.

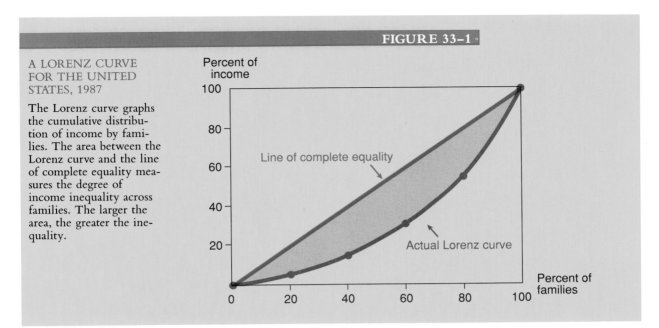

FIGURE 33–1

A LORENZ CURVE FOR THE UNITED STATES, 1987

The Lorenz curve graphs the cumulative distribution of income by families. The area between the Lorenz curve and the line of complete equality measures the degree of income inequality across families. The larger the area, the greater the inequality.

distributed, the closer the actual Lorenz curve is to the line of complete equality. Therefore, one measure of income inequality is the size of the area between these two curves (represented by the shaded area of Figure 33-1). A smaller area denotes less income inequality; a larger area, greater inequality.

YOUR TURN

Suppose income is distributed as unevenly as possible—a single family receives a country's entire income. (a) Draw the Lorenz curve associated with this distribution. (b) Shade the area between this Lorenz curve and the Lorenz curve corresponding to complete equality of income.

A Decline in Income Inequality

The Lorenz curve tracks changes in income inequality over time. When Lorenz curves are plotted for 1929 and 1987, the latter lies closer to the line of complete equality (see Figure 33-2, page 746). The implication is that income was distributed more evenly in 1987 than in 1929. Other indicators reinforce this conclusion. For example, the share of income received by families in the top quintile fell from 54 percent in 1929 to 44 percent in 1987, and the share received by the top 5 percent of families shrank from 30 percent to 17 percent (see Table 33-4, page 746).

The transformation to a more equal distribution of income did not occur gradually; rather, it was accomplished by mid-century. Over the past 40 years the distribution of income has changed very little—the share of income received by the bottom quintile has fluctuated around 5 percent, whereas the share received by the top quintile has remained at just over 40 percent. In fact, if anything, the distribution of income has become less equal in recent years (compare 1987 with 1980). The conclusion to be drawn from Table 33-4 is that the distribution of income became more equal during the first half of this century but that the movement toward greater equality has not continued since that time.

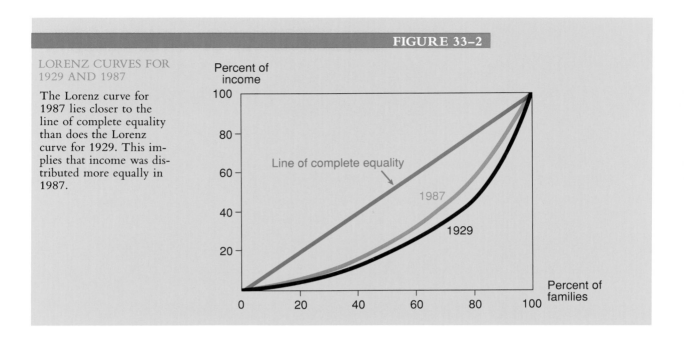

FIGURE 33-2

LORENZ CURVES FOR 1929 AND 1987

The Lorenz curve for 1987 lies closer to the line of complete equality than does the Lorenz curve for 1929. This implies that income was distributed more equally in 1987.

TABLE 33-4

THE DISTRIBUTION OF FAMILY INCOME, VARIOUS YEARS*

Quintile	Percent of income					
	1929	**1935–36**	**1950**	**1965**	**1980**	**1987**
First	}12.5**	4.1	4.5	5.2	5.1	4.6
Second		9.2	12.0	12.2	11.6	10.8
Third	13.8	14.1	17.4	17.8	17.5	16.9
Fourth	19.3	20.9	23.4	23.9	24.3	24.0
Fifth	54.4	51.7	42.7	40.9	41.6	43.7
Total	100.0	100.0	100.0	100.0	100.0	100.0
Top 5 percent	30.0	26.5	17.3	15.5	15.3	16.9

*Before taxes.

**Data unavailable separately for first and second quintiles; 12.5 for both quintiles together.

Sources: U.S. Department of Commerce, *Historical Statistics of the United States, Colonial Times to 1970*, Part 1 (1975), p. 301; *Current Population Reports,* Series P-60, No. 151 (1986), p. 37, and No. 162 (1989), p. 42.

International Comparisons

By constructing separate Lorenz curves for each country, it is possible to compare the distribution of income across countries. For example, Figure 33-3 reveals that income is distributed more equally in Japan than in the United States and, in turn, more equally in the United States than in Honduras. As a general rule, the distribution of income is more equal in industrialized countries (such as Japan and

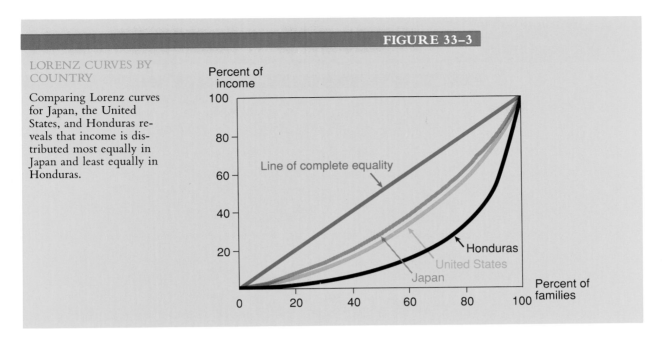

FIGURE 33-3

LORENZ CURVES BY COUNTRY

Comparing Lorenz curves for Japan, the United States, and Honduras reveals that income is distributed most equally in Japan and least equally in Honduras.

the United States) than in less developed countries (such as Honduras). The distribution is also more equal in centrally planned countries (e.g., China and the Soviet Union) than in capitalistic countries.[2]

WHY INCOMES DIFFER

Income inequality can be traced to differences in both wage income and nonwage income. First, wage rates differ. Among the reasons previously cited (in Chapters 29 and 31) are differences in age, human capital, discrimination, unions, and economic rents. Second, for any given wage rate, those who work more hours during the year receive higher wage incomes. Beyond that, families with multiple wage earners tend to earn more than families with a single wage earner.

Wealth is also distributed unevenly. In fact, the distribution of wealth is more unequal than the distribution of income. The wealthiest 2 percent of families hold 26 percent of the nation's wealth.[3] Because greater wealth leads to greater nonwage income—interest, rent, and profit—those with high concentrations of wealth can expect high incomes, even in the absence of work.

As uneven as the distribution of wealth currently is, it is actually more equal today than during the first half of the century. Indeed, the movement to greater equality of wealth contributed directly to greater equality of income. As the wealthy have seen their fortunes shrink, at least in relative terms, their income advantage over the rest of the population has narrowed. In some cases, fortunes have been wiped out, eliminating a family's once-healthy nonwage income (see Exhibit 33-1, page 748).

[2]See Margaret E. Grosh and E. Wayne Nafziger, "The Computation of World Income Distribution," *Economic Development and Cultural Change* (January 1986), pp. 347–359.

[3]U.S. Department of Commerce, *Household Wealth and Asset Ownership: 1984,* Series P-70, No. 7 (1986), p. 53.

EXHIBIT 33–1

THE MIGHTY HATH FALLEN

Nelson Bunker Hunt was once the wealthiest person in the world, with an estimated fortune of $16 billion. At the time, he boasted that "a billion dollars isn't what it used to be." Since then, both his wealth and his attitude have changed.

Hunt lost billions of dollars speculating on commodities, including an unsuccessful attempt in 1979 to corner the market for silver. His losses mounted with the purchase of speculative oil and coal leases. Then, as the price of oil plunged in the 1980s, the value of his oil properties and real estate plummetted. Unable to meet financial commitments, Bunker Hunt defaulted on his loans and in

1988, after a court ordered him to pay damages to a Peruvian silver company, Hunt filed for bankruptcy. Although he remained locked in a court battle, trying to salvage some of his wealth, it was clear that most or all of the $16 billion had been lost. In the process, the distribution of wealth in the country had become a little more equal.

Sources: Adapted from John A. Jenkins, "The Hunt Brothers: Battling a Billion-Dollar Debt," *New York Times Magazine* (September 27, 1987), p. 24; G. C. Hill and Leonard Apcar, "Losing Billions," *The Wall Street Journal* (June 27, 1986), p. 1; *Kansas City Times,* "Two Hunt Brothers File for Bankruptcy Protection," September 22, 1988, p. 1.

THE EFFECT OF TAXATION AND TRANSFERS ON THE DISTRIBUTION OF INCOME

Our discussion of the distribution of income has dealt with income before taxes and before government transfer payments (social security, housing subsidies, and so on). As it turns out, the effect of taxation on the distribution of income is not terribly important. Low- and middle-income families pay about the same percentage of their income in taxes as do high-income families. As a consequence, the after-tax distribution of income is not substantially different from the before-tax distribution.[4]

Means Test

A requirement that a family's income not exceed a certain level; if it does the family is declared ineligible for that particular form of public assistance.

Transfer payments are another story. Many transfer payments are **means-tested:** only families with incomes below a certain level qualify and, among those that qualify, families with the lowest incomes receive the greatest aid. Therefore, these payments disproportionately benefit low-income families. If the value of transfer payments is included, the distribution of income becomes considerably more equal.[5] Figure 33-4 depicts the distribution of income both before and after adjusting for taxes and transfer payments. Almost all the change is due to the effect of transfer payments.

HOW MUCH INCOME INEQUALITY DO WE WANT?

Few advocate complete equality of income. If everyone were guaranteed the same income, what incentive would a person have to work hard, to be diligent, to put in long hours? Why accept a job with a high risk of injury or poor working conditions?

---

[4]In technical terms the current tax system is approximately *proportional.* For evidence of this, see Joseph A. Pechman, *Who Paid the Taxes, 1966–85?* (Washington, DC: The Brookings Institution, 1985), especially pp. 4–5.

[5]According to one study, adjusting for taxes and transfers raised the share of income received by the bottom quintile from 5.4 percent to 12.5 percent in 1972; the share received by the top quintile fell from 41.4 percent to 33.3 percent. See Edgar K. Browning, "The Trend Toward Equality in the Distribution of Net Income," *Southern Economic Journal* (July 1976), p. 914. Other studies find a somewhat smaller effect but agree with the basic conclusion: transfers substantially reduce income inequality.

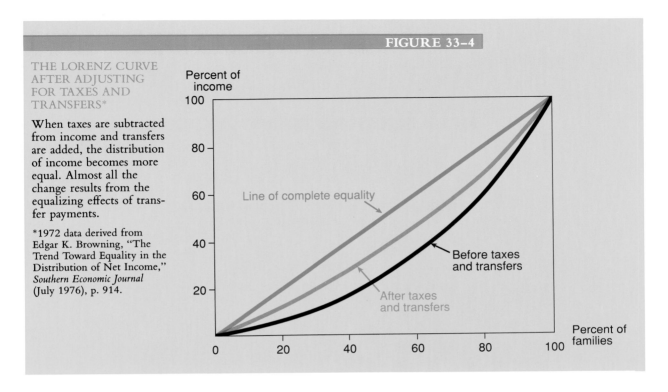

FIGURE 33–4

THE LORENZ CURVE AFTER ADJUSTING FOR TAXES AND TRANSFERS*

When taxes are subtracted from income and transfers are added, the distribution of income becomes more equal. Almost all the change results from the equalizing effects of transfer payments.

*1972 data derived from Edgar K. Browning, "The Trend Toward Equality in the Distribution of Net Income," *Southern Economic Journal* (July 1976), p. 914.

Why work at all? And why should entrepreneurs innovate if they do not receive any reward from the success of a new product or a new technique of production?

Complete equality of income blunts or even eliminates the incentive to use resources efficiently. In turn, if resources remain idle or underused and if new technologies remain undeveloped, the result is a lower level of output. Although everyone gets an equal slice of the economic pie, that pie is likely to be quite skimpy. Equality has a cost.

Conversely, a pure market-based distribution of income—which rewards hard work, long hours, unpleasant employment, and innovation—encourages economic efficiency. By compensating resources on the basis of how much they contribute, such a system promotes maximum production. On the other hand, the resulting distribution of income is cold and impersonal. If rewards are based solely on one's contribution to output, those who do not contribute do not eat. Pity those unable to work—the young, the old, the ill, the physically impaired. Unless they have substantial nonwage income or someone to look after them, they may not survive.

Almost everyone agrees that such a distribution of income is intolerable and that those unable to make it on their own warrant public assistance. The thorny issues concern the magnitude of public support and its distribution. Who should receive assistance and how much? What form should the assistance take? How should the revenues necessary to fund this support be raised? As low-income families receive transfer payments, the distribution of income becomes more equal. How much equality do we want? These are all issues within the realm of *normative economics*.

To achieve greater equality, the government taxes income, transferring funds to the poor. But taxes reduce the effective reward for productive activities (work, innovation, and the like), thereby discouraging such activities among the general population. Similarly, transfer payments blunt work incentives of the poor. Because of such disincentives, a policy of taxation and transfers reduces economic efficiency and therefore the level of output. In other words, the government faces a trade-off between economic efficiency and equality of income: greater equality can be achieved only by accepting a lower level of output.

As an analogy, consider the transfer of water from one barrel, mostly full, to a second barrel, mostly empty, using a leaky bucket.[6] In the transfer, water that spills is lost. How much water (income) we choose to transfer likely depends on the size of the leak (the efficiency loss). If the leak is small, we may prefer large transfers, bringing the water levels in the two barrels close together. But if the leak is great, then so much water would be lost in the transfer that we may accept considerable inequality. The optimal amount of redistribution ultimately depends on (a) the size of the leak and (b) the importance one attaches to greater equality.

A distinction must also be made between *equality of outcomes* and *equality of opportunities.* Equal opportunity means that all start the race with an equal chance to win. Equal outcomes mean that all share the prize equally. Different outcomes may be viewed as more acceptable when they reflect differences in effort rather than unfair opportunity. If two people have equal labor-market skills but one works longer and harder than the second, should we really be bothered that income of the first is greater? Isn't income inequality more objectionable where it results from one individual starting with a big advantage over the other?

Those who emphasize equal opportunity tend to favor programs that give disadvantaged individuals a greater chance to succeed, as opposed to greater income per se. Such programs include breaking down entry barriers to certain occupations, facilitating worker mobility, attacking discrimination, bringing higher education within the reach of the poor, and providing good nutrition for children and expectant mothers.

Because views of equality vary across individuals, as does the emphasis placed on equality, there is no consensus concerning the proper role of government in the redistribution of income. Traditionally, however, the bulk of government support has been aimed at people near or below the *poverty line.* Before considering specific programs to alter the distribution of income, it is appropriate to take a look at the principal target of these programs—the poor.

POVERTY

There are alternative views of poverty. Some define poverty in *relative* terms—for example, those in the bottom 20 percent of the income distribution or those whose income is less than 50 percent of the median income. The problem with such definitions is that they ignore changes in living standards due to economic growth. Even if each family's purchasing power were to double, so that it could buy twice as much as before, poverty as just defined would not diminish. Indeed, if the poor were, by definition, those in the bottom quintile of the income distribution, the war on poverty would be doomed to failure. No matter how much income a country has or how it is divided, there must always be a bottom quintile.

Because of shortcomings in the concept of relative poverty, many prefer to define poverty in *absolute* terms—that is, in terms of how much income is required to maintain some minimum standard of living. According to this concept, one first determines how much income is required to buy basic goods and services. Those whose incomes fall below this level—the **poverty line**—are classified as poor. Note

Poverty Line
A level of income below which a family is classified as poor. The poverty line is based on the cost of those items deemed necessary to maintain a minimally acceptable standard of living.

---

[6]This example comes from Arthur Okun, *Equality and Efficiency: The Big Tradeoff* (Washington, DC: The Brookings Institution, 1975).

that when poverty is defined in absolute terms, the percentage of the population counted as poor may change over time even if the distribution of income remains constant. In particular, rising incomes tend to reduce poverty—other things equal—whereas falling incomes increase poverty.

THE OFFICIAL POVERTY LINE

The United States government relies on the concept of absolute poverty. It first began calculating poverty lines in 1964 based on estimates by the U.S. Department of Agriculture of the cost of an "economy food plan."[7] According to earlier research by the Department of Agriculture, families with three or more members spent an average of one-third of their income on food. Therefore, the poverty line for these families was set equal to three times the cost of the economy food plan. For smaller families the food budget was slightly less than one-third of income; therefore, a larger multiple was used. Because food budgets vary with family size, poverty lines also depend on family size. Poverty lines are updated each year to reflect changes in the cost of living as measured by the Consumer Price Index. The poverty lines for 1987 are presented in Table 33-5.[8]

Based on these figures, 32.5 million people in the United States were living in poverty, or about 13.5 percent of the population. Some argue, however, that the situation was actually worse—that government statistics understate poverty. They note that some individuals with incomes above the poverty line have high medical expenses, heavy debts, or other obligations that prevent them from achieving a minimally acceptable standard of living. If such individuals were counted as poor, the poverty rate would be substantially higher.

Others take the opposite position, contending that poverty is less severe than official figures indicate. One reason is that poverty statistics are based solely on money income. They exclude noncash government support—what are called **in-kind transfers.** Among the common in-kind transfers are food stamps, housing assistance, and free or subsidized medical care. If the value of in-kind transfers were counted as income, fewer families would have incomes below the poverty line. For

In-Kind Transfers
Transfer payments that consist of goods and services rather than cash. Included are food, public housing, and medical care.

TABLE 33-5	
POVERTY LINES BY FAMILY SIZE, 1987	
Number of persons in family	**Poverty line**
One	$ 5,778
Two	7,397
Three	9,056
Four	11,611
Five	13,737
Six	15,509
Seven	17,649
Eight	19,515
Nine or more	23,105

Source: U.S. Department of Commerce, *Current Population Reports*, Series P-60, No. 163 (1989), p. 157.

[7]The Department of Agriculture calculates the cost of four different food plans: economy, low-cost, moderate-cost, and liberal. The economy plan is the most basic—that is, least generous.

[8]Actually, poverty lines or, as they are sometimes called, "poverty indexes," also vary with the age of household head and location (urban or rural). The numbers in Table 33-5 are weighted averages.

example, had the market value of in-kind transfers been included, the poverty rate in 1987 would have fallen from 13.5 percent to 8.5 percent. Also excluded from income is the rental value of owner-occupied housing. A family that owns its dwelling needs less income to achieve a given standard of living than a family that rents. Had imputed rents been counted as income for homeowners, poverty statistics would have declined even further.

What this points out is that any definition of poverty is arbitrary. How much poverty a country has depends on how one defines poverty. The official measure of poverty is used not because it is perfect but because some measure had to be chosen. Once a measure is selected, it can help identify the poor and track changes in their numbers over time. This may help the government fashion antipoverty programs and measure their success (or lack of success) in alleviating poverty.

WHO ARE THE POOR?

There is no simple profile of the poor. The poor are young and old, male and female, members of every race. They inhabit every state, live in cities and on farms. Yet, even though poverty permeates our entire society, it is not distributed evenly across groups.

As Table 33-6 indicates, blacks are three times as likely to be poor as whites, and poverty among Hispanics is almost as great as among blacks. Poverty is least likely in married-couple families and most likely in families without a husband present. Poverty is more common for children than for adults, as more than one-fifth of the population 14 and younger lives in poverty.

By contrast, the poverty rate among the elderly is *below* the national average. This is a relatively recent development (see Figure 33-5). In 1966, the poverty rate for those 65 and older was almost twice the national average. Since then, poverty has

TABLE 33-6	

THE DISTRIBUTION OF POVERTY, 1987

Group	Percent below the poverty line
All persons	13.5
White	10.5
Black	33.1
Hispanic	28.2
Age of person	
Under 15	21.4
15 to 24	15.7
25 to 44	10.2
45 to 54	8.1
55 to 59	9.8
60 to 64	10.8
65 and over	12.2
All families	10.8
Married-couple families	6.0
Male head, no wife	12.5
Female head, no husband	34.3
All unrelated individuals	20.8

Source: U.S. Department of Commerce, *Current Population Reports*, Series P-60, No. 163 (1989).

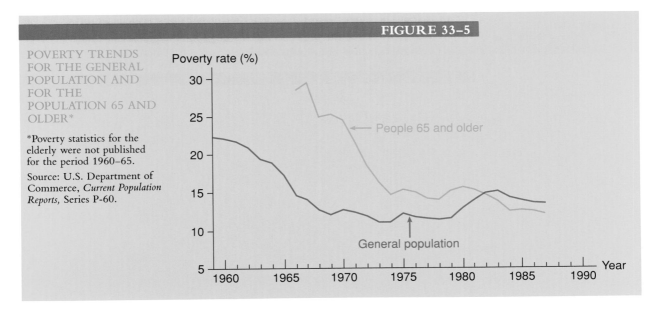

FIGURE 33–5

POVERTY TRENDS FOR THE GENERAL POPULATION AND FOR THE POPULATION 65 AND OLDER*

*Poverty statistics for the elderly were not published for the period 1960–65.

Source: U.S. Department of Commerce, *Current Population Reports,* Series P-60.

fallen faster for the elderly than for any other age group. This is due in part to increased social spending on the elderly. For instance, social security benefits have increased faster than wages over this period. Other forms of income, including pensions and interest, have also increased substantially. Because wealth is concentrated in the hands of the elderly,[9] they have been the principal beneficiaries of increased wealth in the economy.

If in-kind transfers are included, the relative gains of the elderly are even more dramatic—since in-kind transfers (notably medical care) are heavily skewed in favor of the aged. When in-kind transfers are considered income, the poverty rate among the elderly falls to 2 percent, compared to 16 percent for young children (see Table 33-7). This is not to deny that many elderly live substandard lives. What it does

TABLE 33-7

POVERTY RATES IF IN-KIND TRANSFERS ARE COUNTED
AS INCOME, 1987*

Age group	Percent below the poverty line
All persons	8.5
Under 6 years	15.7
6 to 17 years	12.1
18 to 24 years	11.9
25 to 44 years	7.1
45 to 64 years	6.1
65 years and over	2.1

*Based on the market value of in-kind transfers.

Source: U.S. Bureau of the Census, *Estimates of Poverty Including the Value of Noncash Benefits: 1987,* Technical Paper 58, 1988, p. 5.

[9]The median net worth in 1984 was $32,667 for all households but $60,266 for households whose head was 65 or older. See U.S. Department of Commerce, *Household Wealth,* p. 4.

indicate is that the elderly are no longer the most impoverished age group. That distinction now belongs to children.

TRENDS IN POVERTY

Between 1959 and 1969 the overall poverty rate fell from 22.4 percent to 12.1 percent (see Figure 33-5). This was due in part to a strengthening economy. As employment and wages increased, poverty eased. Transfer payments also increased rapidly during this period, and some analysts credit them with contributing to the decline.

After showing little movement during the 1970s, the poverty rate started rising during the early 1980s. This reflected a combination of forces. First, the economy experienced its most severe downturn since the Great Depression. Many workers lost their jobs or had their hours of work cut back, pushing additional families below the poverty line. Second, the percentage of families headed by single females was growing. As previously noted, this is the family arrangement with the highest incidence of poverty. Critics of the Reagan Administration also attribute some of the increased poverty to a reorientation of spending by the federal government away from social programs and toward defense. They claim that budget cutbacks in social programs allowed too many families to fall through the government's *safety net*.

Do Transfers Reduce Poverty?

Not everyone accepts the preceding argument.[10] Some contend that transfer programs have actually promoted poverty by discouraging labor supply. Because the level of transfer payments is based on a family's income, individuals who work, and therefore earn wage income, are *rewarded* by having their transfer payments reduced or even eliminated. Once the lost transfer payments are factored in, work often loses its appeal. In extreme cases the government may reduce transfer payments on a dollar-for-dollar basis—an additional dollar of wage income leads to a one-dollar loss of transfer payments. In that event, additional work fails to increase income at all. Instead of encouraging individuals to work, gain experience, and ultimately pull themselves out of poverty, the government fosters reliance on transfer programs.

Critics of transfer programs also observe that until recently many states denied welfare payments to families as long as an able-bodied male was present. Such a provision encouraged the breakup of families, which in turn increased poverty. According to this view, the increase in the percentage of families headed by single females is, at least in part, the direct consequence of past transfer programs.

Even supporters of transfer payments concede that these programs have adverse incentives. What is at issue is the magnitude of these effects. Those favoring increased government support tend to downplay the disincentive effects, arguing that on balance transfer payments reduce poverty. Others disagree. Because there is no consensus on the impact of transfer programs, there is also no agreement on whether scaling back these programs has contributed to poverty. What is clear is that the downward trend in poverty had ended by the early 1970s. Although the poverty rate has declined slightly in recent years, it is higher today than 20 years ago.

---

[10]See Lowell Gallaway and Richard Vedder, *Paying People to Be Poor,* National Center for Policy Analysis, Policy Report No. 121, February 1986; James Gwartney and Thomas S. McCaleb, "Have Antipoverty Programs Increased Poverty?" *Cato Journal* (Spring/Summer, 1985), pp. 1–16.

Conflicting Views of Poverty

> See-saw, Margery Daw,
> Jacky shall have a new master;
> Jacky shall have but a penny a day,
> Because he can't work any faster.

The success and even appropriateness of transfer programs depend on why people are poor. Does their poverty result from a lack of effort on their part—not working or not working any faster? If it does, concern about work disincentives is well placed. Alternatively, if poverty arises because of an inability to work, then disincentive effects are unimportant. Programs that provide income to individuals incapable of working unambiguously reduce poverty. The debate over how transfer payments affect poverty is thus colored by one's view of whether poverty is due to inadequate effort or to factors beyond an individual's control.

The truth lies somewhere between these two extremes. Some poverty reflects the underutilization of labor market skills; other poverty is rooted in causes unrelated to labor markets—old age, illness, disability, and others. What this suggests is that different antipoverty programs may be appropriate for different families, depending on the family's situation. In particular, it may be appropriate to differentiate between families that can substantially contribute to their own support and those that cannot.

Recent government policy has moved in this direction. For instance, during the 1980s many states began requiring able-bodied adults to work in order to be eligible for transfer payments. Such a system, workfare, is designed not only to address work disincentives but to lay the groundwork for the working poor to pull themselves out of poverty. Those on workfare often receive remedial education, training, and childcare assistance. Once employed, they also gain valuable experience, working skills, and sometimes enhanced self-esteem. Such gains, it is hoped, will ultimately enable the person to become self-sufficient. To date, state workfare programs have met with mixed success (see Exhibit 33-2, page 756).

In 1988, Congress enacted legislation to implement workfare on a national basis by 1993. Single parents with children over the age of three will be required to work or to participate in approved training and education programs in order to remain eligible for government support. In families with two parents, support will be conditional on at least one parent searching for a job and, until one is found, spending a minimum of 16 hours per week performing some government or community service.

For those capable of working there is no doubt that work and job-market skills reduce one's chance of being poor. Among families where the household head works year round, the poverty rate is less than four percent (see Table 33-8, page 756). The poverty rate is much higher when the household head works only part year and higher still when the head fails to work at all. Poverty is similarly related to education. Those who fail to finish high school are about five times as likely to be poor as those with at least one year of college. The implication is that, for those who are employable, education, workfare, and other programs that enhance workers' skills may alleviate poverty.

Workfare
A program in which low-income individuals receive government support in return for agreeing to work.

Is Poverty Chronic?

Employment or additional skills may be the ticket for some low-income families, but for others work is not an option. For them, escaping poverty is more difficult. Lacking the means to earn income, they tend to remain poor year after year. But

---

EXHIBIT 33–2

TWO VIEWS OF
WORKFARE:
"IT HELPS ME" . . .
"IT'S A WASTE"

Yvette Burgos, 25, Boston, three children, 10 years on welfare, trained under Massachusetts' new education and training program and placed with a nonprofit firm, Boston Fuel Consortium. Now, office manager:

I had nothing to do before. Now, I look forward to every day of getting to work and knowing that other people are relying on me. I enjoy getting up and putting on makeup and dressing for work.

It helps me to know that I can do things. My kids like having a working mother. We were close, but we're much closer now. They respect me, and they're proud of what I've done. So am I. I could not have dreamed things would ever be this good for us.

I feel free—free to be what I want and do what I want and buy what I want. I'm on a tight budget, but before I was really on a tight budget. I couldn't do anything.

Peggy Deno, 37, San Diego, three children, more than 10 years on welfare, on workfare training last year, still looking for a job:

I believe workfare is a waste of the taxpayers' money. They put you on a video thing and have you fill out job applications. It's common-sense stuff. Most people in my class didn't want to work. I turned down a job assembling electronic components because they don't want to pay more than $4 an hour. I've worked in electronics before and don't think I should have to start as a trainee.

I'd rather be making it on my own, but when I go back to work, I want to tell welfare where to go.

Peggy Deno and family.

Source: Richard Alm, et al., "States Refocus Welfare, With Eye on 'Real' Jobs," *U.S. News & World Report,* October 28, 1985, p. 58. Copyright October 28, 1985, U.S. News & World Report; reprinted by permission.

TABLE 33-8

POVERTY RATES AMONG FAMILIES BY EMPLOYMENT STATUS AND EDUCATION OF HOUSEHOLD HEAD, 1987

Employment status or education	Poverty rate (%)
Employment status in 1987	
Did not work	25.3
Worked fewer than 50 weeks	19.9
Worked at least 50 weeks	3.4
Full time	2.7
Education*	
Elementary: No years completed	41.0
1 to 7 years	27.4
8 years	17.1
High school: 1 to 3 years	18.8
4 years	9.3
College: 1 year or more	3.7

*Education series are for household heads 25 and older.

Source: U.S. Department of Commerce, *Current Population Reports,* Series P-60, No. 161 (1988), p. 36.

how much poverty is long-term or chronic, and how much is transistory? If policymakers want to combat poverty, they must understand its nature.

To shed light on this issue, one study tracked 5000 families over a ten-year period.[11] It found that most poverty is transitory. Of those who were poor at some time during the ten years, most were poor two years or less. Poor law students became rich lawyers. Unemployed poor became employed nonpoor. Single adults (and their children) escaped poverty when they married or remarried. Yet, interspersed among the temporary poor was a small pool of chronic poor. About 2.6 percent of the people were poor in at least eight of the ten years.

The picture that emerges is of two groups of poor. For the larger group, poverty is short-term. It often results from temporary illness, marital breakups, job loss, or other setbacks. For such individuals, transfer payments are a temporary crutch; they do not lead to long-term welfare dependency. At the same time, there is a small mass of chronic poor. For them, transfer payments provide more than temporary relief; they are a principal source of long-term income.

In conclusion, the poor are not a monolithic group. They differ in age, race, and family arrangement. Some are readily employable; others are not. Some remain poor briefly; others never escape poverty. There is no single cause of poverty and therefore no single solution. It is for this reason that the government has a variety of programs to assist the poor.

MAJOR ANTIPOVERTY PROGRAMS

Scores of government programs affect poverty, from tax laws that encourage business to expand hiring to college loans that enable students to increase their earnings power. Even general economic policy—including government spending, taxation, and monetary policy—impacts poverty by influencing the level of economic activity. In fact, some argue that a strong economy is the single most-effective weapon against poverty.

Although programs such as those just cited may reduce poverty, the government's *war on poverty* has been waged primarily with (a) *employment and training programs* (designed to increase labor income of unemployed and low-skilled workers) and (b) *transfer programs* (designed to redistribute income from the population at large to those segments deemed to have special needs).

EMPLOYMENT AND TRAINING PROGRAMS

Government training programs are designed to impart valuable skills to workers so they may earn sufficient wage income to support themselves and their families. These programs have often failed to achieve their objectives. Many early programs were criticized as cost-ineffective, since only a small portion of program costs were devoted to training. Furthermore, the skills imparted to workers were not always the ones sought by employers. Many workers either failed to complete their training or failed to obtain jobs once the training was completed.

More recently, training programs have increased the percentage of funding devoted to training (rather than to administration, supplies, and so forth) and have attempted to work in conjunction with private employers. For example, the Job Training Partnership Act (JTPA) of 1982 established Private Industry Councils

---

[11]Greg J. Duncan, et al., *Years of Poverty, Years of Plenty: The Changing Fortunes of American Workers and Families* (Ann Arbor, MI: Institute for Social Research, 1984).

(PICs) through which representatives of the local business community attempt to identify the skills required in the local labor market. Although some fault the distribution of funds (states where workers already enjoy high wages receive more funding than low-wage states),[12] programs such as JTPA should enable the government to do a better job of matching worker skills to available jobs.

An alternative to training workers for jobs in the private sector is for the government itself to employ these workers through public employment programs. Such jobs are often criticized as "make work." In other words, it is alleged that these workers are not producing valuable goods and services. There is also some question as to how many new jobs are created. When the federal government provided state and local governments with funds to create additional public-sector jobs, studies found that state and local governments used some of this funding to employ workers they would have hired anyway. Thus, there was only a modest expansion of public-sector jobs. Furthermore, some of those employed by the government would have been able to find jobs in the private sector, meaning that public-sector jobs were crowding out private-sector jobs. For such reasons, the government in recent years has shied away from public employment programs, emphasizing instead expanded employment in the private sector.

TRANSFER PROGRAMS

Social Insurance
Transfer programs based on some criteria other than income (e.g., retirement or unemployment).
Public Assistance/Welfare
Transfer programs that are means-tested—that is, available only to low-income families.

Government transfer programs fall into two categories—(a) social insurance and (b) public assistance or welfare. Social insurance programs are available to individuals regardless of their income. Examples are social security and unemployment insurance, which provide benefits to rich and poor alike. In contrast, welfare programs are means-tested—only low-income families qualify. As a result, the poor receive a greater share of welfare payments than social insurance payments. In other words, welfare programs are more effective at redistributing income to the poor. The major transfer programs are listed in Table 33-9.

Social Insurance

Social Security and Medicare   The single largest transfer program is Old Age, Survivors, and Disability Insurance (OASDI) or, as it is commonly called, *social security*.[13] Established in 1935, social security has expanded greatly over time. In 1991, an estimated 40 million beneficiaries will receive cash payments totalling $262 billion, or roughly five percent of GNP. Beneficiaries include retired workers 62 and older; disabled workers; and spouses, children, and survivors of insured workers.

In 1965, the federal government increased its commitment to retired and disabled workers by creating *medicare*. Also included in the medicare program are victims of end-stage renal (kidney) disease. Medicare's main component, hospital insurance, pays for care provided in hospitals and in various other health facilities. In addition, those who qualify for medicare may purchase heavily subsidized health insurance that pays most of the cost of physician services, laboratory fees, and medical equipment. Medicare is the largest and most expensive of the transfer programs providing in-kind benefits.

---

[12]See James F. Ragan and Daniel J. Slottje, "Problems with Allocating Federal Grants on the Basis of Unemployment Statistics," Working Paper No. 8713, Southern Methodist University, December 1987.

[13]Sometimes the term "social security" is used more broadly to include medicare as well as OASDI.

TABLE 33-9			
MAJOR TRANSFER PROGRAMS			
		Expenditures (billions of dollars)	
Program	**Date enacted**	**1988**	**1991***
Social insurance			
Cash benefits:			
Social security (OASDI)	1935	$219	$262
Unemployment insurance (UI)	1935	15	16
In-kind benefits:			
Medicare	1965	79	107
Public assistance (welfare)			
Cash benefits:			
Aid to Families with Dependent Children (AFDC)	1935	20	19
Supplemental Security Income (SSI)	1972	12	14
In-kind benefits:			
Medicaid	1965	55	72
Food stamps, nutrition assistance	1964	20	22
Housing assistance	1937	14	17

*Estimated.

Source: Executive Office of the President, *Budget of the United States Government, Fiscal Year 1990.*

Both social security and medicare are financed by a payroll tax. In 1989, employers and employees each paid a tax of 7.51 percent of the worker's first $48,000 in wages and salaries. In other words, a worker earning $10,000 in 1989 paid $751 in taxes for social security and medicare; a worker making $48,000 or more paid $3604.80 (7.51 percent of $48,000). In each case the employer was required to match this tax. Thus, the combined employer-employee tax was as high as $7209.60 for some workers.

Social security benefits and taxes are determined by Congress. Currently, both monthly benefits and the tax base ($48,000 in 1989) are indexed to inflation—they rise in response to higher prices. But benefits and taxes can be changed at any time. When the postwar baby boom retires next century and the ratio of retirees to workers rises, it may be necessary to further increase taxes, to reduce benefits, or to otherwise adjust the system so that taxes will be sufficient to support benefits. Over the near term, however, social security is considered sound and, for many Americans, remains a major source of income (see Exhibit 7-1).

Unemployment Insurance Unemployment insurance benefits are available to jobless workers who qualify for regular or extended unemployment insurance (UI) programs. Because these programs are administered by states, eligibility requirements and the level of benefits vary from state to state. Under the regular UI program, workers receive benefits for up to 26 weeks. Workers in states with high unemployment rates may also qualify for the extended UI program, which provides benefits for up to 13 additional weeks (39 weeks total). UI benefits are financed by a payroll tax levied on employers.

TABLE 33-10	
AVERAGE AFDC PAYMENT BY STATE, MARCH 1989	
State	**Payment per family**
Low-payment states	
Alabama	$114
Mississippi	120
Louisiana	168
Texas	168
High-payment states	
New York	518
Connecticut	585
California	611
Alaska	687

Source: U.S. Department of Health and Human Services, Office of Family Assistance, unpublished data, 1989.

Public Assistance

Aid to Families with Dependent Children   Through Aid to Families with Dependent Children (AFDC), federal, state, and local governments provide assistance to low-income families with children. Although the federal government pays for over half the cost of this program, individual states determine the level of benefits. For example, in 1989 the average monthly payment per family was $611 in California, but only $114 in Alabama (see Table 33-10). Because the poor of the various states are treated differently, some have criticized AFDC as inequitable.

In the past, AFDC has also been criticized for encouraging family breakups. In some states the presence of an able-bodied male was sufficient to disqualify the family from AFDC. For a program that is supposed to help the children of low-income families, discouraging the father from living with them may actually worsen their plight. Recognizing this, Congress reformed the AFDC program in 1988 and now requires that states extend eligibility to two-parent families.

Supplemental Security Income   Low-income individuals who are aged, blind, or disabled may also qualify for cash assistance under Supplemental Security Income (SSI). The basic SSI program is paid for by the federal government out of general tax revenues; some states supplement these federal payments.

In-Kind Benefits   In addition to cash support, low-income families receive various types of noncash or in-kind benefits. In fact, the government spends twice as much on in-kind transfers to the poor as on cash transfers. Among the major in-kind benefits are health care (medicaid), food (through food stamps, child nutrition programs, and the distribution of surplus foods), and housing assistance (including public housing and rent subsidies).

NEGATIVE INCOME TAX

Some have proposed scrapping the myriad of public assistance programs and replacing them with a negative income tax—a single program for subsidizing low-income families. One version of the negative income tax, called the Family

Assistance Plan, was endorsed by President Richard Nixon and passed the House of Representatives before being killed by the Senate. Presidents Ford and Carter later proposed their own variants of the negative income tax, again without success.

The program favored by these presidents is called a negative income tax because families with incomes below a certain level would receive a subsidy or *negative tax* from the federal government. For example, a family of four might be guaranteed a minimum income of $8000 per year. If the family had no earned income, the government would provide the full $8000. But if the family received income from other sources (e.g., work), it would be viewed as less needy and therefore receive a lower level of support.

If the family earned $3000 in wage income, the government might reduce the subsidy by $2000. In that event the family would face an implicit tax rate of 2/3, meaning that the government reduces its subsidy by an amount equal to two-thirds the family's earned income.[14] Even though the family's wage income would rise from $0 to $3000, its total income (earned income plus subsidy) would increase by only $1000—from $8000 to $9000 (see Table 33-11).

Subsequent increases in income would further reduce the subsidy until it was eventually phased out. Beyond that point, the family would be required to start paying taxes—that is, its income would be subject to a positive tax rather than a negative tax. The point at which the negative income tax ends and a positive income tax begins is called the break-even income. Its value is given by the following formula:

$$\text{break-even income} = \frac{\text{guaranteed annual income}}{\text{implicit tax rate}}$$

In the preceding example, the break-even income would be $8000/(2/3) = $12,000. Families with incomes below $12,000 would receive government assistance through the negative income tax; families with incomes above $12,000 would be taxpayers.

Those favoring a negative income tax argue that it would eliminate inequitable treatment of the poor by ensuring that income assistance is uniform across states. They also claim that it would be easier to administer than the present mix of programs. On the other hand, even supporters of a negative income tax concede that it probably would be more costly than current public assistance programs and that it would fail to eliminate the work disincentives plaguing these programs, although in many cases it would reduce existing disincentives.

TABLE 33-11			
A HYPOTHETICAL NEGATIVE INCOME-TAX PLAN*			
Earned income	Subsidy (NIT)	Implicit tax	Total income
$ 0	$8,000	$ 0	$ 8,000
3,000	6,000	2,000	9,000
6,000	4,000	4,000	10,000
9,000	2,000	6,000	11,000
12,000	0	8,000	12,000

*Assumes a maximum subsidy of $8000 and an implicit tax rate of two-thirds.

[14]The term "benefit reduction rate" is sometimes used in place of "implicit tax rate."

Work disincentives arise for two reasons. First, a negative income tax reduces the cost of not working by guaranteeing some minimum income to those who do not work. Second, it reduces the effective benefit of work—wage income minus the implicit tax. Given an implicit tax rate of 2/3, a worker earning $4.50 per hour would actually net only $1.50 per hour once the lost subsidy is factored in. By reducing the effective rate of compensation, the negative income tax decreases the willingness of people to accept employment.

The work disincentive could be reduced by lowering the implicit tax rate. For example, cutting the implicit tax rate from 2/3 to 1/3 would effectively double the rate of compensation. Each hour worked would increase total income by $3.00 rather than by $1.50. This would encourage additional workers to accept employment, but it would also increase the number of families receiving a negative income tax. Given an implicit tax rate of 1/3, the break-even income would rise to $24,000. In other words, families whose income falls between $12,000 and $24,000—families whose need is less severe—would now be receiving government support. This could add considerably to the cost of the program. In fact, a major reason that Congress failed to enact a negative income-tax program was its belief that any negative income tax would either seriously discourage work or carry a high price tag. Neither option was considered attractive.

Although a negative income tax has not been implemented, dissatisfaction with welfare programs has prompted reforms at both the federal and state levels. The trend at present appears to be for the government to provide greater assistance in the form of day care, transportation, training, and health insurance but to expect greater work efforts from able-bodied adults who receive this assistance. Those capable of holding a job are now generally required either to look for work or to undergo the training and education that may ultimately lead to employment. If the number of poor with jobs can be increased, that would allow the government to concentrate on those individuals unable to support themselves.

SUMMARY

1. Income is distributed unevenly in the United States. When arranged in order of income, the top 20 percent of families receive more than 40 percent of total income; the bottom 20 percent receive less than 5 percent.
2. One way to measure income inequality is with a Lorenz curve, which measures the cumulative distribution of income across families. The Lorenz curve indicates that the distribution of income is more equal now than it was during the first half of the century.
3. Income inequality is due to differences in both wage and nonwage income. Families that receive higher wage rates, work more hours, and have multiple wage earners tend to earn greater wage income than other families. Similarly, families with greater wealth tend to receive more nonwage income.
4. Taxes do not substantially alter the distribution of income, but transfer payments do. Because many transfer payments are geared to the low-income population, if the value of transfers is included the distribution of income becomes considerably more equal.
5. There is a trade-off between equality of income and economic efficiency. Programs designed to transfer income to the low-income population lead to lower levels of output. The issues of how much income equality a society should have and how best to achieve that equality fall within the realm of normative economics.
6. The U.S. government began calculating its official *poverty line* in 1964, based on the cost of food. Poverty lines are now updated annually based on increases in the general cost of living.
7. In the United States, approximately one person in seven lives below the poverty line. Although the rate of poverty declined sharply in the 1960s, it stabilized in the 1970s and increased during the early 1980s.

8. Poverty rates are higher than average for children, blacks, Hispanics, and female-headed households. They are lower than average for the elderly, the well educated, and families with a working head.

9. Some argue that greater transfer payments are needed to reduce poverty. In contrast, others claim that past transfer programs have contributed to poverty by reducing the incentive to work and by encouraging family breakups. Recent reforms have attempted to address these concerns by promoting work among the able-bodied poor (through workfare programs) and by extending eligibility to two-parent families.

10. Although some poverty is chronic, most poverty is short-lived. It results from temporary illness, marital breakups, job loss, or other setbacks. For such individuals, transfer payments do not lead to long-term welfare dependency.

11. The government's main weapons against poverty have been employment and training programs and transfer programs. Training programs are designed to impart valuable labor-market skills to workers so they may pull themselves out of poverty. In contrast, public employment programs directly create government jobs for the disadvantaged or unemployed worker. Because many question the value of public employment work, these programs have fallen out of favor in recent years.

12. Transfer programs provide either social insurance or public assistance. Social insurance programs include social security, medicare, and unemployment insurance. They provide income, regardless of need, to persons who satisfy certain criteria (e.g., retirement, disability, or unemployment). Public assistance or welfare programs provide income only to families below a certain income. Some public assistance programs provide cash (e.g., AFDC and Supplemental Security Income); others provide in-kind (noncash) benefits (e.g., food stamps, housing assistance, and medical care).

13. In place of public assistance programs, some advocate a negative income tax. This would provide a subsidy to low-income families, the value of which would be reduced as earned income increased. A negative income tax would be easier to administer than present programs and would eliminate the inequitable treatment of the poor across states. On the other hand, it would probably be costlier than present programs and would not eliminate work disincentives.

KEY TERMS

Lorenz curve
means test
poverty line
in-kind transfers
workfare

social insurance
public assistance/welfare
negative income tax
implicit tax rate
break-even income

STUDY QUESTIONS AND PROBLEMS

1. The following table contains data on the distribution of income in 1987 broken down by race.

	Percent of income	
Quintile	Whites	Blacks
First	5.1	3.3
Second	11.2	8.7
Third	17.0	15.5
Fourth	23.8	25.1
Fifth	42.9	47.4
Total	100.0	100.0

a. Construct the cumulative distribution of income for each race.

b. Draw the corresponding Lorenz curves.

c. For which group is income distributed more equally?

2. The United States has an estate tax but, because of a generous exemption, only large estates are subject to the tax. Thus, only the property of wealthy individuals is taxed before being transferred to heirs. How does this tax on inherited wealth affect the distribution of income? Why does it have this effect?

3. The United States is a rich country. Why doesn't the government guarantee everyone an income above the poverty line?

4. What is the difference between relative poverty and absolute poverty? On which is the government's poverty line based? How was the government's poverty line originally constructed?

5. Why do some claim that the government's count of poverty is too low? Why do others claim that it is too high?

6. How would more rapid economic growth affect poverty? Is growth by itself likely to eliminate poverty? Explain.

7. Why do you think poverty is more severe for blacks than for whites?

8. If you picture the average senior citizen as poor and much worse off than the general population—then you're 15 years out of date.[15]

Do you agree with this statement? Compare poverty rates of the elderly and the rest of the population, both now and 15 to 20 years ago.

9. (a) Would free public housing reduce poverty, as measured by the government? Explain. (b) Would free day care and job training for the poor affect the rate of poverty? Why?

10. (a) What are the major social insurance programs? (b) What are the major public assistance programs? (c) Which programs are reserved exclusively for those with low income?

11. On what basis has the AFDC program been criticized?

12.

Earned income	NIT	Implicit tax	Total income
$ 0	$6000	$ 0	$6000
2000	4500	1500	6500
4000	3000	3000	7000
6000	1500	4500	7500
8000	0	6000	8000

Based on the preceding table, find the values of the implicit tax rate, the guaranteed annual income, and the break-even income.

13. Consider a negative income tax with a guaranteed annual income of $6000 and an implicit tax rate of 1/2.

a. What would be the total income of a family that earned $8000?

b. What would be the break-even income?

c. If the government cut the guaranteed annual income to $3000, how would this alter the break-even income?

---

[15]Michael Boskin, quoted in Joan Berger, "The New Old," *Business Week,* November 25, 1985, p. 140.

ANSWERS TO YOUR TURN

(a) The Lorenz curve would lie along the outer edge of the box. It would correspond to the horizontal axis until point *A,* and then jump to point *B.* (b) The area of inequality would be represented by the shaded triangle.

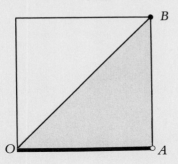

SELECTED REFERENCES

Danziger, Sheldon, Robert Haveman, and Robert Plotnick, "How Income Transfers Affect Work, Savings and the Income Distribution," *Journal of Economic Literature* (September 1981), pp. 975–1028. Analyzes the effects of transfer programs.

Duncan, Greg J., et al., *Years of Poverty, Years of Plenty: The Changing Fortunes of American Workers and Families* (Ann Arbor, MI: Institute for Social Research, 1984). Examines 5000 families, tracking changes in income and poverty.

Executive Office of the President, *Budget of the United States Government, Fiscal Year 1991* (Washington, DC: GPO, 1990). Discusses transfer programs and their budgets.

Murray, Charles, *Losing Ground* (New York: Basic Books, 1984). Studies poverty and the programs intended to reduce it.

Okun, Arthur, *Equality and Efficiency: The Big Tradeoff* (Washington, DC: The Brookings Institution, 1975). Discusses the conflicting goals of income equality and economic efficiency.

PART IX

OTHER
ISSUES

CHAPTER 34

EXTERNALITIES, THE ENVIRONMENT, AND NONRENEWABLE NATURAL RESOURCES

When the Exxon Valdez *ran aground in Prince William Sound, Alaska, Exxon lost nearly 11 million gallons of oil; society lost a good deal more. In addition to the wildlife lost to the oil spill and the damage to the beaches, Alaska's fishing industry was devastated. As this incident painfully illustrates, the impacts of some economic activities, including the production and transportation of crude oil, extend well beyond the marketplace. Where this is true, private markets fail to produce socially optimal outcomes.*

Chapter 34 examines both the reasons for this type of market failure and the proposed solutions, paying special attention to environmental issues. How pure an environment does society want, and how can it best achieve this goal? After addressing this issue, the chapter turns to another environmental concern: the depletion of nonrenewable natural resources. Are we in danger of soon running out of oil, natural gas, and other critical raw materials?

When the 987-foot *Exxon Valdez* ran aground south of the oil terminus of Valdez, it touched off the worst-case scenario that environmentalists had predicted and once again brought into the nation's living rooms the stark images of a recurring marine nightmare: A stricken ship hemorrhaging its oleaginous cargo. Pathetic, oil-smothered sea birds and mammals, many of them doomed. Fisheries poisoned, livelihoods threatened, beaches befouled, residents furious. . . . The 11-million-gallon spill, largest in U.S. history, [will] decimate this year's $100 million seafood harvest in the sound and will seriously harm a once unspoiled aquatic ecosystem.[1]

---

[1]Michael Satchell with Steve Lindbeck, "Tug of War Over Oil Drilling," *U.S. News & World Report,* April 10, 1989, p. 47.

768

EXTERNALITIES

Externalities arise when the actions of consumers or producers affect third parties—individuals who do not directly participate in the production or consumption of a particular good. The name "externality" was chosen because parties external to market transactions are affected by these transactions. Alternatively, externalities are often called *spillovers* to signify that the consequences of production or consumption "spill over" to affect third parties.

Externalities may be either positive (**external benefits**) or negative (**external costs**). For example, a private utility seeking to generate electricity may dam a river and, as a side effect, homeowners downstream may suffer less flood damage and farmers less crop damage. In that event, even though the utility was not motivated by an altruistic desire to help homeowners and farmers, these parties nonetheless benefit from the utility's decision to build a dam. Similarly, as a homeowner you benefit if your neighbors plant trees and flowers and otherwise beautify the neighborhood. In addition to any scenic benefits you enjoy, your property value appreciates as your neighborhood becomes more attractive.

Alternatively, if your neighbors start raising pigs, collecting junk cars, and hosting loud parties, their actions reduce the value of your property—that is, impose external costs on you. Other sources of external costs include buildings that block your view, barking dogs, toxic wastes, and cigarette smoke (see Exhibit 34-1, page 770).

Externalities are an example of market failure: the failure of free markets to allocate resources in a socially optimal manner. In particular, the tendency is for too many resources to be devoted to the production of goods associated with negative externalities and not enough resources devoted to the production of goods having positive externalities. The following section explains why externalities lead to market failure and why government intervention offers the potential to improve resource allocation.

PROMOTING POSITIVE EXTERNALITIES

Vaccines protect individuals from measles and other communicable diseases. As such, they benefit those receiving the vaccine. But they also benefit individuals who are not themselves inoculated. As additional people receive the vaccine, the likelihood diminishes that an unprotected individual will come into contact with someone carrying the disease.

The market demand for vaccinations is based on the **private benefits** of the vaccine—that is, the benefits to the individuals receiving it. In contrast, society's demand for vaccinations is determined by the **social benefits** of the vaccine, which include the benefits derived by those who are not inoculated as well as by those who are. Because the social benefits exceed the private benefits, society's demand for vaccinations lies to the right of the market demand (see Figure 34-1, page 771).

The equilibrium level of vaccinations is Q_{priv}, given by the intersection of market demand and supply. Q_{priv} is not socially optimal, however, inasmuch as

Positive Externalities (External Benefits) Benefits received but not paid for by third parties as a result of others' production or consumption.
Negative Externalities (External Costs) Uncompensated costs imposed on third parties as a result of consumption or production by other individuals or firms.

Private Benefits The benefits received by those consuming or producing a good.
Social Benefits Private benefits plus external benefits.

EXHIBIT 34–1

A RIGHT TO SMOKE?

Smokers often argue that they have the right to smoke tobacco. Although smoking may shorten their lives, they contend that the decision is theirs to make. More and more, nonsmokers are contesting that claim, asserting instead that they have the right to a smoke-free environment. To quote the surgeon general: "The right of smokers to smoke ends where their behavior affects the health and well-being of others."

Does passive smoking—involuntarily inhaling others' smoke—harm nonsmokers? The National Academy of Sciences examined the evidence, issuing a report in late 1986. More recently, the surgeon general issued a separate report. Major conclusions of these two reports include the following.

1. Passive smoking kills approximately 2400 nonsmokers annually. Along with asbestos, involuntary smoking is the major cause of deaths from airborne pollution.
2. Passive smoking significantly increases the risks of asthma, bronchitis, and pneumonia in children and may stunt development of their lungs.
3. Smoke may irritate the eyes, nose, and throat of nonsmokers, causing headaches, sore throats, and other adverse reactions.

In addition, other studies conclude that employees who smoke inflict costs on their employers through increased absenteeism and higher insurance rates and that the taxes of nonsmokers help finance the medical treatment of smokers. For these reasons, smoking generates substantial external costs.

In the aftermath of these reports, nonsmokers have become more militant in their opposition to smoking, and governments and private companies have responded by imposing added restrictions on smokers. Smoking is now prohibited in most public buildings and many offices as well as on flights of two hours or less. Northwest Airlines gained notoriety in 1988 when it became the first airline to prohibit smoking on all its domestic flights. Even in restaurants and other establishments that still allow smoking, nonsmokers have won nonsmoking sections. While the battle for control of the air continues, nonsmokers appear to be gaining ground. As their rights expand, the external costs of smoking will lessen.

Sources: Adapted from Charles LeMaistre, "Nobody Is Safe If a Smoker Is Around," *New York Times,* January 4, 1987, p. 2F; Lois Therrien, "In More and More Places, Smoking Causes Fines," *Business Week,* December 29, 1986, p. 40; Laura Mansnerus and Katherine Roberts, "Smoking's Effect on Nonsmokers," *New York Times,* November 16, 1986, p. 7E.

---

private markets ignore external benefits. From the perspective of society, vaccinations should continue until Q_{soc}, which is where the benefit to society of another vaccination equals the cost of another vaccination. In other words, *when positive externalities are present, markets lead to an underallocation of resources. Because private markets ignore external benefits, they produce less than the socially optimal level of output.*

To correct for this underallocation of resources, the government could induce additional individuals to receive the vaccine. One way to accomplish this is to subsidize the vaccine, thereby driving the price paid by consumers below the price received by producers. In particular, consumers would be willing to buy Q_{soc} vaccinations at a price of P_3 while producers would be willing to sell this quantity for a price of P_2. Both conditions can be satisfied if the government absorbs the difference between these two prices—for instance, by offering producers a supplemental payment of $P_2 - P_3$ per unit of vaccine. In summary, where positive externalities exist, subsidies offer a way to expand production and, in principle, to achieve the socially optimal level of output.

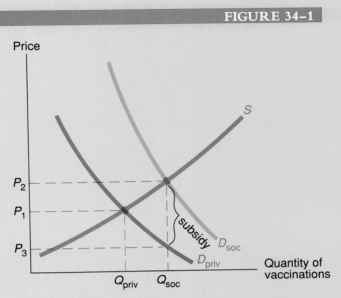

FIGURE 34-1

CORRECTING FOR AN UNDERALLOCATION OF RESOURCES

The market demand for vaccinations, D_{priv}, is based on the private benefits accruing to those vaccinated. If left to the market, the number vaccinated is Q_{priv}, determined by the intersection of market demand and supply. Q_{priv} is less than the socially optimal number of vaccinations, Q_{soc}, because consumers ignore the external benefits accruing to those not vaccinated. To achieve the optimal number of vaccinations, the government offers a subsidy of $P_2 - P_3$ for each vaccination.

RESPONDING TO NEGATIVE EXTERNALITIES

Where externalities are negative, markets lead to an overallocation of resources. Because markets ignore external costs, more output is produced than is socially optimal. As an illustration, consider a perfectly competitive industry whose firms dump raw sewage into a nearby river. To them, the river is a free good—a dumping ground they do not have to pay to use. But whereas disposal is costless to individual firms, it imposes significant costs on other members of society. It kills fish, causes health problems in humans, spoils recreational facilities along the river, and increases water purification costs for towns downstream that draw their drinking water from the river. Because of these external costs, the **private costs** of production—those actually incurred by the firms—are less than the **social costs** of production.

To maximize profit, each firm produces up to the point where the price it receives for its product equals the cost to the firm of producing another unit—that is, price equals marginal private cost (MPC). But when production is accompanied by external costs, as in our example, marginal social cost (MSC) is higher than marginal private cost. This implies that the cost to society of producing another unit of output exceeds its value. In other words, given negative externalities each firm produces more than socially optimal. This is shown in Figure 34-2 (page 772).

Figure 34-3 (page 772) illustrates negative externalities for the industry. S_{priv} is the supply curve for the industry in the absence of government intervention— obtained by aggregating the marginal cost curve of each firm (MPC). Given demand

Private Costs
The costs incurred by those producing or consuming a good.
Social Costs
Private costs plus external costs.

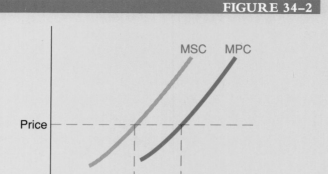

FIGURE 34–2

OVERPRODUCTION BY A POLLUTING FIRM

Because a firm does not pay external costs, these costs do not enter its production decision. Instead, a competitive firm produces up to the point where price equals marginal private cost, q_{priv}. From the perspective of society, all production costs should be considered, including external costs. Therefore, the socially optimal level of output for the firm is q_{soc}, where price equals marginal social cost.

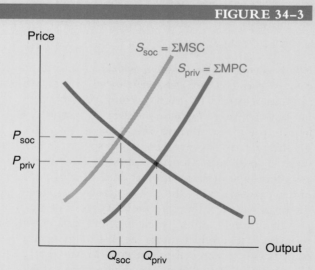

FIGURE 34–3

CORRECTING FOR AN INDUSTRY'S EXCESS PRODUCTION

When firms pay only the private costs of production, industry supply is given by S_{priv}. In equilibrium, firms produce Q_{priv} output and charge price P_{priv}. From society's perspective, there is too much output and too low a price because external costs have been ignored. But when external costs are forced on producers—that is, when costs are internalized—then market supply is reduced to S_{soc} and excess production is eliminated.

for the industry's product, market output is Q_{priv}. This is more than the socially optimal amount of output because it ignores the external costs of production. Instead, society seeks Q_{soc} output, given by the intersection of market demand and S_{soc}. It is here that price equals marginal social cost.

Note that the market price, P_{priv}, is too *low*. Because the market does not force firms to pay the full costs of production, they charge consumers an artificially low price. Had firms been required to pay the full social cost of production, the price would be P_{soc}. This is one instance where a low price is not socially beneficial: it contributes to excess consumption of this product at the expense of other products that do not have negative externalities.

One solution to this problem is to increase production costs to the firm. For example, the government could force or induce polluting firms to clean up the river or to dispose of their wastes in ways other than by dumping them into the river. Such actions would **internalize** the firms' pollution costs—that is, force the firms to absorb these costs rather than shift them on to third parties. As production costs increased, firms would raise price and consumers would reduce their consumption. If economic costs were fully internalized, price would rise to P_{soc} and the overallocation of resources to this industry would cease. Various proposals for internalizing costs are considered following a brief discussion of environmental problems.

Internalize Costs
To shift external costs from third parties back to those parties directly responsible for the costs.

THE ENVIRONMENT

Although the preceding example illustrates negative externalities by considering industrial pollution, it is important to realize that businesses are not the only sources of pollution. Almost one-half of the government facilities recently inspected were in violation of environmental laws. The Department of Defense alone generated more hazardous waste than the five largest chemical companies.[2] Consumers also pollute the environment through their garbage, fires, and automobiles. If environmental policy is to be effective, it must consider all sources of pollution, not just industrial pollution.

Table 34-1 (page 774) reveals information on the origins of six major air pollutants. As indicated, for most pollutants industrial waste is not the major source of pollution. For both lead emissions and carbon monoxide the principal culprit is transportation, primarily automobile travel.

Statistics on environmental quality are compiled by the United States Environmental Protection Agency (EPA), the organization responsible for monitoring pollution levels and enforcing the Clean Air Act, the Clean Water Act, and other environmental laws. EPA statistics paint a mixed picture of the environment. For example, a substantial number of citizens live in communities that are not in compliance with air quality standards (see Table 34-2, page 774). On the other hand, air quality has generally improved since 1978. Perhaps most impressive, emissions of lead are down 94 percent. This is due primarily to the introduction of unleaded gasoline in 1975, a reduction in the lead content of leaded gasoline, and a requirement that new automobiles be equipped with catalytic converters.

The pollutant most commonly in violation of air quality standards is ozone, the major component of what is commonly called "smog." In 1987, more than

[2]Murray L. Weidenbaum, *Rendezvous with Reality: The American Economy After Reagan* (New York: Basic Books, 1988), p. 220.

TABLE 34-1

MAJOR AIR POLLUTANTS BY SOURCE

Pollutant	Source of pollutant (%)					
	Transportation	Fuel combustion	Industrial processes	Solid waste	Miscellaneous	Total
Total suspended particulate (TSP)	20	26	36	4	14	100
Sulfur dioxide (SO_2)	5	80	15	0	0	100
Carbon monoxide (CO)	66	12	8	3	11	100
Nitrogen oxide (NO)*	43	53	3	0.5	0.5	100
Volatile organic compound (VOC)**	31	12	42	3	12	100
Lead (Pb)	37	6	25	32	0	100

*Leads to the formation of the pollutant nitrogen dioxide.

**Contributes to ozone pollution.

Source: U.S. Environmental Protection Agency, *National Air Quality and Emissions Trends Report, 1987* (1989), Chapter 3.

TABLE 34-2

AIR POLLUTION STANDARDS AND COMPLIANCE*

Pollutant	Standard**		Percent of population in counties not in compliance, 1987	National reduction of pollutant, 1978–1987 (percent)
Particulate matter (PM_{10})	50	ug/m³	9	23***
Sulfur dioxide (SO_2)	0.03	ppm	1	17
Carbon monoxide (CO)	9	ppm	12	25
Nitrogen dioxide (NO_2)	0.053	ppm	3	8
Ozone (O_3)	0.12	ppm	36	16****
Lead (Pb)	1.5	ug/m³	1	94

*National Ambient Air Quality Standards.

**ug/m³ = micrograms per cubic meter
ppm   = parts per million

***Reduction for total suspended particulate.

****Because of a calibration change in 1979, data for prior years are not strictly comparable; over the period 1979–1987, ozone pollution was reduced by 17 percent.

Source: U.S. Environmental Protection Agency, *National Air Quality and Emissions Trends Report, 1987* (1989).

one-third of the population lived in counties that were not in compliance with ozone standards. The problem was especially severe in Los Angeles, where readings were nearly three times the EPA standard.

LEGISLATIVE STANDARDS

Before placing too much emphasis on pollution levels or rates of compliance, it is important to ask how environmental standards are set. Under current policy, standards are often arbitrarily determined by Congress. For example, the current ozone standard is 0.12 parts per million, not to be exceeded for more than one hour per year. Prior to 1979, the standard was 0.08 parts per million; in 1971, the standard was even more stringent. The standard has been eased over time in part because of political pressure from cities not in compliance and in part because some recent scientific studies conclude that exposure to ozone at the rate of 0.30 parts per million, more than double the current standard, poses health problems only for those engaged in strenuous activities.[3] There is no compelling reason why the standard is 0.12 parts per million rather than 0.08 or 0.16; 0.12 is simply the figure chosen by Congress.

Along with air quality standards, Congress set a deadline for compliance with these standards. The initial deadline, stipulated by the Clean Air Act of 1970, was 1975. The deadline was later extended to 1987 and then 1988. When asked why the initial deadline of 1975 was selected, Senator Edmund Muskie, sponsor of the bill, admitted that the deadline was arbitrary, chosen without taking into account "economic and technological feasibility."[4] In that light, it is perhaps not surprising that Congress has chosen to revise it.

COST-BENEFIT ANALYSIS

Even though arbitrary standards do promote a cleaner environment, most economists criticize them as simplistic. Such standards may promote either too little environmental quality or too much.

How, you might ask, can the environment be too clean? The answer is that environmental purity carries a cost: resources used to reduce pollution are not available for other activities. Over a recent ten-year period, pollution-control expenditures were estimated to be roughly $1 trillion (see Table 34-3, page 776). Had spending on environmental quality been reduced, the country could have produced more cars, housing, and education. Alternatively, if additional resources had been diverted to pollution control, we would have a cleaner environment but fewer other goods. In other words, the cost of a cleaner environment is the output that is sacrificed in order to achieve higher environmental standards.

Cost-Benefit Analysis
A framework for comparing the costs and benefits of a particular activity (e.g., to determine the optimal level of that activity).

How much pollution is optimal? Although there are different frameworks with which to address this question, most economists emphasize **cost-benefit analysis,** in which the costs to society of a cleaner environment are weighed against the benefits. The benefits include better health (e.g., fewer illnesses and lower medical expenses), reduced crop damage, additional wildlife, and improved recreational facilities. As a general rule, the marginal benefits of pollution control decline as the level of pollution is reduced. When pollution is unchecked, even a slight improvement generates substantial benefits. But as pollution abatement continues, further gains in health, crop yield, wildlife population, and quality of recreational sites tend to taper off. This is illustrated in Figure 34-4 (page 776) by a declining marginal benefit curve.

[3]Melinda Warren and Kenneth Chilton, *Clearing the Air: Regulating Ozone in the Public Interest* (St. Louis: Center for the Study of American Business, 1988), p. 1.

[4]Murray L. Weidenbaum, *Business, Government, and the Public*, 3rd ed. (Englewood Cliffs, NJ: Prentice-Hall, 1986), p. 89.

	TABLE 34-3		

ESTIMATED TOTAL POLLUTION ABATEMENT EXPENDITURES,
1979–1988 (in billions of 1988 dollars)

Program	Operation/maintenance	Capital costs	Total costs
Air pollution	$244.9	$279.6	$ 524.5
Water pollution	157.0	230.0	387.0
Solid waste	128.6	27.6	156.2
Toxic substances	5.6	7.1	12.7
Drinking water	8.2	8.0	16.2
Noise	4.0	6.7	10.7
Pesticides	2.5	0.1	2.6
Land reclamation	7.0	20.9	27.9
Total	$557.8	$580.0	$1137.8

Source: U.S. Council on Environmental Quality, *Environmental Quality, 1980* (1980), p. 397, restated in 1988 dollars.

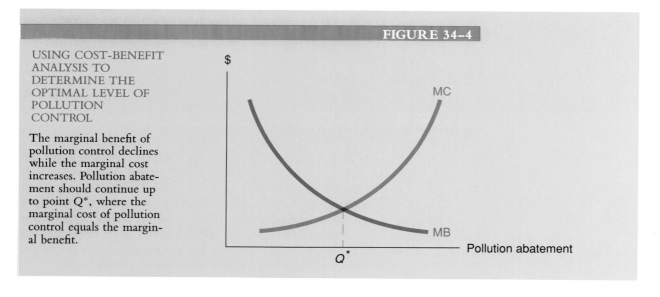

FIGURE 34–4

USING COST-BENEFIT ANALYSIS TO DETERMINE THE OPTIMAL LEVEL OF POLLUTION CONTROL

The marginal benefit of pollution control declines while the marginal cost increases. Pollution abatement should continue up to point Q*, where the marginal cost of pollution control equals the marginal benefit.

In contrast, the marginal cost of pollution abatement increases. Initial reductions in pollution are often easy, requiring only modest adjustments. But as firms tackle the more difficult pollution problems, further progress often requires installing costly equipment and altering production processes. As an example of how costs accelerate, consider the paper industry. The cost of eliminating 95 percent of the industry's water pollution was estimated to be $3 billion, compared to a cost of $7.8 billion to eliminate 98 percent of the pollution.[5] In other words, the cost of an incremental 3-percent improvement in water quality was more than the total cost of eliminating the first 95 percent of the pollution.

[5]Murray L. Weidenbaum, "Benefit-Cost Analysis of Government Regulation," *Toxic Substances Journal* (Autumn 1980), pp. 91–102.

From an economic perspective, the optimal amount of pollution control is the amount for which the marginal cost of reducing pollution equals the marginal benefit. Until this point is reached (point Q^* in Figure 34-4), the benefits of additional pollution control exceed the added costs. Beyond this point further reductions in pollution cost more than they yield in benefits.

Environmentalists sometimes oppose cost-benefit analysis for fear that, once the costs of pollution abatement are recognized, environmental standards will be relaxed. But this will be true only if environmental standards are excessive to begin with. In many instances, cost-benefit analysis leads to tougher standards. For example, a cost-benefit study was responsible for the EPA reducing the lead content in gasoline from 1.1 gram per gallon to 0.1 gram. According to this study, over the period 1985–1992, the lower lead content will yield $6.7 billion more in benefits than in costs.[6]

The primary difficulty in implementing cost-benefit analysis is obtaining reliable figures on costs and benefits. Alternative assumptions often yield conflicting estimates. With additional research, differences in estimates can sometimes be narrowed, but not eliminated. Accordingly, there may be different projections of the optimal amount of pollution. Thus, even with cost-benefit analysis some subjectivity is involved. Still, cost-benefit analysis provides useful information and a rational approach for formulating environmental policy. It is likely to achieve a higher level

---

YOUR TURN   COMPARING THE COSTS AND BENEFITS OF POLLUTION CONTROL

The widget industry currently generates 6 tons of air pollutants per month. The following table depicts the total costs and benefits to society of reducing pollution to lower levels.

Level of pollution (tons/mo)	Total benefit of reducing pollution to this level (millions of $/mo)	Total cost of reducing pollution to this level (millions of $/mo)
5	$15	$ 2
4	25	5
3	32	11
2	37	21
1	40	36
0	42	60

a. What is the marginal cost of reducing pollution from 5 tons per month to 4? What is the marginal benefit? What does this say about the current level of pollution (6 tons per month)?

b. Congress is considering a limit of 2 tons per month. Would this be preferable to the current level of pollution? Explain.

c. From an economic perspective, what is the optimal level of pollution? Show how you derived the answer.

d. If Congress wished to maximize air quality in this industry, how much pollution should it allow per month? Why is this not the economically optimal level of pollution?

---

[6]Ralph A. Luken, "Weighing the Benefits of Clean-up Rules Against Their Costs," *EPA Journal* (March 1988), pp. 9–12.

of social welfare than arbitrary standards, chosen without reference to economic costs and benefits.

WAYS TO REDUCE POLLUTION

In addition to selecting acceptable levels of pollution, the government must also decide how to attack pollution. It can rely on voluntary compliance, require that firms take specific actions to eliminate pollution, tax either the pollution itself or the product that generates pollution, subsidize pollution-control equipment, or even sell firms the right to emit a limited amount of pollution. Because the costs and success of these different approaches often vary, it is important to examine the strengths and weaknesses of each.

Voluntary Compliance

The government could appeal to the social conscience of individuals and firms, as it does when it asks them to prevent forest fires, to refrain from littering, and to dispose of chemicals responsibly. As long as the cost of compliance is low, compliance may be substantial. But as the cost rises, fewer and fewer parties are willing to contribute to a clean environment.

Firms that voluntarily use resources to reduce pollution increase their costs of production and earn lower profits than had they ignored pollution. In competitive industries, these lost profits are the difference between a firm remaining in business and closing its doors—since only firms that produce at the lowest possible cost can survive in the long run. In other words, firms that ignore pollution have lower costs and therefore can drive so-called "socially responsible" firms out of business. As an example of this, consider the economic demise of Larry Daniels (Exhibit 34-2).

Direct Regulation

Rather than rely on voluntary compliance, the government sometimes resorts to direct regulation—what is commonly referred to as "command and control." Firms and consumers are ordered to adhere to certain specific requirements. Those that do not are subject to fines and imprisonment. The government relies on direct regulation when it mandates that new cars must have catalytic converters and burn unleaded gasoline. Similarly, the government could attack the problem of contaminated fish by banning the use of chlordane or requiring that fish with high concentrations be removed from the market.

Cost Effective
Achieving a given objective (e.g., the elimination of a certain volume of pollution) at the lowest cost possible.

The problem with direct regulation is that, in many cases, it is not **cost effective.** It prevents firms and consumers from achieving a given reduction in pollution using other, less costly techniques. For example, direct regulations often tie a firm to the best present technology even if superior technologies, which would permit the firm to reduce pollution more efficiently, become available in the future. Not only does this impose unnecessary costs on firms (once these technologies are available), it blunts the incentives of entrepreneurs to develop new technologies to deal with pollution.

At other times, the government fails even to take advantage of the best present technology. For example, the 1977 amendments to the Clean Air Act require power plants to install scrubbers on their new coal-powered boilers to remove from 70 to 90 percent of the sulphur in the stack gas. This rule applies regardless of the sulphur content of the coal. The rule is inefficient because it precludes power plants from

---

EXHIBIT 34–2

TRUST ME, THEY'RE CLEAN

Larry Daniels, a commercial fisherman in New Madrid, Missouri, had just come home with the day's catch when he got a letter from state health officials warning that many species of fish in the Mississippi and Missouri rivers were contaminated with chlordane, a toxic pesticide. Daniels promptly dumped his catch—350 pounds of carp, catfish and drum—into a trash can. Then he closed his fish market and never reopened it. "I was not going to sell fish if it was hazardous to people, especially children. I just didn't want to contribute to any kid getting cancer down the road."

The highest level of chlordane was found in carp and catfish in the Mississippi at St. Louis. The fish there contained 1389 parts of chlordane for each billion parts of fish. The U.S. Food and Drug Administration warns against eating fish containing chlordane at levels higher than 300 parts per billion. Chlordane is suspected of causing cancer; it is known to cause chronic liver damage and may damage the immune and nervous systems.

Four blocks from Daniels' closed fish market . . . Fred Moore is busy catching and selling fish. "I can't tell any difference in my business," he said. Don Whitehead, manager of the R & R Fish Market in St. Charles, said he sold catfish and buffalo from the nearby Missouri River, as well as fish from Kentucky. Customers don't ask whether the fish may be contaminated with chlordane, he said. "They aren't going to hurt you any worse than smoking cigarettes."

State officials say they are most concerned that some fishermen or market owners are mislabeling fish to circumvent the health advisory. "Everywhere you go, you now see signs saying 'Ohio River fish,'" Robinson said. "I don't believe it at all. The Ohio River is a long way away, and it's just not practical for most small merchants to bring in large shipments of fish from there." At a meeting in Charleston, Missouri, to explain the health advisory to commercial fishermen, Crellin said, he overheard a fisherman asking a friend how to spell "Kentucky" because he wanted to put that label on his fish.

Daniels, the fisherman in New Madrid, said his family had scraped by on food stamps until he found a job as a truck driver several weeks ago. He said he had no regrets about his decision. "A lot of guys around here are still fishing and selling them," he said. "It's just like selling marijuana to kids. There's a lot of people who do it, but that doesn't mean it's right. People can continue to eat the fish, but not from me, they won't."

Source: Marjorie Mandel, "Contaminated Fish May Be Mislabelled," *St. Louis Post Dispatch*, May 3, 1987, pp. 1–6. Reprinted by permission.

---

using alternatives that are less costly than scrubbing. In particular, for many utilities it would be less costly to burn untreated low-sulphur coal or to burn moderate-sulphur coal whose sulphur content has been reduced through a washing process. Both methods would eliminate *more* sulphur from the air than scrubbing the gas of high-sulphur coal. Thus, the 1977 amendments increase the cost of generating electricity while sacrificing air quality.

Apparently, Congress was aware of the consequences of its actions but succumbed to political pressures. Had Congress allowed power plants to reduce sulphur emission by switching to low-sulphur coal (which is produced in the western United States), employment in eastern coal fields (whose coal has a high sulphur content) would have contracted. For that reason, representatives of the eastern coal-producing states opposed universal limits on sulphur emissions (e.g., 1.2 pounds of sulphur per million BTUs of energy) and instead pushed through legislation that forces utilities to scrub all coal, even low-sulphur western coal.[7]

---

[7]Lester B. Lave, "Coal and the Clean Air Act," in S. Fred Singer, ed., *Free Market Energy* (New York: Universe Books, 1984), pp. 181–85.

Effluent Fees

Effluent Fee

A charge or tax levied on each unit of a pollutant emitted into the environment.

Because of the inefficiency of direct regulation, economists generally favor market-based strategies to reduce pollution. One of these is the **effluent fee,** which is a tax per unit of pollutant. By making pollution costly to the firm, the effluent fee gives the firm an incentive to curb its pollution. In particular, the firm will continue to eliminate pollution as long as this is less costly than paying the effluent fee. Unlike direct regulation, the effluent fee provides producers with an incentive to reduce pollution at the lowest possible cost—whether this entails installing specific pollution-control equipment, switching to a cleaner fuel, or recycling (see Exhibit 34-3). Thus, the effluent fee is cost effective.

One drawback of an effluent fee is that it requires continuous monitoring of pollution levels—to keep track of the amount of pollution emitted by each company so that taxes can be assessed. Monitoring is also required with direct regulation, to determine whether companies are complying with the law, but the government can get by with spot (random) monitoring. Because monitoring uses up resources, the added monitoring costs associated with an effluent fee increase the cost of this method of pollution control. But, as a practical matter, monitoring costs are often modest.

An Output Tax

Instead of taxing pollution directly, an alternative is to tax the products responsible for that pollution. For example, if the production of steel contributes to air pollution, the government could levy a tax on each ton of steel produced. This would reduce the output of steel and, in turn, the amount of pollution generated by the steel industry.

An output tax has one advantage over an effluent fee. Because the tax is levied on production—rather than on the level of pollution—it does not require monitoring pollution. On the other hand, the output tax has a major drawback: it does not

---

EXHIBIT 34-3

TURNING SLUDGE INTO DOLLARS

Firms voluntarily recycle waste when it is profitable to do so. But when a cheaper alternative is available to the firm (e.g., emitting waste into the environment), the firm has no incentive to recycle. The situation changes, however, if the firm is assessed a tax on its emissions. In particular, such a tax increases the benefits of recycling, since the recycled waste escapes taxation.

As the cost of waste disposal has increased, due in part to higher taxes, recycling has become more common. A chemical company that had been discharging 35,000 tons of flyash each year located a company that was willing to use flyash in the cement blocks it manufactured. In another instance, a timber company developed a procedure for converting its wastes into products such as

vegetable wax. Finally, consider the chemical company that had been generating 1000 cubic yards of calcium fluoride sludge each month. By combining this sludge with yet another waste product, the company was able to produce synthetic fluorspar, an input it previously had been purchasing from other companies.

In summary, whenever technologically feasible, companies have responded to higher disposal costs by recycling their waste products. They have done so not out of a sense of social responsibility but rather out of a more basic motive—making profits.

Source: Adapted from Murray L. Weidenbaum, *Rendezvous with Reality: The American Economy After Reagan* (New York: Basic Books, 1988), p. 218.

reduce the amount of pollution per unit of output. For example, steel companies would have no incentive to burn low-sulphur coal, install scrubbers, or otherwise reduce the amount of pollution per ton of steel. Unlike an emission fee, an output tax does not reward companies for switching to a less-polluting technique of production. Therefore, for a given level of output, the amount of pollution is greater if an output tax is used rather than an effluent fee.

Subsidizing Pollution Control

In addition to reducing pollution through taxes, the government sometimes uses subsidies to encourage pollution abatement. By bearing part of the cost of pollution-control equipment, the government reduces the cost to firms of eliminating pollution. By itself, this is not likely to have much impact. If compliance remains voluntary, firms have no economic incentive to install pollution-control equipment, even if the government foots most of the bill. On the other hand, when firms are forced to curtail pollution (e.g., as a result of direct regulation), subsidies reduce the costs to firms.

But this simply means that pollution-control costs are passed on to third parties—in this case, taxpayers. Therefore, those who create pollution do not bear the full consequences of their actions. In addition, to the extent subsidies keep the private cost of production below the social cost, firms continue to charge less than the socially optimal amount for their product and therefore consumers purchase more output than is socially optimal.

Another criticism of pollution-abatement subsidies concerns their cost effectiveness. By reducing the relative cost of pollution-control equipment, subsidies encourage firms to attack pollution by purchasing additional equipment, even though alternative approaches (e.g., switching to a cleaner fuel) may have a lower social cost. In summary, pollution-control subsidies are criticized as inequitable (for shifting pollution costs to third parties), inefficient (in the sense of permitting excess production of the polluting product), and cost ineffective (for failing to reduce pollution at the lowest cost).

Assigning Property Rights

In attacking pollution, it is important to recognize why private markets fail to produce the socially optimal amount of pollution. Markets fail because property rights are not clearly defined or enforced. Do smokers have the right to exhale cigarette smoke into the air, or do nonsmokers have the right to a smoke-free environment? To whom does a river belong—to a firm seeking to dispose of its waste products or to swimmers and fishermen? Unless such issues are resolved, economic agents will continue to make conflicting claims on the environment.

On the other hand, if property rights were spelled out, the courts could assess damages against those who violate others' rights. For example, if swimmers and fishermen owned the rights to a river, a firm could not legally discharge its wastes there unless it obtained permission of the swimmers and fishermen—something they would not give unless they were paid sufficiently to compensate for any damages caused by the firm's pollution. If the firm dumped pollutants into the river without obtaining permission, the swimmers and fishermen could sue for damages.

Although assigning property rights and seeking court enforcement is one remedy to the problem of pollution, this approach has problems of its own. The litigation process is costly and time-consuming. Beyond that, the burden of proof is on the plaintiff. For example, the swimmers must demonstrate that they were harmed by the pollution, provide evidence of the extent of their damages, and prove that the damages resulted from the acts of the defendant-firm. Even if the plaintiffs prevail, they may be unable to collect the full damages if the award exceeds the firm's ability to pay. For such reasons, many believe that lawsuits are not the most effective way to reduce pollution.

Selling Rights to Pollute

Instead of giving swimmers and fishermen the rights to a river, an alternative is to assign firms the right to pollute. Although this is a controversial proposal, especially to those who view pollution as a moral rather than economic issue, economists defend this approach on various grounds. First, the government can limit pollution to what it considers the optimal level by selling only enough **pollution rights** to create this amount of pollution. Second, as with a pollution tax, selling rights to pollute would generate revenues for the government. These could be used for such projects as developing new pollution-control technologies and cleaning up the environment. Finally, if firms were required to buy a permit for each unit of pollution emitted, they would have an incentive to reduce pollution, since each unit eliminated voluntarily would mean one less permit to buy. Moreover, in eliminating that pollution, firms would be motivated to use the least-costly approach available. Thus, a **market for pollution rights** would be cost effective.

Figure 34-5 illustrates how a market for pollution rights would work. The supply of pollution rights is perfectly inelastic, reflecting the fact that the government has decided to limit pollution to the level Q^*. The demand curve is downward sloping because firms respond to an increased price of pollution rights by reducing emissions—substituting pollution control for pollution rights. If the demand curve for pollution rights is given by D_1, the government sells pollution rights at a price of P_1 and collects $P_1 \times Q^*$ in revenues.

Pollution Right
A permit that entitles its bearer to emit one unit of a certain pollutant into the environment.

Market for Pollution Rights
A market in which pollution rights are bought and sold, at prices determined by the supply of and demand for these permits.

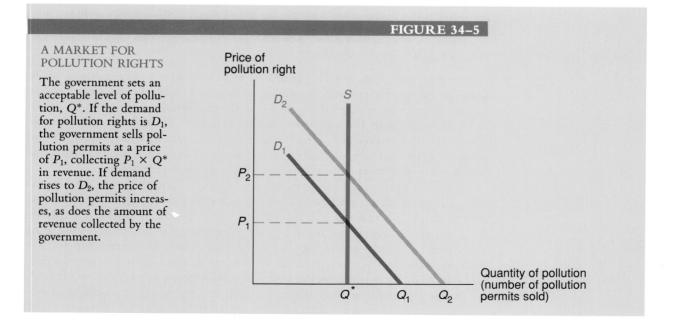

FIGURE 34–5

A MARKET FOR POLLUTION RIGHTS

The government sets an acceptable level of pollution, Q^*. If the demand for pollution rights is D_1, the government sells pollution permits at a price of P_1, collecting $P_1 \times Q^*$ in revenue. If demand rises to D_2, the price of pollution permits increases, as does the amount of revenue collected by the government.

Over time, demand for pollution rights may increase as additional firms locate along the river. This raises the price of pollution rights, thereby generating more revenues for the government—but the level of pollution remains unchanged. Despite firms' greater desire to pollute, the quality of the environment does not deteriorate. Note that had firms been allowed to pollute at will, they would have created Q_1 pollution given the demand curve D_1 and Q_2 pollution given demand curve D_2. Thus a market for pollution rights reduces pollution from the market level (Q_1 or Q_2) to that level determined to be socially acceptable (Q^*).

Emissions Trading   Although currently there is no market for pollution rights—in which the government sells firms a license to pollute—the EPA is experimenting with several variations on this theme. Under its emissions trading program, companies that reduce pollution by more than the amount required earn emission reduction credits (ERCs), which may be used in certain circumstances to offset deficiencies in pollution control elsewhere. Two components of emissions trading are *offsets* and *bubbles*.

Offsets

Reductions in pollution beyond the amount required of one firm (or plant) that are used to permit a second firm (or plant) in the same area to increase its pollution.

Offsets are used in areas of the country not yet in compliance with air quality standards. New firms are allowed to enter the area, and existing firms to expand, provided that they can induce other firms in the area to reduce their pollution by an even larger amount. In other words, firms that need pollution credits (ERCs) can buy these credits from other firms that are willing, for a price, to *overcomply* with their own pollution standards. Offsets can also be used by a firm to increase pollution at one of its plants in exchange for tightening up pollution control at another plant. Thus, offsets allow continued economic growth in an area while, at the same time, improving air quality standards. This is more attractive than the alternative of banning all new sources of pollution, and thereby stifling economic growth.

Another virtue of offsets is that they take advantage of the fact that pollution control is less costly in some firms than in others. For example, according to one study the costs of eliminating an additional ton of hydrocarbons ranged from $41 at a gasoline terminal to $16,500 at a spray-painting operation.[8] By allowing more hydrocarbons to be released from spray painting—provided that fewer hydrocarbons are released from gas terminals—offsets reduce the costs of achieving a given level of pollution control. The major difference between a policy of offsets and the previously discussed market for pollution rights is that, with offsets, revenues from the sale of pollution rights accrue to the firm reducing pollution, rather than to the government.

Bubble

An imaginary enclosure around one or more plants that becomes the basis for a firm's pollution-control requirements. In particular, a firm is allowed to exceed pollution-control standards at individual points in the bubble provided that these excesses are offset elsewhere within the same bubble.

Unlike offsets, which may be traded between firms, **bubbles** accommodate emissions trading within a single firm. When the Clean Air Act was initially enforced, emissions requirements were established for each source of pollution within a plant—that is, for every valve, smokestack, and other outlet for air pollution. A problem with this strategy was that it failed to account for the fact that reducing pollution was less costly at some ports than others. Therefore, the initial approach was not cost effective. Aware of this, in 1979 the EPA began implementing its bubble policy, under which a firm could create, subject to government approval, an imaginary bubble encompassing one or more of its plants.

Once a bubble is established, the firm sums emissions requirements for the individual sources of pollution to obtain a cumulative limit for the bubble. The firm

[8]P. Ginberg and G. Schaumburg, *Economic Incentive Systems for the Control of Hydrocarbon Emissions from Stationary Sources*, Report to the Council on Environmental Quality, 1980.

is then allowed to exceed pollution standards at individual points provided that these excesses are offset at other points. In effect, the bubble permits the firm to spread pollution control across all sources in such a way that it can minimize the cost of achieving the specified level of pollution control.

In 1986, the EPA tightened its requirements for creating bubbles by mandating that the total emissions from a bubble be 20 percent below the sum of the limits for the individual sources of pollution. For example, if a firm had ten sources of pollution, each permitted to discharge one ton of hydrocarbons, the total amount of hydrocarbons allowed under the new bubble policy would be eight tons. It has been estimated that, in their first twelve years of existence, bubbles and other forms of emissions trading saved firms well in excess of $4 billion.[9]

YOUR TURN   THE ADVANTAGES OF A BUBBLE

A power plant operates two boilers, the second of which has advanced pollution-control equipment. The following table depicts the costs of reducing pollution to specified levels for each of the boilers.

	Total cost of reducing pollution to this level (millions of dollars)	
Tons of pollution per month	**Boiler 1**	**Boiler 2**
10	$ 4	$1
9	7	2
8	11	3
7	16	4
6	22	5
5	29	6
4	37	8

a. Assume the government requires that each boiler limit its pollution to 8 tons per month. What is the total cost to the firm of bringing both its boilers into compliance?

b. The government now agrees to consider both boilers as part of the same bubble. If the allowable level of pollution for this bubble is 16 tons per month, what is the least-costly way to meet this requirement? How much can the firm save each month, compared to the previous limit of 8 tons of pollution per boiler?

c. Suppose the government, as a condition for bringing both boilers under the same bubble, demands that the bubble generate no more than 14 tons of pollution per month. Should the firm accept the government's offer, or is it better off under the old standard that allowed 8 tons of pollution from each boiler (16 tons total)? Explain.

Summary and Implications

Table 34-4 summarizes certain alternative ways of reducing pollution. Of the various approaches, voluntary compliance is often the least effective. Those who take it upon themselves to reduce pollution incur greater costs than those who ignore the problem. This puts so-called "socially responsible" firms at a cost disadvantage; in

---

[9]Robert W. Hahn and Gordon L. Hester, "The Market for Bads: EPA's Experience with Emissions Trading," *Regulation* (Number 3/4, 1987), p. 50.

TABLE 34-4

SUMMARY OF ALTERNATIVE METHODS FOR REDUCING POLLUTION

Program	Requires continuous monitoring	Tends to be cost effective	Generates revenue for the government	Comment
Voluntary compliance	No	No	No	Generally ineffective.
Direct regulation	No	No	No	Politically popular.
Effluent fee	Yes	Yes	Yes	Provides a market incentive to reduce pollution.
Output tax	No	No	Yes	Does not reduce the amount of pollution per unit of output.
Pollution-control subsidy	No	No	No	Shifts pollution-control cost to third parties.
Market for pollution rights	Yes	Yes	Yes	Keeps pollution at socially acceptable levels regardless of the demand to pollute.

competitive industries, they will be unable to compete in the long run with firms that ignore pollution.

Aware of the limits of voluntary compliance, the government relies heavily on direct regulation, whereby the government dictates exactly what firms and consumers must do to combat pollution. Where a particular pollutant is judged so harmful that its socially optimal level is zero, direct regulation is often the easiest way to halt emissions of this pollutant. Another advantage of direct regulation is that continuous monitoring of pollution levels is unnecessary. On the other hand, direct regulation suffers a number of major shortcomings. Foremost is the fact that it is not cost effective. Because of its rigid nature, firms and consumers are prevented from using less costly approaches to reduce pollution. Where direct regulation mandates a specific technology, it also blunts the incentive to develop new technologies to deal with pollution. Finally, with direct regulation, firms have no incentive to reduce pollution beyond the level dictated by the government.

Sometimes the government couples direct regulation with pollution-control subsidies, so that firms will not have to bear the full cost of reducing pollution. But this merely shifts the cost from polluters to taxpayers. Subsidizing pollution-control equipment also tends to be cost ineffective because it discourages firms from using alternative approaches to pollution control (e.g., burning cleaner fuels) even when they are less costly to society.

Economists generally favor a market-based approach to pollution control—for example, imposing effluent fees or instituting a market for pollution rights. An advantage of both effluent fees and pollution rights is that they provide an incentive to reduce pollution at the lowest cost possible. A drawback, usually minor, is that they require continuous monitoring of pollution levels. Although there is currently no formal market for pollution rights—in which the government sells a license to pollute—the EPA does allow emissions trading, which is the basic feature of the market for pollution rights.

An alternative to the effluent fee is a tax on the output of the polluting company. This leads to a reduction in output and therefore in pollution but, unlike the effluent fee, offers firms no incentive to reduce the amount of pollution per unit of output.

SOME COMPLICATIONS

Cross-Media Pollution

> It is entirely possible that somewhere in the country, toxic metals are being removed from the air, transferred to a waste water stream, removed again by water pollution controls, converted to a sludge, shipped to an incinerator and returned to the air.[10]

To be most effective, the government's attack on pollution must be integrated. Society gains little if pollution is simply transferred from one medium (e.g., air) to another medium (water or land). We must concern ourselves with what happens to pollution after it is removed from a particular medium. It was this realization that led to the creation of the EPA in 1970. In justifying the new agency, President Nixon argued that

> The environment must be perceived as a single interrelated system. . . . [We need to] examine interactions among forms of pollution and identify where on the ecological chain interdiction would be most appropriate.[11]

But if the EPA was founded on the principle of integration, it has had limited success fostering that principle. The agency must administer a dozen separate laws, each addressing its own set of problems and espousing its own goals. Sometimes the requirements of one law are at cross purposes with a second law. Moreover, much pollution control remains within the province of states and local communities, which often vacillate in their approach to pollution control (see Exhibit 34-4). The country has a long way to go before its environmental policy can be considered integrated and consistent.

The International Nature of Pollution

As challenging as it is to develop an integrated national approach to pollution, devising an integrated global approach is even more difficult. Yet such an approach is important inasmuch as all countries share a common environment. Production or consumption in one country often creates pollution elsewhere. For example, winds blow sulphur dioxide from Mexican smelters into the United States, while different winds carry the sulphur dioxide emitted by U.S. utilities into Canada. In each case the result is acid rain, which kills fish and destroys lakes and forests in the recipient country. Similarly, the chlorofluorocarbons (CFCs) and halons that countries pump into the air deplete the earth's protective ozone layer and intensify ultraviolet radiation, thereby increasing the risks of skin cancer and other health problems. Yet another concern is the *greenhouse effect*. The burning of fossil fuels has increased the concentration of carbon dioxide in the atmosphere, which is expected to increase global temperatures, alter rain patterns, and raise sea levels.

---

[10]Lee M. Thomas, Administrator of the EPA, quoted in *New York Times*, "Some Solutions to Pollution Aren't the Final Word," May 11, 1986, p. 5E.

[11]Council on Environmental Quality, *Environmental Quality, 1985* (1986) (Washington, DC: GPO), p. 10.

EXHIBIT 34–4

DISPOSING OF GARBAGE

Twenty years ago, most small communities on rural Long Island got rid of their garbage the old-fashioned way: they burned it. The smoldering fires sent spires of sooty smoke drifting across the countryside. Concerned about air pollution, New York State officials banned the open burning of municipal garbage in 1967 and encouraged the towns to dispose of their waste in what was thought to be a more environmentally sound manner: the so-called sanitary landfill.

One such disposal site sits atop a pine-studded ridge near Southampton on eastern Long Island. Beneath the landfill, a plume of toxic heavy metals and carcinogenic vinyl chlorides is seeping through the porous soil at the rate of a foot a day, contaminating ground water, ruining residential wells and threatening marine life just a half mile away. Already the town of Southampton has spent more than $2 million to cap and line part of the landfill and to supply water to residents whose wells it has contaminated.

Ordinary household garbage, not industrial pollution, is to blame, although rumors have circu-

lated that commercial or industrial waste was occasionally dumped at the site. "Heavy metals can be leached from things like batteries and old electrical parts," said Steven Meger, an environmental planner with The Group for the South Fork, a local environmental organization. "And vinyl chlorides can come from the plastic in various household products."

"We're a little more enlightened now, and we realize burying wasn't such a good idea," said Robert A. Becherer, a regional hazardous waste engineer with the New York Department of Environmental Conservation in Stony Brook. "So now we're going back to burning—but hopefully it'll be a little cleaner and more controlled this time."

Some scientists, however, point to a new risk—that burning from resource recovery units could spew dioxin, among other chemical contaminants, into the air.

Source: Thomas J. Knudson, "A Landfill Haunts the Island," *New York Times,* May 11, 1986, p. 5E. Copyright © 1986 by The New York Times Company. Reprinted by permission.

"Yes, We've Been Regulars Since Way Back in 1988, when the "Greenhouse Effect" First Kicked in. How about You? This Your First Trip To Alaska?..."

Source: With permission of the *Star Tribune.*

Given the global nature of these problems, an effective response requires the concentrated actions of a significant number of nations. Fortunately, there are signs that some progress is being made. Since 1972, a number of world conferences have been called to deal specifically with environmental issues. More than 30 nations have signed a treaty negotiated in 1987 that calls for countries to reduce emissions of CFCs to one-half their 1986 levels and to freeze consumption of halons. Similarly, a

1988 agreement among 25 industrial nations, including the United States, limits emissions of nitrogen oxide to their 1987 levels. At a minimum, there appears to be a heightened awareness of the fact that global problems require global solutions.

NONRENEWABLE NATURAL RESOURCES

The availability of natural resources would be of interest even in the absence of environmental problems, but in fact the two are related. The greenhouse effect alluded to earlier is the direct consequence of burning fossil fuels. By replacing coal with natural gas and other cleaner sources of energy, less carbon dioxide would be emitted into the air, thereby lessening the damage. Similarly, substituting low-sulphur coal for high-sulphur coal would mitigate the problem of acid rain.

But if switching to cleaner sources of energy offers a way to curb pollution, it raises other concerns. Many sources of energy, including natural gas, are *nonrenewable*. In contrast to, say, timber—whose current supply can be replaced by planting new trees—once we exhaust the earth's supply of natural gas it is gone. Many nonenergy natural resources are also nonrenewable, from asbestos to zinc. This has created concern that the present generation is squandering the earth's natural resources, leaving behind a world in which future generations will have to worry not only about pollution but also about how to maintain consumption in the face of declining resources.

The "energy crisis" of the 1970s, and the country's newly discovered vulnerability to foreign supplies of energy, only intensified fears that the country was running out of resources. Reinforcing this view, the government ran "public-service" messages encouraging conservation, prohibited the use of natural gas for certain activities, and established programs to regulate the price and distribution of oil and natural gas. At the same time, some organizations were predicting that certain resources would soon be depleted. For example, in 1976 the American Electric Power Company ran advertisements claiming that in twelve years "America will be out of oil and gas."[12]

The predicted event did not materialize. In fact, in 1988 America had enough natural gas to last another twelve years—through the year 2000. This raises a number of important issues. How were we able to postpone depletion of our stock of natural gas past 1988? Can we do it again in the year 2000? What led to the shortage of natural gas and other materials in the 1970s? Did the government's regulation of the oil and natural gas industries ameliorate the energy problem? How did government controls affect the country's dependence on foreign sources of energy?

WHY THE END NEVER COMES

Expected Life (of a resource)
Proven reserves divided by consumption.

Proven Reserves
The amount of a natural resource that has been discovered and that producers are willing to extract given current costs and prices.

Periodically, statistics are compiled on the **expected life** of various resources. In 1976, such statistics placed the expected life of natural gas at twelve years. To see what these statistics do and do not mean, it is important to understand how they are constructed. The expected life of natural gas is based on its **proven reserves,** which in the United States amounted to 228 trillion cubic feet in 1976. U.S. consumption of natural gas that year amounted to 19.5 trillion cubic feet. Simple division reveals that if this rate of consumption were maintained, proven reserves would be depleted in twelve years.

---

[12]Arnold Hite, "Chicken Little Was Wrong About Oil, Too," *Wall Street Journal*, February 3, 1988, p. 20.

But proven reserves do not include all of a resource that is locked in the earth. Rather, proven reserves refer to the quantity of a resource that has been discovered and that producers are willing to extract given current prices and technology. Extraction costs depend on the size of a deposit and its purity. They also vary with its location. A certain amount of a resource may lie near the earth's surface, easily accessible. Other deposits may be buried miles under ground or beneath the ocean floor. In addition, it may be necessary to transport some deposits great distances across hostile terrain before reaching the market. For such reasons, some deposits are too costly to extract at present prices. These deposits are not counted as *proven reserves*.

As the price of a resource rises, and a larger quantity can be profitably extracted, proven reserves increase. (Oil that costs $25 per barrel to produce will not be part of proven reserves when the price is $20 per barrel but will be when the price is $30.) Proven reserves also expand when extraction costs decline (e.g., due to a technological advance or government tax incentives). Finally, proven reserves increase as exploration leads to the discovery of new deposits of the reserve. In other words, proven reserves fluctuate over time.

Given this responsiveness in proven reserves, statistics on the expected life of various resources can be misleading. They should not be interpreted as indicating the date when the stock of a resource will be depleted. As a resource becomes more scarce, its price tends to rise. Not only does this directly increase proven reserves, it triggers additional exploration and provides added incentives to develop new, cost-saving technologies. These will further boost proven reserves. In fact, proven reserves often *increase* over time, as new reserves are added faster than current reserves are depleted.

There is a second reason why statistics on the expected life of a resource understate the actual remaining life, and that relates to demand. If the relative price of a resource rises, those using the resource will switch to substitutes. Other things equal, this will reduce consumption of the resource, slowing the rate at which it is depleted. In other words, as a resource becomes more scarce, the resulting higher price not only spurs exploration and production of the resource, it also curtails consumption. Both effects extend the resource's expected life. Because estimates of the expected life ignore the market responses of producers and consumers, they paint an unduly pessimistic picture of when, if ever, a given resource will be depleted. Accordingly, we can be quite confident that natural gas will be available well past the year 2000.

EXPLAINING THE SHORTAGES OF RAW MATERIALS

The 1970s were a decade of shortages. The recession that began in late 1973 is frequently attributed to shortages of raw materials, which forced companies to curtail production and lay off employees. In addition, natural gas was in short supply throughout the decade, especially during the winter of 1976–77. What accounted for these shortages? If prices adjust to reflect the relative scarcity of raw materials, as argued in the preceding section, then why were shortages not quickly eliminated?

The answer is that prices were *not* allowed to adjust. During much of this period the government artificially kept the prices of many raw materials below the market level, predictably creating a shortage (see Figure 34-6, page 790). From 1971–74, prices of goods and materials were subject to controls of various degree. During part of this period prices were frozen; at other times prices were allowed to rise, but only

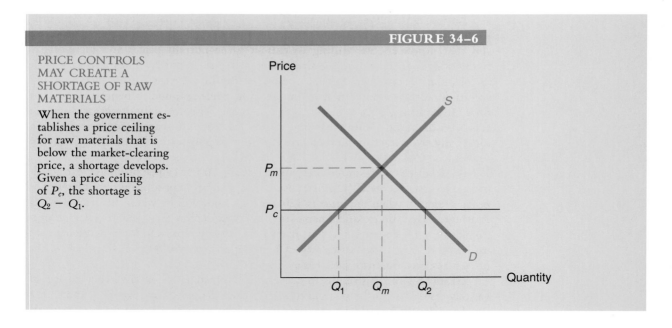

FIGURE 34–6

PRICE CONTROLS
MAY CREATE A
SHORTAGE OF RAW
MATERIALS

When the government es-
tablishes a price ceiling
for raw materials that is
below the market-clearing
price, a shortage develops.
Given a price ceiling
of P_c, the shortage is
$Q_2 - Q_1$.

by a limited amount. As demand for raw materials increased, due to a strengthening
economy, pressure on prices mounted. Soon market prices were above controlled
prices and, when that happened, firms were unable to obtain the quantities of raw
materials they sought.

Price controls for natural gas have a much longer history. They were initiated in
1954 and continue even today for certain categories of natural gas, although controls
for most categories have been phased out in accordance with the Natural Gas Policy
Act of 1978. Despite differences in the way controls on natural gas were set up, their
effect was the same as for other products: *when controls keep a price below its market
level, shortages develop.*

In the case of natural gas, shortages did not occur immediately. Given the heavy
fixed costs of drilling for natural gas and the modest variable costs of operating
existing wells, producers continued to sell large volumes of gas from existing wells,
despite the imposition of controls. But controls did slow new drilling and
exploration, threatening to create severe shortages in the future. Aware of this, the
government attempted to fine-tune controls by allowing higher price ceilings on *new*
wells (those drilled after a certain date) and on so-called "high-cost" wells. This
mitigated some of the adverse effects on exploration and production, although it
increased the complexity of price controls. For example, when the policy of partial
decontrol of natural gas went into effect in 1979, there were 25 separate categories
of natural gas, with different schedules for decontrol and with prices ranging from
$.20 per million BTUs to $2.24.[13]

Despite such variations in the price-control program, its basic purpose was to
keep the price of natural gas below its market-clearing level. As such, the shortages
that developed were inevitable. The lesson of the shortages was not, as some
inferred, that the country was running out of natural gas. Instead, the message was

[13]Same as 4, p. 120.

that when the price of natural gas (or any other good) is not allowed to rise to its market-clearing level, some consumers will be frustrated in their attempts to buy the good.

PRICE CONTROLS AND IMPORTED OIL

Oil was also subject to price controls, but for the most part the country avoided oil shortages by increasing its imports from abroad. Thus the primary consequence of price controls on oil was to increase our dependence on foreign oil. To understand this, it is necessary to know how these controls were implemented.

The Energy Policy and Conservation Act of 1975 established price controls for domestically produced oil. Because only domestic oil was controlled, refiners that purchased foreign oil were forced to pay the higher world price. Unless something was done, this would put them at a cost disadvantage compared to refiners with access to domestic oil. To eliminate this distortion, the Energy Policy and Conservation Act also instituted an **entitlement program** designed to equalize the price of all oil sold in the United States. Refiners that wanted to buy price-controlled U.S. oil were first required to purchase entitlements from the government, giving them the authority to buy this oil. On the other hand, refiners that purchased the higher-priced imported oil were given a subsidy, financed by the entitlement fees. By adjusting entitlement fees and subsidies, the government established an effective common price for all domestic refiners, regardless of where they actually purchased their oil.

Entitlement Program
A system for allocating oil to U.S. refiners that consisted of entitlement fees (taxes) on domestic oil and subsidies on imported oil. Once the entitlement fees and subsidies were taken into account, all refiners faced the same effective price for their oil.

Because of the entitlement program, U.S. consumers were able to buy oil for less than the world price. This increased the quantity of oil demanded by U.S. consumers and reduced their incentive to conserve oil. At the same time, because U.S. producers were forced to accept less than the world price, they reduced the amount of oil they were willing to supply. Thus, the government's price-control program increased U.S. consumption of oil while simultaneously reducing U.S. production. Because the shortfall between domestic production and consumption is met through imports, the net effect of price controls on oil was to increase U.S. demand for imported oil, thereby increasing the country's vulnerability to OPEC.

Price controls on oil were abolished in 1981. The immediate effect was to allow the price of oil to rise in the United States, stimulating greater conservation by U.S. consumers and greater production and exploration by U.S. producers. These actions helped curb demand for imported oil and contributed to the pressure already being exerted on OPEC, as higher oil prices reduced worldwide consumption of oil and increased the supply of oil from non-OPEC countries. As the power of OPEC waned, oil prices plunged so that, despite the lifting of controls, oil prices in the United States dropped below their 1981 levels.

In summary, the history of price controls on oil and natural gas indicates that controls distort incentives for production and consumption. Controls either lead to shortages, as in the case of natural gas, or increase our dependence on foreign producers, as in the case of oil. Rather than being a solution to an "energy crisis," price controls prolong the crisis.

SUMMARY

1. Externalities arise when the actions of producers or consumers affect third parties. Because markets ignore external benefits and costs, they fail to produce the socially

optimal amount of output. Where externalities are positive, markets produce less output than socially desired; where externalities are negative, markets produce too much output.

2. In an attempt to move market output toward the socially optimal level, the government often subsidizes goods having external benefits while taxing goods having external costs. Taxes and other added costs are an attempt to internalize costs—to shift them back to those parties that create the external costs.

3. One of the major negative externalities is pollution. In an attempt to reduce pollution, the government has imposed various legislative standards for environmental quality. Although these standards reduce pollution, they are often arbitrary. As such, they may fail to achieve the optimal level of pollution.

4. From an economic perspective, society should continue to reduce pollution until the marginal cost of pollution control equals the marginal benefit. The cost of pollution control is measured in terms of the output that is given up in order to obtain a cleaner environment.

5. Voluntary compliance is generally not an effective way to reduce pollution because it imposes costs on those who clean up the environment. Accordingly, the government relies more heavily on the command-and-control approach of direct regulation, whereby firms and consumers must follow certain rigid requirements for reducing pollution. A drawback of direct regulation is that it prevents firms and consumers from using alternative, less-costly techniques.

6. In place of direct regulation, economists generally prefer an effluent fee, which is a tax on each unit of pollution. The effluent fee provides firms and consumers an incentive to reduce pollution as efficiently as possible.

7. Alternatively, instead of taxing pollution, the government could tax the product that causes the pollution. The weakness of this approach is that firms and consumers have no incentive to reduce the amount of pollution per unit of output.

8. The government sometimes subsidizes the pollution-control equipment it requires firms to buy in order to ease the burden on these firms. But this merely transfers the cost of pollution control to the taxpayer and, by reducing the price firms charge, increases consumption of the polluting product. Finally, subsidies encourage firms to attack pollution by purchasing additional pollution-control equipment when alternative, more-efficient approaches are available.

9. Yet another approach is to establish a market for pollution rights, in which firms can buy the right to emit a certain level of pollution into the environment. Although the government does not presently sell pollution rights, it does allow firms that exceed pollution standards to sell pollution credits (what are, in effect, pollution rights) to other firms or to use these credits internally for offsetting pollution excesses elsewhere in the plant. An advantage of this approach is that it reduces pollution in those areas where it can be eliminated most efficiently.

10. Because the pollution removed from one medium is often deposited elsewhere, environmental policy must be integrated across the different media if it is to be truly effective. Given the global nature of many environmental problems, it is also desirable that environmental policy be integrated across countries.

11. Although many resources are nonrenewable, this does not imply that their supplies are fixed. *Proven reserves* of a resource—the amount producers are willing to extract—increase as the price of the resource rises, as extraction costs fall, and as new deposits are discovered. Accordingly, the proven reserves at a given point in time should not be interpreted as indicating when, if ever, a resource will be depleted. Indeed, proven reserves commonly rise over time, despite continued consumption.

12. Past shortages of natural gas in the United States were due to price controls and were not a sign that natural gas would soon be depleted. Until 1981, price controls were also imposed on oil produced in the United States. These controls reduced domestic exploration and production of oil, blunted incentives to conserve oil, and consequently increased the country's demand for imported oil.

KEY TERMS

externalities

positive externalities/external
  benefits

negative externalities/external
  costs

private benefits

social benefits

private costs

social costs

internalize costs

cost-benefit analysis

cost effective

effluent fee

pollution rights

market for pollution rights

offsets

bubbles

expected life (of a resource)

proven reserves

entitlement program

STUDY QUESTIONS AND PROBLEMS

1. (a) Demand for college education depends on the price of that education. Draw the market demand curve for college education. (b) Many scholars believe that a highly educated population benefits all of society (e.g., by promoting medical advances and more rapid technological growth). Assuming this is true, draw society's demand curve for college education. (c) Based on the preceding demand curves, as well as on the supply curve, indicate the equilibrium level of college education and the socially optimal level. (d) What can the government do to foster the socially optimal level of education?

2. The country's air and water cannot be made too clean. We should demand that they be restored to their original, pristine state.

   Explain why you do or do not agree.

3. Why is government action generally necessary to reduce pollution? Why don't firms and consumers take it upon themselves to stop polluting?

4. Production of a good raises the concentration level of an airborne pollutant from 5 parts per million to 10 parts per million. An economic study estimates that the social costs and benefits of reducing pollution from current levels are as follows:

Concentration (parts per million)	Total benefit	Total cost
9	$24,000	$ 10,000
8	44,000	25,000
7	60,000	45,000
6	72,000	70,000
5	80,000	100,000

   a. A local politician argues that firms should be forced to restore air quality to its previous level (5 parts per million). Explain why you do or do not agree.
   b. Assuming that the preceding estimates are correct, what is the socially optimal concentration of the pollutant? Explain.
   c. Assume the benefits of reducing pollution are actually twice as great as estimated. How does this affect your conclusion about the optimal concentration of the pollutant?
   d. If a new technology makes it less costly to remove the pollutant, how will this affect the optimal concentration of the pollutant?

5. Some of Vermont's landfills were leaking toxic substances, so in 1987 the state passed a law requiring landfill operators to install liners to prevent leakage. The state also levied a new tax of $2.40 per cubic yard of trash deposited in any Vermont landfill.

    a. The higher costs of operating landfills led to substantially higher prices for garbage pickup. Although some consumers and businesses protested, economists argued that the previous rates had been too low. In what sense is it possible to pay too little for a service?

    b. How does raising the cost of using a landfill affect the incentive to recycle trash? Explain.

    c. In another provision of the law, the government of Vermont agreed to subsidize recycling. On what economic grounds can this subsidy be criticized?

6. Copper smelters produce sulphur dioxide. To reduce emissions of this pollutant, the government could either tax firms on the volume of copper they produce or on their emissions of sulphur dioxide.

    a. In what sense is the emissions tax preferable?

    b. The copper tax has one modest advantage over the emissions tax. What is it?

7. Suppose the mayor of New York City receives five proposals for reducing carbon monoxide in the city: (i) appealing to residents of the city to curb unnecessary automobile use, (ii) imposing a tax of $5 per day on all vehicles operating in New York City, (iii) requiring meters on all vehicles in order to measure carbon monoxide emissions and then charging the owners an amount based on the level of emissions, (iv) banning the use of all cars and trucks every Monday, (v) subsidizing all train travel to and from the city and reducing subway fares in the city to $.10.

    a. Which proposal is likely to be the least effective at reducing emissions of carbon monoxide?

    b. Which proposal could be criticized for shifting to taxpayers the cost of controlling pollution?

    c. Which proposal is an example of direct regulation?

    d. Which proposal makes use of an effluent fee?

8. (a) What is an EPA *bubble*? (b) Why do economists prefer the bubble policy to the command-and-control approach of direct regulation?

9. The Bureau of Mines reports that world reserves of bauxite (aluminum ore) increased from 5.7 billion metric tons in 1965 to 21.8 billion metric tons in 1987. How is this possible? Given the consumption of aluminum that occurred over this period, how could society end up with more of this exhaustible resource in 1987?

10. Explain how each of the following would affect proven reserves of the particular natural resource:

    a. a *windfall profits* tax on oil, which decreases the effective price that oil companies receive for selling a barrel of oil

    b. a subsidy that suddenly makes it profitable to extract low-grade iron ore

    c. the discovery of a major gold deposit in Alaska

    d. a technological advance that lowers the cost of extracting diamonds

11. Suppose the government forces U.S. titanium producers to slash the price of their product.

    a. How will this affect (i) domestic production of titanium and (ii) demand for imported titanium?

    b. Assuming that the United States buys enough titanium to affect the world price, how will price controls on U.S. producers affect the world price of titanium?

ANSWERS TO YOUR TURN

COMPARING THE COSTS AND BENEFITS OF POLLUTION CONTROL
(a) MC = $3 million; MB = $10 million; the current level of pollution is higher than socially optimal. (b) Yes. The total benefit of reducing pollution to 2 tons per month exceeds the cost of doing so by $16 million ($37 million minus $21 million). (c) The optimal level of pollution is 3 tons per month. This is the lowest level of pollution for which the marginal benefit of reducing pollution exceeds the marginal cost. (Alternatively, 3 tons of pollution occurs where the difference between the total benefits of reducing pollution and the total cost is maximized: TB − TC = $21 million.) (d) Zero pollution. The marginal cost of reducing pollution to less than 3 tons per month exceeds the marginal benefit.

ANSWERS TO YOUR TURN

THE ADVANTAGE OF A BUBBLE
(a) $14 million (i.e., $11 million plus $3 million). (b) The firm can reduce its pollution-control expenditures to $9 million per month by allowing boiler 1 to emit 10 tons of pollution while limiting boiler 2 to 6 tons of pollution. Compared to the previous limit (a), this results in a cost savings of $5 million per month. (c) The firm should accept the government's offer. The cost of satisfying the 14-ton limit is $13 million ($7 million for boiler 1 and $6 million for boiler 2). This is $1 million less than the cost of limiting pollution each month to 8 tons per boiler. Even though the firm is now producing 2 fewer tons of pollution each month, it is able to reduce its pollution-control expenditures because it now has discretion over how it reduces pollution.

SELECTED REFERENCES

Council on Environmental Quality, *Environmental Quality* (Washington, DC: GPO). Discusses environmental legislation, cost-benefit analysis, and such environmental problems as acid rain and the greenhouse effect—the annual report of the President's Council on Environmental Quality.

Robert W. Hahn and Gordon L. Hester, "The Market for Bads: EPA's Experience with Emissions Trading," *Regulation* (Number 3/4, 1987), pp. 48–53. Analyzes the EPA's emissions trading program.

S. Fred Singer, ed., *Free Market Energy* (New York: Universe Books, 1984). Examines U.S. energy policy and its alternatives.

U.S. Environmental Protection Agency, *National Air Quality and Emissions Trends Report* (Washington, DC: GPO). Details progress and problems in complying with air quality standards.

Melinda Warren and Kenneth Chilton, *Clearing the Air: Regulating Ozone in the Public Interest* (St. Louis: Center for the Study of American Business, 1988). Discusses the history, costs, and benefits of the Clean Air Act.

CHAPTER 35

AGRICULTURE

The Bucks have survived, but some of their neighbors have not. As recently as 1986, an estimated 37,000 farms were insolvent (their debt exceeded assets). An even larger number were burdened by heavy debt and low income.[2] With so many farmers unable to repay their loans, rural bank failures soared. Financial distress in rural America reached its highest level since the Great Depression.

Yet despite the recent hardship endured by a substantial minority of farmers, the economic situation of the average farmer has actually improved this century. Indeed, during much of the preceding two decades the average income of farm families has been at least as high as the average income of nonfarm families. Recent pockets of financial distress in agriculture have come in the face of long-term progress, at least as measured on a per-farm basis.

After examining long-term trends in agriculture, including changes in aggregate farm income and income per farmer, Chapter 35 addresses the recent financial distress of some of the nation's farmers. We then consider the rationale for government involvement, analyze the impact of current farm programs—from propping up prices to subsidizing foreign sales of U.S. farm products—and discuss recent proposals to reduce the role of government in agriculture, now that average farm incomes have improved.

Joe Buck and his son James harvested 1200 acres of wheat this summer on their farm in northern Oklahoma. By December, they will have collected nearly $75,000 in direct government subsidy payments—a third of their operating income for the year. "No two ways about it. The check's like welfare," James Buck said. "Nobody likes to take welfare, but you got to do it to survive."[1]

---

[1]Keith Schneider, "The Subsidy 'Addiction' on the Farms," New York Times, September 13, 1987, p. 5E.

[2]See U.S. Department of Agriculture, Farm Sector Review, 1986 (1988), p. 40.

SOME BACKGROUND

Agriculture is a key sector of the United States economy. When defined broadly to include the production and sale of food and fiber, agriculture accounts for one-sixth of the country's output and provides employment for over 20 million workers.[3] In terms of world trade, United States agriculture is even more important, helping to feed and clothe the world's population. For some commodities, including coarse grains and soybeans, the United States accounts for over one-half the world's exports. Because the United States sells more agricultural products to foreign countries than it imports, agriculture has helped to keep the country's trade deficit from becoming even larger.

Agricultural industries tend to be highly competitive. Most have a large number of producers, and entry into and exit from the industry is generally easy. In the case of major crops, including wheat and corn, hundreds of thousands of different farmers supply the market. For a given grade of product, output is homogeneous— buyers do not care from whom they purchase the product. Finally, information on price, supply, and other pertinent data is readily available to both buyers and sellers. Under such conditions, individual buyers and sellers are price takers. Although government intervention sometimes affects market supply or demand or impedes market adjustment, behavior of prices and incomes can be explained, especially over long periods, by the forces of supply and demand.

TRENDS IN AGRICULTURE

To examine developments in agriculture, it is necessary to consider both the aggregate income of all farmers and the average income per farmer. Due largely to changes in the farm population, the two series have moved in opposite directions. While aggregate income of farmers has decreased sharply, average income per farmer has drifted higher during much of the century.

CHANGES IN NET FARM INCOME

Net Farm Income
The total revenue generated by a nation's farms minus farm production costs.

Net farm income is a measure of the aggregate income of all farmers. Defined as the total revenue from farming minus production costs, net farm income has fallen by 50 percent since 1945 after accounting for inflation (see Figure 35-1, page 798). As a percentage of national income, the decline has been even steeper—from 6.8 percent in 1945 to 1.0 percent in 1988.

Over the same period that net farm income has fallen, the relative price of farm products has also eroded. That is, the price of farm products has increased more slowly than prices in general (see Figure 35-2, page 799). Both developments can be explained in terms of supply and demand.

---

[3]U.S. Department of Agriculture, *Farm Sector Review, 1986,* p. 43.

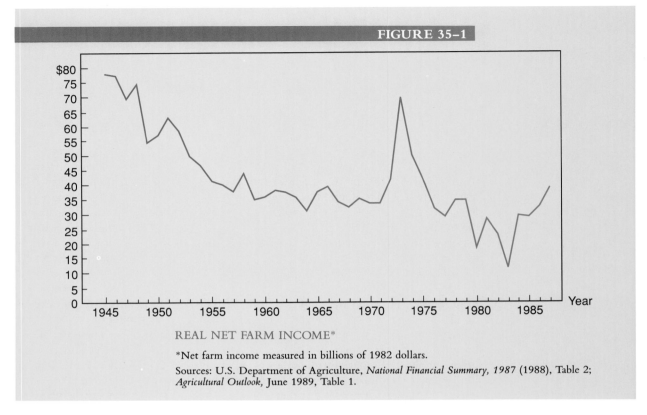

FIGURE 35-1

REAL NET FARM INCOME*

*Net farm income measured in billions of 1982 dollars.

Sources: U.S. Department of Agriculture, *National Financial Summary, 1987* (1988), Table 2; *Agricultural Outlook,* June 1989, Table 1.

Central to this story is the dramatic growth in farm productivity. Higher-yielding crops have been continually introduced, along with more-effective herbicides and pesticides. Advances in machinery, livestock genetics, and farm management have further increased output per farmer. Since the end of World War II, output per hour of labor has increased by an average of 5.4 percent per year in agriculture, compared to only 1.9 percent per year in the nonfarm business sector. Because greater productivity permits greater output, the supply of agricultural products has grown rapidly.

At the same time, demand for agricultural products has increased only modestly. This is due principally to a low income elasticity of demand for food—estimated to be about 0.1 to 0.2.[4] That is, a ten-percent increase in income leads consumers to increase their food purchases by only one or two percent. Although consumers could buy ten percent more of all goods, including food, they modify their spending patterns. As incomes rise, consumers devote relatively less of their budget to food and relatively more to the purchase of automobiles, stereo equipment, vacations, and other nonagricultural products. In other words, demand for agricultural products has increased more slowly than income; demand for nonagricultural products has increased more rapidly.

The uneven growth in supply and demand is illustrated in Figure 35-3. Because the supply of agricultural products has outstripped demand, the relative price of

[4]See Charles Schultze, *The Distribution of Farm Subsidies: Who Gets the Benefits?* (Washington, DC: The Brookings Institution, 1971); P.S. George and G.A. King, *Consumer Demand for Food Commodities in the United States,* Giannini Foundation Monograph No. 26, University of California, Berkeley, 1971.

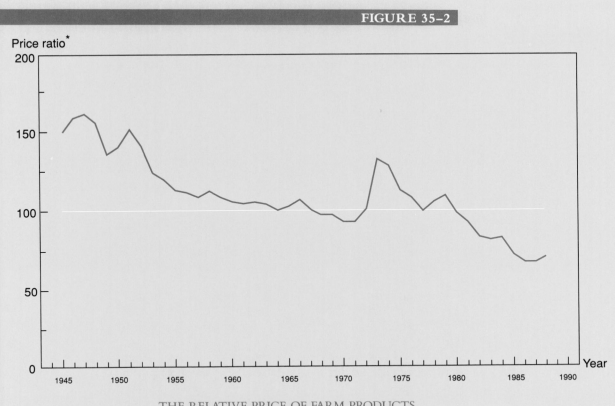

FIGURE 35–2

THE RELATIVE PRICE OF FARM PRODUCTS

*Index of Prices Received by Farmers divided by the Consumer Price Index. The base year 1967 equals 100.

Sources: U.S. Department of Commerce, *Historical Statistics of the United States,* 1975, Table K 353; U.S. Department of Agriculture, *Agricultural Prices, Annual Summary,* various issues; U.S. Department of Labor, *Consumer Price Index,* 1989.

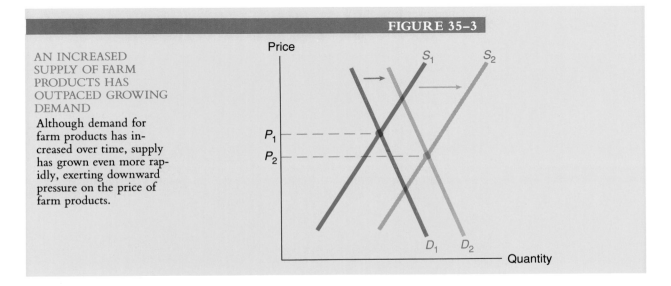

FIGURE 35–3

AN INCREASED SUPPLY OF FARM PRODUCTS HAS OUTPACED GROWING DEMAND

Although demand for farm products has increased over time, supply has grown even more rapidly, exerting downward pressure on the price of farm products.

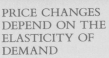

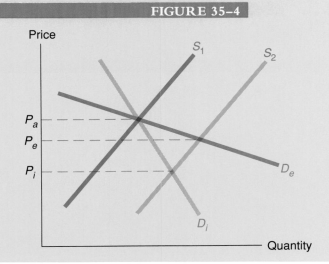

FIGURE 35–4

PRICE CHANGES DEPEND ON THE ELASTICITY OF DEMAND
Other things equal, increased supply reduces price by a relatively greater amount the less elastic is demand. For example, an increase in supply from S_1 to S_2 reduces price to P_e if demand is D_e; but given the relatively less elastic demand curve D_i, price plummets to P_i.

agricultural products has fallen over time. Accentuating this decline has been the low price elasticity of demand for agricultural products. If demand were elastic, an increase in supply would have only a modest effect on price. But because demand is inelastic, price must fall by a relatively large amount to restore equilibrium (see Figure 35-4). According to one widely cited study, the aggregate elasticity of demand for farm products has averaged 0.2 in the short run and 0.5 in the long run.[5] Other things equal, prices would have to fall by five percent in the short run (two percent in the long run) just to increase quantity demanded by one percent.

The inelastic demand for farm products has, in turn, had adverse consequences for net farm income. Given an inelastic demand curve, a lower price reduces the total revenue of farm products (see Figure 35-5). Therefore, despite increasing output, farmers have received lower receipts for the sale of their output. Although productivity advances have helped to keep costs in check, they have not been sufficient to offset the decline in total revenues. As a consequence, net farm income has fallen over time.

In summary, the decline in net farm income can be explained as follows.

1. Supply has grown faster than demand, forcing down the relative price of farm products.
2. Because demand is inelastic, lower prices have resulted in lower revenues for farmers.
3. In the absence of cost savings to fully offset the lower total revenues, net farm income has fallen.

YOUR TURN

Although the long-term trend is for vastly greater supply, sometimes bad weather and other natural disasters reduce supply in the short run. How would a reduction in supply affect price and total revenue of farmers?

[5]These figures are averages for the years 1950–1982. See Luther Tweeten, "Economic Instability in Agriculture: the Contributions of Prices, Government Programs and Exports," *American Journal of Agricultural Economics* (December 1983), Table 1.

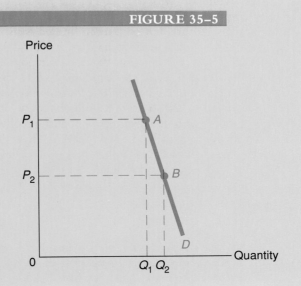

FIGURE 35-5

A LOWER PRICE MEANS LESS TOTAL REVENUE WHEN DEMAND IS INELASTIC

Because demand is inelastic, a reduction in price from P_1 to P_2 lowers total revenue. In other words, the total revenue associated with P_2 (given by the rectangle $0P_2BQ_2$) is less than the total revenue associated with P_1 (given by rectangle $0P_1AQ_1$).

LEAVING THE FARM

Economic theory predicts adjustment: if resources earn less in an industry than they could elsewhere, the resource owners will transfer these resources to the industries offering higher returns. Given developments in agriculture—declining prices and shrinking net farm income—one would therefore predict that resources would leave agriculture.

As Table 35-1 illustrates, labor mobility in agriculture has been substantial. The farm population has declined from 30 million at the turn of the century to about 5 million today. In percentage terms, the exodus from farming has been even more

TABLE 35-1

THE DWINDLING FARM POPULATION

	The U.S. farm population*	
Year	Total (in millions)	As a percent of total population
1900	29.9	41.9
1910	32.1	34.9
1920	32.0	30.2
1930	30.5	24.9
1940	30.5	23.2
1950	23.0	15.3
1960	15.6	8.7
1970	9.7	4.8
1980	6.1	2.7
1988	5.0	2.0

*The definition of "farm" was changed in 1977, leading to a modest reduction in the size of the "farm population" after this date.

Sources: U.S. Department of Commerce, *Historical Statistics of the United States,* Part 2 (1975), p. 457, *Current Population Reports,* Series P-27, (1989), p. 1.

dramatic, with the share of the population engaged in farming falling from over 40 percent in 1900 to a current value of 2 percent. Land has also been withdrawn from agriculture, but on a more limited basis. Unless farmland is located close to urban areas or production facilities, it typically has a low opportunity cost.

At the same time that the farm population has decreased, a growing share of the income received by farm families has come from *off-farm* sources (e.g., wages from nonfarm employment or rent from nonfarm real estate). Indeed, off-farm income of farm operators now exceeds net farm income. In summary, many farmers have adjusted to the decline in net farm income by leaving agriculture entirely, and those who remain have reduced their reliance on farming as a source of income. This adjustment has been painful for some, but has alleviated financial pressures for those who remain in farming.

CHANGES IN THE AVERAGE INCOME OF FARM OPERATORS

Even though net farm income has decreased over the past 50 years, the farm population has declined even more dramatically, meaning that there are fewer farmers to share in that income. In addition, off-farm income has grown substantially for farm operators. For these reasons, the decline in net farm income has not resulted in lower incomes on a per-farm basis. Indeed, in 1972, for the first time ever, the average income of farm families surpassed that of nonfarm families (see Figure 35-6). The situation was reversed in the 1980s, as short-term financial pressures developed in agriculture. But by the latter half of the decade farmers were, on average, doing at least as well as their nonfarm counterparts. Given estimates that farmers earned only about 40 percent as much as nonfarmers during the 1930s, the economic plight of farmers has eased considerably.

If Figure 35-6 illustrates the general improvement in the average income of farmers, it also demonstrates the extreme variability of farm incomes. The movements in this series are due almost entirely to fluctuations in the incomes of farmers rather than the incomes of nonfarmers. Because the 1970s were unusually prosperous years for agriculture and the early 1980s posed unusually severe financial pressures, it is useful to look more closely at developments during this period in order to see how rapidly conditions in agriculture can change.

GOOD TIMES, BAD TIMES

World demand for U.S. agricultural products soared during the 1970s, due to a number of factors, including rapid income growth in developing countries and easy credit to finance purchases of farm products. In addition, the value of the dollar declined during the early 1970s, making imports from the United States less expensive. At the same time, the supply of food in other countries was adversely affected by a number of developments—from crop failures in the Soviet Union to the disappearance of anchovies off the coast of Peru. As a result, U.S. exports of farm products increased, both in total volume and as a share of world exports. After netting out for the effects of inflation, U.S. farm exports were almost three times greater in 1980 than in 1970.

This export boom triggered a run-up in the price of farmland. Given the increased demand for farm output, demand for land needed to produce this output also increased. Because real assets, including land, are viewed as a hedge against inflation, the inflationary environment of the 1970s further boosted demand for

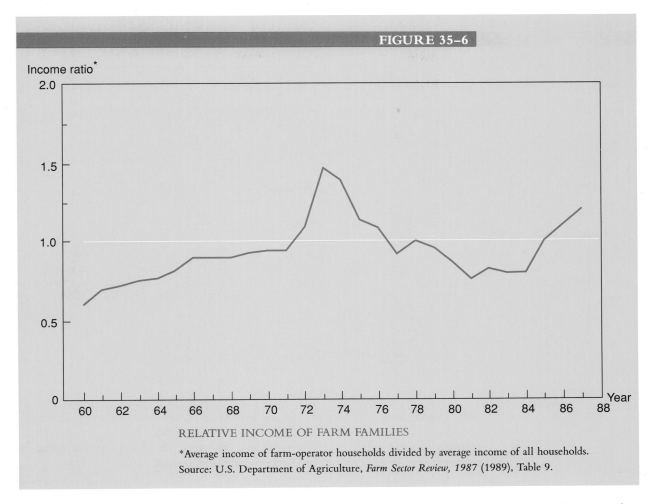

FIGURE 35–6

Income ratio*

RELATIVE INCOME OF FARM FAMILIES

*Average income of farm-operator households divided by average income of all households.
Source: U.S. Department of Agriculture, *Farm Sector Review, 1987* (1989), Table 9.

farmland. As a result, the price of farmland rose steadily during the 1970s (see Figure 35-7, page 804).

With the expectation that land prices would continue to rise, many farmers borrowed heavily to purchase additional farmland, despite high interest rates. But, as Figure 35-7 illustrates, the value of farmland headed south in the 1980s. Those same forces of supply and demand, which had been so kind to U.S. farmers in the previous decade, turned decidedly negative. A severe global recession in the early 1980s slowed demand for farm products, and debtor nations found it more difficult to buy on credit. Also, the dollar appreciated during the early 1980s, raising the price of imports from the United States. On top of this, foreign governments increased their subsidies to agriculture, thereby boosting foreign supply of farm products. Many nations that imported food during the 1970s became net exporters during the 1980s. As a result of these forces, U.S. exports of farm products declined during the early and mid-1980s.

With the export market shrinking and inflation subsiding, demand for farmland withered. Farmers who had borrowed heavily in expectation of rising land prices were squeezed by heavy debt and plunging land values. In many instances, farmers' equity turned negative—their liabilities exceeded the value of their assets. In other cases, equity remained positive but income, which had fallen as agricultural markets

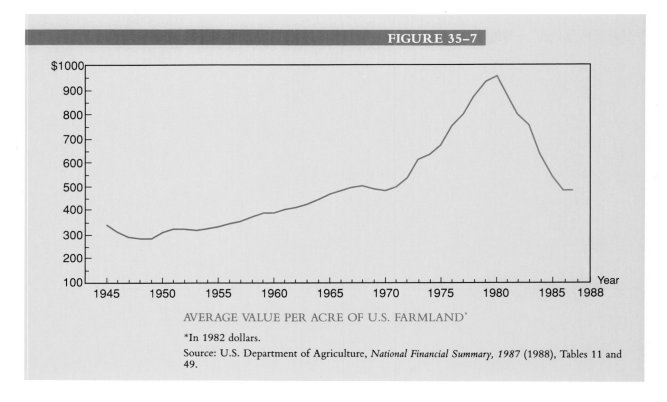

FIGURE 35–7

AVERAGE VALUE PER ACRE OF U.S. FARMLAND*

*In 1982 dollars.

Source: U.S. Department of Agriculture, *National Financial Summary, 1987* (1988), Tables 11 and 49.

deteriorated, was now too low to meet interest obligations. Although financial conditions improved in the late 1980s, as recently as 1986 about 16 percent of the nation's farmers were experiencing "financial stress" and hoping for either a strengthening in agricultural markets or government assistance.[6]

SHOULD GOVERNMENT BE IN AGRICULTURE?

Over the past 60 years, the government has funded dozens of programs designed to help farmers. Before examining the consequences of specific programs, it is appropriate to first ask why the government is so heavily involved in agriculture. Government intervention has been defended on various grounds; among the major arguments offered are the following.

Reduction of Risk

Farming is characterized by a high degree of risk and uncertainty. Bad weather may wipe out a farmer's entire crop. On the other hand, universally favorable conditions may lead to bumper crops, which depress price and the aggregate income of farmers. Embargoes, trade disputes, and other political events may limit demand for U.S. farm products, while foreign subsidies swell world supply. Given inelastic product demand, such changes in market conditions are likely to lead to wide gyrations in the prices of farm products and the incomes of farmers. Some contend that price

---

[6]This figure comes from U.S. Department of Agriculture, *Farm Sector Review, 1986*, p. 41. As defined by the Department of Agriculture, "financial distress" exists when a farmer's debt exceeds 40 percent of asset values and the farmer's income is insufficient to meet financial obligations.

instability harms consumers, while income instability harms farmers. In their view, government intervention is necessary to smooth movements in prices and income.

Those critical of this argument counter that, even if stability is desired, government intervention is unnecessary. They point to the availability of private insurance against crop failure, futures markets to protect against a decline in product price, and other market instruments to reduce risk. Farmers' limited reliance on such market instruments is attributed to the fact that the government is heavily involved in stabilizing price and income and providing relief in the aftermath of natural disasters. For example, in 1988, the government provided $4 billion in aid to drought-stricken farmers. Clearly, the expectation of continued government assistance has reduced farmers' incentives to use crop insurance and other market instruments. But could private markets alone adequately reduce risk, or is some government intervention necessary? On this issue there is no consensus.

The Family Farm

Government intervention has also been defended as necessary to save *the family farm.* To quote one analyst:

> Farming occupies an honored place in our culture. Even big-city sophisticates who would sooner die than attend a Grange Hall dance find it reassuring to know that somewhere out there honest folk are working the earth much as it has been worked for centuries.[7]

Those who embrace this view find it tragic that families are driven from their farms despite their long hours and hard work. Some seek government protection of these individuals and preservation of their lifestyle.

Others argue that the government should support low-income farmers, just as it supports low-income nonfarmers, but reject pleas to save the family farm. They note that large corporate farms are generally more efficient than small family operations and, where that is true, saving the family farm is inefficient from an economic perspective—it leads to a higher cost of producing agricultural output. Why, they ask, should inefficient producers be sheltered from competition?

Income Support

Average income historically has been lower for those in farming although, as Figure 35-6 demonstrates, this is no longer always the case. But even when the average income of farmers is high, the distribution of income among farmers is highly unequal. In particular, in most years the incidence of poverty is greater for those who farm than for the rest of the population.[8] For this reason, some favor government intervention in agriculture as a means of alleviating poverty.

The problem with this argument is that subsidizing an entire industry benefits *all* producers in the industry. In particular, subsidizing agriculture not only makes poor farmers less poor, it makes wealthy farmers more wealthy. It is difficult to defend on equity grounds a policy that indiscriminately increases incomes of all producers in an industry, regardless of their need.

[7]Gregg Easterbrook, "Making Sense of Agriculture," *The Atlantic Monthly,* July 1985, p. 63.

[8]In 1987, for the first time ever, the poverty rate of the farm population dropped below the poverty rate of the nonfarm population (12.6 percent versus 13.5 percent).

Externalities

Farming sometimes has adverse effects on the rest of society. Animal waste, fertilizer, and soil runoff contaminate water supplies while pesticides pose health risks in humans. Because of such externalities, government intervention can be justified as a means of protecting the public health and the environment. As a side effect, the government's presence may also alter income of farmers.

GOVERNMENT FARM PROGRAMS

While debate continues over the proper scope of government intervention, one thing is clear: the government is heavily involved in agriculture. The government-run **Commodity Credit Corporation (CCC)** purchases surplus products from farmers, extends loans to farmers on highly favorable terms, and offers other assistance. Net outlays by the CCC have fluctuated between $12 billion and $26 billion per year since 1985. The total cost of government intervention is even greater when one considers the higher prices consumers pay as a result of this intervention.

Government involvement in agricultural markets can be traced back to the Great Depression, which hit the farm economy especially hard. Given the competitive nature of agriculture and the noncompetitive nature of many nonagricultural markets, prices of farm products fell more precipitously than those of nonfarm products. The government responded by buying surplus crops to prevent agricultural prices from declining further. Since then the government has experimented with a number of different farm programs. Most of them fall into one or more of the following categories: (a) price supports, (b) supply restrictions, (c) demand expansion, and (d) direct payments.

Price Supports

Price supports are designed to artificially raise the prices received by farmers. If the government views the equilibrium price as too low, it can set a price floor above this figure. The government supports (or maintains) the price floor by agreeing to buy any output offered at this price.

As a practical matter, price supports are often accomplished through the use of **nonrecourse loans.** The government, through the CCC, loans farmers money with the farm commodity serving as collateral. For example, the government might loan a farmer $3 per bushel of wheat. If the market price exceeds $3, the farmer can always sell his wheat and repay the loan. But if the price falls below $3, the farmer simply turns his wheat over to the government, and the loan is forgiven. This latter option, the nonrecourse feature of the loan, guarantees the wheat farmer a minimum of $3 per bushel of wheat.

Whenever price supports exceed the equilibrium level, they result in a surplus (see Figure 35-8). Consumers respond to the higher price by reducing their consumption, while farmers increase their production. To maintain the support price, the government is forced to buy the surplus. Although this may help farmers in the short run, it poses long-term problems. As surpluses mount over time, they become increasingly costly to store. And what is to become of these surpluses? If they are dumped on the market in the future, they will depress prices at that time—high prices in the present come at the expense of lower prices in the future. Price supports, by themselves, do not provide a lasting solution to farmers' problems.

Commodity Credit Corporation (CCC)
A government agency that purchases surplus commodities from farmers.

Price Support
A minimum price guaranteed by the government. The government preserves the minimum price by agreeing to buy any output offered at this price.

Nonrecourse Loan
A government loan that a farmer may, at his discretion, either repay or cancel. To cancel, the farmer transfers ownership of the commodity to the government, keeping whatever funds the government has loaned him.

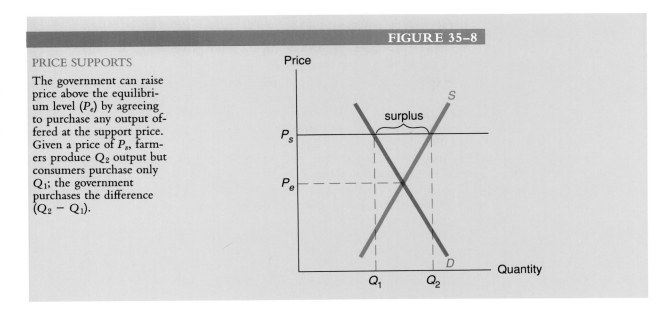

FIGURE 35-8

PRICE SUPPORTS

The government can raise price above the equilibrium level (P_e) by agreeing to purchase any output offered at the support price. Given a price of P_s, farmers produce Q_2 output but consumers purchase only Q_1; the government purchases the difference ($Q_2 - Q_1$).

Supply Restrictions

Aware of this price-support dilemma, the government has designed a number of programs that reduce the supply of agricultural products. As Figure 35-9 illustrates, a lower supply can increase price without contributing to a surplus. Supply restrictions have taken several forms. Under the *Acreage Reduction Program,* farmers must "set aside" or remove a certain amount of land from the production of a particular crop (e.g., 20 percent) in order to qualify for the support price. Farmers who withdraw additional land may qualify for extra payments. Other programs remove land from production for environmental reasons. For example, the *Conserva-*

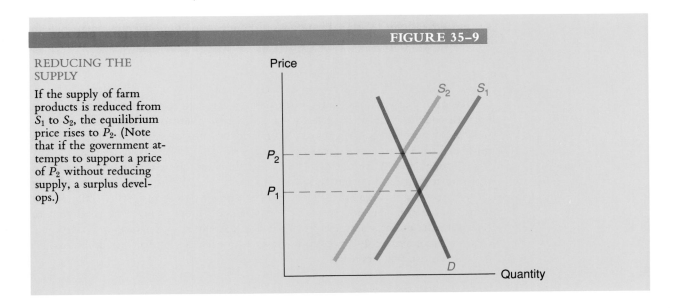

FIGURE 35-9

REDUCING THE SUPPLY

If the supply of farm products is reduced from S_1 to S_2, the equilibrium price rises to P_2. (Note that if the government attempts to support a price of P_2 without reducing supply, a surplus develops.)

tion Reserve Program pays farmers to idle their highly erodible land, thereby reducing soil runoff and water pollution.

In 1983, the government experimented by making noncash payments to farmers who limited their planting of certain crops. Under the *Payment-in-Kind (PIK)* program, farmers who pulled some of their land from production were given some of the government's surplus crops. Farmers viewed the terms of payment so attractive that nearly 80 million acres of cropland were idled that year. More cropland was taken out of production in the United States than was planted in western Europe![9]

Although removing land from production reduces output, it is important to realize that the reduction in output is often modest. Land differs in fertility. When farmers are paid to remove 20 percent of their land from production, they withdraw the 20 percent that is least productive. Moreover, now that they are devoting less land to production, they tend to use it more intensively. That is, on the acres planted they increase the application of fertilizer, herbicides, labor, and farm machinery. As a consequence, despite using 20 percent less land, farmers may produce only slightly less output.

Some commodities are covered by **marketing orders,** which are more severe than land restrictions in the sense that they tell the farmer how much output may be sold rather than how much land may be used. In some years California lemon growers have been forced to watch more than one-half of their lemon crop rot because the Department of Agriculture, which enforces the marketing orders, would not allow them to sell additional lemons.

The preceding example illustrates one of the major criticisms of supply restrictions—they are inefficient. Either resources are left idle, instead of producing output, or output is produced but never brought to market. In either case society fails to take full advantage of its resources.

A second criticism of supply restrictions is that they often disrupt rural communities. If farmers plant fewer acres, they need less fertilizer, chemicals, machinery, and other resources. Those businesses that sell such products see their sales fall and, in turn, they lose money. Many who sell farm inputs are forced out of business, not only directly harming them but also weakening the communities they serve (see Exhibit 35-1). Therefore, although supply restrictions may benefit farmers, they harm other segments of the economy.

Marketing Order
A directive, enforced by the Department of Agriculture, limiting the quantity of a product that each producer may sell on the market.

Demand Expansion

Unlike supply restrictions, policies that bolster demand for farm products increase both the equilibrium price and quantity. These programs therefore offer government a way to increase farm revenues without creating surpluses. Accordingly, such programs have been popular with politicians as well as farmers.

Through food stamps, the school lunch program, and assorted other measures, the government has boosted domestic demand for food; but, with consumption in the United States already high by world standards, such programs offer only a limited potential. An economist at Chase Econometrics once estimated that to eliminate the country's annual corn surplus, each man, woman, and child would have to eat an extra 1 1/2 pounds of corn flakes each day or drink an additional 50 gallons of corn whiskey each year.

---

[9]Council of Economic Advisers, *Economic Report of the President, 1987,* p. 149.

EXHIBIT 35–1

THE FALLOUT FROM ACREAGE RESTRICTIONS

Ike Cox thinks the government has gone too far in paying farmers not to grow. Government acreage cutbacks will cause Cox, co-owner of CTL Supply, to lose 25 percent of his grain-storage and seed business this year.

Cox and other small-town farm suppliers are not alone. Many of the nation's largest agribusiness companies—and even some farm groups—are reversing their positions on acreage setasides, arguing that the United States quickly could become a second-rate agricultural power unless farmers are allowed to plant more to meet rising export demand.

The loss of status as the world's dominant grain exporter would send severe shocks through the U.S. economy. Midwestern cities would be hit especially hard because a large part of their economies are tied to farming and grain exports.

In Kansas City, a permanent decline in U.S. grain exports would slash business for the huge terminal elevators that dot the industrial district, reduce traffic on the railroads, and slow wheat trading at the Kansas City Board of Trade. Combine manufacturing in Independence, just now coming alive after a long shutdown, again could flounder. And the emergence of agricultural biotechnology companies in the Kansas City area could be nipped in the bud.

Farmers in Cox's territory, Harrison County, have flocked into the government's Conservation Reserve Program. For about $60 an acre per year from Uncle Sam, or $600 for the next 10 years, growers in the county have agreed to plant native grass or trees on 58,000 acres. That's about 22 percent of Harrison County's cropland. So Harrison County farmers will need a lot less fertilizer, seed, and chemicals in the next decade. And they won't need nearly as much room to store their smaller harvests.

Unless farmers are encouraged to plant more acres, the rural economy may never recover from the farm crises of the mid-'80s, the critics say. That will permanently shrink the tax bases of the rural towns, and services will suffer. Cox points to a University of Missouri-Columbia study showing that the programs will cut $15 million a year out of the economy of northern Missouri because farmers will need fewer farm supplies. "Those dollars aren't going to be going through the economy here," Cox said, "It's going to hurt a lot more people than they think."

Source: Dirck Steimel, "Dwindling Acres: Have We Gone Too Far?" *The Kansas City Star*, February 28, 1988, pp. 1-11j. Reprinted by permission; *The Kansas City Star*, © 1988.

Given that consumers in the United States cannot eat (much less drink) farmers to prosperity, the government has emphasized programs designed to increase the exports of farm products. Such programs include negotiating reductions in other countries' trade barriers, making loans to less developed countries, and offering export subsidies that reduce the relative price of U.S. products in world markets. Sometimes the United States government buys directly from farmers and then sells to foreign countries at a lower price. For example, the federal government sold sugar to China for less than one-third of what it had paid U.S. sugar growers. And, because of grain subsidies, it has been widely observed that you can buy U.S. wheat for less in Moscow than in Kansas City.

Herein lies a major criticism of U.S. policy. Export programs cannot be judged simply in terms of the volume of food exports. Where the United States pays three times the world price to export sugar, rice, butter, and other commodities, that policy can hardly be termed a success. The costs of export programs must be weighed against the benefits and, unfortunately, the costs often dominate.

Given the limited market for U.S. food, both domestically and internationally, some place more confidence in programs designed to stimulate nontraditional uses of agricultural output. For example, the U.S. government sponsors research to develop nonfood products from corn and other crops and to spur demand for these products. Thanks to government support, billions of bushels of corn have been converted into the fuel methanol. And because methanol is relatively pollution-free, environmental regulations may lead to its expanded use in the future. Other uses for corn include disposable bottles, plastic sheeting, and even gas filters (see Exhibit 35-2). Similarly, sunflowers, once used mainly to produce bird food, are involved in the manufacture of fuel, fabric, and acoustical tile. Such nontraditional markets may offer farmers the opportunity to more fully participate in the country's economic growth.

Direct Payments

Target Price
A minimum price guaranteed by the government. If the market price falls below the target price, the government reimburses farmers for the difference.

Deficiency Payment
A supplemental payment that farmers receive for each unit of output they produce, equal to the difference between the target price and the market price. If the market price exceeds the target price, there is no deficiency payment.

A drawback of the three preceding approaches—price supports, supply restrictions, and demand expansion—is that, in the process of aiding farmers, the government raises the price of agricultural products. Thus, farmers are helped at the expense of consumers. An alternative approach is for the government to make direct payments to farmers without raising prices. Under its **target price** program, the government guarantees farmers a minimum price for their product, a so-called "target price." But, unlike the price support program, the government does not promise to buy surplus commodities. Instead, farmers sell their commodities on the market, receiving supplemental government payments whenever the market price falls below the target price.

This program is illustrated in Figure 35-10. Given a target price of P_t, farmers produce Q_t output. But consumers are prepared to pay only P_m for this level of output, so the government makes up the difference. That is, for each unit sold, farmers receive a price of P_m from consumers and a **deficiency payment** of $P_t - P_m$ from the government. Total deficiency payments received by farmers amount to $(P_t - P_m) \times Q_t$, represented by the shaded area of Figure 35-10.

Deficiency payments depress the price consumers pay for farm products. In the absence of government intervention the price would have been P_e rather than P_m. It

EXHIBIT 35–2

NEW MARKETS FOR CORN

Corn is replacing petroleum not just in gas tanks, but also in homes, factories, and other industrial applications. Already corn is used in the manufacture of adhesives, chemical additives, de-icing materials, and plastic bags. Scientists have discovered that products currently made from petroleum can alternatively be produced from corn starch. As technology improves, some scientists believe the United States may eventually produce all its plastics from corn. This would consume an extra three billion bushels of corn each year (about one-third the current U.S. corn crop), while saving a billion barrels of oil.

Because corn-based products are biodegradable, decomposing much more rapidly than petroleum-based products, this substitution would benefit the environment. Another obvious advantage to oil-importing countries, such as the United States, is that such developments would reduce dependence on foreign oil. For such reasons, research into the creation of new, agriculturally based products offers the possibility of not only helping farmers but benefiting society as well.

Source: Adapted from Keith Schneider, "New Invention from the Cornfield," *New York Times*, January 10, 1988, p. 36E.

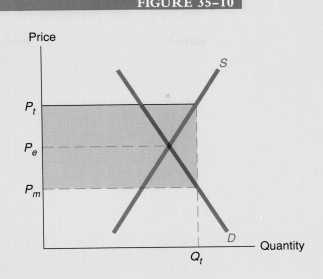

FIGURE 35–10

TARGET PRICES AND
DEFICIENCY
PAYMENTS

If the government sets a
target price of P_t, farmers
produce Q_t output. When
the farmers bring this
quantity to the market,
they find that consumers
are willing to pay only
P_m. To supplement this
low price, the government
makes a deficiency pay-
ment of $P_t - P_m$ for each
unit produced. Altogether,
farmers receive deficiency
payments of $(P_t - P_m) \times$
Q_t, represented by the
shaded area.

does not follow, however, that direct payments to farmers are socially beneficial.
The funds needed to make these payments must be raised through taxes. Moreover,
deficiency payments promote an overallocation of resources to agriculture. In terms
of Figure 35-10, the last unit produced has a value of P_m (the price consumers are
willing to pay for it), but the cost of producing that last unit is P_t. Thus, deficiency
payments induce farmers to produce output whose value to society is less than the
cost of producing it.

CRITICISMS OF U.S. FARM POLICY

> U.S. agricultural programs have resulted in enormous budgetary costs, benefits that do
> not reach those most in need, huge surpluses of farm products, major trade disputes with
> other countries, and great harm to well-functioning international markets.[10]

The government's farm policy has been criticized on several counts. Some argue that
its costs outweigh benefits, others that it provides benefits to the wrong farmers.
These and other criticisms are explored in the following section.

High Costs

Apart from administrative costs, the costs of farm programs include inefficient use of
resources. These costs are ultimately borne by consumers (in the form of higher
prices) and by taxpayers. According to a study by the U.S. Department of
Agriculture, each dollar of cash income that the government transfers to farmers
costs consumers and taxpayers as much as five dollars.[11] Because farmers gain less
than the rest of society loses, farm programs reduce the average standard of living.

[10]Council of Economic Advisers, *Economic Report of the President, 1987,* p. 147.
[11]Council of Economic Advisers, *Economic Report of the President, 1986,* p. 155.

Distribution of Benefits

High costs, by themselves, do not imply that farm programs are inappropriate. Even though average income is reduced, these programs may effectively reduce poverty and narrow the distribution of income. If these are socially desirable goals, then farm programs may be an important element of the government's social policy.

But critics reject this argument, noting that farm programs are not an efficient way of reaching those in need. Because government support is based on the level of production, benefits go primarily to large farms. In 1987, farms with less than $40,000 in sales (generally run by part-time farmers) received an average of about $2000 in direct government payments; farms with $40,000 to $99,999 in sales (mostly family farms) received just under $15,000. In contrast, farms with sales of at least $500,000 received farm subsidies amounting to $46,000 (see Table 35-2).

Because operators of large farms generally have higher incomes than those of small farms, and a lower incidence of poverty, output-based programs tend to provide the greatest assistance to those least in need. In some cases, large farms collect massive subsidies. For example, a California superfarm recently received $20 million in agricultural subsidies while an Illinois utility, which grew corn on the side, was paid over $0.5 million.[12] In light of such payments, it is difficult to defend current farm policy on distributional grounds. Nor can it be defended as a means to assist those suffering financial distress. Financial problems have been more common among small farms, yet they receive less support than large farms. In summary, whether need is defined in terms of income or financial distress, those receiving most of the government support are those least in need!

A Growing Elasticity of Demand

According to some studies, the elasticity of demand for agricultural products has increased over time. This primarily reflects the increasingly international nature of agricultural markets and the fact that foreign demand is more elastic than domestic demand. As the share of agricultural output exported increases—as occurred during the 1970s and late 1980s—the average elasticity of demand for U.S. agricultural products increases.

TABLE 35-2

NET FARM INCOME AND DIRECT GOVERNMENT PAYMENT BY SIZE OF FARM OPERATION, 1987

Farms with sales of	Average net farm income*	Average direct government payment
Less than $ 40,000	$ 516	$ 2,002
$ 40,000 to $ 99,999	18,713	14,913
$100,000 to $249,999	51,749	26,170
$250,000 to $499,999	128,678	38,360
$500,000 and over	738,132	46,073

*Before inventory adjustment.

Source: U.S. Department of Agriculture, *National Financial Summary, 1987* (1988), Tables 37 and 38.

---

[12]*The New York Times,* "Big Farms to Get Huge Payments Under New Bill," July 27, 1986, p. 11; Keith Schneider, "The Subsidy 'Addiction' on the Farms," *New York Times,* September 13, 1987, p. 5E.

Although aggregate demand for farm products remains inelastic, demand for some individual products has apparently become elastic. For example, over the period 1976–1982, the long-run elasticity of demand for soybeans was estimated to be 1.2.[13] In that event, restrictions limiting supply are likely to be inappropriate in the long run. For products whose demand is elastic, supply restrictions *depress* revenues of farmers.

Government Programs as a Cost of Production

Even where farm programs increase the revenues of farmers, they simultaneously inflate production costs. Programs that increase the income generated per acre of farmland increase demand for that land, driving up its price. In other words, the future value of government support becomes *capitalized* or built into the price of the land. Although this benefits those who own the land prior to the announcement of these programs, it does not help those who later buy or rent this land, since they must pay more to use the land. For such farmers, the benefits of farm programs are completely offset by higher land costs. Thus, government farm programs do not increase the profitability of farming, they merely increase the wealth of the initial land owners.

Instability

Another criticism of government policy is that, despite an apparent goal of stabilizing prices and incomes, the result may be greater instability. For example, some point to trade embargoes, in which U.S. farm exports are withheld from foreign markets for political reasons. In addition to any short-term effect, this creates the impression that the United States is an unreliable supplier. Critics also note that farm policy is reversed over time and that, at any moment, policy is often inconsistent. For instance, agricultural research is supported in order to increase supply while acreage reserve programs and set-asides are implemented to reduce supply. Given such conflicting signals and uncertainty about what the government plans for the future, some view government as a source of instability.

ALTERNATIVE PROPOSALS

Given such criticisms, many favor less government intervention in agriculture and greater reliance on markets. Except for environmental issues, some see no compelling reason for the government's presence. To them, the issue is how to remove the government without further harming farmers. One proposal is to eliminate future subsidies while, at the same time, providing current farmers a one-time, lump-sum payment to compensate for the loss of future support. This would be less costly in the long run than present policy, would benefit consumers by reducing prices, and would eliminate overproduction in agriculture.

Others accept continued government involvement in agriculture, but argue that it should take a different form. Among the proposals currently debated are decoupling and targeting.

---

[13]Same as 5.

Decoupling

Under decoupling, payments to farmers would be independent of their level of production. For example, government support might consist of a fixed payment to all present farmers or a payment of so much per acre, regardless of how the land is used (even if it leaves agriculture). With government support no longer linked to production, farmers would have no incentive to produce more than the equilibrium quantity of output, thereby relieving the government of the commitment to buy surplus output. Moreover, because farmers would no longer receive prices in excess of market levels, resources would not be overallocated to agriculture. Those resources remaining in agriculture would be there because their value in agriculture exceeds their value in other industries.

Targeting

Current farm policy is indiscriminate, providing support to all farmers regardless of their need. Some propose targeting assistance to certain categories of farmers—for example, limiting support to impoverished farmers or small family farms. Although this could lower the cost to taxpayers by reducing the number of farmers eligible for support, it would still be inefficient in the sense that it subsidizes high-cost farmers. This latter effect could be mitigated by targeting aid to those farmers willing to leave agriculture. By subsidizing retraining and migration, the government could help those unable to earn an adequate living from farming to transfer to other industries. This would also lessen the hardship associated with resource adjustment from agriculture.

SUMMARY

1. Agriculture is an essential industry, accounting for one-sixth of U.S. output. Because the United States exports more farm products than it imports, agriculture has prevented the trade deficit from becoming even larger.
2. Demand for farm products has grown slowly, due to a low income elasticity of demand. At the same time, productivity advances have sparked rapid growth in the supply of farm products. Because of the more rapid growth in supply, the relative price of farm products has eroded over time.
3. Because aggregate demand for farm products is inelastic, the growth in supply has reduced total revenues from farming. Because costs have not fallen commensurately, net farm income has also declined.
4. Despite the reduction in net farm income, a declining farm population has kept the average income of farmers from drifting lower. Increased income from off-farm activities has also helped farm families. In the 1970s, for the first time ever, average income of farm families exceeded average income of nonfarm families. Although this situation was reversed during the early 1980s, recent statistics suggest that average farm income is again comparable to average nonfarm income.
5. The economic situation of farmers is much more volatile than that of the nonfarm population. With exports booming, farm incomes rose to record levels in the 1970s and the value of farmland soared. But as market conditions deteriorated, the 1980s brought lower incomes and new financial pressures. Farmers who borrowed heavily in anticipation of continued appreciation of land values were squeezed by declining land values and high interest obligations.
6. The government is heavily involved in agriculture. Through the Commodity Credit Corporation, it supports above-equilibrium prices for some products by purchasing surplus output. The government also restricts supply [e.g., by paying farmers to take land

out of production or, in extreme cases, by limiting the amount of output they can sell (through marketing orders)]. This raises the price received by farmers but disrupts rural communities and forces society to forgo output that could be produced.

7. Other government programs raise price by spurring demand for U.S. farm products, both here and abroad. In addition to increasing food consumption, the government promotes nonfood uses of agricultural products.

8. Target prices provide another form of government support. When the market price is less than the target price, the government reimburses farmers for the difference by making *deficiency payments.*

9. U.S. farm policy is criticized for raising taxes and inflating prices paid by consumers. And while farm programs provide some aid to low-income farmers, high-income farmers receive larger subsidies. Therefore, current policy is an inefficient way to reduce rural poverty and to narrow the distribution of income.

10. Farm programs inflate the cost of farming by driving up land prices. Because farm programs increase the income generated per acre of farmland, they raise the value of that land and therefore the cost of using it. These added costs offset the higher revenues generated by farm programs.

11. Some critical of current farm policy want to limit government support to certain groups of farmers (targeting) or make that support independent of the level of production (decoupling). The latter option has the advantage of eliminating the incentive to overproduce. Others seek the complete withdrawal of government from agriculture, perhaps after first compensating farmers for the loss of future subsidies.

KEY TERMS

net farm income
Commodity Credit Corporation
   (CCC)
price support

nonrecourse loan
marketing order
target price
deficiency payment

STUDY QUESTIONS AND PROBLEMS

1. As incomes increase, does demand grow more rapidly for agricultural or nonagricultural products? Other things equal, how does this uneven growth in demand affect the relative price of agricultural products?

2. How does rapid technological growth in agriculture affect (a) the price consumers pay for food and (b) the total revenue derived from farming?

3. How could the government reduce its stockpile of surplus agricultural products? List three reasonable alternatives.

4. Describe each of the following programs: Acreage Reduction Program, Conservation Reserve Program, and Payment-in-Kind. What common element do the three programs share?

5. (a) What is a target price? (b) How does it differ from a support price? (c) How does it affect the amount of resources devoted to agriculture? Why?

6. Explain how each of the following programs affects the volume of agricultural output: (a) support prices, (b) supply restrictions, (c) demand expansion, and (d) target prices.

7. Other things equal, how is the volume of U.S. agricultural exports affected by each of the following factors?
   a. the value of the dollar
   b. income growth in developing countries
   c. agricultural subsidies of foreign governments
   d. export subsidies of the U.S. government
   e. crop failures overseas
   f. policies restricting U.S. farm output

8. According to a 1980 congressional study:

   Urban expansion is devouring farmland at a dangerous rate. . . . Between 9000 and 14,000 acres of farmland are being converted daily to nonfarm uses.

   The study recommended that farmland be protected and that development be discouraged. Suppose the study's recommendations were adopted (e.g., through legislation penalizing the use of land for nonagricultural purposes).
   a. How would this legislation affect the distribution of resources between the agricultural and nonagricultural sectors?
   b. How would it affect the volume of farm output? How would it affect nonfarm output?
   c. What can we infer from the fact that urban users of land are prepared to pay a higher price than farmers?
   d. Do you think legislation discouraging the withdrawal of land from agriculture would benefit or harm society? Explain.
9. Comment on how supply restrictions affect the total revenue of farmers (a) if demand is elastic and (b) if demand is inelastic. For most agricultural products is demand elastic or inelastic?
10. There is a temptation to speak of "the farm problem" as if all farmers face the same problem. Why is this inappropriate? What insights do we gain by recognizing differences among farmers?
11. Do you think that current farm policy has generally benefited farmers? Why or why not?

ANSWER TO YOUR TURN

A reduction in supply would raise price and, given an inelastic product demand, increase total revenue of farmers.

SELECTED REFERENCES

Michael T. Belongia, "The Farm Sector in the 1980s: Sudden Collapse or Steady Downturn?" *Federal Reserve Bank of St. Louis Review* (November 1986), pp. 17–25. Analyzes short-term and long-term problems of farmers.

Council of Economic Advisors, "Income Transfers to Agriculture," *Economic Report of the President, 1986,* Chapter 4 (1986). Discusses financial problems of farmers and major farm programs.

Council of Economic Advisors, "Toward Agricultural Policy Reform," *Economic Report of the President, 1987,* Chapter 5 (1987). Examines the structure of farms and the rationale for government involvement in agriculture.

Gail L. Cramer and Clarence W. Jensen, *Agricultural Economics and Agribusiness,* 3rd ed. (New York: Wiley & Sons, 1985), Chapter 12. Analyzes proposals for increasing income of farmers.

Mark Drabenstott, "U.S. Agriculture: the International Dimension," *Federal Reserve Bank of Kansas City Economic Review* (November 1985), pp. 3–8. Tracks the export performance of U.S. farm products.

Thomas Gale Moore, "Farm Policy: Justifications, Failures and the Need for Reform," *Federal Reserve Bank of St. Louis Review* (October 1987), pp. 5–12. Presents a critical analysis of farm policy and prospects for reform.

John B. Penson, Jr., Rulon D. Pope, and Michael L. Cook, *Introduction to Agricultural Economics* (Englewood Cliffs, NJ: Prentice-Hall, 1986), Chapter 10. Studies farm policy and the importance of elasticities.

PART X

THE
WORLD
ECONOMY

CHAPTER 36

INTERNATIONAL TRADE

International trade touches all our lives. Some, like Sheila Jackson, benefit from the lower prices and greater selection made possible by trade. Others, including Maria Sanchez, lose their jobs as a result of trade, as consumers substitute foreign products for domestic products. Although Maria's opposition to imports is understandable, it is important to ask how the benefits of trade stack up against the costs. If benefits dominate, trade is advantageous to society; if costs dominate, trade is harmful.

    Before considering why countries trade or, in some cases, why they erect barriers to impede trade, some background is in order. How extensive is world trade? With whom does the United States trade? And what does the U.S. import and export?

"There's nothing wrong with imports," said Sheila Jackson. "I buy American goods when they have a good price, but I've got three kids at home. I can't be wasting my money. These shoes came from Korea, and they didn't cost an arm and a leg."

Maria Sanchez has a different attitude. She lost her job of seven years when the Town and Country Shoe Factory recently closed its doors in Sedalia, Missouri. Some of the jobs were shifted to factories in Arkansas, but some were lost to producers overseas. Maria is still bitter. Although she has since found another job, the pay is lower. "You know, if they had kept foreign shoes out of the country, I might still have my old job."

PATTERNS OF TRADE

International Trade

World trade is dominated by large industrial nations. Of the $2.7 trillion exported in 1988, the eight largest trading nations accounted for nearly 60 percent of exports (see Table 36-1). Three countries alone—West Germany, the United States, and Japan—were responsible for one-third of all trade. Because developing countries have lower levels of output, they generally play a much smaller role in world trade; yet even here there are exceptions. Hong Kong and Korea have grown so rapidly that, despite their developing status, each contributes about 2 percent of world trade.[1]

TABLE 36-1

MERCHANDISE EXPORTS, 1988 (by country)

Country	Exports		
	In billions of dollars	**As percent of country's GNP**	**As percent of world exports**
Industrial countries			
West Germany	$323	26.8	12.0
United States	322	6.6	11.9
Japan	265	9.3	9.8
France	168	16.8**	6.2
United Kingdom	145	19.3**	5.4
Italy	129	14.9**	4.8
Canada	117	24.8	4.3
Netherlands	103	45.7	3.8
Developing countries			
Hong Kong	63	N/A*	2.3
Korea	61	39.9**	2.3
South Africa	22	27.9**	0.8
Malaysia	21	64.9	0.8
Thailand	16	25.0**	0.6

*N/A = not available.

**Figure is for 1987.

Source: International Monetary Fund, *International Financial Statistics* (July 1989). Reprinted by permission.

[1] All the trade statistics of this chapter refer to *merchandise trade*—the exchange of *goods* between countries. An alternative way of measuring trade is to include the value of services as well as goods. Unfortunately, statistics on services are less readily available. Data on the volume of world trade are published only on a merchandise basis and, even in the United States, merchandise trade data are more detailed and more current than data that include services.

As Table 36-1 shows, countries vary greatly in terms of their share of output exported. The Netherlands and Korea export 40 percent or more of their gross national product (GNP), and Malaysia exports 65 percent. In contrast, the United States exports only 7 percent of its GNP to other countries.

Because the United States is a large, diverse country blessed with abundant natural resources, much of its trade is internal. Southern oil-producing states send heating oil to the North. Coastal states ship seafood inland. Agricultural states produce the food and fiber to feed and clothe urban residents. As a consequence of its diverse production, the United States relies less on international trade than most other countries. Yet despite exporting relatively little of its output, the United States, because it produces more output than any other country, still accounts for 12 percent of world exports. As of 1988, only West Germany had as large a share of world exports.

Trade by the United States

As Table 36-2 illustrates, the United States trades with countries around the world. A large share of its exports go to its neighbors in North America, especially Canada, its top foreign buyer. Other major buyers of U.S. products are the large industrial nations, including Japan, the United Kingdom, and West Germany. In turn, the

TABLE 36-2

THE UNITED STATES PATTERN OF TRADE, 1988
(by region and country)

Region/country	Exports to (billions of dollars)	Imports from (billions of dollars)
Africa	$ 7.4	$ 10.9
Egypt	2.3	0.2
South Africa	1.7	1.5
Asia	99.7	190.7
Japan	37.7	89.8
Australia, Oceania	8.2	4.8
Australia	7.1	3.6
Europe	91.6	102.7
United Kingdom	18.4	18.0
West Germany	14.3	26.5
France	10.1	12.2
Italy	6.8	11.6
Soviet Union	2.8	0.6
North America	98.0	110.4
Canada	70.9	81.5
Mexico	20.6	23.3
South America	15.1	21.8
Brazil	4.3	9.3
Venezuela	4.6	5.2

Source: U.S. Department of Commerce, *Survey of Current Business* (April 1989).

Trade Deficit
The amount by which a country's imports exceed its exports.

United States tends to buy heavily from those countries that are its best customers. Lately however, the United States has been buying more foreign products than it has been selling—that is importing more than it exports (see Figure 36-1). The **trade deficit** for 1988 alone amounted to $128 billion. Approximately 40 percent of this deficit was attributable to a trade imbalance with Japan.

Table 36-3 (page 822) shows the U.S. trade pattern in terms of the products exported and imported. The United States is a leading producer of capital goods. In recent years it has been exporting roughly $15-$20 billion each in aircraft and computers in addition to a large volume of other machinery. Another major source of exports is industrial materials and supplies, including coal, ores, and metal scrap. In many years the United States also exports large quantities of agricultural products, especially grains and soybeans; however, export volume varies considerably from year to year, depending on world supply and demand.

The United States is a major importer of petroleum and petroleum products, although it has reduced its purchases somewhat. In 1980, approximately 30 percent of imports were petroleum; eight years later the figure was less than 10 percent. Other major imports include automobiles, telecommunications equipment, semiconductors, clothing, footwear, and steel.

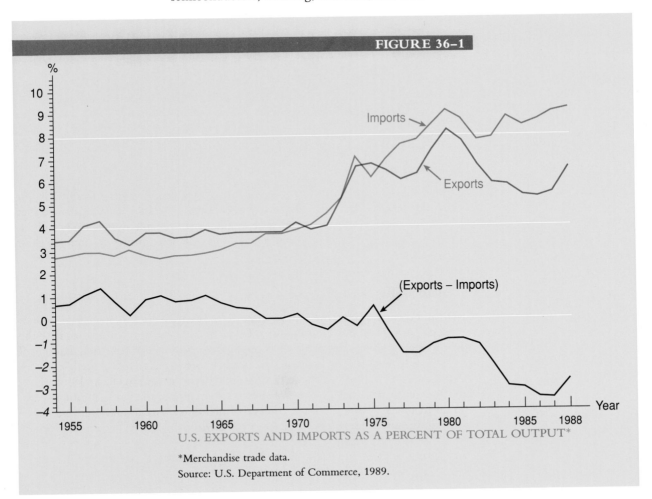

FIGURE 36–1

U.S. EXPORTS AND IMPORTS AS A PERCENT OF TOTAL OUTPUT*

*Merchandise trade data.
Source: U.S. Department of Commerce, 1989.

TABLE 36-3

U.S. EXPORTS AND IMPORTS, 1988
(by type of product)

Product	Exports		Imports	
	In billions of dollars	**As percent of exports**	**In billions of dollars**	**As percent of imports**
Food, feed, beverages	$ 33.2	10.3	$ 25.0	5.6
Industrial materials*	83.0	25.8	117.0	26.0
Petroleum	N/A**	N/A**	39.4	8.8
Capital goods***	111.6	34.7	101.4	22.6
Autos	32.6	10.2	88.1	19.6
Consumer goods***	23.8	7.4	96.4	21.4
Other	37.4	11.6	21.8	4.8
TOTAL	$321.6	100.0	$449.7	100.0

*Includes petroleum.
**N/A = not available.
***Excludes autos.
Source: U.S. Department of Commerce, *Survey of Current Business* (April 1989).

REASONS FOR TRADE

The preceding section documents the volume and pattern of international trade but does not address the fundamental question of why nations trade. Trade occurs so that nations may obtain goods not otherwise available or available domestically only at higher cost. In either case, trade permits the citizens of a country to increase their consumption and enjoy a higher standard of living.

Access to Different Goods and Resources

As rich and diverse as it is, the United States is incapable of producing certain goods and does a poor job of producing others. The United States simply does not have the right climate for growing bananas and coffee beans. Nor does it have rich deposits of every mineral. Among the minerals not currently produced in the United States are graphite, from which pencils, brake linings, and lubricants are made, and strontium, which is used in the manufacture of color television picture tubes, pigments, and ceramic magnets. Other strategic minerals, including bauxite and alumina (from which aluminum is manufactured), are produced domestically but reserves are so low that imports are necessary unless the U.S. is prepared to drastically scale back its consumption of these minerals. Table 36-4 highlights the U.S. import reliance on various minerals.

Most other countries are even more dependent on imports than is the United States. If each country were isolated and forced to make do with its natural mix of

TABLE 36-4			

NET IMPORT RELIANCE OF THE UNITED STATES FOR SELECTED MINERALS

Mineral	Import reliance*	Mineral	Import reliance*
Arsenic	100	Tantalum	92
Columbium	100	Diamond	89
Graphite	100	Fluorspar	88
Manganese	100	Pt-group metals	88
Mica	100	Cobalt	86
Strontium	100	Tungsten	80
Yttrium	100	Chromium	75
Gem stones	99	Nickel	74
Bauxite and alumina	97	Tin	73

*Imports minus exports as a percentage of U.S. consumption (adjusted for changes in mineral stocks).

Source: U.S. Bureau of Mines, *Mineral Commodity Summaries, 1988*, p. 2.

resources, standards of living would fall throughout the world, since consumption would be limited to those goods that could be produced within the country. U.S. citizens would be forced to give up their coffee, Ugandans their modern machinery. Trade makes such sacrifices unnecessary—it opens the door to products not otherwise available. By trading coffee beans and machinery, U.S. consumers can enjoy one of their favorite beverages; Ugandans can obtain modern equipment.

Absolute Advantage

Even when two countries are capable of producing the same products, trade may still be advantageous because of differences in resource endowments. Saudi Arabia and the United States can both produce oil and grain but, given Saudi Arabia's rich pools of easily accessible oil and its relatively barren soil, oil is less costly to produce in Saudia Arabia and grain is less costly to produce in the United States. Because of such cost differences, Saudi Arabia has found it profitable to export oil and import grain. Conversely, the United States has found that it benefits from trading grain for oil.

Similar cost differences exist for other products and other countries. Canada, blessed with natural resources, is a low-cost source of timber and many minerals. Japan, on the other hand, is poor in terms of natural resources but has an industrious, highly skilled work force. This permits it to produce electronic and other hi-tech equipment at a lower cost than Canada. As a result, the two countries have discovered that each benefits if Canada trades natural resources to Japan for VCRs, cameras, and compact disc players.

An example will help illustrate the mutual gains from trade. To keep things simple, we limit the example to two countries and two goods and assume that labor is the only resource used in production. In the United States each worker can produce either 3 computers or 200 pairs of shoes. In Italy each worker can produce either 1 computer of 300 pairs of shoes. According to these numbers, the United States can produce computers using fewer resources than Italy (one-third of a worker per computer in the United States versus an entire worker in Italy). Italy, on the other hand, can produce shoes using fewer resources than the United States. Because

Absolute Advantage
The ability to produce a particular good using fewer resources than a second country (i.e., a lower ratio of resources to output).

of these differences in resource costs, the United States is said to have an **absolute advantage** in the production of computers and Italy an absolute advantage in the production of shoes.

Given these differences in costs, both countries can gain from trade. To understand this, consider what happens when the United States transfers a worker from the shoe industry to the computer industry. Production of computers increases by 3 units, but 200 fewer pairs of shoes are produced (see Table 36-5, top line). Consider resource reallocation in the opposite direction in Italy. If one worker is switched from the computer industry to the shoe industry, Italy turns out 1 less computer but an additional 300 pairs of shoes. The bottom line of Table 36-5 indicates the net effect of this reallocation of labor within the two countries: the net production of computers in the two countries increases by 2 units; the net production of shoes rises by 100 pairs.

In other words, if Italy specializes in the production of shoes—producing more shoes than will be consumed in Italy—and the United States specializes in the production of computers, the two countries will end up with more computers *and* more shoes! By concentrating production in that country where production costs are lower (where absolute advantage exists), the two countries expand world output. In turn, if this extra output is divided between the two countries (more on this later), the average standard of living will rise in each country. Even though both countries can produce both goods, because costs differ there are economic reasons for specialization and trade.

Comparative Advantage

The preceding discussion assumed that each country enjoys an absolute advantage in the production of one good. But what if the same country can produce each good using fewer resources than the other country? Your initial response may be that, in such an instance, gains from trade would be impossible. Why would a country import a good that it could produce with fewer resources? But as David Ricardo demonstrated almost 180 years ago, specialization and trade may still be advantageous provided that opportunity costs differ by country.

To see this, we interchange two numbers from the preceding example. Suppose that each worker in the United States can produce either 3 computers or *300* pairs of

---

TABLE 36-5

GAINS FROM SPECIALIZATION AND TRADE—THE CASE OF ABSOLUTE ADVANTAGE

Country	Change in output	
	Computers	**Pairs of shoes**
United States	+ 3	− *200*
Italy	− *1*	+ 300
Net effect	+ 2	+ 100

By transferring one worker from the shoe industry to the computer industry, the United States produces 3 more computers but 200 fewer pairs of shoes. Italy transfers one worker from the computer industry to the shoe industry, producing 1 less computer but an additional 300 pairs of shoes. The net effect of this reallocation of resources is to produce 2 more computers and an additional 100 pairs of shoes.

shoes and that each worker in Italy can produce either 1 computer or *200* pairs of shoes. Based on these new numbers, the United States enjoys an absolute advantage in the production of both goods. Even so, both countries can benefit if the United States specializes in the production of computers, Italy specializes in the production of shoes, and the United States trades computers to Italy for shoes. We first show that this is true and then explain why.

Again the experiment consists of reallocating resources within the two countries. Let the United States move one worker from the production of shoes to computers while Italy moves two workers in the opposite direction, away from computers and into the shoe industry.[2] As Table 36-6 illustrates, production of computers rises by 3 units in the United States and falls by 2 units in Italy. Production of shoes falls by 300 pairs in the United States but rises by 400 pairs in Italy. Altogether, the two countries now have one extra computer and an additional 100 pairs of shoes. As in the first example, specialization and trade permit the two countries to expand their joint production and therefore to have greater output.

The reason that specialization and trade are mutually advantageous is that the *relative* cost of the two goods differs by country. The United States has a big absolute advantage in the production of computers—each worker produces 3 times as many computers in the United States as in Italy. In contrast, the absolute advantage in shoes is much smaller—each worker produces only 1.5 times as many shoes in the United States as in Italy. By specializing in computers, the United States can take advantage of its relatively larger absolute advantage in this industry.

This is perhaps easiest to understand by comparing the opportunity cost of computers in the two countries. In the United States the opportunity cost of 3 computers is 300 pairs of shoes or, equivalently, the opportunity cost of 1 computer is 100 pairs of shoes. Therefore, when measured by opportunity cost the cost of producing a computer is lower in the United States—the United States sacrifices only 100 pairs of shoes whereas Italy would have to sacrifice 200 pairs. Because the

TABLE 36-6

GAINS FROM SPECIALIZATION AND TRADE—THE CASE OF COMPARATIVE ADVANTAGE

Country	Change in output	
	Computers	Pairs of shoes
United States	+ 3	− *300*
Italy	− *2*	+ 400
Net effect	+ 1	+ 100

The United States transfers one worker from the shoe industry to the computer industry; Italy transfers two workers from the computer industry to the shoe industry. This reallocation leads to greater output of computers (since the increased production in the United States exceeds the loss in Italy) and greater output of shoes (since the increased production in Italy exceeds the loss in the United States).

---

[2]A larger number of workers was transferred in Italy because workers are less productive there—that is, more workers are required to produce a given volume of output. The conclusion of this example—that specialization and trade permit greater output of both goods—does not hinge on twice as many workers being reallocated in Italy. To prove this to yourself, rework the example transferring 2 workers in the United States and 5 workers in Italy, or 3 workers in the United States and 5 in Italy.

Comparative Advantage
The ability to produce a particular good at a lower opportunity cost than a second country.

Law of Comparative Advantage
Total output is maximized when countries specialize in the production of those goods for which they have a comparative advantage.

opportunity cost of producing computers is lower in the United States, the United States is said to have a **comparative advantage** in the production of computers.

Conversely, the opportunity cost of producing shoes must be lower in Italy. If Italy sacrifices more shoes per computer, it must sacrifice fewer computers for a given quantity of shoes. For example, to produce 200 pairs of shoes Italy must forgo only 1 computer whereas the United States must give up 2 computers. Therefore, Italy has a comparative advantage in the production of shoes. Equivalently, the United States has a comparative *dis*advantage in the production of shoes.

To be advantageous, trade does not require that each country have an absolute advantage in the production of a different good. All that is necessary is that each country have a *comparative* advantage in the production of a different good. This proposition is known as the **law of comparative advantage,** and it explains why, in the preceding example, trade benefits both the United States and Italy, even though the United States has an absolute advantage in the production of both goods.

YOUR TURN   EQUAL COST RATIOS
In the United States each worker can produce 3 computers or 300 pairs of shoes. In Italy the corresponding numbers are 2 computers or 200 pairs of shoes. (a) In the United States what is the opportunity cost of 1 computer? (b) In Italy what is the opportunity cost of 1 computer? (c) Under these conditions is trade advantageous?

From Production Possibilities to Trading Possibilities

The gains from specialization and trade can also be demonstrated diagrammatically with production possibilities curves. Accordingly, we recast the preceding example in terms of production possibilities curves. To do so, it is first necessary to specify how many workers each country has available for the production of computers or shoes. Let us assume arbitrarily that the United States has 1000 workers available and Italy has 1200.

Based on the preceding assumptions, the production possibilities curves for the two countries are presented in Figure 36-2. The United States can produce 3000 computers and no shoes, 300,000 pairs of shoes and no computers, or such intermediate combinations of the two goods as 2000 computers and 100,000 pairs of shoes. Because of lower output per worker in Italy, the potential output is lower there than in the United States, despite Italy's greater number of workers.

In the absence of trade, each country is constrained to its production possibilities curve. But, as previously indicated, specialization and trade offer the two countries the potential to increase the amount of output available to their citizens. That is, world output will be greater if the two countries trade than if they are self-sufficient (do not trade). How much of this additional output each country gains from trade depends on the **terms of trade**—the rate at which imported and exported goods are exchanged. This is determined by the relative price of these goods. For example, if the price of a computer is 150 times greater than the price of a pair of shoes, the terms of trade are 150 pairs of shoes for each computer.

The terms of trade are constrained by the opportunity cost in each country. Given the fact that the opportunity cost of producing 1 computer is 100 pairs of shoes in the United States and 200 pairs of shoes in Italy, the terms of trade must

Terms of Trade
The amount of one good that must be given up to obtain a unit of a second good.

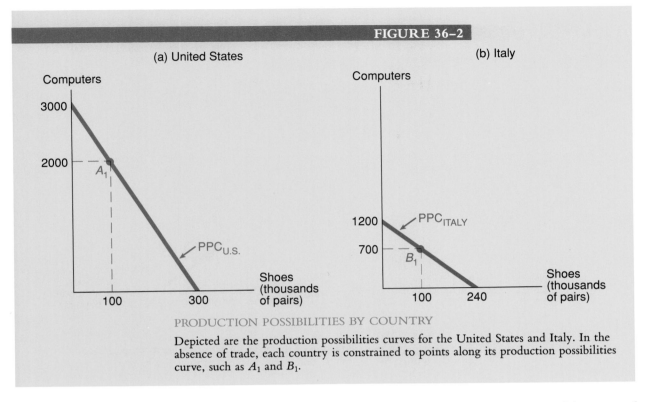

FIGURE 36–2

(a) United States

(b) Italy

PRODUCTION POSSIBILITIES BY COUNTRY

Depicted are the production possibilities curves for the United States and Italy. In the absence of trade, each country is constrained to points along its production possibilities curve, such as A_1 and B_1.

Trading Possibilities Curve

A line showing the combinations of two goods a country may obtain by producing the good for which it has a comparative advantage and trading it for the other good.

settle somewhere between 100 and 200 pairs of shoes per computer. If the terms of trade were less than 100 pairs of shoes per computer, the United States would refuse to export computers; if the terms of trade were more than 200 pairs of shoes per computer, Italy would refuse to export shoes. For concreteness, assume the terms of trade are 150 pairs of shoes per computer.[3]

Once the terms of trade are known, it is possible to construct a nation's **trading possibilities curve,** which indicates the combinations of the two goods available to it through trade. For example, consider the options available to the United States if it specializes in producing computers (the good for which it has a comparative advantage). By devoting all its resources to the production of computers, it can produce 3000 computers (and no shoes). If the U.S. trades one computer to Italy it ends up with 2999 computers and 150 pairs of shoes. If it trades 1000 computers it ends up with 2000 computers and 150,000 pairs of shoes. These and other options are depicted on the trading possibilities curve in Figure 36-3(a), page 828.

Note that points on the trading possibilities curve lie *beyond* the production possibilities curve—trade enables a country to obtain additional output. Had the United States insisted on self-sufficiency it could have reached point A_1—corresponding to 2000 computers and 100,000 pairs of shoes—but it could not have obtained more of one good without giving up some of the other. With trade, however, greater quantities of both goods become feasible. For example, with trade

---

[3]Determination of the terms of trade depends on how prices are set. In the absence of government intervention, the price of each good—and therefore the terms of trade—is determined by world supply and demand for each good. For simplicity, we assume that neither country constitutes a large enough segment of the world market to affect prices.

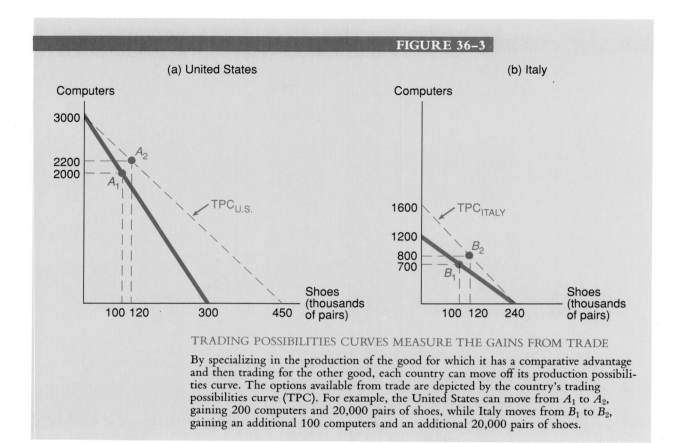

FIGURE 36-3

(a) United States

(b) Italy

TRADING POSSIBILITIES CURVES MEASURE THE GAINS FROM TRADE

By specializing in the production of the good for which it has a comparative advantage and then trading for the other good, each country can move off its production possibilities curve. The options available from trade are depicted by the country's trading possibilities curve (TPC). For example, the United States can move from A_1 to A_2, gaining 200 computers and 20,000 pairs of shoes, while Italy moves from B_1 to B_2, gaining an additional 100 computers and an additional 20,000 pairs of shoes.

the United States can obtain 2200 computers and 120,000 pairs of shoes (point A_2). Compared to point A_1, the United States gains 200 computers and 20,000 pairs of shoes.

Similarly, trade benefits Italy, bringing previously unattainable options within reach (see Figure 36-3b). For instance, with trade Italy can move from point B_1 to point B_2, in the process gaining 100 computers and 20,000 pairs of shoes. As a consequence of trade, both countries obtain greater quantities of both goods. Thus, specialization and trade allow both countries to enjoy higher standards of living than would be possible in the absence of trade.

SOME QUALIFICATIONS

In illustrating the gains from trade, the preceding discussion made a number of simplifying assumptions. These do not alter the basic conclusion—that trade can be mutually advantageous—but they do have implications concerning the extent of trade and the magnitude of the gains from trade. To understand this we relax two of the preceding assumptions.

Increasing Costs

One simplifying asumption was that the costs of production are constant. In particular, the opportunity cost of one computer was assumed to be the same no matter how many computers a country produces. It was this assumption that caused the production possibilities curve to be a straight line. If the opportunity cost of producing a good increases with the amount produced (that is, if production possibilities curves have their traditional bowed shape), trade may, after some point, cease to be advantageous.

For example, if the cost of producing a pair of shoes rises in Italy with the number of shoes produced, beyond some point it may cost the United States more to import additional shoes than to produce them domestically (i.e., in the United States). Once that point is reached, shoe imports will cease. Thus, increasing production costs may lead to *incomplete specialization*—the United States still produces extra computers, which it trades to Italy for shoes, but it also produces a portion of the shoes consumed in the United States. Similarly, rising computer costs in the United States may prompt Italy to produce computers as well as import them. In summary, the volume of trade is likely to be less when the opportunity cost of producing a good is increasing rather than constant.

Transaction Costs

The preceding discussion also ignored transaction costs, including the cost of transporting computers to Italy and shoes to the United States.[4] The presence of transaction costs alters the terms of trade. For example, after netting out for transaction costs, the United States might receive only 140 pairs of shoes for each computer while Italy may have to give up 160 pairs of shoes to obtain a computer. The difference (20 pairs of shoes) reflects the costs of moving the goods between the two countries. Although transaction costs reduce the gains from trade, trade remains advantageous. Even with transaction costs, it costs the United States less to import shoes than to produce them in the United States and it costs Italy less to import computers than to produce them in Italy.

LIMITING TRADE

Free Trade
Trade that is free of artificial barriers that would restrict the movement of goods between countries.

Despite large potential gains from *unrestricted* or **free trade,** nations often erect barriers to impede trade. What are the major trade barriers? What are their consequences? And why do nations impose them?

ARTIFICIAL BARRIERS TO TRADE

In contrast to natural barriers to trade, notably transaction costs, artificial barriers consist of government programs to obstruct the movement of goods across national borders. Sometimes a government limits exports in the belief that they would compromise national security. But, with this one exception, trade barriers are aimed at slowing or eliminating *imports.* Among the major barriers to imports are tariffs, import quotas, voluntary export restrictions, and antidumping laws.

Tariffs

Tariff (duty)
A tax levied on an imported product.

A **tariff** (or **duty**) is a tax levied on an imported good. Because it increases the cost of selling the good, it reduces foreign supply. When the tariff is set high enough, it

---

[4]See Chapter 2 for a review of transaction costs.

Prohibitive Tariff
A tariff set so high that it prevents the sale of a foreign product in the country imposing the tariff.

Nonprohibitive Tariff
A tariff that reduces but does not eliminate foreign sales in the country imposing the tariff.

drives foreign producers from the country's market entirely. Such a tariff is called a **prohibitive tariff.** For example, during the 1988 presidential primaries, one candidate raised the prospect of slapping a tax on Hyundais to increase the price of this small Korean automobile to $48,000. At such a price, imports of the car would dry up completely.

More commonly, tariffs are nonprohibitive—that is, they reduce foreign supply but do not eliminate it. The effects of a nonprohibitive tariff are illustrated in Figure 36-4. $D_{U.S.}$ is the demand by U.S. consumers for the product in question and $S_{U.S.}$ is the supply of U.S. producers. In the absence of a tariff, the product sells at the world price of P_w.[5] At this price, U.S. consumers buy Q_1^c units of output, domestic (U.S.) producers sell Q_1^d units, and foreign producers make up the difference. That is, imports amount to $Q_1^c - Q_1^d$.

Now suppose the U.S. government levies a tariff of t dollars per unit on all imports. This raises the price for U.S. consumers to $P_w + t$, causing them to reduce their purchases to Q_2^c. Domestic producers respond to the higher price by boosting output to Q_2^d, with the government collecting $t \times (Q_2^c - Q_2^d)$ in taxes from foreign producers (represented by the shaded rectangle in Figure 36-4).

The tariff harms U.S. consumers, who now receive less output and must pay a higher price. It also hurts foreign producers, who lose sales in the United States without benefitting from the higher price there. (The increased price foreign producers receive is fully offset by the tariff they must pay.) On the other hand, the tariff benefits U.S. producers and workers in the protected industry. U.S. producers receive a higher price for their product and, because of reduced foreign selling, increase their output. With domestic production expanding, demand for U.S. workers in the industry rises, putting upward pressure on wages and employment in the industry.

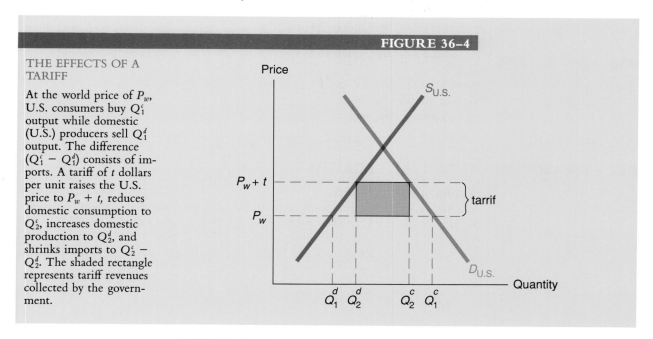

FIGURE 36-4

THE EFFECTS OF A TARIFF

At the world price of P_w, U.S. consumers buy Q_1^c output while domestic (U.S.) producers sell Q_1^d output. The difference $(Q_1^c - Q_1^d)$ consists of imports. A tariff of t dollars per unit raises the U.S. price to $P_w + t$, reduces domestic consumption to Q_2^c, increases domestic production to Q_2^d, and shrinks imports to $Q_2^c - Q_2^d$. The shaded rectangle represents tariff revenues collected by the government.

[5]The United States is assumed to be such a small part of the world market that it is a price taker. Although this assumption is not necessary, it simplifies the analysis.

To determine a tariff's net effect on the U.S. economy, it is necessary to compare the benefits of those gaining from the tariff with the costs of those losing. When that is done, the tariff must be judged a failure: losses exceed benefits. This is because the tariff, like other trade barriers, leads to a misallocation of resources within the United States. Too many resources are pulled into the protected industry (in response to artificially high prices there), leaving too few resources for other industries. In effect, resources are drawn away from industries in which the United States has a comparative advantage and diverted to industries in which the United States has a comparative disadvantage.

It is important to recognize that a tariff does not increase total output of the economy. Increased production in the protected industry comes at the expense of lower output in other industries—output that society values more highly. Overall, tariffs reduce the value of output produced by a country.

Import Quotas

Import Quota

A restriction setting a maximum limit on the amount of a product that may be legally imported into a country.

An **import quota** is a restriction limiting the quantity of a product that may be legally imported into a country. The effects of a quota are in many ways similar to those of a tariff: it reduces imports, increases domestic production, raises price, harms consumers, and benefits domestic producers in the protected industry. This can be understood with the aid of Figure 36-5, which examines the consequences of a sugar quota.

If U.S. consumers can buy sugar at a world price of 7 cents per pound, they will consume 11 million tons of sugar annually. Of that total, 3 million tons will be produced domestically and 8 million tons imported. Now consider what happens if Congress decides to protect the U.S. sugar industry by establishing an import quota

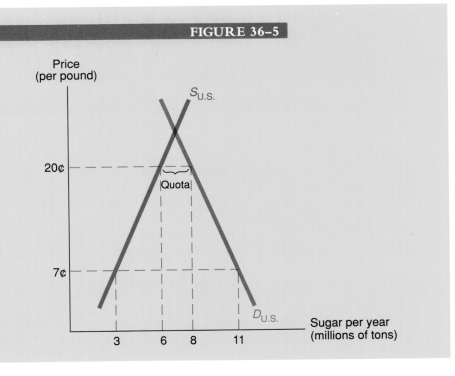

FIGURE 36–5

THE EFFECTS OF A QUOTA

At the world price of 7 cents per pound, U.S. consumers purchase 11 million tons of sugar annually. Domestic production accounts for 3 million tons, imports for the remaining 8 million tons. An annual quota of 2 million tons causes the gap between domestic consumption and domestic production to shrink to 2 million tons, which occurs when the U.S. price rises to 20 cents per pound. Of the 8 million tons of sugar demanded at 20 cents per pound, 6 million tons are supplied domestically.

of 2 million tons of sugar per year. With less imported sugar now available, U.S. consumers bid up the price of sugar, until the quantity of sugar available for sale in the United States (domestic sugar plus foreign sugar) equals the quantity demanded. That is, the price rises until the gap between domestic supply and demand narrows to 2 million tons. This occurs at a price of 20 cents per pound. At this price, U.S. consumers want to buy 8 million tons and U.S. producers want to sell 6 million tons. Once the 2 million tons of imports are included, the amount of sugar available in the United States coincides with the amount demanded.

The U.S. sugar industry reaps the benefits of Congressional intervention; consumers bear the costs. Sheltered from competition, sugar growers can sell twice as much output while receiving a premium of 13 cents per pound above the world price. Consumers receive less sugar despite paying more for it. As with a tariff, consumers lose more than producers gain; society is made worse off. Resources are drawn into the sugar industry to produce, at costs of up to 20 cents per pound, sugar that is available at 7 cents per pound. This means fewer resources are available to other industries to produce output that would be more valuable than the added sugar.

Despite the similarities with tariffs, quotas are in some ways even more damaging. First, they restrict imports to a given level no matter how strong demand is for the product. If domestic demand increases over time, quotas allow domestic prices to rise and the gap between domestic and world prices to widen. In contrast, with tariffs, increased demand leads to increased imports, sheltering consumers from higher prices. Second, tariffs have the advantage of raising revenue for the government. Both tariffs and quotas increase the price that foreign producers receive for selling in the domestic economy. With tariffs the price hike is taxed away; with quotas it accrues to foreign producers. In other words, a tariff generates revenues for the government, revenues that can be spent on the country's citizens, whereas a quota transfers these revenues to foreign producers.

Voluntary Export Restrictions

Voluntary Export Restriction
An agreement by one country to limit exports to a second country.

A **voluntary export restriction** is, in essence, a quota by a different name. A foreign country promises not to export more than a specified volume of output to the domestic country. In other words, imports into the domestic country are limited to a prescribed amount. But this is exactly what a quota does. Therefore, the effects of a voluntary export restriction are identical to those of an import quota.

Voluntary export restrictions are voluntary in the same sense that a holdup victim voluntarily parts with his money. Because it is not in the best interests of a nation to limit its exports, it will do so only reluctantly, as a means of heading off even more stringent export restrictions. For example, Japan agreed to limit exports of automobiles to the United States not because it wanted to sell fewer automobiles there but because it wanted to avoid the more severe quotas Congress was proposing.

Antidumping Laws

Dumping
A practice in which a producer sells its product at a lower price in a foreign market than at home.

Dumping occurs when a company sells a good at a lower price in a foreign country than at home.[6] For example, companies in Japan have been accused of dumping computer chips in the United States and European companies of dumping steel. Antidumping laws are designed to halt this practice (e.g., to force Japanese

---

[6]Alternatively, dumping is sometimes defined as selling in a foreign market for *less than cost.*

companies to raise the price of the computer chips they sell in the United States). As with tariffs and quotas, domestic producers benefit from the higher prices while consumers suffer.

Dumping may occur for several reasons. To begin with, the government of the companies engaged in dumping may subsidize their exports. For example, the Japanese government may defray the costs of chips exported to the United States. Japanese companies can then sell their chips for less in the United States because costs are lower there. In that event, the lower price in the United States is a gift to U.S. consumers from the Japanese government—U.S. consumers get their chips at less than cost, with the Japanese government (or more accurately Japanese taxpayers) footing the bill. Because the Japanese are paying for U.S. consumption, the standard of living in Japan falls while the standard of living in the United States rises. Although U.S. chip manufacturers are adversely affected, the United States as a whole benefits from Japanese subsidies.

An alternative reason for dumping is to create monopoly power. For instance, Japanese chip makers may be willing temporarily to sell at a loss in an attempt to drive American chip makers out of business—a practice known as *predatory pricing*. Once their American competitors are eliminated, the Japanese chip makers can then increase chip prices and earn monopoly profits. In that event, dumping would have a detrimental long-run effect on the U.S. economy.

But even if Japanese chip makers were so motivated, it is not clear that such a scheme could succeed. First, competition from non-American chip makers would prevent chip prices from soaring. Second, if prices did rise, U.S. producers would have an incentive to reenter the chip industry. In any event, most economists contend that dumping is not motivated by predatory pricing and that, as a consequence, antidumping laws are neither necessary nor desirable.

THE COST OF TRADE BARRIERS IN THE UNITED STATES

By restricting trade, the United States government raises prices to consumers and reduces their standard of living. But by how much are consumers affected? The answer varies by product, depending on the amount of *protection* afforded a particular industry. It has been estimated that, because of trade barriers, U.S. consumers pay an additional $5 per sweater and an extra $3 per box of candy (see Table 36-7).

TABLE 36-7			
THE EFFECTS OF TRADE RESTRICTIONS ON PRICE			
Good	Free-market price	Price with trade restraints	Price increase
Sweater	$20	$25	$5
Rubber boots	10	12	2
Leather dress gloves	33	40	7
Vinyl handbag	10	12	2
Leather handbag	40	44	4
Teddy bear	8	10	2
Clock radio	30	32	2
Box candy	2	5	3

Source: Clyde Farnsworth, "Trying to Shield Injured American Industries," *New York Times,* January 18, 1987, p. 5E. Copyright © 1987 by The New York Times Company.Reprinted by permission.

TABLE 36-8			
THE COSTS OF SAVING JOBS IN PROTECTED INDUSTRIES			
Industry	Jobs saved	Total cost (millions of dollars)	Cost per job saved (dollars)
Book manufacturing	5,000	$ 500	$ 100,000
Benzenoid chemicals	300	2,650	>1,000,000
Glassware	1,000	200	200,000
Rubber footwear	7,800	230	30,000
Nonrubber footwear	12,700	700	55,000
Ceramic tiles	850	116	135,000
Orange juice	2,200	525	240,000
Canned tuna	1,200	91	76,000
Textiles, apparel	640,000	27,000	42,000
Carbon steel	9,000	6,800	750,000
Automobiles	55,000	5,800	105,000
Maritime industries	11,000	3,000	270,000
Sugar	15,300	930	60,000
Dairy products	25,000	5,500	220,000

Source: Adapted from Gary Clyde Hufbauer, Diane T. Berliner, and Kimberly Ann Elliott, *Trade Protection in the United States: 31 Case Studies* (Washington, DC: Institute for International Economics), Tables 1.1 and 1.2. Copyright © 1986 by the Institute for International Economics. Reprinted by permission.

Automobile prices have been inflated by more than $1000. According to the Institute for International Economics, trade restrictions cost U.S. consumers more than $65 billion annually.

Protectionism
Sheltering domestic industries from foreign competition through tariffs, quotas, or other programs that limit imports.

Another way to measure the cost of **protectionist** policies is in terms of the added costs to consumers per job created in the protected industry. For instance, in the textile and apparel industries—where the most jobs have been saved—consumers pay an additional $27 billion per year to preserve 640,000 jobs. That works out to approximately $42,000 per year for a job that pays less than half that amount. In some industries the cost per job saved is hundreds of thousands of dollars (see Table 36-8). If the government wishes to help workers in industries facing foreign competition, there are clearly less costly ways of providing relief.

EXPLAINING THE PRESENCE OF TRADE BARRIERS

If trade barriers reduce a country's standard of living, then why would a country impose them? Several explanations are relevant. We begin by analyzing some of the most frequently cited arguments for limiting imports. Some have merit, some do not. We follow with a discussion of the political factors that shape trade legislation.

COMMON ARGUMENTS FOR RESTRICTING TRADE

National Defense

Free trade increases a country's output but not necessarily its well-being. To dramatize this point, suppose the United States has a comparative advantage in the production of wheat and the Soviet Union a comparative advantage in producing military hardware. In that event, the total output of wheat and weapons is maximized when the United States specializes in the production of wheat, exporting wheat to the Soviet Union in return for military hardware. Yet even though specialization and trade lead to greater output for both countries, the United States, for strategic reasons, is likely to find this arrangement unacceptable. In the event of hostilities, the Soviet Union might prove an unreliable supplier of weapons. Moreover, Soviet dominance in this industry would likely give it added political clout in the world. Therefore, most citizens would agree that it is in the best interests of the United States to produce its military hardware despite the fact that this policy reduces the output available to its citizens. A lower standard of living is considered a small price to pay for added national security.

Because national defense is generally accepted as a legitimate reason to protect an industry that does not have a comparative advantage, industries seeking relief from foreign competition often couch their requests in terms of national defense. Before agreeing to shelter an industry from foreign competition, the government must determine whether this industry truly is vital to national defense and whether the benefits of a stronger defense are worth the costs. If not, protection is legitimate only when it can be justified on other grounds.

Infant Industry

The infant-industry argument offers a second reason to protect a domestic industry. According to this argument, average costs of production typically are high during the transitional period in which an industry is established, but fall as the industry matures. That means an industry just starting in one country, say Mexico, may find it difficult to compete with other countries where the industry is well established and costs are lower. But if the Mexican industry were given an opportunity to mature, its costs might drop to the point where it could compete in foreign and domestic markets without government protection. Once established, the Mexican industry might have a comparative advantage. If the Mexican government believes this is likely to be the case, it has reason to provide temporary relief—either restricting imports of the good into Mexico or subsidizing the industry until it is strong enough to stand on its own.

Although this argument has logic, the assumptions on which it is based should be underscored. The first assumption is that the country has a comparative advantage in the production of the good that will be manifested only after the industry is mature. Without this eventual comparative advantage, the argument collapses. The risk then is that the government will shelter industries that will never have a comparative advantage and can never make it on their own.

Another assumption is that the government will provide only *temporary* relief, since the mature industry will be able to compete without government assistance. From a practical standpoint, history teaches that once an industry receives government relief, it is difficult to wean. The U.S. government has nursed the book manufacturing industry since 1891 and the maritime industry since 1789; neither is yet willing to stand alone.

Finally, the infant-industry argument is premised on the assumption that a country is just entering an established market. For industrial countries, such as the United States, it is difficult to justify this assumption. Some industries, however, have devised creative ways of repackaging the infant-industry argument. For instance, U.S. automobile manufacturers convinced Congress that, even though theirs was a mature industry, they needed "breathing room" to become proficient in the small-car market, which was dominated by foreign producers. This was the reason the U.S. government pressured Japan into limiting automobile exports to the United States (see Exhibit 36-1).

Retaliation

Some proponents of trade barriers argue that they support free trade in principle but that free trade is not an option. Foreign countries restrict our exports and, when they do, we must retaliate by limiting their exports to our country. If they won't play fair, why should we?

EXHIBIT 36-1

RESTRICTING IMPORTS OF JAPANESE CARS

U.S. automobile producers suffered record losses in 1980. Misreading the market and failing to foresee higher gasoline prices, they continued to produce large cars at a time when consumers wanted smaller, more fuel-efficient vehicles. Because foreign companies were producing the type of vehicles consumers wanted, the import share of the automobile market zoomed. With the 1980 recession compounding their woes, U.S. automobile producers turned to Congress for relief. What they needed, said automotive executives, was a chance to restructure, time to design a more-efficient fleet of cars—General Motors' chairman suggested two or three years. Once that was accomplished, they assured Congress, automakers would be ready to go head-to-head with foreign producers without government protection.

Because the Japanese were the principal exporter of small cars, bills were introduced in Congress to limit the number of Japanese cars entering the United States. Facing prospects of severe import restrictions, the Japanese government reluctantly entered negotiations with the U.S. government to reduce the number of cars exported to the United States. On May 1, 1981, the two governments announced that Japan would "voluntarily" limit exports to the United States for the next three years. The cap for the first year would be 1.68 million cars, with caps for future years to be negotiated.

As the flow of cars from Japan slowed, waiting lists developed and consumers began offering dealers as much as $2500 above list price to obtain Japanese cars. Soon the Japanese companies raised car prices and, as they did, their American counterparts followed suit. The U.S. International Trade Commission estimates that the voluntary export restrictions raised the average price of Japa-

nese cars by $185 in 1981, $359 in 1982, $831 in 1983, and $1300 in 1984. The corresponding increases in domestic car prices were $78, $170, $426, and $659. The Commission estimates that, from May 1981 through 1984, U.S. consumers paid an additional $15.8 billion for new cars as a result of export restrictions. An alternative agency, the International Monetary Fund, puts the cost at $17 billion. Despite these studies, Japan was pressured to extend the export restrictions, which it did, although raising the export cap to 1.85 million cars in 1984 and to 2.3 million cars in 1986.

With less competition from Japan and a generally improving economy during the 1980s, profits of U.S. automobile companies soared to record levels. Chrysler became so profitable that it made its chairman, Lee Iacocca, the country's highest paid executive. The companies had downsized their fleets, dramatically increasing fuel efficiency, and car sales were strong. So in 1988, after seven years of export restrictions and the emergence of a leaner, more-efficient automobile industry in the United States, American automobile companies clearly had the "breathing room" they had requested. Yet, rather than agree to the elimination of the export restrictions, executives at Ford and Chrysler petitioned for *tougher* restrictions, asking that the number of Japanese cars admitted to the United States be reduced by 26 percent, to 1.7 million vehicles. As a compromise, the 2.3 million cap was extended for another year.

Sources: Adapted from Arthur Denzau, *Made in America* (St. Louis: Center for the Study of American Business, 1986); Art Pine, "Study Says Curb on Japan's Cars Lifts U.S. Prices," *The Wall Street Journal,* February 14, 1985, p. 3; *New York Times,* "Why Choke Japanese Auto Imports?" December 13, 1987, p. 24E; Melinda Guiles and Gregory Witcher, "U.S. Auto Makers Are Unhappy," *The Wall Street Journal,* February 1, 1988, p. 34.

Critics of this argument point out that not only does retaliation harm the country that initially erected trade barriers, it also harms the country that retaliates. Just as the benefits of trade accrue to both countries, the costs of every reduction in trade are borne by both countries. Some liken retaliation to the situation in which one passenger shoots a hole in a boat and a second passenger, to get even, adds a second hole.

There is, however, one case where retaliation could prove beneficial, and that is where the second country's retaliation proves so onerous that the first country agrees to roll back its trade barriers provided that the second country does likewise. In other words, retaliation could improve the bargaining position of the second country and lead to the eventual elimination of the trade barrier that triggered the retaliation. But this is a risky game to play. The first country may instead respond to the retaliation by erecting additional barriers, further harming both countries. In fact, historically retaliation often leads to trade wars—such as the one that deepened the Great Depression.

Increasing Employment

Some support trade restrictions as a means of expanding a country's employment, and as Table 36-8 shows, trade restrictions have created jobs in protected industries. *But trade restrictions do not increase total employment in the country. Increased employment in protected industries comes at the expense of lower employment in other industries.*

A reduction in foreign cars entering the United States reduces maritime employment in San Francisco and other port cities and eliminates jobs at dealerships selling imported cars. Similarly, import restrictions that force U.S. computer makers to pay three times the world price for computer chips—in order to increase employment in the domestic chip industry—make U.S. computers more costly, thus reducing the number of computers purchased and dragging down employment in the computer industry. Beyond that, if the United States buys less from other countries they in turn have fewer dollars to buy U.S. products. As a consequence, U.S. exports fall, leading to lower employment in export industries. Some studies suggest that trade restrictions actually *reduce* total employment. One such study estimates that each $10 billion in imports costs the United States 179,000 jobs but that an equal volume of exports creates 193,000 jobs, for a net gain of 14,000 jobs.[7] In summary, import restrictions alter the distribution of jobs across industries, but they do not increase employment in the country.

Low Foreign Wages

Another bogus argument for restricting imports is that U.S. workers cannot compete with cheap foreign labor. Wages average close to $10 per hour in the United States but less than $1 per hour in many developing countries. Given wage differences of this magnitude, how can U.S. workers possibly compete? Unless the United States restricts imports, this argument continues, wages in the United States will be driven down to foreign levels, thereby depressing the U.S. standard of living.

A major flaw in this argument is that it neglects productivity differences across countries. Compared to workers in less developed countries, U.S. workers have more education and training, greater amounts of capital to work with, and more-advanced

---

[7]Richard Belous and Andrew Wyckoff, "Trade Has Job Winners Too," *Across the Board* (September 1987), pp. 53–55.

technologies. Therefore, U.S. workers can produce more output per hour. As long as their greater productivity offsets their higher wages, U.S. workers will not be at a competitive disadvantage.

A simple example illustrates this point. Suppose shoe workers in the United States are paid $8 per hour. If it takes a worker 2 hours to produce a pair of shoes, the labor cost per pair of shoes manufactured in the United States is $16 (see Table 36-9). Now suppose workers in Korea receive $1 per hour but require 16 hours to produce a pair of shoes. Then the labor cost per pair of shoes is also $16. Although wages are 8 times higher in the United States, U.S. productivity is also 8 times higher. Therefore, U.S. shoe workers are not at a competitive disadvantage compared to Korean shoe workers.

Of course, productivity differences vary by industry. In the aircraft industry, U.S. workers may be 20 times more productive; in the textile industry, they may be only twice as productive. If wages are 8 times higher in the United States for both industries, the United States and Korea each gain if the United States exports aircraft to Korea and imports textiles. Observe that higher textile wages in the United States are not the reason the United States imports textiles—wages in the aircraft industry are also higher in the United States, yet the United States exports aircraft. The United States imports textiles because the U.S. productivity advantage in textiles is small whereas the U.S. productivity advantage in the aircraft industry is large. In other words, the United States comparative advantage lies in the aircraft industry, Korea's in the textile industry. To shelter U.S. textile workers from competition means forgoing the gains of trade and therefore reducing the standard of living in the United States, not raising it.

Cheap foreign labor has sometimes induced U.S. companies to move their operations to foreign soil, but such moves are not always a success. Unless the wage advantage of foreign workers offsets their productivity disadvantage, labor costs are no lower in foreign countries. Other disadvantages of foreign operations include greater transportation costs to U.S. markets and communications problems. For such reasons, some companies that left the United States in hope of paring costs have since returned (see Exhibit 36-2).

THE POLITICS OF SPECIAL INTERESTS

If trade barriers were erected only where they benefit society (e.g., for reasons of national defense), many industries would lose their protection from foreign competition. But, as a practical matter, trade restrictions are often based on political considerations rather than public interest. Trade benefits certain groups even if it harms society in general. For instance, steel workers, their companies, and steel-producing states (such as Pennsylvania) all gain from legislation that keeps foreign steel out of the United States. Because of these gains, they all lobby Congress for protective legislation.

Even though such legislation harms more people than it helps, it is unlikely to meet organized opposition. Consumers—who must pay the higher prices for cars, refrigerators, and other goods that use steel—are unlikely to associate these higher prices with protection for the steel industry. Therefore, they are unlikely to complain about this protection. Higher steel prices also reduce employment in other industries in the United States. According to one study, for each job created in the steel industry as a result of import restrictions, higher steel prices eliminate three

TABLE 36-9

A HIGHER WAGE RATE DOES NOT IMPLY HIGHER PRODUCTION COSTS

Country	Hours of labor per pair of shoes	Labor cost per hour (wage rate)	Labor cost per pair of shoes
United States	2	$8	$16
Korea	16	1	16

The labor cost per pair of shoes is the same in the United States as in Korea despite a higher wage rate in the United States ($8 versus $1). This is because U.S. workers are more productive, requiring just 2 hours to produce a pair of shoes, rather than 16.

EXHIBIT 36–2

THE TRAIN COMES HOME

Chesterfield Township, Michigan—When Lionnel Trains shut down its sprawling plant here, fired all but five of its 350 factory workers and moved its manufacturing to Tijuana, Mexico, the toy-train maker thought that it was on to a no-lose proposition: 55-cent-an-hour wages. It wasn't. Quality, supply, labor and communications problems made the move a fiasco. Lionel couldn't fill two-thirds of its orders, and complaints poured in from dealers and customers. It wound up with big losses.

Last April, not quite three years later, the company completed its return to this pro-union industrial area 30 miles north of Detroit. It leased back the plant that it had sold and rehired many of its former workers. It's making money again. Gloats the township supervisor, James Pollard: "Here was the industry that left Michigan for the green grass of a foreign country. And it turned out that the grass was brown."

Lionel isn't the only company to find that the pastures of Mexico, Taiwan and other havens of low-cost labor aren't so verdant. While companies in the shoe, textile, clothing and electronics industries continue to go offshore, a handful of companies in industries ranging from high technology to sporting goods are taking another look at manufacturing in the U.S. And some longtime importers are concluding that increased automation and a weaker dollar enable them to manufacture products more cheaply here.

"First you say, 'Gee whiz. It's cheaper to make it over there,' " says Robert Burrows, the president of Rawlings Sporting Goods Co. of St. Louis. But such expenses as inventory, customs and transpor-

tation costs, he says, create "a lot of pitfalls"—sometimes enough to offset the labor savings. Distance adds a myriad of headaches: Suppliers 10,000 miles away can't fill orders quickly; checking on a production run is tougher; and the long lag between orders and deliveries makes forecasting even dicier than usual.

Lionel dispatched only a few managers in Tijuana with the idea of hiring and training the rest locally. It quickly found that it couldn't, and it wound up spending thousands of dollars a month on air fare and housing to send down engineers. Lionel also didn't foresee the long waiting lists at the Tijuana telephone company; for a year, Lionel had to operate with only two phone lines. Nor did it realize that there were no Mexican subcontractors for important plating processes; it had to shuttle parts to California subcontractors and back. "It started to seem ridiculous," an engineering executive says.

Meanwhile, the problems were causing sales and public-relations nightmares at Michigan headquarters. Lionel could deliver only one-third of its orders, and it lost shelf space to competitors. But Lionel was determined not to lose its 90% share of the high-priced collector-train business, and it realized that Tijuana might never make those trains well. So it rehired 50 workers last fall to make them in Michigan. Soon after, the entire train line was back, too.

Source: Cynthia Mitchell, "Coming Home: Some Firms Resume Manufacturing in U.S.," *The Wall Street Journal,* October 14, 1986, pp. 1 and 31. Reprinted by permission of *The Wall Street Journal;* ©Dow Jones & Company, 1986. All rights reserved.

jobs in steel-using industries.[8] But the three workers who lose their jobs or are never hired are probably unaware of the cause of their joblessness.

Moreover, those harmed by import restrictions—consumers who must pay the higher prices and workers in other industries who lose their jobs—are widely dispersed throughout the economy. Therefore, even if these consumers and workers are aware of the adverse effects of import restrictions, it is difficult for them to organize and fight such restrictions. In this event, politicians face intense pressure from the steel lobby to keep foreign steel out of the country but little pressure from other groups to let it in. Politicians also realize that by voting for such legislation they are likely to receive the support of a grateful steel industry during the next political campaign while losing few if any votes as a result of protectionist steel legislation (the treatment of steel imports is unlikely to be a high priority for anyone not associated with the steel industry). For such reasons, politicians stand to reap political benefits from the passage of special-interest trade legislation.

Politicians may also have a genuine concern for workers displaced by imports. Even though a more-open trade policy would benefit society as a whole, Congress may want to shield current steel workers from the pain and lost income associated with job loss. But there are less costly ways of accomplishing this than erecting import barriers. Workers who lose their jobs due to imports can be provided job training and placement services and given financial assistance until alternative employment is found. Indeed, various pieces of legislation, including the 1988 Trade Act, contain such provisions. The fact that Congress chooses to erect trade barriers in the face of such trade assistance suggests that political considerations remain a major force in crafting trade legislation.

A HISTORY OF TARIFFS IN THE UNITED STATES

The rate at which imports are taxed has varied widely over time (see Figure 36-6). The average tariff rate peaked at more than 60 percent following the Tariff of Abominations (in 1828) and then moved erratically lower until 1861 when, in an effort to finance the Civil War, it was again raised. Protectionist sentiment remained strong over the next 70 years except for a brief return to more-open trade during the Woodrow Wilson Presidency. In 1930, Congress enacted the Smoot-Hawley Tariff, once again pushing the tariff rate above 60 percent. Foreign countries retaliated and U.S. exports plunged. Rather than expanding employment, as its sponsors had promised, the Smoot-Hawley Tariff contributed to the highest unemployment rate in U.S. history.

After being swept into office in 1932, President Franklin Roosevelt pressed Congress to reform trade policy. Congress responded by enacting the Reciprocal Trade Agreement Act of 1934, which gave the president the power to negotiate bilaterally with other countries to reduce tariff rates by as much as 50 percent. The next major development occurred in 1947, when the United States joined other nations in establishing the **General Agreement on Tariffs and Trade (GATT)**. With more than 90 nations presently agreeing to abide by its rules, GATT provides a mechanism for resolving trade disputes and negotiating a reduction in trade barriers. Of the various "rounds" of negotiations sponsored by GATT, the Kennedy Round and Tokyo Round were particularly successful in reducing tariff rates. Today the

GATT
An international agreement promoting more-open trade policy and providing the machinery to settle trade disputes among participating nations.

[8]Arthur Denzau, *How Import Restraints Reduce Employment* (St. Louis: Center for the Study of American Business, 1987).

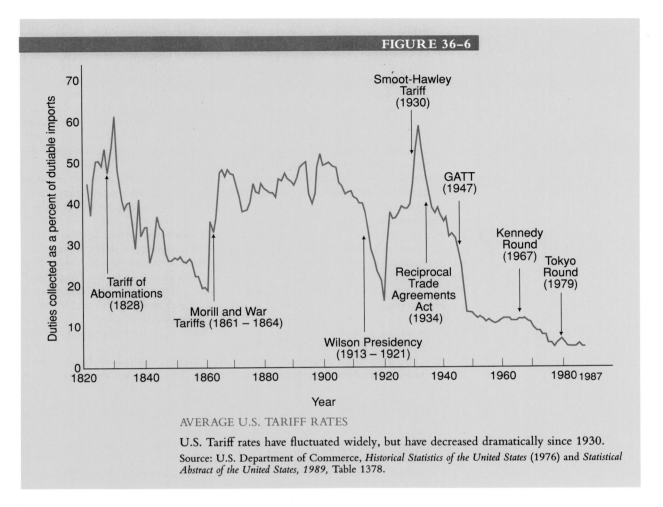

FIGURE 36-6

AVERAGE U.S. TARIFF RATES

U.S. Tariff rates have fluctuated widely, but have decreased dramatically since 1930.

Source: U.S. Department of Commerce, *Historical Statistics of the United States* (1976) and *Statistical Abstract of the United States, 1989,* Table 1378.

average U.S. tariff rate is close to 5 percent, as low as it has ever been in the country's history.

Although the United States has clearly moved toward a policy of freer trade over the past 60 years, the decline in the tariff rate overstates the strength of that movement. Other forms of protection, including voluntary export restrictions and antidumping laws, have become more common in recent years. Politicians continue to face pressure from special-interest groups, and much of the public remains ignorant of the costs of trade barriers. Even though the costs to society exceed the benefits, the benefits are more visible. Despite nearly universal condemnation by economists, protectionism remains alive.

SUMMARY

1. Despite exporting less than ten percent of its output, the United States, as the world's largest producer, plays a major role in world trade. One-third of all exports come from the United States, West Germany, or Japan.
2. Most of the United States trade is with other industrial countries, including Canada, its largest buyer. The United States is a leading exporter of capital goods and a major importer of petroleum.

3. Although countries sometimes trade to gain access to goods and resources not otherwise available to the country, most trade is based on the principle of comparative advantage. Even if two countries produce the same goods, each can benefit from specializing in the production of that good for which it has a comparative advantage (lower opportunity cost) and then trading this good to the other country. Specialization and trade lead to greater output of each good and therefore to a higher standard of living in each country.

4. Despite the potential gains from trade, nations often restrict imports. Among the major trade barriers are tariffs, import quotas, voluntary export restrictions, and antidumping laws. Each of these barriers reduces imports, leads to higher prices in the domestic country, expands domestic production, and pares domestic consumption of the good. A nonprohibitive tariff also generates revenue for the government.

5. Trade barriers lead to a misallocation of resources, causing a country to divert resources from industries where it enjoys a comparative advantage to industries where it is a relatively high-cost producer. In the United States, trade restrictions cost consumers tens of billions of dollars annually.

6. The national-defense and infant-industry arguments provide two potentially valid reasons for restricting trade. If a nation considers an industry vital for national defense, protection may be warranted despite the cost it imposes on consumers. Protection may also be justified where a nation's emerging (infant) industry is forced to compete with mature industries of other countries. If the industry ultimately will have a comparative advantage once it matures, temporary protection provides the industry time to establish itself and to reduce its costs to the point where it can compete without government assistance.

7. Trade restrictions have also been defended on the basis of increasing employment and sheltering workers from low-wage foreign labor, but these arguments are not valid. Although import restrictions save jobs in protected industries, they reduce employment in other industries—total employment does not increase. The low-wage argument ignores productivity differences across countries. When U.S. workers are more productive, they can compete with lower-paid foreign workers.

8. Trade barriers often result from political pressure applied by groups that stand to gain from such barriers. Although the social costs of protection exceed its benefits, the costs are less visible and more widely dispersed throughout the country. Therefore, opposition to trade barriers is difficult to organize.

9. The average U.S. tariff rate has fallen from over 60 percent, following the Smoot-Hawley Tariff of 1930, to close to 5 percent today. Although this signals a move to a more-open trade policy, protectionism remains a powerful force. In fact, nontariff barriers have increased in recent years.

KEY TERMS

trade deficit	prohibitive tariff
absolute advantage	nonprohibitive tariff
comparative advantage	import quota
law of comparative advantage	voluntary export restrictions
terms of trade	dumping
trading possibilities curve	protectionism
free trade	General Agreement on Tariffs
tariff (duty)	and Trade (GATT)

STUDY QUESTIONS AND PROBLEMS

1. Explain why nations trade.
2. Would you expect the United States or Honduras to have an absolute advantage in producing precision machinery? Which is likely to have an absolute advantage in growing bananas? Explain your reasoning.

3. In Korea each unit of labor can produce 2 computers or 4 VCRs. In the United States each unit of labor can produce 3 computers or 5 VCRs. Both countries experience constant costs of production.
   a. Which country has an absolute advantage in producing computers?
   b. Which country has an absolute advantage in producing VCRs?
   c. Within Korea what is the opportunity cost of producing 100 VCRs?
   d. Within the United States what is the opportunity cost of producing 100 VCRs?
   e. Which country has a comparative advantage in producing VCRs?
   f. Which country should specialize in producing VCRs?
   g. Which country should specialize in producing computers?
4. In Canada each unit of a resource can produce either 1 bushel of wheat or 2 boxes of apples.
   a. Assuming that Canada has 1 million units of the resource, draw its production possibilities curve.
   b. If the terms of trade with the United States are 1 bushel of wheat for 3 boxes of apples, should Canada specialize in the production of apples or wheat?
   c. Draw the trading possiblities curve for Canada.
5. How does a sugar quota affect employment in (a) the domestic sugar industry and (b) the domestic candy industry? Justify your answers.
6. In what ways are quotas and nonprohibitive tariffs similar? In what ways are they different?
7. The following diagram shows the supply by U.S. producers and demand by U.S. consumers for rubber ducks. The world price is $4.

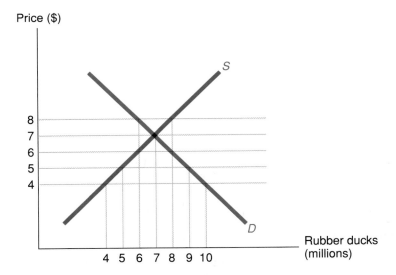

   a. If there is free trade, how many rubber ducks will the United States produce and how many will it import?
   b. If a quota of 2 million ducks is established, what will be the price of rubber ducks in the United States?
   c. Given this quota, how many rubber ducks will the United States produce and how many will it import?
   d. If the quota is replaced with a prohibitive tariff, what will happen to the price of rubber ducks in the United States?

8. An oil import fee has two things going for it: (a) it reduces U.S. dependence on foreign oil and (b) it increases employment in oil-producing states—and therefore in the country as a whole.
   Evaluate this argument. Would taxing oil imports reduce the amount of foreign oil entering the United States? Would it expand total U.S. employment? Explain.

9. If trade restrictions harm more people than they benefit, why don't voters pressure Congress to remove them?

(a) 100 pairs of shoes. (b) 100 pairs of shoes. (c) No. Because the opportunity cost is the same for each country, specialization and trade would not boost total output of the two countries.

CHAPTER 37

THE INTERNATIONAL FINANCIAL SYSTEM

The actual rate of exchange is largely governed by the expected behavior of the country's monetary authority.

—DENNIS H. ROBERTSON, 1922

We have learned that trade—be it local, interregional, or international—extends the principle of specialization and division of labor and thereby promotes higher living standards. We all benefit from a thriving international economy. One of the key considerations that differentiates international trade from domestic trade is that different nations have different currencies. If you buy a Kodak camera made in the United States, the seller wants to be paid in U.S. currency—dollars. If you purchase a Nikon camera from Japan, the seller wants to be paid in the Japanese currency—yen. By the same token, the Japanese importer of luxury U.S. automobiles must pay in dollars.

In Chapter 37, we study the financial aspects of international economics. We begin by looking at the foreign exchange market and analyzing the causes and consequences of changing exchange rates. The debate over fixed versus floating exchange rates is outlined. We then turn to a discussion of the international economic accounts of a nation—its balance of payments. The large international trade deficits of the United States during the 1980s are analyzed. We conclude the chapter with an overview of the international debt problem of the less developed countries (LDCs).

THE FOREIGN EXCHANGE MARKET

Foreign Exchange Market
The market in which the currencies of different countries are bought and sold.

Foreign Exchange Rate
The amount of another country's money that residents of a country can obtain in exchange for one unit of their own money; the price at which one country's currency may be traded for foreign currency.

The **foreign exchange market** is the market in which such national currencies as dollars, yen, deutsche marks, pesos, and lire are exchanged. The price at which such currencies are exchanged is the **foreign exchange rate.** Activity in the foreign exchange market has expanded enormously in recent decades as the result of rapid growth of merchandise trade, tourism, and especially international **capital flows**— acquisition of real and financial assets across national borders. Several major U.S. banks maintain inventories of *foreign exchange* in the form of foreign-denominated currencies held in branch or correspondent banks in foreign cities. Americans generally may obtain this foreign exchange from home town banks that, in turn, purchase it from large New York banks.

A foreign exchange rate exists between each pair of nations that engage in international commerce. A sample of dollar exchange rates for selected foreign currencies at several points in time is illustrated in Table 37-1, where each exchange rate is quoted as the number of units of foreign currency per U.S. dollar. Hence, the exchange rates listed indicate the *value of the U.S. dollar* measured in units of foreign currency. For example, at the end of 1988 the U.S. dollar was exchangeable for 126 Japanese yen and 6.06 French francs. With the exception of the U.S.-England exchange rate, this is the way exchange rates are conventionally quoted in this country. Note, however, that international currency values are reciprocal in nature. If the dollar is worth 126 yen, the yen is equivalent to $0.00794, or about eight-tenths of a penny. Likewise, if the dollar is worth £0.552, the British pound is valued at $1.81.

Currency Depreciation
A decline in the international value of the currency; the currency buys fewer units of foreign currency.

Currency Appreciation
An increase in the international value of the currency; the currency buys more units of foreign currency.

Floating Exchange Rates
Exchange rates that are allowed to change daily in response to market forces of supply and demand.

Fixed Exchange Rates
A system in which governments intervene aggressively to keep exchange rates at certain levels rather than permitting them to float in response to market forces.

As Table 37-1 indicates, exchange rates vary considerably over time. At the end of 1988, for example, the U.S. dollar was worth fewer French francs, Japanese yen, and German deutsche marks than at the end of 1983. The dollar **depreciated** against the franc, yen, and deutsche mark—meaning that the value of the dollar declined. These foreign currencies **appreciated** (became worth more) against the dollar. On the other hand, the dollar *appreciated* against the Mexican peso in the same period. The peso *depreciated* vis-à-vis the dollar.[1]

Since the early 1970s, most major currencies have been **floating**—exchange rates have been allowed to change from day to day in the marketplace, sometimes by a substantial amount. Prior to the early 1970s, governments aggressively intervened in foreign exchange markets to **fix** or **peg** exchange rates at prearranged levels. The exchange rate is not a matter of indifference to the nations involved. In fact, important disputes have sometimes arisen as a result of the decisions of some nations

[1]Because exchange rates are reciprocal in nature and can be quoted either in units of foreign currency per unit of domestic currency or units of domestic currency per unit of foreign currency, one is easily confused. To minimize confusion, think first in terms of the value of the currency in the *denominator* of the quotation. If the U.S.-Japan exchange rate moves from 120 yen/dollar to 130 yen/dollar, the dollar clearly appreciates—it becomes worth more yen. Hence, the yen depreciates against the dollar. If you are told that the U.S.-England exchange rate moves from $1.50/£ to $1.70/£, you can clearly see that the pound appreciates as it becomes worth more dollars. Hence, the dollar depreciates.

TABLE 37-1						

FOREIGN EXCHANGE RATES WITH THE UNITED STATES FOR SELECTED NATIONS
(end-of-year quotations)

			Units of foreign currency per dollar			
Country	**Currency unit**	**Symbol**	**1973**	**1978**	**1983**	**1988**
Austria	Schilling	S	19.9	13.7	19.3	12.6
Canada	Dollar	$	1.00	1.19	1.24	1.19
France	Franc	Fr	4.71	4.18	8.34	6.06
Italy	Lira	L	608	830	1660	1306
Japan	Yen	¥	280	195	232	126
Mexico	Peso	$	12.5	22.7	144	2281
Switzerland	Franc	SFr	3.24	1.62	2.18	1.50
West Germany	Deutsche mark	DM	3.20	2.12	2.39	1.78
United Kingdom	Pound	£	0.425	0.517	0.637	0.552

Source: International Monetary Fund, *International Financial Statistics,* 1989.

to intervene to influence the level of the exchange rate. Before we examine the ramifications of changing exchange rates, however, let us analyze the factors that determine the level of the exchange rate at a given point in time and the forces that cause it to change over time.

EXCHANGE RATE DETERMINATION IN A REGIME OF FREELY FLOATING RATES

The foreign exchange market is a good example of a highly competitive market. There are many buyers and sellers, each relatively small compared to the total market. Total *daily* worldwide foreign exchange market transactions typically exceed $200 billion. In a system of *freely floating exchange rates,* governments abstain from intervention in the foreign exchange market and permit exchange rates to be driven entirely by the forces of the free market. Like prices in the wheat market and other auction markets, the impersonal forces of supply and demand determine the exchange rate. Today, even when governments occasionally intervene, the volume of such activity tends to be rather small relative to the amount of private activity.

Consider the determination of the U.S. exchange rate with Japan as illustrated in Figure 37-1 (page 848). In the analysis we explain the value of the U.S. dollar. In the event we want to find the price of apples, we find out the number of units of money per apple. By the same token, we express the value of the U.S. dollar in terms of the number of units of foreign currency such as yen. The units on the horizontal axis are the quantity of dollars. The vertical axis expresses the value or price of the dollar. The supply and demand curves represent the flow of dollars supplied and demanded each period. In the figure, the supply and demand curves for dollars intersect to determine an equilibrium exchange rate of 130 yen per dollar.

What forces lie behind the supply and demand curves for dollars? The demand for dollars stems from Japanese buyers of American goods and services, U.S.

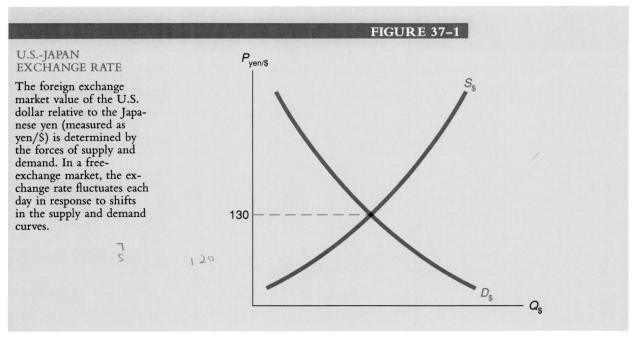

FIGURE 37-1

U.S.-JAPAN EXCHANGE RATE

The foreign exchange market value of the U.S. dollar relative to the Japanese yen (measured as yen/$) is determined by the forces of supply and demand. In a free-exchange market, the exchange rate fluctuates each day in response to shifts in the supply and demand curves.

financial assets such as stocks and bonds, and real assets such as land, office buildings, and factories. Because the Japanese buyers must pay for these American items with dollars, they demand U.S. dollars, selling their yen in exchange. The demand curve in Figure 37-1 is downward sloping because, *given all other factors,* a decline in the U.S. dollar makes everything purchased in America cheaper to potential Japanese buyers. For example, if the dollar were to depreciate from 200 yen to 120 yen, a $3 U.S. bushel of wheat would decline in price in Japan from 600 yen to 360 yen (ignoring transportation costs, and so forth).

The supply curve of dollars in Figure 37-1 comes from Americans seeking to purchase Japanese goods and services, financial assets, and real assets. Because Americans must pay for the Japanese transactions in yen, they must sell dollars to obtain yen and finance the transactions. The supply curve of dollars corresponds to a demand curve for yen.[2] The supply curve in Figure 37-1 slopes upward because, *given other factors,* an increase in the value of the dollar (measured in yen) reduces the price of Japanese goods, services, and assets in the United States. A Nikon camera selling for 100,000 yen in Tokyo costs an American $400 if the dollar exchanges for 250 yen but costs $800 if the dollar fetches only 125 yen. Since a stronger dollar

---

[2]One could draw a corresponding figure to accompany Figure 37-1 in which the exchange rate is expressed as $/Yen rather than Yen/$. The horizontal axis would be labeled as Q_{yen} and the supply and demand schedules would be in yen rather than in dollars. The $D¥$ in such a figure would correspond to the $S_\$$ in our Figure 37-1—Americans selling dollars to buy yen to make payment in Japan. The $S¥$ in this hypothetical figure would be related to the $D_\$$ in our Figure 37-1—Japanese selling yen to buy dollars to make payment in the United States. The equilibrium exchange rate in this hypothetical figure, given the equilibrium rate in Figure 37-1 of 130¥/$, would be $.00769/¥.

[3]Technically, this assumes that American demand for Japanese products is relatively elastic with respect to the price in dollars. If, instead, we continue to purchase roughly the same amount of Japanese items in spite of a lower dollar price to Americans owing to a stronger dollar, we would actually need to supply fewer dollars at higher exchange rates. In the short run, the supply curve may be negatively sloped since people do not respond fully at once to a more favorable price. In the longer run, economists believe the supply curve is upward sloping as illustrated because American demand for imported goods and services is highly responsive to the price in dollars.

reduces the cost of Japanese items to Americans, we tend to respond to a higher dollar by supplying more dollars to finance enlarged purchases.[3]

FORCES CAUSING CHANGES IN EXCHANGE RATES

Price changes in competitive markets are precipitated by shifts in supply and demand curves. Any factor that results in a shift in the supply or demand curve of Figure 37-1 produces a change in the U.S.-Japan exchange rate. Fundamental factors causing shifts in the supply and demand curves and thereby inducing changes in exchange rates include changes in relative price levels, income levels, and real interest rates in the countries involved. Also, changes in consumer preferences and development of new products for export markets can initiate changes in supply and demand curves in foreign exchange markets, thereby producing a change in exchange rates. Speculators' anticipations of forthcoming changes in these fundamental factors also influence current exchange rates. In the long run, these preferences, product development, and relative price level behavior in nations are powerful forces that influence the exchange rate. In the medium run, relative income levels of nations are important, and relative interest rate behavior seems to exert a powerful short-run influence on the exchange rate. Hour-to-hour and day-to-day exchange-rate movements are often precipitated by activity of foreign-exchange market speculators.

Relative Price Level Behavior and Exchange Rates

Assume the U.S.-Japan exchange rate is initially 130 yen/$, with supply and demand curves for dollars ($S_\$^1$ and $D_\$^1$) intersecting at A in Figure 37-2 (page 850). Now assume the price level increases by 20 percent in Japan but remains constant in the United States. Clearly, American goods and services are now relatively more attractive to both Japanese and Americans at each and every exchange rate. The increased willingness of the Japanese to purchase American items shifts the demand curve for dollars from $D_\$^1$ to $D_\$^2$. This would move the equilibrium to B in the figure, indicating an appreciation of the dollar (depreciation of the yen). Also, because American goods now look relatively more attractive to Americans at each and every exchange rate, the willingness to import from Japan is reduced and the supply curve of dollars decreases—shifts leftward from $S_\$^1$ to $S_\$^2$. This indicates a further appreciation of the dollar, the new equilibrium being at C in the figure and the exchange rate reaching 150 yen per dollar.

The analysis suggests that countries with high inflation will experience depreciation of their currencies in the foreign exchange market. Indeed, the two countries depicted in Table 37-1 that exhibited the most rapid inflation during 1973–1988—Mexico and Italy—also experienced the most severe depreciation of their currencies against the dollar in that period. Mexico, which experienced extremely high inflation, saw the peso lose more than 99 percent of its value vis-à-vis the U.S. dollar in that period. Equivalently stated, the U.S. dollar appreciated more than one-hundred fold against the Mexican peso.

Purchasing Power Parity Theory (PPP)
Theory that the exchange rate between any two national currencies adjusts to reflect changes in the relative price levels in the two nations.

The Purchasing Power Parity Theory (PPP)   Building on the preceding analysis, the **purchasing power parity theory (PPP)** postulates that exchange rates adjust to offset different rates of inflation in two countries. If the U.S.-Japan exchange rate is initially in equilibrium at 150 yen/$ and the U.S. price level then doubles relative to the price level in Japan, PPP theory predicts that the dollar will depreciate sufficiently to restore purchasing power parity. That is, PPP predicts the dollar will

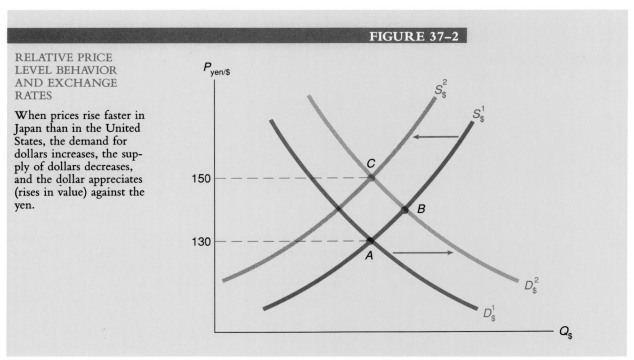

FIGURE 37–2

RELATIVE PRICE
LEVEL BEHAVIOR
AND EXCHANGE
RATES

When prices rise faster in
Japan than in the United
States, the demand for
dollars increases, the supply of dollars decreases,
and the dollar appreciates
(rises in value) against the
yen.

depreciate by 50 percent (i.e., fall by half) to a level of 75 yen per dollar. If the dollar
fell by less than 50 percent, Japanese products would look more attractive relative to
American products—both to Japanese and to Americans—than was the case prior to
the price level disturbance. American imports from Japan would increase and U.S.
exports to Japan would decline, exerting downward pressure on the U.S. dollar until
it had restored purchasing power parity by declining 50 percent.[4]

Under highly restrictive and very unrealistic conditions, PPP would always
precisely hold. Suppose only two countries exist—the United States and Turkey.
Suppose these nations produce one homogeneous product for export—wheat.
Suppose wheat costs $3 per bushel in the United States and 3000 lire per bushel in
Turkey. Then the U.S.-Turkey exchange rate must be 1000 lire per dollar. The
wheat must cost the same to an American or a Turk whether purchased at home or
abroad. Otherwise, one country's wheat industry would be forced out of business. If
American wheat were to rise to $6 per bushel while Turkish wheat remains at 3000
lire, the dollar would depreciate from 1000 lire to 500 lire. This example reflects the
fundamental intuition behind PPP theory.

Adapting this framework to the real world, we must recognize that many
products are not homogeneous in nature. When the dollar falls and Toyotas become
more expensive relative to Fords, Americans continue to purchase Toyotas (though
presumably in reduced quantities) because of perceived quality differences and other
reasons. Also, a nation's price level includes many nontradeable goods and services,
whereas only tradeable items are strictly relevant to PPP. Prices of tradeable and

[4]Hence, PPP implies that domestic inflation does not impair a nation's long-run competitive position in
world markets if freely floating exchange rates prevail. The exchange rate is alleged to move precisely to
compensate for inflation differences among nations, thus leaving each nation's products relatively
unchanged in price in foreign markets. If—when U.S. prices double and an American Cadillac increases
in price from $25,000 to $50,000—the dollar falls from 3 deutsche marks to 1.5 deutsche marks, the
Cadillac continues to sell for 75,000 DM in Germany. Suppose in Germany, where the price level
remains constant, a Mercedes-Benz sells for 90,000 DM. The decline in the U.S. dollar raises its price in
the United States from $30,000 to $60,000—the same percentage price increase experienced by the
Cadillac and other U.S. goods.

nontradeable goods do not necessarily move together over time. In episodes of severe inflation, PPP theory seems to work well in accounting for exchange-rate movements. For example, the U.S. dollar depreciated sharply against the deutsche mark and yen in the late 1970s because the U.S. inflation rate considerably exceeded that of Germany and Japan. However, in the low-inflation environment of the 1980s, PPP pretty much collapsed as an explanation of exchange-rate movements. As an example, during 1980–1985, the U.S. dollar *appreciated* strongly against the yen and mark. PPP would have called for a modest *depreciation* of the dollar in that period inasmuch as U.S. inflation was slightly greater than that of Japan and Germany. Then, in 1985–1988, the dollar fell sharply, even though PPP would have called for a very modest decline. PPP clearly broke down in the 1980s, and you will understand why from the analysis that follows. Don't count PPP out yet, though! It is likely to stage a comeback the next time severe inflation rears its ugly head.

Relative Income Levels and Exchange Rates

Assume output and income in the United States rise while in Germany they remain stagnant. American demand for goods and services—both domestically produced and imported—expands while German demand remains flat. As a result, the U.S. dollar tends to depreciate against the deutsche mark. Paradoxically, growth of domestic income leads to a weaker currency if other factors are held constant.[5] This principle is illustrated in Figure 37-3.

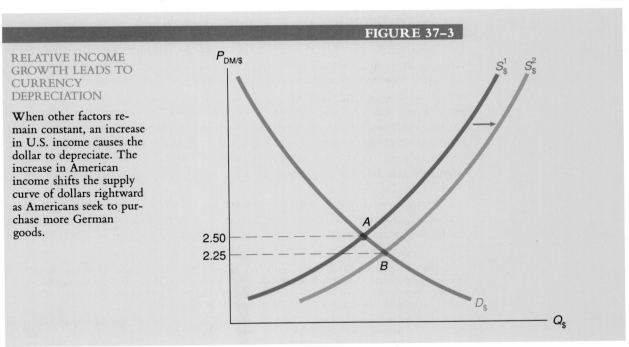

FIGURE 37–3

RELATIVE INCOME GROWTH LEADS TO CURRENCY DEPRECIATION

When other factors remain constant, an increase in U.S. income causes the dollar to depreciate. The increase in American income shifts the supply curve of dollars rightward as Americans seek to purchase more German goods.

[5]However, we must qualify this point. Quite often, strong income growth leads to an increase in real interest rates as domestic demand for loans escalates and the central bank moves to tighten credit to restrain economic activity. As we shall see, higher real interest rates tend to cause currency *appreciation* by attracting foreign funds to purchase the high-yielding domestic securities. Hence, we can say that relative income growth leads to currency depreciation *unless* it also leads to higher relative real interest rates. Other things equal, higher income growth leads to currency depreciation—but in the real world other things are not always equal.

Initially, supply and demand curves for dollars are represented by $S_\$^1$ and $D_\$$, with equilibrium at A and the exchange rate at 2.50 deutsche marks per dollar. Then U.S. income growth induces Americans to purchase more imported goods as well as domestic goods. To purchase more German goods, Americans must sell more dollars for marks. The $S_\$$ curve shifts rightward to $S_\$^2$, moving the equilibrium to B. In Figure 37-3, the dollar depreciates to 2.25 deutsche marks. Since German income is constant, German demand for U.S. goods and services remains unchanged. Hence, the demand curve for dollars in the figure remains unchanged. The expansion in relative U.S. income causes a depreciation of the dollar and an increase in the U.S. international trade deficit as imports into the United States expand.[6]

During 1985–1988, the U.S. experienced a declining dollar accompanied by a burgeoning deficit of our trade balance (exports minus imports). This was partially attributable to the fact that U.S. income expanded more rapidly than the income of such major trading partners as Japan and Germany. During this period the Reagan Administration became quite concerned about the falling dollar and the huge trade deficit. Rather than deliberately introducing contractionary policies in the United States to reduce income and thereby help arrest the falling dollar, U.S. officials pleaded with Japan and European nations to stimulate their domestic economies. In terms of Figure 37-3, such measures would raise the demand curve for dollars and thereby strengthen the dollar in foreign exchange markets. At the same time, such measures would stimulate American exports, thereby reducing the American trade deficit.

Relative Real Interest Rates and Exchange Rates

In recent years, changes in relative interest rates among countries—especially changes in real (inflation-adjusted) interest rates—have played an increasingly important role in precipitating changes in exchange rates. There exists a huge pool of liquid funds (so-called "hot money") that has grown enormously in the past 20 years. These funds are owned by banks, other financial and nonfinancial firms, and wealthy individuals eager to invest such funds in the financial centers exhibiting the most attractive rates of return. As relative real rates of return among nations change, these funds are likely to be shifted from nation to nation.[7] To illustrate the effect of a change in real interest rates upon the U.S.-France exchange rate, consider Figure 37-4.

Suppose initially we are at A in Figure 37-4, the exchange rate being 6 francs per dollar. Suppose the American central bank—the Federal Reserve—tightens credit and raises interest rates (nominal and real) in the United States. To take

---

[6]If German income expanded in line with U.S. income, the demand curve for dollars would shift rightward as Germans stepped up their purchases of American items. Hence, both the supply and demand curves in Figure 37-3 would increase over time (shifting rightward) and the exchange rate and the U.S. trade balance with Germany would remain approximately unchanged.

[7]Actually, a rational investor must consider the change in the exchange rate that is likely to occur while the funds are invested as well as the yield differential in deciding the most profitable country in which to invest. If a country is expected to experience significant depreciation of its currency in the exchange market because of domestic inflation or other reasons, it may have difficulty attracting investors (foreign or domestic) even if its yields are considerably higher than those in other nations. Would an American investor have done well buying Mexican securities yielding 30 percent in 1983 (see Table 37-1)? It is the differential between the yield available in country X and the expected net-percentage-exchange market depreciation of the currency of country X that the rational investor must focus on and compare with similar measures for countries Y and Z. If U.S. securities are yielding two percent more than German securities but the dollar is expected to depreciate against the deutsche mark at an annual rate of two percent, American and German investors are indifferent between U.S. and German securities.

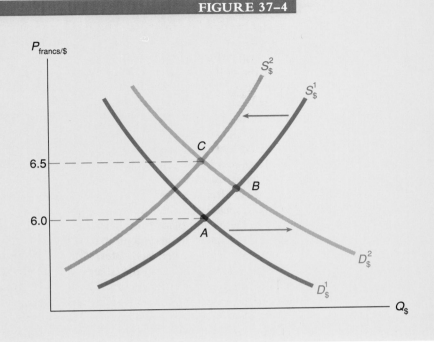

FIGURE 37–4

THE EFFECT OF HIGHER U.S. REAL INTEREST RATES ON THE DOLLAR

An increase in American real interest rates increases the demand for dollars as foreigners seek to purchase American bonds and other interest-bearing assets. Also, the supply of dollars shifts leftward as Americans become less interested in foreign securities. Via these forces, higher American real interest rates cause the dollar to appreciate.

advantage of more attractive yields here, French investors buy an increased amount of U.S. securities. This increases the demand for dollars to $D_\$^2$, which would move the equilibrium to B in the figure, causing the dollar to appreciate. Also, American investors become less inclined to purchase French securities. Hence, they offer fewer dollars for francs, and the supply curve in the figure decreases to $S_\$^2$. The new equilibrium is at C, the dollar having appreciated to 6.5 francs due to the increase in real American yields.[8] Higher real interest rates, given other factors, make for a strong currency in the foreign exchange market.

The volume of financial capital ("hot money") worldwide has expanded more rapidly in recent decades than has the volume of import and export activity. This may help to explain the increased responsiveness of exchange rates to real interest rate differentials. It may also help to account for the weakening of PPP as a factor in exchange-rate movements during the 1980s. The other factor accounting for the decline in PPP is the fact that inflation has been relatively subdued since the 1970s. Since price levels among nations have not diverged as much in the 1980s as in the 1970s, other factors have naturally assumed increased relative importance in explaining exchange-rate movements.

Speculation and Exchange-Rate Movements

Foreign-Exchange Market Speculators
Individuals and firms that buy and sell foreign currencies with the intent of profiting from exchange-rate movements.

Intra-day and day-to-day exchange-rate movements are often driven by speculative transactions. **Speculators** buy or sell foreign currencies solely to profit from

---

[8] If interest rates increase solely because of higher expected inflation, there is no increase in real interest rates and probably no additional net capital inflow and no appreciation of the dollar. The higher nominal rate of return is roughly offset by expected depreciation of the dollar. Much of the change in relative interest rates in countries exhibiting modest inflation in recent years has been real rather than nominal, however. When U.S. interest rates declined sharply in 1985–88, most of the decline was reflected in lower real interest rates. This helped to account for a sustained depreciation of the U.S. dollar.

exchange-rate changes. Speculators are often exporters, importers, and others who want foreign currencies for fundamental reasons but alter the *timing* of their foreign exchange transactions in expectation that the exchange rate will move in a certain direction. Suppose a U.S. exporter of mainframe computers receives payments denominated in French francs. If the exporter expects the franc to rise (appreciate) against the dollar in the next week, the exporter may wait to convert the francs to dollars. If so, this exporter is acting as a speculator.

Speculators essentially attempt to forecast movements in the factors that drive exchange rates and then act upon these forecasts. For example, if speculators believe the U.S. dollar will fall because of an impending increase in U.S. inflation not yet recognized by the market, the speculators sell dollars now, hoping to repurchase them later at a lower price. Likewise, if news is released indicating that U.S. real interest rates are likely to rise, speculators purchase dollars immediately in hopes of selling them after they appreciate. Each hour of the day, as relevant new information is released, speculators seize upon the information to forecast likely future exchange-rate movements and place their bets accordingly.

There is some disagreement about the effects of currency speculation on the stability of foreign exchange rates. Some economists believe such speculation destabilizes markets by causing sharp, disruptive exchange-rate movements not attributable to fundamental factors. Other economists point out that if speculators correctly forecast the direction of the fundamental factors driving exchange rates, they simply take actions that move the exchange rate in the direction it is bound to move in any event. If so, speculators are really serving to smooth exchange-rate movements. Nevertheless, central banks around the world have frequently intervened in foreign exchange markets in recent years in an attempt to prevent disruptive exchange-rate changes not believed to be justified by fundamental considerations. For example as the U.S. dollar appreciated strongly against the yen and deutsche mark in mid-1989, central banks sold billions of dollars in exchange for foreign currencies in an attempt to hold down the surging dollar.

YOUR TURN   Suppose the German central bank (the Bundesbank) surprises financial markets by sharply raising its discount rate (i.e., the interest rate it charges German commercial banks). Analyze the impact of this announcement on the U.S.-German exchange rate, expressed as deutsche marks per dollar.

An Analysis of the Gyrating Dollar, 1975–1988

The *dancing dollar* has experienced innumerable short-term movements in recent years. More significantly, there were three major sustained swings of the dollar during 1975–1988, as illustrated in Figure 37-5. These swings include the substantial depreciation of the dollar during the late 1970s, the sustained bull market in the dollar during the first half of the 1980s, and the sharp fall of the dollar during 1985–1988. Using our new framework of analysis, we now attempt to account for these three major swings in exchange rates.

The Great Depreciation of 1975–1979   The American inflation rate ratcheted upward from less than two percent in 1964 to double-digit levels by 1980. Several events in this period contributed to the massive increase in the underlying rate of inflation. These include the overheating of the U.S. economy associated with the

FIGURE 37–5

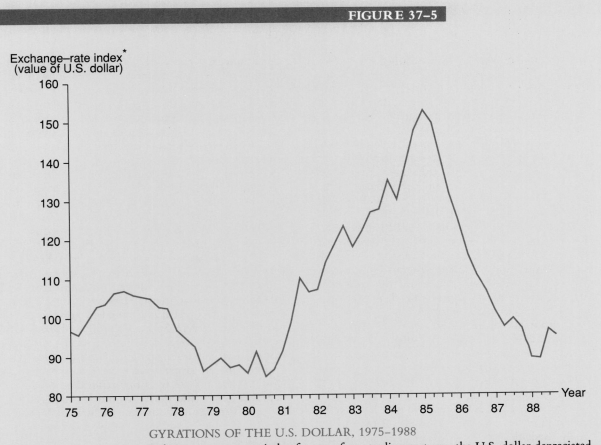

Exchange–rate index*
(value of U.S. dollar)

GYRATIONS OF THE U.S. DOLLAR, 1975–1988

Relative to a currency index for ten of our trading partners, the U.S. dollar depreciated
in the late 1970s. The dollar appreciated dramatically from late 1980 until early 1985,
then fell again during 1985–1988. By early 1988, the dollar reached levels similar to
those experienced at the beginning of the decade.

*A multilateral trade-weighted value of the U.S. dollar against currencies of the G-10 countries
(i.e., United Kingdom, Germany, Japan, France, Canada, Italy, Netherlands, Belgium, Sweden,
Switzerland; March 1973 = 100).

Source: Board of Governors of the Federal Reserve System.

escalation of the Vietnam War (1965–1969), two dramatic increases in the price of
imported oil (1974 and 1979), and an excessively stimulative U.S. monetary policy
in the late 1970s. By the late 1970s, money supply growth was surging and inflation
was solidly in the double-digit range. Because inflation was more subdued in most
other nations, PPP theory predicts that the dollar should have fallen—and it did! By
the end of the decade of the 1970s, the dollar stood at roughly 1.8 German deutsche
marks, 240 Japanese yen, and 1.60 Swiss francs—down sharply from 1970
quotations of 3.65 deutsche marks, 358 yen, and 4.30 francs, respectively. American
real interest rates were low (usually negative) and falling as inflation escalated in the
late 1970s. Also, U.S. income was rising strongly as we approached the peak of the
business cycle at the end of the decade. It is clear that the three fundamental factors

EXHIBIT 37-1

THE CHANGING FACTORS DRIVING EXCHANGE-RATE SPECULATION

A myriad of factors can motivate speculators to turn bullish or bearish on a particular currency in the foreign exchange market. It is interesting to note how the particular information deemed most crucial by such speculators changes over time.

In the late 1970s, U.S. inflation was raging and many questioned the extent to which the U.S. government was willing to pay the price to defeat it. Each month, foreign exchange speculators watched for the release of the official price indexes—the Consumer Price Index, the Producer Price Index, and the GNP deflator. In the 1970s, purchasing power parity theory (PPP) provided a fairly reliable model for exchange-rate movements. If the monthly price indexes revealed that inflation was running higher than expected, speculators would immediately sell dollars on the basis that import and export activity would ultimately produce a depreciation of the dollar.

During the 1980s, PPP broke down as a reliable tracker of exchange-rate movements. Capital flows based on real interest rate levels assumed a larger role in explaining exchange rates. In late 1979, the Fed moved to a policy of targeting money supply growth at reasonably low levels, allowing interest rates to seek whatever levels were compatible with the modest growth of the money supply. Speculators turned their attention to the weekly money supply announcement that flashed across the ticker at 2:00 p.m. EST each Thursday. If the announced money supply exceeded market expectations, speculators anticipated a tightening of Fed policy to get back on the money target. This suggested that interest rates (nominal and real) would have to rise, thus inducing an inflow of

capital and an appreciation of the dollar. Hence, speculators purchased dollars immediately upon the announcement, causing the dollar to quickly firm up. If the money supply announcement came in below expectations, speculators immediately sold dollars to take advantage of an expected easing of monetary policy and a resulting decline in U.S. interest rates and the U.S. dollar.

By the mid-1980s, the Fed had abandoned its experiment with monetarism and speculators had abandoned their fascination with the money supply. In this period (1983–1987) the U.S. trade deficit increased sharply—chiefly in response to the enormous 1980–1985 appreciation of the U.S. dollar and the faster growth of income in America relative to Europe and developing nations. After early 1985, the dollar began to depreciate in foreign exchange markets. However, in 1986 and 1987, the trade deficit continued to grow in spite of the falling dollar. Speculators focused attention on the monthly release of information revealing the most recent trade figures. If the trade deficit figure came in larger than expected, speculators would dump dollars in anticipation that a further depreciation in the dollar would be required in order to turn around our trade deficit. In January 1988, when the new figures showed an unexpectedly large decline in the trade deficit, the dollar rallied sharply as speculators turned bullish en masse.

Based on your observation of the evening news and your reading of the daily newspaper, what chief indicators are the foreign exchange market speculators watching this year?

(relative inflation rates, income levels, and real interest rates) do an excellent job of tracking the depreciation of the U.S. dollar in the late 1970s.

The Bull Market in the Dollar, 1980–1985   In the early 1980s, the United States experienced a dramatic increase in interest rates, which remained well above ten percent for several years. At the same time, the U.S. inflation rate came down much faster than anyone had expected (twelve percent in 1980 to about four percent by early 1983). As a result, real interest rates swung dramatically upward from the negative rates of the late 1970s to virtually unprecedented positive levels of six to ten percent in the early 1980s. This increase in real interest rates helped to trigger a large net inflow of capital into U.S. financial markets. Part of the upsurge in real

EXHIBIT 37–2

THE ROLE OF FEDERAL BUDGET DEFICITS IN THE BOOMING DOLLAR OF 1980–1985

Many economists believe that the massive increase in federal budget deficits in the United States during the early 1980s was a major cause of the *soaring dollar* of 1980–1985. By driving up U.S. interest rates, these deficits predictably induced a large net inflow of capital into the United States, thus bidding up the dollar. The strong dollar meant that U.S. goods were very expensive in foreign markets and foreign goods were unusually cheap here. This worked a severe hardship on the U.S. agricultural and manufacturing sectors in general and on workers and firms in American export- and import-competing industries in particular. Many, therefore, blamed the U.S. trade deficits of the 1980s and the structural unemployment in American manufacturing industries as well as the distress in agriculture on the federal budget deficits.

However, the Reagan Administration and quite a few economists offered an alternative explanation. By reducing taxes, pursuing a policy of deregulating business, and generally attempting to unleash the forces of *free enterprise,* the Administration allegedly made America a more desirable place in which to invest. In this view, real interest rates in the United States were high in the 1980s not because of large budget deficits, but because of increased real returns anticipated as a result of beneficial Reagan Administration policies. In this light, the trade deficits cannot be viewed as entirely negative. They are portrayed as an inevitable side effect of the increased preference on the part of the rest of the world to invest in American assets.

Also, it can be stated that, for investment purposes, the political climate in other regions worsened. For example, a socialist regime came to power in France. And political and economic conditions deteriorated in Latin American nations after 1982, which led to the increased perception that funds invested there might be confiscated or otherwise rendered nonrepayable. The United States was increasingly pronounced a "safe haven" in which to invest during 1980–1985. A good part of the capital inflow, therefore, was not strictly attributable to the higher real interest rates in the United States.

This episode is a good example of the disagreement among economists on issues with strong political implications. Critics of the Reagan Administrations emphasize the role of the budget deficits as outlined in the first paragraph. Supporters of the Administration's policies downgrade the role of deficits and emphasize the factors outlined in the second paragraph. It is worth mentioning, however, that the first Reagan Administration's chief economist during 1982–1984, Martin Feldstein, voiced strong opposition to the deficits. Perhaps in part because his advice was ignored, he resigned and returned to his academic position at Harvard.

interest rates was probably due to the burgeoning federal budget deficits of the early 1980s. In addition, in early 1981, the first Reagan Administration inaugurated a pro-business agenda that contributed to the improving perception of America as an excellent environment in which to invest. Also contributing to the capital inflow was the deterioration of economic and political conditions in Latin America and the consequent emergence of the United States as a relatively *safe haven* in which to invest.

In its latter stages, the rising dollar was probably boosted to unrealistically high levels by the *bandwagon effect,* in which speculators sometimes contribute to excessive movements in exchange rates by purchasing currencies that have already appreciated strongly because of fundamental factors. By early 1985, the U.S. dollar had risen by more than 50 percent on average compared to its 1979–1980 levels. As a predictor of exchange rates, PPP collapsed in this period. Although the U.S. inflation rate was subdued in the 1980–1985 period, it remained higher than that of most of our trading partners. Hence, PPP called for a modest depreciation of the dollar. Also, because domestic income grew much faster in the United States than in other industrial countries after 1982, this also should have depreciated the dollar. Instead, we got an enormous *rise* in the dollar—and must look to the massive net capital inflow due to high real American interest rates for the explanation.

The Fall in the Dollar, 1985–1988   The more recent and substantial decline in the dollar cannot be explained fully by the three fundamental factors. Inflation remained quite subdued in the United States, so PPP forces can only account for a very minor portion of the dollar's depreciation. Stronger income growth in the U.S. than in other nations helps to account partially for the falling dollar. Also, the yield differential favoring the United States, though still positive, declined. After 1986, the falling dollar seems to have been driven significantly by speculative forces responding to several seemingly intractable problems in the United States. The U.S. trade deficits increased rapidly after 1983 and the United States emerged for the first time in 70 years as a net debtor in global financial markets—our obligations to foreigners exceeding our assets abroad. A growing awareness of the lack of political will in this country to come to grips with the large structural budget deficit may have contributed to the speculative attack on the dollar. By late 1987 and early 1988, the second Reagan Administration became concerned that the dollar was falling too rapidly and perhaps too far. The United States arranged for international cooperation among central banks to support the dollar and limit its depreciation. In 1987, for example, governments collectively purchased approximately $100 billion of U.S. currency in foreign exchange markets to prevent additional weakness in the dollar.

CONSEQUENCES OF EXCHANGE-RATE CHANGES

Changes in exchange rates may significantly affect a nation's standard of living and such key macroeconomic variables as the unemployment rate and the inflation rate. Moreover, changes in exchange rates may affect income distribution, helping certain groups in society while simultaneously impairing others. For these reasons, nations are sometimes reluctant to accept changes in exchange rates, even when they are dictated by the fundamental forces analyzed in this chapter. Consider the consequences of currency appreciation and depreciation.

Effects of the Strong Dollar, 1980–1985

There were both positive and negative influences stemming from the sustained appreciation of the U.S. dollar. On the positive side, the rising dollar unleashed powerful disinflationary forces that helped to bring down the U.S. inflation rate from more than twelve percent in 1980 to less than four percent during 1983–1986. Appreciation of the dollar reduces the cost in dollars of imports into the United States. To the extent that imports enter into our price indexes, this directly reduces the U.S. price level. More important, it places increased pressure on U.S. manufacturing firms to hold down wages and prices in order to remain competitive in world markets. Concurrently, a strong dollar—by making foreign products look attractive to Americans and by raising the prices of American products abroad—redirects some of the demand for American products to products produced abroad. This effect is often considered disadvantageous because it worsens our trade deficit and increases our unemployment rate. A positive side effect, however, is that it helps to reduce U.S. inflation by reducing aggregate demand for American goods and services.

The masses of American consumers experience an improvement in their standard of living because of the availability of cheaper foreign-produced goods. The U.S. **terms of trade**—the ratio of the price of U.S. exports to the price of U.S. imports—improves as each unit of our exports pays for a larger amount of imported goods.[9] American tourists abroad benefit as the dollar purchases more units of foreign currencies. Those Americans engaged in import businesses reap an obvious gain as the American cost of foreign items declines.

On the other hand, there are many people—some domestic, some foreign—who suffer from a strong dollar. American losers are concentrated in the U.S. export and import-competing industries. Examples include workers and firms in the auto, steel, textile, heavy machinery, computer, and agricultural sectors. it was estimated that more than one million American workers lost their jobs in the early 1980s because of the strong dollar. This led to powerful sentiment in the United States for legislation restricting the free flow of imports into this country. In addition, some U.S. firms relocated production facilities from domestic to foreign locations to benefit from the greater purchasing power of the dollar abroad.

The strong dollar of 1980–1985 also had negative implications for foreign nations. To prevent their currencies from falling excessively against the dollar, many European nations maintained interest rates at higher levels than they normally would have preferred. As a result, economic activity in Europe was abnormally sluggish for several years following the worldwide recession of 1981–1983. Unemployment remained above ten percent in some European nations. Since OPEC requires that oil payments be made in dollars, the booming dollar boosted oil prices sharply for many oil-importing countries. This created an effect similar to (though somewhat milder than) the shocks administered by the OPEC oil price hikes of the 1970s. Finally, LDC debtor nations such as Brazil and Mexico, whose debts are denominated in dollars, found it more difficult to meet payments on their debts because of the high cost of the dollar.

Effects of the Falling Dollar, 1985–1988

By raising the cost of imports, reducing the pressure on American industries to hold the line on wages and prices, and raising foreign (and American) demand for U.S. goods and services, a depreciation of the U.S. dollar tends to unleash inflationary forces.[10]

Terms of Trade The ratio of the average price of a country's exports to the average price of its imports.

---

[9]A nation's terms of trade is defined at the ratio of the price of its exports divided by the price of its imports, both measured in units of domestic currency. When the U.S. dollar appreciates, the dollar price of U.S. wheat in America stays the same while the dollar price of an imported Toyota falls. Fewer bushels of American wheat are needed to purchase one imported Toyota. This favorable change in the U.S. terms of trade associated with a rising dollar increases the overall American standard of living.

[10]It should be noted that the consequences of a rising dollar are not perfectly symmetrical with the effects of a falling dollar. As the dollar declined following early 1985—tending to place Japanese exporters at a disadvantage in selling to U.S. markets—many Japanese manufacturing firms reduced prices (in yen) to offset the rising cost of the yen to Americans. These Japanese firms were sometimes willing to sharply reduce profit margins to protect established markets. Hence, even though the dollar fell against the yen by roughly 50 percent from the second half of 1984 to the beginning of 1988, Japanese-made Hondas and Toyotas increased in price only by about 20 percent in U.S. markets. The halving of the value of the dollar against the yen would have doubled the U.S. price of these cars if the Japanese automobile manufacturers had neither implemented cost-cutting measures nor accepted lower profit margins on their cars.

"You hate me when I'm strong and despise me when I'm weak."

By permission of Bill Mauldin and Wil-Jo Associates.

U.S. export- and import-competing industries are stimulated by a falling dollar, though with a significant time lag. Beginning in 1988, U.S. exports began to increase strongly. This led to a welcome revival in the long-depressed U.S. manufacturing sector.

The masses of American consumers are hurt by the falling dollar as the array of cheap foreign autos, electronics goods, and other imports are stripped away. The increased cost of imports (and domestic goods) tends to reduce real wages and the standard of living of Americans. The decline in the dollar adversely affects the U.S. terms of trade as more bushels of U.S. wheat are required to pay for each Nikon camera from Japan. Hence, a net loss accrues to U.S. society. That is, the aggregate cost imposed on the masses of losers by the falling dollar exceeds the aggregate benefits accruing to the minority of individuals engaged in the sectors directly exposed to foreign competition.

GOVERNMENT INTERVENTION IN FOREIGN EXCHANGE MARKETS

Exchange-rate movements exert major effects—some *good,* some *bad.* In addition, highly variable exchange rates can increase risk and therefore discourage international economic activity. Therefore, it is not surprising that there is a fair amount of sentiment for governments to intervene to limit exchange-rate movements or to prevent them from changing at all.

Why Do Governments Intervene in Foreign Exchange Markets?

In principle, governments may directly intervene in foreign exchange markets either to attempt to smooth excessive short-term changes in exchange rates or to attempt to push the rate in a direction perceived to be in the government's interest. If exchange rates are highly unstable, a case can be made for government activity to stabilize rates. Highly volatile exchange rates increase the risk of entering into international transactions and are therefore thought to inhibit the volume of trade. However, critics of government intervention doubt that governments know better than speculators what the *correct* exchange rate is at any point in time. Unless speculators are on average losing money, they are right most of the time. This means, on average, that speculators are purchasing currencies that are too weak and selling currencies that are too strong, thereby serving to stabilize movements in exchange rates.

Governments also intervene to influence exchange rates for other, more selfish reasons. We have analyzed how changes in exchange rates benefit some groups and harm others. Over the years, the Japanese government has frequently intervened to hold down the yen (i.e., to support the U.S. dollar or keep it from declining). This activity can probably be explained by the political power of the electronics, automobile, and other Japanese export industries that prosper from strong sales in American markets. A strongly appreciating yen—though it benefits the great masses of Japanese consumers—reduces the state of prosperity in the powerful Japanese export industries. Apparently these industries have more political clout than the less-organized masses of Japanese consumers. In the colorful language of international finance, such politically motivated interventionist actions in foreign exchange markets by governments have earned the floating exchange-rate system the moniker **dirty float.** [11]

SHOULD WE RETURN TO A SYSTEM OF FIXED EXCHANGE RATES?

The experience with floating exchange rates since the early 1970s has not been as free of problems as early supporters of floating rates had expected. Exchange-rate fluctuations have been quite volatile at times—considerably more volatile than expected. For example, the dollar's decline in the late 1970s was probably of greater magnitude than fundamental factors dictated, as was the dollar's appreciation in 1984–early 1985, and in 1989. Contrary to the belief of many early advocates of floating rates, implementation of floating rates has not allowed countries to ignore external considerations and to set macroeconomic policy solely on the basis of domestic goals. As noted earlier, for instance, European nations kept interest rates high in spite of depressed economic activity during 1982–1985 to prevent their currencies from depreciating excessively against the dollar. And the United States did the same thing in the winter of 1987–1988 to guard against a feared additional decline in the dollar. Also, trade protectionist sentiment was stronger in the United States in the 1980s than at any time since the 1930s. Some economists and officials

---

[11] These activities by the Japanese government might correctly be regarded by American manufacturing firms and workers as a form of trade restriction against U.S. products: If, by purchasing dollars (selling yen), the Japanese government keeps the dollar five percent higher than it would otherwise be, it is making American products artificially expensive in Japan and Japanese products artificially cheap in the United States by roughly five percent.

therefore advocate a return to the system of fixed exchange rates that prevailed during 1944–1973. In fact, many nations currently have fixed exchange rates with certain close trading partners.[12] For these reasons, a brief analysis of the workings of fixed exchange rates is pertinent.

The Bretton-Woods System of the Adjustable Peg, 1944–1973

The **adjustable-peg system** was established at an international conference held at Bretton Woods, New Hampshire, in 1944. In the agreement, each nation's government or central bank was required to intervene in the foreign exchange market to *peg* the exchange rate at a specific level known as **parity** or **par value** for an indefinite period of time. For many years, the U.S.-England exchange rate parity was established at $2.80 per £.[13] The government of England kept the pound from depreciating below $2.80 by using its **international reserves** to purchase its own currency in the foriegn exchange market. These reserves consisted primarily of the British central bank's holdings of gold and U.S. dollars. Figure 37-6 illustrates how this system functioned.

International Reserves
A government's stock of foreign currencies and gold available to support the country's currency in the foreign exchange market.

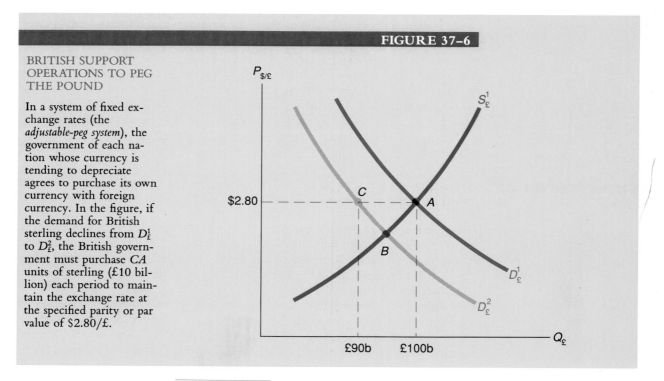

FIGURE 37–6

BRITISH SUPPORT OPERATIONS TO PEG THE POUND

In a system of fixed exchange rates (the *adjustable-peg system*), the government of each nation whose currency is tending to depreciate agrees to purchase its own currency with foreign currency. In the figure, if the demand for British sterling declines from $D_£^1$ to $D_£^2$, the British government must purchase *CA* units of sterling (£10 billion) each period to maintain the exchange rate at the specified parity or par value of $2.80/£.

---

[12]As of the end of 1988, some 35 nations (mostly LDCs) pegged their currencies to the dollar. Fourteen nations tied their currencies to the French franc; 42 nations pegged themselves to other currencies or baskets of currencies. A group of eight members of the European Monetary System (EMS) fix their exchange rate with each other, allowing the whole bloc to float against the dollar, yen, and other independently floating currencies. The EMS members currently consist of Belgium, Denmark, France, Germany, Ireland, Italy, Luxembourg, and the Netherlands.

[13]Technically, this parity was established by each nation defining the value of its currency unit in terms of gold. If the U.S. official gold price were $35/ounce and the British official price were £12.5/ounce, the par value would be established at $2.80/£ (since $35 and £12.5 are equivalent). If England were to raise its gold price to £14.6, it would devalue the pound and reduce the par value exchange rate to $2.40/£. This is precisely what England did in 1967.

Suppose England manages to set the par value at exactly the intersection of $S_£^1$ and $D_£^1$ (i.e., *$2.80/£*)—exactly the level at which a free float would have established the exchange rate. No intervention is needed initially. However, the supply and demand curves do not remain fixed, but instead are constantly shifting about. Suppose the demand schedule for sterling shifts down to $D_£^2$ due to a recession in America or a price level increase in England. In a free float, the pound would depreciate to a new equilibrium (point *B* in Figure 37-6). However, the British central bank is obligated to prevent this from happening. It can do this for awhile by purchasing the excess supply of sterling each period (*CA* or £10 billion in the figure). Essentially, in purchasing the surplus sterling, the Bank of England shifts the demand curve back to $D_£^1$ to maintain the pound at $2.80.

As this British currency support operation continues, the British government's stock of international reserves decreases. At some point speculators anticipate that the government will run out of ammunition (gold and dollars) and will be forced to devalue the pound to a sustainable level—approximately in line with the intersection of $S_£^1$ and $D_£^2$ (i.e., point *B*) in Figure 37-6. This is what happened in 1967, when England devalued the pound from $2.80 to $2.40, or by roughly 15 percent. When speculators foresee the likelihood of devaluation, they sell sterling in large quantities—thus shifting the $S_£$ schedule sharply rightward. This creates a much larger excess supply of sterling, forcing the government to give up the game. The pound is devalued—and the government now pegs the pound at the new, lower level for an indefinite period.

To avoid the preceding devaluation scenario in the first place, nations with chronically weak currencies (England, France, Italy) were tempted to try to move the equilibrium rate back to the original par values by highly destructive measures. These measures include such trade restrictions as quotas and tariffs and such domestic austerity programs as higher taxes, reduced government outlays, and higher interest rates fostered by the central bank. In terms of Figure 37-6, austerity programs in England would shift the $S_£$ schedule leftward by reducing British incomes and the demand for imports. By depressing the domestic price level, such measures would improve the competitive posture of British goods in world markets and shift the $D_£$ schedule rightward. A ten-percent tariff imposed by Britain on imported items would reduce the willingness of British citizens to import, thus shifting the $S_£$ schedule leftward. Any of these destructive measures would help sustain the exchange rate at its par value.

Criticisms of the Adjustable-Peg Exchange-Rate System   The chief criticism of the adjustable-peg system is that it forced countries with chronically weak currencies to implement policies that created high unemployment, slow growth, financial distress, and international trade restrictions. In many cases, monetary and fiscal policies were being set on the basis of international considerations rather than on domestic needs. Of course, when the British pound was weak, some other currency—the dollar, yen, or deutsche mark—must have been strong. The strong-currency nation could in principle have helped by boosting its own economy, thereby boosting demand for imports and strengthening the weak currency's position in the foreign exchange market. Unfortunately, the strong-currency nations tended to view the situation as strictly the problem of the weak-currency nation. Therefore, the burden of adjustment typically was placed entirely upon the weak-currency nation.

The fixed exchange-rate system of 1944–1973 was dubbed the "adjustable-peg system" because of the periodic realignments of the level at which the exchange rate was pegged. Critics of this system argued that it is eminently more sensible to let the exchange rate freely adjust to resolve a disequilibrium of the type illustrated in Figure 37-6 than to resort to such destructive measures as trade barriers and increased domestic unemployment in a largely futile effort to restore the equilibrium exchange rate to the glorified par value level. Typically such measures only *delayed* the exchange rate adjustment in any event. Nations with **overvalued currencies** (i.e., exchange rates held above market equilibrium levels—such as England in the preceding example) clearly experience less agony through letting their currencies depreciate than by attempting to become competitive by pushing down the nation's entire structure of costs and prices via restrictive monetary and fiscal policies.[14]

By the early 1970s, the divergence of inflation rates and other imbalances among nations had become quite substantial. The adjustable-peg system was no longer viable because the volume of international reserves held by weak-currency nations (including the United States) was insufficient to maintain fixed parities for long periods of time. Exchange rates were unpegged—set free—and have been floating ever since. The floating system now in place is not utopian—it does not solve all our international problems. But most economists believe that the floating system is better equipped to deal with the increasing volume of international economic activity and the shocks that from time to time hit the global economy than the adjustable-peg exchange rate system that preceded it. It is unlikely we will return to fixed exchange rates in the near future.

THE BALANCE OF PAYMENTS

Balance of Payments
A statistical tabulation of a nation's transactions with other countries for a given period.

A nation's **balance of payments** is a statistical tabulation of all transactions between that nation and the rest of the world for a given year. Transactions that give rise to payments to the rest of the world are recorded as debits (−); transactions that generate receipts from the rest of the world are recorded as credits (+). The balance of payments include transactions made by individuals, firms, and governments.

The overall balance of payments accounts include the *current account* and the *capital account.* Both accounts are influenced by government transactions as well as by transactions of private entities. Table 37-2 outlines the components of the U.S. balance of payments in 1988.

The Current Account

Balance of Trade
The difference between the value of a nation's exports and imports of merchandise or goods; one component of the balance of payments.

The **current account** includes trade in currently produced goods and services, where *services* is broadly interpreted. The current account is dominated by the **balance of trade,** which is the net difference between merchandise exports and merchandise imports. Line 3 reveals that the United States ran a "balance of trade" deficit of some $127 billion in 1988. The U.S. trade deficit figure, released monthly by the Department of Commerce, has been one of the most eagerly observed

---

[14]The ultimate example of this folly, in the eyes of most economists, was "Mr. Churchill's mistake" of 1925. During World War I (1914–1918), British prices had risen considerably faster than those in the United States and other nations. Exchange rates were floated during 1919–1925 and the pound depreciated sharply as predicted by PPP theory. But in early 1925 Winston Churchill (the British Chancellor of the Exchequer) decided to return to the prewar parity of $4.86/£. This put England at a large competitive disadvantage and almost destroyed its export industries. For many years, the British unemployment rate never fell below ten percent.

TABLE 37-2	
THE U.S. BALANCE OF PAYMENTS, 1988 (billions of dollars)	

Current account

1. Merchandise exports	+ 319.3
2. Merchandise imports	− 446.5
3. Balance of trade	− 127.2
4. Net travel and transportation	− 2.6
5. Net military transactions	− 4.6
6. Net income from foreign investments	+ 22.5
7. Balance on goods and services	− 111.9
8. Unilateral transfers (net)	− 14.7
9. Balance on current account	− 126.5

Capital account

Private

10. Change in U.S. private assets abroad	− 81.5
11. Change in foreign assets in U.S.	+ 180.4
12. Net private capital flows	+ 98.9

Government

13. Change in U.S. government assets abroad	− 0.6
14. Change in foreign government assets in U.S.	+ 38.9
15. Net government capital flows	+ 38.3
16. Balance on capital account	+ 137.2
17. Statistical discrepancy (lines 9 + 16, with sign reversed)	− 10.7
18. **Total balance of payments**	**0**

Source: Adapted from Department of Commerce, *Survey of Current Business,* June 1989.

economic statistics in recent years. Its release sometimes triggers large changes in foreign exchange rates as well as changes in prices in U.S. financial markets, including the stock market.

Several other items included in the current account are conceptually regarded as exports and imports of *services,* and are listed for 1988 in lines 4–6 of Table 37-2. An American tourist who buys a meal in London or pays a hotel bill in Paris contributes to our current account deficit in the same way as an American who buys an imported VCR. So does an American importer who utilizes foreign-owned ships to transport cargo. Foreigners make corresponding transactions in the United States, but line 4 indicates a small U.S. deficit on travel and transportation. Similarly, U.S. military activities abroad contribute to the deficit (line 5). Income flowing from past American investment abroad (plants, real estate, securities) is conceptually treated as payment for use of the services of U.S. capital. Of course, foreign nations have also accumulated vast assets in this country, from which they earn a rapidly growing income. In 1988, the table (line 6) indicates a significant net positive balance of $22.5 billion from such flows in favor of the United States. When these net exports of U.S. services (lines 4, 5, 6) are added to our trade balance (line 3), we arrive at the "balance on goods and services." Line 7 indicates a deficit of $111.9 billion for 1988 on goods and services.

Finally, we consider "unilateral transfers." Income earners may send money to family or friends abroad. Charitable organizations send aid to famine-stricken regions of the world. The U.S. government provides foreign aid to low-income nations. Net unilateral transfers from the United States amounted to almost $15 billion in 1988 (line 8). When net unilateral transfers are added to the balance on goods and services, we obtain the current account balance (line 9). The 1988 current account deficit was $126.5 billion.

Capital Account

The **capital account** tallies up changes in foreign assets—securities, real estate, checking accounts, and the like—owned by Americans and subtracts changes in the stock of similar American assets owned by foreigners. These changes in net foreign assets, known as *capital flows*, may be attributable either to governments or to private parties. Private capital flows have traditionally dominated government capital flows. Table 37-2 indicates that foreign private investors purchased $180.4 billion of additional U.S. assets in 1988, whereas Americans purchased $81.5 billion of new foreign assets. This indicates a net private capital *inflow* of $98.9 billion (line 12). In addition, governments (U.S. and foreign) purchased (net) about $38 billion of U.S. assets (line 15). This activity is explained by the desire of governments in 1988 to support the U.S. dollar in order to prevent its further depreciation in foreign exchange markets. Central banks (especially foreign) purchased dollars in exchange markets and typically placed the funds in U.S. checking accounts or U.S. government securities.

When private and government capital flows are combined, we obtain line 16—the net balance on capital account. Note that this item ($137.2 billion) fails to precisely offset the deficit balance on current account ($126.5 billion). In principle, this is impossible because each event generating a credit (+) for the United States gives rise to a corresponding transaction generating a debit (−). For example, when a U.S. computer manufacturer (IBM) makes a $100 million shipment to Canada, "merchandise exports" rise $100 million (line 1). But the Canadian importer pays for the shipment by writing a check on its account in a U.S. bank (line 11 declines by $100 million) or perhaps by making payment to IBM's bank account in Toronto, in which case U.S. private assets abroad increase $100 million (line 10).

The failure of the capital account balance to precisely offset the current account balance is attributable to imperfections inherent in compiling the balance of payments. The Department of Commerce may have accurate data on the value of U.S. imports of Hyundais from Korea, but the method of payment may not be known. In this event, imports are recorded as a debt item (line 2) but the corresponding credit item is simply recorded under "statistical discrepancy" (line 17). Hence, most of the *statistical discrepancy* derives from unrecorded capital movements. Note in Table 37-2 that the "total balance of payments" is precisely zero. In a trivial accounting sense, each nation's total balance of payments is zero.

THE U.S. TRADE DEFICIT

If each nation's balance of payments is always zero, why worry? What's all the talk about a U.S. balance of payments problem? International payments imbalances imply problems with the *composition* of the overall international accounts. Hardship in certain sectors of the economy may be occurring. Alternatively, the composition may be unsustainable and problems may occur later when inevitable adjustments are made. For example, suppose a highly developed nation is enjoying an artificially high standard of living by purchasing and enjoying five percent more goods and services each year than it produces. Suppose it accomplishes this feat by running a $200 billion trade deficit—importing $200 billion more goods and services each year than it exports. It finances the trade deficit via net annual capital inflows of $200 billion. That is, foreigners are purchasing the nation's assets (on balance) and granting loans to it.

This may be fun while it lasts, but it seems unlikely that such a policy can be continued for 100 years. At some point, foreigners will grow weary or leery of investing and lending additional funds. At this point, the nation in question will have to eliminate its trade deficit by bringing imports and exports into alignment. In fact, if the rest of the world not only refuses to loan new money but also decides to cash in some of its accumulated IOUs, the nation will have to run a trade surplus. It will have to reduce significantly its standard of living by purchasing and enjoying fewer goods than it produces (i.e., by achieving a trade surplus and by using the proceeds to pay off some of the external debt).

The U.S. experienced huge international deficits in its trade, goods and services, and current accounts in the 1980s. The profile of these deficits is illustrated in Figure 37-7 (page 868). These deficits increased in magnitude during 1981–1987, but have declined somewhat since mid-1987.

The United States as an International Debtor

From approximately World War I until the mid-1980s, the United States was a net creditor in global markets. This means that the sum of all foreign investments accumulated by Americans—foreign stocks, bonds, real estate, and so forth—exceeded the corresponding stock of American assets owned by foreigners. As a result of the capital inflows of the 1980s and the trade deficits that accompanied them (Figure 37-7), the United States in 1984 became a net debtor for the first time in roughly 70 years. In fact, during the decade of the 1980s, the United States moved from being the largest creditor nation in the world to the largest debtor.

Thoughtful economists worry that this might be a lot like "enjoy now, pay later"—the quintessential "fool's paradise." If foreigners decide they have overinvested in American assets and begin to liquidate some of their IOUs, the United States will be forced to run trade surpluses. Hence, a potential scenario for the 1990s could be just the reverse of the experience of the 1980s. We may be forced to tighten our belts and accept a lower standard of living. That is, we Americans may be forced to acquire *fewer* goods and services than we collectively produce, using the revenues from our trade surplus to pay off the foreigners who cash in their IOUs.[15] If foreign willingness to hold American assets decreases precipitously, the dollar would

[15]One cannot be certain when this reversal will occur, but the distressing thing is that the situation is to a large extent now outside of American control. Capital flows depend on the fragile concept of investor psychology as well as upon relative real rates of return in nations. They also depend on a *portfolio equilibrium concept,* in which investors seek to diversify assets by placing a balanced amount of funds in several different countries. Martin Feldstein and numerous other economists believe the United States will be forced by events to run trade surpluses in the 1990s. See Feldstein, "Correcting the Trade Deficit," *Foreign Affairs,* Spring 1987, pp. 795–806.

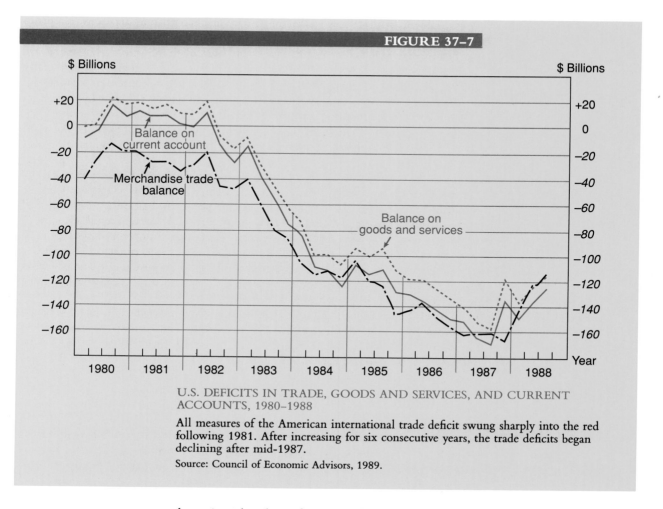

FIGURE 37–7

U.S. DEFICITS IN TRADE, GOODS AND SERVICES, AND CURRENT ACCOUNTS, 1980–1988

All measures of the American international trade deficit swung sharply into the red following 1981. After increasing for six consecutive years, the trade deficits began declining after mid-1987.

Source: Council of Economic Advisors, 1989.

depreciate sharply in foreign exchange markets. By stimulating U.S. exports and slowing imports, the falling dollar would be the chief mechanism through which the turnaround in our current account would occur. Unfortunately, a rapid fall of the dollar would cause domestic problems such as higher inflation.

THE LDC DEBT CRISES

Less developed countries (LDCs) typically have inadequate domestic savings with which to finance economic growth. Such nations as Brazil, Mexico, and Argentina rely on the export of raw materials and international borrowing to obtain funds for investment in infrastructure and plant and equipment. The United States, for example, was an international debtor nation during most of our history until World War I. We borrowed from the rest of the world to finance the expansion of railroads and other infrastructure. Hence, one normally expects such LDC nations as Brazil, Mexico, Argentina, and Peru to be net debtors. Developed nations often regard the LDCs—which typically exhibit low wages and often are well endowed with natural resources—as attractive places to lend and invest.

Much of the LDC debt problem today can be traced to decisions made in the 1970s. In that decade, raw material prices rose sharply, boosting export revenues of the LDCs. Real interest rates in the United States and other creditor nations were low, significantly easing the burden of debtors. LDCs faced few problems in meeting interest payments. From the vantage point of the 1970s, LDC prosperity seemed easy to sustain. Given this environment, many LDCs—especially Latin American nations—sought a major expansion in credit, and the large American banks were eager to accommodate. Some of these funds were used for legitimate investment projects; others were utilized to finance ventures of questionable merit.

The LDC debt crisis was triggered by a series of shocks in the first half of the decade of the 1980s. These shocks severely reduced the ability of many LDCs to meet the interest payments on their debts. First, a severe worldwide recession occurred during 1981–1983. This resulted in a major drop in LDC exports demanded by industrial nations. Also, prices of raw materials dropped sharply, ensuring a severe contraction in the revenues generated by LDC exports.

Second, real interest rates in developed countries (the lending nations) increased sharply and remained high for several years, especially in the United States. Recall that debtors come under increased pressure when real interest rates rise. Third, the U.S. dollar increased dramatically in foreign exchange markets during 1980–1985. Since many LDC debts are denominated in dollars, the increased cost of obtaining dollars tended to exacerbate the LDC debt problem.

In 1982, Mexico declared that it was unable to meet payments on its debt to the United States. In ensuing years, Argentina, Brazil, Peru, and the Philippines encountered similar problems. The interim *remedy* has been to postpone payments and *renegotiate* the loans on scaled-back terms. The enormous LDC debts and the difficulties in meeting payments continue to constitute a serious problem for many large American banks. Several of these banks have loans outstanding to LDCs in amounts equal to 200 percent or more of bank capital or net worth. This means in principle that wholesale default on the LDC debt could bankrupt several of our largest banks, perhaps touching off a major financial panic in the process.

None of the parties involved would benefit from widespread default. The LDCs themselves would lose heavily, inasmuch as they would be sealed off from future credit. For this reason there is no choice but for the LDC nations, the U.S. government, and international financial institutions to achieve maximum cooperation to manage the debt crisis. In the late 1980s, several U.S. banks acknowledged the reduced prospects for full loan repayments by sharply increasing loan-loss reserve provisions. Although such provisions reduced bank earnings temporarily, they implicitly acknowledged an emerging political reality—that many of the loans will never be repaid in full and that banks will be forced to take losses resulting from their decisions to make the loans.

A fundamental solution to the debt crisis requires that the LDCs generate a healthy surplus in their international trade accounts and use the proceeds to work down the debts by meeting interest and amortization expenses. Two basic avenues can contribute to this result. First, the LDCs can attempt to bring about a real depreciation of their currencies in foreign exchange markets via austerity programs and other measures in order to boost export sales. Unfortunately, such measures typically involve reducing standards of living of the populace in the short run. The living standards in LDCs are already grim and have declined significantly in the 1980s. Real wages in Mexico, for example, declined by roughly 50 percent in the decade of the 1980s. Second, the industrial nations can boost the export sales of the LDC nations by implementing stimulative macroeconomic measures to strengthen aggregate demand in the developed nations.

By mid-1989, the LDC debt amounted to roughly $1300 billion, with annual interest expense in the $100 billion range, or about 25 percent of annual export revenues of the LDCs. The LDC debt crisis eased somewhat in the 1985–1989 period as the dollar and U.S. interest rates declined and economic activity in the industrial nations strengthened. As we enter the 1990s, the situation continues to simmer. Many LDCs remain vulnerable to any severe weakening of worldwide economic activity or major increase in interest rates in the creditor nations. The LDC debt crisis may be exacerbated by strong protectionist sentiment in the United States and Europe, and by the desire of the U.S. to bring down its own huge trade deficit and reduce its role as an international debtor.

SUMMARY

1. The foreign exchange market is the market in which the various national currencies are exchanged. The exchange rate is the price at which these currencies are exchanged. Exchange rates may be quoted as the number of units of foreign currency per unit of domestic currency or as units of domestic currency per unit of foreign currency. If the dollar is worth one-half of one pound sterling, the pound is worth two dollars.

2. Since the early 1970s, exchange rates have been unpegged and allowed to float in the market, although with occasional intervention by governments. Exchange rates change daily, sometime by a significant amount. If a currency rises in value or becomes worth more units of foreign currency, it is said to *appreciate*. If a currency falls in value, it *depreciates*.

3. The fundamental economic forces that cause changes in exchange rates are changes in relative price levels, relative incomes, and relative real interest rates among countries. Given other factors, the U.S. dollar appreciates against the German deutsche mark if the U.S. price level rises more slowly than the German price level, if U.S. income expands more slowly than German income, and if U.S. real interest rates increase relative to those in Germany.

4. Speculators attempt to forecast the behavior of the fundamental determinants underlying exchange rates and act according to these forecasts. For example, if speculators anticipate an increase in the Federal Reserve discount rate, they will foresee higher U.S. yields and thus immediately purchase dollars with yen, deutsche marks, and other currencies. Speculative activity is responsible for a major portion of intra-day exchange-rate movements. Interest rate movements are also reflected very quickly in exchange-rate changes. Relative income changes among nations influence exchange rates over a somewhat longer horizon and relative price level behavior is a long-run determinant of exchange rates.

5. The three fundamental determinants help to explain three major swings in the value of the U.S. dollar—the depreciation of 1975–1979, the rising dollar of 1980–1985, and the falling dollar of 1985–1988. The falling dollar of the 1970s is explained largely by the high U.S. inflation rate compared to that of other nations. Booming U.S. income and low real interest rates in the United States also explain the dollar's sustained depreciation. The soaring dollar of the 1980–1985 period was fueled principally by an enormous change in the net flow of capital in favor of the United States owing to sharply higher real interest rates here and the perception of this country as a favorable place to invest. The falling dollar of the late 1980s is not so clearly explained by fundamental factors. It is true that income expanded more rapidly at home than abroad and that the net real yield advantage here decreased. However, these factors are insufficient to account for the magnitude of the decline of the dollar. Speculation against the dollar accounts for much of the depreciation, especially after 1986.

6. A change in exchange rates has important implications for a nation's economy. When the dollar appreciates, domestic inflation is held down and the nation's terms of trade improve as each unit of our exports pays for more imports. However, exports are slowed, imports

are stimulated, and real domestic income is redistributed from those whose livelihood depends on the prosperity of the manufacturing and agricultural sectors to the masses of consumers who benefit from cheap imports. A depreciation of the dollar has the opposite consequences. Domestic inflation is boosted and the terms of trade worsen. The trade balance is tilted in the direction of a smaller deficit or larger surplus as exports increase relative to imports. Workers and firms in the sectors exposed to foreign competition benefit while the masses of consumers suffer a reduction in their real incomes because of higher prices of imports and, ultimately, domestic goods.

7. Governments sometimes intervene directly in foreign exchange markets to intentionally influence exchange rates. Hence, the system in place since the early 1970s has been a *managed float* and not a totally *free float*. Since governments sometimes intervene to deliberately manipulate the exchange rate in a direction perceived to be in that government's interest and contrary to the interest of other nations, the system has been dubbed the "dirty float."

8. During 1944–1973, world trade was based on a fixed exchange-rate system known as the "adjustable peg." Each nation agreed to support ("peg") its own currency when it tended to depreciate via direct purchases of the currency in the foreign exchange market. The knowledge that exchange rates would be constant from week to week was thought to be beneficial to a thriving system of trade. Unfortunately, nations whose currencies were prone to depreciate were forced to bear the entire burden of the adjustment to the disequilibrium. Strong-currency nations typically refused to alter their policies. Weak-currency nations were forced to either implement restrictive trade measures or attempt to force down their domestic price structure to regain competitiveness. Barring successful correction of balance of payments deficits via these measures, nations could only throw in the towel and devalue—peg their currency at a new, lower value relative to other nations.

9. A nation's balance of payments is an organized tabulation of its financial transactions with other nations. The *current account* summarizes all transactions in currently produced goods and services. The *capital account* tabulates capital movements across borders—changes in holdings of such assets as real estate, securities, and bank accounts between countries. Except for a statistical discrepancy owing to imperfection in data collection, the capital account and the current account sum to zero. That is, the overall balance of payments is always zero.

10. In the 1980s, the United States experienced burgeoning deficits in its international balance on merchandise trade, goods and services, and current accounts. This implies an equivalent offsetting change in the capital account—a massive net inflow of foreign capital. This reversed the experience of the previous seven decades, in which the United States exhibited persistent surpluses in current account and was a net exporter of capital to the rest of the world. This role reversal is basically attributable to a major increase in the desire to invest funds in the United States in the 1980s. This, in turn, is accounted for chiefly by the phenomenal increase in real interest rates in this country in the early 1980s.

KEY TERMS

foreign exchange market	terms of trade
foreign exchange rate	dirty float
capital flows	adjustable-peg system
currency depreciation	parity or par value
currency appreciation	international reserves
floating exchange rates	overvalued currencies
fixed exchange rates	balance of payments
purchasing power parity theory (PPP)	current account
	balance of trade
foreign exchange market speculators	capital account

STUDY QUESTIONS AND PROBLEMS

1. What does it mean to say the U.S. dollar "depreciates" in foreign exchange markets? If the U.S. exchange rate with Italy moves from 1600 lire per dollar to 2000 lire per dollar, does the dollar appreciate or depreciate? What about the lira?

2. Focusing on the United States-Italy exchange rate, draw appropriate supply and demand curves and label them and the axes. Explain the reasons for the slopes of the supply and demand curves. What is the equilibrium exchange rate in your drawing?

3. Consider the United States-France exchange rate, expressed as francs per dollar. Analyze the effects of each of the following events on the value of the dollar, assuming other factors remain constant. Utilize the appropriate supply–demand framework.
   a. Income in France rises.
   b. The Fed raises U.S. interest rates.
   c. The U.S. price level rises five percent.
   d. Adidas (in France) introduces a highly attractive new line of tennis shoes.
   e. The U.S. announces new tariffs on all French goods.
   f. A new "buy-American" ethic is promoted in this country.
   g. U.S. budget deficits are eliminated.

4. Explain the purchasing power parity theory of foreign exchange rates and the intuition underlying it. Why do you suppose PPP does a better job of tracking the U.S.-Mexico exchange rate in the 1980s than the U.S.-Japan exchange rate?

5. Under what set of conditions would purchasing power parity exchange rates always precisely prevail? Explain.

6. Suppose you are employed by an investment bank as a foreign-exchange-rate analyst. The investment bank is involved in taking positions in various currencies. New U.S. inflation figures have been released, and they reveal that inflation is running lower than expected. What advice would you give your investment bank?

7. Explain the rationale underlying the following: "The policy of the Japanese central bank of supporting the dollar or holding down the yen via direct foreign exchange market transactions is equivalent to Japan placing a tariff on U.S. goods."

8. Explain why a depreciating or appreciating U.S. dollar affects the U.S. inflation rate.

9. Given that a strong dollar in foreign exchange markets holds down U.S. inflation and raises our standard of living, why would anyone oppose measures that cause the dollar to appreciate strongly?

10. Using a supply and demand framework, show how a government in a pegged exchange-rate system prevents the exchange rate from fluctuating. Why might the government at some point be unable to continue to do this?

11. Do you feel governments should intervene to *manage* the exchange rate or withdraw and permit a *free float*? Defend your answer.

12. What are the drawbacks of the Bretton-Woods adjustable-peg exchange-rate system of 1944–1973? Why was it abandoned? Should we return to it in the 1990s?

13. In what sense can one say that the large U.S. trade deficits of the 1980s were a "bad" thing? A "good" thing?

14. Outline the causes and consequences of the simmering LDC debt crises. What steps could the United States take to ease the burden of this debt and make it easier for the LDCs to meet their payments?

ANSWERS TO YOUR TURN

The announcement indicates to the world financial community that German short-term interest rates will be increasing. This will ultimately cause the deutsche mark to appreciate (dollar to depreciate) as net demand for German securities (and deutsche marks) increases. Also, the announcement signals the German intent to keep inflation in check, which is bullish for the deutsche mark. For these reasons, speculators will immediately buy marks (sell dollars) upon the announcement. The mark will appreciate and the dollar will depreciate.

SELECTED REFERENCES

Economic Report of the President (Washington, DC: U.S. Government Printing Office, published annually). This document analyzes recent international financial developments as they pertain to the U.S. economy.

Kreinin, Mordechai E., *International Economics: A Policy Approach,* 5th ed. (New York: Harcourt Brace Jovanovich, 1987). This textbook in international economics amplifies on the topics presented in this chapter. See especially chapters 2, 3, 4, and 7.

Lindert, Peter H., *International Economics,* 8th ed. (Homewood, IL: Richard D. Irwin, 1986). This international economics textbook covers all the issues analyzed in this chapter.

CHAPTER 38

THE ECONOMICS OF LESS DEVELOPED COUNTRIES

From our individual points of view, the earth seems large. Even in our own neighborhoods there are people we do not know and places we are not invited to go, so people and places in other countries seem unrelated to us. But from the cosmic viewpoint evoked by Whitman and Stevenson, the whole earth is best thought of as a spaceship and the earth's whole population as fellow passengers. The spaceship metaphor expresses the essential unity of the human race. The earth seems immense to individuals, but it is unimaginably small in relation to the whole of creation. And human communities, even those that have existed for a few thousand years, are very recent events in a universe perhaps 15 billion years old. In light of the stupendous size and age of the universe, our earth is miniscule and all of human life very recent and fleeting. Wisdom requires us to be sensitive to the human condition in all segments of our small planet-spaceship.

One thought ever at the fore—
That in the Divine Ship, the World, breasting Time and Space,
All peoples of the globe together sail, sail the same voyage,
Are bound to the same destination.

—WALT WHITMAN

We travel together, passengers on a little spaceship, dependent on its vulnerable reserves of air and soil; all committed for our safety to its security and peace; preserved from annihilation only by the care, the work, and I will say the love we give our fragile craft. We cannot maintain it half fortunate, half miserable, half confident, half despairing, half slave to the ancient enemies of man. . . . No craft, no crew can travel safely with such vast contradictions. On their resolution depends the survival of us all.

—ADLAI STEVENSON

THE DIVISION OF THE WORLD INTO DEVELOPED AND LESS DEVELOPED COUNTRIES

Less Developed Countries (LDCs) Countries in which living standards are low because modern technology generally has not been applied to production processes.

The economic principles discussed in this book are applicable everywhere; nevertheless most of their applications and factual content relate to the United States, which is one of about 25 economically *developed* countries. In these countries science-based technology is applied to production processes in all major sectors (agriculture, industry, and services) and, as a consequence, production per worker is high. The high output per worker is the fundamental reason why economic well-being is generally high in developed countries.

In contrast, most of the people on the earth today live in countries that have not yet applied technology to production problems in all sectors. In these **less developed countries (LDCs),** production per worker is generally low and, consequently, levels of economic well-being are low. Chapter 38 analyzes the economics of the LDCs.

CLASSIFYING COUNTRIES BY LEVELS OF OUTPUT PER PERSON

There are approximately 165 countries in the world. Of these, 129 in 1986 had populations in excess of 1 million persons. Table 38-1 (pages 876–77) arranges 110 of these countries from low to high per-capita production (comparative production data are inadequate for 19 other countries, so their positions are approximate). The table gives the six categories into which the World Bank divides the 129 countries: low-income, lower middle-income, upper middle-income, high-income oil exporters, industrial market economies, and nonreporting nonmembers of the World Bank.[1] There is widespread agreement that all the low-income and lower middle-income countries, most of the upper middle-income countries, and a few of the nonreporting nonmember countries are LDCs. The industrial market countries, a few of the upper middle-income countries, and a few of the nonreporting nonmember countries are developed countries.

Table 38-1 also gives the population of each country. In 1986, approximately three-quarters of the world's population lived in LDCs. This means that the economics discussed in this chapter is relevant for three-quarters of the human race.

The countries are ranked by level of per-capita production, not by total production, because we are interested in the economic well-being of people. Although total production (GNP) in China or India is much larger than in Sweden or Denmark, the level of economic well-being is not nearly as high. Total

---

[1]The World Bank (also known as the International Bank for Reconstruction and Development) is the major international institution involved in economic development. It is an important source of finance for development and for research into development problems. (Most statistical data used in this chapter are taken from its extremely valuable annual *World Development Report.)* The World Bank was created in 1944 at the same time as the International Monetary Fund. Both have their headquarters in Washington, D.C.

TABLE 38-1

POPULATION AND PER-CAPITA PRODUCTION, 1986

Countries	Population (millions) mid-1986	Per-capita output (1986 dollars)	Countries	Population (millions) mid-1986	Per-capita output (1986 dollars)
Low-income economies	**2,493.0**	**270**	Chad	5.1	—
Ethiopia	43.5	120	*Guinea*	6.3	—
Bhutan	1.3	150	*Kampuchea*	—	—
Burkina Faso	8.1	150	Lao PDR	3.7	—
Nepal	17.0	150	*Vietnam*	63.3	—
Bangladesh	103.2	160	**Lower middle-income**	**691.2**	**750**
Malawi	7.4	160	Liberia	2.3	460
Zaire	31.7	160	Yemen, PDR	2.2	470
Mali	7.6	180	Indonesia	166.4	490
Burma	38.0	200	Yemen, Arab Republic	8.2	550
Mozambique	14.2	210	Philippines	57.3	560
Madagascar	10.6	230	Morocco	22.5	590
Uganda	15.2	230	Bolivia	6.6	600
Burundi	4.8	240	Zimbabwe	8.7	620
Tanzania	23.0	250	Nigeria	103.1	640
Togo	3.1	250	Dominican Republic	6.6	710
Niger	6.6	260	Papua New Guinea	3.4	720
Benin	4.2	270	Côte d'Ivoire	10.7	730
Somalia	5.5	280	Honduras	4.5	740
Central African Republic	2.7	290	Egypt, Arab Republic	49.7	760
India	781.4	290	Nicaragua	3.4	790
Rwanda	6.2	290	Thailand	52.6	810
China	1054.0	300	El Salvador	4.9	820
Kenya	21.2	300	Botswana	1.1	840
Zambia	6.9	300	Jamaica	2.4	840
Sierra Leone	3.8	310	Cameroon	10.5	910
Sudan	22.6	320	Guatemala	8.2	930
Haiti	6.1	330	Congo, People's Republic	2.0	990
Pakistan	99.2	350	Paraguay	3.8	1,000
Lesotho	1.6	370	Peru	19.8	1,090
Ghana	13.2	390	Turkey	51.5	1,110
Sri Lanka	16.1	400	Tunisia	7.3	1,140
Mauritania	1.8	420	Ecuador	9.6	1,160
Senegal	6.8	420	Mauritius	1.0	1,200
Afghanistan	—	—			

production may be a good indicator of national power (China is probably a more *powerful* country than Sweden) but not of economic well-being.

Table 38-2 (page 878) narrows our focus to 33 countries that together account for about three-fourths of the world's population.[2] As before, the countries are

---

[2]Each of these 33 countries has a population in excess of 20 million. Only 6 countries with populations in excess of 20 million are not included here: North Korea, Poland, Rumania, USSR, Vietnam, and Yugoslavia.

Countries	Population (millions) mid-1986	Per-capita output (1986 dollars)	Countries	Population (millions) mid-1986	Per-capita output (1986 dollars)
Colombia	29.0	1,230	United Arab Emirates	1.4	14,680
Chile	12.2	1,320	*Libya*	3.9	—
Costa Rica	2.6	1,480			
Jordan	3.6	1,540	**Industrial market economies**	**741.6**	**12,960**
Syrian Arab Republic	10.8	1,570	Spain	38.7	4,860
Lebanon	—	—	Ireland	3.6	5,070
			New Zealand	3.3	7,460
Upper middle-income	**577.2**	**1,890**	Italy	57.2	8,550
			United Kingdom	56.7	8,870
Brazil	138.4	1,810			
Malaysia	16.1	1,830	Belgium	9.9	9,230
South Africa	32.3	1,850	Austria	7.6	9,990
Mexico	80.2	1,860	Netherlands	14.6	10,020
Uruguay	3.0	1,900	France	55.4	10,720
			Australia	16.0	11,920
Hungary	10.6	2,020			
Poland	37.5	2,070	Germany, Federal Republic	60.9	12,080
Portugal	10.2	2,250	Finland	4.9	12,160
Yugoslavia	23.3	2,300	Denmark	5.1	12,600
Panama	2.2	2,330	Japan	121.5	12,840
			Sweden	8.4	13,160
Argentina	31.0	2,350			
Korea, Republic of	41.5	2,370	Canada	25.6	14,120
Algeria	22.4	2,590	Norway	4.2	15,400
Venezuela	7.8	2,920	United States	241.6	17,480
Gabon	1.0	3,080	Switzerland	6.5	17,680
Greece	10.0	3,680	**Nonreporting nonmembers**	**367.3**	**—**
Oman	1.3	4,980	*Albania*	3.0	—
Trinidad and Tobago	1.2	5,360	*Angola*	9.0	—
Israel	4.3	6,210	*Bulgaria*	9.0	—
Hong Kong	5.4	6,910	*Cuba*	10.2	—
			Czechoslovakia	15.5	—
Singapore	2.6	7,410			
Iran, Islamic Republic	45.6	—	*German Democratic Republic*	16.6	—
Iraq	16.5	—	*Korea, Democratic Republic of*	20.9	—
Romania	22.9	—	*Mongolia*	2.0	—
			USSR	281.1	—
High-income oil exporters	**19.1**	**6,740**			
Saudi Arabia	12.0	6,950			
Kuwait	1.8	13,890			

Source: World Bank, *World Development Report, 1988.*

arranged in order from low to high per-capita incomes in 1986. While there is no universally acceptable criterion by which to classify a country as developed or less developed, there is widespread agreement with the classification of these 33 large countries as 25 LDCs and 8 developed countries.

The figures in Table 38-2 show an enormous range in per-capita production, from Ethiopia and Bangladesh at the *poor* extreme to Canada and the United States

TABLE 38-2

PER-CAPITA PRODUCTION FOR SELECTED COUNTRIES, 1986

Countries	In U.S. dollars (using market exchange rate)	Index relative to U.S. =100 (using market exchange rate)	Index relative to U.S. =100 (using purchasing power exchange rate)
Less developed			
Ethiopia	120	0.7	2.4
Bangladesh	160	0.9	5.1
Zaire	160	0.9	1.3
Burma	200	1.1	4.3
Tanzania	250	1.4	3.2
India	290	1.7	6.0
Kenya	300	1.7	4.5
China	300	1.7	7.0
Sudan	320	1.8	4.3
Pakistan	350	2.0	9.0
Indonesia	490	2.8	9.7
Philippines	560	3.2	10.7
Morocco	590	3.4	9.9
Nigeria	640	3.7	4.2
Egypt	760	4.3	9.0
Thailand	810	4.6	14.4
Turkey	1110	6.4	19.7
Colombia	1230	7.0	20.1
Brazil	1810	10.4	24.8
South Africa	1850	10.6	28.5
Mexico	1860	10.6	29.5
Argentina	2350	13.4	25.9
Korea	2370	13.6	23.3
Algeria	2590	14.8	15.7
Iran	—	—	30.5
Developed			
Spain	4860	27.8	49.1
Italy	8550	48.9	57.5
Britain	8870	50.7	67.7
France	10,720	61.3	77.8
Germany	12,080	69.1	79.9
Japan	12,840	73.5	69.6
Canada	14,120	80.8	90.6
United States	17,480	100.0	100.0

Source: Adapted from World Bank, *World Development Report, 1988.*

at the *rich* extreme. These production differences are an indication that the levels of economic well-being also show an enormous range.

Notice that the range of incomes *within* the LDC category is wider than the range within the developed country category. That is, the differences in economic performance between say Ethiopia and Algeria, countries within the less-developed category, are much larger than the differences between say Spain and the United States, countries within the developed country category.

The per-capita income figures used to arrange the countries from poor to rich are all expressed in U.S. dollars. In Chapter 9 you learned how GNP is measured in the United States. The per-capita income figure for the United States is found simply by dividing the 1986 U.S. GNP figure by the 1986 U.S. population. The figures for the other countries in Table 38-2 require an additional step. Because each country has its own currency, its per-capita GNP is first reckoned using its own currency. Then these figures must be converted into U.S. dollars before a country can be ranked in the table. For example, India's GNP is measured using the Indian currency, the rupee. Dividing this GNP figure by India's population gives India's per-capita GNP in rupees. But comparison with other countries requires all figures to be in the same currency units. India's per-capita GNP in rupees is converted into its dollar equivalent using the 1986 dollar–rupee exchange rate (about 12 rupees to the dollar). A similar procedure is used for all the other countries. (Each value in column two of Table 38-2 is obtained using existing exchange rates.) To facilitate comparisons, column three sets the United States at 100 percent and lists all other countries relative to the United States. Thus, for example, the table shows Brazil's per-capita production to be 10.4 percent of U.S. per-capita production.

This standard comparison makes the gaps between a poor country like India and a rich country like the United States appear very large. Specifically, it appears that 1986 average incomes in the United States were about 60 times larger than in India ($17,480/$290 = 60)! We hope you suspect that there is something unrealistic about this. Imagine your parents offering to give you $290 to live on for the next year. This would be your entire income. Is it realistic to think that you could survive for a whole year on so little?

MEASURING GAPS USING PURCHASING-POWER EXCHANGE RATES

Research has shown that the exchange rates used for the preceding comparisons systematically underestimate the real production that takes place in the LDCs. The exchange rate of about 12 rupees per U.S. dollar turns out to be an unrealistic estimate of the real purchasing power of the rupee in India. In other words, 12 rupees in India actually purchase more than 1 dollar purchases in the United States. In fact, the evidence is that 12 rupees buy about three times more than 1 dollar purchases—that is, three times more than the exchange rate indicates.

Exchange rates are heavily influenced by the market prices of the goods that enter international trade, but not by the prices of goods and services that cannot enter international trade (e.g., haircuts and housing). Compared to goods traded internationally, nontradable goods and services are relatively low-priced and relatively abundant in LDCs.

Because the exchange-rate method of measuring income gaps leads to serious problems, a major effort has been made to obtain more realistic comparisons.[3] The

---

[3]The International Comparison Project has been a joint responsibility of the United Nations Statistical Office, the World Bank, and researchers at the University of Pennsylvania. It began with detailed purchasing-power comparisons of just 6 countries for 1967, but its coverage has grown over time to include 60 countries for 1980—and work continues.

result of this effort is **purchasing-power exchange rates (PP)**, which take into account the purchasing power of a country's currency over the entire range of goods and services. These purchasing-power exchange rates are then used to make the conversions to U.S. dollars. The results for 1985 are given in column four of Table 38-2, again with the United States set at 100 percent and all other countries listed relative to the United States. The table shows that India's per-capita GNP is 6.0 percent of U.S. GNP (about 1/17), not the 1.7 percent (about 1/60) derived earlier. Such purchasing-power based comparisons are the best available estimates of the real differences in per-capita GNP.

Although the relative gaps between poor and rich countries are smaller using the PP exchange rates rather than the standard exchange rates, they are still quite large. The poorest countries in Africa and Asia have average incomes that are less than 5 percent of the U.S. level. The large developed countries of western Europe have per-capita production levels 10 to 12 times higher than the India-Bangladesh-Pakistan levels.

How the Gaps Emerged

How did these differences in living standards emerge? Why is per-capita production so much higher in developed countries? The short answer to these complex questions is that over the last 100–150 years or so the developed countries have experienced more rapid rates of growth in per-capita production than the LDCs.

Even small differences in rates of growth can result in wide gaps after only a century or so. To understand this we must first review the simple math of growth rates (sometimes called the simple math of *compound interest*). Table 38-3 gives the results of various annual rates of growth over selected time periods. For example, an initial sum of $1 million growing at 2 percent per year compounded once each year increases to $2.7 million after 50 years, $7.2 million after 100 years, and $52.5 million after 200 years. Also indicated for each growth rate is the *doubling time*: the number of years required for a quantity to double.[4] Anything growing at 2 percent per year doubles in only 35 years. For illustrative purposes, a growth rate of 7 percent is included; this rate has a doubling time of only 10 years. After 100 years, anything growing at 7 percent is 868 times larger than when it started. It is obvious that no economy can grow at 7 percent per year for very long. The basic point stressed here is that even *low* growth rates extended for a century or more lead to extremely large increases.

We can now use this information to explore the emergence of the gaps between rich countries and LDCs. It is clear that today's gap of, say, 12 to 1 between developed countries and LDCs could emerge after only 100 years from even small differences in growth rates. If two countries start at the same productivity level but the first does not grow at all and the second grows at 2 percent, the second will produce at a level 7.2 times higher after only 100 years. It is almost certain that 100 years ago the European countries that are developed today already had somewhat higher output per capita than the Asian countries that are less developed today. Assume the gap 100 years ago was already 2 to 1. If in the last 100 years the

---

[4]The so-called "Rule of 70" can be used to approximate the doubling time. When the number 70 is divided by a growth rate, the result is the approximate doubling time. For example, something growing at 3 percent doubles in just over 23 years (70/3 = 23.3).

TABLE 38-3					
CONSEQUENCES OF VARIOUS RATES OF GROWTH*					
Year	**0%**	**1%**	**2%**	**3%**	**7%**
0	1.0	1.0	1.0	1.0	1.0
10	1.0	1.1	1.2	1.3	2.0
50	1.0	1.6	2.7	4.4	29.5
100	1.0	2.7	7.2	19.2	867.7
200	1.0	7.3	52.5	369.4	752931.6
Doubling times (years)		69.7	35.0	23.4	10.2

*The table indicates how much one unit grows when compounded at various growth rates for various lengths of time. One unit may be viewed as millions of dollars, thousand of people, and so forth.

European countries grew at 1.8 percent while the Asian LDCs were stagnant, the 12 to 1 gap we now observe would emerge. We conclude that the current gaps between developed countries and LDCs are probably best understood as the consequence of a speeding up in growth rates in developed countries in the last century or so, causing them to move far ahead of the relatively stagnant LDCs.

The Industrial Revolution began in Britain about 200 years ago and then spread out from Britain to a number of other European countries, and to Europe's offshoots abroad—Canada, the United States, Australia, and New Zealand.[5] These countries—plus Japan with its spectacular economic performance over the last century—are today's developed countries. In contrast, the LDCs are those countries—containing about three-quarters of the world's current population—that have not yet experienced fully the application of science-based technology to production.[6]

CHARACTERISTICS OF LESS DEVELOPED COUNTRIES

The major characteristic of LDCs—that which distinguishes them from the developed countries—is the low level of production and income per person. But money figures on per-capita production (and income) are inadequate to convey the level of economic well-being. For example, hundreds of millions of people in LDCs suffer from poor health and inadequate education.

One of the saddest facts about LDCs is their high infant mortality rate, defined as the number of babies who die before their first birthday per 1000 live births. Table 38-4 (page 882) gives the extremely high levels in many LDCs. Related to infant mortality is short *life expectancy,* measured as the number of years a newborn can expect to live given current patterns of mortality. In the poorest LDCs life expectancies are in the 45–50 year range; without exception the developed countries have life expectancies in excess of 70 years. Not given in the table are improvements in these indices during recent decades. As bad as health conditions are in LDCs, they are better now than they used to be.

[5]It is now recognized that we should speak of both an "industrial" and an "agricultural" revolution in Britain and other developed countries. Agricultural productivity increased as a consequence of increasing knowledge of plants, animals, fertilizers, and so forth.
[6]The classic treatment of these topics is Simon Kuznets, *Modern Economic Growth: Rate, Structure and Spread* (New Haven, CT: Yale University Press, 1966).

	TABLE 38-4				

SOME INDICATORS OF ECONOMIC WELL-BEING FOR SELECTED
COUNTRIES, 1986

Countries	Infant mortality (deaths per 1000 births)	Life expectancy (years)	Calories (% of requirements)	Secondary enrollment (% of age group)	Per-capita energy consumption (kg of oil equivalent/year)
Less developed					
Ethiopia	155	46	93	12	21
Bangladesh	121	50	81	18	46
Zaire	100	52	96	57	73
Burma	64	59	117	24	76
Tanzania	108	53	98	3	35
India	86	57	96	35	208
China	34	69	111	39	532
Kenya	74	57	83	20	100
Sudan	108	49	90	19	58
Pakistan	111	52	95	17	205
Indonesia	87	57	110	39	213
Philippines	46	63	104	65	180
Morocco	85	60	105	31	246
Nigeria	104	51	86	29	134
Egypt	88	61	126	62	577
Thailand	41	64	105	30	325
Turkey	79	65	123	42	750
Colombia	47	65	110	50	728
Brazil	65	65	106	35	830
South Africa	74	61	118		2470
Mexico	48	68	126	55	1235
Argentina	33	70	119	70	1427
Korea	25	69	118	94	1408
Algeria	77	62	115	45	1034
Iran	109	59	118	46	958
Developed					
Spain	11	76	143	91	1928
Italy	10	77	140	75	2539
Britain	9	75	128	89	3802
France	8	77	139	96	3640
Germany	9	75	130	74	4464
Japan	6	78	113	96	3186
Canada	8	76	130	103	8945
United States	10	75	137	99	7193

Sources: Adapted from World Bank, *World Development Report, 1986* and *1988.*

Relatively high infant mortality and short life expectancy are due in part to unsafe water and inadequate food. Whereas most people living in developed countries take for granted clean drinking water and sanitary waste disposal, it has been estimated that one-fourth of the world's population lack such resources. The situation is particularly bad in rural areas of Africa and Asia, where perhaps four-fifths of the inhabitants lack access to clean water.[7]

It is not easy to summarize the food situation in the LDCs. Calorie supply as a percentage of essential calorie requirements is given in Table 38-4. These figures cannot take into account either seasonal differences in food availability or, more importantly, unequal distribution of food to persons in LDCs. Thus even when an LDC's figure is above 100 percent, it is certain that some inadequate nutrition exists. And, clearly, when an LDC's figure is near or below 100 percent, serious nutrition problems exist. This and other information support the conclusion that hundreds of millions of people have inadequate amounts of nutrients (calories, proteins, vitamins, and minerals) during all or part of the year.

Parents in LDCs have inadequate access to schooling for their children. Whereas in developed countries almost all the secondary school-age population is enrolled in secondary school, in most LDCs secondary enrollments are much lower (Table 38-4). Primary school-age enrollments in LDCs (not given) have increased dramatically in recent decades, but caution is appropriate when using these figures because they are unable to measure the quality of the educational services available. In many extremely poor LDCs the *teachers* in primary schools are themselves just primary school graduates with scant additional training. Unlike developed countries, most teachers in LDCs are not college graduates. In addition, the facilities and educational materials available to the students are often severely limited in both quantity and quality. So the educational services available to primary students may not be as adequate as the enrollment numbers seem to indicate.

Energy consumption per person is very low in LDCs. Table 38-4 gives the annual per-capita "oil-equivalent" energy consumption. Firewood and such traditional fuels as dung used in LDCs are not included in the totals because of measurement problems; however, their inclusion would not change the overall picture. The gap between developed countries and LDCs shown by these figures is staggering. In many LDCs there is a serious shortage of fuelwoods, with hundreds of millions of persons depending on wood that is being cut faster than it can be replaced.[8] In the developed countries, the gargantuan energy appetite is a matter of grave economic and ecological concern. A large share of these energy needs are met by *exhaustible* fossil fuels that ultimately must be replaced by other energy sources. In addition, we now know that the carbon dioxide resulting from the combustion of fossil fuels exceeds the biosphere's ability to recycle, thus causing the *greenhouse effect* and consequent rise in atmospheric temperature. To the extent that increased productivity and incomes in LDCs are accompanied by increased use of exhaustible fossil fuels, as is highly likely, these problems will only increase. Clearly, the energy problems on spaceship earth require attention.

POPULATION GROWTH IS RAPID IN LDCs

The Demographic Transition

We now turn to perhaps the most important characteristic of LDCs—their rapid population growth. Before discussing LDC population problems in some

---

[7]Lester R. Brown et al., *State of the World 1986* (New York: Norton, 1986), pp. 167–68.
[8]Same as 7, Ch. 5, "Reforesting the Earth."

Demographic Transition
The transition from a society experiencing high birth and death rates to low birth and death rates; in the transition, the decline in birthrates lags the decline in death rates, leading to rapid population growth.

detail, a little population history is in order. Such population history is referred to as the **demographic transition,** and is illustrated in Figure 38-1. Until recent centuries, in all countries birth and death rates were high, with birthrates exceeding death rates by only a very small amount—so world population growth was very slow. For most of human history, zero population growth was the rule rather than the exception. In other words, Phase 1 in Figure 38-1 encompasses most of human history. The phase lasted for thousands of years, right up to recent times.

Today a number of developed countries are experiencing little or no population growth; in these countries birth and death rates are approximately equal to each other, with both at low levels. Such countries are already in Phase 3, having completed the demographic transition from a traditional society in which both birth and death rates are high and approximately equal to each other (Phase 1) to a modern developed society in which both birth and death rates are low and approximately equal to each other (Phase 3). For such developed countries, Phase 2 generally lasted a century or two, during which the gap between birth and death rates was probably not as large as shown in the figure.

The basic fact about the present world population is that most developed countries have completed the demographic transition from high birth and death rates to low birth and death rates, but most LDCs are only part way through the transition. LDC death rates have fallen, but LDC birthrates have not yet fallen sufficiently to approximately equal the lower death rates—so population in most LDCs is growing rapidly. In terms of Figure 38-1, today's LDCs are still in Phase 2. Some LDCs (e.g., those in sub-Saharan Africa) are in the early part of the phase, with birthrates still at traditionally high levels, while many other LDCs are in the latter part of the phase, with birthrates falling but remaining significantly above death rates.

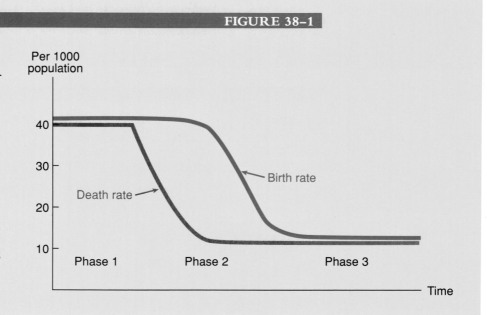

FIGURE 38–1

DEMOGRAPHIC TRANSITION

In the first phase of development, both birthrates and death rates are high and zero population growth prevails. In the second phase, the declining death rate precedes the declining birthrate, and population growth is rapid. In the final phase, the birthrate declines sufficiently to dramatically slow population growth. Economically advanced nations are in phase three; LDCs are in phase two.

Because the population cannot grow indefinitely on a finite planet, birthrates and death rates must eventually come into approximate equality. This means that for the world as a whole, and for each country, Phase 2 must be a temporary phase. Much depends on how long it takes for LDCs to complete the demographic transition and move into Phase 3.[9]

Why Population Grows Rapidly in LDCs

Table 38-5 (page 886) reports prospective average annual population growth rates for the period 1986–2000. The rates exceed 2 percent in 16 of the 25 LDCs, leading as we saw earlier to doubling in 35 years. Only in relatively high-income Argentina and Korea, and in China with its intrusive government, is the rate less than 1.6 percent. Extremely high rates, in excess of 3 percent per year (leading to doubling in less than 25 years), occur in numerous African LDCs. In no LDC in the table is the expected rate below 1.1 percent. In sharp contrast, in *none* of the developed countries is the expected rate higher than 0.7 percent. These different population growth rates sharply divide developed countries and LDCs.

Population is growing rapidly in LDCs because births exceed deaths. Table 38-5 gives birthrates and death rates for 1986. In recent decades—with the introduction of modern medicine and improved transportation that reduce deaths from periodic famines—LDC death rates have fallen. Population is growing rapidly in LDCs at present because of the gap between the unchanged high birthrates and the now lower death rates (Phase 2).

Why are birthrates still high in LDCs? It had been thought that parents in LDCs had more children than they wanted because of their lack of knowledge about contraceptives or because of limited availability of contraceptives. If it were indeed the case that the *actual* number of children exceeds the *desired* number of children, the increased provision of contraceptives would bring about a reduction of the population growth rate. For this reason, many early population-control programs focused on making contraceptives available. But we now know that a more fundamental reason exists. Parents may *desire* many children because children become productive at an early age or because having many children ensures that one or more survives into adulthood to be able to look after the parents in their old age. In the absence of anything like a social security system, in most traditional societies aged parents are looked after by their children. Thus, high fertility rates are *traditional.* For countless generations parents had to conceive and bear many children to ensure that some of the babies would survive high infant and child mortality and become adults. In summary, rapid population growth in LDCs occurs not because parents have more children than they want but because parents want a large number of children.

This is both good news and bad news. The good news is that *if* parents have many children in order to increase the probability that one or more become adults, the decrease in infant and child mortality seen in recent years will by itself eventually cause the desired number of children to decrease as parents come to understand and act upon the knowledge that they do not need six or eight children

---

[9]It is useful to make clear why the low birth and death rates of Phase 3 are desirable. A long average life expectancy requires a low death rate. To the extent that societies prefer long lives over short lives, death rates must be low. But the finite nature of the planet requires essentially zero population growth. So birthrates must equal death rates, and must therefore also be low.

	TABLE 38-5				
	POPULATION CHARACTERISTICS FOR SELECTED COUNTRIES*				
Countries	Population (millions)		Expected growth rate 1986–2000 (%)	Birth rate (per 1000)	Death rate (per 1000)	Dependency rate
	1986	2000				
Less developed						
Ethiopia	43	65	2.9	47	19	96
Bangladesh	103	145	2.5	41	15	89
Zaire	32	48	3.0	45	15	96
Burma	38	52	2.3	33	10	85
Tanzania	23	37	3.4	50	15	100
India	781	1002	1.8	32	12	79
China	1054	1279	1.4	19	7	54
Kenya	21	36	3.9	52	12	122
Sudan	23	34	2.9	45	16	92
Pakistan	99	150	3.0	47	15	89
Indonesia	166	207	1.8	28	11	79
Philippines	57	76	2.3	35	7	79
Morocco	22	30	2.2	33	10	92
Nigeria	103	164	3.3	50	16	104
Egypt	50	67	2.2	34	10	82
Thailand	53	65	1.6	25	7	69
Turkey	51	67	1.9	29	8	75
Colombia	29	37	1.8	27	7	69
Brazil	138	180	1.9	29	8	69
South Africa	32	45	2.3	34	10	82
Mexico	80	107	2.1	29	6	85
Argentina	31	36	1.1	23	9	67
Korea	41	49	1.2	20	6	56
Algeria	22	33	2.9	40	9	104
Iran	46	69	3.0	41	10	89
Developed						
Spain	39	41	0.4	13	9	54
Italy	57	58	0.1	10	10	49
Britain	57	58	0.1	13	12	54
France	55	58	0.4	14	10	52
Germany	61	59	−0.3	10	12	43
Japan	121	129	0.5	12	7	47
Canada	26	28	0.7	15	7	47
United States	242	263	0.6	16	9	52

*Population for the year 1986 is actual; population for the year 2000 is projected. The final three columns reflect data for 1986.
Source: Adapted from World Bank, *World Development Report, 1988.*

to be sure of having one or two survive to become adults. The bad news is that it is harder to bring about the reductions in desired family size than it is to provide contraceptives.

Consequences of Rapid Population Growth

Rapid population growth has several important economic consequences. The first is that it causes a high **dependency rate,** defined as the number of nonworkers per 100 workers in the population. Table 38-5 shows the dependency rate based on the assumption that persons aged 15–64 are "workers" and persons aged 0–14 and above 64 are "nonworkers." The dependency rate is much higher for LDCs than for developed countries, because in a rapidly growing population a relatively large proportion of its members are young. (In LDCs the increased proportion of persons aged 0–14 more than makes up for the reduced proportion aged 64 and older.) The table shows that 100 workers in the poorest LDCs must support about twice as many dependents as do 100 workers in developed countries. The LDCs' low ratio of workers to total population in conjunction with the low output per worker causes the low output/population ratio (the low per-capita income) that characterizes LDCs.

A second economic consequence of rapid population growth is the existence of **population momentum,** which is defined as the tendency of a population to continue to increase even after the replacement level of fertility has been reached. The **replacement level of fertility** occurs when two parents replace themselves with two children. Most LDCs have fertility rates far above the replacement level: parents generally have more than two children. LDC populations are expected to grow rapidly for a long time to come because their fertility rates will be above replacement levels for a long time to come. But even if LDC fertility rates decreased immediately to the replacement level—so that beginning now all future couples would limit themselves to two children—the population would continue growing for a long time because of the disproportionately large number of youngsters (potential parents) already alive. Thus rapid population growth in the past guarantees some population growth in the future. Just as a fast-moving train does not stop immediately when its brakes are applied, a population does not stop growing immediately even when all couples decide to limit themselves to two children. Moving trains and rapidly growing populations have momentum.

The World Bank has estimated the magnitude of population momentum—the increase in population that would occur during the period from 1985 until population growth ceased—on the unrealistically optimistic assumption that the replacement level of fertility was reached in 1985. In none of the 25 LDCs we have been examining is the estimated population increase after 1985 less than 50 percent. In fully 18 of the 25 countries the increase is at least 80 percent. This is a truly dismaying prospect. It means that even with the most optimistic scenario imaginable, LDCs will have to cope with much larger populations in the near future.

The third important economic consequence of rapid population growth is that it causes a rapid growth in the labor force. We learn in the next section that this alone can slow down the growth of labor productivity—output per man-hour—which is the basic source of improved economic well-being.

The upshot of this discussion is that rapid population growth is a serious problem for LDCs and that a slowing down of the population growth rate would make a contribution to economic well-being.[10]

---

[10]While most of us can agree that birthrates must fall, there is now and perhaps will continue to be substantial disagreement about the morality, the legality, and the practicality of the various means capable of bringing this about (e.g., various methods of contraception or abortion).

Dependency rate
The number of people not working per 100 workers in the population.

Population Momentum
The tendency of population to continue to increase even when the average couple bears two children; this phenomenon is attributable to the disproportionate number of youth in the population.

Replacement Level of Fertility
The fertility level that exactly "replaces" the parents—that is, two children per couple.

THE AGRICULTURAL (RURAL) SECTOR IS IMPORTANT IN LDCs

The economic structure of the LDCs differs from the economic structure of the developed countries. By "structure" economists mean the relative importance of an economy's major sectors (agriculture, industry, and services) in production and employment. We limit the discussion here to agriculture's share of total labor force. Table 38-6 gives the percentage of each country's labor force engaged in agriculture.

The pattern is clear: the lower a country's per-capita income the greater the percentage of its labor force engaged in agriculture. In the poorest LDCs, more than 80 percent of the labor force is engaged in agriculture; in the richest developed countries, less than 10 percent is in agriculture.

The fundamental reason for this is consumer demand. When per-capita production and incomes are low, people spend large proportions of their low incomes on agricultural products. Thus, in poor countries agriculture accounts for large proportions of both production and consumption. International trade can modify the rigid link between a nation's production and consumption, but only infrequently can this cause the pattern to be broken.

The data in Table 38-6 are cross-sectional data: they show the pattern by providing information about the countries at a given time (1986). The pattern also exists as a given country develops through time. As economic development occurs and per-capita production and income increase, the proportion of income spent on agricultural products decreases. This is reflected in a decreased proportion of a country's labor force and GNP in agriculture.[11] For example, in the United States in 1850, 50 percent of the labor force was engaged in agriculture. As per-capita production and incomes grew after 1850, the proportion in agriculture decreased to its current low level. The inverse relationship between per-capita income and the relative importance of the agricultural sector, both cross-sectional and over time, is one of the most characteristic phenomena of development. There have been no exceptions to it.

Note that these structural patterns refer to proportions, not absolute amounts. While the proportion of GNP accounted for by agriculture shrinks, the absolute amount of agricultural output increases. And while the proportion of the labor force in agriculture shrinks, for a long time the absolute number of workers in agriculture increases. As mentioned, in the United States the proportion of the labor force in agriculture decreased from 1850 to the present, but the absolute number of people in agriculture (and the absolute number of farms) increased until 1910–1920. Only since then have both the proportion and the absolute numbers in agriculture declined. Today's LDCs are still in the pre-1910 U.S. phase: the proportion of the labor force in LDC agriculture will decrease as per-capita output grows, but the absolute numbers in agriculture will increase for a long time to come. This means that the kind of agricultural development that has been occurring in the United States (for the last 60 years) and in other developed countries—with decreasing numbers in agriculture accompanied by increasing average farm size—will not occur in LDCs in the near future. In the LDCs, increasing numbers of people will make

---

[11]The corollary is that development is associated with increased proportions of a country's labor force and GNP in industry and services. This is the reason that economic development is sometimes referred to as "industrialization."

TABLE 38-6

RELATIVE IMPORTANCE OF AGRICULTURE, SELECTED COUNTRIES

Countries	1986 per-capita production (in dollars)	Percent of labor force in agriculture
Less developed		
Ethiopia	120	80
Bangladesh	160	75
Zaire	160	72
Burma	200	53
Tanzania	250	86
India	290	70
Kenya	300	81
China	300	74
Sudan	320	71
Pakistan	350	55
Indonesia	490	57
Philippines	560	52
Morocco	590	46
Nigeria	640	68
Egypt	760	46
Thailand	810	71
Turkey	1,110	58
Colombia	1,230	34
Brazil	1,810	31
South Africa	1,850	17
Mexico	1,860	37
Argentina	2,350	13
Korea	2,370	36
Algeria	2,590	31
Iran	—	36
Developed		
Spain	4,860	17
Italy	8,550	12
Britain	8,870	3
France	10,720	9
Germany	12,080	6
Japan	12,840	11
Canada	14,120	5
United States	17,480	4

Source: Adapted from World Bank, *World Development Report, 1988.*

their living in agriculture; the tendency will be for rural density (the population/ land area ratio) to increase. This means that much of the agricultural research relevant to developed countries with lots of land and few workers is not relevant to LDCs with their prospective increases in rural densities.

GROWTH THEORY FOR LDCs

Causes of Outward Shift of the PPC

The production possibilities curve (PPC) was used in Chapter 2 to illustrate certain economic principles; you should review this material at this time. You will recall that at a given moment in time (or a period of time short enough that changes in the quantity or quality of inputs are not significant) a country has a *given* amount of natural resources, capital, and labor, and a given level of technology. The PPC shows the maximum amounts of goods (output) that can be produced with these given inputs and technology. If the available inputs are not all employed, or are employed inefficiently, then actual production takes place at a point inside the PPC.

The PPC was also used to show that choices must be made. If a country is producing efficiently at a point on the PPC, it can achieve an increase in production of one good only by decreasing production of the other. One choice illustrated in Chapter 2 is particularly relevant here. If the two goods on the axes of the PPC are consumer goods and investment goods, the PPC shows that to increase the production of investment goods requires a decrease in the production of consumer goods. Current consumption is reduced to allow increased production of investment goods, more rapid economic growth and, consequently, larger future consumption. (As a practical matter, consumption in LDCs is often so low that it is quite difficult to reduce it further.) The increased production of investment goods causes an outward shift of the next period's PPC because there is an increased quantity of capital available for production in the next time period.

The PPC can also illustrate economic growth. If over time the quantity or quality of the inputs increases, or the level of technology increases, the PPC shifts outward. This means that more can be produced—the production possibilities have increased.

Note that an increase in GNP does not by itself mean that economic well-being has improved. We saw earlier that GNP per capita, not GNP by itself, is the appropriate indicator of economic well-being. If over a period of time both GNP and population increase by the same proportion, we can say that economic growth (measured by the outward shift of the PPC) has occurred but that economic well-being has not increased. For well-being to increase, GNP must grow more rapidly than population grows. This means that the outward shift of the PPC must be due predominantly to increases in factors other than the quantity of labor—that is, to increases in the nonhuman inputs or increases in technology.

Natural Resources

We now take a closer look at the increases in natural resources, capital, labor, and technology that will cause economic well-being in LDCs to improve. It is not possible here to deal adequately with natural resource issues in LDCs. Many LDCs clearly face critical problems with large populations in relation to their natural resource base.

There is a sense in which a country's natural resources are *fixed*. A country has a given surface area on which to catch sunlight and rainfall, and given mineral deposits. An *increase* in the natural resource input to production really means an increase in the proportion of the surface area used for economic production or an increase in the rate at which the fixed natural-resource deposits are depleted. In the short run an increased utilization of natural resources causes GNP to increase. But we must distinguish GNP increases sustainable over long periods of time from GNP increases not sustainable over long periods. To do this we must distinguish between *exhaustible* and *nonexhaustible* natural resources.

Coal and petroleum are exhaustible natural resources. An increase in the rate at which such resources are mined from geological deposits causes GNP to increase, but the resources cannot be mined forever. The depletion of exhaustible resources eventually requires finding alternative resources or reducing consumption. A critical problem for every society is achieving an optimal rate of depletion of exhaustible natural resources.

Forests and bodies of water are nonexhaustible natural resources, provided they are properly managed. Timber and fish are goods that can be harvested from such resources. If the harvest of timber from the forest or of fish from the sea does not exceed the regenerative powers of the forest or deplete the breeding population of fish, we obtain a sustainable flow of such goods. An important task for every society is to create a decision-making environment in which yields do not exceed sustainable levels.

In some densely populated LDCs it will be difficult to increase the rate of utilization of natural resources. For example, all available land may already be in use for agricultural production. But even when resources appear abundant, great caution must be exercised. The clearing of tropical forests to obtain land for raising crops or animals can easily lead to soil erosion. And the destruction of tropical forests in LDCs influences global climate by reducing the biosphere's ability to recycle carbon dioxide.

Capital

Recall that when economists speak of "capital" they mean such material objects as trucks, tractors, computers, roads, irrigation systems, and electricity-generation facilities. It is growth in this real capital that allows workers to be more productive and that supports higher levels of economic well-being.

It is important not to exaggerate the role of capital accumulation as a source of economic growth in LCDs. The rapid increase in Europe's production after World War II following the rebuilding of war-damaged capital caused just such an exaggeration. The productive capital of Europe had been very heavily damaged by the war. After the war this capital was restored in just a few years, partly due to U.S. assistance via the Marshall Plan. GNP in Europe expanded quite rapidly, causing economists and others to place great emphasis on physical capital as a cause of growth and perhaps not enough emphasis on other essential inputs in the production process. Early foreign-aid programs to assist LDCs placed much emphasis on increasing the physical capital of LDCs, but GNP in LDCs did not rise rapidly as it had in Europe. Only later was it realized that re-equipping workers in Europe who already had experience with capital was quite different from equipping workers in LDCs who had no previous industrial experience. Economists now pay increased attention to the human factor in the production process in LDCs.

Labor

In most cases, an increase in the number of workers causes an increase in output. But if an increase in labor input is not accompanied by increases in other cooperating inputs (natural resources and capital), there will not be a proportional increase in output. Put more precisely, a ten-percent increase in labor input results in *less* than a ten-percent increase in output, other things equal. By itself, population (and labor force) growth leads to increases in GNP *and decreases in GNP per capita*. This, of course, is the primary reason why rapid population growth can be a serious problem. A famous economist once remarked that each new person (worker) in the economy comes with two hands—but not with a combine harvester or with farmland or other natural resources.

There is sometimes uninformed talk of "a shortage of labor" in LDCs. This reflects either an inappropriate focus on GNP rather than GNP per capita as the best indicator of economic well-being or a failure to recognize that an increase in labor, while leading to a GNP increase, leads to a *decrease* in GNP per capita. Developed countries are developed precisely because they exhibit high ratios of capital and other inputs per unit of labor—that is, because labor is in short supply relative to capital and other resources. To the extent that individual economic well-being is an appropriate goal, a small amount of labor relative to capital and other inputs is exactly what LDCs should strive for because this is what makes productivity and living standards high.

So far we have been talking about the quantity of labor. We must also talk about the quality of labor—because production is related to both the quantity and the quality of workers. Healthy, well-trained workers can produce more than unhealthy, poorly trained workers. In general, workers in developed countries are both healthier and better trained than workers in LDCs. Expenditures that increase the health and training of workers increase the productivity of the workers. Because expenditures of this sort have basically the same output-increasing impact as expenditures on physical capital, such expenditures on improving the health and training of workers are called "human-capital investments." In summary, increases in labor quality brought about by investments in improved health and education lead to increases in GNP per capita. A major part of development efforts in LDCs must be directed toward increasing the quality of labor.

Technology

Along with natural resources, capital, and labor, the level of technology available at a given time determines the production possibilities of a country. The major contributing factor to economic development in recent centuries has been the application of science-based technology to production processes. The developed countries have applied modern technology to all or most of their production processes, the LDCs have not. The application of technology is the main reason why the developed countries are not still LDCs.

Because of the enormous backlog of existing technology, the LDCs are in the favorable position of being able to adopt already existing technology rather than having to invent it. This is fortunate because many of the LDCs are so small that it is unlikely they would be efficient producers of new technology. However, the possibility of being able to adopt existing technology should not be exaggerated. Much of the available technology is not suited to LDCs. For example, much of the agricultural technology developed for the large-farm environment of developed countries is not applicable in the crowded, small-farm environment of most LDCs. Thus it is necessary to adapt the existing technology to the requirements of the

LDC. Another way of saying this is that the LDCs need *appropriate* technology, not necessarily the latest technology.

Each LDC must determine effective methods by which to obtain and implement appropriate technology. A variety of methods are available: sending capable students abroad to learn about improved technology, striking deals with multinational corporations whereby they invest in LDCs, implementing improved technology, transferring skills to LDC managers and workers, and establishing indigenous institutions capable of using basic science (probably produced almost exclusively in developed countries or larger LDCs) as a foundation for designing improved technology.

LDC DEVELOPMENT POLICIES

We have seen that increasing the productivity of a country's labor force is the essence of its economic development. The preceding discussion of the major factors in economic growth leads to the conclusion that LDC governments must encourage the wise use of natural resources, the accumulation of both physical and human capital, and the adoption of improved technology. Here we mention certain other specific requirements: LDC governments must maintain law and order, must genuinely desire widespread increases in economic well-being, must carry out needed public investments, and must adopt appropriate domestic and international economic policies.

Basic Requirements

The most basic governmental function is to maintain law and order. An efficient economy requires at least minimal personal security. If the police, army, or bands of armed civilians routinely extort resources from others, the incentive to produce and invest is severely disrupted or eliminated. In some LDCs such minimum security does not exist. Where this is the case, the first developmental step is clear.

LDC governments must be committed to improving the economic well-being of all citizens, not just a few. This commitment is far from universal in LDCs. Some societies are run by elites (oligarchies) interested solely in self-aggrandizement. In such societies the governments do not use available resources to make the needed investments in social overhead capital like education and public health. It is unrealistic to expect significant increases in the economic well-being of the poor majority in such societies so long as the government acts in this fashion. Another way of saying this is that existence of a responsive political system—one in which government officials are genuinely committed to the needs and interests of the masses—may be a necessary condition for economic development.

But even assuming an LDC's government maintains law and order and is committed to promoting widespread economic development, it is still essential that it make wise public investments and implement appropriate economic policies. Good intentions are not enough. Some LDC governments ostensibly committed to economic development adhere to policies that systematically stifle incentives to save, invest, and produce efficiently. The economic principles you have learned from this textbook—especially the microeconomics concerning the role of markets in coordinating the behavior of buyers and sellers—are frequently ignored by governments otherwise intent on economic development.

The ideal case is that an LDC's government has both good intentions and good policies. The worst case scenario is that an LDC's government has both bad intentions and bad policies. The intermediate cases are difficult to rank. Perhaps cases where bad intentions are accompanied by (inadvertent) good policies are better than cases of good intentions accompanied by bad policies.

Public Investments

Many productive investments can be undertaken only by government authorities. When the benefits are widespread and payments cannot efficiently be collected from individual beneficiaries (e.g., roads, education, public health, agricultural research and extension), public investment is required. These investments in *social overhead capital* must be financed out of the limited resources available to governments through taxation, and from internal and external borrowing. Careful analysis of the possible benefits and costs of potential public investment projects is required to obtain the greatest possible impact on economic development through available public resources. Choices must be made between additional investments in education, transportation, and so forth. Efficiency requires that, say, $10 million not be spent on a particular road project if the same expenditure on an education project would have a greater impact on development. Of course, an efficient use of government resources is easy to recommend, but difficult to achieve, even in developed countries!

Appropriate Economic Policies

In addition to its own expenditures, LDC governments must put in place appropriate domestic and international economic policies. Economic life consists literally of millions of individual decisions about working, saving, investing, consuming, conceiving children, and so on. You have learned in earlier chapters how prices influence individual decisions and in turn how individual decisions influence prices. When actual prices accurately reflect the values of resources and goods, the decisions taken by individuals are appropriate from both individual and social perspectives. When actual prices do not reflect such values, private decisions cannot lead to socially optimal results. In short, appropriate government policy includes *getting prices right* and allowing private decision makers to act in light of those correct prices. Governments must ensure that their taxing and subsidy policies move prices in appropriate directions.

Appropriate *domestic economic policies* are crucial. For example, if governmental intervention keeps prices below equilibrium, shortages result. This often happens with food prices in LDCs. LDC governments often act to keep the price of food low; this increases consumption and reduces the incentive for LDC farmers to produce. (Incidentally, this is the opposite of what frequently happens in developed countries where government intervention keeps food prices *above* equilibrium, causing surpluses.)

Prices of such inputs as labor and capital influence the techniques used in production. Often LDC governments act to keep the price of labor high and the price of capital low. Such price distortions result in the choice of production techniques that use too little labor and too much capital—exactly the opposite of the appropriate combination in LDCs, given that labor is quite plentiful in LDCs.

Appropriate *international economic policies* are also crucial. An overvalued exchange rate—putting too high a price on the LDC's own currency or, said the other way, putting too low a price on foreign currency—reduces the incentives for LDC exporters to export and increases the incentives to import. Eliminating the distortion caused by an overvalued exchange rate can simultaneously increase exports and reduce imports.

A case can be made that relative prices inside an LDC should reflect relative prices on the world market. Only in this way are the LDC's resources allocated according to comparative advantage. Following comparative advantage means that a country imports those goods and services that are cheaper on the world market than at home and exports to the world market those goods and services more valuable abroad than at home. Such policy instruments as taxes (including import tariffs), subsidies, and exchange rates influence relative prices directly; such instruments as import and export quotas influence relative prices indirectly. Use of such policy instruments in a manner that does not cause domestic relative prices to diverge from world-market prices is called outward-oriented trade strategy. At the opposite extreme, use of such instruments to cause domestic relative prices to diverge from world prices—thereby inducing domestic production of substitutes for imports rather than of export goods—is called inward-oriented trade strategy.

Recent research has compared the impact of these two strategies. Forty-one countries were classified according to the strategies they followed: strongly outward oriented, moderately outward oriented, moderately inward oriented, and strongly inward oriented. The results were unambiguous. The highest growth rates for both total production and production per person were experienced by countries following a *strongly outward-oriented strategy*. The growth rates were lower the more the strategy departed from a *strongly outward-oriented approach*. The lowest rates were experienced by nations following a *strongly inward-oriented approach*.[12]

ROLE OF DEVELOPED COUNTRIES IN THE DEVELOPMENT OF LDCs

Finally, we return to the theme with which we began this chapter: All people are fellow passengers on spaceship earth. So how can those in the developed parts of the craft help those still in less-developed parts?

The image of the development process underlying this chapter is that decisions made by the LDC's own government and by the LDC's private citizens are primary determinants of the LDC's economic performance. (Exhibit 38-1, page 896, summarizes a competing image of the development process.) While the main burden is therefore on the LDC itself, developed countries can do two things to help speed up the development process. Developed countries can help LDCs accumulate more rapidly the resources needed for economic development and can help LDCs achieve an efficient allocation of available resources in production by adhering to liberal international trade policies—that is, by abandoning all impediments to free trade.

---

[12]World Bank, *World Development Report 1987*, Ch. 5, "Trade Policy and Industrialization" (Washington, DC: World Bank, 1987).

EXHIBIT 38–1

LENIN'S EXPLOITATION THEORY

There is another theory of economic development, one that views LDCs as victims of decisions made and actions taken by outsiders. This theory blames developed countries for the poverty of LDCs.

Briefly, the theory begins with Karl Marx's prediction that the impoverishment of the workers in capitalist countries will eventually lead to revolutions that will end private ownership of the means of production and establish socialist economies in place of capitalism. But the predicted overthrow of capitalism did not take place in the 70 years following Marx's prediction. Lenin explained the delay in the predicted revolutions in capitalist countries by arguing that developed capitalist countries had exploited LDCs. In effect, the conditions in developed countries that would otherwise have led to revolutions had been temporarily alleviated by developed countries enriching themselves by "ripping-off" LDCs, either through colonial exploitation or through international trade and investment linkages from which developed countries benefitted most.

This Leninist theory links most or a large part of the poverty in today's LDCs to contacts with developed capitalist countries and to the LDCs' own capitalism (private ownership of natural resources, capital goods, and so forth).[13] This theory leads to the policy prescription that LDCs must eliminate domestic capitalism and severely limit all international economic contacts with developed capitalist countries. This Leninist theory implies that, from the LDC perspective, help from developed countries should be limited to resource transfers to LDC governments. Private investment by developed countries in LDCs, in this view, should be prohibited by the LDCs.[14]

[13]These ideas are sometimes labeled "Marxism-Leninism," but this label inappropriately links Marx with Lenin. Whereas Lenin argued that economic development in LDCs was hindered by colonialism and other contacts with developed capitalist countries, Marx recognized the net beneficial impact on LDCs of such contacts. On this important topic, see Bill Warren, *Imperialism: Pioneer of Capitalism* (London: New Left Books, 1980).

[14]Citizens of both developed countries and LDCs must be sensitive to their possible biases. As citizens of a developed country, we are possibly biased against the Leninist view because it would make us uncomfortable to think that the economic success of the United States was causally linked to any lack of economic success in LDCs. On the other hand, citizens of LDCs may be attracted to the Leninist theory because it blames their poverty on outsiders and not on defective political institutions and other factors inside their own societies.

Developed Countries as Sources of Investment Funds

Earlier we mentioned the great importance of LDC investment in human and physical capital to increase production. In most LDCs these investments are constrained by limits on the LDC's available savings. Developed countries can foster both public and private net transfers of resources to LDCs. When savings from developed countries can be transferred to LDCs, accumulation of human and physical capital in LDCs is speeded up.[15]

Private investment resources can flow to LDCs via direct investments by private firms, including investments by multinational corporations (firms with production facilities in more than one country). LDCs must negotiate good agreements with

[15]In the absence of international economic contacts, a country's investment is limited by its own saving. But if a country can import more than it exports, it can invest more than it saves. It seems *natural* that a poor country should be enabled to invest more than it saves by becoming able to import more than it exports—that is, by running a trade deficit financed by savings transfers from other countries. Resources can be transferred from rich countries to LDCs to support higher investment in LDCs if LDCs run trade deficits and developed countries run trade surpluses. (Seen in this light, the United States trade deficit of the 1980s—a case of a developed country absorbing savings from the rest of the world—seems *unnatural.*)

multinationals not only to obtain capital and technology, but to ensure development and training of LDC human resources. Private investment resources can also flow via loans to the LDC from private banks. (On this latter topic, see the discussion of the world debt problem in Chapter 37.)

Public investment resources can flow bilaterally (directly from the developed country to the LDC) or multilaterally (e.g., from developed countries to the World Bank and then from the World Bank to the LDC). Public resources are especially important in assisting LDC governments to provide the needed infrastructure: transportation, education, health, and agricultural research. These public resources for development are sometimes termed "foreign aid." In recent years U.S. foreign aid for economic development has been in the range of $7–$10 billion per year.[16]

Developed Countries as Liberal Trading Partners

Finally, although it is less dramatic than contributing to the flow of resources and technology to LDCs, developed countries can contribute to an efficient allocation of all productive resources in both LDCs and developed countries by adhering to a liberal international trading regime. As resources and technology accumulate in LDCs, comparative advantage shifts. LDCs move beyond being exporters of primary products into labor-intensive manufactured goods, and later into a full range of manufactured goods. This means that LDCs will gain comparative advantage in sectors hitherto important in developed countries. For both LDCs and developed countries to achieve the benefits that come from an efficient worldwide allocation of resources, it is necessary that reallocations occur in developed countries. Some industries in developed countries must diminish or perhaps even disappear. Although economic theory shows that the developed country as a whole gains from such reallocation, particular sectors may suffer losses. Steps taken in developed countries to facilitate such efficient reallocations simultaneously increase the economic well-being of developed countries and contribute importantly to economic development of LDCs.

SUMMARY

1. Less developed countries (LDCs) account for about three-fourths of the world's population. This proportion will increase in the decades ahead because of the more rapid population growth in LDCs.
2. Countries can be ranked according to production per person. The LDCs are countries in which production per person is low. Low production (economic output) per worker is the basic cause of low levels of economic well-being in LDCs.
3. When the gaps between developed countries and LDCs are measured using actual exchange rates, the gaps appear unrealistically large. Purchasing-power exchange rates show the gaps to be much smaller, but there still is a large difference between the economic well-being of rich and poor nations. The gaps between today's developed countries and LDCs emerged over the last two centuries as a consequence of the speeding-up of growth rates in the now-developed countries.

---

[16]Many citizens of the United States appear to think that the United States gives a lot of economic aid to LDCs, and many think a reduction of foreign aid would make a substantial contribution to reducing the federal deficit. In reality, foreign economic aid represents less than one percent of federal expenditures, and its complete elimination would make only a modest contribution to solving the deficit problem. Foreign aid is an easy target because citizens of LDCs do not vote in U.S. elections. It is important that those who do vote and who are interested in promoting the economic development of LDCs have a correct understanding of the importance and the limited magnitude of U.S. foreign aid.

4. The lower level of economic well-being in LDCs is characterized by high infant mortality, short life expectancy, unsafe water supplies, inadequate food for hundreds of millions of people, and inadequate access to decent housing, educational opportunities, and medical services. In recent decades, many LDCs have been successful in increasing the levels of economic well-being available to their populations, but rapid rates of per-capita output growth over extended periods of time are still needed to eliminate poverty.

5. An especially important characteristic of LDCs is rapid population growth due to the large gap between birth and death rates. The demographic transition from high birth and death rates to low birth and death rates is not yet complete in LDCs. Death rates have decreased in recent decades but birth rates are often still at high traditional levels. Population will continue to grow until birthrates decrease and again become equal to death rates.

6. Rapid population growth causes a high dependency rate (many dependents per each 100 workers). Past rapid growth ensures a large population increase in the future because of population momentum. Rapid population growth slows down the growth of worker productivity by slowing the accumulation of both human and nonhuman capital, and by increasing the pressure on limited amounts of natural resources.

7. Agriculture is the dominant sector in LDCs. The lower a country's per-capita production, the greater the relative importance of agriculture. As per-capita production rises, the relative importance of agriculture shrinks. Because of the enormous size of agriculture and rapid growth of population, the absolute numbers of people in agriculture will rise in the years ahead—further complicating the problems of agricultural development.

8. Output per worker is a function of the quantities of nonhuman inputs available per worker and the level of technology. Development requires increased inputs per worker and improved technology.

9. LDC governments must intend to promote widespread economic development and must adopt economic policies that promote it. If either element is missing, growth will be slow or nonexistent. Development problems are so serious that if the LDC's government is uninterested in development, the problems will not be tackled. But good intentions are not enough; good intentions accompanied by inappropriate economic policies stifle progress.

10. LDC governments need appropriate domestic economic policies and programs. Government must provide the social infrastructure for development and create an economic environment in which private sector decisions about childbearing, saving, investment, and production lead to increases in economic well-being.

11. LDC governments need appropriate international economic policies. These policies must foster appropriate specialization according to comparative advantage and create an environment that attracts useful direct foreign (multinational corporation) investment and foreign lending.

12. The United States and other developed countries can contribute to LDC development by public (government-to-government) resource transfers, but probably more importantly by adhering to liberal international economic policies that encourage efficient international specialization. This means that developed countries must be willing to restructure their own economies to accommodate more imports from and more exports to LDCs.

KEY TERMS

less developed countries (LDCs)
purchasing-power exchange rates (PP)
infant mortality rate
demographic transition

dependency rate
population momentum
replacement level of fertility
outward-oriented trade strategy
inward-oriented trade strategy

STUDY QUESTIONS AND PROBLEMS

1. Approximately what proportion of the human race lives in LDCs? Are there any large countries (with, say, more than 20 million citizens) that are difficult to classify as either developed or less developed? If so, why?

2. Per-capita income comparisons using market exchange rates exaggerate the gaps between LDCs and developed countries. The richest countries appear 50–60 times better off than the poorest countries. Why does this happen? When purchasing-power exchange rates are used, how large does the gap between rich and poor appear? Why do the magnitudes of the gaps change so much when purchasing-power exchange rates are used?

3. Have the current income gaps between the rich and poor countries emerged because growth rates in rich countries speeded up, because growth rates in LDCs slowed down, or for some other reason? Discuss.

4. If GNP grows at 2 percent per year, how many years will it take for GNP to double? If population grows at 1 percent for 100 years, by how much will it expand?

5. Is population in LDCs growing fast because birthrates have risen or because death rates have fallen? What is the relationship between life expectancy and death rates? Why is the dependency rate high in LDCs?

6. Why is the agricultural sector so large in LDCs?

7. What is the distinction between exhaustible and nonexhaustible natural resources?

8. What historical experience after World War II caused the role of capital in the development process to be exaggerated?

9. What steps can developed countries take to help speed up development in LDCs?

10. What measures can LDCs themselves implement to bolster growth?

SELECTED REFERENCES

Lester R. Brown et al., *State of the World 1986* (New York: Norton, 1986).

Simon Kuznets, *Modern Economic Growth: Rate, Structure and Spread* (New Haven, CT: Yale University Press, 1966).

Robert Summers and Alan Heston, "A New Set of International Comparisons of Real Product and Price Level Estimates for 130 Countries, 1950–1985," *Review of Income and Wealth,* March 1988, pp. 1–25.

Bill Warren, *Imperialism: Pioneer of Capitalism* (London: New Left Books, 1980).

World Bank, *World Development Report* (Washington, DC: World Bank, published annually).

CHAPTER 39

GROWTH AND REFORM IN THE SOVIET AND CHINESE COMMAND ECONOMIES

Gorbachev is agitating for economic reforms that involve some very capitalist concepts, like prices and profits. In China, Deng Xiaoping has already introduced similar reforms. The free market, or at least a freer market, is an idea that has been lost and found.

[1]Robert J. Samuelson

The Soviet Bloc nations, China, and many less developed countries regulate their economies to a much greater degree than the capitalist economies due to a combination of socialist ideology derived from Marxian economics and a sense of haste in promoting economic growth. Starting in the 1930s with Stalin's development push in the Soviet Union, many countries have attempted to spur growth and catch up with the advanced industrial countries by adopting elements of the command economy. They have used central government direction to answer the basic economic questions of what goods to produce, how, and for whom in a way that favored investment over consumption and that stressed large industrial projects to take advantage of economies of scale.

Although the use of the command economy in the Stalinist model for development did, for a time, give rise to high growth rates in socialist countries, there has been widespread stagnation lately and a growing recognition that they are falling behind their capitalist rivals. Why are there general shortages and long queues for consumer goods? Why has there been such a problem with innovation and the adoption of new technology? Why are socialist economists lately talking more about the merits of markets and enterprise autonomy? Why does the leader of the Soviet Union say that socialism is at stake in his reform effort? Are the communist countries really turning to capitalism for help?

---

[1]Robert J. Samuelson, *Newsweek* (February 9,1987), p. 54.

This last chapter will attempt to answer these questions. It develops further the analysis of economic systems discussed in Chapter 2, concentrating here on command economies. It covers the origin of the actual policies and regulations used in present day command economies, focusing on the Soviet Union and China. It analyzes the problems and circumstances that are forcing implementation of reforms in these countries. Finally, the chapter considers the prospects for success of the reforms.

ORIGINS OF THE COMMAND ECONOMY

When the Bolsheviks under Vladimir Lenin seized power in Russia in 1917, they were reversing the sequence of revolution that had been predicted by Karl Marx in the previous century. The revolution had been predicted to take place only after **capitalism** had provided the productive and political bases for it. There was supposed to have been a highly developed and productive industrial system in place with a dissatisfied class of industrial workers, the *proletariat*, ready to revolt. Instead, Lenin and his successor, Joseph Stalin, had to construct a Marxian-type economy on the foundations of poverty. Later, in 1949, the Chinese communists under Mao Tse-tung took power in China, another underdeveloped country.

In these large, backward, and war-ravaged countries, socialism came to be equated with a full-blown **command economy** with bureaucratic planning and state ownership of industry. Lenin, Stalin, and Mao were applying Marxist ideology using both his critique of capitalism and his description of the ideal of future communism. At the same time, they were attempting to develop the Russian and Chinese economies as rapidly as possible under the strict control of their communist parties. Stalin expressed this sense of haste in speaking of overtaking and surpassing his capitalist rivals in ten years: "Either we do it or they will crush us."[2]

MARXIAN ECONOMICS

Critique of Capitalism

Marx had three fundamental criticisms of capitalism: it was unjust, inhuman, and wasteful. With capitalists owning the means of production (factories and machines), the workers were forced to hire themselves out. The injustice of this unequal situation was that the workers were not paid all of the resulting output. According to Marx's **labor theory of value,** the profit and interest earned by capital owners were

Capitalism
An economic system in which property is privately owned and markets rather than central authorities coordinate economic decisions.

Command Economy
An economic system in which property is publicly owned and central authorities coordinate economic decisions.

---

[2]Gur Ofer, "Soviet Economic Growth: 1928–1985," *Journal of Economic Literature* (December 1987), p. 1798. [Original source: Joseph S. Berliner, "The Economics of Overtaking and Surpassing," in Henry Rovsovsky, ed., *Industrialization in Two Systems: Essays in Honor of Alexander Gerschenkron* (NY: Wiley, 1966) p. 161.]

Labor Theory of Value
The view associated with Marx that labor is the only factor of production capable of producing value so that the value of every commodity is determined by the amount of labor embodied in it.

not legitimate payments for factor services but an unearned "surplus" extracted from the workers. Wages were deliberately kept low and workers kept under control by the threat of unemployment. Capitalists supposedly maintained an "army of the unemployed" in order to make the threat credible. Because of this Marxian scenario of capitalist exploitation, communists objected to the principle of private property and to workers being hired by others. The accumulation of capital through personal saving in order to invest for private gain was scorned. Inequality and unemployment were not to be tolerated.

Marx considered capitalism inhuman because workers were alienated from their jobs and were not able to realize their full potential as creative human beings. In Marx's view, capitalists organized their factories in such a way as to increase their domination and control over the work force. A strict division of labor served to downgrade the skills and cheapen the labor of the mass of workers, while at the same time worker solidarity was suppressed by dividing workers into types (skilled/non-skilled, mental/manual) with different pay and status. Therefore, people, who by nature should obtain most of their satisfaction from work, were forced to toil like machines for a dominating class of capitalists. Communists vowed to replace capitalism's individualism and concern with self-interest with a collectivist vision; they wanted to create a new type of worker who would care more about the society than about himself.

Finally, Marx saw capitalism as wasteful because of the business cycle and because of inefficient coordination in the marketplace. The business cycle was attributed to workers' low incomes and subsequent underconsumption. The resulting surplus goods and unemployment were endemic to the system and a tragic waste of resources. With regard to markets, Marx saw at least one advantage of the capitalist system: competition drove capitalists to constantly search for new technology and to increase society's capability to produce (though much of the new technology might be designed just to get rid of pesky workers or to gain better control over them).

But, in general, Marxists view the market as chaotic. Planning is done in capitalist economies by monopolistic corporations that deny consumers sovereignty through advertising and other forms of manipulation. However, even large corporations cannot be sure of a market for their products. To Marxists, government planning is a better way to coordinate production and avoid depressions.

Socialism and Communism

Proletariat
The working class under capitalism consisting of people who own only their own labor as opposed to the capitalist (or bourgeoisie) class of property and capital owners.

Marx foresaw a revolution by the **proletariat** against the dominating capitalist class that would not take place unless and until capitalism had become fully developed. Full development meant the possibility of abundant output and an end to economic suffering. As capitalism matured, however, he predicted that workers as a class would become progressively worse off and more united in their solidarity. At the same time, capitalist strife and competition over falling profits would cause the system to self-destruct. Marx thought that private property rights, so important for competitive markets, would be viewed by the proletariat as a hindrance to further economic progress. The result would be a socialist revolution as workers sought a better way of organizing the economy and society.

Communist Utopia
The Marxian conception of a future ideal society without economic classes or the division of labor and with all people realizing their full potential as creative human beings.

Why was socialism supposed to be better? Marx envisioned an eventual **communist utopia** that would take the productive forces created by the capitalists and, through redistribution and planning, enhance them. This would enable workers to realize their full human powers. Given the foundation of abundance created by capitalism, there would be the possibility of a new era without economic suffering and classes.[3] All workers would do enjoyable work (no one relegated to menial labor!) and participate fully in decision making on the key issue of what to produce.

There is very little, however, in Marx's writings or in the vast Marxist literature on what the actual organization of such a society might look like. One may presume that markets, accumulation of vast wealth, and working for others, as elements of capitalism, would be out. Cooperation would replace specialization and competition in the market. **Material incentives**, especially the profit motive, were scorned as bourgeois and as unnecessary because the **moral incentive** of working for the future of communism was sufficient reason for hard work. Workers would compete for medals of recognition for model workers rather than striving for cash bonuses. No "unearned" income from capitalist investment would be allowed. *How* and *for whom* were answered by the slogan: "From each according to his ability, to each according to his needs." This was, and is, not much to go on in setting up the socialist economy—which was meant to be the intermediate stage to full communism—except that workers could still be paid according to their individual work effort.

Revolution in Backward Areas

What a **socialist economy** came to mean in the Soviet Union of Stalin, and later in China, was a command economy dominated by the communist party. The backward conditions in the Soviet Union and China have had as much to do with determining the shape of this **Stalinist growth model** as has Marxist ideology. Without a large proletariat and without a large party backing them, Lenin, and Stalin after him, created the centralized communist party as a "dictatorship of the proletariat" that was supposed to retain power until an actual proletariat arose. The Leninist concentration of political power continued in the nations of the Soviet bloc and China and was instrumental in developing and maintaining their centralized economic coordination. This centralized system was supposed to be better than the decentralized and democratic system of capitalism at defining clear growth goals for the economy and focusing the nation's resources toward their achievement. Time and effort would not be wasted on gathering popular consent for tough economic measures promoting growth. In particular, the lack of political opposition enabled the communist parties to pursue two major unpopular elements of the *Stalinist growth model:* the collectivization of agriculture (which resulted in a disastrous famine in the Soviet Union during the 1930s) and the promotion of investment in heavy industry over consumption.

THE STALINIST GROWTH MODEL

The main objective of the Stalinist growth model as applied in the Soviet Union, China, and their allies was to develop the national economy as quickly as possible in order to catch up with the leading capitalist countries. All the nation's main resources were to be state-owned so they could be mobilized toward this end.

Material Incentives
A reward system that promotes desirable behavior by giving the recipient a greater claim over material goods than one who has performed less well.

Moral Incentives
A reward system that promotes desirable behavior by appealing to the recipient's responsibility to society and by raising the recipient's social stature within the community.

Socialist Economy
To Marx, an intermediate stage of communism in which workers are paid according to their work; identified with the Stalinist growth model in the Soviet bloc and China.

Stalinist Growth Model
A combination of the command economy and centralized political control used to pursue rapid economic growth by collectivizing agriculture and concentrating investment on heavy industry.

---

[3]And, because Marx viewed the state as an arm of class power, the disappearance of the capitalist class meant that the state could wither away.

The Ideal of Central Planning

Five-Year Plan
A document that lays out the strategies and growth targets for economic development in the Stalinist growth model; supporting one-year plans include specific directives for enterprise production and commodity allocation.

Central planning in the Stalinist growth model substituted coordination by central authorities for coordination provided by the market in a capitalist system.[4] First, professional planners were to explore the alternatives available to society and weigh them relative to national objectives, putting the results into a **five-year plan.** Second, once the strategic decisions were made, it was just a matter of making up the detailed *one-year plans* and administratively directing the various production enterprises to fulfill the plans. The managers of enterprises were responsible both for reporting faithfully on their production capacity and for meeting mandatory plan targets, which were orders from above concerning inputs and outputs. It was assumed that the planners would have available the tremendous amount of detailed information about the economy necessary to make the system work. In any event, it was thought that consumer needs could be kept simple—a one-color toothbrush would do for all. (Just as Henry Ford once said, "Customers can have any color car they want, as long as it's black.")

According to the Stalinist growth model, there would be no market trade in capital goods. These goods were to be allocated to enterprises as needed according to the plan. There would be no problem of mutual inconsistency of producer and consumer decisions because the planners would strike a so-called "material balance" to equate supply and demand (something done automatically by the *invisible hand* in a market economy) and to ensure that there were no shortages of commodities or waste of resources. To achieve balance for a particular item (e.g., cold-rolled sheet steel), the planners would have to know the output capacities of all the nation's steel mills as well as the steel inputs necessary for all other industries to meet their planned outputs. The steel available would be allocated based on those planned outputs. Since the planners were attempting to carry out this task for all goods, the annual plans became extremely complex. They also were often incomplete and unrealistic, leaving much room for interpretation.

One important objective of central planning was to force society to save as much as possible and to invest the funds according to central priorities. This was to be accomplished partly by holding down consumption and partly by generating a surplus of funds from the agricultural sector. The payoff for the sacrifice of present consumption was to come in future abundance. It was argued that only a socialist country would be able to adopt such a farsighted strategy. The surplus accruing from agriculture was to be obtained by paying farmers low prices and selling food at high prices. All investment decisions would be made by the state with funding via state budget grants or state bank loans. The top priority for investment in the Stalinist growth model became large-scale heavy industry, since it appeared that this is what the advanced countries relied on for their high productivity, seemingly benefiting from generous economies of scale.[5]

Among the advantages cited for central planning were the absence of the misallocations associated with externalities, monopoly power, and inequalities that plague capitalist systems. Planners would be able to "internalize" both negative and positive externalities or spillovers to produce the socially optimum output. Further,

---

[4]See Chapter 2 for a description of the difference between the command and capitalist systems.
[5]It should be noted that large-scale industry was to create an important missing prerequisite of socialism—the proletariat as the largest element of society—since the proletariat of capitalist systems was defined as the workers in large-scale industries. By the same token, collectivizing agriculture was to convert the peasants to employees and therefore make them a part of the proletariat.

the state would produce the desired amount of public goods. Despite the emphasis on large-scale enterprises, there were to be no adverse effects associated with monopoly. Managers would not use their power in a self-interested way to maximize profits but would follow the plan and minimize costs. Finally, without a property-owning capitalist class, there would be little income inequality and no poverty.

How the Stalinist Growth Model Worked

No country that has adopted the Stalinist growth model, including the Soviet Union itself, has ever been able to put all its desired ideological and practical features into force. There has never been a complete absence of markets. As discussed in Exhibit 2-2, even Lenin was forced into a temporary compromise of his anticapitalist principles. His New Economic Policy in the 1920s restored some markets, allowed private farming on nationalized land, and encouraged private enterprise in light industry and services. Many communist leaders look back to Lenin's New Economic Policy as justification for their present reforms. Stalin ended this experiment with markets in the 1930s by forcing the peasants onto collective farms (and removing private ownership from the economy) and by instituting central planning with the first in a series of five-year plans. After that, the model included only a vestige of a market in that workers were paid in money and purchased some of their goods in stores (with the plan providing for only a limited choice). Many items, however, including housing and medical care, were either delivered in kind or were highly subsidized. Workers generally were able to choose their jobs, although there was some use of direct labor allocation.

Despite the relative prevalence of in-kind distribution, the envisioned equal income distribution has never been achieved. For one thing, material incentives in the form of wage differentials were necessary to get certain jobs done. For another, there were extra rewards (including access to special shops with goods unavailable to ordinary citizens) for those holding status in the party, the arts, and the professions. The ruling parties in both China and the Soviet Union have had to wage ideological battles against those leftists who demand more egalitarianism.[6] The rulers' argument has been that the present systems are socialist and not fully communist, so that the proper distribution principle is "from each according to his ability, to each according to his work."

Another important compromise that appears to violate stated Marxist ideals has been the development of a large bureaucracy in each of the command economies. Given the Leninist objective of securing socialist political gains by maintaining tight political and economic control (which goes back to Lenin), there has been a notable lack of democratic involvement in decision making. Part of the extraordinary strife observed in China during the Cultural Revolution of the 1960s and 1970s was due to Chairman Mao's effort to control the bureaucracy while leaving the single-party state intact. However, he failed to find a middle ground between centralized command and the market for coordinating economic activity.

The Soviet model of a command economy, despite Western expectations to the contrary, was quite successful for a time in mobilizing resources for growth. In the 1950s, Soviet leader Nikita Khrushchev was able to make his threat to "bury" the capitalist countries seem plausible. There were notable successes in science and space, as well as enviable increases in the output of basic industrial materials. Many

---

[6]This was the main policy plank of the famous Chinese "Gang of Four" followers of Mao Tse-Tung (including Mao's wife), who were arrested, tried, and imprisoned after Mao's death.

TABLE 39-1

GROWTH RATES IN REAL GROSS NATIONAL PRODUCT, 1961–1988

Area and country	1961–1965 (annual average)	1966–1970 (annual average)	1971–1975 (annual average)	1976–1982 (annual average)	1983	1984	1985	1986	1987	1988*
Developed countries	5.3	4.6	3.0	3.3	2.7	4.7	3.2	2.8	3.1	3.0
United States	4.6	3.0	2.2	2.3	3.6	6.8	3.4	2.8	3.4	3.8
Japan	12.4	11.0	4.3	4.5	3.2	5.1	4.7	2.5	4.4	5.4
European community	4.9	4.6	2.9	3.0	1.5	2.4	2.4	2.6	2.7	2.5
Developing countries	5.3	5.8	5.7	4.0	.5	2.8	1.7	4.0	3.3	(**)
Communist countries	4.4	5.0	4.2	2.7	2.7	2.3	2.3	4.1	1.1	(**)
U.S.S.R.	4.7	5.0	3.1	2.1	3.3	1.4	0.8	3.9	0.7	2.0
Eastern Europe	3.9	3.8	4.9	1.2	1.8	3.6	0.8	3.0	0.6	2.1
China	− 0.2	8.3	5.5	6.2	9.1	12.0	12.0	7.5	9.5	9.0

*Preliminary estimates.
**Not available.

Source: *Economic Report of the President, 1988* and *1989.*

newly independent developing countries looked to the Soviet Union as a model for successful development. In China, centralized planning and state ownership was used to end widespread hunger and bring basic services to the people. By achieving a magnitude of forced saving consistent with the Stalinist growth model, China was able to devote 30 percent of its GNP to investment and to increase the share of industrial production in total output much faster than other very poor developing countries.

However, despite high investment and the mobilization by the state of other resources in the economies using the Stalinist model, growth began to fall short of their governments' rosy projections. Table 39-1 shows Western estimates of growth rates, comparing the command economies to both developed and developing countries (LDCs). The table's estimates for the Soviet Union are far lower than those published by the Soviet government. Only recently have the Soviets begun to concede that Western estimates are closer to what actual growth has been. Even by Western estimates, China's growth has been quite rapid. The negative growth in 1961–1965 was due to Mao's poorly conceived Great Leap Forward. The data from the 1980s reflect the success of recent reforms, but per-capita output remains very low. China has seen the economies of its market-oriented neighbors surge ahead (e.g., Table 38-1 shows China with annual per-capita production of just $300 compared to Korea's $2370).

For its part, the Soviet Union is not willing to accept that it is now just another slow-growing mature economy, since its output per capita is only one-half that of the United States. Soviet citizens complain about the system's failure to provide adequate food, clothing, housing, and medical care. In addition, with slower growth the Soviet Union finds it difficult to maintain the high level of military expenditures necessary to maintain its superpower status.

SLOW GROWTH IN COMMAND ECONOMIES

It has become increasingly evident to new leaders in both the Soviet Union and China that their economies will fall further behind unless drastic changes are made in the command system inherited from the past. Developing countries are now more interested in emulating the success of capitalistic nations. The major command economies have lost prestige. Why have growth rates slowed in the command economies? In general terms, the technological progress characteristic of growth in capitalistic economies has been missing in those countries using the Stalinist growth model. All sectors have suffered from the widespread shortages and inefficient use of resources associated with centralized planning and ownership. Gorbachev has said that the vast central planning system in Moscow is no longer stimulating the economy but rather is serving as a "braking mechanism."

Costs were incurred and expenditures delayed in the effort to catch up quickly. Agriculture, consumer goods, and the infrastructure (transportation, services, and the like) have all been neglected in the haste to build a heavy industrial sector. One of the main reasons for agricultural shortages and food rationing in the Soviet Union is the lack of adequate transportation and storage facilities and the subsequent high level of spoilage. In effect, the countries using the Stalinist growth model borrowed from the future in their impatience to grow. Interest on the "loan" is now being paid in the form of increased costs (e.g., high transportation costs).[7]

NEGLECT OF AGRICULTURE

In agriculture, the Stalinist model calls for collectivization (state farms and communes) and central planning in an attempt to ensure an adequate food supply and to generate a surplus with which to invest in industry. But agriculture has lagged badly as neglect, poor incentives, and the inefficiency of faraway planning have taken their toll. The United States manages to feed itself and produce a large surplus for export with only 2 percent of its population on farms. In contrast, the Soviet Union has been unable to feed its own people and must import food even though 20 percent of its population works on farms. Economies of scale from large farming operations turned out to be small; the surplus to be extracted has turned into a costly subsidy system designed to keep food prices low in urban areas. That is, instead of paying low prices at the farm and selling at high prices in state food stores (thus generating surplus state revenue for use in industry), the state has been paying low prices and charging even lower prices (thus using state revenue for a subsidy). This is illustrated in Figure 39-1 (page 908). The subsidy on bread has been so high in the Soviet Union that farmers have found it profitable to sell their grain at the state procurement price and buy cheap bread in the shops to feed to their livestock.

Not all command economies have collectivized agriculture as extensively as the Soviet Union and China. And even the Soviet Union and China have allowed the collective farmers to work their own small private plots and to sell their output in a limited free market. It is reported that with only about 3 percent of the Soviet Union's arable land the peasants, on their private plots, produce about 25 percent of the country's total crop output and about 30 percent of the total milk and meat output.[8]

---

[7]Same as 3, pp. 1801–1826; a discussion of the Stalinist growth model and the cost of haste in development.
[8]Data cited in Marshall Goldman, *Gorbachev's Challenge: Economic Reform in the Age of High Technology* (New York: Norton, 1987), pp. 33–34.

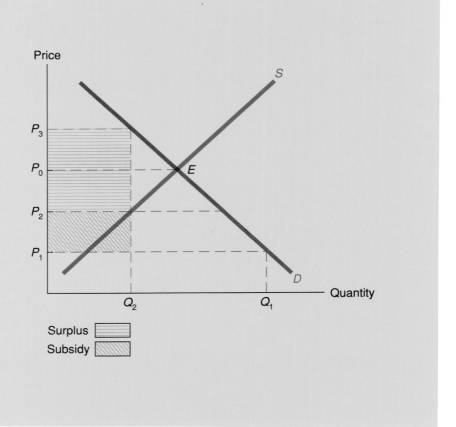

FIGURE 39–1

AGRICULTURAL
SURPLUSES AND
SUBSIDIES

Assume this market for agricultural goods has an equilibrium price P_0. Countries using the Stalinist growth model tried to extract a surplus of revenues from the agricultural sector by setting the price paid to farmers at a low P_2 and charging consumers P_3. The low price to farmers resulted in low output, which Stalin and Mao attempted to prevent (by collectivizing in order to reap economies of scale). Over time, planned revenue surpluses became subsidies as retail prices were held down (some remaining unchanged for more than 50 years). In Figure 39-1, the farmers continued to receive the low price P_2 while consumers paid an even lower price P_1 for food items. The low quantity available (Q_2) must be rationed as long as price is held below P_3.

Surplus ▭
Subsidy ▨

OVERRELIANCE ON EXTENSIVE GROWTH

Through inertia, the economy continued to develop to a large degree on an extensive basis, orientated toward drawing additional labor and material resources into production. As a consequence, the growth rate of labor productivity and certain other indices of efficiency dropped substantially. Attempts to rectify the problem through new construction exacerbated the problem of balance. The national economy, which has vast resources, ran into resource shortages. A gap formed between social requirements and the achieved level of production, between effective demand and the amount of goods available to meet that demand.[9]

Inadequate Technological Progress

Gorbachev, in the preceeding quotation, points out one source of the Soviet Union's slow growth. There has been a failure to move, as the more advanced capitalist countries have, away from what he calls an "extensive" basis for growth to an "intensive" one. Chapter 2 pointed out that economic growth, represented by the outward shift of the country's production possibilities curve (PPC), occurs when a

[9]Mikhail Gorbachev in *Pravda,* February 26, 1986, as quoted in Theodore Draper, "Soviet Reformers: From Lenin to Gorbachev," *Dissent* (Summer 1987), p. 301.

Extensive Growth
An outward shift of a country's production possibilities curve over time due to increases in natural resources, labor, and capital goods.

Intensive Growth
An outward shift of a country's production possibilities curve over time brought about by technological progress.

country increases its resources or develops new technologies. A country that relies mainly on drawing ever-increasing amounts of natural resources, labor, and capital goods into production in order to keep its PPC shifting outward is engaged in **extensive growth.** In contrast, **intensive growth** relies on technological progress to shift the PPC. With the application of new technology, existing resources can be used more intensively. The record shows that the Soviet Union and other countries following the Stalinist growth model have been unable to develop and apply new technology at a sustained level. And, since they also have run into limits on increasing resource inputs, their growth rates have faltered. As Figure 39-2 illustrates, technological progress is the key to future growth.

With regard to increasing noncapital resources, the Soviet Union at first was able to increase labor force supplies by transferring workers from agriculture to

FIGURE 39-2

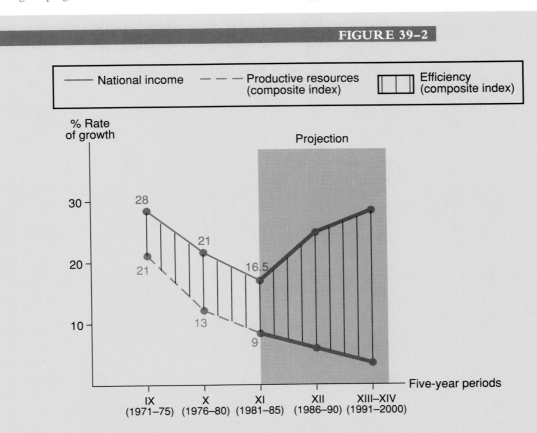

SOURCES OF GROWTH IN SOVIET NATIONAL INCOME

Figure 39-2 illustrates how contributions to growth from increased resources have fallen off. The solid color line reflects official Soviet data on the percentage growth in its national income over certain five-year periods. The broken color line represents growth rates of productive resources (composite index). The solid vertical lines between the two color lines form an area that measures productivity growth or growth attributable to technological process. For example, of the officially reported 16.5 percent cumulative growth from 1981–1985, 9 percent was due to increased resources and 7.5 percent to technological progres.

Source: Abel Aganbegyan, *The Challenge of Perestroika* (Bloomington, IN: Indiana University Press, 1988), Figure 2. Copyright 1988, University of Indiana Press; reprinted by permission.

industry and by increasing labor participation rates. However, population growth has declined recently and labor surpluses in agriculture have tended to disappear. The easy growth in natural resource inputs, at least in the Soviet Union, also appear to have ended as the exploration for new sources increasingly must involve more inhospitable and costly areas.

Misplaced Investment

The success in generating high levels of national saving for investing in capital goods has been one of the hallmarks of command economies. But central planners have had great difficulty making the high investment work as a vehicle for rapid technological progress. Too much of the Soviet Union's research and development is conducted in institutions separate from the producing enterprises, making it difficult to move innovations to the shop floor. Also, there are problems in getting existing state enterprises to apply new technology to the production process. Therefore, the planners tend to put new technology predominantly into newly constructed factories. But given the slow pace of project completion—brought about by the absence of appropriate financial incentives and the fact that builders are judged on the basis of how much work they have in progress rather than on the amount completed—too much of the country's investment funds are tied up in construction. In addition, extensive growth via investment without technological progress implies diminishing returns to additional capital accumulation. Therefore, investment must be continually increased or growth rates will fall even further.

The imbalance that Gorbachev refers to in the quotation is the high-investment ratio and accompanying low consumption to total output ratio typical of command economies. The problem with this imbalance is that the low output of consumption goods makes it difficult to provide the material incentives now deemed necessary to spur Soviet workers and managers.

POOR PLANNING IN INDUSTRY

Overuse of Central Planning

The planning system itself is widely recognized to be a major contributor to the slower growth of command economies. Excessive control from the center not only represses initiative, especially by enterprise managers, but also results in misallocation of both investment goods and current inputs and outputs. The system bogs down due to the sheer scale of the detailed decision making necessary for running a large complex economy. It has proved impossible, even with computers, for those at the top to collect, process, and check all requisite information for their planning and coordination tasks. There is also the typical inflexibility of a bureaucracy. Such a system might work under Stalin when there were just a few priorities involving standardized goods and simple mass-production processes. However, it is not suited to the modern economy's multiple priorities and rapid technological and social changes. The result is inefficiency and production at a point inside the economy's production possibilities curve.

An example of how central planning generates inefficiency and waste is the case of a furniture factory in Western Siberia that wants to produce its own particleboard on-site in the future, rather than having to depend on shipments from afar that must be arranged by various central-planning agencies in Moscow. Instead of obtaining timber products from local sources, the enterprise must wait while these raw materials are transported thousands of miles from forests in the European part of the country. Meanwhile, *other* planning agencies in Moscow that control the timber in Siberia ship timber products of the same type to the European part of the country—a costly transfer, and one that taxes an overburdened rail system.[10]

Deficient Enterprise Management

Under the state ownership of enterprises in the Stalinist growth model, there is no separation of ownership and management. In a market system, an identification of the interests of owners and hired management promotes efficiency since the capitalist owners have a strong profit motive. In the Stalinist system, such an identification means enterprise managers pay too much attention to the wishes of higher bureaucrats (who represent the state as owner) and not enough to the needs of customers. The result is inefficiency and waste of resources.

Managers in the Stalinist system are in strict control of their enterprises. Because they have the power to frustrate national plans and objectives and because there is no market pressure to restrain their self-interest, enterprise managers are appointed from above and kept under strict control by government and party bureaucrats. But proper control of enterprises (and workers) has proved elusive in the Stalinist system. Being under the thumb of the bureaucracy, managers exhibit a lack of responsibility and initiative. Their self-interest in protecting their positions makes them cautious. They contribute to inefficiency by not minimizing costs and by not producing the right goods, of the right quality, at the right time. The problem is not just to produce more goods, but to produce goods that people want. With few goods to buy and little chance of being fired for laziness, workers have little incentive to work hard. Soviet workers have a saying: "They pretend to pay us and we pretend to work."

A major problem is that the five-year and one-year plans have not provided proper guidelines for production. A manager's performance is judged primarily on his or her ability to fulfill annual targets for quantity or total value of output. The fact that the targets are annual ones leads to shortsightedness. Useful longer-run innovations in products or processes are not undertaken because this would interfere with getting the immediate job done. Quality suffers too, since managers know how difficult it is to measure quality. They know that they are seldom disciplined for poor quality. The feedback in a market system that allows the customer to dictate demands to the producer is missing, so shoddy goods pile up in warehouses. Prime Minister Lubomir Strougal of Czechoslovakia has admitted that warehouses in his country hold $3.5 billion worth of unwanted goods.[11] Judging managers simply on the basis of total value of output produced also means that it is seldom in a manager's self-interest to reduce costs. Since inputs and workers might turn out to be in short supply, managers tend to hoard whatever they can get. Workers end up underemployed.

Low prices and wages may also encourage the hoarding of resources. To a manager in a command economy, however, funds are not a problem since he or she can count on being provided with whatever amount is necessary for meeting the

---

[10]From Daniel Ford, "A Reporter at Large: Rebirth of a Nation," *New Yorker* (March 28, 1988), p. 61.
[11]Cited in "Prague's Long Winter, Still No Spring," *The Economist* (August 13, 1988), pp. 34–40.

EXHIBIT 39–1

THE VOLGA PIPE MILL

In place of the market, with its fine nuances, the Soviets designed a remarkably simple planning system. Instead of profits, the main criterion for success was quantity. The more a worker or a manager produced, the better. Given the poorly trained work and managerial forces available at the time, this was a rather ingenious way to use a large but unskilled labor force to achieve an unprecedented rate of economic growth.

Frequently, the emphasis on quantity proved to be too simplistic. A standard other than absolute quantity alone ultimately became necessary. Many enterprises produced a diverse collection of goods that did not lend themselves to one overriding index which could be specified in units like tons or meters. If an enterprise that produced both light and heavy products was assigned a target in tons, it tended to produce only the heavier item and ignore the lighter merchandise. In an effort to circumvent such bias, Soviet planners designed a performance measurement system based on the gross value of production measured in rubles (VAL). Products, regardless of size or weight, would be added together to determine a firm's ruble output.

While the VAL system had its advantages, it also had its shortcomings. Pricing in the Soviet Union operates on a cost-plus basis. Given the relative absence of competitive pricing and concerns about finding willing purchasers, the Soviet manager is able to price his goods with full allowance for the cost of his input regardless of how high that might be. Even more, the Soviet

manager actually has an incentive to seek out the most costly raw materials and components available. As factory managers quickly came to realize, under the VAL system the more expensive the inputs, the higher the gross value of output in rubles. In practice, this has resulted in the excessive use of raw materials.

Viktor G. Afanasyev, the editor in chief of *Pravda,* has provided a common example of how irksome and wasteful the VAL system can be. The Volga Pipe Mill was producing thin rolled pipe that was equal in strength to thick rolled pipe, but weighed one-half as much. Potentially the switch to such pipe could save the Soviet Union hundreds of millions of rubles and tens of thousands of tons of high-quality alloy steel each year. But because the Volga Pipe Mill product sells for less, its VAL was 10 percent less and as a consequence "its wages, reserves, bonuses and all the rest of its rewards to the producers have fallen by 15 percent, 'fallen,' but in actual fact, its labor productivity has increased."

But VAL's perniciousness does not end there. No one wants to use the Volga Pipe Plant's pipe. Builders refuse to use thin rolled pipe because it is cheap and no construction unit in its right mind will use cheap products because its VAL will also suffer.

Source: Reprinted from *Gorbachev's Challenge: Economic Reform in the Age of High Technology,* pp. 20–22, by Marshall I. Goldman, by permission of W. W. Norton & Company, Inc. Copyright © 1987 by W. W. Norton & Company, Inc.

Soft-Budget Constraint
An essentially unlimited budget enjoyed by enterprises, which can fall back on the state for subsidies and tax breaks to bail out unprofitable operations.

plan. That is, enterprises face a so-called soft-budget constraint. The plan may specify a spending limit, but it is negotiable. Unprofitable firms are not allowed to fail. Many bad investments and other decisions are simply allowed to stand. At the same time, profits in a command system are confiscated by the state as owner of the enterprise and, therefore, do not act as an incentive to the managers. Managers look for their rewards and security by satisfying the wishes of the bureaucracy above them.

One consequence of the general lack of quality and variety in the goods of the command economies is a stunted foreign trade sector. There had been a tendency to go it alone anyway, given the dislike for capitalist states and the desire to prove the superiority of socialism. In addition, competition and marketing was seen as "capitalistic." The Soviet Union, although a major industrial power, exports few manufactured items and must import food. This tendency toward self-sufficiency has pervaded its whole economy. Enterprise managers, industrial ministries, and regions all have tried to produce their own supplies due to the need to meet the plan and the unreliable source of inputs provided by the bureaucracy. In China, Mao actually encouraged regional self-sufficiency to reduce the central bureaucracy's power.

Distorted Prices Under Central Planning

Most prices in command economies are set by the central planners and generally have only a tenuous relationship to the scarcity values that prices in free markets reflect. A major reason for such price distortions is that prices are seldom changed and, over time, get out of line. Price stability for individual commodities is viewed as a desirable goal. Another major contributor to price distortions is the normal practice of setting commodity prices equal to long-run industry average costs. With long-run costs as the standard, prices are not adjusted for changes in supply and demand conditions. Besides, prices equal to long-run average costs are unlikely to give the proper signals to producers. In a market economy, profit-maximizing firms produce an output that equates marginal cost with the market price. When supply and demand changes cause market prices to deviate from average costs, changes in profits signal entry into and exit from the industry. In command economies, the lack of a real profit motive and the setting of prices by bureaucracy limit such responses.

Many prices end up either too high or too low. One reason for the high prices of some goods is that enterprises are tempted to downgrade product quality in meeting their plan targets. Consumers then see the price as too high given the quality. Excess goods pile up. Generally, however, command economies are plagued with shortages and with prices too low to clear the market. Goods in short supply that are not directly allocated or rationed by the planners go to whoever is first in line or to whoever has an "in" with the producer. Producers operate in sellers' markets in which buyers must seek out and perhaps bribe sellers in order to obtain the product. Instead of hiring salespersons to market their products, enterprises must employ so-called "expediters" to search out essential inputs.

There are numerous features of command economies in addition to artificially low prices that contribute to the predominance of such sellers' markets. In the producer goods sector, *soft budgets* at enterprises lead to an unlimited demand for capital and other inputs; there is no real penalty for investment failure or for cost overruns. There is also no financial constraint on investment, since the funds are either free (government grants) or available at low cost (due to below-market interest rates at state banks). In the consumer goods sector, sales taxes are supposed to be set to bring low retail prices up to market-clearing levels, but this is seldom done. (For many goods, low prices are maintained as a subsidy for consumers.) In addition, planners have allowed total wages to rise faster than total consumer goods production, which contributes to excess demand. The typical condition of shortage caused by the combination of low planned output and high demand in consumer markets is illustrated in Figure 39-3 (page 914). The common complaint of workers in command economies is that, although they have the money, there is nothing in the shops to spend it on.

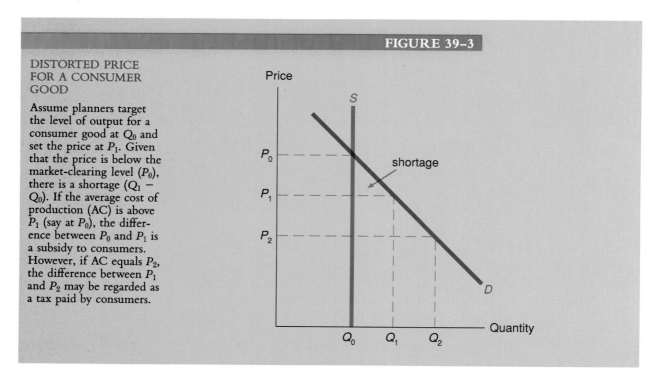

FIGURE 39-3

DISTORTED PRICE FOR A CONSUMER GOOD

Assume planners target the level of output for a consumer good at Q_0 and set the price at P_1. Given that the price is below the market-clearing level (P_0), there is a shortage ($Q_1 - Q_0$). If the average cost of production (AC) is above P_1 (say at P_0), the difference between P_0 and P_1 is a subsidy to consumers. However, if AC equals P_2, the difference between P_1 and P_2 may be regarded as a tax paid by consumers.

REFORM IN TODAY'S COMMAND ECONOMIES

Reform in command economies has a long history, including retreats from the haste of the growth effort and from the attempts to run the economy as "one vast corporation." There has often been a questioning of the origin and necessity of the repressive features of the Stalinist growth model. The political break from the Soviet Union by Yugoslavia and China led to experiments in worker management of enterprises in the former and to Mao's struggles against the dominance of central officialdom in the latter. In the countries remaining in the Soviet orbit, there have been continuous adjustments to the system. For example, there have been recurring shifts in emphasis between material and moral incentives. There was discussion in the Soviet Union and China as early as the 1950s about increasing the role of markets. But until recently, reform mainly has involved efforts to make the command system work better by tightening discipline or decentralizing within the bureaucratic system. As the Chinese say about this record: "We relax control, and get chaos; we recentralize, and get inertia." Hungary, however, did go further by dropping mandatory plan targets for enterprises in 1968 without causing chaos.

ELEMENTS IN REFORM PROGRAMS

With the new reform-minded leadership in China (1978) and in the Soviet Union (1985), serious efforts are underway to loosen bureaucratic control and to attempt market-type decentralization. The general aims of reform are to achieve greater efficiency, reduce waste, and ensure that production reflects the needs of customers and not just plan fulfillment. Once the burden of central planning is eased, managers and workers are expected to show more individual initiative. The resulting increased technological innovation will raise the standard of living. How is all this to be accomplished? Partly by redirecting investment away from heavy industry. And although Chinese and Soviet reforms differ in many details, the common elements include:

1. greater reliance on material incentives to direct economic activity
2. concessions to the private sector
3. increased enterprise autonomy in the state sector

Increasing Material Incentives

In emphasizing material incentives, reformers in command economies are seeking better ways of tying rewards to productivity in order to encourage more productive work. In doing so, they are making full use of the motto "to each according to his contribution." Arguing that the time has passed for merely exhorting people to work hard, Soviet leader Gorbachev has called for a powerful system of incentives to get "all workers to fully reveal their capability, work fruitfully and use resources most effectively." To achieve this

> the system of pay and labor incentives must be arranged in a new way. It is particularly important that the actual pay of every worker be closely linked to his personal contribution to the end result, and that no limit be set on it. There is only one criteria of justice: whether or not it is earned.[12]

So this is the promise to workers: if you work harder, the rewards will be greater. And the rewards can be greater in the future because greater effort will increase productivity. However, long accustomed to a system that neither rewards hard work nor penalizes low effort, workers in the command economies may not increase their effort until there are more goods in the shops. It should be noted that enterprise profits are to play an important role in the new system of material incentives. Both workers and managers will be able to earn cash bonuses if profits increase.

Allowing More Private Economic Activity

A movement toward a more market-oriented rural sector led the reform effort in China. Success there has carried the reform to the rest of the economy. Farms in China had been forcibly collectivized into very large communes. Although the incomes of peasants had depended on how well the commune did as a whole, a firm link between the individual farmer's remuneration and his output was never developed. The reforms accomplished this first by raising agricultural prices to encourage production and second by establishing a **responsibility system.** Rural families were allocated a portion of the collective land on 15-year leases (later increased to 50 years) for which they are responsible for profits and losses. Rather than assigning production quotas to the millions of new farm units, there was a switch to indirect market methods (higher prices) of assuring the nation's food supply. The questions of *what, how,* and *for whom* began to be decided by the market rather than by a mandatory plan. However, the Chinese government still fixes important prices and still faces a dismantling of expensive but extremely popular food subsidies.

Responsibility System
An institutional arrangement designed to tie monetary rewards more closely to work actually performed; in practice in Chinese agriculture, a system of family farming based on long-term leases of land.

---

[12]Secretary Gorbachev to the Communist Party Central Committee in 1987; quoted approvingly by conservative American economist Paul Craig Roberts in *Business Week,* September 9, 1987.

As a result of the Chinese agricultural reforms, farm output doubled and peasant incomes nearly tripled. In turn, higher farm income greatly buoyed rural industry and trade. China's experience in diminishing its food problem by reforming rural areas first appears to be convincing the Soviet Union to put more emphasis on agriculture in its own reform efforts. Although conditions are quite different, the Soviet Union is hoping for similar success from long-term leases of land and implementation of markets.

Both the Chinese and the Soviets also have made new concessions to private enterprise and markets in such nonagricultural sectors as small-scale consumer goods and services, which are relatively neglected in the Soviet growth model. (See an example of the new private enterprise in Exhibit 2-2.) As in agriculture, it is individual and family firms that are contemplated—although there has been some ideological shift away from the traditional prohibition against private hiring of outside workers. As in agriculture, the autonomy of small firms and cooperatives from the central plan and the opportunity to work for their own reward in the market should bring increased production and efficiency.

To some extent, the concessions to private activity are just a legal recognition of, and an attempt to bring under state control, a large existing *underground* or *secondary economy* that increasingly has been diverting people's efforts from the planned economy. Interestingly, western-style income taxes are being introduced to capture revenues from underground activity. It is very likely that private enterprise will continue to be highly circumscribed in both countries by bureaucratic regulation and will be in the shadow of what will remain a large state-owned sector. There will be very little of the privatization of state-owned industry that has been so popular in western Europe.

Encouraging Autonomy for State Enterprises

It is in the sector of large state-owned enterprises where most of the targets of reform lie. China has been struggling the longest trying to extend the responsibility system that worked so well in rural areas to state-owned industry. Under the responsibility (or what the Soviets refer to as "self-finance") system, managers are given more autonomy, meaning that they can make decisions with minimal interference from either planners or party. The idea is that managers can make better use of their own local information to answer the questions of *what* and *how* than can the central planners. Instead of having to fulfill the mandatory production targets of the state plan, enterprises are supposed to produce for the market.

Managers are being told to use their new decision-making autonomy to maximize profits. This is supposed to make managers more innovative and more attentive to costs and quality. Such a switch in behavior and motivation comes fairly easily in agriculture and small business, where the family is a natural profit or income maximizer. It is more difficult to expect a similar change in behavior on the part of state enterprise managers accustomed to following the plan and depending on the bureaucracy for help.

Reformers are instituting other basic changes that should help managers begin to look to the market for direction. In the first place, the practice of confiscating enterprise profits is being replaced with a system that allows enterprises to use some of their profits for reinvestment or for bonuses (material incentives) for managers and workers. In the second place, planning staffs are being reduced in recognition that it is not enough just to abolish mandatory plans but that at least some of the meddlesome bureaucrats must disappear. The number to be "let go" in the Soviet Union is one-half the total central planning staff, approximately 50,000 persons.

How are managers to be restrained from abusing the new powers vested in the enterprises? One of the new market-type constraints is to be the "discipline" imposed by the potential for failure and bankruptcy as in the capitalist system. Bad decisions that result in losses are no longer to be met with an unlimited safety net as in the days of soft budgets. Managers may also be constrained in the future by an increased decision-making role of workers, who may begin to elect managers (Yugoslavia has been trying labor-managed firms). A worker who risks losing his job due to failure can no longer think of an enterprise in trouble as "no concern of mine."

MIXING MARKET COORDINATION AND PLANNING

One major question about the reforms is to what extent the command economies will actually rely on the market to answer the questions of *what, how,* and *for whom.* That is, what will be the role of the central planning bureaucracy in the reformed system? It seems clear that for markets to bring increased efficiency, the role of the bureaucracy in the economy must be limited. There has been talk of confining planners to long-term strategic planning. In addition, many more goods than at present must be traded in markets, enterprises must be guided by the incentive of profit maximization, and competition must increase.

Creating Markets

Markets must be created so that most goods are available for purchase at market-determined prices rather than being centrally allocated. Otherwise, enterprise managers will continue to look to the bureaucracy for allocations of cheap inputs and for a place to dump their output instead of responding to market signals. Both the Soviet Union and China have a tradition of free markets for the produce harvested from the private plots of farmers. Now they are moving to set up new markets for other goods and services. The Soviets are planning what they call a "market in means of production," in which state enterprises make contracts establishing deliveries and prices for goods traded between them without the interference of the bureaucracy. The state is to obtain its goods via state orders for which enterprises are to compete. So far, however, the bureaucrats have maintained their control over Soviet enterprises by substituting large state orders for the old mandatory production targets, leaving little production for the market. In China, new markets have been created for state enterprises by the adoption of a two-tier pricing system that allows the sale of production above plan quotas at market-determined prices. The old fixed prices are still used for production delivered to the state. A continued reduction in the state quotas in this two-tier system would increase enterprise exposure to market forces.

Increasing the Role of Profits

Market efficiency also depends on managers giving primary attention to maximizing profits. They will not if they still feel bound by a plan. Even if planning ceases to be "mandatory," managers may still feel it is in their best interests to satisfy the desires of those above them. If this is so, then the plan fulfillment will continue to be more

EXHIBIT 39–2

A SOCIALIST STOCK MARKET?

In 1984, the World Bank suggested that China institute a joint-stock system of ownership for state enterprises as a way of inspiring workers and staff to work hard. Cooperative-type enterprises had already been allowed to issue shares in China. The suggestion to extend this authorization to state enterprises drew both positive and negative responses. In October 1986, three economists from Beijing were invited to New York to give reports on the suggestion.

Ma Bin and Hong Zhunyan list five reasons given by those in favor of the joint-stock system. First, the presence of nonstate shareholders enables management to be separated from ownership and frees enterprise decision making from state administration. Second, once individual workers and staff become shareholders, their economic fate becomes integrated with that of the enterprise. Third, the experience of advanced capitalist countries shows that an ill-managed state enterprise often starts to improve once it has been sold to private joint-stock companies. Fourth, the joint-stock system will help channel consumers' saving to investment in fixed assets. Fifth, under the joint-stock system, the performance of stocks will serve to guide investment. Since Marx once said that dispersed ownership reduces the power of individual capitalists, many believe shareholding conforms with Marxism.

Ma and Hong speculate that what is behind the idea of introducing the joint-stock system is the capitalist economic view that only with private ownership is it possible for consumers to obtain maximum consumption. But Ma and Hong argue that this would block the road to communism. Marx meant to eliminate capitalist private ownership and the system of man exploiting man. In addition, Ma and Hong worry about some people owning more shares than others and this leading to class polarization when increased profits are distributed. They conclude that "[the joint-stock system] does not apply to the actual conditions of China." They recommend instead a merit pay system based on the principle "to each according to his work" to inspire workers.

Xu Jing'an, in arguing for a joint-stock system, says that under the current system widespread investment mistakes are covered up by the fact that ill-run enterprises can be protected administratively. In contrast, a stock-share system makes investors assume responsibility for any lack of profitability of their investment from the very beginning. In addition, shareholding by wage-earning workers gives them an additional tie with their enterprise. As the proverb goes: "When you have cargo in a ship, the ebb and flow of the tide arouses your concern." Xu says that the biggest obstacle to implementation of share ownership is the resistance of traditional ideas. "Socialism needs to forge ahead," he says, "and it is up to us to break new paths."

Sources: Adapted from Ma Bin and Hong Zhunyan, "Enlivening Large State Enterprises: Where Is the Motive Force?" and Xu Jing'an, "The Stock-Share System: A New Avenue for China's Economic Reform," *Journal of Comparative Economics* (September 1987), pp. 503–514.

important than profits. One reason managers may feel more loyalty to the plan is that they may continue to be appointed by the planners above them. Or managers might find it easier to make a profit by negotiating with those above them rather than by hunting for customers in the market. For example, if tax rates remain variable, bureaucrats will still have the discretion to reduce rates to help out an enterprise. Credit may also be negotiable. Both China and the Soviet Union have said that, in the future, enterprises must depend on the banking system rather than on government grants to finance extra investment. Credit would be granted on the basis of profitability, thus abolishing the soft budget. But if the credit system remains centralized under the control of the old bureaucracy and if a private capital market is not established, nothing much will change. Unprofitable firms will still be able to negotiate their way out of bankruptcy.

Enterprise profits are to come, in part at least, from selling goods in free markets. For the system to work, however, prices must be correct so that profits properly reflect enterprise efforts in cost-cutting and innovation. Prices will not be correct if price setting by central authorities continues or if enterprises are still required to set prices equal to long-run average costs. Only prices determined by the market will carry the necessary information about product demands and input scarcities that can be relied on to direct production decisions by the enterprises. Although price reform is proceeding slowly in the command economies and is meeting opposition, there appears to be a recognition that it is a vital part of any reform program.

Allowing Competition

Probably the most difficult problem in ensuring that markets operate efficiently is making managers competitive. This will be especially difficult in the reformed command economies where government-created monopolies have been the norm and competition is seen as destructive. If the bureaucracy controls the entry of new state firms, it is unlikely that existing enterprises will have to worry about competition from this source. Conceivably, private firms and cooperatives could effectively compete among themselves and with state enterprises, especially in the service sector. This competition is not likely to be very effective if such firms need a license from the bureaucracy or credit from the state bank in order to enter the market.[13] One solution is to open the economy to foreign trade, which can bring both competition and exposure to world prices that reflect world scarcities. The Soviet Union has made some moves in this direction, and China's opening to the rest of the world has been one of the most dramatic aspects of its reform.

OPPOSITION TO REFORM

Ideology and Reform

Ideological opposition to reform arises because reform, to the extent it uses market decentralization to bolster efficiency, calls into question the ideals of socialism embodied in the Stalinist growth model. Increased enterprise autonomy and dependence on markets deny to socialism the necessity of mandatory planning. Concessions to private activity negate the interpretation of socialism as a system without private ownership. The turn toward material incentives seems to negate the moral thrust of Marxism. There are many in China and in the Soviet Union who wish to see the reform movement slowed and who would prefer to strengthen central planning. In answer, reform advocates cite the example of Lenin's New Economic Policy, which also used capitalistic methods to improve efficiency. Like Lenin, these advocates may also view this backsliding as just a temporary retreat on the way to true socialism.

---

[13]For example, some budding entrepreneur may wish to open an ice cream shop in a small city that already has one such shop. Management of the shop in place may appeal to the licensing bureau to not grant the license on the basis that the new shop will take some of its business away. If competition is not seen as beneficial, the appeal is likely to be granted. Control by the government of licensing new businesses is also a problem in many western mixed economies and is often an item on the deregulation agenda.

Experience has shown that serious opposition to reform can arise when some of the features that Marxists complain about in market economies—such as inequality, unemployment, and inflation—begin to appear. The Chinese have been urged by their leaders to become rich; Gorbachev (in the quotation cited earlier) implied that there would be no limit to individual incomes as long as they were *earned*. There has always been inequality in command economies, of course, but under the reforms there would likely be more instances of conspicuous wealth. There will be the tendency in communist countries to label this "money grubbing" and to stop the activities giving rise to wealth. Cuba's leader, Fidel Castro, has recently abolished new farmers' markets on the basis that people were using them to get ahead financially.

The gradual nature of the reforms favored so far by Soviet and Chinese leaders may itself contribute to inequality. During the transition away from the command economy, officials who control scarce supplies of still price-controlled items are able to exact kickbacks and other favors. In addition, the communist party elite and their families are likely to be better positioned than others to take advantage of the new opportunities for private enterprise. Demands for action against such corruption and nepotism were an important element in the spring 1989 democracy demonstrations in China. Students asked for publication of the salaries and assets of government leaders and their children.

In addition, reform requires that poor performance be penalized. Workers in unprofitable enterprises could end up earning less than others who hold the same job in profitable ones, violating the principle of equal pay for equal work. Low profits and failing firms would lead to layoffs. Officially, command economies have not admitted to unemployment, but reform requires that surplus labor move to where it is needed. This restructuring means many more people will be "between jobs." Inflation is also likely to emerge as formerly repressed prices are raised to reflect supply and demand in markets. There is also the real possibility that the large industrial enterprises created by the planners may abuse their monopolistic power to raise prices. So far, however, it has been the unwinding of the subsidies to housing and food inherent in the low prices on these items that has sparked the most vigorous and politically threatening opposition to reform. Poland's Solidarity trade union was formed originally to protest such price increases. More recently, student demonstrators in China asked for continued price ceilings on consumer goods.

The Politics of Reform

The workers who will be more at risk of job loss and who will have to pay more for necessities constitute one "vested interest" resisting change. The reforms violate the old Stalinist social contract in which the workers traded political obedience for security (life-time employment, subsidized food) and for freedom from hard work (being paid regardless of effort). Another vested interest is the bureaucracy itself, which stands to lose many of its perquisites. Moreover, the bureaucrats themselves are also losing positions and influence in the command economies. Even enterprise managers may oppose reform because of a reluctance to accept responsibility despite the prospects of greater reward.

In the Soviet Union, Gorbachev has attempted to generate support for his reforms in the general population to get around the ideological opposition and to counter the vested interests. A campaign of openness called *glasnost* has encouraged people to learn about the repressive history of the Stalinist system and to criticize officials who block reform. History examinations were actually canceled in Soviet schools in 1988 because the existing textbooks were no longer considered truthful. In addition, the Soviet people are beginning to question the traditional, repressive political centralization of the Stalinist system. Gorbachev has called for democratization of the system, but plans on retaining the preeminent role of the Communist Party. In 1989, the first contested elections in the Soviet Union since 1917 were held for seats in a new legislative body (most candidates were members of the Communist Party). Some eastern European countries are taking democratization even further by allowing candidates from competing parties. China's reformers have depended more on the direct benefits of reform (higher incomes, more goods) to build support for further reform. However, the massive Chinese demonstrations in favor of democracy and freedom in 1989 showed that improved living standards may still leave people dissatisfied.

THE OUTLOOK FOR REFORM

The Record of Reform

Will the reforms succeed in getting the command economies back on track in their effort to catch up with the capitalist countries? Or will there be a reversion to the highly centralized Stalinist growth model? The record so far is not clear. The opponents of reform cite the problems of price instability and unemployment inherent in any serious restructuring program in their denunciation of reform. After the 1968 reform in Hungary, such tendencies led to some return of bureaucratic regulation; but in China, the early reforms in agriculture and the two-tier price system in industry created tendencies that encouraged continued movement toward the use of market forces. A huge constituency in favor of reform was created when Chinese peasants were given higher prices and their own land to farm. By the late 1980s, however, China was forced to slow its progress toward the market system due to protests against a 20-percent inflation rate, which was blamed on price reform.

Neither China nor the Soviet Union has adopted a complete and comprehensive reform package with a clear vision as to the future direction of their economic systems. The concessions to private enterprise, increased enterprise autonomy, and free markets have been more or less ad hoc measures to avert crises. The Chinese have been more forthright in their enthusiasm for the market system, whereas the Soviets emphasize the strengthening of socialism. Consider this statement by Gorbachev to Soviet Bloc leaders: "Some of you look to markets as a lifesaver for your economies; but comrades," he warned, "you should not think about lifesavers but about the ship, and the ship is socialism."[14] Gorbachev holds out the possibility of a more cooperative and humane socialism with less bureaucratic repression than in socialism as defined by Stalin. It is ironic that what he advocates is close to the "socialism with a human face" that was crushed by Soviet troops in Czechoslovakia in 1968. Gorbachev and his supporters have also decided to downplay the notion of an eternal antagonism between capitalism and communism based on class conflict. They are eager to remove obstacles to the trade and joint ventures that bring in western technology.

---

[14]Quoted in Robert Bazell, "Silicon Gulag," *New Republic* (June 6, 1988), pp. 10–11.

The indecisiveness of China's leaders on the future pace and scope of reform and the evident power struggle among the leadership during the spring of 1989 helped foster massive nationwide demonstrations. When these were finally brutally suppressed, it was evident that the hard-liners in favor of continuing the political and cultural dominance of the communist party had prevailed. Although the leaders maintain to the rest of the world that they still want reform and openness, it is uncertain what effect the repression will have on the willingness of foreigners to continue investment and trade contacts.

The Challenges Ahead

A crucial element for success in reform of the command economies is whether there is an increase in technological progress. If growth is to be switched to an intensive mode, annual plan targets and hasty growth must be de-emphasized. This may mean a short-term reduction in the availability of products—which often dissatisfied customers anyway—as the newly autonomous enterprise managers initiate innovations in products and processes. The command economies (and the mature capitalist economies) must compete with the Japans of the world in moving scientific breakthroughs from laboratory to factory. This requires a freedom of information and a climate of entrepreneurship that reformers recognize as missing in the highly-centralized Stalinist system. The Stalinist system has discouraged risk-taking and has abhorred the chaos of the marketplace. But that chaos represents a sort of continuing revolution within the market system that produces change. In addition, innovation is often the result of individual dissent from accepted ways of doing things. This tends not to be tolerated, much less fostered, in the Stalinist system where political power is monopolized by the communist party.

The reformers are imposing a profit motive on the newly autonomous enterprise managers in order to stimulate innovation and technological progress. The Soviets have high hopes that their managers can be turned into entrepreneurs. One Soviet economist has predicted that by 1995 managers "should have overcome the psychological barrier connected with the veneration of higher [bureaucrats], having learned to make their own decisions concerning commercial activities."[15] But if profits are to emit a proper signal, price reform is needed. With prices reflecting scarcity, the managers' pursuit of profits in markets could alleviate the problems of chronic shortages in the command economies. Higher living standards manifested by plentiful consumer goods could end the worker alienation and unrest in command economies that was supposed to exist only under capitalism. Government regulation could be more indirect, with monetary policy implemented to control inflation, unemployment insurance to alleviate the hardship associated with layoffs, and antitrust measures to deal with monopoly power.

CONCLUSION

Will the reformed command economies be transformed into capitalist economies characterized by consumer sovereignty, profit maximization by private owners, and distribution of goods based on ability to pay? Given the statements of the reformers, this is unlikely. There will still be more planning and arbitrary bureaucratic

---

[15]Makarov, Valary L., "On the Strategy for Implementing Economic Reform in the USSR," *American Economic Review* (May 1988), p. 459.

regulation than in the capitalist mixed economies, which have recently moved toward deregulating and privatizing state enterprises. The shortages in the system are used by some to justify continued bureaucratic control; they argue that the short supplies must be directly allocated at fixed prices. (Many in the United States also favored fixed prices and direct allocation during the 1970s "gasoline shortages.") And there will still be a temptation to use the power of the state to pursue the Marxian vision of socialism and eventual communism. This ideological force will tend to reduce reliance on the creative powers of the market. The potential problem of a partial and hesitant reform away from centralized control toward the use of market forces, however, is that enterprises could act contrary to reasonable plans and at the same time fail to respond to market signals. Inefficiency and slow growth could continue. The command economies could end up with the worst of both worlds.

SUMMARY

1. The command economy originated in countries that were in a hurry to catch up economically with the advanced capitalist countries. The Marxian utopian vision and critique of capitalism provided the ideological base for the system.
2. Building socialism in the backward countries where Marxian revolutions first took place came to mean a highly centralized political and economic system with state ownership of the means of production and central planning. This Stalinist growth model involved collectivization of agriculture and concentration on heavy industry.
3. The main impetus behind the recent reform efforts in the command economies is the slow growth in these countries and a recognition that they are falling further behind their capitalist rivals. The Stalinist growth model no longer appears to be an attractive development alternative to capitalism.
4. Growth rates have slowed in the command economies that use the Stalinist growth model, as centralized planning and state ownership have led to inefficiency and waste of resources. In addition, because technological progress has lagged, command economies have failed to make the switch from an *extensive* mode of growth to an *intensive* one.
5. Agriculture has fared poorly in command economies due to poor incentives and the inefficiency of faraway planning. Economies of scale have not been as great as expected. Instead of the expected surplus of revenues from agriculture, there are costly food subsidies for urban workers. Reform in agriculture requires ownership changes and higher prices.
6. The planning system contributes to slower growth in command economies through over-centralization of decision making and through bureaucratization of decision implementation. Central control represses initiative. Quality suffers as enterprises concentrate on annual *quantity* targets. A soft budget means no penalty for failure.
7. Most prices in command economies are centrally set and generally differ from market-clearing levels. Prices are set equal to long-run industry average costs and are often held constant for long periods. Financial restraints on demand are weak, so shortages are common and enterprises operate in a sellers' market.
8. Reforms in command economies are designed to increase efficiency by making concessions to the private and cooperative sectors, by increasing enterprise autonomy, and by relying more on material incentives. There is to be less central direction of the economy and more use of market forces to direct economic activity.
9. Increasing the reliance on markets to answer the questions of *what, how,* and *for whom* in command economies requires that markets be created with prices that reflect supply and demand forces, that managers give primary attention to maximizing profits, and that enterprises become competitive. The bureaucracy must concentrate on strategic planning.

10. China and the Soviet Union have not yet adopted comprehensive reform packages, and there is little indication of the nature of mixed economic system the command economies will become. These countries still are tempted to use the power of the state to pursue fast growth and the Marxian vision of socialism. They are likely to have more state ownership and central regulation than the capitalist mixed economies.

KEY TERMS

capitalism
command economy
labor theory of value
proletariat
communist utopia
material incentives
moral incentives
socialist economy

Stalinist growth model
five-year plan
extensive growth
intensive growth
soft-budget constraint
responsibility system
glasnost

STUDY QUESTIONS AND PROBLEMS

1. Reform of agriculture in command economies may include the leasing of formerly collective land to individual farmers. What difference would it make concerning the amount of investment farmers are willing to undertake whether the lease is for 15 years or 50 years?
2. Why do producers generally operate in a "buyers' market" in capitalist countries, instead of in the "sellers' market" that is so prevalent in the command economies?
3. Identify the tax or subsidy in the following situations:
   a. Potatoes have a fixed price of 1 ruble per kilogram and the average cost of production is 1.75 rubles.
   b. The fixed price of vodka is 10.50 rubles per one-half liter and the average cost is 1.25 rubles.
4. In each of the following cases, indicate whether growth is extensive or intensive:
   a. The labor force increases by 10 percent.
   b. Investment causes the capital stock to rise by 5 percent.
   c. A new technique is discovered for producing steel pipe that reduces required materials.

SELECTED REFERENCES

Aganbegyan, Abel, *The Challenge of Perestroika* (Bloomington, IN: Indiana University Press, 1988).

Goldman, Marshall, *Gorbachev's Challenge: Economic Reform in the Age of High Technology* (New York: Norton, 1987).

Kornai, Janos, "The Hungarian Reform Process," *Journal of Economic Literature* (December 1986), pp. 1687–1737.

Ofer, Gur, "Soviet Economic Growth: 1928–1985," *Journal of Economic Literature* (December 1987), pp. 1767–1833.

Perkins, Dwight Heald, "Reforming China's Economic System," *Journal of Economic Literature* (June 1988), pp. 601–645.

Wu, Jinglian, and Bruce L. Reynolds, "Choosing a Strategy for China's Reform," *American Economic Review* (May 1988), pp. 461–466.

Schnitzer, Martin C., *Comparative Economic Systems,* 4th ed. (Cincinnati: Southwestern, 1987).

GLOSSARY OF MARGIN DEFINITIONS

Absolute Advantage
The ability to produce a particular good using fewer resources than a second country (i.e., a lower ratio of resources to output). *824*

Accounting Profit
Total revenue minus accounting costs. (Because accountants and economists measure costs differently, accounting profit differs from economic profit.) *515*

Affirmative Action
A policy designed to increase the representation of women or minorities (e.g., to increase their relative employment). *715*

Aggregate Demand Curve
The aggregate demand curve shows the quantity of the nation's output demanded at each possible price level. *165*

Aggregate Supply Curve
The aggregate supply curve shows the quantity of the nation's output supplied at each possible price level. *166*

Antitrust Policy
Government laws and procedures designed to shape market structure and influence the behavior of firms. *623*

Assets
Items that the firm owns and claims that the firm has upon entities external to the firm. *130*

Automatic Stabilizer
A feature of the economy that acts automatically to inhibit economic fluctuations without discretionary policy changes being implemented. *227*

Autonomous Consumption
The portion of consumption that is independent of disposable income; consumer expenditures that would occur in the event that disposable income were zero. *210*

Average Cost Pricing
A regulatory procedure intended to equate price with average cost, and thereby limit the firm to normal profits. *650*

Average Product of Labor
Total product divided by the quantity of labor, holding capital constant. *518*

Average Tax Rate
The percentage of total income paid in taxes. *149*

Balance of Payments
A statistical tabulation of a nation's transactions with other countries for a given period. *864*

Balance of Trade
The difference between the value of a nation's exports and imports of merchandise or goods; one component of the balance of payments. *864*

Balance Sheet
A financial report listing a firm's assets and liabilities at a moment in time. *130*

Bank Assets
Items a bank owns. *286*

Bank Balance Sheet
A statement of a bank's assets, liabilities, and capital accounts (or net worth). *285*

Bank Liabilities
Items a bank owes; the debts of the bank. *286*

Barter
A system of exchange whereby goods and services are traded directly without the use of money. *56*

Black Market
A market in which goods are bought and sold at prices above the legal maximum. *84*

**Board of Governors
(of the Federal Reserve System)**
Key seven-person board that dominates the decision-making process in conducting monetary policy. *303*

Bracket Creep
The tendency for inflation to automatically push

individuals into higher marginal and average tax rates in an unindexed income-tax system. *268*

Break-Even Income
The level of income at which the government's subsidy disappears and beyond which the family must start paying income tax. *761*

Break-Even Income Level
Income level at which consumption equals income; income level at which saving is zero. *211*

Bubble
An imaginary enclosure around one or more plants that becomes the basis for a firm's pollution-control requirements. In particular, a firm is allowed to exceed pollution-control standards at individual points in the bubble provided that these excesses are offset elsewhere within the same bubble. *783*

Budget Deficit
The shortfall of federal receipts relative to expenditures, measured at an annual rate. *438*

Budget Line
A line indicating all combinations of two goods that can be purchased with an income, given the price of each good. *507*

Capital
Machines, structures, and other inputs produced by humans. *3*

Capital Accounts *286*
The difference between a bank's assets and its liabilities; indicates owners' equity stake in the bank. *286*

Capital Deepening
Expansion in the average amount of capital goods per worker. An important source of productivity growth. *473*

Capital Goods
Output used to produce other goods. *38*

Capitalism
An economic system in which property is privately owned and markets rather than central authorities coordinate economic decisions. *901*

Capture Hypothesis
The claim that regulators promote the interests of the industry they regulate rather than protecting the public. *644*

Cartel
An organization of producers that is designed to set price and output for its members. *604*

Classical Economics
Viewpoint that dominated economic thinking before Keynes. It held that market prices would quickly adjust to boost the economy out of recession, and therefore government intervention in the macroeconomy was unnecessary. *413*

Classical Range
The vertical portion of the aggregate supply curve. Firms are incapable of expanding output because the economy is operating at maximum capacity. *258*

Closed Shop
A work arrangement that permits a company to hire only those workers who are currently members of a union. *673*

Collective Bargaining
The process through which unions and management negotiate wages, fringe benefits, and nonmonetary terms of employment. *678*

Command Economy
An economic system in which property is publicly owned and central authorities coordinate economic decisions. *41, 901*

Commodity Credit Corporation (CCC) *806*
A government agency that purchases surplus commodities from farmers. *806*

Common Stock
A certificate of partial ownership of a corporation that gives its holder a vote in the selection of the firm's directors and a residual claim on the assets and profits of the firm. *120*

Communist Utopia
The Marxian conception of a future ideal society without economic classes or the division of labor and with all people realizing their full potential as creative human beings. *902*

Comparable Worth
A doctrine that each job has an intrinsic value, independent of labor supply and demand, and that jobs with similar intrinsic values have similar (comparable) worth. *710*

Comparative Advantage
The ability of one country to produce a particular good at a lower opportunity cost than a second country. *46, 826*

Compensating Wage Differential
The wage premium a worker receives for a job with

undesirable characteristics, to compensate for those characteristics. *669*

Complementary Goods
Goods that are consumed together. Two goods are complements when an increase in the price of one good reduces demand for the other. *69, 102*

Complementary Inputs
Inputs that are complements in production; an increase in the price of one reduces demand for the other. *693*

Conglomerate Merger
A merger between companies in unrelated markets. *628*

Constant-Cost Industry
An industry in which input prices (and therefore cost curves) remain unchanged as the industry expands. *561*

Constant Returns to Scale
A situation in which long-run average cost does not change with the level of output. *528*

Consumer Equilibrium
A situation in which the consumer is obtaining the maximum total utility consistent with a given income (budget). *491, 508*

Consumer Goods
Output consumed directly, rather than used to produce other goods. *38*

Consumer Price Index
The most widely quoted index of U.S. prices; based on the market basket of goods and services purchased by a typical household. *392*

Consumer Sovereignty
The principle that consumers, through spending decisions, determine how much of each good is produced. *41*

Consumer Surplus
The difference between the maximum amount a consumer is willing to pay for a given quantity of a good and the amount actually paid. *495*

Consumption Expenditures
Household expenditures on all goods and services except housing; consists of household expenditures on durable goods, nondurables, and services. *189*

Consumption Function
The relationship between consumer expenditures and disposable income, holding all other determinants of consumer spending constant. *210*

Convergence Principle
Tendency of industrial nations with relatively low living standards to grow more rapidly than more affluent nations, thereby reducing the gap in living standards. *468*

Copyright
An exclusive right, granted by the government, to publish, copy, or sell a piece of music, art, or literature. *573*

Corporate Bond
An IOU or evidence of debt issued by a corporation that carries a specified schedule of interest payments to be made to the bondholder (lender) and a date for redemption of the principal. *126*

Corporation
A firm that takes the form of an independent legal entity with ownership divided into shares and each owner's liability limited to his or her investment in the firm. *117*

Cost Effective
Achieving a given objective (e.g., the elimination of a certain volume of pollution) at the lowest cost possible. *778*

Cost-Benefit Analysis
A framework for comparing the costs and benefits of a particular activity (e.g., to determine the optimal level of that activity). *775*

Crowding In
The favorable effect of increased deficits upon investment spending owing to the stimulative effect upon aggregate demand, output, and the utilization rate of capital equipment. *455*

Crowding Out
The adverse effect of increased deficits on investment spending owing to the negative effect of higher interest rates associated with the larger deficits. *454*

Crowding-In Effect
The tendency for an expansionary fiscal policy to induce an *increase* in investment spending by stimulating sales growth and utilization rate of existing plant and equipment. *227*

Crowding-Out Effect
The tendency for an expansionary fiscal policy to induce an offsetting reduction in investment spending by raising interest rates. *227*

Crude Quantity Theory
The proposition that velocity is constant in the short run and that aggregate demand (PY) and the price level vary proportionally with the money supply. *333*

Currency Appreciation
An increase in the international value of the currency; the currency buys more units of foreign currency. *846*

Currency Depreciation
A decline in the international value of the currency; the currency buys fewer units of foreign currency. *846*

Customer Discrimination
A preference of consumers to be served by members of a particular group (e.g., males). *712*

Cyclical Deficit
The portion of the actual deficit attributable to a shortfall of actual GNP relative to full-employment GNP. *446*

Cyclical Unemployment
Unemployment attributable to inadequate aggregate demand; the difference between the actual unemployment rate and the unemployment rate associated with full employment. *369*

Decreasing-Cost Industry
An industry in which input prices decrease as the industry expands. *561*

Deficiency Payment
A supplemental payment that farmers receive for each unit of output they produce, equal to the difference between the target price and the market price. If the market price exceeds the target price, there is no deficiency payment. *810*

Demand Curve
A diagram showing the relationship between the price of a good and the quantity demanded per period of time, other things equal. *68*

Demand Schedule
A table showing the relationship between the price of a good and the quantity demanded per period of time, other things equal. *68*

Demographic Transition
The transition from a society experiencing high birth and death rates to low birth and death rates; in the transition, the decline in birthrates lags the decline in death rates, leading to rapid population growth. *884*

Dependency Rate
The number of people not working per 100 workers in the population. *887*

Depreciation
The value of the nation's capital equipment that is used up in a given period, normally one year; indicates how much investment is needed to keep the nation's capital stock intact. *196*

Depression
A very severe and prolonged economic downturn. *177*

Depression Range
The flat portion of the aggregate supply curve. More output can be called forth at the existing price level because substantial idle plant capacity exists and qualified workers are available to firms at existing wages. *257*

Deregulation
The removal of government regulations. *638*

Derived Demand
The demand for a resource; determined by (derived from) the demand for the product it produces. *662*

Discount Rate
The interest rate charged on loans to financial institutions made by the Federal Reserve. *303, 346*

Diseconomies of Scale
A situation in which long-run average cost rises with the level of output. *530*

Disequilibrium
A state of imbalance; a market is in disequilibrium when the quantity demanded does not coincide with the quantity supplied. *78*

Disequilibrium Price
Any price for which the quantity demanded differs from the quantity supplied. *78*

Dumping
A practice in which a producer sells its product at a lower price in a foreign market than at home. *832*

Economic Good
A good that is scarce. At a price of zero the amount of the good desired exceeds the quantity available. *4*

Economic Growth
The ability of a country to produce greater levels of output—represented by an outward shift of its production possibilities curve. *38, 462*

Economic Profit
Total revenue minus the total cost of production (implicit as well as explicit). *514, 736*

Economic Regulation
The regulation of specific industries, designed to influence such outcomes as price, service, and number of producers in an industry. *638*

Economic Rent
The premium received by a resource in excess of its opportunity cost. *734*

Economic Rent of a Worker
The return to a scarce natural talent; the difference

between the wage received (because of that talent) and the wage available in the best alternative line of work. *666*

Economic System
An institutional arrangement for determining what goods are produced, how they are produced, and for whom. *40*

Economics
The study of how scarce resources are allocated among competing uses. *5*

Economies of Scale
A situation in which long-run average cost declines as the firm increases its level of output. *528*

Efficient Production
Achieving maximum feasible output from a given amount of resources. *35*

Effluent Fee
A charge or tax levied on each unit of a pollutant emitted into the environment. *780*

Elastic Demand
Demand is elastic when $E_d > 1$. *93*

Employee Discrimination
A preference of employees to work with members of the same group (e.g., other males) and to avoid contact with different workers (e.g., women). *712*

Entitlement Program
A system for allocating oil to U.S. refiners that consisted of entitlement fees (taxes) on domestic oil and subsidies on imported oil. Once the entitlement fees and subsidies were taken into account, all refiners faced the same effective price for their oil. *791*

Entrepreneur
An individual who organizes resources for production, introduces new products or techniques of production, and reaps the rewards/bears the consequences of such endeavors. *3*

Equilibrium
A state of balance; a market is in equilibrium when the quantity demanded equals the quantity supplied. *77*

Equilibrium Output
The level of GNP at which aggregate demand is equal to GNP; the level of output toward which the economy tends to settle. *221, 236*

Equilibrium Price
The price for which the quantity demanded equals the quantity supplied. *77*

Excess Reserves
The amount by which the reserves of a financial institution exceed its required reserves. *287*

Expected Life (of a resource)
Proven reserves divided by consumption. *788*

Explicit Costs
Direct payments made to others for the resources they own. *513*

Extensive Growth
An outward shift of a country's production possibilities curve over time due to increases in natural resources, labor, and capital goods. *909*

External Benefits. *See* Positive Externalities

External Costs. *See* Negative Externalities

Fallacy of Composition
Falsely concluding that what is true for the individual must be true for the group. *11*

Featherbedding
Restrictive work practices of unions designed to force a company to hire more labor than desired at the union wage rate. *677*

Federal Funds Market
Market in which banks trade their excess reserve deposits (with the Fed) on a one-day basis. *346*

Federal Funds Rate
The interest rate on loans made among financial institutions in the federal funds market. *346*

Federal Open Market Committee (FOMC)
The committee responsible for determining the basic thrust of monetary policy and conducting open market operations; consists of the seven members of the Board of Governors and five of the twelve Federal Reserve Bank presidents. *303*

Federal Reserve System (the Fed) *301*
The central bank of the United States; the organization responsible for conducting monetary policy by influencing the supply of money and credit and the level of interest rates. *301*

Fiat Money
Money that attains its value by government decree; it has little value as a commodity. All U.S. currency and coins today are fiat money. *283*

Fiscal Policy
The deliberate manipulation of federal expenditures

and taxes for the purpose of influencing economic activity. *168*

Fisher Effect
The effect that higher expected inflation has in inducing higher interest rates. *351*

Five-Year Plan
A document that lays out the strategies and growth targets for economic development in the Stalinist growth model; supporting one-year plans include specific directives for enterprise production and commodity allocation. *904*

Fixed Costs
Costs that are independent of the level of production. *520*

Fixed Exchange Rates
A system in which governments intervene aggressively to keep exchange rates at certain levels rather than permitting them to float in response to market forces. *846*

Floating Exchange Rates
Exchange rates that are allowed to change daily in response to market forces of supply and demand. *846*

Foreign Exchange Market
The market in which the currencies of different countries are bought and sold. *846*

Foreign Exchange Market Speculators
Individuals and firms that buy and sell foreign currencies with the intent of profiting from exchange-rate movements. *853*

Foreign Exchange Rate
The amount of another country's money that residents of a country can obtain in exchange for one unit of their own money; the price at which one country's currency may be traded for foreign currency. *846*

Free Good
A good that is not scarce. *4*

Free Trade
Trade that is free of artificial barriers that would restrict the movement of goods between countries. *829*

Frictional Unemployment
Unemployment due to normal job search by individuals who have quit their jobs, are initially entering the labor force, or are reentering the labor force. *367*

Full Employment
Situation in which economy operates at lowest unemployment rate possible without setting off a boost in inflation; probably corresponds to an unemployment rate of 5 or 5.5 percent. *169*

Full-Bodied Money
A form of money whose value in exchange (as money) is equivalent to its value as a commodity. *283*

Full-Employment Level of Output
The level of GNP the economy would produce if its labor and other resources were fully employed. *238*

GATT
An international agreement promoting more-open trade policy and providing the machinery to settle trade disputes among participating nations. *840*

Gentlemen's Agreement
An informal understanding among members of a group to pursue practices that are in the best interests of the group. *605*

GNP Deflator
A price index constructed by taking a weighted average of prices of all goods and services that enter into the nation's gross national product; it reveals the change since the base year in the cost of purchasing the items that constitute the nation's GNP. *198, 392*

Government Purchases
Federal, state, and local government spending on final goods and services, including costs of hiring government employees but excluding government transfer payments. *141, 192*

Government Transfer Payments
Expenditures by government for which no goods or services are concurrently received by the government. *142, 192*

Gross Investment (*I*)
The total value of all investment goods produced in the economy during a specific time period, normally one year. *190*

Gross National Product
The value of the output of all final goods and services produced during a specific period (usually one year). *14, 170, 186*

Herfindahl Index
A measure of market concentration obtained by squaring the market share of each firm in the industry and then summing these numbers. *616*

Hidden Unemployed
Discouraged workers who stop seeking work and are not counted as unemployed. *367*

Horizontal Merger
A merger between companies in the same market. *628*

Hostile Takeover
A merger accomplished by purchasing controlling interest directly from the stockholders of the target firm, against the wishes of its management. *122*

Human Capital
The knowledge and skills acquired by workers, principally through education and training. *473, 666*

Hypothesis
A proposition concerning a particular relationship or event—often part of a theory. *8*

Impact Lag
The time period that elapses between the point at which a new policy is implemented and when the policy begins to influence economic activity. *421*

Implementation Lag
The time period that elapses between the point at which a need for policy change is recognized and when the change in policy is implemented. *421*

Implicit Costs
The opportunity costs of using resources already owned by the firm. *514*

Implicit Tax Rate
The amount by which the government reduces its subsidy in response to another dollar of earned income—that is, the change in subsidy divided by the change in earned income. *761*

Import Quota
A restriction limiting the amount of a foreign good that may enter a country legally. *48, 831*

Impure Inflation
The *real-world* type of inflation in which *relative* prices of goods and services are changing while the general level of prices increases. *403*

Income Effect
The change in quantity demanded of a good that results from a change in purchasing power (when the price of the good changes). *498*

Income Effect (for labor)
The change in the amount of labor supplied that can be attributed to a change in income. A higher income increases the demand for leisure, reducing the hours of work. *663*

Income Statement
A financial report showing the revenues, costs, and profits from the firm's activities over a specified period of time. *132*

Increasing-Cost Industry
An industry in which input prices increase as the industry expands. *561*

Independent Goods
Goods for which the cross elasticity of demand is zero. *102*

Indexation
Widespread use of escalator clauses that tie wages, rents, and other prices directly to the nation's price index in order to reduce the redistributive effects of inflation. *405*

Indifference Curve
A curve depicting all combinations of two goods to which an individual is indifferent—that is, all combinations that have the same total utility. *504*

Indifference Map
A set of indifference curves. *505*

Individual Retirement Account (IRA)
Voluntary, tax-deductible, self-managed retirement savings program authorized by legislation in the early 1980s to promote the incentive to save. *268*

The Industry's Long-Run Supply Curve
A curve indicating the relationship between the price of a good and the amount supplied by the industry after the entry of new firms to the industry or the exit of existing firms. *561*

The Industry's Short-Run Supply Curve
A curve indicating the relationship between the price of a good and the amount supplied by the industry in the short run. (In the short run the number of firms in the industry is fixed.) *557*

Inefficient Production
Producing less than maximum output due to leaving resources idle or using them ineffectively. *35*

Inelastic Demand
Demand is inelastic when $E_d < 1$. *93*

Inferior Good
A good for which demand falls in response to a higher income. *69*

Inflation
A sustained increase in the aggregate price level; a persistent decline in the value of the monetary unit (e.g., the dollar). *167, 391*

Inflation Rate
The rate at which a nation's average prices rise over time. *8*

Inflationary Gap
The amount by which equilibrium GNP exceeds the full-employment GNP level; occurs when aggregate expenditures are excessive relative to the capacity to produce goods and services. *246*

In-Kind Transfers
Transfer payments that consist of goods and services rather than cash. Included are food, public housing, and medical care. *751*

Innovation
The application of new technical knowledge to such economic processes as production and distribution. *470*

Intensive Growth
An outward shift of a country's production possibilities curve over time brought about by technological progress. *909*

Interest Income
The payments received by lenders for the use of their funds (expressed in dollars). *725*

Interest Rate
The price paid for the use of lenders' funds (expressed in percentage terms). *344, 725*

Intergenerational Burden
The costs imposed by the current generation upon future generations by bequeathing an inadequate capital stock. *442*

Intermediate Target
A variable (such as the money supply or interest rates) the Fed attempts to control in the short run in order to influence such ultimate objectives as unemployment and inflation rates. *316*

Internalize Costs
To shift external costs from third parties back to those parties directly responsible for the costs. *773*

International Reserves
A government's stock of foreign currencies and gold available to support the country's currency in the foreign exchange market. *862*

International Trade
The exchange of goods or resources between countries. *44*

Invention
The discovery of new knowledge. *470*

Isocost Line
A line showing all the combinations of capital and labor that can be purchased with a given amount of money. *537*

Isoquant
A curve depicting the various input combinations that are capable of producing a given level of output when used efficiently. *536*

Keynesians
Economists who, like Keynes, believe that a capitalistic economy does not tend automatically toward a full-employment equilibrium; hence, activist monetary and fiscal policies are advocated. *261, 416*

Kinked Demand Curve
The demand curve facing an oligopolist if rivals in the industry match the firm's price reductions but ignore its price increases. *600*

Labor
The physical and mental abilities of workers. *3*

Labor Force
Those individuals 16 years of age and over who are counted as either employed or unemployed. *365, 702*

Labor Force Participation Rate
The percentage of the working-age population that is in the labor force. *367, 702*

Labor Theory of Value
The view associated with Marx that labor is the only factor of production capable of producing value so that the value of every commodity is determined by the amount of labor embodied in it. *901*

Land
A country's natural resources. *3*

Law of Comparative Advantage
Total output is maximized when countries specialize in the production of those goods for which they have a comparative advantage. *826*

Law of Diminishing Marginal Utility
The proposition that marginal utility of a good eventually declines as consumption of the good increases. *491*

Law of Increasing Costs
The hypothesis that the opportunity cost of a good rises as the quantity of the good produced increases. *35*

Less Developed Countries (LDCs)
Countries in which living standards are low because modern technology generally has not been applied to production processes. *875*

Liabilities
Debts of the firm or claims that outsiders have on the firm. *130*

Liquidity
The ease and willingness with which one may convert an asset into money when one needs cash. Savings accounts are highly liquid; land is not. *282*

Loanable Funds Model
A model that explains interest rates in terms of the demand for and supply of lenders' funds. According to this model, the interest rate is the price paid for the use of these funds. *725*

Long Run
A period of time long enough to change the quantities of all inputs. *104, 517*

Long-Run Average Cost Curve
A curve revealing the lowest cost per unit at which a firm can produce each level of output, given sufficient time to change all inputs. *527*

Lorenz Curve
A diagram illustrating the cumulative distribution of income by families. *744*

Luxury
A good for which the income elasticity of demand is greater than 1. *101*

Macroeconomics
The study of the aggregate economy. *14*

Marginal Analysis
An examination of what occurs when current conditions change. *7*

Marginal Cost Pricing
A regulatory procedure intended to equate price with marginal cost, and thereby promote efficient allocation of resources. *650*

Marginal Factor Cost
The increase in the total cost of an input associated with using an additional unit of the input. *686*

Marginal Product of Labor
The increase in output associated with a one-unit increase in labor, holding capital constant. *518*

Marginal Productivity Theory of Income Distribution
The theory that income is distributed to factors of production according to each factor's marginal revenue product. In particular, the theory predicts that each input will be paid an amount equal to its marginal revenue product. *697*

Marginal Propensity to Consume (MPC)
The ratio of the change in consumption to the change in disposable income that induces the change in consumption; the slope of the consumption function. *210*

Marginal Propensity to Save (MPS)
The ratio of the change in saving to the change in disposable income that induces the change in saving; the slope of the saving function. *211*

Marginal Revenue
The increase in total revenue associated with a one-unit increase in output. *551*

Marginal Revenue Product of Labor
The increase in total revenue to a firm resulting from the hiring of an additional unit of labor. *660*

Marginal Tax Rate
The percentage of an *additional* dollar of income paid in taxes. *149*

Marginal Utility
The extra satisfaction (change in total utility) from consuming one more unit of a good. *489*

Market
A mechanism through which buyers and sellers are brought together for the purpose of exchanging some good or resource. *41*

Market Concentration Ratio
The percentage of industry sales attributable to the four largest firms in an industry. *613*

Market Demand Curve
A curve showing the relationship between the price of a good and the total quantity demanded by all consumers in the market (per period of time); obtained by summing the demand curves of individual consumers. *499*

Market Demand for Labor
The relationship between the wage rate and the total amount of labor demanded by all firms in the labor market (other things equal). *662*

Market Failure
A situation in which unrestricted markets produce either more or less of a good than is socially optimal. *61*

Market Period
A period of time during which the quantity supplied cannot be changed—represented by a perfectly inelastic supply curve. *104*

Market for Pollution Rights
A market in which pollution rights are bought and sold, at prices determined by the supply of and demand for these permits. *782*

Market Structure
The distinguishing characteristics of a market, including

number of firms, the similarity of the products they sell, and the ease with which new firms can enter the market. *543*

Market Supply of Labor
The relationship between the wage rate and the total amount of labor supplied to the market (other things equal). *664*

Marketing Order
A directive, enforced by the Department of Agriculture, limiting the quantity of a product that each producer may sell on the market. *808*

Material Incentives
A reward system that promotes desirable behavior by giving the recipient a greater claim over material goods than one who has performed less well. *903*

Means Test
A requirement that a family's income not exceed a certain level; if it does the family is declared ineligible for that particular form of public assistance. *748*

Microeconomics
The study of the individual units that comprise the economy. *14*

Minimum Efficient Scale
The level of output at which economies of scale end. *528*

Mixed Economy
An economic system that mixes pure capitalism and a command economy. Some resources are owned privately, others publicly. Some economic decisions are made in markets, others by central authorities. *41*

Model
A formal presentation of a theory, often mathematical or graphical. *8*

Monetarism
The viewpoint that monetary instability is the dominant cause of output fluctuations and that money supply growth is the dominant cause of inflation. *338*

Monetarists
Economists who share the view that money exerts a dominant effect on economic activity and that a capitalistic economy has an effective self-regulating mechanism. Activist policies are thought to hinder these corrective mechanisms and to destabilize economic activity, and are therefore rejected. *261, 416*

Monetary Aggregates
The various measures of the nation's money supply, including M-1, M-2, M-3, and L. *282*

Monetary Policy
The use of certain economic tools by the Federal Reserve

System to alter availability of credit, level of interest rates, and supply of money in order to influence economic activity. *168*

Money
Anything widely accepted as payment for goods and services; any generally accepted medium of exchange. *279*

Monopolistic Competition
A market structure characterized by a large number of firms selling distinct (differentiated) products and in which entry into and exit from the industry is easy. *589*

Monopoly
An industry with only one seller. There are no good substitutes for the product of the monopolist. *571*

Monopoly Power
The ability of a firm to influence output price by changing the amount it sells. Any firm facing a downward-sloping demand curve has some monopoly power. *571*

Monopsonist
The only buyer of a particular input. *686*

Moral Incentives
A reward system that promotes desirable behavior by appealing to the recipient's responsibility to society and by raising the recipient's social stature within the community. *903*

Multiplier
The ratio of the change in equilibrium output to the original change in spending (C, I, G, or net exports) that caused the change in output. *223*

Mutual Interdependence
An interrelationship among producers. Firms, aware that their actions affect others in the industry, make decisions only after taking into account how rivals are likely to respond. *598*

M-1
Demand deposits and other checkable accounts plus currency and coins in the hands of the public; the narrow medium of exchange or *transactions* measure of money. *279*

National Debt
The total stock of bonds and other federal government IOUs outstanding; the sum of past federal budget deficits minus the sum of past surpluses. *438*

National Income (NY)
The aggregate income received by the resource owners of land, labor, capital, and entrepreneurship; equal to GNP minus the sum of depreciation and indirect business taxes. *197*

National Income Accounting
The set of rules and procedures used to measure the total flow of output produced by a nation, together with the income generated by this production. *186*

Natural Monopoly
An industry characterized by extensive economies of scale. The total cost of producing a given output is minimized when only one firm is in the industry. *585*

Natural Rate of Unemployment
The minimum sustainable unemployment rate below which inflation tends to accelerate; the percentage of the labor force either frictionally or structurally unemployed. *371*

Necessity
A good for which the income elasticity of demand is greater than 0 but less than 1. *101*

Negative Externalities (External Costs)
Uncompensated costs imposed on third parties as a result of consumption or production by other individuals or firms. *137, 769*

Negative Income Tax
A program in which families with low incomes would receive a negative tax (i.e., subsidy). That subsidy would be reduced as the family's income from other sources increased. *761*

Net Farm Income
The total revenue generated by a nation's farms minus farm production costs. *797*

Net Investment
The net addition to the nation's capital stock in a given period; gross investment minus depreciation. *190*

Net National Product (NNP)
Gross national product minus a depreciation allowance for the value of capital goods wearing out during the period. *196*

Net Worth
The difference between a firm's assets and its liabilities; net worth is the residual equity or claim of the owners of the firm. *131*

Nominal Interest Rate
The interest rate measured in actual dollars borrowers must pay; the actual interest rate. *727*

Nonprohibitive Tariff
A tariff that reduces but does not eliminate foreign sales in the country imposing the tariff. *830*

Nonrecourse Loan
A government loan that a farmer may, at his discretion, either repay or cancel. To cancel, the farmer transfers ownership of the commodity to the government, keeping whatever funds the government has loaned him. *806*

Normal Good
A good for which demand increases in response to a higher income. *69*

Normal Range
The upward-sloping portion of the aggregate supply curve; to induce more production, higher prices are required. *258*

Normative Economics
Deals with value judgments. *13*

Offsets
Reductions in pollution beyond the amount required of one firm (or plant) that are used to permit a second firm (or plant) in the same area to increase its pollution. *783*

Okun's Law
Estimated relationship between the unemployment rate and the national loss of output; each one percent of unemployment above the natural unemployment rate is associated with a 2.5 percent gap between actual and potential GNP. *375*

Oligopoly
A market structure in which a small number of firms dominates the industry; other firms are kept out through barriers to entry. *598*

Open Market Operations
Buying and selling of U.S. government securities by the Fed with a view toward influencing monetary and credit conditions. *309*

Open Shop
A work arrangement in which employees cannot be compelled to join a union, even if one has been chosen to represent the company's work force. *673*

Opportunity Cost
The best alternative to the option chosen. *5*

Other Things (being) Equal
A condition in which only the specific variables under consideration change; all other variables remain constant. *10*

Output Gap
The magnitude by which actual GNP falls short of potential GNP. *375*

Partnership
An unincorporated firm with two or more owners who have unlimited liability for the firm's debts. *118*

Patent
An exclusive right, granted by the government, to market a product or process for 17 years. *572*

Pay Gap
The difference in pay between two groups, traditionally specified in percentage terms. *705*

Perfectly Elastic Demand
A demand that is infinitely responsive to price—represented by a horizontal demand curve. *95*

Perfectly Elastic Supply
A supply that is infinitely responsive to price—represented by a horizontal supply curve. *103*

Perfectly Inelastic Demand
A demand that is totally unresponsive to price—represented by a vertical demand curve. *94*

Perfectly Inelastic Supply
A supply that is totally unresponsive to price—represented by a vertical supply curve. *103*

Personal Disposable Income (Y_d)
Income in the hands of individuals after deducting income taxes; income available to households to spend and save. *197*

Phillips Curve
A graph illustrating the relationship between the unemployment rate and the rate of inflation. *378*

Policy Ineffectiveness Theorem
Proposition advocated by proponents of REM or new classical macroeconomics that only *surprise* or *unanticipated* policies have an effect on such real economic variables as output and employment. *427*

Pollution Right
A permit that entitles its bearer to emit one unit of a certain pollutant into the environment. *782*

Population Momentum
The tendency of population to continue to increase even when the average couple bears two children; this phenomenon is attributable to the disproportionate number of youth in the population. *887*

Positive Economics
Involves statements based on fact. *13*

Positive Externalities (External Benefits)
Benefits received but not paid for by third parties as a result of others' production or consumption. *139, 769*

Positive Time Preference
A preference to consume now rather than wait. *725*

Potential GNP
The level of GNP the nation would produce under conditions of full employment. Potential GNP rises over time because of growth in the labor force and productivity. *170, 239*

Poverty Line
A level of income below which a family is classified as poor. The poverty line is based on the cost of those items deemed necessary to maintain a minimally acceptable standard of living. *750*

Predatory Pricing
A practice whereby one or more firms temporarily reduce price in order to drive weaker firms from the industry and then raise price once these competitors have been eliminated. *623*

Present Value
The value now of one or a series of payments to be received in the future; often referred to as the *discounted present value* of future payments. *127*

Price Ceiling
The maximum legal price that may be charged for a good. *81*

Price Discrimination
The practice of selling a good at different prices that are not attributable to differences in cost. *579*

Price Floor
The minimum legal price that must be paid for a good. *81*

Price Index
A weighted average of the prices of goods and services expressed in relation to a base year value of 100. *391*

Price Leadership
A practice in certain oligopolistic industries whereby one firm initiates price changes and other firms in the industry follow its lead. *606*

Price Support
A minimum price guaranteed by the government. The government preserves the minimum price by agreeing to buy any output offered at this price. *806*

Price System
A mechanism for coordinating economic decisions in which prices are determined in markets and used to allocate resources and output. *58*

Price Taker
An economic unit that has no control over price. The perfectly competitive firm is a price taker in the product market. *546*

Price-Cap Regulation
A form of regulation limiting the price a firm may charge (but not limiting allowable profits). *651*

Prime Loan Rate
A benchmark bank loan rate that is widely publicized and used as a standard by which other bank loan rates are set. *345*

Private Benefits
The benefits received by those consuming or producing a good. *769*

Private Costs
The costs incurred by those producing or consuming a good. *771*

Privatization
Transferring production of a good from the public sector to the private sector. *652*

Producer Price Index
A price index based on a large sample of materials and goods purchased by firms; formerly known as the wholesale price index. *392*

Product Market
A market in which a particular good or service is bought and sold. *55*

Production Function
A relationship indicating the maximum amount of output that can be produced per period with various quantities of inputs and a given technology. *517*

Production Possibilities Curve
A line revealing the maximum combinations of two goods that can be produced with a given quantity of resources, assuming that technology is fixed. *34*

Productive Efficiency
An industry's output is produced at the lowest cost possible. *564*

Productivity Growth
Expansion of output and real income per hour of work; the main source of rising living standards. *463*

Progressive Tax
The fraction of income paid in tax rises as income rises. *145*

Prohibitive Tariff
A tariff set so high that it prevents the sale of a foreign product in the country imposing the tariff. *830*

Proletariat
The working class under capitalism consisting of people who own only their own labor as opposed to the capitalist (or bourgeoisie) class of property and capital owners. *902*

Proportional Tax
The fraction of income paid in tax remains constant at all income levels. *145*

Proprietorship
A firm owned by a single individual who has unlimited liability for the firm's debts. *117*

Protectionism
Sheltering domestic industries from foreign competition through tariffs, quotas, or other programs that limit imports. *834*

Proven Reserves
The amount of a natural resource that has been discovered and that producers are willing to extract given current costs and prices. *788*

Public Assistance/Welfare
Transfer programs that are means-tested—that is, available only to low-income families. *758*

Public Good
A good or service that cannot be provided for one person without being available to others, and once provided for one person can be provided for others at no additional cost. *139*

Public Interest Theory of Regulation
The theory that regulation is a response to market failure and therefore designed to benefit society. *640*

Purchasing Power Parity Theory (PPP)
Theory that the exchange rate between any two national currencies adjusts to reflect changes in the relative price levels in the two nations. *849*

Pure Capitalism
An economic system in which property is privately owned and markets rather than central authorities coordinate economic decisions. *41*

Pure Economic Rent
The payment for using a resource that is fixed in supply. *731*

Pure Inflation
A hypothetical type of inflation in which all prices increase at exactly the same rate so there is no change in *relative* prices among goods and services. *403*

Quantity Demanded
The amount of a good that consumers wish to buy at a particular price. *67*

Quantity Supplied
The amount of a good that firms wish to sell at a particular price. *73*

Rate Base
The value of a firm's capital, as determined by a regulatory commission. *651*

Rate of Return
The annual return received on a firm's capital (or rate base), expressed as a percentage of the firm's capital. *651*

Rate-of-Return Regulation
A form of regulation limiting a firm to a prescribed rate of return on its capital (rate base). *650*

Rational Behavior
Acting in a manner consistent with a decision maker's objectives. *6*

Rational Expectations Macroeconomics (REM) or New Classical Macroeconomics
Modern school of economists that emphasizes the effectiveness of market forces pushing the economy toward full employment and views discretionary stabilization policies as being ineffective. *423*

Real Deficit
The actual deficit adjusted for the net balance sheet gain experienced by government because of inflation; actual deficit minus the inflation rate times the net federal debt outstanding. *453*

Real GNP
GNP adjusted for inflation; the value of gross national product in constant prices. *170*

Real Interest Rate
The nominal (actual) interest rate minus the expected rate of inflation. *357, 728*

Recession
A period of time in which a nation's real output declines. *170*

Recessionary Gap
The amount by which equilibrium GNP falls short of the full-employment GNP level; the amount of additional output required to generate full employment. *239*

Recognition Lag
The time period that elapses between the point at which a change in policy is needed and when the need is recognized by policymakers. *421*

Regressive Tax
The fraction of income paid in tax declines as income rises. *146*

Rent Seeking
The use of scarce resources in an attempt to secure a monopoly and therefore earn monopoly profits. *584*

Replacement Level of Fertility
The fertility level that exactly "replaces" the parents—that is, two children per couple. *887*

Required Reserves
The minimum amount of reserves a financial institution is required to hold based on the institution's deposit liabilities and the percentage reserve requirement set by the Fed. *286*

Reserve Requirements
The percentage of deposits that financial institutions are required by the Fed to hold in the form of reserves—cash and deposits at the Fed. *286, 312*

Reserves
Cash holdings of a financial institution plus its deposit at the Federal Reserve. *286*

Resource (factor) Market
A market in which a particular resource (factor of production) is bought and sold. *55*

Resources
Inputs (land, capital, and labor) used to produce goods and services. *3*

Responsibility System
An institutional arrangement designed to tie monetary rewards more closely to work actually performed; in practice in Chinese agriculture, a system of family farming based on long-term leases of land. *915*

Ricardian-Equivalence Theorem
Hypothesis that increased federal budget deficits induce an equivalent increase in private saving, thus leaving the gross pool of saving (government plus private) unaltered. If valid, most of the alleged adverse consequences of budget deficits are nonexistent. *272*

Right-to-Work Laws
Legislation enacted by certain states to require open shops (i.e., to outlaw compulsory union membership). *673*

Risk of Default
The probability that a borrower will fail to meet its interest obligations or repay the loan. *730*

Roundabout Production
The process of obtaining capital and using it to produce consumer goods rather than producing consumer goods directly, without capital. *725*

Rule of Reason
The doctrine that all monopolies are not illegal, only monopolies that have engaged in unreasonable behavior. *627*

Say's Law
The view that production creates its own demand because it generates an equivalent amount of income with which the output may be purchased. *413*

Scarcity of Resources
Insufficient resources are available to produce all goods and services desired by consumers. *5*

Schumpeter-Galbraith Hypothesis
The claim that innovation occurs more rapidly when firms are large in size and comprise a substantial share of the market. *608*

Screening Hypothesis
The claim that employers make hiring decisions on the basis of a person's education but that education does not make a worker more productive. *667*

Self-Correcting Mechanism
The forces in the economy that tend to push equilibrium output toward the full-employment output level in the absence of government implementation of monetary and fiscal policies to stabilize economic activity. *242*

Short Run
A period of time so short that the quantities of some inputs cannot be changed. *104, 516*

Shortage
The amount by which quantity demanded exceeds quantity supplied at a given price. *77*

Shutting Down
Temporarily halting operations; producing no output in the current period. This limits the firm's loss to its fixed costs. *549*

Social Benefits
Private benefits plus external benefits. *769*

Social Costs
Private costs plus external costs. *771*

Social Insurance
Transfer programs based on some criteria other than income (e.g., retirement or unemployment). *758*

Social Regulation
Broad-based regulations designed to improve the environment and to enhance health and safety. *638*

Socialist Economy
To Marx, an intermediate stage of communism in which workers are paid according to their work; identified with the Stalinist growth model in the Soviet bloc and China. *903*

Soft-Budget Constraint
An essentially unlimited budget enjoyed by enterprises, which can fall back on the state for subsidies and tax breaks to bail out unprofitable operations. *912*

Special Interest Theory of Regulation
The theory that regulation is designed to protect special interest groups at the expense of the public. *640*

Specialization
An arrangement in which persons or countries concentrate on the production of a limited number of goods or activities, rather than becoming self-sufficient. *44*

Stabilization Policies
Government programs designed to prevent serious economic downturns and rapid inflation by influencing the nation's aggregate demand curve. *168*

Stagflation
A situation in which sluggish or declining output is accompanied by strong inflation. *174*

Stalinist Growth Model
A combination of the command economy and centralized political control used to pursue rapid economic growth by collectivizing agriculture and concentrating investment on heavy industry. *903*

Standard of Living
The average output or real income per person; annual output divided by the population. *463*

Structural Deficit or High-Employment Deficit
The deficit that would prevail under conditions of full employment; depends on legislated programs and tax rates, not on economic activity. *447*

Structural Unemployment
Unemployment due to structural changes in the economy; the portion of unemployment accounted for by those out of work for long periods because their skills do not match those required for available jobs. *368*

Substitute Goods
Goods that are substitutable in consumption. Two goods are substitutes when an increase in the price of one good increases demand for the other. *69, 102*

Substitute Inputs
Inputs that are substitutes in production; an increase in the price of one increases demand for the other. *693*

Substitution Effect
The change in quantity demanded of a good due to a change in the price of that good relative to its substitutes. *498*

Substitution Effect (for labor)
The change in the amount of labor supplied that can be attributed to a change in the opportunity cost of leisure. By increasing the opportunity cost of leisure, a higher wage rate induces an individual to substitute work for leisure. *663*

Sunk Cost
A cost that has already been incurred and cannot be recovered. *532*

Superiority Hypothesis
The claim that large oligopolistic producers captured sizable market shares due to their superior efficiency (lower cost curves). *630*

Supply Curve
A diagram showing the relationship between the price of a good and the quantity supplied per period of time, other things equal. *73*

Supply Schedule
A table showing the relationship between the price of a good and the quantity supplied per period of time, other things equal. *73*

Supply-Side Economics
School of economics that emphasizes the importance of promoting policies to shift the aggregate supply curve rightward by implementing measures that boost the incentive to work, produce, save, and invest. *179, 264*

Surplus
The amount by which quantity supplied exceeds quantity demanded at a given price. *77*

Target Price
A minimum price guaranteed by the government. If the market price falls below the target price, the government reimburses farmers for the difference. *810*

Tariff (duty)
A tax levied on an imported product. *829*

Tax Incidence
The distribution of the tax burden—that is, who ultimately pays the tax. *105, 146*

Technology
The body of knowledge encompassing techniques for transforming resources into output. *34*

Terms of Trade
The amount of one good that must be given up to obtain a unit of a second good. *826*

Terms of Trade
The ratio of the average price of a country's exports to the average price of its imports (both prices measured in units of domestic currency). *859*

Theory
A formulation of underlying relationships in an attempt to explain certain phenomena. *8*

Theory of Occupational Crowding
A theory that the lower wages of women (or minority workers) result from their being denied entrance into certain high-paying occupations and, instead, their being crowded into other occupations, thereby depressing wages in those occupations. *710*

Total Revenue
The price of a good times the quantity sold ($TR = P \times Q$). *96*

Total Utility
The total amount of satisfaction received from all the units consumed of a good. *489*

Trade Deficit
The amount by which a country's imports exceed its exports. *821*

Trading Possibilities Curve
A line showing the combinations of two goods a country may obtain by producing the good for which it has a comparative advantage and trading it for the other good. *827*

Transaction Costs
The costs associated with the exchange of a good or resource. *47*

Transactions Demand for Money
Money held to finance a stream of expenditures that does not coincide precisely in time with the receipt of funds such as paychecks. *328*

Treasury Bill Yield
The yield on safe, short-term government securities known as Treasury bills. *345*

Trust
A combination of companies acting in concert in order to increase control of an industry. *623*

Unemployment Rate
Percentage of the labor force that is unemployed:
$$\frac{\text{unemployment}}{\text{labor force}} \times 100. \quad 366, 717$$

Union
An organization of workers that negotiates on a collective basis (as one body) in order to increase the bargaining power of the workers. *671*

Union Shop
A work arrangement that requires employees to join a union within a certain period of time after they are hired. *673*

Unit Elastic Demand
Demand is unit elastic when $E_d = 1$. *521*

Variable Costs
Costs that increase as the level of production rises. *521*

Velocity
The number of times annually that an *average dollar* is spent on final goods and services; the ratio of the nominal GNP to the money supply. *325*

Vertical Merger
A merger between a company supplying an input and a company buying it. *628*

Voluntary Export Restriction
An agreement by one country to limit exports to a second country. *832*

Wealth Effect
The effect that a change in the nation's price level exerts on consumption, aggregate demand, and equilibrium output by changing the real value of such financial assets as money, savings accounts, and government bonds held by individuals. *215, 239*

Workfare
A program in which low-income individuals receive government support in return for agreeing to work. *755*

SUBJECT/NAME INDEX

Note: Page numbers followed by an "n" indicate terms found in footnotes. Page numbers followed by an "r" indicate names found in the Selected References section.

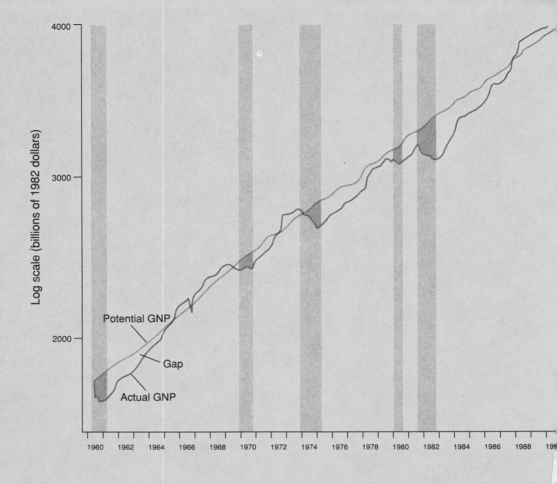

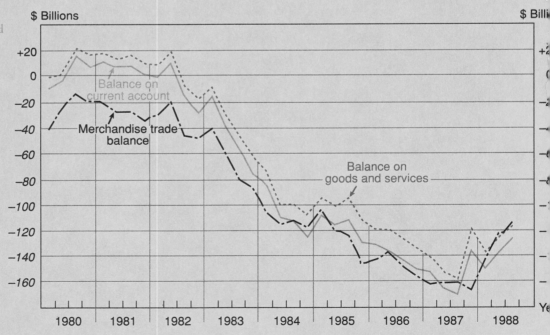